HUMAN KNOWLEDGE

Classical and Contemporary Approaches

THIRD EDITION

Edited by

Paul K. Moser

Arnold vander Nat

New York   Oxford
OXFORD UNIVERSITY PRESS
2003

Oxford University Press

Oxford   New York
Auckland   Bangkok   Buenos Aires   Cape Town
Chennai   Dar es Salaam   Delhi   Hong Kong   Istanbul   Karachi
Kolkata   Kuala Lumpur   Madrid   Melbourne   Mexico City   Mumbai   Nairobi
São Paulo   Shanghai   Singapore   Taipei   Tokyo   Toronto

and an associated company in Berlin

Published by Oxford University Press, Inc.
198 Madison Avenue, New York, New York 10016
http://www.oup-usa.org

Oxford is a registered trademark of Oxford University Press

ISBN: 0-19-514966-1

Printing number: 9 8 7 6 5 4 3 2 1

Printed in the United States of America
on acid-free paper

For our daughters
Anna, Colleen, Laura, and Meghan

Contents

PART II   CONTEMPORARY SOURCES

Preface

This book contains readings on the theory of knowledge that represent the most influential classical and contemporary philosophical approaches. It includes philosophical approaches to human knowledge from the following periods, standpoints, and groups: Ancient Greek Philosophy (Plato, Aristotle, Sextus Empiricus); Medieval Philosophy (Augustine, Aquinas); Early Modern Philosophy (Descartes, Leibniz, Locke, Berkeley, Hume, Reid, Kant); Classical Pragmatism and Anglo-American Empiricism (James, Russell, Ayer, Lewis, Carnap, Quine, Rorty); and various other influential Anglo-American philosophers (Wittgenstein, Moore, Strawson, Chisholm, Putnam, Kripke, etc.). The selections are nontechnical and readable by typical undergraduate philosophy students. Given the diversity of its selections, the book can be adapted to various philosophical perspectives and emphases.

The book's General Introduction introduces some of the major philosophical problems about human knowledge. Each of the book's main sections is introduced by a special introduction. In addition, the book includes bibliographies corresponding to each of its main sections. Consequently, the book will serve as a comprehensive textbook for any academic course, undergraduate or graduate, that deals with the major philosophical approaches to human knowledge.

The first and second editions of this book benefited from suggestions from many people, including William P. Alston, Alvin I. Goldman, Mark Henninger, Brian McLaughlin, Alfred Mele, Jeffrey Tlumak, and Frank Yartz. This third edition benefited, in addition, from comments from several referees for Oxford University Press. Our research assistant at Loyola University of Chicago, Blaine Swen, provided very helpful services in the preparation of the manuscript. We thank all these people and the Oxford editorial staff, especially Robert Miller, Senior Philosophy Editor. Loyola University of Chicago supplied an excellent environment for work on this edition.

Chicago, Illinois   P.K.M.
                                                                                                         A.v.d.N.

General Introduction

Human Knowledge: Its Nature, Sources, and Limits

Paul K. Moser and Arnold vander Nat

This General Introduction will identify some of the central concepts and problems of the theory of knowledge, that is, epistemology. Its aim will be not so much to suggest answers to the main questions of epistemology as to raise these questions and to draw some important distinctions for an adequate epistemology.

Epistemologists typically investigate such general questions as: (i) What is human knowledge? Specifically, what are its essential components? (ii) What are the sources, or origins, of human knowledge? Does all human knowledge originate in sensation, or does some of it originate independently of sensory experience? In short, *how* do we know anything? (iii) What is the scope, or extent, of human knowledge? *Can* we have knowledge? If so, *does* anyone actually have it? In addition, is all human knowledge restricted to what is currently perceived? Can we have knowledge of the past, the future, or the unperceived present? Such questions about the nature, sources, and limits of human knowledge motivate epistemology, past and present.

The traditional view of human propositional knowledge, originating in Plato's *Meno* and *Theaetetus*, acknowledges three essential, or required, components of such knowledge. These components are captured by the view that knowledge is, inherently, justified true belief. The following section presents various approaches to the belief, truth, and justification components of knowledge.

I. THE NATURE OF KNOWLEDGE

Philosophers ordinarily distinguish different kinds of human knowledge: including empirical (or, a posteriori) knowledge, nonempirical (or, a priori) knowledge, knowledge by description (a sort of propositional knowledge), knowledge by acquaintance (a sort of nonpropositional knowledge), and knowledge of *how* to do something. Some philosophers, however, argue that certain of these alleged kinds of knowledge (for example, a priori knowledge) simply do not exist, or that some are reducible to more basic kinds (for instance, that knowing how is reducible to propositional knowledge *that* something is the case). We shall briefly characterize some of the kinds of knowledge in question.

Empirical (or, a posteriori) knowledge depends for its evidence, or justification, on sensory experience. Nonempirical (or, a priori) knowledge, in contrast, depends for its evidence not

1

on sensory experience, but solely on what Kant and others have called "pure reason" or "pure understanding." Contemporary understanding of the distinction between a priori and a posteriori knowledge comes mainly from Kant's *Critique of Pure Reason* (1781), but versions of the distinction precede Kant in the writings of, for example, Leibniz and Hume.

Philosophers do not share a uniform account of the actual conditions under which sensory experience yields the kind of evidence appropriate to empirical knowledge. Similarly, they lack a uniform account of the specific essential conditions for nonempirical knowledge. Knowledge of physical objects is, however, a standard example of empirical knowledge, whereas knowledge of logical and mathematical truths is a standard instance of nonempirical knowledge. Our knowledge of logical and mathematical truth apparently does not depend for its evidence on sensory experience. The relevant philosophical problem, however, is to explain exactly how one can come to have justified belief and knowledge (as at least justified true belief) independently of evidence from sensory experience. We shall discuss this matter in a later section on the sources of knowledge.

Bertrand Russell, in his selection in Part II, distinguishes propositional knowledge by description from nonpropositional knowledge by acquaintance. He also distinguishes knowledge of *truths* (that is, true propositions) from knowledge of *things* (that is, nonpropositional objects). Knowledge of things can be either knowledge of things by acquaintance or knowledge of things by description. Knowledge by description essentially involves knowledge of a truth, that is, knowledge *that* something is the case. Knowledge by acquaintance, in contrast, is based on direct nonpropositional awareness of something and does not essentially involve knowledge of a truth. You are acquainted, for instance, with the color of these printed words as you read them, and, more generally, with the perceptual features of physical objects when you attend to them. The familiar notion of knowing a *person* seems equivalent neither to Russell's notion of knowledge by acquaintance nor his notion of knowledge by description. Knowing a person, as typically understood, essentially involves both an acquaintance with a person and knowledge of some truths about that person.

This General Introduction focuses on propositional knowledge, knowledge *that* something is the case. Philosophers traditionally have held that the various sorts of propositional knowledge have a common core of necessary features. We turn now to such features.

1. The Belief Condition

Knowledge and belief are related to one another straightforwardly. Knowledge requires belief, but belief does not require knowledge. We ordinarily deny that someone can know, for example, that there are nine planets without believing this. Sometimes, however, people believe things that they do not know or that are even false. Knowledge is belief of a special kind, belief satisfying certain conditions. These necessary conditions for knowledge, on the traditional approach, are the *truth* of what is believed and the *justification*, or evidence, for what is believed.

Our main concern, we noted, is with *propositional knowledge*, that is, knowing that something is the case: knowing, for example, that there are nine planets. Correspondingly, our main concern is with *propositional belief*: belief, for example, that there are nine planets. Talk of *propositional belief* suggests a view that belief is something *related* to an *object* of belief, a proposition. Mere terminological choice cannot, however, decide issues about what belief actually is. Since an account of the nature of belief is a complicated matter, we shall have to be content here with presenting only some of the important relevant distinctions.

Philosophers often distinguish *occurrent* belief from *standing*, or *nonoccurrent*, belief. Occurrent belief, on a straightforward construal, requires one's current assent to the proposition believed. If the assent is conscious, the belief is an *overt*, or *explicit*, occurrent belief; if the assent is unconscious, the belief is an *implicit* occurrent belief. For example, we might consciously consider whether the book before us is ours and conclude that it is. We then have an overt occurrent belief that the book before us is ours. In contrast, we might be engrossed in reading a book and reflexively reach to turn the page. We then have the implicit occurrent belief that we have arrived at the bottom of the page and there is additional material to be read on the next page. The latter belief is implicit, as our overt beliefs are here concerned just with what we are reading. Much of the time, apparently, we hold implicit and overt occurrent beliefs.

Not all our beliefs are occurrent beliefs, whether overt or implicit. We believe, for example, that the Earth is round and that $2+2=4$. Such beliefs are rarely occurrent, but are typically *standing* beliefs: They are beliefs that do not essentially involve current assent, either overt or implicit, to the propositions believed. Given all that one has learned and not forgotten since birth, one's set of standing beliefs is usually large. Standing beliefs are not implicit occurrent beliefs, as one is capable of entertaining only a very limited number of beliefs at any given time. One consideration in favor of standing beliefs is that we do not cease to believe that $2+2=4$, for instance, merely because we now happen to be thinking of something else.

What exactly are beliefs? There are two noteworthy views on this matter: a *dispositional view* and a *state-object view*. The dispositional view is that beliefs are just *dispositions to behave in a certain way*. Two leading proponents of this view are Charles Peirce and Gilbert Ryle. Believing that the drink before me is poisoned is, on the dispositional view, just to be disposed to act in a manner appropriate to its being poisoned: for example, to be disposed to avoid drinking the beverage at all cost and to prevent others from drinking it too.

The dispositional view is arguably commendable to the extent that it agrees with what we actually hold true of beliefs. We all have a great many dispositions to behave in certain ways; as a result, our actions are fairly predictable, at least in general terms. Identifying beliefs with dispositions to behave gives beliefs a degree of concreteness that on another view they might lack. If, furthermore, beliefs are just dispositions to act, then one would expect beliefs to figure in the motivating forces of our actions; and they apparently do. One would also expect standing beliefs to be nonoccurrent in much the way that dispositions are often unactivated, and they typically are.

The view that beliefs are just dispositions to act faces a notable difficulty. We normally appeal to our beliefs, including their propositional content indicated by a "that" clause, to *explain* why we do what we do. We say, for instance, that Smith drank the beverage *because* he believed that he was thirsty and *because* he believed that drinking it would quench his thirst without causing harm. Given the dispositional view, one will propose, correspondingly, that Smith drank the beverage because doing so was part of a disposition of his to behave in certain ways. The latter proposal fails, however, to account for the role of the relevant propositional content in Smith's behavior: namely, the belief-content that he, Smith, was thirsty, and that drinking the beverage would quench his thirst. Explanation of actions by means of beliefs makes crucial reference to propositional content, but the dispositional view of belief does not accommodate such explanation. In omitting propositional content, the dispositional view omits what seems crucial to beliefs and their role in the explanation of actions.

We can illustrate the problem by noting that the actions we are disposed to take, when we have a belief, should be *appropriate* to the belief. Whether our actions are thus appropriate depends on what our beliefs are *about*, what their propositional content is. Jones, for example, knowingly drank the poisoned beverage, appropriately, because she believed that an antidote was readily available and that this behavior would impress her friends. It seems that for explanatory purposes a dispositional account of belief must make reference to the very sort of *belief-content* it aims to omit. At a minimum, proponents of the dispositional view owe us an account of how this problem is avoidable.

The second noteworthy view about the nature of belief is the *state-object view*. Belief, on this view, consists of a special relation between a person and an *object of belief*. There is, on the one hand, a person's state of believing (sometimes unmanifested), and on the other, an object of belief—what is believed. To believe that the Earth is round, on the present view, is to be related in a special manner to a particular object of belief. What, however, *is* this object of belief? Furthermore, what exactly is the special relation in question?

The objects of belief, according to a prominent view stemming from Gottlob Frege, are *abstract propositions*. Abstract propositions, on this view, are nonphysical entities that exist independently of anyone's thinking of them. They are thus similar to numbers and other mathematical objects as portrayed by Platonists. The special relation of believing, according to a prominent view, is a certain *propositional attitude*, involving some degree of confidence toward the relevant propositional object of belief. Leading proponents of such a variation on the state-object view include Frege, Bertrand Russell, and G. E. Moore.[1] This variation is compatible with the general view that believing is an attitude directed toward an object of belief. It provides, in addition, an answer to part of the problem of how two persons—even persons separated by a long period of time—can believe *the same thing*: for example, that the Earth is round. Each person has *access* to one and the same abstract proposition, and each can have the attitude of believing toward that proposition.

Some noteworthy difficulties remain. One problem concerns the supposed realm of abstract nonphysical propositions, which many proponents regard as eternal, infinite in number, and accessible by a mere act of the mind. Some philosophers, especially those with physicalist inclinations, have doubts about the existence of such a realm, and they regard the presumed special relation of believers to that Platonic realm as mysterious at best. The view in question bears on the problem of the intersubjectivity of belief, but it needs an account that adds to its intelligibility and plausibility, thereby removing its mystery.

An alternative view is that the objects of belief are *sentences*. Proponents of this view include Rudolf Carnap, Israel Scheffler, and W. V. Quine.[2] Let us distinguish between a sentence *token* and a sentence *type*. A sentence token is just the concrete physical sentence resulting from someone's speaking or writing at a particular time. A sentence type, in contrast, is the abstract class of all such sentence utterances or inscriptions that, roughly speaking, have the same form. Each utterance of "It is hot," for example, is a member of the abstract class of all such utterances, and is thus a token of that sentence type.

If the objects of belief are sentence tokens, the belief relation between a person and an object of belief will not be automatically problematic. Concrete physical occurrences are the sort of things that one can be intelligibly related to in various ways, for example, causally. There is, however, a difficulty facing this view. If the objects of belief are concrete inscriptions and utterances, then a person not now related to such tokens does not currently believe *anything*; for there is then no object of belief for that person. This is a troublesome result, on the assumption that there can be beliefs in the absence of physical inscriptions and utterances.

Perhaps the objects of belief are sentence *types*. The difficulty at hand would be avoidable in that case. Even if a person is not now related to a particular inscription or utterance, an abstract sentence-type can still be the object of belief if the person bears a belief relation to it. Do abstract sentence-types, however, actually exist? If so, can a person have a belief relation to such an abstract entity? In particular, can one have such a belief relation without having a similar relation to a physical *token* of the relevant type? If not, the presumed role of abstract sentence *types* is perhaps eliminable.

Another problem confronts the view that objects of belief are sentence types. Many people who do not speak English evidently share some of our beliefs, for example, the belief that the Earth is round. The sentence type *The Earth is round* is apparently different from the sentence type *La terre est ronde*. Perhaps, then, one should either deny that a French-speaking person believes that the Earth is round or enlarge the class of tokens that belong to a sentence type. What, however, would be the criterion for augmenting sentence types? Can we include the motions of someone who speaks a sign language? What of mere grammatical variations, including those characterizing familiar synonymous sentences? Such cases may require a criterion about *expressing the same proposition*—something sentential theories of belief aim to avoid.

Let us turn to a traditional view on the objects of belief, a view suggested by Aristotle, certain medieval scholastics, Descartes, Locke, Hume, Kant, Noam Chomsky, and Jerry Fodor. This view takes the objects of belief to be *mental propositions* that are different from abstract propositions. They are the *thoughts* we think as we go about our daily business—or even when we do nothing at all. Sometimes we *express* our thoughts in words or in some other manner, but usually our thoughts are unexpressed. Mental propositions are private objects in that they belong to the mental life of an individual and have no existence apart from it.

The mental-propositions view can account for the distinction between occurrent and standing beliefs by identifying standing beliefs with mental propositions *stored in memory*. Unlike the dispositional view, it can accommodate the common opinion that we act as we do because we believe what we do. Unlike the abstract-object view, the mental-propositions view avoids problems involving a realm of Platonic objects existing independently of our thoughts. Because mental propositions are particulars in the mental life of a person, the belief relation between a person and an object of belief is not especially problematic. Unlike the sentential-object view, the mental-propositions view allows that the objects of belief, being particular mental propositions, can be expressed in various natural languages and manners—and may even be altogether unexpressed.

Some difficulties remain. One issue concerns what exactly mental propositions are. The reply that they are thoughts does not help, because a similar unanswered issue applies to thoughts: What exactly are thoughts? The private nature of mental propositions raises another question: If mental propositions are the private thoughts of an individual, how can we account for the presumed fact that some people believe *the same thing*? In what way, specifically, can two people have the same private thought (or even similar private thoughts)? A related question is: How can there be verbal communication between individuals if thoughts are private? (Wittgenstein raised the latter question, among others, in his discussion of private languages.)

One might distinguish between mental-proposition *tokens* and *types*, while acknowledging that the objects of belief are mental-proposition tokens and that two people *believe the same thing* if the objects of their beliefs belong to the same mental-proposition type. Believing the same thing thus involves type identity of belief, not token identity. The objects of belief here are not abstract types; so the belief relation is less problematic than that characterized by some Platonic views. In addition, the criterion for inclusion in a mental-proposition type can avoid the problem that there are many ways to assert the same thing, at least if mental-proposition types and tokens are independent of particular manners of expression. The latter topic raises complex questions that we cannot pursue here.

We have contrasted dispositional and state-object views of belief. A state-object view is, however, compatible with the position that beliefs are, *in a way*, dispositional. A state-object view may imply that one has a disposition to act owing to one's having a belief relation to some object of belief. The belief, for instance, that there is a tiger in the next room, when conjoined with other beliefs (such as that tigers often eat people), typically generates a disposition to avoid entering the room and a disposition to warn others. The belief that there is a tiger in the next room also typically generates a disposition to *assent*, at least under appropriate circumstances, to the assertion that there is a tiger in the next room. A state-object view can acknowledge that beliefs are dispositional in those respects, but would deny that beliefs are *just* dispositions to act. Such a view, in addition, needs to maintain a distinction between dispositional believing and a mere disposition to believe.

We undertook a discussion of views on the nature of belief because belief is a necessary component of knowledge. Let us turn now to two other necessary conditions for knowledge: truth and justification.

2. The Truth Condition

You know that all college professors are brilliant only if it is *true* that all college professors are brilliant. If there is one dull college professor, you do not *know* that all college professors are brilliant. Knowledge thus has a truth requirement. It is not the case, then, that astronomers before Copernicus *knew* that the earth is flat. Since it is false that the earth is flat, nobody knows that the earth is flat. One might, however, believe—even justifiably believe—that the earth is flat; for neither mere belief nor justifiable belief requires truth. Knowledge without truth is impossible, according to the traditional conception of knowledge.

We still need an answer to Pontius Pilate's vexing question: What is truth? This question does not ask what the criteria, or standards, for discerning truth are. Criteria for discerning truth concern our ways of *finding out* what is true. Pilate's question, however, apparently concerns the nature of truth, that is, what constitutes truth. We might recast Pilate's question as: What does it mean to say that something is true? One might know what it means to say that something is true, but have no criterion enabling oneself to find out whether a particular proposition is true. We shall outline some prominent theories about what truth is, including correspondence, coherence, and pragmatic theories. (We shall use the terms "proposition" and "statement" interchangeably, even though some writers maintain a distinction.)

a. Truth and Correspondence

Since the time of Aristotle, many philosophers (including G. E. Moore, Bertrand Russell, the early Ludwig Wittgenstein, and J. L. Austin) have held that truth consists in a correspondence relation between sentence-like truth-bearers and features of the actual world. A correspondence theory of truth implies that true statements represent how the world is in virtue of their "corresponding" to some aspects of the actual world, to some actually existing situation. This is an approach to what constitutes truth, not to how we discern that a statement is true.

Proponents of a correspondence theory have faced problems in formulating an account of the kind of correspondence definitive of truth. The key issue concerns the exact sense in which a true statement—say, the statement that this is an epistemology book—*corresponds* to reality? It is difficult to pin down the relevant sense of correspondence; at least, no precise account of correspondence has come to be widely accepted by philosophers.[3] Correspondence cannot be literal "picturing," or "mirroring," of the world by true statements, because many true statements are not literal pictures of what they signify. Consider the following: true statements involving unrealized conditions ("If I were a brain surgeon, I would make more money than I do as a philosophy professor"); true statements about normative considerations ("A wealthy American ought to donate at least $10 to assist starving people overseas"); and true propositions about other sorts of special, apparently nonempirical considerations ("$2+3=5$" and "Not both P and not-P"). Such truths evidently do not literally picture what they are true of, or what makes them true. It is unclear, in any case, how exactly, or in what precise sense, they "correspond" to what they are true of. Proponents of a correspondence theory must identify the kind of correlation definitive of truths of the sorts in question.[4]

Problems concerning the nature of correspondence have led J. L. Mackie and others to endorse the following "simple" view of truth: To say that a statement is true is to say that whatever in the making of the statement is stated to obtain does obtain.[5] This view is reminiscent of Aristotle's remark, in Book IV of his *Metaphysics*, that truth is a statement of what is that it is or a statement of what is not that it is not. Mackie opposes F. P. Ramsey's influential "redundancy" view of truth, the view that the predicate "is true" is eliminable because it adds nothing to the statements to which it is applied.[6] Given the simple view, Mackie denies that the statement that S is true is nothing but a reaffirmation of the statement that S. Truth, according to the simple view, is a distinctive relation—a relation identified by the simple view—between a statement and an actual situation; and a statement that does not ascribe truth (such as S) does not automatically ascribe the truth relation in question. The simple view is a minimal correspondence theory in that it characterizes truth as relational between a statement and an actual situation.

Alfred Tarski's influential "semantic approach" to truth is, according to some philosophers, a correspondence approach to truth. Tarski introduced the following principle not as a definition of truth but as an adequacy condition that must be met by any acceptable definition of truth: X is true if and only if P (where "P" stands for a declarative sentence, and "X" stands for the name of that sentence.)[7] Given Tarski's condition, the sentence "All students are studious" is true if and only if all students are studious. What follows "if and only if" in Tarski's adequacy condition connotes an actual situation to which the relevant true sentence is appropriately related. As a result, various philosophers have regarded Tarski's condition as specifying a correspondence requirement on truth. Philosophers still disagree, however, over whether Tarski offers a correspondence approach to truth. There are, in any case, two notable differences between Tarski and Mackie on truth: Whereas Tarski restricts truth-bearers to sentences, Mackie does not; and whereas Tarski is doubtful of achieving a uniform definition for ordinary, nonformal uses of "truth," Mackie is not.

Even if we had the needed account of the correspondence definitive of truth, we would still face a difficult question in joining this account with a claim to knowledge. How can one ever know that a correspondence relation holds between a statement and the world? More specifically, how can one be justified in believing that such a relation holds? If we know that truth is correspondence, then to know that a proposition is true, we must know that a correspondence relation obtains. Does such knowledge require that we compare a proposition with the way the world is, to determine that the former corresponds to the latter? If so, must we then have, at least if we are to show that we have such knowledge, an independent means of access to the way the world is, a means that does not essentially involve acceptance of propositions about the world? Do we actually have any such means of access? Some philosophers find, on the basis of those questions, that a correspondence theory of truth raises problems when conjoined with claims to knowledge.

It is false that a correspondence relation definitive of truth will obtain only if one *knows* that this relation obtains. According to any version of the correspondence theory, a statement can be true because of its correspondence to the way things are even if no one knows that this relation obtains. The correspondence relation definitive of truth, according to correspondence theorists, is not an epistemic, knowledge-dependent relation. The previous questions arise only when one seeks, in the context of an epistemology, to determine whether a correspondence relation obtains.

b. Truth and Coherence

A coherence theory of truth attempts to characterize truth without reliance on talk of statement-world correspondence relations. According to such a theory, to say that a statement is true is to say that it "coheres" with a specific comprehensive system of statements. The general idea is that a set of statements' being suitably interconnected or systematic (that is, "coherent") is definitive of truth. This approach to truth was endorsed by Spinoza, Hegel, and Brand Blanshard, among others.[8] Blanshard explicitly identified coherence as not only a test of truth but also what is "constitutive" of truth. Logical implication, the strongest kind of coherence, is the kind of coherence to which Blanshard appealed in characterizing truth. Coherentists about truth typically regard the system of mathematical truths as offering a paradigm of a coherent system yielding truth.

A coherence theory of truth requires an explanation of what coherence is and of what kind of comprehensive system a true proposition must cohere with. The main assumption of a coherence theory of truth is that truth is a comprehensive system of interconnected statements or propositions. On the strictest notion of coherence as logical implication, the claim that a statement coheres with a set of other statements means that the truth of that statement either guarantees, or is guaranteed by, the truth of a member or members of the set.

A problem of circularity arises here if one defines "truth" in terms of coherence, and then defines "coherence" in such a way that the relevant notion of truth is presupposed. A coherentist about truth might define "coherence" by means of a list of *formal* inferences, that is, grammatically defined forms of inference (such as "If *P* then *Q*, and *P*; therefore, *Q*") that do not presuppose the notion of truth in question. We shall then need to know, however, why we should accept *those* formal inferences rather than some others, such as Affirming the Consequent. One might argue that a coherentist about truth cannot justify a list of inference forms without relying on a notion of implication that presupposes the notion of truth in question. Whatever the fate of this problem, the trademark of coherentism about truth is that it does not define "truth" in terms of a special relation between propositions (or statements) and the nonpropositional world, but rather in terms of systematic interconnectedness of propositions (or statements).

What kind of system of propositions must a true belief cohere with? Does each person's set of beliefs constitute a true-making set, that is, a system coherence with which is sufficient for truth? Many, if not most, individuals have inconsistent sets of beliefs; so an affirmative answer would have the implication that a proposition and its denial are both true. A similar implication follows from the view that a particular community's set of believed propositions qualifies as a true-making system. It would not help to restrict the view in question to those propositions agreed on by all the members of a community. We can easily imagine another community, all of whose members agree on numerous opposite propositions. Some coherentists about truth have held that a true-making system need only be *consistent*. Why, however, should a formally consistent system of propositions be regarded as definitively true-making? For any such system, we can generally construct an opposing consistent system consisting largely of denials of the members of the first system. At a minimum, coherentists owe us a list of conditions for a true-making coherent system

Coherentism about truth is not a theory about the standards for *finding out* what is true. It is a theory of the nature of truth: truth as appropriately interconnected propositions. There are some notable consequences of coherentism about truth when it is conjoined with an epistemology. An epistemology involving a coherence theory of truth, unlike one involving a correspondence theory, will not require that a knower must know that a correspondence relation holds between a proposition and the world. Given such an epistemology, one can come to know that a particular proposition is true by means of knowing that this proposition coheres with a specified comprehensive set of propositions. Why, however, should the recognition of such coherence be taken as adequate for knowledge of *how things actually are*?

It seems that the relevant comprehensive set of propositions must be intimately connected, in some determinate way, with actual states of affairs. Otherwise, truth and knowledge will be divorced from the way the world actually is. It is arguable that coherence (among propositions or beliefs) by itself is inadequate for the sort of truth required by knowledge, for such coherence by itself may have nothing to do with what is factual (as in the case of obviously far-fetched but coherent science fiction). Proponents of coherentism about truth, therefore, owe us an explanation of the essential connection between coherence and how things are. Indeed, the formulation of this explanation is a crucial problem facing coherentism about truth.

c. Truth and Pragmatic Value

According to pragmatism about truth, to say that a proposition is true is to say that it is useful in a certain way. Pragmatist theories of truth emerge from the writings of William James and John Dewey, although Charles Peirce deserves credit for founding the philosophical movement now called "pragmatism." Both James and Dewey emphasized that the kind of usefulness definitive of truth is not identical with what we ordinarily call "usefulness." In *The Meaning of Truth*, James characterized pragmatists' talk of truth as talk of the "workableness" of ideas, and added that the relevant workableness consists in the "assimilation" and "verification" of ideas. He evidently had in mind the *cognitive* usefulness of a proposition in unifying our experience of the world.[9] Peirce and Dewey identified truth with "the opinion which is fated to be ultimately agreed to by all who investigate."[10] The common theme of the pragmatist approaches of James, Peirce, and Dewey is that truth consists in a certain kind of validation or verification of ideas, and that such validation or verification determines the "pragmatic" value of an idea.

The relevant notion of cognitive usefulness is not satisfactorily elaborated by Peirce, James, or Dewey. At times they appear to identify truth with a kind of verification or "warranted assertibility." They seem to hold that any proposition suitably conducive to a unified, or coherent, account of our experience qualifies as true. In fact, they evidently assume that such conduciveness to a unified account is definitive of truth.

Many philosophers have faulted pragmatism about truth for confusing matters of justification (or, warrant) and matters of truth. Pragmatists must explain why *false* propositions (as normally so construed) cannot have impeccable pragmatic value involving their being useful in unifying our experience and even "ultimately agreed to by all who investigate." We need, in particular, an account of the alleged necessary connection between what is pragmatically valuable, in virtue of verification, and what is factual. Our ordinary use of "true" allows for validated beliefs that are, unknown to us, not actually true. The history of science offers many cases illustrating this point in favor of fallibilism about verification. Many comprehensive explanatory systems—for example, the pre-Copernican Ptolemaic model of the universe—in fact include false propositions. How, then, can one plausibly say that cognitive usefulness is definitive of truth? Pragmatists, in any case, have not offered a unified argument favoring a necessary connection between what has pragmatic value and what is factual.

A related problem is that what is cognitively use*ful* relative to one set of explanatory assumptions is often cognitively use*less* relative to a different set of assumptions. Should we say that truth, like cognitive usefulness, is relative to a set of explanatory assumptions? Many philosophers would resist an affirmative answer.

If truth is cognitive usefulness in unifying experience, then one can come to know that a proposition is true by coming to know that it is cognitively useful. Cognitive usefulness is, however, relative to a set of explanatory assumptions, and when these assumptions are false, a proposition can be cognitively useful even if false. When these assumptions are false, a person's knowledge that a proposition is cognitively useful will not automatically be sufficient for knowing that the proposition is true. Perhaps supporters of pragmatism about truth will reject the notions of truth and falsity at work here. In doing so, however, they will be offering a major departure from how we ordinarily understand truth and falsity. At a minimum, we need considerable argument supporting such a departure.

d. Kinds and Concepts of Truth

Since the time of Aristotle philosophers have distinguished between *necessary* and *contingent* truths, and since Kant's time philosophers have distinguished between *analytic* and *synthetic* truths and between *a priori* and *a posteriori* truths. A proposition is necessarily true just in case it is not possibly false. Leibniz characterized logically necessarily true propositions as propositions true *in all possible worlds*. The truths of logic and mathematics, according to many philosophers, are paradigm instances of logically necessary truths. Contingently true propositions, in contrast, are true propositions that are possibly false. Leibniz characterized these as propositions true in the actual world but not in all possible worlds. The truths of the natural sciences, according to many philosophers, are paradigm instances of contingent truths.

Analytically true propositions, according to Kant, "express nothing in the predicate but what has been already actually thought in the concept of the subject, though not so distinctly or with the same (full) consciousness" (*Prolegomena*, 2a). We might say, accordingly, that analytically true propositions are true solely in virtue of the meanings of their constituent terms. Such propositions cannot be denied without inconsistency. Two of Kant's examples of analytic truths are: "All bodies are extended" and "Gold is a yellow metal." Propositions are synthetically true, in contrast, if they are true but not analytically true, that is, not true just in virtue of the meaning of their terms. Synthetically true propositions might be true in virtue of observable situations in the world. Some paradigm instances of synthetic truths are so-called *empirical* truths, the truths of experience: "Some babies are bald" and "Some philosophers are obscure." The denial of such synthetic truths clearly does not involve inconsistency.

A priori truths are truths knowable or justifiable independently of sensory experience. The truths of logic are standard examples of truths that are a priori (and analytic and necessary, for that matter). A posteriori (or, empirical) truths are truths that can be known or justified only on the basis of sensory experience. The truths of the natural sciences are standard examples of truths that are a posteriori (and synthetic and contingent, for that matter). Saul Kripke (in his selection in Part II) and others have argued, however, that some contingent truths can be known a priori.[11]

We have, then, distinctions between necessary and contingent propositions, between analytic and synthetic propositions, and between a priori and a posteriori propositions. How exactly are these categories of propositions related? Some philosophers, including A. J. Ayer, have claimed that a proposition is a priori only if it is necessary and analytic, and that a proposition is necessary only if analytic. Kant, however, claimed that some synthetic truths "carry with them necessity, which cannot be obtained from experience" (*Prolegomena*, 2c). Some of Kant's examples come from mathematics: for instance, "A straight line is the shortest path between two points." Kant held that such synthetic truths can be known a priori, that is, solely by pure understanding and pure reason without reliance on support from particular sensory experiences. The question whether there are synthetic a priori truths is, however, still controversial among philosophers.

The analytic-synthetic distinction has been a point of dispute among contemporary philosophers since 1951, when W. V. Quine published his famous challenge to the distinction. (See Quine's "Two Dogmas of Empiricism," reprinted below.) Quine's challenge is based on arguments showing that none of the prominent accounts of analyticity (up to 1951) is ultimately satisfactory, owing to unacceptable obscurity or circularity. Since 1951 there have been numerous attempts to undercut Quine's challenge. Some of these attempts try to give clear noncircular criteria for a proposition's being analytically true, while others question the need for such clear criteria.[12]

A philosopher might be a pluralist about the nature of truth, offering different analyses and criteria for different kinds of truth. For instance, one might be a correspondence theorist concerning observational synthetic truths and a coherence theorist (or, alternatively, a pragmatist) concerning theoretical synthetic truths and analytic truths. Such a pluralistic approach would require a precise explanation of the combined theories, and its philosophical attractiveness would depend on its success in answering the questions we have raised.

Our survey of various approaches to truth suggests a general lesson. Even if philosophers can agree on some general, rather vague notion of truth, some different philosophers evidently use different specific concepts of truth: for example, correspondence, coherentist, and pragmatist concepts. This lesson supports a kind of conceptual relativism about specific notions of truth in circulation. Such relativism opposes uncritical talk of "the" notion of truth, on the ground that there evidently is no such singular thing—at least if a specific notion is at issue. Conceptual relativism does not, however, entail substantive relativism implying that whatever a person or a group believes is automatically true; it allows for nonrelativist notions of truth. Variability in notions of truth does not make mere (shared) belief a sufficient condition of actual truth. In particular, conceptual relativism about truth does not require an "anything goes" attitude toward truth.[13]

3. The Justification Condition

Knowledge, as standardly characterized, is not simply true belief. Some true beliefs result just from lucky guesswork and thus do not qualify as knowledge. A groundless conjecture, in other words, might be true and be believed by a person but still not be knowledge. Knowledge requires that a belief condition and a truth condition be satisfied, but also requires that the satisfaction of the belief condition be "appropriately related" to the satisfaction of the truth condition. This is a general way of characterizing the justification condition for knowledge. *Epistemic* justification is just the kind of justification appropriate to knowledge. A more specific characterization states that a knower must have an *adequate indication* that a known proposition is true. If such adequate indication is *evidence* indicating that a proposition is true, we have a traditional view of justification as evidence, a view suggested by Plato and Kant, among others. On this view, true beliefs qualifying as knowledge must be based on justifying reasons, or evidence.

Contemporary epistemologists acknowledge the possibility of justified false beliefs, and this view is called *fallibilism* about justification. Fallibilism allows, for instance, that the Ptolemaic astronomers before Copernicus were justified in holding their geocentric model of the universe, even though it was a false model. Justifying support for a proposition, according to most contemporary epistemologists, need not logically entail the proposition justified; it need not be such that necessarily if the justifying proposition is true, then the justified proposition is true too. When justifying support does logically entail what it justifies, *deductive* justification obtains. For instance, the propositions that *all Olympian gods are mythical* and that *Apollo is an Olympian god* can provide deductive support for my belief that Apollo is mythical. Those supporting propositions logically guarantee that my belief about Apollo is true, in that it is logically impossible for them to be true while my belief about Apollo is false.

Inductive justification does not logically entail what it justifies. It obtains when if the justifying support is true, then the justified proposition is, to some extent, *probably* true. Contemporary epistemologists do not share a uniform account of the kind of probability characteristic of inductive justification. They do agree, however, that epistemic justification is typically *defeasible* in this respect: Justifying support for a proposition for a person can cease to be justifying for that person when that person acquires additional evidence. Your justification, for example, for thinking that there is a large pool of water on the road ahead can be defeated by new evidence acquired upon approaching the relevant spot on the road.

Many philosophers hold that our beliefs about the external world, including our beliefs about household physical objects, are justified inductively and defeasibly. Some skeptics contend, in opposition, that our beliefs about the external world are unjustified, on the twofold ground that we do not have logically entailing, conclusive evidence for them, and our inductive evidence is unreliable. Contemporary nonskeptics typically concede that our ordinary beliefs about physical objects are not supported by logically conclusive evidence, but they do not share a unified response to the skeptical challenge that inductive evidence is unreliable.

Some skeptics have used a "regress argument" to contend that we are not justified in believing anything about the external, conceiving-independent world.[14] The question motivating this argument is whether (and, if so, how) we are justified in holding any belief entailing the existence of an external world, including physical objects, *on the basis of* other beliefs. Such justification of beliefs on the basis of other beliefs would involve *inferential justification*. A skeptic's use of the regress argument aims to show that each of the available accounts of inferential justification fails, and that such justification is not available.

Consider an example. While walking along the beach, we decide that swimming would be enjoyable, but that the dangers of swimming now are serious. Our belief that swimming now is dangerous gets support from other beliefs we have. We believe, in particular, that (a) local weather reports predict lightning storms today in our area, (b) there are threatening cumulonimbus clouds overhead, and (c) the local weather reports and the presence of the cumulonimbus clouds are reliable indicators of lightning in the very near future. Our belief that swimming now is dangerous gets support from our belief that (a), (b), and (c) are true. What supports (a), (b), and (c) for us? Other beliefs we have will provide support, continuing the chain of inferential justification. Part of the support for (a) might be that (d) we talked with our friends about today's weather reports. Part of the support for (b) might be our belief that (e) we apparently see dark thunderclouds overhead. Our support for (d) and (e) might be likewise inferential, thereby extending the chain of inferential justification.

The skeptic's initial worry is: If one's belief that external objects exist is supposedly justified on the basis of another belief, how is the latter, allegedly justifying belief itself justified? Is it justified by a further belief? If so, how is the latter belief itself justified? We seem threatened by an endless regress of required justifying beliefs—a regress too complex to employ in our actual everyday reasoning. We must, then, either accept the skeptical conclusion that inferential justification is unavailable or show how to handle the threatening regress.

Nonskeptical epistemologists have offered four main replies to the regress problem: infinitism, coherentism, foundationalism, and contextualism.

a. Infinitism

The first reply, *epistemic infinitism*, proposes that regresses of inferential justification are infinite, but that this does not preclude genuine justification. Our belief that swimming is dangerous now, according to this reply, would be justified by belief (a), belief (a) would be justified by belief (d), belief (d) would be justified by another belief, and so on without end. Such infinitism has attracted very few proponents, but it was supported (at least in 1868) by Charles Peirce, the founder of American pragmatism.[15] Infinitism states that inferential justification can come from an infinite regress of supporting beliefs.

Some epistemologists, including skeptics, argue that infinite chains of supposedly inferential justification cannot yield genuine justification. They claim that no matter how far back we go in an infinite regress, we find only beliefs that are *conditionally* justified: justified *if*, and *only if*, their supporting beliefs are justified. The supporting beliefs themselves are at most conditionally justified too: justified if, and only if, their supporting beliefs are justified. At every point in the endless chain, we find a belief that is *merely* conditionally justified, not actually justified.

Another consideration is that one's having an infinity of supporting beliefs apparently requires an infinite amount of time, because the formation of each of the supporting beliefs takes some time. We humans, however, do not have an infinite amount of time. It is doubtful, therefore, that our actual justification rests on infinite regresses of justifying beliefs. At a minimum, the proponent of infinite has some explaining to do.

b. Coherentism

A second nonskeptical reply to the regress problem is *epistemic coherentism*: the view that all justification is inferential and systematic in virtue of "coherence relations" among beliefs.

Inferential justification, on this view, terminates not in a single belief, but in a system or network of beliefs with which the justified proposition coheres. Epistemic coherentism denies that justification is linear in the way suggested by infinitism. Epistemic coherentism, involving a coherence theory of justification, is not the same as a coherence theory of *truth*. Coherentism about truth, as noted previously, aims to specify the meaning of "truth," or the essential nature of truth. A coherence theory of justification, in contrast, seeks to explain the kind of justification appropriate to knowledge.[16]

Proponents of epistemic coherentism must answer two questions: First, what kind of coherence is essential to justified belief? Second, what kind of belief system must a justified belief cohere with? Concerning the first question, many coherentists acknowledge logical entailment and explanation as coherence relations among beliefs. Explanatory coherence relations obtain when some of one's beliefs effectively explain why some other of one's beliefs are true. My belief that it is raining outside, for instance, might effectively explain the truth of my belief that my office windows are wet. Concerning the second question, not just any belief system will confer epistemic justification. Some belief systems, such as those consisting of science-fiction propositions, are obviously erroneous, and thus are unable to confer epistemic justification. Whatever one's answers to the previous two questions, epistemic coherentism implies that the justification of any belief depends on that belief's coherence relations to other beliefs. Coherentism is thus systematic, stressing the role of interconnectedness of beliefs in justification.

Some skeptics will ask why we should regard coherence among one's beliefs as a reliable indication of empirical truth, of how things actually are in the empirical world. A more common specific objection is the following so-called *isolation objection* to epistemic coherentism: Epistemic coherentism entails that one can be epistemically justified in accepting a contingent empirical proposition that is incompatible with, or at least improbable given, one's total empirical evidence.[17] Proponents of this objection do not restrict empirical evidence to empirical propositions believed or accepted by a person.

The isolation objection applies to epistemic coherentism once the scope of empirical evidence goes beyond the propositions believed or accepted by a person. Suppose, for example, that one's empirical evidence includes the subjective nonpropositional contents (for example, visual images) of one's *non*belief sensory awareness-states, such as one's seeming to perceive something or one's feeling a pain. If there are such contents, then they, being nonpropositional, are not among what one believes or accepts. One might accept that one is having a particular visual image, but this would not entail that the image itself is a proposition one accepts. If we include the nonpropositional contents of nonbelief sensory states in one's empirical evidence, the isolation objection will bear directly on coherence theories of justification. Coherence theories, by definition, make justification depend just on coherence relations among propositions one believes or accepts. They thus neglect the evidential significance of the nonpropositional contents of nonbelief sensory states. Proponents of coherentism have not offered a uniform resolution of the problem raised by the isolation objection.

c. Foundationalism

A third nonskeptical reply to the regress problem is *epistemic foundationalism*. Foundationalism about epistemic justification states that such justification has a two-tier structure: Some instances of justification are noninferential, or foundational, and all other instances of justification are inferential, or nonfoundational, in that they derive ultimately from foundational justification. This structural view was proposed in Aristotle's *Posterior Analytics* as a view about knowledge. It received an extreme formulation in Descartes's *Meditations*, where it is supplemented with the assumption that foundations of knowledge must be certain. In addition, foundationalism is represented, in one form or another, in the twentieth-century epistemological works of Bertrand Russell, C. I. Lewis, and Roderick Chisholm, among many others.[18]

Versions of foundationalism about justification differ on the explanation of noninferential, foundational justification and on the explanation of how justification can be transmitted from foundational beliefs to nonfoundational beliefs. Some philosophers, following Descartes, have assumed that foundational beliefs must be *certain* (for example, indubitable or infallible). That assumption underlies *radical* foundationalism, a view requiring that foundational beliefs be certain and that such beliefs guarantee the certainty or the truth of the nonfoundational beliefs they support. Two considerations explain why radical foundationalism is now unpopular. First, very few, if any, of our perceptual beliefs are certain. Second, the beliefs that might be candidates for certainty (for example, the belief that I am thinking) are insufficiently informative to guarantee the certainty or the truth of our highly specific inferential beliefs concerning the external world (for example, beliefs about physics, chemistry, and biology).[19]

Most contemporary foundationalists accept *modest* foundationalism, the view that foundational beliefs need not possess or yield certainty and need not deductively support justified nonfoundational beliefs. Foundationalists typically characterize a *noninferentially justified, foundational* belief as a belief whose epistemic justification does not derive from other beliefs; but they leave open whether the *causal* basis of foundational beliefs includes other beliefs. They typically hold, in addition, that foundationalism is an account of a belief's (or a proposition's) *having* justification for a person, not of one's *showing* that a belief has justification or is true.

Modest foundationalists have offered three main approaches to noninferential, foundational justification: (a) self-justification, (b) justification by nonbelief, nonpropositional experiences, and (c) justification by a reliable nonbelief origin of a belief. Recent proponents of self-justification have included Roderick Chisholm and C. J. Ducasse.[20] They hold that a foundational belief can justify itself, apart from any evidential support from something else. In contrast, proponents of foundational justification by nonbelief experiences disavow literal self-justification. They hold, following C. I. Lewis, that foundational perceptual beliefs can be justified by nonbelief sensory or perceptual experiences (for example, my nonbelief experience involving seeming to see a desk) that either make true, are best explained by, or otherwise support those foundational beliefs (for example, the belief that there is, or at least appears to be, a desk here).[21] Proponents of foundational justification by reliable origins hold that noninferential justification depends on nonbelief belief-forming processes (for example, perception, memory, introspection) that are truth-conducive to some extent, in virtue of tending to produce true rather than false beliefs.[22] Such *reliabilism* invokes, as a justifier, the reliability of a belief's nonbelief origin, whereas the previous view invokes the particular sensory experiences underlying a foundational belief. Despite disagreement here, proponents of modest foundationalism typically agree that noninferential justification, at least in most cases, can be defeated upon expansion of one's justified beliefs.

Wilfrid Sellars and Laurence BonJour have offered an influential argument against claims to noninferential justification.[23] They have argued that one cannot be noninferentially epistemically justified in holding any beliefs, on the ground that one is epistemically justified in holding a belief only if one has good reason to think that the belief is true. The latter ground, they claim, entails that the justification of an alleged foundational belief will actually depend on an argument of the following form:

(i)   My foundational belief that *P* has feature *F*.
(ii) Beliefs having feature *F* are likely to be true.
(iii) Hence, my foundational belief that *P* is likely to be true.

If the justification of one's foundational beliefs depends on such an argument, those beliefs will not be foundational after all. Their justification will then depend on the justification of other beliefs: the beliefs represented by the premises of the argument (i)–(iii).

The view that the justification of one's belief that P requires one's being *justified in believing* premises (i) and (ii) is too demanding. Given that requirement, you will be justified in believing that P only if you are justified in believing that your belief that P has feature F. Given those requirements, you will be justified in believing that (i) your belief that P has F only if you are justified in believing an additional proposition: that (ii) your belief that (i) has F. Given the requirements in question, we have no nonarbitrary way to block the implication that similar requirements apply not only to this latter proposition—namely, (ii)—but also to each of the ensuing infinity of required justified beliefs. We seem, however, not to have the required infinity of increasingly complex justified beliefs.

If justificational support for a belief must be accessible to the believer, that accessibility should not itself be regarded as requiring further justified belief. Current debates over *internalism* and *externalism* regarding epistemic justification concern what sort of access, if any, one must have to the support for one's justified beliefs. Internalism incorporates an accessibility requirement, of some sort, on what provides justification, whereas externalism does not. Debates about internalism and externalism are prominent in contemporary epistemology.[24]

Foundationalists must specify the conditions for noninferential justification and the conditions for the transmission of justification from foundational beliefs to inferentially justified, nonfoundational beliefs. Modest foundationalists acknowledge nondeductive, merely probabilistic connections that transfer justification. They have not, however, reached agreement on the exact nature of such connections. Some modest foundationalists hold that some kind of "inference to a best explanation" can account for transmission of justification in many cases. The belief, for example, that there is a computer before me can, in certain circumstances, provide a best explanation of various foundational beliefs about my perceptual inputs. This, however, is a controversial matter among contemporary epistemologists.

Versions of foundationalism that restrict noninferential justification to subjective beliefs about what one *seems* to see, hear, feel, smell, and taste confront a special problem. Those versions must explain how such subjective beliefs can provide justification for beliefs about conceiving-independent physical objects. Such subjective beliefs do not logically entail beliefs about physical objects. Since extensive hallucination is always possible, it is possible that one's subjective beliefs are true while the relevant beliefs about physical objects are false. This consideration challenges foundationalists endorsing *linguistic phenomenalism*, the view that statements about physical objects can be translated without loss of meaning into logically equivalent statements merely about subjective states characterized by subjective beliefs.[25] Perhaps a foundationalist can invoke a set of nondeductive relations to explain how subjective beliefs can justify beliefs about physical objects, although no set of such relations has attracted widespread acceptance from foundationalists.[26] Some versions of foundationalism allow for the noninferential justification of beliefs about physical objects, and thus avoid the problem at hand.

d. Contextualism

A fourth nonskeptical reply to the regress problem is epistemic contextualism.[27] Wittgenstein set forth a central tenet of contextualism with his claim that "at the foundation of well-founded belief lies belief that is not founded" (*On Certainty*, §253). If we construe Wittgenstein's claim as stating that at the foundation of justified beliefs lie beliefs that are unjustified, we have an alternative to infinitism, coherentism, and foundationalism. In any context of inquiry, according to contextualism, people simply assume (the acceptability of) some propositions as starting points for inquiry. These "contextually basic" propositions, while themselves lacking evidential support, can support other propositions. Contextualists emphasize that contextually basic propositions can vary from social group to social group, and from context to context— for example, from moral inquiry to physical inquiry. What functions as an unjustified justifier in one context need not in another.

Contextualism faces a problem arising from its view that unjustified beliefs can provide epistemic justification for other beliefs. We need to avoid the implausible view that just *any* unjustified belief, however obviously false or contradictory, can provide justification in certain contexts. If just any unjustified proposition can serve as a justifier, we shall be able to justify anything we want. Even if we typically take certain things for granted in certain contexts, this does not support the view that there are unjustified justifiers. Perhaps the things typically taken for granted are actually supportable by good reasons. If they are not supportable, we need some way to distinguish them from unjustified beliefs that cannot transmit justification to other beliefs. Contextualists must explain, then, how an unjustified belief—but not just any unjustified belief—can provide inferential justification for other beliefs. Contextualists have not reached agreement on the needed explanation.

In sum, the regress problem for inferential justification seems resilient. Infinitism, coherentism, foundationalism, or contextualism may provide a viable solution to the problem, but only after a resolution of the problems noted above. Many contemporary epistemologists acknowledge the importance, if not the sufficiency, of coherence relations of some sort for the justification of beliefs about the external world. Some philosophers have tried to combine a restricted coherence theory of justification with a foundationalist account of immediate justification. A coherence theory of justification has the virtue of explaining the justification of our highly theoretical beliefs, whereas foundationalism preserves the justificatory significance of our sensory states. The combining of these two theories is perhaps an effective approach to the regress problem, but we shall not pursue that topic here.

Some recent philosophers have proposed that we reject anything like the traditional justification condition for knowledge. They recommend a *causal theory of knowing* according to which you know that *P* if you believe that *P*, *P* is true, and your believing that *P* is causally produced and sustained by the fact that makes *P* true.[29] A causal theory of knowing admits of variations, but faces problems, in any manifestation, from knowledge of universal propositions. Perhaps we know, for example, that all books have been written by humans, but our believing this seems not to be causally supported by the fact that all books have been written by humans. It is questionable whether the latter fact produces any beliefs. We need an explanation of how a causal theory can account for knowledge of such universal propositions.

4. The Fourth Condition

We have seen that there is no widespread agreement on what precisely the key components of knowledge are, even if there is a considerable agreement that knowledge requires justified true belief. Traditionally, many philosophers assumed that justified true belief is sufficient as well as necessary for knowledge. This is a minority position now, mainly because of the "Gettier counterexamples" to this view. In 1963 Edmund Gettier published an influential challenge to the view that if you have a justified true belief that *P*, then you know that *P*. One of Gettier's counterexamples to this view is as follows:

> Smith and Jones have applied for the same job. Smith is justified in believing that (a) Jones will get the job, and that (b) Jones has ten coins in his pocket. On the basis of (a) and (b) Smith infers, and thus is justified in believing, that (c) the person who will get the job has ten coins in his pocket. As it turns out, Smith himself actually gets the job, and he happens to have ten coins in his pocket. So, although Smith is justified in believing the true proposition (c), Smith does not know that (c).

Gettier-style counterexamples are cases where one has a justified true belief that *P* but lacks knowledge that *P*. The Gettier problem is the problem of finding a modification of, or an alternative to, the traditional justified-true-belief analysis that avoids difficulties from Gettier-style counterexamples.

After three decades of vigorous research, contemporary epistemologists have still not come up with a widely accepted solution to the Gettier problem.[30] Many epistemologists take the main lesson of Gettier-style counterexamples to be that propositional knowledge requires a fourth condition, beyond the justification, belief, and truth conditions. Some philosophers have claimed, in opposition, that Gettier's counterexamples are defective because they rely on the false principle that *false* evidence can justify one's beliefs. There are, however, examples similar to Gettier's that do not rely on this principle. (See the selection by Richard Feldman on the Gettier problem in Part II.)

One prominent fourth condition consists of a "defeasibility condition" requiring that the justification appropriate to knowledge be "undefeated" in that an appropriate subjunctive conditional concerning defeaters of justification be true of that justification. A simple defeasibility condition requires of one's knowing that *P* that there be no true proposition, *Q*, such that if *Q* became justified for one, *P* would no longer be justified for one. If Smith knows that Jeanne removed books from the library, then Smith's coming to believe with justification that Jeanne's identical twin removed books from the library would not defeat the justification for Smith's belief regarding Jeanne herself. A different approach avoids subjunctive conditionals of that sort, claiming that propositional knowledge requires justified true belief sustained by the collective totality of actual truths. This approach requires a precise account of when justification is defeated and restored.[31]

The importance of the Gettier problem arises from the importance of a precise understanding of the nature, or the essential components, of propositional knowledge. A precise understanding of the nature of knowledge arguably requires a Gettier-resistant account of knowledge. It may be, nonetheless, that conceptual relativism applies to knowledge, that some philosophers work with different specific notions of knowledge. That hypothesis merits more attention than it has attracted from contemporary epistemologists.

II. THE SOURCES OF KNOWLEDGE

Certain propositions seem to have a privileged epistemological status. Consider the following:

(a) Every event has a cause.
(b) An object cannot be in two places at the same time.
(c) Two objects cannot be in exactly the same place at the same time.
(d) The shortest distance between two points is a straight line.
(e) Every line has one line parallel to it through a given point.
(f) Between every two points there is a spatial separation.
(g) Nihil ex nihilo fit. (Nothing comes from nothing.)
(h) Nothing can be utterly annihilated.
(i) In every change there is something permanent.
(j) Space and its objects extend in height, breadth, and width.

Perhaps such propositions are epistemologically special in that they are both a priori and nonanalytic, that is, synthetic. They are arguably a priori inasmuch as they are evidently not learned or justified on the basis of experience (in the way empirical generalizations are). They are arguably nonanalytic in that they evidently have descriptive content of a sort foreign to analytic propositions.

We need not grant, for current purposes, that propositions (a)–(j) are actually both nonanalytic and known a priori. We should consider, however, various philosophical positions seeking to explain how there could be synthetic a priori propositions. The issue is how it is *possible* that one knows nondefinitional, synthetic propositions independently of sensory experience. In short, how can there be *synthetic* a priori propositions?

Rationalists and empiricists have given opposing accounts of the propositions in question, rationalists emphasizing the role of reason, and empiricists the role of sensory experience. Let us define the *empirical use of reason* as either episodes of thinking about the objects of sensory experience or episodes of deductive or inductive reasoning from premises derived ultimately from the former episodes of thinking. Let us define the *nonempirical use of reason* as episodes of thinking other than the empirical use of reason. An inductive inference based on observation (reports) is an empirical use of reason, whereas an awareness just of the relation between certain innate ideas (if there be such) is a nonempirical use of reason.

Core Rationalism is, let us say, the following position:

(1)   We have knowledge of reality through the nonempirical use of reason.

Core Empiricism, in contrast, is the following position:

(2)   We have knowledge of reality, but we do not have such knowledge through the nonempirical use of reason.

These definitions presuppose a distinction between knowledge and knowledge *of reality*. They do not entail, however, that all knowledge arrived at by the nonempirical use of reason is a priori in its origin; they allow that some such knowledge is occasioned by sensory experience. (We discuss these points below.) Core Rationalism and Core Empiricism differ from some other characterizations of rationalism and empiricism, and will classify some philosophers contrary to some familiar schemes. Aristotle, for example, qualifies as a rationalist rather than an empiricist, and Kant ends up as an empiricist rather than a rationalist. Let us turn to different versions of Core Rationalism and Core Empiricism.[32]

a. Rationalism

Plato and other adherents of Platonism espoused a version of Core Rationalism known as *Platonic Rationalism*. They gave the following answer to the question of how a priori knowledge is possible: Reality in itself consists of Forms, that is, eternal, universal, unchanging entities accessible to reason. Reality exhibits, moreover, a rational structure arising from the logical relations among the Forms. This rational structure, like the Forms themselves, is accessible to reason. The Forms exist independently of the sensory world of material objects, the latter world being only a shadowy reflection of the real world of the Forms. Through the use of reason, we apprehend *directly* the rational structure of reality. Inasmuch as the Forms exist independently of the sensory world of material objects, this apprehension of reality is independent of sensory experience.[33]

Platonic Rationalism offers the following explanation: Propositions (a)–(j) describe the rational structure of the world of Forms. Because we have an a priori apprehension of this structure, we know a priori that these special propositions are true. We rationally intuit, for instance, the Form *Eventness* and the Form *Causality*, and we rationally intuit that these Forms are related. This intuition gives rise to the apprehension of the truth of the proposition that every event is caused. Platonic Rationalism thus postulates an immediate acquaintance, through reason, with the rational structure of reality itself. We may call this acquaintance a *rational intuition*. This intuition gives rise to the apprehension of the truth of the special propositions. Platonic Rationalism characterizes rational intuition as *a priori*, that is, independent of sensory experience.

Aristotle, Thomas Aquinas, and some other medieval scholastics held an alternative to Platonic Rationalism. Their version of Core Rationalism is *Aristotelian Rationalism*. Instead of holding the realm of Forms to be separate from the world of physical objects, this position asserts that the Forms exist *in* physical objects, as an essential part of them. The apprehension of the Forms and their interrelations through rational intuition does not occur a priori. Because the Forms cannot exist apart from physical objects, rational intuition of them is possible only through the occasion of sensory experience.[34] For example, one perceives an event through sensory experience, and rationally intuits the Forms *Eventness* and *Causality* and their relations. Such rational intuition is not possible without the occasion of such sensory experience.

Aristotelian Rationalism has affinities with Platonic Rationalism in its account of propositions (a)–(j). The apprehension of the truth of these propositions follows upon the rational intuition of a relation of Forms. An important difference between the two accounts is that Aristotelian Rationalism, unlike Platonic Rationalism, holds rational intuition to be *empirical* in requiring the occasion of sensory experience. It is consistent, however, to say that some knowledge of reality is acquired only on the occasion of sensory experience (and is thus empirical) but that such knowledge is acquired through a nonempirical use of reason (as in the case of rationally intuiting the relationships among the Forms).[35]

A third version of Core Rationalism, espoused by Descartes and Leibniz, is *Classical Rationalism*. This position reverses the order of apprehension. Rather than positing a rational intuition of universal Forms as a basis for knowledge of propositions (a)–(j), Classical Rationalism holds that we begin with a priori knowledge of such propositions. It claims, for example, that we know from the start the truth of the causal principle that every event is caused. Such knowledge, according to Classical Rationalism, gives us a priori insight into the way reality itself is structured.

How exactly can we have a priori knowledge of propositions (a)–(j)? The answer proposed by Classical Rationalism is *Concept Innatism*: Certain concepts and propositions are *innate* in us. We possess these concepts from birth, and we can apprehend a priori how they are related to each other. Relevant concepts include those of *event, cause, location, time, extension, self, substance, quality, unity, plurality, negation, necessity,* and *perfection*. If these concepts are innate, and we have an a priori apprehension of how they are related, then we also have an a priori apprehension that certain propositions containing these concepts are true. Classical Rationalism holds that beliefs based on such a priori apprehension constitute a priori knowledge. (Rationalism is distinguishable from particular implementations of it, such as Concept Innatism. We shall see that Concept Innatism is logically consistent with empiricism).

We have considered some different types of rationalism in connection with how they explain the possibility of nonanalytic a priori knowledge. Let us consider some types of empiricism.

b. Empiricism

Core Empiricism states that we cannot have knowledge of reality through the nonempirical use of reason. If we cannot have knowledge of reality through the nonempirical use of reason, then we are incapable of knowledge of reality by rational intuition or by innate universal principles. If there is any knowledge of reality, according to Core Empiricism, it derives from *sensory experience* and the empirical use of reason—and from these alone. Core Empiricism holds that we do indeed have knowledge, and characteristically it holds that we have knowledge of reality as well.

Most empiricists are *Concept Empiricists*, holding that all concepts are directly or indirectly acquired through sensory experience. All simple concepts, and many complex concepts, are evidently acquired through direct sensory experience. This includes such concepts as *purple, sweet, cat, curved, house,* and *orange juice*. Concept Empiricism implies that such complex concepts as *electricity, star, government, god, unicorn,* and *atom*, although not themselves directly acquired from experience, consist entirely of parts that are so acquired. Concept Empiricism by itself imposes no special conditions regarding the nature of concept acquisition through sensory experience.[36] It is rather a general alternative to Concept Innatism, the view that we possess certain concepts innately. Concept Empiricism and Core Empiricism, in addition, are mutually independent positions.

The strongest version of Core Empiricism is *Logical Positivism*. Its central tenet is the

Verification Principle: A nonanalytic proposition is *meaningful* if and only if it is verifiable or falsifiable solely on the basis of sensory experience.[37] The meaningfulness of analytic propositions, according to many logical positivists, is just a matter of logic or the rules of language use. Logical positivists sometimes endorse a *phenomenalist condition*: Meaningful propositions must be reducible to observational propositions concerning particulars. The relevant observational propositions must be directly verifiable or falsifiable solely by reference to phenomenal items of sensation, such as colors, shapes, tastes, sounds, smells, textures, or warmths.[38] David Hume and J. S. Mill are forerunners of twentieth-century Logical Positivism, proponents of which include Bertrand Russell, Rudolf Carnap, and A. J. Ayer.

Classical Empiricism is more moderate than Logical Positivism. It consists of Core Empiricism in conjunction with Concept Empiricism. Adherents include John Locke and most contemporary empiricists. According to Concept Empiricism, statements are meaningful if and only if their nonlogical terms express genuine concepts. All genuine concepts, according to this view, derive ultimately from sensory experience and therefore have some kind of empirical content. Meaningful statements, therefore, must have empirical content and must be confirmable or falsifiable by direct sensory experience.[39]

Classical Empiricism espouses a weakened version of the Verification Principle of Logical Positivism. It requires not that meaningful statements be reducible to observational propositions, but only that they have empirical content and can be supported or falsified through sensory experience. The weakened criterion of meaningfulness permits the entertainment of such metaphysical statements as "The world is spiritual in nature," "Matter is composed of atoms," and "The human mind is innately endowed with a language of thought" (provided that the terms used express genuine concepts). Logical Positivists reject such statements as devoid of meaning, whereas Classical Empiricists concern themselves with the empirically testable consequences of such statements.

Logical Positivism and Classical Empiricism oppose the possibility of nonanalytic a priori knowledge, affirming that only analytic propositions can be known a priori. One can imagine the opposite of any proposition that is nonanalytic; so, according to those positions, one can know such a proposition only on the basis of experience. Each of the special propositions (a)–(j), according to Logical Positivism and Classical Empiricism, either is not a priori or is analytic. Proposition (a) is not a priori, propositions (b) and (c) are analytic, and so forth.

Most empiricists are Concept Empiricists, but some empiricists are not. One form of Core Empiricism holds that some concepts are innate. Let us call this position *Nativistic Empiricism*. Immanuel Kant held this position, as do many contemporary philosophers. If certain concepts are innate, then we can affirm propositions involving just these concepts a priori, having apprehended the relationships among these concepts a priori. Can such propositions also be the objects of a priori knowledge? Even if we consider such propositions to be a priori knowable,[40] it does not follow that in fact they are. It follows only that these propositions are a priori beliefs, believed independently of any sensory experience.

Even if one were to grant that propositions (a)–(j) are known a priori, would such knowledge be *knowledge of the real world*? Classical Rationalism says yes, but Nativistic Empiricism says no. Nativistic Empiricism asserts that there are innate concepts, that some of our beliefs are therefore a priori, but that these beliefs do not constitute knowledge of the real world. According to Nativistic Empiricism, propositions (a)–(j) are cases of a priori belief, and some are even cases of knowledge, but they are not knowledge of reality. If such cases are not knowledge of reality, then what are they knowledge of? Kant held that the propositions in question are knowledge of *the world of experience*. The world of experience is such that every event is caused, and we know this. The world of experience, in addition, is such that every line has one line parallel to it through a given point, and we know this, and so on. Kant held, however, that we have no knowledge of the conceiving-independent, real world.

III. THE LIMITS OF KNOWLEDGE

A question of central importance to epistemology is: What is the *scope* of human knowledge? The more restricted we take the limits of knowledge to be, the more skeptical we are. Skepticism about the scope of knowledge comes in various forms and strengths. Two prominent types are *knowledge-skepticism* and *justification-skepticism*. Unrestricted knowledge-skepticism entails that no one knows anything, whereas unrestricted justification-skepticism entails that no one is justified in believing anything. (The points we shall make about knowledge-skepticism have direct analogues for justification-skepticism.)

The strongest form of knowledge-skepticism claims that it is *impossible*, in some sense, for us to know anything. Less extremely, a knowledge-skeptic may hold that we do not in fact know anything (granting that it is *possible* for us to know something). More moderately, a knowledge-skeptic might maintain that we do not know anything with *certainty*, construing certainty as either indubitability (immunity to doubt), infallibility (immunity to error), or irrevisability (immunity to revision). An interesting question for any variant of knowledge-skepticism is: What is the epistemic status of the skeptical claim itself? Skeptics will be threatened by self-referential inconsistency if they maintain that they *know* that their skeptical claim is true. The epistemic status of that skeptical claim, then, must be weaker than knowledge.

Many knowledge-skeptics have been less than thoroughgoing in their skepticism, having been content to doubt only a certain kind of knowledge: knowledge of the external world, knowledge of the future, or knowledge of other minds. These skeptics restrict their skepticism to a specific subject-matter, while leaving open the issue of whether we have knowledge of other areas. One advantage of such *limited* skepticism is that it can typically avoid the afore-mentioned problem of self-referential inconsistency.

Arguments in support of the various sorts of skepticism are many and diverse.[41] One skeptical argument that deserves comment is "the argument from error." This argument assumes that if your present cognitive state is indistinguishable from another state that does not qualify as knowledge (for example, a state where you were in error about something), then your present state is not actually a state of knowledge. Descartes presents a version of this argument when he questions whether there is any relevant qualitative difference between his waking perceptual states and his dream states. Skeptics deny that one can identify the relevant difference (and even that the difference exists), and therefore claim that we do not have knowledge.

Another difficult skeptical argument, originating in ancient Greece, merits attention: the Problem of the Criterion. The problem is generated by two general questions: (i) What do we know? and (ii) How do we know anything? Question (i) asks about the extent of our knowledge, while question (ii) asks about the defining criteria of knowledge. The dilemma is that without an answer to question (i) we evidently cannot answer question (ii), and without an answer to question (ii) we cannot answer question (i).

The sixteenth-century skeptic Michel de Montaigne states a version of the Problem of the Criterion as follows:

> To adjudicate [between the true and the false] among the appearances of things, we need to have a distinguishing method; to validate this method we need to have a justifying argument; but to validate this justifying argument we need the very method at issue. And there we are, going round on the wheel.[42]

Does the Problem of the Criterion show that knowledge is impossible? Some skeptics think so. The problem, in any case, raises this question: How can we specify *what* we know without having specified *how* we know, and how can we specify *how* we know without having specified *what* we know? Is there any reasonable way out of this threatening circle? This is one of the most difficult epistemological problems, and an epistemology should offer a defensible solution to it.

Contemporary epistemology lacks a widely accepted reply to the Problem of the Criterion. One influential reply, from Roderick Chisholm, rules out skepticism from the start, with the assumption that we do know some specific propositions about the external world. Chisholm endorses a *particularist* reply that begins with an answer to the question of what we know. Such a reply seems to beg a key question against the skeptic. A *methodist* reply to the Problem of the Criterion begins with an answer to the question of how we know. Such a reply risks divorcing knowledge from our considered judgments about particular cases of knowledge. It must, in any case, avoid begging key questions raised by skeptics.

Let us consider another skeptical argument.[43] Suppose that you are a *realist* claiming knowledge that external, mind-independent objects exist, and that you take such knowledge to entail that it is objectively the case that external objects exist. Suppose also that you regard yourself as having a cogently sound argument for your claim to knowledge that external objects exist.

Your argument, let us suppose, takes the following form:

1. If one's belief that *P* has feature *F*, then one knows that *P*.
2. My belief that external objects exist has *F*.
3. Hence, I know that external objects exist.

Even critics of realism can grant premise 1, if only for the sake of argument. Premise 1 may be an implication of what a realist *means* by "knows that *P*".

Feature *F* can incorporate any of a number of familiar well-foundedness (or, justifiedness) properties: either (a) suitable doxastic coherence, (b) maximal explanatory efficacy, (c) undefeated self-evidentness, (d) consistent predictive success, (e) uncontested communal acceptance, (f) causal sustenance by such a (presumably reliable) belief-forming process as perception, memory, introspection, or testimony, (g) adequate theoretical elegance in terms of such virtuous characteristics as simplicity and comprehensiveness, (h) survival value in the evolutionary scheme of things, or (i) some combination of (a)–(h).

If knowledge involves more than objectively true belief, as it does on standard conceptions, then *F* will be a complex property, involving the property of being objectively true plus some additional property. The additional property, on standard conceptions of knowledge, incorporates a well-foundedness feature of some sort (and sometimes a no-defeaters restriction on that feature to handle the aforementioned Gettier problem). Let us call this *the well-foundedness component of F*. A well-foundedness feature serves to distinguish knowledge from true belief due simply to such a coincidental phenomenon as lucky guesswork. Such a feature may be regarded as making a belief "likely to be true" to some extent. An *internalist* well-foundedness feature is accessible—directly or indirectly—to the knower for whom it yields likelihood of truth; an *externalist* well-foundedness feature is not.

If knowledge that *P* entails that it is objectively the case—or objectively true—that *P*, the relevant kind of likelihood of truth must entail likelihood of what is objectively true, or objectively the case. Whether internalist or externalist, a well-foundedness feature must yield likelihood of what is objectively the case. It must indicate with some degree of likelihood what is the case conceiving-independently. A well-foundedness component of *F* violating this requirement will fail to distinguish knowledge from true belief due simply to lucky guesswork.

Premise 2 generates a problem motivating skepticism about realism concerning external objects. It affirms (i) that your belief that external objects exist is objectively true, and (if you hold that knowledge has a well-foundedness component) (ii) that a well-foundedness feature indicates with some degree of likelihood that external objects exist. A skeptic can raise this question:

Q1. What non-question-begging reason, if any, have we to affirm that your belief that external objects exist is objectively true?

Being a realist committed to a well-foundedness component of knowledge, you will naturally appeal to your preferred well-foundedness component of F to try to answer this question. You will answer that the satisfaction of the conditions for that well-foundedness component gives the needed reason to affirm that your belief is true.

For any well-foundedness component a realist offers, a skeptic will raise the following challenge:

Q2. What non-question-begging reason, if any, have we to affirm that the satisfaction of the conditions for that well-foundedness component of F is actually indicative, to any extent, of what is objectively the case?

Realists might reply that it is true in virtue of what they mean by "indicative of what is objectively the case" that their preferred well-foundedness component is indicative of what is objectively the case. This move uses definitional (or, conceptual) considerations to answer skeptics, but actually fails to answer their main concern.

The main skeptical concern is just this:

Q3. What non-question-begging reason, if any, have we to affirm that the satisfaction of the conditions for a preferred well-foundedness component of F—including the satisfaction of conditions definitive of what a realist means by "indicative of what is objectively the case"—is ever a genuinely reliable means of representational access to what is objectively the case?

In other words, what non-question-begging reason, if any, have we to affirm that some claim satisfying the conditions for a preferred well-foundedness component (for example, the claim that external objects exist) is actually objectively true? We can grant realists their preferred definition of "indicative of what is the case," but then raise Q3. A skeptic will raise Q3 once a realist appeals to a well-foundedness component of F.

Invoking your preferred well-foundedness component to defend realism against Q3 would be question-begging. The reliability of your preferred well-foundedness component is under question now; and begging this question offers no cogent support for realism. If, for instance, you hold that coherent belief is indicative of objective truth, you cannot now simply presume that coherent belief is indicative of objective truth. The key issue is whether coherent belief (or any similar well-foundedness component) is actually indicative of objective truth. Perhaps *given* your preferred well-foundedness component, that well-foundedness component is itself well-founded. This consideration, however, does nothing to answer Q3. Q3 asks what non-question-begging reason, if any, we have to regard your preferred well-foundedness component as ever being a reliable means to objective truth. In effect: Apart from appeal to (the reliability of) your preferred well-foundedness component, what reason have we to regard that component as ever being a reliable means to objective truth (for example, objective truth regarding your belief that external objects exist)?

Q3 allows for fallibilism about well-foundedness: the view that a well-founded belief can be false. In addition, Q3 need not assume that evidence on which a claim is well-founded must logically entail (or, deductively support) that claim; nor does it require that we take a controversial stand on purely conceptual disputes over the exact conditions for epistemic justification. These are some virtues of Q3 as a challenge to realism.

The non-question-begging reason sought by Q3 will not simply presume a realism-favoring answer to a skeptic's familiar questions about reliability. Some of these familiar questions concern the reliability, in any actual case, of our belief-forming processes (for example, perception, introspection, judgment, memory, testimony) that sometimes produce belief in the existence of external objects. Some other familiar questions concern the reliability, in any actual case, of suitably coherent, explanatorily efficacious, or predictively successful belief regarding the existence of external objects. Each of the well-foundedness properties noted previously will attract such a question about reliability from a skeptic. A skeptic will thus be unmoved by observations concerning the simplicity and comprehensiveness provided by realism about external objects. The application of Q3 will ask for a non-question-begging reason to affirm that the simplicity and comprehensiveness provided by such realism is ever a reliable means to objectively true belief. Any higher-order use of a well-foundedness component—to support a well-foundedness component—meets the same fate as first-order use; for Q3 applies equally to any higher-order use.

A skeptic does not demand that realists give a cogent argument without using any premises. That demand would be empty. The challenge is rather: Give a cogent non-question-begging reason to hold that your belief that external objects exist is a case where a belief satisfying your preferred well-foundedness component is an objectively true belief. The demand is just that realists forgo the use of *question-begging* premises—premises that beg relevant questions about reliability motivating skepticism. Q1–Q3 illustrate some standard skeptical questions. Mere soundness of argument is not at issue; cogent non-question-begging soundness is.

Skeptics can invoke a familiar epistemological consideration, if only for the sake of argument. Cognitively relevant access to anything by humans depends on such belief-forming processes as perception, introspection, judgment, memory, testimony, intuition, and common sense. Such processes are subject to question via Q3, and cannot deliver non-question-begging support for their own reliability. We cannot assume a position independent of our own cognitively relevant processes to deliver a non-question-begging indication of the reliability of those processes. This seems to be the human cognitive predicament, and no realist has shown how we can escape it. This consideration favors the conclusion that we must take skepticism seriously.

We cannot, it seems, effectively rely on our eyesight, for example, to test the objective reliability of our own eyesight. The familiar Snellen test for vision thus cannot effectively measure objectively reliable vision. The Snellen chart tests the function of the fovea, the most sensitive part of the retina. Clinical use of this chart assumes that the component letters, "E," "F," "P," "T," etc.—which subtend an angle of five minutes of arc at the eye's nodal point—can be identified "appropriately" by the "normal eye." Tests are typically given at a distance of six meters, or twenty feet. At this distance, the light rays from the chart's letters are roughly parallel, and the perceiver does not—or at least should not—have to strive to focus. If a perceiver seated six meters from the chart reads the line of letters subtending a visual angle of five minutes at six meters, we say that her vision is 6/6, or (in the foot-oriented USA) 20/20. The numerator of the fraction indicates the distance at which the test is given. The denominator denotes the distance at which the smallest letters read subtend a visual angle of five minutes.

We cannot plausibly hold without argument that 6/6 vision, by the standard of the Snellen test, qualifies as objectively reliable vision, vision conducive to objectively true visual beliefs. Testing for visual acuity relies on a standard of "normal vision" determined by reference to how the "typical human eye" actually operates in resolving the Snellen letters. The standard set by the subtending of a visual angle of five minutes arises from what is, liberally speaking, visually typical among the community of human visual perceivers. The "typical" human perceiver, loosely speaking, clearly sees—without blurring, fuzziness, or duplication—three bars of an inverted "E" when she is standing six meters from the Snellen chart. Such visual experience, according to the Snellen test, is the standard for "normal vision."

Vision normal by the Snellen standard does not obviously qualify as objectively reliable or truth-conducive in a way pertinent to skepticism about realism. Normal vision by the Snellen standard is based on an assumed statistical average concerning human visual perceivers, not on considerations purporting to indicate objective reliability of vision. A skeptic, in accord with Q3, will naturally question whether that statistical average is ever a reliable means to conceiving-independent reality. We cannot presume the reliability of our vision to provide non-question-begging reasons in favor of the reliability of our vision.

The lesson here is general: We cannot effectively rely on the deliverances of our belief-forming processes (for example, perception, introspection, judgment, memory, testimony, intuition, and common sense) to test the reliability of those processes regarding their accessing conceiving-independent facts. Appeal to the deliverances of those processes would beg the key question against an inquirer doubtful of the reliability of those deliverances and processes. The belief-forming processes in question need testing, with respect to their reliability, to provide non-question-begging support for a realist's claim to objective truth. A question-begging reason will settle nothing in the dispute between skeptics and realists.

Questions under dispute in a philosophical context cannot attract non-question-begging answers from mere presumption of the correctness of a disputed answer. If we allow such question-begging in general, we can support *any* disputed position we prefer: Simply beg the key question in any dispute regarding the preferred position. Given that strategy, argument becomes superfluous in the way circular argument is typically pointless. Question-begging strategies promote an undesirable arbitrariness in philosophical debate. They are thus rationally inconclusive relative to the questions under dispute. What is question-begging is always relative to a context of disputed issues, a context that is not necessarily universally shared.[44]

A pragmatic defense of realism in terms of a belief's overall utility will not succeed. A variation on Q3 applies directly: What non-question-begging reason, if any, have we to affirm that a belief's overall pragmatic utility is ever a genuinely reliable means of access to what is objectively the case? It does no good to note that it is pragmatically useful to regard pragmatic utility as a reliable means to objective truth. A skeptic seeks non-question-begging reasons. Given the aforementioned human cognitive predicament, we can offer little hope for the needed non-question-begging support on pragmatic grounds.

Skeptics doubtful of the correctness of realism need not be idealists holding that an individual's mental activity creates all objects. They rather can hold that we lack non-question-begging reasons to endorse—to any degree—idealism as well as realism. The burden of cogent argument is now on the realist's shoulders. A key question is whether any segment of the history of epistemology enables one to discharge that burden. The subsequent selections in epistemology serve as guideposts in the quest for an answer to this and related questions concerning human knowledge.

NOTES

1. See Frege, "Thoughts," in Nathan Salmon and Scott Soames, eds., *Propositions and Attitudes* (Oxford: Oxford University Press, 1988), pp. 33–55; and Frege, "On Sense and Reference," in Peter Geach and Max Black, eds., *Translations from the Philosophical Writings of Gottlob Frege* (Oxford: Basil Blackwell, 1960), pp. 56–78. See also Russell, "On Propositions: What They Are and How They Mean," in Russell, *Logic and Knowledge*, ed. Robert Marsh (London: Allen and Unwin, 1956), pp. 283–320; and Moore, *Some Main Problems of Philosophy* (London: Allen and Unwin, 1953), pp. 52–71, 252–260.

2. See Carnap, *Meaning and Necessity*, 2d ed. (Chicago: University of Chicago Press, 1956), pp. 53–63; Scheffler, *The Anatomy of Inquiry* (New York: Knopf, 1963), pp. 102–110; and Quine, *Word and Object* (Cambridge: MIT Press, 1960), p. 208. For some discussion, see Michael Corrado, "On Believing Inscriptions to Be True," *Philosophy and Phenomenological Research* 36 (1975), 59–73, and Paul Moser, "Types, Tokens, and Propositions: Quine's Alternative to Propositions," *Philosophy and Phenomenological Research* 44 (1984), 361–375.

3. For discussion of some alternative approaches to correspondence, see A. N. Prior, "Correspondence Theory of Truth," in *The Encyclopedia of Philosophy*, ed. Paul Edwards (New York: Macmillan,

1967), Volume II, pp. 223–32; D. J. O'Connor, *The Correspondence Theory of Truth* (London: Hutchinson University Library, 1975); Susan Haack, *Philosophy of Logics* (Cambridge: Cambridge University Press, 1979), chapter 7; and Richard Kirkham, *Theories of Truth* (Cambridge: MIT Press, 1992), chapter 4.

4. Some correspondence theorists restrict the relevant correspondence relation to true *atomic* statements: such statements as "Gottlob is dour" and "Laura pets Fido", in terms of which nonatomic statements have their truth-values determined. See Haack, *Philosophy of Logics*, chapter 7, for discussion of this restriction.

5. See Mackie, *Truth, Probability, and Paradox* (Oxford: Clarendon Press, 1973), chapter 2. Cf. Paul Moser, *Knowledge and Evidence* (Cambridge: Cambridge University Press, 1989), pp. 23–35.

6. On Ramsey's redundancy view, see Ramsey, "Facts and Propositions," in his *The Foundations of Mathematics* (London: Routledge & Kegan Paul, 1931). Cf. Paul Horwich, *Truth* (Oxford: Basil Blackwell, 1990).

7. See Tarski, "The Semantic Conception of Truth and the Foundations of Semantics," *Philosophy and Phenomenological Research* 4 (1944), 341–75. Cf. Tarski, "The Concept of Truth in Formalized Languages," in his *Logic, Semantics, Metamathematics* (Oxford: Clarendon Press, 1956), pp. 152–278.

8. For support for the view that Spinoza and Hegel endorsed coherence theories of the nature of truth, see Ralph Walker, *The Coherence Theory of Truth* (London: Routledge, 1989), chapters 3, 5. On Blanshard's coherentism about truth, see Blanshard, *The Nature of Thought* (London: Allen and Unwin, 1939), Volume II, pp. 260, 268. For a survey of some prominent coherence accounts of truth, see Alan White, "Coherence Theory of Truth," in *The Encyclopedia of Philosophy*, Volume II, pp. 130–33, and Nicholas Rescher, *The Coherence Theory of Truth* (Oxford: Clarendon Press, 1973), chapter 1.

9. For some of the details of James' pragmatist theory of truth, see Paul Moser, "William James' Theory of Truth," *Topoi* 2 (1983), 217–22. For an alternative interpretation, see H. S. Thayer, Introduction to James' *The Meaning of Truth* (Cambridge: Harvard University Press, 1975), pp. xxvi–xlii, and idem, "James' Theory of Truth: A Reply," *Topoi* 2 (1983), 223–26.

10. Peirce, "How to Make Our Ideas Clear," in Justus Buchler, ed., *Philosophical Writings of Peirce* (New York: Dover, 1955), p. 38. Cf. Dewey, *Logic: The Theory of Inquiry* (New York: Holt, Rinehart, and Winston, 1938), p. 345. On Peirce's later views on truth, see C. J. Misak, *Truth and the End of Inquiry: A Peircean Account of Truth* (Oxford: Clarendon Press, 1991), pp. 35–45.

11. On various approaches to the a priori, see Paul Moser, ed., *A Priori Knowledge* (Oxford: Oxford University Press, 1987).

12. Some replies to Quine's challenge are: Paul Grice and P. F. Strawson, "In Defense of a Dogma," *The Philosophical Review* 65 (1956), 141–51; Hilary Putnam, "Analyticity and Apriority: Beyond Wittgenstein and Quine," in Putnam, *Realism and Reason, Philosophical Papers, Volume 3* (Cambridge: Cambridge University Press, 1983), pp. 115–38; and Paul Moser, *Philosophy After Objectivity* (New York: Oxford University Press, 1993), chapter 3.

13. For discussion of conceptual relativism about truth, see Moser, *Philosophy After Objectivity*, chapter 4.

14. See, for instance, I. T. Oakley, "An Argument for Scepticism Concerning Justified Belief," *American Philosophical Quarterly* 13 (1976), 221–28.

15. See Peirce, "Questions Concerning Certain Faculties Claimed for Man," in Philip Wiener, ed., *Charles S. Peirce: Selected Writings* (New York: Dover, 1966), pp. 15–38.

16. Recent proponents of epistemic coherentism, of one version or another, include: Wilfrid Sellars, "Epistemic Principles," in H.-N. Castañeda, ed., *Action, Knowledge, and Reality* (Indianapolis, Ind.: Bobbs-Merrill, 1975), pp. 332–48; Nicholas Rescher, *Cognitive Systematization* (Oxford: Blackwell, 1979); Keith Lehrer, *Theory of Knowledge* (Boulder, Colo.: Westview, 1990); and Laurence BonJour, *The Structure of Empirical Knowledge* (Cambridge: Harvard University Press, 1985).

17. For various approaches to the isolation objection, see Paul Moser, "Lehrer's Coherentism and the Isolation Objection," in J. W. Bender, ed., *The Current State of the Coherence Theory* (Dordrecht: Reidel, 1989), pp. 29–37.

18. For a survey and bibliography of recent work on foundationalism, see Timm Triplett, "Recent Work on Foundationalism," *American Philosophical Quarterly* 27 (1990), 93–116. See also the essay by Ernest Sosa in Part II, and Robert Audi, "Foundationalism, Coherentism, and Epistemological Dogmatism," in J. E. Tomberlin, ed., *Philosophical Perspectives, 2: Epistemology* (Atascadero, Calif.: Ridgeview, 1988), pp. 407–42.

19. For discussion of some prominent views on the certainty of beliefs, see Robert Meyers, *The Like-*

lihood of Knowledge (Dordrecht: Reidel, 1988), chapter 3; and William Alston, *Epistemic Justification* (Ithaca, N.Y.: Cornell University Press, 1989), chapters 10, 11.

20. See Chisholm, "Theory of Knowledge in America," in Chisholm, *The Foundations of Knowing* (Minneapolis: University of Minnesota Press, 1982); and Ducasse, "Propositions, Truth, and the Ultimate Criterion of Truth," in Ducasse, *Truth, Knowledge, and Causation* (London: Routledge and Kegan Paul, 1968).

21. See Lewis, *An Analysis of Knowledge and Valuation* (LaSalle, Ill.: Open Court, 1946). For variations in accord with modest foundationalism, see Alan Goldman, *Empirical Knowledge* (Berkeley: University of California Press, 1988), and Paul Moser, *Knowledge and Evidence* (Cambridge: Cambridge University Press, 1989).

22. The view that reliable belief-forming processes confer epistemic justification is called *reliabilism*. Proponents of one version or another include Alvin Goldman, *Epistemology and Cognition* (Cambridge: Harvard University Press, 1986); William Alston, *Epistemic Justification* (Ithaca, N.Y.: Cornell University Press, 1989); and Ernest Sosa, *Knowledge in Perspective* (Cambridge: Cambridge University Press, 1991).

23. See their works cited in note 16.

24. See the selection by Alston in Part II. See also Alston, *Epistemic Justification*, chapters 8, 9.

25. For discussion of various versions of phenomenalism, see James Cornman, *Perception, Common Sense, and Science* (New Haven, Conn.: Yale University Press, 1975); and Richard Fumerton, *Metaphysical and Epistemological Problems of Perception* (Lincoln: University of Nebraska Press, 1985). See also Roderick Chisholm, *Perceiving: A Philosophical Study* (Ithaca, N.Y.: Cornell University Press, 1957), pp. 189–97.

26. For support for such nondeductive relations, see Roderick Chisholm, *Theory of Knowledge*, 2d ed. (Englewood Cliffs, N.J.: Prentice Hall, 1977); and James Cornman, *Skepticism, Justification, and Explanation* (Dordrecht: Reidel, 1980).

27. Contextualism was suggested by Ludwig Wittgenstein's *On Certainty* (New York: Harper and Row, 1969), and formulated explicitly by David Annis, "A Contextualist Theory of Epistemic Justification," *American Philosophical Quarterly* 15 (1978), 213–19 (reprinted in Part II). Another influential proponent of contextualism is Richard Rorty, *Philosophy and the Mirror of Nature* (Princeton, N.J.: Princeton University Press, 1979). For discussion of Rorty's contextualism, see Moser, *Knowledge and Evidence*, chapter 4; and Sosa, *Knowledge in Perspective*, chapter 6.

28. See, for example, James Cornman, *Skepticism, Justification, and Explanation* (Dordrecht: Reidel, 1980).

29. For one of the first causal theories, see Alvin Goldman, "A Causal Theory of Knowing," *The Journal of Philosophy* 64 (1976), 357–72.

30. For a survey and an assessment of many recent efforts to handle Gettier's counterexamples, see Robert Shope, *The Analysis of Knowing* (Princeton, N.J.: Princeton University Press, 1983). See also the selection by John Pollock in Part II; and Robert Shope, "Conditions and Analyses of Knowledge," in Paul K. Moser, ed., *The Oxford Handbook of Epistemology* (New York: Oxford University Press, 2003).

31. For relevant discussion, see Moser, *Knowledge and Evidence*, chapter 6. The approach there has affinities with the selection by Pollock in Part II.

32. Both Core Rationalism and Core Empiricism are versions of *antiskepticism*, the position that it is indeed possible to know certain things, and that generally people in fact do have some knowledge. This position does not rule out a partial skepticism with respect to certain kinds of knowledge. Plato, for example, was skeptical with respect to empirical knowledge, and Kant was skeptical with respect to knowledge of the external world. We shall return to the topic of skepticism.

33. In Plato's theory of the precognition of the Forms, the soul prior to birth communes with, or directly apprehends, the Forms and thereby comes to know the intelligible structure of reality. This apprehension is an intuition unmediated by concepts. After birth the apprehension ceases to be an immediate intuition and becomes instead a recollection.

34. Many Medievals endorsed a doctrine of *abstraction*, whereby the mind abstracts the (intelligible) Form of an object from the sensory qualities the object possesses. The Form thus abstracted elicits *concepts* in the mind.

35. It would be inappropriate to define *rationalism* as the position that we have a priori knowledge of the world, that is, knowledge independent of sensory experience. Such a definition would require that Aristotelian Rationalism be called *empiricism*. Some species of rationalism entail that sensory experience is required to occasion knowledge.

36. Compare, for instance, the moderate position of John Locke and the more radical position of David

Hume. Locke holds that our concepts arise from full-blown sensory experience, that is, from experience resulting from (as post-Kantian philosophers would put it) sensory material that the perceptual machinery of the mind has already synthesized. According to Locke, the concepts of space, time, substance, and causality are derived from such full-blown sensory experience. Hume, in contrast, attempts to derive the latter concepts from the individual sense-data entering into the construction of sensory experience.

37. That Logical Positivism entails Concept Empiricism follows from the fact that if there were innate concepts, there would be propositions consisting of them whose meaningfulness does not depend on empirical verifiability or falsifiability.

38. The defining tenet of verificationism is the so-called Principle of Verification: The sense of a proposition is the method of its (empirical) verification. Owing to the influence of Ludwig Wittgenstein and the Vienna Circle, which included Moritz Schlick, Otto Neurath, Rudolf Carnap, Kurt Gödel and others, verificationism flourished during the 1920's and 30's. Because of difficult questions about the exact nature of verification, and about how the Principle of Verification is itself verified, verificationism soon lost its appeal. On this topic, see the selection by A. J. Ayer in Part II. See also the historical discussions of verificationism in Milton Munitz, *Contemporary Analytic Philosophy* (New York: Macmillan, 1981), chapter 6, and J. Alberto Coffa, *The Semantic Tradition from Kant to Carnap: To the Vienna Station* (Cambridge: Cambridge University Press, 1991).

39. For some Concept Empiricists (namely, the Aristotelian Rationalists) the meaningfulness of propositions does not result from their having some empirical content, but results instead from the non-empirical meaning of concepts that accompany sensory experience.

40. There evidently are no examples of propositions which we consider to be self-evident and which we *consider* not to be knowledge, or which we consider to be false. That is, all such self-evident propositions are considered to be true.

41. For an overview of skeptical arguments, see Nicholas Rescher, *Scepticism: A Critical Reappraisal* (Oxford: Basil Blackwell, 1980); Peter D. Klein, *Certainty: A Refutation of Scepticism* (Minneapolis: University of Minnesota Press, 1981); and Barry Stroud, *The Significance of Philosophical Scepticism* (Oxford: Oxford University Press, 1984). See also Peter Klein, "Skepticism," in Paul K. Moser, ed., *The Oxford Handbook of Epistemology* (New York: Oxford University Press, 2003).

42. Montaigne, *The Essays of Montaigne* (New York: Modern Library, 1933) p. 544, quoted in Nicholas Rescher, *Methodological Pragmatism* (Oxford: Basil Blackwell, 1977), p. 17. Rescher's book offers a pragmatist resolution of the Problem of the Criterion. For a widely discussed alternative resolution, see Roderick Chisholm, "The Problem of the Criterion," in Chisholm, *The Foundations of Knowing* (Minneapolis: University of Minnesota Press, 1982), chapter 5. For an attempt to dissolve the problem, see Robert Amico, *The Problem of the Criterion* (Lanham, Md.: Rowman and Littlefield, 1993).

43. The argument is discussed in detail in Paul Moser, *Philosophy After Objectivity* (New York: Oxford University Press, 1993).

44. For doubts about any purely formal criterion of vicious circularity in argument, see Roy Sorensen, " '*P*, Therefore, *P*' Without Circularity," *The Journal of Philosophy* 88 (1991), 245–66.

PART I
CLASSICAL SOURCES

Greek and Medieval Sources

Western epistemology originated in ancient Greece, in the writings of Plato and Aristotle. Like various other ancient Greek philosophers, Plato and Aristotle pursued philosophical questions about the nature, sources, and limits of human knowledge. They examined issues about (a) the essential features of knowledge, (b) the origins of knowledge, and (c) the extent of knowledge.

Disclaiming knowledge of the changeable sensory realm, Plato and Aristotle restricted knowledge to the realm of immutable Forms. Plato held that the Forms occupy a realm independent of sensory objects, whereas Aristotle maintained that the Forms were instantiated by sensory objects. The following selections from Plato and Aristotle represent their views on the nature of knowledge. As an alternative to the nonskeptical accounts of Plato and Aristotle, the selection from Sextus Empiricus represents Greek skepticism at its most challenging. If the arguments presented by Sextus are sound, then the epistemological views of Plato and Aristotle are misguided, and we should be doubtful toward claims to knowledge. The constant recurrence of themes from Plato, Aristotle, and Sextus Empiricus in the subsequent history of epistemology testifies to the enduring philosophical significance of their selections included here.

The selections from Plato's *Meno*, *Phaedo*, *Republic*, and *Theaetetus* represent the most important themes in Plato's epistemology. Two of these themes are noteworthy here. First, in the *Meno*, *Phaedo*, and *Theaetetus*, Plato introduces a notion of knowledge as justified true belief, as true belief "tied down," or supported, by reason or explanation (*logos*). This notion was widely accepted in the history of epistemology (with some exceptions) until 1963 when Edmund Gettier published his influential article, "Is Justified True Belief Knowledge?" (reprinted in Part II). Second, in the *Republic*, Plato affirms that knowledge is only of what is unchangeable. Plato's view of the immutability of objects of knowledge prompted both a denial of sensory knowledge and a doctrine of knowledge of the Forms by recollection. If what is known cannot change, then knowledge of sensory objects is ruled out, as all sensory objects are changeable.

A difficult question for the supporter of Plato's view is: Why should we accept that knowledge is only of what is immutable (in particular, the Forms)? This question is not persuasively answered in Plato's writings. One might argue on Plato's behalf that only immutable things are *real*, and that knowledge is only of what is real, since knowledge is only of what is true. Such argument will lead, however, only to the question of why we should hold that only immutable things are real, or why we should deny that there are truths about changeable sensory objects. Perhaps Plato simply presumed that knowledge must be of a kind of perfect reality not subject to change.

Given his skepticism about sensory knowledge, Plato tried to explain how one can have knowledge of nonsensory Forms, Forms not residing in the world of sensory experience. The explanation in the *Meno* and the *Phaedo* relies on a theory of recollection implying that our current knowledge of such Forms as equality and rectangularity arises from our recalling knowledge of the Forms that we had acquired before our embodied existence. Plato argues, on this basis, for the pre-existence of the soul. Since our knowledge of the Forms cannot arise from present sensory experience, Plato contends, it must come from our prior existence; therefore, our souls existed before embodiment. Such an argument figured in Plato's attempt to explain *a priori* knowledge of the immutable forms.

The selections from Aristotle's *Posterior Analytics* and *De Anima* develop some of the epistemological themes introduced by Plato. Aristotle continues, for example, with the Platonic assumption that knowledge is only of what is immutable. Aristotle endorses, on the basis of this assumption, that knowledge is only of Forms. Aristotle's Forms, although immutable, are not Plato's Forms. Aristotle's Forms exist in physical objects, not in a Platonic realm independent of the sensory world. Aristotle holds that knowledge of the Forms is not itself sensory, but is always occasioned by sensory experience.

In the selections from the *De Anima*, Aristotle focuses on the nature of sensory perception, the different kinds of sensory objects, the relation between perceiving and thinking, and the role of the mind in perceptual knowledge. Aristotle draws his famous distinction between the *common sensibles* and the *special objects* of sense. The common sensibles are sensory objects perceivable by all the senses: for example, movement, rest, number, figure, magnitude. The special objects of sense are perceivable by only a single sense: for example, color by sight, sound by hearing, flavor by taste.

Aristotle draws his influential distinction between the passive and the active mind. The passive mind is the mind as *acted upon* by something capable of being thought. The active mind is the mind as that which "makes all things," the mind as that which synthesizes, analyzes, and judges. Aristotle characterizes the passive mind as the place of the Forms *potentially*, but not *actually*. The active mind, in contrast, is the place of the Forms as "abstracted" from sensory particulars (to borrow some familiar interpretive language from Thomas Aquinas). When there is perceptual knowledge due to such abstraction, according to Aristotle, the mind and the object of knowledge are "identical." The kind of identity relevant here is a topic of dispute among commentators. The epistemological views of Aristotle were, nonetheless, to have a major influence on the philosophy of Thomas Aquinas about 1500 years later.

In the selection from the *Posterior Analytics*, Aristotle aims to characterize the structure of human knowledge. He begins with an examination of the nature of knowledge acquired by argument, or demonstration. He claims that the premises of demonstrative knowledge must be true, immediate, and better known than the conclusions derived. Seeking to avoid an endless regress of required premises, Aristotle maintains that some knowledge is not demonstrative (that is, not based on premises) and that this nondemonstrative knowledge underlies our demonstrative knowledge. This view has earned Aristotle recognition as the originator of epistemic foundationalism. (See the General Introduction for discussion of foundationalism.)

Throughout the *Posterior Analytics*, Aristotle aims to distinguish genuine knowledge from mere opinion. Aristotle emphasizes that knowledge is of that which is necessary, that which could not be otherwise. (Recall Plato's view that knowledge is of only what is immutable.) Aristotle holds that to have knowledge of a thing is to know its *essence*, to know *why it is*. This view leads Aristotle to examine knowledge of causation, and to introduce his famous distinction between four sorts of causation: formal, material, efficient, and final causation.

In sum, the selections from Aristotle represent his theory of perceptual knowledge, his foundationalism, his essentialism, and his theory of causation.

In the *Outlines of Pyrrhonism*, Sextus Empiricus presents numerous arguments in support of skepticism, the view that we should suspend judgment on all matters inasmuch as conflicting judgments are equally probable. The suspending of all judgment is a state of "mental rest" where nothing is affirmed or denied. Sextus characterizes the method of skepticism as that of "opposing to every proposition an equal proposition." This involves the raising of considerations indicating that no member of a set of conflicting propositions takes precedence in virtue of superior probability.

The goal of the skeptical method is to avoid "dogmatism" and to achieve the "untroubled and tranquil" mental condition of quietude. Three arguments presented by Sextus are noteworthy, owing to their influence on the history of epistemology. First, in Chapter 15 of Book I, Sextus presents the famous regress argument in support of skepticism. The gist of the argument is that any argument adduced in support of a claim needs a further argument, and the latter argument needs another, and so on ad infinitum; consequently, we should suspend judgment on all matters inasmuch as we possess no starting point for convincing argument. Sextus suggests that the only way out of such a regress is by circular reasoning, which is as objectionable as an endless regress of reasons. Second, in Chapter 4 of Book II, Sextus presents the notorious Problem of the Criterion. He claims that in a dispute between a skeptic and a nonskeptic regarding the existence of a criterion of truth, we must possess an accepted criterion of truth in order to adjudicate the dispute, *and* we must first decide the dispute over the existence of a criterion of truth in order to arrive at the criterion needed to adjudicate the aforementioned dispute. Sextus concludes that since this dispute reduces to a form of circular reasoning, the search for a criterion of truth is impracticable. Third, in Chapter 15 of Book II, Sextus presents a skeptical argument against induction, an argument foreshadowing David Hume's famous skepticism about induction. The argument objects to any attempt to establish a universal judgment on the basis of particular instances, on the ground that such an inductive inference will rely on a review of either all or some of the particular instances. A review of only some, according to the argument, is inadequate, because some of the particulars omitted by the review may conflict with the universal judgment; and a review of all is no more helpful, as we are unable to canvass the indefinite number of relevant particulars. Sextus concludes that induction is invalid.

The *Outlines of Pyrrhonism* offers the first comprehensive defense of thoroughgoing skepticism. Even if the arguments presented by Sextus are ultimately unconvincing, they deserve attention because of their influence on the history of epistemology.

Medieval epistemology developed in the well-defined shadow of ancient Greek epistemology, particularly the epistemology of Plato and Aristotle. The following medieval selections come from Augustine and Thomas Aquinas, the leading epistemologists of the time between Sextus Empiricus and Descartes. Augustine, at the very beginning of the medieval era, opposed the epistemological views of the Greek skeptics who formed the New Academy as a continuation of Plato's earlier Academy. Aquinas, toward the end of the medieval era, developed views stemming from Aristotle's nonskeptical epistemology. Augustine devotes more effort to opposing skepticism than does Aquinas, perhaps because the issue of skepticism was more pressing during the time of Augustine than during the time of Aquinas. The later Christian medievals typically regarded skepticism as having been adequately refuted by Augustine and like-minded philosophers.

The issue of the relation between matters of reason and matters of faith was just as prominent during the time of Aquinas as it was in Augustine's day. Such Christian philosophers as Augustine and Aquinas used philosophical reasoning to support what they deemed orthodox Christian theology. In many cases it is unclear where medieval philosophers draw the line between philosophy and theology. Various commentators refer to the philosophy of Aquinas as *natural theology*. Medieval Christian philosophers were, however, sometimes careful to specify which parts of their intellectual systems came from divine revelation in the scriptures and which parts came from reasoning in support of such revelation. We can regard the latter parts as philosophy rather than theology if we wish to preserve a distinction between philosophy and theology. The following medieval selections, in any case, are decidedly epistemological and thus more philosophical than theological.

The selections from Augustine's *Contra Academicos* (*Against the Academicians*) and *De Civitas Dei* (*The City of God*) represent Augustine's major arguments against the Greek skeptics of the New Academy. Augustine characterizes the skepticism of the New Academy as the view that everything is uncertain, and that a wise person should not assent to anything. This is the sort of skepticism defend by Sextus Empiricus. In opposition to such skepticism, Augustine develops several influential arguments, two of which merit comment here. First, replying to various skeptical arguments against the reliability of sensory perception, Augustine argues that the senses are not to be blamed simply because they permit unreliable images in people who are mentally abnormal or asleep. He finds no reason to attribute what the mind of an abnormal or sleeping person fabricates to the mind of a person who is rational or awake. Augustine adds that one will not be deceived if one gives assent to the senses only to the extent that one affirms how things *appear to oneself*. He thus challenges the skeptic to refute the person who says the following: "I know that this appears white to me; I know that my hearing is delighted with this; I know that this has an agreeable odor; I know that this tastes sweet to me; I know that this feels cold to me." Second, Augustine offers an argument that foreshadows Descartes's use of the *cogito* as a starting point against the skeptic. Regarding the presumed truth that he exists, Augustine claims to have no fear of the skeptical threat, "What if you are deceived?" If he himself is deceived, Augustine explains, then he exists, since one who does not exist cannot be deceived. Augustine therefore claims certainty for the belief that he exists, and concludes that thoroughgoing skepticism has been refuted.

In the selections from the *Summa Theologiae*, Thomas Aquinas considers the following epistemological questions: (1) Does the soul know material things through the intellect? (2) Is intellectual knowledge taken from sensible things? (3) Can the intellect actually understand anything without relying on sensory images? (4) Does the intellect understand material things by abstraction from sensory images? (5) Do species (that is, intentional images) abstracted from sensory images stand in relation to the intellect as *that which is understood*? (6) Do universals have priority in intellectual knowledge? (7) Does the intellect understand by combining and separating? In answering these questions, Aquinas often compares and contrasts his views with those of Plato, Aristotle, and Augustine, and frequently elaborates favorably on positions introduced by Aristotle. Regarding the question whether intellectual knowledge is taken from sensory things, for example, Aquinas begins by restating arguments from Augustine and Plato that conclude that we cannot acquire truth from the corporeal senses. In accord with Aristotle, however, Aquinas favors the view that the beginning of our knowledge is in the senses. Denying that sensation is the complete cause of intellectual knowledge, Aquinas endorses Aristotle's suggestion that an intellectual function higher than sensation— the active mind of Aristotle's *De Anima*—makes sensory images intelligible by abstraction. The following selections from Aquinas elaborate on this Aristotelian view by specifying the role of mental images, universals, and abstraction in knowledge.

1 / Plato (c. 427–c. 347 B.C.)

MENO

MEN. Yes, Socrates: but what do you mean by saying that we do not learn, and that what we call learning is only a process of recollection? Can you teach me how this is?

SOC. I told you, Meno, just now that
82 you were a rogue, and now you ask whether I can teach you, when I am saying that there is no teaching, but only recollection; and thus you imagine that you will expose me in a contradiction.

MEN. Indeed, Socrates, I protest that I had no such intention. I only asked the question from habit; but if you can prove to me that what you say is true, I wish that you would.

SOC. It will be no easy matter, but I am willing to do my best for you. Suppose that
b you call one of your numerous attendants, whichever you like, that I may demonstrate on him.

MEN. Certainly. Come hither, boy.

SOC. He is Greek, and speaks Greek, does he not?

MEN. Yes, indeed; he was born in the house.

SOC. Attend now, and observe whether he learns of me or only remembers.

MEN. I will.

SOC. Tell me, boy, do you know that a figure like this is a square?

BOY. I do.

SOC. And you know that a square figure has these four lines equal?

BOY. Certainly.
c SOC. And these lines which I have

drawn through the middle of the square are also equal?

BOY. Yes.

SOC. A square may be of any size?

BOY. Certainly.

SOC. And if one side of the figure be two feet long, and the other side two feet, how much will the whole be? Let me explain: if in one direction the space was two feet long, and in the other direction one foot, the whole space would be two feet taken once?

BOY. Yes.

SOC. But since this side is also two d feet, there are twice two feet?

BOY. There are.

SOC. Then the square is twice two feet?

BOY. Yes.

SOC. And how many are twice two feet? Count and tell me.

BOY. Four, Socrates.

SOC. And might there not be another figure twice as large as this, but of the same kind, and having like this all the lines equal?

BOY. Yes.

SOC. And how many feet will that be?

BOY. Eight feet.

SOC. And now try and tell me the length of the line which forms the side of that double square: this is two feet—what e will that be?

BOY. Clearly, Socrates, it will be double.

1. *Meno* 81e–86b; *Phaedo,* 74a–77a, 100b–101e: *Republic,* Book VI: 507b–511e, Book VII: 514a–518d: *Theaetetus.* 187a–202d, 206c–210d from *The Dialogues of Plato,* 4th ed. translated by Benjamin Jowett (Oxford: Clarendon Press, 1953). Reprinted by permission of Oxford University Press.

SOC.   Do you observe, Meno, that I am not teaching the boy anything, but only asking him questions; and now he fancies that he knows how long a line is necessary in order to produce a figure of eight square feet; does he not?

MEN.   Yes.

SOC.   And does he really know?

MEN.   Certainly not.

SOC.   He fancies that because the square is double, the line is double?

MEN.   True.

SOC.   Now see him being brought step
83 by step to recollect in regular order. *(To the boy.)* Tell me, boy, do you assert that a double space comes from a double line? Remember that I am not speaking of an oblong, but of a figure equal every way, and twice the size of this—that is to say of eight feet; and I want to know whether you still say that a double square comes from a double line?

BOY.   Yes.

SOC.   But does this line become doubled if we add another such line here?

BOY.   Certainly.

SOC.   And four such lines, you say, will make a space containing eight feet?

BOY.   Yes.

SOC.   Let us describe such a figure: Would you not say that this is the figure of eight feet?
b   BOY.   Yes.

SOC.   And are there not these four divisions in the figure, each of which is equal to the figure of four feet?

BOY.   True.

SOC.   And is not that four times four?

BOY.   Certainly.

SOC.   And four times is not double?

BOY.   No, indeed.

SOC.   But how much?

BOY.   Four times as much.
c   SOC.   Therefore the double line, boy, has given a space, not twice, but four times as much.

BOY.   True.

SOC.   Four times four are sixteen—are they not?

BOY.   Yes.

SOC.   What line would give you a space

of eight feet—for that gives a fourfold space, of sixteen feet, does it not?

BOY.   Yes.

SOC.   And the space of four feet is made from this half line?

BOY.   Yes.

SOC.   Good; and is not a space of eight feet twice the size of this, and half the size of the other?

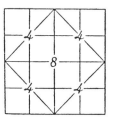

BOY.   Certainly.

SOC.   Such a space, then, will be made out of a line greater than this one, and less than that one?

BOY.   Yes; I think so.   d

SOC.   Very good; I like to hear you say what you think. And now tell me, is not this a line of two feet and that of four?

BOY.   Yes.

SOC.   Then the line which forms the side of the eight feet space ought to be more than this line of two feet, and less than the other of four feet?

BOY.   It ought.

SOC.   Try and see if you can tell me how much it will be.   e

BOY.   Three feet.

SOC.   Then if we add a half to this line of two, that will be the line of three. Here are two and there is one; and on the other side, here are two also and there is one; and that makes the figure of which you speak?

BOY.   Yes.

SOC.   But if there are three feet this way and three feet that way, the whole space will be three times three feet?

BOY.   This is evident.

SOC.   And how much are three times three feet?

BOY.   Nine.

SOC.   And what was to be the number of feet in the doubled square?

BOY.   Eight.

SOC. Then the eight foot space is not made out of a line of three feet?

BOY. No.

84 SOC. But from what line?—tell me exactly; and if you would rather not reckon, try and show me the line.

BOY. Indeed, Socrates, I do not know.

SOC. Do you see, Meno, what advances he has made in his power of recollection? He did not know at first, and he does not know now, what is the side of a figure of eight feet: but then he thought that he knew, and answered confidently as if he knew, and felt no difficulty; now he feels a difficulty, and neither knows nor fancies

b that he knows.

MEN. True.

SOC. Is he not better off in knowing his ignorance?

MEN. I think that he is.

SOC. If we have made him doubt, and given him the "torpedo's shock," have we done him any harm?

MEN. I think not.

SOC. We have certainly, as would seem, assisted him in some degree to the discovery of the truth; and now he will wish to remedy his ignorance, but then he would have been ready to tell all the world again

c and again that the double space should have a double side.

MEN. True.

SOC. But do you suppose that he would ever have started to inquire into or to learn what he fancied that he knew, though he was really ignorant of it, until he had fallen into perplexity under the idea that he did not know, and had desired to know?

MEN. I think not, Socrates.

SOC. Then he was the better for the torpedo's touch?

MEN. I think so.

SOC. Mark now the further development. I shall only ask him, and not teach

d him, and he shall share the inquiry with me; and do you watch and see if you find me telling or explaining anything to him, instead of eliciting his opinion. Tell me, boy, is not this a square of four feet which I have drawn?

BOY. Yes.

SOC. And now I add another square equal to the former one?

BOY. Yes.

SOC. And a third, which is equal to either of them?

BOY. Yes.

SOC. Suppose that we fill up the vacant corner?

BOY. Very good.

SOC. Here, then, there are four equal spaces?

BOY. Yes.   e

SOC. And how many times larger is this space than this other?

BOY. Four times.

SOC. But we wanted one only twice as large, as you will remember.

BOY. True.

SOC. Now, does not this line, reaching from corner to corner, bisect each of these 85 spaces?

BOY. Yes.

SOC. And are there not here four equal lines which contain this space?

BOY. There are.

SOC. Look and see how much this space is.

BOY. I do not understand.

SOC. Has not each interior cut off half of the four spaces?

BOY. Yes.

SOC. And how many such spaces are there in this section?

BOY. Four.

SOC. And how many in this?

BOY. Two.

SOC. And four is how many times two?

BOY. Twice.

SOC. So that this space is of how many feet?

BOY. Of eight feet.   b

SOC. And from what line do you get this figure?

BOY. From this.

SOC. That is, from the line which extends from corner to corner of the figure of four feet?

BOY. Yes.

SOC. And that is the line which the learned call the diagonal. And if this is the proper name, then you, Meno's slave, are prepared to affirm that the double space is the square of the diagonal?

BOY. Certainly, Socrates.

SOC. What do you say of him, Meno? Were not all these answers given out of his own head?

c   MEN. Yes, they were all his own.

SOC. And yet, as we were just now saying, he did not know?

MEN. True.

SOC. But still he had in him those notions of his—had he not?

MEN. Yes.

SOC. Then he who does not know may still have true notions of that which he does not know?

MEN. Apparently.

SOC. And at present these notions have just been stirred up in him, as in a dream; but if he were frequently asked the same questions, in different forms, he would d know as accurately as anyone at last?

MEN. I dare say.

SOC. Without anyone teaching him he will recover his knowledge for himself, if he is merely asked questions?

MEN. Yes.

SOC. And this spontaneous recovery of knowledge in him is recollection?

MEN. True.

SOC. And this knowledge which he now has must he not either have acquired at some time, or else possessed always?

MEN. Yes.

SOC. But if he always possessed this knowledge he would always have known; or if he has acquired the knowledge he e could not have acquired it in this life, unless he has been taught geometry. And he may be made to do the same with all geometry and every other branch of knowledge; has anyone ever taught him all this? You must know about him, if, as you say, he was born and bred in your house.

MEN. And I am certain that no one ever did teach him.

SOC. And yet he has these notions?

MEN. The fact, Socrates, is undeniable.

SOC. But if he did not acquire them in this life, then he must have had and learned 86 them at some other time?

MEN. Clearly he must.

SOC. Which must have been the time when he was not a man?

MEN. Yes.

SOC. And if there are always to be true notions in him, both while he is and while he is not a man, which only need to be awakened into knowledge by putting questions to him, his soul must remain always possessed of this knowledge; for he must always either be or not be a man.

MEN. Obviously.

SOC. And if the truth of all things al- b ways exists in the soul, then the soul is immortal. Wherefore be of good cheer, and try to discover by recollection what you do not now know, or rather what you do not remember.

PHAEDO

74   Now consider this question. We affirm, do we not, that there is such a thing as equality, not of one piece of wood or stone or similar material thing with another, but that, over and above this, there is absolute equality? Shall we say so?

Say so, yes, replied Simmias, and swear b to it, with all the confidence in life.

And do we know the nature of this absolute existence?

To be sure, he said.

And whence did we obtain our knowledge? Did we not see equalities of material things, such as pieces of wood and stones, and conceive from them the idea of an equality which is different from them? For you will acknowledge that there is a difference? Or look at the matter in another way:—Do not the same pieces of wood or stone appear to one man equal, and to another unequal?

That is certain.

c But did pure equals ever appear to you unequal? or equality the same as inequality?

Never, Socrates.

Then these equal objects are not the same with the idea of equality?

I should say, clearly not, Socrates.

And yet from these equals, although differing from the idea of equality, you obtained the knowledge of that idea?

Very true, he said.

Which might be like, or might be unlike them?

Yes.

But that makes no difference: so long as from seeing one thing you conceive another, d whether like or unlike, there must surely have been an act of recollection?

Very true.

But what would you say of equal portions of wood or other material equals? and what is the impression produced by them? Are they equals in the same sense in which absolute equality is equal? or do they fall short of this perfect equality in a measure.

Yes, he said, in a very great measure too.

And must we not allow, that when a man, looking at any object, reflects "the thing which I see aims at being like some other thing, but falls short of and cannot be like e that other thing, and is inferior," he who so reflects must have had a previous knowledge of that to which the other, although similar, was inferior?

Certainly.

And has not this been our own case in the matter of equals and of absolute equality?

Precisely.

Then we must have known equality previously to the time when we first saw the 75 material equals, and reflected that they all strive to attain absolute equality, but fall short of it?

Very true.

And we recognize also that we have only derived this conception of absolute equality, and can only derive it, from sight or touch, or from some other of the senses, which are all alike in this respect?

Yes, Socrates, for the purposes of the present argument, one of them is the same as the other.

From the senses then is derived the conception that all sensible equals aim at an absolute equality of which they fall short?

Yes. b

Then before we began to see or hear or perceive in any way, we must have had a knowledge of absolute equality, or we could not have referred to that standard the equals which are derived from the senses?—for to that they all aspire, and of that they fall short.

No other inference can be drawn from the previous statements.

And did we now begin to see and hear and have the use of our other senses as soon as we were born?

Certainly.

Then we must have acquired the knowl- c edge of equality at some previous time?

Yes.

That is to say, before we were born, I suppose?

It seems so.

And if we acquired this knowledge before we were born, and were born having the use of it, then we also knew before we were born and at the instant of birth not only the equal or the greater or the less, but all other such ideas; for we are not speaking d only of equality, but of beauty, goodness, justice, holiness, and of all which we stamp with the name of absolute being in the dialectical process, both when we ask and when we answer questions. Of all this we affirm with certainty that we acquired the knowledge before birth?

We do.

But, if after having acquired, we have not on each occasion forgotten what we acquired, then we must always come into life having this knowledge, and shall have it always as long as life lasts—for knowing is the acquiring and retaining knowledge and not losing it. Is not the loss of knowledge, Simmias, just what we call forgetting?

e   Quite true, Socrates.

But if this knowledge which we acquired before birth was lost by us at birth, and if afterwards by the use of the senses we recovered what we previously knew, will not the process which we call learning be a recovering of knowledge which is natural to us, and may not this be rightly termed recollection?

Very true.

76   So much is clear—that when we perceive something, either by the help of sight, or hearing, or some other sense, that perception can lead us to think of some other thing like or unlike which is associated with it but has been forgotten. Whence, as I was saying, one of two alternatives follows:—either we all have this knowledge at birth, and continue to know through life; or, after birth, those who are said to learn only recollect, and learning is simply recollection.

Yes, that is quite true, Socrates.

And which alternative, Simmias, do you prefer? Have we the knowledge at our birth,
b   or do we recollect afterwards things which we knew previously to our birth?

I cannot decide at the moment.

At any rate you can decide whether he who has knowledge will or will not be able to render an account of his knowledge? What do you say?

Certainly, he will.

But do you think that every man is able to give an account of the matters about which we were speaking a moment ago?

Would that they could, Socrates, but I much rather fear that tomorrow, at this time, there will no longer be anyone alive who is able to give an account of them such as ought to be given.

Then you are not of opinion, Simmias,   c
that all men know these things.

Certainly not.

They are in process of recollecting that which they learned before?

Certainly.

But when did our souls acquire this knowledge?—clearly not since we were born as men?

Certainly not.

And therefore, previously?

Yes.

Then, Simmias, our souls must also have existed without bodies before they were in the form of man, and must have had intelligence.

Unless indeed you suppose, Socrates, that all knowledge is given us at the very moment of birth; for this is the only time which remains.

Yes, my friend, but if so, when, pray, do   d
we lose it? for it is not in us when we are born—that is admitted. Do we lose it at the moment of receiving it, or if not at what other time?

No, Socrates, I perceive that I was unconsciously talking nonsense.

Then may we not say, Simmias, that if there do exist these things of which we are always talking, absolute beauty and goodness, and all that class of realities; and if to this we refer all our sensations and with this compare them, finding the realities to be   e
pre-existent and our own possession—then just as surely as these exist, so surely must our souls have existed before our birth? Otherwise our whole argument would be worthless. By an equal compulsion we must believe both that these realities exist, and that our souls existed before our birth; and if not the realities, then not the souls.

Yes, Socrates; I am convinced that there is precisely the same necessity for the one as for the other; and the argument finds a safe refuge in the position that the existence   77
of the soul before birth cannot be separated from the existence of the reality of which you speak. For there is nothing which to my mind is so patent as that beauty, goodness, and the other realities of which you were

just now speaking, exist in the fullest possible measure; and I am satisfied with the proof.

. . . .

100b There is nothing new, he said, in what I am about to tell you; but only what I have been always and everywhere repeating in the previous discussion and on other occasions: I shall try to show you the sort of causation which has occupied my thoughts. I shall have to go back to those familiar theories which are in the mouth of everyone, and first of all assume that there is an absolute beauty and goodness and greatness, and the like; grant me these and admit that they exist, and I hope to be able to show you the nature of cause, and to prove the immortality of the soul.

c Cebes said: You may proceed at once with the proof, for I grant you this.

Well, he said, then I should like to know whether you agree with me in the next step; for I cannot help thinking that if there be anything beautiful other than absolute beauty it is beautiful only in so far as it partakes of absolute beauty—and I should say the same of everything. Do you agree in this notion of the cause?

Yes, he said, I agree.

He proceeded: I no longer looked for, nor can I understand, those other ingenious causes which are alleged; and if a person says to me that the bloom of colour, or

d form, or any such thing is a source of beauty, I dismiss all that, which is only confusing to me, and simply and singly, and perhaps foolishly, hold and am assured in my own mind that nothing makes a thing beautiful but the presence or participation of beauty in whatever way or manner obtained; for as to the manner I am uncertain, but I stoutly contend that by beauty all beautiful things become beautiful. This appears to me to be the safest answer which I can give, either to myself or to another, and to this I cling, in the persuasion that this principle will never be overthrown, and that to myself or to anyone who asks the

e question, I may safely reply, That by beauty

beautiful things become beautiful. Do you not agree with me?

I do.

And that by greatness things become great and greater greater, and by smallness the less become less?

True.

Then if a person were to remark that A is taller by a head than B, and B less by a head than A, you would refuse to admit his statement, and would stoutly contend that what you mean is only that the greater is 101 greater by, and by reason of, greatness, and the less is less only by, and by reason of, smallness. I imagine you would be afraid of a counter-argument that if the greater is greater and the less less by the head, then, first, the greater is greater and the less less by the same thing; and, secondly, the greater man is greater by the head which is itself small, and so you get the monstrous absurdity that a man is great by something b small. You would be afraid of this, would you not?

Indeed I should, said Cebes, laughing.

In like manner you would think it dangerous to say that ten exceeded eight by, and by reason of, two; but would say by, and by reason of, number; or you would say that two cubits exceed one cubit not by a half, but by magnitude?—for there is the same danger in all these cases.

Very true, he said.

Again, would you not be cautious of affirming that the addition of one to one, or c the division of one, is the cause of two? And you would loudly asseverate that you know of no way in which anything comes into existence except by participation in the distinctive reality of that in which it participates, and consequently as far as you know, the only cause of two is the participation in duality—this is the way to make two, and the participation in unity is the way to make one. You would say: 'I will let alone all subtleties like these of division and addition—wiser heads than mine may answer them; inexperienced as I am, and ready to start, as the proverb says, at my own shadow, I cannot afford to give up the

d sure ground of the original postulate.' And
if anyone fastens on you there, you would
not mind him, or answer him until you
could see whether the consequences which
follow agree with one another or not, and
when you are further required to give an
account of this postulate, you would give it
in the same way, assuming some higher
postulate which seemed to you to be the
best founded, until you arrived at a satis-
e factory resting-place; but you would not
jumble together the fundamental principle
and the consequences in your reasoning,

like the eristics—at least if you wanted to
discover real existence. Not that this confusion signifies to them, who probably
never care or think about the matter at all,
for they have the wit to be well pleased
with themselves however thorough may be
the muddle of their ideas.

But you, if you are a philosopher, will
certainly do as I say.   102

What you say is most true, said Simmias
and Cebes, both speaking at once.

.   .   .   .   .   .

REPUBLIC

507 Yes, I said, but I must first come to an
b understanding with you, and remind you of
what I have mentioned in the course of this
discussion, and at many other times.

What?

The old story, that there are many beautiful things and many good. And again there
is a true beauty, a true good; and all other
things to which the term *many* has been applied, are now brought under a single idea,
and, assuming this unity, we speak of it in
every case as *that which really is*.

Very true.

The many, as we say, are seen but not
known, and the Ideas are known but not
seen.

c Exactly.

And what is the organ with which we see
the visible things?

The sight, he said.

And with the hearing, I said, we hear, and
with the other senses perceive the other objects of sense?

True.

But have you remarked that sight is by
far the most costly and complex piece of

workmanship which the artificer of the
senses ever contrived?

Not exactly, he said.

Then reflect: have the ear and voice need
of any third or additional nature in order
that the one may be able to hear and the d
other to be heard?

Nothing of the sort.

No indeed, I replied, and the same is true
of most, if not all, the other senses—you
would not say that any of them requires
such an addition?

Certainly not.

But you see that without the addition of
some other nature there is no seeing or being seen?

How do you mean?

Sight being, as I conceive, in the eyes,
and he who has eyes wanting to see; colour
being also present in the objects, still unless
there be a third nature specially adapted to
the purpose, sight, as you know, you see e
nothing and the colours will be invisible.

Of what nature are you speaking?

Of that which you term light, I replied.

True, he said.

508 Then the bond which links together the sense of sight and the power of being seen, is of an evidently nobler nature than other such bonds—unless sight is an ignoble thing?

Nay, he said, the reverse of ignoble.

And which, I said, of the gods in heaven would you say was the lord of this element? Whose is that light which makes the eye to see perfectly and the visible to appear?

I should answer, as all men would, and as you plainly expect—the sun.

May not the relation of sight to this deity be described as follows?

How?

Neither sight nor the organ in which it resides, which we call the eye, is the sun?

b No.

Yet of all the organs of sense the eye is the most like the sun?

By far the most like.

And the power which the eye possesses is a sort of effluence which is dispensed from the sun?

Exactly.

Then the sun is not sight, and the author of sight who is recognized by sight?

True, he said.

And this, you must understand, is he whom I call the child of the good, whom the good begat in his own likeness, to be in c the visible world, in relation to sight and the things of sight, what the good is in the intellectual world in relation to mind and the things of mind:

Will you be a little more explicit? he said.

Why, you know, I said, that the eyes, when a person directs them towards objects on which the light of day is no longer shining, but the moon and stars only, see dimly, d and are nearly blind; they seem to have no clearness of vision in them?

Very true.

But when they are directed towards objects on which the sun shines, they see clearly and there is sight in them?

Certainly.

And the soul is like the eye: when resting upon that on which truth and being shine, the soul perceives and understands, and is radiant with intelligence; but when turned towards the twilight and to those things which come into being and perish, then she has opinion only, and goes blinking about, and is first of one opinion and then of another, and seems to have no intelligence?

Just so.

Now, that which imparts truth to the known and the power of knowing to the e knower, is, as I would have you say, the Idea of good, and this Idea, which is the cause of science and of truth, you are to conceive as being apprehended by knowledge, and yet, fair as both truth and knowledge are, you will be right to esteem it as different from these and even fairer; and as in the previous 509 instance light and sight may be truly said to be like the sun and yet not to be the sun, so in this other sphere science and truth may be deemed to be like the good, but it is wrong to think that they are the good; the good has a place of honour yet higher.

What a wonder of beauty that must be, he said, which is the author of science and truth, and yet surpasses them in beauty; for you surely cannot mean to say that pleasure is the good?

God forbid, I replied; but may I ask you to consider the image in another point of view?

In what point of view?   b

You would say, would you not, that the sun is not only the author of visibility in all visible things, but of generation and nourishment and growth, though he himself is not generation?

Certainly.

In like manner you must say that the good not only infuses the power of being known into all things known, but also bestows upon them their being and existence, and yet the good is not existence, but lies far beyond it in dignity and power.

Glaucon said, with a ludicrous earnestness: By the light of heaven, that is far beyond indeed!   c

Yes, I said, and the exaggeration may be set down to you; for you made me utter my fancies.

And pray continue to utter them; at any rate let us hear if there is anything more to be said about the similitude of the sun.

Yes, I said, there is a great deal more.

Then omit nothing, however slight.

I expect that I shall omit a great deal, I said, but shall not do so deliberately, as far as present circumstances permit.

I hope not, he said.

d   You have to imagine, then, that there are two ruling powers, and that one of them is set over the intellectual world, the other over the visible. I do not say heaven, lest you should fancy that I am playing upon the name (οὐρανός, ὁρατός). May I suppose that you have the distinction of the visible and intelligible fixed in your mind?

I have.

Now take a line which has been cut into two unequal parts, and divide each of them again in the same proportion, and suppose the two main divisions to answer, one to the visible and the other to the intelligible, and

e   then compare the subdivisions in respect of their clearness and want of clearness, and you will find that the first section in the

510 sphere of the visible consists of images. And by images I mean, in the first place, shadows, and in the second place, reflections in water and in solid, smooth and polished bodies and the like: Do you understand?

Yes, I understand.

Imagine, now, the other section, of which this is only the resemblance, to include the animals which we see, and every thing that grows or is made.

Very good.

Would you not admit that both the sections of this division have different degrees of truth, and that the copy is to the original as the sphere of opinion is to the sphere of knowledge?

b   Most undoubtedly.

Next proceed to consider the manner in which the sphere of the intellectual is to be divided.

In what manner?

Thus:—There are two subdivisions, in the lower of which the soul, using as images those things which themselves were reflected in the former division, is forced to base its enquiry upon hypotheses, proceeding not towards a principle but towards a

conclusion; in the higher of the two, the soul proceeds *from* hypotheses, and goes up to a principle which is above hypotheses, making no use of images as in the former case, but proceeding only in and through the Ideas themselves.

I do not quite understand your meaning, he said.

Then I will try again; you will understand   c me better when I have made some preliminary remarks. You are aware that students of geometry, arithmetic, and the kindred sciences assume the odd and the even and the figures and three kinds of angles and the like in their several branches of science; these are their hypotheses, which they and everybody are supposed to know, and therefore they do not deign to give any account of them either to themselves or others; but they begin with them, and go on until they arrive at last, and in a consistent   d manner, at the solution which they set out to find?

Yes, he said, I know.

And do you not know also that although they make use of the visible forms and reason about them, they are thinking not of these, but of the ideals which they resemble; not of the figures which they draw, but of the absolute square and the absolute diameter, and so on—the forms which they draw or make, and which themselves have shadows and reflections in water, are in turn   e converted by them into images; for they are really seeking to behold the things themselves, which can only be seen with the eye of the mind?

That is true.   511

And this was what I meant by a subdivision of the intelligible, in the search after which the soul is compelled to use hypotheses; not ascending to a first principle, because she is unable to rise above the region of hypothesis, but employing now as images those objects from which the shadows below were derived, even these being deemed clear and distinct by comparison with the shadows.

I understand, he said, that you are speak-   b ing of the province of geometry and the sister arts.

And when I speak of the other division of the intelligible, you will understand me to speak of that other sort of knowledge which reason herself attains by the power of dialectic, using the hypotheses not as first principles, but literally as hypotheses—that is to say, as steps and points of departure into a world which is above hypotheses, in order that she may soar beyond them to the first principle of the whole; and clinging to this and then that which depends on this, by successive steps she descends again without c the aid of any sensible object, from Ideas, through Ideas, and in Ideas she ends.

I understand you, he replied; not perfectly, for you seem to me to be describing a task which is really tremendous; but, at any rate, I understand you to say that that part of intelligible Being, which the science of dialectic contemplates, is clearer than that which falls upon the arts, as they are termed, which take hypotheses as their principles; and though the objects are of such a kind that they must be viewed by the un-
d derstanding, and not by the senses, yet, because they start from hypotheses and do not ascend to a principle, those who contemplate them appear to you not to exercise the higher reason upon them, although when a first principle is added to them they are cognizable by the higher reason. And the habit which is concerned with geometry and the cognate sciences I suppose that you would term understanding and not reason, as being intermediate between opinion and reason.

You have quite conceived my meaning, I said; and now, corresponding to these four divisions, let there be four faculties in the soul—reason answering to the highest, un-
e derstanding to the second, faith (or conviction) to the third, and perception of shadows to the last—and let there be a scale of them, and let us suppose that the several faculties have clearness in the same degree that their objects have truth.

I understand, he replied, and give my assent, and accept your arrangement.

.   .   .   .   .   .

514   And now, I said, let me show in a figure how far our nature is enlightened or unen-

lightened:—Behold! human beings housed in an underground cave, which has a long entrance open towards the light and as wide as the interior of the cave; here they have been from their childhood, and have their legs and necks chained, so that they cannot b move and can only see before them, being prevented by the chains from turning round their heads. Above and behind them a fire is blazing at a distance, and between the fire and the prisoners there is a raised way; and you will see, if you look, a low wall built along the way, like the screen which marionette players have in front of them, over which they show the puppets.

I see.

And do you see, I said, men passing along the wall carrying all sorts of vessels, c and statues and figures of animals made of 515 wood and stone and various materials, which appear over the wall? While carrying their burdens, some of them, as you would expect, are talking, others silent.

You have shown me a strange image, and they are strange prisoners.

Like ourselves, I replied; for in the first place do you think they have seen anything of themselves, and of one another, except the shadows which the fire throws on the opposite wall of the cave?

How could they do so, he asked, if b throughout their lives they were never allowed to move their heads?

And of the objects which are being carried in like manner they would only see the shadows?

Yes, he said.

And if they were able to converse with one another, would they not suppose that the things they saw were the real things?

Very true.

And suppose further that the prison had an echo which came from the other side, would they not be sure to fancy when one of the passers-by spoke that the voice which they heard came from the passing show?

No question, he replied.

To them, I said, the truth would be liter- c ally nothing but the shadows of the images.

That is certain.

And now look again, and see in what

manner they would be released from their bonds, and cured of their error, whether the process would naturally be as follows. At first, when any of them is liberated and compelled suddenly to stand up and turn his neck round and walk and look towards the light, he will suffer sharp pains; the glare will distress him, and he will be unable to see the realities of which in his former state he had seen the shadows; and then conceive some-

d one saying to him that what he saw before was an illusion, but that now, when he is approaching nearer to being and his eye is turned towards more real existence, he has a clearer vision,—what will be his reply? And you may further imagine that his instructor is pointing to the objects as they pass and requiring him to name them,—will he not be perplexed? Will he not fancy that the shadows which he formerly saw are truer than the objects which are now shown to him.

Far truer.

e And if he is compelled to look straight at the light, will he not have a pain in his eyes which will make him turn away to take refuge in the objects of vision which he can see, and which he will conceive to be in reality clearer than the things which are now being shown to him?

True, he said.

And suppose once more, that he is reluctantly dragged up that steep and rugged ascent, and held fast until he is forced into the presence of the sun himself, is he not likely

516 to be pained and irritated? When he approaches the light his eyes will be dazzled, and he will not be able to see anything at all of what are now called realities.

Not all in a moment, he said.

He will require to grow accustomed to the sight of the upper world. And first he will see the shadows best, next the reflections of men and other objects in the water, and then the objects themselves; and, when he turned to the heavenly bodies and the heaven itself, he would find it easier to gaze upon the light of

b the moon and the stars at night than to see the sun or the light of the sun by day?

Certainly.

Last of all he will be able to see the sun, not turning aside to the illusory reflections of him in the water, but gazing directly at him in his own proper place, and contemplating him as he is.

Certainly.

He will then proceed to argue that this is he who gives the seasons and the years, and is the guardian of all that is in the visible world, and in a certain way the cause of all things which he and his fellows have been c accustomed to behold?

Clearly, he said, he would arrive at this conclusion after what he had seen.

And when he remembered his old habitation, and the wisdom of the cave and his fellow-prisoners, do you not suppose that he would felicitate himself on the change, and pity them?

Certainly, he would.

And if they were in the habit of conferring honours among themselves on those who were quickest to observe the passing shadows and to remark which of them went before and which followed after and which d were together, and who were best able from these observations to divine the future, do you think that he would be eager for such honours and glories, or envy those who attained honour and sovereignty among those men? Would he not say with Homer,

"Better to be a serf, labouring for a landless master,"

and to endure anything, rather than think as they do and live after their manner?

Yes, he said, I think that he would con- e sent to suffer anything rather than live in this miserable manner.

Imagine once more, I said, such a one coming down suddenly out of the sunlight, and being replaced in his own seat; would he not be certain to have his eyes full of darkness?

To be sure, he said.

And if there were a contest, and he had to compete in measuring the shadows with the prisoners who had never moved out of the cave, while his sight was still weak, and 517 before his eyes had become steady (and the time which would be needed to acquire this new habit of sight might be very considerable), would he not make himself ridiculous? Men would say to him that he had returned from the place above with his eyes ruined; and that it was better not even to think of ascending; and if anyone tried to loose another and lead him up to the light, let them only catch the offender, and they would put him to death.

No question, he said.

b This entire allegory, I said, you may now append, dear Glaucon, to the previous argument; the prison-house is the world of sight, the light of the fire is the power of the sun, and you will not misapprehend me if you interpret the journey upwards to be the ascent of the soul into the intellectual world according to my surmise, which, at your desire, I have expressed—whether rightly or wrongly God knows. But, whether true or false, my opinion is that in the world of knowledge the Idea of good appears last of all, and is seen only with c an effort; although, when seen, it is inferred to be the universal author of all things beautiful and right, parent of light and of the lord of light in the visible world, and the immediate and supreme source of reason and truth in the intellectual; and that this is the power upon which he who would act rationally either in public or private life must have his eye fixed.

I agree, he said, as far as I am able to understand you.

Moreover, I said, you must agree once more, and not wonder that those who attain to this vision are unwilling to take any part in human affairs; for their souls are ever d hastening into the upper world where they desire to dwell; which desire of theirs is very natural, if our allegory may be trusted.

Yes, very natural.

And is there anything surprising in one who passes from divine contemplations to the evil state of man, appearing grotesque and ridiculous; if, while his eyes are blinking and before he has become accustomed to the surrounding darkness, he is compelled to fight in courts of law, or in other places, about the images or the shadows of images of justice, and must strive against e some rival about opinions of these things which are entertained by men who have never yet seen the true justice?

Anything but surprising, he replied.

Anyone who has common sense will re- 518 member that the bewilderments of the eyes are of two kinds and arise from two causes, either from coming out of the light or from going into the light, and, judging that the soul may be affected in the same way, will not give way to foolish laughter when he sees anyone whose vision is perplexed and weak; he will first ask whether that soul of man has come out of the brighter life and is unable to see because unaccustomed to the dark, or having turned from darkness to the day is dazzled by excess of light. And he will count the one happy in his condition and state of be- b ing, and he will pity the other; or, if he have a mind to laugh at the soul which comes from below into the light, this laughter will not be quite so laughable as that which greets the soul which returns from above out of the light into the cave.

That, he said, is a very just distinction.

But then, if I am right, certain professors of education must be wrong when they say that they can put a knowledge into the soul which was not there before, like sight into c blind eyes.

They undoubtedly say this, he replied.

Whereas our argument shows that the power and capacity of learning exists in the soul already; and that just as if it were not possible to turn the eye from darkness to light without the whole body, so too the instrument of knowledge can only by the movement of the whole soul be turned from the world of becoming to that of being, and learn by degrees to endure the sight of being, and of the brightest and best of being, or in other words, of the good.   d

Very true.

And must there not be some art which will show how the conversation can be affected in the easiest and quickest manner; an art which will not implant the faculty of sight, for that exists already, but will set it straight when it has been turned in the wrong direction, and is looking away from the truth?

. . . .

THEAETETUS

187   SOC.   But the original aim of our discussion was to find out rather what knowledge is than what it is not; at the same time
we have made some progress, for we no
longer seek for knowledge in perception at
all, but in that other process, however
called, in which the mind is alone and engaged with being.

THEAET.   All that, Socrates, if I am not
mistaken, is called thinking or opining.

b   SOC.   You conceive truly. And now, my
friend, please to begin again at this point;
and having wiped out of your memory all
that has proceded, see if you have arrived
at any clearer view, and once more say what
is knowledge.

THEAET.   I cannot say, Socrates, that
all opinion is knowledge, because there may
be a false opinion; but I will venture to assert, that knowledge is true opinion: let this
then be my reply; and if this is hereafter
disproved, we must try to find another.

SOC.   That is the way in which you
ought to answer, Theaetetus, and not in
c   your former hesitating strain, for if we are
bold we shall gain one of two advantages;
either we shall find what we seek, or we
shall be less likely to think that we know
what we do not know—in either case we
shall be richly rewarded. And now, what are
you saying?—Are there two sorts of opinion, one true and the other false; and do you
define knowledge to be the true?

THEAET.   Yes, according to my present
view.

SOC.   Is it still worth our while to resume the discussion touching opinion?

THEAET.   To what are you alluding?

d   SOC.   There is a point which troubles
me, as it has often done before; my discussion with myself or with others has left me
in great perplexity about the nature or origin
of the mental experience to which I refer.

THEAET.   Pray what is it?

SOC.   How a man can form a false
opinion. But I am even now in doubt
whether we ought to leave this question or
examine it by another method than we used
a short time ago.

THEAET.   Begin again, Socrates,—at
least if you think that there is the slightest
necessity for doing so. Were not you and
Theodorus just now remarking very truly,
that in discussions of this kind we may take
our own time?

SOC.   You are quite right, and perhaps   e
there will be no harm in retracing our steps
and beginning again. Better a little which is
well done, than a great deal imperfectly.

THEAET.   Certainly.

SOC.   Well, and what is the difficulty?
Do we not speak of false opinion, and say
that one man holds a false and another a
true opinion, as though there were some
natural distinction between them?

THEAET.   We certainly say so.

SOC.   And we can at least say that all   188
things, and each thing severally, are either
known or not known. I leave out of view
the intermediate conceptions of learning
and forgetting, because they have nothing
to do with our present question.

THEAET.   There can be no doubt, Socrates, if you exclude these, that there is no
other alternative but knowing or not knowing a thing.

SOC.   That point being now determined, must we not say that he who had an
opinion, must either know or not know that
to which his opinion refers?

THEAET.   He must.

SOC.   Moreover, he who knows, cannot   b
not know, and he who does not know, cannot know, one and the same thing?

THEAET.   Of course.

SOC.   What shall we say then? When a
man has a false opinion does he think that
which he knows to be some other thing

which he knows, and knowing both, is he at the same time ignorant of both?

THEAET. That, Socrates, is impossible.

SOC. But perhaps he thinks of something which he does not know as some other thing which he does not know; for example, he knows neither Theaetetus nor Socrates, and yet he fancies that Theaetetus is Socrates, or Socrates Theaetetus?

c THEAET. How can he?

SOC. But surely he cannot suppose something which he *knows* to be a thing which he does not know, or what he does not know to be what he knows?

THEAET. That would be monstrous.

SOC. How, then, is false opinion formed? For if all things are either known or unknown, there can be no opinion which is not comprehended under this alternative; and within it we can find no scope for false opinion.

THEAET. Most true.

SOC. Suppose that we remove the question out of the sphere of knowing or not knowing, into that of being and not-being.

d THEAET. What do you mean?

SOC. May we not suspect the simple truth to be that he who thinks on any subject that which *is not,* will necessarily think what is false, whatever in other respects may be the state of his mind?

THEAET. That, again, is not unlikely, Socrates.

SOC. Then suppose some one to say to us, Theaetetus:—Is it possible for any man to think, as you now say, that which *is not,* either as a self-existent substance or as a predicate of something else? And suppose that we answer, "Yes, he can, when in

e thinking he thinks what is not true."—That will be our answer?

THEAET. Yes.

SOC. But is there any parallel to this?

THEAET. What do you mean?

SOC. Can a man see something and yet see nothing?

THEAET. Impossible.

SOC. But if he sees any one thing, he sees something that exists. Do you suppose

that what is one is ever to be found among non-existing things?

THEAET. I do not.

SOC. He then who sees some one thing, sees something which is?

THEAET. Apparently.

SOC. And he who hears anything, hears some one thing,—a thing which *is?* 189

THEAET. Yes.

SOC. And he who touches anything, touches something which is one and therefore is?

THEAET. That again is true.

SOC. And does not he who thinks, think some one thing?

THEAET. Certainly.

SOC. And does not he who thinks some one thing, think something which is?

THEAET. I agree.

SOC. Then he who thinks of that which b is not, thinks of nothing?

THEAET. Apparently not.

SOC. And he who thinks of nothing, does not think at all?

THEAET. That seems clear.

SOC. Then no one can think that which is not, either as a self-existent substance or as a predicate of something else?

THEAET. Apparently not.

SOC. Then to think falsely is different from thinking that which is not?

THEAET. It would seem so.

SOC. Then false opinion has no existence in us, either in this way, or in that which we took a short time before.

THEAET. Certainly not.

SOC. But may not the following be the description of what we express by this name?

THEAET. What?

SOC. May we not suppose that false opinion or thought is a sort of heterodoxy; a person may make an exchange in his c mind, and say that one real object is another real object. For thus he thinks that which is, but he puts one thing in place of another, and missing the aim of his thoughts, he may be truly said to have false opinion.

THEAET. Now you appear to me to have spoken the exact truth: when a man puts the base in the place of the noble, or the noble in the place of the base, then he has truly false opinion.

SOC.   I see, Theaetetus, that your fear has disappeared, and that you are beginning to despise me.

THEAET.   What makes you say so?

SOC.   You think, if I am not mistaken, that your "truly false" is safe from censure, and that I shall never ask whether there can be a swift which is slow, or a heavy which is light, or any other self-contradictory thing, which works, not according to its own nature, but according to that of its opposite. But I will not insist upon this, for I do not wish needlessly to discourage you. And so you are satisfied that false opinion is heterodoxy, or the thought of something else?

THEAET.   I am.

SOC.   It is possible then upon your view for the mind to conceive of one thing as another?

THEAET.   True.

SOC.   But must not the mind, or thinking power, which misplaces them, have a conception either of both objects or of one of them?

THEAET.   Certainly; either together or in succession.

SOC.   Very good. And do you mean by conceiving, the same which I mean?

THEAET.   What is that?

SOC.   I mean the conversation which the soul holds with herself in consideration of anything. I speak of what I scarcely understand; but the soul when thinking appears to me to be just talking—asking questions of herself and answering them, affirming and denying. And when she has arrived at a decision, either gradually or by a sudden impulse, and has at last agreed, and does not doubt, this is called her opinion. I say, then, that to form an opinion is to speak, the opinion is a word spoken,—I mean, to oneself and in silence, not aloud or to another: What think you?

THEAET.   I agree.

SOC.   Then when any one thinks of one thing as another, he is saying to himself that one thing is another?

THEAET.   Yes.

SOC.   But do you ever remember saying to yourself that the noble is certainly base, or the unjust just: or, in a word, have you ever attempted to convince yourself that one thing is another? Nay, not even in sleep, did you ever venture to say to yourself that odd is undoubtedly even, or anything of the kind?

THEAET.   Never.

SOC.   And do you suppose that any other man, either in his senses or out of them, ever seriously tried to persuade himself that an ox is a horse, or that two are one?

THEAET.   Certainly not.

SOC.   But if thinking is talking to oneself, no one speaking and thinking of two objects, and apprehending them both in his soul, will say and think that the one is the other of them, and I must add, that you too had better let the word "other" alone [i.e. not insist that "one" and "other" are the same.] I mean to say, that no one thinks the noble to be base or anything of the kind.

THEAET.   I will pass the word "other," Socrates; and I agree to what you say.

SOC.   If a man has both of them in his thoughts, he cannot think that the one of them is the other?

THEAET.   So it seems.

SOC.   Neither, if he has one of them only in his mind and not the other, will he ever think that one is the other?

THEAET.   True; for we should have to suppose that he apprehends that which is not in his thoughts at all.

SOC.   Then no one who has either both or only one of the two objects in his mind can think that the one is the other. And therefore, he who maintains that false opinion is heterodoxy is talking nonsense; for neither in this, any more than in the two previous ways, can false opinion exist in us.

THEAET.   No.

SOC.   But if, Theaetetus, this experience is not shown to be real, we shall be driven into many absurdities.

THEAET.   What are they?

SOC.   I will not tell you until I have endeavoured to consider the matter from every point of view. For I should be ashamed of us if we were driven in our perplexity to admit the absurd consequences of which I speak. But if we find the solution, and get away from them, we may regard them only as the difficulties of others, and the ridicule will not attach to us. On the other hand, if we utterly fail, I suppose that we must be humble, and allow the argument to trample us under foot, as the sea-sick passenger is trampled upon by the sailor, and to do anything to us. Listen, then, while I tell you how I hope to find a way out of our difficulty.

THEAET.   Let me hear.

SOC.   I think that we were wrong in denying that a man could think what he knew to be what he did not know; and that there is a way in which such a deception is possible.

THEAET.   You mean to say, as I suspected at the time when we made that denial, that I may know Socrates, and at a distance see someone who is unknown to me, and suppose him to be Socrates whom I know—then the deception will occur?

SOC.   But has not that position been relinquished by us, because involving the absurdity that we should know and not know the things which we know?

THEAET.   True.

SOC.   Let us make the assertion in another form, which may or may not have a favourable issue; but as we are in a great strait, every argument should be turned over and tested. Tell me, then, whether I am right in saying that you may learn a thing which at one time you did not know?

THEAET.   Certainly you may.

SOC.   And another and another?

THEAET.   Yes.

SOC.   I would have you imagine, then, that there exists in the mind of man a block of wax, which is of different sizes in different men; harder, moister, and having more or less of purity in one than another, and in some of an intermediate quality.

THEAET.   I see.

SOC.   Let us say that this tablet is a gift of Memory, the mother of the Muses; and that when we wish to remember anything which we have seen, or heard, or thought in our own minds, we hold the wax to the perceptions and thoughts, and in that material receive the impression of them as from the seal of a ring; and that we remember and know what is imprinted as long as the image lasts; but when the image is effaced, or cannot be taken, then we forget and do not know.

THEAET.   Very good.

SOC.   Now, when a person has this knowledge, and is considering something which he sees or hears, may not false opinion arise in the following manner?

THEAET.   In what manner?

SOC.   When he thinks what he knows, sometimes to be what he knows, and sometimes to be what he does not know. We were wrong before in denying the possibility of this.

THEAET.   And how would you amend the former statement?

SOC.   I should begin by making a list of the the impossible cases which must be excluded. (1) No one can think one thing to be another when he does not perceive either of them, but has the memorial or seal of both of them in his mind; nor can any mistaking of one thing for another occur, when he only knows one, and does not know, and has no impression of the other; nor can he think that one thing which he does not know is another thing which he does not know, or that what he does not know is what he knows; nor (2) that one thing which he perceives is another thing which he perceives, or that something which he perceives is something which he does not perceive; or that something which he does not perceive is something else which he does not perceive; or that something which he does not perceive is something which he perceives; nor again (3) can he think that something which he knows and perceives, and of which he has the impression coinciding with sense, is something else which he knows and perceives, and of which he has the impression coinciding with sense;—this last case, if possible, is still more inconceivable than the others; nor (4) can he think that something which he knows and perceives, and of which he has the memo-

rial in good order, is something else which
he knows; nor if his mind is thus furnished,
can he think that a thing which he knows
and perceives is another thing which he per-
c ceives; or that a thing which he does not
know and does not perceive, is the same as
another thing which he does not know and
does not perceive, is the same as another
thing which he does not know and does not
perceive;—nor again, can he suppose that a
thing which he does not know and does not
perceive is the same as another thing which
he does not know; or that a thing which he
does not know and does not perceive is another thing which he does not perceive:—
All these utterly and absolutely exclude the
possibility of false opinion. The only cases,
if any, which remain, are the following.

THEAET. What are they? If you tell
me, I may perhaps understand you better;
but at present I am unable to follow you.

SOC. A person may think that some
thing which he knows, or which he perceives and does not know, are some other
things which he knows and perceives; or
that some things which he knows and per-
d ceives, are other things which he knows and
perceives.

THEAET. I understand you less than
ever now.

SOC. Hear me once more, then:—I,
knowing Theodorus, and remembering in
my own mind what sort of person he is, and
also what sort of person Theaetetus is, at
one time see them, and at another time do
not see them, and sometimes I touch them,
and at another time not, or at one time I
may hear them or perceive them in some
other way, and at another time not perceive
you, but still I remember you, and know
you in my own mind.

e THEAET. Very true.

SOC. Then, first of all, I want you to
understand that a man may or may not perceive sensibly that which he knows.

THEAET. True.

SOC. And that which he does not know
will sometimes not be perceived by him and
sometimes will be perceived and only
perceived?

THEAET. That is also true.

SOC. See whether you can follow me 193
better now: Socrates can recognize Theodorus and Theaetetus, but he sees neither of
them, nor does he perceive them in any
other way; he cannot then by any possibility
imagine in his own mind that Theaetetus is
Theodorus. Am I not right?

THEAET. You are quite right.

SOC. Then that was the first case of
which I spoke.

THEAET. Yes.

SOC. The second case was, that I,
knowing one of you and not knowing the
other, and perceiving neither, can never
think him whom I know to be him whom I
do not know.

THEAET. True.   b

SOC. In the third case, not knowing
and not perceiving either of you, I cannot
think that one of you whom I do not know
is the other whom I do not know. I need not
again go over the catalogue of excluded
cases, in which I cannot form a false opinion about you and Theodorus, either when
I know both or when I am in ignorance of
both, or when I know one and not the other.
And the same of perceiving: do you understand me?

THEAET. I do.

SOC. The only possibility of erroneous
opinion is, when knowing you and Theodorus, and having on the waxen block the
impression of both of you given as by a c
seal, but seeing you imperfectly and at a
distance, I am eager to assign the right impression of memory to the right visual impression, and to fit this into its own print,
in order that recognition may take place; but
if I fail and transpose them, putting the foot
into the wrong shoe—that is to say, putting
the vision of either of you on to the wrong
impression, or if my mind, like the sight in d
a mirror, which is transferred from right to
left, err by reason of some similar affection,
then "heterodoxy" and false opinion ensue.

THEAET. Yes, Socrates, you have described the nature of opinion with wonderful exactness.

SOC. Or again, when I know both of
you, and perceive as well as know one of
you, but not the other, and my knowledge

of him does not accord with perception—that was the case put by me just now which you did not understand.

THEAET. No, I did not.

SOC. I meant to say, that when a person knows and perceives one of you, and his knowledge coincides with his perception, he will never think him to be some other person, whom he knows and perceives, and the knowledge of whom coincides with his perception—for that also was a case supposed.

THEAET. True.

SOC. But there was an omission of the further case, in which, as we now say, false opinion may arise, when knowing both, and seeing, or having some other sensible perception of both, I fail in holding the seal over against the corresponding sensation; like a bad archer, I miss and fall wide of the mark—and this is called falsehood.

THEAET. Yes; it is rightly so called.

SOC. When, therefore, perception is present to one of the seals or impressions but not to the other, and the mind fits the seal of the absent perception on the one which is present, in any case of this sort the mind is deceived; in a word, if our view is sound, there can be no error or deception about things which a man does not know and has never perceived, but only in things which are known and perceived; in these alone opinion turns and twists about, and becomes alternately true and false;—true when the seals and impressions of sense meet straight and opposite—false when they go awry and are crooked.

THEAET. And is not that, Socrates, nobly said?

SOC. Nobly! yes; but wait a little and hear the explanation, and then you will say so with more reason; for to think truly is noble and to be deceived is base.

THEAET. Undoubtedly.

SOC. And the origin of truth and error, men say, is as follows:—When the wax in the soul of any one is deep and abundant, and smooth and perfectly tempered, then the impressions which pass through the senses and sink into the heart of the soul, as Homer says in a parable, meaning to indicate the likeness of the soul to wax (κήρ κηρός) these, I say, being pure and clear, and having a sufficient depth of wax, are also lasting, and minds such as these easily learn and easily retain, and are not liable to confuse the imprints of sensations, but have true thoughts; for, having clear impressions well spaced out, they can quickly "say what they are,"—that is, distribute them into their proper places on the block. And such men are called wise. Do you agree?

THEAET. Entirely.

SOC. But when the heart of anyone is shaggy—a quality which the all-wise poet commends—or muddy and of impure wax, or very soft, or very hard, then there is a corresponding defect in the mind; the soft are good at learning, but apt to forget, and the hard are the reverse; the shaggy and rugged and gritty, or those who have an admixture of earth or dung in their composition, have the impressions indistinct, as also the hard, for there is no depth in them; and the soft too are indistinct, for their impressions are easily confused and effaced. Yet greater is the indistinctness when they are all jostled together in a little soul, which has no room. These are the natures which are prone to false opinion; for when they see or hear or think of anything, they are slow in assigning the right objects to the right impressions—in their stupidity they confuse them, and are apt to see and hear and think amiss—and such men are said to be deceived in their knowledge of objects, and ignorant.

THEAET. No man, Socrates, can say anything truer than that.

SOC. Then now we may admit the existence of false opinion in us?

THEAET. Certainly.

SOC. And of true opinion also?

THEAET. Yes.

SOC. We have at length satisfactorily proven that beyond a doubt there are these two sorts of opinion.

THEAET. Undoubtedly.

SOC. Alas, Theaetetus, what a tiresome creature is a man who is fond of talking!

THEAET. What makes you say so?

SOC. Because I am disheartened at my

own stupidity and tiresome garrulity; for what other term will describe the habit of a man who is always arguing on all sides of a question; whose dullness cannot be convinced, and who will never leave off?

THEAET. But what puts you out of heart?

SOC. I am not only out of heart, but in positive despair; for I do not know what to answer if anyone were to ask me:—O Socrates, have you indeed discovered that false opinion arises neither in the comparison of
d   perceptions with one another nor yet in thought, but in the linking of thought with perception? Yes, I shall say, with the complacence of one who thinks that he has made a noble discovery.

THEAET. I see no reason why we should be ashamed of our demonstration, Socrates.

SOC. He will say: You mean to argue that the man whom we only think of and do not see, cannot be confused with the horse which we do not see or touch, but only think and do not perceive? That I believe to be my meaning, I shall reply.

THEAET. Quite right.

e   SOC. Well, then, he will say, according to that argument, the number eleven, which is only thought, can never be mistaken for twelve, which is only thought: How would you answer him?

THEAET. I should say that a mistake may very likely arise between the eleven or twelve which are seen or handled, but that no similar mistake can arise between the eleven and twelve which are in the mind.

SOC. Well, but do you think that no one ever put before his own mind five and seven,—I do not mean five or seven men or
196   other such objects, but five or seven in the abstract, which, as we say, are recorded on the waxen block, and in which false opinion is held to be impossible;—did no man ever ask himself how many these numbers make when added together, and answer that they are eleven, while another thinks that they are twelve, or would all agree in thinking and saying that they are twelve?

b   THEAET. Certainly not; many would think that they are eleven, and in the higher numbers the chance of error is greater still; for I assume you to be speaking of numbers in general.

SOC. Exactly; and I want you to consider whether this does not imply that the twelve in the waxen block are supposed to be eleven?

SOC. Then do we not come back to the old difficulty? For he who makes such a mistake does think one thing which he knows to be another thing which he knows; but this, as we said, was impossible, and afforded an irresistible proof of the non-   c existence of false opinion, because otherwise the same person would inevitably know and not know the same thing at the same time.

THEAET. Most true.

SOC. Then false opinion cannot be explained as a confusion of thought and sense, for in that case we could not have been mistaken about pure conceptions of thought; and thus we are obliged to say, either that false opinion does not exist, or that a man may not know that which he knows;—which alternative do you prefer?

THEAET. It is hard to determine, Socrates.

SOC. And yet the argument will   d scarcely admit of both. But, as we are at our wits' end, suppose that we do a shameless thing?

THEAET. What is it?

SOC. Let us attempt to explain what it is like "to know."

THEAET. And why should that be shameless?

SOC. You seem not to be aware that the whole of our discussion from the very beginning has been a search after knowledge, of which we are assumed not to know the nature.

THEAET. Nay, but I am well aware.

SOC. And is it not shameless when we do not know what knowledge is, to be explaining the verb "to know"? The truth is, Theaetetus, that we have long been infected   e with logical impurity. Thousands of times have we repeated the words "we know," and "do not know," and "we have or have not science or knowledge," as if we could understand what we are saying to one another, even while we remain ignorant about knowledge; and at this moment we are using the words "we understand," "we are ignorant," as though we could still employ them when deprived of knowledge or science.

THEAET. But if you avoid these expressions, Socrates, how will you ever argue at all?

197 SOC. I could not, being the man I am. The case would be different if I were a true hero of dialectic: and O that such an one were present! for he would have told us to avoid the use of these terms; at the same time he would not have spared in you and me the faults which I have noted. But, seeing that we are no great wits, shall I venture to say what knowing is? for I think that the attempt may be worth making.

THEAET. Then by all means venture, and no one shall find fault with you for using the forbidden terms.

SOC. You have heard the common explanation of the verb "to know"?

THEAET. I think so, but I do not remember it at the moment.

b SOC. They explain the word "to know" as meaning "to have knowledge."

THEAET. True.

SOC. I propose that we make a slight change, and say "to possess" knowledge.

THEAET. How do the two expressions differ?

SOC. Perhaps there may be no difference; but still I should like you to hear my view, that you may help me to test it.

THEAET. I will, if I can.

SOC. I should distinguish "having" from "possessing": for example, a man may buy and keep under his control a garment which he does not wear; and then we should say, not that he has, but that he possess the garment.

THEAET. It would be the correct expression.

c SOC. Well, may not a man "possess" and yet not "have" knowledge in the sense of which I am speaking? As you may suppose a man to have caught wild birds— doves or any other birds—and to be keeping them in an aviary which he has constructed at home; we might say of him in one sense, that he always has them because he possesses them, might we not?

THEAET. Yes.

SOC. And yet, in another sense, he has none of them; but they are in his power, and he has got them under his hand in an enclosure of his own, and can take and have them whenever he likes;—he can catch any which he likes, and let the bird go again, and he may do so as often as he pleases.   d

THEAET. True.

SOC. Once more, then, as in what preceded we made a sort of waxen tablet in the mind, so let us now suppose that in the mind of each man there is an aviary of all sorts of birds—some flocking together apart from the rest, others in small groups, others solitary, flying anywhere and everywhere.

THEAET. Let us imagine such an aviary—and what is to follow?   e

SOC. We may suppose that the birds are kinds of knowledge, and that when we were children, this receptacle was empty; whenever a man has gotten and detained in the enclosure a kind of knowledge, he may be said to have learned or discovered the thing which is the subject of the knowledge; and this is to know.

THEAET. Granted.

SOC. And further, when any one 198 wishes to catch any of these knowledges or sciences, and having taken, to hold it, and again to let them go, how will he express himself?—will he describe the "catching" of them and the original "possession" in the same words? I will make my meaning clearer by an example:—You admit that there is an art of arithmetic?

THEAET. To be sure.

SOC. Conceive this as an attempt to capture knowledge of every species of the odd and even.

THEAET. I follow.

SOC. Having the use of the art, the arithmetician, if I am not mistaken, has the conceptions of number under his hand, and b can transmit them to another.

THEAET. Yes.

SOC. And when transmitting them he

may be said to teach them, and when receiving to learn them, and when having them in possession in the aforesaid aviary he may be said to know them.

THEAET. Exactly.

SOC. Attend to what follows: must not the perfect arithmetician know all numbers, for he has the science of all numbers in his mind?

THEAET. True.

c   SOC. And he can reckon abstract numbers in his head, or things about him which are numerable?

THEAET. Of course he can.

SOC. And to reckon is simply to consider how much such and such a number amounts to?

THEAET. Very true.

SOC. And so he appears to be searching into something which he knows, as if he did not know it, for we have already admitted that he knows all numbers;—you have heard these perplexing questions raised?

THEAET. I have.

d   SOC. May we not pursue the image of the doves, and say that the chase after knowledge is of two kinds? One kind is prior to possession and for the sake of possession, and the other for the sake of taking and holding in the hands that which is possessed already. And thus, when a man had learned and known something long ago, he may resume and get hold of the knowledge which he has long possessed, but has not at hand in his mind.

THEAET. True.

e   SOC. That was my reason for asking how we ought to speak when an arithmetician sets about numbering, or a grammarian about reading? Shall we say, that although he knows, he comes back to himself on such an occasion to learn what he already knows?

THEAET. It would be too absurd, Socrates.

SOC. Shall we say then that he is going to read or number what he does not know, although we have admitted that he knows 199 all letters and all numbers?

THEAET. That, again, would be an absurdity.

SOC. Then shall we say that we care nothing about the mere names—any one may twist and turn the words "knowing" and "learning" in any way which he likes; but that since we have made a clear distinction between the possession of knowledge and the having or using it, we do assert that a man cannot not possess that which he possesses; and, therefore, in no case can a man not know that which he knows, but he may get a false opinion about it; for he may have the knowledge, not of this particular thing, b but of some other;—when the various numbers and forms of knowledge are flying about in the aviary, and wishing to capture a certain sort of knowledge out of the general store, he may take the wrong one by mistake. Thus it is that he may think eleven to be twelve, getting hold, as it were, of the ring-dove which he had in his mind, when he wanted the pigeon.

THEAET. A very rational explanation.

SOC. But when he catches the one which he wants, then he is not deceived, and has an opinion of what is; and thus both false and true opinion may exist, and the difficulties which were previously raised c disappear. I dare say that you agree with me, do you not?

THEAET. Yes.

SOC. And so we are rid of the difficulty of a man's not knowing what he knows, for we are not driven to the inference that he does not possess what he possesses, whether he be or be not deceived. And yet I fear that a greater difficulty is looking in at the window.

THEAET. What is it?

SOC. How can the exchange of one knowledge for another ever become false opinion?

THEAET. What do you mean?

SOC. In the first place, how can a man d who has the knowledge of anything be ignorant of that which he knows, not by reason of ignorance, but by reason of his own knowledge? And, again, is it not an extreme absurdity that he should suppose another thing to be this, and this to be another thing;—that, having knowledge present with him in his mind, he should still know nothing and be ignorant of all things?—you might as well argue that ignorance may make a man know, and blindness make him see, as that knowledge can make him ignorant.

e   THEAET. Perhaps, Socrates, we may have been wrong in making only forms of knowledge our birds: whereas there ought to have been forms of ignorance as well, flying about together in the mind, and then he who sought to take one of them might sometimes catch a form of knowledge, and sometimes a form of ignorance; and thus he would have a false opinion from ignorance, but a true one from knowledge, about the same thing.

200   SOC. I cannot help praising you, Theaetetus, and yet I must beg you to reconsider your words. Let us grant what you say—then, according to you, he who takes ignorance will have a false opinion—am I right?

THEAET. Yes.

SOC. He will certainly not think that he has a false opinion?

THEAET. Of course not.

SOC. He will think that his opinion is true, and he will fancy that he knows the things about which he has been deceived?

THEAET. Certainly.

SOC. Then he will think that he has captured a knowledge and not an ignorance?

THEAET. Clearly.

SOC. And thus, after going a long way b round, we are once more face to face with our original difficulty. The hero of dialectic will retort upon us:—"O my excellent friends," he will say, laughing, "if a man knows the specimen of ignorance and also that of knowledge, can he think that one of them which he knows is the other which he knows? or, if he knows neither of them, can he think that the one which he knows not is another which he knows not? or, if he knows one and not the other, can he think the one which he knows to be the one which he does not know? or the one which he does

not know to be the one which he knows? or will you proceed to tell me that there are other knowledges which know the types of knowledge and ignorance, and which the owner keeps in some other aviaries or graven on waxen blocks according to your c foolish images, and which he may be said to know while he possess them, even though he have them not at hand in his mind? And thus, in a perpetual circle, you will be compelled to go round and round, and you will make no progress." What are we to say in reply, Theaetetus?

THEAET. Indeed, Socrates, I do now know what we are to say.

SOC. Are not his reproaches just, and does not the argument truly show that we d are wrong in seeking for false opinion until we know what knowledge is; that must be first ascertained; then, the nature of false opinion?

THEAET. I cannot but agree with you, Socrates, so far as we have yet gone.

SOC. Then, once more, what shall we say that knowledge is?—for we are not going to lose heart as yet.

THEAET. Certainly, I shall not lose heart, if you do not.

SOC. What definition will be most consistent with our former views?

THEAET. I cannot think of any but our e old one, Socrates.

SOC. What was it?

THEAET. Knowledge was said by us to be true opinion; and true opinion is surely unerring, and the results which follow from it are all noble and good.

SOC. He who led the way into the river, Theaetetus, said "The experiment will show"; and perhaps if we go forward in the 201 search, we may stumble upon the thing which we are looking for; but if we stay where we are, nothing will come to light.

THEAET. Very true; let us go forward and try.

SOC. The trail soon comes to an end, for a whole profession is against us.

THEAET. How is that, and what profession do you mean?

SOC. The profession of the great wise

ones who are called orators and lawyers; for these persuade men by their art and make them think whatever they like, but they do b not teach them. Do you imagine that there are any teachers in the world so clever as to be able to impart the full truth about past acts of robbery or violence, to men who were not eye-witnesses, while a little water is flowing in the clepsydra?

THEAET. Certainly not, they can only persuade them.

SOC. And would you not say that per-suading them is making them have an opinion?

THEAET. To be sure.

SOC. When, therefore, judges are justly persuaded about matters which you can know only by seeing them, and not in any other way, and when thus judging of them from report they attain a true opinion about c them, they judge without knowledge, and yet are rightly persuaded, if they have judged well.

THEAET. Certainly.

SOC. And yet, O my friend, if true opinion in law courts and knowledge are the same, the perfect judge could not have judged rightly without knowledge; and therefore I must infer that they are not the same.

THEAET. There is a distinction, Soc-rates, which I have heard made by someone else, but I had forgotten it. He said that true d opinion, combined with reason, was knowl-edge, but that the opinion which had no rea-son was out of the sphere of knowledge; and that things of which there is no rational account are not knowable—such was the singular expression which he used—and that things which have a reason or expla-nation are knowable.

SOC. Excellent; but then, how did he distinguish between things which are and are not "knowable"? I wish that you would repeat to me what he said, and then I shall know whether you and I have heard the same tale.

THEAET. I do not know whether I can recall it; but if another person would tell me, I think that I could follow him.

SOC. Let me give you, then, a dream in return for a dream:—Methought that I e too had a dream, and I heard in my dream that the primeval letters or elements out of which you and I and all other things are compounded, have no reason or explana- 202 tion; you can only name each of them in-dividually, but no predicate can be either affirmed or denied of them, for in the one case existence, in the other non-existence is already implied, neither of which must be added, if you mean to speak of this or that thing by itself alone. It should not be called "itself," or "that," or "each," or "alone," or "this," or the like; for these go about every-where and are applied to all things, but are distinct from them; whereas if the first ele-ments can be described, and had a definition of their own, they would be spoken of apart from all else. But none of these primeval b elements can be defined; they can only be named, for they have nothing but a name; whereas the things which are compounded of them, as they themselves are complex, are defined by a combination of names, for the combination of names is the essence of a definition. Thus, then, the elements or let-ters are only objects of perception, and can-not be defined or known; but the syllables or combinations of them are known and ex-pressed, and are apprehended by true opin-ion. When, therefore, any one forms the true opinion of anything without rational expla-nation, you may say that his mind is truly exercised, but has no knowledge; for he who cannot give and receive a reason for a c thing, has no knowledge of that thing; but when he adds rational explanation, then, he is perfected in knowledge and may be all that I have been denying of him. Was that the form in which the dream appeared to you?

THEAET. Precisely.

SOC. And you allow and maintain that true opinion, combined with definition or rational explanation, is knowledge?

THEAET. Exactly.

SOC. Then may we assume, Theaete-tus, that today, and in this casual manner, we have found a truth which in former d times many wise men have grown old and have not found?

THEAET. At any rate, Socrates, I am satisfied with the present statement.

. . . .

206 SOC. . . . do not let us lose sight of the question before us . . . , which is the mean-
c ing of the statement, that right opinion with rational definition of explanation is the most perfect form of knowledge.

THEAET. We must not.

SOC. Well, and what does the author of this statement mean by the term "explanation"? I think we have a choice of three meanings.

THEAET. What are they?

d SOC. In the first place, the meaning may be, manifesting one's thought by the voice with verbs and nouns, imaging an opinion in the stream which flows from the lips, as in a mirror or water. Does not this appear to you to be one kind of explanation?

THEAET. Certainly; he who so manifests his thought, is said to explain himself.

SOC. But then, every one who is not born deaf or dumb is able sooner or later to manifest what he thinks of anything; and if so, all those who have a right opinion about
e anything will also have right explanation; nor will right opinion be anywhere found to exist apart from knowledge.

THEAET. True.

SOC. Let us not, therefore, hastily charge him who gave his account of knowledge with uttering an unmeaning word; for perhaps he did not intend to say this, but that when a person was asked what was the
207 nature of anything, he should be able to answer his questioner by giving the elements of the thing.

THEAET. As for example, Socrates . . . ?

SOC. As, for example, when Hesiod says that a wagon is made up of a hundred planks. Now, neither you nor I could describe all of them individually; but if any one asked what is a wagon, we should be content to answer that a wagon consists of wheels, axle, body, rims, yoke.

THEAET. Certainly.

SOC. And our opponent will probably laugh at us, just as he would if we professed to be grammarians and to give a grammatical account of the name of Theaetetus, and yet could only tell the syllables and not the letters of your name. We might hold a true b opinion and make a correct statement; but *knowledge*, he could claim, is not attained until, combined with true opinion, there is an enumeration of the elements out of which anything is composed, as, I think, has already been remarked.

THEAET. It has.

SOC. In the same way, he might claim that while we merely have true opinion about the wagon, a man who can describe c its essence by an enumeration of the hundred planks, adds rational explanation to true opinion, and instead of opinion has art and knowledge of the nature of a wagon, in that he attains to the whole through the elements.

THEAET. And do you not agree in that view, Socrates?

SOC. Tell me, my friend, whether the view is yours—whether you admit the resolution of all things into their elements to be a rational explanation of them, and the consideration of them in syllables or larger combinations of them to be irrational—so that we can inquire whether that view is right. d

THEAET. Indeed I admit it.

SOC. Well, and do you conceive that a man has knowledge of any element who at one time affirms and at another time denies that element of something, or thinks that the same thing is composed of different elements at different times?

THEAET. Assuredly not.

SOC. And do you not remember that in your case and in that of others this often occurred at first in the process of learning to read?

THEAET. You mean that we often put different letters into the same syllables, and e gave the same letter sometimes to the proper syllable, sometimes to a wrong one.

SOC. Yes.

THEAET. To be sure; I perfectly remember, and I am very far from supposing that they who are in this condition have knowledge.

SOC. When a person at that stage of learning writes the name of Theaetetus, and thinks that he ought to write and does write 208 *Th* and *e;* but, again, meaning to write the name of Theodorus, thinks that he ought to write and does write *T* and *e*—can we suppose that he knows the first syllables of your two names?

THEAET. We have already admitted that such a one has not yet attained knowledge.

SOC. And in like manner he may enumerate without knowing them the second and third and fourth syllables of your name?

THEAET. He may.

SOC. And in that case, when he has written the syllables in order, since he can enumerate all the letters he will have written "Theaetetus" with right opinion?

THEAET. Clearly.

SOC. But although we admit that he b has right opinion, he will still be without knowledge?

THEAET. Yes.

SOC. And yet he will have explanation, as well as right opinion, for he knew his way through the letters when he wrote; and this we admit to be explanation.

THEAET. True.

SOC. Then, my friend, there is such a thing as right opinion united with definition or explanation, which should still not be called knowledge.

THEAET. It would seem so.

SOC. And what we fancied to be a perfect definition of knowledge is a dream c only. But perhaps we had better not say so as yet, for were there not three senses of "explanation", one of which must, as we said, be adopted by him who maintains knowledge to be true opinion combined with rational explanation? And very likely there may be found some one who will not prefer this but the third.

THEAET. Your reminder is just; there is still one sense remaining. The first was the image or expression of the mind in speech; the second, which has just been mentioned, is a way of reaching the whole by an enumeration of the elements. But what is the third?

SOC. That which would occur to many

people: ability to tell the mark or sign of difference which distinguishes the thing in question from all others.

THEAET. Can you give me any example of such a definition?

SOC. As, for example, in the case of d the sun, I think that you would be contented with the statement that the sun is the brightest of the heavenly bodies which revolve about the earth.

THEAET. Certainly.

SOC. Understand why: The reason is, as we were just now saying, that if you get at the difference and distinguishing characteristic of each thing, then, as many persons affirm, you will secure its explanation; but while you lay hold only of the common and not of the characteristic quality, your explanation will relate to all things to which this common quality belongs.

THEAET. I understand you, and it is in e my judgement correct to call this definition [or explanation].

SOC. But he, who having right opinion about anything, can find out the difference which distinguishes it from other things will have come to *know* that of which before he had only an opinion.

THEAET. Yes; that is what we are maintaining.

SOC. Nevertheless, Theaetetus, on a nearer view, I find myself quite disappointed; the picture, which at a distance was not so bad, has now become altogether unintelligible.

THEAET. What do you mean?

SOC. I will endeavour to explain: I will 209 suppose myself to have true opinion of you, and if to this I add your definition, then I have knowledge, but if not, opinion only.

THEAET. Yes.

SOC. The definition was assumed to be the interpretation of your difference.

THEAET. True.

SOC. But when I had only opinion, I had no conception of your distinguishing characteristics.

THEAET. I suppose not.

SOC. Then I must have conceived of some general or common nature which no more belonged to you than to another. b

THEAET. True.

SOC.   Tell me, now: How in that case could I have formed a judgement of you any more than of any one else? Suppose that I imagine Theaetetus to be a man who has nose, eyes, and mouth, and every other member complete; how would that enable me to distinguish Theaetetus from Theodorus, or from some outer barbarian?

THEAET.   How could it?

SOC.   Or if I had further conceived of you, not only as having nose and eyes, but
c as having a snub nose and prominent eyes, should I have any more notion of you than of myself and others who resemble me?

THEAET.   Certainly not.

SOC.   Surely I can have no conception of Theaetetus until your snub-nosedness has left an impression on my mind different from the snub-nosedness of all others whom I have ever seen, and until your other peculiarities have a like distinctness; and so when I meet you tomorrow the right opinion will be recalled?

THEAET.   Most true.

d SOC.   Then right opinion also implies the perception of differences?

THEAET.   Clearly.

SOC.   What meaning, then, remains for the reason or explanation which we are told to add to right opinion? If the meaning is, that we should form an extra opinion of the way in which something differs from another thing, the proposal is ridiculous.

THEAET.   How so?

SOC.   We are bidden to acquire a right opinion of the differences which distinguish one thing from another, which is just what we already have, and so we go round and round; the revolution of the scytal, or pestle,
e or any other rotatory machine, in the same circles, is as nothing compared with such a requirement; and we may be truly described as the blind directing the blind; for to add those things which we already have, in order that we may learn what we already think, is like a soul utterly benighted.

THEAET.   Tell me; what were you going to say just now, when you asked the question?

SOC.   If, my boy, the argument, in speaking of adding the definition, had used the word to "know," and not merely "have an opinion" of the difference, this which is the most promising of all the definitions of knowledge would have come to a pretty end, for to know is surely to acquire knowledge.

THEAET.   True.   210

SOC.   And so, when the question is asked, What is knowledge? this fair argument will answer "Right opinion with knowledge"—knowledge, that is, of difference, for this, as the said argument maintains, is adding the definition.

THEAET.   That seems to be true.

SOC.   But how utterly foolish, when we are asking what is knowledge, that the reply should only be, right opinion with knowledge whether of difference or of anything else! And so, Theaetetus, knowledge is neither sensation nor true opinion, nor yet definition and explanation accompanying and added to true opinion?   b

THEAET.   I suppose not.

SOC.   And are you still in labour and travail, my dear friend, or have you brought all that you have to say about knowledge to the birth?

THEAET.   I am sure, Socrates, that you have elicited from me a good deal more than ever was in me.

SOC.   And does not my art show that you have brought forth wind, and that the offspring of your brain are not worth bringing up?

THEAET.   Very true.

SOC.   But if, Theaetetus, you should ever conceive afresh, you will be all the better for the present investigation, and if not, c
you will be soberer and humbler and gentler to other men, and will be too modest to fancy that you know what you do not know. These are the limits of my art; I can no further go, nor do I know aught of the things which great and famous men know or have known in this or former ages. The office of a midwife I, like my mother, have received from God; she delivered women, and I deliver men; but they must be young and noble and fair.   d

2 / Aristotle (384–322 B.C.)
POSTERIOR ANALYTICS

BOOK I

1 **71ª** All instruction given or received by way of argument proceeds from pre-existent knowledge. This becomes evident upon a survey of all the species of such instruction. The mathematical sciences and all other speculative disciplines are acquired in this way, and so are the two forms of dialectical 5 reasoning, syllogistic and inductive; for each of these latter makes use of old knowledge to impart new, the syllogism assuming an audience that accepts its premises, induction exhibiting the universal as implicit in the clearly known particular. Again, the persuasion exerted by rhetorical arguments is in principle the same, since they use either example, a kind of induction, or enthy- 10 meme, a form of syllogism.

The pre-existent knowledge required is of two kinds. In some cases admission of the fact must be assumed, in others comprehension of the meaning of the term used, and sometimes both assumptions are essential. Thus, we assume that every predicate can be either truly affirmed or truly denied of any subject, and that "triangle" means so and so; as regards "unit" we have to make 15 the double assumption of the meaning of the word and the existence of the thing. The reason is that these several objects are not equally obvious to us. Recognition of a truth may in some cases contain as factors both previous knowledge and also knowledge acquired simultaneously with that rec-

ognition—knowledge, this latter, of the particulars actually falling under the universal and therein already virtually known. For ex- 20 ample, the student knew beforehand that the angles of every triangle are equal to two right angles; but it was only at the actual moment at which he was being led on to recognize this as true in the instance before him that he came to know "this figure inscribed in the semicircle" to be a triangle. For some things (viz. the singulars finally reached which are not predicable of anything else as subject) are only learnt in this way, i.e., there is here no recognition through a middle of a minor term as subject to a major. Before he was led on to recognition or before he actually drew a conclu- 25 sion, we should perhaps say that in a manner he knew, in a manner not.

If he did not in an unqualified sense of the term *know* the existence of this triangle, how could he *know* without qualification that its angles were equal to two right angles? No: clearly he *knows* not without qualification but only in the sense that he *knows* universally. If this distinction is not drawn, we are faced with the dilemma in the *Meno*: either a man will learn nothing or what he already knows; for we cannot 30 accept the solution which some people offer. A man is asked, "Do you, or do you not, know that every pair is even?" He says he does know it. The questioner then produces a particular pair, of the existence, and so a *fortiori* of the evenness, of which he

Reprinted from *Analytica Posteriora*, I. 1–3 (71a–73a20), I.9 (75b35–76a30), 1.31 (87b25–88a15), 1.33 (88b30–89b5), II.1–2 (89b20–90a30), II.19 (99b15–100b15). From *The Oxford Translation of Aristotle*, vol 1, translated by G. R. G. Mure, edited by W. D. Ross (Oxford: Oxford University Press, 1928). Reprinted by permission of Oxford University Press.

was unaware. The solution which some people offer is to assert that they do not know that every pair is even, but only that everything which they know to be a pair is **71ᵇ** even: yet what they know to be even is that of which they have demonstrated evenness, i.e., what they made the subject of their premiss, viz. not merely every triangle or number which they know to be such, but any and every number or triangle without reservation. For no premiss is ever couched in the form "every number which you know to be such," or "every rectilinear figure which you know to be such": the predicate 5 is always construed as applicable to any and every instance of the thing. On the other hand, I imagine there is nothing to prevent a man in one sense knowing what he is learning, in another not knowing it. The strange thing would be, not if in some sense he knew what he was learning, but if he were to know it in that precise sense and manner in which he was learning it.

2 We suppose ourselves to possess unqualified scientific knowledge of a thing, as opposed to knowing it in the accidental way 10 in which the sophist knows, when we think that we know the cause on which the fact depends, as the cause of that fact and of no other, and, further, that the fact could not be other than it is. Now that scientific knowing is something of this sort is evident— witness both those who falsely claim it and those who actually possess it, since the former merely imagine themselves to be, while the latter are also actually, in the condition described. Consequently the proper object 15 of unqualified scientific knowledge is something which cannot be other than it is.

There may be another manner of knowing as well—that will be discussed later. What I now assert is that at all events we do know by demonstration. By demonstration I mean a syllogism productive of scientific knowledge, a syllogism, that is, the grasp of which is *eo ipso* such knowledge. Assuming then that my thesis as to the nature of scientific knowing is correct, the 20 premisses of demonstrated knowledge must be true, primary, immediate, better known than and prior to the conclusion, which is further related to them as effect to cause. Unless these conditions are satisfied, the basic truths will not be "appropriate" to the conclusion. Syllogism there may indeed be without these conditions, but such syllogism, not being productive of scientific knowledge, will not be demonstration. The premisses must be true: for that which is 25 non-existent cannot be known—we cannot know, e.g., that the diagonal of a square is commensurate with its side. The premisses must be primary and indemonstrable; otherwise they will require demonstration in order to be known, since to have knowledge, if it be not accidental knowledge, of things which are demonstrable, means precisely to have a demonstration of them. The premisses must be the causes of the conclu- 30 sion, better known than it, and prior to it; its causes, since we possess scientific knowledge of a thing only when we know its cause: prior, in order to be causes; antecedently known, this antecedent knowledge being not our mere understanding of the meaning, but knowledge of the fact as **72ᵃ** well. Now "prior" and "better known" are ambiguous terms, for there is a difference between what is prior and better known in the order of being and what is prior and better known to man. I mean that objects nearer to sense are prior and better known to man; objects without qualification prior and better are those further from sense. Now the most universal causes are furthest from sense and particular causes are nearest 5 to sense, and they are thus exactly opposed to one another. In saying that the premisses of demonstrated knowledge must be primary, I mean that they must be the "appropriate" basic truths, for I identify primary premiss and basic truth. A "basic truth" in a demonstration is an immediate proposition. An immediate proposition is one which has no other proposition prior to it. A proposition is either part of an enunciation, e.g., it predicates a single attribute of a single subject. If a proposition is dialect- 10 ical, it assumes either part indifferently; if it is demonstrative, it lays down one part to the definite exclusion of the other because

that part is true. The term "enunciation" de-notes either part of a contradiction indiffer-ently. A contradiction is an opposition which of its own nature excludes a middle. The part of a contradiction which conjoins a predicate with a subject is an affirmation;
15 the part disjoining them is a negation. I call an immediate basic truth of syllogism a "thesis" when, though it is not susceptible of proof by the teacher, yet ignorance of it does not constitute a total bar to progress on the part of the pupil: one which the pupil must know if he is to learn anything what-ever is an axiom. I call it an axiom because there are such truths and we give them the name of axioms *par excellence.* If a thesis
20 assumes one part or the other of an enun-ciation, i.e., asserts either the existence or the non-existence of a subject, it is a hy-pothesis; if it does not so assert, it is a def-inition. Definition *is* a "thesis" or a "laying something down," since the arithmetician lays it down that to be a unit is to be quan-titatively indivisible; but it is not a hypoth-esis, for to define what a unit is is not the same as to affirm its existence.
25   Now since the required ground of our knowledge—i.e., of our conviction—of a fact is the possession of such a syllogism as we call demonstration, and the ground of the syllogism is the facts constituting its premisses, we must not only know the pri mary premisses—some if not all of them—beforehand, but know them better than the conclusion: for the cause of an attribute's inherence in a subject always itself inheres in the subject more firmly than that attrib-ute: e.g., the cause of our loving anything is dearer to us than the object of our love.
30 So since the primary premisses are the cause of our knowledge—i.e. of our con-viction—it follows that we know them bet-ter—that is, are more convinced of them—than their consequences, precisely because our knowledge of the latter is the effect of our knowledge of the premisses. Now a man cannot believe in anything more than in the things he knows, unless he has either actual knowledge of it or something better than actual knowledge. But we are faced

with this paradox if a student whose belief 35 rests on demonstration has not prior knowl-edge: a man must believe in some, if not all, of the basic truths more than in the con-clusion. Moreover, if a man sets out to ac-quire the scientific knowledge that comes through demonstration, he must not only have a better knowledge of the basic truths and a firmer conviction of them than of the connexion which is being demonstrated: 72ᵇ more than this, nothing must be more cer-tain or better known to him than these basic truths in their character as contradicting the fundamental premisses which lead to the opposed and erroneous conclusion. For in-deed the conviction of pure science must be unshakable.

Some hold that, owing to the necessity of 3 knowing the primary premisses, there is no scientific knowledge. Others think there is, but that all truths are demonstrable. Neither doctrine is either true or a necessary deduc-tion from the premisses. The first school, assuming that there is no way of knowing other than by demonstration, maintain that an infinite regress is involved, on the ground that if behind the prior stands no primary, we could not know the posterior through 10 the prior (wherein they are right, for one cannot traverse an infinite series): if on the other hand they say the series termi nates and there are primary premisses, yet these are unknowable because incapable of demonstration, which according to them is the only form of knowledge. And since thus one cannot know the primary premisses, knowledge of the conclusions which follow from them is not pure scientific knowledge nor properly knowing at all, but rests on the mere supposition that the premisses are 15 true. The other party agree with them as re-gards knowing, holding that it is only pos-sible by demonstration, but they see no dif-ficulty in holding that all truths are demonstrated, on the ground that demon-stration may be circular and reciprocal.
    Our own doctrine is that not all knowl-edge is demonstrative: on the contrary, knowledge of the immediate premisses is 20

independent of demonstration. (The necessity of this is obvious; for since we must know the prior premisses from which the demonstration is drawn, and since the regress must end in immediate truths, those truths must be indemonstrable.) Such, then, is our doctrine, and in addition we maintain that besides scientific knowledge there is its originative source which enables us to recognize the definitions.

25   Now demonstration must be based on premisses prior to and better known than the conclusion; and the same things cannot simultaneously be both prior and posterior to one another: so circular demonstration is clearly not possible in the unqualified sense of "demonstration," but only possible if "demonstration," be extended to include that other method of argument which rests on a distinction between truths prior to us

30   and truths without qualification prior, i.e. the method by which induction produces knowledge. But if we accept this extension of its meaning, our definition of unqualified knowledge will prove faulty; for there seem to be two kinds of it. Perhaps, however, the second form of demonstration, that which proceeds from truths better known to us, is not demonstration in the unqualified sense of the term.

The advocates of circular demonstration are not only faced with the difficulty we have just stated: in addition their theory reduces to the mere statement that if a thing exists, then it does exist—an easy way of

35   proving anything. That this is so can be clearly shown by taking three terms, for to constitute the circle it makes no difference whether many terms or few or even only two are taken. Thus by direct proof, if A is, B must be; if B is, C must be; therefore if A is, C must be. Since then—by the circular

73ᵃ   proof—if A is, B must be, and if B is, A must be, A may be substituted for C above. Then "if B is, A must be" = "if B is, C must be," which above gave the conclusion "if A is, C must be": but C and A have been identified. Consequently the upholders of

15   circular demonstration are in the position of saying that if A is, A must be—a simple

way of proving anything. Moreover, even such circular demonstration is impossible except in the case of attributes that imply one another, viz. "peculiar" properties.

Now, it has been shown that the positing of one thing—be it one term or one premiss—never involves a necessary consequent: two premisses constitute the first and small-   10 est foundation for drawing a conclusion at all and therefore *a fortiori* for the demonstrative syllogism of science. If, then, A is implied in B and C, and B and C are reciprocally implied in one another and in A, it is possible, as has been shown in my writings on the syllogism, to prove all the assumptions on which the original conclusion rested, by circular demonstration in the first   15 figure. But it has also been shown that in the other figures either no conclusion is possible, or at least none which proves both the original premisses. Propositions the terms of which are not convertible cannot be circularly demonstrated at all, and since convertible terms occur rarely in actual demonstrations, it is clearly frivolous and impossible to say that demonstration is reciprocal and that therefore everything can   20 be demonstrated.

·   ·   ·   ·   ·   ·   ·

It is clear that if the conclusion is to show   **9   75ᵇ** an attribute inhering as such, nothing can be demonstrated except from its "appropriate" basic truths. Consequently a proof even from true, indemonstrable, and immediate   40 premisses does not constitute knowledge. Such proofs are like Bryson's method of squaring the circle; for they operate by taking as their middle a common character—a   **76ᵃ** character, therefore, which the subject may share with another—and consequently they apply equally to subjects different in kind. They therefore afford knowledge of an attribute only as inhering accidentally, not as belonging to its subject as such: otherwise they would not have been applicable to another genus.

Our knowledge of any attribute's connexion with a subject is accidental unless we know that connexion through the middle   5 term in virtue of which it inheres, and as an inference from basic premises essential and "appropriate" to the subject—unless we know, e.g., the property of possessing angles equal to two right angles as belonging to that subject in which it inheres essentially, and as inferred from basic premises essential and "appropriate" to that subject: so that if that middle term also belongs essentially to the minor, the middle must belong to the same kind as the major and minor terms. The only exceptions to this rule 10 are such cases as theorems in harmonics which are demonstrable by arithmetic. Such theorems are proved by the same middle terms as arithmetical properties, but with a qualification—the fact falls under a separate science (for the subject genus is separate), but the reasoned fact concerns the superior science, to which the attributes essentially belong. Thus, even these apparent excep- 15 tions show that no attribute is strictly demonstrable except from its "appropriate" basic truths, which, however, in the case of these sciences have the requisite identity of character.

It is no less evident that the peculiar basic truths of each inhering attribute are indemonstrable; for basic truths from which they might be deduced would be basic truths of all that is, and the science to which they belonged would possess universal sovereignty. This is so because he knows better whose knowledge is deducted from higher 20 causes, for his knowledge is from prior premises when it derives from causes themselves uncaused: hence, if he knows better than others or best of all, his knowledge would be science in a higher or the highest degree. But, as things are, demonstration is not transferable to another genus, with such exceptions as we have mentioned of the application of geometrical demon- 25 strations to theorems in mechanics or optics, or of arithmetical demonstrations to those of harmonics.

It is hard to be sure whether one knows or not; for it is hard to be sure whether one's knowledge is based on the basic truths appropriate to each attribute—the differentia of true knowledge. We think we have sci-

entific knowledge if we have reasoned from true and primary premises. But that is not so: the conclusion must be homogeneous with the basic facts of the science.   30

. . . . . .

Scientific knowledge is not possible through 31 the act of perception, even if perception as a faculty is of "the such" and not merely of a "this somewhat," yet one must at any rate actually perceive a "this somewhat," and at a definite present place and time: but that 30 which is commensurately universal and true in all cases one cannot perceive, since it is not "this" and it is not "now"; if it were, it would not be commensurately universal— the term we apply to what is always and everywhere. Seeing, therefore, that demonstrations are commensurately universal and universals imperceptible, we clearly cannot obtain scientific knowledge by the act of 35 perception: nay, it is obvious that even if it were possible to perceive that a triangle has its angles equal to two right angles, we should still be looking for a demonstration— we should not (as some say) possess knowledge of it; for perception must be of a particular, whereas scientific knowledge involves the recognition of the commensurate universal. So if we were on the moon, and saw the earth shutting out the sun's light, 40 we should not know the cause of the 88ᵇ eclipse: we should perceive the present fact of the eclipse, but not the reasoned fact at all, since the act of perception is not of the commensurate universal. I do not, of course, deny that by watching the frequent recurrence of this event we might, after tracking the commensurate universal, possess a demonstration, for the commensurate universal is elicited from the several groups of singulars.

The commensurate universal is precious 5 because it makes clear the cause; so that in the case of acts like these which have a cause other than themselves universal knowledge is more precious than sense-perceptions and than intuition. (As regards primary truths there is of course a different account to be given.) Hence it is clear that knowledge of things demonstrable cannot

10 be acquired by perception, unless the term perception is applied to the possession of scientific knowledge through demonstration. Nevertheless certain points do arise with regard to connexions to be proved which are referred for their explanation to a failure in sense-perception: there are cases when an act of vision would terminate our inquiry, not because in seeing we should be knowing, but because we should have elicited the universal from seeing; if, for ex-

15 ample, we saw the pores in the glass and the light passing through, the reason of the kindling would be clear to us because we should at the same time see it in each instance and intuit that it must be so in all instances.

.   .   .   .

33 88ᵇ Scientific knowledge and its object differ from opinion and the object of opinion in that scientific knowledge is commensurately universal and proceeds by necessary connexions, and that which is necessary cannot be otherwise. So though there are things which are true and real and yet can be oth-

35 erwise, *scientific knowledge* clearly does not concern them: if it did, things which can be otherwise would be incapable of being otherwise. Nor are they any concern of *rational intuition*—by rational intuition I mean an originative source of scientific knowledge—

89ᵃ nor of indemonstrable knowledge, which is the grasping of the immediate premiss. Since then rational intuition, science, and opinion, and what is revealed by these terms, are the only things that can be "true," it follows that it is *opinion* that is concerned with that which may be true or false, and can be otherwise: opinion in fact is the

5 grasp of a premiss which is immediate but not necessary. This view also fits the observed facts, for opinion is unstable, and so is the kind of being we have described as its object. Besides, when a man thinks a truth incapable of being otherwise he always thinks that he knows it, never that he opines it. He thinks that he opines when he

10 thinks that a connexion, though actually so, may quite easily be otherwise; for he believes that such is the proper object of opin-

ion, while the necessary is the object of knowledge.

In what sense, then, can the same thing be the object of both opinion and knowledge? And if any one chooses to maintain that all that he knows he can also opine, why should not opinion be knowledge? For he that knows and he that opines will follow the same train of thought through the same middle terms until the immediate premises are reached: because it is possible to opine 15 not only the fact but also the reasoned fact, and the reason is the middle term; so that, since the former knows, he that opines also has knowledge.

The truth perhaps is that if a man grasp truths that cannot be other than they are, in the way in which he grasps the definitions through which demonstrations take place, he will have not opinion but knowledge: if on the other hand he apprehends these attributes as inhering in their subjects, but not in virtue of the subjects' substance and essential nature, he possesses opinion and not 20 genuine knowledge; and his opinion, if obtained through immediate premises, will be both of the fact and of the reasoned fact: if not so obtained, of the fact alone. The object of opinion and knowledge is not quite identical; it is only in a sense identical, just as the object of true and false opinion is in a sense identical. The sense in which some maintain that true and false opinion can 25 have the same object leads them to embrace many strange doctrines, particularly the doctrine that what a man opines falsely he does not opine at all. There are really many senses of "identical," and in one sense the object of true and false opinion can be the same, in another it cannot. Thus, to have a true opinion that the diagonal is commen- 30 surate with the side would be absurd: but because the diagonal with which they are both concerned is the same, the two opinions have objects so far the same: on the other hand, as regards their essential definable nature these objects differ. The identity of the objects of knowledge and opinion is similar. Knowledge is the apprehension of, e.g., the attribute "animal" as incapable of being otherwise, opinion the apprehension

35 of "animal" as capable of being otherwise—
e.g., the apprehension that animal is an element in the essential nature of man is
knowledge; the apprehension of animal as
predicable of man but not as an element in
man's essential nature is opinion: man is the
subject in both judgments, but the mode of
inherence differs.

This also shows that one cannot opine
and know the same thing simultaneously;
for then one would apprehend the same
89ᵇ thing as both capable and incapable of being otherwise—an impossibility. Knowledge and opinion of the same thing can co-
exist in two different people in the sense we
have explained, but not simultaneously in
the same person. That would involve a
man's simultaneously apprehending, e.g.,
(1) that man is essentially animal—i.e., can-
5 not be other than animal—and (2) that man
is not essentially animal, that is, we may
assume, may be other than animal.

Further consideration of modes of thinking
and their distribution under the heads of discursive thought, intuition, science, art, practical wisdom, and metaphysical thinking,
belongs rather partly to natural science,
partly to moral philosophy.

.   .   .   .

BOOK II

1 89ᵇ The kinds of question we ask are as many
as the kinds of things which we know. They
are in fact four:—(1) whether the connexion
of an attribute with a thing is a fact, (2)
25 what is the reason of the connexion, (3)
whether a thing exists, (4) what is the nature
of the thing. Thus, when our question concerns a complex of thing and attribute and
we ask whether the thing is thus or otherwise qualified—whether, e.g., the sun suffers eclipse or not—then we are asking as
to the fact of a connexion. That our inquiry
ceases with the discovery that the sun does
suffer eclipse is an indication of this; and if
we know from the start that the sun suffers
eclipse, we do not inquire whether it does
so or not. On the other hand, when we know

the fact we ask the reason; as, for example,
when we know that the sun is being
eclipsed and that an earthquake is in pro-   30
gress, it is the reason of eclipse or earthquake into which we inquire.

Where a complex is concerned, then,
those are the two questions we ask; but for
some objects of inquiry we have a different
kind of question to ask, such as whether
there is or is not a centaur or a God. (By
"is or is not" I mean "is or is not without
further qualification"; as opposed to "is or
is not (e.g.) white.") On the other hand,
when we have ascertained the thing's existence, we inquire as to its nature, asking,
for instance, "what, then, is God?" or "what
is man?"   35

These, then, are the four kinds of ques-   2
tion we ask, and it is in the answers to these
questions that our knowledge consists.

Now when we ask whether a connexion
is a fact, or whether a thing without qualification is, we are really asking whether the
connexion or the thing has a "middle"; and
when we have ascertained either that the
connexion is a fact or that the thing is—i.e.,
ascertained either the partial or the unqualified being of the thing—and are proceeding 90ᵃ
to ask the reason of the connexion or the
nature of the thing, then we are asking what
the "middle" is.

(By distinguishing the fact of the connexion and the existence of the thing as respectively the partial and the unqualified being of the thing, I mean that if we ask "does
the moon suffer eclipse?" or "does the
moon wax?" the question concerns a part of
the thing's being; for what we are asking in
such questions is whether a thing is this or
that, i.e. has or has not this or that attribute:
whereas, if we ask whether the moon or
night exists, the question concerns the unqualified being of a thing.)

We conclude that in all our inquiries we   5
are asking either whether there is a "middle" or what the "middle" is: for the "middle" here is precisely the cause, and it is the
cause that we seek in all our inquiries.
Thus, "Does the moon suffer eclipse?"
means "Is there or is there not a cause producing eclipse of the moon?" and when we

have learnt that there is, our next question is, "What then, is this cause?"; for the cause through which a thing *is*—not *is this or that,* i.e., has this or that attribute, but with-

10 out qualification *is*—and the cause through which it is—not *is* without qualification, but *is this or that* as having some essential attribute or some accident—are both alike the "middle." By that which *is* without qualification I mean the subject, e.g., moon or earth or sun or triangle; by that which a subject *is* (in the partial sense) I mean a property, e.g., eclipse, equality or inequality, interposition or non-interposition. For in

15 all these examples it is clear that the nature of the thing and the reason of the fact are identical: the question "What is eclipse?" and its answer "The privation of the moon's light by the interposition of the earth" are identical with the question "What is the reason of eclipse?" or "Why does the moon suffer eclipse?" and the reply "Because of the failure of light through the earth's shutting it out." Again, for "What is a concord? A commensurate numerical ratio of a high and a low note," we may substitute "What

20 reason makes a high and a low note concordant? Their relation according to a commensurate numerical ratio." "Are the high and the low note concordant?" is equivalent to "Is their ratio commensurate?"; and when we find that it is commensurate, we ask "What, then, is their ratio?"

Cases in which the "middle" is sensible

25 show that the object of our inquiry is always the "middle"; we inquire, because we have not perceived it, whether there is or is not a "middle" causing e.g. an eclipse. On the other hand, if we were on the moon we should not be inquiring either as to the fact or the reason, but both fact and reason would be obvious simultaneously. For the act of perception would have enabled us to know the universal too; since, the present fact of an eclipse being evident, perception

30 would then at the same time give us the present fact of the earth's screening the sun's light, and from this would arise the universal.

Thus, as we maintain, to know a thing's nature is to know the reason why it is; and this is equally true of things in so far as they

are said without qualification to *be* as opposed to being possessed of some attribute, and in so far as they are said to be possessed of some attribute such as equal to two right angles, or greater or less.

. . . .

We must now start afresh and consider **8 93ᵃ** which of these conclusions are sound and which are not, and what is the nature of definition, and whether essential nature is in any sense demonstrable and definable or in none.

Now to know its essential nature is, as we said, the same as to know the cause of a thing's existence, and the proof of this de- 5 pends on the fact that a thing must have a cause. Moreover, this cause is either identical with the essential nature of the thing or distinct from it; and if its cause is distinct from it, the essential nature of the thing is either demonstrable or indemonstrable. Consequently, if the cause is distinct from the thing's essential nature and demonstration is possible, the cause must be the middle term, and, the conclusion proved being universal and affirmative, the proof is in the first figure. So the method just examined of proving it through another essential nature would be one way of proving essential nature, because a conclusion containing essen- 10 tial nature must be inferred through a middle which is an essential nature just as a "peculiar" property must be inferred through a middle which is a "peculiar" property; so that of the two definable natures of a single thing this method will prove one and not the other.

Now it was said before that this method could not amount to demonstration of essential nature—it is actually a dialectical proof of it—so let us begin again and ex- 15 plain by what method it can be demonstrated. When we are aware of a fact we seek its reason, and though sometimes the fact and the reason dawn on us simultaneously, yet we cannot apprehend the reason a moment sooner than the fact; and clearly in just the same way we cannot apprehend a thing's definable form without apprehending that it exists, since while we are igno- 20 rant whether it exists we cannot know its essential nature. Moreover we are aware whether a thing exists or not sometimes through apprehending an element in its character, and sometimes accidentally, as, for example, when we are aware of thunder as a noise in the clouds, of eclipse as a privation of light, or of man as some species of animal, or of the soul as a self-moving thing. As often as we have accidental 25 knowledge that the thing exists, we must be in a wholly negative state as regards awareness of its essential nature; for we have not got genuine knowledge even of its existence, and to search for a thing's essential nature when we are unaware that it exists is to search for nothing. On the other hand, whenever we apprehend an element in the thing's character there is less difficulty. Thus it follows that the degree of our knowledge of a thing's essential nature is determined by the sense in which we are aware that it exists. Let us then take the fol-30 lowing as our first instance of being aware of an element in the essential nature. Let A be eclipse, C the moon, B the earth's acting as a screen. Now to ask whether the moon is eclipsed or not is to ask whether or not B has occurred. But that is precisely the same as asking whether A has a defining condition; and if this condition actually exists, we assert that A also actually exists. Or again we may ask which side of a contradiction the defining condition necessitates: does it make the angles of a triangle equal or not equal to two right angles? When we 35 have found the answer, if the premises are immediate, we know fact and reason together; if they are not immediate, we know the fact without the reasons, as in the following example: let C be the moon, A eclipse, B the fact that the moon fails to produce shadows though she is full and though no visible body intervenes between us and her. Then if B, failure to produce 93b shadows in spite of the absence of an intervening body, is attributable to C, and A, eclipse, is attributable to B, it is clear that the moon is eclipsed, but the reason why is not yet clear, and we know that eclipse exists, but we do not know what its essential

nature is. But when it is clear that A is attributable to C and we proceed to ask the reason of this fact, we are inquiring what is 5 the nature of B: is it the earth's acting as a screen, or the moon's rotation or her extinction? But B is the definition of the other term, viz., in these examples, of the major term A; for eclipse is constituted by the earth acting as a screen. Thus, (1) "What is thunder?" "The quenching of fire in cloud," and (2) "Why does it thunder?" "Because fire is quenched in the cloud," are equivalent. Let C be cloud, A thunder, B the 10 quenching of fire. Then B is attributable to C, cloud, since fire is quenched in it; and A, noise, is attributable to B; and B is assuredly the definition of the major term A. If there be a further mediating cause of B, it will be one of the remaining partial definitions of A.

We have stated then how essential nature 15 is discovered and becomes known, and we see that, while there is no syllogism—i.e., no demonstrative syllogism—of essential nature, yet it is through syllogism, viz. demonstrative syllogism, that essential nature is exhibited. So we conclude that neither can the essential nature of anything which has a cause distinct from itself be known without demonstration, nor can it be demonstrated; and this is what we contended in our preliminary discussions.

. . . .

We think we have scientific knowledge 1 94a when we know the cause, and there are four causes: (1) the definable form, (2) an antecedent which necessitates a consequent, (3) the efficient cause, (4) the final cause. Hence each of these can be the middle term of a proof, for (a) though the inference from antecedent to necessary consequent does not hold if only one premise is assumed— 25 two is the minimum—still when there are two it holds on condition that they have a single common middle term. So it is from the assumption of this single middle term that the conclusion follows necessarily. The following example will also show this. Why is the angle in a semicircle a right angle?— or from what assumption does it follow that it is a right angle? Thus, let *A* be right angle, *B* the half of two right angles, *C* the angle in a semicircle. Then *B* is the cause in virtue of which *A*, right angle, is attributable to *C*, the angle in a semicircle, since *B* = *A* and the other, viz. *C*, = *B*, for *C* is half of two right angles. Therefore it *is* the assumption of *B*, the half of two right angles, from which it follows that *A* is attributable to *C*, i.e. that the angle in a semicircle is a right angle. Moreover, *B* is identical with *(b)* the defining form of *A*, since it is what *A*'s definition signifies. Moreover, the formal cause has already been shown to be the middle. *(c)* "Why did the Athenians become involved in the Persian war?" means "What cause originated the waging of war against the Athenians?" and the answer is, "Because they raided Sardis with the Eretrians," since this originated the war. Let *A* be war, *B* unprovoked raiding, *C* the Athenians. Then *B*, unprovoked raiding, is true of *C*, the Athenians, and *A* is true of *B*, since men make war on the unjust aggressor. So *A*, having war waged upon them, is true of *B*, the initial aggressors, and *B* is true of *C*, the Athenians, who were the aggressors. Hence here too the cause—in this case the efficient cause—is the middle term. *(d)* This is no less true where the cause is the final cause. E.g. why does one take a walk after supper? For the sake of one's health. Why does a house exist? For the preservation of one's goods. The end in view is in the one case health, in the other preservation. To ask the reason why one must walk after supper is precisely to ask to what end one must do it. Let *C* be walking after supper, *B* the non-regurgitation of food, *A* health. Then let walking after supper possess the property of preventing food from rising to the orifice of the stomach, and let this condition be healthy; since it seems that *B*, the non-regurgitation of food, is attributable to *C*, taking a walk, and that *A*, health, is attributable to *B*. What, then, is the cause through which *A*, the final cause, inheres in *C*? It is *B*, the non-regurgitation of food; but *B* is a kind of definition of *A*, for *A* will be explained by it. Why is *B* the cause of *A*'s belonging to *C*? Because to be in a condition such as *B* is to be in health. The definitions must be transposed, and then the detail will become clearer. Incidentally, here the order of coming to be is the reverse of what it is in proof through the efficient cause: in the efficient order the middle term must come to be first, whereas in the teleological order the minor, *C*, must first take place, and the end in view comes last in time.

The same thing may exist for an end and be necessitated as well. For example, light shines through a lantern (1) because that which consists of relatively small particles necessarily passes through pores larger than those particles—assuming that light does issue by penetration—and (2) for an end, namely to save us from stumbling. If, then, a thing can exist through two causes, can it come to be through two causes—as for instance if thunder be a hiss and a roar necessarily produced by the quenching of fire, and also designed, as the Pythagoreans say, for a threat to terrify those that lie in Tartarus? Indeed, there are very many such cases, mostly among the processes and products of the natural world; for nature, in different senses of the term "nature," produces now for an end, now by necessity.

Necessity too is of two kinds. It may work in accordance with a thing's natural tendency, or by constraint and in opposition to it; as, for instance, by necessity a stone is borne both upwards and downwards, but not by the same necessity.

Of the products of man's intelligence some are never due to chance or necessity but always to an end, as for example a house or a statue; others, such as health or safety, may result from chance as well.

It is mostly in cases where the issue is indeterminate (though only where the production does not originate in chance, and the end is consequently good), that a result is due to an end, and this is true alike in nature or in art. By chance, on the other hand, nothing comes to be for an end.

. . . .

As regards syllogism and demonstration, the definition of, and the conditions required to produce each of them, are now clear, and with that also the definition of, and the conditions required to produce, demonstrative knowledge, since it is the same as demonstration. As to the basic premises, how they become known and what is the developed state of knowledge of them is made clear by raising some preliminary problems.

20   We have already said that scientific knowledge through demonstration is impossible unless a man knows the primary immediate premises. But there are questions which might be raised in respect of the apprehension of these immediate premises: one might not only ask whether it is of the same kind as the apprehension of the conclusions, but also whether there is or is not scientific knowledge of both; or scientific knowledge of the latter, and of the former a different kind of knowledge: and, further, whether the developed states of knowledge
25 are not innate but come to be in us, or are innate but at first unnoticed. Now it is strange if we possess them from birth: for it means that we possess apprehensions more accurate than demonstration and fail to notice them. If on the other hand we acquire them and do not previously possess them, how could we apprehend and learn without a basis of preexistent knowledge?
30 For that is impossible, as we used to find in the case of demonstration. So it emerges that neither can we possess them from birth, nor can they come to be in us if we are without knowledge of them to the extent of having no such developed state at all. Therefore we must possess a capacity of some sort, but not such as to rank higher in accuracy than these developed states. And this at least is an obvious characteristic of
35 all animals, for they possess a congenital discriminative capacity which is called sense-perception. But though sense-perception is innate in all animals, in some the sense-impression comes to persist, in others it does not. So animals in which this persistence does not come to be have either no knowledge at all outside the act of perceiving, or no knowledge of objects of which no impression persists; animals in

which it does come into being have perception and can continue to retain the sense-impression in the soul: and when such persistence is frequently repeated a further distinction at once arises between those which out of the persistence of such sense-impression develop a power of systematizing them and those which do not. So out of sense-perception comes to be what we call memory, and out of frequently repeated memories of the same thing develops experience; for a number of memories constitute a single experience. From experience again—i.e., from the universal now stabilized in its entirety within the soul, the one beside the many which is a single identity within them all—originate the skill of the craftsman and the knowledge of the man of science, skill in the sphere of coming to be and science in the sphere of being.

We conclude that these stages of knowledge are neither innate in a determinate form, nor developed from other higher states of knowledge, but from sense-perception. It is like a rout in battle stopped by first one man making a stand and then another, until the original formation has been restored. The soul is so constituted as to be capable of this process.

Let us now restate the account given already, though with insufficient clearness. When one of a number of logically indiscriminable particulars has made a stand, the earliest universal is present in the soul: for though the act of sense-perception is of the particular, its content is universal—is man, for example, not the man Callias. A fresh stand is made among these rudimentary universals, and the process does not cease until the indivisible concepts, the true universals, are established; e.g., such and such a species of animal is a step towards the genus animal, which by the same process is a step towards a further generalization.

Thus it is clear that we must get to know the primary premises by induction: for the method by which even sense-perception implants the universal is inductive. Now of the thinking states by which we grasp truth, some are unfailingly true, others admit of error—opinion, for instance, and calcula-

tion, whereas scientific knowing and intuition are always true: further, no other kind of thought except intuition is more accurate than scientific knowledge, whereas primary premisses are more knowable than demonstrations, and all scientific knowledge is dis-
10 cursive. From these considerations it follows that there will be no scientific knowledge of the primary premisses, and since except intuition nothing can be truer than scientific knowledge, it will be intuition that apprehends the primary premisses—

a result which also follows from the fact that demonstration cannot be the originative source of demonstration, nor, consequently, scientific knowledge of scientific knowledge. If, therefore, it is the only other kind of true thinking except scientific knowing, intuition will be the originative source of 15 scientific knowledge. And the originative source of science grasps the original basic premiss, while science as a whole is similarly related as originative source to the whole body of fact.

DE ANIMA

BOOK II

. . . .

5 Having made these distinctions let us now speak of sensation in the widest sense. Sensation depends, as we have said, on a process of movement or affection from without, for it is held to be some sort of change
35 of quality. Now some thinkers assert that
417ᵃ like is affected only by like; in what sense this is possible and in what sense impossible, we have explained in our general discussion of acting and being acted upon.

Here arises a problem: why do we not perceive the sense themselves as well as the external objects of sense, or why without the stimulation of external objects do they
5 not produce sensation, seeing that they contain in themselves fire, earth, and all the other elements, which are the direct or indirect objects of sense? It is clear that what is sensitive is so only potentially, not actually. The power of sense is parallel to what

is combustible, for that never ignites itself spontaneously, but requires an agent which has the power of starting ignition; otherwise it could have set itself on fire, and would not have needed actual fire to set it ablaze.

In reply we must recall that we use the word "perceive" in two ways, for we say 10 (a) that what has the power to hear or see, "sees" or "hears," even though it is at the moment asleep, and also (b) that what is actually seeing or hearing, "sees" or "hears." Hence "sense" too must have two meanings, sense potential, and sense actual. Similarly "to be a sentient" means either (a) to have a certain power or (b) to manifest a certain activity. To begin with, for a time, 15 let us speak as if there were no difference between (1) being moved or affected, and (2) being active, for a movement is a kind of activity—an imperfect kind, as has elsewhere been explained. Everything that is acted upon or moved is acted upon by an agent which is actually at work. Hence it is

De Anima, II.5–6 (416b30–418a25), III.3–6 (427a15–430b30), III.8 (431a20–432a10). From *The Oxford Translation of Aristotle*, vol. 3, translated by J. A. Smith, edited by W. D. Ross (Oxford: Oxford University Press, 1931). Reprinted by permission of Oxford University Press.

20   that in one sense, as has already been stated, what acts and what is acted upon are like, in another unlike, i.e. prior to and during the change the two factors are unlike, after it like.

But we must now distinguish not only *between* what is potential and what is actual but also different senses in which things can be said to be potential or actual; up to now we have been speaking as if each of these phrases had only one sense. We can speak of something as "a knower" either *(a)* as when we say that man is a knower, meaning that man falls within the class of beings that

25   know or have knowledge, or *(b)* as when we are speaking of a man who possesses a knowledge of grammar; each of these is so called as having in him a certain potentiality, but there is a difference between their respective potentialities, the one *(a)* being a potential knower, because his kind or matter is such and such, the other *(b)*, because he can in the absence of any external counteracting cause realize his knowledge in actual knowing at will. This implies a third meaning of "a knower" *(c)*, one who is already realizing his knowledge—he is a knower in actuality and in the most proper sense is

30   knowing, e.g. this A. Both the former are potential knowers, who realize their respective potentialities, the one *(a)* by change of quality, i.e. repeated transitions from one state to its opposite under instruction, the

417ᵇ   other *(b)* by the transition from the inactive possession of sense or grammar to their active exercise. The two kinds of transition are distinct.

Also the expression "to be acted upon" has more than one meaning; it may mean either *(a)* the extinction of one of two contraries by the other, or *(b)* the maintenance of what is potential by the agency of what is actual and already like what is acted upon, with such likeness as is compatible

5   with one's being actual and the other potential. For what possesses knowledge becomes an actual knower by a transition which is either not an alteration of it at all (being in reality a development into its true self or actuality) or at least an alteration in

a quite different sense from the usual meaning.

Hence it is wrong to speak of a wise man as being "altered" when he uses his wisdom, just as it would be absurd to speak of a builder as being altered when he is using his skill in building a house.

What in the case of knowing or under-   10 standing leads from potentiality to actuality ought not to be called teaching but something else. That which starting with the power to know learns or acquires knowledge through the agency of one who actually knows and has the power of teaching either *(a)* ought not to be said to "be acted upon" at all *or (b)* we must recognize two   15 senses of alteration, viz. (1) the substitution of one quality for another, the first being the contrary of the second, or (2) the development of an existent quality from potentiality in the direction of fixity or nature.

In the case of what is to possess sense, the first transition is due to the action of the male parent and takes place before birth so that at birth the living thing is, in respect of sensation, at the stage which corresponds to the *possession* of knowledge. Actual sensation corresponds to the stage of the exercise of knowledge. But between the two cases compared there is a difference; the   20 objects that excite the sensory powers to activity, the seen, the heard, etc., are outside. The ground of this difference is that what actual sensation apprehends is individuals, while what knowledge apprehends is universals, and these are in a sense within the soul. That is why man can exercise his knowledge when he wishes, but his sensation does not depend upon himself—a sensible object must be there. A similar state-   25 ment must be made about our *knowledge* of what is sensible—on the same ground, viz. that the sensible objects are individual and external.

A later more appropriate occasion may be found thoroughly to clear up all this. At   30 present it must be enough to recognize the distinctions already drawn; a thing may be said to be potential in either of two senses, *(a)* in the sense in which we might say of a boy that he may become a general or *(b)* in the sense in which we might say the same **418ᵃ** of an adult, and there are two corresponding senses of the term "a potential sentient." There are no separate names for the two stages of potentiality; we have pointed out that they are different and how they are different. We cannot help using the incorrect terms "being acted upon or altered" of the two transitions involved. As we have said, what has the power of sensation is potentially like what the perceived object is actually; that is, while at the beginning of the process of its being acted upon the two interacting factors are dissimilar, at the end 5 the one acted upon is assimilated to the other and is identical in quality with it.

6 In dealing with each of the senses we shall have first to speak of the objects which are perceptible by each. The term "object of sense" covers three kinds of objects, two kinds of which are, in our language, directly perceptible, while the remaining one is only incidentally perceptible. Of the first two 10 kinds one *(a)* consists of what is perceptible by a single sense, the other *(b)* of what is perceptible by any and all of the senses. I call by the name of special object of this or that sense that which cannot be perceived by any other sense than that one and in respect of which no error is possible; in this sense colour is the special object of sight, sound of hearing, flavour of taste. Touch, indeed, discriminates more than one set of 15 different qualities. Each sense has one kind of object which it discerns, and never errs in reporting that what is before it is colour or sound (though it may err as to what it is that is coloured or where that is, or what it is that is sounding or where that is). Such objects are what we propose to call the special objects of this or that sense.

"Common sensibles" are movement, rest, number, figure, magnitude; these are not peculiar to any one sense, but are common to all. There are at any rate certain kinds of movement which are perceptible both by touch and by sight.

20 We speak of an incidental object of sense

where e.g. the white object which we see is the son of Diares; here because "being the son of Diares" is incidental to the directly visible white patch we speak of the son of Diares as being (incidentally) perceived or seen by us. Because this is only incidentally an object of sense, it in no way as such affects the senses. Of the two former kinds, both of which are in their own nature perceptible by sense, the first kind—that of special objects of the several senses—constitute *the* objects of sense in the strictest sense of the term and it is to them that in 25 the nature of things the structure of each several sense is adapted.

. . . . . .

BOOK III

. . . . . .

There are two distinctive peculiarities by **427ᵃ 3** reference to which we characterize the soul—(1) local movement and (2) thinking, discriminating, and perceiving. Thinking both speculative and practical is regarded as akin to a form of perceiving; for in the one as well as the other the soul discriminates 20 and is cognizant of something which *is*. Indeed the ancients go so far as to identify thinking and perceiving; e.g., Empedocles says "For 'tis in respect of what is present that man's wit is increased," and again "Whence it befalls them from time to time to think diverse thoughts," and Homer's phrase "For suchlike is man's mind" means 25 the same. They all look upon thinking as a bodily process like perceiving, and hold that like is *known* as well as *perceived* by like, as I explained at the beginning of our discussion. Yet they ought at the same time to have accounted for error also; for it is more **427ᵇ** intimately connected with animal existence and the soul continues longer in the state of error than in that of truth. They cannot escape the dilemma: either (1) whatever seems is true (and there are some who accept this) or (2) error is contact with the unlike; for that is the opposite of the knowing of like by like.

5   But it is a received principle that error as well as knowledge in respect to contraries is one and the same.

That perceiving and practical thinking are not identical is therefore obvious; for the former is universal in the animal world, the latter is found in only a small division of it. Further, speculative thinking is also distinct from perceiving—I mean that in which we
10   find rightness and wrongness—rightness in prudence, knowledge, true opinion, wrongness in their opposites; for perception of the special objects of sense is always free from error, and is found in all animals, while it is possible to think falsely as well as truly, and thought is found only where there is discourse of reason as well as sensibility.
15   For imagination is different from either perceiving or discursive thinking, though it is not found without sensation, or judgement without it. That this activity is not the same kind of thinking as judgement is obvious. For imagining lies within our own power whenever we wish (e.g. we can call up a picture, as in the practice of mnemonics by the use of mental images), but in forming
20   opinions we are not free: we cannot escape the alternative of falsehood or truth. Further, when we think something to be fearful or threatening, emotion is immediately produced, and so too with what is encouraging; but when we merely imagine we remain as unaffected as persons who are looking at a painting of some dreadful or encouraging scene. Again within the field of judgement
25   itself we find varieties—knowledge, opinion, prudence, and their opposites; of the differences between these I must speak elsewhere.

Thinking is different from perceiving and is held to be in part imagination, in part judgement: we must therefore first mark off the sphere of imagination and then speak of
428ᵃ judgement. If then imagination is that in virtue of which an image arises for us, excluding metaphorical uses of the term, is it a single faculty or disposition relative to images, in virtue of which we discriminate and are either in error or not? The faculties in virtue of which we do this are sense, opinion, science, intelligence.

That imagination is not sense is clear 5 from the following considerations: Sense is either a faculty or an activity, e.g. sight or seeing: imagination takes place in the absence of both, as e.g. in dreams. (2) Again, sense is always present, imagination not. If actual imagination and actual sensation were the same, imagination would be found in all the brutes: this is held not to be the 10 case; e.g. it is not found in ants or bees or grubs. (3) Again, sensations are always true, imaginations are for the most part false. (4) Once more, even in ordinary speech, we do not, when sense functions precisely with regard to its object, say that we imagine it to be a man, but rather when there is some failure of accuracy in its exercise. And (5), as we were saying before, visions appear to 15 us even when our eyes are shut. Neither is imagination *any* of the things that are never in error: e.g. knowledge or intelligence; for imagination may be false.

It remains therefore to see if it is opinion, for opinion may be either true or false.

But opinion involves belief (for without 20 belief in what we opine we cannot have an opinion), and in the brutes though we often find imagination we never find belief. Further, every opinion is accompanied by belief, belief by conviction, and conviction by discourse of reason: while there are some of the brutes in which we find imagination, without discourse of reason. It is clear then that imagination cannot, again, be (1) opinion *plus* sensation, or (2) opinion mediated 25 by sensation, or (3) a blend of opinion and sensation; this is impossible both for these reasons and because the content of the supposed opinion cannot be different from that of the sensation (I mean that imagination must be the blending of the perception of white with the opinion that it is white: it could scarcely be a blend of the opinion that 30 it is good with the perception that it is **428ᵇ** white): to imagine is therefore (on this view) identical with the thinking of exactly the same as what one in the strictest sense perceives. But what we imagine is sometimes false though our contemporaneous judgement about it is true; e.g. we imagine the sun to be a foot in diameter though we are convinced that it is larger than the inhabited part of the earth, and the following dilemma presents itself. Either *(a)* while the fact has not changed and the observer has neither forgotten nor lost belief in the true opinion which he had, that opinion had disappeared, or *(b)* if he retains it then his opinion is at once true and false. A true opinion, however, becomes false only when the fact alters without being noticed.

Imagination is therefore neither any of the states enumerated, nor compounded out of them.

But since when one thing has been set in motion another thing may be moved by it, and imagination is held to be a movement and to be impossible without sensation, i.e., to occur in beings that are percipient and to have for its content what can be perceived, and since movement may be produced by actual sensation and that movement is necessarily similar in character to the sensation itself, this movement must be (1) necessarily *(a)* incapable of existing apart from sensation, *(b)* incapable of existing except when we perceive, (2) such that in virtue of its possession that in which it is found may present various phenomena both active and passive, and (3) such that it may be either true or false.

The reason of the last characteristic is as follows. Perception (1) of the special objects of sense is never in error or admits the least possible amount of falsehood. (2) That of the concomitance of the objects concomitant with the sensible qualities comes next: in this case certainly we may be deceived; for while the perception that there is white before us cannot be false, the perception that what is white is this or that may be false. (3) Third comes the perception of the universal attributes which accompany the concomitant objects to which the special sensibles attach (I mean e.g. of movement and magnitude); it is in respect of these that the greatest amount of sense-illusion is possible.

The motion which is due to the activity of sense in these three modes of its exercise will differ from the activity of sense; (1) the first kind of derived motion is free from er-

ror while the sensation is present; (2) and (3) the others may be erroneous whether it is present or absent, especially when the object of perception is far off. If then imagination presents no other features than those enumerated and is what we have described, then imagination must be a movement resulting from an actual exercise of a power of sense.

As sight is the most highly developed sense, the name φαντασία (imagination) has been formed from φάος (light) because it is not possible to see without light.

And because imaginations remain in the organs of sense and resemble sensations, animals in their actions are largely guided by them, some (i.e. the brutes) because of the non-existence in them of mind, others (i.e. men) because of the temporary eclipse in them of mind by feeling or disease or sleep.

About imagination, what it is and why it exists, let so much suffice.

Turning now to the part of the soul with which the soul knows and thinks (whether this is separable from the others in definition only, or spatially as well) we have to inquire (1) what differentiates this part, and (2) how thinking can take place.

If thinking is like perceiving, it must be either a process in which the soul is acted upon by what is capable of being thought, or a process different from but analogous to that. The thinking part of the soul must therefore be, while impassible, capable of receiving the form of an object; that is, must be potentially identical in character with its object without being the object. Mind must be related to what is thinkable, as sense is to what is sensible.

Therefore, since everything is a possible object of thought, mind in order, as Anaxagoras says, to dominate, that is, to know, must be pure from all admixture; for the copresence of what is alien to its nature is a hindrance and a block: it follows that it too, like the sensitive part, can have no nature of its own, other than that of having a certain capacity. Thus that in the soul which is called mind (by mind I mean that whereby

the soul thinks and judges) is, before it thinks, not actually any real thing. For this reason it cannot reasonably be regarded as blended with the body: if so, it would ac-
25 quire some quality, e.g. warmth or cold, or even have an organ like the sensitive faculty: as it is, it has none. It was a good idea to call the soul "the place of forms," though (1) this description holds only of the intellective soul, and (2) even this is the forms only potentially, not actually.

Observation of the sense-organs and their
30 employment reveals a distinction between the impassibility of the sensitive and that of the intellective faculty. After strong stimulation of a sense we are less able to exercise it than before, as e.g. in the case of a loud sound we cannot hear easily immediately
429ᵇ after, or in the case of a bright colour or a powerful odour we cannot see or smell, but in the case of mind thought about an object that is highly intelligible renders it more and not less able afterwards to think objects that are less intelligible: the reason is that while the faculty of sensation is dependent upon the body, mind is separable from it.

5 Once the mind has become each set of its possible objects, as a man of science has, when this phrase is used of one who is actually a man of science (this happens when he is now able to exercise the power on his own initiative), its condition is still one of potentiality, but in a different sense from the potentiality which preceded the acquisition of knowledge by learning or discovery: the mind too is then able to think *itself*.

10 Since we can distinguish between a spatial magnitude and what it is to be such, and between water and what it is to be water, and so in many other cases (though not in all; for in certain cases the thing and its form are identical), flesh and what it is to be flesh are discriminated either by different faculties, or by the same faculty in two different states: for flesh necessarily involves matter and is like what is snub-nosed, a *this* in a *this*. Now it is by means of the sensitive faculty that we discriminate the hot and the
15 cold, i.e. the factors which combined in a certain ratio constitute flesh: the essential character of flesh is apprehended by some-

thing different either wholly separate from the sensitive faculty or related to it as a bent line to the same line when it has been straightened out.

Again in the case of abstract objects what is straight is analogous to what is snub-nosed; for it necessarily implies a continuum as its matter: its constitutive essence is different, if we may distinguish between straightness and what is straight: let us take 20 it to be two-ness. It must be apprehended, therefore, by a different power or by the same power in a different state. To sum up, in so far as the realities it knows are capable of being separated from their matter, so it is also with the powers of mind.

The problem might be suggested: if thinking is a passive affection, then if mind is simple and impassible and has nothing in common with anything else, as Anaxagoras says, how can it come to think at all? For interaction between two factors is held to 25 require a precedent community of nature between the factors. Again it might be asked, is mind a possible object of thought to itself? For if mind is thinkable *per se* and what is thinkable is in kind one and the same, then either *(a)* mind will belong to everything, or *(b)* mind will contain some element common to it with all other realities which makes them all thinkable.

(1) Have not we already disposed of the difficulty about interaction involving a com- 30 mon element, when we said that mind is in a sense potentially whatever is thinkable, though actually it is nothing until is has thought? What it thinks must be in it just as characters may be said to be on a writing- 430ᵃ table on which as yet nothing actually stands written: this is exactly what happens with mind.

(2) Mind is itself thinkable in exactly the same way as its objects are. For *(a)* in the case of objects which involve no matter, what thinks and what is thought are identical; for speculative knowledge and its object are identical. (Why mind is not always thinking we must consider later) *(b)* In the 5 case of those which contain matter each of the objects of thought is only potentially present. It follows that while *they* will not

have mind in them (for mind is a potentiality of them only in so far as they are capable of being disengaged from matter) mind may yet be thinkable.

10 5 Since in every class of things, as in nature as a whole, we find two factors involved, (1) a matter which is potentially all the particulars included in the class, (2) a cause which is productive in the sense that it makes them all (the latter standing to the former, as e.g. an art to its material), these distinct elements must likewise be found within the soul.

And in fact mind as we have described it is what it is by virtue of becoming all 15 things, while there is another which is what it is by virtue of making all things: this is a sort of positive state like light; for in a sense light makes potential colours into actual colours.

Mind in this sense of it is separable, impassible, unmixed, since it is in its essential nature activity (for always the active is superior to the passive factor, the originating force to the matter which it forms).

20 Actual knowledge is identical with its object: in the individual, potential knowledge is in time prior to actual knowledge, but in the universe as a whole it is not prior even in time. Mind is not at one time knowing and at another not. When mind is set free from its present conditions it appears as just what it is and nothing more: this alone is immortal and eternal (we do not, however, remember its former activity because, while 25 mind in this sense is impassible, mind as passive is destructible), and without it nothing thinks.

6 The thinking then of the simple objects of thought is found in those cases where falsehood is impossible: where the alternative of true or false applies, there we always find a putting together of objects of thought in a quasi-unity. As Empedocles said that "where heads of many a creature sprouted 30 without necks" they afterwards by Love's power were combined, so here too objects of thought which were given separate are combined, e.g. "incommensurate" and "di-

agonal"; if the combination be of objects past or future the combination of thought includes in its content the date. For false- **430ᵇ** hood always involves a synthesis; for even if you assert that what is white is not white you have included not-white in the synthesis. It is possible also to call all these cases division as well as combination. However that may be, there is not only the true or false assertion that Cleon is white but also the true or false assertion that he *was* or *will* 5 *be* white. In each and every case that which unifies is mind.

Since the word "simple" has two senses, i.e. may mean either *(a)* "not capable of being divided" or *(b)* "not actually divided," there is nothing to prevent mind from knowing what is undivided, e.g. when it apprehends a length (which is actually undivided) and that in an undivided time; for the time is divided or undivided in the same manner as the line. It is not possible, then, to tell 10 what part of the line it was apprehending in each half of the time: the object has no actual parts until it has been divided: if in thought you think each half separately, then by the same act you divide the time also, the half-lines becoming as it were new wholes of length. But if you think it as a whole consisting of these two possible parts, then also you think it in a time which corresponds to both parts together. (But what is not quantitatively but qualitatively 15 simple is thought in a simple time and by a simple act of the soul.)

But that which mind thinks and the time in which it thinks are in this case divisible only incidentally and not as such. For in them too there is something indivisible (though, it may be, not isolable) which gives unity to the time and the whole of length; and this is found equally in every continuum whether temporal or spatial.

Points and similar instances of things that 20 divide, themselves being indivisible, are realized in consciousness in the same manner as privations.

A similar account may be given of all other cases, e.g., how evil or black is cognized; they are cognized, in a sense, by means of their contraries. That which cog-

nizes must have an element of potentiality
in its being, and one of the contraries must
be in it. But if there is anything that has no
25 contrary, then it knows itself and is actually
and possesses independent existence.

Assertion is the saying of something concerning something, e.g. affirmation, and is
in every case either true or false; this is not
always the case with mind: the thinking of
the definition in the sense of the constitutive
essence is never in error nor is it the assertion of something concerning something,
but, just as while the seeing of the special
object of sight can never be in error, the
belief that the white object seen is a man
30 may be mistaken, so too in the case of objects which are without matter.

.   .   .   .

431ᵇ 20 Let us now summarize our results about
soul, and repeat that the soul is in a way all
existing things; for existing things are either
sensible or thinkable, and knowledge is in
a way what is knowable, and sensation is in
a way what is sensible: in *what* way we
must inquire.

Knowledge and sensation are divided to
correspond with the realities, potential
25 knowledge and sensation answering to potentialities, actual knowledge and sensation
to actualities. Within the soul the faculties

of knowledge and sensation are *potentially*
these objects, the one what is knowable, the
other what is sensible. They must be either
the things themselves or their forms. The
former alternative is of course impossible:
it is not the stone which is present in the
soul but its form.

It follows that the soul is analogous to   **432ᵃ**
the hand; for as the hand is a tool of tools,
so the mind is the form of forms and sense
the form of sensible things.

Since according to common agreement
there is nothing outside and separate in
existence from sensible spatial magnitudes,
the objects of thought are in the sensible
forms., viz. both the abstract objects and   5
all the states and affections of sensible
things. Hence (1) no one can learn or understand anything in the absence of sense,
and (2) when the mind is actively aware
of anything it is necessarily aware of it
along with an image: for images are like
sensuous contents except in that they contain no matter.

Imagination is different from assertion
and denial: for what is true or false involves
a synthesis of concepts. In what will the primary concepts differ from images? Must we   10
not say that neither these nor even our other
concepts are images, though they necessarily involve them?

3 / Sextus Empiricus (A.D. 175?–225?)
OUTLINES OF PYRRHONISM

BOOK I

Chapter 4—What Scepticism Is

8 Scepticism is an ability, or mental attitude, which opposes appearances to judgements in any way whatsoever, with the result that, owing to the equipollence of the objects and reasons thus opposed, we are brought firstly to a state of mental suspense and next to a state of "unperturbedness" or quietude.

9 Now we call it an "ability" not in any subtle sense, but simply in respect of its "being able." By "appearances" we now mean the objects of sense-perception, whence we contrast them with the objects of thought or "judgements." The phrase "in any way whatsoever" can be connected either with the word "ability," to make us take the word "ability," as we said, in its simple sense, or with the phrase "opposing appearances to judgements"; for inasmuch as we oppose these in a variety of ways—appearances to appearances, or judgements to judgements, or *alternando* appearances to judgements,— in order to ensure the inclusion of all these antitheses we employ the phrase "in any way whatsoever." Or, again, we join "in any way whatsoever" to "appearances and judgements" in order that we may not have to inquire how the appearances appear or how the thought-objects are judged, but may take these terms in the simple sense.

10 The phrase "opposed judgements" we do not employ in the sense of negations and affirmations only but simply as equivalent to "conflicting judgements." "Equipollence" we use of equality in respect of probability and improbability, to indicate that no one of the conflicting judgements takes precedence of any other as being more probable. "Suspense" is a state of mental rest owing to which we neither deny nor affirm anything. "Quietude" is an untroubled and tranquil condition of soul. And how quietude enters the soul along with suspension of judgement we shall explain in our chapter (XII) "Concerning the End."

·   ·   ·   ·   ·   ·

Chapter 6—Of the Principles of Scepticism

12 The originating cause of Scepticism is, we say, the hope of attaining quietude. Men of talent, who were perturbed by the contradictions in things and in doubt as to which of the alternatives they ought to accept, were led on to inquire what is true in things and what false, hoping by the settlement of this question to attain quietude. The main basic principle of the Sceptic system is that of opposing to every proposition an equal proposition; for we believe that as a consequence of this we end by ceasing to dogmatize.

·   ·   ·   ·   ·   ·

Chapter 10—Do the Sceptics Abolish Appearances?

19 Those who say that "the Sceptics abolish appearances," or phenomena, seem to me to

Outlines of Pyrrhonism, Book I: 4.8–10, 6.12, 10.19–20, 13.31–34, 14.36, 14.91–107, 14.112–34, 15.164–77; Book II: 3.14–17, 4.18–20, 6.48, 6.55–60, 7.70–75, 7.79, 15.204; Book III: 32.280–81. Excerpted by permission of the publishers and the Loeb Classical Library from Sextus Empiricus, *Outlines of Pyrrhonism*, translated by R. G. Bury (Cambridge, Mass.: Harvard University Press, 1933).

be unacquainted with the statements of our School. For, as we said above, we do not overthrow the affective sense-impressions which induce our assent voluntarily; and these impressions are "the appearances." And when we question whether the underlying object is such as it appears, we grant the fact that it appears, and our doubt does not concern the appearance itself but the account given of that appearance,—and that is a different thing from questioning the ap-

20 pearance itself. For example, honey appears to us to be sweet (and this we grant, for we perceive sweetness through the senses), but whether it is also sweet in its essence is for us a matter of doubt, since this is not an appearance but a judgement regarding the appearance. And even if we do actually argue against the appearances, we do not propound such arguments with the intention of abolishing appearances, but by way of pointing out the rashness of the Dogmatists; for if reason is such a trickster as to all but snatch away the appearances from under our very eyes, surely we should view it with suspicion in the case of things non-evident so as not to display rashness by following it.

. . . .

Chapter 13—Of the General Modes Leading to Suspension of Judgement

31 Now that we have been saying that tranquillity follows on suspension of judgement, it will be our next task to explain how we arrive at this suspension. Speaking generally, one may say that it is the result of setting things in opposition. We oppose either appearances to appearances or objects

32 of thought to objects of thought or *alternando*. For instance, we oppose appearances to appearances when we say "The same tower appears round from a distance, but square from close at hand"; and thoughts to thoughts, when in answer to him who argues the existence of Providence from the order of the heavenly bodies we oppose the fact that often the good fare ill and the bad fare well, and draw from this

33 the inference that Providence does not exist. And thoughts we oppose to appearances, as

when Anaxagoras countered the notion that snow is white with the argument, "Snow is frozen water, and water is black; therefore snow also is black." With a different idea we oppose things present sometimes to things past or future, as for instance, when someone propounds to us a theory which we are unable to refute, we say to him in 34 reply, "Just as, before the birth of the founder of the School to which you belong, the theory it holds was not as yet apparent as a sound theory, although it was really in existence, so likewise it is possible that the opposite theory to that which you now propound is already really existent, though not yet apparent to us, so that we ought not as yet to yield assent to this theory which at the moment seems to be valid."

. . . . . .

Chapter 14—Concerning the Ten Modes

The usual tradition amongst the older Scep- 36 tics is that the "modes" by which "suspension" is supposed to be brought about are ten in number;

. . . . . .

The *Third Mode* is, we say, based on differences in the senses. That the senses differ from one another is obvious. Thus, to the 92 eye paintings seem to have recesses and projections, but not so to the touch. Honey, too, seems to some pleasant to the tongue but unpleasant to the eyes; so that it is impossible to say whether it is absolutely pleasant or unpleasant. The same is true of sweet oil, for it pleases the sense of smell but displeases the taste. So too with spurge: 93 since it pains the eyes but causes no pain to any other part of the body, we cannot say whether, in its real nature, it is absolutely painful or painless to bodies. Rain-water, too, is beneficial to the eyes but roughens the wind-pipe and the lungs; as also does olive-oil, though it mollifies the epidermis. The cramp-fish, also, when applied to the extremities produces cramp, but it can be applied to the rest of the body without hurt. Consequently we are unable to say what is the real nature of each of these things, although it is possible to say what each thing at the moment appears to be.

94   A longer list of examples might be given, but to avoid prolixity, in view of the plan of our treatise, we will say just this. Each of the phenomena perceived by the senses seems to be a complex: the apple, for example, seems smooth, odorous, sweet and yellow. But it is non-evident whether it really possesses these qualities only; or whether it has but one quality but appears varied owing to the varying structure of the sense-organs; or whether, again, it has more qualities than are apparent, some of which 95 elude our perception. That the apple has but one quality might be argued from what we said above regarding the food absorbed by bodies, and the water sucked up by trees, and the breath in flutes and pipes and similar instruments; for the apple likewise may be all of one sort but appear different owing to differences in the sense-organs in which 96 perception takes place. And that the apple may possibly possess more qualities than those apparent to us we argue in this way. Let us imagine a man who possesses from birth the senses of touch, taste and smell, but can neither hear nor see. This man, then, will assume that nothing visible or audible has any existence, but only those three kinds of qualities which he is able to ap- 97 prehend. Possibly, then, we also, having only our five senses, perceive only such of the apple's qualities as we are capable of apprehending; and possibly it may possess other underlying qualities which affect other sense-organs, though we, not being endowed with those organs, fail to apprehend the sense-objects which come through them.

98   "But," it may be objected, "Nature made the senses commensurate with the objects of sense." What kind of "Nature"? we ask, seeing that there exists so much unresolved controversy amongst the Dogmatists concerning the reality which belongs to Nature. For he who decides the question as to the existence of Nature will be discredited by them if he is an ordinary person, while if he is a philosopher he will be a party to the controversy and therefore himself subject to judgement and not a judge. If however, it is possible that only those qualities which we 99 seem to perceive subsist in the apple, or that a greater number subsist, or, again, that not even the qualities which affect us subsist, then it will be non-evident to us what the nature of the apple really is. And the same argument applies to all the other objects of sense. But if the senses do not apprehend external objects, neither can the mind apprehend them; hence, because of this argument also, we shall be driven, it seems, to suspend judgement regarding the external underlying objects.

In order that we may finally reach sus- 100 pension by basing our argument on each sense singly, or even by disregarding the senses, we further adopt the *Fourth Mode* of suspension. This is the Mode based, as we say, on the "circumstances," meaning by "circumstances" conditions or dispositions. And this Mode, we say, deals with states that are natural or unnatural, with waking or sleeping, with conditions due to age, motion or rest, hatred or love, emptiness or fulness, drunkenness or soberness, predispositions, confidence or fear, grief or joy. Thus, according as the mental state is nat- 101 ural or unnatural, objects produce dissimilar impressions, as when men in a frenzy or in a state of ecstasy believe they hear daemons' voices, while we do not. Similarly they often say that they perceive an odour of storax or frankincense, or some such scent, and many other things, though we fail to perceive them. Also, the same water which feels very hot when poured on inflamed spots seems lukewarm to us. And the same coat which seems of a bright yellow colour to men with blood-shot eyes does not appear so to me. And the same honey seems to me sweet, but bitter to men 102 with jaundice. Now should anyone say that it is an intermixture of certain humours which produces in those who are in an unnatural state improper impressions from the underlying objects, we have to reply that, since healthy persons also have mixed humours, these humours too are capable of causing the external objects—which really are such as they appear to those who are said to be in an unnatural state—to appear

103 other than they are to healthy persons. For to ascribe the power of altering the underlying objects to those humours, and not to these, is purely fanciful; since just as healthy men are in a state that is natural for the healthy but unnatural for the sick, so also sick men are in a state that is unnatural for the healthy but natural for the sick, so that to these last also we must give credence as being, relatively speaking, in a natural state.

104   Sleeping and waking, too, give rise to different impressions, since we do not imagine when awake what we imagine in sleep, nor when asleep what we imagine when awake; so that the existence or non-existence of our impressions is not absolute but relative, being in relation to our sleeping or waking condition. Probably, then, in dreams we see things which to our waking state are unreal, although not wholly unreal; for they exist in our dreams, just as waking realities exist although non-existent in dreams.

105   Age is another cause of difference. For the same air seems chilly to the old but mild to those in their prime; and the same colour appears faint to older men but vivid to those in their prime; and similarly the same sound

106 seems to the former faint, but to the latter clearly audible. Moreover, those who differ in age are differently moved in respect of choice and avoidance. For whereas children—to take a case—are all eagerness for balls and hoops, men in their prime choose other things, and old men yet others. And from this we conclude that differences in age also cause different impressions to be produced by the same underlying objects.

107   Another cause why the real objects appear different lies in motion and rest. For those objects which, when we are standing still, we see to be motionless, we imagine to be in motion when we are sailing past them.

.   .   .   .

112   Seeing then that the dispositions also are the cause of so much disagreement, and that

men are differently disposed at different times, although, no doubt, it is easy to say what nature each of the underlying objects appears to each man to possess, we cannot go on to say what its real nature is, since the disagreement admits in itself of no settlement. For the person who tries to settle it is either in one of the afore-mentioned dispositions or in no disposition whatsoever. But to declare that he is in no disposition at all—as, for instance, neither in health nor sickness, neither in motion nor at rest, of no definite age, and devoid of all the other dispositions as well—is the height of absurdity. And if he is to judge the sense-impressions while he is in some one disposition, he will be a party to the disagreement, and, moreover, he will not be an impartial judge of the external underlying 113 objects owing to his being confused by the dispositions in which he is placed. The waking person, for instance, cannot compare the impressions of sleepers with those of men awake, nor the sound person those of the sick with those of the sound; for we assent more readily to things present, which affect us in the present, than to things not present.

In another way, too, the disagreement of 114 such impressions is incapable of settlement. For he who prefers one impression to another, or one "circumstance" to another, does so either uncritically and without proof or critically and with proof; but he can do this neither without these means (for then he would be discredited) nor with them. For if he is to pass judgement on the impressions he must certainly judge them by a criterion; this criterion, then, he will declare 115 to be true, or else false. But if false, he will be discredited; whereas, if he shall declare it to be true, he will be stating that the criterion is true either without proof or with proof. But if without proof, he will be discredited; and if with proof, it will certainly be necessary for the proof also to be true, to avoid being discredited. Shall he, then, affirm the truth of the proof adopted to establish the criterion after having judged it or without judging it? If without judging, 116 he will be discredited; but after judging, plainly he will say that he has judged it by a criterion; and of that criterion we shall ask for a proof, and of that proof again a criterion. For the proof always requires a criterion to confirm it, and the criterion also a proof to demonstrate its truth; and neither can a proof be sound without the previous existence of a true criterion nor can the criterion be true without the previous confir-

117 mation of the proof. So in this way both the criterion and the proof are involved in the circular process of reasoning, and thereby both are found to be untrustworthy: for since each of them is dependent on the credibility of the other, the one is lacking in credibility just as much as the other. Consequently, if a man can prefer one impression to another neither without a proof and a criterion nor with them, then the different impressions due to the differing conditions will admit of no settlement; so that as a result of this Mode also we are brought to suspend judgement regarding the nature of external realities.

118   The *Fifth Argument* (or *Trope*) is that based on positions, distances, and locations; for owing to each of these the same objects appear different; for example, the same porch when viewed from one of its corners appears curtailed, but viewed from the middle symmetrical on all sides; and the same ship seems at a distance to be small and stationary, but from close at hand large and in motion: and the same tower from a distance appears round but from a near point quadrangular.

119   These effects are due to distances; among effects due to locations are the following: the light of a lamp appears dim in the sun but bright in the dark; and the same oar bent when in the water but straight when out of the water; and the egg soft when inside the fowl but hard when in the air; and the jacinth fluid when in the lynx but hard when in the air; and the coral soft when in the sea but hard when in the air; and sound seems to differ in quality according as it is produced in a pipe, or in a flute, or simply in the air.

120   Effects due to positions are such as these: the same painting when laid flat appears smooth, but when inclined forward at a cer-

tain angle it seems to have recesses and prominences. The necks of doves, also, appear different in the hue according to the differences in the angle of inclination.

121   Since, then, all apparent objects are viewed in a certain place, and from a certain distance, or in a certain position, and each of these conditions produces a great divergency in the sense-impressions, as we mentioned above, we shall be compelled by this Mode also to end up in suspension of judgement. For in fact anyone who purposes to give the preference to any of these impressions will be attempting the impossible. For

122 if he shall deliver his judgement simply and without proof, he will be discredited; and should he, on the other hand, desire to adduce proof, he will confute himself if he says that the proof is false, while if he asserts that the proof is true he will be asked for a proof of its truth, and again for a proof of this latter proof, since it also must be true, and so on *ad infinitum*. But to produce

123 proofs to infinity is impossible; so that neither by the use of proofs will he be able to prefer one sense-impression to another. If, then, one cannot hope to pass judgement on the afore-mentioned impressions either with or without proof, the conclusion we are driven to is suspension; for while we can, no doubt, state the nature which each object appears to possess as viewed in a certain position or at a certain distance or in a certain place, what its real nature is we are, for the foregoing reasons, unable to declare.

124   The *Sixth Mode* is that based on admixtures, by which we conclude that, because none of the real objects affects our senses by itself but always in conjunction with something else, though we may possibly be able to state the nature of the resultant mixture formed by the external object and that along with which it is perceived, we shall not be able to say what is the exact nature of the external reality in itself. That none of the external objects affects our sense by itself but always in conjunction with something else, and that, in consequence, it assumes a different appearance, is, I imagine, quite obvious. Thus, our own complexion is

125 of one hue in warm air, of another in cold,

and we should not be able to say what our complexion really is, but only what it looks like in conjunction with each of these conditions. And the same sound appears of one sort in conjunction with rare air and of another sort with dense air; and odours are more pungent in a hot bath-room or in the sun than in chilly air; and a body is light when immersed in water but heavy when surrounded by air.

126   But to pass on from the subject of external admixture,—our eyes contain within themselves both membranes and liquids. Since, then, the objects of vision are not perceived apart from these, they will not be apprehended with exactness; for what we perceive is the resultant mixture, and because of this the sufferers from jaundice see everything yellow, and those with bloodshot eyes reddish like blood. And since the same sound seems of one quality in open places, of another in narrow and winding places, and different in clear air and in murky air, it is probable that we do not apprehend the sound in its real purity; for the ears have crooked and narrow passages, which are also befogged by vaporous effluvia which

127   are said to be emitted by the regions of the head. Moreover, since there reside substances in the nostrils and in the organs of taste, we apprehend the objects of taste and of smell in conjunction with these and not in their real purity. So that, because of these admixtures, the senses do not apprehend the exact quality of the external real objects.

128   Nor yet does the mind apprehend it, since, in the first place, its guides, which are the senses, go wrong; and probably, too, the mind itself adds a certain admixture of its own to the messages conveyed by the senses; for we observe that there are certain humours present in each of the regions which the Dogmatists regard as the seat of the "Ruling Principle"—whether it be the brain or the heart, or in whatever according to this Mode also we see that, owing to our inability to make any statement about the real nature of external objects, we are compelled to suspend judgement.

129   The *Seventh Mode* is that based, as we said, on the quantity and constitution of the underlying objects, meaning generally by "constitution" the manner of composition. And it is evident that by this Mode also we are compelled to suspend judgement concerning the real nature of the objects. Thus, for example, the filings of a goat's horn appear white when viewed simply by themselves and without combination, but when combined in the substance of the horn they look black. And silver filings appear black when they are by themselves, but when united to the whole mass they are sensed as white. And chips of the marble of Taenarum 130 seem white when planed, but in combination with the whole block they appear yellow. And pebbles when scattered apart appear rough, but when combined in a heap they produce the sensation of softness. And hellebore if applied in a fine and powdery state produces suffocation, but not so when it is coarse. And wine strengthens us when 131 drunk in moderate quantity, but when too much is taken it paralyses the body. So likewise food exhibits different effects according to the quantity consumed; for instance, it frequently upsets the body with indigestion and attacks of purging because of the large quantity taken. Therefore in these cases, too, we shall be able to describe the quality of the shaving of the horn and of the compound made up of many shavings, and that of the particle of silver and of the compound of many particles, and that of the silver of Taenarean marble and of the compound of many such small pieces, and the relative qualities of the pebbles, the hellebore, the wine and the food,—but when it comes to the independent and real nature of the objects, this we shall be unable to describe because of the divergency in the sense-impressions which is due to the combinations.

As a general rule, it seems that wholesome things become harmful when used in 133 immoderate quantities, and things that seem hurtful when taken to excess cause no harm when in minute quantities. What we observe in regard to the effects of medicines is the best evidence in support of our statement; for there the exact blending of the simple drugs makes the compound wholesome, but

when the slightest oversight is made in the measuring, as sometimes happens, the compound is not only unwholesome but frequently even most harmful and deleterious. Thus the argument from quantities and
134 compositions causes confusion as to the real nature of the external substances. Probably, therefore, this Mode also will bring us round to suspension of judgement, as we are unable to make any absolute statement concerning the real nature of external objects.

.   .   .   .

Chapter 15—Of the Five Modes

164 The later Sceptics hand down Five Modes leading to suspension, namely these: the first based on discrepancy, the second on regress *ad infinitum,* the third on relativity,
165 the fourth on hypothesis, the fifth on circular reasoning. That based on discrepancy leads us to find that with regard to the object presented there has arisen both amongst ordinary people and amongst the philosophers an interminable conflict because of which we are unable either to choose a thing or
166 reject it, and so fall back on suspension. The Mode based upon regress *ad infinitum* is that whereby we assert that the thing adduced as a proof of the matter proposed needs a further proof, and this again another, and so on *ad infinitum*, so that the consequence is suspension, as we possess
167 no starting-point for our argument. The Mode based upon relativity, as we have already said, is that whereby the object has such or such an appearance in relation to the subject judging and to the concomitant percepts, but as to its real nature we suspend
168 judgement. We have the Mode based on hypothesis when the Dogmatists, being forced to recede *ad infinitum*, take as their starting-point something which they do not establish by argument but claim to assume as granted
169 simply and without demonstration. The Mode of circular reasoning is the form used when the proof itself which ought to establish the matter of inquiry requires confirmation derived from that matter; in this case, being unable to assume either in order

to establish the other, we suspend judgement about both.

That every matter of inquiry admits of being brought under these Modes we shall show briefly in this way. The matter pro- 170 posed is either a sense-object or a thought-object, but whichever it is, it is an object of controversy; for some say that only sensibles are true, others only intelligibles, others that some sensible and some intelligible objects are true. Will they then assert that the controversy can or cannot be decided? If they say it cannot, we have it granted that we must suspend judgement; for concerning matters of dispute which admit of no decision it is impossible to make an assertion. But if they say that it can be decided, we ask by what is it to be decided. For example, in the case of the sense-object (for we 171 shall base our argument on it first), is it to be decided by a sense-object or a thought-object? For if they say by a sense-object, since we are inquiring about sensibles that object itself also will require another to confirm it; and if that too is to be a sense-object, it likewise will require another for its confirmation, and so on *ad infinitum*. And if the sense-object shall have to be de- 172 cided by a thought-object, then, since thought-objects also are controverted, this being an object of thought will need examination and confirmation. Whence then will it gain confirmation? If from an intelligible object, it will suffer a similar regress *ad infinitum*; and if from a sensible object, since an intelligible was adduced to establish the sensible and a sensible to establish the intelligible, the Mode of circular reasoning is brought in.

If, however, our disputant, by way of es- 173 cape from this conclusion, should claim to assume as granted and without demonstration some postulate for the demonstration of the next steps of his argument, then the Mode of hypothesis will be brought in, which allows no escape. For if the author of the hypothesis is worthy of credence, we shall be no less worthy of credence every time that we make the opposite hypothesis. Moreover, if the author of the hypothesis assumes what is true he causes it to be suspected by assuming it by hypothesis rather than after proof; while if it is false, the

174 foundation of his argument will be rotten. Further, if hypothesis conduces at all to proof, let the subject of inquiry itself be assumed and not some other thing which is merely a means to establish the actual subject of the argument; but if it is absurd to assume the subject of inquiry, it will also be absurd to assume that upon which it depends.

175 It is also plain that all sensibles are relative; for they are relative to those who have the sensations. Therefore it is apparent that whatever sensible object is presented can easily be referred to one of the Five Modes. And concerning the intelligible object we argue similarly. For if it should be said that it is a matter of unsettled controversy, the necessity of our sus-

176 pending judgement will be granted. And if, on the other hand, the controversy admits of decision, then if the decision rests on an intelligible object we shall be driven to the regress *ad infinitum*, and to circular reasoning if it rests on a sensible; for since the sensible again is controverted and cannot be decided by means of itself because of the regress *ad infinitum*, it will require the

177 intelligible object, just as also the intelligible will require the sensible. For these rea sons, again, he who assumes anything by hypothesis will be acting illogically. Moreover, objects of thought, or intelligibles, are relative; for they are so named on account of their relation to the person thinking, and if they had really possessed the nature they are said to possess, there would have been no controversy about them. Thus the intelligible also is referred to the Five Modes, so that in all cases we are compelled to suspend judgement concerning the object presented.

Such then are the Five Modes handed down amongst the later Sceptics; but they propound these not by way of superseding the Ten Modes but in order to expose the rashness of the Dogmatists with more variety and completeness by means of the Five in conjunction with the Ten.

.   .   .   .

BOOK II

Chapter 3—Of the Criterion

But first we must notice that the word "cri- 14 terion" is used both of that by which, as they say, we judge of reality and nonreality, and of that which we use as the guide of life; and our present task is to discuss the so-called criterion of truth, since we have already dealt with the criterion in its other sense in our discourse "On Scepticism."

The criterion, then, with which our ar- 15 gument is concerned, has three several meanings—the general, the special, and the most special. In the "general" sense it is used of every standard of apprehension, and in this sense we speak even of physical organs, such as sight, as criteria. In the "special" sense it includes every technical standard of apprehension, such as the rule and compass. In the "most special" sense it includes every technical standard of apprehension of a non-evident object; but in this application ordinary standards are not regarded as criteria but only logical standards and those which the Dogmatists employ for the judging of truth. We propose, 16 therefore, in the first place to discuss the logical criterion. But the logical criterion also may be used in three senses—of the agent, or the instrument, or the "according to what"; the agent, for instance, may be a man, the instrument either sense-perception or intelligence, and the "according to what" the application of the impression "according to" which the man proceeds to judge by means of one of the aforesaid instruments.

It was appropriate, I consider, to make 17 these prefatory observations so that we may realize what is the exact subject of our discourse; and it remains for us to proceed to our counterstatement aimed against those who rashly assert that they have apprehended the criterion of truth, and we will begin with the dispute which exists about this question.

Chapter 4—Does a Criterion of Truth Really Exist?

18 Of those, then, who have treated of the criterion some have declared that a criterion exists—the Stoics, for example, and certain others—while by some its existence is denied, as by the Corinthian Xeniades, amongst others, and by Xenophanes of Colophon, who says—"Over all things opinion bears sway"; while we have adopted suspension of judgement as to whether it does
19 or does not exist. This dispute, then, they will declare to be either capable or incapable of decision; and if they shall say it is incapable of decision they will be granting on the spot the propriety of suspension of judgement, while if they say it admits of decision, let them tell us whereby it is to be decided, since we have no accepted criterion, and do not even know, but are still inquiring, whether any criterion exists. Be-
20 sides, in order to decide the dispute which has arisen about the criterion, we must possess an accepted criterion by which we shall be able to judge the dispute; and in order to possess an accepted criterion, the dispute about the criterion must first be decided. And when the argument thus reduces itself to a form of circular reasoning the discovery of the criterion becomes impracticable, since we do not allow them to adopt a criterion by assumption, while if they offer to judge the criterion by a criterion we force them to a regress *ad infinitum*. And furthermore, since demonstration requires a demonstrated criterion, while the criterion requires an approved demonstration, they are forced into circular reasoning.

.   .   .   .

Chapter 6—Of the Criterion "By Means of Which" (or Instrument)

48 Concerning this criterion the controversy which exists amongst the Dogmatists is fierce and, one may say, unending. We, however,—with a view here also to a systematic treatment,—maintain that inasmuch as Man is, according to them, the criterion "By whom" matters are judged, and Man (as they also themselves agree) can have no other instrument by means of which he will be able to judge except sense and intellect, then if we shall show that he is unable to judge by means of either sense alone or intellect alone or both conjoined, we shall have given a concise answer to all the individual opinions; for they can all, as it seems, be referred to these three rival theories. Let us begin with the senses.   49

.   .   .   .   .   .

Even were one to concede that the sense- 55
impressions of those in a natural state are reliable, and those of men in a non-natural condition unreliable, even so the judgement of external real objects by means of the senses alone will be found to be impossible. For certainly the sense of sight, even when it is in a natural state, pronounces the same tower to be at one time round, at another square; and the sense of taste declares the same food to be unpleasant in the case of those full-fed, but pleasant in the case of those who are hungry; and the sense of hearing likewise perceives the same sound as loud by night but as faint by day; and the sense 56
of smell regards the same objects as malodorous in the case of most people, but not so in the case of tanners; and the same sense of touch feels warmth in the outer hall, when we enter the bath-rooms, but cold when we leave them. Therefore, since even when in a natural state the senses contradict themselves, and their dispute is incapable of decision, seeing that we possess no accepted criterion by means of which it can be judged, the same perplexities must necessarily follow. Moreover, of the establishment of this conclusion we may derive still further arguments from our previous discussion of the Modes of Suspension. Hence it would probably be untrue to say that sense-perception alone is able to judge real external objects.

Let us, then, proceed in our exposition to 57
the intellect. Now those who claim that we should attend to the intellect only in our judgement of things will, in the first place, be unable to show that the existence of intellect is apprehensible. For when Gorgias,

in denying that anything exists, denies also the existence of intellect, while some declare that it has real existence, how will they decide this contradiction? Not by the intellect, for so they will be assuming the matter in question; nor yet by anything else, since, as they assert, according to our present assumption there exists nothing else by means of which objects are judged. So then the problem as to whether intellect does or does not exist will not admit of decision or apprehension; and from this it follows, as a corollary, that in the judgement of objects we ought not attend to the intellect alone, which has not as yet been apprehended.

58   But let it be granted that the intellect has been apprehended, and let us agree, by way of assumption, that it really exists; I still affirm that it cannot judge objects. For if it does not even discern itself accurately but contradicts itself about its own existence and the mode of its origin and the position in which it is placed, how can it be able to

59   apprehend anything else accurately? And even if it be granted that the intellect is capable of judging objects, we shall not discover how to judge according to it. For since there exists great divergence in respect of the intellect—for the intellect of Gorgias, according to which he states that nothing exists, is one kind, and another kind is that of Heracleitus, according to which he declares that all things exist, and another that of those who say that some things do and others do not exist—we shall have no means of deciding between these divergent intellects, nor shall we be able to assert that

60   it is right to take this man's intellect as our guide but not that man's. For if we venture to judge by any one intellect, by thus agreeing to assent to one side in the dispute we shall be assuming the matter in question; while if we judge by anything else, we shall be falsifying the assertion that one ought to judge objects by the intellect alone.

.   .   .   .

63   The only remaining alternative is judgement by means of both senses and intellect. But this again is impossible; for not only do the senses not guide the intellect to appre-

hension, but they even oppose it. For it is certain, at any rate, that from the fact that honey appears bitter to some and sweet to others, Democritus declared that it is neither sweet nor bitter, while Heracleitus said that it is both. And the same account may be given of all the other senses and sensibles. Thus, when it starts out from the sense, the intellect is compelled to make diverse and conflicting statements; and this is alien to a criterion of apprehension.

.   .   .   .   .   .

Chapter 7—Of the Criterion "According to Which"

Let us consider next the Criterion "Accord- 70 ing to which," as they say, objects are judged. In the first place, then, we may say this of it, that "presentation" is inconceivable. They declare that "presentation" is an impression on "the regent part." Since, then, the soul, and the regent part, is breath or something more subtle than breath, as they affirm, no one will be able to conceive of an impression upon it either by way of depression and eminence, as we see in the case of seals, or by way of the magical "alteration" they talk about; for the soul will not be able to conserve the remembrance of all the concepts that compose an art, since the pre-existing concepts are obliterated by the subsequent "alterations." Yet even if 71 "presentation" could be conceived, it would still be non-apprehensible; for since it is an affection of the regent part, and the regent part, as we have shown, is not apprehended, neither shall we apprehend its affection.

Further, even were we to grant that the 72 "presentation" is apprehended, objects cannot be judged according to it; for the intellect, as they assert, does not make contact with external objects and receive presentations by means of itself but by means of the senses, and the senses do not apprehend external real objects but only, if at all, their own affections. So then the presentation will be that of the affection of the sense, which is different from the external reality; for honey is not the same as my feeling of sweetness nor gall the same as my feeling of bitterness,

but a different thing. And if this affection
73 differs from the external real object, the presentation will not be that of the external reality but of something else which is different
therefrom. If, therefore, the intellect judges
according to this, it judges badly and not according to reality. Consequently, it is absurd
to say that external objects are judged according to the presentation.
74   Nor, again, is it possible to assert that the
soul apprehends external realities by means
of the affections of sense owing to the similarity of the affections of the senses to the
external real objects. For how is the intellect
to know whether the affections of the senses
are similar to the objects of sense when it
has not itself encountered the external objects, and the senses do not inform it about
their real nature but only about their own
affections, as I have argued from the Modes
75 of Suspension? For just as the man who
does not know Socrates but has seen a picture of him does not know whether the picture is like Socrates, so also the intellect
when it gazes on the affections of the senses
but does not behold the external objects will
not so much as know whether the affections
of the senses are similar to the external realities. So that not even on the ground of
resemblance will he be able to judge these
objects according to the presentation.

.   .   .   .   .   .

79   This is enough to say now, in our outline
sketch, with reference to the criterion "According to which," as it was said, objects are
judged. But one should notice that we do not
propose to assert that the criterion of truth is
unreal (for that would be dogmatism); but
since the Dogmatists appear to have established plausibly that there really is a criterion of truth, we have set up counter-
arguments which appear to be plausible; and
though we do not positively affirm either that
they are true or that they are more plausible
than their opposites, yet because of the apparently equal plausibility of these arguments and of those propounded by the Dogmatists we deduce suspension of judgement.

.   .   .   .   .   .

Chapter 15—Concerning Induction

It is also easy, I consider, to set aside the   204
method of induction. For, when they propose to establish the universal from the particulars by means of induction, they will effect this by a review either of all or of some
of the particular instances. But if they review some, the induction will be insecure,
since some of the particulars omitted in the
induction may contravene the universal;
while if they are to review all, they will be
toiling at the impossible, since the particulars are infinite and indefinite. Thus on both
grounds, as I think, the consequence is that
induction is invalidated.

.   .   .   .   .   .

BOOK III

Chapter 32—Why the Sceptic Sometimes Purposely Propounds Arguments Which Are Lacking in Power of Persuasion

The Sceptic, being a lover of his kind, de-   280
sires to cure by speech, as best he can, the
self-conceit and rashness of the Dogmatists.
So, just as the physicians who cure bodily
ailments have remedies which differ in
strength, and apply the severe ones to those
whose ailments are severe and the milder to
those mildly affected.—So too the Sceptic
propounds arguments which differ in   281
strength, and employs those which are
weighty and capable by their stringency of
disposing of the Dogmatists' ailment, self-
conceit, in cases where the mischief is due
to a severe attack of rashness, while he employs the milder arguments in the case of
those whose ailment of conceit is superficial
and easy to cure, and whom it is possible
to restore to health by milder methods of
persuasion. Hence the adherent of Sceptic
principles does not scruple to propound at
one time arguments that are weighty in their
persuasiveness, and at another time such as
appear less impressive,—and he does so on
purpose, as the latter are frequently sufficient to enable him to effect his object.

.   .   .   .

4 / Augustine (A.D. 354–430)
CONTRA ACADEMICOS

BOOK II

V.11. The Academicians are of the opinion that knowledge cannot be attained by man in so far as those things are concerned which pertain to philosophy—for Carneades said he did not care about other matters—and yet that man can be wise and that the whole duty of a wise man is accomplished in seeking truth, a statement which was also made by you, Licentius, in your argument; the conclusion is that the wise man should not assent to anything; for the fact that it is wrong for a wise man to assent to things that are uncertain, makes it necessary that he be in error. And they not only said that everything is uncertain but they even supported their statement by very forceful arguments. But they seemed to have appropriated the idea that truth cannot be grasped, from that definition of Zeno, the Stoic, who said that that can be apprehended as true which has been so deeply impressed upon the mind from the source from which it came, that it could not proceed from that from which it did not come. To express it more briefly and clearly, truth can be grasped by those signs which whatever is false cannot have. They emphasized this precisely in order to prove conclusively that it cannot be found. From this source have arisen the dissensions of philosophers, the unreliability of the senses, vain imaginations and frenzies, sophistical syllogisms and sorites in defense of that cause. And since they had learned from this same Zeno, that nothing is more disgraceful than to conjecture, they very cleverly inferred that if nothing can actually be known and if it is dis-

graceful to express an opinion, then the wise man should never approve of anything.

12. From this cause great odium was excited against them; of the logical consequence seemed to be that he who would not assent to anything would not accomplish anything. Hence the Academicians seemed to portray your wise man as always sleeping and neglecting all his duties since they thought he never gave assent to anything. Hereupon, by introducing a kind of probability which they even mentioned as being similar to truth, they maintained that the wise man was in no way negligent in his duties since he had that which he was striving for; truth, however, lay hidden, being either crushed or obscured because of the darkness of our nature or the similarity existing in all things, although they said that the very withholding and, as it were, suspension of assent was, indeed, the great achievement of the wise man.

. . . .

BOOK III

X.23. You say that nothing can be apprehended in philosophy and, in order to spread your opinion far and wide, you make use of the disputes and contentions of philosophers and you think that these dissensions furnish arms for you against them. For how shall we determine the strife between Democritus and the earlier natural philosophers about one world and innumerable worlds when no harmony could subsist between him and Epicurus,

From *Against the Academicians* (Book II: v.11–12; Book III: x.23, xi.24–26), edited by Mary Garvey. Copyright © 1978, Marquette University Press. Reprinted by permission of the publisher.

his successor? For when that lover of pleasure does not allow his atoms, his little maidservants, so to speak, that is, the little bodies which he joyfully embraces in the darkness, to hold their course, but permits them of their own accord to deviate here and there into strange bypaths, he has squandered his entire patrimony through contentions. But this is of no concern to me. For if it belongs to wisdom to know any of these things, it cannot be hidden from the wise man. If, however, it is something else, the wise man knows that type of wisdom and despises such things as these. And yet, I who am still far removed from the likeness of a wise man, know something about those physical phenomena. For I hold as certain either that there is or is not one world; and if there is not one, there are either a finite or an infinite number of worlds. Carneades would teach that that opinion resembles what is false. I likewise know that this world of ours has been so arranged either because of the nature of bodies or by some providence, and that it either always was and will be or that it began to exist and will by no means cease existing, or that it does not have its origin in time but will have an end, or that it has started to remain in existence and will remain but not forever, and I know innumerable physical phenomena of this type. For those disjunctions are true nor can anyone confuse them with any likeness to what is false. But take something for granted, says the Academician. I do not wish to do so; for that is to say: abandon what you know; say what you do not know. But opinion is uncertain. Assuredly it is better that it be uncertain than that it be destroyed; it surely is clear; it certainly now can be called false or true. I say that I know this opinion. Prove to me that I do not know them, you who do not deny that such matters pertain to philosophy and who maintain that none of these things can be known; say that those disjunctive ideas are either false or have something in common with what is false from which they cannot altogether be distinguished.

XI. 24. Whence, he says, do you know that this world exists if the senses are untrustworthy? Your methods of reasoning have never been able to disprove the power of the senses in such a way as to convince us that nothing is seen and you certainly have never dared to try such a thing, but you have exerted yourself to persuade us urgently that (a thing) can be otherwise than it seems. And so I call this entire thing, whatever it is, which surrounds us and nourishes us, this object, I say, which appears before my eyes and which I perceive is made up of earth and sky, or what appears to be earth and sky, the world. If you say nothing is seen by me, I shall never err. For he is in error who rashly proves what seems to him. For you say that what is false can be seen by those perceiving it; you do not say that nothing is seen. Certainly every reason for arguing will be removed when it pleases you to settle the point, if we not only know nothing but if nothing is even seen by us. If, however, you deny that this object which appears to me is the world, you are making it a controversy in regard to a name since I said that I called it the world.

25. If you are asleep, you will say, is that also the world, which you see? I have already said I call only that the world, which appears to me to be such. But if it pleases me to call only that the world, which is seen by those who are awake or even by those who are rational, prove this if you can, that those who are asleep and are raving are not raving and sleeping in the world. Therefore I say this: that entire mass of bodies and that contrivance in which we exist whether sleeping, or raging, or awake, or rational, either is one or is not one. Explain how that opinion can be false. For if I am asleep, it can follow that I said nothing; or even if the words have escaped from the mouth of a person who is asleep, as often happens, it can follow that I did not speak here, nor while sitting in this way, nor to those who were listening; but it cannot follow that this is false. Nor do I say that I apprehended this because I am awake. For you can say that this could appear to me even if I were asleep and therefore this can bear a close resemblance to what is false. But if there are one and six worlds, it is evident to me, no matter in what condition I may be, that there are seven worlds, and I am not rash in asserting that I know it. Therefore, show me either that this logical conclusion or those disjunctions mentioned above in regard to sleep or madness or unreliability of the

senses can be false, and I shall grant that I have been defeated if I remember them when I have been awakened. For I believe it is sufficiently evident that those things which appear false through sleep and an abnormal condition of the mind are those things which have reference to the senses of the body; for that three threes are nine and represent the square of intelligible numbers is necessary or would be true even though the human race were lying prostate. And yet I also see that many things can be said in favor of the senses themselves, which we have not found refuted by the Academicians. For I think that the senses are not to be blamed because they permit false and frenzied mental images or because in sleep we see things which are not true. If indeed the senses have reported the truth to those who are awake and who are rational, what the mind of a sleeping or insane person may fabricate for itself is not to be attributed to them.

26. It now remains for us to inquire whether the senses report the truth when they give information. Suppose that some Epicurean should say: "I have no complaint to make in regard to the senses; for it is unjust to demand more of them than they can give; moreover whatever the eyes can see they see in a reliable manner." Then is what they see in regard to an oar in the water true? It certainly is true. For when the reason is added for its appearing thus, if the oar dipped in the water seemed straight, I should rather blame my eyes for the false report. For they did not see what should have been seen when such causes arose. What need is there of many illustrations? This can also be said of the movement of towers, of the feathers of birds, of innumerable other things. "And yet I am deceived if I give my assent," someone says. Do not give assent any further than to the extent that you can persuade yourself that it appears true to you, and there is no deception. For I do not see how the Academician can refute him who says: "I know that this appears white to me, I know that my hear-

ing is delighted with this, I know that this has an agreeable odor, I know that this tastes sweet to me. I know that this feels cold to me." Tell us rather whether the leaves of the wild olive trees, which the goat so persistently desires, are by their very nature bitter. O foolish man! Is not the goat more reasonable? I do not know how they seem to the goat, but they are bitter to me. What more do you ask for? But perhaps there is also some one to whom they do not taste bitter. Do you trouble yourself about this? Did I say they were bitter to everyone? I said they were bitter to me and I do not always maintain this. For what if for some reason or other a thing which now tastes sweet to a person should at another time seem bitter to him? I say this, that when a person tastes something, he can honestly swear that he knows it is sweet to his palate or the contrary, and that no trickery of the Greeks can dispossess him of that knowledge. For who would be so bold as to say to me when I am longing for something with great pleasure: Perhaps you do not taste it, but this is only a dream? Do I offer any opposition to him? But still that would give me pleasure even in my sleep. Therefore no likeness to what is false obscures that which I have said I know, and both the Epicurean and the Cyrenaics may say many other things in favor of the senses against which I have heard that the Academicians have not said anything. But why should this concern me? If they so desire and if they can, let them even do away with the argument with my approbation. Whatever argument they raise against the senses has no weight against all philosophers. For there are those who admit that whatever the mind receives through a sense of the body, can beget opinion, but they deny (that it can beget) knowledge which, however, they wish to be confined to the intellect and to live in the mind, far removed from the senses. And perhaps that wise man whom we are seeking is in their number. But we shall say more about this at another time.

DE CIVITAS DEI

BOOK XI

26. We are and we know that we are, and we love this existing and knowing. Regarding these three things I have just mentioned, no falsity disguised as truth disturbs us. For we do not come in contact with them through any bodily sense, as we do those things outside of us, as colors by seeing, sounds by hearing, odors by smelling, tastes by tasting, what is hard and soft by touching. There, we perceive in our mind mental images resembling those sensible things, we hold them in memory, and through them we are excited to desire those sensible things. But here without any deceitful mental images or phantasms. I am most certain that I am, I know, and I love.

Concerning these truths, I fear no arguments of the Academy's skeptics, who say "What if you are deceived?" For if I am deceived, I am. For he who does not exist can in no way be deceived. Therefore, I exist if I am deceived.

Since I exist if I am deceived, how can I be deceived about my existence when it is certain that I exist if I am deceived? Since, therefore, even if I were deceived, it would still be I who was deceived, without a doubt I would not be deceived in this—that I know that I exist. Consequently, I am also not deceived in knowing that I know. For as I know that I am, I know also this, that I know.

And when I love these two, being and knowing, I add that love as a third thing of equal importance to those things which I know. For I am not deceived that I love when I am not deceived in the things that I love. And even if they were false, it would be true that I love false things. For how would it be right to reprehend me and right to prohibit me from the love of false things, if it were false that I love them? But since those things I love are true and certain, who will doubt that when these things are loved, the love of them is true and certain?

From *De Civitas Dei*, translated by Mark Henninger (previously unpublished). Reprinted by permission of the translator.

5 / Thomas Aquinas (1225–1274)
SUMMA THEOLOGIAE

Questions 84. How the Soul, While Joined to the Body, Knows Material Things

Article 1. Does the Soul Know Material Things Through the Intellect?

The first point:[1] It would seem that the soul does not know material things through the intellect. For Augustine says[2] that *material things cannot be understood by the intellect nor a body seen except by the senses.* Again he says[3] that we have intellectual vision only of those things that really exist in the soul. But material things are not of this kind. Therefore the soul cannot know them through the intellect.

2. Again, as sense knowledge is to intelligible objects, so is intellectual knowledge to sensible objects. But the soul, by means of sense knowledge, can in no way know spiritual realities, and intelligible objects are of this kind. Neither therefore can the soul in any way know material things by means of the intellect, since such things belong to the order of sensible objects.

3. Again, the objects of intellectual knowledge are necessary and always the same. But all material realities are changeable and not always the same. Therefore the soul through the intellect cannot know material things.

On the other hand, there is the fact that demonstrative knowledge is found in the intellect. Had the intellect no knowledge of material things, it could not have demonstrative knowledge of them. Thus there would be no natural science dealing with changeable material beings.

Reply: For evidence on this question we should note that the earliest philosophers who inquired into the nature of things thought there was nothing in the world except material reality. Since they recognized that all material things are changeable and thought of them as being in continual flux, they concluded that we can have no certainty about the truth of things. For what is in continual flux cannot be known with certainty—it will have disappeared before the mind can discern it. Heraclitus said, *It is impossible to step twice into the same river,* so Aristotle reports.[4]

Coming after these men, Plato, trying to save the fact that we can have certitude in knowing the truth, maintained that there were, in addition to the material things around us, another class of beings, separate from matter and change, which he called Ideas or Forms. By participation in these, all singular, sensible objects around us get their designation as "man," "horse," etc. Accordingly, Plato held that demonstrative knowledge, definitions, and everything else pertaining to the activity of the intellect has reference, not to sensible material things around us, but to separate immaterial objects somewhere else. Thus the soul would understand, not the material things around us, but their immaterial Forms.

This may be shown to be false for two reasons. Because first, since the Ideas are immaterial and unchanging, demonstrative knowledge of change and matter (such as is characteristic of natural science) would be ruled out, as would any demonstration in terms of material or changeable explanatory principles.

From *Summa Theologiae*, (Questions 84, articles 1, 6, 7; Question 85, articles 1–3, 5), edited by T. Gilby. Copyright © 1964, Blackfriars. Reprinted by permission of the Blackfriars.

Because secondly it would seem ludicrous, in seeking knowledge of things that are evident to us, to bring in as a means other realities which could not be of the essence of these evident things since they are of an essentially different order. Thus even if these immaterial substances were known, we would not thereby be able to know anything about the sensible things around us.

It would seem that, in this matter, Plato strayed from the truth because—aware that all knowledge comes by way of likenesses—he believed the form of the thing known must necessarily be in the knower exactly as it is in the thing known. Now he recognized that the form of a thing understood is in the intellect in a universal, immaterial, and unchanging way. This is apparent from the mode of operation of the intellect, which must understand in terms of universality and at least some sort of necessity; for ways of acting correspond to the form of the agent. Thus Plato concluded that the things understood must exist in themselves in this same way, namely, in an immaterial and unchanging way.

But there is no necessity for this. Even in sensible things we observe that the same form can be in different sensible objects in different ways; for instance, whiteness can be more intense in one thing than another, and whiteness can be associated with sweetness in one thing but not in another. Furthermore, the same is true of the form of a sensible object: it exists in a different way in the thing outside than it does in sense knowledge, which receives sensible forms without their matter—for instance, the colour of gold without the gold itself. Similarly, the intellect receives material and changeable species of material things in an immaterial and unchanging way, in accord with its nature; for things are received in a subject according to the nature of the subject.

We must conclude, therefore, that the soul knows material things through the intellect with a knowledge that is immaterial, universal and necessary.

Hence: 1. Augustine's words must be understood as referring to that by which the intellect knows, not to what it knows. For the intellect does know material things intellectually, but not by means of material things or

material and corporeal likenesses of things: rather, by immaterial, intellectual species which can really exist in the soul.

2. As Augustine notes,[5] it is not correct to say, as the senses know only material things, so the intellect knows only spiritual things—the consequence would be that God and the angels could not know material realities. The reason for the difference is that a lower power does not extend as far as a higher, but a greater power can do what belongs to a lesser—and do it better.

3. Every change presupposes something unchanging: in a qualitative change the underlying substance remains unchanged, and in a substantial change primary matter remains the same. Again, even in changeable things there are unchanging relations—for instance, although Socrates is not always seated, whenever he does sit it is unchangeably true that he remains in one place. Thus it follows that there is nothing against having an unchanging demonstrative knowledge of changeable things.

. . . .

Article 6. Is Intellectual Knowledge Taken From Sensible Things?

The first point:[6] 1. It would seem that intellectual knowledge is not taken from sensible things. For Augustine says[7] that *we cannot expect to acquire the pure truth from the corporeal senses,* and he proves this in two ways. First, from the fact that *whatever a corporeal sense attains is changing, and this without any lapse of time; but if something does not remain the same, it cannot be perceived.* Secondly, from the fact that *everything that we sense by means of the body we also receive in images, even when the things are not present to the senses (as for instance in sleep or in a rage). Yet we cannot distinguish by means of the senses whether we are perceiving the sensible things themselves or false images, and nothing can be perceived which is indistinguishable from what is false.*

He thus concludes that truth cannot be expected from the senses. But intellectual knowledge does apprehend the truth. Therefore intellectual knowledge should not be looked for from the senses.

2. Again, Augustine says,[8] *We must not*

think that the body can make an impression on the spirit, as though the spirit were to be subject, like matter, to the body's action; for that which acts is in every way more excellent than that on which it acts. From which he concludes that *the body does not cause its image in the spirit, but the spirit causes it in itself.* Therefore intellectual knowledge is not derived from sensible things.

3. Again, an effect does not go beyond the reach of its cause. But, since we understand some things which cannot be perceived by the senses, intellectual knowledge does go beyond sensible things. Therefore intellectual knowledge is not derived from sensible things.

On the other hand, Aristotle proves[9] that the beginning of our knowledge is in the senses.

Reply: On this question there were among the philosophers three opinions. Democritus held that *there is no other cause, for any of our knowledge, than the fact that images come into our souls from the bodies of which we think,* according to Augustine.[10] Aristotle also remarks[11] that Democritus held that knowledge comes about *by means of images and emanations.*

The reason for this position was that neither Democritus nor the other ancient natural philosophers distinguished between intellect and sense, according to Aristotle.[12] Thus, since a change is effected in the senses by the sensible object, they thought that all our knowledge comes about merely by such a change effected by sensible objects. And it was this change that Democritus claimed is brought about by emanations of images.

Plato, on the other hand, held that the intellect is distinct from the senses, and indeed that it is an immaterial faculty which does not use a corporeal organ when it acts. Now since the incorporeal cannot be affected by the corporeal, Plato also held that intellectual knowledge does not come about by a change effected in the intellect by sensible things, but rather by participation in separate intelligible forms, as mentioned earlier. He further held that the senses are independently operating faculties; thus even the senses themselves—since they are spiritual faculties—are not affected by sensible objects. Instead, the organs of the senses are affected by sensible things, and the soul is somehow awakened by this change to form within itself the images of sensible objects.

Augustine seems to touch on this opinion when he says[13] that *the body does not feel, but the soul by means of the body, which it makes use of as a kind of messenger to reproduce within itself what is announced from without.*

Thus, according to the opinion of Plato, intellectual knowledge does not start from sensible knowledge, nor does sensible knowledge itself proceed totally from sensible things. Rather, sensible objects awaken the sensible soul to sense and, similarly, the senses awaken the intellectual soul to understand.

Aristotle, finally, proceeded along a middle course. With Plato he agreed in holding that the intellect is distinct from the senses, but he did not hold that the senses have a proper activity without communication with the body.[14] Thus for him sensation is not an activity of the soul alone but of the body-soul composite, and the same is true of all the activities of the sensible part of man. Accordingly, since there is no difficulty in the fact that sensible objects outside the soul should have an effect on the composite, Aristotle was in agreement with Democritus to this extent: the activities of the sensible part are brought about by an impression made on the senses by sensible objects—not by means of an emanation, as Democritus held, but by some kind of activity. (Democritus, indeed, held that every action is produced by an influx of atoms.[15])

On the other hand, Aristotle held that the intellect does have an activity in which the body does not communicate.[16] But nothing corporeal can make an impression on an incorporeal thing. Therefore, to cause an intellectual activity, according to Aristotle, a mere impression made by sensible bodies is not enough—something of a higher order is required because *the active is superior to the passive factor,* as he says.[17]

Nevertheless, this does not imply that our intellectual activity is caused merely by an impression from things of a higher order as Plato held. That higher, superior agent which Aristotle calls the agent intellect—spoken of earlier[18]—by a process of abstraction makes images received from the senses actually intelligible.

According to this, then, intellectual activity is caused by the senses by way of these images. However, since these images are not capable of effecting a change in the possible intellect but must be made actually intelligible by the agent intellect, it is not right to say that sensible knowledge is the total and complete cause of intellectual knowledge—better to say it is somehow the material of the cause.

Hence: 1. Augustine's words there should be understood in the sense that truth is not to be looked for entirely from the senses. For the light of the agent intellect is required for us to know the truth found in changeable things in an unchanging way, and to distinguish real things from likenesses of things.

2. Augustine is not there speaking of intellectual knowledge, but of knowledge in the imagination. And since according to Plato's view the faculty of imagination has an activity belonging to the soul alone, Augustine uses the same argument to show that bodies do not impress their likenesses on the imagination (the soul does this itself) that Aristotle uses[19] to prove that the agent intellect is immaterial—namely, that *the active is superior to the passive factor.*

Without doubt we must suppose, according to this view, not only a passive, but also an active capacity in the imagination. However, if we hold, according to the view of Aristotle,[20] that the activity of the imagination belongs to the composite, there is no difficulty. For a sensible body is "superior" to an organ of an animal to the extent that in comparison with the organ, it is a being actual relative to a being potential, even as a coloured object is with respect to the potentially coloured pupil of the eye.

It could nevertheless be said that, although the primary change in the imagination is produced by changes coming from sensible objects—*imagination is a movement resulting from an actual exercise of a sense faculty*[21]—still there is an activity of the soul in man which, by separating and joining, forms different images of things (even of things not re-

ceived from the senses), and Augustine's words can be taken as referring to this.

3. Sense knowledge is not the whole cause of intellectual knowledge, and it is thus no cause for wonder if intellectual knowledge goes beyond sense knowledge.

Article 7. Can the Intellect, Using Only the Species it Has and not Turning to Sense Images, Actually Understand?

The first point:[22] 1. It would seem that the intellect could actually understand by means of the species it has, without turning to sense images. For the intellect is placed in a state of actuality by an informing species. But for the intellect, being in a state of actuality is precisely the act of understanding. Therefore species suffice to make the intellect actually understood, without any turning to sense images.

2. Again, the imagination is more dependent on the senses than is the intellect upon imagination. But the faculty of imagination can exercise its act in the absence of sensible objects. Therefore *a fortiori* the intellect can actually understand without turning to sense images.

3. Again, there are no sense images of incorporeal beings since the imagination does not transcend the world of time and extension. If, therefore, our intellect could not actually understand a thing without turning to sense images, it would follow that it could not understand anything incorporeal. But this is clearly false since we understand truth itself, as well as God and the angels.

On the other hand, Aristotle claims[23] that *the soul never thinks without an image.*

Reply: It is impossible for our intellect, in its present state of being joined to a body capable of receiving impressions, actually to understand anything without turning to sense images. This is evident on two counts. First, because, since it is a faculty which does not use a corporeal organ, the intellect would be in no sense impeded by an injury to a corporeal organ if for its act another act of a faculty that does use a corporeal organ were not required. But the senses, the imagination, and the other faculties of the sense part of man do use corporeal organs. Hence it is obvious that, for the intellect actually to understand (not only in acquiring new knowledge but also in using knowledge already acquired), acts of the imagination and the other faculties are necessary.

We see, in fact, that if acts of the imagination are impeded by an injury to its organ—for instance, in a seizure—or, similarly, if acts of sense memory are impeded—for instance, in coma—a man is impeded from actually understanding even things which he had known before.

The second count is this. As anyone can experience for himself, if he attempts to understand anything, he will form images for himself which serve as examples in which he can, as it were, look at what he is attempting to understand. This is the reason, indeed, why, when we want to help someone understand something, we propose examples to him so that he can form images for himself in order to understand.

The reason for all this is that cognitive faculties are proportioned to their objects. For instance, an angel's intellect, which is totally separate from corporeal reality, has as its proper object intelligible substances separate from corporeal reality, and it is by means of these intelligible objects that it knows material realities. The proper object of the human intellect, on the other hand, since it is joined to a body, is a nature of "whatness" found in corporeal matter—the intellect, in fact, rises to the limited knowledge it has of invisible things by way of the nature of visible things. But by definition a nature of this kind exists in an individual which has corporeal matter, for instance, it is of the nature of stone that it should exist in this or that particular stone, or of the nature of horse that it should exist in this or that particular horse, etc. Thus the nature of stone or any other material reality cannot be known truly and completely except in so far as it exists in a particular thing. Now we apprehend the particular through the senses and imagination. Therefore if it is actually to understand its proper object, then the intellect must needs turn to sense images in order to look at universal natures existing in particular things.

Whereas if the proper object of our intellect were an immaterial form, or if the natures of

sensible things subsisted apart from particulars, as the Platonists think, it would not be necessary for our intellect when understanding always to be turning to sense images.

Hence: 1. Species stored up in the possible intellect remain there in a habitual way when the intellect is not actually understanding, as was said above.[24] Thus, in order for us actually to understand, a mere storing of species is not sufficient: we must also use them, and indeed in accord with the things of which they are images, which are natures existing in particulars.

2. Since the sense image is itself a likeness of a particular thing, the imagination does not need a further likeness of a particular, as does the intellect.

3. We know incorporeal realities, which have no sense images, by analogy with sensible bodies, which do have images, just as we understand truth in the abstract by a consideration of things in which we see truth. God we know, according to Dionysius,[25] as cause about which we ascribe the utmost perfection and negate any limit. Furthermore, we cannot, in our present state, know other incorporeal substances except negatively and by analogy with corporeal realities. Thus when we understand anything of these beings, we necessarily have to turn to images of sensible bodies even though they do not themselves have such images.

Question 85. The Mode and Order of Understanding

Article 1. Does our Intellect Understand Material, Corporeal Realities by Abstraction from Sense Images?

The first point:[26] 1. It would seem that our intellect does not understand material and corporeal realities by abstraction from sense images. For if one understands an object otherwise than as it really is then he is in error. But the forms of material things are not abstract, set apart from the particulars represented by sense images. Therefore if we understand in abstraction species from sense images, our intellect will be in error.

2. Again, material things are natural things, requiring matter in their definition. Now nothing can be understood without something

which is required for its definition. Hence material things cannot be understood without matter. But matter is the principle of individuation. Therefore material things cannot be understood by abstracting the universal from the particular, which is the same as abstracting species from sense images.

3. Again, Aristotle says[27] that sense images have the same relation to the intellectual soul that colour has to sight. But seeing does not take place by abstracting images from colours, but by colours being impressed on the sight. Neither, therefore, does understanding happen by way of something being abstracted from sense images, but by an impression made on the intellect by sense images.

4. Again, as Aristotle says,[28] in the intellectual soul there are two faculties: namely, the possible and the agent intellects. But the function of the possible intellect is not that of abstracting species from images but of receiving species already abstracted. Neither, however, does it seem to be the function of the agent intellect: it has the same relation to sense images that light has to colours, which is not that of abstracting anything from colours but rather of streaming out to them. Therefore in no way do we understand by abstracting from sense images.

5. Again, Aristotle says[29] that the intellect *thinks the forms in the images.* Not, therefore, by abstracting them.

On the other hand, Aristotle says[30] that *as realities are separable from matter, so is it with their being understood.* Therefore material realities must be understood precisely as abstracted or set apart from matter and from material likenesses such as sense images.

Reply: As was said earlier,[31] knowable objects are proportioned to knowing faculties, and there are three levels of such faculties. First, one kind of cognitive faculty is the form of a corporeal organ: such is sense. Accordingly, the object of every sense faculty is a form existing in corporeal matter, and so, since this sort of matter is the principle of individuation, all the faculties of the sense part of man only know particulars.

A second kind of cognitive faculty is neither the form of a corporeal organ nor in any way joined to corporeal matter; such is an angel's intellect. Accordingly, its object is a form subsisting without matter, for although angels can know material things, they see them only in something immaterial, namely either in themselves or in God.

The human intellect stands in the middle. It is not the form of an organ, although it is a faculty of the soul which is the form of a body, as is clear from what was said earlier.[32] Accordingly, it is proper for it to know forms which, in fact, exist individually in corporeal matter, yet not precisely as existing in such or such individual matter. Now to know something which in fact exists in individuated matter, but not as existing in such or such matter is to abstract a form from individual matter, represented by sense images. Thus we have to say that our intellect understands material things by abstraction from sense images.

Through material things known in this way we come to a limited knowledge of immaterial realities, just as, in the contrary way, angels know material realities by way of the immaterial.

Now Plato, paying attention only to the immateriality of the human intellect and not to the fact that it is somehow joined to a body, held that the object of the intellect is immaterial Ideas, and that we understand, as we have mentioned,[33] not by abstraction, but by participation in abstract entities.

Hence: 1. Abstraction occurs in two ways: one, by way of combining and separating, as when we understand one not to be in another or to be separate from it; two, by way of a simple and absolute consideration, as when we understand one without considering the other at all.

And so although for the intellect in the first way to abstract objects which in reality are not abstract is not without falsehood, it is not in the second way, as clearly appears with sensible realities. For example, were we to understand or say that colour does not exist in a coloured body, or that it exists apart from it, there would be falsehood in the opinion or statement. Whereas were we to consider colour and its properties, without any consideration of the apple which has colour, and go on to express verbally what we thus understand, the opinion or statement would be without falsehood. For being an apple is not part of the definition of colour, and thus nothing prevents colour from being understood apart from the apple being understood.

I claim likewise that whatever pertains to the definition of any species of material reality, for instance stone or man or horse, can be considered without individuating conditions which are no part of the definition of the species. And this is what I mean by abstracting the universal from the particular, the idea from sense images, to consider the nature of a species without considering individuating conditions represented by sense images.

Therefore when it is said that that understanding is false which understands a thing other than as it is, the statement is true if "other than" refers to the thing understood. For the understanding is false whenever one understands a thing to be other than it is; hence the understanding would be false if one should so abstract the species of stone from matter that he would understand it to exist apart from matter, as Plato held.

The proposition, however, would not be true if "other than" were taken as referring to the one understanding. For there is no falsity if the mode of understanding in the one who understands is different from the mode of existing in the thing—a thing understood is in the one who understands in an immaterial way, according to the mode of the intellect, and not in a material way, according to the mode of a material reality.

2. Some have thought that the species of a natural thing is all form, that matter is not a part of the species; but if this were so, matter would not be included in definitions of natural things.

Another way of speaking is thus required, distinguishing between two kinds of matter, *common* and *designated* or *individual: common* would be, for instance, flesh and bones, and *individual* this flesh and these bones. The intellect abstracts the species of a natural thing from individual sensible matter, but not from common sensible matter. Thus it abstracts the species of man from this flesh and these bones which do not pertain to the definition of the specific nature—they are, rather, as Aristotle

says,[34] parts of the individual. The specific nature therefore can be considered without them. However, the species of man cannot be abstracted by the intellect from flesh and bones as such.

Mathematical species, on the other hand, can be abstracted by the intellect from both individual and common *sensible matter*—though not from common (but only individual) *intelligible matter*. For *sensible matter* means corporeal matter as underlying sensible qualities—hot and cold, hard and soft, etc.—whereas *intelligible matter* means substance as underlying quantity. Now it is obvious that quantity inheres in substance, before sensible qualities do. Hence quantities—numbers, dimensions, shapes (which are boundaries of quantities)—can be considered apart from sensible qualities, and this is precisely to abstract them from sensible matter. They cannot, however, be considered apart from an understanding of *some* substance as underlying quantity—which would be to abstract them from common intelligible matter—though they can be considered apart from this or that substance—which is to abstract them from individual intelligible matter.

Finally, some things—such as being, oneness, potentiality and actuality, etc.—can be abstracted even from common intelligible matter, as is evident in immaterial substances.

Plato, however, since he gave no consideration to the two modes of abstraction mentioned above, held that all the things we have spoken of as abstracted by the intellect exist in reality as abstract entities.

3. Colours, as existing in individual corporeal matter, have the same mode of existence as the faculty of sight. Consequently, they can impress their likeness on sight. Sense images, on the contrary, since they are likenesses of individuals and exist in corporeal organs, do not have the same mode of existence as the human intellect—as is obvious from what has been said. Consequently, they cannot, of their own power, make an impression on the possible intellect.

However, in virtue of the agent intellect and by its turning to sense images (which, in turn, represent the realities of which they are images), a likeness is effected in the possible intellect, but only with respect to the specific nature. And it is thus that species are said to be abstracted from sense images, and not as though a form, numerically the same as the one that existed before in the sense images, should now come to exist in the possible intellect in the way in which a body is taken from one place and transferred to another.

4. Sense images are illuminated by the agent intellect and further, by its power, species are abstracted from them. They are illuminated because sense images, by the power of the agent intellect, are rendered apt to have intellectual intentions or species abstracted from them, just as man's sense part receives heightened power from being joined to his intellectual part. The agent intellect, moreover, abstracts species from images, in that by its power we can consider specific natures without individuating conditions, and it is by likenesses of these natures that the possible intellect is informed.

5. Our intellect both abstracts species from sense images—in so far as it considers the natures of things as universal—and yet, at the same time, understands these in sense images, since it cannot understand even the things from which it abstracts species without turning to sense images, as mentioned before.[35]

Article 2. Do Species Abstracted from Sense Images Stand in Relation to Our Intellect as What is Understood?

The first point:[36] 1. It would seem that species abstracted from sense images do stand in relation to our intellect as *that which* is understood. For what is actually understood exists in the one who understands; it is, in fact, identical with the intellect as actualized. But of the thing understood there is nothing in the intellect which understands except the abstracted species. Therefore this species is what is actually understood.

2. Again, what is actually understood must exist in something, or else it would simply not exist. But it does not exist in anything outside the soul, for, since things outside the soul are material, nothing in them can be what is actually understood. Therefore it follows by exclusion that what is actually understood is in the intellect, and thus that is nothing other than the species mentioned.

3. Again, Aristotle says[37] that *spoken words are the symbols of things experienced in the soul.* But words signify things understood, since we use words precisely to signify what we understand. Therefore things experienced in the soul, namely species, are the things actually understood.

On the other hand, a species has the same relation to the intellect as a sensible image to the senses. But sensible images are not *what* is sensed; they are rather *that by which* sensation takes place. Therefore the species is not *what* is understood, but *that by which* the intellect understands.

Reply: Some have held that our cognitive faculties know only what is experienced within them, for instance, that the senses perceive only the impressions made on their organs. According to this opinion the intellect understands only what is experienced within it, i.e., the species received in it. Thus, again according to this opinion, these species are *what* is understood.

The opinion, however, is obviously false for two reasons. First, because the things we understand are the same as the objects of science. Therefore, if the things we understand were only species existing in the soul, it would follow that none of the sciences would be concerned with things existing outside the soul, but only with species existing in the soul. (It may be recalled how the Platonists held that all the sciences are concerned with Ideas, which they said were things actually understood.)

Second, because a consequence would be the error of the ancient philosophers who said that *all appearances are true,*[38] implying that contradictory opinions could at the same time be true. For if a faculty knows only what is experienced within it, that only is what it can discern. Now a thing "appears" in accord with the way a cognitive faculty is affected. Therefore the discernment of a cognitive faculty will always judge a thing to be what it discerns, namely, what is experienced within it; and accordingly every judgment will be true.

For instance, if the sense of taste perceives only what is experienced within it, then when a man whose sense of taste is healthy discerns that honey is sweet, his judgment will be true. Similarly, if a sick man, whose sense of taste is affected, experiences honey as bitter, his judgment will be true. For each makes his judgment as his sense of taste is affected. It will thus follow that every opinion—and indeed every perception of any kind—has an equal claim to truth.

We must say, therefore, that species stands in relation to the intellect as *that by which* the intellect understands. To make the matter clear: although there are two kinds of activity[39]—one that remains within the agent (e.g., seeing or understanding), and one that passes over into a thing outside (e.g., heating or cutting)—nevertheless each is produced in accord with a form. Now just as the form from which an activity extending to a thing outside proceeds is like the object of the activity (for instance, the heat of a heater is like that of the thing heated), so also, in a similar way, the form from which an activity remaining within an agent proceeds is a likeness of the object. Thus it is according to a likeness of a visible thing that the faculty of sight sees, and likewise a likeness of a thing understood, i.e., a species, is the form according to which the intellect understands.

However, since the intellect reflects upon itself, by such reflection it understands both its own understanding and the species by which it understands. Thus species are secondarily that which is understood. But what is understood first is the reality of which a particular species is a likeness.

This is, in fact, already evident in the opinion of the ancient philosophers who held that *like is known by like.*[40] For they held that the soul would know solids that are outside it by means of solids within it, etc. Thus if we understand the species of a solid instead of actual solid materials—according to Aristotle's teaching,[41] *it is not the stone which is present in the soul but its form*—it will follow that by means of species the soul knows things which are outside the soul.

Hence: 1. What is understood is in the one who understands by means of its likeness. This is the meaning of the saying that what is actually understood is identical with the intellect as actualized, in so far as a likeness of the thing

understood is the form of the intellect, just as a likeness of a sensible reality is the form of a sense when actualized. Hence it does not follow that an abstracted species is what is actually understood, but only that it is a likeness of it.

2. The phrase "what is actually understood" involves two points: namely, the thing which is understood and the being understood. And likewise in the term "abstracted universal" there are two, namely, the nature of a thing and its state of abstraction or universality. Thus the nature, to which "being understood" and "being abstracted" (or the intention of universality) are applied, exists only in individuals, whereas "being understood" and "being abstracted" (or the intention of universality) exist in the intellect.

We can more easily see this by comparison with the senses. For instance, the sense of sight sees the colour of an apple but not its characteristic scent. Thus if one asks: Where does this colour, which is seen apart from the scent, exist?, it is obvious, on one hand, that the colour seen exists only in the apple, but on the other that being perceived without the scent can be attributed to it only with respect to sight, in so far as in the sense of sight there is a likeness of the one but not of the other.

Similarly, humanity, when understood, exists only in this or that human being, but its being apprehended without individuating conditions (i.e., its "being abstracted" and the consequent intention of universality) can be attributed to humanity only as perceived by the intellect where there is a likeness of the specific nature, but not of individuating conditions.

3. In the sense part of man there are two kinds of activity. One takes place by way of a change effected from outside, thus the activity of the senses is fully carried out through a change effected by sensible objects. The other activity is a "formation" by which the faculty of imagination formulates for itself a model of something absent or even of something never seen.

Now both of these activities are joined in the intellect. For, first, there is indeed an effect produced in the possible intellect in so far as it is informed by a species; and then, secondly, when it is thus informed, it formulates either a definition or else an affirmative or negative statement, which is then signified by words. Thus the meaning which a name signifies is a definition, and an enunciation or proposition signifies the intellect's combining or separating. Therefore words do not signify the effects produced in the possible intellect but those things which the intellect formulates for itself in order to understand things outside.

Article 3. Do things That Are More Universal Have Priority in Our Intellectual Knowledge?

The first point.[42] It would seem that things which are more universal do not have priority in our intellectual knowledge. For things which are first known and better known by nature are known later and less well by us. But universal entities by nature have priority, since *one thing is said to be "prior" to another when the sequence of their being cannot be reversed.*[43] Therefore universal entities come later in our intellect's knowledge.

2. Again, with respect to ourselves, complex realities have priority over simple realities. But universal entities are more simple. Therefore in us their knowledge comes later.

3. Again, Aristotle says[44] that we know the thing defined before we know the elements of a definition. But things with greater universality are elements in the definition of the less universal; for instance, *animal* is an element in the definition of man. Therefore in us the knowledge of the more universal comes later.

4. Again, we come to principles and causes by way of effects. But universal entities are among these principles. Therefore universal entities are known later by us.

On the other hand, Aristotle says[45] that *we must advance from generalities to particulars.*

Reply: Two points must be considered with respect to our intellect's knowledge. The first, that intellectual knowledge has its origin partially in sense knowledge. Thus, since singulars are the object of the senses, universals of the intellect, our knowledge of singular things must come before our knowledge of things as universal.

The second, that we should recall how the intellect goes from potentiality to actuality. But anything that goes from potentiality to actuality arrives at incomplete actuality (midway between potentiality and actuality) before it arrives at complete actuality. Now the complete actuality at which the intellect arrives is complete knowledge, in which things are known definitely and distinctly, whereas its incomplete actuality is imperfect knowledge, where things are known indistinctly and confusedly. (For what is known in this way is partly actually known, partly only potentially known.) Thus Aristotle says[46] that *what is to us plain and obvious at first is rather confused masses, the elements and principles of which become known to us later by analysis.*

Now it is evident that knowing something which contains many aspects without having a precise knowledge of each of them is a rather confused knowledge of the thing. But both a "universal whole" (which contains its "parts" or particulars virtually) and an "integral whole" can be known in this way—each can be known in a confused way, without the parts being known distinctly. On the other hand, to have distinct knowledge of what is contained in a universal whole is to have knowledge of something less universal. For instance, knowing animals indistinctly means knowing the class "animal," whereas knowing animals distinctly means knowing animals as rational or non-rational—it means knowing, for instance, man or lion.

Therefore knowing "animal," comes within the scope of our intellect before knowing the class "man," and the same is true in any comparison of something more universal with something less universal.

Since the senses, like the intellect, go from potentiality to actuality, the same order of knowledge is also apparent in them. For we discern, with the senses, the more before the less general, both with respect to space and with respect to time. With respect to space, for instance, when a thing is seen from a distance, it is recognized as a body before it is recognized as an animal, as an animal before being recognized as a man, and as a man before Socrates or Plato. So also with respect to time, thus a child in the beginning distinguishes man from non-man before he distinguishes this man from that one; as Aristotle says,[47] *a child starts by calling all men "father," but later on distinguishes between each of them.*

The reason for this is evident. For anyone who knows something indistinctly is in a state of potentiality with respect to knowing the principle of distinction—for instance, one who knows a class is in a state of potentiality with respect to knowing a specific difference. Thus it is evident that indistinct knowledge is midway between potentiality and actuality.

In conclusion then, we must say that in us the knowledge of singulars precedes the knowledge of universals in so far as sense knowledge precedes intellectual knowledge. But both in the senses and in the intellect more general precedes less general knowledge.

Hence: 1. The universal can be considered in two ways. First, a universal nature can be considered together with the intention of universality. Now since the intention of universality—i.e., the fact that one and the same thing has a relation to many particulars—comes from the intellect's abstraction, in this consideration the universal must be posterior. Thus Aristotle says[48] that *the universal, "animal," must be treated either as nothing at all or as a later product.*

According to Plato, however, who maintained that universals were subsistent, the universal would come before particulars in this consideration. For according to him particulars only exist by participation in subsistent universals, called Ideas.

Secondly, a universal can be considered with respect to the nature itself (e.g., of animality or humanity) as found in particulars. In this sense we must say that the order of nature is of two kinds. One is the way of generation or time according to which things that are imperfect and potential come first. In this sense the more general is by nature first, as is apparent in an obvious way in the generation of a human *via* an animal, for in the uterus there is first generated an animal and then a human being.[49] The second is the order of perfection, of "nature's intention," in which actuality is by nature prior, simply speaking, to potentiality, and the perfect to the imperfect. In this sense the less general is by nature prior to the more general—man to animal, for instance: for the intention of nature, in the process mentioned, is not to stop with the generation of an animal, but to go on to the generation of man.

2. A more general universal is related to the less general both as whole and as part. As whole, in so far as the more universal virtually contains both the less universal and other things—for instance, *animal* contains not only *man* but also *horse*. As part, on the other hand, in so far as the less general contains in its definition both the more general and other things; for instance, *man* contains not only *animal* but also *rational.*

Thus, in our knowledge, "animal" considered in itself comes before "man"; but our knowledge of man precedes our knowledge of the fact that "animal" is an element in the definition of man.

3. A part can be known in two ways. First, absolutely, as it is in itself; and in this sense nothing prevents our knowing parts before we know the whole (e.g., stones before knowing a house). Secondly, as parts of this particular whole; and in this sense we must know the whole before the parts. For instance, we know a house in a confused way before we distinguish its individual parts.

Accordingly we have to say that the elements in a definition, the defining factors, considered absolutely, are known before the thing defined, otherwise this would not be clarified by using them. However, as parts of the definition they are known later; for instance, we know man in a confused way before we know how to distinguish all the elements in the definition of man.

4. The universal, when taken together with the intention of universality, is admittedly a *principle of knowledge*, in the sense namely that the intention of universality is a consequence of the fact that our intellect understands by way of abstraction. However, there is no necessary reason why every principle of knowledge should also be a *principle of being* (as Plato thought), since we sometimes know causes through their effects and substances by way of accidents. Therefore the universal, taken in this sense (and according to the opin-

ion of Aristotle), is neither a principle of being nor a substance.[50]

On the other hand, if we consider the natures corresponding to class and sub-class as these are found in individuals, then in a sense they stand in relation to the individuals as their *formal principle*, since singularity is accounted for by matter, the specific nature by form.

Note however that within this formal principle the class aspect is related to the sub-class aspect as *material principle*, for the class-nature is taken from what is material in a thing, the sub-class-nature from what is formal—for instance, "animal" from the sense part of man, "human" from the intellectual. Consequently the ultimate "intention of nature" is concerned with the specific nature, not with the individual or class, since form is the goal of generation (matter entering in as required by the form).

Finally, it is not necessary that the knowledge of every principle and cause be posterior in us: sometimes we come to know unknown effects through causes that are sensible, sometimes the reverse is true.

. . . .

Article 5. Does Our Intellect Understand by Combining and Separating?

The first point:[51] 1. It would seem that our intellect does not understand by combining and separating. For combining and separating can only take place with respect to more than one thing. But the intellect cannot understand more than one thing at a time. Therefore it cannot understand by combining and separating.

2. Again, every combination or separation has attached to it either present, past or future time. But the intellect abstracts from time as from other particular conditions. Therefore the intellect does not understand by combining and separating.

3. Again, the intellect understands by assimilation to things. But combinations and separations are not found in things, for, in things, there is nothing but the reality signified by subject and predicate, and it is one and the same if a combination is a true one.

On the other hand, words signify the intellect's conceptions, according to Aristotle.[52] But there are combinations and separations of words, as appears in affirmative and negative statements. Therefore the intellect combines and separates.

Reply: The human intellect must understand by combining and separating. For, in so far as the human intellect goes from potentiality to actuality, it has a certain similarity to realities in the world of generation and corruption, which are not fully completed from the outset but achieve completeness step by step. So also the human intellect does not immediately, in first apprehending a thing, have complete knowledge; rather, it first apprehends only one aspect of the thing—namely, its whatness, which is the primary and proper object of the intellect—and only then can it understand the properties, accidents, and relationships incidental to the thing's essence. Accordingly, it must necessarily either combine one apprehension with another or separate them, or else it must go from one combination or separation to another (which is the process of reasoning).

The intellects of God and the angels, on the other hand, are like incorruptible realities which do have their total perfection immediately and from the outset; thus the intellects of God and the angels have a completely perfect knowledge of a thing from the outset. Therefore, in knowing the whatness of a thing, they know at the same time all the things that we are able to know by combining, separating, and reasoning.

Thus the human intellect knows by combining, separating, and reasoning. The intellects of God and the angels, on the other hand, know combinations, separations, and processes of reasoning by way of a simple understanding of what things are, not by way of combining, separating, and reasoning.

Hence: 1. The intellect's combinations and separations come about by way of a comparison or contrast. The intellect thus knows several objects by combining and separating in the same way that it compares or contrasts things.

2. The intellect, while it does abstract from sense images, nevertheless cannot actually understand except by turning to sense images, as mentioned above. And it is by reason of that aspect in which it turns to images that time is attached to the intellect's combinations and separations.

3. The likeness of a thing is received in the intellect according to the mode of the intellect, not according to the mode of the thing. Thus, although there is something in the thing that corresponds to the combination or separation in the intellect, its state in the thing is not the same as in the intellect. For the human intellect's proper object is the whatness of a material thing, and this whatness is subject to the senses and imagination.

Now there are two kinds of composition in material things. The first, of form and matter— corresponding to this in the intellect is the combination in which a "universal whole" is attributed to one of its "parts" or particulars (in so far as the class aspect is taken from a thing's common matter and the specific difference from the form, whereas the particular aspect is taken from individual matter). The second, of subject or substance and accident; corresponding to this composition in reality is the intellectual combination in which an accident is attributed to its subject, as in the sentence, "Man is white."

Nevertheless, the intellectual combinations differ from the real compositions, since the things combined in reality are distinct, whereas intellectual combination signifies the identity of the things combined. For the intellect's combination is not such as to say that "man is whiteness"; rather it says that "man is white," i.e., "has whiteness," and it is the same subject which *is* man and *has* whiteness. So also with respect to the composition of form and matter: "animal" signifies "that which has sensation"; "rational," "that which has an intellectual nature"; "man," "that which has both"; "Socrates," "that which has all these, together with individual matter"— and it is because of this relation of identity that our intellect attributes one to the other in its combinations.

NOTES

1. Cf. *De veritate* X, 4
2. *Soliloquies* X, 6. PL 32, 888
3. *De Genesi ad litteram* XII, 24. PL 34, 474
4. *Metaphysics* IV, 5. 1010a13

5. *De civitate Dei* XXII, 29. PL 41, 800
6. Cf. *De veritate* X, 6. *Quodl.* VIII, 2, 1. *Compend. Theol. 81*
7. *Lib.* 83 *quast.* 9. PL 40, 13
8. *De Genesi ad litteram* XII, 16. PL 34, 467
9. *Metaphysics* I, I. 981a2; *Posterior Analytics* II, 15. 100a3
10. *Epist.* 118, *ad Dioscurum* 4. PL 33, 446
11. *De divinatione per sommum* 2. 464a5
12. *De Anima* III, 3. 427a17
13. *De Genesi ad litteram* XII, 24. PL 34, 475
14. Cf. *De somno* 454a7
15. Aristotle, *De generatione* I, 8. 324b5
16. *De Anima* III, 4. 429a24
17. Ibid. III, 5. 430a18
18. Ia. 73, 3–4
19. *De Anima* III, 5. 430a18
20. Ibid. I, I. 430a5
21. Ibid. III, 3. 429a1
22. Cf. II *Sent.* 20, 2, 2 ad 3. *De veritate* X. 2 ad 7. *In De memor.* 3
23. *De Anima* III, 7. 431a16
24. Ia. 79. 6
25. *De divinis nominibus* I, 5. PG 3. 593
26. Cf. Ia. 12. 4. *CG* II, 77. *In Meta.* II, lect. 1
27. *De Anima* III, 7. 431a14
28. *De Anima* III, 5. 430a14
29. Ibid. III, 7. 431b2
30. Ibid. III, 4. 429b21
31. Ia. 84. 7
32. Ia. 76. 1
33. Ia. 84. 1
34. *Metaphysics* VI, 10. 1035b28
35. Ia. 84. 7
36. Cf. *De veritate* X, 9. *CG* IV, II. *In De Anima* III, *lect.* 8
37. *Peri Hermeneias* I, 1. 16a3
38. Aristotle, *Metaphysics* III, 5. 1009a8
39. Aristotle, *Metaphysics* VIII, 8. 1050a23
40. Aristotle, *De Anima* 1. 2 & 5. 404b17; 409b25
41. Ibid. III, 8. 431b29
42. Cf. *In Physic.* 1. *lect.* 1; *In Poster.* 1, *lect.* 4
43. Aristotle, *Categories* 12, 14a29
44. *Physics* 1, *lect.* 1. 184b11
45. *Physics* 1, *lect.* 1. 184b24
46. *Physics* 1, *lect.* 1. 184a21
47. *Physics* 1, *lect.* 1. 184b11
48. *De Anima* I, 1. 402b8
49. *De generatione animal.* II, 3. 736a36–b3; "That they [the male seed and the embryo in the female] possess the nutritive soul is plain. As they develop they also acquire the sensitive soul in virtue of which an animal is an animal; e.g., an animal does not become at the same time an animal and a man."
50. *Metaphysics* VI, 13. 1038
51. Cf. Ia. 14, 14; 16. 2; 58, 3; 4
52. *Peri Hermeneias* I, 1. 16a3

GREEK AND MEDIEVAL SOURCES: BIBLIOGRAPHY

General

Beare, J. I. *Greek Theories of Elementary Cognition.* Oxford, 1906.

Carré, M. *Realism and Nominalism.* Oxford, 1946.

Copleston, F. C. *A History of Medieval Philosophy,* London, 1972.

Dodds, C. R. *The Greeks and the Irrational.* Berkeley, Calif., 1951.

Everson, S., ed. *Epistemology.* Cambridge, Eng., 1990.

Gilson, E. *Reason and Revelation in the Middle Ages.* New York, 1938.

Guthrie, W. K. *A History of Greek Philosophy,* 5 vols. Cambridge, Eng., 1962–79.

Hintikka, J. "Time, Truth, and Knowledge in Ancient Greek Philosophy." *American Philosophical Quarterly* 4 (1967): 1–14.

Schofield, M., M. Burnyeat, and J. Barnes, eds. *Doubt and Dogmatism.* Oxford, 1980.

Stough, C. *Greek Scepticism.* Berkeley, Calif., 1969.

Plato

Cornford, F. M. *Plato's Theory of Knowledge.* London, 1935.

Crombie, I. M. *An Examination of Plato's Doctrines.* Vol. 2, *Plato on Knowledge and Reality.* London, 1963.

Gulley, N. *Plato's Theory of Knowledge.* London, 1962.

Kraut, R., ed. *The Cambridge Companion to Plato.* Cambridge, Eng., 1992.

Malcolm, J. *Plato on the Self-Predication of Forms.* Oxford, 1991.

Moravcsik, J. M. *Plato and Platonism.* Oxford, 1992.

Robinson, R. *Plato's Earlier Dialectic,* 2nd ed. Oxford, 1953.

Ross, W. D. *Plato's Theory of Ideas.* Oxford, 1952.

Runciman, W. G. *Plato's Later Epistemology.* Cambridge, Eng., 1962.

Vlastos, G., ed. *Plato.* Vol. 1, *Metaphysics and Epistemology,* New York, 1971.

White, N. P. *Plato on Knowledge and Reality.* Indianapolis, Ind., 1976.

Aristotle

Ackrill, J. L. *Aristotle the Philosopher.* Oxford, 1981.

Barnes, J., et al., eds. *Articles on Aristotle,* Vol. 1, *Science.* London, 1978.

Cherniss, H. *Aristotle's Criticism of Plato and the Early Academy.* Baltimore, 1944.

Fine, G. *On Ideas: Aristotle's Criticism of Plato's Theory of Forms.* Oxford, 1993.

Hintikka, J. "On the Ingredients of an Aristotelian Science." *Nous* 6 (1972): 55–69.

Irwin, T. *Aristotle's First Principles.* Oxford, 1988.

Lewis, F. *Substance and Predication in Aristotle.* Cambridge, Eng., 1991.

McKeon, R. "Aristotle's Conception of the Development and the Nature of Scientific Method." *Journal for the History of Ideas* 8 (1947): 3–44.

McKirahan, R. *Principles and Proofs: Aristotle's Theory of Demonstrative Science.* Princeton, N.J., 1992.

Moravcsik, J. M., ed. *Aristotle: A Collection of Critical Essays.* New York, 1967.

Nussbaum, M. C., and A. O. Rorty, eds. *Essays on Aristotle's De Anima.* Oxford, 1992.

Ross, W. D. *Aristotle,* 5th ed. New York, 1959.

Solmsen, E. *Aristotle's System of the Physical World.* Ithaca, N.Y., 1960.

Sorabji, R. *Necessity, Cause, and Blame: Perspectives on Aristotle's Theory.* Ithaca, N.Y., 1980.

Sextus Empiricus

Annas, J., and J. Barnes. *The Modes of Scepticism.* Cambridge, Eng., 1985.

Barnes, J. *The Toils of Scepticism.* Cambridge, Eng., 1990.

Bevan, E. R. *Stoics and Sceptics.* Oxford, 1913.

Chisholm, R. M. "Sextus Empiricus and Modern Empiricism." *Philosophy of Science* 8 (1941): 371–84.

Hallie, P., ed. *Scepticism, Man, and God: Selections from the Major Writings of Sextus Empiricus.* Middletown, Conn. 1964.

Maccoll, N. *The Greek Sceptics, from Pyrrho to Sextus.* London, 1869.

Patrick, M. M. *Sextus Empiricus and Greek Scepticism.* Cambridge, Eng., 1889.

Zeller, E. *The Stoics, Epicureans, and Sceptics.* New York, 1962.

Augustine

Abercrombie, N. *St. Augustine and French Classical Thought.* Oxford, 1938.
Bourke, V. J. *Augustine's Quest of Wisdom.* Milwaukee, Wis., 1945.
———. *Augustine's View of Reality.* Villanova, Pa., 1964.
Brown, P. *St. Augustine of Hippo: A Biography.* London, 1967.
Gilson, E. *The Christian Philosophy of St. Augustine.* New York, 1960.
Kirwan, C. *Augustine.* London, 1989.
Markus, R. A., ed. *Augustine: A Collection of Critical Essays.* New York, 1972.
Matthews, G. *Thought's Ego in Augustine and Descartes.* Ithaca, N.Y., 1992.

Nash, R. H. *The Light of the Mind: Augustine's Theory of Knowledge.* Lexington, Ky., 1969.

Thomas Aquinas

Bourke, V. J. *Aquinas' Search for Wisdom.* Milwaukee, Wis., 1965.
Copleston, F. C. *Aquinas.* Baltimore, 1970.
Davies, B. *The Thought of Thomas Aquinas.* Oxford, 1992.
Gilson, E. *The Christian Philosophy of St. Thomas Aquinas.* New York, 1956.
Hoenen, P. *Reality and Judgment According to St. Thomas.* Chicago, 1952.
Kenny, A. *Aquinas.* Oxford, 1984.
———. *Aquinas on Mind.* London, 1993.
———. *The Five Ways.* London. 1969.
———, ed. *Aquinas: A Collection of Critical Essays.* New York, 1969.

Early Modern Sources

The early period of modern philosophy begins with the philosophy of René Descartes and ends with the philosophy of Immanuel Kant. This period is *classical modern philosophy*, covering roughly the years 1600–1800. The central issue distinguishing classical modern philosophy from medieval philosophy is its rejection of the Aristotelian Rationalism that dominated the medieval period. Classical modern philosophers typically rejected the view that knowledge of reality is obtained through the *direct* awareness of the Forms that constitute the essence of the objects of sense. They replaced that view with the position that we *indirectly represent* the world through sensory experience and conceptualization. This is a significant difference. In medieval philosophy the frame of reference involves a human mind that has access in its apprehension to reality itself. In classical modern philosophy the frame of reference involves a human mind restricted in its direct apprehension to the confines of the human mind itself. In classical modern philosophy the dominant theme is that of a mind shut off from direct access to the reality lying beyond it, but finding within itself the basis for knowledge of the world.

Classical modern philosophers typically rejected Aristotelian Rationalism in one of two ways: They adopted an alternative form of rationalism, or they adopted some form of empiricism. The rationalists characteristically proposed that we possess *innate ideas*, and that, being aware of their logical relationships, we have *a priori* knowledge of the world as it really is. The empiricists rejected both the older Greek-medieval doctrine of the rational intuition of Forms and the later rationalist doctrine of innate ideas. (An exception is Kant, who did not reject the doctrine of innate ideas.) The empiricists proposed that all our ideas have their origin in sensory experience, and that there is no a priori knowledge of the world as it really is. In the following selections, the rationalists are represented by Descartes and Leibniz, and the empiricists are represented by Locke, Berkeley, Hume, Reid, and Kant. (The General Introduction commented on various forms of rationalism and empiricism.)

Descartes's solution to the problem of specifying the conditions for knowledge is stated in his *principle of the clear and distinct (relation of) ideas*: We know that a proposition is true if and only if we clearly and distinctly perceive the *ideas* comprising the proposition to be related as the proposition indicates. This principle plays a prominent role in Descartes's *Meditations on First Philosophy*, where Descartes presents his famous *Method of Doubt*. In order to discover, from among the many propositions the mind considers, which propositions (if any) can be known with absolute certainty, Descartes proposes that we begin by provisionally doubting everything we formerly believed. Such doubt is to be all inclusive; no proposition whatever is immune from this universal suspension of assent. If after such a strategy some propositions cannot be doubted, then, Descartes concludes, we shall know with certainty that those propositions are true. This method leads Descartes to rediscover Augustine's *cogito argument*, that, since he cannot doubt that he exists, he knows with certainty that he exists. (See the section on Greek and medieval sources for Augustine's argument.)

The discovery of the *cogito* leads Descartes to propose the aforementioned principle of clarity and distinctness as the general criterion for absolute certainty and knowledge. Since, however, provisional universal doubt must extend to this principle itself, Descartes proceeds to establish the existence of a God whose reliability will guarantee the certain truth of this principle. The logical problem with Descartes's reasoning here is notorious. The problem concerns his apparently arguing in a vicious circle: In order to establish the principle of clarity and distinctness, Descartes appeals to the existence of a reliable God; but in order to establish the existence of God, Descartes appeals to the principle of clarity and distinctness. This problem requires, at the least, a reformulation of the Method of Doubt, and it may affect the merits of the principle of clarity and distinctness itself.

The selections from *An Essay Concerning Human Understanding* represent the empiricism of John Locke. Locke holds that the mind, though possessing several natural abilities and manners of operation, is initially like a *tabula rasa*, a blank tablet on which no concepts have yet been written. Through abstraction from sensory experience, according to Locke, the mind gradually comes to have concepts, concepts manipulated by the mind according to its natural abilities and manners of operation.

The selections present Locke's treatment of the influential distinction between the primary and secondary qualities possessed by objects. Locke focuses on the corresponding distinction between ideas of primary qualities and ideas of secondary qualities, the former being *applied spatiotemporal concepts*, and the latter being the *actual sensory features* in sensory experience. Examples of the first kind of idea are such concepts as *square, moving, divided in three parts*, and *on top of*. Examples of the second kind of idea are such featured sensations as a particular shade of red, a particular termination of particular color fields (that is, a sensory shape), and a particular degree of a certain taste. Locke held that the ideas of primary qualities that objects produce in us *resemble* corresponding properties of those objects, whereas the ideas of secondary qualities that objects produce in us do not in any way resemble those objects.

Locke's position on the criterion of knowledge is similar to Descartes's: We know that a proposition is true if and only if we are aware of the "agreement" between the ideas that make up the proposition. Locke notes the limited extent to which we have knowledge of external objects, including knowledge of their existence and knowledge of their actual constitution. He finds that most of our beliefs concerning "the regular proceedings of causes and effects in the ordinary course of nature" fall under the category of beliefs based on probability.

Leibniz wrote his *New Essays on the Human Understanding* as a reply to Locke's *Essay*. This work is thus a commentary by a prominent rationalist on a classic statement of empiricism. Leibniz focuses on the question whether the mind is originally a *tabula rasa* that does not innately possess certain ideas and principles. He argues that with respect to general truths, experience can only supply specific examples, and cannot establish the universal necessity of such truths as those found in mathematics, logic, metaphysics, and ethics. Leibniz concludes that "their proof can only come from internal principles which are called innate." He notes, however, that we should not expect to find such principles within us in any obvious way. These principles are innate in the way that certain "inclinations, dispositions, habits, or natural capacities" are innate.

Locke had argued against innate ideas and principles, partly on the ground that many people are not at all aware of any such principles or ideas. Against this argument, Leibniz notes that even Locke must hold that many things are present in us without our conscious awareness—habits and memories being obvious examples. Leibniz cites the innumerable "insensible perceptions" in us at every moment without our conscious awareness: for example, the unconscious perceptions of familiar sounds, sights, and feelings that become apparent to us when our attention is directed to them or when they cease to exist. Leibniz's point neither establishes rationalism nor refutes empiricism, but it does challenge one argument Locke had used against the doctrine of innate ideas.

One of Berkeley's main concerns in his book, *A Treatise Concerning the Principles of Human Knowledge*, was to expound his position of Idealism. We commonly believe that the ordinary objects around us have their existence independently of our perception of them. This belief, according to Berkeley, involves a plain contradiction. The objects in question are the things we perceive, and what we perceive are our ideas. Ideas cannot exist without being perceived by some mind. The ordinary objects around us, therefore, cannot exist without being perceived by some mind. Berkeley thus held that the ordinary objects around us are *ideas* in our minds; they are nothing but sensory perceptions. In sum, *esse est percipi*, to be is to be perceived. Concerning what happens to objects that we cease to perceive for the moment, Berkeley held that "so long as they are not actually perceived by me or do not exist in my mind or that of any other created spirit, they must either have no existence at all or else subsist in the mind of some eternal spirit."

Berkeley rejected Locke's distinction between primary and secondary qualities and ideas. If there is no external world, then there is no external world that our ideas of primary qualities resemble. Besides, asserted Berkeley, there is no difference between those ideas called primary and those called secondary, inasmuch as all ideas are particular and determinate perceptions: They are sensory impressions or the traces thereof in memory or imagination. Since Berkeley thus rejected the possibility of abstract ideas, he could not allow a distinction between ideas of primary quality and ideas of secondary quality to be based on the Lockean distinction between concepts and the featured sensations to which they apply.

The selections from *An Inquiry Concerning Human Understanding* present Hume's main contributions to the theory of knowledge. Hume noted that general truths (of the form "All S are P") divide into the class of Relations of Ideas and the class of Matters of Fact. The former are propositions we judge true just in virtue of the meaning of the terms involved; the latter are propositions we judge true in virtue of our experience. Whereas many earlier philosophers had concerned themselves primarily with knowledge concerning relation of ideas, Hume concerned himself with knowledge of general matters of fact. Matters of fact are what Hume calls "cause and effect relations." Propositions concerning "cause and effect relations" (for example, the proposition that fire burns paper) express correlations in our experience between one kind of event and another.

Hume introduces the notion of "the relation of cause and effect." This relation is the form of reasoning known as *induction*, reasoning from a number of particular examples to the general conclusion that the matter is always so. Hume's main contentions were the following: (1) *All judgments concerning general matters of fact have no basis other than inductive reasoning from particular cases.* (2) *Inductive reasoning cannot be demonstrated to be correct.* While Locke had anticipated these points to some extent, most philosophers before Hume had failed to find a problem where Hume definitely found one.

The selections from *An Inquiry into the Human Mind* highlight Thomas Reid's attack on what he calls the *doctrine of ideas*, a doctrine he takes to form the basis of the philosophies of Descartes, Malebranche, Locke, Berkeley, and Hume. This doctrine is the view that the objects we perceive and think about are not physical objects that exist outside of us, but are rather the sensory impressions and ideas that exist within our own minds. The skeptical arguments Hume presented in his *Treatise* had a strong effect on Reid. Not only did Reid thereby come to reject the Idealism of Berkeley, (which he had once espoused), but he went further to reject the entire doctrine of ideas.

In the selections that follow, we see how Reid distinguishes between, on the one hand, *sensation* and the impressions and ideas it involves, and, on the other hand, *perception*, through which we know external physical objects and their qualities. For example, the sensory impressions we have of colors make us perceive the physical objects before us as well as the color qualities those objects really have. This distinction agrees well with *common sense*. Ordinary people are confident that the things they see and feel and smell are real and have an existence in the external world and have the qualities that we perceive them to have. Throughout the *Inquiry*, Reid emphasizes—and became well-known for doing so—the critical role of common sense: the verdicts of common sense are to be upheld, and where philosophy and common sense conflict, philosophy must give way.

The General Introduction classified Kant as a *Nativistic Empiricist*. Kant agreed with the rationalists that we have some a priori synthetic knowledge, taking examples from mathematics and physics. Kant was, however, impressed with Hume's skeptical conclusions concerning cause and effect. He concluded that a priori synthetic knowledge would not be possible *if* synthetic knowledge were determined solely by factors that the objects of experience brought to the mind. Kant proposed what he called a *Copernican Revolution*: He postulated that our synthetic knowledge was partly determined by certain conditions that the mind imposes on the objects of experience (not just conditions that the objects of experience impose on the mind). The former conditions, he held, account for the a priori character of some synthetic knowledge.

The selections from the *Prolegomena to Any Future Metaphysics* state what Kant regarded as a priori conditions that the mind imposes on objects of experience. First, some of the a priori conditions pertain to the manner or arrangement of sensory experience. Sensory experience is *spatial* in character: The objects that we experience exist in space. The mind, according to Kant, contributes this characteristic of experience. Sensory experience is also *temporal*: The objects that we experience exist through time. This, too, the mind contributes, according to Kant. Second, some of the *a priori* conditions pertain to our conceptualization, our understanding of the objects that sensory experience presents. These conditions include such categories as *substance*, *cause*, *unity*, *possibility*, and others. Kant holds that these conditions, although they result in a priori knowledge, are not to be regarded as characterizing the world *in itself*. Space, time, substance, cause, unity, possibility, and so on, characterize only the world *as experienced*. This qualification, given the taxonomy of our General Introduction, disqualifies Kant as a rationalist.

6 / René Descartes (1596–1650)
MEDITATIONS ON FIRST PHILOSOPHY

MEDITATION I

It is now some years since I detected how many were the false beliefs that I had from my earliest youth admitted as true, and how doubtful was everything I had since constructed on this basis; and from that time I was convinced that I must once for all seriously undertake to rid myself of all the opinions which I had formerly accepted, and commence to build anew from the foundation, if I wanted to establish any firm and permanent structure in the sciences. But as this enterprise appeared to be a very great one, I waited until I had attained an age so mature that I could not hope that at any later date I should be better fitted to execute

Meditations on First Philosophy, I, II, III, IV, VI (in parts). From *Philosophical Works of Descartes*, translated by Elizabeth S. Haldane and G. R. T. Ross, Cambridge University Press. Copyright © 1911, by Cambridge University Press. Reprinted by permission of the publisher.

my design. This reason caused me to delay so long that I should feel that I was doing wrong were I to occupy in deliberation the time that yet remains to me for action. To-day, then, since very opportunely for the plan I have in view I have delivered my mind from every care [and am happily agitated by no passions] and since I have procured for myself an assured leisure in a peaceable retirement, I shall at last seriously and freely address myself to the general upheaval of all my former opinions.

Now for this object it is not necessary that I should show that all of these are false—I shall perhaps never arrive at this end. But inasmuch as reason already persuades me that I ought no less carefully to withhold my assent from matters which are not entirely certain and indubitable than from those which appear to me manifestly to be false, if I am able to find in each one some reason to doubt, this will suffice to justify my rejecting the whole. And for that end it will not be requisite that I should examine each in particular, which would be an endless undertaking; for owing to the fact that the destruction of the foundations of necessity brings with it the downfall of the rest of the edifice, I shall only in the first place attack those principles upon which all my former opinions rested.

All that up to the present time I have accepted as most true and certain I have learned either from the senses or through the senses; but it is sometimes proved to me that these senses are deceptive, and it is wiser not to trust entirely to any thing by which we have once been deceived.

But it may be that although the senses sometimes deceive us concerning things which are hardly perceptible, or very far away, there are yet many others to be met with as to which we cannot reasonably have any doubt, although we recognise them by their means. For example, there is the fact that I am here, seated by the fire, attired in a dressing gown, having this paper in my hands and other similar matters. And how could I deny that these hands and this body are mine, were it not perhaps that I compare myself to certain persons, devoid of sense, whose cerebella are so troubled and clouded by the violent vapours of black bile, that they constantly assure us that they think they are

kings when they are really quite poor, or that they are clothed in purple when they are really without covering, or who imagine that they have an earthenware head or are nothing but pumpkins or are made of glass. But they are mad, and I should not be any the less insane were I to follow examples so extravagant.

At the same time I must remember that I am a man, and that consequently I am in the habit of sleeping, and in my dreams representing to myself the same things or sometimes even less probable things, than do those who are insane in their waking moments. How often has it happened to me that in the night I dreamt that I found myself in this particular place, that I was dressed and seated near the fire, whilst in reality I was lying undressed in bed! At this moment it does indeed seem to me that it is with eyes awake that I am looking at this paper; that this head which I move is not asleep, that it is deliberately and of set purpose that I extend my hand and perceive it; what happens in sleep does not appear so clear nor so distinct as does all this. But in thinking over this I remind myself that on many occasions I have in sleep been deceived by similar illusions, and in dwelling carefully on this reflection I see so manifestly that there are no certain indications by which we may clearly distinguish wakefulness from sleep that I am lost in astonishment. And my astonishment is such that it is almost capable of persuading me that I now dream.

Now let us assume that we are asleep and that all these particulars, e.g. that we open our eyes, shake our head, extend our hands, and so on, are but false delusions; and let us reflect that possibly neither our hands nor our whole body are such as they appear to us to be. At the same time we must at least confess that the things which are represented to us in sleep are like painted representations which can only have been formed as the counterparts of something real and true, and that in this way those general things at least, i.e. eyes, a head, hands, and a whole body, are not imaginary things, but things really existent. For, as a matter of fact, painters, even when they study with the greatest skill to represent sirens and satyrs by forms the most strange and extraordinary, cannot give them natures which are entirely new, but merely make a certain medley of the members of different animals: or if their imagination is extravagant enough to invent something so novel that nothing similar has ever before been seen, and that then their work represents a thing purely fictitious and absolutely false, it is certain all the same that the colours of which this is composed are necessarily real. And for the same reason, although these general things, to wit, [a body], eyes, a head, hands, and such like, may be imaginary, we are bound at the same time to confess that there are at least some other objects yet more simple and more universal, which are real and true; and of these just in the same way as with certain real colours, all these images of things which dwell in our thoughts, whether true and real or false and fantastic, are formed.

To such a class of things pertains corporeal nature in general, and its extension, the figure of extended things, their quantity or magnitude and number, as also the place in which they are, the time which measures their duration, and so on.

That is possibly why our reasoning is not unjust when we conclude from this that Physics, Astronomy, Medicine, and all other sciences which have as their end the consideration of composite things, are very dubious and uncertain; but that Arithmetic, Geometry, and other sciences of that kind which only treat of things that are very simple and very general, without taking great trouble to ascertain whether they are actually existent or not, contain some measure of certainty and an element of the indubitable. For whether I am awake or asleep, two and three together always form five, and the square can never have more than four sides, and it does not seem possible that truths so clear and apparent can be suspected of any falsity [or uncertainty].

Nevertheless I have long had fixed in my mind the belief that an all-powerful God existed by whom I have been created such as I am. But how do I know that He has not brought it to pass that there is no earth, no heaven, no extended body, no magnitude, no place, and that nevertheless [I possess the perceptions of all these things and that] they seem to me to exist just exactly as I now see them? And, besides, as I sometimes imagine that oth-

ers deceive themselves in the things which they think they know best, how do I know that I am not deceived every time that I add two and three, or count the sides of a square, or judge of things yet simpler, if anything simpler can be imagined? But possibly God has not desired that I should be thus deceived, for He is said to be supremely good. If, however, it is contrary to His goodness to have made me such that I constantly deceive myself, it would also appear to be contrary to His goodness to permit me to be sometimes deceived, and nevertheless I cannot doubt that He does permit this.

There may indeed be those who would prefer to deny the existence of a God so powerful, rather than believe that all other things are uncertain. But let us not oppose them for the present, and grant that all that is here said of a God is a fable; nevertheless in whatever way they suppose that I have arrived at the state of being that I have reached—whether they attribute it to fate or to accident, or make out that it is by a continual succession of antecedents, or by some other method—since to err and deceive oneself is a defect, it is clear that the greater will be the probability of my being so imperfect as to deceive myself ever, as is the Author to whom they assign my origin the less powerful. To these reasons I have certainly nothing to reply, but at the end I feel constrained to confess that there is nothing in all that I formerly believed to be true, of which I cannot in some measure doubt, and that not merely through want of thought or through levity, but for reasons which are very powerful and maturely considered; so that henceforth I ought not the less carefully to refrain from giving credence to these opinions than to that which is manifestly false, if I desire to arrive at any certainty [in the sciences].

But it is not sufficient to have made these remarks, we must also be careful to keep them in mind. For these ancient and commonly held opinions still revert frequently to my mind, long and familiar custom having given them the right to occupy my mind against my inclination and rendered them almost masters of my belief; nor will I ever lose the habit of deferring to them or of placing my confidence in them, so long as I consider them as they really are, i.e. opinions in some measure doubtful, as I have just shown, and at the same time highly probable, so that there is much more reason to believe in than to deny them. That is why I consider that I shall not be acting amiss, if, taking of set purpose a contrary belief, I allow myself to be deceived, and for a certain time pretend that all these opinions are entirely false and imaginary, until at last, having thus balanced my former prejudices with my latter [so that they cannot divert my opinions more to one side than to the other], my judgment will no longer be dominated by bad usage or turned away from the right knowledge of the truth. For I am assured that there can be neither peril nor error in this course, and that I cannot at present yield too much to distrust, since I am not considering the question of action, but only of knowledge.

I shall then suppose, not that God who is supremely good and the fountain of truth, but some evil genius not less powerful than deceitful, has employed his whole energies in deceiving me; I shall consider that the heavens, the earth, colours, figures, sound, and all other external things are nought but the illusions and dreams of which this genius has availed himself in order to lay traps for my credulity; I shall consider myself as having no hands, no eyes, no flesh, no blood, nor any senses, yet falsely believing myself to possess all these things; I shall remain obstinately attached to this idea, and if by this means it is not in my power to arrive at the knowledge of any truth, I may at least do what is in my power [i.e. suspend my judgment], and with firm purpose avoid giving credence to any false thing, or being imposed upon by this arch deceiver, however powerful and deceptive he may be. But this task is a laborious one, and insensibly a certain lassitude leads me into the course of my ordinary life. And just as a captive who in sleep enjoys an imaginary liberty, when he begins to suspect that his liberty is but a dream, fears to awaken, and conspires with these agreeable illusions that the deception may be prolonged, so insensibly of my own accord I fall back into my former opinions, and I dread awakening from this slumber, lest the laborious wakefulness which would follow the tranquil-

ity of this repose should have to be spent not in daylight, but in the excessive darkness of the difficulties which have just been discussed.

MEDITATION II

The Meditation of yesterday filled my mind with so many doubts that it is no longer in my power to forget them. And yet I do not see in what manner I can resolve them; and, just as if I had all of a sudden fallen into very deep water, I am so disconcerted that I can neither make certain of setting my feet on the bottom, nor can I swim and so support myself on the surface. I shall nevertheless make an effort and follow anew the same path as that on which I yesterday entered, i.e. I shall proceed by setting aside all that in which the least doubt could be supposed to exist, just as if I had discovered that it was absolutely false; and I shall ever follow in this road until I have met with something which is certain, or at least, if I can do nothing else, until I have learned for certain that there is nothing in the world that is certain. Archimedes, in order that he might draw the terrestrial globe out of its place, and transport it elsewhere, demanded only that one point should be fixed and immoveable; in the same way I shall have the right to conceive high hopes if I am happy enough to discover one thing only which is certain and indubitable.

I suppose, then, that all the things that I see are false; I persuade myself that nothing has ever existed of all that my fallacious memory represents to me. I consider that I possess no senses; I imagine that body, figure, extension, movement and place are but the fictions of my mind. What, then, can be esteemed as true? Perhaps nothing at all, unless that there is nothing in the world that is certain.

But how can I know there is not something different from those things that I have just considered, of which one cannot have the slightest doubt? Is there not some God, or some other being by whatever name we call it, who puts these reflections into my mind? That is not necessary, for is it not possible that I am capable of producing them myself? I myself, am

I not at least something? But I have already denied that I had senses and body. Yet I hesitate, for what follows from that? Am I so dependent on body and senses that I cannot exist without these? But I was persuaded that there was nothing in all the world, that there was no heaven, no earth, that there were no minds, nor any bodies: was I not then likewise persuaded that I did not exist? Not at all; of a surety I myself did exist since I persuaded myself of something [or merely because I thought of something]. But there is some deceiver or other, very powerful and very cunning, who ever employs his ingenuity in deceiving me. Then without doubt I exist also if he deceives me, and let him deceive me as much as he will, he can never cause me to be nothing so long as I think that I am something. So that after having reflected well and carefully examined all things, we must come to the definite conclusion that this proposition: I am, I exist, is necessarily true each time that I pronounce it, or that I mentally conceive it.

.   .   .   .

But what then am I? A thing which thinks. What is a thing which thinks? It is a thing which doubts, understands, [conceives], affirms, denies, wills, refuses, which also imagines and feels.

Certainly it is no small matter if all these things pertain to my nature. But why should they not so pertain? Am I not that being who now doubts nearly everything, who nevertheless understands certain things, who affirms that one only is true, who denies all the others, who desires to know more, is averse from being deceived, who imagines many things, sometimes indeed despite his will, and who perceives many likewise, as by the intervention of the bodily organs? Is there nothing in all this which is as true as it is certain that I exist, even though I should always sleep and though he who has given me being employed all his ingenuity in deceiving me? Is there likewise any one of these attributes which can be distinguished from my thought, or which might be said to be separated from myself? For it is so evident of itself that it is I who doubts, who understands, and who desires, that there is no reason here to add anything to explain it. And

I have certainly the power of imagining likewise; for although it may happen (as I formerly supposed) that none of the things which I imagine are true, nevertheless this power of imagining does not cease to be really in use, and it forms part of my thought. Finally, I am the same who feels, that is to say, who perceives certain things, as by the organs of sense, since in truth I see light, I hear noise, I feel heat. But it will be said that these phenomena are false and that I am dreaming. Let it be so; still it is at least quite certain that it seems to me that I see light, that I hear noise and that I feel heat. That cannot be false; properly speaking it is what is in me called feeling; and used in this precise sense that is no other thing than thinking.

From this time I begin to know what I am with a little more clearness and distinction than before; but nevertheless it still seems to me, and I cannot prevent myself from thinking, that corporeal things, whose images are framed by thought, which are tested by the senses, are much more distinctly known than that obscure part of me which does not come under the imagination. Although really it is very strange to say that I know and understand more distinctly these things whose existence seems to me dubious, which are unknown to me, and which do not belong to me, than others of the truth of which I am convinced, which are known to me and which pertain to my real nature, in a word, than myself. But I see clearly how the case stands: my mind loves to wander, and cannot yet suffer itself to be retained within the just limits of truth. Very good, let us once more give it the freest rein, so that, when afterwards we seize the proper occasion for pulling up, it may the more easily be regulated and controlled.

Let us begin by considering the commonest matters, those which we believe to be the most distinctly comprehended, to wit, the bodies which we touch and see; not indeed bodies in general, for these general ideas are usually a little more confused, but let us consider one body in particular. Let us take, for example, this piece of wax: it has been taken quite freshly from the hive, and it has not yet lost the sweetness of the honey which it contains; it still retains somewhat of the odour of the flowers from which it has been culled; its colour, its figure, its size are apparent; it is hard, cold, easily handled, and if you strike it with the finger, it will emit a sound. Finally all the things which are requisite to cause us distinctly to recognise a body, are met with in it. But notice that while I speak and approach the fire what remained of the taste is exhaled, the smell evaporates, the colour alters, the figure is destroyed, the size increases, it becomes liquid, it heats, scarcely can one handle it, and when one strikes it, no sound is emitted. Does the same wax remain after this change? We must confess that it remains; none would judge otherwise. What then did I know so distinctly in this piece of wax? It could certainly be nothing of all that the senses brought to my notice, since all these things which fall under taste, smell, sight, touch, and hearing, are found to be changed, and yet the same wax remains.

Perhaps it was what I now think, viz. that this wax was not that sweetness of honey, nor that agreeable scent of flowers, nor that particular whiteness, nor that figure, nor that sound, but simply a body which a little while before appeared to me as perceptible under these forms, and which is now perceptible under others. But what, precisely, is it that I imagine when I form such conceptions? Let us attentively consider this, and, abstracting from all that does not belong to the wax, let us see what remains. Certainly nothing remains excepting a certain extended thing which is flexible and moveable. But what is the meaning of flexible and moveable? Is it not that I imagine that this piece of wax being round is capable of becoming square and of passing from a square to a triangular figure? No, certainly it is not that, since I imagine it admits of an infinitude of similar changes, and I nevertheless do not know how to compass the infinitude by my imagination, and consequently this conception which I have of the wax is not brought about by the faculty of imagination. What now is this extension? Is it not also unknown? For it becomes greater when the wax is melted, greater when it is boiled, and greater still when the heat increases; and I should not conceive [clearly] according to truth what wax is, if I did not think that even this piece that we are considering is capable of receiving more vari-

ations in extension than I have ever imagined. We must then grant that I could not even understand through the imagination what this piece of wax is, and that it is my mind alone which perceives it. I say this piece of wax in particular, for as to wax in general it is yet clearer. But what is this piece of wax which cannot be understood excepting by the [understanding or] mind? It is certainly the same that I see, touch, imagine, and finally it is the same which I have always believed it to be from the beginning. But what must particularly be observed is that its perception is neither an act of vision, nor of touch, nor of imagination, and has never been such although it may have appeared formerly to be so, but only an intuition of the mind, which may be imperfect and confused as it was formerly, or clear and distinct as it is at present, according as my attention is more or less directed to the elements which are found in it, and of which it is composed.

Yet in the meantime I am greatly astonished when I consider [the great feebleness of mind] and its proneness to fall [insensibly] into error; for although without giving expression to my thoughts I consider all this in my own mind, words often impede me and I am almost deceived by the terms of ordinary language. For we say that we see the same wax, if it is present, and not that we simply judge that it is the same from its having the same colour and figure. From this I should conclude that I knew the wax by means of vision and not simply by the intuition of the mind; unless by chance I remember that, when looking from a window and saying I see men who pass in the street, I really do not see them, but infer that what I see is men, just as I say that I see wax. And yet what do I see from the window but hats and coats which may cover automatic machines? Yet I judge these to be men. And similarly solely by the faculty of judgment which rests in my mind, I comprehend that which I believed I saw with my eyes.

A man who makes it his aim to raise his knowledge above the common should be ashamed to derive the occasion for doubting from the forms of speech invented by the vulgar; I prefer to pass on and consider whether I had a more evident and perfect conception of what the wax was when I first perceived it, and when I believed I knew it by means of the external senses or at least by the common sense as it is called, that is to say by the imaginative faculty, or whether my present conception is clearer now that I have most carefully examined what it is, and in what way it can be known. It would certainly be absurd to doubt as to this. For what was there in this first perception which was distinct? What was there which might not as well have been perceived by any of the animals? But when I distinguish the wax from its external forms, and when, just as if I had taken from it its vestments, I consider it quite naked, it is certain that although some error may still be found in my judgment, I can nevertheless not perceive it thus without a human mind.

But finally what shall I say of this mind, that is, of myself, for up to this point I do not admit in myself anything but mind? What then, I who seem to perceive this piece of wax so distinctly, do I not know myself, not only with much more truth and certainty, but also with much more distinctness and clearness? For if I judge that the wax is or exists from the fact that I see it, it certainly follows much more clearly that I am or that I exist myself from the fact that I see it. For it may be that what I see is not really wax, it may also be that I do not possess eyes with which to see anything; but it cannot be that when I see, or (for I no longer take account of the distinction) when I think I see, that I myself who think am nought. So if I judge that the wax exists from the fact that I touch it, the same thing will follow, to wit, that I am; and if I judge that my imagination, or some other cause, whatever it is, persuades me that the wax exists, I shall still conclude the same. And what I have here remarked of wax may be applied to all other things which are external to me [and which are met with outside of me]. And further, if the [notion or] perception of wax has seemed to me clearer and more distinct, not only after the sight or the touch, but also after many other causes have rendered it quite manifest to me, with how much more [evidence] and distinctness must it be said that I now know myself, since all the reasons which contribute to the knowledge of wax, or any other body whatever, are yet better proofs of the nature of my mind! And there are so many

other things in the mind itself which may contribute to the elucidation of its nature, that those which depend on body such as these just mentioned, hardly merit being taken into account.

But finally here I am, having insensibly reverted to the point I desired, for, since it is now manifest to me that even bodies are not properly speaking known by the senses or by the faculty of imagination, but by the understanding only, and since they are not known from the fact that they are seen or touched, but only because they are understood, I see clearly that there is nothing which is easier for me to know than my mind. But because it is difficult to rid oneself so promptly of an opinion to which one was accustomed for so long, it will be well that I should halt a little at this point, so that by the length of my meditation I may more deeply imprint on my memory this new knowledge.

MEDITATION III

I shall now close my eyes. I shall stop my ears. I shall call away all my senses. I shall efface even from my thoughts all the images of corporeal things, or at least (for that is hardly possible) I shall esteem them as vain and false; and thus holding converse only with myself and considering my own nature, I shall try little by little to reach a better knowledge of and a more familiar acquaintanceship with myself. I am a thing that thinks, that is to say, that doubts, affirms, denies, that knows a few things, that is ignorant of many [that loves, that hates], that wills, that desires, that also imagines and perceives; for as I remarked before, although the things which I perceive and imagine are perhaps nothing at all apart from me and in themselves, I am nevertheless assured that these modes of thought that I call perceptions and imaginations, inasmuch only as they are modes of thought, certainly reside [and are met with] in me.

And in the little that I have just said, I think I have summed up all that I really know, or at least all that hitherto I was aware that I knew. In order to try to extend my knowledge further, I shall now look around more carefully and see whether I cannot still discover in myself some other things which I have not hitherto perceived. I am certain that I am a thing which thinks; but do I not then likewise know what is requisite to render me certain of a truth? Certainly in this first knowledge there is nothing that assures me of its truth, excepting the clear and distinct perception of that which I state, which would not indeed suffice to assure me that what I say is true, if it could ever happen that a thing which I conceived so clearly and distinctly could be false; and accordingly it seems to me that already I can establish as a general rule that all things which I perceive very clearly and very distinctly are true.

At the same time I have before received and admitted many things to be very certain and manifest, which yet I afterwards recognised as being dubious. What then were these things? They were the earth, sky, stars and all other objects which I apprehended by means of the senses. But what did I clearly [and distinctly] perceive in them? Nothing more than that the ideas or thoughts of these things were presented to my mind. And not even now do I deny that these ideas are met with in me. But there was yet another thing which I affirmed, and which, owing to the habit which I had formed of believing it, I thought I perceived very clearly, although in truth I did not perceive it at all, to wit, that there were objects outside of me from which these ideas proceeded, and to which they were entirely similar. And it was in this that I erred, or, if perchance my judgment was correct, this was not due to any knowledge arising from my perception.

But when I took anything very simple and easy in the sphere of arithmetic or geometry into consideration, e.g. that two and three together made five, and other things of the sort, were not these present to my mind so clearly as to enable me to affirm that they were true? Certainly if I judged that since such matters could be doubted, this would not have been so for any other reason than that it came into my mind that perhaps a God might have endowed me with such a nature that I may have been deceived even concerning things which seemed to me most manifest. But every time that this preconceived opinion of the sovereign power

of a God presents itself to my thought, I am constrained to confess that it is easy to Him, if He wishes it, to cause me to err, even in matters in which I believe myself to have the best evidence. And, on the other hand, always when I direct my attention to things which I believe myself to perceive very clearly, I am so persuaded of their truth that I let myself break out into words such as these: Let who will deceive me, He can never cause me to be nothing while I think that I am, or some day cause it to be true to say that I have never been, it being true now to say that I am, or that two and three make more or less than five, or any such thing in which I see a manifest contradiction. And, certainly, since I have no reason to believe that there is a God who is a deceiver, and as I have not yet satisfied myself that there is a God at all, the reason for doubt which depends on this opinion alone is very slight, and so to speak metaphysical. But in order to be able altogether to remove it, I must inquire whether there is a God as soon as the occasion presents itself; and if I find that there is a God, I must also inquire whether He may be a deceiver; for without a knowledge of these two truths I do not see that I can ever be certain of anything.

And in order that I may have an opportunity of inquiring into this in an orderly way [without interrupting the order of meditation which I have proposed to myself, and which is little by little to pass from the notions which I find first of all in my mind to those which I shall later on discover in it] it is requisite that I should here divide my thoughts into certain kinds, and that I should consider in which of these kinds there is, properly speaking, truth or error to be found. Of my thoughts some are, so to speak, images of the things, and to these alone is the title "idea" properly applied; examples are my thought of a man or of a chimera, of heaven, of an angel, or [even] of God. But other thoughts possess other forms as well. For example in willing, fearing, approving, denying, though I always perceive something as the subject of the action of my mind, yet by this action I always add something else to the idea which I have of that thing; and of the thoughts of this kind some are called volitions or affections, and other judgments.

Now as to what concerns ideas, if we consider them only in themselves and do not relate them to anything else beyond themselves, they cannot properly speaking be false; for whether I imagine a goat or a chimera, it is not less true that I imagine the one than the other. We must not fear likewise that falsity can enter into will and into affections, for although I may desire evil things, or even things that never existed, it is not the less true that I desire them. Thus there remains no more than the judgments which we make, in which I must take the greatest care not to deceive myself. But the principal error and the commonest which we may meet with in them, consists in my judging that the ideas which are in me are similar or conformable to the things which are outside me; for without doubt if I considered the ideas only as certain modes of my thoughts, without trying to relate them to anything beyond, they could scarcely give me material for error.

But among these ideas, some appear to me to be innate, some adventitious, and others to be formed [or invented] by myself; for, as I have the power of understanding what is called a thing, or a truth, or a thought, it appears to me that I hold this power from no other source than my own nature. But if I now hear some sound, if I see the sun, or feel heat, I have hitherto judged that these sensations proceeded from certain things that exist outside of me; and finally it appears to me that sirens, hippogryphs, and the like, are formed out of my own mind. But again I may possibly persuade myself that all these ideas are of the nature of those which I term adventitious, or else that they are all innate, or all fictitious: for I have not yet clearly discovered their true origin.

And my principal task in this place is to consider, in respect to those ideas which appear to me to proceed from certain objects that are outside me, what are the reasons which cause me to think them similar to these objects. It seems indeed in the first place that I am taught this lesson by nature; and, secondly, I experience in myself that these ideas do not depend on my will nor therefore on myself—for they often present themselves to my mind in spite of my will. Just now, for instance, whether I will or whether I do not will, I feel heat, and thus I persuade myself that this feeling, or at least this idea of heat, is produced in me by some-

thing which is different from me, i.e. by the heat of the fire near which I sit. And nothing seems to me more obvious than to judge that this object imprints its likeness rather than anything else upon me.

Now I must discover whether these proofs are sufficiently strong and convincing. When I say that I am so instructed by nature, I merely mean a certain spontaneous inclination which impels me to believe in this connection, and not a natural light which makes me recognise that it is true. But these two things are very different; for I cannot doubt that which the natural light causes me to believe to be true, as, for example, it has shown me that I am from the fact that I doubt, or other facts of the same kind. And I possess no other faculty whereby to distinguish truth from falsehood, which can teach me that what this light shows me to be true is not really true, and no other faculty that is equally trustworthy. But as far as [apparently] natural impulses are concerned, I have frequently remarked, when I had to make active choice between virtue and vice, that they often enough led me to the part that was worse; and this is why I do not see any reason for following them in what regards truth and error.

And as to the other reason, which is that these ideas must proceed from objects outside me, since they do not depend on my will, I do not find it any the more convincing. For just as these impulses of which I have spoken are found in me, notwithstanding that they do not always concur with my will, so perhaps there is in me some faculty fitted to produce these ideas without the assistance of any external things, even though it is not yet known by me; just as, apparently, they have hitherto always been found in me during sleep without the aid of any external objects.

And finally, though they did proceed from objects different from myself, it is not a necessary consequence that they should resemble these. On the contrary, I have noticed that in many cases there was a great difference between the object and its idea. I find, for example, two completely diverse ideas of the sun in my mind; the one derives its origin from the senses, and should be placed in the category of adventitious ideas; according to this idea the sun seems to be extremely small; but the other is derived from astronomical reasonings, i.e. is elicited from certain notions that are innate in me, or else it is formed by me in some other manner; in accordance with it the sun appears to be several times greater than the earth. These two ideas cannot, indeed, both resemble the same sun, and reason makes me believe that the one which seems to have originated directly from the sun itself, is the one which is most dissimilar to it.

All this causes me to believe that until the present time it has not been by a judgment that was certain [or premeditated], but only by a sort of blind impulse that I believed that things existed outside of, and different from me, which, by the organs of my senses, or by some other method whatever it might be, conveyed these ideas or images to me [and imprinted on me their similitudes].

But there is yet another method of inquiring whether any of the objects of which I have ideas within me exist outside of me. If ideas are only taken as certain modes of thought, I recognise amongst them no difference or inequality, and all appear to proceed from me in the same manner; but when we consider them as images, one representing one thing and the other another, it is clear that they are very different one from the other. There is no doubt that those which represent to me substances are something more, and contain so to speak more objective reality within them [that is to say, by representation participate in a higher degree of being or perfection] than those that simply represent modes or accidents; and that idea again by which I understand a supreme God, eternal, infinite, [immutable], omniscient, omnipotent, and Creator of all things which are outside of Himself, has certainly more objective reality in itself than those ideas by which finite substances are represented.

Now it is manifest by the natural light that there must at least be as much reality in the efficient and total cause as in its effect. For, pray, whence can the effect derive its reality, if not from its cause? And in what way can this cause communicate this reality to it, unless it possessed it in itself? And from this it follows, not only that something cannot proceed from nothing, but likewise that what is more perfect—that is to say, which has more reality within itself—cannot proceed from the less perfect. And this is not only evidently true of those effects which possess actual or formal reality, but also of the ideas in which we consider merely what is termed objective reality. To take an example, the stone which has not yet existed not only cannot now commence to be unless it has been produced by something which possesses within itself, either formally or eminently, all that enters into the composition of the stone [i.e. it must possess the same things or other more excellent things than those which exist in the stone] and heat can only be produced in a subject in which it did not previously exist by a cause that is of an order [degree or kind] at least as perfect as heat, and so in all other cases. But further, the idea of heat, or of a stone, cannot exist in me unless it has been placed within me by some cause which possesses within it at least as much reality as that which I conceive to exist in the heat or the stone. For although this cause does not transmit anything of its actual or formal reality to my idea, we must not for that reason imagine that it is necessarily a less real cause; we must remember that [since every idea is a work of the mind] its nature is such that it demands of itself no other formal reality than that which it borrows from my thought, of which it is only a mode [i.e. a manner or way of thinking]. But in order that an idea should contain some one certain objective reality rather than another, it must without doubt derive it from some cause in which there is at least as much formal reality as this idea contains of objective reality. For if we imagine that something is found in an idea which is not found in the cause, it must then have been derived from nought; but however imperfect may be this mode of being by which a thing is objectively [or by representation] in the understanding by its ideas, we cannot certainly say that this mode of being is nothing, nor, consequently, that the idea derives its origin from nothing.

Nor must I imagine that, since the reality that I consider in these ideas is only objective, it is not essential that this reality should be formally in the causes of my ideas, but that it is sufficient that it should be found objectively. For just as this mode of objective existence pertains to ideas by their proper nature, so does the mode of formal existence pertain to the causes of those ideas (this is at least true of the first and principal) by the nature peculiar to them. And although it may be the case that one idea gives birth to another idea, that cannot continue to be so indefinitely; for in the end we must reach an idea whose cause shall be so to speak an archetype, in which the whole reality [or perfection] which is so to speak objectively [or by representation] in these ideas is contained formally [and really]. Thus the light of nature causes me to know clearly that the ideas in me are like [pictures or] images which can, in truth, easily fall short of the perfection of the objects from which they have been derived, but which can never contain anything greater or more perfect.

And the longer and the more carefully that I investigate these matters, the more clearly and distinctly do I recognise their truth. But what am I to conclude from it all in the end? It is this, that if the objective reality of any one of my ideas is of such a nature as clearly to make me recognise that it is not in me either formally or eminently, and that consequently I cannot myself be the cause of it, it follows of necessity that I am not alone in the world, but that there is another being which exists, or which is the cause of this idea. On the other hand, had no such an idea existed in me, I should have had no sufficient argument to convince me of the existence of any being beyond myself; for I have made very careful investigation everywhere and up to the present time have been able to find no other ground.

But of my ideas, beyond that which represents me to myself, as to which there can here be no difficulty, there is another which represents a God, and there are others representing corporeal and inanimate things, others angels, others animals, and others again which represent to me men similar to myself.

As regards the ideas which represent to me other men or animals, or angels, I can however easily conceive that they might be formed by an admixture of the other ideas which I have of myself, of corporeal things, and of God, even although there were apart from me neither men nor animals, nor angels, in all the world.

And in regard to the ideas of corporeal objects, I do not recognise in them anything so great or so excellent that they might not have possibly proceeded from myself; for if I consider them more closely, and examine them individually, as I yesterday examined the idea of wax, I find that there is very little in them which I perceive clearly and distinctly. Magnitude or extension in length, breadth, or depth, I do so perceive; also figure which results from a termination of this extension, the situation which bodies of different figure preserve in relation to one another, and movement or change of situation; to which we may also add substance, duration, and number. As to other things such as light, colours, sounds, scents, tastes, heat, cold, and the other tactile qualities, they are thought by me with so much obscurity and confusion that I do not even know if they are true or false, i.e. whether the ideas which I form of these qualities are actually the ideas of real objects or not [or whether they only represent chimeras which cannot exist in fact]. For although I have before remarked that it is only in judgments that falsity, properly speaking, or formal falsity, can be met with, a certain material falsity may nevertheless be found in ideas, i.e. when these ideas represent what is nothing as though it were something. For example, the ideas which I have of cold and heat are so far from clear and distinct that by their means I cannot tell whether cold is merely a privation of heat, or heat a privation of cold, or whether both are real qualities, or are not such. And inasmuch as [since ideas resemble images] there cannot be any ideas which do not appear to represent some things, if it is correct to say that cold is merely a privation of heat, the idea which represents it to me as something real and positive will not be improperly termed false, and the same holds good of other similar ideas.

To these it is certainly not necessary that I should attribute any author other than myself. For if they are false, i.e. if they represent things which do not exist, the light of nature shows me that they issue from nought, that is to say, that they are only in me in so far as something is lacking to the perfection of my nature. But if they are true, nevertheless because they exhibit so little reality to me that I cannot even clearly distinguish the thing represented from non-being, I do not see any reason why they should not be produced by myself.

As to the clear and distinct idea which I have of corporeal things, some of them seem as though I might have derived them from the idea which I possess of myself, as those which I have of substance, duration, number, and such like. For [even] when I think that a stone is a substance, or at least a thing capable of existing of itself, and that I am a substance also, although I conceive that I am a thing that thinks and not one that is extended, and that the stone on the other hand is an extended thing which does not think, and that thus there is a notable difference between the two conceptions—they seem, nevertheless, to agree in this, that both represent substances. In the same way, when I perceive that I now exist and further recollect that I have in former times existed, and when I remember that I have various thoughts of which I can recognise the number, I acquire ideas of duration and number which I can afterwards transfer to any object that I please. But as to all the other qualities of which the ideas of corporeal things are composed, to wit, extension, figure, situation and motion, it is true that they are not formally in me, since I am only a thing that thinks; but because they are merely certain modes of substance [and so to speak the vestments under which corporeal substance appears to us] and because I myself am also a substance, it would seem that they might be contained in me eminently.

Hence there remains only the idea of God, concerning which we must consider whether it is something which cannot have proceeded from me myself. By the name God I understand a substance that is infinite [eternal, immutable], independent, all-knowing, all-powerful, and by which I myself and everything else, if anything else does exist, have been created. Now all these characteristics are such that the more diligently I attend to them, the less do they appear capable of proceeding from me alone; hence, from what has been already said, we must conclude that God necessarily exists.

For although the idea of substance is within me owing to the fact that I am substance, nevertheless I should not have the idea of an infinite substance—since I am finite—if it had not proceeded from some substance which was veritably infinite.

. . . .

MEDITATION IV

I have been well accustomed these past days to detach my mind from my senses, and I have accurately observed that there are very few things that one knows with certainty respecting corporeal objects, that there are many more which are known to us respecting the human mind, and yet more still regarding God Himself; so that I shall now without any difficulty abstract my thoughts from the consideration of [sensible or] imaginable objects, and carry them to those which, being withdrawn from all contact with matter, are purely intelligible. And certainly the idea which I possess of the human mind inasmuch as it is a thinking thing, and not extended in length, width and depth, nor participating in anything pertaining to body, is incomparably more distinct than is the idea of any corporeal thing. And when I consider that I doubt, that is to say, that I am an incomplete and dependent being, the idea of a being that is complete and independent, that is of God, presents itself to my mind with so much distinctness and clearness—and from the fact alone that this idea is found in me, or that I who possess this idea exist, I conclude so certainly that God exists, and that my existence depends entirely on Him in every moment of my life—that I do not think that the human mind is capable of knowing anything with more evidence and certitude. And it seems to me that I now have before me a road which will lead us from the contemplation of the true God (in whom all the treasures of science and wisdom are contained) to the knowledge of the other objects of the universe.

For, first of all, I recognise it to be impossible that He should ever deceive me; for in all fraud and deception some imperfection is to be found, and although it may appear that the power of deception is a mark of subtilty or power, yet the desire to deceive without doubt testifies to malice or feebleness, and accordingly cannot be found in God.

In the next place I experienced in myself a certain capacity for judging which I have doubtless received from God, like all the other things that I possess; and as He could not desire to deceive me, it is clear that He has not given me a faculty that will lead me to err if I use it aright.

. . . .

Whereupon, regarding myself more closely, and considering what are my errors (for they alone testify to there being any imperfection in me), I answer that they depend on a combination of two causes, to wit, on the faculty of knowledge that rests in me, and on the power of choice or of free will—that is to say, of the understanding and at the same time of the will. For by the understanding alone I [neither assert nor deny anything, but] apprehend the ideas of things as to which I can form a judgment. But no error is properly speaking found in it, provided the word error is taken in its proper signification. . . .

. . . .

From all this I recognise that the power of will which I have received from God is not of itself the source of my errors—for it is very ample and very perfect of its kind—any more than is the power of understanding; for since I understand nothing but by the power which God has given me for understanding, there is no doubt that all that I understand, I understand as I ought, and it is not possible that I err in this. Whence then come my errors? They come from the sole fact that since the will is much wider in its range and compass than the understanding, I do not restrain it within the same bounds, but extend it also to things which I do not understand: and as the will is of itself indifferent to these, it easily falls into error and sin, and chooses the evil for the good, or the false for the true.

. . . .

. . . it seems to me that I have not gained little by this day's Meditation, since I have discovered the source of falsity and error. And certainly there can be no other source than that which I have explained; for as often as I so restrain my will within the limits of my knowledge that it forms no judgment except on matters which are clearly and distinctly represented to it by the understanding, I can never be deceived; for every clear and distinct conception is without doubt something, and hence cannot derive its origin from what is nought, but must of necessity have God as its author—God, I say, who being supremely perfect, cannot be the cause of any error; and consequently we must conclude that such a conception [or such a judgment] is true. Nor have I only learned to-day what I should avoid in order that I may not err, but also how I should act in order to arrive at a knowledge of the truth; for without doubt I shall arrive at this end if I devote my attention sufficiently to those things which I perfectly understand; and if I separate from these that which I only understand confusedly and with obscurity. To these I shall henceforth diligently give heed.

. . . .

MEDITATION VI

. . . But now that I begin to know myself better, and to discover more clearly the author of my being, I do not in truth think that I should rashly admit all the matters which the senses seem to teach us, but, on the other hand, I do not think that I should doubt them all universally.

And first of all, because I know that all things which I apprehend clearly and distinctly can be created by God as I apprehend them, it suffices that I am able to apprehend one thing apart from another clearly and distinctly in order to be certain that the one is different from the other, since they may be made to exist in separation at least by the omnipotence of God; and it does not signify by what power this separation is made in order to compel me to judge them to be different: and, therefore, just because I know certainly that I exist, and that meanwhile I do not remark that any other thing necessarily pertains to my nature or essence, excepting that I am a thinking thing, I rightly conclude that my essence consists solely in the fact that I am a thinking thing [or a substance whose whole essence or nature is to think]. And although possibly (or rather certainly, as I shall say in a moment) I possess a body with which I am very intimately conjoined, yet because, on the one side, I have a clear and distinct idea of myself inasmuch as I am only a thinking and unextended thing, and as, on the other, I possess a distinct idea of body, inasmuch as it is only an extended and unthinking thing, it is certain that this I [that is to say, my soul by which I am what I am], is entirely and absolutely distinct from my body, and can exist without it.

I further find in myself faculties employing modes of thinking peculiar to themselves, to wit, the faculties of imagination and feeling, without which I can easily conceive myself clearly and distinctly as a complete being; while, on the other hand, they cannot be so conceived apart from me, that is without an intelligent substance in which they reside, for [in the notion we have of these faculties, or, to use the language of the Schools] in their formal concept, some kind of intellection is comprised, from which I infer that they are distinct from me as its modes are from a thing. I observe also in me some other faculties such as that of change of position, the assumption of different figures and such like, which cannot be conceived, any more than can the preceding, apart from some substance to which they are attached, and consequently cannot exit without it; but it is very clear that these faculties, if it be true that they exist, must be attached to some corporeal or extended substance, and not to an intelligent substance, since in the clear and distinct conception of these there is some sort of extension found to be present, but no intellection at all. There is certainly further in me a certain passive faculty of perception, that is, of receiving and recognising the ideas of sensible things, but this would be useless to me [and I could in no way avail myself of it], if there were not either in me or in some other thing another active faculty capable of forming and producing these ideas. But this active faculty cannot exist in me [inasmuch as I am a thing that thinks] seeing that it does not presuppose thought, and also that those ideas are often produced in me without my contributing in any way to the same, and often even against my will; it is thus necessarily the case that the faculty resides in some substance different from me in which all the reality which is objectively in the ideas that are produced by this faculty is formally or eminently contained, as I remarked before. And this substance is either a body, that is, a corporeal nature in which there is contained formally [and really] all that which is objectively [and by representation] in those ideas, or it is God Himself, or some other creature more noble than body in which that same is contained eminently. But, since God is no deceiver, it is very manifest that He does not communicate to me these ideas immediately and by Himself, nor yet by the intervention of some creature in which their reality is not formally, but only eminently, contained. For since He has given me no faculty to recognise that this is the case, but, on the other hand, a very great inclination to believe [that they are sent to me or] that they are conveyed to me by corporeal objects, I do not see how He could be defended from the accusation of deceit if these ideas were produced by causes other than corporeal objects. Hence we must allow that corporeal things exist. However, they are perhaps not exactly what we perceive by the senses, since this comprehension by the senses is in many instances very obscure and confused; but we must at least admit that all things which I conceive in them clearly and distinctly, that is to say, all things which, speaking generally, are comprehended in the object of pure mathematics, are truly to be recognised as external objects.

As to other things, however, which are either particular only, as, for example, that the sun is of such and such a figure, etc., or which are less clearly and distinctly conceived, such as light, sound, pain and the like, it is certain that although they are very dubious and uncertain, yet on the sole ground that God is not a deceiver, and that consequently He has not permitted any falsity to exist in my opinion which He has not likewise given me the faculty of correcting, I may assuredly hope to conclude that I have within me the means of arriving at the truth even here. . . .

7 / John Locke (1632–1704)
AN ESSAY CONCERNING HUMAN UNDERSTANDING

BOOK I
NEITHER PRINCIPLES NOR IDEAS ARE INNATE

Chapter I

No Innate Speculative Principles

1. It is an established opinion amongst some men, that there are in the understanding certain *innate principles*; some primary notions, κοιναὶ ἔννοιαι, characters, as it were stamped upon the mind of man; which the soul receives in its very first being, and brings into the world with it. It would be sufficient to convince unprejudiced readers of the falseness of this supposition, if I should only show (as I hope I shall in the following parts of this Discourse) how men, barely by the use of their natural faculties, may attain to all the knowledge they have, without the help of any innate impressions; and may arrive at certainty, without any such original notions or principles. For I imagine any one will easily grant that it would be impertinent to suppose the ideas of colours innate in a creature to whom God hath given sight, and a power to receive them by the eyes from external objects: and no less unreasonable would it be to attribute several truths to the impressions of nature, and innate characters, when we may observe in ourselves faculties fit to attain as easy and certain knowledge of them as if they were originally imprinted on the mind.

But because a man is not permitted without censure to follow his own thoughts in the search of truth, when they lead him ever so little out of the common road, I shall set down the reasons that made me doubt of the truth of that opinion, as an excuse for my mistake, if I be in one; which I leave to be considered by those who, with me, dispose themselves to embrace truth wherever they find it.

2. There is nothing more commonly taken for granted than that there are certain *principles,* both *speculative* and *practical* (for they speak of both), universally agreed upon by all mankind: which therefore, they argue, must needs be the constant impressions which the souls of men receive in their first beings, and which they bring into the world with them, as necessarily and really as they do any of their inherent faculties.

3. This argument, drawn from universal consent, has this misfortune in it, that if it were true in matter of fact, that there were certain truths wherein all mankind agreed, it would not prove them innate, if there can be any other way shown how men may come to that universal agreement, in the things they do consent in, which I presume may be done.

4. But, which is worse, this argument of universal consent, which is made use of to prove innate principles, seems to me a demonstration that there are none such because there are none to which all mankind give an universal assent. I shall begin with the speculative, and instance in those magnified princi-

An Essay Concerning Human Understanding, Book I: i.1–5; Book II: i.1–6, ii.1–3, viii. 7–10, 13–21, ix. 1–4, 8–9, xi. 1,4,6,8,9, xxxiii. 5–7; Book III: i.1–3, ii. 1–2, iii. 6–9; Book IV: i. 1–8, ii. 1–5, 14, v. 1–6, xi. 1–5, xiv. 3–4, xv. 1–3, xvi. 5–8, 12. From *An Essay Concerning Human Understanding,* edited by A. C. Fraser (Oxford: Clarendon Press, 1894). Copyright 1894, Clarendon Press. Reprinted by permission of the publisher.

ples of demonstration, "Whatsoever is, is," and "It is impossible for the same thing to be and not to be;" which, of all others, I think have the most allowed title to innate. These have so settled a reputation of maxims universally received, that it will no doubt be thought strange if any one should seem to question it. But yet I take liberty to say, that these propositions are so far from having an universal assent, that there are a great part of mankind to whom they are not so much as known.

5. For, first, it is evident, that all children and idiots have not the least apprehension or thought of them. And the want of that is enough to destroy that universal assent which must needs be the necessary concomitant of all innate truths: it seeming to me near a contradiction to say, that there are truths imprinted on the soul, which it perceives or understands not: imprinting, if it signify anything, being nothing else but the making certain truths to be perceived. For to imprint anything on the mind without the mind's perceiving it, seems to me hardly intelligible. If therefore children and idiots have souls, have minds, with those impressions upon them, *they* must unavoidably perceive them, and necessarily know and assent to these truths; which since they do not, it is evident that there are no such impressions. For if they are not notions naturally imprinted, how can they be innate? and if they are notions imprinted, how can they be unknown? To say a notion is imprinted on the mind, and yet at the same time to say that the mind is ignorant of it, and never yet took notice of it, is to make this impression nothing. No proposition can be said to be in the mind which it never yet knew, which it was never yet conscious of. For if any one may, then, by the same reason, all propositions that are true, and the mind is capable ever of assenting to, may be said to be in the mind, and to be imprinted: since, if any one can be said to be in the mind, which it never yet knew, it must be only because it is capable of knowing it; and so the mind is of all truth it ever shall know. Nay, thus truths may be imprinted on the mind which it never did, nor ever shall know; for a man may live long, and die at last in ignorance of many truths which his mind was capable of knowing, and that with certainty. So that if the capacity of know-

ing be the natural impression contended for, all the truths a man ever comes to know will, by this account, be every one of them innate; and this great point will amount to no more, but only to a very improper way of speaking: which, whilst it pretends to assert the contrary, says nothing different from those who deny innate principles. For nobody, I think, ever denied that the mind was capable of knowing several truths. The capacity, they say, is innate; the knowledge acquired. But then to what end such contest for certain innate maxims? If truths can be imprinted on the understanding without being perceived, I can see no difference there can be between any truths the mind is *capable* of knowing in respect of their original: they must all be innate or all adventitious: in vain shall a man go about to distinguish them. He therefore that talks of innate notions in the understanding, cannot (if he intend thereby any distinct sort of truths) mean such truths to be in the understanding as it never perceived, and is yet wholly ignorant of. For if these words "to be in the understanding" have any propriety, they signify to be understood. So that to be in the understanding, and not to be understood; to be in the mind and never to be perceived, is all one as to say anything is and is not in the mind or understanding. If therefore these two propositions, "Whatsoever is, is," and "It is impossible for the same thing to be and not to be," are by nature imprinted, children cannot be ignorant of them: infants, and all that have souls, must necessarily have them in their understandings, know the truth of them, and assent to it.

·   ·   ·   ·   ·   ·

BOOK II
OF IDEAS

Chapter I

Of Ideas in General and Their Original

1. Every man being conscious to himself that he thinks; and that which his mind is applied about whilst thinking being the *ideas* that are there, it is past doubt that men have in their minds several ideas,—such as are those expressed by the words

whiteness, hardness, sweetness, thinking, motion, man, elephant, army, drunkenness, and others: it is in the first place then to be inquired, *How he comes by them?*

I know it is a received doctrine, that men have native ideas, and original characters, stamped upon their minds in their very first being. This opinion I have at large examined already; and, I suppose what I have said in the foregoing Book will be much more easily admitted, when I have shown whence the understanding may get all the ideas it has; and by what ways and degrees they may come into the mind;—for which I shall appeal to every one's own observation and experience.

2. Let us then suppose the mind to be, as we say, white paper, void of all characters, without any ideas:—How comes it to be furnished? Whence comes it by that vast store which the busy and boundless fancy of man has painted on it with an almost endless variety? Whence has it all the *materials* of reason and knowledge? To this I answer, in one word, from EXPERIENCE. In that all our knowledge is founded; and from that it ultimately derives itself. Our observation employed either, about external sensible objects, or about the internal operations of our minds perceived and reflected on by ourselves, is that which supplies our understandings with all the *materials* of thinking. These two are the fountains of knowledge, from whence all the ideas we have, or can naturally have, do spring.

3. First, our Senses, conversant about particular sensible objects, do convey into the mind several distinct perceptions of things, according to those various ways wherein those objects do affect them. And thus we come by those *ideas* we have of *yellow, white, heat, cold, soft, hard, bitter, sweet,* and all those which we call sensible qualities; which when I say the senses convey into the mind, I mean, they from external objects convey into the mind what produces there those perceptions. This great source of most of the ideas we have, depending wholly upon our senses, and derived by them to the understanding, I call SENSATION.

4. Secondly, the other fountain from which experience furnisheth the understanding with ideas is,—the perception of the operations of our own mind within us, as it is employed

about the ideas it has got;—which operations, when the soul comes to reflect on and consider, do furnish the understanding with another set of ideas, which could not be had from things without. And such are *perception, thinking, doubting, believing, reasoning, knowing, willing,* and all the different actings of our own minds;—which we being conscious of, and observing in ourselves, do from these receive into our understandings as distinct ideas as we do from bodies affecting our senses. This source of ideas every man has wholly in himself, and though it be not sense, as having nothing to do with external objects, yet it is very like it, and might properly enough be called *internal sense.* But as I call the other Sensation, so I call this REFLECTION, the ideas it affords being such only as the mind gets by reflecting on its own operations within itself. By reflection then, in the following part of this discourse, I would be understood to mean, that notice which the mind takes of its own operations, and the manner of them, by reason whereof there come to be ideas of these operations in the understanding. These two, I say, viz. external material things, as the objects of SENSATION, and the operations of our own minds within, as the objects of REFLECTION, are to me the only originals from whence all our ideas take their beginnings. The term *operations* here I use in a large sense, as comprehending not barely the actions of the mind about its ideas, but some sort of passions arising sometimes from them, such as is the satisfaction or uneasiness arising from any thought.

5. The understanding seems to me not to have the least glimmering of any ideas which it doth not receive from one of these two. *External objects* furnish the mind with the ideas of sensible qualities, which are all those different perceptions they produce in us; and *the mind* furnishes the understanding with ideas of its own operations.

These, when we have taken a full survey of them, and their several modes, combinations, and relations, we shall find to contain all our whole stock of ideas; and that we have nothing in our minds which did not come in one of these two ways. Let any one examine his own thoughts, and thoroughly search into his understanding; and then let him tell me, whether all the original ideas he has there, are any other than of the objects of his senses, or of the operations of his mind, considered as objects of his reflection. And how great a mass of knowledge soever he imagines to be lodged there, he will, upon taking a strict view, see that he has not any idea in his mind but what one of these two have imprinted;—though perhaps, with infinite variety compounded and enlarged by the understanding, as we shall see hereafter.

6. He that attentively considers the state of a child, at his first coming into the world, will have little reason to think him stored with plenty of ideas, that are to be the matter of his future knowledge. It is *by degrees* he comes to be furnished with them. And though the ideas of obvious and familiar qualities imprint themselves before the memory begins to keep a register of time or order, yet it is often so late before some unusual qualities come in the way, that there are few men that cannot recollect the beginning of their acquaintance with them. And if it were worth while, no doubt a child might be so ordered as to have but a very few, even of the ordinary ideas, till he were grown up to a man. But all that are born into the world, being surrounded with bodies that perpetually and diversely affect them, variety of ideas, whether care be taken of it or not, are imprinted on the minds of children. Light and colours are busy at hand everywhere, when the eye is but open; sounds and some tangible qualities fail not to solicit their proper senses, and force an entrance to the mind;—but yet, I think, it will be granted easily, that if a child were kept in a place where he never saw any other but black and white till he were a man, he would have no more ideas of scarlet or green, than be that from his childhood never tasted an oyster, or a pine-apple, has of those particular relishes.

. . . .

Chapter II

Of Simple Ideas

The better to understand the nature, manner, and extent of our knowledge, one thing is carefully to be observed concerning the ideas we have; and that is, that some of them are *simple* and some *complex.*

Though the qualities that affect our senses are, in the things themselves, so united and blended, that there is no separation, no distance between them; yet it is plain, the ideas they produce in the mind enter by the senses simple and unmixed. For, though the sight and touch often take in from the same object, at the same time, different ideas;—as a man sees at once motion and colour; the hand feels softness and warmth in the same piece of wax: yet the simple ideas thus united in the same subject, are as perfectly distinct as those that come in by different senses. The coldness and hardness which a man feels in a piece of ice being as distinct ideas in the mind as the smell and whiteness of a lily; or as the taste of sugar, and smell of a rose. And there is nothing that can be plainer to a man than the clear and distinct perception he has of those simple ideas; which, being each in itself uncompounded, contains in it nothing but *one uniform appearance, or conception in the mind,* and is not distinguishable into different ideas.

2. These simple ideas, the materials of all our knowledge, are suggested and furnished to the mind only by those two ways above mentioned, viz. sensation and reflection. When the understanding is once stored with these simple ideas, it has the power to repeat, compare, and unite them, even to an almost infinite variety and so can make at pleasure new complex ideas. But it is not in the power of the most exalted wit, or enlarged understanding, by any quickness or variety of thought, to *invent* or *frame* one new simple idea in the mind, not taken in by the ways before mentioned: nor can any force of the understanding *destroy* those that are there. The dominion of man, in this little world of his own understanding being muchwhat the same as it is in the great world of visible things; wherein his power, however managed by art and skill, reaches no farther than to compound and divide the materials that are made to his hand; but can do nothing towards the making the least particle of new matter, or destroying one atom of what is already in being. The same inability will every one find in himself, who shall go about to fashion in his understanding one simple idea, not received in by his senses from external objects, or by reflection from the operations of his own mind about them. I would have any one try to fancy any taste which had never affected his palate; or frame the idea of a scent he had never smelt:

and when he can do this, I will also conclude that a blind man hath ideas of colours, and a deaf man true distinct notions of sounds.

3. This is the reason why—though we cannot believe it impossible to God to make a creature with other organs, and more ways to convey into the understanding the notice of corporeal things than those five, as they are usually counted, which he has given to man— yet I think it is not possible for any *man* to imagine any other qualities in bodies, howsoever constituted, whereby they can be taken notice of, besides sounds, tastes, smells, visible and tangible qualities. And had mankind been made but with four senses, the qualities then which are the objects of the fifth sense had been as far from our notice, imagination, and conception, as now any belonging to a sixth, seventh, or eighth sense can possibly be;— which, whether yet some other creatures, in some other parts of this vast and stupendous universe, may not have, will be a great presumption to deny. He that will not set himself proudly at the top of all things, but will consider the immensity of this fabric, and the great variety that is to be found in this little and inconsiderable part of it which he has to do with, may be apt to think that, in other mansions of it, there may be other and different intelligent beings, of whose faculties he has as little knowledge or apprehension as a worm shut up in one drawer of a cabinet hath of the senses or understanding of a man; such variety and excellency being suitable to the wisdom and power of the Maker. I have here followed the common opinion of man's having but five senses; though, perhaps, there may be justly counted more;—but either supposition serves equally to my present purpose.

. . . .

Chapter VIII

Some Further Considerations Concerning Our Simple Ideas of Sensation

. . . . . .

7. To discover the nature of our *ideas* the better, and to discourse of them intelligibly, it will be convenient to distinguish them *as they are ideas or perceptions in our minds; and as*

they are modifications of matter in the bodies that cause such perceptions in us: that so we may not think (as perhaps usually is done) that they are exactly the images and resemblances of something inherent in the subject; most of those of sensation being in the mind no more the likeness of something existing without us, than the names that stand for them are the likeness of our ideas, which yet upon hearing they are apt to excite in us.

8. Whatsoever the mind perceives *in itself,* or is the immediate object of perception, thought, or understanding, that I call *idea;* and the power to produce any idea in our mind, I call *quality* of the subject wherein that power is. Thus a snowball having the power to produce in us the ideas of white, cold, and round,—the power to produce those ideas in us, as they are in the snowball. I call qualities; and as they are sensations or perceptions in our understandings. I call them ideas; which *ideas,* if I speak of sometimes as in the things themselves, I would be understood to mean those qualities in the objects which produce them in us.

9. Qualities thus considered in bodies are, *First,* such as are utterly inseparable from the body, in what state soever it be; and such as in all the alterations and changes it suffers, all the force can be used upon it, it constantly keeps; and such as sense constantly finds in every particle of matter which has bulk enough to be perceived; and the mind finds inseparable from every particle of matter, though less than to make itself singly be perceived by our senses: v.g. Take a grain of wheat, divide it into two parts; each part has still solidity, extension, figure, and mobility: divide it again, and it retains still the same qualities; and so divide it on, till the parts become insensible; they must retain still each of them all those qualities. For division (which is all that a mill, or pestle, or any other body, does upon another, in reducing it to insensible parts) can never take away either solidity, extension, figure, or mobility from any body, but only makes two or more distinct separate masses of matter, of that which was but one before; all which distinct masses, reckoned as so many distinct bodies, after division, make a certain number.

These I call *original* or *primary qualities* of

body, which I think we may observe to produce simple ideas in us, viz. solidity, extension, figure, motion or rest, and number.

10. *Secondly,* such qualities which in truth are nothing in the objects themselves but powers to produce various sensations in us by their primary qualities, i.e. by the bulk, figure, texture, and motion of their insensible parts, as colours, sounds, tastes, etc. These I call *secondary qualities.* To these might be added a *third* sort, which are allowed to be barely powers; though they are as much real qualities in the subject as those which I, to comply with the common way of speaking, call qualities, but for distinction, secondary qualities. For the power in fire to produce a new colour, or consistency, in *wax* or *clay,*—by its primary qualities, is as much a quality in fire, as the power it has to produce in *me* a new idea or sensation of warmth or burning, which I felt not before,—by the same primary qualities, viz. the bulk, texture, and motion of its insensible parts.

. . . .

13. . . . . let us suppose at present that the different motions and figures, bulk and number, of such particles, affecting the several organs of our senses, produce in us those different sensations which we have from the colours and smells of bodies; v.g. that a violet, by the impulse of such insensible particles of matter, of peculiar figures and bulks, and in different degrees and modifications of their motions, causes the ideas of the blue colour, and sweet scent of that flower to be produced in our minds. It being no more impossible to conceive that God should annex such ideas to such motions, with which they have no similitude, than that he should annex the idea of pain to the motion of a piece of steel dividing our flesh, with which that idea hath no resemblance.

14. What I have said concerning colours and smells may be understood also of tastes and sounds, and other the like sensible qualities; which, whatever reality we by mistake attribute to them, are in truth nothing in the objects themselves, but powers to produce various sensations in us; and depend on those primary qualities, viz. bulk, figure, texture, and motion of parts as I have said.

15. From whence I think it easy to draw this

observation,—that the ideas of primary qualities of bodies are resemblances of them, and their patterns do really exist in the bodies themselves, but the ideas produced in us by these secondary qualities have no resemblance of them at all. There is nothing like our ideas, existing in the bodies themselves. They are, in the bodies we denominate from them, only a power to produce those sensations in us: and what is sweet, blue, or warm in idea, is but the certain bulk, figure, and motion of the insensible parts, in the bodies themselves, which we call so.

16. Flame is denominated hot and light; snow, white and cold; and manna, white and sweet, from the ideas they produce in us. Which qualities are commonly thought to be the same in those bodies that those ideas are in us, the one that perfect resemblance of the other, as they are in a mirror, and it would by most men be judged very extravagant if one should say otherwise. And yet he that will consider that the same fire that, at one distance produces in us the sensation of warmth, does, at a nearer approach, produce in us the far different sensation of pain, ought to bethink himself what reason he has to say—that this idea of warmth, which was produced in him by the fire, is *actually in the fire*; and his idea of pain, which the same fire produced in him the same way, is *not* in the fire. Why are whiteness and coldness in snow, and pain not, when it produces the one and the other idea in us; and can do neither, but by the bulk, figure, number, and motion of its solid parts?

17. The particular bulk, number, figure, and motion of the parts of fire or snow are really in them,—whether any one's senses perceive them or no: and therefore they may be called *real* qualities, because they really exist in those bodies. But light, heat, whiteness, or coldness, are no more really in them than sickness or pain is in manna. Take away the sensation of them; let not the eyes see the light or colours, nor the ears hear sounds; let the palate not taste, nor the nose smell, and all colours, tastes, odours, and sounds, *as they are such particular ideas,* vanish and cease, and are reduced to their causes, i.e. bulk, figure, and motion of parts.

18. A piece of manna of a sensible bulk is

able to produce in us the idea of a round or square figure; and by being removed from one place to another, the idea of motion. This idea of motion represents it as it really is in manna moving: a circle or square are the same, whether in idea or existence, in the mind or in the manna. And this, both motion and figure, are really in the manna, whether we take notice of them or no: this everybody is ready to agree to. Besides, manna, by the bulk, figure, texture, and motion of its parts, has a power to produce the sensations of sickness, and sometimes of acute pains or gripings in us. That these ideas of sickness and pain are *not* in the manna, but effects of its operations on us, and are nowhere when we feel them not; this also every one readily agrees to. And yet men are hardly to be brought to think that sweetness and whiteness are not really in manna; which are but the effects of the operations of manna, by the motion, size, and figure of its particles, on the eyes and palate: as the pain and sickness caused by manna are confessedly nothing but the effects of its operations on the stomach and guts, by the size, motion, and figure of its insensible parts, (for by nothing else can a body operate, as has been proved): as if it could not operate on the eyes and palate, and thereby produce in the mind particular distinct ideas, which in itself it has not, as well as we allow it can operate on the guts and stomach, and thereby produce distinct ideas, which in itself it has not. These ideas, being all effects of the operations of manna on several parts of our bodies, by the size, figure, number, and motion of its parts;—why those produced by the eyes and palate should rather be thought to be really in the manna, than those produced by the stomach and guts; or why the pain and sickness, ideas that are the effect of manna, should be thought to be nowhere when they are not felt; and yet the sweetness and whiteness, effects of the same manna on other parts of the body, by ways equally as unknown, should be thought to exist in the manna, when they are not seen or tasted, would need some reason to explain.

19. Let us consider the red and white colours in porphyry. Hinder light from striking on it, and its colours vanish; it no longer produces any such ideas in us; upon the return of light it produces these appearances on us again. Can any one think any real alterations are made in the porphyry by the presence or absence of light; and that those ideas of whiteness and redness are really in porphryry in the light, when it is plain *it has no colour in the dark?* It has, indeed, such a configuration of particles, both night and day, as are apt, by the rays of light rebounding from some parts of that hard stone, to produce in us the idea of redness, and from others the idea of whiteness; but whiteness or redness are not in it at any time, but such a texture that hath the power to produce such a sensation in us.

20. Pound an almond, and the clear white colour will be altered into a dirty one, and the sweet taste into an oily one. What real alteration can the beating of the pestle make in any body, but an alteration of the texture of it?

21. Ideas being thus distinguished and understood, we may be able to give an account how the same water, at the same time, may produce the idea of cold by one hand and of heat by the other: whereas it is impossible that the same water, if those ideas were really in it, should at the same time be both hot and cold. For, if we imagine *warmth*, as it is in our hands, to be nothing but a certain sort and degree of motion in the minute particles of our nerves or animal spirits, we may understand how it is possible that the same water may, at the same time, produce the sensations of heat in one hand and cold in the other; which yet *figure* never does, that never producing the idea of a square by one hand which has produced the idea of a globe by another. But if the sensation of heat and cold be nothing but the increase or diminution of the motion of the minute parts of our bodies, caused by the corpuscles of any other body, it is easy to be understood, that if that motion be greater in one hand than in the other; if a body be applied to the two hands, which has in its minute particles a greater motion than in those of one of the hands, and a less than in those of the other, it will increase the motion of the one hand and lessen it in the other; and so cause the different sensations of heat and cold that depend thereon.

.   .   .   .

Chapter IX

Of Perception

1. *Perception*, as it is in the first faculty of the mind exercised about our ideas; so it is the first and simplest idea we have from reflection, and is by some called thinking in general. Though thinking, in the propriety of the English tongue, signifies that sort of operation in the mind about its ideas, wherein the mind is active; where it, with some degree of voluntary attention, considers anything. For in bare naked perception, the mind is, for the most part, only passive; and what it perceives, it cannot avoid perceiving.

2. What perception is, every one will know better by reflecting on what he does himself, when he sees, hears, feels, &c., or thinks, than by any discourse of mine. Whoever reflects on what passes in his own mind cannot miss it. And if he does not reflect, all the words in the world cannot make him have any notion of it.

3. This is certain, that whatever alterations are made in the body, if they reach not the mind; whatever impressions are made on the outward parts, if they are not taken notice of within, there is no perception. Fire may burn our bodies with no other effect than it does a billet, unless the motion be continued to the brain, and there the sense of heat, or idea of pain, be produced in the mind; wherein consists actual perception.

4. How often may a man observe in himself, that whilst his mind is intently employed in the contemplation of some objects, and curiously surveying some ideas that are there, it takes no notice of impressions of sounding bodies made upon the organ of hearing, with the same alteration that uses to be for the producing the idea of sound? A sufficient impulse there may be on the organ; but it not reaching the observation of the mind, there follows no perception: and though the motion that uses to produce the idea of sound be made in the ear, yet no sound is heard. Want of sensation, in this case, is not through any defect in the organ, or that the man's ears are less affected than at other times when he does hear: but that which uses to produce the idea, though conveyed in by the usual organ, not being taken notice of

in the understanding, and so imprinting no idea in the mind, there follows no sensation. So that wherever there is sense or perception, there some idea is actually produced, and present in the understanding.

. . . . . .

8. We are further to consider concerning perception, that the ideas we receive by sensation are often, in grown people, altered by the judgment, without our taking notice of it. When we set before our eyes a round globe of any uniform colour, v.g. gold, alabaster, or jet, it is certain that the idea thereby imprinted on our mind is of a flat circle, variously shadowed, with several degrees of light and brightness coming to our eyes. But we having, by use, been accustomed to perceive what kind of appearance convex bodies are wont to make in us; what alterations are made in the reflections of light by the difference of the sensible figures of bodies;—the judgment presently, by an habitual custom, alters the appearances into their causes. So that from that which is truly variety of shadow or colour, collecting the figure, it makes it pass for a mark of figure, and frames to itself the perception of a convex figure and an uniform colour; when the idea we receive from thence is only a plane variously coloured, as is evident in painting. To which purpose I shall here insert a problem of that very ingenious and studious promoter of real knowledge, the learned and worthy Mr. Molineux, which he was pleased to send me in a letter some months since; and it is this:—"Suppose a man *born* blind, and now adult, and taught by his *touch* to distinguish between a cube and a sphere of the same metal, and nighly of the same bigness, so as to tell, when he felt one and the other, which is the cube, which the sphere. Suppose then the cube and sphere placed on a table, and the blind man be made to see: *quare*, whether *by his sight, before he touched them*, he could now distinguish and tell which is the globe, which the cube?" To which the acute and judicious proposer answers, "Not. For, though he has obtained the experience of how a globe, how a cube affects his touch, yet he has not yet obtained the experience, that what affects his touch so or so, must affect his sight so or so; or that a protu-

berant angle in the cube, that pressed his hand unequally, shall appear to his eye as it does in the cube."—I agree with this thinking gentleman, whom I am proud to call my friend, in his answer to this problem; and am of opinion that the blind man, at first sight, would not be able with certainty to say which was the globe, which the cube, whilst he only saw them; though he could unerringly name them by his touch, and certainly distinguish them by the difference of their figures felt. This I have set down, and leave with my reader, as an occasion for him to consider how much he may be beholden to experience, improvement, and acquired notions, where he thinks he had not the least use of, or help from them. And the rather, because this observing gentleman further adds, that "having, upon the occasion of my book, proposed this to divers very ingenious men, he hardly ever met with one that at first gave the answer to it which he thinks true, till by hearing his reasons they were convinced."

9. But this is not, I think, usual in any of our ideas, but those received by sight. Because sight, the most comprehensive of all our senses, conveying to our minds the ideas of light and colours, which are peculiar only to that sense; and also the far different ideas of space, figure, and motion, the several varieties whereof change the appearances of its proper object, viz. light and colours; we bring ourselves by use to judge of the one by the other. This, in many cases by a settled habit,—in things whereof we have frequent experience, is performed so constantly and so quick, which is an idea formed by our judgment; so that one, viz. that of sensation, serves only to excite the other, and is scarce taken notice of itself;—as a man who reads or hears with attention and understanding, takes little notice of the characters or sounds, but of the ideas that are excited in him by them.

. . . .

Chapter XI

Of Discerning and Other Operations of the Mind

1. Another faculty we may take notice of in our minds is that of *discerning and distinguishing* between the several ideas it has. It is not enough to have a confused perception of something in general. Unless the mind had a distinct perception of different objects and their qualities, it would be capable of very little knowledge, though the bodies that affect us were as busy about us as they are now, and the mind were continually employed in thinking. On this faculty of distinguishing one thing from another depends the evidence and certainty of several, even very general, propositions, which have passed for innate truths;—because men, overlooking the true cause why those propositions find universal assent, impute it wholly to native uniform impressions; whereas it in truth depends upon this clear discerning faculty of the mind, whereby it *perceives* two ideas to be the same, or different. But of this more hereafter.

. . . .

4. The COMPARING them one with another, in respect of extent, degrees, time, place, or any other circumstances, is another operation of the mind about its ideas, and is that upon which depends all that large tribe of ideas comprehended under *relation;* which, of how vast an extent it is, I shall have occasion to consider hereafter.

. . . .

6. The next operation we may observe in the mind about its ideas is COMPOSITION, whereby it puts together several of those simple ones it has received from sensation and reflection, and combines them into complex ones. Under this of composition may be reckoned also that of *enlarging*, wherein, though the composition does not so much appear as in more complex ones, yet it is nevertheless a putting several ideas together, though of the same kind. Thus, by adding several units together, we make the idea of a dozen; and putting together the repeated ideas of several perches, we frame that of a furlong.

. . . .

8. When children have, by repeated sensations, got ideas fixed in their memories, they begin by degrees to learn the use of signs. And when they have got the skill to apply the organs of speech to the framing of articulate

sounds, they begin to make use of words, to signify their ideas to others. These verbal signs they sometimes borrow from others, and sometimes make themselves, as one may observe among the new and unusual names children often give to things in the first use of language.

9. The use of words then being to stand as outward marks of our internal ideas, and those ideas being taken from particular things, if every particular idea that we take in should have a distinct name, names must be endless. To prevent this, the mind makes the particular ideas received from particular objects to become general; which is done by considering them as they are in the mind such appearances,—separate from all other existences, and the circumstances of real existence, as time, place, or any other concomitant ideas. This is called ABSTRACTION, whereby ideas taken from particular beings become general representatives of all of the same kind; and their names general names, applicable to whatever exists conformable to such abstract ideas. Such precise, naked appearances in the mind, without considering how, whence, or with what others they came there, the understanding lays up (with names commonly annexed to them) as the standards to rank real existences into sorts, as they agree with these patterns, and to denominate them accordingly. Thus the same colour being observed to-day in chalk or snow, which the mind yesterday received from milk, it considers that appearance alone, makes it a representative of all of that kind; and having given it the name *whiteness*, it by that sound signifies the same quality wheresoever to be imagined or met with: and thus universals, whether ideas or terms, are made.

. . . . . .

Chapter XXXIII

Of the Association of Ideas

5. Some of our ideas have a *natural* correspondence and connexion one with another: it is the office and excellency of our reason to trace the seed, and hold them together in that union and correspondence which is founded in their peculiar beings. Besides this, there is another connexion of ideas wholly owing to *chance* or *custom*. Ideas that in themselves are

not all of kin, come to be so united in some men's minds that it is very hard to separate them; they always keep in company, and the one no sooner at any time comes into the understanding, but its associate appears with it; and if they are more than two which are thus united, the whole gang, always inseparable, show themselves together.

6. This strong combination of ideas, not allied by nature, the mind makes in itself either voluntarily or by chance; and hence it comes in different men to be very different, according to their different inclinations, education, interests, &c. *Custom* settles habits of thinking in the understanding, as well as of determining in the will, and of motions in the body: all which seems to be but trains of motions in the animal spirits, which, once set a going, continue in the same steps they have been used to; which, by often treading, are worn into a smooth path, and the motion in it becomes easy, and as it were natural. As far as we can comprehend thinking, thus ideas seem to be produced in our minds; or, if they are not, this may serve to explain their following one another in an habitual train, when once they are put into their track, as well as it does to explain such motions of the body. A musician used to any tune will find that, let it but once begin in his head, the ideas of the several notes of it will follow one another orderly in his understanding, without any care or attention, as regularly as his fingers move orderly over the keys of the organ to play out the tune he has begun, though his unattentive thoughts be elsewhere a wandering. Whether the natural cause of these ideas, as well as of that regular dancing of his fingers be the motion of his animal spirits, I will not determine, how probable soever, by this instance, it appears to be so: but this may help us a little to conceive of intellectual habits, and of the tying together of ideas.

7. That there are such associations of them made by custom, in the minds of most men, I think nobody will question, who has well considered himself or others; and to this, perhaps, might be justly attributed most of the sympathies and antipathies observable in men, which work as strongly, and produce as regular effects as if they were natural; and are therefore called so, though they at first had no other orig-

inal but the accidental connexion of two ideas, which either the strength of the first impression, or future indulgence so united, that they always afterwards kept company together in that man's mind, as if they were but one idea. I say most of the antipathies, I do not say all; for some of them are truly natural, depend upon our original constitution, and are born with us; but a great part of those which are counted natural, early, impressions, or wanton fancies at first, which would have been acknowledged the original of them, if they had been warily observed. A grown person surfeiting with honey no sooner hears the name of it, but his fancy immediately carries sickness and qualms to his stomach, and he cannot bear the very idea of it; other ideas of dislike, and sickness, and vomiting, presently accompany it, and he is disturbed; but he knows from whence to date this weakness, and can tell how he got this indisposition. Had this happened to him by an over-dose of honey when a child, all the same effects would have followed; but the cause would have been mistaken, and the antipathy counted natural.

.   .   .   .

BOOK III
OF WORDS

Chapter I

Of Words or Language in General

1. God, having designed man for a sociable creature, made him not only with an inclination, and under a necessity to have fellowship with those of his own kind, but furnished him also with language, which was to be the great instrument and common tie of society. Man, therefore, had by nature his organs so fashioned, as to be fit to frame articulate sounds, which we call words. But this was not enough to produce language; for parrots, and several other birds, will be taught to make articulate sounds distinct enough, which yet by no means are capable of language.

2. Besides articulate sounds, therefore, it was further necessary that he should be able to use these sounds as signs of internal conceptions; and to make them stand as marks for the ideas within his own mind, whereby they might be made known to others, and the thoughts of men's minds be conveyed from one to another.

3. But neither was this sufficient to make words so useful as they ought to be. It is not enough for the perfection of language, that sounds can be made signs of ideas, unless those signs can be so made use of as to comprehend several particular things: for the multiplication of words would have perplexed their use, had every particular thing need of a distinct name to be signified by. To remedy this inconvenience, language had yet a further improvement in the use of *general terms*, whereby one word was made to mark a multitude of particular existences: which advantageous use of sounds was obtained only by the difference of the ideas they were made signs of: those names becoming general, which are made to stand for *general ideas*, and those remaining particular, where the *ideas* they are used for are *particular*.

.   .   .   .   .   .

Chapter II

Of the Significance of Words

1. Man, though he have great variety of thoughts, and such from which others as well as himself might receive profit and delight; yet they are all within his own breast, invisible and hidden from others, nor can of themselves be made to appear. The comfort and advantage of society not being to be had without communication of thoughts, it was necessary that man should find out some external sensible signs, whereof those invisible ideas, which his thoughts are made up of, might be made known to others. For this purpose nothing was so fit, either for plenty or quickness, as those articulate sounds, which with so much ease and variety he found himself able to make. Thus we may conceive how *words*, which were by nature so well adapted to that purpose, came to be made use of by men as the signs of their ideas; not by any natural connexion that there is between particular articulate sounds and certain ideas, for then there would be but one language amongst all men; but by a voluntary imposition, whereby such a word is made

arbitrarily the mark of such an idea. The use, then, of words, is to be sensible marks of ideas; and the ideas they stand for are their proper and immediate signification.

2. The use men have of these marks being either to record their own thoughts, for the assistance of their own memory; or, as it were, to bring out their ideas, and lay them before the view of others: words, in their primary or immediate signification, stand for nothing but *the ideas in the mind of him that uses them*, how imperfectly soever or carelessly those ideas are collected from the things which they are supposed to represent. When a man speaks to another, it is that he may be understood: and the end of speech is, that those sounds, as marks, may make known his ideas to the hearer. That then which words are the marks of are the ideas of the speaker: nor can any one apply them as marks, immediately, to anything else but the ideas that he himself hath: for this would be to make them signs of his own conceptions, and yet apply them to other ideas; which would be to make them signs and not signs of his ideas at the same time; and so in effect to have no signification at all. Words being voluntary signs, they cannot be voluntary signs imposed by him on things he knows not. That would be to make them signs of nothing, sounds without signification. A man cannot make his words the signs either of qualities in things, or of conceptions in the mind of another, whereof he has none in his own. Till he has some ideas of his own, he cannot suppose them to correspond with the conceptions of another man; nor can he use any signs for them: for thus they would be the signs of he knows not what, which is in truth to be the signs of nothing. But when he represents to himself other men's ideas by some of his own, if he consent to give them the same names that other men do, it is still to his own ideas; to ideas that he has, and not to ideas that he has not.

.   .   .   .

Chapter III

Of General Terms

6. The next thing to be considered is.—How general words come to be made. For, since all things that exist are only particulars, how come

we by general terms; or where find we those general names they are supposed to stand for? Words become general by being made the signs of general ideas: and ideas become general, by separating from them the circumstances of time and place, and any other ideas that may determine them to this or that particular existence. By this way of abstraction they are made capable of representing more individuals than one; each of which having in it a conformity to that abstract idea, is (as we call it) of that sort.

7. But, to deduce this is a little more distinctly, it will not perhaps be amiss to trace our notions and names from their beginning, and observe by what degrees we proceed, and by what steps we enlarge our ideas from our first infancy. There is nothing more evident, than that the ideas of the persons children converse with (to instance in them alone) are, like the persons themselves, only particular. The ideas of the nurse and the mother are well framed in their minds; and, like pictures of them there, represent only those individuals. The names they first gave to them are confined to these individuals; and the names of *nurse* and *mamma*, the child uses, determine themselves to those persons. Afterwards, when time and larger acquaintance have made them observe that there are a great many other things in the world, that in some common agreements of shape, and several other qualities, resemble their father and mother, and those persons they have been used to, they frame an idea, which they find those many particulars do partake in; and to that they give, with others, the name *man*, for example. And thus they come to have a general name, and a general idea. Wherein they make nothing new; but only leave out the complex idea they had of Peter and James, Mary and Jane, that which is peculiar to each, and retain only what is common to them all.

8. By the same way that they come by the general name and idea of *man*, they easily advance to more general names and notions. For, observing that several things that differ from their idea of man, and cannot therefore be comprehended under that name, have yet certain qualities wherein they agree with man, by retaining only those qualities, and uniting them into one idea, they have again another and

more general idea; to which having given a name they make a term of a more comprehensive extension: which new idea is made, not by any new addition, but only as before, by leaving out the shape, and some other properties signified by the name man, and retaining only a body, with life, sense, and spontaneous motion, comprehended under the name animal.

9. That this is the way whereby men first formed general ideas, and general names to them I think is so evident, that there needs no other proof of it but the considering of a man's self, or others, and the ordinary proceedings of their minds in knowledge. And he that thinks *general natures* or *notions* are anything else but such abstract and partial ideas of more complex ones, taken at first from particular existences, will, I fear, be at a loss where to find them. For let any one effect, and then tell me, wherein does his idea of *man* differ from that of *Peter* and *Paul*, or his idea of *horse* from that of *Bucephalus*, but in the leaving out something that is peculiar to each individual, and retaining so much of those particular complex ideas of several particular existences as they are found to agree in? Of the complex ideas signified by the names *man* and *horse*, leaving out but those particulars wherein they differ, and retaining only those wherein they agree, and of those making a new distinct complex idea, and giving the name *animal* to it, one has a more general term, that comprehends with man several others creatures. Leave out the idea of *animal*, sense and spontaneous motion, and the remaining complex idea, made up of the remaining simple ones of body, life, and nourishment, becomes a more general one, under the more comprehensive term, *vivens*. And, not to dwell longer upon this particular, so evident in itself; by the same way the mind proceeds to *body, substance*, and at last to *being, thing*, and such universal terms, which stand for any of our ideas whatsoever. To conclude: this whole mystery of genera and species, which make such a noise in the schools, and are with justice so little regarded out of them, is nothing else but *abstract ideas*, more or less comprehensive, with names annexed to them. In all which, this is constant and unvariable, that every more general term stands for such an idea, and is but a part of any of those contained under it.

. . . .

BOOK IV
OF KNOWLEDGE AND
PROBABILITY

Chapter I

Of Knowledge in General

1. Since the mind, in all its thoughts and reasonings, hath no other immediate object but its own ideas, which it alone does or can contemplate, it is evident that our knowledge is only conversant about them.

2. *Knowledge* then seems to me to be nothing but *the perception of the connexion of and agreement, or disagreement and repugnancy of any of our ideas*. In this alone it consists. Where this perception is, there is knowledge, and where it is not, there, though we may fancy, guess, or believe, yet we always come short of knowledge. For when we know that white is not black, what do we else but perceive, that these two ideas do not agree? When we possess ourselves with the utmost security of the demonstration, that the three angles of a triangle are equal to two right ones, what do we more but perceive, that equality to two right ones does necessarily agree to, and is inseparable from, the three angles of a triangle?

3. But to understand a little more distinctly wherein this agreement or disagreement consists, I think we may reduce it all to these four sorts:

 I.   *Identity*, or *diversity*.
 II.   *Relation*.
 III. *Co-existence*, or *necessary connexion*.
 IV.   *Real existence*.

4. *First*, as to the first sort of agreement or disagreement, viz. *identity* or *diversity*. It is the first act of the mind, when it has any sentiments or ideas at all, to perceive its ideas; and so far as it perceives them, to know each what it is, and thereby also to perceive their difference, and that one is not another. This is so

absolutely necessary, that without it there could be no knowledge, no reasoning, no imagination, no distinct thoughts at all. By this the mind clearly and infallibly perceives each idea to agree with itself, and to be what it is; and all distinct ideas to disagree, i.e. the one not to be the other: and this it does without pains, labour, or deduction; but at first view, by its natural power of perception and distinction. And though men of art have reduced this into those general rules, *What is, is*, and *It is impossible for the same thing to be and not to be*, for ready application in all cases, wherein there may be occasion to reflect on it: yet it is certain that the first exercise of this faculty is about particular ideas. A man infallibly knows, as soon as ever he has them in his mind, that the ideas he calls *white* and *round* are the very ideas they are; and that they are not other ideas which he calls *red* or *square*. Nor can any maxim or proposition in the world make him know it clearer or surer than he did before, and without any such general rule. This then is the first agreement or disagreement which the mind perceives in its ideas; which it always perceives at first sight: and if there ever happen any doubt about it, it will always be found to be about the names, and not the ideas themselves, whose identity and diversity will always be perceived, as soon and clearly as the ideas themselves are: nor can it possibly be otherwise.

5. *Secondly*, the next sort of agreement or disagreement the mind perceives in any of its ideas may, I think, be called *relative*, and is nothing but the perception of the *relation* between any two ideas, of what kind soever, whether substances, modes, or any other. For, since all distinct ideas must eternally be known not to be the same, and so be universally and constantly denied one of another, there could be no room for any positive knowledge at all, if we could not perceive any relation between our ideas, and find out the agreement or disagreement they have one with another, in several ways the mind takes of comparing them.

6. *Thirdly*, the third sort of agreement or disagreement to be found in our ideas, which the perception of the mind is employed about, is *co-existence* or *non-co-existence* in the *same*

subject; and this belongs particularly to substances. Thus when we pronounce concerning gold, that it is fixed, our knowledge of this truth amounts to no more but this, that fixedness, or a power to remain in the fire unconsumed, is an idea that always accompanies and is joined with that particular sort of yellowness, weight, fusibility, malleableness, and solubility in *aqua regia*, which make our complex idea signified by the word gold.

7. *Fourthly*, the fourth and last sort is that of *actual real existence* agreeing to any idea.

Within these four sorts of agreement or disagreement is, I suppose, contained all the knowledge we have, or are capable of. For all the inquiries we can make concerning any of our ideas, all that we know or can affirm concerning any of them, is, That it is, or is not, the same with some other; that it does or does not always co-exist with some other idea in the same subject; that it has this or that relation with some other idea; or that it has a real existence without the mind. Thus, "blue is not yellow," is of identity. "Two triangles upon equal bases between two parallels are equals," is of relation. "Iron is susceptible of magnetical impressions," is of co-existence. "God is," is of real existence. Though identity and co-existence are truly nothing but relations, yet they are such peculiar ways of agreement or disagreement of our ideas, that they deserve well to be considered as distinct heads, and not under relation in general; since they are so different grounds of affirmation and negation, as will easily appear to any one, who will but reflect on what is said in several places of this *Essay*.

I should now proceed to examine the several degrees of our knowledge, but that it is necessary first, to consider the different acceptations of the word *knowledge*.

8. There are several ways wherein the mind is possessed of truth; each of which is called knowledge.

I. There is *actual knowledge*, which is the present view the mind has of the agreement or disagreement of any of its ideas, or of the relation they have one to another.

II. A man is said to know any proposition, which having been once laid before his thoughts, he evidently perceived the agreement or disagreement of the ideas whereof it consists; and so lodged it in his memory, that whenever that proposition comes again to be reflected on, he, without doubt or hesitation, embraces the right side, assents to, and is certain of the truth of it. This, I think, one may call *habitual knowledge*. And thus a man may be said to know all those truths which are lodged in his memory, by a foregoing clear and full perception, whereof the mind is assured past doubt as often as it has occasion to reflect on them. For our finite understandings being able to think clearly and distinctly but on one thing at once, if men had no knowledge of any more than what they actually thought on, they would all be very ignorant: and he that knew most, would know but one truth, that being all he was able to think on at one time.

. . . .

Chapter II

Of the Degrees of Our Knowledge

1. All our knowledge consisting, as I have said, in the view the mind has of its own ideas, which is the utmost light and greatest certainty we, with our faculties, and in our way of knowledge, are capable of, it may not be amiss to consider a little the degrees of its evidence. The different clearness of our knowledge seems to me to lie in the different way of perception the mind has of the agreement or disagreement of any of its ideas. For if we will reflect on our own ways of thinking, we will find, that sometimes the mind perceives the agreement or disagreement of two ideas *immediately by themselves*, without the intervention of any other: and this I think we may call *intuitive knowledge*. For in this the mind is at no pains of proving or examining, but perceives the truth as the eye doth light, only by being directed towards it. Thus the mind perceives that *white* is not *black*, that a *circle* is not a *triangle*, that *three* are more than *two* and equal to *one and two*. Such kinds of truths the mind perceives at the first sight of the ideas together, by bare intuition; without the intervention of any other idea: and this kind of knowledge is the clearest and most certain that human frailty is capable of. This part of knowl-

edge is irresistible, and, like bright sunshine, forces itself immediately to be perceived, as soon as ever the mind turns its view that way; and leaves no room for hesitation, doubt, or examination, but the mind is presently filled with the clear light of it. *It is on this intuition that depends all the certainty and evidence of all knowledge;* which certainty every one finds to be so great, that he cannot imagine, and therefore not require a greater: for a man cannot conceive himself capable of a greater certainty than to know that any idea in his mind is such as he perceives it to be: and that two ideas, wherein he perceives a difference, are different and not precisely the same. He that demands a greater certainty than this, demands he knows not what, and shows only that he has a mind to be a sceptic, without being able to be so. Certainty depends so wholly on this intuition, that, in the next degree of knowledge which I call demonstrative, this intuition is necessary in all the connexions of the intermediate ideas, without which we cannot attain knowledge and certainty.

2. The next degree of knowledge is, where the mind perceives the agreement or disagreement of any ideas, but not immediately. Though wherever the mind perceives the agreement or disagreement of any of its ideas, there be certain knowledge; yet it does not always happen, that the mind sees that agreement or disagreement, which there is between them, even where it is discoverable; and in that case remains in ignorance, and at most gets no further than a probable conjecture. The reason why the mind cannot always perceive presently the agreement or disagreement of two ideas, is, because those ideas, concerning whose agreement or disagreement the inquiry is made, cannot by the mind be so put together as to show it. In this case then, when the mind cannot so bring its ideas together as by their immediate comparison, and as it were juxta-position or application one to another, to perceive their agreement or disagreement, it is fain, *by the intervention of other ideas* (one or more, as it happens) to discover the agreement or disagreement which it searches; and this is that which we call *reasoning*. Thus, the mind being willing to know the agreement or disagreement in bigness between the three angles of a tri-

angle and two right ones, cannot by an immediate view and comparing them do it: because the three angles of a triangle cannot be brought at once, and be compared with any other one, or two, angles; and so of this the mind has no immediate, no intuitive knowledge. In this case the mind is fain to find out some other angles, to which the three angles of a triangle have an equality; and, finding those equal to two right ones, comes to know their equality to two right ones.

3. Those intervening ideas, which serve to show the agreement of any two others, are called *proofs*; and where the agreement and disagreement is by this means plainly and clearly perceived, it is called *demonstration*; it being *shown* to the understanding, and the mind made to see that it is so. A quickness in the mind to find out these intermediate ideas (that shall discover the agreement or disagreement of any other), and to apply them right, is, I suppose, that which is called *sagacity*.

4. This knowledge, by intervening proofs, though it be certain, yet the evidence of it is not altogether so clear and bright, nor the assent so ready, as in intuitive knowledge. For, though in demonstration the mind does at last perceive the agreement or disagreement of the ideas it considers: yet it is not without pains and attention: there must be more than one transient view to find it. A steady application and pursuit are required to this discovery: and there must be a progression by steps and degrees, before the mind can in this way arrive at certainty, and come to perceive the agreement or repugnancy between two ideas that need proofs and the use of reason to show it.

5. Another difference between intuitive and demonstrative knowledge is, that, though in the latter all doubt be removed when, by the intervention of the intermediate ideas, the agreement or disagreement is perceived, yet before the demonstration there was a doubt; which in intuitive knowledge cannot happen to the mind that has its faculty of perception left to a degree capable of distinct ideas; no more than it can be a doubt to the eye (that can distinctly see white and black), whether this ink and this paper be all of a colour. If there be sight in the eyes, it will, at first glimpse, without hesitation, perceive the words printed on this paper dif-

ferent from the colour of the paper; and so if the mind have the faculty of distinct perception, it will perceive the agreement or disagreement of those ideas that produce intuitive knowledge. If the eyes have lost the faculty of seeing, or the mind of perceiving, we in vain inquire after the quickness of sight in one, or clearness of perception in the other.

. . . .

14. These two, viz. intuition and demonstration, are the degrees of our *knowledge*; whatever comes short of one of these, with what assurance soever embraced, is but *faith* or *opinion*, but not knowledge, at least in all general truths. There is, indeed, another perception of the mind, employed about the *particular existence of finite beings without us*, which, going beyond bare probability, and yet not reaching perfectly to either of the foregoing degrees of certainty, passes under the name of *knowledge*. There can be nothing more certain than that the idea we receive from an external object is in our minds: this is intuitive knowledge. But whether there by anything more than barely that idea in our minds; whether we can thence certainly infer the existence of anything without us, which corresponds to that idea, is that whereof some men think there may be a question made; because men may have such ideas in their minds, when no such thing exists, no such object affects their senses. But yet here I think we are provided with an evidence that puts us past doubting. For I ask any one, Whether he be not invincibly conscious to himself of a different perception, when he looks on the sun by day, and thinks on it by night: when he actually tastes wormwood, or smells a rose, or only thinks on that savour or odour? We as plainly find the difference there is between any idea revived in our minds by our own memory, and actually coming into our minds by our senses, as we do between any two distinct ideas. If any one say, a dream may do the same thing, and all these ideas may be produced in us without any external objects; he may please to dream that I make him this answer:—I. That it is no great matter, whether I remove his scruple or no: where all is but dream, reasoning and arguments are of no use, truth and knowledge nothing. 2. That I believe

he will allow a very manifest difference between dreaming of being in the fire, and being actually in it. But yet if he be resolved to appear so sceptical as to maintain, that what I call being actually in the fire is nothing but a dream; and that we cannot thereby certainly know, that any such thing as fire actually exists without us: I answer, That we certainly finding that pleasure or pain follows upon the application of certain objects to us, whose existence we perceive, or dream that we perceive, by our senses; this certainty is as great as our happiness or misery, beyond which we have no concernment to know or to be. So that, I think, we may add to the two former sorts of knowledge this also, of the existence of particular external objects, by that perception and consciousness we have of the actual entrance of ideas from them, and allow these three degrees of knowledge, viz. *intuitive, demonstrative*, and *sensitive*: in each of which there are different degrees and ways of evidence and certainty.

.   .   .   .

Chapter V

Of Truth in General

1. What is truth? was an inquiry many ages since; and it being that which all mankind either do, or pretend to search after, it cannot but be worth our while carefully to examine wherein it consists; and so acquaint ourselves with the nature of it, as to observe how the mind distinguishes it from falsehood.

2. Truth, then, seems to me, in the proper import of the word, to signify nothing but *the joining or separating of Signs, as the Things signified by them do agree or disagree one with another*. The joining or separating of signs here meant, is what by another name we call *proposition*. So that truth properly belongs only to propositions: whereof there are two sorts, viz. mental and verbal; as there are two sorts of signs commonly made use of, viz. ideas and words.

3. To form a clear notion of truth, it is very necessary to consider truth of thought, and truth of words, distinctly one from another: but yet it is very difficult to treat of them asunder. Because it is unavoidable, in treating of mental propositions, to make use of words: and then

the instances given of mental propositions cease immediately to be barely mental, and become verbal. For a *mental proposition* being nothing but a bare consideration of the ideas, as they are in our minds, stripped of names, they lose the nature of purely mental propositions as soon as they are put into words.

4. And that which makes it yet harder to treat of mental and verbal propositions separately is, that most men, if not all, in their thinking and reasonings within themselves, make use of words instead of ideas; at least when the subject of their meditation contains in it complex ideas. . . .

5. But to return to the consideration of truth: we must, I say, observe two sorts of propositions that we are capable of making:—

First, *Mental*, wherein the ideas in our understandings are without the use of words put together, or separated, by the mind perceiving or judging of their agreement or disagreement.

Secondly, *Verbal* propositions, which are words, the signs of our ideas, put together or separated in affirmative or negative sentences. By which way of affirming or denying, these signs, made by sounds, are, as it were, put together or separated one from another. So that proposition consists in joining or separating signs; and truth consists in the putting together or separating those signs, according as the things which they stand for agree or disagree.

6. Every one's experience will satisfy him, that the mind, either by perceiving, or supposing, the agreement or disagreement of any of its ideas, does tacitly within itself put them into a kind of proposition affirmative or negative; which I have endeavoured to express by the terms putting together and separating. But this action of the mind, which is so familiar to every thinking and reasoning man is easier to be in his head the idea of two lines, viz. the side and diagonal of a square, whereof the diagonal is an inch long, he may have the idea also of the division of that line into a certain number of equal parts; v.g. into five, ten, a hundred, a thousand, or any other number, and may have the idea of that inch line being divisible, or not divisible, into such equal parts, as a certain number of them will be equal to the sideline. Now, whenever he perceives, believes, or supposes such a kind of divisibility

to agree or disagree to his idea of that line, he, as it were, joins or separates those two ideas, viz. the idea of that line, and the idea of that kind of divisibility; and so makes a mental proposition, which is true or false, according as such a kind of divisibility, a divisibility into such *aliquot* parts, does really agree to that line or no. When ideas are so put together, or separated in the mind, as they or the things they stand for do agree or not, that is, as I may call it, *mental truth*. But *truth of words* is something more; and that is the affirming or denying of words one of another as the ideas they stand for agree or disagree: and this again is twofold; either purely verbal and trifling, which I shall speak of (chap. viii), or real and instructive; which is the object of that real knowledge which we have spoken of already.

.   .   .   .   .   .

Chapter XI

Of Our Knowledge of the Existence of Other Things

1. The knowledge of our own being we have by intuition. The existence of a God, reason clearly makes known to us, as has been shown.

The knowledge of the existence of *any other thing* we can have only by *sensation*: for there being no necessary connexion of real existence with any *idea* a man hath in his memory; nor of any other existence but that of God with the existence of any particular man: no particular man can know the existence of any other being, but only when, by actual operating upon him, it makes itself perceived by him. For, the having the idea of anything in our mind, no more proves the existence of that thing, than the picture of a man evidences his being in the world, or the visions of a dream make thereby a true history.

2. It is therefore the *actual receiving* of ideas from without that gives us notice of the existence of other things, and makes us know, that something doth exist at that time without us which causes that idea in us; though perhaps we neither know nor consider how it does it. For it takes not from the certainty of our senses, and the ideas we receive by them, that we know not the manner wherein they are produced: v.g. whilst I write this, I have, by the paper affecting my eyes, that idea produced in my mind, which, whatever object causes, I call *white*; by which I know that that quality or accident (i.e. whose appearance before my eyes always causes that idea) doth really exist, and hath a being without me. And of this, the greatest assurance I can possibly have, and to which my faculties can attain, is the testimony of my eyes, which are the proper and sole judges of this thing; whose testimony I have reason to rely on as so certain, that I can no more doubt, whilst I write this, that I see white and black, and that something really exists that causes that sensation in me, than that I write or move my hand; which is a certainty as great as human nature is capable of, concerning the existence of anything, but a man's self alone, and of God.

3. The notice we have by our senses of the existing of things without us, though it be not altogether so certain as our intuitive knowledge, or the deductions of our reason employed about the clear abstract ideas of our own minds; yet it is an assurance that deserves the name of *knowledge*. If we persuade ourselves that our faculties act and inform us right concerning the existence of those objects that affect them, it cannot pass for an ill-grounded confidence: for I think nobody can, in earnest, be so sceptical as to be uncertain of the existence of those things which he sees and feels. At least, he that can doubt so far (whatever he may have with his own thoughts), will never have any controversy with me; since he can never be sure I say anything contrary to his own opinion. As to myself, I think God has given me assurance enough of the existence of things without me: since, by their different application, I can produce in myself both pleasure and pain, which is one great concernment of my present state. This is certain: the confidence that our faculties do not herein deceive us, is the greatest assurance we are capable of concerning the existence of material beings. For we cannot act anything but by our faculties; nor talk of knowledge itself, but by the help of those faculties which are fitted to apprehend even what knowledge is.

But besides the assurance we have from our senses themselves, that they do not err in the information they give us of the existence of things without us, when they are affected by them, we are further confirmed in this assurance by other concurrent reasons:—

4. I. It is plain those perceptions are produced in us by exterior causes affecting our senses: because those that want the *organs* of any sense, never can have the ideas belonging to that sense produced in their minds. This is too evident to be doubted: and therefore we cannot but be assured that they come in by the organs of that sense, and no other way. The organs themselves, it is plain, do not produce them: for then the eyes of a man in the dark would produce colours, and his nose smell roses in the winter: but we see nobody gets the relish of a pineapple, till he goes to the Indies, where it is, and tastes it.

5. II. Because sometimes I find that *I cannot avoid the having those ideas produced in my mind*. For though, when my eyes are shut, or windows fast, I can at pleasure recall to my mind the ideas of light, or the sun, which former sensations had lodged in my memory; so I can at pleasure lay by *that* idea, and take into my view that of the smell of a rose, or taste of sugar. But, if I turn my eyes at noon towards the sun, I cannot avoid the ideas which the light or sun then produces in me. So that there is a manifest difference between the ideas laid up in my memory (over which, if they were there only, I should have constantly the same power to dispose of them and lay them by at pleasure), and those which force themselves upon me, and I cannot avoid having. And therefore it must needs be some exterior cause, and the brisk acting of some objects without me, whose efficacy I cannot resist, that produces those ideas in my mind, whether I will or no. Besides, there is nobody who doth not perceive the difference in himself between contemplating the sun, as he hath the idea of it in his memory, and actually looking upon it: of which two, his perception is so distinct, that few of his ideas are more distinguishable one from another. And therefore he hath certain knowledge that they are not *both* memory, or the actions of his mind, and fancies only within him; but that actual seeing hath a cause without.

· · · · · · ·

Chapter XIV

Of Judgment

3. The faculty which God has given man to supply the want of clear and certain knowledge, in cases where that cannot be had, is *judgment*: whereby the mind takes its ideas to agree or disagree; or, which is the same, any proposition to be true or false, without perceiving a demonstrative evidence in the proofs. The mind sometimes exercises this judgment out of necessity, where demonstrative proofs and certain knowledge are not to be had; and sometimes out of laziness, unskilfulness, or haste, even where demonstrative and certain proofs are to be had. Men often stay not warily to examine the agreement or disagreement of two ideas, which they are desirous or concerned to know; but, either incapable of such attention as is requisite in a long train of gradations, or impatient of delay, lightly cast their eyes on, or wholly pass by the proofs; and so, without making out the demonstration, determine of the agreement or disagreement of two ideas, as it were by a view of them as they are at a distance, and take it to be the one or the other, as seems most likely to them upon such a loose survey. This faculty of the mind, when it is exercised immediately about things, is called *judgment*; when about truths delivered in words, is most commonly called *assent* or *dissent*: which being the most usual way, wherein the mind has occasion to employ this faculty, I shall, under these terms, treat of it, as least liable in our language to equivocation.

4. Thus the mind has two faculties conversant about truth and falsehood:—

First, *knowledge*, whereby it certainly *perceives*, and is undoubtedly satisfied of the agreement or disagreement of any ideas.

Secondly, *judgment*, which is the putting ideas together, or separating them from one another in the mind, when their certain agreement or disagreement is not perceived, but *presumed* to be so; which is, as the word imports, taken to be so before it certainly appears. And if it so unites or separates them as in reality things are, it is right judgment.

Chapter XV

Of Probability

1. As *demonstration* is the showing the agreement or disagreement of two ideas, by the intervention of one or more proofs, which have a constant, immutable, and visible connexion one with another; so *probability* is nothing but the appearance of such an agreement or disagreement, by the intervention of proofs, whose connexion is not constant and immutable, or at least is not perceived to be so, but is, or appears for the most part to be so, and is enough to induce the mind to judge the proposition to be true or false, rather than the contrary. For example: in the demonstration of it a man perceives the certain, immutable connexion there is of equality between the three angles of a triangle, and those intermediate ones which are made use of to show their equality to two right ones; and so, by an intuitive knowledge of the agreement or disagreement of the intermediate ideas in each step of the progress, the whole series is continued with an evidence, which clearly shows the agreement or disagreement of those three angles in equality to two right ones: and thus he has certain knowledge that it is so. But another man, who never took the pains to observe the demonstration, hearing a mathematician, a man of credit, affirm the three angles of a triangle to be equal to two right ones, assents to it, i.e. receives it for true: in which case the foundation of his assent is the probability of the thing; the proof being such as for the most part carries truth with it: the man on whose testimony he receives it, not being wont to affirm anything contrary to or besides his knowledge, especially in matters of this kind: so that that which causes his assent to this proposition, that the three angles of a triangle are equal to two right ones, that which makes him take these ideas to agree, without knowing them to do so, is the wonted veracity of the speaker in other cases, or his supposed veracity in this.

2. Our knowledge, as has been shown, being very narrow, and we not happy enough to find certain truth in everything which we have occasion to consider; most of the propositions we think, reason, discourse—nay, act upon, are

such as we cannot have undoubted knowledge of their truth: yet some of them border so near upon certainty, that we make no doubt at all about them; but assent to them as firmly, and act, according to that assent, as resolutely as if they were infallibly demonstrated, and that our knowledge of them was perfect and certain. But there being degrees herein, from the very neighbourhood of certainty and demonstration, quite down to improbability and unlikeness, even to the confines of impossibility; and also degrees of assent from full assurance and confidence, quite down to conjecture, doubt, and distrust: I shall come now (having, as I think, found out *the bounds of human knowledge and certainty*), in the next place, to consider *the several degrees and grounds of probability and assent or faith.*

3. Probability is likeliness to be true, the very notation of the word signifying such a proposition for which there be arguments or proofs to make it pass, or be received for true. The entertainment the mind gives this sort of propositions is called *belief, assent,* or *opinion,* which is the admitting or receiving any proposition for true, upon arguments or proofs that are found to persuade us to receive it as true, without certain knowledge that it is so. And herein lies the difference between *probability* and *certainty, faith,* and *knowledge,* that in all the parts of knowledge there is intuition; each immediate idea, each step has its visible and certain connexion; in belief, not so. That which makes me believe, is something extraneous to the thing I believe; something not evidently joined on both sides to, and so not manifestly showing the agreement or disagreement of those ideas that are under consideration.

.   .   .   .

Chapter XVI

Of the Degrees of Assent

.   .   .   .

5. But to return to the grounds of assent, and the several degrees of it, we are to take notice, that the propositions we receive upon inducements of *probability* are of *two sorts:* either concerning some particular existence, or, as it is usually termed, matter of fact, which,

falling under observation, is capable of human testimony; or else concerning things, which, being beyond the discovery of our senses, are not capable of any such testimony.

6. Concerning the *first* of these, viz. *particular matter of fact*.

I. Where any particular thing, consonant to the constant observation of ourselves and others in the like case, comes attested by the concurrent reports of all that mention it, we receive it as easily, and build as firmly upon it, as if it were certain knowledge; and we reason and act thereupon with as little doubt as if it were perfect demonstration. Thus, if all Englishmen, who have occasion to mention it, should affirm that it froze in England the last winter, or that there were swallows seen there in the summer, I think a man could almost as little doubt of it as that seven and four are eleven. The first, therefore, and *highest degree of probability*, is, when the general consent of all men, in all ages, as far as it can be known, concurs with a man's constant and never-failing experience in like cases, to confirm the truth of any particular matter of fact attested by fair witnesses: such are all the stated constitutions and properties of bodies, and the regular proceedings of causes and effects in the ordinary course of nature. This we call an argument from the nature of things themselves. For what our own and other men's *constant observation* has found always to be after the same manner, that we with reason conclude to be the effect of steady and regular causes; though they come not within the reach of our knowledge. Thus, that fire warmed a man, made lead fluid, and changed the colour or consistency in wood or charcoal; that iron sunk in water, and swam in quicksilver: these and the like propositions about particular facts, being agreeable to our constant experience, as often as we have to do with these matters; and being generally spoke of (when mentioned by others) as things found constantly to be so, and therefore not so much as controverted by anybody—we are put past doubt that a relation affirming any such thing to have been, or any predication that it will happen again in the same manner, is very true. These *probabilities* rise so near to *certainty*, that they govern our thoughts as absolutely, and influence all our ac-

tions as fully, as the most evident demonstration; and in what concerns us we make little or no difference between them and certain knowledge. Our belief, thus grounded, rises to *assurance*.

7. II. The *next degree of probability* is, when I find by my own experience, and the agreement of all others that mention it, a thing to be for the most part so, and that the particular instance of it is attested by many and undoubted witnesses: v.g. history giving us such an account of men in all ages, and my own experience, as far as I had an opportunity to observe, confirming it, that most men prefer their private advantage to the public: if all historians that write of Tiberius, say that Tiberius did so, it is extremely probable. And in this case, our assent has a sufficient foundation to raise itself to a degree which we may call *confidence*.

8. III. In things that happen indifferently, as that a bird should fly this or that way; that it should thunder on a man's right or left hand, &c., when any particular matter of fact is vouched by the concurrent testimony of unsuspected witnesses, there our assent is also *unavoidable*. Thus: that there is such a city in Italy as Rome: that about one thousand seven hundred years ago, there lived in it a man, called Julius Caesar: that he was a general, and that he won a battle against another, called Pompey. This, though in the nature of the thing there be nothing for nor against it, yet being related by historians of credit, and contradicted by no one writer a man cannot avoid believing it, and can as little doubt of it as he does of the being and actions of his own acquaintance, whereof he himself is a witness.

.   .   .   .

12. [*Secondly*] The probabilities we have hitherto mentioned are only such as concern matter of fact, and such things as are capable of observation and testimony. There remains that other sort, concerning which men entertain opinions with variety of assent, though *the things be such, that falling not under the reach of our senses, they are not capable of testimony*. Such are, 1. The existence, nature and operations of finite immaterial beings without us; as spirits, angels, devils, &c. Or the existence of material beings which, either for their

smallness in themselves or remoteness from us, our senses cannot take notice of—as, whether there be any plants, animals, and intelligent inhabitants in the planets, and other mansions of the vast universe. 2. Concerning the manner of operation in most parts of the works of nature: wherein, though we see the sensible effects, yet their causes are unknown, and we perceive not the ways and manner how they are produced. We see animals are generated, nourished, and move; the loadstone draws iron; and the parts of a candle, successively melting, turn into flame, and give us both light and heat. These and the like effects we see and know: but the causes that operate, and the manner they are produced in, we can only guess and probably conjecture. For these and the like, coming not within the scrutiny of human senses, cannot be examined by them, or be attested by anybody; and therefore can appear more or less probable, only as they more or less agree to truths that later established in our minds, and as they hold proportion to other parts of our knowledge and observation. *Analogy* in these matters is the only help we have, and it is from that alone we draw all our grounds of probability. Thus, observing that the bare rubbing of two bodies violently one upon another, produces heat, and very often fire itself, we have reason to think, that what we call *heat* and *fire* consists in a violent agitation of the imperceptible minute parts of the burning matter.

. . . .

8 / Gottfried Leibniz (1646–1716)
NEW ESSAYS ON THE HUMAN UNDERSTANDING

INTRODUCTION

As the *Essay on the Understanding*, by an illustrious Englishman, is one of the best and most highly esteemed works of the present time, I have resolved to make some remarks upon it, because, having for a long time given considerable attention to the same subject and to most of the matters with which the essay deals, I have thought that this would be a good occasion for publishing some of my opinions under the title of *New Essays on the Understanding*, in the hope that my thoughts will obtain a favourable reception through appearing in such good company. I have hoped also to be able to profit by the work of another, not only in the way of lessening my own work (as in fact it is less trouble to follow the thread of a good author than to work on entirely untrodden ground), but also in the way of adding something to what he has given us, which is always easier than making an independent beginning. For I think I have removed some difficulties which he left entirely alone. Thus his reputation is helpful to me: and besides, being disposed to do justice and very far from wishing to lessen the esteem in which his work is held, I would increase his reputation, if my approval

New Essays on the Human Understanding: Introduction, in *The Monadology and Other Philosophical Writings*, edited by Robert Latta (Oxford: Clarendon Press, 1948), 357–385. Copyright © 1948, Clarendon Press. Reprinted by permission of the publisher.

have any weight. It is true that I often differ from him in opinion; but, far from denying the worth of famous writers, we bear witness to it by making known in what respect and for what reasons we differ from their opinion, when we think it necessary to prevent their authority from prevailing against reason on some important points; and besides, in replying to such excellent men, we make it easier for the truth to be accepted, and it is to be supposed that it is principally for truth that they are working.

In fact, although the author of the *Essay* says a thousand fine things of which I cordially approve, our systems greatly differ. His has more relation to Aristotle and mine to Plato, although in many things both of us have departed from the doctrine of these two ancient writers. He is more popular, and I for my part am sometimes compelled to be a little more *acroamatic* and abstract, which is not of advantage to me, especially when a living language is used. But I think that by introducing two speakers, one of whom expounds opinions taken from this author's *Essay*, while the other adds my observations, I show the relation between us in a way that will be more satisfactory to the reader than if I had put down mere remarks, the reading of which would have been constantly interrupted by the necessity of turning to his book in order to understand mine. Nevertheless it will be well also to compare our writings sometimes, and not to judge of his opinions except from his own work, although I have usually retained his expressions. It is true that owing to the limitations involved in following the thread of another person's argument and making remarks upon it, I have been unable even to think of achieving the graceful turns of which dialogue is susceptible; but I hope that the matter will make up for the defects of the style.

The differences between us have regard to subjects of some importance. There is the question whether the soul, in itself, is entirely empty, like a writing-tablet on which nothing has yet been written *(tabula rasa)*, (which is the opinion of Aristotle and of the author of the *Essay*), and whether everything that is inscribed upon it comes solely from the senses and experience; or whether the soul originally contains the principles of several notions and doctrines, which are merely roused on certain occasions by external objects, as I hold along with Plato and even with the Schoolmen, and with all those who interpret in this sense the passage of St. Paul (Romans, ii. 15), in which he shows that the law of God is written in men's hearts. The Stoics called these principles προλήψεις, that is, fundamental assumptions or what we take for granted beforehand. Mathematicians call them *common notions* (κοιναὶ ἔννοιαι). Modern philosophers give them other excellent names; and, in particular, Julius Scaliger named them *semina aeternitatis item zopyra*, as much as to say, living fires, flashes of light *[traits lumineux]*, hidden within us but appearing at the instance of the senses, like the sparks which come from the steel when it strikes the flint. And not without reason it is thought that these flashes *[éclats]* indicate something divine and eternal, which appears above all in necessary truths. Hence there arises another question, whether all truths are dependent on experience, that is, on induction and instances; or whether there are some which have yet another foundation. For if some events can be foreseen before we have made any trial of them, it is manifest that we contribute to them something of our own. The senses, although they are necessary for all our actual acquiring of knowledge, are by no means sufficient to give us the whole of our knowledge, since the senses never give anything but instances, that is to say particular or individual truths. Now all the instances which confirm a general truth, however numerous they may be, are not sufficient to establish the universal necessity of this same truth; for it does not at all follow that what has happened will happen in the same way. For example, the Greeks, the Romans, and all the other peoples of the earth, as it was known to the ancients, always observed that before twenty-four hours have passed, day changes into night and night into day. But they would have been wrong if they had thought that the same rule is observed everywhere else, for since that time, the opposite has been experienced by people on a visit to Nova Zembla. And he would still be wrong who should think that, in our regions at least, it is a necessary and eternal truth that shall endure for ever, since we must hold that the earth and the sun itself do not exist necessarily, and that perhaps there will come a time when this beautiful star with its whole system will no longer exist, at least in its present form. Whence it seems that necessary truths, such as we find in pure mathematics and especially in arithmetic and geometry, must have principles whose proof does not depend upon instances nor, consequently, upon the witness of the senses, although without the senses it would never have come into our heads to think of them. This is a point which should be carefully noted, and it is one which Euclid so well understood that he often proves by reason that which is evident enough through experience and through sense-images. Logic also, along with metaphysics and ethics *[la morale]*, of which the one forms natural theology and the other natural jurisprudence, are full of such truths; and consequently their demonstration can come only from the inner principles which are called innate. It is true we must not imagine that we can read these eternal laws of reason in the soul as in an open book, as the edict of the praetor may be read on his *album* without trouble or investigation; but it is enough that we can discover these laws in ourselves by means of attention, for which opportunities are furnished by the senses; and the success of experiments serves also as a confirmation of reason, somewhat as in arithmetic "proofs" are useful in helping us to avoid errors of calculation when the process is a long one. In this also lies the difference between human knowledge and that of the lower animals. The lower animals are purely empirical and direct themselves by particular instances alone; for, so far as we can judge, they never succeed in forming necessary propositions; while men, on the other hand, have the capacity for demonstrative science. It is also on this account that the power of making *concatenations* [of ideas] which the lower animals possess is something inferior to the reason which is in men. The concatenations [of ideas] made by the lower animals are simply like those of mere empirics, who maintain that what has sometimes happened will happen again in a case which resembles the former in characteristics which strike them, although they are incapable of judging whether or not the same reasons hold

good in both cases. That is why it is so simple a matter for men to entrap animals, and so easy for mere empirics to make mistakes. From this making of mistakes even persons who have become skillful through age and experience are not exempt, when they trust too much to their past experience, as some have done in civil and military affairs; because enough consideration is not given to the fact that the world changes and that men become more skilful by finding countless new contrivances, while on the other hand the stags or the hares of our time do not become more full of shifts than those of former times. The concatenations [of ideas] in the lower animals are only a shadow of reasoning, that is to say they are only connexions of imagination and passings from one image to another, because in new circumstances which seem to resemble others which have occurred before we expect anew what we at other times found along with them, as if things were actually connected together because their images are connected in memory. It is true that reason also leads us to expect, as a rule, that there will occur in the future what is in harmony with a long experience of the past, but this is, nevertheless, not a necessary and infallible truth; and our forecast may fail when we least expect it, because the reasons which have hitherto justified it no longer operate. And on this account the wisest people do not trust altogether to experience, but try, so far as possible, to get some hold of the reason of what happens, in order to decide when exceptions must be made. For reason is alone capable of laying down trustworthy rules and of supplying what is lacking in those which were not trustworthy, by stating the exception to them, and in short of finding sure connexions in the force of necessary consequences; and this often enables us to foresee the event without having to experience the sense-connexions of images, to which the animals are confined, so that that which shows that the sources *[principes]* of necessary truths are within us also distinguishes man from the lower animals.

Perhaps our able author may not entirely differ from me in opinion. For after having devoted the whole of his first book to the rejection of innate knowledge *[lumières]*, understood in a certain sense, he nevertheless admits, at the beginning of the second book and in those which follow, that the ideas which do not originate in sensation come from reflexion. Now reflexion is nothing but an attention to that which is in us, and the senses do not give us what we already bring with us. That being so, can it be denied that there is much that is innate in our mind [esprit], since we are, so to speak, innate to ourselves, and since in ourselves there are being, unity, substance, duration, change, activity [action], perception, pleasure and a thousand other objects of our intellectual ideas? And as these objects are immediate objects of our understanding and are always present (although they cannot always be consciously perceived [aperçus] because of our distractions and wants), why should it be surprising that we say that these ideas, along with all that depends on them, are innate in us? Accordingly I have taken as illustration a block of veined marble, rather than a block of perfectly uniform marble or than empty tablets, that is to say, what is called by philosophers *tabula rasa*. For if the soul were like these empty tablets, truths would be in us as the figure of Hercules is in a block of marble, when the block of marble is indifferently capable of receiving this figure or any other. But if there were in the stone veins, which should mark out the figure of Hercules rather than other figures, the stone would be more determined towards this figure, and Hercules would somehow be, as it were, innate in it, although labour would be needed to uncover the veins and to clear them by polishing and thus removing what prevents them from being fully seen. It is thus that ideas and truths are innate in us, as natural inclinations, dispositions, habits or powers [virtualités], and not as activities [actions], although these powers [virtualités] are always accompanied by some activities [actions], often imperceptible, which correspond to them.

Our able author seems to maintain that there is in us nothing *virtual*, and even nothing of which we are not always actually conscious. But this cannot be understood in a strict sense; otherwise his opinion would be too paradoxical, since, for instance, we are not always conscious of acquired habits and of the things stored in our memory, and, indeed, they do not always come to our aid when we require them,

although we often bring them back easily into our mind on some slight occasion which recalls them to us, as we need only the beginning of a song in order to remember it. Our author also limits his thesis in other places, saying that there is in us nothing of which we have not at least been conscious [aperçus] formerly. But in addition to the fact that nobody can, through reason alone, be quite certain how far our past *apperceptions* have extended, for we may have forgotten them, especially in light of the Platonic doctrine of reminiscence, which, though a myth, contains, in part at least, nothing incompatible with bare reason—in addition, I say, to this fact, why must everything be acquired by us through apperception of external things, and why should it be impossible to unearth anything in ourselves? Is our soul, then, so empty that, beyond images borrowed from outside, it is nothing? That, I am sure, is not a view which our judicious author can approve. And where shall we find tablets which have not some variety in themselves? For there is never such a thing as a perfectly unbroken [uni] and uniform surface. Why, then, should not we also be able to provide ourselves with some sort of thought out of our own inner being, when we deliberately try to penetrate its depths? Thus I am led to believe that his opinion on this point is not fundamentally different from mine, or rather from the common opinion, inasmuch as he recognizes two sources of our knowledge, the senses and reflexion.

I do not know that it will be so easy to reconcile him with us and with the Cartesians, when he maintains that the mind does not always think, and especially that it is without perception when we sleep without dreaming: and he holds that, since bodies can exist without motion, souls might also quite well exist without thinking. But here I reply in a way somewhat different from that which is usual; for I maintain that, naturally, a substance cannot exist without activity [action], and indeed that there never is a body without motion. Experience is already in my favour as regards this, and to be persuaded of it one has only to refer to the book of the illustrious Mr. Boyle against an absolute rest. But I think that reason also supports it, and this is one of the proofs which I use to overthrow the theory of atoms.

Besides there are countless indications which lead us to think that there is at every moment an infinity of *perceptions* within us, but without apperception and without reflexion; that is to say, changes in the soul itself of which we are not conscious *[s'apercevoir]*, because the impressions are either too small and too numerous or too closely combined *[trop unies]*, so that each is not distinctive enough by itself, but nevertheless in combination with others each has its effect and makes itself felt, at least confusedly, in the whole. Thus it is that, through being accustomed to it, we take no notice of the motion of a mill or a waterfall when we have for some time lived quite near them. Not that this motion does not continually affect our organs, nor that something does not pass into the soul, which responds to it because of the harmony of the soul and the body, but these impressions which are in the soul and in the body, having lost the attractions of novelty, are not strong enough to attract our attention and our memory, busied with more engrossing objects. For all attention requires memory, and often when we are not, so to speak, admonished and warned to take notice of some of our present perceptions, we let them pass without reflexion and even without observing them; but if some one directs our attention to them immediately afterwards, and for instance bids us notice some sound that has just been heard, we remember it, and we are conscious that we had some feeling of it at the time. Thus there were perceptions of which we were not immediately conscious *[s'apercevoir]*, apperception arising in this case only from our attention being directed to them after some interval, however small. And for an even better understanding of the *petites perceptions* which we cannot individually distinguish in the crowd, I am wont to employ the illustration of the moaning or sounds of the sea, which we notice when we are on the shore. In order to hear this sound as we do, we must hear the parts of which the whole sound is made up, that is to say the sounds which come from each wave, although each of these little sounds makes itself known only in the confused combination of all the sounds taken together, that is to say, in the moaning of the sea, and no one of the sounds would be observed if the wave which makes it

were alone. For we must be affected a little by the motion of this wave, and we must have some perception of each of these sounds, however little they may be; otherwise we should not have the perception of a hundred thousand waves, for a hundred thousand nothings cannot make something. We never sleep so profoundly as not to have some feeble and confused feeling, and we should never be wakened by the greatest noise in the world if we had not some perception of its beginning which is small, just as we should never break a cord by the greatest effort in the world, if it were not strained and stretched a little by less efforts, though the small extension they produce is not apparent.

These *petites perceptions* have thus through their consequences an influence greater than people think. It is they that form this something I know not what, these tastes, these images of sense-qualities, clear in combination but confused in parts, these impressions which surrounding bodies make upon us, who contain infinity, this connexion which each being has with all the rest of the universe. It may even be said that in consequence of these *petites perceptions* the present is big with the future and laden with the past, that there is a conspiration of all things (σύμπνοια πάντα), as Hippocrates said, and that in the least of substances eyes as penetrating as those of God might read the whole succession of the things of the universe.

Quae sint, quae fuerint, quae futura trahantur.

These unconscious *[insensible]* perceptions also indicate and constitute the identity of the individual, who is characterized by the traces of expressions of his previous states which these unconscious perceptions preserve, as they connect his previous states with his present state; and these unconscious perceptions may be known by a higher mind *[esprit]*, although the individual himself may not be conscious of them, that is to say, though he may no longer have a definite recollection of them. But they [these perceptions] furnish also the means of recovering this recollection, when it is needed, through periodic developments which may some day occur. That is why death, owing to these perceptions, can only be a sleep, and cannot even last as a sleep, for in animals perceptions merely cease to be distinct [distingué] enough, and are reduced to a state of confusion, in which consciousness [aperception] is suspended, but which cannot last for ever, not to speak here of man who must have great privileges in this regard in order to keep his personality.

Further, the unconscious [insensible] perceptions explain that wonderful pre-established harmony of body and soul, and indeed of all Monads or simple substances, which takes the place of the untenable theory of the influence of one upon another, and which, in the opinion of the author of the most excellent of Dictionaries, exalts the greatness of the Divine perfections beyond what has ever been conceived. After this I should add little, if I were to say that it is these *petites perceptions* which *determine* us on many occasions without our thinking it, and which deceive people by the appearance of an *indifference of equilibrium*, as if, for instance, we were completely indifferent whether to turn to the right or to the left. It is also unnecessary for me to point out here, as I have done in the book itself, that they cause that *uneasiness* which I show to consist in something which differs from pain only as the small from the great, and which nevertheless often constitutes our desire and even our pleasure, giving to it a kind of stimulating relish. It is also due to these unconscious [insensible] parts of our conscious [sensible] perceptions that there is a relation between these perceptions of colour, heat, and other sensible qualities, and the motions in bodies which correspond to them; while the Cartesians, along with our author, in spite of all his penetration, regard the perceptions we have of these qualities as arbitrary, that is to say, as if God had given them to the soul according to His good pleasure, without regard to any essential relation between the perceptions and their objects; an opinion which surprises me, and which seems to me not very worthy of the wisdom of the Author of things, who does nothing without harmony and without reason.

In a word, *unconscious [insensible] perceptions* are of as great use in pneumatics as imperceptible *[insensible]* corpuscles are in physics; and it is as unreasonable to reject the one as the other on the ground that they are beyond the reach of our senses. Nothing takes place all at once, and it is one of my great maxims, one among the most completely verified of maxims, that *nature never makes leaps;* which I called the *law of continuity* when I spoke of it in the first *Nouvelles de la République des Lettres;* and the use of this law in physics is very considerable: it is to the effect that we always pass from small to great, and vice versa, through that which is intermediate in degrees as in parts; and that a motion never immediately arises from rest nor is immediately reduced to rest, but comes or goes through a smaller motion, just as we never completely traverse any line or length without having traversed a smaller line, although hitherto those who have laid down the laws of motion have not observed this law, and have thought that a body can in a moment receive a motion contrary to that which it had immediately before. And all this leads us to think that *noticeable perceptions* also come by degrees from those which are too small to be noticed. To think otherwise is to know little of the illimitable fineness [subtilité] of things, which always and everywhere contains [enveloppe] an actual infinity.

I have also noticed that, in virtue of imperceptible [insensible] variations, two individual things cannot be perfectly alike, and that they must always differ more than *numero*. This makes an end of "the empty tablets of the soul," "a soul without thought," "a substance without activity" [action], "the void in space," "atoms," and even particles not actually divided in matter, "absolute rest," "complete uniformity in one part of time, place or matter," "perfect globes of the second element, arising from original perfect cubes," and a thousand other fictions of philosophers, which come from their incomplete notions and which the nature of things does not admit of, and which are made passable by our ignorance and the slight attention we give to the imperceptible [insensible], but which cannot be made tolerable unless in the limited sense of abstractions of the mind, which protests that it does not deny what it sets aside and thinks ought not to come into any present consideration. Otherwise, if we seriously meant this, namely that the things of which we are not conscious [*s'apercevoir*] are neither in the soul nor in the body, we should err in philosophy as is done in statecraft [*politique*], when no account is taken of τόμικρόν, imperceptible [*insensible*] progressions; but on the other hand an abstraction is not an error, provided we know that what we ignore is actually there. So mathematicians make use of abstractions when they speak of the perfect lines which they ask us to consider, the uniform motions and other regular effects, although *matter* (that is to say, the intermingling of the effects of the surrounding infinite) always makes some exception. We proceed thus in order to discriminate conditions [*considérations*] from one another and in order to reduce effects to their grounds [*raisons*], as far as possible, and to foresee some of their consequences: for the more we are careful to neglect none of the conditions which we can control, the more does practice correspond to theory. But it belongs only to the supreme reason, which nothing escapes, to comprehend distinctly all the infinite and to see all grounds [*raisons*] and all consequences. All that we can do as regards infinities is to recognize them confusedly and to know at least distinctly that they are there: otherwise we have a very poor idea of the beauty and greatness of the universe, and also we cannot have a sound physics, which explains the nature of bodies in general, and still less a sound pneumatics, which includes the knowledge of God, of souls, and of simple substances in general.

This knowledge of unconscious [*insensible*] perceptions serves also to explain why and how no two souls, human or other, of one and the same kind, ever come perfectly alike from the hands of the Creator, and each has always from the first a reference to the point of view it will have in the universe. But this indeed follows already from what I observed regarding two individuals, namely, that their *difference* is always *more than a numerical one*. There is also another important point, as to which I must differ, not only from the opinions of our author, but also from those of the majority of modern writers. I believe, with the majority of the ancients, that all superhuman spirits [*génies*], all souls, all created simple substances are always

combined with a body, and that there never are souls entirely separated [from body]. I have a priori reasons for this, but it will also be found that the doctrine is of advantage in this respect, that it solves all the philosophical difficulties about the state of souls, about their perpetual preservation, about their immortality and about their working; for the difference between one state of the soul and another never is and never has been anything but a difference between the more and the less conscious [*sensible*], the more and the less perfect, or vice versa, and thus the past or the future state of the soul is as explicable as its present state. The slightest reflexion makes it sufficiently evident that this is in accordance with reason, and that a leap from one state to another infinitely different state could not be natural. I am surprised that the philosophic schools have without reason given up natural explanation, and have deliberately plunged themselves into very great difficulties and given occasion for the apparent triumphs of freethinkers [*esprits forts*], all of whose arguments fall at once through this explanation of things, according to which there is no more difficulty in conceiving the preservation of souls (or rather, as I think, of the animal), than there is in the change of the caterpillar into the butterfly, and in the preservation of thought during sleep, to which Jesus Christ has divinely likened death. But then I have already said that no sleep can last for ever; and it will last for the shortest time or almost not at all in the case of rational souls, which are destined always to preserve the personal character [*personnage*] which has been given them in the City of God, and consequently to retain memory; and this is so, in order that they may be more susceptible of punishments and rewards. And I add further that no derangement of its visible organs is capable of reducing things to complete confusion in an animal, or of destroying all its organs and depriving the soul of the whole of its organic body and of the ineffaceable remains of all its former impressions. But the ease with which people have given up the ancient doctrine that the angels have ethereal [*subtils*] bodies connected with them (which has been confounded with the corporeality of the angels themselves), the introduction of supposed unembodied [*sé-*

parés] intelligences among created things (to which Aristotle's theory of intelligences that make the skies revolve has greatly contributed), and finally the ill-considered opinion people have held that we cannot believe in the preservation of the souls of the lower animals without falling into metempsychosis and making them go *[promener]* from body to body, and the perplexity in which people have been through not knowing what to do with them, have, in my opinion, led to the neglect of the natural way of explaining the preservation of the soul. This has done great injury to natural religion and has led a good many to believe that our immortality is only a miraculous grace of God; and our celebrated author also speaks of it with some doubt, as I shall mention presently. But it were well if all those who are of this opinion had spoken about it as wisely and as sincerely as he; for it is to be feared that a good many people who speak of immortality through grace, do so only to save appearances, and are at bottom nearly of the same opinion as those Averroists and some erring Quietists, who imagine an absorption of the soul and its reunion with the ocean of divinity, a notion which perhaps my system alone clearly shows to be impossible.

9 / George Berkeley (1685–1753)
A TREATISE CONCERNING THE PRINCIPLES OF HUMAN KNOWLEDGE

6. In order to prepare the mind of the reader for the easier conceiving what follows, it is proper to premise somewhat, by way of Introduction, concerning the nature and abuse of Language. But the unravelling this matter leads me in some measure to anticipate my design, by taking notice of what seems to have had a chief part in rendering speculation intricate and perplexed, and to have occasioned innumerable errors and difficulties in almost all parts of knowledge. And that is the opinion that the mind hath a power of framing *abstract* ideas or notions of things. He who is not a perfect stranger to the writings and disputes of philosophers must needs acknowledge that no small part of them are spent about abstract ideas. These are in a more especial manner thought to be the object of those sciences which go by the name of logic and metaphysics, and of all that which passes under the notion of the most abstracted and sublime learning; in all which one shall scarce find any question handled in such a manner as does not suppose their existence in the mind, and that it is well acquainted with them.

7. It is agreed on all hands that the *qualities* or *modes* of things do never really exist each of them apart by itself, and separated from all others, but are mixed, as it were, and blended together, several in the same object. But, we are told, the mind, being able to consider each quality singly, or abstracted from those other qualities with which it is united, does by that means frame to itself *abstract ideas*. For ex-

A Treatise Concerning the Principles of Human Knowledge, Introduction: 6–10, 11, 12; Part 1: 1–36. From *The Works of George Berkeley*, edited by A. C. Fraser (Oxford: Clarendon Press, 1901). Copyright © 1901, Clarendon Press. Reprinted by permission of the publisher.

ample, there is conceived by sight an object extended, coloured, and moved: this mixed or compound idea the mind resolving into its simple, constituent parts, and viewing each by itself, exclusive of the rest, does frame the abstract ideas of extension, colour, and motion. Not that it is possible for colour or motion to exist without extension; but only that the mind can frame to itself by abstraction the idea of colour exclusive of extension, and of motion exclusive of both colour and extension.

8. Again, the mind having observed that in the particular extensions perceived by sense there is something common and alike in all, and some other things peculiar, as this or that figure or magnitude, which distinguish them one from another, it considers apart, or singles out by itself, that which is common; making thereof a most abstract idea of extension; which is neither line, surface, nor solid, nor has any figure or magnitude, but is an idea entirely prescinded from all these. So likewise the mind, by leaving out of the particular colours perceived by sense that which distinguishes them one from another, and retaining that only which is common to all, makes an idea of colour in abstract; which is neither red, nor blue, nor white, nor any other determinate colour. And, in like manner, by considering motion abstractedly, not only from the body moved, but likewise from the figure it describes, and all particular directions and velocities, the abstract idea of motion is framed; which equally corresponds to all particular motions whatsoever that may be perceived by sense.

9. And as the mind frames to itself abstract ideas of *qualities* or *modes*, so does it, by the same precision, or mental separation, attain abstract ideas of the more compounded *beings* which include several coexistent qualities. For example, the mind having observed that Peter, James, and John resemble each other in certain common agreements of shape and other qualities, leaves out of the complex or compound idea it has of Peter, James, and any other particular man, that which is peculiar to each, retaining only what is common to all, and so makes an abstract idea, wherein all the particulars equally partake; abstracting entirely from and cutting off all those circumstances and differences which might determine it to any particular existence. And after this manner it is said we come by the abstract idea of *man*, or, if you please, humanity, or human nature; wherein it is true there is included colour, because there is no man but has some colour, but then it can be neither white, nor black, nor any particular colour, because there is no one particular colour wherein all men partake. So likewise there is included stature, but then it is neither tall stature, nor low stature, nor yet middle stature, but something abstracted from all these. And so of the rest. Moreover, there being a great variety of other creatures that partake in some parts, but not all, of the complex idea of man, the mind, leaving out those parts which are peculiar to men, and retaining those only which are common to all the living creatures, frames the idea of *animal*; which abstracts not only from all particular men, but also all birds, beasts, fishes, and insects. The constituent parts of the abstract idea of animal are body, life, sense, and spontaneous motion. By *body* is meant body without any particular shape or figure, there being no one shape or figure common to all animals; without covering, either of hair, or feathers, or scales, &c., nor yet naked: hair, feathers, scales, and nakedness being the distinguishing properties of particular animals, and for that reason left out of the abstract idea. Upon the same account, the spontaneous motion must be neither walking, nor flying, nor creeping; it is nevertheless a motion, but what that motion is it is not easy to conceive.

10. Whether others have this wonderful faculty of abstracting their ideas, they best can tell. For myself, [I dare be confident I have it not.] I find indeed I have a faculty of imagining, or representing to myself, the ideas of those particular things I have perceived, and of variously compounding and dividing them. I can imagine a man compounding and dividing them. I can imagine a man with two heads; or the upper parts of a man joined to the body of a horse. I can consider the hand, the eye, the nose, each by itself abstracted or separated from the rest of the body. But then whatever hand or eye I imagine, it must have some particular shape and colour. Likewise the idea of man that I frame to myself must be either of a white, or a black, or a tawny, a straight, or a

crooked, a tall, or a low, or a middle-sized man. I cannot by any effort of thought conceive the abstract idea above described. And it is equally impossible for me to form the abstract idea of motion distinct from the body moving, and which is neither swift nor slow, curvilinear nor rectilinear; and the like may be said of all other abstract general ideas whatsoever. To be plain, I own myself able to abstract in one sense, as when I consider some particular parts or qualities separated from others, with which, though they are united in some object, yet it is possible they may really exist without them. But I deny that I can abstract from one another, or conceive separately, those qualities which it is impossible should exist so separated; or that I can frame a general notion, by abstracting from particulars in the manner aforesaid—which last are the two proper acceptations of *abstraction*. And there is ground to think most men will acknowledge themselves to be in my case. The generality of men which are simple and illiterate never pretend to abstract notions. It is said they are difficult, and not to be attained without pains and study. We may therefore reasonably conclude that, if such there be, they are confined only to the learned.

11. ... it seems that a word becomes general by being made the sign, not of an abstract general idea, but of several particular ideas, any one of which it indifferently suggests to the mind. For example, when it is said "the change of motion is proportional to the impressed force," or that "whatever has extension is divisible," these propositions are to be understood of motion and extension in general; and nevertheless it will not follow that they suggest to my thoughts an *idea* of motion without a body moved, or any determinate direction and velocity; or that I must conceive an *abstract general idea* of extension, which is neither line, surface, nor solid, neither great nor small, black, white, nor red, nor of any other determinate colour. It is only implied that whatever particular motion I consider, whether it be swift or slow, perpendicular, horizontal, or oblique, or in whatever object, the axiom concerning it holds equally true. As does the other of every particular extension; it matters not whether line, surface, or solid, whether of this or that magnitude or figure.

12. By observing how ideas become general, we may the better judge how words are made so. And here it is to be noted that I do not deny absolutely there are *general ideas*, but only that there are any *abstract general ideas*. For, in the passages we have quoted wherein there is mention of general ideas, it is always supposed that they are formed by abstraction, after the manner set forth in sections 8 and 9. Now, if we will annex a meaning to our words, and speak only of what we can conceive, I believe we shall acknowledge that an idea, which considered in itself is particular, becomes general, by being made to represent or stand for all other particular ideas of the same sort. To make this plain by an example: Suppose a geometrician is demonstrating the method of cutting a line in two equal parts. He draws, for instance, a black line of an inch in length: this, which in itself is a particular line, is nevertheless *with regard to its signification* general; since, as it is there used, it represents all particular lines whatsoever; so that what is demonstrated of it is demonstrated of all lines, or, in other words, of a line in general. And, as *that particular line* becomes general by being made a sign, so the *name* line, which taken absolutely is particular, by being a sign, is made general. And as the former owes its generality, not to its being the sign of an abstract or general line, but of all particular right lines that may possibly exist, so the latter must be thought to derive its generality from the same cause, namely, the various particular lines which it indifferently denotes.

PART I

1. It is evident to any one who takes a survey of the *objects of human knowledge*, that they are either *ideas* actually imprinted on the senses; or else such as are perceived by attending to the passions and operations of the mind; or lastly, *ideas* formed by help of memory and imagination—either compounding, dividing, or barely representing those originally perceived in the aforesaid ways. By sight I have the ideas of light and colours, with their several degrees and variations. By touch I perceive hard and

soft, heat and cold, motion and resistance; and of all these more and less either as to quantity or degree. Smelling furnishes me with odours; the palate with tastes; and hearing conveys sounds to the mind in all their variety of tone and composition.

And as several of these are observed to accompany each other, they come to be marked by one name, and so to be reputed as one *thing*. Thus, for example, a certain colour, taste, smell, figure and consistence having been observed to go together, are accounted one distinct thing, signified by the name apple; other collections of ideas constitute a stone, a tree, a book, and the like sensible things; which as they are pleasing or disagreeable excite the passions of love, hatred, joy, grief, and so forth.

2. But, besides all that endless variety of ideas or objects of knowledge, there is likewise Something which knows or perceives them; and exercises divers operations, as willing, imagining, remembering, about them. This perceiving, active being is what I call *mind, spirit, soul,* or *myself.* By which words I do not denote any one of my ideas, but a thing entirely distinct from them, wherein they exist, or, which is the same thing, whereby they are perceived; for the existence of an idea consists in being perceived.

3. That neither our thoughts, nor passions, nor ideas formed by the imagination, exist without the mind is what everybody will allow. And to me it seems no less evident that the various sensations or ideas imprinted on the Sense, however blended or combined together (that is, whatever objects they compose), cannot exist otherwise than in a mind perceiving them. I think an intuitive knowledge may be obtained of this, by any one that shall attend to what is meant by the term *exist* when applied to sensible things. The table I write on I say exists; that is, I see and feel it: and if I were out of my study I should say it existed; meaning thereby that if I was in my study I might perceive it, or that some other spirit actually does perceive it. There was an odour, that is, it was smelt; there was a sound, that is, it was heard; a colour or figure, and it was perceived by sight or touch. This is all that I can understand by these and the like expres-

sions. For as to what is said of the *absolute* existence of unthinking things, without any relation to their being perceived, that is to me perfectly unintelligible. Their *esse* is *percipi*; nor is it possible they should have any existence out of the minds or thinking things which perceive them.

4. It is indeed an opinion strangely prevailing amongst men, that houses, mountains, rivers, and in a world all sensible objects, have an existence, natural or real, distinct from their being perceived by the understanding. But, with how great an assurance and acquiescence soever this Principle may be entertained in the world, yet whoever shall find in his heart to call it in question may, if I mistake not, perceive it to involve a manifest contradiction. For, what are the forementioned objects but the things we perceive by sense? and what do we perceive besides our own ideas or sensations? and is it not plainly repugnant that any one of these, or any combination of them, should exist unperceived?

5. If we thoroughly examine this tenet it will, perhaps, be found at bottom to depend on the doctrine of *abstract ideas*. For can there be a nicer strain of abstraction than to distinguish the existence of sensible objects from their being perceived, so as to conceive them existing unperceived? Light and colours, heat and cold, extension and figures—in a word the things we see and feel—what are they but so many sensations, notions, ideas, or impressions on the sense? and is it possible to separate, even in thought, any of these from perception? For my part, I might as easily divide a thing from itself. I may, indeed, divide in my thoughts, or conceive apart from each other, those things which perhaps I never perceived by sense so divided. Thus, I imagine the trunk of a human body without the limbs, or conceive the smell of a rose without thinking on the rose itself. So far, I will not deny, I can abstract; if that may properly be called *abstraction* which extends only to the conceiving separately such objects as it is possible may really exist or be actually perceived asunder. But my conceiving or imagining power does not extend beyond the possibility of real existence or perception. Hence, as it is impossible for me to see or feel anything without an actual sensation of that thing, so is

it impossible for me to conceive in my thoughts any sensible thing or object distinct from the sensation or perception of it. In truth, the object and the sensation are the same thing, and cannot therefore be abstracted from each other.

6. Some truths there are so near and obvious to the mind that a man need only open his eyes to see them. Such I take this important one to be, viz. that all the choir of heaven and furniture of the earth, in a word all those bodies which compose the mighty frame of the world, have not any subsistence without a mind; that their *being* is to be perceived or known; that consequently so long as they are not actually perceived by me, or do not exist in my mind, or that of any other created spirit, they must either have no existence at all, or else subsist in the mind of some Eternal Spirit: it being perfectly unintelligible, and involving all the absurdity of abstraction, to attribute to any single part of them an existence independent of a spirit.

To be convinced of which, the reader need only reflect, and try to separate in his own thoughts the *being* of a sensible thing from its *being perceived.*

7. From what has been said it is evident there is not any other Substance than *Spirit*, or that which perceives. But, for the fuller proof of this point, let it be considered the sensible qualities are colour, figure, motion, smell, taste, and such like, that is, the ideas perceived by sense. Now, for an idea to exist in an unperceiving thing is a manifest contradiction; for to have an idea is all one as to perceive: that therefore wherein colour, figure, and the like qualities exist must perceive them. Hence it is clear there can be no unthinking substance or *substratum* of those ideas.

8. But, say you, though the ideas themselves do not exist without the mind, yet there may be things like them, whereof they are copies or resemblances; which things exist without the mind, in an unthinking substance. I answer, an idea can be like nothing but an idea; a colour or figure can be like nothing but another color or figure. If we look but ever so little into our thoughts, we shall find it impossible for us to conceive a likeness except only between our ideas. Again, I ask whether those supposed *originals*, or external things, of which our ideas are the pictures or representations, be themselves perceivable or no? If they are, then *they* are ideas, and we have gained our point: but if you say they are not, I appeal to any one whether it be sense to assert a colour is like something which is invisible; hard or soft, like something which is intangible; and so of the rest.

9. Some there are who make a distinction betwixt *primary* and *secondary* qualities. By the former they mean extension, figure, motion, rest, solidity or impenetrability, and number; by the latter they denote all other sensible qualities, as colours, sounds, tastes, and so forth. The ideas we have of these last they acknowledge not to be the resemblances of anything existing without the mind, or unperceived; but they will have our ideas of the *primary qualities* to be patterns or images of things which exist without the mind, in an unthinking substance which they call Matter. By Matter, therefore, we are to understand an inert, senseless substance, in which extension, figure, and motion do actually subsist. But it is evident, from what we have already shewn, that extension, figure, and motion are only ideas existing in the mind, and that an idea can be like nothing but another idea; and that consequently neither they nor their archetypes can exist in an unperceiving substance. Hence, it is plain that the very notion of what is called *Matter* or *corporeal substance*, involves a contradiction in it. Insomuch that I should not think it necessary to spend more time in exposing its absurdity. But, because the tenet of the existence of Matter seems to have taken so deep a root in the minds of philosophers, and draws after it so many ill consequences, I choose rather to be thought prolix and tedious than omit anything that might conduce to the full discovery and extirpation of that prejudice.

10. They who assert that figure, motion, and the rest of the primary or original qualities do exist without the mind, in unthinking substances, do at the same time acknowledge that colours, sounds, heat, cold, and suchlike secondary qualities, do not; which they tell us are sensations, existing in the mind alone, that depend on and are occasioned by the different size, texture, and motion of the minute parti-

cles of matter. This they take for an undoubted truth, which they can demonstrate beyond all exception. Now, if it be certain that those *original* qualities are inseparably united with the other sensible qualities, and not, even in thought, capable of being abstracted from them, it plainly follows that *they* exist only in the mind. But I desire any one to reflect, and try whether he can, by any abstraction of thought, conceive the extension and motion of a body without all other sensible qualities. For my own part, I see evidently that it is not in my power to frame an idea of a body extended and moving, but I must withal give it some colour or other sensible quality, which is acknowledged to exist only in the mind. In short, extension, figure, and motion, abstracted from all other qualities, are inconceivable. Where therefore the other sensible qualities are, there must these be also, to wit, in the mind and nowhere else.

11. Again, *great* and *small, swift* and *slow*, are allowed to exist nowhere without the mind; being entirely relative, and changing as the frame or position of the organs of sense varies. The extension therefore which exists without the mind is neither great nor small, the motion neither swift nor slow; that is, they are nothing at all. But, say you, they are extension in general, and motion in general. Thus we see how much the tenet of extended moveable substances existing without the mind depends on that strange doctrine of *abstract ideas*. And here I cannot but remark how nearly the vague and indeterminate description of Matter, or corporeal substance, which the modern philosophers are run into by their own principles, resembles that antiquated and so much ridiculed notion of *materia prima*, to be met with in Aristotle and his followers. Without extension solidity cannot be conceived: since therefore it has been shewn that extension exists not in an unthinking substance, the same must also be true of solidity.

12. That *number* is entirely the creature of the mind, even though the other qualities be allowed to exist without, will be evident to whoever considers that the same thing bears a different denomination of number as the mind views it with different respects. Thus, the same extension is one, or three, or thirty-six, according as the mind considers it with reference to a yard, a foot, or an inch. Number is so visibly relative, and dependent on men's understanding, that it is strange to think how any one should give it an absolute existence without the mind. We say one book, one page, one line, etc.; all these are equally units, though some contain several of the others. And in each instance, it is plain, the unit relates to some particular combination of ideas *arbitrarily* put together by the mind.

13. Unity I know some will have to be a simple or uncompounded idea, accompanying all other ideas into the mind. That I have any such idea answering the word *unity* I do not find; and if I had, methinks I could not miss finding it; on the contrary, it should be the most familiar to my understanding, since it is said to accompany all other ideas, and to be perceived by all the ways of sensation and reflexion. To say no more, it is an *abstract idea*.

14. I shall farther add, that, after the same manner as modern philosophers prove certain sensible qualities to have no existence in Matter, or without the mind, the same thing may be likewise proved of all other sensible qualities whatsoever. Thus, for instance, it is said that heat and cold are affections only of the mind, and not at all patterns of real beings, existing in the corporeal substances which excite them; for that the same body which appears cold to one hand seems warm to another. Now, why may we not as well argue that figure and extension are not patterns or resemblances of qualities existing in Matter; because to the same eye at different stations, or eyes of a different texture at the same station, they appear various, and cannot therefore be the images of anything settled and determinate without the mind? Again, it is proved that sweetness is not really in the sapid thing; because the thing remaining unaltered the sweetness is changed into bitter, as in case of a fever or otherwise vitiated palate. Is it not as reasonable to say that motion is not without the mind; since if the succession of ideas in the mind become swifter, the motion, it is acknowledged, shall appear slower, without any alteration in any external object?

15. In short, let any one consider those arguments which are thought manifestly to prove

that colours and tastes exist only in the mind, and he shall find they may with equal force be brought to prove the same thing of extension, figure, and motion. Though it must be confessed this method of arguing does not so much prove that there is no extension or colour in an outward object, as that we do not know by sense which is the true extension or colour of the object. But the arguments foregoing plainly shew it to be impossible that any colour or extension at all, or other sensible quality whatsoever, should exist in an unthinking subject without the mind, or in truth that there should be any such thing as an outward object.

16. But let us examine a little the received opinion. It is said extension is a *mode* or *accident* of Matter; and that Matter is the *substratum* that supports it. Now I desire that you would explain to me what is meant by Matter's *supporting* extension. Say you, I have no idea of Matter, and therefore cannot explain it. I answer, though you have no positive, yet, if you have any meaning at all, you must at least have a relative idea of Matter, though you know not what it is, yet you must be supposed to know what relation it bears to accidents, and what is meant by its supporting them. It is evident *support* cannot here be taken in its usual or literal sense, as when we say that pillars support a building. In what sense therefore must it be taken? For my part, I am not able to discover any sense at all that can be applicable to it.

17. If we inquire into what the most accurate philosophers declare themselves to mean by *material substance*, we shall find them acknowledge they have no other meaning annexed to those sounds but the idea of Being in general, together with the relative notion of its supporting accidents. The general idea of Being appeareth to me the most abstract and incomprehensible of all other; and as for its supporting accidents, this, as we have just now observed, cannot be understood in the common sense of those words: it must therefore be taken in some other sense, but what that is they do not explain. So that when I consider the two parts or branches which make the signification of the words *material substance*, I am convinced there is no distinct meaning annexed to them. But why should we trouble ourselves any farther, in discussing this material *substratum* or

support of figure and motion and other sensible qualities? Does it not suppose they have an existence without the mind? And is not this a direct repugnancy, and altogether inconceivable?

18. But, though it were possible that solid, figured, moveable substances may exist without the mind, corresponding to the ideas we have of bodies, yet how is it possible for us to know this? Either we must know it by Sense or by Reason. As for our senses, by them we have the knowledge only of our sensations, ideas, or those things that are immediately perceived by sense, call them what you will: but they do not inform us that things exist without the mind, or unperceived, like to those which are perceived. This the materialists themselves acknowledge.—It remains therefore that if we have any knowledge at all of external things, it must be by reason inferring their existence from what is immediately perceived by sense. But I do not see what reason can induce us to believe the existence of bodies without the mind, from what we perceive, since the very patrons of Matter themselves do not pretend there is any necessary connexion betwixt them and our ideas? I say it is granted on all hands (and what happens in dreams, frensies, and the like, puts it beyond dispute) that it is possible we might be affected with all the ideas we have now, though no bodies existed without resembling them. Hence it is evident the supposition of external bodies is not necessary for the producing our ideas; since it is granted they are produced sometimes, and might possibly be produced always, in the same order we see them in at present, without their concurrence.

19. But, though we might possibly have all our sensations without them, yet perhaps it may be thought easier to conceive and explain the manner of their production, by supposing external bodies in their likeness rather than otherwise; and so it might be at least probable there are such things as bodies that excite their ideas in our minds. But neither can this be said. For, though we give the materialists their external bodies, they by their own confession are never the nearer knowing how our ideas are produced; since they own themselves unable to comprehend in what manner body can act upon spirit, or how it is possible it should imprint any idea in the mind. Hence it is evident the

production of ideas or sensations in our minds, can be no reason why we should suppose Matter or corporeal substances; since that is acknowledged to remain equally inexplicable with or without this supposition. If therefore it was possible for bodies to exist without the mind, yet to hold they do so must needs be a very precarious opinion; since it is to suppose, without any reason at all, that God has created innumerable beings that are entirely useless, and serve to no manner of purpose.

20. In short, if there were external bodies, it is impossible we should ever come to know it; and if there were not, we might have the very same reasons to think there were that we have now. Suppose—what no one can deny possible—an intelligence, without the help of external bodies, to be affected with the same train of sensations or ideas that you are, imprinted in the same order and with like vividness in his mind. I ask whether that intelligence hath not all the reason to believe the existence of Corporeal Substances, represented by his ideas, and exciting them in his mind, that you can possibly have for believing the same thing? Of this there can be no question. Which one consideration were enough to make any reasonable person suspect the strength of whatever arguments he may think himself to have, for the existence of bodies without the mind.

21. Were it necessary to add any farther proof against the existence of Matter, after what has been said, I could instance several of those errors and difficulties (not to mention impieties) which have sprung from that tenet. It has occasioned numberless controversies and disputes in philosophy, and not a few of far greater moment in religion. But I shall not enter into the detail of them in this place, as well because I think arguments a posteriori are unnecessary for confirming what has been, if I mistake not, sufficiently demonstrated a priori, as because I shall hereafter find occasion to speak somewhat of them.

22. I am afraid I have given cause to think I am needlessly prolix in handling this subject. For, to what purpose is it to dilate on that which may be demonstrated with the utmost evidence in a line or two, to anyone that is capable of the least reflexion? It is but looking into your own thoughts, and so trying whether you can conceive it possible for a sound, or figure, or motion, or colour to exist without the mind or unperceived. This easy trial may perhaps make you see that what you contend for is a downright contradiction. Insomuch that I am content to put the whole upon this issue:— If you can but conceive it possible for one extended moveable substance, or in general for any one idea, or anything like an idea, to exist otherwise than in a mind perceiving it, I shall readily give up the cause. And, as for all that compages of external bodies you contend for, I shall grant you its existence, though you cannot either give me any reason why you believe it exists, or assign any use to it when it is supposed to exist. I say, the bare possibility of your opinions being true shall pass for an argument that it is so.

23. But, say you, surely there is nothing easier than for me to imagine trees, for instance, in a park, or books existing in a closet, and nobody by to perceive them. I answer, you may so, there is no difficulty in it. But what is all this, I beseech you, more than framing in your mind certain ideas which you call *books* and *trees,* and at the same time omitting to frame the idea of any one that may perceive them? But do not you yourself perceive or think of them all the while? This therefore is nothing to the purpose: it only shews you have the power of imagining, or forming ideas in your mind; but it does not shew that you can conceive it possible the objects of your thought may exist without the mind. To make out this, it is necessary that you conceive them existing unconceived or unthought of; which is a manifest repugnancy. When we do our utmost to conceive the existence of external bodies, we are all the while only contemplating our own ideas. But the mind, taking no notice of itself, is deluded to think it can and does conceive bodies existing unthought of, or without the mind, though at the same time they are apprehended by, or exist in, itself. A little attention will discover to any one the truth and evidence of what is here said, and make it unnecessary to insist on any other proofs against the existence of *material substance.*

24. Could men but forbear to amuse themselves with words, we should, I believe, soon come to an agreement in this point. It is very

obvious, upon the least inquiry into our own thoughts, to know whether it be possible for us to understand what is meant by the *absolute existence of sensible objects in themselves*, or *without the mind*. To me it is evident those words mark out either a direct contradiction, or else nothing at all. And to convince others of this, I know no readier or fairer way than to entreat they would calmly attend to their own thoughts; and if by this attention the emptiness or repugnancy of those expressions does appear, surely nothing more is requisite for their conviction. It is on this therefore that I insist, to wit, that the *absolute existence of unthinking things* are words without a meaning, or which include a contradiction. This is what I repeat and inculcate, and earnestly recommend to the attentive thoughts of the reader.

25. All our ideas, sensations, notions, or the things which we perceive, by whatsoever names they may be distinguished, are visibly inactive: there is nothing of power or agency included in them. So that one idea or object of thought cannot produce or make any alteration in another. To be satisfied of the truth of this, there is nothing else requisite but a bare observation of our ideas. For, since they and every part of them exist only in the mind, it follows that there is nothing in them but what is perceived: but whoever shall attend to his ideas, whether of sense or reflexion, will not perceive in them any power or activity; there is, therefore, no such thing contained in them. A little attention will discover to us that the very being of an idea implies passiveness and inertness in it; insomuch that it is impossible for an idea to do anything, or, strictly speaking, to be the cause of anything: neither can it be the resemblance or pattern of any active being, as is evident from sect. 8. Whence it plainly follows that extension, figure, and motion cannot be the cause of our sensations. To say, therefore, that these are the effects of powers resulting from the configuration, number, motion, and size of corpuscles, must certainly be false.

26. We perceive a continual succession of ideas; some are anew excited, others are changed or totally disappear. There is therefore *some* cause of these ideas, whereon they depend, and which produces and changes them.

That this cause cannot be any quality or idea or combination of *ideas*, is clear from the preceding section. It must therefore be a *substance*; but it has been shewn that there is no corporeal or material substance: it remains therefore that the cause of ideas is an incorporeal active substance or Spirit.

27. A Spirit is one simple, undivided, active being—as it perceives ideas it is called the *understanding*, and as it produces or otherwise operates about them it is called the *will*. Hence there can be no *idea* formed of a soul or spirit; for all ideas whatever, being passive and inert (vid. sect. 25), they cannot represent unto us, by way of image or likeness, that which acts. A little attention will make it plain to any one, that to have an idea which shall be *like* that active Principle of motion and change of ideas is absolutely impossible. Such is the nature of Spirit, or that which acts, that it cannot be of itself perceived, but only by the effects which it produceth. If any man shall doubt of the truth of what is here delivered, let him but reflect and try if he can frame the idea of any power or active being; and whether he has ideas of two principal powers, marked by the names *will* and *understanding*, distinct from each other, as well as from a third idea of Substance or Being in general, with a relative notion of its supporting or being the subject of the aforesaid powers—which is signified by the name *soul* or *spirit*. This is what some hold; but, so far as I can see, the words *will, understanding, mind, soul, spirit*, do not stand for different ideas, or, in truth, for any idea at all, but for something which is very different from ideas, and which, being an agent, cannot be like unto, or represented by, any idea whatsoever. Though it must be owned at the same time that we have some *notion* of soul, spirit, and the operations of the mind, such as willing, loving, hating—inasmuch as we know or understand the meaning of these words.

28. I find I can excite ideas in my mind at pleasure, and vary and shift the scene as often as I think fit. It is no more than *willing*, and straightway this or that idea arises in my fancy; and by the same power it is obliterated and makes way for another. This making and unmaking of ideas doth very properly denominate the mind active. Thus much is certain and

grounded on experience: but when we talk of unthinking agents, or of exciting ideas exclusive of volition, we only amuse ourselves with words.

29. But, whatever power I may have over my own thoughts, I find the ideas actually perceived by Sense have not a like dependence on *my* will. When in broad daylight I open my eyes, it is not in my power to choose whether I shall see or no, or to determine what particular objects shall present themselves to my view: and so likewise as to the hearing and other senses; the ideas imprinted on them are not creatures of *my* will. There is therefore some other Will or Spirit that produces them.

30. The ideas of Sense are more strong, lively, and distinct than those of the Imagination; they have likewise a steadiness, order, and coherence, and are not excited at random, as those which are the effects of human wills often are, but in a regular train or series—the admirable connexion whereof sufficiently testifies the wisdom and benevolence of its Author. Now the set rules, or established methods, wherein the Mind we depend on excites in us the ideas of Sense, are called *the laws of nature*; and these we learn by experience, which teaches us that such and such ideas are attended with such and such other ideas, in the ordinary course of things.

31. This gives us a sort of foresight, which enables us to regulate our actions for the benefit of life. And without this we should be eternally at a loss: we could not know how to act anything that might procure us the least pleasure, or remove the least pain of sense. That food nourishes, sleep refreshes, and fire warms us; that to sow in the seedtime is the way to reap in the harvest; and in general that to obtain such or such ends, such or such means are conducive—all this we know, not by discovering any *necessary connexion* between our ideas, but only by the observation of the *settled laws* of nature; without which we should be all in uncertainty and confusion, and a grown man no more know how to manage himself in the affairs of life than an infant just born.

32. And yet this consistent uniform working, which so evidently displays the Goodness and Wisdom of that Governing Spirit whose Will constitutes the laws of nature, is so far from leading our thoughts to Him, that it rather sends them wandering after second causes. For, when we perceive certain ideas of Sense constantly followed by other ideas, and we know this is not of our own doing, we forthwith attribute power and agency to the ideas themselves, and make one the cause of another, than which nothing can be more absurd and unintelligible. Thus, for example, having observed that when we perceive by sight a certain round luminous figure, we at the same time perceive by touch the idea or sensation called heat, we do from thence conclude the sun to be the *cause* of heat. And in like manner perceiving the motion and collision of bodies to be attended with sound, we are inclined to think the latter the *effect* of the former.

33. The ideas imprinted on the Senses by the Author of nature are called *real things*: and those excited in the imagination, being less regular, vivid, and constant, are more properly termed *ideas* or *images of* things, which they copy and represent. But then our *sensations*, be they never so vivid and distinct, are nevertheless ideas: that is, they exist in the mind, or are perceived by it, as truly as the ideas of its own framing. The ideas of Sense are allowed to have more reality in them, that is, to be more strong, orderly, and coherent than the creatures of the mind; but this is no argument that they exist without the mind. They are also less dependent on the spirit or thinking substance which perceives them, in that they are excited by the will of another and more powerful Spirit: yet still they are *ideas*: and certainly no idea, whether faint or strong, can exist otherwise than in a mind perceiving it.

34. Before we proceed any farther it is necessary we spend some time in answering Objections which may probably be made against the Principles we have hitherto laid down. In doing of which, if I seem too prolix to those of quick apprehensions, I desire I may be excused, since all men do not equally apprehend things of this nature; and I am willing to be understood by every one.

First, then, it will be objected that by the foregoing principles all that is real and substantial in nature is banished out of the world, and instead thereof a chimerical scheme of *ideas* takes place. All things that exist exist only in the mind; that is, they are purely notional. What therefore becomes of the sun, moon, and stars? What must we think of houses, rivers, mountains, trees, stones; nay, even of our own bodies? Are all these but so many chimeras and illusions on the fancy?— To all which, and whatever else of the same sort may be objected, I answer, that by the Principles premised we are not deprived of any one thing in nature. Whatever we see, feel, hear, or any wise conceive or understand, remains as secure as ever, and is as real as ever. There is a *rerum natura*, and the distinction between realities and chimeras retains its full force. This is evident from sect. 29, 30, and 33, where we have shewn what is meant by *real things*, in opposition to *chimeras* or *ideas of our own framing*; but then they both equally exist in the mind, and in that sense are alike *ideas*.

35. I do not argue against the existence of any one thing that we can apprehend, either by sense or reflection. That the things I see with my eyes and touch with my hands do exist, really exist, I make not the least question. The only thing whose existence we deny is that which *philosophers* call Matter or corporeal substance. And in doing of this there is no damage done to the rest of mankind, who, I dare say, will never miss it. The Atheist indeed will want the colour of an empty name to support his impiety; and the Philosophers may possibly find they have lost a great handle for trifling and disputation. But that is all the harm that I can see done.

36. If any man thinks this detracts from the existence or reality of things, he is very far from understanding what hath been premised in the plainest terms I could think of. Take here an abstract of what has been said:—There are spiritual substances, minds, or human souls, which will or excite ideas in themselves at pleasure; but these are faint, weak, and unsteady in respect of others they perceive by sense: which, being impressed upon them according to certain rules or laws of nature, speak themselves the effects of a Mind more powerful and wise than human spirits. These latter are said to have *more reality* in them than the former;—by which is meant that they are more affecting, orderly, and distinct, and that they are not fictions of the mind perceiving them. And in this sense the sun that I see by day is the real sun, and that which I imagine by night is the idea of the former. In the sense here given of *reality*, it is evident that every vegetable, star, mineral, and in general each part of the mundane system, is as much a *real being* by our principles as by any other. Whether others mean anything by the term *reality* different from what I do, I entreat them to look into their own thoughts and see.

10 / **David Hume** (1711–1776)
AN ENQUIRY CONCERNING HUMAN UNDERSTANDING

SECTION II

Of the Origin of Ideas

11 Every one will readily allow, that there is a considerable difference between the perceptions of the mind, when a man feels the pain of excessive heat, or the pleasure of moderate warmth, and when he afterwards recalls to his memory this sensation, or anticipates it by his imagination. These faculties may mimic or copy the perceptions of the senses; but they never can entirely reach the force and vivacity of the original sentiment. The utmost we say of them, even when they operate with greatest vigour, is, that they represent their object in so lively a manner, that we could *almost* say we feel or see it: But, except the mind be disordered by disease or madness, they never can arrive at such a pitch of vivacity, as to render these perceptions altogether undistinguishable. All the colours of poetry, however splendid, can never paint natural objects in such a manner as to make the description be taken for a real landskip. The most lively thought is still inferior to the dullest sensation.

We may observe a like distinction to run through all the other perceptions of the mind. A man in a fit of anger, is actuated in a very different manner from one who only thinks of that emotion. If you tell me, that any person is in love, I easily understand your meaning, and form a just conception of his situation; but never can mistake that conception for the real disorders and agitations of the passion. When we reflect on our past sentiments and affections, our thought is a faithful mirror, and copies its objects truly; but the colours which it employs are faint and dull, in comparison of those in which our original perceptions were clothed. It requires no nice discernment or metaphysical head to mark the distinction between them.

Here therefore we may divide all the per- 12 ceptions of the mind into two classes or species, which are distinguished by their different degrees of force and vivacity. The less forcible and lively are commonly denominated *Thoughts* or *Ideas*. The other species want a name in our language, and in most others; I suppose, because it was not requisite for any, but philosophical purposes, to rank them under a general term of appellation. Let us, therefore, use a little freedom, and call them *Impressions;* employing that word in a sense somewhat different from the usual. By the term *impression*, then, I mean all our more lively perceptions, when we hear, or see, or feel, or love, or hate, or desire, or will. And impressions are distinguished from ideas, which are the less lively perceptions, of

An Enquiry Concerning Human Understanding, II, III, IV, V, VII (in part), edited by L. A. Selby-Bigge, 3rd ed. revised by P. H. Nidditch. Copyright © 1975, Oxford University Press. Reprinted by permission of Oxford University Press.

which we are conscious, when we reflect on any of those sensations or movements above mentioned.

13   Nothing, at first view, may seem more unbounded than the thought of man, which not only escapes all human power and authority, but is not even restrained within the limits of nature and reality. To form monsters, and join incongruous shapes and appearances, costs the imagination no more trouble than to conceive the most natural and familiar objects. And while the body is confined to one planet, along which it creeps with pain and difficulty; the thought can in an instant transport us into the most distant regions of the universe; or even beyond the universe, into the unbounded chaos, where nature is supposed to lie in total confusion. What never was seen, or heard of, may yet be conceived; nor is any thing beyond the power of thought, except what implies an absolute contradiction.

But though our thought seems to possess this unbounded liberty, we shall find, upon a nearer examination, that it is really confined within very narrow limits, and that all this creative power of the mind amounts to no more than the faculty of compounding, transposing, augmenting, or diminishing the materials afforded us by the senses and experience. When we think of a golden mountain, we only join two consistent ideas, *gold*, and *mountain*, with which we were formerly acquainted. A virtuous horse we can conceive; because, from our own feeling, we can conceive virtue; and this we may unite to the figure and shape of a horse, which is an animal familiar to us. In short, all the materials of thinking are derived either from our outward or inward sentiment: the mixture and composition of these belongs alone to the mind and will. Or, to express myself in philosophical language, all our ideas or more feeble perceptions are copies of our impressions or more lively ones.

14   To prove this, the two following arguments will, I hope, be sufficient. First, when we analyze our thoughts or ideas, however compounded or sublime, we always find that they resolve themselves into such simple ideas as were copied from a precedent feeling or sentiment. Even those ideas, which, at first view, seem the most wide of this origin, are found, upon a nearer scrutiny, to be derived from it. The idea of God, as meaning an infinitely intelligent, wise, and good Being, arises from reflecting on the operations of our own mind, and augmenting, without limit, those qualities of goodness and wisdom. We may prosecute this enquiry to what length we please; where we shall always find, that every idea which we examine is copied from a similar impression. Those who would assert that this position is not universally true nor without exception, have only one, and that an easy method of refuting it; by producing that idea, which, in their opinion, is not derived from this source. It will then be incumbent on us, if we would maintain our doctrine, to produce the impression, or lively perception, which corresponds to it.

15   Secondly. If it happen, from a defect of the organ, that a man is not susceptible of any species of sensation, we always find that he is as little susceptible of the correspondent ideas. A blind man can form no notion of colours; a deaf man of sounds. Restore either of them that sense in which he is deficient; by opening this new inlet for his sensations, you also open an inlet for the ideas; and he finds no difficulty in conceiving these objects. The case is the same, if the object, proper for exciting any sensation, has never been applied to the organ. A Laplander or Negro has no notion of the relish of wine. And though there are few or no instances of a like deficiency in the mind, where a person has never felt or is wholly incapable of a sentiment or passion that belongs to his species; yet we find the same observation to take place in a less degree. A man of mild manners can form no idea of inveterate revenge or cruelty; nor can a selfish heart easily conceive the heights of friendship and generosity. It is readily allowed, that other beings may possess many senses of which we can have no conception; because the ideas of them have never been introduced to us in the only manner by which an idea can have access

to the mind, to wit, by the actual feeling and sensation.

16   There is, however, one contradictory phenomenon, which may prove that it is not absolutely impossible for ideas to arise, independent of their correspondent impressions. I believe it will readily be allowed, that the several distinct ideas of colour, which enter by the eye, or those of sound, which are conveyed by the ear, are really different from each other; though, at the same time, resembling. Now if this be true of different colours, it must be no less so of the different shades of the same colour; and each shade produces a distinct idea, independent of the rest. For if this should be denied, it is possible, by the continual gradation of shades, to run a colour insensibly into what is most remote from it; and if you will not allow any of the means to be different, you cannot, without absurdity, deny the extremes to be the same. Suppose, therefore, a person to have enjoyed his sight for thirty years, and to have become perfectly acquainted with colours of all kinds except one particular shade of blue, for instance, which it never has been his fortune to meet with. Let all the different shades of that colour, except that single one, be placed before him, descending gradually from the deepest to the lightest; it is plain that he will perceive a blank, where the shade is wanting, and will be sensible that there is a greater distance in that place between the contiguous colours than in any other. Now I ask, whether it be possible for him, from his own imagination, to supply this deficiency, and raise up to himself the idea of that particular shade, though it had never been conveyed to him by his senses? I believe there are few but will be of opinion that he can: and this may serve as a proof that the simple ideas are not always, in every instance, derived from the correspondent impressions; though this instance is so singular, that it is scarcely worth our observing, and does not merit that for it alone we should alter our general maxim.

17   Here, therefore, is a proposition, which not only seems, in itself, simple and intelligible; but, if a proper use were made of it, might render every dispute equally intelligible, and banish all that jargon, which has so long taken possession of metaphysical reasonings, and drawn disgrace upon them. All ideas, especially abstract ones, are naturally faint and obscure: the mind has but a slender hold of them: they are apt to be confounded with other resembling ideas; and when we have often employed any term, though without a distinct meaning, we are apt to imagine it has a determinate idea annexed to it. On the contrary, all impressions, that is, all sensations, either outward or inward, are strong and vivid; the limits between them are more exactly determined: nor is it easy to fall into any error or mistake with regard to them. When we entertain, therefore, any suspicion that a philosophical term is employed without any meaning or idea (as is but too frequent), we need but enquire, *from what impression is that supposed idea derived?* And if it be impossible to assign any, this will serve to confirm our suspicion. By bringing ideas into so clear a light we may reasonably hope to remove all dispute, which may arise, concerning their nature and reality.[1]

SECTION III

Of the Association of Ideas

It is evident that there is a principle of connexion between the different thoughts or ideas of the mind, and that, in their appearance to the memory or imagination, they introduce each other with a certain degree of method and regularity. In our more serious thinking or discourse that is so observable, that any particular thought, which breaks in upon the regular tract or chain of ideas, is immediately remarked and rejected. And even in our wildest and most wandering reveries, nay in our very dreams, we shall find, if we reflect, that the imagination ran not altogether at adventures, but that there was still a connexion upheld among the different ideas, which succeeded each other. Were the loosest and freest conversation to be transcribed, there would immediately be observed something which connected it in all its transitions. Or where this is wanting, the person who broke the thread of discourse might still inform you, that there had secretly revolved in his mind a succession of thought, which had gradually led him from the subject of conversation. Among different languages, even where we cannot suspect the least connexion or communication, it is found, that the words, expressive of ideas, the most compounded, do yet nearly correspond to each other: a certain proof that the simple ideas, comprehended in the compound ones, were bound together by some universal principle, which had an equal influence on all mankind.

19   Though it be too obvious to escape observation, that different ideas are connected together; I do not find that any philosopher has attempted to enumerate or class all the principles of association; a subject, however, that seems worthy of curiosity. To me, there appear to be only three principles of connexion among ideas, namely, *Resemblance, Contiguity* in time or place, and *Cause* or *Effect*.

That these principles serve to connect ideas will not, I believe, be much doubted. A picture naturally leads our thoughts to the original:[2] the mention of one apartment in a building naturally introduces an enquiry or discourse concerning the others:[3] and if we think of a wound, we can scarcely forbear reflecting on the pain which follows.[4] But that this enumeration is complete, and that there are no other principles of association except these, may be difficult to prove to the satisfaction of the reader, or even to a man's own satisfaction. All we can do, in such cases, is to run over several instances, and examine carefully the principle which binds the different thoughts to each other, never stopping till we render the principle as general as possible.[5] The more instances we examine, and the more care we employ, the more assurance shall we acquire, that the enumeration, which we form from the whole, is complete and entire.

SECTION IV

Sceptical Doubts Concerning the Operations of the Understanding

Part 1

All the objects of human reason or enquiry   20 may naturally be divided into two kinds, to wit, *Relations of Ideas*, and *Matters of Fact*. Of the first kind are the sciences of Geometry, Algebra, and Arithmetic; and in short, every affirmation which is either intuitively or demonstratively certain. *That the square of the hypothenuse is equal to the square of the two sides*, is a proposition which expresses a relation between these figures. *That three times five is equal to the half of thirty*, expresses a relation between these numbers. Propositions of this kind are discoverable by the mere operation of thought, without dependence on what is anywhere existent in the universe. Though there never were a circle or triangle in nature, the truths demonstrated by Euclid would for ever retain their certainty and evidence.

Matters of fact, which are the second ob-   21 jects of human reason, are not ascertained in the same manner; nor is our evidence of their truth, however great, of a like nature with the foregoing. The contrary of every matter of fact is still possible; because it can never imply a contradiction, and is conceived by the mind with the same facility and distinctness, as if ever so comfortable to reality. *That the sun will not rise tomorrow* is no less intelligible a proposition, and implies no more contradiction, than the affirmation, *that it will rise*. We should in vain, therefore, attempt to demonstrate its falsehood. Were it demonstratively false, it would imply a contradiction, and could never be distinctly conceived by the mind.

It may, therefore, be a subject worthy of curiosity, to enquire what is the nature of that evidence which assures us of any real existence and matter of fact, beyond the present testimony of our senses, or the records of our memory. This part of philosophy, it is observable, has been little cultivated, either by the ancients or moderns; and therefore our doubts and errors, in the prosecution of so important an enquiry, may be the more excusable; while we march through such difficult paths without any guide or direction. They may even prove useful, by exciting curiosity, and destroying that implicit faith and security, which is the bane of all reasoning and free enquiry. The discovery of defects in the common philosophy, if any such there be, will not, I presume, be a discouragement, but rather an incitement, as is usual, to attempt something more full and satisfactory than has yet been proposed to the public.

22   All reasonings concerning matter of fact seem to be founded on the relation of *Cause and Effect*. By means of that relation alone we can go beyond the evidence of our memory and senses. If you were to ask a man, why he believes any matter of fact, which is absent; for instance, that his friend is in the country, or in France; he would give you a reason; and this reason would be some other fact; as a letter received from him, or the knowledge of his former resolutions and promises. A man finding a watch or any other machine in a desert island, would conclude that there had once been men in that island. All our reasonings concerning fact are of the same nature. And here it is constantly supposed that there is a connexion between the present fact and that which is inferred from it. Were there nothing to bind them together, the inference would be entirely precarious. The hearing of an articulate voice and rational discourse in the dark assures us of the presence of some person: Why? because these are the effects of the human make and fabric, and closely connected with it. If we anatomize all the other reasonings of this nature, we shall find that they are founded on the relation of cause and effect, and that this relation is either near or remote, direct or collateral. Heat and light are collateral effects of fire, and the one effect may justly be inferred from the other.

23   If we would satisfy ourselves, therefore, concerning the nature of that evidence, which assures us of matters of fact, we must enquire how we arrive at the knowledge of cause and effect.

I shall venture to affirm, as a general proposition, which admits of no exception, that the knowledge of this relation is not, in any instance, attained by reasonings a priori; but arises entirely from experience, when we find that any particular objects are constantly conjoined with each other. Let an object be presented to a man of ever so strong natural reason and abilities; if that object be entirely new to him, he will not be able, by the most accurate examination of its sensible qualities, to discover any of its causes or effects. Adam, though his rational faculties be supposed, at the very first, entirely perfect, could not have inferred from the fluidity and transparency of water that it would suffocate him, or from the light and warmth of fire that it would consume him. No object ever discovers, by the qualities which appear to the senses, either the causes which produced it, or the effects which will arise from it; nor can our reason, unassisted by experience, ever draw any inference concerning real existence and matter of fact.

This proposition, *that causes and effects* 24 *are discoverable, not by reason but by experience*, will readily be admitted with regard to such objects, as we remember to have once been altogether unknown to us; since we must be conscious of the utter inability, which we then lay under, of foretelling what would arise from them. Present two smooth pieces of marble to a man who has no tincture of natural philosophy; he will never discover that they will adhere together in such a manner as to require great force to separate them in a direct line, while they make so small a resistance to a lateral pressure. Such events, as bear little analogy to the common course of nature, are also readily confessed to be known only by experience; nor does any man imagine that the explosion of gunpowder, or the attraction of a loadstone, could ever be discovered by arguments a priori. In like manner, when an effect is supposed to depend upon an intricate machinery or secret structure of parts, we make no difficulty in attributing all our knowledge of it to experience. Who will assert that he can give the ultimate reason, why milk or bread is proper nourishment for a man, not for a lion or a tiger?

But the same truth may not appear, at first sight, to have the same evidence with regard to events, which have become familiar to us from our first appearance in the world, which bear a close analogy to the whole course of nature, and which are supposed to depend on the simple qualities of objects, without any secret structure of parts. We are apt to imagine that we could discover these effects by the mere operation of our reason, without experience. We fancy, that were we brought on a sudden into this world, we could at first have inferred that one Billiard-ball would communicate motion to another upon impulse; and that we needed not to have waited for the event, in order to pronounce with certainty concerning it. Such is the influence of custom, that, where it is strongest, it not only covers our natural ignorance, but even conceals itself, and seems not to take place, merely because it is found in the highest degree.

25   But to convince us that all the laws of nature, and all the operations of bodies without exception, are known only by experience, the following reflections may, perhaps, suffice. Were any object presented to us, and were we required to pronounce concerning the effect, which will result from it, without consulting past observation; after what manner, I beseech you, must the mind proceed in this operation? It must invent or imagine some event, which it ascribes to the object as its effect; and it is plain that this invention must be entirely arbitrary. The mind can never possibly find the effect in the supposed cause, by the most accurate scrutiny and examination. For the effect is totally different from the cause, and consequently can never be discovered in it. Motion in the second Billiard-ball is a quite distinct event from motion in the first; nor is there anything in the one to suggest the smallest hint of the other. A stone or piece of metal raised into the air, and left without any support, immediately falls: but to consider the matter a priori, is there anything

we discover in this situation which can beget the idea of a downward, rather than an upward, or any other motion, in the stone or metal?

And as the first imagination or invention of a particular effect, in all natural operations, is arbitrary, where we consult not experience; so must we also esteem the supposed tie or connexion between the cause and effect, which binds them together, and renders it impossible that any other effect could result from the operation of that cause. When I see, for instance, a Billiard-ball moving in a straight line towards another, even suppose motion in the second ball should by accident be suggested to me, as the result of their contact or impulse; may I not conceive, that a hundred different events might as well follow from that cause? May not both these balls remain at absolute rest? May not the first ball return in a straight line, or leap off from the second in any line or direction? All these suppositions are consistent and conceivable. Why then should we give the preference to one, which is no more consistent or conceivable than the rest? All our reasonings a priori will never be able to show us any foundation for this preference.

In a word, then, every effect is a distinct event from its cause. It could not, therefore, be discovered in the cause, and the first invention or conception of it, a priori, must be entirely arbitrary. And even after it is suggested, the conjunction of it with the cause must appear equally arbitrary; since there are always many other effects, which, to reason, must seem fully as consistent and natural. In vain, therefore, should we pretend to determine any single event, or infer any cause or effect, without the assistance of observation and experience.

Hence we may discover the reason why 26 no philosopher, who is rational and modest, has ever pretended to assign the ultimate cause of any natural operation, or to show distinctly the action of that power, which produces any single effect in the universe. It is confessed, that the utmost effort of human reason is to reduce the principles, productive of natural phenomena, to a greater simplicity, and to resolve the many particular effects into a few general causes, by means of reasonings from analogy, experience, and observation. But as to the causes of these general causes, we should in vain attempt their discovery; nor shall we ever be able to satisfy ourselves, by any particular explication of them. These ultimate springs and principles are totally shut up from human curiosity and enquiry. Elasticity, gravity, cohesion of parts, communication of motion by impulse; these are probably the ultimate causes and principles which we shall ever discover in nature; and we may esteem ourselves sufficiently happy, if, by accurate enquiry and reasoning, we can trace up the particular phenomena to, or near to, these general principles. The most perfect philosophy of the natural kind only staves off our ignorance a little longer: as perhaps the most perfect philosophy of the moral or metaphysical kind serves only to discover larger portions of it. Thus the observation of human blindness and weakness is the result of all philosophy, and meets us at every turn, in spite of our endeavours to elude or avoid it.

27   Nor is geometry, when taken into the assistance of natural philosophy, ever able to remedy this defect, or lead us into the knowledge of ultimate causes, by all that accuracy of reasoning for which it is so justly celebrated. Every part of mixed mathematics proceeds upon the supposition that certain laws are established by nature in her operations; and abstract reasonings are employed, either to assist experience in the discovery of these laws, or to determine their influence in particular instances, where it depends upon any precise degree of distance and quantity. Thus, it is a law of motion, discovered by experience, that the moment or force of any body in motion is in the compound ratio or proportion of its solid contents and its velocity; and consequently, that a small force may remove the greatest obstacle or raise the greatest weight, if, by any contrivance or machinery, we can increase the velocity of that force, so as to make it an overmatch for its antagonist. Geometry assists us in the application

of this law, by giving us the just dimensions of all the parts and figures which can enter into any species of machine; but still the discovery of the law itself is owing merely to experience, and all the abstract reasonings in the world could never lead us one step towards the knowledge of it. When we reason a priori, and consider merely any object or cause, as it appears to the mind, independent of all observation, it never could suggest to us the notion of any distinct object, such as its effect; much less, show us the inseparable and inviolable connexion between them. A man must be very sagacious who could discover by reasoning that crystal is the effect of heat, and ice of cold, without being previously acquainted with the operation of these qualities.

Part II

But we have not yet attained any tolerable satisfaction with regard to the question first proposed. Each solution still gives rise to a new question as difficult as the foregoing, and leads us on to farther enquiries. When it is asked, *What is the nature of all our reasonings concerning matter of fact?* the proper answer seems to be, that they are founded on the relation of cause and effect. When again it is asked, *What is the foundation of all our reasonings and conclusions concerning that relation?* it may be replied in one word, Experience. But if we still carry on our sifting humour, and ask, *What is the foundation of all conclusions from experience?* this implies a new question, which may be of more difficult solution and explication. Philosophers, that give themselves airs of superior wisdom and sufficiency, have a hard task when they encounter persons of inquisitive dispositions, who push them from every corner to which they retreat, and who are sure at last to bring them to some dangerous dilemma. The best expedient to prevent this confusion, is to be modest in our pretensions; and even to discover the difficulty ourselves before it is objected to us. By this means, we may make a kind of merit of our very ignorance.

I shall content myself, in this section, with an easy task, and shall pretend only to give a negative answer to the question here proposed. I say then, that, even after we have experience of the operations of cause and effect, our conclusions from that experience are *not* founded on reasoning, or any process of the understanding. This answer we must endeavour both to explain and to defend.

29 It must certainly be allowed, that nature has kept us at a great distance from all her secrets, and has afforded us only the knowledge of a few superficial qualities of objects; while she conceals from us those powers and principles on which the influence of these objects entirely depends. Our senses inform us of the colour, weight, and consistence of bread; but neither sense nor reason can ever inform us of those qualities which fit it for the nourishment and support of a human body. Sight or feeling conveys an idea of the actual motion of bodies; but as to that wonderful force or power, which would carry on a moving body for ever in a continued change of place, and which bodies never lose but by communicating it to others; of this we cannot form the most distant conception. But notwithstanding this ignorance of natural powers and principles, we always presume, when we see like sensible qualities, that they have like secret powers, and expect that effects, similar to those which we have experienced, will follow from them. If a body of like colour and consistence with that bread, which we have formerly eat, be presented to us, we make no scruple of repeating the experiment, and foresee, with certainty, like nourishment and support. Now this is a process of the mind or thought, of which I would willingly know the foundation. It is allowed on all hands that there is no known connexion between the sensible qualities and the secret powers; and consequently, that the mind is not led to form such a conclusion concerning their constant and regular conjunction, by anything which it knows of their nature. As to past *Experience*, it can be allowed to give *direct* and *certain* information of those precise objects only, and that precise period

of time, which fell under its cognizance: but why this experience should be extended to future times, and to other objects, which for aught we know, may be only in appearance similar, this is the main question on which I would insist. The bread, which I formerly eat, nourished me; that is, a body of such sensible qualities was, at that time, endued with such secret powers: but does it follow, that other bread must also nourish me at another time, and that like sensible qualities must always be attended with like secret powers? The consequence seems no-wise necessary. At least, it must be acknowledged that there is here a consequence drawn by the mind; that there is a certain step taken; a process of thought, and an inference, which wants to be explained. These two propositions are far from being the same, *I have found that such an object has always been attended with such an effect*, and *I foresee, that other objects, which are, in appearance, similar, will be attended with similar effects*. I shall allow, if you please, that the one proposition may justly be inferred from the other: I know, in fact, that it always is inferred. But if you insist that the inference is made by a chain of reasoning, I desire you to produce that reasoning. The connexion between these propositions is not intuitive. There is required a medium, which may enable the mind to draw such an inference, if indeed it be drawn by reasoning and argument. What that medium is, I must confess, passes my comprehension; and it is incumbent on those to produce it, who assert that it really exists, and is the origin of all our conclusions concerning matter of fact.

This negative argument must certainly, in 30 process of time, become altogether convincing, if many penetrating and able philosophers shall turn their enquiries this way and no one be ever able to discover any connecting proposition or intermediate step, which supports the understanding in this conclusion. But as the question is yet new, every reader may not trust so far to his own penetration, as to conclude, because an argument escapes his enquiry, that therefore it does not really exist. For this reason it may be requisite to venture upon a more difficult task; and enumerating all the branches of human knowledge, endeavour to show that none of them can afford such an argument.

All reasonings may be divided into two kinds, namely, demonstrative reasoning, or that concerning relations of ideas, and moral reasoning, or that concerning matter of fact and existence. That there are no demonstrative arguments in the case seems evident; since it implies no contradiction that the course of nature may change, and that an object, seemingly like those which we have experienced, may be attended with different or contrary effects. May I not clearly and distinctly conceive that a body, falling from the clouds, and which, in all other respects, resembles snow, has yet the taste of salt or feeling of fire? Is there any more intelligible proposition than to affirm, that all the trees will flourish in December and January, and decay in May and June? Now whatever is intelligible, and can be distinctly conceived, implies no contradiction, and can never be proved false by any demonstrative argument or abstract reasoning a priori.

If we be, therefore, engaged by arguments to put trust in past experience, and make it the standard of our future judgement, these arguments must be probable only, or such as regard matter of fact and real existence, according to the division above mentioned. But that there is no argument of this kind, must appear, if our explication of that species of reasoning be admitted as solid and satisfactory. We have said that all arguments concerning existence are founded on the relation of cause and effect; that our knowledge of that relation is derived entirely from experience; and that all our experimental conclusions proceed upon the supposition that the future will be conformable to the past. To endeavour, therefore, the proof of this last supposition by probable arguments, or arguments regarding existence, must be evidently going in a circle, and taking that for granted, which is the very point in question.

31   In the reality, all arguments from expe-

rience are founded on the similarity which we discover among natural objects, and by which we are induced to expect effects similar to those which we have found to follow from such objects. And though none but a fool or madman will ever pretend to dispute the authority of experience, or to reject that great guide of human life, it may surely be allowed a philosopher to have so much curiosity at least as to examine the principle of human nature, which gives this mighty authority to experience, and makes us draw advantage from that similarity which nature has placed among different objects. From causes which appear *similar* we expect similar effects. This is the sum of all our experimental conclusion. Now it seems evident that, if this conclusion were formed by reason, it would be as perfect at first, and upon one instance, as after ever so long a course of experience. But the case is far otherwise. Nothing so like as eggs; yet no one, on account of this appearing similarity, expects the same taste and relish in all of them. It is only after a long course of uniform experiments in any kind, that we attain a firm reliance and security with regard to a particular event. Now where is that process of reasoning which, from one instance, draws a conclusion, so different from that which it infers from a hundred instances that are nowise different from that single one? This question I propose as much for the sake of information, as with an intention of raising difficulties. I cannot find, I cannot imagine any such reasoning. But I keep my mind still open to instruction, if any one will vouchsafe to bestow it on me.

Should it be said that, from a number of uniform experiments, we *infer* a connexion between the sensible qualities and the secret powers; this, I must confess, seems the same difficulty, couched in different terms. The question still recurs, on what process of argument this *inference* is founded? Where is the medium, the interposing ideas, which join propositions so very wide of each other? It is confessed that the colour, consistence, and other sensible qualities of bread appear not, of themselves, to have any connexion with the secret powers of nour-   32 ishment and support. For otherwise we could infer these secret powers from the first appearance of these sensible qualities, without the aid of experience; contrary to the sentiment of all philosophers, and contrary to plain matter of fact, Here, then, is our natural state of ignorance with regard to the powers and influence of all objects. How is this remedied by experience? It only shows us a number of uniform effects, resulting from certain objects, and teaches us that those particular objects, at that particular time, were endowed with such powers and forces. When a new object, endowed with similar sensible qualities, is produced, we expect similar powers and forces, and look for a like effect. From a body of like colour and consistence with bread we expect like nourishment and support. But this surely is a step or progress of the mind, which wants to be explained. When a man says, *I have found, in all past instances, such sensible qualities conjoined with such secret powers:* And when he says, *Similar sensible qualities will always be conjoined with similar secret powers*, he is not guilty of a tautology, nor are these propositions in any respect the same. You say that the one proposition is an inference from the other. But you must confess that the inference is not intuitive; neither is it demonstrative: Of what nature is it, then? To say it is experimental, is begging the question. For all inferences from experience suppose, as their foundation, that the future will resemble the past, and that similar powers will be conjoined with similar sensible qualities. If there be any suspicion that the course of nature may change, and that the past may be no rule for the future, all experience becomes useless, and can give rise to no inference or conclusion. It is impossible, therefore, that any arguments from experience can prove this resemblance of the past to the future; since all these arguments are founded on the supposition of that resemblance. Let the course of things be allowed hitherto ever so regular; that alone, without some new argument or inference, proves not that, for the future, it will continue so. In vain do you pretend to have learned the na-

ture of bodies from your past experience. Their secret nature, and consequently all their effects and influence, may change, without any change in their sensible qualities. This happens sometimes, and with regard to some objects: Why may it not happen always, and with regard to all objects? What logic, what process of argument secures you against this supposition? My practice, you say, refutes my doubts. But you mistake the purport of my question. As an agent, I am quite satisfied in the point; but as a philosopher, who has some share of curiosity, I will not say scepticism, I want to learn the foundation of this inference. No reading, no enquiry has yet been able to remove my difficulty, or give me satisfaction in a matter of such importance. Can I do better than propose the difficulty to the public, even though, perhaps, I have small hopes of obtaining a solution? We shall at least, by this means, be sensible of our ignorance, if we do not augment our knowledge.

I must confess that a man is guilty of 33 unpardonable arrogance who concludes, because an argument has escaped his own investigation, that therefore it does not really exist. I must also confess that, though all the learned, for several ages, should have employed themselves in fruitless search upon any subject, it may still, perhaps, be rash to conclude positively that the subject must, therefore, pass all human comprehension. Even though we examine all the sources of our knowledge, and conclude them unfit for such a subject, there may still remain a suspicion, that the enumeration is not complete, or the examination not accurate. But with regard to the present subject, there are some considerations which seem to remove all this accusation of arrogance or suspicion of mistake.

It is certain that the most ignorant and stupid peasants—nay infants, nay even brute beasts—improve by experience, and learn the qualities of natural objects, by observing the effects which result from them. When a child has felt the sensation of pain from touching the flame of a candle, he will be careful not to put his hand near any candle; but will expect a similar effect from a cause which is similar in its sensible qualities and appearance. If you assert, therefore, that the understanding of the child is led into this conclusion by any process of argument or ratiocination, I may justly require you to produce that argument; nor have you any pretence to refuse so equitable a demand. You cannot say that the argument is abstruse, and may possibly escape your enquiry; since you confess that it is obvious to the capacity of a mere infant. If you hesitate, therefore, a moment, or if, after reflection, you produce any intricate or profound argument, you, in a manner, give up the question, and confess that it is not reasoning which engages us to suppose the past resembling the future, and to expect similar effects from causes which are, to appearance, similar. This is the proposition which I intended to enforce in the present section. If I be right, I pretend not to have made any mighty discovery. And if I be wrong, I must acknowledge myself to be indeed a very backward scholar, since I cannot now discover an argument which, it seems, was perfectly familiar to me long before I was out of my cradle.

SECTION V

Sceptical Solution of These Doubts

Part I

. . . .

35   Suppose a person, though endowed with the strongest faculties of reason and reflection, to be brought on a sudden into this world; he would, indeed, immediately observe a continual succession of objects, and one event following another; but he would not be able to discover anything farther. He would not, at first, by any reasoning, be able to reach the idea of cause and effect; since the particular powers, by which all natural operations are performed, never appear to the senses; nor is it reasonable to conclude, merely because one event, in one instance,

precedes another, that therefore the one is the cause, the other the effect. Their conjunction may be arbitrary and casual. There may be no reason to infer the existence of one from the appearance of the other. And in a word, such a person, without more experience, could never employ his conjecture or reasoning concerning any matter of fact, or be assured of anything beyond what was immediately present to his memory and senses.

Suppose, again, that he has acquired more experience, and has lived so long in the world as to have observed similar objects or events to be constantly conjoined together; what is the consequence of this experience? He immediately infers the existence of one object from the appearance of the other. Yet he has not, by all his experience, acquired any idea or knowledge of the secret power by which the one object produces the other; nor is it, by any process of reasoning, he is engaged to draw this inference. But still he finds himself determined to draw it: And though he should be convinced that his understanding has no part in the operation, he would nevertheless continue in the same course of thinking. There is some other principle which determines him to form such a conclusion.

This principle is Custom or Habit. For 36 wherever the repetition of any particular act or operation produces a propensity to renew the same act or operation, without being impelled by any reasoning or process of the understanding, we always say, that this propensity is the effect of *Custom*. By employing that word, we pretend not to have given the ultimate reason of such a propensity. We only point out a principle of human nature, which is universally acknowledged, and which is well known by its effects. Perhaps we can push our enquiries no farther, or pretend to give the cause of this cause; but must rest contented with it as the ultimate principle, which we can assign, of all our conclusions from experience. It is sufficient satisfaction, that we can go so far, without repining at the narrowness of our faculties because they will carry us no farther. And it is certain we here advance a very intelligible proposition at least, if not a true one, when we assert that, after the constant conjunction of two objects—heat and flame, for instance, weight and solidity—we are determined by custom alone to expect the one from the appearance of the other. This hypothesis seems even the only one which explains the difficulty, why we draw, from a thousand instances, an inference which we are not able to draw from one instance, that is, in no respect, different from them. Reason is incapable of any such variation. The conclusions which it draws from considering one circle are the same which it would form upon surveying all the circles in the universe. But no man, having seen only one body move after being impelled by another, could infer that every other body will move after a like impulse. All inferences from experience, therefore, are effects of custom, not of reasoning.[7]

Custom, then, is the great guide of human life. It is that principle alone which renders our experience useful to us, and makes us expect, for the future, a similar train of events with those which have appeared in the past. Without the influence of custom, we should be entirely ignorant of every matter of fact beyond what is immediately present to the memory and senses. We should never know how to adjust means to ends, or to employ our natural powers in the production of any effect. There would be an end at once of all action, as well as of the chief part of speculation.

37   But here it may be proper to remark, that though our conclusions from experience carry us beyond our memory and senses, and assure us of matters of fact which happened in the most distant places and most remote ages, yet some fact must always be present to the senses or memory, from which we may first proceed in drawing these conclusions. A man, who should find in a desert country the remains of pompous buildings, would conclude that the country had, in ancient times, been cultivated by civilized inhabitants; but did nothing of this nature occur to him, he could never form such an inference. We learn the events of former ages from history; but then we must

peruse the volumes in which this instruction is contained, and thence carry up our inferences from one testimony to another, till we arrive at the eyewitnesses and spectators of these distant events. In a word, if we proceed not upon some fact, present to the memory or senses, our reasonings would be merely hypothetical; and however the particular links might be connected with each other, the whole chain of inferences would have nothing to support it, nor could we ever, by its means, arrive at the knowledge of any real existence. If I ask why you believe any particular matter of fact, which you relate, you must tell me some reason; and this reason will be some other fact, connected with it. But as you cannot proceed after this manner, *in infinitum*, you must at last terminate in some fact, which is present to your memory or senses; or must allow that your belief is entirely without foundation.

What, then, is the conclusion of the 38 whole matter? A simple one; though, it must be confessed, pretty remote from the common theories of philosophy. All belief of matter of fact or real existence is derived merely from some object, present to the memory or senses, and a customary conjunction between that and some other object. Or in other words; having found, in many instances, that any two kinds of objects—flame and heat, snow and cold—have always been conjoined together; if flame or snow be presented anew to the senses, the mind is carried by custom to expect heat or cold, and to *believe* that such a quality does exist, and will discover itself upon a nearer approach. This belief is the necessary result of placing the mind in such circumstances. It is an operation of the soul, when we are so situated, as unavoidable as to feel the passion of love, when we receive benefits; or hatred, when we meet with injuries. All these operations are a species of natural instincts, which no reasoning or process of the thought and understanding is able either to produce or to prevent.

At this point, it would be very allowable for us to stop our philosophical researches. In most questions we can never make a single step farther; and in all questions we must terminate here at last, after our most restless and curious enquiries. But still our curiosity will be pardonable, perhaps commendable, if it carry us on to still farther researches, and make us examine more accurately the nature of this *belief*, and of the *customary conjunction*, whence it is derived. By this means we may meet with some explications and analogies that will give satisfaction; at least to such as love the abstract sciences, and can be entertained with speculations, which, however accurate, may still retain a degree of doubt and uncertainty. As to readers of a different taste; the remaining part of this section is not calculated for them, and the following enquiries may well be understood, though it be neglected.

.   .   .   .   .   .

SECTION VII

Of the Idea of Necessary Connection

Part I

49   There are no ideas, which occur in metaphysics, more obscure and uncertain, than those of *power, force, energy* or *necessary connexion*, of which it is every moment necessary for us to treat in all our disquisitions. We shall, therefore, endeavour, in this section, to fix, if possible, the precise meaning of these terms, and thereby remove some part of that obscurity, which is so much complained of in this species of philosophy.

It seems a proposition, which will not admit of much dispute, that all our ideas are nothing but copies of our impressions, or, in other words, that it is impossible for us to *think* of anything, which we have not antecedently *felt*, either by our external or internal senses. I have endeavoured[8] to explain and prove this proposition, and have expressed my hopes, that, by a proper application of it, men may reach a greater clearness and precision in philosophical reasonings, than what they have hitherto been able to attain. Complex ideas may, perhaps, be well known by definition, which is nothing but an enumeration of those parts or simple ideas, that compose them. But when we have pushed up definitions to the most simple ideas, and find still some ambiguity and obscurity; what resource are we then possessed of? By what invention can we throw light upon these ideas, and render them altogether precise and determinate to our intellectual view? Produce the impressions or original sentiments, from which the ideas are copied. These impressions are all strong and sensible. They admit not of ambiguity. They are not only placed in a full light themselves, but may throw light on their correspondent ideas, which lie in obscurity. And by this means, we may, perhaps, attain a new microscope or species of optics, by which, in the moral sciences, the most minute, and most simple ideas may be so enlarged as to fall readily under our apprehension, and be equally known with the grossest and most sensible ideas, that can be the object of our enquiry.

To be fully acquainted, therefore, with   50 the idea of power or necessary connexion, let us examine its impression; and in order to find the impression with greater certainty, let us search for it in all the sources, from which it may possibly be derived.

When we look about us towards external objects, and consider the operation of causes, we are never able, in a single instance, to discover any power or necessary connexion; any quality, which binds the effect to the cause, and renders the one an infallible consequence of the other. We only find, that the one does actually, in fact, follow the other. The impulse of one billiard-ball is attended with motion in the second. This is the whole that appears to the *outward* senses. The mind feels no sentiment or *inward* impression from this succession of objects: Consequently, there is not, in any single, particular instance of cause and effect, any thing which can suggest the idea of power or necessary connexion.

From the first appearance of an object, we never can conjecture what effect will result from it. But were the power of energy of any cause discoverable by the mind, we could foresee the effect, even without experience; and might, at first, pronounce with certainty concerning it, by the mere dint of thought and reasoning.

In reality, there is no part of matter, that does ever, by its sensible qualities, discover any power or energy, or give us ground to imagine, that it could produce any thing, or be followed by any other object, which we could denominate its effect. Solidity, extension, motion; these qualities are all complete in themselves, and never point out any other event which may result from them. The scenes of the universe are continually shifting, and one object follows another in an uninterrupted succession; but the power or force, which actuates the whole machine, is entirely concealed from us, and never discovers itself in any of the sensible qualities of body. We know, that, in fact, heat is a constant attendant of flame; but what is the connexion between them, we have no room so much as to conjecture or imagine. It is impossible, therefore, that the idea of power can be derived from the contemplation of bodies, in single instances of their operation; because no bodies ever discover any power, which can be the original of this idea.[9]

51   Since, therefore, external objects as they appear to the senses, give us no idea of power or necessary connexion, by their operation in particular instances, let us see, whether this idea be derived from reflection on the operations of our own minds, and be copied from any internal impression. It may be said, that we are every moment conscious of internal power; while we feel, that, by the simple command of our will, we can move the organs of our body, or direct the faculties of our mind. An act of volition produces motion in our limbs, or raises a new idea in our imagination. This influence of the will we know by consciousness. Hence we acquire the idea of power or energy; and are certain, that we ourselves and all other intelligent beings are possessed of power. This idea, then, is an idea of reflection, since it arises from reflecting on the operations of our own mind, and on the command which is exercised by will, both

over the organs of the body and faculties of the soul.

.   .   .   .

Part II

But to hasten to a conclusion of this argu-   58
ment, which is already drawn out to too great a length: We have sought in vain for an idea of power or necessary connexion in all the sources from which we could suppose it to be derived. It appears that, in single instances of the operation of bodies, we never can, by our utmost scrutiny, discover any thing but one event following another; without being able to comprehend any force or power by which the cause operates, or any connexion between it and its supposed effect. The same difficulty occurs in contemplating the operations of mind on body—where we observe the motion of the latter to follow upon the volition of the former, but are not able to observe or conceive the tie which binds together the motion and volition, or the energy by which the mind produces this effect. The authority of the will over its own faculties and ideas is not a whit more comprehensible: So that, upon the whole, there appears not, throughout all nature, any one instance of connexion which is conceivable by us. All events seem entirely loose and separate. One event follows another, but we never can observe any tie between them. They seem *conjoined*, but never *connected*. And as we can have no idea of any thing which never appeared to our outward sense or inward sentiment, the necessary conclusion *seems* to be that we have no idea of connexion or power at all, and that these words are absolutely without any meaning, when employed either in philosophical reasonings or common life.

But there still remains one method of   59
avoiding this conclusion, and one source which we have not yet examined. When any natural object or event is presented, it is impossible for us, by any sagacity or penetration, to discover, or even conjecture, without experience, what event will result from it, or to carry our foresight beyond that object which is immediately present to the memory and senses. Even after one instance

or experiment, where we have observed a particular event to follow upon another, we are not entitled to form a general rule, or foretell what will happen in like cases; it being justly esteemed an unpardonable temerity to judge of the whole course of nature from one single experiment, however accurate or certain. But when one particular species of event has always, in all instances, been conjoined with another, we make no longer any scruple of foretelling one upon the appearance of the other, and of employing that reasoning, which can alone assure us of any matter of fact or existence. We then call the one object, *Cause*: the other, *Effect*. We suppose that there is some connexion between them; some power in the one, by which it infallibly produces the other, and operates with the greatest certainty and strongest necessity.

It appears, then, that this idea of a necessary connexion among events arises from a number of similar instances which occur of the constant conjunction of these events; nor can that idea ever be suggested by any one of these instances, surveyed in all possible lights and positions. But there is nothing in a number of instances, different from every single instance, which is supposed to be exactly similar, except only, that after a repetition of similar instances, the mind is carried by habit, upon the appearance of one event, to expect its usual attendant, and to believe that it will exist. This connexion, therefore, which we *feel* in the mind, this customary transition of the imagination from one object to its usual attendant, is the sentiment or impression from which we form the idea of power or necessary connexion. Nothing farther is in the case. Contemplate the subject on all sides; you will never find any other origin of that idea. This is the sole difference between one instance, from which we can never receive the idea of connexion, and a number of similar instances, by which it is suggested. The first time a man saw the communication of motion by impulse, as by the shock of two billiard balls, he could not pronounce that the one event was *connected*: but only that it was *conjoined* with the other. After he has

observed several instances of this nature, he then pronounces them to be *connected*. What alteration has happened to give rise to this new idea of *connexion*! Nothing but that he now *feels* these events to be *connected* in his imagination, and can readily foretell the existence of one from the appearance of the other. When we say, therefore, that one object is connected with another, we mean only that they have acquired a connexion in our thought, and give rise to this inference, by which they become proofs of each other's existence: A conclusion which is somewhat extraordinary, but which seems founded on sufficient evidence. Nor will its evidence be weakened by any general diffidence of the understanding, or sceptical suspicion concerning every conclusion which is new and extraordinary. No conclusions can be more agreeable to scepticism than such as make discoveries concerning the weakness and narrow limits of human reason and capacity.

And what stronger instance can be produced of the surprising ignorance and weakness of the understanding than the present? For surely, if there be any relation among objects which it imports to us to know perfectly, it is that of cause and effect. On this are founded all our reasonings concerning matter of fact or existence. By means of it alone we attain any assurance concerning objects which are removed from the present testimony of our memory and senses. The only immediate utility of all sciences, is to teach us, how to control and regulate future events by their causes. Our thoughts and enquiries are, therefore, every moment, employed about this relation: Yet so imperfect are the ideas which we form concerning it, that it is impossible to give any just definition of cause, except what is drawn from something extraneous and foreign to it. Similar objects are always conjoined with similar. Of this we have experience. Suitably to this experience, therefore, we may define a cause to be *an object, followed by another, and where all the objects similar to the first are followed by objects similar to the second.* Or in other words *where, if the first object had not been,*

60

the second never had existed. The appearance of a cause always conveys the mind, by a customary transition, to the idea of the effect. Of this also we have experience. We may, therefore, suitably to this experience, form another definition of cause, and call it, *an object followed by another, and whose appearance always conveys the thought to that other.* But though both these definitions be drawn from circumstances foreign to the cause, we cannot remedy this inconvenience, or attain any more perfect definition, which may point out that circumstance in the cause, which gives it a connexion with its effect. We have no idea of this connexion, nor even any distinct notion what it is we desire to know, when we endeavour at a conception of it. We say, for instance, that the vibration of this string is the cause of this particular sound. But what do we mean by that affirmation? We either mean *that this vibration is followed by this sound, and that all similar vibrations have been followed by similar sounds*: Or, *that this vibration is followed by this sound, and that upon the appearance of one the mind anticipates the senses, and forms immediately an idea of the other.* We may consider the relation of cause and effect in either of these two lights; but beyond these, we have no idea of it.[10]

61   To recapitulate, therefore, the reasonings of this section: Every idea is copied from some preceding impression or sentiment; and where we cannot find any impression, we may be certain that there is no idea. In all single instances of the operation of bodies or minds, there is nothing that produces any impression, nor consequently can suggest any idea, of power or necessary connexion. But when many uniform instances appear, and the same object is always followed by the same event; we then begin to entertain the notion of cause and connexion. We then *feel* a new sentiment or impression, to wit, a customary connexion in the thought or imagination between one object and its usual attendant; and this sentiment is the original of that idea which we seek for. For as this idea arises from a number of similar instances, and not from any single

instance, it must arise from that circumstance, in which the number of instances differ from every individual instance. But this customary connexion or transition of the imagination is the only circumstance in which they differ. In every other particular they are alike. The first instance which we saw of motion communicated by the shock of two billiard balls (to return to this obvious illustration) is exactly similar to any instance that may, at present, occur to us: except only, that we could not, at first, *infer* one event from the other; which we are enabled to do at present, after so long a course of uniform experience. I know not whether the reader will readily apprehend this reasoning. I am afraid that, should I multiply words about it, or throw it into a greater variety of lights, it would only become more obscure and intricate. In all abstract reasonings there is one point of view which, if we can happily hit, we shall go farther towards illustrating the subject than by all the eloquence and copious expression in the world. This point of view we should endeavour to reach, and reserve the flowers of rhetoric for subjects which are more adapted to them.

NOTES

1. It is probable that no more was meant by those, who denied innate ideas, than that all ideas were copies of our impressions; though it must be confessed, that the terms, which they employed, were not chosen with such caution, nor so exactly defined, as to prevent all mistakes about their doctrine. For what is meant by *innate*? If innate be equivalent to natural, then all the perceptions and ideas of the mind must be allowed to be innate or natural, in whatever sense we take the latter word, whether in opposition to what is uncommon, artificial, or miraculous. If by innate be meant, contemporary to our birth, the dispute seems to be frivolous; nor is it worth while to enquire at what time thinking begins, whether before, at, or after our birth. Again, the word *idea*, seems to be commonly taken in a very loose sense, by Locke and others; as standing for any of our perceptions, our sensations and passions, as

well as thoughts. Now in this sense, I should desire to know, what can be meant by asserting, that self-love, or resentment of injuries, or the passion between the sexes is not innate!

But admitting these terms, *impressions* and *ideas*, in the sense above explained, and understanding by *innate*, what is original or copied from no precedent perception, then may we assert that all our impressions are innate, and our ideas not innate.

To be ingenuous, I must own it to be my opinion, that Locke was betrayed into this question by the schoolmen, who, making use of undefined terms, draw out their disputes to a tedious length, without ever touching the point in question. A like ambiguity and circumlocution seem to run through that philosopher's reasonings on this as well as most other subjects.

2. Resemblance.

3. Contiguity.

4. Cause and effect.

5. For instance, Contrast or Contrariety is also a connexion among Ideas: but it may, perhaps, be considered as a mixture of *Causation* and *Resemblance*. Where two objects are contrary, the one destroys the other, that is, the cause of its annihilation, and the idea of the annihilation of an object, implies the idea of its former existence.

6. The word, Power, is here used in a loose and popular sense. The more accurate explication of it would give additional evidence to this argument. See Section VII.

7. Nothing is more usual than for writers, even, or *moral, political*, or *physical* subjects, to distinguish between *reason* and *experience*, and to suppose, that these species of argumentation are entirely different from each other. The former are taken for the mere result of our intellectual faculties, which, by considering a priori the nature of things, and examining the effects, that must follow from their operation, establish particular principles of science and philosophy. The latter are supposed to be derived entirely from sense and observation, by which we learn what has actually resulted from the operation of particular objects, and are thence able to infer, what will, for the future, result from them. Thus, for instance, the limitations and restraints of civil government, and a legal constitution, may be defended, either from *reason*, which reflecting on the great frailty and corruption of human nature, teaches, that no man can safely be trusted with unlimited authority; or from *experience* and history, which inform us of the enormous abuses, that ambition, in every age and country, has been found to make of so imprudent a confidence.

The same distinction between reason and experience is maintained in all our deliberations concerning the conduct of life; while the experienced statesman, general, physician, or merchant is trusted and followed; and the unpracticed novice, with whatever natural talents endowed, neglected and despised. Though it be allowed, that reason may form very plausible conjectures with regard to the consequences of such a particular conduct in such particular circumstances; it is still supposed imperfect, without the assistance of experience, which is alone able to give stability and certainty to the maxims, derived from study and reflection.

But notwithstanding that this distinction be thus universally received, both in the active and speculative scenes of life, I shall not scruple to pronounce, that it is, at bottom, erroneous, at least, superficial.

If we examine those arguments, which, in any of the sciences above mentioned, are supposed to be the mere effects of reasoning and reflection, they will be found to terminate, at last, in some general principle or conclusion, for which we can assign no reason but observation and experience. The only difference between them and those maxims, which are vulgarly esteemed the result of pure experience, is, that the former cannot be established without some process of thought, and some reflection on what we have observed, in order to distinguish its circumstances, and trace its consequences: Whereas in the latter, the experienced event is exactly and fully similar to that which we infer as the result of any particular situation. The history of a Tiberius or a Nero makes us dread a like tyranny, were our monarchs freed from the restraints of laws and senates: But the observation of any fraud or cruelty in private life is sufficient, with the aid of a little thought, to give us the same apprehension; while it serves as an instance of the general corruption of human nature, and shows us the danger which we must incur by reposing an entire confidence in mankind. In both cases, it is experience which is ultimately the foundation of our inference and conclusion.

There is no man so young and unexperienced, as not to have formed, from observation, many general and just maxims concerning human affairs and the conduct of life; but it must be confessed, that, when a man comes to put these in practice, he will

be extremely liable to error, till time and farther experience both enlarge these maxims,
and teach him their proper use and application. In every situation or incident, there are
many particular and seemingly minute circumstances, which the man of greatest talents is, at first, apt to overlook, though on
them the justness of his conclusions, and
consequently the prudence of his conduct,
entirely depend. Not to mention, that, to a
young beginner, the general observations
and maxims occur not always on the proper
occasions, nor can be immediately applied
with due calmness and distinction. The truth
is, an unexperienced reasoner could be no
reasoner at all, were he absolutely unexperienced; and when we assign that character to
any one, we mean it only in a comparative
sense, and suppose him possessed of experience, in a smaller and more imperfect
degree.

8. Section II.

9. Mr. Locke, in his chapter of power, says that,
finding from experience, that there are several new productions in matter, and concluding that there must somewhere be a power
capable of producing them, we arrive at last
by this reasoning at the idea of power. But
no reasoning can ever give us a new, original, simple idea; as this philosopher himself
confesses. This, therefore, can never be the
origin of that idea.

10. According to these explications and definitions, the idea of *power* is relative as much
as that of *cause*: and both have a reference
to an effect, or some other event constantly
conjoined with the former. When we consider the *unknown* circumstances of an object, by which the degree or quantity of its
effect is fixed and determined, we call that
its power. And accordingly, it is allowed by
all philosophers, that the effect is the measure of the power. But if they had any idea
of power, as it is in itself, why could not they
measure it in itself? The dispute whether the
force of a body in motion be as its velocity,
or the square of its velocity: this dispute, I
say, needed not be decided by comparing its
effects in equal or unequal times: but by a
direct mensuration and comparison.

As to the frequent use of the words.
Force, Power, Energy, etc., which every
where occur in common conversation, as
well as in philosophy: that is no proof, that
we are acquainted, in any instance, with the
connecting principle between cause and effect, or can account ultimately for the production of one thing by another. These
words, as commonly used, have very loose
meaning annexed to them: and their ideas
are very uncertain and confused. No animal
can put external bodies in motion without
the sentiment of a *nisus* or endeavour, and
every animal has a sentiment or feeling
from the stroke or blow of an external object, that is in motion. These sensations,
which are merely animal, and from which
we can a priori draw no inference, we are
apt to transfer to inanimate objects, and to
suppose, that they have some such feelings,
whenever they transfer or receive motion.
With regard to energies, which are exerted,
without or annexing to them any idea of
communicated motion, we consider only the
constant experienced conjunction of the
events: and as we *feel* a customary connexion between the ideas, we transfer that feeling to the objects; as nothing is more usual
than to apply to external bodies every internal sensation, which they occasion.

11 / Thomas Reid (1710–1796)
INQUIRY INTO THE HUMAN MIND

CHAPTER V. OF TOUCH

Section VIII. Of the Systems of Philosophers Concerning the Senses.

All the systems of philosophers about our senses and their objects have split upon this rock, of not distinguishing properly sensations which can have no existence but when they are felt, from the things suggested by them. Aristotle—with as distinguishing a head as ever applied to philosophical disquisitions—confounds these two; and makes every sensation to be the form, without the matter, of the thing perceived by it. As the impression of a seal upon wax has the form of the seal but nothing of the matter of it, so he conceived our sensations to be impressions upon the mind, which bear the image, likeness, or form of the external thing perceived, without the matter of it. Colour, sound, and smell, as well as extension, figure, and hardness, are, according to him, various forms of matter: our sensations are the same forms imprinted on the mind, and perceived in its own intellect. It is evident from this, that Aristotle made no distinction between primary and secondary qualities of bodies, although that distinction was made by Democritus, Epicurus, and others of the ancients.

Des Cartes, Malebranche, and Locke, revived the distinction between primary and secondary qualities; but they made the secondary qualities mere sensations, and the primary ones resemblances of our sensations. They maintained that colour, sound, and heat, are not anything in bodies, but sensations of the mind; at the same time, they acknowledged some particular texture or modification of the body to be the cause or occasion of those sensations; but to this modification they gave no name. Whereas, by the vulgar, the names of colour, heat, and sound, are but rarely applied to the sensations, and most commonly to those unknown causes of them, as hath been already explained. The constitution of our nature leads us rather to attend to the things signified by the sensation than to the sensation itself, and to give a name to the former rather than to the latter. Thus we see, that, with regard to secondary qualities, these philosophers thought with the vulgar, and with common sense. Their paradoxes were only an abuse of words; for when they maintain, as an important modern discovery, that there is no heat in the fire, they mean no more, than that the fire does not feel heat, which every one knew before.

With regard to primary qualities, these philosophers erred more grossly. They indeed believed the existence of those qualities; but they did not at all attend to the sensations that suggest them, which, having no names, have been as little considered as if they had no existence. They were aware that figure, extension, and hardness, are perceived by means of sensations of touch; whence they rashly concluded, that these sensations must be images and resemblances of figure, extension, and hardness.

The received hypothesis of ideas naturally led them to this conclusion: and indeed cannot consist with any other; for, according to that hypothesis, external things must be perceived by means of images of them in the mind; and what can those images of external things in the

From *The Works of Thomas Reid*, 7th ed., ed. William Hamilton. Edinburgh: MacLachlan and Stewart, 1872.

mind be, but the sensations by which we perceive them?

This, however, was to draw a conclusion from a hypothesis against fact. We need not have recourse to any hypothesis to know what our sensations are, or what they are like. By a proper degree of reflection and attention we may understand them perfectly, and be as certain that they are not like any quality of body, as we can be, that the toothache is not like a triangle. How a sensation should instantly make us conceive and believe the existence of an external thing altogether unlike to it, I do not pretend to know; and when I say that the one suggests the other, I mean not to explain the manner of their connection, but to express a fact, which every one may be conscious of—namely, that, by a law of our nature, such a conception and belief constantly and immediately follow the sensation.

.   .   .   .

CHAPTER VI. OF SEEING

Section III. Of the Visible Appearances of Objects.

In this section we must speak of things which are never made the object of reflection, though almost every moment presented to the mind. Nature intended them only for signs; and in the whole course of life they are put to no other use. The mind has acquired a confirmed and inveterate habit of inattention to them; for they no sooner appear, than quick as lightning the thing signified succeeds, and engrosses all our regard. They have no name in language; and, although we are conscious of them when they pass through the mind, yet their passage is so quick and so familiar, that it is absolutely unheeded; nor do they leave any footsteps of themselves, either in the memory or imagination. That this is the case with regard to the sensations of touch, hath been shewn in the last chapter; and it holds no less with regard to the visible appearances of objects.

I cannot therefore entertain the hope of being intelligible to those readers who have not, by pains and practice, acquired the habit of dis-

tinguishing the appearance of objects to the eye, from the judgment which we form by sight of their colour, distance, magnitude, and figure.

The only profession in life wherein it is necessary to make this distinction, is that of painting. The painter hath occasion for an abstraction, with regard to visible objects, somewhat similar to that which we here require: and this indeed is the most difficult part of his art. For it is evident, that, if he could fix in his imagination the visible appearance of objects, without confounding it with the things signified by that appearance, it would be as easy for him to paint from the life, and to give every figure its proper shading and relief, and its perspective proportions, as it is to paint from a copy. Perspective, shading, giving relief, and colouring, are nothing else but copying the appearance which things make to the eye. We may therefore borrow some light on the subject of visible appearance from this art.

Let one look upon any familiar object, such as a book, at different distances and in different positions: is he not able to affirm, upon the testimony of his sight, that it is the same book, the same object, whether seen at the distance of one foot or of ten, whether in one position or another; that the colour is the same, the dimensions the same, and the figure the same, as far as the eye can judge? This surely must be acknowledged. The same individual object is presented to the mind, only placed at different distances and in different positions. Let me ask, in the next place, Whether this object has the same appearance to the eye in these different distances? Infallibly it hath not. For,

First, However certain our judgment may be that the colour is the same, it is as certain that it hath not the same appearance at different distances. There is a certain degradation of the colour, and a certain confusion and indistinctness of the minute parts, which is the natural consequence of the removal of the object to a greater distance. Those that are not painters, or critics in painting, overlook this; and cannot easily be persuaded, that the colour of the same object hath a different appearance at the distance of one foot and of ten, in the shade and in the light. But the masters in painting know how, by the degradation of the colour and the confusion of the minute parts, figures which are upon the same canvas, and at the same distance from the eye, may be made to represent objects which are at the most unequal distances. They know how to make the objects appear to be of the same colour, by making their pictures really of different colours, according to their distances or shades.

Secondly, Every one who is acquainted with the rules of perspective, knows that the appearance of the figure of the book must vary in every different position: yet if you ask a man that has no notion of perspective, whether the figure of it does not appear to his eye to be the same in all its different positions? he can with a good conscience affirm that it does. He hath learned to make allowance for the variety of visible figure arising from the difference of position, and to draw the proper conclusions from it. But he draws these conclusions so readily and habitually, as to lose sight of the premises: and therefore where he hath made the same conclusion, he conceives the visible appearance must have been the same.

Thirdly, Let us consider the apparent magnitude or dimensions of the book. Whether I view it at the distance of one foot or of ten feet, it seems to be about seven inches long, five broad, and one thick. I can judge of these dimensions very nearly by the eye, and I judge them to be the same at both distances. But yet it is certain, that, at the distance of one foot, its visible length and breadth is about ten times as great as at the distance of ten feet; and consequently its surface is about a hundred times as great. This great change of apparent magnitude is altogether overlooked, and every man is apt to imagine, that it appears to the eye of the same size at both distances. Further, when I look at the book, it seems plainly to have three dimensions, of length, breadth, and thickness: but it is certain that the visible appearance hath no more than two, and can be exactly represented upon a canvas which hath only length and breadth.

In the last place, does not every man, by sight, perceive the distance of the book from his eye? Can he not affirm with certainty, that in one case it is not above one foot distant, that in another it is ten? Nevertheless, it appears certain, that distance from the eye is no immediate object of sight. There are certain things in the visible appearance, which are signs of distance from the eye, and from which, as we shall afterwards shew, we learn by experience to judge of that distance within certain limits; but it seems beyond doubt, that a man born blind, and suddenly made to see, could form no judgment at first of the distance of the objects which he saw.

The young man couched by Cheselden thought, at first, that everything he saw touched his eye, and learned only by experience to judge of the distance of visible objects.

I have entered into this long detail, in order to shew that the visible appearance of an object is extremely different from the notion of it which experience teaches us to form by sight; and to enable the reader to attend to the visible appearance of colour, figure, and extension, in visible things, which is no common object of thought, but must be carefully attended to by those who would enter into the philosophy of this sense, or would comprehend what shall be said upon it. To a man newly made to see, the visible appearance of objects would be the same as to us; but he would see nothing at all of their real dimensions, as we do. He could form no conjecture, by means of his sight only, how many inches or feet they were in length, breadth, or thickness. He could perceive little or nothing of their real figure; nor could he discern that this was a cube, that a sphere; that this was a cone, and that a cylinder. His eye could not inform him that this object was near, and that more remote. The habit of a man or of a woman, which appeared to us of one uniform colour, variously folded and shaded, would present to his eye neither fold nor shade, but variety of colour. In a word, his eyes, though ever so perfect, would at first give him almost no information of things without him. They would indeed present the same appearances to him as they do to us, and speak the same language; but to him it is an unknown language; and, therefore, he would attend only to the signs, without knowing the signification of them, whereas to us it is a language perfectly familiar; and, therefore, we take no notice of the signs, but attend only to the thing signified by them.

Section IV. That Colour Is a Quality of Bodies, Not a Sensation of the Mind.

By colour, all men, who have not been tutored by modern philosophy, understand, not a sensation of the mind, which can have no existence when it is not perceived, but a quality or modification of bodies, which continues to be the same whether it is seen or not. The scarlet-rose which is before me, is still a scarlet-rose when I shut my eyes, and was so at midnight when no eye saw it. The colour remains when the appearance ceases; it remains the same when the appearance changes. For when I view this scarlet-rose through a pair of green spectacles, the appearance is changed; but I do not conceive the colour of the rose changed. To a person in the jaundice, it has still another appearance; but he is easily convinced that the change is in his eye, and not in the colour of the object. Every different degree of light makes it have a different appearance, and total darkness takes away all appearance, but makes not the least change in the colour of the body. We may, by a variety of optical experiments, change the appearance of figure and magnitude in a body, as well as that of colour; we may make one body appear to be ten. But all men believe, that, as a multiplying glass does not really produce ten guineas out of one, nor a microscope turn a guinea into a ten-pound piece, so neither does a coloured glass change the real colour of the object seen through it, when it changes the appearance of that colour.

The common language of mankind shews evidently, that we ought to distinguish between the colour of a body, which is conceived to be a fixed and permanent quality in the body, and the appearance of that colour to the eye, which may be varied a thousand ways, by a variation of the light, of the medium, or of the eye itself. The permanent colour of the body is the cause which, by the mediation of various kinds or degrees of light, and of various transparent bodies interposed, produces all this variety of appearances. When a coloured body is presented, there is a certain apparition to the eye, or to the mind, which we have called *the ap-pearance of colour*. Mr. Locke calls it *an idea*; and, indeed, it may be called so with the greatest propriety. This idea can have no existence but when it is perceived. It is a kind of thought, and can only be the act of a percipient or thinking being. By the constitution of our nature, we are led to conceive this idea as a sign of something external, and are impatient till we learn its meaning. A thousand experiments for this purpose are made every day by children, even before they come to the use of reason. They look at things, they handle them, they put them in various positions, at different distances, and in different lights. The ideas of sight, by these means, come to be associated with, and readily to suggest, things external, and altogether unlike them. In particular, that idea which we have called *the appearance of colour*, suggests the conception and belief of some unknown quality in the body which occasions the idea; and it is to this quality, and not to the idea, that we give the name of *colour*.* The various colours, although in their nature equally unknown, are easily distinguished when we think or speak of them, by being associated with the ideas which they excite. In like manner, gravity, magnetism, and electricity, although all unknown qualities, are distinguished by their different effects. As we grow up, the mind acquires a habit of passing so rapidly from the ideas of sight to the external things suggested by them, that the ideas are not in the least attended to, nor have they names given them in common language.

When we think or speak of any particular colour, however simple the notion may seem to be which is presented to the imagination, it is really in some sort compounded. It involves an unknown cause and a known effect. The name of *colour* belongs indeed to the cause only, and not to the effect. But as the cause is unknown, we can form no distinct conception of it but by its relation to the known effect; and, therefore, both go together in the imagination, and are so closely united, that they are mistaken for one simple object of thought. When I would conceive those colours of bodies which we call *scarlet* and *blue*—if I conceived them only as unknown qualities, I could perceive no distinction between the one and the other. I must, therefore, for the sake of distinction, join to each of them, in my imagination, some effect or some relation that is peculiar; and the most obvious distinction is, the appearance which one and the other makes to the eye. Hence the appearance is, in the imagination, so closely united with the quality called *a scarlet-colour*, that they are apt to be mistaken for one and the same thing, although they are in reality so different and so unlike, that one is an idea in the mind, and the other is a quality of body.

I conclude, then, that colour is not a sensation, but a secondary quality of bodies, in the sense we have already explained; that it is a certain power or virtue in bodies, that in fair daylight exhibits to the eye an appearance which is very familiar to us, although it hath no name. Colour differs from other secondary qualities in this, that, whereas the name of the quality is sometimes given to the sensation which indicates it, and is occasioned by it, we never, as far as I can judge, give the name of *colour* to the sensation, but to the quality only. Perhaps the reason of this may be that the appearances of the same colour are so various and changeable, according to the different modifications of the light, of the medium, and of the eye, that language could not afford names for them. And, indeed, they are so little interesting that they are never attended to, but serve only as signs to introduce the things signified by them. Nor ought it to appear incredible, that appearances so frequent and so familiar should have no names, nor be made objects of thought; since we have before shewn that this is true of many sensations of touch, which are no less frequent nor less familiar.

Section V. An Inference from the Preceding.

From what hath been said about colour, we may infer two things. The first is, that one of the most remarkable paradoxes of modern philosophy, which hath been universally esteemed as a great discovery, is, in reality, when examined to the bottom, nothing else but an abuse of words. The paradox I mean is, That colour is not a quality of bodies, but only an idea in the mind. We have shewn, that the word *colour*, as used by the vulgar, cannot signify an idea in the mind, but a permanent quality of body. We have shewn that there is really a permanent quality of body, to which the common use of this word exactly agrees. Can any stronger proof be desired, that this quality is that to which the vulgar give the name of *colour?* If it should be said, that this quality, to which we give the name of *colour*, is unknown to the vulgar, and, therefore, can have no name among them, I answer, it is, indeed, known only by its effects—that is, by its exciting a certain idea in us; but are there not numberless qualities of bodies which are known only by their effects, to which, notwithstanding, we find it necessary to give names? Medicine alone might furnish us with a hundred instances of this kind. Do not the words *astringent, narcotic, epispastic, causlic*, and innumerable others, signify qualities of bodies, which are known only by their effects upon animal bodies? Why, then, should not the vulgar give a name to a quality, whose effects are every moment perceived by their eyes? We have all the reason, therefore, that the nature of the thing admits, to think that the vulgar apply the name of *colour* to that quality of bodies which excites in us what the philosophers call the *idea of colour*. And that there is such a quality in bodies, all philosophers allow, who allow that there is any such thing as body. Philosophers have thought fit to leave that quality of bodies which the vulgar call *colour*, without a name, and to give the name of *colour* to the idea or appearance, to which, as we have shewn, the vulgar give no name, because they never make it an object of thought or reflection. Hence it appears, that when philosophers affirm that colour is not in bodies, but in the mind, and the vulgar affirm that colour is not in the mind, but is a quality of bodies, there is no difference between them about things, but only about the meaning of a word.

The vulgar have undoubted right to give names to things which they are daily conversant about; and philosophers seem justly chargeable with an abuse of language, when they change the meaning of a common word, without giving warning.

If it is a good rule, to think with philosophers and speak with the vulgar, it must be right to speak with the vulgar when we think with them, and not to shock them by philosophical paradoxes, which, when put into common language, express only the common sense of mankind.

If you ask a man that is no philosopher what colour is, or what makes one body appear white, another scarlet, he cannot tell. He leaves that inquiry to philosophers, and can embrace any hypothesis about it, except that of our modern philosophers, who affirm that colour is not in body, but only in the mind.

. . . . . .

We desire, therefore, with pleasure, to do justice to the doctrine of Locke, and other modern philosophers, with regard to colour and other secondary qualities, and to ascribe to it its due merit, while we beg leave to censure the language in which they have expressed their doctrine. When they had explained and established the distinction between the appearance which colour makes to the eye, and the modification of the coloured body which, by the laws of nature, causes that appearance, the question was, whether to give the name of *colour* to the cause or to the effect? By giving it, as they have done, to the effect, they set philosophy apparently in opposition to common sense, and expose it to the ridicule of the vulgar. But had they given the name of *colour* to the cause, as they ought to have done, they must then have affirmed, with the vulgar, that colour is a quality of bodies; and that there is neither colour nor anything like it in the mind. Their language, as well as their sentiments, would have been perfectly agreeable to the common apprehensions of mankind, and true Philosophy would have joined hands with Common Sense. As Locke was no enemy to common sense, it may be presumed, that, in this instance, as in some others, he was seduced by some received hypothesis; and that this was actually the case, will appear in the following section.

Section VI. That None of Our Sensations Are Resemblances of Any of the Qualities of Bodies.

A second inference is, that, although colour is really a quality of body, yet it is not repre-

sented to the mind by an idea or sensation that resembles it; on the contrary, it is suggested by an idea which does not in the least resemble it. And this inference is applicable, not to colour only, but to all the qualities of body which we have examined.

It deserves to be remarked, that, in the analysis we have hitherto given of the operations of the five senses, and of the qualities of bodies discovered by them, no instance hath occurred, either of any sensation which resembles any quality of body, or of any quality of body whose image or resemblance is conveyed to the mind by means of the senses.

There is no phænomenon in nature more unaccountable than the intercourse that is carried on between the mind and the external world—there is no phænomenon which philosophical spirits have shewn greater avidity to pry into, and to resolve. It is agreed by all, that this intercourse is carried on by means of the senses; and this satisfies the vulgar curiosity, but not the philosophic. Philosophers must have some system, some hypothesis, that shews the manner in which our senses make us acquainted with external things. All the fertility of human invention seems to have produced only one hypothesis for this purpose, which, therefore, hath been universally received; and that is, that the mind, like a mirror, receives the images of things from without, by means of the senses; so that their use must be to convey these images into the mind.

Whether to these images of external things in the mind, we give the name of *sensible forms*, or *sensible species*, with the Peripatetics, or the name *of ideas of sensation*, with Locke; or whether, with later philosophers, we distinguish *sensations*, which are immediately conveyed by the senses, from *ideas of sensation*, which are faint copies of our sensations retained in the memory and imagination; these are only differences about words. The hypothesis I have mentioned is common to all these different systems.

The necessary and allowed consequence of this hypothesis is, *that no material thing, nor any quality of material things, can be conceived by us, or made an object of thought, until its image is conveyed to the mind by means of the senses.* We shall examine this hypothesis particularly afterwards, and at this time only observe, that, in consequence of it, one would naturally expect, that to every quality and attribute of body we know or can conceive, there should be a sensation corresponding, which is the image and resemblance of that quality; and that the sensations which have no similitude or resemblance to body, or to any of its qualities, should give us no conception of a material world, or of anything belonging to it. These things might be expected as the natural consequences of the hypothesis we have mentioned.

Now, we have considered, in this and the preceding chapters, Extension, Figure, Solidity, Motion, Hardness, Roughness, as well as Colour, Heat, and Cold, Sound, Taste, and Smell. We have endeavoured to shew that our nature and constitution lead us to conceive these as qualities of body, as all mankind have always conceived them to be. We have likewise examined with great attention the various sensations we have by means of the five senses, and are not able to find among them all one single image of body, or of any of its qualities. From whence, then, come those images of body and of its qualities into the mind? Let philosophers resolve this question. All I can say is, that they come not by the senses. I am sure that, by proper attention and care, I may know my sensations, and be able to affirm with certainty what they resemble, and what they do not resemble. I have examined them one by one, and compared them with matter and its qualities; and I cannot find one of them that confesses a resembling feature.

A truth so evident as this—that our sensations are not images of matter, or of any of its qualities—ought not to yield to a hypothesis such as that above-mentioned, however ancient, or however universally received by philosophers; nor can there be any amicable union between the two. This will appear by some reflections upon the spirit of the ancient and modern philosophy concerning sensation.

During the reign of the Peripatetic philosophy, our sensations were not minutely or accurately examined. The attention of philosophers, as well as of the vulgar, was turned to the things signified by them: therefore, in consequence of the common hypothesis, it was taken for granted, that all the sensations we have from external things, are the forms or images of these external things. And thus the truth we have mentioned yielded entirely to the hypothesis, and was altogether suppressed by it.

Des Cartes gave a noble example of turning our attention inward, and scrutinizing our sensations; and this example hath been very worthily followed by modern philosophers, particularly by Malebranche, Locke, Berkeley, and Hume. The effect of this scrutiny hath been, a gradual discovery of the truth above-mentioned—to wit, the dissimilitude between the sensations of our minds, and the qualities or attributes of an insentient inert substance, such as we conceive matter to be. But this valuable and useful discovery, in its different stages, hath still been unhappily united to the ancient hypothesis—and from this inauspicious match of opinions, so unfriendly and discordant in their natures, have arisen those monsters of paradox and scepticism with which the modern philosophy is too justly chargeable.

Locke saw clearly, and proved incontestably, that the sensations we have by taste, smell, and hearing, as well as the sensations of colour, heat, and cold, are not resemblances of anything in bodies; and in this he agrees with Des Cartes and Malebranche. Joining this opinion with the hypothesis, it follows necessarily, that three senses of the five are cut off from giving us any intelligence of the material world, as being altogether inept for that office. Smell, and taste, and sound, as well as colour and heat, can have no more relation to body, than anger or gratitude; nor ought the former to be called qualities of body, whether primary or secondary, any more than the latter. For it was natural and obvious to argue thus from that hypothesis: If heat, and colour, and sound are real qualities of body, the sensations by which we perceive them must be resemblances of those qualities; but these sensations are not resemblances; therefore, those are not real qualities of body.

We see, then, that Locke, having found that the ideas of secondary qualities are no resemblances, was compelled, by a hypothesis common to all philosophers, to deny that they are real qualities of body. It is more difficult to assign a reason why, after this, he should call them *secondary qualities*; for this name, if I mistake not, was of his invention. Surely he did not mean that they were secondary qualities of the mind; and I do not see with what propriety, or even by what tolerable license, he could call them secondary qualities of body, after finding that they were no qualities of body at all. In this, he seems to have sacrificed to Common Sense, and to have been led by her authority even in opposition to his hypothesis. The same sovereign mistress of our opinions that led this philosopher to call those things secondary qualities of body, which, according to his principles and reasonings, were no qualities of body at all, hath led, not the vulgar of all ages only, but philosophers also, and even the disciples of Locke, to believe them to be real qualities of body—she hath led them to investigate, by experiments, the nature of colour, and sound, and heat, in bodies. Nor hath this investigation been fruitless, as it must have been if there had been no such thing in bodies; on the contrary, it hath produced very noble and useful discoveries, which make a very considerable part of natural philosophy. If, then, natural philosophy be not a dream, there is something in bodies which we call *colour*, and *heat*, and *sound*. And if this be so, the hypothesis from which the contrary is concluded, must be false: for the argument, leading to a false conclusion, recoils against the hypothesis from which it was drawn, and thus directs its force backward. If the qualities of body were known to us only by sensations that resemble them, then colour, and sound, and heat could be no qualities of body; but these are real qualities of body; and, therefore, the qualities of body are not known only by means of sensations that resemble them.

.   .   .   .

Section VII. Of Visible Figure and Extension.

Although there is no resemblance, nor, as far as we know, any necessary connection, between that quality in a body which we call its *colour*, and the appearance which that colour makes to the eye, it is quite otherwise with regard to its *figure* and *magnitude*. There is certainly a resemblance, and a necessary connection, between the visible figure and magnitude

of a body, and its real figure and magnitude; no man can give a reason why a scarlet colour affects the eye in the manner it does; no man can be sure that it affects his eye in the same manner as it affects the eye of another, and that it has the same appearance to him as it has to another man;—but we can assign a reason why a circle placed obliquely to the eye, should appear in the form of an ellipse. The visible figure, magnitude, and position may, by mathematical reasoning, be deduced from the real; and it may be demonstrated, that every eye that sees distinctly and perfectly, must, in the same situation, see it under this form, and no other. Nay, we may venture to affirm, that a man born blind, if he were instructed in mathematics, would be able to determine the visible figure of a body when its real figure, distance, and position, are given. Dr. Saunderson understood the projection of the sphere, and perspective. Now, I require no more knowledge in a blind man, in order to his being able to determine the visible figure of bodies, than that he can project the outline of a given body, upon the surface of a hollow sphere, whose centre is in the eye. This projection is the visible figure he wants: for it is the same figure with that which is projected upon the *tunica retina* in vision.

A blind man can conceive lines drawn from every point of the object to the centre of the eye, making angles. He can conceive that the length of the object will appear greater or less, in proportion to the angle which it subtends at the eye; and that, in like manner, the breadth, and in general the distance, of any one point of the object from any other point, will appear greater or less, in proportion to the angles which those distances subtend. He can easily be made to conceive, that the visible appearance has no thickness, any more than a projection of the sphere, or a perspective draught. He may be informed, that the eye, until it is aided by experience, does not represent one object as nearer or more remote than another. Indeed, he would probably conjecture this of himself, and be apt to think that the rays of light must make the same impression upon the eye, whether they come from a greater or a less distance.

These are all the principles which we suppose our blind mathematician to have; and these he may certainly acquire by information and reflection. It is no less certain, that, from these principles, having given the real figure and magnitude of a body, and its position and distance with regard to the eye, he can find out its visible figure and magnitude. He can demonstrate in general, from these principles, that the visible figure of all bodies will be the same with that of their projection upon the surface of a hollow sphere, when the eye is placed in the centre. And he can demonstrate that their visible magnitude will be greater or less, according as their projection occupies a greater or less part of the surface of this sphere.

To set this matter in another light, let us distinguish betwixt the *position* of objects with regard to the eye, and their *distance* from it. Objects that lie in the same right line drawn from the centre of the eye, have the same position, however different their distances from the eye may be: but objects which lie in different right lines drawn from the eye's centre, have a different position; and this difference of position is greater or less in proportion to the angle made at the eye by the right lines mentioned. Having thus defined what we mean by the position of objects with regard to the eye, it is evident that, as the real figure of a body consists in the situation of its several parts with regard to one another, so its visible figure consists in the position of its several parts with regard to the eye; and, as he that hath a distinct conception of the situation of the parts of the body with regard to one another, must have a distinct conception of its real figure; so he that conceives distinctly the position of its several parts with regard to the eye, must have a distinct conception of its visible figure. Now, there is nothing, surely, to hinder a blind man from conceiving the position of the several parts of a body with regard to the eye, any more than from conceiving their situation with regard to one another; and, therefore, I conclude, that a blind man may attain a distinct conception of the visible figure of bodies.

.   .   .   .

Section VIII. Some Queries Concerning Visible Figure Answered.

It may be asked, What kind of thing is this visible figure? Is it a Sensation, or an Idea? If it is an idea, from what sensation is it copied? These questions may seem trivial or imperti-nent to one who does not know that there is a tribunal of inquisition erected by certain modern philosophers, before which everything in nature must answer. The articles of inquisition are few indeed, but very dreadful in their consequences. They are only these: Is the prisoner an Impression or an Idea? If an idea, from what impression copied? Now, if it appears that the prisoner is neither an impression, nor an idea copied from some impression, immediately, without being allowed to offer anything in arrest of judgment, he is sentenced to pass out of existence, and to be, in all time to come, an empty unmeaning sound, or the ghost of a departed entity.

Before this dreadful tribunal, cause and effect, time and place, matter and spirit, have been tried and cast: how then shall such a poor flimsy form as visible figure stand before it? It must even plead guilty, and confess that it is neither an impression nor an idea. For, alas! it is notorious, that it is extended in length and breadth; it may be long or short, broad or narrow, triangular, quadrangular, or circular; and, therefore, unless ideas and impressions are extended and figured, it cannot belong to that category.

If it should still be asked, To what category of beings does visible figure then belong? I can only, in answer, give some tokens, by which those who are better acquainted with the categories, may chance to find its place. It is, as we have said, the position of the several parts of a figured body with regard to the eye. The different positions of the several parts of the body with regard to the eye, when put together, make a real figure, which is truly extended in length and breadth, and which represents a figure that is extended in length, breadth, and thickness. In like manner, a projection of the sphere is a real figure, and hath length and breadth, but represents the sphere, which hath three dimensions. A projection of the sphere, or a perspective view of a palace, is a representative in the very same sense as visible figure is; and wherever they have their lodgings in the categories, this will be found to dwell next door to them.

It may farther be asked, Whether there be any sensation proper to visible figure, by which it is suggested in vision?—or by what means it is presented to the mind? This is a question of some importance, in order to our having a distinct notion of the faculty of seeing: and to give all the light to it we can, it is necessary to compare this sense with other senses, and to make some suppositions, by which we may be enabled to distinguish things that are apt to be confounded, although they are totally different.

There are three of our senses which give us intelligence of things at a distance: smell, hearing, and sight. In smelling and in hearing, we have a sensation or impression upon the mind, which, by our constitution, we conceive to be a sign of something external: but the position of this external thing, with regard to the organ of sense, is not presented to the mind along with the sensation. When I hear the sound of a coach, I could not, previous to experience, determine whether the sounding body was above or below, to the right hand or to the left. So that the sensation suggests to me some external object as the cause or occasion of it; but it suggests not the position of that object, whether it lies in this direction or in that. The same thing may be said with regard to smelling. But the case is quite different with regard to seeing. When I see an object, the appearance which the colour of it makes, may be called *the sensation*, which suggests to me some external thing as its cause; but it suggests likewise the individual direction and position of this cause with regard to the eye. I know it is precisely in such a direction, and in no other. At the same time, I am not conscious of anything that can be called *sensation*, but the sensation of colour. The position of the coloured thing is no sensation; but it is by the laws of my constitution presented to the mind along with the colour, without any additional sensation.

Let us suppose that the eye were so constituted that the rays coming from any one point of the object were not, as they are in our eyes, collected in one point of the *retina*, but diffused over the whole: it is evident to those who understand the structure of the eye, that such an eye as we have supposed, would shew the colour of a body as our eyes do, but that it would neither shew figure nor position. The operation of such an eye would be precisely similar to that of hearing and smell; it would give no perception of figure or extension, but merely of colour. Nor is the supposition we

have made altogether imaginary: for it is nearly the case of most people who have cataracts, whose crystalline, as Mr. Cheselden observes, does not altogether exclude the rays of light, but diffuses them over the *retina*, so that such persons see things as one does through a glass of broken gelly: they perceive the colour, but nothing of the figure or magnitude of objects.

Again, if we should suppose that smell and sound were conveyed in right lines from the objects, and that every sensation of hearing and smell suggested the precise direction or position of its object; in this case, the operations of hearing and smelling would be similar to that of seeing: we should smell and hear the figure of objects, in the same sense as now we see it; and every smell and sound would be associated with some figure in the imagination, as colour is in our present state.

We have reason to believe, that the rays of light make some impression upon the *retina*; but we are not conscious of this impression; nor have anatomists or philosophers been able to discover the nature and effects of it; whether it produces a vibration in the nerve, or the motion of some subtile fluid contained in the nerve, or something different from either, to which we cannot give a name. Whatever it is, we shall call it the *material impression*; remembering carefully, that it is not an impression upon the mind, but upon the body; and that it is no sensation, nor can resemble sensation, any more than figure or motion can resemble thought. Now, this material impression, made upon a particular point of the *retina*, by the laws of our constitution, suggests two things to the mind—namely, the colour and the position of some external object. No man can give a reason why the same material impression might not have suggested sound, or smell, or either of these, along with the position of the object. That it should suggest colour and position, and nothing else, we can resolve only into our constitution, or the will of our Maker. And since there is no necessary connection between these two things suggested by this material impression, it might, if it had so pleased our Creator, have suggested one of them without the other. Let us suppose, therefore, since it plainly appears to be possible, that our eyes had been so framed as to suggest to us the position of the object, without suggesting colour, or any other quality: What is the consequence of this supposition? It is evidently this, that the person endued with such an eye, would perceive the visible figure of bodies, without having any sensation or impression made upon his mind. The figure he perceives is altogether external; and therefore cannot be called an impression upon the mind, without the grossest abuse of language. If it should be said, that it is impossible to perceive a figure, unless there be some impression of it upon the mind, I beg leave not to admit the impossibility of this without some proof: and I can find none. Neither can I conceive what is meant by an impression of figure upon the mind. I can conceive an impression of figure upon wax, or upon any body that is fit to receive it; but an impression of it upon the mind, is to me quite unintelligible; and, although I form the most distinct conception of the figure, I cannot, upon the strictest examination, find any impression of it upon my mind.

If we suppose, last of all, that the eye hath the power restored of perceiving colour, I apprehend that it will be allowed, that now it perceives figure in the very same manner as before, with this difference only, that colour is always joined with it.

In answer, therefore, to the question proposed, there seems to be no sensation that is appropriated to visible figure, or whose office it is to suggest it. It seems to be suggested immediately by the material impression upon the organ, of which we are not conscious: and why may not a material impression upon the *retina* suggest visible figure, as well as the material impression made upon the hand, when we grasp a ball, suggests real figure? In the one case, one and the same material impression, suggests both colour and visible figure; and in the other case, one and the same material impression suggests hardness, heat, or cold, and real figure, all at the same time.

We shall conclude this section with another question upon this subject. Since the visible figure of bodies is a real and external object to the eye, as their tangible figure is to the touch, it may be asked, Whence arises the difficulty of attending to the first, and the facility of attending to the last? It is certain that the first is more frequently presented to the eye, than the last is to the touch; the first is as distinct and

determinate an object as the last, and seems in its own nature as proper for speculation. Yet so little hath it been attended to, that it never had a name in any language, until Bishop Berkeley gave it that which we have used after his example, to distinguish it from the figure which is the object of touch.

The difficulty of attending to the visible figure of bodies, and making it an object of thought, appears so similar to that which we find in attending to our sensations, that both have probably like causes. Nature intended the visible figure as a sign of the tangible figure and situation of bodies, and hath taught us, by a kind of instinct, to put it always to this use. Hence it happens, that the mind passes over it with a rapid motion, to attend to the things signified by it. It is as unnatural to the mind to stop at the visible figure, and attend to it, as it is to a spherical body to stop upon an inclined plane. There is an inward principle, which constantly carries it forward, and which cannot be overcome but by a contrary force.

There are other external things which nature intended for signs; and we find this common to them all, that the mind is disposed to overlook them, and to attend only to the things signified by them. Thus there are certain modifications of the human face, which are natural signs of the present disposition of the mind. Every man understands the meaning of these signs, but not one of a hundred ever attended to the signs themselves, or knows anything about them. Hence you may find many an excellent practical physiognomist who knows nothing of the proportions of a face nor can delineate or describe the expression of any one passion.

An excellent painter or statuary can tell, not only what are the proportions of a good face, but what changes every passion makes in it. This, however, is one of the chief mysteries of his art, to the acquisition of which infinite labour and attention, as well as a happy genius, are required; but when he puts his art in practice, and happily expresses a passion by its proper signs, every one understands the meaning of these signs, without art, and without reflection.

What has been said of painting, might easily be applied to all the fine arts. The difficulty in them all consists in knowing and attending to those natural signs whereof every man understands the meaning.

We pass from the sign to the thing signified, with ease, and by natural impulse; but to go backward from the thing signified to the sign, is a work of labour and difficulty. Visible figure, therefore, being intended by nature to be a sign, we pass on immediately to the thing signified, and cannot easily return to give any attention to the sign.

. . . .

Section XX. *Of Perception in General.*

Sensation, and the perception of external objects by the senses, though very different in their nature, have commonly been considered as one and the same thing. The purposes of common life do not make it necessary to distinguish them, and the received opinions of philosophers tend rather to confound them; but, without attending carefully to this distinction, it is impossible to have any just conception of the operations of our senses. The most simple operations of the mind, admit not of a logical definition: all we can do is to describe them, so as to lead those who are conscious of them in themselves, to attend to them, and reflect upon them; and it is often very difficult to describe them so as to answer this intention.

The same mode of expression is used to denote sensation and perception; and, therefore, we are apt to look upon them as things of the same nature. Thus, *I feel a pain; I see a tree*: the first denoteth a sensation, the last a perception. The grammatical analysis of both expressions is the same: for both consist of an active verb and an object. But if we attend to the things signified by these expressions, we shall find that, in the first, the distinction between the act and the object is not real but grammatical; in the second, the distinction is not only grammatical but real.

The form of the expression, *I feel pain*, might seem to imply that the feeling is something distinct from the pain felt; yet, in reality, there is no distinction. As *thinking a thought* is an expression which could signify no more than *thinking*, so *feeling a pain* signifies no more than *being pained*. What we have said of pain is applicable to every other mere sensa-

tion. It is difficult to give instances, very few of our sensations having names; and, where they have, the name being common to the sensation, and to something else which is associated with it. But, when we attend to the sensation by itself, and separate it from other things which are conjoined with it in the imagination, it appears to be something which can have no existence but in a sentient mind, no distinction from the act of the mind by which it is felt.

Perception, as we here understand it, hath always an object distinct from the act by which it is perceived; an object which may exist whether it be perceived or not. I perceive a tree that grows before my window; there is here an object which is perceived, and an act of the mind by which it is perceived; and these two are not only distinguishable, but they are extremely unlike in their natures. The object is made up of a trunk, branches, and leaves; but the act of the mind by which it is perceived hath neither trunk, branches, nor leaves. I am conscious of this act of my mind, and I can reflect upon it; but it is too simple to admit of an analysis, and I cannot find proper words to describe it. I find nothing that resembles it so much as the remembrance of the tree, or the imagination of it. Yet both these differ essentially from perception: they differ likewise one from another. It is in vain that a philosopher assures me, that the imagination of the tree, the remembrance of it, and the perception of it, are all one, and differ only in degree of vivacity. I know the contrary; for I am as well acquainted with all the three as I am with the apartments of my own house. I know this also, that the perception of an object implies both a conception of its form, and a belief of its present existence. I know, moreover, that this belief is not the effect of argumentation and reasoning; it is the immediate effect of my constitution.

I am aware that this belief which I have in perception stands exposed to the strongest batteries of scepticism. But they make no great impression upon it. The sceptic asks me, Why do you believe the existence of the external object which you perceive? This belief, sir, is none of my manufacture; it came from the mint of Nature; it bears her image and superscription; and, if it is not right, the fault is not mine:

I even took it upon trust, and without suspicion. Reason, says the sceptic, is the only judge of truth, and you ought to throw off every opinion and every belief that is not grounded on reason. Why, sir, should I believe the faculty of reason more than that of perception?—they came both out of the same shop, and were made by the same artist; and if he puts one piece of false ware into my hands, what should hinder him from putting another?

Perhaps the sceptic will agree to distrust reason, rather than give any credit to perception. For, says he, since, by your own concession, the object which you perceive, and that act of your mind by which you perceive it, are quite different things, the one may exist without the other; and, as the object may exist without being perceived, so the perception may exist without an object. There is nothing so shameful in a philosopher as to be deceived and deluded; and, therefore, you ought to resolve firmly to withhold assent, and to throw off this belief of external objects, which may be all delusion. For my part, I will never attempt to throw it off; and, although the sober part of mankind will not be very anxious to know my reasons, yet, if they can be of use to any sceptic, they are these:—

First, because it is not in my power: why, then, should I make a vain attempt? It would be agreeable to fly to the moon, and to make a visit to Jupiter and Saturn; but, when I know that Nature has bound me down by the law of gravitation to this planet which I inhabit, I rest contented, and quietly suffer myself to be carried along in its orbit. My belief is carried along by perception, as irresistibly as my body by the earth. And the greatest sceptic will find himself to be in the same condition. He may struggle hard to disbelieve the informations of his senses, as a man does to swim against a torrent; but, ah! it is in vain. It is in vain that he strains every nerve, and wrestles with nature, and with every object that strikes upon his senses. For, after all, when his strength is spent in the fruitless attempt, he will be carried down the torrent with the common herd of believers.

Secondly, I think it would not be prudent to throw off this belief, if it were in my power. If Nature intended to deceive me, and impose upon me by false appearances, and I, by my great cunning and profound logic, have discovered the imposture, prudence would dictate to me, in this case, even to put up [with] this indignity done me, as quietly as I could, and not to call her an impostor to her face, lest she should be even with me in another way. For what do I gain by resenting this injury? You ought at least not to believe what she says. This indeed seems reasonable, if she intends to impose upon me. But what is the consequence? I resolve not to believe my senses. I break my nose against a post that comes in my way; I step into a dirty kennel; and, after twenty such wise and rational actions, I am taken up and clapped into a mad-house. Now, I confess I would rather make one of the credulous fools whom Nature imposes upon, than of those wise and rational philosophers who resolve to withhold assent at all this expense. If a man pretends to be a sceptic with regard to the informations of sense, and yet prudently keeps out of harm's way as other men do, he must excuse my suspicion, that he either acts the hypocrite, or imposes upon himself. For, if the scale of his belief were so evenly poised as to lean no more to one side than to the contrary, it is impossible that his actions could be directed by any rules of common prudence.

Thirdly, Although the two reasons already mentioned are perhaps two more than enough, I shall offer a third. I gave implicit belief to the informations of Nature by my senses, for a considerable part of my life, before I had learned so much logic as to be able to start a doubt concerning them. And now, when I reflect upon what is past, I do not find that I have been imposed upon by this belief. I find that without it I must have perished by a thousand accidents. I find that without it I should have been no wiser now than when I was born. I should not even have been able to acquire that logic which suggests these sceptical doubts with regard to my senses. Therefore, I consider this instinctive belief as one of the best gifts of Nature. I thank the Author of my being, who bestowed it upon me before the eyes of my reason were opened, and still bestows it upon me, to be my guide where reason leaves me in the dark. And now I yield to the direction of my senses, not from instinct only, but from confidence and trust in a faithful and beneficent Monitor, grounded upon the experience of his paternal care and goodness.

In all this, I deal with the Author of my being, no otherwise than I thought it reasonable to deal with my parents and tutors. I believed by instinct whatever they told me, long before I had the idea of a lie, or thought of the possibility of their deceiving me. Afterwards, upon reflection, I found they had acted like fair and honest people, who wished me well. I found that, if I had not believed what they told me, before I could give a reason of my belief, I had to this day been little better than a changeling. And although this natural credulity hath sometimes occasioned my being imposed upon by deceivers, yet it hath been of infinite advantage to me upon the whole; therefore, I consider it as another good gift of Nature. And I continue to give that credit, from reflection, to those of whose integrity and veracity I have had experience, which before I gave from instinct.

There is a much greater similitude than is commonly imagined, between the testimony of nature given by our senses, and the testimony of men given by language. The credit we give to both is at first the effect of instinct only. When we grow up, and begin to reason about them, the credit given to human testimony is restrained and weakened, by the experience we have of deceit. But the credit given to the testimony of our senses, is established and confirmed by the uniformity and constancy of the laws of nature.

Our perceptions are of two kinds: some are natural and original; others acquired, and the fruit of experience. When I perceive that this is the taste of cyder, that of brandy; that this is the smell of an apple, that of an orange; that this is the noise of thunder, that the ringing of bells; this the sound of a coach passing, that the voice of such a friend: these perceptions, and others of the same kind, are not original—they are acquired. But the perception which I have, by touch, of the hardness and softness of bodies, of their extension, figure, and motion, is not acquired—it is original.

In all our senses, the acquired perceptions are many more than the original, especially in sight. By this sense we perceive originally the visible figure and colour of bodies only, and their visible place: but we learn to perceive by the eye, almost everything which we can perceive by touch. The original perceptions of this sense serve only as signs to introduce the acquired.

The signs by which objects are presented to us in perception, are the language of Nature to man; and as, in many respects, it hath great affinity with the language of man to man, so particularly in this, that both are partly natural and original, partly acquired by custom. Our original or natural perceptions are analogous to the natural language of man to man, of which we took notice in the fourth chapter; and our acquired perceptions are analogous to artificial language, which, in our mother-tongue, is got very much in the same manner with our acquired perceptions—as we shall afterwards more fully explain.

.   .   .   .   .   .

12 / Immanuel Kant (1724–1804)
PROLEGOMENA TO ANY FUTURE METAPHYSICS

PROLEGOMENA

Preamble on the Peculiarities of All Metaphysical Cognition

1. Of the Sources of Metaphysics

If it becomes desirable to formulate any cognition as science, it will be necessary first to determine accurately those peculiar features which no other science has in common with it, constituting its characteristics; otherwise the boundaries of all sciences become confused, and none of them can be treated thoroughly according to its nature.

The characteristics of a science may consist of a simple difference of object, or of the sources of cognition, or of the kind of cognition, or perhaps of all three conjointly. On this, therefore, depends the idea of a possible science and its territory.

First, as concerns the sources of metaphysical cognition, its very concept implies that they cannot be empirical. Its principles (including not only its maxims but its basic notions) must never be derived from experience. It must not be physical but metaphysical knowledge, viz., knowledge lying beyond experience. It can therefore have for its basis neither external experience, which is the source of physics proper, nor internal, which is the basis of empirical psychology. It is therefore *a priori* knowledge, coming from pure Understanding and pure Reason.

But so far Metaphysics would not be distinguishable from pure Mathematics; it must therefore be called pure philosophical cognition; and for the meaning of this term I refer to the Critique of the Pure Reason (II. "Method of Transcendentalism," chap. I., sec. i), where the distinction between these two employments of the reason is sufficiently explained. So far concerning the sources of metaphysical cognition.

2. Concerning the Kind of Cognition Which Can Alone Be Called Metaphysical

a. Of the Distinction Between Analytical and Synthetical Judgments in General. The peculiarity of its sources demands that metaphysical cognition must consist of nothing but *a priori* judgments. But whatever be their origin, or their logical form, there is a distinction in judgments, as to their content, according to which they are either merely explicative, adding nothing to the content of the cognition, or expansive, increasing the given cognition: the former may be called analytical, the latter synthetical, judgments.

Analytical judgments express nothing in the predicate but what has been already actually thought in the concept of the subject, though not so distinctly or with the same (full) consciousness. When I say: All bodies are extended, I have not amplified in the least my concept of body, but have only analysed it, as extension was really thought to belong to that

Prolegomena to Any Future Metaphysics, sections 1, 2, 5, 6–11; Remark II; sections 18–26, 32–35. Reprinted with permission of Open Court Publishing Company from Immanual Kant, *Prolegomena to Any Future Metaphysics*, edited by Paul Carus. Copyright © 1949 by Open Court Publishing Company.

concept before the judgment was made, though it was not expressed; this judgment is therefore analytical. On the contrary, this judgment, All bodies have weight, contains in its predicate something not actually thought in the general concept of the body; it amplifies my knowledge by adding something to my concept, and must therefore be called synthetical.

b. The Common Principle of All Analytical Judgments Is the Law of Contradiction. All analytical judgments depend wholly on the Law of Contradiction, and are in their nature *a priori* cognitions, whether the concepts that supply them with matter be empirical or not. For the predicate of an affirmative analytical judgment is already contained in the concept of the subject, of which it cannot be denied without contradiction. In the same way its opposite is necessarily denied of the subject in an analytical, but negative, judgment, by the same Law of Contradiction. Such is the nature of the judgments: all bodies are extended, and no bodies are unextended (i.e., simple).

For this very reason all analytical judgments are *a priori* even when the concepts are empirical, as, for example, Gold is a yellow metal; for to know this I require no experience beyond my concept of gold as a yellow metal: it is, in fact, the very concept, and I need only analyse it, without looking beyond it elsewhere.

c. Synthetical Judgments Require a Different Principle from the Law of Contradiction. There are synthetical *a posteriori* judgments of empirical origin; but there are also others which are proved to be certain *a priori*, and which spring from pure Understanding and Reason. Yet they both agree in this, that they cannot possibly spring from the principle of analysis, viz., the law of contradiction, alone; they require a quite different principle, though, from whatever they may be deduced, they must be subject to the law of contradiction, which must never be violated, even though everything cannot be deduced from it. I shall first classify synthetical judgments.

1. Empirical judgments are always synthetical. For it would be absurd to base an analytical judgment on experience, as our concept suffices for the purpose without requiring any testimony from experience. That body is extended, is a judgment established *a priori*, and

not an empirical judgment. For before appealing to experience, we already have all the conditions of the judgment in the concept, from which we have but to elicit the predicate according to the law of contradiction, and thereby to become conscious of the necessity of the judgment, which experience could not even teach us.

2. Mathematical judgments are all synthetical. This fact seems hitherto to have altogether escaped the observation of those who have analysed human reason; it even seems directly opposed to all their conjectures, though incontestably certain, and most important in its consequences. For as it was found that the conclusions of mathematicians all proceed according to the Law of Contradiction (as is demanded by all apodeictic certainty), men persuaded themselves that the fundamental principles were known from the same law. This was a great mistake, for a synthetical proposition can indeed be comprehended according to the law of contradiction, but only by presupposing another synthetical proposition from which it follows, but never in itself.

First of all, we must observe that all proper mathematical judgments are *a priori*, and not empirical, because they carry with them necessity, which cannot be obtained from experience. But if this be not conceded to me, very good; I shall confine my assertion to *pure Mathematics*, the very notion of which implies that it contains pure *a priori* and not empirical cognitions.

It might at first be thought that the proposition $7 + 5 = 12$ is a mere analytical judgment, following from the concept of the sum of seven and five, according to the Law of Contradiction. But on closer examination it appears that the concept of the sum of $7 + 5$ contains merely their union in a single number, without its being at all thought what the particular number is that unites them. The concept of twelve is by no means thought by merely thinking of the combination of seven and five; and analyse this possible sum as we may, we shall not discover twelve in the concept. We must go beyond these concepts, by calling to our aid some concrete image *(Anschauung)*, i.e., either our five fingers, or five points (as Segner has it in his Arithmetic), and we must add successively the units of the five, given in some concrete image *(Anschauung)*, to the concept of seven. Hence our concept is really amplified by the proposition $7 + 5 = 12$, and we add to the first a second, not thought in it. Arithmetical judgments are therefore synthetical, and the more plainly according as we take larger numbers; for in such cases it is clear that, however closely we analyse our concepts without calling visual images *(Anschauung)* to our aid, we can never find the sum by such mere dissection.

All principles of geometry are no less analytical. That a straight line is the shortest path between two points, is a synthetical proposition. For my concept of straight contains nothing of quantity, but only a quality. The attribute of shortness is therefore altogether additional, and cannot be obtained by any analysis of the concept. Here, too, visualisation *(Anschauung)* must come to aid us. It alone makes the synthesis possible.

Some other principles, assumed by geometers, are indeed actually analytical, and depend on the law of contradiction; but they only serve, as identical propositions, as a method of concatenation, and not as principles, e.g., a = a, the whole is equal to itself, or $a + b > a$, the whole is greater than its part. And yet even these, though they are recognised as valid from mere concepts, are only admitted in mathematics, because they can be represented in some visual form *(Anschauung)*.

. . . .

The General Problem: How is Cognition from Pure Reason Possible?

5. We have above learned the significant distinction between analytical and synthetical judgments. The possibility of analytical propositions was easily comprehended, being entirely founded on the Law of Contradiction. The possibility of synthetical *a posteriori* judgments, of those which are gathered from experience, also requires no particular explanation; for experience is nothing but a continual synthesis of perceptions. There remain therefore only synthetical propositions *a priori*, of which the possibility must be sought or investigated, because they must depend upon other principles than the Law of Contradiction.

But here we need not first establish the possibility of such propositions so as to ask whether they are possible. For there are enough of them which indeed are of undoubted certainty, and as our present method is analytical, we shall start from the fact, that such synthetical but purely rational cognition actually exists; but we must now inquire into the reason of this possibility, and ask, *how* such cognition is possible, in order that we may from the principles of its possibility be enabled to determine the conditions of its use, its sphere and its limits. The proper problem upon which all depends, when expressed with scholastic precision, is therefore:

How are synthetic propositions a priori possible?

For the sake of popularity I have above expressed this problem somewhat differently, as an inquiry into purely rational cognition, which I could do for once without detriment to the desired comprehension, because, as we have only to do here with metaphysics and its sources, the reader will, I hope, after the foregoing remarks, keep in mind that when we speak of purely rational cognition, we do not mean analytical, but synthetical cognition.[1]

Metaphysics stands or falls with the solution of this problem: its very existence depends upon it. Let any one make metaphysical assertions with ever so much plausibility, let him overwhelm us with conclusions, if he has not previously proved able to answer this question satisfactorily, I have a right to say: this is all vain baseless philosophy and false wisdom. You speak through pure reason, and claim, as it were to create cognitions *a priori* by not only dissecting given concepts, but also by asserting connexions which do not rest upon the law of contradiction, and which you believe you conceive quite independently of all experience; how do you arrive at this, and how will you justify your pretensions? An appeal to the consent of the common sense of mankind cannot be allowed; for that is a witness whose authority depends merely upon rumor. Says Horace:

Quodcunque ostendis mihi sic, incredulus odi.
To all that which thou provest me thus, I refuse to give credence.

The answer to this question, though indispensable, is difficult; and though the principal reason that it was not made long ago is, that the possibility of the question never occurred to anybody, there is yet another reason, which is this, that a satisfactory answer to this one question requires a much more persistent, profound, and painstaking reflexion, than the most diffuse work on Metaphysics, which on its first appearance promised immortality to its author. And every intelligent reader, when he carefully reflects what this problem requires, must at first be struck with its difficulty, and would regard it as insoluble and even impossible, did there not actually exist pure synthetical cognitions *a priori*. This actually happened to David Hume, though he did not conceive the question in its entire universality as is done here, and as must be done, should the answer be decisive for all Metaphysics. For how is it possible, says that acute man, that when a concept is given me, I can go beyond it and connect with it another, which is not contained in it, in such a manner as if the latter necessarily belonged to the former? Nothing but experience can furnish us with such connexions (thus he concluded from the difficulty which he took to be an impossibility), and all that vaunted necessity, or, what is the same thing, all cognition assumed to be *a priori*, is nothing but a long habit of accepting something as true, and hence of mistaking subjective necessity for objective.

.　.　.　.　.　.　.

FIRST PART OF THE TRANSCENDENTAL PROBLEM

How Is Pure Mathematics Possible?

6. Here is a great and established branch of knowledge, encompassing even now a wonderfully large domain and promising an unlimited extension in the future. Yet it carries with it thoroughly apodeictical certainty, i.e., absolute necessity, which therefore rests upon no empirical grounds. Consequently it is a pure product of reason, and moreover is thoroughly synthetical. [Here the question arises:]

"How then is it possible for human reason to produce a cognition of this nature entirely *a priori*?"

Does not this faculty [which produces math-

ematics], as it neither is nor can be based upon experience, presuppose some ground of cognition *a priori*, which lies deeply hidden, but which might reveal itself by these its effects, if their first beginnings were but diligently ferreted out?

7. But we find that all mathematical cognition has this peculiarity: it must first exhibit its concept in a visual form (*Anschauung*) and indeed *a priori*, therefore in a visual form which is not empirical, but pure. Without this mathematics cannot take a single step; hence its judgments are always visual, viz., "intuitive"; whereas philosophy must be satisfied with discursive judgments from mere concepts, and though it may illustrate its doctrines through a visual figure, can never derive them from it. This observation on the nature of mathematics gives us a clue to the first and highest condition of its possibility, which is, that some nonsensuous visualisation (called pure intuition, or *reine Anschauung*) must form its basis, in which all its concepts can be exhibited or constructed, *in concreto* and yet *a priori*. If we can find out this pure intuition and its possibility, we may thence easily explain how synthetical propositions *a priori* are possible in pure mathematics, and consequently how this science itself is possible. Empirical intuition [viz., sense perception] enables us without difficulty to enlarge the concept which we frame of an object of intuition [or sense-perception], by new predicates, which intuition [i.e., sense perception] itself presents synthetically in experience. Pure intuition [viz., the visualisation of forms in our imagination, from which every thing sensual, i.e., every thought of material qualities, is excluded] does so likewise, only with this difference, that in the latter case the synthetical judgment is *a priori* certain and apodeictical, in the former, only *a posteriori* and empirically certain; because this latter contains only that which occurs in contingent empirical intuition, but the former, that which must necessarily be discovered in pure intuition. Here intuition, being an intuition *a priori*, is *before all experience*, viz., before any perception of particular objects, inseparably conjoined with its concept.

8. But with this step our perplexity seems rather to increase than to lessen. For the ques-

tion now is, "How is it possible to intuite [in a visual form] anything *a priori?*" An intuition [viz., a visual sense perception] is such a representation as immediately depends upon the presence of the object. Hence it seems impossible to intuite from the outset *a priori*, because intuition would in that event take place without either a former or a present object to refer to, and by consequence could not be intuition. Concepts indeed are such, that we can easily form some of them *a priori*, viz., such as contain nothing but the thought of an object in general; and we need not find ourselves in an immediate relation to the object. Take, for instance, the concepts of Quantity, of Cause, etc. But even these require, in order to make them understood, a certain concrete use—that is, an application to some sense experience *(Anschauung)*, by which an object of them is given us. But how can the intuition of the object [its visualisation] precede the object itself?

9. If our intuition [i.e., our sense experience] were perforce of such a nature as to represent things as they are in themselves, there would not be any intuition *a priori*, but intuition would be always empirical. For I can only know what is contained in the object in itself when it is present and given to me. It is indeed even then incomprehensible how the visualising *(Anschauung)* of a present thing should make me know this thing as it is in itself, as its properties cannot migrate into my faculty of representation. But even granting this possibility, a visualising of that sort would not take place *a priori*, that is, before the object were presented to me; for without this latter fact no reason of a relation between my representation and the object can be imagined, unless it depend upon a direct inspiration.

Therefore in one way only can my intuition *(Anschauung)* anticipate the actuality of the object, and be a cognition *a priori*, viz.: if my intuition contains nothing but the form of sensibility, antedating in my subjectivity all the actual impressions through which I am affected by objects. For that objects of sense can only be intuited according to this form of sensibility I can know *a priori*. Hence it follows: that propositions, which concern this form of sensuous intuition only, are possible and valid for objects of the senses; as also, conversely, that

intuitions which are possible *a priori* can never concern any other things than objects of our senses.

10. Accordingly, it is only the form of sensuous intuition by which we can intuite things *a priori*, but by which we can know objects only as they *appear* to us (to our senses), not as they are in themselves; and this assumption is absolutely necessary if synthetical propositions *a priori* be granted as possible, or if, in case they actually occur, their possibility is to be comprehended and determined beforehand.

Now, the intuitions which pure mathematics lays at the foundation of all its cognitions and judgments which appear at once apodeictic and necessary are Space and Time. For mathematics must first have all its concepts in intuition, and pure mathematics in pure intuition, that is, it must construct them. If it proceeded in any other way, it would be impossible to make any headway, for mathematics proceeds, not analytically by dissection of concepts, but synthetically, and if pure intuition be wanting, there is nothing in which the matter for synthetical judgments *a priori* can be given. Geometry is based upon the pure intuition of space. Arithmetic accomplishes its concept of number by the successive addition of units in time; and pure mechanics especially cannot attain its concepts of motion without employing the representation of time. Both representations, however, are only intuitions; for if we omit from the empirical intuitions of bodies and their alterations (motion) everything empirical, or belonging to sensation, space and time still remain, which are therefore pure intuitions that lie *a priori* at the basis of the empirical. Hence they can never be omitted, but at the same time, by their being pure intuitions *a priori*, they prove that they are mere forms of our sensibility, which must precede all empirical intuition, or perception of actual objects, and conformably to which objects can be known *a priori*, but only as they appear to us.

11. The problem of the present section is therefore solved. Pure mathematics, as synthetical cognition *a priori*, is only possible by referring to no other objects than those of the senses. At the basis of their empirical intuition lies a pure intuition (of space and of time) which is *a priori*. This is possible, because the

latter intuition is nothing but the mere form of sensibility, which precedes the actual appearance of the objects, in that it, in fact, makes them possible. Yet this faculty of intuiting *a priori* affects not the matter of the phenomenon (that is, the sense element in it, for this constitutes that which is empirical), but its form, viz., space and time. Should any man venture to doubt that these are determinations adhering not to things in themselves, but to their relation to our sensibility, I should be glad to know how it can be possible to know the constitution of things *a priori*, viz., before we have any acquaintance with them and before they are presented to us. Such, however, is the case with space and time. But this is quite comprehensible as soon as both count for nothing more than formal conditions of our sensibility, while the objects count merely as phenomena; for then the form of the phenomenon, i.e., pure intuition, can by all means be represented as proceeding from ourselves, that is, *a priori*.

. . . .

Remark II.

Whatever is given us as object, must be given us in intuition. All our intuition however takes place by means of the senses only; the understanding intuites nothing, but only reflects. And as we have just shown that the senses never and in no manner enable us to know things in themselves, but only their appearances, which are mere representations of the sensibility, we conclude that "all bodies, together with the space in which they are, must be considered nothing but mere representations in us, and exist nowhere but in our thoughts." You will say: Is not this manifest idealism?

Idealism consists in the assertion, that there are none but thinking beings, all other things, which we think are perceived in intuition, being nothing but representations in the thinking beings, to which no object external to them corresponds in fact. Whereas I say, that things as objects of our senses existing outside us are given, but we know nothing of what they may be in themselves, knowing only their appearances, i.e., the representations which they cause in us by affecting our senses. Consequently I grant by all means that there are bod-

ies without us, that is, things which, though quite unknown to us as to what they are in themselves, we yet know by the representations which their influence on our sensibility procures us, and which we call bodies, a term signifying merely the appearance of the thing which is unknown to us, but not therefore less actual. Can this be termed idealism? It is the very contrary.

Long before Locke's time, but assuredly since him, it has been generally assumed and granted without detriment to the actual existence of external things, that many of their predicates may be said to belong not to the things in themselves, but to their appearances, and to have no proper existence outside our representation. Heat, color, and taste, for instance, are of this kind. Now, if I go farther, and for weighty reasons rank as mere appearances the remaining qualities of bodies also, which are called primary, such as extension, place, and in general space, with all that which belongs to it (impenetrability or materiality, space, etc.)—no one in the least can adduce the reason of its being inadmissible. As little as the man who admits colors not to be properties of the object in itself, but only as modifications of the sense of sight, should on that account be called an idealist, so little can my system be named idealistic, merely because I find that more, nay,

All the properties which constitute the intuition of a body belong merely to its appearance.

The existence of the thing that appears is thereby not destroyed, as in genuine idealism, but it is only shown, that we cannot possibly know it by the senses as it is in itself.

I should be glad to know what my assertions must be in order to avoid all idealism. Undoubtedly, I should say, that the representation of space is not only perfectly conformable to the relation which our sensibility has to objects—that I have said—but that it is quite similar to the object,—an assertion in which I can find as little meaning as if I said that the sensation of red has a similarity to the property of vermilion, which in me excites this sensation.

. . . .

18. In the first place we must state that, while all judgments of experience (*Erfahrung-*

surtheile) are empirical (i.e., have their ground in immediate sense perception), *vice versa*, all empirical judgments *(empirische Urtheile)* are not judgments of experience, but, besides the empirical, and in general besides what is given to the sensuous intuition, particular concepts must yet be superadded—concepts which have their origin quite *a priori* in the pure understanding, and under which every perception must be first of all subsumed and then by their means changed into experience.

Empirical judgments, so far as they have objective validity, are judgments of experience; but those which are only subjectively valid, I name mere judgments of perception. The latter require no pure concept of the understanding, but only the logical connexion of perception in a thinking subject. But the former always require, besides the representation of the sensuous intuition, particular *concepts originally begotten in the understanding*, which produce the objective validity of the judgment of experience.

All our judgments are at first merely judgments of perception; they hold good only for us (i.e., for our subject), and we do not till afterwards give them a new reference (to an object), and desire that they shall always hold good for us and in the same way for everybody else; for when a judgment agrees with an object, all judgments concerning the same object must likewise agree among themselves, and thus the objective validity of the judgment of experience signifies nothing else than its necessary universality of application. And conversely when we have reason to consider a judgment necessarily universal (which never depends upon perception, but upon the pure concept of the understanding, under which the perception is subsumed), we must consider it objective also, that is, that it expresses not merely a reference of our perception to a subject, but a quality of the object. For there would be no reason for the judgments of other men necessarily agreeing with mine, if it were not the unity of the object to which they all refer, and with which they accord; hence they must all agree with one another.

19. Therefore objective validity and necessary universality (for everybody) are equivalent terms, and though we do not know the object in itself, yet when we consider a judgment as universal, and also necessary, we understand it to have objective validity. By this judgment we cognise the object (though it remains unknown as it is in itself) by the universal and necessary connexion of the given perceptions. As this is the case with all objects of sense, judgments of experience take their objective validity not from the immediate cognition of the object (which is impossible), but from the condition of universal validity in empirical judgments, which, as already said, never rests upon empirical, or, in short, sensuous conditions, but upon a pure concept of the understanding. The object always remains unknown in itself; but when by the concept of the understanding the connexion of the representations of the object, which are given to our sensibility, is determined as universally valid, the object is determined by this relation, and it is the judgment that is objective.

To illustrate the matter: When we say, "the room is warm, sugar sweet, and wormwood bitter,"[2]—we have only subjectively valid judgments. I do not at all expect that I or any other person shall always find it as I now do; each of these sentences only expresses a relation of two sensations to the same subject, to myself, and that only in my present state of perception; consequently they are not valid of the object. Such are judgments of perception. Judgments of experience are of quite a different nature. What experience teaches me under certain circumstances, it must always teach me and everybody; and its validity is not limited to the subject nor to its state at a particular time. Hence I pronounce all such judgments as being objectively valid. For instance, when I say the air is elastic, this judgment is as yet a judgment of perception only—I do nothing but refer two of my sensations to one another. But, if I would have it called a judgment of experience, I require this connexion to stand under a condition, which makes it universally valid. I desire therefore that I and everybody else should always connect necessarily the same perceptions under the same circumstances.

20. We must consequently analyse experience in order to see what is contained in this product of the senses and of the understanding, and how the judgment of experience itself is possible. The foundation is the intuition of

which I become conscious, i.e., perception *(perceptio)*, which pertains merely to the senses. But in the next place, there are acts of judging (which belong only to the understanding). But this judging may be twofold—first, I may merely compare perceptions and connect them in a particular state of my consciousness; or, secondly, I may connect them in consciousness generally. The former judgment is merely a judgment of perception, and of subjective validity only: it is merely a connexion of perceptions in my mental state, without reference to the object. Hence it is not, as is commonly imagined, enough for experience to compare perceptions and to connect them in consciousness through judgment; there arises no universality and necessity, for which alone judgments can become objectively valid and be called experience.

Quite another judgment therefore is required before perception can become experience. The given intuition must be subsumed under a concept, which determines the form of judging in general relatively to the intuition, connects its empirical consciousness in consciousness generally, and thereby procures universal validity for empirical judgments. A concept of this nature is a pure *a priori* concept of the Understanding, which does nothing but determine for an intuition the general way in which it can be used for judgments. Let the concept be that of cause, then it determines the intuition which is subsumed under it, e.g., that of air, relative to judgments in general viz., the concept of air serves with regard to its expansion in the relation of antecedent to consequent in a hypothetical judgment. The concept of cause accordingly is a pure concept of the understanding, which is totally disparate from all possible perception, and only serves to determine the representation subsumed under it, relatively to judgments in general, and so to make a universally valid judgment possible.

Before, therefore, a judgment of perception can become a judgment of experience, it is requisite that the perception should be subsumed under some such a concept of the understanding; for instance, air ranks under the concept of causes, which determines our judgment about it in regard to its expansion as hypothetical.[3] Thereby the expansion of the air is represented not as merely belonging to the perception of the air in my present state or in several states of mine, or in the state of perception of others, but as belonging to it necessarily. The judgment, "the air is elastic," becomes universally valid, and a judgment of experience, only by certain judgments preceding it, which subsume the intuition of air under the concept of cause and effect: and they thereby determine the perceptions not merely as regards one another in me, but relatively to the form of judging in general, which is here hypothetical, and in this way they render the empirical judgment universally valid.

If all our synthetical judgments are analysed so far as they are objectively valid, it will be found that they never consist of mere intuitions connected only (as is commonly believed) by comparison into a judgment; but that they would be impossible were not a pure concept of the understanding superadded to the concepts abstracted from intuition, under which concept these latter are subsumed, and in this manner only combined into an objectively valid judgment. Even the judgments of pure mathematics in their simplest axioms are not exempt from this condition. The principle, "a straight line is the shortest between two points," presupposes that the line is subsumed under the concept of quantity, which certainly is no mere intuition, but has its seat in the understanding alone, and serves to determine the intuition (of the line) with regard to the judgments which may be made about it, relatively to their quantity, that is, to plurality (as *judicia plurativa*).[4] For under them it is understood that in a given intuition there is contained a plurality of homogenous parts.

21. To prove, then, the possibility of experience so far as it rests upon pure concepts of the understanding *a priori*, we must first represent what belongs to judgments in general and the various functions of the understanding, in a complete table. For the pure concepts of the understanding must run parallel to these functions, as such concepts are nothing more than concepts of intuitions in general, so far as these are determined by one or other of these functions of judging, in themselves, that is, necessarily and universally. Hereby also the *a priori* principles of the possibility of all expe-

rience, as of an objectively valid empirical cognition, will be precisely determined. For they are nothing but propositions by which all perception is (under certain universal conditions of intuition) subsumed under those pure concepts of the understanding.

21a. In order to comprise the whole matter in one idea, it is first necessary to remind the reader that we are discussing not the origin of experience, but of that which lies in experience. The former pertains to empirical psychology, and would even then never be adequately explained without the latter, which belongs to the Critique of cognition, and particularly of the understanding.

Experience consists of intuitions, which belong to the sensibility, and of judgments, which are entirely a work of the understanding. But the judgments, which the understanding forms alone from sensuous intuitions, are far from being judgments of experience. For in the one case the judgment connects only the perceptions as they are given in the sensuous intuition while in the other the judgments must express what experience in general, and not what the mere perception (which possesses only subjective validity) contains. The judgment of experience must therefore add to the sensuous intuition and its logical connexion in a judgment (after it has been rendered universal by comparison) something that determines the synthetical judgment as necessary and therefore as universally valid. This can be nothing else than that concept which represents the intuition as determined in itself with regard to one form of judgment rather than another, viz., a concept of that synthetical unity of intuitions which can only be represented by a given logical function of judgments.

22. The sum of the matter is this: the business of the senses is to intuit—that of the understanding is to think. But thinking is uniting representations in one consciousness. This union originates either merely relative to the subject, and is accidental and subjective, or is absolute, and is necessary or objective. The union of representations in one consciousness is judgment. Thinking therefore is the same as judging, or referring representations to judgments in general. Hence judgments are either merely subjective, when representations are re-

LOGICAL TABLE OF JUDGMENTS

1	2
As to Quantity	*As to Quality*
Universal	Affirmative
Particular	Negative
Singular	Infinite
3	**4**
As to Relation	*As to Modality*
Categorical	Problematical
Hypothetical	Assertorical
Disjunctive	Apodeictical

TRANSCENDENTAL TABLE OF THE PURE CONCEPTS OF THE UNDERSTANDING

1	2
As to Quantity	*As to Quality*
Unity (the Measure)	Reality
Plurality (the Quantity)	Negation
Totality (the Whole)	Limitation
3	**4**
As to Relation	*As to Modality*
Substance	Possibility
Cause	Existence
Community	Necessity

PURE PHYSIOLOGICAL TABLE OF THE UNIVERSAL PRINCIPLES OF THE SCIENCE OF NATURE

1	2
Axioms of Intuition	Anticipations of Perception
3	**4**
Analogies of Experience	Postulates of Empirical Thinking Generally

ferred to a consciousness in one subject only, and united in it, or objective, when they are united in a consciousness generally, that is, necessarily. The logical functions of all judgments are but various modes of uniting representations in consciousness. But if they serve for concepts, they are concepts of their necessary union in a consciousness, and so principles of objectively valid judgments. This union in a consciousness is either analytical by identity, or synthetical, by the combination and addition of various representations one to another. Experience consists in the synthetical connexion of phenomena (perceptions) in consciousness, so far as this connexion is necessary. Hence the pure concepts of the understanding are those under which all perceptions must be subsumed ere they can serve for judgments of experience, in which the synthetical unity of the perceptions is represented as necessary and universally valid.[5]

23. Judgments, when considered merely as the condition of the union of given representations in a consciousness, are rules. These rules, so far as they represent the union as necessary, are rules *a priori*, and so far as they cannot be deduced from higher rules, are fundamental principles. But in regard to the possibility of all experience, merely in relation to the form of thinking in it, no conditions of judgments of experience are higher than those which bring the phenomena, according to the various form of their intuition, under pure concepts of the understanding, and render the empirical judgment objectively valid. These concepts are therefore the *a priori* principles of possible experience.

The principles of possible experience are then at the same time universal laws of nature, which can be cognised *a priori*. And thus the problem in our second question, "How is the pure Science of Nature possible?" is solved. For the system which is required for the form of a science is to be met with in perfection here, because, beyond the above-mentioned formal conditions of all judgments in general offered in logic, no others are possible, and these constitute a logical system. The concepts grounded thereupon, which contain the *a priori* conditions of all synthetical and necessary judgments, accordingly constitute a transcendental system. Finally the principles, by means of which all phenomena are subsumed under these concepts, constitute a physical system, that is, a system of nature, which precedes all empirical cognition of nature, makes it even possible, and hence may in strictness be denominated the universal and pure science of nature.

24. The first one [6] of the physiological principles subsumes all phenomena, as intuitions in space and time, under the concept of Quantity, and is so far a principle of the application of Mathematics to experience. The second one subsumes the empirical element, viz., sensation, which denotes the real in intuitions, not indeed directly under the concept of quantity, because sensation is not an intuition that contains either space or time, though it places the respective object into both. But still there is between reality (sense-representation) and the zero, or total void of intuition in time, a difference which has a quantity. For between every given degree of light and of darkness, between every degree of heat and of absolute cold, between every degree of weight and of absolute lightness, between every degree of occupied space and of totally void space, diminishing degrees can be conceived, in the same manner as between consciousness and total unconsciousness (the darkness of a psychological blank) ever diminishing degrees obtain. Hence there is no perception that can prove an absolute absence of it; for instance, no psychological darkness that cannot be considered as a kind of consciousness, which is only outbalanced by a stronger consciousness. This occurs in all cases of sensation, and so the understanding can anticipate even sensations, which constitute the peculiar quality of empirical representations (appearances), by means of the principle: "that they all have (consequently that what is real in all phenomena has) a degree." Here is the second application of mathematics *(mathesis intensorum)* to the science of nature.

25. Anent the relation of appearances merely with a view to their existence, the determination is not mathematical but dynamical, and can never be objectively valid, consequently never fit for experience, if it does not come under *a priori* principles by which the cognition of experience relative to appearances becomes even possible. Hence appearances must be subsumed under the concept of Substance, which is the foundation of all determination of existence, as a concept of the thing itself; or secondly—so far as a succession is found among phenomena, that is, an event—under the concept of an Effect with reference to Cause; or lastly—so far as coexistence is to be known objectively, that is, by a judgment of experience—under the concept of Community (action and reaction). Thus *a priori* principles form the basis of objectively valid, though empirical judgments, that is, of the possibility of

experience so far as it must connect objects as existing in nature. These principles are the proper laws of nature, which may be termed dynamical.

Finally the cognition of the agreement and connexion not only of appearances among themselves in experience, but of their relation to experience in general, belongs to the judgments of experience. This relation contains either their agreement with the formal conditions, which the understanding cognises, or their coherence with the materials of the senses and of perception, or combines both into one concept. Consequently it contains Possibility, Actuality, and Necessity according to universal laws of nature; and this constitutes the physical doctrine of method, or the distinction of truth and of hypotheses, and the bounds of the certainty of the latter.

26. The third table of Principles drawn from the nature of the understanding itself after the critical method, shows an inherent perfection, which raises it far above every other table which has hitherto though in vain been tried or may yet be tried by analysing the objects themselves dogmatically. It exhibits all synthetical *a priori* principles completely and according to one principle, viz., the faculty of judging in general, constituting the essence of experience as regards the understanding, so that we can be certain that there are no more such principles, which affords a satisfaction such as can never be attained by the dogmatical method. Yet is this not all: there is a still greater merit in it.

We must carefully bear in mind the proof which shows the possibility of this cognition *a priori*, and at the same time limits all such principles to a condition which must never be lost sight of, if we desire it not to be misunderstood, and extended in use beyond the original sense which the understanding attaches to it. This limit is that they contain nothing but the conditions of possible experience in general so far as it is subjected to laws *a priori*. Consequently I do not say, that things *in themselves* possess a quantity, that their actuality possesses a degree, their existence a connexion of accidents in a substance, etc. This nobody can prove, because such a synthetical connexion from mere concepts, without any reference to sensuous intuition on the one side, or con-

nexion of it in a possible experience on the other, is absolutely impossible. The essential limitation of the concepts in these principles then is: That all things stand necessarily *a priori* under the afore-mentioned conditions, as objects of experience only.

. . . .

32. Since the oldest days of philosophy inquirers into pure reason have conceived, besides the things of sense, or appearances (phenomena), which make up the sensible world, certain creations of the understanding (*Verstandeswesen*), called noumena, which should constitute an intelligible world. And as appearance and illusion were by those men identified (a thing which we may well excuse in an undeveloped epoch), actuality was only conceded to the creations of thought.

And we indeed, rightly considering objects of sense as mere appearances, confess thereby that they are based upon a thing in itself, though we know not this thing in its internal constitution, but only know its appearances, viz., the way in which our senses are affected by this unknown something. The understanding therefore, by assuming appearances, grants the existence of things in themselves also, and so far we may say, that the representation of such things as form the basis of phenomena, consequently of mere creations of the understanding, is not only admissible, but unavoidable.

Our critical deduction by no means excludes things of that sort (noumena), but rather limits the principles of the Aesthetic (the science of the sensibility) to this, that they shall not extend to all things, as everything would then be turned into mere appearance, but that they shall only hold good of objects of possible experience. Hereby then objects of the understanding are granted, but with the inculcation of this rule which admits of no exception: "that we neither know nor can know anything at all definite of these pure objects of the understanding, because our pure concepts of the understanding as well as our pure intuitions extend to nothing but objects of possible experience, consequently to mere things of sense, and as soon as we leave this sphere these concepts retain no meaning whatever."

33. There is indeed something seductive in

our pure concepts of the understanding, which tempts us to a transcendent use,—a use which transcends all possible experience. Not only are our concepts of substance, of power, of action, of reality, and others, quite independent of experience, containing nothing of sense appearance, and so apparently applicable to things in themselves (noumena), but, what strengthens this conjecture, they contain a necessity of determination in themselves, which experience never attains. The concept of cause implies a rule, according to which one state follows another necessarily; but experience can only show us, that one state of things often, or at most, commonly, follows another, and therefore affords neither strict universality, nor necessity.

Hence the Categories seem to have a deeper meaning and import than can be exhausted by their empirical use, and so the understanding inadvertently adds for itself to the house of experience a much more extensive wing, which it fills with nothing but creatures of thought, without ever observing that it has transgressed with its otherwise lawful concepts the bounds of their use.

34. Two important, and even indispensable though very dry, investigations had therefore become indispensable in the Critique of Pure Reason,—viz., the two chapters "Vom Schematismus der reinen Verstandsbegriffe," and "Vom Grunde der Unterscheidung ailer Verstandesbegriffe überhaupt in Phänomena und Noumena." In the former it is shown, that the senses furnish not the pure concepts of the understanding *in concreto*, but only the schedule for their use, and that the object conformable to it occurs only in experience (as the product of the understanding from materials of the sensibility). In the latter it is shown, that, although our pure concepts of the understanding and our principles are independent of experience, and despite of the apparently greater sphere of their use, still nothing whatever can be thought by them beyond the field of experience, because they can do nothing but merely determine the logical form of the judgment relatively to given intuitions. But as there is no intuition at all beyond the field of the sensibility, these pure concepts, as they cannot possibly be exhibited *in concreto*, are void of all meaning; conse-

quently all these noumena, together with their complex, the intelligible world,[7] are nothing but representation of a problem, of which the object in itself is possible, but the solution, from the nature of our understanding, totally impossible. For our understanding is not a faculty of intuition, but of the connexion of given intuitions in experience. Experience must therefore contain all the objects for our concepts; but beyond it no concepts have any significance, as there is no intuition that might offer them a foundation.

35. The imagination may perhaps be forgiven for occasional vagaries, and for not keeping carefully within the limits of experience, since it gains life and vigor by such flights, and since it is always easier to moderate its boldness, than to stimulate its languor. But the understanding which ought to *think* can never be forgiven for indulging in vagaries; for we depend upon it alone for assistance to set bounds, when necessary, to the vagaries of the imagination.

But the understanding begins its aberrations very innocently and modestly. It first elucidates the elementary cognitions, which inhere in it prior to all experience, but yet must always have their application in experience. It gradually drops these limits, and what is there to prevent it, as it has quite freely derived its principles from itself? And then it proceeds first to newly-imagined powers in nature, then to beings outside nature; in short to a world, for whose construction the materials cannot be wanting, because fertile fiction furnishes them abundantly, and though not confirmed, is never refuted, by experience. This is the reason that young thinkers are so partial to metaphysics of the truly dogmatical kind, and often sacrifice to it their time and their talents, which might be otherwise better employed.

But there is no use in trying to moderate these fruitless endeavors of pure reason by all manner of cautions as to the difficulties of solving questions so occult, by complaints of the limits of our reason, and by degrading our assertions into mere conjectures. For if their impossibility is not distinctly shown, and reason's cognition of its own essence does not become a true science, in which the field of its right use is distinguished, so to say, with mathematical certainty from that of its worthless and idle use, these fruitless efforts will never be abandoned for good.

NOTES

1. It is unavoidable that as knowledge advances, certain expressions which have become classical, after having been used since the infancy of science, will be found inadequate and unsuitable, and a newer and more appropriate application of the terms will give rise to confusion. [This is the case with the term "analytical."] The analytical method, so far as it is opposed to the synthetical, is very different from that which constitutes the essence of analytical propositions: it signifies only that we start from what is sought, as if it were given, and ascend to the only conditions under which it is possible. In this method we often use nothing but synthetical propositions, as in mathematical analysis, and it were better to term it the regressive method, in contradistinction to the synthetic or progressive. A principle part of Logic too is distinguished by the name of Analytics, which here signifies the logic of truth in contrast to Dialectics, without considering whether the cognitions belonging to it are analytical or synthetical.

2. I freely grant that these examples do not represent such judgments of perception as ever could become judgments of experience, even though a concept of the understanding were superadded, because they refer merely to feeling, which everybody knows to be merely subjective, and which of course can never be attributed to the object, and consequently never become objective. I only wished to give here an example of a judgment that is merely subjectively valid, containing no ground for universal validity, and thereby for a relation to the object. An example of the judgments of perception, which become judgments of experience by superadded concepts of the understanding, will be given in the next note.

3. As an easier example, we may take the following: "When the sun shines on the stone, it grows warm." This judgment, however often I and others may have perceived it, is a mere judgment of perception, and contains no necessity; perceptions are only usually conjoined in this manner. But if I say, "The sun warms the stone," I add to the perception a concept of the understanding, viz., that of cause, which con-

nects with the concept of sunshine that of heat as a necessary consequence, and the synthetical judgment becomes of necessity universally valid, viz., objective, and is converted from a perception into experience.

4. This name seems preferable to the term *particularia*, which is used for these judgments in logic. For the latter implies the idea that they are not universal. But when I start from unity (in single judgments) and so proceed to universality, I must not [even indirectly and negatively] imply any reference to universality. I think plurality merely without universality, and not the exception from universality. This is necessary, if logical considerations shall form the basis of the pure concepts of the understanding. However, there is no need of making changes in logic.

5. But how does this proposition, "that judgments of experience contain necessity in the synthesis of perceptions," agree with my statement so often before inculcated, that "experience as cognition *a posteriori* can afford contingent judgments only"? When I say that experience teaches me something, I mean only the perception that lies in experience—for example, that heat always follows the shining of the sun is contained indeed in the judgment of experience (by means of the concept of cause), yet is a fact not learned by experience; for conversely, experience is first of all generated by this addition of the concept of the understanding (of cause) to perception. How perception attains this addition may be seen by referring in the *Critique* itself to the section on the Transcendental faculty of Judgment [viz., in the first, *Von dem Schematismus der reinen Verstandsbefriffe*].

6. The three following paragraphs will hardly be understood unless reference be made to what the *Critique* itself says on the subject of the Principles; they will, however, be of service in giving a general view of the Principles, and in fixing the attention on the main points.

7. We speak of the "intelligible world," not (as the usual expression is) "intellectual world." For cognitions are intellectual through the understanding, and refer to our world of sense also; but objects, so far as they can be represented merely by the understanding, and to which none of our sensible intuitions can refer, are termed "intelligible." But as some possible intuition must correspond to every object, we would have to assume an understanding that intuites things immediately; but of such we have not the least notion, nor have we of the *things of the understanding [Verstandeswesen]*, to which it should be applied.

EARLY MODERN SOURCES: BIBLIOGRAPHY

General

Bennett, J. *Locke, Berkeley, Hume: Central Themes.* Oxford, 1971.

Collins, J. *British Empiricists: Locke, Berkeley, Hume.* New York, 1967.

Popkin, R. H. *The History of Skepticism from Erasmus to Spinoza.* Berkeley, Calif., 1979.

Schacht, R. *Classical Modern Philosophers: Descartes to Kant.* London, 1984.

Yolton, J. W. *Perceptual Acquaintance from Descartes to Reid.* Oxford, 1984.

Descartes

Cottingham, J. *Cambridge Companion to Descartes.* Cambridge, Eng., 1992.

Doney, W., ed. *Descartes: A Collection of Critical Essays.* New York, 1967.

Frankfurt, H. *Demons, Dreamers, and Madmen: The Defense of Reason in Descartes's "Meditations."* Indianapolis, Ind., 1970.

Garber, D. *Descartes's Metaphysical Physics.* Chicago, 1992.

Gaukroger, S. *Cartesian Logic: An Essay on Descartes's Conception of Inference.* Oxford, 1989.

Hooker, M., ed. *Descartes: Critical and Interpretive Essays.* Baltimore, 1978.

Kenny, A. *Descartes: A Study of His Philosophy.* New York, 1968.

Schouls, P. *The Imposition of Method: A Study of Descartes and Locke.* Oxford, 1980.

Sesonke, A. and N. Fleming, eds. *Meta-Meditations: Studies in Descartes.* Belmont, Calif., 1965.

Sorell, T. *Descartes.* Oxford, 1987.

Van Cleve, J. "Foundationalism, Epistemic Principles, and the Cartesian Circle." *The Philosophical Review* 88 (1979): 55–91.

Voss, S., ed. *Essays on the Philosophy and Science of Rene Descartes.* Oxford, 1993.

Williams, B. *Descartes: The Project of Pure Enquiry.* Harmondsworth, Eng., 1978.

Wilson, M. *Descartes.* London, 1978.

Leibniz

Broad, C. D. *Leibniz.* Cambridge, Eng., 1975.

Frankfurt, H., ed. *Leibniz: A Collection of Critical Essays.* New York, 1972.

Hooker, M., ed. *Leibniz: Critical and Interpretive Essays.* Minneapolis, 1982.

Ishiguro, H. *Leibniz's Philosophy of Logic and Language.* Cambridge, Eng., 1990.

Jolley, N. *Leibniz and Locke: A Study of the New Essays on Human Understanding.* Oxford, 1984.

———. *The Light of the Soul: Theories of Ideas in Leibniz, Malebranche, and Descartes.* Oxford, 1990.

Mates, B. *The Philosophy of Leibniz.* Oxford, 1986.

Parkinson, G. H. *Logic and Reality in Leibniz's Metaphysics.* Oxford, 1965.

Rescher, N. *The Philosophy of Leibniz.* Totowa, N.J., 1979.

Russell, B. *A Critical Exposition of the Philosophy of Leibniz.* Cambridge, Eng., 1900.

Locke

Ayers, M. *Locke.* London, 1991.

Bennett, J. *Locke, Berkeley, Hume.* Oxford, 1971.

Dunn, J. *Locke.* Oxford, 1984.

Gibson, J. *Locke's Theory of Knowledge and Its Historical Relations.* Cambridge, Eng., 1960.

Mackie, I. L. *Problems from Locke.* Oxford, 1976.

Mandelbaum, M. "Locke's Realism." In *Philosophy, Science, and Sense Perception.* Baltimore, 1964.

Martin, C. B., and D. M. Armstrong, eds. *Locke and Berkeley: A Collection of Critical Essays.* New York, 1968.

O'Connor, D. J. *John Locke.* London, 1952.

Schouls, P. *The Imposition of Method: A Study of Descartes and Locke.* Oxford, 1980.

Tipton, I. C., ed. *Locke on Human Understanding.* Oxford, 1977.

Woolhouse, R. S. *Locke.* Minneapolis, 1985.

Yolton, J. *John Locke and the Way of Ideas.* Oxford, 1956.

———. *Locke and the Compass of Human Understanding.* Cambridge, Eng., 1970.

———, ed. *John Locke: Problems and Perspectives.* Cambridge, Eng., 1969.

Berkeley

Bennett, J. *Locke, Berkeley, Hume.* Oxford, 1971.

Engle, G. W. and G. Taylor, eds. *Berkeley's Prin-*

ciples of Human Knowledge: Critical Studies. Belmont, Calif., 1968.

Luce, A. A. *Berkeley's Immaterialism.* New York, 1945.

Martin, C. B., and D. M. Armstrong, eds. *Locke and Berkeley: A Collection of Critical Essays.* New York, 1968.

Pitcher, G. *Berkeley.* London, 1977.

Tipton, I. C. *Berkeley: The Philosophy of Immaterialism.* London, 1974.

Turbayne, C. M., ed. *Berkeley: Critical and Interpretive Essays.* Minneapolis, 1982.

Warnock, G. J. *Berkeley.* Baltimore, 1953.

Hume

Ayer, A. J. *Hume.* New York, 1980.

Bennett, J. *Locke, Berkeley, Hume.* Oxford, 1971.

Chappell, V. C., ed. *Hume: A Collection of Critical Essays.* New York, 1966.

Flew, A. *Hume's Philosophy of Belief.* London, 1961.

Fogelin, R. J. *Hume's Skepticism in the Treatise of Human Nature.* London, 1985.

Livingston, D. W., and J. T. King, eds. *Hume: A Re-evaluation.* New York, 1976.

Pears, D., ed. *David Hume: A Symposium.* London, 1963.

Pears, D. *Hume's System: An Examination of the First Book of His Treatise.* Oxford, 1990.

Penelhum, T. *Hume.* London, 1975.

Stove, D. C. *Probability and Hume's Inductive Scepticism.* Oxford, 1973.

Strawson, G. *The Secret Connexion: Causation, Realism, and David Hume.* Oxford, 1989.

Stroud, B. *Hume.* London, 1977.

Reid

Gallie, R. *Thomas Reid and "the Way of Ideas".* Boston, 1989.

Lehrer, K. *Thomas Reid.* London, 1989.

Wolterstorff, N. *Thomas Reid and the Story of Epistemology.* New York, 2001.

Kant

Allison, H. *Kant's Transcendental Idealism.* New Haven, Conn., 1983.

Beck, L. W., ed. *Kant Studies Today.* La Salle, Ill., 1969.

————, ed. *Kant's Theory of Knowledge.* Dordrecht, 1974.

Bennett, J. *Kant's Analytic.* Cambridge, Eng., 1966.

————. *Kant's Dialectic.* Cambridge, Eng., 1974.

Bird, G. *Kant's Theory of Knowledge.* London, 1962.

Buchdahl, G. *Kant and the Dynamics of Reason.* Oxford, 1992.

Dryer, D. P. *Kant's Solution for Verification in Metaphysics.* London, 1966.

Guyer, P. *Kant and the Claims of Knowledge.* Cambridge, Eng., 1987.

————, ed. *Cambridge Companion to Kant.* Cambridge, Eng., 1992.

Kant, I. *Critique of Pure Reason,* trans. N. K. Smith. New York, 1965.

Körner, S. *Kant.* Baltimore, 1955.

Mohanty, J. N., and R. W. Shahan, eds. *Essays on Kant's Critique of Pure Reason.* Norman, Okla., 1982.

Paton, H. J. *Kant's Metaphysics of Experience.* London, 1936.

Smith, N. Kemp. *A Commentary to Kant's "Critique of Pure Reason."* London, 1929.

Strawson, P. F. *The Bounds of Sense.* London, 1966.

Walker, R. C. *Kant.* London, 1978.

————, ed. *Kant on Pure Reason.* Oxford, 1982.

Weldon, T. D. *Kant's Critique of Pure Reason.* Oxford, 1958.

Wolff, R. P. *Kant's Theory of Mental Activity.* Cambridge, Mass., 1963.

————, ed. *Kant: A Collection of Critical Essays.* New York, 1967.

PART II
CONTEMPORARY
SOURCES

Pragmatism and Empiricism

Twentieth-century Anglo-American epistemology began with the critical reaction of Bertrand Russell and G. E. Moore to Kantian and Hegelian idealism at Oxford and Cambridge. In *My Philosophical Development* (London, 1959), Russell comments as follows:

> It was towards the end of 1898 that Moore and I rebelled against both Kant and Hegel. Moore led the way, but I followed closely in his footsteps. I think that the first published account of the new philosophy was Moore's article in *Mind* [1899] on "The Nature of Judgment." Although neither he nor I would now adhere to all the doctrines in this article, I, and I think he, would still agree with its negative part, i.e., with the doctrine that fact is in general independent of experience. (p. 42)

Following Moore, Russell opposed the kind of idealism entailing that "there can be nothing which is not experienced or experience" (p. 107). Russell and Moore were *realists* about facts, owing to their view that facts are generally independent of experience and other mental activity.

In opposing idealism, Russell and Moore claimed to have *knowledge* of mind-independent facts. Their claim to such knowledge rested on *empiricism*: the view that the empirical evidence of the senses—for example, visual, auditory, tactile, or gustatory experiences—is a crucial sort of evidence appropriate to genuine knowledge. Russell's empiricism is more explicit than Moore's. In *The Problems of Philosophy* (London, 1912), Russell claims:

> Nothing can be known to *exist* except by the help of experience. That is to say, if we wish to prove that something of which we have no direct experience exists, we must have among our premises the existence of one or more things of which we have direct experience. Our belief that the Emperor of China exists, for example, rests upon testimony, and testimony consists, in the last analysis, of sense-data seen or heard in reading or being spoken to. (pp. 74–75)

Russell sides with such empiricists as Locke, Berkeley, and Hume against the rationalist view that a priori knowledge—knowledge independent of specific experience—can yield knowledge of what actually exists. Russell sides with such rationalists as Descartes and Leibniz, however, on the point that logical principles—whether deductive or inductive—are not known on the basis of support from experience. All support from experience, Russell claims, *presupposes* logical principles. Russell does allow, nonetheless, that our knowledge of logical principles is elicited or caused by experience. He thus permits a distinction between the warrant and the cause of a belief. Russell claims, in *The Problems of Philosophy,* that "all knowledge which asserts existence is empirical, and the only a priori knowledge concerning existence is hypothetical, giving connexions among things that exist or may exist, but not giving actual existence" (p. 75). Russell's empiricism is thus moderate, allowing for some a priori knowledge.

The selections in this section represent empiricism of one species or another. The selections by James, Lewis, and Carnap represent combinations of empiricism and pragmatism, the latter view maintaining that considerations about purpose satisfaction figure importantly in knowledge or at least rational belief.

The empiricism of Russell was taken to an extreme by various logical positivists, originally represented in the early 1920s by the group of philosophers, logicians, mathematicians, and scientists who called themselves "the Vienna Circle." The members of the circle, including Rudolf Carnap and A. J. Ayer, shared an interest in certain philosophical and scientific problems, and favored an approach to these problems that was analytical, scientific, and antimetaphysical. They aimed to use modern logic (deriving from Frege and Russell) and various analytical techniques to restrict philosophical pursuits to the advancement of "scientific" knowledge, thereby banishing metaphysical concerns from philosophy.

Ludwig Wittgenstein influenced the philosophical views of the Vienna Circle. In his *Tractatus Logico-Philosophicus* (1921), Wittgenstein enunciated the following doctrines attractive to the antimetaphysical members of the circle:

4.11 The totality of true propositions is the whole of natural sciences (or the whole corpus of the natural sciences).
4.112 Philosophy aims at the logical clarification of thoughts. Philosophy is not a body of doctrine but an activity. . . . Philosophy does not result in "philosophical propositions" but rather in the clarification of propositions.
6.53 The correct method in philosophy would really be the following: to say nothing except what can be said, i.e., propositions of natural science—i.e., something that has nothing to do with philosophy—and then, whenever someone else wanted to say something metaphysical, to demonstrate to him that he had failed to give a meaning to certain signs in his propositions. . . .

The members of the circle focused—typically with favor—on such antimetaphysical theses of the *Tractatus,* rather than on its avowed mysticism: "6.522. There are, indeed, things that cannot be put into words. They *make themselves manifest.* They are what is mystical." The circle also welcomed Wittgenstein's view that knowledge of logical propositions is not a special kind of metaphysical knowledge about the world. Wittgenstein proposed the following: "The propositions of logic are tautologies. . . . Therefore the propositions of logic say nothing. (They are the analytic propositions.)" (6.1–6.11).

The defining tenet of logical positivism is a principle of verification regarding meaning and understanding—a principle not found in the *Tractatus* itself. The *Tractatus* had endorsed the following view of understanding: "4.024. To understand a proposition means to know what is the case if it is true. (One can understand it, therefore, without knowing whether it is true.)" By the late 1920s, however, Wittgenstein was endorsing a verification principle regarding meaning and understanding. In late 1929 Wittgenstein claimed:

. . . if I can never verify the sense of a proposition completely, then I cannot have meant anything by the proposition either. Then the proposition signifies nothing whatever. In order to determine the sense of a proposition, I should have to know a very specific procedure for when to count the proposition as verified. (*Wittgenstein and the Vienna Circle,* ed. B. F. McGuinness (Oxford, 1979), p. 47)

A characterization of meaning and understanding in terms of verification and justification surfaces in some of Wittgenstein's works in the late 1920s and early 1930s. In his *Philosophical Remarks* (ca. 1930), Wittgenstein states that "to understand the sense of a proposition means to know how the issue of its truth or falsity is to be decided" (p. 77). In his *Philosophical Grammar* (ca. 1933), Wittgenstein remarks that "it is what is regarded as the justification of an assertion that constitutes the sense of the assertion" (I, sec. 40).

In the early 1930s a number of logical positivists endorsed a principle of verification regarding meaning. We can put the verification principle succinctly: The meaning of a proposition is its method of verification. The Vienna Circle construed the relevant method of verification as a method of justification, or confirmation, in terms of *observable* events or situations. They thus held that every meaningful claim could be expressed in terms of observational claims, that is, claims susceptible to confirmation or disconfirmation on the basis of observation.

The main problems facing logical positivism concern the status of the verification principle. One problem is that some meaningful claims seem not to admit of a "method of verification." Consider, for example, the claim that an omnipotent being exists: a being sufficiently powerful to accomplish anything that can be coherently described. Presumably we understand this claim, but we have no method of confirmation or disconfirmation for it. We lack a method of verification, but the claim in question still seems meaningful—at least by ordinary standards. If we weaken conditions for verification, to allow for the desired method, we shall disable the principle of verification from excluding metaphysical claims as meaningless.

Does the principle of verification itself admit of a method of verification resting on observational evidence? This seems doubtful. Our observational evidence deriving from sensory experience fails to provide a straightforward method of verification for the verification principle itself. Perhaps, then, the verification principle is meaningless by its own standard for meaningfulness. In his anthology *Logical Positivism* (New York, 1959), A. J. Ayer treats this self-referential difficulty as follows:

> The Vienna Circle tended to ignore this difficulty: but it seems to me fairly clear that what they were in fact doing was to adopt the verification principle as a convention. They were propounding a definition of meaning which accorded with common usage in the sense that it set out the conditions that are in fact satisfied by statements which are regarded as empirically informative. Their treatment of *a priori* statements was also intended to provide an account of the way in which statements actually function. To this extent their work was descriptive; it became prescriptive with the suggestion that only statements of these two kinds should be regarded as either true or false, and that only statements which were capable of being either true or false should be regarded as literally meaningful. (p. 15)

Carnap had also suggested that the verification principle was a "convention" resting on a choice about how to use certain language.

The role of convention in the epistemology of the Vienna Circle led to a kind of pragmatism—an emphasis on purpose-relative considerations in epistemology. This is understandable because questions about which linguistic conventions to adopt are naturally understood as questions about which conventions best serve one's linguistic and theoretical purposes. The pragmatism in question also appears in such classical American philosophers as William James and C. I. Lewis.

James expounded pragmatism regarding truth and rational belief. He offered his pragmatic account of truth as capturing "the meaning" of "truth." In a chapter of *Pragmatism* (New York, 1907) titled "Pragmatism's Conception of Truth," James writes:

> True ideas are those that we can assimilate, validate, corroborate, and verify. . . . That is the practical difference it makes to us to have true ideas; that, therefore, is the meaning of truth, for it is all that truth is known as. (p. 97)

Some philosophers have objected that James simply confuses what it is for a claim to be *true* and what it is for a claim to be *verified*. These philosophers typically cite cases where a claim is true but not verifiable. Consider, for example, the status of the claim that the Earth is round before this could be verified.

James is unmoved. In a 1904 essay, "A World of Pure Experience," James invokes his "pragmatic method":

> When a dispute arises, that ["pragmatic"] method consists in auguring what practical consequences would be different if one side rather than the other were true. If no difference can be

thought of, the dispute is a quarrel over words. What then would the self-transcendency [of true ideas] affirmed to exist in advance of all experiential mediation or termination, be *known as*? What would it practically result in for *us*, were it true?

Given this pragmatic method, James infers that a dispute over the nature of truth (e.g., whether truth is independent of verification) is an empty verbal matter if unaccompanied by a difference in practical consequences.

In "The Will to Believe," James examines the role of volition in human belief-formation, arguing that our "passional tendencies and volitions" do influence our beliefs and that this is unobjectionable in certain cases. James's thesis is: "Our passional nature not only lawfully may, but must, decide an option between propositions, whenever it is a genuine option that cannot by its nature be decided on intellectual grounds; for to say, under such circumstances, "Do not decide, but leave the question open," is itself a passional decision—just like deciding yes or no—and is attended with the same risk of losing the truth. James notes that "Acquire truth!" and "Avoid error!" are two different commands for would-be knowers, and that choosing between them can substantially determine one's strategy for belief formation. Strict commitment to the avoidance of error, for instance, may result in one's not taking any risk to acquire truth. James claims that one's views about our duty concerning the acquisition of truth or the avoidance of error are expressions of one's "passional life."

James acknowledges a "right" or a "freedom" to believe with regard to "living options" that one's intellect cannot resolve by itself. Applying this "right" to the question of God's existence, James asserts: "When I look at the religious question as it really puts itself to concrete men . . . then [the] command that we shall put a stopper on our heart, instincts, and courage, and *wait*—this command . . . seems to me the queerest idol ever manufactured in the philosophic cave." James evidently intends his point to be general, applying to any "living option" that intellectual considerations cannot resolve by themselves. James's emphasis on volitional factors in acceptable belief formation is characteristic of certain species of pragmatism. His principle of the "freedom" (or "will") to believe" represents a distinctive kind of pragmatism about acceptable belief.

The selection by Bertrand Russell, "Appearance, Reality, and Knowledge by Acquaintance," introduces the epistemologically important distinction between "appearance" and "reality," between how things appear to be and how they really are. Russell contends that we have immediate sensory knowledge only of "sense-data," such things as colors, sounds, smells, and textures. He denies that we have immediate knowledge of actual physical objects, but raises the troublesome question of the relation between sense-data and physical objects. Russell explores this question in connection with the views of Berkeley and Leibniz, and expresses doubt about the effectiveness of philosophy in providing a defensible answer.

Russell regarded sense-data as the epistemological basis of all our knowledge of the external world, and as something known by "acquaintance." Russell distinguishes between knowledge *by acquaintance* and knowledge *by description*, and between knowledge of things and knowledge of true propositions. Knowledge of things can be either knowledge of things by acquaintance or knowledge of things by description. Knowledge by description requires knowledge of a true proposition—knowledge *that* something is the case. Knowledge by acquaintance, in contrast, consists of direct nonpropositional awareness of something, not of knowledge of truths.

In his 1911 essay "Knowledge by Acquaintance and Knowledge by Description," Russell states that "to say that S has acquaintance with O is essentially the same thing as to say that O is presented to S." Russell would say that you are acquainted with the color of these printed words as you read them. Such acquaintance, Russell held, underlies all of our empirical knowledge. In the selection reprinted here, Russell acknowledges acquaintance with such universals, or general ideas, as whiteness and diversity, and he endorses the following principle about understanding: "Every proposition which we can understand must be composed wholly of constituents with which we are acquainted."

After 1918 Russell abandoned sense-data as the objects of cognition, and sensations as a special kind of cognition. He came to reject the view that in visual color experience, for example, there is a *subject* related via awareness to a patch of color. Russell claimed that the subject is a "logical fiction," much like mathematical points and instants. Having rejected the subject as an actually existing thing, Russell also rejected a distinction between sensations and sense-data. The sensation of a patch of color is, on this view, no different from the patch of color. Such sensation thus does not qualify as a kind of knowledge. Much of Russell's epistemological work after 1918 seeks an explanation of awareness, acquaintance, and empirical evidence without appeal to sense-data—and often with help from John Watson's behaviorism about psychological phenomena.

In "Verification and Philosophy," A. J. Ayer represents the logical positivism inspired by the Vienna Circle. He offers the principle of verification as a criterion for meaningful propositions, as a criterion for determining when an indicative sentence expresses a proposition. Ayer proposes that a statement expressed by a sentence is literally meaningful if and only if it is either analytic or empirically verifiable. He offers a distinction between strong and weak verifiability in order to permit that meaning can derive from probabilistic support from experience. Ayer holds, nonetheless, that some empirical propositions can be strongly, or conclusively, verified by experience; these are "basic" propositions that refer only to the sensory content of a single experience and that can be mistaken only in a verbal sense.

Ayer illustrates that his original principle of verification is vague and that its vagueness makes it too liberal for the antimetaphysical purposes of logical positivism. He proposes, however, that a principle of verification can serve as a criterion for literal meaning, the kind of meaning possessed only by something that is true or false. Ayer's principle of verification is offered as a definition, not an empirical hypothesis, regarding literal meaning. Ayer explores the implications of his verificationist account of meaning for a priori propositions, propositions about the past and about other minds, and ethical judgments.

Ayer explains the philosophical value of Bertrand Russell's theory of descriptions, in connection with the question of whether statements about material things can be translated, without loss of meaning, into statements about sensory experiences. Ayer denies that such a translation is available but acknowledges the possibility of a schema showing what relations between sensory contents must obtain for statements about material things to be true. Ayer denies, however, that philosophy can justify our scientific or commonsense beliefs, on the ground that their justification is an empirical matter of the kind unsettled by a priori philosophy.

In "The Pragmatic Element in Knowledge," C. I. Lewis contends that knowledge has an ineliminable pragmatic component. This pragmatic component is an element of "active interpretation" that supposedly resides in all knowledge. In sensory, empirical knowledge, we use interpretation via concepts to organize and to characterize input from sensation. Lewis regards the distinguishing feature of pragmatism as its emphasis on a knower's act of interpretation relative to the data of sensation.

Truths about experience, according to Lewis's pragmatism, are always expressed by, and thus depend on, a conceptual system chosen on pragmatic grounds. Lewis explains:

[T]he point of the pragmatic theory is . . . the responsiveness of truth to human bent or need, and the fact that in some sense it is made by mind. . . . [T]he interpretation of experience must always be in terms of categories and concepts which the mind itself determines. There may be alternative conceptual systems, giving rise to alternative descriptions of experience, which are equally objective and equally valid, if there be not some purely logical defect in these categorial conceptions. When this is so, choice will be determined, consciously or unconsciously, on pragmatic grounds. . . . [T]he pragmatic element in knowledge concerns the choice in application of conceptual modes of interpretation. (*Mind and the World-Order* (New York, 1929), pp. 271–72; cf. p. 257).

Lewis holds that all interpretation includes an experience-independent, a priori element and that this interpretive element receives support not from experience, but from pragmatic factors—for example, "some demand or purpose of the mind itself."

Lewis argues that empirical knowledge consists of three elements: the immediate data of sensation, the concept or category under which those data are subsumed, and the mental act that interprets the data by means of the concept. Both Lewis and James hold that apart from an act of interpretation, one's experience would be the "buzzing, blooming confusion of the infant." An act of interpretation, on their view, enables such confusion to become an ordered world of experience. Lewis takes pains to defend the independence of a purely sensory, "given" element in experience. As a pragmatist, however, he highlights the pragmatic basis for the application of concepts to the data given in experience. Concepts, on his view, are "instruments of interpretation." Lewis sums up his view thus: "Wherever such criteria as comprehensiveness and simplicity, or serviceability for the control of nature, or conformity to human bent and human ways of acting play their part in the determination of such conceptual instruments, there is a pragmatic element in knowledge."

Often we do seek a pragmatic rationale for a manner of interpretation. We then wonder about the practical consequences of wielding certain concepts (or, ways of classifying), relative to our explanatory purposes. Such a pragmatic rationale concerns the instrumental effectiveness of certain concepts in achieving our theoretical purposes, whatever those purposes happen to be. Can there be a rationale for concepts that is not pragmatic? Have pragmatists overlooked a cognitive basis for choosing concepts that is not merely pragmatic? *Perhaps* we can assess concepts relative to something more objective and less variable, namely, relative to the reliability of their portrayal of the objective, conceiving-independent world. Some philosophers hold that the latter kind of assessment, in terms of objective reliability, is distinctively "epistemological" and that a merely pragmatic rationale can be (and often is) irrelevant to such epistemological assessment. The underlying assumption is that epistemological assessment is centrally concerned with objective, purpose-independent truth and reliable indications of such truth. Pragmatic success can sometimes get by with beliefs that are unreliable and even false— such as when it is convenient for our purposes to maintain an unreliable, false view on something.

If we can make sense of talk of objective, purpose-independent correctness, we can distinguish epistemological from pragmatic assessment. A notion of purpose-independent correctness can allow that what set of concepts we wield in theorizing often depends on our purposes in theorizing. The key issue now is, however, whether it makes sense to talk of the purpose-independent correctness of concepts. The rough idea from the critic of pragmatism is this: The external world is featured in certain mind-independent ways (e.g., many of its objects have "natural" boundaries), and our classificatory concepts can be more or less accurate, or reliable, in how they "fit" the mind-independent features of the external world. If we can make sense of such talk of accurate fitting, we can acknowledge a distinctively epistemological concern: Do our concepts accurately fit the external world? Here we have an issue of crucial importance in epistemology.

In his 1936 essay "Testability and Meaning," Carnap identified one purpose-relative consideration in epistemology as follows:

Suppose a sentence *S* is given, some test-observations for it have been made, and *S* is confirmed by them in a certain degree. Then it is a matter of practical decision whether we will consider that degree as high enough for our acceptance of S . . . Although our decision is based upon the observations made so far, nevertheless it is not uniquely determined by them. There is no general rule to determine our decision. Thus the acceptance and the rejection of a (synthetic) sentence always contains a *conventional component*.

This view entails only that our decisions about rational acceptance have an ineliminable conventional component, not that they are wholly conventional.

By 1950, the year "Empiricism, Semantics, and Ontology" appeared, Carnap's pragmatism was explicit. Realists about the external world typically affirm that there really are observable spatiotemporal things and events, whereas subjective idealists question the reality of the thing world itself. The controversy between realists and idealists began with the origins of philosophy itself. In "Empiricism, Semantics, and Ontology," Carnap gives the controversy a pragmatic reading:

> Those who raise the question of the reality of the thing world itself have perhaps in mind not a theoretical question . . . , but rather a practical question, a matter of practical decision concerning the structure of our language. We have to make the choice whether or not to accept and use the forms of expression in the [linguistic] framework in question.

Carnap acknowledges that "the thing language" efficiently serves many purposes of everyday life and that it is advisable to accept the thing language on this pragmatic basis. He rejects, however, any suggestion that such a pragmatic basis can provide confirming evidence for "the reality" of the thing world. A statement of the reality of the total system of certain entities (e.g., spatiotemporal things), according to Carnap, is a "pseudo-statement without cognitive content." Questions about the total system of certain entities—what Carnap calls "external questions"—make sense, on this view, only as *practical* questions about whether to adopt certain ways of using language.

By the 1950s the logical positivists of the 1920s had moved toward pragmatism in epistemology. In doing so, they were reviving themes from an American movement that antedated the Vienna Circle.

Prominent twentieth-century empiricists before 1950 typically accepted an analytic-synthetic distinction: a distinction between propositions true just in virtue of meaning (or definition) and propositions true in virtue of considerations other than meaning (such as observable phenomena). Corresponding to this distinction, empiricists typically drew a distinction between empirical (a posteriori) knowledge and nonempirical (a priori) knowledge. A common view among empiricists was that all a priori knowledge is knowledge of analytic truths, that there can be no a priori knowledge of synthetic truths. Ayer, for example, had argued for a linguistic conception of the a priori implying that the truths of logic and mathematics are a priori in that we cannot deny them without violating the rules governing our use of language. Ayer argued that the analyticity of the truths of logic and mathematics is the only good explanation of their being knowable a priori and that we can have no a priori knowledge of empirical reality or of synthetic truths.

In 1951, W. V. Quine published "Two Dogmas of Empiricism," challenging the following so-called dogmas of modern empiricism: belief in a dichotomy between analytic and synthetic truths, and belief in reductionism according to which every meaningful sentence is equivalent to some sentence whose terms refer to immediate sensory experience. Quine argues that any suitable appeal to analyticity in epistemology presupposes a notion of *cognitive synonymy* that is no more intelligible than talk of analyticity itself. One class of analytic statements—so-called *logically true* statements—does not attract this objection from Quine. Such statements, represented by "No unmarried man is married," remain true under all reinterpretations of their nonlogical components.

A second class of statements, represented by "No bachelor is married," does invite Quine's objection. Some philosophers hold that the members of the latter class reduce to logical truths by substituting synonyms for synonyms—for example, "unmarried man" for "bachelor." Other philosophers have talked instead of reducing the second class of analytic statements to the first *by definition*. They rely on the proposal that we *define* "bachelor" as "unmarried man." Quine objects to such talk of definition, claiming that it typically rests on an inadequately explained notion of synonymy concerning what is defined and certain antecedent linguistic usage. The presumed notion of *synonymy*, according to Quine, needs clarification no less than does the notion of analyticity.

Quine anticipates an effort to explain analyticity via a verification theory of meaning. An analytic truth, on this view, is a statement confirmed "no matter what," that is, "come what may." Quine endorses *epistemic holism* instead: the view that statements are confirmed or disconfirmed not individually on the basis of experience, but only as a "field." Given Quine's holism, any statement can be accepted come what may as long as we revise—perhaps drastically—other parts of our field of accepted statements. Epistemic holism entails that no statement is in principle beyond revisability. Quine thus concludes that the verification approach to analyticity relies on an implausibly atomistic approach to confirmation and disconfirmation.

Quine denies that we need analyticity to account for the meaningfulness of logical and mathematical truths. Their meaningfulness can be regarded as deriving from their figuring in the natural sciences for the implication of various observationally testable statements. Logical and mathematical truths, on this view, are not divorced from empirical content; they rather participate, if indirectly, in the empirical content of various observational statements. Similarly, we do not need analyticity to explain the *necessity* of logical and mathematical truths. Necessity, on this view, is just a matter of our current unwillingness to dispense with certain statements at the center of our web of belief. Two important effects of dispensing with the two dogmas are a breaking down of the long-standing distinction between speculative metaphysics and empirical science and a move toward the sort of pragmatism found in James.

In "Pragmatism, Relativism, and Irrationalism," Richard Rorty proposes that such pragmatists as James and Dewey should not be regarded as offering a distinctive "theory of knowledge." They rather held, according to Rorty, that traditional epistemology-oriented philosophy is seriously misguided and thus should be replaced by concerns about the actual cultural practices that gave rise to our use of such terms as "knowledge," "justification," and "truth." Rorty offers three sloganistic characterizations of the pragmatism of James and Dewey. (1) It is wrong to think of either knowledge, justification, or truth as having an essence. (2) There is no epistemological difference between truth about what *ought to be* and truth about what *is*, nor any metaphysical difference between facts and values. (3) There are no constraints on inquiry besides conversational ones, i.e., constraints supplied by the views of our fellow inquirers. Given (3), it is incorrect to hold that there are constraints on inquiry supplied, for instance, by the nature of physical objects, the human mind, or language. Rorty contends that the sort of pragmatism involving (1)–(3) does not entail relativism or irrationalism.

13 / William James (1842–1910)
THE WILL TO BELIEVE

In the recently published Life by Leslie Ste-phen of his brother, Fitz-James, there is an ac-count of a school to which the latter went when he was a boy. The teacher, a certain Mr. Guest, used to converse with his pupils in this wise: "Gurney, what is the difference between justi-fication and santification?—Stephen, prove the omnipotence of God!" etc. In the midst of our Harvard freethinking and indifference we are prone to imagine that here at your good old orthodox College conversation continues to be somewhat upon this order; and to show you that we at Harvard have not lost all interest in these vital subjects, I have brought with me to-night something like a sermon on justification by faith to read to you,—I mean an essay in justification *of* faith, a defence of our right to adopt a believing attitude in religious matters, in spite of the fact that our merely logical in-tellect may not have been coerced. "The Will to Believe," accordingly, is the title of my paper.

I have long defended to my own students the lawfulness of voluntarily adopted faith; but as soon as they have got well imbued with the logical spirit, they have as a rule refused to admit my contention to be lawful philosophi-cally, even though in point of fact they were personally all the time chock-full of some faith or other themselves. I am all the while, how-ever, so profoundly convinced that my own po-sition is correct, that your invitation has seemed to me a good occasion to make my statements more clear. Perhaps your minds will be more open than those with which I have hitherto had to deal. I will be as little technical as I can, though I must begin by setting up some technical distinctions that will help us in the end.

I

Let us give the name of *hypothesis* to anything that may be proposed to our belief; and just as the electricians speak of live and dead wires, let us speak of any hypothesis as either *live* or *dead*. A live hypothesis is one which appeals as a real possibility to him to whom it is pro-posed. If I ask you to believe in the Mahdi, the notion makes no electric connection with your nature,—it refuses to scintillate with any cred-ibility at all. As an hypothesis it is completely dead. To an Arab, however (even if he be not one of the Mahdi's followers), the hypothesis is among the mind's possibilities: it is alive. This shows that deadness and liveness in an hypothesis are not intrinsic properties, but re-lations to the individual thinker. They are mea-sured by his willingness to act. The maximum of liveness in an hypothesis means willingness to act irrevocably. Practically, that means be-lief; but there is some believing tendency wherever there is willingness to act at all.

Next, let us call the decision between two hypotheses an *option*. Options may be of sev-eral kinds. They may be—(1), *living* or *dead*; (2), *forced* or *avoidable*; (3), *momentous* or *trivial*; and for our purposes we may call an option a *genuine* option when it is of the forced, living, and momentous kind.

From William James, *The Will to Believe and Other Essays*. New York: Dover Publications, 1956. Reprinted by permission of Dover Publications, Inc. This essay was published originally in *New World* 5 (June 1896), 327–47.

1. A living option is one in which both hypotheses are live ones. If I say to you: "Be a theosophist or be a Mohammedan," it is probably a dead option, because for you neither hypothesis is likely to be alive. But if I say: "Be an agnostic or be a Christian," it is otherwise: trained as you are, each hypothesis makes some appeal, however small, to your belief.

2. Next, if I say to you: "Choose between going out with your umbrella or without it," I do not offer you a genuine option, for it is not forced. You can easily avoid it by not going out at all. Similarly, if I say, "Either love me or hate me," "Either call my theory true or call it false," your option is avoidable. You may remain indifferent to me, neither loving nor hating, and you may decline to offer any judgment as to my theory. But if I say, "Either accept this truth or go without it," I put on you a forced option, for there is no standing place outside of the alternative. Every dilemma based on a complete logical disjunction, with no possibility of not choosing, is an option of this forced kind.

3. Finally, if I were Dr. Nansen and proposed to you to join my North Pole expedition, your option would be momentous; for this would probably be your only similar opportunity, and your choice now would either exclude you from the North Pole sort of immortality altogether or put at least the chance of it into your hands. He who refuses to embrace a unique opportunity loses the prize as surely as if he tried and failed. *Per contra*, the option is trivial when the opportunity is not unique, when the stake is insignificant, or when the decision is reversible if it later prove unwise. Such trivial options abound in the scientific life. A chemist finds an hypothesis live enough to spend a year in its verification: he believes in it to that extent. But if his experiments prove inconclusive either way, he is quit for his loss of time, no vital harm being done.

It will facilitate our discussion if we keep all these distinctions well in mind.

II

The next matter to consider is the actual psychology of human opinion. When we look at certain facts, it seems as if our passional and volitional nature lay at the root of all our convictions. When we look at others, it seems as if they could do nothing when the intellect had once said its say. Let us take the latter facts up first.

Does it not seem preposterous on the very face of it to talk of our opinions being modifiable at will? Can our will either help or hinder our intellect in its perceptions of truth? Can we, by just willing it, believe that Abraham Lincoln's existence is a myth, and that the portraits of him in McClure's Magazine are all of some one else? Can we, by any effort of our will, or by any strength of wish that it were true, believe ourselves well and about when we are roaring with rheumatism in bed, or feel certain that the sum of the two one-dollar bills in our pocket must be a hundred dollars? We can *say* any of these things, but we are absolutely impotent to believe them; and of just such things is the whole fabric of the truths that we do believe in made up,—matters of fact, immediate or remote, as Hume said, and relations between ideas, which are either there or not there for us if we see them so, and which if not there cannot be put there by any action of our own.

In Pascal's *Thoughts* there is a celebrated passage known in literature as Pascal's wager. In it he tries to force us into Christianity by reasoning as if our concern with truth resembled our concern with the stakes in a game of chance. Translated freely his words are these: You must either believe or not believe that God is—which will you do? Your human reason cannot say. A game is going on between you and the nature of things which at the day of judgment will bring out either heads or tails. Weigh what your gains and your losses would be if you should stake all you have on heads, or God's existence: if you win in such case, you gain eternal beatitude; if you lose, you lose nothing at all. If there were an infinity of chances, and only one for God in this wager, still you ought to stake your all on God; for though you surely risk a finite loss by this procedure, any finite loss is reasonable, even a certain one is reasonable, if there is but the possibility of infinite gain. Go, then, and take holy water, and have masses said; belief will come and stupefy your scruples,—*Cela vous fera croire et vous abêtira*. Why should you not? At bottom, what have you to lose?

You probably feel that when religious faith expresses itself thus, in the language of the gaming-table, it is put to its last trumps. Surely Pascal's own personal belief in masses and holy water had far other springs; and this celebrated page of his is but an argument for others, a last desperate snatch at a weapon against the hardness of the unbelieving heart. We feel that a faith in masses and holy water adopted willfully after such a mechanical calculation would lack the inner soul of faith's reality; and if we were ourselves in the place of the Deity, we should probably take particular pleasure in cutting off believers of this pattern from their infinite reward. It is evident that unless there be some pre-existing tendency to believe in masses and holy water, the option offered to the will by Pascal is not a living option. Certainly no Turk ever took to masses and holy water on its account; and even to us Protestants these means of salvation seem such foregone impossibilities that Pascal's logic, invoked for them specifically, leaves us unmoved. As well might the Mahdi write to us, saying, "I am the Expected One whom God has created in his effulgence. You shall be infinitely happy if you confess me; otherwise you shall be cut off from the light of the sun. Weigh, then, your infinite gain if I am genuine against your finite sacrifice if I am not!" His logic would be that of Pascal; but he would vainly use it on us, for the hypothesis he offers us is dead. No tendency to act on it exists in us to any degree.

The talk of believing by our volition seems, then, from one point of view, simply silly. From another point of view it is worse than silly, it is vile. When one turns to the magnificent edifice of the physical sciences, and sees how it was reared; what thousands of disinterested moral lives of men lie buried in its mere foundations; what patience and postponement, what choking down of preference, what submission to the icy laws of outer fact are wrought into its very stones and mortar; how absolutely impersonal it stands in its vast augustness,—then how besotted and contemptible seems every little sentimentalist who comes blowing his voluntary smoke-wreaths, and pre-

tending to decide things from out of his private dream! Can we wonder if those bred in the rugged and manly school of science should feel like spewing such subjectivism out of their mouths? The whole system of loyalties which grow up in the schools of science go dead against its toleration; so that it is only natural that those who have caught the scientific fever should pass over to the opposite extreme, and write sometimes as if the incorruptibly truthful intellect ought positively to prefer bitterness and unacceptableness to the heart in its cup.

> It fortifies my soul to know
> That, though I perish, Truth is so—

sings Clough, while Huxley exclaims: "My only consolation lies in the reflection that, however bad our posterity may become, so far as they hold by the plain rule of not pretending to believe what they have no reason to believe, because it may be to their advantage so to pretend [the word 'pretend' is surely here redundant], they will not have reached the lowest depth of immorality." And that delicious *enfant terrible* Clifford writes: "Belief is desecrated when given to unproved and unquestioned statements for the solace and private pleasure of the believer. . . . Whoso would deserve well of his fellows in this matter will guard the purity of his belief with a very fanaticism of jealous care, lest at any time it should rest on an unworthy object, and catch a stain which can never be wiped away. . . . If [a] belief has been accepted on insufficient evidence [even though the belief be true, as Clifford on the same page explains] the pleasure is a stolen one. . . . It is sinful because it is stolen in defiance of our duty to mankind. That duty is to guard ourselves from such beliefs as from a pestilence which may shortly master our own body and then spread to the rest of the town. . . . It is wrong always, everywhere, and for every one, to believe anything upon insufficient evidence."

III

All this strikes one as healthy, even when expressed, as by Clifford, with somewhat too much of robustious pathos in the voice. Free-will and simple wishing do seem, in the matter of our credences, to be only fifth wheels to the coach. Yet if any one should thereupon assume that intellectual insight is what remains after wish and will and sentimental preference have taken wing, or that pure reason is what then settles our opinions, he would fly quite as directly in the teeth of the facts.

It is only our already dead hypotheses that our willing nature is unable to bring to life again. But what has made them dead for us is for the most part a previous action of our willing nature of an antagonistic kind. When I say "willing nature," I do not mean only such deliberate volitions as may have set up habits of belief that we cannot now escape from,—I mean all such factors of belief as fear and hope, prejudice and passion, imitation and partisanship, the circumpressure of our caste and set. As a matter of fact we find ourselves believing, we hardly know how or why. Mr. Balfour gives the name of "authority" to all those influences, born of the intellectual climate, that make hypotheses possible or impossible for us, alive or dead. Here in this room, we all of us believe in molecules and the conservation of energy, in democracy and necessary progress, in Protestant Christianity and the duty of fighting for "the doctrine of the immortal Monroe," all for no reasons worthy of the name. We see into these matters with no more inner clearness, and probably with much less, than any disbeliever in them might possess. His unconventionality would probably have some grounds to show for its conclusions; but for us, not insight, but the *prestige* of the opinions, is what makes the spark shoot from them and light up our sleeping magazines of faith. Our reason is quite satisfied, in nine hundred and ninety-nine cases out of every thousand of us, if it can find a few arguments that will do to recite in case our credulity is criticised by some one else. Our faith is faith in some one else's faith, and in the greatest matters this is most the case. Our belief in truth itself, for instance, that there is a truth, and that our minds and it are made for each other,—what is it but a passionate affirmation of desire, in which our social system backs us up? We want to have a truth; we want to believe that our

experiments and studies and discussions must put us in a continually better and better position towards it; and on this line we agree to fight out our thinking lives. But if a pyrrhonistic sceptic asks us *how we know* all this, can our logic find a reply? No! certainly it cannot. It is just one volition against another,—we willing to go in for life upon a trust or assumption which he, for his part, does not care to make.[1]

As a rule we disbelieve all facts and theories for which we have no use. Clifford's cosmic emotions find no use for Christian feelings. Huxley belabors the bishops because there is no use for sacerdotalism in his scheme of life. Newman, on the contrary, goes over to Romanism, and finds all sorts of reasons good for staying there, because a priestly system is for him an organic need and delight. Why do so few "scientists" even look at the evidence for telepathy, so called? Because they think, as a leading biologist, now dead, once said to me, that even if such a thing were true, scientists ought to band together to keep it suppressed and concealed. It would undo the uniformity of Nature and all sorts of other things without which scientists cannot carry on their pursuits. But if this very man had been shown something which as a scientist he might *do* with telepathy, he might not only have examined the evidence, but even have found it good enough. This very law which the logicians would impose upon us—if I may give the name of logicians to those who would rule out our willing nature here—is based on nothing but their own natural wish to exclude all elements for which they, in their professional quality of logicians, can find no use.

Evidently, then, our non-intellectual nature does influence our convictions. There are passional tendencies and volitions which run before and others which come after belief, and it is only the latter that are too late for the fair; and they are not too late when the previous passional work has been already in their own direction. Pascal's argument, instead of being powerless, then seems a regular clincher, and is the last stroke needed to make our faith in masses and holy water complete. The state of things is evidently far from simple; and pure insight and logic, whatever they might do ideally, are not the only things that really do produce our creeds.

IV

Our next duty, having recognized this mixed-up state of affairs, is to ask whether it be simply reprehensible and pathological, or whether, on the contrary, we must treat it as a normal element in making up our minds. The thesis I defend is, briefly stated, this: *Our passional nature not only lawfully may, but must, decide an option between propositions, whenever it is a genuine option that cannot by its nature be decided on intellectual grounds; for to say, under such circumstances, "Do not decide, but leave the question open," is itself a passional decision,—just like deciding yes or no,—and is attended with the same risk of losing the truth.* The thesis thus abstractly expressed will, I trust, soon become quite clear. But I must first indulge in a bit more of preliminary work.

V

It will be observed that for the purposes of this discussion we are on "dogmatic" ground,—ground, I mean, which leaves systematic philosophical scepticism altogether out of account. The postulate that there is truth, and that it is the destiny of our minds to attain it, we are deliberately resolving to make, though the sceptic will not make it. We part company with him, therefore, absolutely at this point. But the faith that truth exists, and that our minds can find it, may be held in two ways. We may talk of the *empiricist* way and of the *absolutist* way of believing in truth. The absolutists in this matter say that we not only can attain to knowing truth, but we can *know when* we have attained to knowing it; while the empiricists think that although we may attain it, we cannot infallibly know when. To *know* is one thing, and to know for certain *that* we know is another. One may hold to the first being possible without the second; hence the empiricists and

the absolutists, although neither of them is a sceptic in the usual philosophic sense of the term, show very different degrees of dogmatism in their lives.

If we look at the history of opinions, we see that the empiricist tendency has largely prevailed in science, while in philosophy the absolutist tendency has had everything its own way. The characteristic sort of happiness, indeed, which philosophies yield has mainly consisted in the conviction felt by each successive school or system that by it bottom-certitude had been attained. "Other philosophies are collections of opinions, mostly false; *my* philosophy gives standing-ground forever,"—who does not recognize in this the key-note of every system worthy of the name? A system, to be a system at all, must come as a *closed* system, reversible in this or that detail, per chance, but in its essential features never!

Scholastic orthodoxy, to which one must always go when one wishes to find perfectly clear statement, has beautifully elaborated this absolutist conviction in a doctrine which it calls that of "objective evidence." If, for example, I am unable to doubt that I now exist before you, that two is less than three, or that if all men are mortal than I am mortal too, it is because these things illumine my intellect irresistibly. The final ground of this objective evidence possessed by certain propositions is the *adaequatio intellectûs nostri cum rê.* The certitude it brings involves an *aptitudinem ad extorquendum certum assensum* on the part of the truth envisaged, and on the side of the subject a *quietem in cognitione*, when once the object is mentally received, that leaves no possibility of doubt behind; and in the whole transaction nothing operates but the *entitas ipsa* of the object and the *entitas ipsa* of the mind. We slouchy modern thinkers dislike to talk in Latin,—indeed, we dislike to talk in set terms at all; but at bottom our own state of mind is very much like this whenever we uncritically abandon ourselves: You believe in objective evidence, and I do. Of some things we feel that we are certain; we know, and we know that we do know. There is something that gives a click inside of us, a bell that strikes twelve, when the hands of our mental clock have swept the dial and meet over the meridian hour. The greatest empiricists among us are only empiricists on reflection: when left to their instincts, they dogmatize like infallible popes. When the Cliffords tell us how sinful it is to be Christians on such "insufficient evidence," insufficiency is really the last thing they have in mind. For them the evidence is absolutely sufficient, only it makes the other way. They believe so completely in an anti-christian order of the universe that there is no living option: Christianity is a dead hypothesis from the start.

VI

But now, since we are all such absolutists by instinct, what in our quality of students of philosophy ought we to do about the fact? Shall we espouse and indorse it? Or shall we treat it as a weakness of our nature from which we must free ourselves, if we can?

I sincerely believe that the latter course is the only one we can follow as reflective men. Objective evidence and certitude are doubtless very fine ideals to play with, but where on this moonlit and dream-visited planet are they found? I am, therefore, myself a complete empiricist so far as my theory of human knowledge goes. I live, to be sure, by the practical faith that we must go on experiencing and thinking over our experience, for only thus can our opinions grow more true; but to hold any one of them—I absolutely do not care which—as if it never could be reinterpretable or corrigible, I believe to be a tremendously mistaken attitude, and I think that the whole history of philosophy will bear me out. There is but one indefectibly certain truth, and that is the truth that pyrrhonistic scepticism itself leaves standing,—the truth that the present phenomenon of consciousness exists. That, however, is the bare starting-point of knowledge, the mere admission of a stuff to be philosophized about. The various philosophies are but so many attempts at expressing what this stuff really is. And if we repair to our libraries what disagreement do we discover! Where is a certainly true answer found? Apart from abstract propositions of comparison (such as two and two are the same

as four), propositions which tell us nothing by themselves about concrete reality, we find no proposition ever regarded by any one as evidently certain that has not either been called a falsehood, or at least had its truth sincerely questioned by some one else. The transcending of the axioms of geometry, not in play but in earnest, by certain of our contemporaries (as Zöllner and Charles H. Hinton), and the rejection of the whole Aristotelian logic by the Hegelians, are striking instances in point.

No concrete test of what is really true has ever been agreed upon. Some make the criterion external to the moment of perception, putting it either in revelation, the *consensus gentium*, the instincts of the heart, or the systematized experience of the race. Others make the perceptive moment its own test,—Descartes, for instance, with his clear and distinct ideas guaranteed by the veracity of God; Reid with his "common-sense"; and Kant with his forms of synthetic judgment *a priori*. The inconceivability of the opposite; the capacity to be verified by sense; the possession of complete organic unity or self-relation, realized when a thing is its own other,—are standards which, in turn, have been used. The much lauded objective evidence is never triumphantly there; it is a mere aspiration or *Grenzbegriff*, marking the infinitely remote ideal of our thinking life. To claim that certain truths now possess it, is simply to say that when you think them true and they *are* true, then their evidence is objective, otherwise it is not. But practically one's conviction that the evidence one goes by is of the real objective brand, is only one more subjective opinion added to the lot. For what a contradictory array of opinions have objective evidence and absolute certitude been claimed! The world is rational through and through,—its existence is an ultimate brute fact; there is a personal God,—a personal God is inconceivable; there is an extra-mental physical world immediately known,—the mind can only know its own ideas; a moral imperative exists,—obligation is only the resultant of desires; a permanent spiritual principle is in every one,—there are only shifting states of mind; there is an endless chain of causes,—there is an absolute first cause; an eternal necessity,—a freedom; a purpose,—no purpose;

a primal One,—a primal Many; a universal continuity,—an essential discontinuity in things; an infinity,—no infinity. There is this,—there is that; there is indeed nothing which some one has not thought absolutely true, while his neighbor deemed it absolutely false; and not an absolutist among them seems ever to have considered that the trouble may all the time be essential, and that the intellect, even with truth directly in its grasp, may have no infallible signal for knowing whether it be truth or no. When, indeed, one remembers that the most striking practical application to life of the doctrine of objective certitude has been the conscientious labors of the Holy Office of the Inquisition, one feels less tempted than ever to lend the doctrine a respectful ear.

But please observe, now, that when as empiricists we give up the doctrine of objective certitude, we do not thereby give up the quest or hope of truth itself. We still pin our faith on its existence, and still believe that we gain an ever better position towards it by systematically continuing to roll up experiences and think. Our great difference from the scholastic lies in the way we face. The strength of his system lies in the principles, the origin, the *terminus a quo* of his thought; for us the strength is in the outcome, the upshot, the *terminus ad quem*. Not where it comes from but what it leads to is to decide. It matters not to an empiricist from what quarter an hypothesis may come to him: he may have acquired it by fair means or by foul; passion may have whispered or accident suggested it; but if the total drift of thinking continues to confirm it, that is what he means by its being true.

VII

One more point, small but important, and our preliminaries are done. There are two ways of looking at our duty in the matter of opinion,—ways entirely different, and yet ways about whose difference the theory of knowledge seems hitherto to have shown very little concern. *We must know the truth*; and *we must avoid error*:—these are our first and great commandments as would-be knowers; but they are two separable laws. Although it may indeed happen that when we believe the truth *A*, we escape as an incidental consequence from believing the falsehood *B*, it hardly ever happens that by merely disbelieving *B* we necessarily believe *A*. We may in escaping *B* fall into believing other falsehoods, *C* or *D*, just as bad as *B*; or we may escape *B* by not believing anything at all, not even *A*.

Believe truth! Shun error!—these, we see, are two materially different laws; and by choosing between them we may end by coloring differently our whole intellectual life. We may regard the chase for truth as paramount, and the avoidance of error as secondary; or we may, on the other hand, treat the avoidance of error as more imperative, and let truth take its chance. Clifford, in the instructive passage which I have quoted, exhorts us to the latter course. Believe nothing, he tells us, keep your mind in suspense forever, rather than by closing it on insufficient evidence incur the awful risk of believing lies. You, on the other hand, may think that the risk of being in error is a very small matter when compared with the blessings of real knowledge, and be ready to be duped many times in your investigation rather than postpone indefinitely the chance of guessing true. I myself find it impossible to go with Clifford. We must remember that these feelings of our duty about either truth or error are in any case only expressions of our passional life. Biologically considered, our minds are as ready to grind out falsehood as veracity, and he who says, "Better go without belief forever than believe a lie!" merely shows his own preponderant private horror of becoming a dupe. He may be critical of many of his desires and fears, but this fear he slavishly obeys. He cannot imagine any one questioning its binding force. For my own part, I have also a horror of being duped; but I can believe that worse things than being duped may happen to a man in this world: so Clifford's exhortation has to my ears a thoroughly fantastic sound. It is like a general informing his soldiers that it is better to keep out of battle forever than to risk a single wound. Not so are victories either over enemies or over nature gained. Our errors are surely not such awfully solemn things. In a world where we are so certain to incur them in spite of all our caution, a certain lightness of heart seems healthier than this excessive nervousness on their behalf. At any rate, it seems the fittest thing for the empiricist philosopher.

VIII

And now, after all this introduction, let us go straight at our question. I have said, and now repeat it, that not only as a matter of fact do we find our passional nature influencing us in our opinions, but that there are some options between opinions in which this influence must be regarded both as an inevitable and as a lawful determinant of our choice.

I fear here that some of you my hearers will begin to scent danger, and lend an inhospitable ear. Two first steps of passion you have indeed had to admit as necessary,—we must think so as to avoid dupery, and we must think so as to gain truth; but the surest path to those ideal consummations, you will probably consider, is from now onwards to take no further passional step.

Well, of course, I agree as far as the facts will allow. Wherever the option between losing truth and gaining it is not momentous, we can throw the chance of *gaining truth* away, and at any rate save ourselves from any chance of *believing falsehood*, by not making up our minds at all till objective evidence has come. In scientific questions, this is almost always the case; and even in human affairs in general, the need of acting is seldom so urgent that a false belief to act on is better than no belief at all. Law courts, indeed, have to decide on the best evidence attainable for the moment, because a judge's duty is to make law as well as to ascertain it, and (as a learned judge once said to me) few cases are worth spending much time over: the great thing is to have them decided on *any* acceptable principle, and got out of the way. But in our dealings with objective nature we obviously are recorders, not makers, of the truth; and decisions for the mere sake of deciding promptly and getting on to the next business would be wholly out of place. Throughout the breadth of physical nature facts are what they are quite independently of us,

and seldom is there any such hurry about them that the risks of being duped by believing a premature theory need be faced. The questions here are always trivial options, the hypotheses are hardly living (at any rate not living for us spectators), the choice between believing truth or falsehood is seldom forced. The attitude of sceptical balance is therefore the absolutely wise one if we would escape mistakes. What difference, indeed, does it make to most of us whether we have or have not a theory of the Röntgen rays, whether we believe or not in mind-stuff, or have a conviction about the causality of conscious states? It makes no difference. Such options are not forced on us. On every account it is better not to make them, but still keep weighing reasons *pro et contra* with an indifferent hand.

I speak, of course, here of the purely judging mind. For purposes of discovery such indifference is to be less highly recommended, and science would be far less advanced than she is if the passionate desires of individuals to get their own faiths confirmed had been kept out of the game. See for example the sagacity which Spencer and Weismann now display. On the other hand, if you want an absolute duffer in an investigation, you must, after all, take the man who has no interest whatever in its results: he is the warranted incapable, the positive fool. The most useful investigator, because the most sensitive observer, is always he whose eager interest in one side of the question is balanced by an equally keen nervousness lest he become deceived.[2] Science has organized this nervousness into a regular *technique*, her so-called method of verification; and she has fallen so deeply in love with the method that one may even say she has ceased to care for truth by itself at all. It is only truth as technically verified that interests her. The truth of truths might come in merely affirmative form, and she would decline to touch it. Such truth as that, she might repeat with Clifford, would be stolen in defiance of her duty to mankind. Human passions, however, are stronger than technical rules. *Le coeur a ses raisons*, as Pascal says, *que la raison ne connalt pas*; and however indifferent to all but the bare rules of the game the umpire, the abstract intellect, may be, the concrete players who furnish him the materials to judge of are usually, each one of them, in love with some pet "live hypothesis" of his own. Let us agree, however, that wherever there is no forced option, the dispassionately judicial intellect with no pet hypothesis, saving us, as it does, from dupery at any rate, ought to be our ideal.

The question next arises: Are there not somewhere forced options in our speculative questions, and can we (as men who may be interested at least as much in positively gaining truth as in merely escaping dupery) always wait with impunity till the coercive evidence shall have arrived? It seems *a priori* improbable that the truth should be so nicely adjusted to our needs and powers as that. In the great boarding-house of nature, the cakes and the butter and the syrup seldom come out so even and leave the plates so clean. Indeed, we should view them with scientific suspicion if they did.

IX

Moral questions immediately present themselves as questions whose solution cannot wait for sensible proof. A moral question is a question not of what sensibly exists, but of what is good, or would be good if it did exist. Science can tell us what exists; but to compare the *worths*, both of what exists and of what does not exist, we must consult not science, but what Pascal calls our heart. Science herself consults her heart when she lays it down that the infinite ascertainment of fact and correction of false belief are the supreme goods for man. Challenge the statement, and science can only repeat it oracularly, or else prove it by showing that such ascertainment and correction bring man all sorts of other goods which man's heart in turn declares. The question of having moral beliefs at all or not having them is decided by our will. Are our moral preferences true or false, or are they only odd biological phenomena, making things good or bad for *us*, but in themselves indifferent? How can your pure intellect decide? If your heart does not *want* a world of moral reality, your head will assuredly never make you believe in one. Mephistophe-

lian scepticism, indeed, will satisfy the head's play-instincts much better than any rigorous idealism can. Some men (even at the student age) are so naturally cool-hearted that the moralistic hypothesis never has for them any pungent life, and in their supercilious presence the hot young moralist always feels strangely ill at ease. The appearance of knowingness is on their side, of *naïveté* and gullibility on his. Yet, in the inarticulate heart of him, he clings to it that he is not a dupe, and that there is a realm in which (as Emerson says) all their wit and intellectual superiority is no better than the cunning of a fox. Moral scepticism can no more be refuted or proved by logic than intellectual scepticism can. When we stick to it that there *is* truth (be it of either kind), we do so with our whole nature, and resolve to stand or fall by the results. The sceptic with his whole nature adopts the doubting attitude; but which of us is the wiser, Omniscience only knows.

Turn now from these wide questions of good to a certain class of questions of fact, questions concerning personal relations, states of mind between one man and another. *Do you like me or not?*—for example. Whether you do or not depends, in countless instances, on whether I meet you half-way, am willing to assume that you must like me, and show you trust and expectation. The previous faith on my part in your liking's existence is in such cases what makes your liking come. But if I stand aloof, and refuse to budge an inch until I have objective evidence, until you shall have done something apt, as the absolutists say, *ad extorquendum assensum meum*, ten to one your liking never comes. How many women's hearts are vanquished by the mere sanguine insistence of some man that they *must* love him! He will not consent to the hypothesis that they cannot. The desire for a certain kind of truth here brings about that special truth's existence; and so it is in innumerable cases of other sorts. Who gains promotions, boons, appointments, but the man in whose life they are seen to play the part of live hypotheses, who discounts them, sacrifices other things for their sake before they have come, and takes risks for them in advance? His faith acts on the powers above him as a claim, and creates its own verification.

A social organism of any sort whatever,

large or small, is what it is because each member proceeds to his own duty with a trust that the other members will simultaneously do theirs. Wherever a desired result is achieved by the co-operation of many independent persons, its existence as a fact is a pure consequence of the precursive faith in one another of those immediately concerned. A government, an army, a commercial system, a ship, a college, an athletic team, all exist on this condition, without which not only is nothing achieved, but nothing is even attempted. A whole train of passengers (individually brave enough) will be looted by a few highwaymen, simply because the latter can count on one another, while each passenger fears that if he makes a movement of resistance, he will be shot before any one else backs him up. If we believed that the whole car-full would rise at once with us, we should each severally rise, and train-robbing would never even be attempted. There are, then, cases where a fact cannot come at all unless a preliminary faith exists in its coming. *And where faith in a fact can help create the fact*, that would be an insane logic which should say that faith running ahead of scientific evidence is the "lowest kind of immorality" into which a thinking being can fall. Yet such is the logic by which our scientific absolutists pretend to regulate our lives!

X

In truths dependent on our personal action, then, faith based on desire is certainly a lawful and possibly an indispensable thing.

But now, it will be said, these are all childish human cases, and have nothing to do with great cosmical matters, like the question of religious faith. Let us then pass on to that. Religions differ so much in their accidents that in discussing the religious question we must make it very generic and broad. What then do we now mean by the religious hypothesis? Science says things are; morality says some things are better than other things; and religion says essentially two things.

First, she says that the best things are the more eternal things, the overlapping things, the

things in the universe that throw the last stone, so to speak, and say the final word. "Perfection is eternal,"—this phrase of Charles Secrétan seems a good way of putting this first affirmation of religion, an affirmation which obviously cannot yet be verified scientifically at all.

The second affirmation of religion is that we are better off even now if we believe her first affirmation to be true.

Now, let us consider what the logical elements of this situation are *in case the religious hypothesis in both its branches be really true.* (Of course, we must admit that possibility at the outset. If we are to discuss the question at all, it must involve a living option. If for any of you religion be a hypothesis that cannot, by any living possibility be true, then you need go no farther. I speak to the "saving remnant" alone.) So proceeding, we see, first, that religion offers itself as a *momentous* option. We are supposed to gain, even now, by our belief, and to lose by our non-belief, a certain vital good. Secondly, religion is a *forced* option, so far as that good goes. We cannot escape the issue by remaining sceptical and waiting for more light, because, although we do avoid error in that way *if religion be untrue*, we lose the good, *if it be true*, just as certainly as if we positively chose to disbelieve. It is as if a man should hesitate indefinitely to ask a certain woman to marry him because he was not perfectly sure that she would prove an angel after he brought her home. Would he not cut himself off from that particular angel-possibility as decisively as if he went and married some one else? Scepticism, then, is not avoidance of option; it is option of a certain particular kind of risk. *Better risk loss of truth than chance of error,*—that is your faith-vetoer's exact position. He is actively playing his stake as much as the believer is; he is backing the field against the religious hypothesis, just as the believer is backing the religious hypothesis against the field. To preach scepticism to us as a duty until "sufficient evidence" for religion be found, is tantamount therefore to telling us, when in presence of the religious hypothesis, that to yield to our fear of its being error is wiser and better than to yield to our hope that it may be true. It is not intellect against all passions, then; it is only intellect with one passion laying down its law. And by what, forsooth, is the supreme wisdom of this passion warranted? Dupery for dupery, what proof is there that dupery through hope is so much worse than dupery through fear? I, for one, can see no proof; and I simply refuse obedience to the scientist's command to imitate his kind of option, in a case where my own stake is important enough to give me the right to choose my own form of risk. If religion be true and the evidence for it be still insufficient, I do not wish, by putting your extinguisher upon my nature (which feels to me as if it had after all some business in this matter), to forfeit my sole chance in life of getting upon the winning side,—that chance depending, of course, on my willingness to run the risk of acting as if my passional need of taking the world religiously might be prophetic and right.

All this is on the supposition that it really may be prophetic and right, and that, even to us who are discussing the matter, religion is a live hypothesis which may be true. Now, to most of us religion comes in a still further way that makes a veto on our active faith even more illogical. The more perfect and more eternal aspect of the universe is represented in our religions as having personal form. The universe is no longer a mere *It* to us, but a *Thou*, if we are religious; and any relation that may be possible from person to person might be possible here. For instance, although in one sense we are passive portions of the universe, in another we show a curious autonomy, as if we were small active centres on our own account. We feel too, as if the appeal of religion to us were made to our own active goodwill, as if evidence might be forever withheld from us unless we met the hypothesis half-way. To take a trivial illustration: just as a man who in a company of gentlemen made no advances, asked a warrant for every concession, and believed no one's word without proof, would cut himself off by such churlishness from all the social rewards that a more trusting spirit would earn,— so here, one who should shut himself up in snarling logicality and try to make the gods extort his recognition willy-nilly, or not get it at all, might cut himself off forever from his only opportunity of making the gods' acquaintance. This feeling, forced on us we know not

whence, that by obstinately believing that there are gods (although not to do so would be so easy both for our logic and our life) we are doing the universe the deepest service we can, seems part of the living essence of the religious hypothesis. If the hypothesis *were* true in all its parts, including this one, then pure intellectualism, with its veto on our making willing advances, would be an absurdity; and some participation of our sympathetic nature would be logically required. I, therefore, for one, cannot see my way to accepting the agnostic rules for truth-seeking, or wilfully agree to keep my willing nature out of the game. I cannot do so for this plain reason, that *a rule of thinking which would absolutely prevent me from acknowledging certain kinds of truth if those kinds of truth were really there, would be an irrational rule.* That for me is the long and short of the formal logic of the situation, no matter what the kinds of truth might materially be.

I confess I do not see how this logic can be escaped. But sad experience makes me fear that some of you may still shrink from radically saying with me, *in abstracto*, that we have the right to believe at our own risk any hypothesis that is live enough to tempt our will. I suspect, however, that if this is so, it is because you have got away from the abstract logical point of view altogether, and are thinking (perhaps without realizing it) of some particular religious hypothesis which for you is dead. The freedom to "believe what we will" you apply to the case of some patent superstition; and the faith you think of is the faith defined by the schoolboy when he said, "Faith is when you believe something that you know ain't true." I can only repeat that this is misapprehension. *In concreto*, the freedom to believe can only cover living options which the intellect of the individual cannot by itself resolve; and living options never seem absurdities to him who has them to consider. When I look at the religious question as it really puts itself to concrete men, and when I think of all the possibilities which both practically and theoretically it involves, then this command that we shall put a stopper on our heart, instincts, and courage, and *wait*—acting of course meanwhile more or less as if religion were *not* true³—till doomsday, or till such time as our intellect and senses working together may have raked in evidence enough,—this command, I say, seems to me the queerest idol ever manufactured in the philosophic cave. Were we scholastic absolutists, there might be more excuse. If we had an infallible intellect with its objective certitudes, we might feel ourselves disloyal to such a perfect organ of knowledge in not trusting to it exclusively, in not waiting for its releasing word. But if we are empiricists, if we believe that no bell in us tolls to let us know for certain when truth is in our grasp, then it seems a piece of idle fantasticality to preach so solemnly our duty of waiting for the bell. Indeed, we *may* wait if we will,—I hope you do not think that I am denying that,—but if we do so, we do so at our peril as much as if we believed. In either case *we act*, taking our life in our hands. No one of us ought to issue vetoes to the other, nor should we bandy words of abuse. We ought, on the contrary, delicately and profoundly to respect one another's mental freedom: then only shall we bring about the intellectual republic; then only shall we have that spirit of inner tolerance without which all our outer tolerance is soulless, and which is empiricism's glory; then only shall we live and let live, in speculative as well as in practical things.

I began by a reference to Fitz-James Stephen; let me end by a quotation from him. "What do you think of yourself? What do you think of the world? . . . These are questions with which all must deal as it seems good to them. They are riddles of the Sphinx, and in some way or other we must deal with them. . . . In all important transactions of life we have to take a leap in the dark. . . . If we decide to leave the riddles unanswered, that is a choice; if we waver in our answer, that, too, is a choice: but whatever choice we make, we make it at our peril. If a man chooses to turn his back altogether on God and the future, no one can prevent him; no one can show beyond reasonable doubt that he is mistaken. If a man thinks otherwise and acts as he thinks, I do not see that any one can prove that *he* is mistaken. Each must act as he thinks best; and if he is wrong, so much the worse for him. We stand on a mountain pass in the midst of whirling snow and blinding mist, through which we get glimpses now and then of paths which may be deceptive. If we stand still we shall be frozen to death. If we take the wrong road we shall be dashed to pieces. We do not certainly know whether there is any right one. What must we do? 'Be strong and of good courage.' Act for the best, hope for the best, and take what comes. . . . If death ends all, we cannot meet death better."⁴

NOTES

1. Compare the admirable p. 310 in S. H. Hodgson's *Time and Space,* London, 1865.
2. Compare Wilfrid Ward's essay "The Wish to Believe" in his *Witnesses to the Unseen,* London, 1893.
3. Since belief is measured by action, he who forbids us to believe religion to be true, necessarily also forbids us to act as we should if we did believe it to be true. The whole defence of religious faith hinges upon action. If the action required or inspired by the religious hypothesis is in no way different from that dictated by the naturalistic hypothesis, then religious faith is a pure superfluity, better pruned away, and controversy about its legitimacy is a piece of idle trifling, unworthy of serious minds. I myself believe, of course, that the religious hypothesis gives to the world an expression which specifically determines our reactions, and makes them in a large part unlike what they might be on a purely naturalistic scheme of belief.
4. *Liberty, Equality, Fraternity,* p. 353, 2d ed., London, 1874.

14 / Bertrand Russell (1872–1970)
APPEARANCE, REALITY, AND KNOWLEDGE BY ACQUAINTANCE

I. APPEARANCE AND REALITY

Is there any knowledge in the world which is so certain that no reasonable man could doubt it? This question, which at first sight might not seem difficult, is really one of the most difficult that can be asked. When we have realized the obstacles in the way of a straightforward and confident answer, we shall be well launched on the study of philosophy—for philosophy is merely the attempt to answer such ultimate questions, not carelessly and dogmatically, as we do in ordinary life and even in the sciences, but critically, after exploring all that makes such questions puzzling, and after realizing all the vagueness and confusion that underlie our ordinary ideas.

In daily life, we assume as certain many things which, on a closer scrutiny, are found to be so full of apparent contradictions that only a great amount of thought enables us to know what it is that we really may believe. In the search for certainty, it is natural to begin with our present experiences, and in some sense, no doubt, knowledge is to be derived from them. But any statement as to what it is that our immediate experiences make us know is very likely to be wrong. It seems to me that I am now sitting in a chair, at a table of a certain shape, on which I see sheets of paper with writing or print. By turning my head I see out of the window buildings and clouds and the sun. I believe that the sun is about ninety-three million miles from the earth; that it is a hot globe many times bigger than the earth; that, owing to the earth's rotation, it rises every morning, and will continue to do so for an indefinite time in the future. I believe that, if any other normal person comes into my room, he will see the same chairs and tables and books and papers as I see, and that the table which I see is the same as the table which I feel pressing against my arm. All this seems to be so evident as to be hardly worth stating, except in answer to a man who doubts whether I know anything. Yet all this may be reasonably doubted, and all of it requires much careful discussion before we can be sure that we have stated it in a form that is wholly true.

To make our difficulties plain, let us concentrate attention on the table. To the eye it is oblong, brown and shiny, to the touch it is smooth and cool and hard; when I tap it, it gives out a wooden sound. Any one else who sees and feels and hears the table will agree with this description, so that it might seem as if no difficulty would arise; but as soon as we try to be more precise our troubles begin. Although I believe that the table is "really" of the same colour all over, the parts that reflect the light look much brighter than the other parts, and some parts look white because of reflected light. I know that, if I move, the parts that reflect the light will be different, so that the apparent distribution of colours on the table will change. It follows that if several people are looking at the table at the same moment, no two of them will see exactly the same distri-

From Bertrand Russell, *The Problems of Philosophy,* Oxford: Oxford University Press, 1912. Reprinted by permission of Oxford University Press.

bution of colours, because no two can see it from exactly the same point of view, and any change in the point of view makes some change in the way the light is reflected.

For most practical purposes these differences are unimportant, but to the painter they are all-important: the painter has to unlearn the habit of thinking that things seem to have the colour which common sense says they "really" have, and to learn the habit of seeing things as they appear. Here we have already the beginning of one of the distinctions that cause most trouble in philosophy—the distinction between "appearance" and "reality," between what things seem to be and what they are. The painter wants to know what things seem to be, the practical man and the philosopher want to know what they are; but the philosopher's wish to know this is stronger than the practical man's, and is more troubled by knowledge as to the difficulties of answering the question.

To return to the table. It is evident from what we have found, that there is no colour which preeminently appears to be *the* colour of the table, or even of any one particular part of the table—it appears to be of different colours from different points of view, and there is no reason for regarding some of these as more really its colour than others. And we know that even from a given point of view the colour will seem different by artificial light, or to a colour blind man, or to a man wearing blue spectacles, while in the dark there will be no colour at all, though to touch and hearing the table will be unchanged. This colour is not something which is inherent in the table, but something depending upon the table and the spectator and the way the light falls on the table. When, in ordinary life, we speak of *the* colour of the table, we only mean the sort of colour which it will seem to have to a normal spectator from an ordinary point of view under usual conditions of light. But the other colours which appear under other conditions have just as good a right to be considered real; and therefore, to avoid favouritism, we are compelled to deny that, in itself, the table has any one particular colour.

The same thing applies to the texture. With the naked eye one can see the grain, but otherwise the table looks smooth and even. If we looked at it through a microscope, we should see roughnesses and hills and valleys, and all sorts of differences that are imperceptible to the naked eye. Which of these is the "real" table? We are naturally tempted to say that what we see through the microscope is more real, but that in turn would be changed by a still more powerful microscope. If, then, we cannot trust what we see with the naked eye, why should we trust what we see through a microscope? Thus, again, the confidence in our senses with which we began deserts us.

The *shape* of the table is no better. We are all in the habit of judging as to the "real" shapes of things, and we do this so unreflectingly that we come to think we actually see the real shapes. But, in fact, as we all have to learn if we try to draw, a given thing looks different in shape from every different point of view. If our table is "really" rectangular, it will look, from almost all points of view, as if it had two acute angles and two obtuse angles. If opposite sides are parallel, they will look as if they converged to a point away from the spectator; if they are of equal length, they will look as if the nearer side were longer. All these things are not commonly noticed in looking at a table, because experience has taught us to construct the "real" shape from the apparent shape, and the "real" shape is what interests us as practical men. But the "real" shape is not what we see; it is something inferred from what we see. And what we see is constantly changing in shape as we move about the room; so that here again the senses seem not to give us the truth about the table itself, but only about the appearance of the table. Similar difficulties arise when we consider the sense of touch. It is true that the table always gives us a sensation of hardness, and we feel that it resists pressure. But the sensation we obtain depends upon how hard we press the table and also upon what part of the body we press with; thus the various sensations due to various pressures or various parts of the body cannot be supposed to reveal *directly* any definite property of the table, but at most to be *signs* of some property which perhaps *causes* all the sensations, but is not actually apparent in any of them. And the same applies still more obviously to the sounds which can be elicited by rapping the table.

Thus it becomes evident that the real table, if there is one, is not the same as what we immediately experience by sight or touch or hearing. The real table, if there is one, is not *immediately* known to us at all, but must be an inference from what is immediately known. Hence, two very difficult questions at once arise; namely, (1) Is there a real table at all? (2) If so, what sort of object can it be?

It will help us in considering these questions to have a few simple terms of which the meaning is definite and clear. Let us give the name of "sense-data" to the things that are immediately known in sensation: such things as colours, sounds, smells, hardnesses, roughnesses, and so on. We shall give the name "sensation" to the experience of being immediately aware of these things. Thus, whenever we see a colour, we have a sensation *of* the colour, but the colour itself is a sense-datum, not a sensation. The colour is that *of* which we are immediately aware, and the awareness itself is the sensation. It is plain that if we are to know anything about the table, it must be by means of the sense-data—brown colour, oblong shape, smoothness, etc.—which we associate with the table; but, for the reasons which have been given, we cannot say that the table *is* the sense-data, or even that the sense-data are directly properties of the table. Thus a problem arises as to the relation of the sense-data to the real table, supposing there is such a thing.

The real table, if it exists, we will call a "physical object." Thus we have to consider the relation of sense-data to physical objects. The collection of all physical objects is called "matter." Thus our two questions may be re-stated as follows: (1) Is there any such thing as matter? (2) If so, what is its nature?

The philosopher who first brought prominently forward the reasons for regarding the immediate objects of our senses as not existing independently of us was Bishop Berkeley (1685–1753). His *Three Dialogues Between Hylas and Philonous, in Opposition to Sceptics and Atheists,* undertake to prove that there is no such thing as matter at all, and that the world consists of nothing but minds and their ideas. Hylas has hitherto believed in matter, but he is no match for Philonous, who mercilessly drives him into contradictions and paradoxes, and makes his own denial of matter seem, in the end, as if it were almost common sense. The arguments employed are of very different value: some are important and sound, others are confused or quibbling. But Berkeley retains the merit of having shown that the existence of matter is capable of being denied without absurdity, and that if there are any things that exist independently of us they cannot be the immediate objects of our sensations.

There are two different questions involved when we ask whether matter exists, and it is important to keep them clear. We commonly mean by "matter" something which is opposed to "mind," something which we think of as occupying space and as radically incapable of any sort of thought or consciousness. It is chiefly in this sense that Berkeley denies matter; that is to say, he does not deny that the sense-data which we commonly take as signs of the existence of the table are really signs of the existence of *something* independent of us, but he does deny that this something is non-mental, that it is neither mind nor ideas entertained by some mind. He admits that there must be something which continues to exist when we go out of the room or shut our eyes, and that what we call seeing the table does really give us reason for believing in something which persists even when we are not seeing it. But he thinks that this something cannot be radically different in nature from what we see, and cannot be independent of seeing altogether, though it must be independent of *our* seeing. He is thus led to regard the "real" table as an idea in the mind of God. Such an idea has the required permanence and independence of ourselves, without being—as matter would otherwise be—something quite unknowable, in the sense that we can only infer it, and can never be directly and immediately aware of it.

Other philosophers since Berkeley have also held that, although the table does not depend for its existence upon being seen by me, it does depend upon being seen (or otherwise apprehended in sensation) by *some* mind—not necessarily the mind of God, but more often the whole collective mind of the universe. This they hold, as Berkeley does, chiefly because they think there can be nothing real—or at any rate nothing known to be real—except minds and their thoughts and feelings. We might state the argument by which they support their view in some such way as this: "Whatever can be thought of is an idea in the mind of the person thinking of it; therefore nothing can be thought of except ideas in minds; therefore anything else is inconceivable, and what is inconceivable cannot exist."

Such an argument, in my opinion, is fallacious; and of course those who advance it do not put it so shortly or so crudely. But whether valid or not, the argument has been very widely advanced in one form or another; and very many philosophers, perhaps a majority, have held that there is nothing real except minds and their ideas. Such philosophers are called "idealists." When they come to explaining matter, they either say, like Berkeley, that matter is really nothing but a collection of ideas, or they say, like Leibniz (1646–1716), that what appears as matter is really a collection of more or less rudimentary minds.

But these philosophers, though they deny matter as opposed to mind, nevertheless, in another sense, admit matter. It will be remembered that we asked two questions; namely, (1) Is there a real table at all? (2) If so, what sort of object can it be? Now both Berkeley and Leibniz admit that there is a real table, but Berkeley says it is certain ideas in the mind of God, and Leibniz says it is a colony of souls. Thus both of them answer our first question in the affirmative, and only diverge from the views of ordinary mortals in their answer to our second question. In fact, almost all philosophers seem to be agreed that there is a real table: they almost all agree that, however much our sense-data—colour, shape, smoothness, etc.—may depend upon us, yet their occurrence is a sign of something existing independently of us, something differing, perhaps, completely from our sense-data, and yet to be regarded as causing those sense-data whenever we are in a suitable relation to the real table.

Now obviously this point in which the philosophers are agreed—the view that there *is* a real table, whatever its nature may be—is vitally important, and it will be worth while to consider what reasons there are for accepting this view before we go on to the further question as to the nature of the real table. Our next

chapter, therefore, will be concerned with the reasons for supposing that there is a real table at all.

Before we go farther it will be well to consider for a moment what it is that we have discovered so far. It has appeared that, if we take any common object of the sort that is supposed to be known by the sense, what the senses *immediately* tell us is not the truth about the object as it is apart from us, but only the truth about certain sense-data which, so far as we can see, depend upon the relations between us and the object. Thus what we directly see and feel is merely "appearance," which we believe to be a sign of some "reality" behind. But if the reality is not what appears, have we any means of knowing whether there is any reality at all? And if so, have we any means of finding out what it is like?

Such questions are bewildering, and it is difficult to know that even the strangest hypotheses may not be true. Thus our familiar table, which has roused but the slightest thoughts in us hitherto, has become a problem full of surprising possibilities. The one thing we know about it is that it is not what it seems. Beyond this modest result, so far, we have the most complete liberty of conjecture. Leibniz tells us it is a community of souls; Berkeley tells us it is an idea in the mind of God; sober science, scarcely less wonderful, tells us it is a vast collection of electric charges in violent motion.

Among these surprising possibilities, doubt suggests that perhaps there is no table at all. Philosophy, if it cannot *answer* so many questions as we could wish, has at least the power of *asking* questions which increase the interest of the world, and show the strangeness and wonder lying just below the surface even in the commonest things of daily life.

II. KNOWLEDGE BY ACQUAINTANCE AND KNOWLEDGE BY DESCRIPTION

. . . there are two sorts of knowledge: knowledge of things, and knowledge of truths. . . . We shall be concerned exclusively with knowledge of things, of which in turn we shall have to distinguish two kinds. Knowledge of things, when it is of the kind we call knowledge by *acquaintance,* is essentially simpler than any knowledge of truths, and logically independent of knowledge of truths, though it would be rash to assume that human beings ever, in fact, have acquaintance with things without at the same time knowing some truth about them. Knowledge of things by *description,* on the contrary, always involves, as we shall find in the course of the present chapter, some knowledge of truths as its source and ground. But first of all we must make clear what we mean by "acquaintance" and what we mean by "description."

We shall say that we have *acquaintance* with anything of which we are directly aware, without the intermediary of any process of inference or any knowledge of truths. Thus in the presence of my table I am acquainted with the sense-data that make up the appearance of my table—its colour, shape, hardness, smoothness, etc.; all these things of which I am immediately conscious when I am seeing and touching my table. The particular shade of colour that I am seeing may have many things said about it—I may say that it is brown, that it is rather dark, and so on. But such statements, though they make me know truths *about* the colour, do not make me know the colour itself any better than I did before: so far as concerns knowledge of the colour itself, as opposed to knowledge of truths about it, I know the colour perfectly and completely when I see it, and no further knowledge of it itself is even theoretically possible. Thus the sense-data which make up the appearance of my table are things with which I have acquaintance, things immediately known to me just as they are.

My knowledge of the table as a physical object, on the contrary, is not direct knowledge. Such as it is, it is obtained through acquaintance with the sense-data that make up the appearance of the table. We have seen that it is possible, without absurdity, to doubt whether there is a table at all, whereas it is not possible to doubt the sense-data. My knowledge of the table is of the kind which we shall call "knowledge by description." The table is "the physical object which causes such-and-such sense-data." This *describes* the table by means of the sense-data. In order to know anything at all about the table, we must know truths connecting it with things with which we have acquaintance: we must know that "such-and-such sense-data are caused by a physical object." There is no state of mind in which we are directly aware of the table; all our knowledge of the table is really knowledge of *truths,* and the actual thing which is the table is not, strictly speaking, known to us at all. We know a description, and we know that there is just one object to which this description applies, thought the object itself is not directly known to us. In such a case, we say that our knowledge of the object is knowledge by description.

All our knowledge, both knowledge of things and knowledge of truths, rests upon acquaintance as its foundation. It is therefore important to consider what kinds of things there are with which we have acquaintance.

Sense-data, as we have already seen, are among the things with which we are acquainted; in fact, they supply the most obvious and striking example of knowledge by acquaintance. But if they were the sole example, our knowledge would be very much more restricted than it is. We should only know what is now present to our senses: we could not know anything about the past—not even that there was a past—nor could we know any truths about our sense-data, for all knowledge of truths, as we shall show, demands acquaintance with things which are of an essentially different character from sense-data, the things which are sometimes called "abstract ideas," but which we shall call "universals." We have therefore to consider acquaintance with other things besides sense-data if we are to obtain any tolerably adequate analysis of our knowledge.

The first extension beyond sense-data to be considered is acquaintance by *memory.* It is obvious that we often remember what we have seen or heard or had otherwise present to our senses, and that in such cases we are still immediately aware of what we remember, in spite of the fact that it appears as past and not as present. This immediate knowledge by memory is the source of all our knowledge concerning the past: without it, there could be no knowledge of the past by inference, since we should never know that there was anything past to be inferred.

The next extension to be considered is acquaintance by *introspection*. We are not only aware of things, but we are often aware of being aware of them. When I see the sun, I am often aware of my seeing the sun; thus "my seeing the sun" is an object with which I have acquaintance. When I desire food, I may be aware of my desire for food; thus "my desiring food" is an object with which I am acquainted. Similarly we may be aware of our feeling pleasure or pain, and generally of the events which happen in our minds. This kind of acquaintance, which may be called self-consciousness, is the source of all our knowledge of mental things. It is obvious that it is only what goes on in our own minds that can be thus known immediately. What goes on in the minds of others is known to us through our perception of their bodies, that is, through the sense-data in us which are associated with their bodies. But for our acquaintance with the contents of our own minds, we should be unable to imagine the minds of others, and therefore we could never arrive at the knowledge that they have minds. It seems natural to suppose that self-consciousness is one of the things that distinguish men from animals: animals, we may suppose, though they have acquaintance with sense-data, never become aware of this acquaintance. I do not mean that they *doubt* whether they exist, but that they have never become conscious of the fact that they have sensations and feelings, nor therefore of the fact that they, the subjects of their sensations and feelings, exist.

We have spoken of acquaintance with the contents of our minds as *self*-consciousness, but it is not, of course, consciousness of our *self*: it is consciousness of particular thoughts and feelings. The question whether we are also acquainted with our bare selves, as opposed to particular thoughts and feelings, is a very difficult one, upon which it would be rash to speak positively. When we try to look into ourselves we always seem to come upon some particular thought or feeling, and not upon the "I" which has the thought or feeling. Nevertheless there are some reasons for thinking that we are acquainted with the "I," though the ac-

quaintance is hard to disentangle from other things. To make clear what sort of reason there is, let us consider for a moment what our acquaintance with particular thoughts really involves.

When I am acquainted with "my seeing the sun," it seems plain that I am acquainted with two different things in relation to each other. On the one hand there is the sense-datum which represents the sun to me, on the other hand there is that which sees this sense-datum. All acquaintance, such as my acquaintance with the sense-datum which represents the sun, seems obviously a relation between the person acquainted and the object with which the person is acquainted. When a case of acquaintance is one with which I can be acquainted (as I am acquainted with my acquaintance with the sense-datum representing the sun), it is plain that the person acquainted is myself. Thus, when I am acquainted with my seeing the sun, the whole fact with which I am acquainted is "Self-acquainted-with-sense-datum."

Further, we know the truth "I am acquainted with this sense-datum." It is hard to see how we could know this truth, or even understand what is meant by it, unless we were acquainted with something which we call "I." It does not seem necessary to suppose that we are acquainted with a more or less permanent person, the same to-day as yesterday, but it does seem as though we must be acquainted with that thing, whatever its nature, which sees the sun and has acquaintance with sense-data. Thus, in some sense it would seem we must be acquainted with our Selves as opposed to our particular experiences. But the question is difficult, and complicated arguments can be adduced on either side. Hence, although acquaintance with ourselves seems *probably* to occur, it is not wise to assert that it undoubtedly does occur.

We may therefore sum up as follows what has been said concerning acquaintance with things that exist. We have acquaintance in sensation with the data of the outer senses, and in introspection with the data of what may be called the inner sense—thoughts, feelings, desires, etc.; we have acquaintance in memory with things which have been data either of the outer senses or of the inner sense. Further, it is probable, though not certain, that we have acquaintance with Self, as that which is aware of things or has desires towards things.

In addition to our acquaintance with particular existing things, we also have acquaintance with what we shall call *universals*, that is to say, general ideas, such as *whiteness, diversity, brotherhood*, and so on. Every complete sentence must contain at least one word which stands for a universal, since all verbs have a meaning which is universal. . . . Awareness of universals is called *conceiving*, and a universal of which we are aware is called a *concept*.

It will be seen that among the objects with which we are acquainted are not included physical objects (as opposed to sense-data), nor other people's minds. These things are known to us by what I call "knowledge by description," which we must now consider.

By a "description" I mean any phrase of the form "a so-and-so" or "the so-and-so." A phrase of the form "a so-and-so" I shall call an "ambiguous" description; a phrase of the form "the so-and-so" (in the singular) I shall call a "definite" description. Thus "a man" is an ambiguous description, and "the man with the iron mask" is a definite description. There are various problems connected with ambiguous description, but I pass them by, since they do not directly concern the matter we are discussing, which is the nature of our knowledge concerning objects in cases where we know that there is an object answering to a definite description, though we are not *acquainted* with any such object. This is a matter which is concerned exclusively with *definite* descriptions. I shall therefore, in the sequel, speak simply of "descriptions" when I mean "definite descriptions." Thus a description will mean any phrase of the form "the so-and-so" in the singular.

We shall say that an object is "known by description" when we know that it is "the-so-and-so," i.e. when we know that there is one object, and no more, having a certain property; and it will generally be implied that we do not have knowledge of the same object by acquaintance. We know that the man with the iron mask existed, and many propositions are known about him; but we do not know who he was. We know that the candidate who gets the most votes will be elected, and in this case we

are very likely also acquainted (in the only sense in which one can be acquainted with some one else) with the man who is, in fact, the candidate who will get most votes; but we do not know which of the candidates he is, i.e. we do not know any proposition of the form "A is the candidate who will get most votes" where A is one of the candidates by name. We shall say that we have "merely descriptive knowledge" of the so-and-so when, although we know that the so-and-so exists, and although we may possibly be acquainted with the object which is, in fact, the so-and-so, yet we do not know any proposition "*a* is the so-and-so," where *a* is something with which we are acquainted.

When we say "the so-and-so exists," we mean that there is just one object which is the so-and-so. The proposition "*a* is the so-and-so" means that *a* has the property so-and-so, and nothing else has. "Mr. A. is the Unionist candidate for this constituency" means "Mr. A. is a Unionist candidate for this constituency, and no one else is." "The Unionist candidate for this constituency exists" means "some one is a Unionist candidate for this constituency, and no one else is." Thus, when we are acquainted with an object which is the so-and-so, we know that the so-and-so exists; but we may know that the so-and-so exists when we are not acquainted with any object which we know to be the so-and-so, and even when we are not acquainted with any object which, in fact, is the so-and-so.

Common words, even proper names, are usually really descriptions. That is to say, the thought in the mind of a person using a proper name correctly can generally only be expressed explicitly if we replace the proper name by a description. Moreover, the description required to express the thought will vary for different people, or for the same person at different times. The only thing constant (so long as the name is rightly used) is the object to which the name applies. But so long as this remains constant, the particular description involved usually makes no difference to the truth or falsehood of the proposition in which the name appears.

Let us take some illustrations. Suppose some statement made about Bismarck. Assuming that there is such a thing as direct acquaintance with oneself, Bismarck himself might have used his name directly to designate the particular person with whom he was acquainted. In this case, if he made a judgement about himself, he himself might be a constituent of the judgement. Here the proper name has the direct use which it always wishes to have, as simply standing for a certain object, and not for a description of the object. But if a person who knew Bismarck made a judgement about him, the case is different. What this person was acquainted with were certain sense-data which he connected (rightly, we will suppose) with Bismarck's body. His body, as a physical object, and still more his mind, were only known as the body and the mind connected with these sense-data. That is, they were known by description. It is, of course, very much a matter of chance which characteristics of a man's appearance will come into a friend's mind when he thinks of him; thus the description actually in the friend's mind is accidental. The essential point is that he knows that the various descriptions all apply to the same entity, in spite of not being acquainted with the entity in question.

When we, who did not know Bismarck, make a judgement about him, the description in our minds will probably be some more or less vague mass of historical knowledge—far more, in most cases, than is required to identify him. But, for the sake of illustration, let us assume that we think of him as "the first Chancellor of the German Empire." Here all the words are abstract except "German." The word "German" will, again, have different meanings for different people. To some it will recall travels in Germany, to some the look of Germany on the map, and so on. But if we are to obtain a description which we know to be applicable, we shall be compelled, at some point, to bring in a reference to a particular with which we are acquainted. Such reference is involved in any mention of past, present, and future (as opposed to definite dates), or of here and there, or of what others have told us. Thus is would seem that, in some way or other, a description known to be applicable to a particular must involve some reference to a particular with which we are acquainted, if our knowledge

about the thing described is not to be merely what follows *logically* from the description. For example, "the most long-lived of men" is a description involving only universals, which must apply to some man, but we can make no judgements concerning this man which involve knowledge about him beyond what the description gives. If, however, we say, "The first Chancellor of the German Empire was an astute diplomatist," we can only be assured of the truth of our judgement in virtue of something with which we are acquainted—usually a testimony heard or read. Apart from the information we convey to others, apart from the fact about the actual Bismarck, which gives importance to our judgement, the thought we really have contains the one or more particulars involved, and otherwise consists wholly of concepts.

All names of places—London, England, Europe, the Earth, the Solar System—similarly involve, when used, descriptions which start from some one or more particulars with which we are acquainted. I suspect that even the Universe, as considered by metaphysics, involves such a connexion with particulars. In logic, on the contrary, where we are concerned not merely with what does exist, but with whatever might or could exist or be, no reference to actual particulars is involved.

It would seem that, when we make a statement about something only known by description, we often *intend* to make our statement, not in the form involving the description, but about the actual thing described. That is to say, when we say anything about Bismarck, we should like, if we could, to make the judgement which Bismarck alone can make, namely, the judgement of which he himself is a constituent. In this we are necessarily defeated, since the actual Bismarck is unknown to us. But we know that there is an object B, called Bismarck, and that B was an astute diplomatist. We can thus *describe* the proposition we should like to affirm, namely, "B was an astute diplomatist," where B is the object which was Bismarck. If we are describing Bismarck as "the first Chancellor of the German Empire," the proposition we should like to affirm may be described as "the proposition asserting, concerning the actual object which was the first

Chancellor of the German Empire, that this object was an astute diplomatist." What enables us to communicate in spite of the varying descriptions we employ is that we know there is a true proposition concerning the actual Bismarck, and that however we may vary the description (so long as the description is correct) the proposition described is still the same. This proposition, which is described and is known to be true, is what interests us; but we are not acquainted with the proposition itself, and do not know *it*, though we know it is true.

It will be seen that there are various stages in the removal from acquaintance with particulars: there is Bismarck to people who knew him; Bismarck to those who only know of him through history; the man with the iron mask; the longest-lived of men. These are progressively further removed from acquaintance with particulars; the first comes as near to acquaintance as is possible in regard to another person; in the second, we shall still be said to know "who Bismarck was"; in the third, we do not know who was the man with the iron mask, though we can know many propositions about him which are not logically deducible from the fact that he wore an iron mask; in the fourth, finally, we know nothing beyond what is logically deducible from the definition of the man. There is a similar hierarchy in the region of universals. Many universals, like many particulars, are only known to us by description. But here, as in the case of particulars, knowledge concerning what is known by description is ultimately reducible to knowledge concerning what is known by acquaintance.

The fundamental principle in the analysis of propositions containing descriptions is this: *Every proposition which we can understand must be composed wholly of constituents with which we are acquainted.*

We shall not at this stage attempt to answer all the objections which may be urged against this fundamental principle. For the present, we shall merely point out that, in some way or other, it must be possible to meet these objections, for it is scarcely conceivable that we can make a judgement or entertain a supposition without knowing what it is that we are judging or supposing about. We must attach *some* meaning to the words we use, if we are to speak significantly and not utter mere noise; and the meaning we attach to our words must be something with which we are acquainted. Thus when, for example, we make a statement about Julius Caesar, it is plain that Julius Caesar himself is not before our minds, since we are not acquainted with him. We have in mind some *description* of Julius Caesar: "the man who was assassinated on the Ides of March," "the founder of the Roman Empire," or, perhaps, merely "the man whose name was *Julius Caesar*." (In this last description, *Julius Caesar* is a noise or shape with which we are acquainted.) Thus our statement does not mean quite what it seems to mean, but means something involving, instead of Julius Caesar, some description of him which is composed wholly of particulars and universals with which we are acquainted.

The chief importance of knowledge by description is that it enables us to pass beyond the limits of our private experience. In spite of the fact that we can only know truths which are wholly composed of terms which we have experienced in acquaintance, we can yet have knowledge by description of things which we have never experienced. In view of the very narrow range of our immediate experience, this result is vital, and until it is understood, much of our knowledge must remain mysterious and therefore doubtful.

15 / A. J. AYER (1910–1989)
VERIFICATION AND PHILOSOPHY

THE PRINCIPLE OF VERIFICATION

The principle of verification is supposed to furnish a criterion by which it can be determined whether or not a sentence is literally meaningful. A simple way to formulate it would be to say that a sentence had literal meaning if and only if the proposition it expressed was either analytic or empirically verifiable. To this, however, it might be objected that unless a sentence was literally meaningful it would not express a proposition;[1] for it is commonly assumed that every proposition is either true or false, and to say that a sentence expressed what was either true or false would entail saying that it was literally meaningful. Accordingly, if the principle of verification were formulated in this way, it might be argued not only that it was incomplete as a criterion of meaning, since it would not cover the case of sentences which did not express any propositions at all, but also that it was otiose, on the ground that the question which it was designed to answer must already have been answered before the principle could be applied. It will be seen that when I introduce the principle in this book I try to avoid this difficulty by speaking of "putative propositions" and of the proposition which a sentence "purports to express"; but this device is not satisfactory. For, in the first place, the use of words like "putative" and "purports" seems to bring in psychological considerations into which I do not wish to enter, and secondly, in the case where the "putative proposition" is neither analytic nor empirically verifiable, there would, according to this way of speaking, appear to be nothing that the sentence in question could properly be said to express. But if a sentence expresses nothing there seems to be a contradiction in saying that what it expresses is empirically unverifiable; for even if the sentence is adjudged on this ground to be meaningless, the reference to "what it expresses" appears still to imply that something is expressed.

This is, however, no more than a terminological difficulty, and there are various ways in which it might be met. One of them would be to make the criterion of verifiability apply directly to sentences, and so eliminate the reference to propositions altogether. This would, indeed, run counter to ordinary usage, since one would not normally say of a sentence, as opposed to a proposition, that it was capable of being verified, or, for that matter, that it was either true or false; but it might be argued that such a departure from ordinary usage was justified, if it could be shown to have some practical advantage. The fact is, however, that the practical advantage seems to lie on the other side. For while it is true that the use of the word "proposition" does not enable us to say anything that we could not, in principle, say without it, it does fulfill an important function; for it makes it possible to express what is valid not merely for a particular sentence s but for any sentence to which s is logically equivalent. Thus, if I assert, for example, that the proposition p is entailed by the proposition q I am indeed claiming implicitly that the English sentence s which expresses p can be validly derived from the English sentence r which expresses q, but this is not the whole of my claim.

From A. J. Ayer, *Language, Truth, and Logic*, 2d ed. New York: Dover Publications, 1946. Reprinted by permission of Dover Publications, Inc.

For, if I am right, it will also follow that any sentence, whether of the English or any other language, that is equivalent to *s* can be validly derived, in the language in question, from any sentence that is equivalent to *r;* and it is this that my use of the word "proposition" indicates. Admittedly, we could decide to use the word "sentence" in the way in which we now use the word "proposition," but this would not be conducive to clarity, particularly as the word "sentence" is already ambiguous. Thus, in a case of repetition, it can be said either that there are two different sentences or that the same sentence has been formulated twice. It is in the latter sense that I have so far been using the word, but the other usage is equally legitimate. In either usage, a sentence which was expressed in English would be accounted a different sentence from its French equivalent, but this would not hold good for the new usage of the word "sentence" that we should be introducing if we substituted "sentence" for "proposition." For in that case we should have to say that the English expression and its French equivalent were different formulations of the same sentence. We might indeed be justified in increasing the ambiguity of the word "sentence" in this way if we thereby avoided any of the difficulties that have been thought to be attached to the use of the word "proposition"; but I do not think that this is to be achieved by the mere substitution of one verbal token for another. Accordingly, I conclude that this technical use of the word "sentence," though legitimate in itself, would be likely to promote confusion, without securing us any compensatory advantage.

A second way of meeting our original difficulty would be to extend the use of the word "proposition," so that anything that could properly be called a sentence would be said to express a proposition, whether or not the sentence was literally meaningful. This course would have the advantage of simplicity, but it is open to two objections. The first is that it would involve a departure from current philosophical usage; and the second is that it would oblige us to give up the rule that every proposition is to be accounted either true or false. For while, if we adopted this new usage, we should still be able to say that anything that was either true or false was a proposition, the converse would no longer hold good; for a proposition would be neither true nor false if it was expressed by a sentence which was literally meaningless. I do not myself think that these objections are very serious, but they are perhaps sufficiently so to make it advisable to solve our terminological problem in some other way.

The solution that I prefer is to introduce a new technical term; and for this purpose I shall make use of the familiar word "statement," though I shall perhaps be using it in a slightly unfamiliar sense. Thus I propose that any form of words that is grammatically significant shall be held to constitute a sentence, and that every indicative sentence, whether it is literally meaningful or not, shall be regarded as expressing a statement. Furthermore, any two sentences which are mutually translatable will be said to express the same statement. The word "proposition," on the other hand, will be reserved for what is expressed by sentences which are literally meaningful. Thus, the class of propositions become, in this usage, a subclass of the class of statements, and one way of describing the use of the principle of verification would be to say that it provided a means of determining when an indicative sentence expressed a proposition, or, in other words, of distinguishing the statements that belonged to the class of propositions from those that did not.

It should be remarked that this decision to say that sentences express statements involves nothing more than the adoption of a verbal convention; and the proof of this is that the question, "What do sentences express?" to which it provides an answer is not a factual question. To ask of any particular sentence what it is that it expresses may, indeed, be to put a factual question; and one way of answering it would be to produce another sentence which was a translation of the first. But if the general question, "What do sentences express?" is to be interpreted factually, all that can be said in answer is that, since it is not the case that all sentences are equivalent, there is not any one thing that they all express. At the same time, it is useful to have a means of referring indefinitely to "what sentences express" in cases where the sentences themselves are not particularly specified; and this purpose is served by the introduction of the word "statement" as a technical term. Accordingly, in saying that sentences express statements, we are indicating how this technical term is to be understood, but we are not thereby conveying any factual information in the sense in which we should be conveying factual information if the question we were answering was empirical. This may, indeed, seem a point too obvious to be worth making; but the question, "What do sentences express?" is closely analogous to the question, "What do sentences mean?" and, as I have tried to show elsewhere,[2] the question, "What do sentences mean?" has been a source of confusion to philosophers because they have mistakenly thought it to be factual. To say that indicative sentences mean propositions is indeed legitimate, just as it is legitimate to say that they express statements. But what we are doing, in giving answers of this kind, is to lay down conventional definitions; and it is important that these conventional definitions should not be confused with statements of empirical fact.

Returning now to the principle of verification, we may, for the sake of brevity, apply it directly to statements rather than to the sentences which express them, and we can then reformulate it by saying that a statement is held to be literally meaningful if and only if it is either analytic or empirically verifiable. But what is to be understood in this context by the term "verifiable"? I do indeed attempt to answer this question in the first chapter of this book; but I have to acknowledge that my answer is not very satisfactory.

To begin with, it will be seen that I distinguish between a "strong" and a "weak" sense of the term "verifiable," and that I explain this distinction by saying that "a proposition is said to be verifiable in the strong sense of the term, if and only if its truth could be conclusively established in experience," but that "it is verifiable, in the weak sense, if it is possible for experience to render it probable." And I then give reasons for deciding that it is only the weak sense of the term that is required by my principle of verification. What I seem, however, to have overlooked is that, as I represent them, these are not two genuine alternatives.[3] For I subsequently go on to argue that all empirical propositions are hypotheses which are continually subject to the test of further experience; and from this it would follow not merely that the truth of any such proposition never was conclusively established but that it never could be; for however strong the evidence in its favour, there would never be a point at which it was impossible for further experience to go against it. But this would mean that my "strong" sense of the term "verifiable" had no possible application, and in that case there was no need for me to qualify the other sense of "verifiable" as weak; for on my own showing it was the only sense in which any proposition could conceivably be verified.

If I do not now draw this conclusion, it is because I have come to think that there is a class of empirical propositions of which it is permissible to say that they can be verified conclusively. It is characteristic of these propositions, which I have elsewhere[4] called "basic propositions," that they refer solely to the content of a single experience, and what may be said to verify them conclusively is the occurrence of the experience to which they uniquely refer. Furthermore, I should now agree with those who say that propositions of this kind are "incorrigible," assuming that what is meant by their being incorrigible is that it is impossible to be mistaken about them except in a verbal sense. In a verbal sense, indeed, it is always possible to misdescribe one's experience; but if one intends to do no more than record what is experienced without relating it to anything else, it is not possible to be factually mistaken; and the reason for this is that one is making no claim that any further fact could confute. It is, in short, a case of "nothing venture, nothing lose." It is, however, equally a case of "nothing venture, nothing win," since the mere recording of one's present experience does not serve to convey any information either to any other person or indeed to oneself; for in knowing a basic proposition to be true one obtains no further knowledge than what is already afforded by the occurrence of the relevant experience. Admittedly, the form of words that is used to express a basic proposition may be understood to express something that is informative both to another person and to oneself, but when it is so understood it no longer expresses a basic proposition. It was for this reason, indeed, that I maintained, in the fifth chapter of this book, that there could not be such things as basic propositions, in the sense in which I am now using the term; for the burden of my argument was that no synthetic proposition could be purely ostensive. My reasoning on this point was not in itself incorrect, but I think that I mistook its purport. For I seem not to have perceived that what I was really doing was to suggest a motive for refusing to apply the term "proposition" to statements that "directly recorded an immediate experience"; and this is a terminological point which is not of any great importance.

Whether or not one chooses to include basic statements in the class of empirical propositions, and so to admit that some empirical propositions can be conclusively verified, it will remain true that the vast majority of the propositions that people actually express are neither themselves basic statements, nor deducible from any finite set of basic statements. Consequently, if the principle of verification is to be seriously considered as a criterion of meaning, it must be interpreted in such a way as to admit statements that are not so strongly verifiable as basic statements are supposed to be. But how then is the word "verifiable" to be understood?

It will be seen that, in this book, I begin by suggesting that a statement is "weakly" verifiable, and therefore meaningful, according to my criterion, if "some possible sense-experience would be relevant to the determination of its truth or falsehood." But, as I recognized, this itself requires interpretation; for the word "relevant" is uncomfortably vague. Accordingly, I put forward a second version of my principle, which I shall restate here in slightly different terms, using the phrase "observation-statement," in place of "experiential proposition," to designate a statement "which records an actual or possible observation." In this version, then, the principle is that a statement is verifiable, and consequently meaningful, if some observation-statement can be deduced from it in conjunction with certain other premises, without being deducible from those other premises alone.

I say of this criterion that it "seems liberal enough," but in fact it is far too liberal, since it allows meaning to any statement whatsoever. For, given any statement *"S"* and an observation-statement *"O," "O"* follows from *"S"* and "if *S* then *O*" without following from "if *S* then *O*" alone. Thus, the statements "the Absolute is lazy" and "if the Absolute is lazy, this is white" jointly entail the observation-statement "this is white," and since "this is white" does not follow from either of these premises, taken by itself, both of them satisfy my criterion of meaning. Furthermore, this would hold good for any other piece of nonsense that one cared to put, as an example, in place of "the Absolute is lazy," provided only that it had the grammatical form of an indicative sentence. But a criterion of meaning that allows such latitude as this is evidently unacceptable.[5]

It may be remarked that the same objection applies to the proposal that we should take the possibility of falsification as our criterion. For, given any statement *"S"* and any observation-statement *"O," "O"* will be incompatible with the conjunction of *"S"* and "if *S* then not *O*." We could indeed avoid the difficulty, in either case, by leaving out the stipulation about the other premises. But as this would involve the exclusion of all hypotheticals from the class of empirical propositions, we should escape from making our criteria too liberal only at the cost of making them too stringent.

Another difficulty which I overlooked in my original attempt to formulate the principle of verification is that most empirical propositions are in some degree vague. Thus, as I have remarked elsewhere,[6] what is required to verify a statement about a material thing is never the occurrence of precisely this or precisely that sense-content, but only the occurrence of one or other of the sense-contents that fall within a fairly indefinite range. We do indeed test any such statement by making observations which consist in the occurrence of particular sense-contents; but, for any test that we actually carry out, there is always an indefinite number of other tests, differing to some extent in respect either of their conditions or their results, that would have served the same purpose. And this means that there is never any set of observation-statements of which it can truly be said that precisely they are entailed by any given statement about a material thing.

Nevertheless, it is only by the occurrence of some sense-content, and consequently by the truth of some observation-statement, that any statement about a material thing is actually verified; and from this it follows that every significant statement about a material thing can be represented as entailing a disjunction of observation-statements, although the terms of this disjunction, being infinite, can not be enumerated in detail. Consequently, I do not think that we need be troubled by the difficulty about vagueness, so long as it is understood that when we speak of the "entailment" of observation-statements, what we are considering to be deducible from the premises in question is not any particular observation-statement, but only one or other of a set of such statements, where the defining characteristic of the set is that all its members refer to sense-contents that fall within a certain specifiable range.

There remains the more serious objection that my criterion, as it stands, allows meaning to any indicative statement whatsoever. To meet this, I shall emend it as follows. I propose to say that a statement is directly verifiable if it is either itself an observation-statement, or is such that in conjunction with one or more observation-statements it entails at least one observation-statement which is not deducible from these other premises alone; and I propose to say that a statement is indirectly verifiable if it satisfies the following conditions: first, that in conjunction with certain other premises it entails one or more directly verifiable statements which are not deducible from these other premises alone; and secondly, that these other premises do not include any statement that is not either analytic, or directly verifiable, or capable of being independently established as indirectly verifiable. And I can now reformulate the principle of verification as requiring of a

literally meaningful statement, which is not analytic, that it should be either directly or indirectly verifiable, in the foregoing sense.

It may be remarked that in giving my account of the conditions in which a statement is to be considered indirectly verifiable, I have explicitly put in the proviso that the "other premises" may include analytic statements; and my reason for doing this is that I intend in this way to allow for the case of scientific theories which are expressed in terms that do not themselves designate anything observable. For while the statements that contain these terms may not appear to describe anything that anyone could ever observe, a "dictionary" may be provided by means of which they can be transformed into statements that are verifiable; and the statements which constitute the dictionary can be regarded as analytic. Were this not so, there would be nothing to choose between such scientific theories and those that I should dismiss as metaphysical; but I take it to be characteristic of the metaphysician, in my somewhat pejorative sense of the term, not only that his statements do not describe anything that is capable, even in principle, of being observed, but also that no dictionary is provided by means of which they can be transformed into statements that are directly or indirectly verifiable.

Metaphysical statements, in my sense of the term, are excluded also by the older empiricist principle that no statement is literally meaningful unless it describes what could be experienced, where the criterion of what could be experienced is that it should be something of the same kind as actually has been experienced.[7] But, apart from its lack of precision, this empiricist principle has, to my mind, the defect of imposing too harsh a condition upon the form of scientific theories; for it would seem to imply that it was illegitimate to introduce any term that did not itself designate something observable. The principle of verification, on the other hand, is, as I have tried to show, more liberal in this respect, and in view of the use that is actually made of scientific theories which the other would rule out, I think that the more liberal criterion is to be preferred.

It has sometimes been assumed by my critics that I take the principle of verification to imply that no statement can be evidence for another unless it is a part of its meaning; but this is not the case. Thus, to make use of a simple illustration, the statement that I have blood on my coat may, in certain circumstances, confirm the hypothesis that I have committed a murder, but it is not part of the meaning of the statement that I have committed a murder that I should have blood upon my coat, nor, as I understand it, does the principle of verification imply that it is. For one statement may be evidence for another, and still neither itself express a necessary condition of the truth of this other statement, nor belong to any set of statements which determines a range within which such a necessary condition falls; and it is only in these cases that the principle of verification yields the conclusion that the one statement is part of the meaning of the other. Thus, from the fact that it is only by the making of some observation that any statement about a material thing can be directly verified it follows, according to the principle of verification, that every such statement contains some observation-statement or other as part of its meaning, and it follows also that, although its generality may prevent any finite set of observation-statements from exhausting its meaning, it does not contain anything as part of its meaning that cannot be represented as an observation-statement; but there may still be many observation-statements that are relevant to its truth or falsehood without being part of its meaning at all. Again, a person who affirms the existence of a deity may try to support his contention by appealing to the facts of religious experience; but it does not follow from this that the factual meaning of his statement is wholly contained in the propositions by which these religious experiences are described. For there may be other empirical facts that he would also consider to be relevant; and it is possible that the descriptions of these other empirical facts can more properly be regarded as containing the factual meaning of his statement than the descriptions of the religious experiences. At the same time, if one accepts the principle of verification, one must hold that his statement does not have any other factual meaning than what is contained in at least some of the relevant empirical propositions; and that if it is so interpreted that no possible experience could go to verify it, it does not have any factual meaning at all.

In putting forward the principle of verification as a criterion of meaning, I do not overlook the fact that the word "meaning" is commonly used in a variety of senses, and I do not wish to deny that in some of these senses a statement may properly be said to be meaningful even though it is neither analytic nor empirically verifiable. I should, however, claim that there was at least one proper use of the word "meaning" in which it would be incorrect to say that a statement was meaningful unless it satisfied the principle of verification; and I have, perhaps tendentiously, used the expression "literal meaning" to distinguish this use from the others, while applying the expression "factual meaning" to the case of statements which satisfy my criterion without being analytic. Furthermore, I suggest that it is only if it is literally meaningful, in this sense, that a statement can properly be said to be either true or false. Thus, while I wish the principle of verification itself to be regarded, not as an empirical hypothesis,[8] but as a definition, it is not supposed to be entirely arbitrary. It is indeed open to anyone to adopt a different criterion of meaning and so to produce an alternative definition which may very well correspond to one of the ways in which the word "meaning" is commonly used. And if a statement satisfied such a criterion, there is, no doubt, some proper use of the word "understanding" in which it would be capable of being understood. Nevertheless, I think that, unless it satisfied the principle of verification, it would not be capable of being understood in the sense in which either scientific hypotheses or common-sense statements are habitually understood. I confess, however, that it now seems to me unlikely that any metaphysician would yield to a claim of this kind; and although I should still defend the use of the criterion of verifiability as a methodological principle. I realize that for the effective elimination of metaphysics it needs to be supported by detailed analyses of particular metaphysical arguments.

THE *A PRIORI*

In saying that the certainty of *a priori* propositions depends upon the fact that they are tautologies, I use the word "tautology" in such a way that a proposition can be said to be a tautology if it is analytic; and I hold that a proposition is analytic if it is true solely in virtue of the meaning of its constituent symbols, and cannot therefore be either confirmed or refuted by any fact of experience. It has, indeed, been suggested[9] that my treatment of *a priori* propositions makes them into a sub-class of empirical propositions. For I sometimes seem to imply that they describe the way in which certain symbols are used, and it is undoubtedly an empirical fact that people use symbols in the ways that they do. This is not, however, the position that I wish to hold; nor do I think that I am committed to it. For although I say that the validity of *a priori* propositions depends upon certain facts about verbal usage, I do not think that this is equivalent to saying that they describe these facts in the sense in which empirical propositions may describe the facts that verify them; and indeed I argue that they do not, in this sense, describe any facts at all. At the same time I allow that the usefulness of *a priori* propositions is founded both on the empirical fact that certain symbols are used in the way that they are and on the empirical fact that the symbols in question are successfully applied to our experience; and I try in the fourth chapter of this book to show how this is so.

Just as it is a mistake to identify *a priori* propositions with empirical propositions about language, so I now think that it is a mistake to say that they are themselves linguistic rules.[10] For apart from the fact that they can properly be said to be true, which linguistic rules cannot, they are distinguished also by being necessary, whereas linguistic rules are arbitrary. At the same time, if they are necessary it is only because the relevant linguistic rules are presupposed. Thus, it is a contingent, empirical

fact that the word "earlier" is used in English to mean earlier, and it is an arbitrary, though convenient, rule of language that words that stand for temporal relations are to be used transitively; but, given this rule, the proposition that, if A is earlier than B and B is earlier than C, A is earlier than C becomes a necessary truth. Similarly, in Russell's and Whitehead's system of logic, it is a contingent, empirical fact that the sign "⊃" should have been given the meaning that it has, and the rules which govern the use of this sign are conventions, which themselves are neither true nor false; but, given these rules the *a priori* proposition "q. ⊃ .p ⊃ q" is necessarily true. Being *a priori,* this proposition gives no information in the ordinary sense in which an empirical proposition may be said to give information, nor does it itself prescribe how the logical constant "⊃" is to be used. What it does is to elucidate the proper use of this logical constant; and it is in this way that it is informative.

An argument which has been brought against the doctrine that *a priori* propositions of the form "p entails q" are analytic is that it is possible for one proposition to entail another without containing it as part of its meaning; for it is assumed that this would not be possible if the analytic view of entailment were correct.[11] But the answer to this is that the question whether one proposition is part of the meaning of another is ambiguous. If you say, for example, as I think most of those who raise this objection would, that *q* is not part of the meaning of *p* if it is possible to understand *p* without thinking of *q,* then clearly one proposition can entail another without containing it as part of its meaning; for it can hardly be maintained that anyone who considers a given set of propositions must be immediately conscious of all that they entail. This is, however, to make a point with which I do not think that any upholder of the analytic view of entailment would wish to disagree; for it is common ground that deductive reasoning may lead to conclusions which are new in the sense that one had not previously apprehended them. But if this is admitted by those who say that propositions of the form "p entails q" are analytic, how can they also say that if *p* entails *q* the meaning of *q* is contained in that of *p?* The answer is that they are using a criterion of meaning, whether the verification principle or another, from which it follows that when one proposition entails another the meaning of the second is contained in that of the first. In other words, they determine the meaning of a proposition by considering what it entails; and this is, to my mind, a perfectly legitimate procedure.[12] If this procedure is adopted the proposition that, if p entails q, the meaning of q is contained in that of p, itself becomes analytic; and it is therefore not to be refuted by any such psychological facts as those on which the critics of this view rely. At the same time, it may fairly be objected to it that it does not give us much information about the nature of entailment; for although it entitles us to say that the logical consequences of a proposition are explicative of its meaning, this is only because the meaning of a proposition is understood to depend upon what it entails.

PROPOSITIONS ABOUT THE PAST AND ABOUT OTHER MINDS

By saying of propositions about the past that they are "rules for the prediction of those 'historical' experiences which are commonly said to verify them" I seem to imply that they can somehow be translated into propositions about present or future experiences. But this is certainly incorrect. Statements about the past may be verifiable in the sense that when they are conjoined with other premises of a suitable kind they may entail observation-statements which do not follow from these other premises alone; but I do not think that the truth of any observation-statements which refer to the present or the future is a necessary condition of the truth of any statement about the past. This does not mean, however, that propositions referring to the past cannot be analysed in phenomenal terms; for they can be taken as implying that certain observations would have occurred if certain conditions had been fulfilled. But the trouble is that these conditions never can be fulfilled; for they require of the observer that he should occupy a temporal position that *ex hypothesi* he does not. This difficulty, however, is not a peculiarity of propositions about the

past; for it is true also of unfulfilled conditionals about the present that their protases cannot in fact be satisfied, since they require of the observer that he should be occupying a different spatial position from that which he actually does. But, as I have remarked elsewhere,[13] just as it is a contingent fact that a person happens at a given moment to be occupying a particular position in space, so is it a contingent fact that he happens to be living at a particular time. And from this I conclude that if one is justified in saying that events which are remote in space are observable, in principle, the same may be said of events which are situated in the past.

Concerning the experiences of others I confess that I am doubtful whether the account that is given in this book is correct; but I am not convinced that it is not. In another work, I have argued that, since it is a contingent fact that any particular experience belongs to the series of experiences which constitutes a given person, rather than to another series which constitutes someone else, there is a sense in which "it is not logically inconceivable that I should have an experience that is in fact owned by someone else"; and from this I inferred that the use of "the argument from analogy" might after all be justified.[14] More recently, however, I have come to think that this reasoning is very dubious. For while it is possible to imagine circumstances in which we might have found it convenient to say of two different persons that they owned the same experience, the act is that, according to our present usage, it is a necessary proposition that they do not; and, since this is so, I am afraid that the argument from analogy remains open to the objections that are brought against it in this book. Consequently, I am inclined to revert to a "behaviouristic" interpretation of propositions about other people's experiences. But I own that it has an air of paradox which prevents me from being wholly confident that it is true.[15]

THE EMOTIVE THEORY OF VALUES

The emotive theory of values, which is developed in the sixth chapter of this book, has provoked a fair amount of criticism; but I find that this criticism has been directed more often against the positivistic principles on which the theory has been assumed to depend than against the theory itself.[16] Now I do not deny that in putting forward this theory I was concerned with maintaining the general consistency of my position; but it is not the only ethical theory that would have satisfied this requirement, nor does it actually entail any of the non-ethical statements which form the remainder of my argument. Consequently, even if it could be shown that these other statements were invalid, this would not in itself refute the emotive analysis of ethical judgements; and in fact I believe this analysis to be valid on its own account.

Having said this, I must acknowledge that the theory is here presented in a very summary way, and that it needs to be supported by a more detailed analysis of specimen ethical judgements than I make any attempt to give.[17] Thus, among other things, I fail to bring out the point that the common objects of moral approval or disapproval are not particular actions so much as classes of actions; by which I mean that if an action is labelled right or wrong, or good or bad, as the case may be, it is because it is thought to be an action of a certain type. And this point seems to me important, because I think that what seems to be an ethical judgement is very often a factual classification of an action as belonging to some class of actions by which a certain moral attitude on the part of the speaker is habitually aroused. Thus, a man who is a convinced utilitarian may simply mean by calling an action right that it tends to promote, the general happiness; and in that case the validity of his statement becomes an empirical matter of fact. Similarly, a man who bases his ethical judgements upon his religious views may actually mean by calling an action right or wrong that it is the sort of action that is enjoined or forbidden by some ecclesiastical authority; and this also may be empirically verified. Now in these cases the form of words by which the factual statement is expressed is the same as that which would be used to express a normative statement; and this may to some extent explain why statements which are recognized to be normative are nevertheless often thought to be factual. Moreover, a great many ethical statements contain, as a factual element, some description of the action, or the situation, to which the ethical term in question is being applied. But although there may be a number of cases in which this ethical term is itself to be understood descriptively, I do not think that this is always so. I think that there are many statements in which an ethical term is used in a purely normative way, and it is to statements of this kind that the emotive theory of ethics is intended to apply.

The objection that if the emotive theory was correct it would be impossible for one person to contradict another on a question of value is here met by the answer that what seem to be disputes about questions of value are really disputes about questions of fact. I should, however, have made it clear that it does not follow from this that two persons cannot significantly disagree about a question of value, or that it is idle for them to attempt to convince one another. For a consideration of any dispute about a matter of taste will show that there can be disagreement without formal contradiction, and that in order to alter another man's opinions, in the sense of getting him to change his attitude, it is not necessary to contradict anything that he asserts. Thus, if one wishes to affect another person in such a way as to bring his sentiments on a given point into accordance with one's own, there are various ways in which one may proceed. One may, for example, call his attention to certain facts that one supposes him to have overlooked; and, as I have already remarked, I believe that much of what passes for ethical discussion is a proceeding of this type. It is, however, also possible to influence other people by a suitable choice of emotive language; and this is the practical justification for the use of normative expressions of value. At the same time, it must be admitted that if the other person persists in maintaining his contrary attitude, without however disputing any of the relevant facts, a point is reached at which the discussion can go no further. And in that case there is no sense in asking which of the conflicting views is true. For, since the expression of a value judgement is not a proposition, the question of truth or falsehood does not here arise.

THE NATURE OF PHILOSOPHICAL ANALYSIS

In citing Bertrand Russell's theory of descriptions as a specimen of philosophical analysis, I unfortunately made a mistake in my exposition of the theory. For, having taken the familiar example of "The author of *Waverley* was Scotch," I said that it was equivalent to "One person, and one person only, wrote *Waverley*, and that person was Scotch." But, as Professor Stebbing pointed out in her review of this book, "if the word 'that' is used referentially, then 'that person was Scotch' is equivalent to the whole of the original," and if it is used demonstratively, then the defining expression "is not a translation of the original."[18] The version sometimes given by Russell himself[19] is that "The author of *Waverley* was Scotch" is equivalent to a conjunction of the three propositions "At least one person wrote *Waverley*"; "At most one person wrote *Waverley*"; and "Whoever wrote *Waverley* was Scotch." Professor Moore, however, has remarked[20] that if the words "whoever wrote *Waverley*" are understood "in the most natural way," the first of these propositions is superfluous; for he argues that part of what would ordinarily be meant by saying that whoever wrote *Waverley* was Scotch is that somebody did write *Waverley*. Accordingly, he suggests that the proposition which Russell intended to express by the words "whoever wrote *Waverley* was Scotch" is "one which can be expressed more clearly by the words 'There never was a person who wrote *Waverley* but was not Scotch.' " And even so he does not think that the proposed translation is correct. For he objects that to say of someone that he is the author of a work does not entail saying that he wrote it, since if he had composed it without actually writing it down he could still properly be called its author. To this Russell has replied that it was "the inevitable vagueness and ambiguity of any language used for every-day purposes" that led him to use an artificial symbolic language in *Principia Mathematica,* and that it is in the definitions given in *Principia Mathematica* that the whole of his theory of descriptions consists.[21] In saying this, however, he is, I think, unjust to himself. For it seems to me that one of the great merits of his theory of descriptions is that it does throw light upon the use of a certain class of expressions in ordinary speech, and that this is a point of philosophical importance. For, by showing that expressions like "the present King of France" do not function as names, the theory exposes the fallacy that has led philosophers to believe in "subsistent entities." Thus, while it is unfortunate that the example most frequently chosen to illustrate the theory should contain a minor inaccuracy, I do not think that this seriously affects its value, even in its application to every-day language. For, as I point out in this book, the object of analysing "The author of *Waverley* was Scotch" is not just to obtain an accurate translation of this particular sentence, but to elucidate the use of a whole class of expressions, of which "the author of *Waverley*" serves merely as a typical example.

A more serious mistake than my misrendering of "The author of *Waverley* was Scotch" was my assumption that philosophical analysis consisted mainly in the provision of "definitions in use." It is, indeed, true that what I describe as philosophical analysis is very largely a matter of exhibiting the inter-relationship of different types of propositions;[22] but the cases in which this process actually yields a set of definitions are the exception rather than the rule. Thus the problem of showing how statements about material things are related to observation-statements, which is, in effect, the traditional problem of perception, might be thought to require for its solution that one should indicate a method of translating statements about material things into observation-statements, and thereby furnish what could be regarded as a definition of a material thing. But, in fact, this is impossible; for, as I have already remarked, no finite set of observation statements is ever equivalent to a statement about a material thing. What one can do, however, is to construct a schema which shows what sort of relations must obtain between sense-contents for it to be true, in any given case, that a material thing exists; and while this process cannot, properly speaking, be said to yield a definition, it does have the effect of showing how the one type of statement is related to the other.[23] Similarly, in the field of political philosophy, one will probably not be able to translate statements on the political level into statements about individual persons; for although what is said about a state, for example, is to be verified only by the behaviour of certain individuals, such a statement is usually indefinite in a way that prevents any particular set of statements about the behaviour of individuals from being exactly equivalent to it. Nevertheless, here again it is possible to indicate what types of relations must obtain between individual persons for the political statements in question to be true: so that even if no actual definitions are obtained, the meaning of the political statements is appropriately clarified.

In such cases as these one does indeed arrive at something that approaches a definition in use; but there are other cases of philosophical analysis in which nothing even approaching a definition is either provided or sought. Thus, when Professor Moore suggests that to say that "existence is not a predicate" may be a way of saying that "there is some very important difference between the way in which 'exist' is used in such a sentence as 'Tame tigers exist' and the way in which 'growl' is used in 'Tame tigers growl,' " he does not develop his point by giving rules for the translation of one set of sentences into another. What he does is to remark that whereas it makes good sense to say "All tame tigers growl" or "Most tame tigers growl" it would be nonsense to say "All tame tigers exist" or "Most tame tigers exist,"[24] Now this may seem a rather trivial point for him to make, but in fact it is philosophically illuminating. For it is precisely the assumption that existence is a predicate that gives plausibility to "the ontological argument"; and the ontological argument is supposed to demonstrate the existence of a God. Consequently Moore by pointing out a peculiarity in the use of the word "exist" helps to protect us from a serious fallacy; so that his procedure, though different from that which Russell follows in his theory of descriptions, tends to achieve the same philosophical end.[25]

I maintain in this book that it is not within the province of philosophy to justify our scientific or common-sense beliefs; for their validity is an empirical matter, which cannot be settled by *a priori* means. At the same time, the question of what constitutes such a justification is philosophical, as the existence of "the problem of induction" shows. Here again, what is required is not necessarily a definition. For although I believe that the problems connected with induction can be reduced to the question of what is meant by saying that one proposition is good evidence for another, I doubt if the way to answer this is to construct a formal definition of "evidence." What is chiefly wanted, I think, is an analysis of scientific method, and although it might be possible to express the results of this analysis in the form of definitions, this would not be an achievement of primary importance. And here I may add that the reduction of philosophy to analysis need not be incompatible with the view that its function is to bring to light "the presuppositions of science." For if there are such presuppositions, they can no doubt be shown to be logically involved in the applications of scientific method, or in the use of certain scientific terms.

It used to be said by positivists of the Viennese school that the function of philosophy was not to put forward a special set of "philosophical" propositions, but to make other propositions clear; and this statement has at least the merit of bringing out the point that philosophy is not a source of speculative truth. Nevertheless I now think that it is incorrect to say that there are no philosophical propositions. For, whether they are true or false, the propositions that are expressed in such a book as this do fall into a special category; and since they are the sort of propositions that are asserted or denied by philosophers, I do not see why they should not be called philosophical. To say of them that they are, in some sense, about the usage of words, is, I believe, correct but also inadequate; for certainly not every statement about the usage of words is philosophical.[26] Thus, a lexicographer also seeks to give information about the usage of words, but the philosopher differs from him in being concerned, as I have tried to indicate, not with the use of particular expressions but with classes of expressions; and whereas the propositions of the lexicographer are empirical, philosophical propositions, if they are true, are usually analytic.[27] For the rest I can find no better way of explaining my conception of philosophy than by referring to examples; and one such example is the argument of this book.

NOTES

1. Vide M. Lazerowitz, "The Principle of Verifiability," *Mind*, 1937, pp. 372–78.
2. In *The Foundations of Empirical Knowledge*, pp. 92–104.
3. Vide M. Lazerowitz, "Strong and Weak Verification," *Mind*, 1939, pp. 202–13.
4. "Verification and Experience," *Proceedings of the Aristotelian Society*, vol. XXXVII; cf. also *The Foundations of Empirical Knowledge*, pp. 80–84.
5. Vide I. Berlin, "Verifiability in Principle," *Proceedings of the Aristotelian Society*, vol. XXXIX.
6. *The Foundations of Empirical Knowledge*, pp. 240–41.
7. Cf. Bertrand Russell, *The Problems of Philosophy*, p. 91: "Every proposition which we can understand must be composed wholly of constituents with which we are acquainted." And, if I understand him correctly, this is what Professor W. T. Stace has in mind when he speaks of a "Principle of Observable Kinds." Vide his "Positivism," *Mind*, 1944. Stace argues that the principle of verification "rests upon" the principle of observable kinds, but this is a mistake. It is true that every statement that is allowed to be meaningful by the principle of observable kinds is also allowed to be meaningful by the principle of verification; but the converse does not hold.
8. Both Dr. A. C. Ewing, "Meaninglessness," *Mind*, 1937, pp. 347–64, and Stace, *op. cit.*, take it to be an empirical hypothesis.
9. E.g., by Professor C. D. Broad, "Are There Synthetic *a priori* Truths?" *Supplementary Proceedings of the Ariistotelian Society*, vol. XV.
10. This contradicts what I said in my contribution to a symposium, "Truth by Convention," *Analysis*, vol. 4, nos. 2 and 3; cf. also Norman Malcolm, "Are Necessary Propositions Really Verbal?" *Mind*, 1940, pp. 189–203.
11. Vide A. C. Ewing, "The Linguistic Theory of *a priori* Propositions," *Proceedings of the Aristotelian Society*, 1940; cf. also Professor G. E. Moore, "A Reply to My Critics," *The Philosophy of G. E. Moore*, pp. 575–76, and Professor E. Nagel's review of *The Philosophy of G. E. Moore, Mind*, 1944, p. 64.
12. Cf. Norman Malcolm, "The Nature of Entailment," *Mind*, 1940, pp. 333–47.
13. *The Foundations of Empirical Knowledge*, p. 167; cf. also Professor G. Ryle, "Unverifiability by Me," *Analysis*, vol. 4, no. 1.
14. *The Foundations of Empirical Knowledge*, pp. 168–70.
15. My confidence in it has been somewhat increased by John Wisdom's interesting series of articles "Other Minds," *Mind*, 1940–43. But I am not sure that this is the effect that he intended them to produce.
16. Cf. Sir W. David Ross, *The Foundations of Ethics*, pp. 30–41.
17. I understand that this deficiency has been made good by C. L. Stevenson in his book *Ethics and Language*, but the book was published in America and I have not yet been able to obtain it. There is a review of it by Austin Duncan-Jones in *Mind*, October 1945, and a good indication of Stevenson's line of argument is to be found in his articles "The Emotive Meaning of Ethical Terms," *Mind*, 1937, "Ethical Judgements and Avoidability," *Mind*, 1938, and "Persuasive Definitions," *Mind*, 1938.
18. *Mind*, 1936. p. 358.
19. E.g., in his *Introduction to Mathematical Philosophy*, pp. 172–80.
20. In an article "Russell's Theory of Descriptions," *The Philosophy of Bertrand Russell*, vide especially pp. 179–89.
21. "Reply to Criticisms," *The Philosophy of Bertrand Russell*, p. 690.
22. G. Ryle, *Philosophical Arguments*, Inaugural Lecture delivered before the University of Oxford, 1945.
23. Vide *The Foundations of Empirical Knowledge*, pp. 243–63; and R. B. Braithwaite, "Propositions About Material Objects," *Proceedings of the Aristotelian Society*, vol. XXXVIII.
24. G. E. Moore, "Is Existence a Predicate?," *Supplementary Proceedings of the Aristotelian Society*, 1936. I have made use of the same illustration in my paper "Does Philosophy Analyse Common Sense?," symposium with A. E. Duncan-Jones, *Supplementary Proceedings of the Aristotelian Society*, 1937.
25. I do not wish to imply that Moore himself was solely, or even primarily, concerned with refuting the ontological argument. But I think that his reasoning does achieve this, though not this alone. Similarly Russell's "theory of descriptions" has other uses besides relieving us of "subsistent entities."
26. Vide "Does Philosophy Analyse Common Sense?" and Duncan-Jones's paper on the same subject, *Supplementary Proceedings of the Aristotelian Society*, 1937; cf. also John Wisdom, "Metaphysics and Verification," *Mind*, 1938, and "Philosophy Anxiety and Novelty," *Mind*, 1944.
27. I have put in the qualifying word "usually" because I think that some empirical propositions, such as those that occur in histories of philosophy, may be counted as philosophical. And philosophers use empirical propositions as examples, to serve philosophical ends. But, in so

far as they are not merely historical, I think that the truths discoverable by philosophical methods are analytic. At the same time I should add that the philosopher's business, as Professor Ryle has pointed out to me, is rather to "solve puzzles" than to discover truths.

16 / Clarence Irving Lewis (1883–1965)
THE PRAGMATIC ELEMENT IN KNOWLEDGE

There are three elements in knowledge: the given or immediate data of sense, the concept, and the act which interprets the one by means of the other. In the matrix of thought these are inseparable: they can only be distinguished by analysis. Not all would agree that even just analysis can separate them. In fact, theories of knowledge might be classified by their insistence upon one or another of these three and the attempt to comprehend the other two within it. Emphasis on the given or immediate characterizes the mystic and Bergson's "pure perception." Subordination of the other two to the conceptual element means idealism or some form of rationalism. Pragmatism is distinguished by the fact that it advances the act of interpretation, with its practical consequences, to first place.

If one ask for a rough and ready expression of the pragmatic creed, I suppose one will be likely to receive the answer, "The truth is made by mind." Qualification, of course, is needed at once. There is equal insistence that the making of truth is directed to some practical situation. And a practical situation implies brute fact, something given, as one element of it: the other element is a human being with his needs and interests. If the pragmatist emphasizes the importance of such needs in determining our human truth, it is equally just to remark that, without the brute fact of the given, the problem of meeting these needs would not arise. Nor would there be anything which could determine that one way of meeting them should succeed and another fail. If the pragmatist maintains, then, that the truth is made, at least he does not believe that it is made out of whole cloth.

Moreover, in conceiving that truth and knowledge represent active interpretation by the mind, pragmatism is not alone. Idealism likewise stresses the creativity of thought. Indeed, the idealist outruns the pragmatist in this respect, conceiving that the object, and so the situation to be met by knowing, has ultimately no existence independent of the mind.

The difference between the two—or a difference—lies in this: that for the idealist "mind" means, in the last analysis, generic mind, the common human mind, or the ideal mind imperfectly manifest in us, the Absolute; while for the pragmatist minds are individual, ultimately distinct, and capable of idiosyncrasy. Such personal or racial peculiarities, or differences which time makes in the prevailing temper, may find their expression in the way minds meet the situations which confront them. And so truth may be somewhat personal, and may change with history. It is not rooted in fixed categories which are a priori.

These are, then, the bare fundamentals of the

From *University of California Publications in Philosophy* 6, no. 3 (1926). Reprinted by permission of the University of California Press.

pragmatist position concerning knowledge; that knowledge is an interpretation, instigated by need or interest and tested by its consequences in action, which individual minds put upon something confronting them or given to them. On any theory, it is to be expected that minds will largely coincide and that agreement, for various obvious reasons, will be the rule. But the extent and manner of such coincidence is, for pragmatism, something to be noted in particular cases, not simply the result of universal human reason.

As I have suggested, the validity of this general type of conception can be tested by studying the nature and importance in knowledge of the pragmatic element of interpretation, and its relation to the other two, which we may refer to as "the concept" and "the given" respectively.

Suppose that we take some outstanding example of knowledge, and, using it as a paradigm, attempt thus to assess the significance of interpretation. Whatever example we choose will be of some particular type, and we must be on our guard against mistaking as general features of knowledge what are only typical of special cases. But if, from lack of time, we thus concentrate on a single illustration, it should represent knowledge at its best. For this reason, I propose the example of geometry. Mathematics comes very close to our ideal of knowledge at least in the important respect of relative certainty. And in the whole field of mathematics, geometry offers the best example because of the concreteness of its applications.

The last quarter-century of mathematical study represents the historical fruition of a great many previous researches and discoveries, so that today we can feel much surer that we understand the nature of mathematical knowledge than it ever has been possible for men to feel before. Three important results emerge from this study. The first is the discovery that all mathematics, and not geometry only, can be developed by the deductive method. A relatively few definitions and initial assumptions suffice to give us all the rest of any branch of mathematics, such as complex algebra or projective geometry.

The second of these results is a necessary consequence of the first: all mathematics is abstract in the sense of being independent of any and every possible application, because if all the theorems follow logically from the definitions and postulates, then we can arbitrarily alter the things which we let the terms, such as "point" and "line," mean, without in the least disturbing any step in the proofs. *Whatever* "point" and "line" may mean, given these assumptions about them, these consequences— the rest of the system—must also hold of them, because the theorems follow from the assumptions by pure logic. Thus for any mathematical system, there will be many possible applications, though very likely only one or two of these will have any practical importance. You can let "points" mean the members of a set of clubs governed by certain rules, or you can let them represent what are usually described as "spheres one inch in diameter." Similarly, the a's and b's and x's of complex algebra may represent numerical magnitudes, or we may let them represent the array of points in space. In this last case, both the applications mentioned are practically important.

The third step was the logical culmination indicated by the two preceding. It was discovered that we can dispense, in mathematics, with all the initial assumptions except the definitions. That is, all the truths of mathematics follow from the definitions of the terms used, without any further assumptions whatever except logic or the principles of proof. This third step could only be proved possible by actually carrying it out. The stupendous labor of thus developing the fundamental principles of mathematics merely from exact definitions of terms, by pure logic, was performed by Mr. Russell and Mr. Whitehead in *Principia Mathematica*.

Our main interest in all this is that it definitely proves something that Plato ventured to assert two thousand years ago; that our knowledge of mathematics is quite independent of that sense-experience which suggests it to us and is the practical motive for our study of it. A club of thorough-paced mathematicians could retire from the world of sense, provided that were somehow possible, and not interrupt their discussions in the least. They would need a means of communication, of course, and some sort of counters, such as words or tally-marks, as the common currency of their discussion. But no application to sense-things is otherwise of the least importance to them. Often they do not assign any meaning at all to their a's and b's; the letters themselves are good enough symbols to serve all their interests.

Thus we discover that the content of pure mathematics is simply the deductive or logical order of purely logical entities, a sort of elaborate logical pattern of abstract terms without any denotation at all.

"But," you say, "who wants that kind of mathematics? Who cares whether it is possible or not?" I must not pause to answer that question in detail beyond pointing out the relation which the business of pure mathematics now bears to that of the practical man. The mathematician is a sort of maker of patterns. He keeps a stock of them which is already bigger than anybody has found a need for. He has an infinite number of different geometries, for example, all just as good from his point of view as Euclid, and such curiosities as quaternions and systems containing curves that have no tangents. Mostly he develops these from pure intellectual curiosity. He is exploring the Platonic heavens, and it may seem as important to him as measuring the earth. Sometimes the practical man borrows one of these patterns ready-made and finds for it a previously unsuspected application. Some of the most important advances in physical science have come about in just this way.

But our interest in this lies in the nature which the truth of abstract mathematics is revealed to have. Three points are important:

1. Assuming logic or common modes of valid proof, the truths of mathematics are quite independent of any world of sense, and hence independent of given experience, so far as given experience means perceptible sense-qualities. If there were two mathematical minds, one on the Earth and one on Mars, their experience and their sense-organs might differ in any way you can imagine, and still if only they shared a common logic or modes of valid thinking, all they would need would be some method of communication in order to have all the truths of mathematics in common.

2. In such abstract mathematics, the whole of all truth is open to any logical mind, provided we know precisely what the terms are defined to mean—that is, how they are logically related. To bring out the point, let us contrast mathematical and empirical or sense-knowledge from the point of view of learning. You see this desk. It is a thing of sense. Suppose that we carry away with us whatever knowledge we gain now as we look at it. And then suppose tomorrow someone ask, "Is there a knot on the under surface of the top of this desk?" We do not know. Not only that, but we might be the master minds of all the ages and have thought about it continuously during the interval, and still we could not know. Nothing but a further experience, of us or someone else, could possibly determine the question.

But now suppose that someone write down here the initial principles of some mathematical system—say Euclid's geometry. We may take *that* knowledge away with us, and there is absolutely no mathematical truth of that system which we could not learn merely by thinking about it.

3. An obvious point but for us the most important of all: mathematical truth is a little more certain than almost any other knowledge that we have, precisely for the reason indicated above. We really do not need any further experience to verify it, and no further experience could possibly trip us up and prove us wrong, unless we have been illogical in our thinking. It is the kind of truth called a priori, knowable with certainty in advance of any particular sense-experience whatever.

Admittedly not all mathematical knowledge is of this sort. As soon as we raise practical questions about the application of geometry to space or of algebra to stresses and strains, the situation is quite different and more complex. But pure mathematics is, I think, typical of one element which enters into all knowledge. It is because we have here an almost clean separation of this element that I have chosen this example, which in other respects may be a little difficult and uninteresting.

Mathematics is an illustration of the immensely elaborate body of truth which may rise from pure concepts, from the merely logical relations of terms, and terms which need not have any reference to sense-qualities or experienceable things of any sort. Moreover, the initial meanings or relations of these terms are quite arbitrary. The mathematician makes them what he will. Often he chooses them from intellectual curiosity about their consequences, an interest very much like that in the possible moves in a game of chess. When such relations of a few terms are set up, just as when a few rules are imposed as conditions of the game of chess, the logical consequences to which they give rise are almost inexhaustible and absolutely determined.

Now in all our knowledge—particularly in all science—there is an element of just such logical order which rises from our definitions. An initial definition, as we may see, is always arbitrary in the sense that it cannot be false. In itself it does not tell us whether anything is true or not, or what the nature of existing objects is. It simply exhibits to us a concept or meaning in the speaker's mind which he asks us temporarily to share with him and symbolize by a certain word or phrase. Socially, of course, it is important that such meanings should be common, and that words be used in familiar ways. But if a scientist finds a new concept worth developing, he may invent a technical term or use an old word in a new meaning which he takes care to make clear. That the introduction of concepts which are novel and not generally shared may be of the highest importance is something illustrated by almost every major advance in science. Such an initial concept, whether new or old, is a definite logical structure. It sets up precise relations of certain elements of thought. And that structure—or the combination of a few such conceptual structures—may give rise to logical consequences as elaborate as mathematics or the game of chess.

Indeed, before we set out upon any systematic investigation, we must have such initial concepts in our minds. It does not matter how we get them; we can always change them for any reason, or for no reason if it suits our whim. The *real* reasons why we *do* use certain concepts is, of course, practical. That is another story, which I shall come to. But however we come by such initial meanings, it is obvious that we must have them before we address ourselves to any problem. Until we have principles of classification which serve to distinguish what is material from what is immaterial, what is a force from what is not a force, straight from crooked, rigid from nonrigid, the simultaneous from the successive, and so on—that is, until we have certain definite concepts or meanings in mind, we cannot even approach the problem of acquiring knowledge of any sorts of things to which such concepts might apply. We have no handle to take hold of them by.

And whatever our concepts or meanings may be, there is a truth about them just as absolute and just as definite and certain as in the case of mathematics. In other fields we so seldom try to think in the abstract, or by pure logic, that we do not notice this. But obviously it is just as true. Wherever there is any set of interrelated concepts, there, quite apart from all questions of application or the things we use them for, we have generated a whole complex array of orderly relations or patterns of meaning. And there must be a truth about these—a purely logical truth, *in abstracto*, and a truth which is certain apart from experience—even though this is only a part of the truth which we want to discover, and the rest of it is of a quite different sort which depends upon experience.

Ordinarily we do not separate out this a priori truth, because ordinarily we do not distinguish the purely logical significance of concepts from the application of words to sensible things. In fact it is only the mathematician who is likely to do this at all. But I should like to indicate that this separation is always possible and that it is important for the understanding of knowledge. To this end, let me use the term "concept" for this element of purely logical meaning. We can then discriminate the conceptual element in thought as the element which two minds must have in common—not merely may have or do have but absolutely *must* have in common—when they understand each other.

I suppose it is a frequent assumption that we are able to apprehend one another's meanings because our images and sensations are alike. But a little thought will show that this assumption is very dubious.

Suppose we talk of physical things in physical terms, and our discussion involves physical measurement. Presumably we have the same ideas of feet and pounds and seconds. If not, the thing is hopeless. But in psychological terms, my notion of a foot goes back to some immediate image of visual so-long-ness, or the movements which I make when I put my hands so far apart, or to a relation between these two. Distances in general mean quite complex relationships between such visual perceptions, muscle and contact-sensations, the feeling of fatigue, and so on. Weight goes back to the muscle-sensation which we call in New England the "heft" of the thing. And our direct apprehension of time is that feeling of duration which is so familiar but so difficult to describe.

Now in such terms, will your sensory image of a foot or a pound coincide with mine? I am nearsighted; your eyes are good. Or I might have a peculiarity of the eye muscles so that focusing on near objects would be accompanied by a noticeable feeling of effort, while this is not the case with you. When it comes to reaching, there is the difference in the length of our arms. If we lift a weight, there is the difference in strength between us to take into account. So it is with everything. In acuity of perception and power to discriminate, there is almost always some small difference between the senses of two individuals, and frequently these discrepancies are marked. It is only in rough and ready terms that we can reasonably suppose that our direct perceptions are alike.

Even for large and crude distinctions, what assurance is there that our impressions coincide? No one can look directly into another's mind. The immediate feeling of red or rough can never be transferred from one mind to another. Suppose it should be a fact that I get the sensation you signalize by saying "red" when-

ever I look at what you call "violet," and vice versa. Suppose that in the matter of the immediately apprehended qualia of sensation my whole spectrum should be exactly the reverse of yours. Suppose even that what are for you sensations of pitch, mediated by the ear, were identical with my feelings of color-quality, mediated by the eye. How should we ever find it out? We could discover such peculiarities of mine so long as they did not impair my powers to discriminate and relate as others do.

Psychological differences of individuals are indeed impressive. Long before scientific psychology was thought of, the ancient skeptic had based his argument on them. This is what led Gorgias to say that nothing can be known, and if anything could be known, it could not be communicated. There can be no verification of community between minds so far as it is a question of the feeling side of experience, though the assumption that there is no coincidence here seems fantastic.

Yet Gorgias was quite wrong about the communication of ideas. That your sensations are never quite like mine need in no way impede our common knowledge or the conveying of ideas. Why? Because we shall still agree that there are three feet to the yard, that red is the first band in the spectrum, and that middle C means a vibration of 256 per second. At the end of an hour which feels very long to you and short to me, we can meet by agreement, because our common understanding of that hour is not a feeling of tedium or vivacity, but means sixty minutes, one round of the clock, a pattern of relation which we have established between chronometers and distances and rates of movements, and so forth.

When we want to be sure that we share each other's meanings, we define our terms. Now defining terms makes no direct reference to sense-qualities. We set up logical relations of one term to others. The pictures in the dictionary may help, but they are not necessary. We might suppose that such definition chases one meaning back into other meanings, and these into still others, until finally it is brought to bay in some first (or last) identity of meaning which must be identity of sensation or imagery. But all the words used in defining any term in the dictionary are also themselves defined. There is no set of undefined first terms printed at the beginning. The patterns of logical relationships set up by these interconnected definitions of terms themselves constitute the conceptual meanings of the terms defined.

To sum up this matter: the sharing of ideas does not necessarily depend on any identity of sense-feeling. It requires only a certain fundamental agreement in the way our minds work. Given this basis of logic, the process of coming to possess our meanings—and in that sense, our world—in common is secured by the business of living together and the methods of naming, pointing, and learning by imitation, which exhibit the fundamental habits of the social animal. In the end, the practical criterion of common meaning is congruous behavior. Speech is merely that part of behavior which is most significant for securing the cooperation of others.

But while I have been striving to make it plausible that concepts and common meanings are something apart from immediate sensation, you have been preparing an objection. I am sure. "This concept," you will say, "is a mere abstraction. Nobody has one in his mind without connecting it with his experience of objects; and the principal use of concepts is to apply to and name perceivable things."

I must grant this at once. Indeed it is one of the points I should like to make. The purely logical pattern of meaning is always an abstraction. It is exactly like the concepts of pure mathematics in this respect, though other concepts may often lack the simplicity and exactness of the mathematical. Just as in the case of pure mathematics there is a complex and important set of logical consequences which arise merely from the definitions of terms, so also in the case of concepts in general, the pattern of logical relations which is generated simply through our modes of distinguishing and relating is something intrinsically capable of being separated from all application to things of sense, and would then constitute a definite and considerable body of knowledge which could be learned merely by thinking, without any reference to the external world at all. Indeed we know at once that any sort of definition has logical consequences which can be so learned. When we remember that any science, and even common-sense knowledge, can get under way only through our bringing to experience those initial modes of classification and relation which our definitions embody, we are brought to realize that in physics, or chemistry, or any other department of knowledge, we do not study simply the facts of our given experience. We study in part such facts and in part the consequences of our own logical meanings, though usually without any separation of these two.

In our knowledge of the external world, concepts represent what thought itself brings to experience. The other element is "the given." It represents that part or aspect which is not affected by thought, the "buzzing, blooming confusion," as James called it, on which the infant first opens his eyes.

It is difficult to make a clean separation of what is given in experience from all admixture of conceptual thinking. The given is something less than perception, since perception already involves analysis and relation in recognition. One cannot express the given in language, because language implies concepts, and because the given is just that element which cannot be conveyed from one mind to another, as the qualia of color can never by conveyed to the man born blind. But one can, so to speak, point to the given. There are some of us who enjoy music passively. We just soak it in, as the infant may confront the world in his first conscious perception. We are transported by it, and all thought is put to sleep. Perhaps others tell us that this is a very uncultivated attitude: that we do not hear the music at all but only a glorious noise. What they mean is that we do not analyze our music and identify its pattern of harmony and melody. Well, for us who listen thus passively, music is pure given, while for those who intellectualize it by analysis it may be something more. But that *more* is not given; the mind brings it to the experience. In every experience there is such a given element, though in very few does it have such immediate esthetic character that we are content to remain confronting it without adding to it by thought.

Perhaps you see already that the mere immediacy of such given experience is never what we mean by knowledge. Or rather, I ought to say, it is not what *most* of us mean by knowledge. There are some, as for instance Bergson and the mystics, who reserve the term "knowledge" for precisely such a state of luminous immediacy. In the end, it is fruitless to quarrel about the use of terms; we can only note this curious exception to ordinary parlance, and pass on. For the rest of us, knowledge of things does not mean being sunk in such immediacy, but an attitude in which what is given is interpreted and has some significance for action.

If I bite an apple, what is given is an ineffable taste. But if this is the basis of any knowledge, it is because I interpret this taste as significant of what is not just now given, of the quality of the apple or of another bite. At this moment, your immediate apprehension of this thing which I hold in my hand leads you to say that I have here a sheet of paper. But if this should suddenly explode, or if I should proceed to swallow it and smile, you might revise that judgment and realize that it went quite beyond what was absolutely given in perception. Or we might just now hear a chirring, chugging noise which would lead us to think of an automobile outside. But in that case, we are at once aware how very much we have added to the given by way of interpretation.

If time permitted, I should like to make it clear that a state of pure immediacy in which consciousness would just coincide with the given would always be purely passive, and that thought not only is active interpretation but that such interpretation is always significant of our possible action and of the further experience to which such action would lead. But I can omit this, because it is a thought which William James himself made familiar. At least it will be clear that in the knowledge of objects, as much as in the knowledge of propositions or generalizations, this element of active interpretation must always be present. We do not have any knowledge merely by being confronted with the given. Without interpretation we should remain forever in the buzzing, blooming confusion of the infant. This, I suppose, is the biological significance of thinking. It is an activity by which we adjust ourselves to those aspects of the environment which are *not* immediately apprehended in sensation. Knowledge is always something which can be verified. And in verification we always proceed to something which is not just now presented.

It is upon the manner and the nature of this interpretation which we put upon the given that I should like to concentrate our attention. Clearly it is something which we bring to the experience. It is something we are able to make only because we confront what is presented by the senses with certain ready-made distinctions, relations and ways of classifying. In particular, we impose upon experience certain patterns of temporal relationships, a certain order, which makes one item significant of others. A visually presented quale of the object is a sign of the way it would taste or feel. The taste of it *now* is a sign of the taste of the next bite also. The way yonder door looks to me now is a sign of the distance I must walk to reach it and the position in which I must put my hand to open it. It is by interpretation that the infant's buzzing, blooming confusion gives way to an orderly world of things. Order, or logical pattern, is the essence of understanding. Knowledge arises when some conceptual pattern of relationships is imposed upon the given by interpretation.

Moreover, as we have seen, it is only this conceptual element of order or logical pattern which can be conveyed from one mind to another. All expressible truth about our world is contained in such relations of order, that is, in terms of concepts we find applicable to what is presented in sense.

Now the concepts which we thus impose upon given experience are almost always such as we have formulated only as the need for them arose. Experience itself has instigated our attitudes of interpretation. The secret of them lies in purpose or interest. It is because our concepts have so generally this pragmatic origin that I began with the one illustration where the case is clearly different. Though elementary mathematics is historically rooted in practical need, mathematical concepts have some of them a quite different origin. The mathematician has a whole cupboardful of such conceptual systems for which nobody has found as yet any useful application. *All* concepts have intrinsically the possibility of such separate status; and all truth or knowledge represents an order which is capable of being considered, like mathematical systems, *in abstracto*. The business of learning, and the process by which mind has conquered the world in the name of intelligibility, is not a process in which we have passively absorbed something which experience has presented to us. It is much more truly a process of trial and error in which we have attempted to impose upon experience one interpretation or conceptual pattern after another and, guided by our practical success or failure, have settled down to that mode of constructing it which accords best with our purposes and interests of action.

Moreover, this mode of successful interpretation may not be dictated unambiguously by the content of experience itself. The famous illustration of this fact that William James made use of is probably the best. For a thousand years men interpreted the motions of the heavens in terms of Ptolemy's astronomy, based on a motionless earth. Then gradually this was given up in favor of the Copernican system of moving earth and fixed stars. Those who argued this issue supposed they were discussing a question of empirical fact. We now perceive that such is not the case. All motion is relative. The question what moves and what is motionless in the heavens is one which cannot be settled merely by experience. But one choice of axes is highly convenient, resulting in relatively simple generalizations for the celestial motions and enabling celestial and sublunary phenomena to be reduced to the same equations, while almost unsurmountable complexity and difficulty attend the other choice. Theoretically if any system of motions is describable with respect to one set of axes, it is also describable in terms of any other set which moves with reference to the first according to any general rule. So that the issue between the Ptolemaic and Copernican choice of a frame of motion cannot be decided on the ground that one describes the facts, the other not. Rather the one describes the facts simply and conveniently, the other complexly and most inconveniently. The only issue is pragmatic.

Similarly with the recent controversy between the physics of relativity and the Euclidean-Newtonian mechanics. Perhaps you and I—certainly I—do not understand the intricacies of Einstein, but so much we have gathered; that since all motion is relative, and since, further, whatever happens at some distant point is known to us only by the passage of an effect through space and time, we cannot measure space without some assumption about time, or time without assumptions about space and the laws of matter which govern clocks, and so on. Therefore at the bottom of our interpretation of events in the physical universe there must be some fundamental assumptions, or definitions and criteria, to which empirical evidence cannot simply say yes or no. One set of assumptions—the relativity ones—means a reduction in the number of independent laws but a reorganization of common sense; the other set obviates this change in current notions about space and time but condemns us to forgo the simplification in fundamental principles. The determinable empirical issues, such as the perturbations of Mercury and the bending of light rays, are—so we may venture to think—by themselves not decisive. If there were no other issue, we should find some way to accommodate these recalcitrant facts to the old categories. The really final issues are pragmatic ones such as the comprehensiveness of laws and economy in unverifiable assumption.

From such striking and important illustrations to the humbler affairs of every day is a far cry. And time does not permit the introduction of further examples which might bridge the gap. But does not history go to prove the point? In any given period, there is some body of generally accepted concepts in terms of which men describe and interpret their experience. Later, these may all be strange. If we go back to the Middle Ages or to the civilization of ancient Greece, and try to view the world as men then saw it, only by an effort can we do so. We might expect that the fundamental things—life, mind, matter and force, cause and effect—would be conceived in the same way. Yet it is exactly here that we find the greatest differences.

These facts are familiar to you, and I need not dwell upon them. But perhaps I may pause for a single illustration. Among the ancients, the distinction between the living and the inanimate was generally drawn between those things which were supposed to have a soul which was the cause of their behavior and development, and those which had no such internal principle which explained their movements. "Soul" was thus a synonym for "the vital," and was a principle of nature, coordinate with the mechanical. Why was this principle of distinction later given up? Has it been disproved that all living things have souls? Or that we must grant, in addition to the mechanical causes of the phenomena of life, an internal vital principle which explains development? We can hardly claim so much. Really to explain this change of categories, we must probably reckon, on the one side, with Christianity and similar influences which, when they came, contrasted "soul," as the spiritual principle in man, with the material body. Thus the soul, instead of being conceived as a natural cause of vital phenomena, is now withdrawn from all physical significance. On the other side, the advantage of control which goes with understanding the facts of life, so far as possible, in terms of physics and chemistry has operated to extrude the idea of a soul, as a natural inner principle, from any place in biological conceptions.

With other fundamental concepts, it is much the same. *Words* such as "life," "matter," and "cause," and so on have been used since thought began, but the *meanings* of them have continuously altered. There is hardly a category or principle of explanation which survives from Aristotle or the science of the Middle Ages. Quite literally, men of those days lived in a different world because their instruments of intellectual interpretation were so different. To be sure, the telescope and microscope and the scientific laboratory have played an important part. As time goes on, the body of familiar experience widens. But that hardly accounts for *all* the changed interpretation which history reveals. Not sense observation alone, but accord with human bent and need must be considered. The motive to control external nature and direct our own destiny was always there. Old principles have been abandoned not only when they disagreed with newly discovered fact, but when they proved unnecessarily complex and bungling, or when they failed to emphasize distinctions which men felt to be important.

When things so fundamental as the catego-

ries of space and time, the laws of celestial mechanics, and the principles of physics are discovered to depend in part upon pragmatic choice; when history reveals continuous alteration in our basic concepts, and an alteration which keeps step with changing interests; and when we recognize that without interpretation it is not a world at all that is presented to us, but only, so to speak, the raw material of a world; then may it not plausibly be urged that, throughout the realm of fact, what is flatly given in experience does not completely determine truth—does not unambiguously fix the conceptual interpretation which shall portray it?

In short, if human knowledge at its best, in the applications of mathematics and in the well-developed sciences, is typical of knowledge in general, then the picture we must frame of it is this: that there is in it an element of conceptual interpretation, theoretically always separable from any application to experience and capable of being studied in abstraction. When so isolated, concepts are like the Platonic ideas, purely logical entities constituted by the pattern of their systematic relations. There is another element, the sensuous or given, likewise always separable by abstraction, though we should find it pure only in a mind which did not think but only felt. This given element, or stream of sensation, is what sets the problem of interpretation, when we approach it with our interests of action. The function of thought is to mediate between such interests and the given. Knowledge arises when we can frame the data of sense in a set of concepts which serve as guides for action, just as knowledge of space arises when we can fit a geometrical interpretation upon our direct perception of the spatial. The given experience does not produce the concepts in our minds. If it did, knowledge would be pure feeling, and thought would be superfluous. Nor do the concepts evoke the experience which fits them, or limit it to their pattern. Rather the growth of knowledge is a process of trial and error, in which we frame the content of the given now in one set of concepts, now in another, and are governed in our final decision by our relative success—by the degree to which our most vital needs and interests are satisfied.

If this is a true picture, then there are three

elements in knowledge, or three phases of the relation of mind to the objects of thought. First, there is the kind of knowledge which we have in abstract mathematics, and the kind of truth which concerns purely logical implications. There is this type of truth for all concepts so far as they are precise and clear. Our knowledge of such truth possesses certainty and finality because it requires only clarity of thought and is entirely independent of experience.

This kind of truth can be, and has been, described in two ways, either of which is accurate when we grasp what they mean. First is the way of Plato, who emphasizes the fact that abstract concepts ("ideas" he calls them) are not created by the mind. What he means is that the mathematician, for example, does not create but discovers the truths that he portrays. Before the non-Euclidean geometries or the possibility of curves without tangents was even thought of, the truth about them was forever fixed.

The second way of describing this realm of abstract entities is to note that such pure concepts have no residence outside the mind. Plato's heaven—so we should say from this second point of view—is merely a fiction to emphasize the absoluteness of conceptual truth. Without our thought concepts would remain forever in the dark limbo of nothingness. Moreover, it is their usefulness, their applicability to given experience, which moves us to evoke them. We select, or call down from Plato's heaven, those concepts which meet our needs. Plato said we are "reminded" of them by experience; we are more likely to say that we invent or formulate them ourselves. In either case, two points are to be remarked: first, that the logical relations of—and hence the truth about—any determinate concept is fixed and eternal and independent of experience; second, that *what* concepts we shall use or apply we are left to determine ourselves in the light of our needs and interests.

The second phase of the mind's relation to its objects is the element of the purely given in experience. Of this by itself, there is not truth or knowledge in the ordinary sense. Yet the given has significance. There is something which speaks directly to us in just this presentation of the senses, in that immediacy of color or of sound which one who lacked the appro-priate sense organ could never imagine nor our description conjure up for him. In particular, the immediate has esthetic significance; perhaps it may also have ethical value and religious meaning. But it is not knowledge in the usual meaning of that term, because it is ineffable; because there is nothing in such direct apprehension which calls for verification; because by itself it has no reference to action.

The third element or phase—the element which distinguishes our knowledge of the external world—is the active interpretation which unites the concept and the given. It is such interpretation alone which needs to be verified, or *can* be verified, and the function of it is essentially practical. Truth here is not fixed, because interpretation is not fixed, but is left for trial and error to determine. The criteria of its success are accommodation to our bent and service of our interests. More adequate or simpler interpretation will mean practically truer. Old truth will pass away when old concepts are abandoned. New truth arises when new interpretations are adopted. Attempted modes of understanding may, of course, completely fail and prove flatly false. But where there is more than one interpretation which can frame the given, "truer" will mean only "better." And after all, even flat falsity can only mean a practical breakdown which has proved complete.

At just this point, however, we may easily fall into misapprehension. In speaking thus of "new truth" and "old truth" and of pragmatically "truer" and "falser," I am following a usage which the literature of pragmatism has made familiar. But I think this is a little to be regretted. Most of the paradoxes and many of the difficulties of the pragmatic point of view cluster about this notion that the truth can change. When we see precisely what it is that happens when old modes of interpretation are discarded in favor of new and more successful ones, all these paradoxes will, I think, be found to disappear. What is it that is new in such a case? The given, brute-fact experience which sets the problem of interpretation is not new. And the concepts in terms of which the interpretation, whether old or new, is phrased are—remembering Plato—such that the truth about them is eternal. Obviously what is new is the *application* of the concept, or system of concepts, to experience of just this sort. The concepts are *newly chosen* for interpretation of the given data. That the concepts may also be new in the sense that no one ever thought of them before does not, at bottom, affect the problem at all.

Historically the situation is likely to be slightly more complex: the body of data to be interpreted itself undergoes some alteration. It is possible that old systems of thought should be rejected and replaced by new, simply through reflection and realization of the superior convenience of the novel mode. In fact, this has sometimes happened. But in the more typical case, such change does not take place without the added spur of newly discovered phenomena which complicate the problem of interpretation. The several factors which must be considered are, then: (1) the two sets of concepts, old and new, (2) the expanding bounds of experience in which what is novel had come to light, (3) the conditions of application of the concepts to this new body of total relevant experience.

In the case of the Copernican revolution, it was the invention of the telescope and the increasing accuracy of observation which mainly provided the impetus to reinterpretation. But these new data, though practically decisive, were decisive of simplicity and comprehensiveness only. As we have seen, celestial motions are theoretically as capable of interpretation with respect to axes through the earth as by reference to the fixed stars. Now suppose that mathematicians and astronomers had so much spare time that both these systems had been worked out, for all the data, with some completeness. Which would be the truth about the heavens? Obviously, both. The laws of celestial motion in the two cases would be quite different, and the divergence would extend beyond astronomy to physics. But both would be absolutely and eternally true in their own terms. The one would be better truth, the other worse, from the point of view of workability. But except in the practical sense that we must stick to the one or the other all through and cannot apply them piecemeal, they could not contradict one another.

This situation is not altered by any thought that newly discovered fact may play another than the pragmatic role, and be decisive of truth in a deeper sense. In any case, if old principles were ever true, they must remain true—in terms of the old concepts. To the extent that new evidence can render the old concepts absolutely inapplicable, the "old truth" never was anything but an hypothesis, and is not proved flatly false. It is not, I hope, the point of the pragmatic theory of knowledge to reduce all truths thus to hypothesis. That would be nothing but a cheerful form of skepticism.

Rather the point is—at least the point which I should like to make—that the truths of experience must always be relative to our chosen conceptual systems in terms of which they are expressed; and that amongst such conceptual systems there may be choice in application. Such choice will be determined, consciously or unconsciously, on pragmatic grounds. New facts may cause a shifting of such grounds. When this happens, nothing literally becomes false, and nothing becomes true which was not always true. An old intellectual instrument has been given up. Old concepts lapse and new ones take their place.

It would be a hardy soul who should read the history of science and of common-sense ideas and deny that just this shift of concepts on pragmatic grounds has frequently had important place in the advance of thought. That historically men suppose they are confronted simply with a question of absolute truth when they debate Copernican versus Ptolemaic astronomy, mechanism versus vitalism, relativity versus Newtonian mechanics, and so on, does not remove the possibility that the really decisive issues may often be pragmatic.

Pragmatists have sometimes neglected to draw the distinction between the concept and immediacy, between interpretation and the given, with the result that they may seem to put all truth at once at the mercy of brute-fact experience and within the power of human choice or in a relation of dependence upon human need. But this would be an attempt to have it both ways. The sense in which facts are brute and given cannot be the sense in which the truth about them is alterable to human decision. The separation of the factors is essential. On the one side, we have the abstract concepts themselves, with their logical implications. The truth about these is absolute, and knowledge of them is a priori. On the other side, there is the absolute datum of the given. But it is between these two, in the determination of those concepts which the mind brings to experience as the instruments of its interpretation, that a large part of the problem of fixing the truths of science and our common-sense knowledge has its

place. Wherever such criteria as comprehensiveness and simplicity, or serviceability for the control of nature, or conformity to human bent and human ways of acting play their part in the determination of such conceptual instruments, there is a pragmatic element in knowledge.

17 / Rudolf Carnap (1891–1970)
EMPIRICISM, SEMANTICS, AND ONTOLOGY

1. THE PROBLEM OF ABSTRACT ENTITIES

Empiricists are in general rather suspicious with respect to any kind of abstract entities like properties, classes, relations, numbers, propositions, etc. They usually feel much more in sympathy with nominalists than with realists (in the medieval sense). As far as possible they try to avoid any reference to abstract entities and to restrict themselves to what is sometimes called a nominalistic language, i.e., one not containing such references. However, within certain scientific contexts it seems hardly possible to avoid them. In the case of mathematics, some empiricists try to find a way out by treating the whole of mathematics as a mere calculus, a formal system for which no interpretation is given or can be given. Accordingly, the mathematician is said to speak not about numbers, functions, and infinite classes, but merely about meaningless symbols and formulas manipulated according to given formal rules. In physics it is more difficult to shun the suspected entities, because the language of physics serves for the communication of reports and predictions and hence cannot be

taken as a mere calculus. A physicist who is suspicious of abstract entities may perhaps try to declare a certain part of the language of physics as uninterpreted and uninterpretable, that part which refers to real numbers as space-time coordinates or as values of physical magnitudes, to functions, limits, etc. More probably he will just speak about all these things like anybody else but with an uneasy conscience, like a man who in his everyday life does with qualms many things which are not in accord with the high moral principles he professes on Sundays. Recently the problem of abstract entities has arisen again in connection with semantics, the theory of meaning and truth. Some semanticists say that certain expressions designate certain entities, and among these designated entities they include not only concrete material things but also abstract entities, e.g., properties as designated by predicates and propositions as designated by sentences.[1] Others object strongly to this procedure as violating the basic principles of empiricism and leading back to a metaphysical ontology of the Platonic kind.

It is the purpose of this article to clarify this controversial issue. The nature and implications of the acceptance of a language referring to abstract entities will first be discussed in general; it will be shown that using such a language does not imply embracing a Platonic ontology but is perfectly compatible with empiricism and strictly scientific thinking. Then the special question of the role of abstract entities in semantics will be discussed. It is hoped that the clarification of the issue will be useful to those who would like to accept abstract entities in their work in mathematics, physics, semantics, or any other field; it may help them to overcome nominalistic scruples.

2. LINGUISTIC FRAMEWORKS

Are there properties, classes, numbers, propositions? In order to understand more clearly the nature of these and related problems, it is above all necessary to recognize a fundamental distinction between two kinds of questions concerning the existence or reality of entities. If someone wishes to speak in his language about a new kind of entities, he has to introduce a system of new ways of speaking, subject to new rules; we shall call this procedure the construction of a linguistic *framework* for the new entities in question. And now we must distinguish two kinds of questions of existence: first, questions of the existence of certain entities of the new kind *within the framework;* we call them *internal questions;* and second, questions concerning the existence or reality *of the system of entities as a whole,* called *external questions.* Internal questions and possible answers to them are formulated with the help of the new forms of expressions. The answers may be found either by purely logical methods or by empirical methods, depending upon whether the framework is a logical or a factual one. An external question is of a problematic character which is in need of closer examination.

The world of things

Let us consider as an example the simplest kind of entities dealt with in the everyday language: the spatio-temporally ordered system of observable things and events. Once we have accepted the thing language with its framework for things, we can raise and answer internal questions, e.g., "Is there a white piece of paper on my desk?," "Did King Arthur actually live?," "Are unicorns and centaurs real or merely imaginary?," and the like. These questions are to be answered by empirical investigations. Results of observations are evaluated according to certain rules as confirming or disconfirming evidence for possible answers. (This evaluation is usually carried out, of course, as a matter of habit rather than a deliberate, rational procedure. But it is possible, in a rational reconstruction, to lay down explicit rules for the evaluation. This is one of the main tasks of a pure, as distinguished from a psychological, epistemology.) The concept of reality occurring in these internal questions is an empirical, scientific, non-metaphysical concept. To recognize something as a real thing or event means to succeed in incorporating it into the system of things at a particular space-time position so that it fits together with the other things recognized as real, according to the rules of the framework.

From these questions we must distinquish the external question of the reality of the thing world itself. In contrast to the former questions, this question is raised neither by the man in the street nor by scientists, but only by philosophers. Realists give an affirmative answer, subjective idealists a negative one, and the controversy goes on for centuries without ever being solved. And it cannot be solved because it is framed in a wrong way. To be real in the scientific sense means to be an element of the system; hence this concept cannot be meaningfully applied to the system itself. Those who raise the question of the reality of the thing world itself have perhaps in mind not a theoretical question as their formulation seems to suggest, but rather a practical question, a matter of a practical decision concerning the structure of our language. We have to make the choice whether or not to accept and use the forms of expression in the framework in question.

In the case of this particular example, there is usually no deliberate choice because we all have accepted the thing language early in our lives as a matter of course. Nevertheless, we may regard it as a matter of decision in this sense: we are free to choose to continue using the thing language or not; in the latter case we could restrict ourselves to a language of sense-data and other "phenomenal" entities, or construct an alternative to the customary thing language with another structure, or, finally, we could refrain from speaking. If someone decides to accept the thing language, there is no objection against saying that he has accepted the world of things. But this must not be interpreted as if it meant his acceptance of a *belief* in the reality of the thing world; there is no such belief or assertion or assumption, because it is not a theoretical question. To accept the thing world means nothing more than to accept a certain form of language, in other words, to accept rules for forming statements and for testing, accepting, or rejecting them. The acceptance of the thing language leads, on the basis of observations made, also to the acceptance, belief, and assertion of certain statements. But the thesis of the reality of the thing world cannot be among these statements, because it cannot be formulated in the thing language or, it seems, in any other theoretical language.

The decision of accepting the thing language, although itself not of a cognitive nature, will nevertheless usually be influenced by theoretical knowledge, just like any other deliberate decision concerning the acceptance of linguistic or other rules. The purposes for which the language is intended to be used, for instance, the purpose of communicating factual knowledge, will determine which factors are relevant for the decision. The efficiency, fruitfulness, and simplicity of the use of the thing language may be among the decisive factors. And the questions concerning these qualities are indeed of a theoretical nature. But these questions cannot be identified with the question of realism. They are not yes-no questions but questions of degree. The thing language in the customary form works indeed with a high degree of efficiency for most purposes of everyday life. This is a matter of fact, based upon the content of our experiences. However, it would be wrong to describe this situation by saying: "The fact of the efficiency of the thing language is confirming evidence for the reality of the thing world"; we should rather say instead: "This fact makes it advisable to accept the thing language."

The system of numbers

As an example of a system which is of a logical rather than a factual nature let us take the system of natural numbers. The framework for this system is constructed by introducing into the language new expressions with suitable rules: (1) numerals like "five" and sentence forms like "there are five books on the table"; (2) the general term "number" for the new entities, and sentence forms like "five is a number"; (3) expressions for properties of numbers (e.g., "odd", "prime"), relations (e.g., "greater than"), and functions (e.g., "plus"), and sentence forms like "two plus three is five"; (4) numerical variables (m, n, etc.) and quantifiers for universal sentences ("for every n, . . .") and existential sentences ("there is an n such that . . .") with the customary deductive rules.

Here again there are internal questions. e.g., "Is there a prime number greater than a hundred?" Here, however, the answers are found, not by empirical investigation based on observations, but by logical analysis based on the rules for the new expressions. Therefore the answers are here analytic, i.e., logically true.

What is now the nature of the philosophical question concerning the existence or reality of numbers? To begin with, there is the internal question which, together with the affirmative answer, can be formulated in the new terms, say, by "There are numbers" or, more explicitly, "There is an n such that n is a number." This statement follows from the analytic statement "five is a number" and is therefore itself analytic. Moreover, it is rather trivial (in contradistinction to a statement like "There is a prime number greater than a million," which is likewise analytic but far from trivial), because it does not say more than that the new system is not empty; but this is immediately seen from the rule which states that words like "five" are substitutable for the new variables. Therefore nobody who meant the question "Are there numbers?" in the internal sense would either assert or even seriously consider a negative answer. This makes it plausible to assume that those philosophers who treat the question of the existence of numbers as a serious philosophical problem, and offer lengthy arguments on either side, do not have in mind the internal question. And, indeed, if we were to ask them: "Do you mean the question as to whether the framework of numbers, *if* we were to accept it, would be found to be empty or not?," they would probably reply; "Not at all, we mean a question *prior* to the acceptance of the new framework." They might try to explain what they mean by saying that it is a question of the ontological status of numbers; the question whether or not numbers have a certain metaphysical characteristic called reality (but a kind of ideal reality, different from the material reality of the thing world) or subsistence or status of "independent entities." Unfortunately, these philosophers have so far not given a formulation of their question in terms of the common scientific language. Therefore our judgment must be that they have not succeeded in giving to the external questions and to the possible answers any cognitive content. Unless and until they supply a clear cognitive interpretation, we are justified in our suspicion that their question is a pseudo-question, that is, one disguised in the form of a theoretical question while in fact it is non-theoretical; in the present case it is the practical problem whether or not to incorporate into the language the new linguistic forms which constitute the framework of numbers.

The system of propositions

New variables, *"p", "q"*, etc., are introduced with a rule to the effect that any (declarative) sentence may be substituted for a variable of this kind; this includes, in addition to the sentences of the original thing language, also all general sentences with variables of any kind which may have been introduced into the language. Further, the general term "proposition" is introduced. "*p* is a proposition" may be defined by "*p* or not *p*" (or by any other sentence form yielding only analytic sentences). Therefore, every sentence of the form ". . . is a proposition" (where any sentence may stand in the place of the dots) is analytic. This holds, for example, for the sentence:

   (a) "Chicago is large is a proposition."

(We disregard here the fact that the rules of English grammar require not a sentence but a that-clause as the subject of another sentence; accordingly, instead of *(a)* we should have to say "That Chicago is large is a proposition.") Predicates may be admitted whose argument expressions are sentences; these predicates may be either extensional (e.g., the customary truth-functional connectives) or not (e.g., modal predicates like "possible", "necessary", etc.). With the help of the new variables, general sentences may be formed, e.g.,

   (b) "For every *p*, either *p* or not-*p*."
   (c) "There is a *p* such that *p* is not necessary and not-*p* is not necessary."
   (d) "There is a *p* such that *p* is a proposition."

(c) and *(d)* are internal assertions of existence. The statement "There are propositions" may be meant in the sense of *(d)*; in this case it is analytic (since it follows from *(a)*) and even trivial. If, however, the statement is meant in an external sense, then it is non-cognitive.

It is important to notice that the system of rules for the linguistic expressions of the propositional framework (of which only a few rules have here been briefly indicated) is sufficient for the introduction of the framework. Any further explanations as to the nature of the propositions (i.e., the elements of the system indicated, the values of the variables *"p"*, *"q"*, etc.) are theoretically unnecessary because, if correct, they follow from the rules. For example, are propositions mental events (as in Russell's theory)? A look at the rules shows us that they are not, because otherwise existential statements would be of the form: "If the mental state of the person in question fulfils such and such conditions, then there is a *p* such that . . ." The fact that no references to mental conditions occur in existential statements (like *(c)*, *(d)*, etc.) shows that propositions are not mental entities. Further, a statement of the existence of linguistic entities (e.g., expressions, classes of expressions, etc.) must contain a reference to a language. The fact that no such reference occurs in the existential statements here, shows that propositions are not linguistic entities. The fact that in these statements no reference to a subject (an observer or knower) occurs (nothing like: "There is a *p* which is necessary for Mr. X"), shows that the propositions (and their properties, like necessity, etc.) are not subjective. Although characterizations of these or similar kinds are, strictly speaking, unnecessary, they may nevertheless be practically useful. If they are given, they should be understood, not as ingredient parts of the system, but merely as marginal notes with the purpose of supplying to the reader helpful hints or convenient pictorial associations which may make his learning of the use of the expressions easier than the bare system of the rules would do. Such a characterization is analogous to an extrasystematic explanation which a physicist sometimes gives to the beginner. He might, for example, tell him to imagine the atoms of a gas as small balls rushing around with great speed, or the electromagnetic field and its oscillations as quasi-elastic tensions and vibrations in an ether. In fact, however, all that can accurately be said about atoms or the field is implicitly contained in the physical laws of the theories in question.[2]

The system of thing properties

The thing language contains words like "red," "hard," "stone," "house," etc., which are used for describing what things are like. Now we may introduce new variables, say "*f*," "*g*," etc., for which those words are substitutable and furthermore the general term "property." New rules are laid down which admit sentences like "Red is a property," "Red is a color," "These two pieces of paper have at least one color in common" (i.e., "There is an *f* such that *f* is a color, and . . ."). The last sentence is an internal assertion. It is of an empirical factual nature. However, the external statement, the philosophical statement of the reality of properties—a special case of the thesis of the reality of universals—is devoid of cognitive content.

The systems of integers and rational numbers

Into a language containing the framework of natural numbers we may introduce first the (positive and negative) integers as relations among natural numbers and then the rational numbers as relations among integers. This involves introducing new types of variables, expressions substitutable for them, and the general terms "integer" and "rational number."

The system of real numbers

On the basis of the rational numbers, the real numbers may be introduced as classes of a special kind (segments) of rational numbers (according to the method developed by Dedekind and Frege). Here again a new type of variables is introduced, expressions substitutable for them (e.g., "$\sqrt{2}$"), and the general term "real number."

The spatio-temporal coordinate system for physics

The new entities are the space-time points. Each is an ordered quadruple of four real numbers, called its coordinates, consisting of three spatial and one temporal coordinates. The physical state of spatio-temporal point or region is described either with the help of qualitative predicates (e.g., "hot") or by ascribing numbers as values of a physical magnitude (e.g., mass, temperature, and the like). The step from the system of things (which does not contain space-time points but only extended objects with spatial and temporal relations between them) to the physical coordinate system is again a matter of decision. Our choice of certain features, although itself not theoretical, is suggested by theoretical knowledge, either logical or factual. For example, the choice of real numbers rather than rational numbers or integers as coordinates is not much influenced by the facts of experience but mainly due to considerations of mathematical simplicity. The restriction to rational coordinates would not be in conflict with any experimental knowledge we have, because the result of any measurement is a rational number. However, it would prevent the use of ordinary geometry (which says, e.g., that the diagonal of a square with the side 1 has the irrational value $\sqrt{2}$) and thus lead to great complications. On the other hand, the decision to use three rather than two or four spatial coordinates is strongly suggested, but still not forced upon us, by the result of common observations. If certain events allegedly observed in spiritualistic séances, e.g., a ball moving out of a sealed box, were confirmed beyond any reasonable doubt, it might seem advisable to use four spatial coordinates. Internal questions are here, in general, empirical questions to be answered by empirical investigations. On the other hand, the external questions of the reality of physical space and physical time are pseudo-questions. A question like "Are there (really) space-time points?" is ambiguous. It may be meant as an internal question; then the affirmative answer is, of course, analytic and trivial. Or it may be meant in the external sense: "Shall we introduce such and such forms into our language?"; in this case it is not a theoretical but a practical question, a matter of decision rather than assertion, and hence the proposed formulation would be misleading. Or finally, it may be meant in the following sense: "Are our experiences such that the use of the linguistic forms in questions will be expedient and fruitful?" This is a theoretical question of a factual, empirical nature. But it concerns a matter of degree; therefore a formulation in the form "real or not?" would be inadequate.

3. WHAT DOES ACCEPTANCE OF A KIND OF ENTITIES MEAN?

Let us now summarize the essential characteristics of situations involving the introduction of a new kind of entities, characteristics which are common to the various examples outlined above.

The acceptance of a new kind of entities is represented in the language by the introduction of a framework of new forms of expressions to be used according to a new set of rules. There may be new names for particular entities of the kind in question; but some such names may already occur in the language before the introduction of the new framework. (Thus, for example, the thing language contains certainly words of the type of "blue" and "house" before the framework of properties is introduced; and it may contain words like "ten" in sentences of the form "I have ten fingers" before the framework of numbers is introduced.) The latter fact shows that the occurrence of constants of the type in question—regarded as names of entities

of the new kind after the new framework is introduced—is not a sure sign of the acceptance of the new kind of entities. Therefore the introduction of such constants is not to be regarded as an essential step in the introduction of the framework. The two essential steps are rather the following. First, the introduction of a general term, a predicate of higher level, for the new kind of entities, permitting us to say of any particular entity that it belongs to this kind (e.g., "Red is a *property,*" "Five is a *number*"). Second, the introduction of variables of the new type. The new entities are values of these variables; the constants (and the closed compound expressions, if any) are substitutable for the variables.[3] With the help of the variables, general sentences concerning the new entities can be formulated.

After the new forms are introduced into the language, it is possible to formulate with their help internal questions and possible answers to them. A question of this kind may be either empirical or logical; accordingly a true answer is either factually true or analytic.

From the internal questions we must clearly distinguish external questions, i.e., philosophical questions concerning the existence or reality of the total system of the new entities. Many philosophers regard a question of this kind as an ontological question which must be raised and answered *before* the introduction of the new language forms. The latter introduction, they believe, is legitimate only if it can be justified by an ontological insight supplying an affirmative answer to the question of reality. In contrast to this view, we take the position that the introduction of the new ways of speaking does not need any theoretical justification because it does not imply any assertion of reality. We may still speak (and have done so) of "the acceptance of the new entities" since this form of speech is customary; but one must keep in mind that this phrase does not mean for us anything more than acceptance of the new framework, i.e., of the new linguistic forms. Above all, it must not be interpreted as referring to an assumption, belief, or assertion of "the reality of the entities." There is no such assertion. An alleged statement of the reality of the system of entities is a pseudo-statement without cognitive content. To be sure, we have to face at this point an important question; but it is a practical, not a theoretical question; it is the question of whether or not to accept the new linguistic forms. The acceptance cannot be judged as being either true or false because it is not an assertion. It can only be judged as being more or less expedient, fruitful, conducive to the aim for which the language is intended. Judgments of this kind supply the motivation for the decision of accepting or rejecting the kind of entities.[4]

Thus it is clear that the acceptance of a linguistic framework must not be regarded as implying a metaphysical doctrine concerning the reality of the entities in question. It seems to me due to a neglect of this important distinction that some contemporary nominalists label the admission of variables of abstract types as "Platonism."[5] This is, to say the least, an extremely misleading terminology. It leads to the absurd consequence, that the position of everybody who accepts the language of physics with its real number variables (as a language of communication, not merely as a calculus) would be called Platonistic, even if he is a strict empiricist who rejects Platonic metaphysics.

A brief historical remark may here be inserted. The non-cognitive character of the questions which we have called here external questions was recognized and emphasized already by the Vienna Circle under the leadership of Moritz Schlick, the group from which the movement of logical empiricism originated. Influenced by ideas of Ludwig Wittgenstein, the Circle rejected both the thesis of the reality of the external world and the thesis of its irreality as pseudo-statements,[6] the same was the case for both the thesis of the reality of universals (abstract entities, in our present terminology) and the nominalistic thesis that they are not real and that their alleged names are not names of anything but merely *flatus vocis*. (It is obvious that the apparent negation of a pseudo-statement must also be a pseudo-statement.) It is therefore not correct to classify the members of the Vienna Circle as nominalists, as is sometimes done. However, if we look at the basic anti-metaphysical and pro-scientific attitude of most nominalists (and the same holds for many materialists and realists

in the modern sense), disregarding their occasional pseudo-theoretical formulations, then it is, of course, true to say that the Vienna Circle was much closer to those philosophers than to their opponents.

4. ABSTRACT ENTITIES IN SEMANTICS

The problem of the legitimacy and the status of abstract entities has recently again led to controversial discussions in connection with semantics. In a semantical meaning analysis certain expressions in a language are often said to designate (or name or denote or signify or refer to) certain extra-linguistic entities.[7] As long as physical things or events (e.g., Chicago or Caesar's death) are taken as designata (entities designated), no serious doubts arise. But strong objections have been raised, especially by some empiricists, against abstract entities as designata, e.g., against semantical statements of the following kind:

1. "The word 'red' designates a property of things";
2. "The word 'color' designates a property of properties of things";
3. "The word 'five' designates a number";
4. "The word 'odd' designates a property of numbers";
5. "The sentence 'Chicago is large' designates a proposition."

Those who criticize these statements do not, of course, reject the use of the expressions in question, like "red" or "five"; nor would they deny that these expressions are meaningful. But to be meaningful, they would say, is not the same as having a meaning in the sense of an entity designated. They reject the belief, which they regard as implicitly presupposed by those semantical statements, that to each expression of the types in question (adjectives like "red," numbers like "five," etc.) there is a particular real entity to which the expression stands in the relation of designation. This belief is rejected as incompatible with the basic principles of empiricism or of scientific thinking. Derogatory labels like "Platonic realism," "hypostatization," or " 'Fido'-Fido principle" are attached to it. The latter is the name given by Gilbert Ryle to the criticized belief, which, in his view, arises by a naïve inference of analogy: just as there is an entity well known to me, viz. my dog Fido, which is designated by the name "Fido," thus there must be for every meaningful expression a particular entity to which it stands in the relation of designation or naming, i.e., the relation exemplified by "Fido"-Fido. The belief criticized is thus a case of hypostatization, i.e., of treating as names expressions which are not names. While "Fido" is a name, expressions like "red," "five," etc., are said not to be names, not to designate anything.

Our previous discussion concerning the acceptance of frameworks enables us now to clarify the situation with respect to abstract entities as designata. Let us take as an example the statement:

(a) " 'Five' designates a number."

The formulation of this statement presupposes that our language L contains the forms of expressions which we have called the framework of numbers, in particular, numerical variables and the general term "number." If L contains these forms, the following is an analytic statement in L:

(b) "Five is a number."

Further, to make the statement (a) possible, L must contain an expression like "designates" or "is a name of" for the semantical relation of designation. If suitable rules for this term are laid down, the following is likewise analytic:

(c) " 'Five' designates five."

(Generally speaking, any expression of the form " '...' designates..." is an analytic statement provided the term "..." is a constant in an accepted framework. If the latter condition is not fulfilled, the expression is not a statement.) Since (a) follows from (c) and (b), (a) is likewise analytic.

Thus it is clear that if someone accepts the framework of numbers, then he must acknowledge (c) and (b) and hence (a) as true statements. Generally speaking, if someone accepts a framework for a certain kind of entities, then he is bound to admit the entities as possible designata. Thus the question of the admissibility of entities of a certain type or of abstract entities in general as designata is reduced to the question of the acceptability of the linguistic framework for those entities. Both the nominalistic critics, who refuse the status of designators or names to expressions like "red," "five," etc., because they deny the existence of abstract entities, and the skeptics, who express doubts concerning the existence and demand evidence for it, treat the question of existence as a theoretical question. They do, of course, not mean the internal question; the affirmative answer to *this* question is analytic and trivial and too obvious for doubt or denial, as we have seen. Their doubts refer rather to the system of entities itself; hence they mean the external question. They believe that only after making sure that there really is a system of entities of the kind in question are we justified in accepting the framework by incorporating the linguistic forms into our language. However, we have seen that the external question is not a theoretical question but rather the practical question whether or not to accept those linguistic forms. This acceptance is not in need of a theoretical justification (except with respect to expediency and fruitfulness), because it does not imply a belief or assertion. Ryle says that the "Fido"-Fido principle is "a grotesque theory." Grotesque or not, Ryle is wrong in calling it a theory. It is rather the practical decision to accept certain frameworks. Maybe Ryle is historically right with respect to those whom he mentions as previous representatives of the principle, viz. John Stuart Mill, Frege, and Russell. If these philosophers regarded the acceptance of a system of entities as a theory, an assertion, they were victims of the same old, metaphysical confusion. But it is certainly wrong to regard *my* semantical method as involving a belief in the reality of abstract entities, since I reject a thesis of this kind as a metaphysical pseudo-statement.

The critics of the use of abstract entities in semantics overlook the fundamental difference between the acceptance of a system of entities and an internal assertion, e.g., an assertion that there are elephants or electrons or prime numbers greater than a million. Whoever makes an internal assertion is certainly obliged to justify it by providing evidence, empirical evidence in the case of electrons, logical proof in the case of the prime numbers. The demand for a theoretical justification, correct in the case of internal assertions, is sometimes wrongly applied to the acceptance of a system of entities. Thus, for example, Ernest Nagel asks for "evidence relevant for affirming with warrant that there are such entities as infinitesimals or propositions." He characterizes the evidence required in these cases—in distinction to the empirical evidence in the case of electrons—as "in the broad sense logical and dialectical." Beyond this no hint is given as to what might be regarded as relevant evidence. Some nominalists regard the acceptance of abstract entities as a kind of superstition or myth, populating the world with fictitious or at least dubious entities, analogous to the belief in centaurs or demons. This shows again the confusion mentioned, because a superstition or myth is a false (or dubious) internal statement.

Let us take as example the natural numbers as cardinal numbers, i.e., in contexts like "Here are three books." The linguistic forms of the framework of numbers, including variables and the general term "number," are generally used in our common language of communication; and it is easy to formulate explicit rules for their use. Thus the logical characteristics of this framework are sufficiently clear (while many internal questions, i.e., arithmetical questions, are, of course, still open). In spite of this, the controversy concerning the external question of the ontological reality of the system of numbers continues. Suppose that one philosopher says: "I believe that there are numbers as real entities. This gives me the right to use the linguistic forms of the numerical framework and to make semantical statements about numbers as designata of numerals." His nominalistic opponent replies: "You are wrong; there are no numbers. The numerals may still be used as meaningful expressions. But they are not names, there are no entities designated by them. Therefore the word number and numerical variables must not be used (unless a way were found to introduce them as merely abbreviating devices, a way of translating them into the nominalistic thing language)." I cannot think of any possible evidence that would be regarded as relevant by both philosophers, and

therefore, if actually found, would decide the controversy or at least make one of the opposite theses more probable than the other. (To construe the numbers as classes or properties of the second level, according to the Frege-Russell method, does, of course, not solve the controversy, because the first philosopher would affirm and the second deny the existence of the system of classes or properties of the second level.) Therefore I feel compelled to regard the external question as a pseudo-question, until both parties to the controversy offer a common interpretation of the question as a cognitive question; this would involve an indication of possible evidence regarded as relevant by both sides.

There is a particular kind of misinterpretation of the acceptance of abstract entities in various fields of science and in semantics, that needs to be cleared up. Certain early British empiricists (e.g., Berkeley and Hume) denied the existence of abstract entities on the ground that immediate experience presents us only with particulars, not with universals, e.g., with this red patch, but not with Redness or Color-in-General; with this scalene triangle, but not with Scalene Triangularity or Triangularity-in-General. Only entities belonging to a type of which examples were to be found within immediate experience could be accepted as ultimate constituents of reality. Thus, according to this way of thinking, the existence of abstract entities could be asserted only if one could show either that some abstract entities fall within the given, or that abstract entities can be defined in terms of the types of entity which are given. Since these empiricists found no abstract entities within the realm of sense-data, they either denied their existence, or else made a futile attempt to define universals in terms of particulars. Some contemporary philosophers, especially English philosophers following Bertrand Russell, think in basically similar terms. They emphasize a distinction between the data (that which is immediately given in consciousness, e.g., sense-data, immediately past experiences, etc.) and the constructs based on the data. Existence or reality is ascribed only to the data; the constructs are not real entities; the corresponding linguistic expressions are merely ways of speech not actually designating anything (reminiscent of the nominalists' *flatus vocis*). We shall not criticize here this general conception. (As far as it is a principle of accepting certain entities and not accepting others, leaving aside any ontological, phenomenalistic and nominalistic pseudo-statements, there cannot be any theoretical objection to it.) But if this conception leads to the view that other philosophers or scientists who accept abstract entities thereby assert or imply their occurrence as immediate data, then such a view must be rejected as a misinterpretation. References to space-time points, the electromagnetic field, or electrons in physics, to real or complex numbers and their functions in mathematics, to the excitatory potential or unconscious complexes in psychology, to an inflationary trend in economics, and the like, do not imply the assertion that entities of these kinds occur as immediate data. And the same holds for references to abstract entities as designata in semantics. Some of the criticism by English philosophers against such references give the impression that, probably due to the misinterpretation just indicated, they accuse the semanticist not so much of bad metaphysics (as some nominalists would do) but of bad psychology. The fact that they regard a semantical method involving abstract entities not merely as doubtful and perhaps wrong, but as manifestly absurd, preposterous and grotesque, and that they show a deep horror and indignation against this method, is perhaps to be explained by a misinterpretation of the kind described. In fact, of course, the semanticist does not in the least assert or imply that the abstract entities to which he refers can be experienced as immediately given either by sensation or by a kind of rational intuition. An assertion of this kind would indeed be very dubious psychology. The psychological question as to which kinds of entities do and which do not occur as immediate data is entirely irrelevant for semantics, just as it is for physics, mathematics, economics, etc., with respect to the examples mentioned above.[8]

5. CONCLUSION

For those who want to develop or use semantical methods, the decisive question is not the alleged ontological question of the existence of abstract entities but rather the question whether the use of abstract linguistic forms or, in technical terms, the use of variables beyond those for things (or phenomenal data), is expedient and fruitful for the purposes for which semantical analyses are made, viz. the analysis, interpretation, clarification, or construction of languages of communication, especially languages of science. This question is here neither decided nor even discussed. It is not a question simply of yes or no, but a matter of degree. Among those philosophers who have carried out semantical analyses and thought about suitable tools for this work, beginning with Plato and Aristotle and, in a more technical way on the basis of modern logic, with C. S. Peirce and Frege, a great majority accepted abstract entities. This does, of course, not prove the case. After all, semantics in the technical sense is still in the initial phases of its development, and we must be prepared for possible fundamental changes in methods. Let us therefore admit that the nominalistic critics may possibly be right. But if so, they will have to offer better arguments than they have so far. Appeal to ontological insight will not carry much weight. The critics will have to show that it is possible to construct a semantical method which avoids all references to abstract entities and achieves by simpler means essentially the same results as the other methods.

The acceptance or rejection of abstract linguistic forms, just as the acceptance or rejection of any other linguistic forms in any branch of science, will finally be decided by their efficiency as instruments, the ratio of the results achieved to the amount and complexity of the efforts required. To decree dogmatic prohibitions of certain linguistic forms instead of testing them by their success or failure in practical use, is worse than futile; it is positively harmful because it may obstruct scientific progress. The history of science shows examples of such prohibitions based on prejudices deriving from religious, mythological, metaphysical, or other irrational sources, which slowed up the developments for shorter or longer periods of time. Let us learn from the lessons of history. Let us grant to those who work in any special field of investigation the freedom to use any form of expression which seems useful to them; the work in the field will sooner or later lead to the elimination of those forms which have no useful function. *Let us be cautious in making assertions and critical in examining them, but tolerant in permitting linguistic forms.*

NOTES

1. The terms "sentence" and "statement" are here used synonymously for declarative (indicative, propositional) sentences.
2. In my book *Meaning and Necessity* (Chicago, 1947) I have developed a semantic method which takes propositions as entities designated by sentences (more specifically, as intensions of sentences). In order to facilitate the understanding of the systematic development, I added some informal, extra-systematic explanations concerning the nature of propositions. I said that the term "proposition" "is used neither for a linguistic expression nor for a subjective, mental occurrence, but rather for something objective that may or may not be exemplified in nature. . . . We apply the term 'proposition' to any entities of a certain logical type, namely, those that may be expressed by (declarative) sentences in a language" (p. 27). After some more detailed discussions concerning the relation between propositions and facts, and the nature of false propositions, I added: "It has been the purpose of the preceding remarks to facilitate the understanding of our conception of propositions. If, however, a reader should find these explanations more puzzling than clarifying, or even unacceptable, he may disregard them" (p. 31) (i.e., disregard these extra-systematic explanations, not the whole theory of the propositions as intensions of sentences, as one reviewer understood). In spite of this warning, it seems that some of those readers who were puzzled by the explanations did not disregard them but thought that by raising objections against them they could refute the theory. This is analogous to the procedure of some laymen who, by (correctly) criticizing the ether picture or other visualizations of physical theories, thought they had refuted those theories. Perhaps the discussions in the present paper will help in clarifying the role of the system of linguistic rules for the introduction of a framework for entities on the one hand, and that of extra-systematic explanations concerning the nature of the entities on the other.
3. W. V. Quine was the first to recognize the importance of the introduction of variables as indicating the acceptance of entities. "The ontology to which one's use of language commits him comprises simply the objects that he treats as falling . . . within the range of values of his variables."
4. For a closely related point of view on these questions see the detailed discussions of Herbert Feigl, "Existential Hypotheses," *Philosophy of Science* 17 (1950), 35–62.
5. Paul Bernays, *"Sur le platonisme dans les mathématiques," L'Enseignement math.* 34 (1935), 52–69.
6. See Carnap, *Scheinprobleme in der Philosophie: das Fremdpsychische und der Realismusstreit*, Berlin, 1928. Moritz Schlick, *Positivismus and Realismus*, reprinted in *Gesammelte Aufsätze*, Wien, 1938.
7. See *Meaning and Necessity* (Chicago, 1947). The distinction I have drawn in the latter book between the method of the name-relation and the method of intension and extension is not essential for our present discussion. The term "designation" is used in the present article in a neutral way; it may be understood as referring to the name-relation or to the intension-relation or to the extension-relation or to any similar relations used in other semantical methods.
8. Wilfrid Sellars ("Acquaintance and Description Again," in *Journal of Philosophy*, 46 (1949), 496–504; see pp. 502 f.) analyzes clearly the roots of the mistake "of taking the designation relation of semantic theory to be a reconstruction of *being present to an experience*."

18 / W. V. Quine (1908–2000)
TWO DOGMAS OF EMPIRICISM

Modern empiricism has been conditioned in large part by two dogmas. One is a belief in some fundamental cleavage between truths which are *analytic*, or grounded in meanings independently of matters of fact, and truths which are *synthetic*, or grounded in fact. The other dogma is *reductionism:* the belief that each meaningful statement is equivalent to some logical construct upon terms which refer to immediate experience. Both dogmas, I shall argue, are ill-founded. One effect of abandoning them is, as we shall see, a blurring of the supposed boundary between speculative metaphysics and natural science. Another effect is a shift toward pragmatism.

1. Background for Analyticity

Kant's cleavage between analytic and synthetic truths was foreshadowed in Hume's distinction between relations of ideas and matters of fact, and in Leibniz's distinction between truths of reason and truths of fact. Leibniz spoke of the truths of reason as true in all possible worlds. Picturesqueness aside, this is to say that the truths of reason are those which could not possibly be false. In the same vein we hear analytic statements defined as statements whose denials are self-contradictory. But this definition has small explanatory value; for the notion of self-contradictoriness, in the quite broad sense needed for this definition of analyticity, stands in exactly the same need of clarification as does the notion of analyticity itself. The two notions are the two sides of a single dubious coin.

Kant conceived of an analytic statement as one that attributes to its subject no more than is already conceptually contained in the subject. This formulation has two shortcomings: it limits itself to statements of subject-predicate form, and it appeals to a notion of containment which is left at a metaphorical level. But Kant's intent, evident more from the use he makes of the notion of analyticity than from his definition of it, can be restated thus: a statement is analytic when it is true by virtue of meanings and independently of fact. Pursuing this line, let us examine the concept of *meaning* which is presupposed.

Meaning, let us remember, is not to be identified with naming.[1] Frege's example of "Evening Star" and "Morning Star," and Russell's of "Scott" and "the author of *Waverly*," illustrate that terms can name the same thing but differ in meaning. The distinction between meaning and naming is no less important at the level of abstract terms. The terms "9" and "the number of the planets" name one and the same abstract entity but presumably must be regarded as unlike in meaning; for astronomical observation was needed, and not mere reflection on meanings, to determine the sameness of the entity in question.

The above examples consist of singular terms, concrete and abstract. With general terms, or predicates, the situation is somewhat different but parallel. Whereas a singular term purports to name an entity, abstract or concrete, a general term does not; but a general term is *true* of an entity, or of each of many, or of none.[2] The class of all entities of which a gen-

Reprinted by permission of the publishers from *From a Logical Point of View* by W. V. Quine, Cambridge, Mass.: Harvard University Press, © 1953, 1961 by the President and Fellows of Harvard College; © 1981 by W. V. Quine.

eral term is true is called the *extension* of the term. Now paralleling the contrast between the meaning of a singular term and the entity named, we must distinguish equally between the meaning of a general term and its extension. The general terms "creature with a heart" and "creature with kidneys," for example, are perhaps alike in extension but unlike in meaning.

Confusion of meaning with extension, in the case of general terms, is less common than confusion of meaning with naming in the case of singular terms. It is indeed a commonplace in philosophy to oppose intension (or meaning) to extension, or, in a variant vocabulary, connotation to denotation.

The Aristotelian notion of essence was the forerunner, no doubt, of the modern notion of intension or meaning. For Aristotle it was essential in men to be rational, accidental to be two-legged. But there is an important difference between this attitude and the doctrine of meaning. From the latter point of view it may indeed be conceded (if only for the sake of argument) that rationality is involved in the meaning of the word "man" while two-leggedness is not; but two-leggedness may at the same time be viewed as involved in the meaning of "biped" while rationality is not. Thus from the point of view of the doctrine of meaning it makes no sense to say of the actual individual, who is at once a man and a biped, that his rationality is essential and his two-leggedness accidental or vice versa. Things had essences, for Aristotle, but only linguistic forms have meanings. Meaning is what essence becomes when it is divorced from the object of reference and wedded to the word.

For the theory of meaning a conspicuous question is the nature of its objects: what sort of things are meanings? A felt need for meant entities may derive from an earlier failure to appreciate that meaning and reference are distinct. Once the theory of meaning is sharply separated from the theory of reference, it is a short step to recognizing as the primary business of the theory of meaning simply the synonymy of linguistic forms and the analyticity of statements; meanings themselves, as obscure intermediary entities, may well be abandoned.[3]

The problem of analyticity then confronts us

anew. Statements which are analytic by general philosophical acclaim are not, indeed, far to seek. They fall into two classes. Those of the first class, which may be called *logically true*, are typified by:

(1) No unmarried man is married.

The relevant feature of this example is that it not merely is true as it stands, but remains true under any and all reinterpretations of "man" and "married." If we suppose a prior inventory of *logical* particles, comprising "no," "un-," "not," "if," "then," "and," etc., then in general a logical truth is a statement which is true and remains true under all reinterpretations of its components other than the logical particles.

But there is also a second class of analytic statements, typified by:

(2) No bachelor is married.

The characteristic of such a statement is that it can be turned into a logical truth by putting synonyms for synonyms; thus (2) can be turned into (1) by putting "unmarried man" for its synonym "bachelor." We still lack a proper characterization of this second class of analytic statements, and therewith of analyticity generally, inasmuch as we have had in the above description to lean on a notion of "synonymy" which is no less in need of clarification than analyticity itself.

In recent years Carnap has tended to explain analyticity by appeal to what he calls state-descriptions.[4] A state-description is any exhaustive assignment of truth values to the atomic, or noncompound, statements of the language. All other statements of the language are, Carnap assumes, built up of their component clauses by means of the familiar logical devices, in such a way that the truth value of any complex statement is fixed for each state-description by specifiable logical laws. A statement is then explained as analytic when it comes out true under every state description. This account is an adaptation of Leibniz's "true in all possible words." But note that this version of analyticity serves its purpose only if the atomic statements of the language are, unlike "John is a bachelor" and "John is married," mutually independent. Otherwise there would be a state-description which assigned truth to "John is a bachelor" and to "John is married," and consequently "No bachelors are married" would turn out synthetic rather than analytic under the proposed criterion. Thus the criterion of analyticity in terms of state-descriptions serves only for languages devoid of extra-logical synonym-pairs, such as "bachelor" and "unmarried man"—synonym-pairs of the type which give rise to the "second class" of analytic statements. The criterion in terms of state-descriptions is a reconstruction at best of logical truth, not of analyticity.

I do not mean to suggest that Carnap is under any illusions on this point. His simplified model language with its state-descriptions is aimed primarily not at the general problem of analyticity but at another purpose, the clarification of probability and induction. Our problem, however, is analyticity; and here the major difficulty lies not in the first class of analytic statements, the logical truths, but rather in the second class, which depends on the notion of synonymy.

2. Definition

There are those who find it soothing to say that the analytic statements of the second class reduce to those of the first class, the logical truths, by *definition;* "bachelor," for example, is *defined* as "unmarried man." But how do we find that "bachelor" is defined as "unmarried man"? Who defined it thus, and when? Are we to appeal to the nearest dictionary, and accept the lexicographer's formulation as law? Clearly this would be to put the cart before the horse. The lexicographer is an empirical scientist, whose business is the recording of antecedent facts; and if he glosses "bachelor" as "unmarried man" it is because of his belief that there is a relation of synonymy between those forms, implicit in general or preferred usage prior to his own work. The notion of synonymy presupposed here has still to be clarified, presumably in terms relating to linguistic behavior. Certainly the "definition" which is the lexicographer's report of an observed synonymy cannot be taken as the ground of the synonymy.

Definition is not, indeed, an activity exclusively of philologists. Philosophers and scientists frequently have occasion to "define" a recondite term by paraphrasing it into terms of a more familiar vocabulary. But ordinarily such a definition, like the philologist's, is pure lexicography, affirming a relation of synonymy antecedent to the exposition in hand.

Just what it means to affirm synonymy, just what the interconnections may be which are necessary and sufficient in order that two linguistic forms be properly describable as synonymous, is far from clear; but, whatever these interconnections may be, ordinarily they are grounded in usage. Definitions reporting selected instances of synonymy come then as reports upon usage.

There is also, however, a variant type of definitional activity which does not limit itself to the reporting of preëxisting synonymies. I have in mind what Carnap calls *explication*—an activity to which philosophers are given, and scientists also in their more philosophical moments. In explication the purpose is not merely to paraphrase the definiendum into an outright synonym, but actually to improve upon the definiendum by refining or supplementing its meaning. But even explication, though not merely reporting a preëxisting synonymy between definiendum and definiens, does rest nevertheless on "other" preëxisting synonymies. The matter may be viewed as follows. Any word worth explicating has some contexts which, as wholes, are clear and precise enough to be useful; and the purpose of explication is to preserve the usage of these favored contexts while sharpening the usage of other contexts. In order that a given definition be suitable for purposes of explication, therefore, what is required is not that the definiendum in its antecedent usage be synonymous with the definiens, but just that each of these favored contexts of the definiendum, taken as a whole in its antecedent usage, be synonymous with the corresponding context of the definiens.

Two alternative definientia may be equally appropriate for the purposes of a given task of explication and yet not be synonymous with each other; for they may serve interchangeably within the favored contexts but diverge elsewhere. By cleaving to one of these definientia rather than the other, a definition of explicative kind generates, by fiat, a relation of synonymy between definiendum and definiens which did not hold before. But such a definition still owes its explicative function, as seen, to preëxisting synonymies.

There does, however, remain still an extreme sort of definition which does not hark back to prior synonymies at all: namely, the explicitly conventional introduction of novel notations for purposes of sheer abbreviation. Here the definiendum becomes synonymous with the definiens simply because it has been created expressly for the purpose of being synonymous with the definiens. Here we have a really transparent case of synonymy created by definition; would that all species of synonymy were as intelligible. For the rest, definition rests on synonymy rather than explaining it.

The word "definition" has come to have a dangerously reassuring sound, owing no doubt to its frequent occurrence in logical and mathematical writings. We shall do well to digress now into a brief appraisal of the role of definition in formal work.

In logical and mathematical systems either of two mutually antagonistic types of economy may be striven for, and each has its peculiar practical utility. On the one hand we may seek economy of practical expression—ease and brevity in the statement of multifarious relations. This sort of economy calls usually for distinctive concise notations for a wealth of concepts. Second, however, and oppositely, we may seek economy in grammar and vocabulary; we may try to find a minimum of basic concepts such that, once a distinctive notation has been appropriated to each of them, it becomes possible to express any desired further concept by mere combination and iteration of our basic notations. This second sort of economy is impractical in one way, since a poverty in basic idioms tends to a necessary lengthening of discourse. But it is practical in another way: it greatly simplifies theoretical discourse *about* the language, through minimizing the terms and the forms of construction wherein the language consists.

Both sorts of economy, though prima facie incompatible, are valuable in their separate ways. The custom has consequently arisen of combining both sorts of economy by forging in effect two languages, the one a part of the other. The inclusive language, though redundant in grammar and vocabulary, is economical in message lengths, while the part, called primitive notation, is economical in grammar and vocabulary. Whole and part are correlated by rules of translation whereby each idiom not in primitive notation is equated to some complex built up of primitive notation. These rules of translation are the so-called *definitions* which appear in formalized systems.

They are best viewed not as adjuncts to one language but as correlations between two languages, the one a part of the other.

But these correlations are not arbitrary. They are supposed to show how the primitive notations can accomplish all purposes, save brevity and convenience, of the redundant language. Hence the definiendum and its definiens may be expected, in each case, to be related in one or another of the three ways lately noted. The definiens may be a faithful paraphrase of the definiendum into the narrower notation, preserving a direct synonymy[5] as of antecedent usage; or the definiens may, in the spirit of explication, improve upon the antecedent usage of the definiendum; or finally, the definiendum may be a newly created notation, newly endowed with meaning here and now.

In formal and informal work alike, thus, we find that definition—except in the extreme case of the explicitly conventional introduction of new notations—hinges on prior relations of synonymy. Recognizing then that the notion of definition does not hold the key to synonymy and analyticity, let us look further into synonymy and say no more of definition.

3. Interchangeability

A natural suggestion, deserving close examination, is that the synonymy of two linguistic forms consists simply in their interchangeability in all contexts without change of truth value—interchangeability, in Leibniz's phrase, *salva veritate*.[6] Note that synonyms so conceived need not even be free from vagueness, as long as the vaguenesses match.

But it is not quite true that the synonyms "bachelor" and "unmarried man" are everywhere interchangeable *salva veritate*. Truths which become false under substitution of "unmarried man" for "bachelor" are easily constructed with the help of "bachelor of arts" or "bachelor's buttons"; also with the help of quotation, thus:

"Bachelor" has less than ten letters.

Such counterinstances can, however, perhaps be set aside by treating the phrases "bachelor of arts" and "bachelor's buttons" and the quotation "bachelor" each as a single indivisible word and then stipulating that the interchangeability *salva veritate* which is to be the touchstone of synonymy is not supposed to apply to fragmentary occurrences inside of a word. This account of synonymy, supposing it acceptable on other counts, has indeed the drawback of appealing to a prior conception of "word" which can be counted on to present difficulties of formulation in its turn. Nevertheless some progress might be claimed in having reduced the problem of synonymy to a problem of wordhood. Let us pursue this line a bit, taking "word" for granted.

The question remains whether interchangeability *salva veritate* (apart from occurrences within words) is a strong enough condition for synonymy, or whether, on the contrary, some heteronymous expressions might be thus interchangeable. Now let us be clear that we are not concerned here with synonymy in the sense of complete identity in psychological associations or poetic quality; indeed no two expressions are synonymous in such a sense. We are concerned only with what may be called *cognitive* synonymy. Just what this is cannot be said without successfully finishing the present study; but we know something about it from the need which arose for it in connection with analyticity in section 1. The sort of synonymy needed there was merely such that any analytic statement could be turned into a logical truth by putting synonyms for synonyms. Turning the tables and assuming analyticity, indeed, we could explain cognitive synonymy of terms as follows (keeping to the familiar example): to say that "bachelor" and "unmarried man" are cognitively synonymous is to say no more nor less than that the statement:

(3) All and only bachelors are unmarried men is analytic.[7]

What we need is an account of cognitive synonymy not presupposing analyticity—if we are to explain analyticity conversely with help of cognitive synonymy as undertaken in section 1. And indeed such an independent account of cognitive synonymy is at present up for consideration, namely, interchangeability *salva veritate* everywhere except within words. The question before us, to resume the thread at last, is whether such interchangeability is a sufficient condition for cognitive synonymy. We can quickly assure ourselves that it is, by examples of the following sort. The statement:

(4) Necessarily all and only bachelors are bachelors

is evidently true, even supposing "necessarily" so narrowly construed as to be truly applicable only to analytic statements. Then, if "bachelor" and "unmarried man" are interchangeable *salva veritate*, the result:

(5) Necessarily all and only bachelors are unmarried men

of putting "unmarried man" for an occurrence of "bachelor" in (4) must, like (4), be true. But to say that (5) is true is to say that (3) is analytic, and hence that "bachelor" and "unmarried man" are cognitively synonymous.

Let us see what there is about the above argument that gives it its air of hocus-pocus. The condition of interchangeability *salva veritate* varies in its force with variations in the richness of the language at hand. The above argument supposes we are working with a language rich enough to contain the adverb "necessarily," this adverb being so construed as to yield truth when and only when applied to an analytic statement. But can we condone a language which contains such an adverb? Does the adverb really make sense? To suppose that it does is to suppose that we have already made satisfactory sense of "analytic." Then what are we so hard at work on right now?

Our argument is not flatly circular, but something like it. It has the form, figuratively speaking, of a closed curve in space.

Interchangeability *salva veritate* is meaningless until relativized to a language whose extent is specified in relevant respects. Suppose now we consider a language containing just the following materials. There is an indefinitely large stock of one-place predicates (for example, *"F"* where *"Fx"* means that *x* is a man) and many-place predicates (for example, *"G"* where *"Gxy"* means that *x* loves *y*), mostly having to do with extralogical subject matter. The rest of the language is logical. The atomic sentences consist each of a predicate followed by one or more variables "x", "y", etc.; and the complex sentences are built up of the atomic ones by truth functions ("not," "and," "or," etc.) and quantification.[8] In effect such a language enjoys the benefits also of descriptions and indeed singular terms generally, these being contextually definable in known ways.[9] Even abstract singular terms naming classes, classes of classes, etc., are contextually definable in case the assumed stock of predicates includes the two-place predicate of class membership.[10] Such a language can be adequate to classical mathematics and indeed to scientific discourse generally, except in so far as the latter involves debatable devices such as contrary-to-fact conditionals or modal adverbs like "necessarily."[11] Now a language of this type is extensional, in this sense: any two predicates which agree extensionally (that is, are true of the same objects) are interchangeable *salva veritate*.[12]

In an extensional language, therefore, interchangeability *salva veritate* is no assurance of cognitive synonymy of the desired type. That "bachelor" and "unmarried man" are interchangeable *salva veritate* in an extensional language assures us of no more than that (3) is true. There is no assurance here that the extension agreement of "bachelor" and "unmarried man" rests on meaning rather than merely on accidental matters of fact, as does the extensional agreement of "creature with a heart" and "creature with kidneys."

For most purposes extensional agreement is the nearest approximation to synonymy we need care about. But the fact remains that extensional agreement falls far short of cognitive synonymy of the type required for explaining analyticity in the manner of section 1. The type of cognitive synonymy required there is such as to equate the synonymy of "bachelor" and "unmarried man" with the analyticity of (3), not merely with the truth of (3).

So we must recognize that interchangeability *salva veritate*, if construed in relation to an ex-

tensional language, is not a sufficient condition of cognitive synonymy in the sense needed for deriving analyticity in the manner of section 1. If a language contains an intensional adverb "necessarily" in the sense lately noted, or other particles to the same effect, then interchangeability *salva veritate* in such a language does afford a sufficient condition of cognitive synonymy; but such a language is intelligible only in so far as the notion of analyticity is already understood in advance.

The effort to explain cognitive synonymy first, for the sake of deriving analyticity from it afterward as in section 1, is perhaps the wrong approach. Instead we might try explaining analyticity somehow without appeal to cognitive synonymy. Afterward we could doubtless derive cognitive synonymy from analyticity satisfactorily enough if desired. We have seen that cognitive synonymy of "bachelor" and "unmarried man" can be explained as analyticity of (3). The same explanation works for any pair of one-place predicates, of course, and it can be extended in obvious fashion to many-place predicates. Other syntactical categories can also be accommodated in fairly parallel fashion. Singular terms may be said to be cognitively synonymous when the statement of identity formed by putting "=" between them is analytic. Statements may be said simply to be cognitively synonymous when their biconditional (the result of joining them by "if and only if") is analytic.[13] If we care to lump all categories into a single formulation, at the expense of assuming again the notion of "word" which was appealed to early in this section, we can describe any two linguistic forms as cognitively synonymous when the two forms are interchangeable (apart from occurrences within "words") *salva* (no longer *veritate* but) *analyticate*. Certain technical questions arise, indeed, over cases of ambiguity or homonymy; let us not pause for them, however, for we are already digressing. Let us rather turn our backs on the problem of synonymy and address ourselves anew to that of analyticity.

4. Semantical Rules

Analyticity at first seemed most naturally definable by appeal to a realm of meanings. On refinement, the appeal to meanings gave way to an appeal to synonymy or definition. But definition turned out to be a will-o'-the-wisp, and synonymy turned out to be best understood only by dint of a prior appeal to analyticity itself. So we are back at the problem of analyticity.

I do not know whether the statement "Everything green is extended" is analytic. Now does my indecision over this example really betray an incomplete understanding, an incomplete grasp of the "meanings," of "green" and "extended"? I think not. The trouble is not with "green" or "extended," but with "analytic."

It is often hinted that the difficulty in separating analytic statements from synthetic ones in ordinary language is due to the vagueness of ordinary language and that the distinction is clear when we have a precise artificial language with explicit "semantical rules." This, however, as I shall now attempt to show, is a confusion.

The notion of analyticity about which we are worrying is a purported relation between statements and language: a statement S is said to be *analytic for* a language L, and the problem is to make sense of this relation generally, that is, for variable "S" and "L". The gravity of this problem is not perceptibly less for artificial languages than for natural ones. The problem of making sense of the idiom "S is analytic for L", with variable "S" and "L", retains its stubbornness even if we limit the range of the variable "L" to artificial languages. Let me now try to make this point evident.

For artificial languages and semantical rules we look naturally to the writings of Carnap. His semantical rules take various forms, and to make my point I shall have to distinguish certain of the forms. Let us suppose, to begin with, an artificial language L_0 whose semantical rules have the form explicitly of a specification, by recursion or otherwise, of all the analytic statements of L_0. The rules tell us that such and such statements, and only those, are the analytic statements of L_0. Now here the difficulty is simply that the rules contain the word "analytic," which we do not understand! We understand what expressions the rules attribute analyticity to, but we do not understand what the rules attribute to those expressions. In short, before we can understand a rule which begins "A statement S is analytic for language

L_0 if and only if . . . ," we must understand the general relative term "analytic for"; we must understand "S is analytic for L" where "S" and "L" are variables.

Alternatively we may, indeed, view the so-called rule as a conventional definition of a new simple symbol "analytic-for-L_0", which might better be written unintendentiously as "K" so as not to seem to throw light on the interesting word "analytic." Obviously any number of classes K, M, N, etc. of statements of L_0 can be specified for various purposes or for no purpose; what does it mean to say that K, as against M, N, etc., is the class of the "analytic" statements of L_0?

By saying what statements are analytic "for L_0" we explain "analytic-for-L_0" but not "analytic," not "analytic for." We do not begin to explain the idiom "S is analytic for L" with variable "S" and "L", even if we are content to limit the range of "L" to the realm of artificial languages.

Actually we do know enough about the intended significance of "analytic" to know that analytic statements are supposed to be true. Let us then turn to a second form of semantical rule, which says not that such and such statements are analytic but simply that such and such statements are included among the truths. Such a rule is not subject to the criticism of containing the un-understood word "analytic"; and we may grant for the sake of argument that there is no difficulty over the broader term "true." A semantical rule of this second type, a rule of truth, is not supposed to specify all the truths of the language; it merely stipulates, recursively or otherwise, a certain multitude of statements which, along with others unspecified, are to count as true. Such a rule may be conceded to be quite clear. Derivatively, afterward, analyticity can be demarcated thus: a statement is analytic if it is (not merely true but) true according to the semantical rule.

Still there is really no progress. Instead of appealing to an unexplained word "analytic," we are now appealing to an unexplained phrase "semantical rule." Not every true statement which says that the statements of some class are true can count as a semantical rule—otherwise *all* truths would be "analytic" in the sense of being true according to semantical rules. Semantical rules are distinguishable, apparently, only by the fact of appearing on a page under the heading "Semantical Rules"; and this heading is itself then meaningless.

We can say indeed that a statement is *analytic-for-L₀* if and only if it is true according to such and such specifically appended "semantical rules," but then we find ourselves back at essentially the same case which was originally discussed: "*S* is analytic for *L₀* if and only if . . ." Once we seek to explain "*S* is analytic for *L*" generally for variable "*L*" (even allowing limitation of "*L*" to artificial languages), the explanation "true according to the semantical rules of *L*" is unavailing: for the relative term "semantical rule of" is as much in need of clarification, at least, as "analytic for."

It may be instructive to compare the notion of semantical rule with that of postulate. Relative to a given set of postulates, it is easy to say what a postulate is: it is a member of the set. Relative to a given set of semantical rules, it is equally easy to say what a semantical rule is. But given simply a notation, mathematical or otherwise, and indeed as thoroughly understood a notation as you please in point of the translations or truth conditions of its statements, who can say which of its true statements rank as postulates? Obviously the question is meaningless—as meaningless as asking which points in Ohio are starting points. Any finite (or effectively specifiable infinite) selection of statements (preferably true ones, perhaps) is as much *a* set of postulates as any other. The word "postulate" is significant only relative to an act of inquiry; we apply the word to a set of statements just in so far as we happen, for the year or the moment, to be thinking of those statements in relation to the statements which can be reached from them by some set of transformations to which we have seen fit to direct our attention. Now the notion of semantical rule is as sensible and meaningful as that of postulate, if conceived in a similarly relative spirit—relative, this time, to one or another particular enterprise of schooling unconversant persons in sufficient conditions for truth of statements of some natural or artificial language *L*. But from this point of view no one signalization of a subclass of the truths of *L* is intrinsically more a semantical rule than another; and, if "analytic" means "true by se-

mantical rules," no one truth of *L* is analytic to the exclusion of another.[14]

It might conceivably be protested that an artificial language *L* (unlike a natural one) is a language in the ordinary sense *plus* a set of explicit semantical rules—the whole constituting, let us say, an ordered pair; and that the semantical rules of *L* then are specifiable simply as the second component of the pair *L*. But, by the same token and more simply, we might construe an artificial language *L* outright as an ordered pair whose second component is the class of its analytic statements; and then the analytic statements of *L* become specifiable simply as the statements in the second component of *L*. Or better still, we might just stop tugging at our bootstraps altogether.

Not all the explanations of analyticity known to Carnap and his readers have been covered explicitly in the above considerations, but the extension to other forms is not hard to see. Just one additional factor should be mentioned which sometimes enters: sometimes the semantical rules are in effect rules of translation into ordinary language, in which case the analytic statements of the artificial language are in effect recognized as such from the analyticity of their specified translations in ordinary language. Here certainly there can be no thought of an illumination of the problem of analyticity from the side of the artificial language.

From the point of view of the problem of analyticity the notion of an artificial language with semantical rules is a *feu follet par excellence*. Semantical rules determining the analytic statements of an artificial language are of interest only in so far as we already understand the notion of analyticity; they are of no help in gaining this understanding.

Appeal to hypothetical languages of an artificially simple kind could conceivably be useful in clarifying analyticity, if the mental or behavioral or cultural factors relevant to analyticity—whatever they may be—were somehow sketched into the simplified model. But a model which takes analyticity merely as an irreducible character is unlikely to throw light on the problem of explicating analyticity.

It is obvious that truth in general depends on both language and extralinguistic fact. The statement "Brutus killed Caesar" would be false if the world had been different in certain ways, but it would also be false if the word "killed" happened rather to have the sense of "begat." Thus one is tempted to suppose in general that the truth of a statement is somehow analyzable into a linguistic component and a factual component. Given this supposition, it next seems reasonable that in some statements the factual component should be null; and these are the analytic statements. But, for all its a priori reasonableness, a boundary between analytic and synthetic statements simply has not been drawn. That there is such a distinction to be drawn at all is an unempirical dogma of empiricists, a metaphysical article of faith.

5. The Verification Theory and Reductionism

In the course of these somber reflections we have taken a dim view first of the notion of meaning, then of the notion of cognitive synonymy, and finally of the notion of analyticity. But what, it may be asked, of the verification theory of meaning? This phrase has established itself so firmly as a catchword of empiricism that we should be very unscientific indeed not to look beneath it for a possible key to the problem of meaning and the associated problems.

The verification theory of meaning, which has been conspicuous in literature from Peirce onward, is that the meaning of a statement is the method of empirically confirming or infirming it. An analytic statement is that limiting case which is confirmed no matter what.

As urged in section 1, we can as well pass over the question of meanings as entities and move straight to sameness of meaning, or synonymy. Then what the verification theory says is that statements are synonymous if and only if they are alike in point of method of empirical confirmation or infirmation.

This is an account of cognitive synonymy not of linguistic forms generally, but of statements.[15] However, from the concept of synonymy of statements we could derive the concept of synonymy for other linguistic forms, by considerations somewhat similar to those at the end of section 3. Assuming the notion of

"word," indeed, we could explain any two forms as synonymous when the putting of the one form for an occurrence of the other in any statement (apart from occurrences within "words") yields a synonymous statement. Finally, given the concept of synonymy thus for linguistic forms generally, we could define analyticity in terms of synonymy and logical truth as in section 1. For that matter, we could define analyticity more simply in terms of just synonymy of statements together with logical truth; it is not necessary to appeal to synonymy of linguistic forms other than statements. For a statement may be described as analytic simply when it is synonymous with a logically true statement.

So, if the verification theory can be accepted as an adequate account of statement synonymy, the notion of analyticity is saved after all. However, let us reflect. Statement synonymy is said to be likeness of method of empirical confirmation or infirmation. Just what are these methods which are to be compared for likeness? What, in other words, is the nature of the relation between a statement and the experiences which contribute to or detract from its confirmation?

The most naïve view of the relation is that it is one of direct report. This is *radical reductionism*. Every meaningful statement is held to be translatable into a statement (true or false) about immediate experience. Radical reductionism, in one form or another, well antedates the verification theory of meaning explicitly so called. Thus Locke and Hume held that every idea must either originate directly in sense experience or else be compounded of ideas thus originating; and taking a hint from Tooke we might rephrase this doctrine in semantical jargon by saying that a term, to be significant at all, must be either a name of a sense datum or a compound of such names or an abbreviation of such a compound. So stated, the doctrine remains ambiguous as between sense data as sensory events and sense data as sensory qualities; and it remains vague as to the admissible ways of compounding. Moreover, the doctrine is unnecessarily and intolerably restrictive in the term-by-term critique which it imposes. More reasonably, and without yet exceeding the limits of what I have called radical reductionism, we may take full statements as our significant units—thus demanding that our statements as wholes be translatable into sense-datum language, but not that they be translatable term by term.

This emendation would unquestionably have been welcome to Locke and Hume and Tooke, but historically it had to await an important reorientation in semantics—the reorientation whereby the primary vehicle of meaning came to be seen no longer in the term but in the statement. This reorientation, seen in Bentham and Frege, underlies Russell's concept of incomplete symbols defined in use;[16] also it is implicit in the verification theory of meaning, since the objects of verification are statements.

Radical reductionism, conceived now with statements as units, set itself the task of specifying a sense-datum language and showing how to translate the rest of significant discourse, statement by statement, into it. Carnap embarked on this project in the *Aufbau*.

The language which Carnap adopted as his starting point was not a sense-datum language in the narrowest conceivable sense, for it included also the notations of logic, up through higher set theory. In effect it included the whole language of pure mathematics. The ontology implicit in it (that is, the range of values of its variables) embraced not only sensory events but classes, classes of classes, and so on. Empiricists there are who would boggle at such prodigality. Carnap's starting point is very parsimonious, however, in its extralogical or sensory part. In a series of constructions in which he exploits the resources of modern logic with much ingenuity, Carnap succeeds in defining a wide array of important additional sensory concepts which, but for his constructions, one would not have dreamed were definable on so slender a basis. He was the first empiricist who, not content with asserting the reducibility of science to terms of immediate experience, took serious steps toward carrying out the reduction.

If Carnap's starting point is satisfactory, still his constructions were, as he himself stressed, only a fragment of the full program. The construction of even the simplest statements about the physical world was left in a sketchy state. Carnap's suggestions on this subject were, de-

spite their sketchiness, very suggestive. He explained spatio-temporal point-instants as quadruples of real numbers and envisaged assignment of sense qualities to point-instants according to certain canons. Roughly summarized, the plan was that qualities should be assigned to point-instants in such a way as to achieve the laziest world compatible with our experience. The principle of least action was to be our guide in constructing a world from experience.

Carnap did not seem to recognize, however, that his treatment of physical objects fell short of reduction not merely through sketchiness, but in principle. Statements of the form "Quality q is at point-instant $x;y;z;t$" were, according to his canons, to be apportioned truth values in such a way as to maximize and minimize certain overall features, and with growth of experience the truth values were to be progressively revised in the same spirit. I think this is a good schematization (deliberately oversimplified, to be sure) of what science really does; but it provides no indication, not even the sketchiest, of how a statement of the form "Quality q is at $x;y;z;t$" could ever be translated into Carnap's initial language of sense data and logic. The connective "is at" remains an added undefined connective; the canons counsel us in its use but not in its elimination.

Carnap seems to have appreciated this point afterward; for in his later writings he abandoned all notion of the translatability of statements about the physical world into statements about immediate experience. Reductionism in its radical form has long since ceased to figure in Carnap's philosophy.

But the dogma of reductionism has, in a subtler and more tenuous form, continued to influence the thought of empiricists. The notion lingers that to each statement, or each synthetic statement, there is associated a unique range of possible sensory events such that the occurrence of any of them would add to the likelihood of truth of the statement, and that there is associated also another unique range of possible sensory events whose occurrence would detract from that likelihood. This notion is of course implicit in the verification theory of meaning.

The dogma of reductionism survives in the

supposition that each statement, taken in isolation from its fellows, can admit of confirmation or infirmation at all. My countersuggestion, issuing essentially from Carnap's doctrine of the physical world in the *Aufbau*, is that our statements about the external world face the tribunal of sense experience not individually but only as a corporate body.[17]

The dogma of reductionism, even in its attenuated form, is intimately connected with the other dogma—that there is a cleavage between the analytic and the synthetic. We have found ourselves led, indeed, from the latter problem to the former through the verification theory of meaning. More directly, the one dogma clearly supports the other in this way: as long as it is taken to be significant in general to speak of the confirmation and infirmation of a statement, it seems significant to speak also of a limiting kind of statement which is vacuously confirmed, *ipso facto*, come what may; and such a statement is analytic.

The two dogmas are, indeed, at root identical. We lately reflected that in general the truth of statements does obviously depend both upon language and upon extralinguistic fact; and we noted that this obvious circumstance carries in its train, not logically but all too naturally, a feeling that the truth of a statement is somehow analyzable into a linguistic component and a factual component. The factual component must, if we are empiricists, boil down to a range of confirmatory experiences. In the extreme case where the linguistic component is all that matters, a true statement is analytic. But I hope we are now impressed with how stubbornly the distinction between analytic and synthetic has resisted any straightforward drawing. I am impressed also, apart from prefabricated examples of black and white balls in an urn, with how baffling the problem has always been of arriving at any explicit theory of the empirical confirmation of a synthetic statement. My present suggestion is that it is nonsense, and the root of much nonsense, to speak of a linguistic component and a factual component in the truth of any individual statement. Taken collectively, science has its double dependence upon language and experience; but this duality is not significantly traceable into the statements of science taken one by one.

The idea of defining a symbol in use was, as remarked, an advance over the impossible term-by-term empiricism of Locke and Hume. The statement, rather than the term, came with Bentham to be recognized as the unit accountable to an empiricist critique. But what I am now urging is that even in taking the statement as unit we have drawn our grid too finely. The unit of empirical significance is the whole of science.

6. Empiricism without the Dogmas

The totality of our so-called knowledge or beliefs, from the most casual matters of geography and history to the profoundest laws of atomic physics or even of pure mathematics and logic, is a man-made fabric which impinges on experience only along the edges. Or, to change the figure, total science is like a field of force whose boundary conditions are experience. A conflict with experience at the periphery occasions readjustments in the interior of the field. Truth values have to be redistributed over some of our statements. Reëvaluation of some statements entails reëvaluation of others, because of their logical interconnections—the logical laws being in turn simply certain further statements of the system, certain further elements of the field. Having reëvaluated one statement we must reëvaluate some others, which may be statements logically connected with the first or may be the statements of logical connections themselves. But the total field is so underdetermined by its boundary conditions, experience, that there is much latitude of choice as to what statements to reëvaluate in the light of any single contrary experience. No particular experiences are linked with any particular statements in the interior of the field, except indirectly through considerations of equilibrium affecting the field as a whole.

If this view is right, it is misleading to speak of the empirical content of an individual statement—especially if it is a statement at all remote from the experiential periphery of the field. Furthermore it becomes folly to seek a boundary between synthetic statements, which hold contingently on experience, and analytic statements, which hold come what may. Any statement can be held true come what may, if we make drastic enough adjustments elsewhere in the system. Even a statement very close to the periphery can be held true in the face of recalcitrant experience by pleading hallucination or by amending certain statements of the kind called logical laws. Conversely, by the same token, no statement is immune to revision. Revision even of the logical law of the excluded middle has been proposed as a means of simplifying quantum mechanics; and what difference is there in principle between such a shift and the shift whereby Kepler superseded Ptolemy, or Einstein Newton, or Darwin Aristotle?

For vividness I have been speaking in terms of varying distances from a sensory periphery. Let me try now to clarify this notion without metaphor. Certain statements, though *about* physical objects and not sense experience, seem peculiarly germane to sense experience— and in a selective way: some statements to some experiences, others to others. Such statements, especially germane to particular experiences, I picture as near the periphery. But in this relation of "germaneness" I envisage nothing more than a loose association reflecting the relative likelihood, in practice, of our choosing one statement rather than another for revision in the event of recalcitrant experience. For example, we can imagine recalcitrant experiences to which we would surely be inclined to accommodate our system by reëvaluating just the statement that there are brick houses on Elm Street, together with related statements on the same topic. We can imagine other recalcitrant experiences to which we would be inclined to accommodate our system by reëvaluating just the statement that there are not centaurs, along with kindred statements. A recalcitrant experience can, I have urged, be accommodated by any of various alternative reëvaluations in various alternative quarters of the total system; but, in the cases which we are now imagining, our natural tendency to disturb the total system as little as possible would lead us to focus our revisions upon these specific statements concerning brick houses or centaurs. These state-

ments are felt, therefore, to have a sharper empirical reference than highly theoretical statements of physics or logic or ontology. The latter statements may be thought of as relatively centrally located within the total network, meaning merely that little preferential connection with any particular sense data obtrudes itself.

As an empiricist I continue to think of the conceptual scheme of science as a tool, ultimately, for predicting future experience in the light of past experience. Physical objects are conceptually imported into the situation as convenient intermediaries—not by definition in terms of experience, but simply as irreducible posits[18] comparable, epistemologically, to the gods of Homer. For my part I do, qua lay physicist, believe in physical objects and not in Homer's gods; and I consider it a scientific error to believe otherwise. But in point of epistemological footing the physical objects and the gods differ only in degree and not in kind. Both sorts of entities enter our conception only as cultural posits. The myth of physical objects is epistemologically superior to most in that it has proved more efficacious than other myths as a device for working a manageable structure into the flux of experience.

Positing does not stop with macroscopic physical objects. Objects at the atomic level are posited to make the laws of macroscopic objects, and ultimately the laws of experience, simpler and more manageable; and we need not expect or demand full definition of atomic and subatomic entities in terms of macroscopic ones, any more than definition of macroscopic things in terms of sense data. Science is a continuation of common sense, and it continues the common-sense expedient of swelling ontology to simplify theory.

Physical objects, small and large, are not the only posits. Forces are another example; and indeed we are told nowadays that the boundary between energy and matter is obsolete. Moreover, the abstract entities which are the substance of mathematics—ultimately classes and classes of classes and so on up—are another posit in the same spirit. Epistemologically these are myths on the same footing with physical objects and gods, neither better nor worse except for differences in the degree to which they expedite our dealings with sense experiences.

The over-all algebra of rational and irrational numbers is underdetermined by the algebra of rational numbers, but is smoother and more convenient; and it includes the algebra of rational numbers as a jagged or gerrymandered part.[19] Total science, mathematical and natural and human, is similarly but more extremely underdetermined by experience. The edge of the system must be kept squared with experience; the rest, with all its elaborate myths or fictions, has as its objective the simplicity of laws.

Ontological questions, under this view, are on a par with questions of natural science.[20] Consider the question whether to countenance classes as entities. This, as I have argued elsewhere,[21] is the question whether to quantify with respect to variables which take classes as values. Now Carnap[22] has maintained that this is a question not of matters of fact but of choosing a convenient language form, a convenient conceptual scheme or framework for science. With this I agree, but only on the proviso that the same be conceded regarding scientific hypotheses generally. Carnap[23] has recognized that he is able to preserve a double standard for ontological questions and scientific hypotheses only by assuming an absolute distinction between the analytic and the synthetic; and I need not say again that this is a distinction which I reject.[24]

The issue over there being classes seems more a question of convenient conceptual scheme; the issue over there being centaurs, or brick houses on Elm Street, seems more a question of fact. But I have been urging that this difference is only one of degree, and that it turns upon our vaguely pragmatic inclination to adjust one strand of the fabric of science rather than another in accommodating some particular recalcitrant experience. Conservatism figures in such choices, and so does the quest for simplicity.

Carnap, Lewis, and others take a pragmatic stand on the question of choosing between language forms, scientific frameworks; but their pragmatism leaves off at the imagined boundary between the analytic and the synthetic. In repudiating such a boundary I espouse a more thorough pragmatism. Each man is given a scientific heritage plus a continuing barrage of sensory stimulation; and the considerations which guide him in warping his scientific heritage to fit his continuing sensory promptings are, where rational, pragmatic.

NOTES

1. See Quine, *From a Logical Point of View*, 9.
2. See ibid., pp. 10, 107–115.
3. See ibid., pp. 11f, 48f.
4. Rudolf Carnap, *Meaning and Necessity*, 9ff: "Empiricism, Semantics, and Ontology," 70ff.
5. According to an important variant sense of "definition" the relation preserved may be the weaker relation of mere agreement in reference; see Quine, *From a Logical Point of View*, 132. But definition in this sense is better ignored in the present connection, being irrelevant to the question of synonymy.
6. Cf. Lewis, *Survey of Symbolic Logic*, 373.
7. This is cognitive synonymy in a primary, broad sense. Carnap (*Meaning and Necessity*, 56ff) and Lewis (*Survey of Symbolic Logic*, 83ff) have suggested how, once this notion is at hand, a narrower sense of cognitive synonymy which is preferable for some purposes can in turn be derived. But this special ramification of concept-building lies aside from the present purposes and must not be confused with the broad sort of cognitive synonymy here concerned.
8. Pp. 81ff of Quine, *From a Logical Point of View*, contain a description of just such a language, except that there happens to be just one predicate, the two-place predicate "e."
9. See ibid., pp. 5–8; also pp. 85f, 16ff.
10. See ibid., p. 87.
11. On such devices see also ibid., Essay VIII.
12. This is the substance of Quine, *Mathematical Logic*, *121.
13. The "if and only if" itself is intended in the truth functional sense. See Carnap, *Meaning and Necessity*, 14.
14. The foregoing paragraph was not part of the present essay as originally published. It was prompted by Martin (see Bibliography).
15. The doctrine can indeed be formulated with terms rather than statements as the units. Thus Lewis describes the meaning of a term as "*a criterion in mind*, by reference to which one is able to apply or refuse to apply the expression in question in the case of presented, or imagined, things or situations" (*Survey of Symbolic Logic*, 133).—For an instructive account of the vicissitudes of the verification theory of mean-

ing, centered however on the question of mean-ing*fulness* rather than synonymy and analyticity, see Hempel, "Problems and Changes in the Empiricist Criterion of Meaning" (reprinted above).

16. See *From a Logical Point of View*, 6.
17. This doctrine was well argued by Duhem, 303–328. Or see Lowinger, 132–140.
18. Cf. Quine, *From a Logical Point of View*, 17f.
19. Cf. ibid., p. 18.
20. "L' ontologie fait corps avec la science elle-me'me et ne peut en e'tre seperée." Meyerson, 439.
21. Quine, *From a Logical Point of View*, 12f., 102ff.
22. Carnap, "Empiricism, Semantics, and Ontology."
23. Ibid, p. 32n.
24. For an effective expression of further misgivings over this distinction, see White, "The Analytic and the synthetic."

REFERENCES

Carnap, Rudolf, *Meaning and Necessity* (Chicago: University of Chicago Press, 1947).

——— "Empiricism, Semantics, and Ontology," *Revue internationale de philosophie* 4 (1950): 20–40.

Duhem, Pierre, *La théorie physique: son objet et so structure* (Paris, 1906).

Lewis, C. I., *A Survey of Symbolic Logic* (Berkeley, 1918).

——— *An Analysis of Knowledge and Valuation* (LaSalle, Ill.: Open Court, 1946).

Lowinger, Armand, *The Methodology of Pierre Duhem* (New York, 1941).

Martin, R. M., "On 'analytic'," *Philosophical Studies* 3 (1952). 42–47.

Meyerson, Émile, *Identité et réalité* (Paris, 1908; 4th ed., 1932).

Quine, W. V., *From a Logical Point of View*, rev. ed. (Cambridge, Mass.: Harvard University Press, 1961).

——— *Mathematical Logic* (New York: Norton, 1940; Cambridge: Harvard University Press, 1947; rev. ed., Cambridge: Harvard University press, 1951).

White, Morton, "The Analtyic and the Synthetic: an Untenable Dualism," in Sidney Hook (ed.), *John Dewey: Philosopher of Science and Freedom* (New York: Dial Press, 1950), 316–330.

19 / Richard Rorty
PRAGMATISM, RELATIVISM, AND IRRATIONALISM

PART I: PRAGMATISM

"Pragmatism" is a vague, ambiguous, and over-worked word. Nevertheless, it names the chief glory of our country's intellectual tradition. No other American writers have offered so radical a suggestion for making our future different from our past, as have James and Dewey. At present, however, these two writers are neglected. Many philosophers think that everything important in pragmatism has been preserved and adapted to the needs of analytic philosophy. More specifically, they view pragmatism as having suggested various holistic corrections of the atomistic doctrines of the early logical empiricists. This way of looking at pragmatism is not wrong, as far as it goes. But it ignores what is most important in James and Dewey. Logical empiricism was one variety of standard, academic, neo-Kantian, epistemologically-centered philosophy. The great pragmatists should not be taken as suggesting an holistic variation of this variant, but rather as breaking with the Kantian epistemological tradition altogether. As long as we see James or Dewey as having "theories of truth" or "theories of knowledge" or "theories of morality" we shall get them wrong. We shall ignore their criticisms of the assumption that there ought to *be* theories about such matters. We shall not see how radical their thought was—how deep was their criticism of the attempt, common to Kant, Husserl, Russell, and C. I. Lewis, to make philosophy into a foundational discipline.

One symptom of this incorrect focus is a tendency to overpraise Peirce. Peirce is praised partly because he developed various logical notions and various technical problems (such as the counterfactual conditional) which were taken up by the logical empiricists. But the main reason for Peirce's undeserved apotheosis is that his talk about a general theory of signs looks like an early discovery of the importance of language. For all his genius, however, Peirce never made up his mind what he wanted a general theory of signs *for*, nor what it might look like, nor what its relation to either logic or epistemology was supposed to be. His contribution to pragmatism was merely to have given it a name, and to have stimulated James. Peirce himself remained the most Kantian of thinkers—the most convinced that philosophy gave us an all-embracing ahistorical context in which every other species of discourse could be assigned its proper place and rank. It was just this Kantian assumption that there was such a context, and that epistemology or semantics could discover it, against which James and Dewey reacted. We need to focus on this reaction if we are to recapture a proper sense of their importance.

This reaction is found in other philosophers who are currently more fashionable than James or Dewey—for example, Nietzsche and Heidegger. Unlike Nietzsche and Heidegger, however, the pragmatists did not make the mistake of turning against the community which takes the natural scientist as its moral hero—the

Reprinted by permission of the copyright holder from *Proceedings and Addresses of the American Philosophical Association* 53 (1980), 719–38.

community of secular intellectuals which came to self-consciousness in the Enlightenment. James and Dewey rejected neither the Enlightenment's choice of the scientist as moral example, nor the technological civilization which science had created. They wrote, as Nietzsche and Heidegger did not, in a spirit of social hope. They asked us to liberate our new civilization by giving up the notion of "grounding" our culture, our moral lives, our politics, our religious beliefs, upon "philosophical bases." They asked us to give up the neurotic Cartesian quest for certainty which had been one result of Galileo's frightening new cosmology, the quest for "enduring spiritual values" which had been one reaction to Darwin, and the aspiration of academic philosophy to form a tribunal of pure reason which had been the neo-Kantian response to Hegelian historicism. They asked us to think of the Kantian project of grounding thought or culture in a permanent ahistorical matrix as *reactionary*. They viewed Kant's idealization of Newton, and Spencer's of Darwin, as just as silly as Plato's idealization of Pythagoras, and Aquinas' of Aristotle.

Emphasizing this message of social hope and liberation, however, makes James and Dewey sound like prophets rather than thinkers. This would be misleading. They had things to say about truth, knowledge, and morality, even though they did not have *theories* of them, in the sense of sets of answers to the textbook problems. In what follows, I shall offer three brief sloganistic characterizations of what I take to be their central doctrine.

My first characterization of pragmatism is that it is simply anti-essentialism applied to notions like "truth," "knowledge," "language," "morality," and similar objects of philosophical theorizing. Let me illustrate this by James's definition of "the true" as "what is good in the way of belief." This has struck his critics as not to the point, as unphilosophical, as like the suggestion that the essence of aspirin is that it is good for headaches. James's point, however, was that there *is* nothing deeper to be said: truth is not the sort of thing which *has* an essence. More specifically, his point was that it is no use being told that truth is "correspondence to reality." Given a language and a view of what the world is like, one can, to be sure,

pair off bits of the language with bits of what one takes the world to be in such a way that the sentences one believes true have internal structures isomorphic to relations between things in the world. When we rap out routine undeliberated reports like "This is water," "That's red," "That's ugly," "That's immoral," our short categorical sentences can easily be thought of as pictures, or as symbols which fit together to make a map. Such reports do indeed pair little bits of language with little bits of the world. Once one gets to negative universal hypotheticals, and the like, such pairing will become messy and *ad hoc*, but perhaps it can be done. James's point was that carrying out this exercise will not enlighten us about why truths are good to believe, or offer any clues as to why or whether our present view of the world is, roughly, the one we should hold. Yet nobody would have asked for a "theory" of truth if they had not wanted answers to these latter questions. Those who want truth to have an essence want knowledge, or rationality, or inquiry, or the relation between thought and its object, to have an essence. Further, they want to be able to use their knowledge of such essences to criticize views they take to be false, and to point the direction of progress toward the discovery of more truths. James thinks these hopes are vain. There are no essences anywhere in the area. There is no wholesale, epistemological way to direct, or criticize, or underwrite, the course of inquiry.

Rather, the pragmatists tell us, it is the vocabulary of practise rather than of theory, of action rather than contemplation, in which one can say something useful about truth. Nobody engages in epistemology or semantics because he wants to know how "This is red" pictures the world. Rather, we want to know in what sense Pasteur's views of disease picture the world accurately and Paracelsus' inaccurately, or what exactly it is that Marx pictured more accurately than Machiavelli. But just here the vocabulary of "picturing" fails us. When we turn from individual sentences to vocabularies and theories, critical terminology naturally shifts from metaphors of isomorphism, symbolism, and mapping to talk of utility, convenience, and likelihood of getting what we want. To say that the parts of properly analyzed true sentences are arranged in a way isomorphic to the parts of the world paired with them sounds plausible if one thinks of a sentence like "Jupiter has moons." It sounds slightly less plausible for "The earth goes round the sun," less still for "There is no such thing as natural motion," and not plausible at all for "The universe is infinite." When we want to praise or blame assertions of the latter sort of sentence, we show how the decision to assert them fits into a whole complex of decisions about what terminology to use, what books to read, what projects to engage in, what life to live. In this respect they resemble such sentences as "Love is the only law" and "History is the story of class struggle." The whole vocabulary of isomorphism, picturing, and mapping is out of place here, as indeed is the notion of being true *of objects*. If we ask what objects these sentences claim to be true of, we get only unhelpful repetitions of the subject terms—"the universe," "the law," "history." Or, even less helpfully, we get talk about "the facts," or "the way the world is." The natural approach to such sentences, Dewey tells us, is not "Do they get it right?", but more like "What would it be like to believe that? What would happen if I did? What would I be committing myself to?" The vocabulary of contemplation, looking, *theoria*, deserts us just when we deal with theory rather than observation, with programming rather than input. When the contemplative mind, isolated from the stimuli of the moment, takes large views, its activity is more like deciding what to *do* than deciding that a representation is accurate. James's dictum about truth says that the vocabulary of practice is uneliminable, that no distinction of kind separates the sciences from the crafts, from moral reflection, or from art.

So a second characterization of pragmatism might go like this: there is no epistemological difference between truth about what ought to be and truth about what is, nor any metaphysical difference between facts and values, nor any methodological difference between morality and science. Even nonpragmatists think Plato was wrong to think of moral philosophy as discovering the essence of goodness, and Mill and Kant wrong in trying to reduce moral choice to rule. But every reason

for saying that they were wrong is a reason for thinking the epistemological tradition wrong in looking for the essence of science, and in trying to reduce rationality to rule. For the pragmatists, the pattern of all inquiry—scientific as well as moral—is deliberation concerning the relative attractions of various concrete alternatives. The idea that in science or philosophy we can substitute "method" for deliberation between alternative results of speculation is just wishful thinking. It is like the idea that the morally wise man resolves his dilemmas by consulting his memory of the Idea of the Good, or by looking up the relevant article of the moral law. It is the myth that rationality consists in being constrained by rule. According to this Platonic myth, the life of reason is not the life of Socratic conversation but an illuminated state of consciousness in which one never needs to ask if one has exhausted the possible descriptions of, or explanations for, the situation. One simply arrives at true beliefs by obeying mechanical procedures.

Traditional, Platonic, epistemologically-centered philosophy is the search for such procedures. It is the search for a way in which one can avoid the need for conversation and deliberation and simply tick off the way things are. The idea is to acquire beliefs about interesting and important matters in a way as much like visual perception as possible—by confronting an object and responding to it as programmed. This urge to substitute *theoria* for *phronesis* is what lies behind the attempt to say that "There is no such thing as natural motion" pictures objects in the same way as does "The cat is on the mat." It also lies behind the hope that some arrangement of objects may be found which is pictured by the sentence "Love is better than hate," and the frustration which ensues when it is realized that there may be no such objects. The great fallacy of the tradition, the pragmatists tell us, is to think that the metaphors of vision, correspondence, mapping, picturing, and representation which apply to small, routine assertions will apply to large and debatable ones. This basic error begets the notion that where there are no objects to correspond to we have no hope of rationality, but only taste, passion, and will. When the pragmatist attacks the notion of truth as accuracy of representation he is thus attacking the traditional distinctions between reason and desire, reason and appetite, reason and will. For none of these distinctions make sense unless reason is thought of on the model of vision, unless we persist in what Dewey called "the spectator theory of knowledge."

The pragmatist tells us that once we get rid of this model we see that the Platonic idea of the life of reason is impossible. A life spent representing objects accurately would be spent recording the results of calculations, reasoning through sorites, calling off the observable properties of things, construing cases according to unambiguous criteria, getting things right. Within what Kuhn calls "normal science," or any similar social context, one can, indeed, live such a life. But conformity to *social* norms is not good enough for the Platonist. He wants to be constrained not merely by the disciplines of the day, but by the ahistorical and nonhuman nature of reality itself. This impulse takes two forms—the original Platonic strategy of postulating novel *objects* for treasured propositions to correspond to, and the Kantian strategy of finding *principles* which are definatory of the essence of knowledge, or representation, or morality, or rationality. But this difference is unimportant compared to the common urge to escape the vocabulary and practices of one's own time and find something ahistorical and necessary to cling to. It is the urge to answer questions like "Why believe what I take to be true?" "Why do what I take to be right?" by appealing to something *more* than the ordinary, retail, detailed, concrete reasons which have brought one to one's present view. This urge is common to nineteenth-century idealists and contemporary scientific realists, to Russell and to Husserl; it is definatory of the Western philosophical tradition, and of the culture for which that tradition speaks. James and Dewey stand with Nietzsche and Heidegger in asking us to abandon that tradition, and that culture.

Let me sum up by offering a third and final characterization of pragmatism: it is the doctrine that there are no constraints on inquiry save conversational ones—no wholesale constraints derived from the nature of the objects, or of the mind, or of language, but only those retail constraints provided by the remarks of our fellow-inquirers. The way in which the properly-programmed speaker cannot help believing that the patch before him is red has *no* analogy for the more interesting and controversial beliefs which provoke epistemological reflection. The pragmatist tells us that it is useless to hope that objects will constrain us to believe the truth about them, if only they are approached with an unclouded mental eye, or a rigorous method, or a perspicuous language. He wants us to give up the notion that God, or evolution, or some other underwriter of our present world-picture, has programmed us as machines for accurate verbal picturing, and that philosophy brings self-knowledge by letting us read our own program. The only sense in which we are constrained to truth is that, as Peirce suggested, we can make no sense of the notion that the view which can survive all objections might be false. But objections—conversational constraints—cannot be anticipated. There is no method for knowing *when* one has reached the truth, or when one is closer to it than before.

I prefer this third way of characterizing pragmatism because it seems to me to focus on a fundamental choice which confronts the reflective mind: that between accepting the contingent character of starting-points, and attempting to evade this contingency. To accept the contingency of starting-points is to accept our inheritance from, and our conversation with, our fellow-humans as our only source of guidance. To attempt to evade this contingency is to hope to become a properly-programmed machine. This was the hope which Plato thought might be fulfilled at the top of the divided line, when we passed beyond hypotheses. Christians have hoped it might be attained by becoming attuned to the voice of God in the heart, and Cartesians that it might be fulfilled by emptying the mind and seeking the indubitable. Since Kant, philosophers have hoped that it might be fulfilled by finding the a priori structure of any possible inquiry, or language, or form of social life. If we give up this hope, we shall lose what Nietzsche called "metaphysical comfort," but we may gain a renewed sense of community. Our identification with our community—our society, our political tradition, our intellectual heritage—is heightened when we see this community as *ours* rather than *nature's shaped* rather than *found*, one among many which men have made. In the end, the pragmatists tell us, what matters is our loyalty to other human beings clinging together against the dark, not our hope of getting things right. James, in arguing against realists and idealists that "the trail of the human serpent is over all," was reminding us that our glory is in our participation in fallible and transitory human projects, not in our obedience to permanent nonhuman constraints.

PART II: RELATIVISM

"Relativism" is the view that every belief on a certain topic, or perhaps about *any* topic, is as good as every other. No one holds this view. Except for the occasional cooperative freshman, one cannot find anybody who says that two incompatible opinions on an important topic are equally good. The philosophers who get *called* "relativists" are those who say that the grounds for choosing between such opinions are less algorithmic than had been thought. Thus one may be attacked as a relativist for holding that familiarity of terminology is a criterion of theory-choice in physical science, or that coherence with the institutions of the surviving parliamentary democracies is a criterion in social philosophy. When such criteria are invoked, critics say that the resulting philosophical position assumes an unjustified primacy for "our conceptual framework," or our purposes, or our institutions. The position in question is criticized for not having done what philosophers are employed to do: explain why our framework, or culture, or interests, or language, or whatever, is at last on the right track—in touch with physical reality, or the moral law, or the real numbers, or some other sort of object patiently waiting about to be copied. So the real issue is not between people who think one view as good as another and people who do not. It is between those who think our culture, or purpose, or intuitions cannot be supported except conversationally, and people who still hope for other sorts of support.

If there *were* any relativists, they would, of course, be easy to refute. One would merely use some variant of the self-referential arguments Socrates used against Protagoras. But such neat little dialectical strategies only work against lightly-sketched fictional characters. The relativist who says that we can break ties among serious and incompatible candidates for belief only by "nonrational" or "noncognitive" considerations is just one of the Platonist or Kantian philosopher's imaginary playmates, inhabiting the same realm of fantasy as the solipsist, the skeptic, and the moral nihilist. Disillusioned, or whimsical, Platonists and Kantians occasionally play at being one or another of these characters. But when they do they are never offering relativism or skepticism or nihilism as a serious suggestion about how we might do things differently. These positions are adopted to make *philosophical* points—that is, moves in a game played with fictitious opponents, rather than fellow-participants in a common project.

The association of pragmatism with relativism is a result of a confusion between the pragmatist's attitude toward *philosophical* theories with his attitude towards *real* theories. James and Dewey are, to be sure, metaphilosophical relativists, in a certain limited sense. Namely: they think there is no way to choose, and no point in choosing, between incompatible philosophical theories of the typical Platonic or Kantian type. Such theories are attempts to ground some element of our practices on something external to these practices. Pragmatists think that any such philosophical grounding is, apart from elegance of execution, pretty much as good or as bad as the practice it purports to ground. They regard the project of grounding as a wheel that plays no part in the mechanism. In this, I think, they are quite right. No sooner does one discover the categories of the pure understanding for a Newtonian age than somebody draws up another list that would do nicely for an Aristotelian or an Einsteinian one. No sooner does one draw up a categorical imperative for Christians than somebody draws up one which works for cannibals. No sooner does one develop an evolutionary epistemology which explains why our science is so good than somebody writes a science-fiction story about

bug-eyed and monstrous evolutionary epistemologists praising bug-eyed and monstrous
scientists for the survival value of their monstrous theories. The reason this game is so easy
to play is that none of these philosophical theories have to do much hard work. The real
work has been done by the scientists who developed the explanatory theories by patience
and genius, or the societies which developed
the moralities and institutions in struggle and
pain. All the Platonic or Kantian philosopher
does is to take the finished first-level product,
jack it up a few levels of abstraction, invent a
metaphysical or epistemological or semantical
vocabulary into which to translate it, and an-
nounce that he has *grounded* it.

"Relativism" only seems to refer to a disturbing view, worthy of being refuted, if it concerns *real* theories, not just philosophical theories. Nobody really cares if there are
incompatible alternative formulations of a categorical imperative, or incompatible sets of
categories of the pure understanding. We *do*
care about alternative, concrete, detailed cos-
mologies, or alternative concrete, detailed proposals for political change. When such an alternative is proposed, we debate it, not in terms
of categories or principles but in terms of the
various concrete advantages and disadvantages
it has. The reason relativism is talked about so
much among Platonic and Kantian philosophers is that they think being relativistic about
philosophical theories—attempts to "ground"
first-level theories—leads to being relativistic
about the first-level theories themselves. If anyone really believed that the worth of a theory
depends upon the worth of its philosophical
grounding, then indeed they would be dubious
about physics, or democracy, until relativism in
respect to philosophical theories had been
overcome. Fortunately, almost nobody believes
anything of the sort.

What people do believe is that it would be
good to hook up our views about democracy,
mathematics, physics, God, and everything
else, into a coherent story about how everything hangs together. Getting such a synoptic
view often does require us to change radically
our views on particular subjects. But this holistic process of readjustment is just muddling
through on a large scale. It has nothing to do
with the Platonic-Kantian notion of grounding.
That notion involves finding constraints, demonstrating necessities, finding immutable principles to which to subordinate oneself. When
it turns out that suggested constraints, necessities, and principles are as plentiful as black-
berries, nothing changes except the attitude of
the rest of culture towards the philosophers.
Since the time of Kant, it has become more
and more apparent to nonphilosophers that a
really professional philosopher can supply a
philosophical foundation for just about anything. This is one reason why philosophers
have, in the course of our century, become increasingly isolated from the rest of culture. Our
proposals to guarantee this and clarify that
have come to strike our fellow-intellectuals as
merely comic.

PART III: IRRATIONALISM

My discussion of relativism may seem to have
ducked the real issues. Perhaps nobody is a
relativist. Perhaps "relativism" is *not* the right
name for what so many philosophers find so
offensive in pragmatism. But surely there *is* an
important issue around somewhere. There is
indeed an issue, but it is not easily stated, nor
easily made amenable to argument. I shall try
to bring it into focus by developing it in two
different contexts, one microcosmic and the
other macrocosmic. The microcosmic issue
concerns philosophy in one of its most parochial senses—namely, the activities of the
American Philosophical Association. Our Association has traditionally been agitated by the
question of whether we should be free-
wheeling and edifying, or argumentative and
professional. For my purposes, this boils down
to an issue about whether we can be pragmatists and still be professionals. The macrocosmic issue concerns philosophy in the widest
sense—the attempt to make everything hang
together. This is the issue between Socrates on
the one hand and the tyrants on the other—the
issue between lovers of conversation and lovers
of self-deceptive rhetoric. For my purposes, it
is the issue about whether we can be pragmatists without betraying Socrates, without falling
into irrationalism.

I discuss the unimportant microcosmic issue about professionalism first because it is sometimes confused with the important issue about irrationalism, and because it helps focus that latter issue. The question of whether philosophy professors should edify agitated our Association in its early decades. James thought they should, and was dubious about the growing professionalization of the discipline. Arthur Lovejoy, the great opponent of pragmatism, saw professionalization as an unmixed blessing. Echoing what was being said simultaneously by Russell in England and by Husserl in Germany, Lovejoy urged the sixteenth annual meeting of the APA to aim at making philosophy into a science. He wanted the APA to organize its program into well-structured controversies on sharply defined problems, so that at the end of each convention it would be agreed who had won.[1] Lovejoy insisted that philosophy could either be edifying and visionary *or* could produce "objective, verifiable, and clearly communicable truths," but not both. James would have agreed. He too thought that one could *not* be both a pragmatist and a professional. James, however, saw professionalization as a failure of nerve rather than as a triumph of rationality. He thought that the activity of making things hang together was *not* likely to produce "objective, verifiable, and clearly communicable truths," and that this did not greatly matter.

Lovejoy, of course, won this battle. If one shares his conviction that philosophers should be as much like scientists as possible, then one will be pleased at the outcome. If one does not, one will contemplate the APA in its seventy-sixth year mindful of Goethe's maxim that one should be careful what one wishes for when one is young, for one will get it when one is old. Which attitude one takes will depend upon whether one sees the problems we discuss today as permanent problems for human thought, continuous with those discussed by Plato, Kant, and Lovejoy—or as modern attempts to breathe life into dead issues. On the Lovejoyan account, the gap between philosophers and the rest of high culture is of the same sort as the gap between physicists and laymen. The gap is not created by the artificiality of the problems being discussed, but by the development of technical and precise ways of dealing with real problems. If one shares the pragmatists' anti-essentialism, however, one will tend to see the problems about which philosophers are now offering "objective, verifiable, and clearly communicable" solutions as historical relics, left over from the Enlightenment's misguided search for the hidden essences of knowledge and morality. This is the point of view adopted by many of our fellow-intellectuals, who see us philosophy professors as caught in a time-warp, trying to live the Enlightenment over again.

I have reminded you of the parochial issue about professionalization not in order to persuade you to one side or the other, but rather to exhibit the source of the anti-pragmatist's passion. This is his conviction that conversation necessarily aims at agreement and at rational consensus, that we converse in order to make further conversation unnecessary. The anti-pragmatist believes that conversation only makes sense if something like the Platonic theory of Recollection is right—if we all have natural starting-points of thought somewhere within us, and will recognize the vocabulary in which they are best formulated once we hear it. For only if something like that is true will conversation have a natural goal. The Enlightenment hoped to find such a vocabulary—nature's own vocabulary, so to speak. Lovejoy—who described himself as an "unredeemed *Aufklärer*"—wanted to continue the project. Only if we had agreement on such a vocabulary, indeed, could conversation be reduced to argumentation—to the search for "objective, verifiable, and clearly communicable" solutions to problems. So the anti-pragmatist sees the pragmatist's scorn for professionalism as scorn for consensus, for the Christian and democratic idea that every human has the seeds of truth within. The pragmatist's attitude seems to him elitist and dilettantish, reminiscent of Alcibiades rather than of Socrates.

Issues about relativism and about professionalization are awkward attempts to formulate this opposition. The real and passionate opposition is over the question of whether loyalty to our fellow-humans presupposes that there is something permanent and unhistorical which explains *why* we should continue to converse in the manner of Socrates, something which guarantees convergence to agreement. Because the anti-pragmatist believes that without such an essence and such a guarantee the Socratic life makes no sense, he sees the pragmatist as a cynic. Thus the microcosmic issue about how philosophy professors should converse leads us quickly to the macrocosmic issue: whether one can be a pragmatist without being an irrationalist, without abandoning one's loyalty to Socrates.

Questions about irrationalism have become acute in our century because the sullen resentment which sins against Socrates, which withdraws from conversation and community, has recently become articulate. Our European intellectual tradition is now abused as "merely conceptual" or "merely ontic" or as "committed to abstractions." Irrationalists propose such rubbishy pseudo-epistemological notions as "intuition" or "an inarticulate sense of tradition" or "thinking with the blood" or "expressing the will of the oppressed classes." Our tyrants and bandits are more hateful than those of earlier times because, invoking such self-deceptive rhetoric, they pose as intellectuals. Our tyrants write philosophy in the morning and torture in the afternoon; our bandits alternately read Hölderlin and bomb people into bloody scraps. So our culture clings, more than ever, to the hope of the Enlightenment, the hope that drove Kant to make philosophy formal and rigorous and professional. We hope that by formulating the *right* conceptions of reason, of science, of thought, of knowledge, of morality, the conceptions which express their *essence*, we shall have a shield against irrationalist resentment and hatred.

Pragmatists tell us that this hope is vain. On their view, the Socratic virtues—willingness to talk, to listen to other people, to weigh the consequences of our actions upon other people—are *simply* moral virtues. They cannot be inculcated nor fortified by theoretical research into essence. Irrationalists who tell us to think with our blood cannot be rebutted by better accounts of the nature of thought, or knowledge, or logic. The pragmatists tell us that the

conversation which it is our moral duty to continue is *merely* our project, the European intellectual's form of life. It has no metaphysical nor epistemological guarantee of sucess. Further (and this is the crucial point) *we do not know what "success" would mean except simply "continuance."* We are not conversing because we have a goal, but because Socratic conversation is an activity which is its *own* end. The anti-pragmatist who insists that agreement is its goal is like the basketball player who thinks that the reason for playing the game is to make baskets. He mistakes an essential moment in the course of an activity for the end of the activity. Worse yet, he is like a basketball fan who argues that all men by nature desire to play basketball, or that the nature of things is such that balls can go through hoops.

For the traditional, Platonic or Kantian philosopher, on the other hand, the possibility of *grounding* the European form of life—of showing it to be more than European, more than a contingent human project—seems the central task of philosophy. He wants to show that sinning against Socrates is sinning against our nature, not just against our community. So he sees the pragmatist as an irrationalist. The charge that pragmatism is "relativistic" is simply his first unthinking expression of disgust at a teaching which seems cynical about our deepest hopes. If the traditional philosopher gets beyond such epithets, however, he raises a question which the pragmatist must face up to: the *practical* question of whether the notion of "conversation" *can* substitute for that of "reason." "Reason," as the term is used in the Platonic and Kantian traditions, is interlocked with the notions of truth as correspondence, of knowledge as discovery of essence, of morality as obedience to principle, all the notions which the pragmatist tries to deconstruct. For better or worse, the Platonic and Kantian vocabularies are the ones in which Europe has described and praised the Socratic virtues. It is not clear that we know how to describe these virtues without those vocabularies. So the deep suspicion which the pragmatist inspires is that, like Alcibiades, he is essentially frivolous—that he is commending uncontroversial common goods while refusing to participate in the only activity which can preserve those goods. He seems to be sacrificing our common European project to the delights of purely negative criticism.

The issue about irrationalism can be sharpened by noting that when the pragmatist says "All that can be done to explicate 'truth', 'knowledge', 'morality', 'virtue' is to refer us back to the concrete details of the culture in which these terms grew up and developed," the defender of the Enlightenment takes him to be saying "Truth and virtue are simply what a community agrees that they are." When the pragmatist says "We have to take truth and virtue as whatever emerges from the conversation of Europe," the traditional philosopher wants to know what is so special about Europe. Isn't the pragmatist saying, like the irrationalist, that *we* are in a privileged situation simply by being *us*? Further, isn't there something terribly dangerous about the notion that truth can only be characterized as "the outcome of doing more of what we are doing now"? What if the "we" is the Orwellian state? When tyrants employ Lenin's blood-curdling sense of "objective" to describe their lies as "objectively true," what is to prevent them from citing Peirce in Lenin's defense?[2]

The pragmatist's first line of defense against this criticism has been created by Habermas, who says that such a definition of truth works only for the outcome of *undistorted* conversation, and that the Orwellian state is the paradigm of distortion. But this is *only* a first line, for we need to know more about what counts as "undistorted." Here Habermas goes transcendental and offers principles. The pragmatist, however, must remain ethnocentric and offer examples. He can only say: "undistorted" means employing *our* criteria of relevance, where *we* are the people who have read and pondered Plato, Newton, Kant, Marx, Darwin, Freud, Dewey, etc. Milton's "free and open encounter," in which truth is bound to prevail, must itself be described in terms of examples rather than principles—it is to be more like the Athenian market-place than the council-chamber of the Great King, more like the twentieth century than the twelfth, more like the

Prussian Academy in 1925 than in 1935. The pragmatist must avoid saying, with Peirce, that truth is *fated* to win. He must even avoid saying that the truth *will* win. He can only say, with Hegel, that truth and justice lie in the direction marked by the successive stages of European thought. This is not because he knows some "necessary truths" and cites these examples as a result of this knowledge. It is simply that the pragmatist knows no better way to explain his convictions than to remind his interlocutor of the position they both are in, the contingent starting points they both share, the floating, ungrounded conversations of which they are both members. This means that the pragmatist cannot answer the question "What is so special about Europe?" save by saying "Do you have anything non-European to suggest which meets *our* European purposes better?" He cannot answer the question "What is so good about the Socratic virtues, about Miltonic free encounters, about undistorted communication?" save by saying "What else would better fulfill the purposes *we* share with Socrates, Milton, and Habermas?"

To decide whether this obviously circular response is enough is to decide whether Hegel or Plato had the proper picture of the progress of thought. Pragmatists follow Hegel in saying that "philosophy is its time grasped in thought." Anti-pragmatists follow Plato in striving for an escape from conversation to something atemporal which lies in the background of all possible conversations. I do not think one can decide between Hegel and Plato save by meditating on the past efforts of the philosophical tradition to escape from time and history. One can see these efforts as worthwhile, getting better, worth continuing. Or one can see them as doomed and perverse. I do not know what would count as a noncircular metaphysical or epistemological or semantical argument for seeing them in either way. So I think that the decision has to be made simply by reading the history of philosophy and drawing a moral.

Nothing that I have said, therefore, is an argument in favor of pragmatism. At best, I have merely answered various superficial criticisms which have been made of it. Nor have I dealt with the central issue about irrationalism. I have not answered the deep criticism of pragmatism which I mentioned a few minutes ago: the criticism that the Socratic virtues cannot, as a practical matter, be defended save by Platonic means, that without some sort of metaphysical comfort nobody will be able *not* to sin against Socrates. William James himself was not sure whether this criticism could be answered. Exercising his own right to believe, James wrote: "If this life be not a real fight in which something is eternally gained for the universe by success, it is no better than a game of private theatricals from which we may withdraw at will." "It *feels*," he said, "like a fight."

For us, footnotes to Plato that we are, it *does* feel that way. But if James's own pragmatism were taken seriously, if pragmatism became central to our culture and our self-image, then it would no longer feel that way. We do not know how it *would* feel. We do not even know whether, given such a change in tone, the conversation of Europe might not falter and die away. We just do not know. James and Dewey offered us no guarantees. They simply pointed to the situation we stand in, now that both the Age of Faith and the Enlightenment seem beyond recovery. They grasped our time in thought. We did not change the course of the conversation in the way they suggested we might. Perhaps we are still unable to do so; perhaps we never shall be able to. But we can nevertheless honor James and Dewey for having offered what very few philosophers have succeeded in giving us: a hint of how our lives might be changed.

me see that pragmatists have to answer this question.

General

Aune, B. *Rationalism, Empiricism, and Pragmatism.* New York, 1970.
Coffa, J. A. *The Semantic Tradition from Kant to Carnap: To the Vienna Station.* Cambridge, Eng., 1991.
Morick, H., ed. *Challenges to Empiricism.* Indianapolis, Ind., 1980.
Munitz, M. *Contemporary Analytic Philosophy.* New York, 1981.
Rescher, N. *Methodological Pragmatism.* Oxford, 1977.
Thayer, H. S. *Meaning and Action: A Critical History of Pragmatism,* 2nd ed. Indianapolis, Ind., 1980.

James

Ayer, A. J. *The Origins of Pragmatism: Studies in the Philosophy of Charles Sanders Peirce and William James.* San Francisco, 1968.
Bird, G. *William James.* London, 1986.
James, W. *The Meaning of Truth.* New York, 1909.
———. *Pragmatism.* New York, 1907.
———. *The Will to Believe and Other Essays in Popular Philosophy.* New York, 1897.
Knight, M., ed. *William James: A Selection from His Writings on Psychology.* Baltimore, 1950.
Perry, R. B. *The Thought and Character of William James.* Cambridge, Mass., 1948

Russell

Ayer, A. J. *Bertrand Russell.* Chicago, 1988.
Griffin, N. *Russell's Idealist Apprenticeship.* Oxford, 1991.
Hylton, P. *Russell, Idealism, and the Emergence of Analytic Philosophy.* Oxford, 1990.
Russell, B. *Human Knowledge: Its Scope and Limits.* New York, 1948.
———. *An Inquiry into Meaning and Truth.* London, 1940.
———. *My Philosophical Development.* London, 1959.
———. *The Problems of Philosophy.* London, 1912.
Sainsbury, M. *Russell.* London, 1979.

NOTES

1. See A. O. Lovejoy, "On Some Conditions of Progress in Philosophical Inquiry," *The Philosophical Review*, XXVI (1917): 123–163 (especially the concluding pages). I owe the reference to Lovejoy's paper to Daniel J. Wilson's illuminating "Professionalization and Organized Discussion in the American Philosophical Association, 1900–1922," *Journal of the History of Philosophy*, XVII (1979): 53–69.
2. I am indebted to Michael Williams for making

Savage, C. W., and C. A. Anderson, eds. *Rereading Russell: Essays in Bertrand Russell's Metaphysics and Epistemology.* Minneapolis, 1988.

Ayer

Ayer, A. J. *The Foundations of Empirical Knowledge.* London, 1940.
———. *Language, Truth, and Logic,* 2nd ed. London, 1946.
———. *Probability and Evidence.* New York, 1972.
———. *The Problem of Knowledge.* Baltimore, 1956.
Hahn, L. E., ed. *The Philosophy of A. J. Ayer.* La Salle, Ill., 1992.
Macdonald, G. and C. Wright, eds. *Fact, Science, and Morality: Essays on Ayer's Language, Truth, and Logic.* Oxford, 1987.

Lewis

Ayer, A. J. *Philosophy in the Twentieth Century,* chap. 3. New York, 1982.
Goheen, J. D., and J. L. Mothershead, eds. *Collected Papers of Clarence Irving Lewis.* Stanford, Calif., 1970.
Lewis, C. I. *An Analysis of Knowledge and Valuation.* La Salle, Ill, 1946.
———. *Mind and the World Order.* New York, 1929.
Moser, P. K. "Foundationalism, the Given, and C. I. Lewis." *History of Philosophy Quarterly* 5 (1988): 189–204.
Schilpp, P. A., ed. *The Philosophy of C. I. Lewis.* La Salle, Ill., 1968.

Carnap

Coffa, J. A. *The Semantic Tradition from Kant to Carnap: To the Vienna Station.* Cambridge, Eng., 1991.
Carnap, R. *Meaning and Necessity,* 2nd ed. Chicago, 1956.
———. *Philosophical Foundations of Physics.* New York, 1966.
Hintikka, Jaakko, ed. *Rudolf Carnap, Logical Empiricist.* Dordrecht, 1975.
Schilpp, P. A., ed. *The Philosophy of Rudolf Carnap.* La Salle, Ill, 1963.

Quine

Hookway, C. *Quine.* Cambridge, Eng., 1988.
Quine, W. V. *From a Logical Point of View,* 2nd ed. Cambridge, Mass., 1961.
———. *Ontological Relativity and Other Essays.* New York, 1969.
———. *Pursuit of Truth.* Cambridge, Mass., 1990.
———. *Theories and Things.* Cambridge, Mass., 1981.
Quine, W. V., and J. S. Ullian. *The Web of Belief,* 2nd ed. New York, 1978.
Schilpp, P. A., and L. E. Hahn, eds. *The Philosophy of W. V. Quine.* La Salle, Ill., 1986.

The Analysis of Knowledge

The General Introduction identified the basis for a fourth condition for knowledge, beyond the belief, truth, and justification conditions. This section focuses on the so-called Gettier problem that calls for such a fourth condition. The Gettier problem originates in Edmund Gettier's influential paper "Is Justified True Belief Knowledge?" Gettier presents two examples evidently showing that justified true belief is not sufficient for one's having knowledge. Here is one of Gettier's examples: Smith is justified in believing the false proposition that (a) Jones owns a Ford. On the basis of (a), Smith infers, and thus is justified in believing, that (b) either Jones owns a Ford or Brown is in Barcelona. As it happens, Brown is in Barcelona; so (b) is true. Although Smith is justified in believing the true proposition (b), Smith does not know (b).

Gettier-style counterexamples are cases where a person has justified true belief that P but lacks knowledge that P. In *The Analysis of Knowing* (Princeton, N.J., 1983), Robert Shope suggests the following abstract description of Gettier-style counterexamples to the traditional analysis of knowledge:

> (G) In a Gettier-style counterexample concerning a person, S, and a proposition, P: (1) the truth condition holds regarding P; (2) the belief condition holds regarding P; (3) the justification condition holds regarding P; (4) some proposition, O, is false; (5) either the justification condition holds regarding O, or at least S would be justified in believing O; (6) S does not know P.

The Gettier problem is just the problem of providing an alternative to, or a modification of, the traditional justified-true-belief analysis that avoids difficulties from Gettier-style counterexamples. In solving this problem, one would go a long way toward identifying the logically sufficient conditions for one's having knowledge.

In "An Alleged Defect in Gettier Counter-Examples," Richard Feldman shows that we cannot fault Gettier-style counterexamples on the ground that they rely on the allegedly false principle that false propositions can justify one's belief in other propositions. Feldman offers a counterexample to the justified-true-belief analysis that resembles Gettier's examples but does not rely on the allegedly false principle. Such a counterexample is perhaps the most difficult for the traditional analysis of knowledge.

In "The Gettier Problem," John Pollock contends that the Gettier problem is solved by regarding "objective epistemic justification" as a necessary condition for knowledge. Objective epistemic justification entails justified true belief, but requires that one arrive at true belief "while doing everything right." More precisely: "S is objectively justified in believing P if and only if S instantiates some argument A supporting P which is ultimately undefeated relative to the set of all truths." Pollock takes this characterization to capture the way in which knowledge requires justification that is ultimately undefeated by true defeaters. Pollock explains how his account can accommodate the so-called social aspects of knowledge.

20 / EDMUND GETTIER
IS JUSTIFIED TRUE BELIEF KNOWLEDGE?

Various attempts have been made in recent years to state necessary and sufficient conditions for someone's knowing a given proposition. The attempts have often been such that they can be stated in a form similar to the following:

(a) S knows that P
  IFF
  (i) *P* is true.
  (ii) S believes that P, and
  (iii) S is justified in believing that P.[1]

For example, Chisholm has held that the following gives the necessary and sufficient conditions for knowledge:[2]

(b) S knows that P
  IFF
  (i) S accepts P,
  (ii) S has adequate evidence for P, and
  (iii) P is true.

Ayer has stated the necessary and sufficient conditions for knowledge as follows:[3]

(c) S knows that P
  IFF
  (i) P is true.
  (ii) S is sure that P is true, and
  (iii) S has the right to be sure that P is true.

I shall argue that (a) is false in that the conditions stated therein do not constitute a *sufficient* condition for the truth of the proposition that S knows that P. The same argument will show that (b) and (c) fail if "has adequate evidence for" or "has the right to be sure that" is substituted for "is justified in believing that" throughout.

I shall begin by noting two points. First, in that sense of "justified" in which S's being justified in believing P is a necessary condition of S's knowing that P, it is possible for a person to be justified in believing a proposition which is in fact false. Secondly, for any proposition P, if S is justified in believing P and P entails Q and S deduces Q from P and accepts Q as a result of this deduction, then S is justified in believing Q. Keeping these two points in mind, I shall now present two cases in which the conditions stated in (a) are true for some proposition, though it is at the same time false that the person in question knows that proposition.

CASE I

Suppose that Smith and Jones have applied for a certain job. And suppose that Smith has strong evidence for the following conjunctive proposition:

(d) Jones is the man who will get the job, and Jones has ten coins in his pocket.

Smith's evidence for (d) might be that the president of the company assured him that Jones would in the end be selected, and that he, Smith, had counted the coins in Jones's pocket ten minutes ago. Proposition (d) entails:

(e) The man who will get the job has ten coins in his pocket.

From *Analysis* 23, no. 6 (1963), 121–123. Copyright © 1963, E. L. Gettier. Reprinted by permission of the author.

Let us suppose that Smith sees the entailment from (d) to (e), and accepts (e) on the grounds of (d), for which he has strong evidence. In this case, Smith is clearly justified in believing that (e) is true.

But imagine, further, that unknown to Smith, he himself, not Jones, will get the job. And, also, unknown to Smith, he himself has ten coins in his pocket. Proposition (e) is then true, though proposition (d), from which Smith inferred (e), is false. In our example, then, all of the following are true: (1) (e) is true, (2) Smith believes that (e) is true, and (3) Smith is justified in believing that (e) is true. But it is equally clear that Smith does not *know* that (e) is true; for (e) is true in virtue of the number of coins in Smith's pocket, while Smith does not know how many coins are in Smith's pocket, and bases his belief in (e) on a count of the coins in Jones's pocket, whom he falsely believes to be the man who will get the job.

CASE II

Let us suppose that Smith has strong evidence for the following proposition:

(f)   Jones owns a Ford.

Smith's evidence might be that Jones has at all times in the past within Smith's memory owned a car, and always a Ford, and that Jones has just offered Smith a ride while driving a Ford. Let us imagine, now, that Smith has another friend, Brown, of whose whereabouts he is totally ignorant. Smith selects three place names quite at random and constructs the following three propositions:

(g)   Either Jones owns a Ford, or Brown is in Boston.

(h)   Either Jones owns a Ford, or Brown is in Barcelona.

(i)   Either Jones owns a Ford, or Brown is in Brest-Litovsk.

Each of these propositions is entailed by (f). Imagine that Smith realizes the entailment of each of these propositions he has constructed by (f), and proceeds to accept (g), (h), and (i) on the basis of (f). Smith has correctly inferred (g), (h), and (i) from a proposition for which he has strong evidence. Smith is therefore completely justified in believing each of these three propositions. Smith, of course, has no idea where Brown is.

But imagine now that two further conditions hold. First, Jones does *not* own a Ford, but is at present driving a rented car. And secondly, by the sheerest coincidence, and entirely unknown to Smith, the place mentioned in proposition (h) happens really to be the place where Brown is. If these two conditions hold, then Smith does *not* know that (h) is true, even though (1) (h) is true, (2) Smith does believe that (h) is true, and (3) Smith is justified in believing that (h) is true.

These two examples show that definition (a) does not state a *sufficient* condition for someone's knowing a given proposition. The same cases, with appropriate changes, will suffice to show that neither definition (b) nor definition (c) do so either.

NOTES

1. Plato seems to be considering some such definition at *Theaetetus* 201, and perhaps accepting one at *Meno* 98.
2. Roderick M. Chisholm, *Perceiving: A Philosophical Study.* (Ithaca, N.Y., 1957), 16.
3. A. J. Ayer, *The Problem of Knowledge* (London: 1956).

21 / RICHARD FELDMAN
AN ALLEGED DEFECT IN GETTIER COUNTER-EXAMPLES

A number of philosophers have contended that Gettier counter-examples to the justified true belief analysis of knowledge all rely on a certain false principle. For example, in their recent paper, "Knowledge Without Paradox,"[1] Robert G. Meyers and Kenneth Stern argue that "(c)ounter-examples of the Gettier sort all turn on the principle that someone can be justified in accepting a certain proposition h on evidence p even though p is false."[2] They contend that this principle is false, and hence that the counter-examples fail. Their view is that one proposition, p, can justify another, h, only if p is true. With this in mind, they accept the justified true belief analysis.

D. M. Armstrong defends a similar view in *Belief, Truth and Knowledge*.[3] He writes:

> This simple consideration seems to make redundant the ingenious arguments of . . . Gettier's . . . article. . . . Gettier produces counter-examples to the thesis that justified true belief is knowledge by producing true beliefs based on justifiably believed grounds . . . but where these grounds are in fact *false*. But because possession of such grounds could not constitute possession of *knowledge*, I should have thought it obvious that they are too weak to serve as suitable grounds.[4]

Thus he concludes that Gettier's examples are defective because they rely on the false principle that false propositions can justify one's belief in other propositions. Armstrong's view seems to be that one proposition, p, can justify another, h, only if p is known to be true (unlike Meyers and Stern who demand only that p in fact be true).[5]

I think, though, that there are examples very much like Gettier's that do not rely on this allegedly false principle. To see this, let us first consider one example in the form in which Meyers and Stern discuss it, and then consider a slight modification of it.

> Suppose Mr. Nogot tells Smith that he owns a Ford and even shows him a certificate to that effect. Suppose, further, that up till now Nogot has always been reliable and honest in his dealings with Smith. Let us call the conjunction of all this evidence m. Smith is thus justified in believing that Mr. Nogot who is in his office owns a Ford (r) and, consequently, is justified in believing that someone in his office owns a Ford (h).[6]

As it turns out, though, m and h are true but r is false. So, the Gettier example runs. Smith has a justified true belief in h, but he clearly does not know h.

What is supposed to justify h in this example is r. But since r is false, the example runs afoul of the disputed principle. Since r is false, it justifies nothing. Hence, if the principle is false, the counter-example fails.

We can alter the example slightly, however, so that what justifies h for Smith is true and he knows that it is. Suppose he deduces from m its existential generalization:

From *Australasian Journal of Philosophy* 52, no. 1 (1974), 68–69. Copyright © 1974, *Australasian Journal of Philosophy*. Reprinted by permission of the author and publisher.

(n) There is someone in the office who told Smith that he owns a Ford and even showed him a certificate to that effect, and who up till now has always been reliable and honest in his dealings with Smith.

(n), we should note, is true and Smith knows that it is, since he has correctly deduced it from *m*, which he knows to be true. On the basis of *n* Smith believes *h*—someone in the office owns a Ford. Just as the Nogot evidence, *m*, justified *r*—Nogot owns a Ford—in the original example, *n* justifies *h* in this example. Thus Smith has a justified true belief in *h*, knows his evidence to be true, but still does not know *h*.

I conclude that even if a proposition can be justified for a person only if his evidence is true, or only if he knows it to be true, there are still counter-examples to the justified true belief analysis of knowledge of the Gettier sort. In the above example, Smith reasoned from the proposition *m*, which he knew to be true, to the proposition *n*, which he also knew, to the truth *h;* yet he still did not know *h*. So some examples, similar to Gettier's, do not "turn on the principle that someone can be justified in accepting a certain proposition . . . even though (his evidence) . . . is false."[7]

NOTES

1. Robert G. Myers and Kenneth Stern, "Knowledge Without Paradox," *The Journal of Philosophy* 70, no. 6 (March 22, 1973): 147–60.
2. Ibid., p. 147.
3. D. M. Armstrong, *Belief, Truth and Knowledge* (Cambridge, Eng., 1973).
4. Ibid., p. 152.
5. Armstrong ultimately goes on to defend a rather different analysis.
6. Meyers and Stern, 151.
7. Ibid., p. 147.

22 / John Pollock
THE GETTIER PROBLEM

1. INTRODUCTION

It is rare in philosophy to find a consensus on any substantive issue, but for some time there was almost complete consensus on what is called 'the justified true belief analysis of knowing'. According to that analysis:

S knows P if and only if:

1. P is true;
2. S believes P; and
3. S is justified in believing P.

In the period immediately preceding the publication of Gettier's [1963] landmark article "Is justified true belief knowledge?," this analysis was affirmed by virtually every writer in epistemology. Then Gettier published his article and single-handedly changed the course of epistemology. He did this by presenting two clear and undeniable counterexamples to the justified true belief analysis. Recounting the example given in chapter one, consider Smith who believes falsely but with good reason that Jones owns a Ford. Smith has no idea where

Reprinted by permission of the publisher from John Pollock, *Contemporary Theories of Knowledge* pp. 180–93. Lanham, Md.: Rowman & Littlefield.

Brown is, but he arbitrarily picks Barcelona and infers from the putative fact that Jones owns a Ford that either Jones owns a Ford or Brown is in Barcelona. It happens by chance that Brown is in Barcelona, so this disjunction is true. Furthermore, as Smith has good reason to believe that Jones owns a Ford, he is justified in believing this disjunction. But as his evidence does not pertain to the true disjunct of the disjunction, we would not regard Smith as *knowing* that either Jones owns a Ford or Brown is in Barcelona.

Gettier's paper was followed by a spate of articles attempting to meet his counterexamples by adding a fourth condition to the analysis of knowing. The first attempts to solve the Gettier problem turned on the observation that in Gettier's examples, the epistemic agent arrives at his justified true belief by reasoning from a false belief. That suggested the addition of a fourth condition something like the following:

S's grounds for believing P do not include any false beliefs.[1]

It soon emerged, however, that further counterexamples could be constructed in which knowledge is lacking despite the believer's not inferring his belief from any false beliefs. Alvin Goldman [1976] constructed the following example. Suppose you are driving through the countryside and see what you take to be a barn. You see it in good light and from not too great a distance, it looks the way barns look, and so on. Furthermore, it is a barn. You then have justified true belief that it is a barn. But in an attempt to appear more opulent than they are, the people around here have taken to constructing very realistic barn facades that cannot readily be distinguished from the real thing when viewed from the highway. There are many more barn facades around than real barns. Under these circumstances we would not agree that you know that what you see is a barn, even though you have justified true belief. Furthermore, your belief that you see a barn is not in any way inferred from a belief about the absence of barn facades. Most likely the possibility of barn facades is something that will not even have occurred to you, much less have played a role in your reasoning.

We can construct an even simpler perceptual example. Suppose S sees a ball that looks red to him, and on that basis he correctly judges that it is red. But unbeknownst to S, the ball is illuminated by red lights and would look red to him even if it were not red. Then S does not know that the ball is red despite his having a justified true belief to that effect. Furthermore, his reason for believing that the ball is red does not involve his believing that the ball is not illuminated by red lights. Illumination by red lights is related to his reasoning only as a defeater, not as a step in his reasoning. These examples, or other related examples,[2] indicate that justified true belief can fail to be knowledge because of the truth values of propositions that do not play a direct role in the reasoning underlying the belief. This observation led to a number of "defeasibility" analyses of knowing.[3] The simplest defeasibility analysis would consist of adding a fourth condition requiring that there be no true defeaters. This might be accomplished as follows:

There is no true proposition Q such that if Q were added to S's beliefs then he would no longer be justified in believing P.[4]

But Keith Lehrer and Thomas Paxson [1969] presented the following counterexample to this simple proposal:

Suppose I see a man walk into the library and remove a book from the library by concealing it beneath his coat. Since I am sure the man is Tom Grabit, whom I have often seen before when he attended my classes, I report that I know that Tom Grabit has removed the book. However, suppose further that Mrs. Grabit, the mother of Tom, has averred that on the day in question Tom was not in the library, indeed, was thousands of miles away, and that Tom's identical twin brother, John Grabit, was in the library. Imagine, moreover, that I am entirely ignorant of the fact that Mrs. Grabit has said these things. The statement that she has said these things would defeat any justification I have for believing that Tom Grabit removed the book, according to our present definition of defeasibility. . . .

The preceding might seem acceptable until we finish the story by adding that Mrs. Grabit is a compulsive and pathological liar, that Tom

Grabit is a fiction of her demented mind, and that Tom Grabit took the book as I believed. Once this is added, it should be apparent that I did know that Tom Grabit removed the book. [p. 228]

A natural proposal for handling the Grabit example is that in addition to there being a true defeater there is a true defeater defeater, and that restores knowledge. For example, in the Grabit case it is true that Mrs. Grabit reported that Tom was not in the library but his twin brother John was there (a defeater), but it is also true that Mrs. Grabit is a compulsive and pathological liar and John Grabit is a fiction of her demented mind (a defeater defeater). It is difficult, however, to construct a precise principle that handles these examples correctly by appealing to true defeaters and true defeater defeaters. It will not do to amend the above proposal as follows:

If there is a true proposition Q such that if Q were added to S's beliefs then he would no longer be justified in believing P, then there is also a true proposition R such that if Q and R were both added to S's beliefs then he would be justified in believing P.

The simplest difficulty for this proposal is that adding R may add new reasons for believing P rather than restoring the old reasons. It is not trivial to see how to formulate a fourth condition incorporating defeater defeaters. I think that such a fourth condition will ultimately provide the solution to the Gettier problem, but no proposal of this sort has been worked out in the literature.[5] I will pursue this further in the next section.

2. OBJECTIVE EPISTEMIC JUSTIFICATION

The Gettier problem has spawned a large number of proposals for the analysis of knowledge. As the literature on the problem has developed, the proposals have become increasingly complex in the attempt to meet more and more complicated counterexamples to simpler analyses. The result is that even if some very complex analysis should turn out to be immune from counterexample, it would seem *ad hoc*. We would be left wondering why we employ any such complicated concept. I will suggest that our concept of knowledge is actually a reasonably simple one. The complexities required by increasingly complicated Gettier-type examples are not complexities in the concept of knowledge, but instead reflect complexities in the structure of our epistemic norms.

In the discussion of externalism I commented on the distinction between subjective and objective senses of "should believe" and how that pertains to epistemology. The subjective sense of "should believe" concerns what we should believe given what we actually do believe (possibly incorrectly). The objective sense of "should believe" concerns what we should believe given what is in fact true. But what we should believe given what is true is just the truths, so the objective sense of "should believe" gets identified with truth. The subjective sense, on the other hand, is ordinary epistemic justification. What I now want to suggest, however, is that there is an intermediate sense of "should believe," that might also be regarded as objective but does not reduce to truth.

It is useful to compare epistemic judgments with moral judgments. Focusing on the latter, let us suppose that a person S subjectively should do A. This will be so *for particular reasons*. There may be relevant facts of which the person is not apprised that bear upon these reasons. It might be the case that even in the face of all the relevant facts, S should still do A. That can happen in either of two ways: (1) among the relevant facts may be new reasons for doing A of which S has no knowledge; or (2) the relevant facts may, on sum, leave the original reasons intact. What I have been calling "the objective sense of 'should' " appeals to both kinds of considerations, but there is also an important kind of moral evaluation that appeals only to considerations of the second kind. This is the notion of the original reasons surviving intact, and it provides us with another variety of objective moral evaluation. We appraise a person and his act simultaneously by saying that he has a moral obligation to perform the act (he subjectively should do it) and his moral obligation derives from what are in fact good reasons (reasons withstanding the test of truth). It seems to me that we are often in the position of making such appraisals, although moral language provides us with no simple way of expressing them. The purely objective sense of "should" pertains more to acts than to agents, and hence does not express moral obligation. Therefore, it should not be confusing if I express appraisals of this third variety artificially by saying that S has an *objective obligation* to do A when he has an obligation to do A and the obligation derives from what are in fact good reasons (in the face of all the relevant facts).

How might objective obligation be analyzed? It might at first be supposed that S has an objective obligation to do A if and only if (1) S subjectively should do A, and (2) there is no set of truths X such that if these truths were added to S's beliefs (and their negations removed in those cases in which S disbelieves them) then it would not be true that S subjectively should do A *for the same reason*. This will not quite do, however. It takes account of the fact that moral reasons are defeasible, but it does not take account of the fact that the defeaters are also defeasible. For example, S might spy a drowning man and be in a position to save him with no risk to himself. Then he subjectively should do so. But suppose that, unbeknownst to S, the man is a terrorist who fell in the lake while he was on his way to blow up a bus station and kill many innocent people. Presumably, if S knew that then he would no longer have a subjective obligation to save the man, and so it follows by the proposed analysis that S does not have an objective obligation to save the man. But suppose it is also the case that what caused the man to fall in the lake was that he underwent a sudden religious conversion that persuaded him to give up his evil ways and devote the rest of his life to good deeds. If S knew this, then he would again have a subjective obligation to save the man, for the same reasons as his original reasons, and so he has an objective obligation to save the man. There is, however, no way to accommodate this on the proposed analysis. On that analysis, if a set of truths defeats an obligation, there is no

way to get it undefeated again by appealing to a broader class of truths.

What the analysis of objective obligation should require is that if S were apprised of "enough" truths (all the relevant ones) then he would still be subjectively obligated to do A. This can be cashed out as requiring that there is a set of truths such that if S were apprised of them, then he would be subjectively obligated in the same way as he originally was, and those are all the relevant truths in the sense that if he were to become apprised of any further truths, that would not make any difference. Precisely:

S has an objective obligation to do A if and only if:

1. S subjectively should do A; and
2. there is a set X of truths such that, given any more inclusive set Y of truths, necessarily, if the truths in Y were added to S's beliefs (and their negations removed in those cases in which S disbelieves them) then it would still be true *for the same reason* that S subjectively should do A.

Now let us return to epistemology. An important difference between moral judgments and epistemic judgments is that basic moral judgments concern obligation whereas basic epistemic judgments concern permissibility. This reflects an important difference in the way moral and epistemic norms function. In morality, reasons are reasons for obligations. Anything is permissible that is not proscribed. In epistemology, on the other hand, epistemic justification concerns what beliefs you are permitted to hold (not "obliged to hold"), and reasons are required for permissibility. Thus the analogy between epistemology and morality is not exact. The analogue of objective moral obligation is "objective epistemic permissibility," or as I will say more simply, *objective epistemic justification*. I propose to ignore our earlier concept of objective epistemic justification because it simply reduces to truth. Our new concept of objective epistemic justification can be defined as follows, on analogy to our notion of objective moral obligation:

S is objectively justified in believing P if and only if:

1. S is (subjectively) justified in believing P; and
2. there is a set X of truths such that, given any more inclusive set Y of truths, necessarily, if the truths in Y were added to S's beliefs (and their negations removed in those cases in which S disbelieves them) and S believed P *for the same reason* then he would still be (subjectively) justified in believing P.

Despite the complexity of its definition, the concept of objective epistemic justification is a simple and intuitive one. As is so often the case with technical concepts, the concept is easier to grasp than it is to define. It can be roughly glossed as the concept of getting the right answer while doing everything right. I am construing "S is justified in believing P" in such a way that it entails that S does believe P, so objective justification entails justified belief. It also entails truth, because if P were false and we added $\sim$ P to Y then S would no longer be justified in believing P. Thus, objective epistemic justification entails justified true belief.

My claim is now that objective epistemic justification is very close to being the same thing as knowledge. We will find in section three that a qualification is required to turn objective justification into knowledge, but in the meantime it can be argued that the Gettier problem can be resolved by taking objective epistemic justification to be a necessary condition for knowledge. This enables us to avoid the familiar Gettier-type examples that create difficulties for other analyses of knowledge. Consider one of Gettier's original examples. Jones believes, correctly, that Brown owns a Ford. He believes this on the grounds that he has frequently seen Brown drive a particular Ford, he has ridden in it, he has seen Brown's auto registration which lists him as owning that Ford, and so forth. But unknown to Jones, Brown sold that Ford yesterday and bought a new one. Under the circumstances, we would not agree that Jones now knows that Brown owns a Ford, despite the fact that he has a justified true belief to that effect. This is explained by noting that Jones is not objectively justified in believing that Brown owns a Ford. This is

because there is a truth—namely, that Brown does not own the Ford Jones thinks he owns—such that if Jones became apprised of it then his original reasons would no longer justify him in believing that Jones owns a Ford, and becoming apprised of further truths would not restore those original reasons.

To take a more complicated case, consider Goldman's barn example. Suppose you are driving through the countryside and see what you take to be a barn. You see it in good light and from not too great a distance, and it looks like a barn. Furthermore, it is a barn. You then have justified true belief that it is a barn. But the countryside here is littered with very realistic barn facades that cannot readily be distinguished from the real thing when viewed from the highway. There are many more barn facades than real barns. Under these circumstances we would not agree that you know that what you see is a barn, even though you have justified true belief. This can be explained by noting that if you were aware of the preponderance of barn facades in the vicinity then you would not be justified in believing you see a barn, and your original justification could not be restored by learning other truths (such as that it is really a barn). Consequently, your belief that you see a barn is not objectively justified.[6]

Finally, consider the Grabit example. Here we want to say that I really do know that Tom Grabit stole the book, despite the fact that Mrs. Grabit alleged that Tom was thousands of miles away and his twin brother John was in the library. That she said this is a true defeater, but there is also a true defeater defeater, viz., that Mrs. Grabit is a compulsive and pathological liar and John Grabit is a fiction of her demented mind. If we include *both* of these truths in the set X then I remain justified *for my original reason* in believing that Tom stole the book, so in this case my belief is objectively justified despite the existence of a true defeater.

To a certain extent, I think that the claim that knowledge requires objective epistemic justification provides a solution to the Gettier problem. But it might be disqualified as a solution to the Gettier problem on the grounds that the definition of objective justification is vague in one crucial respect. It talks about being justified, *for the same reason*, in believing P. I think that that notion makes pre-theoretic good sense, but to spell out what it involves requires us to construct a complete epistemological theory. That, I think, is why the Gettier problem has proven so intractable. The complexities in the analysis of knowing all have to do with filling out this clause. The important thing to realize, however, is that these complexities have nothing special to do with knowledge per se. What they pertain to is the structure of epistemic justification and the way in which beliefs come to be justified on the basis of other beliefs and nondoxastic states. Thus even if it is deemed that we have not yet solved the Gettier problem, we have at least put the blame where it belongs—not on knowledge but on the structure of epistemic justification and the complexity of our epistemic norms.

Let us turn then to the task of filling in some of the details concerning epistemic justification. In chapter two, I proposed an analysis of epistemic justification in terms of ultimately undefeated arguments. That analysis proceeded within the context of a subsequently rejected foundationalist theory, but basically the same analysis can be resurrected within direct realism. For this purpose we must take arguments to proceed from internal states (both doxastic and nondoxastic states) to doxastic states, the links between steps being provided by reasons. Within direct realism, reasons are internal states. They are generally doxastic states, but not invariably. At the very least, perceptual and memory states can also be reasons.

Our epistemic norms permit us to begin reasoning from certain internal states without those states being supported by further reasoning. Such states can be called *basic states*. Paramount among these are perceptual and memory states. Arguments must always begin with basic states and proceed from them to nonbasic doxastic states. What we might call *linear arguments* proceed from basic states to their ultimate conclusions through a sequence of steps each consisting of a belief for which the earlier steps provide reasons. It seems likely, however, that we must allow arguments to have more complicated structures than those permitted in linear arguments. Specifically, we must allow

"subsidiary arguments" to occur within the main argument. A subsidiary argument can begin with premises that are merely assumed for the sake of the argument rather than because they have already been justified. For instance, in the forms of conditional proof familiar from elementary logic, in establishing a condition ($P \supset Q$), we may begin by taking P as a premise (even though it has not been previously established), deriving Q from it, and then "discharging" the assumption of the antecedent to obtain the conditional ($P \supset Q$). It seems that something similar occurs in epistemological arguments. We can accommodate this by taking *an argument conditional on a set* X *of propositions* to be an argument beginning not just from basic states but also from doxastic states that consist of believing the members of X. Then an argument that justifies a conclusion for a person may have embedded in it subsidiary arguments that are conditional on propositions the person does not believe. For present purposes we need not pursue all the details of the permissible structures of epistemological arguments, but the general idea of conditional arguments will be useful below.

An argument *supports* a belief if and only if that belief occurs as a step in the argument that does not occur within any subsidiary argument. A person *instantiates* an argument if and only if he is in the basic states from which the argument begins and he believes the conclusion of the argument on the basis of that argument. Typically, in reasoning to a conclusion one will proceed first to some intermediate conclusions from which the final conclusion is obtained. The notion of holding a belief on the basis of an argument is to be understood as requiring that one also believes the intermediate conclusions on the basis of the initial parts of the argument.

Epistemic justification consists of holding a belief on the basis of an ultimately undefeated argument, that is, instantiating an ultimately undefeated argument supporting the belief. To repeat the definition of an ultimately undefeated argument, every argument proceeding from basic states that S is actually in will be *undefeated at level 0* for S. Of course, arguments undefeated at level 0 can embed subsidiary arguments that are conditional on propositions S does not believe. Some arguments will support defeaters for other arguments, so we define an argument to be undefeated at level 1 if and only if it is not defeated by any other arguments undefeated at level 0. Among the arguments defeated at level 0 may be some that supported defeaters for others, so if we take arguments undefeated at level 2 to be arguments undefeated at level 0 that are not defeated by any arguments undefeated at level 1, there may be arguments undefeated at level 2 that were arguments defeated at level 1. In general, we define an argument to be *undefeated at level n+1* if and only if it is undefeated at level 0 and is not defeated by any arguments undefeated at level n. An argument is *ultimately undefeated* if and only if there is some point beyond which it remains permanently undefeated; that is, for some N, the argument remains undefeated at level n for every n>N.

This gives us a picture of the structure of epistemic justification. Many details remain to be filled in, but we can use this picture without further elaboration to clarify the concept of objective epistemic justification. Roughly, a belief is objectively justified if and only if it is held on the basis of some ultimately undefeated argument A, and either A is not defeated by any argument conditional on true propositions not believed by S, or if it is then there are further true propositions such that the initial defeating arguments will be defeated by arguments conditional on the enlarged set of true propositions. This can be made precise by defining an *argument conditional on* Y to be any argument proceeding from basic states S is actually in together with doxastic states consisting of believing members of Y. We then say that an argument instantiated by S (not an argument conditional on Y) is *undefeated at level n+1 relative to* Y if and only if it is undefeated by any argument undefeated at level n relative to Y. An argument is *ultimately undefeated relative to* Y if and only if there is an N such that it is undefeated at level n relative to Y for every n>N. Then the concept of objective epistemic justification can be made more precise as follows:

S is objectively justified in believing P if and only if S instantiates some argument A sup-

porting P which is ultimately undefeated relative to the set of all truths.

I will take this to be my official definition of objective epistemic justification. I claim, then, that the Gettier-style counterexamples to the traditional definition of knowledge can all be met by taking knowledge to require objective epistemic justification. This makes precise the way in which knowledge requires justification that is either undefeated by true defeaters, or if defeated by true defeaters then those defeaters are defeated by true defeater defeaters, and so on.

A common view has been that the reliability of one's cognitive processes is required for knowledge, and thus reliabilism has a place in the analysis of knowledge quite apart from whether it has a place in the analysis of epistemic justification.[7] The observation that knowledge requires objective epistemic justification explains the appeal of the idea that knowledge requires reliability. Nondefeasible reasons logically entail their conclusions, so they are always perfectly reliable, but defeasible reasons can be more or less reliable under various circumstances. Discovering that the present circumstances are of a type in which a defeasible reason is unreliable constitutes a defeater for the use of that reason. Objective justification requires that if a belief is held on the basis of a defeasible reason then there are no true defeaters (or if there are then there are true defeater defeaters, and so on). Thus knowledge automatically requires that one's reasons be reliable under the present circumstances. Reliabilism has a place in knowledge even if it has none in justification. It is worth emphasizing, however, that considerations of reliability are not central to the concept of knowledge. Rather than having to be imposed on the analysis in an *ad hoc* way, they emerge naturally from the observation that knowledge requires objective epistemic justification.

3. Social Aspects of Knowledge

It is tempting to simply identify knowledge with objective epistemic justification. As I have pointed out, objective justification includes justified true belief, and it is immune from

Gettier-style counterexamples. It captures the idea underlying defeasibility analyses. The basic idea is that *believed* defeaters can prevent justification, and defeaters that are true but not believed can prevent knowledge while leaving justification intact. However, there are also some examples that differ in important ways from the Gettier-style examples we have discussed so far, and they are not so easily handled in terms of there being true defeaters. These examples seem to have to do with social aspects of knowing. The philosopher most prominently associated with these examples is Gilbert Harman.[8] One of Harman's examples is as follows:

Suppose that Tom enters a room in which many people are talking excitedly although he cannot understand what they are saying. He sees a copy of the morning paper on a table. The headlines and main story reveal that a famous civil-rights leader has been assassinated. On reading the story he comes to believe it; it is true. . . .

Suppose that the assassination has been denied, even by eyewitnesses, the point of the denial being to avoid a racial explosion. The assassinated leader is reported in good health; the bullets are said, falsely, to have missed him and hit someone else. The denials occurred too late to prevent the original and true story from appearing in the paper that Tom has seen; but everyone else in the room has heard about the denials. None of them know what to believe. They all have information that Tom lacks. Would we judge Tom to be the only one who knows that the assassination has actually occurred? . . . I do not think so.[(1968), p. 172.]

This example cannot be handled in the same way as the Grabit example. As in the Grabit example there is a true defeater, viz., that the news media have reported that the assassination did not occur. But just as in the Grabit example, there is also a true defeater defeater, viz., that the retraction of the original story was motivated by an attempt to avoid race riots and did not necessarily reflect the actual facts. The appeal to true defeaters and true defeater defeaters should lead us to treat this example just like the Grabit example, but that gives the

wrong answer. The Grabit example is one in which the believer has knowledge, whereas the newspaper example is one in which the believer lacks knowledge.

Harman gives a second kind of example in a recent article:

In case one, Mary comes to know that Norman is in Italy when she calls his office and is told he is spending the summer in Rome. In case two, Norman seeks to give Mary the impression that he is in San Francisco by writing her a letter saying so, a letter he mails to San Francisco where a friend then mails it on to Mary. This letter is in the pile of unopened mail on Mary's desk before her when she calls Norman's office and is told he is spending the summer in Rome. In this case (case two), Mary does not come to know that Norman is in Italy.

It is important in this case that Mary could obtain the misleading evidence. If the evidence is unobtainable, because Norman forgot to mail the letter after he wrote it, or because the letter was delivered to the wrong building where it will remain unopened, then it does not keep Mary from knowing that Norman is in Italy. [(1981), p. 164]

Again, there is a true defeater, viz., that the letter reports Norman to be in San Francisco. But there is also a true defeater defeater, viz., that the letter was written with the intention to deceive. So Mary's belief is objectively justified. Nevertheless, we want to deny that Mary knows that Norman is in Italy.

Harman ([1981], p. 164) summarizes these examples by writing, "There seem to be two ways in which such misleading evidence can undermine a person's knowledge. The evidence can either be evidence that it would be possible for the person to obtain himself or herself or evidence possessed by others in a relevant social group to which the person in question belongs." We might distinguish between these two examples by saying that in the first example there is a true defeater that is "common knowledge" in Tom's social group, whereas in the second example there is a true defeater that is "readily available" to Mary. I will loosely style these "common knowledge" and "ready availability" defeaters.

It is worth noting that a common knowledge defeater can be defeated by a defeater defeater that is also common knowledge. For example, if it were common knowledge that the news media was disclaiming the assassination, but also common knowledge that the disclaimer was fraudulent, then Tom would retain his knowledge that the assassination occurred even if he were unaware of both the disclaimer and its fraudulence. The same thing is true of ready availability defeaters. If Norman had a change of heart after sending the false letter and sent another letter explaining the trick he played on Mary, and both letters lay unopened on Mary's desk when she called Norman's office, her telephone call would give her knowledge that Norman is in Italy.

What is more surprising is that common knowledge and ready availability defeaters and defeater defeaters can be combined to result in knowledge. For instance, if Norman's trick letter lays unopened on Mary's desk when she makes the call, she will nevertheless acquire knowledge that Norman is in Italy if Norman is an important diplomat and, unbeknownst to her, the news media have been announcing all day that Norman is in Rome but has been trying to fool people about his location by sending out trick letters. This shows that despite the apparent differences between common knowledge and ready availability defeaters, there must be some kind of connection between them.

My suggestion is that these both reflect a more general social aspect of knowledge. We are "socially expected" to be aware of various things. We are expected to know what is announced on television, and we are expected to know what is in our mail. If we fail to know all these things and that makes a difference to whether we are justified in believing some true proposition P, then our objectively justified belief in P does not constitute knowledge. Let us say that a proposition is *socially sensitive for S* if and only if it is of a sort S is expected to believe when true. My claim is that Harman's examples are best handled by taking them to involve cases in which there are true socially sensitive defeaters. This might be doubted on the grounds that not all readily available truths are socially sensitive. For instance, suppose

that instead of having his trick letter mailed from San Francisco, Norman had a friend secrete it under Mary's doormat. We are not socially expected to check regularly under our doormats, but nevertheless this is something we can readily do and so information secreted under our doormats counts as readily available. It does not, however, defeat knowledge. If the trick letter were secreted under Mary's doormat, we would regard her as knowing that Norman is in Italy. Suppose, on the other hand, that we lived in a society in which it is common to leave messages under doormats and everyone is expected to check his doormat whenever he comes home. In that case, if the trick letter were under Mary's doormat but she failed to check there before calling Norman's office, we would not regard that call as providing her with knowledge. These examples seem to indicate that it is social sensitivity and not mere ready availability that enables a truth to defeat a knowledge claim.

My suggestion is that we can capture the social aspect of knowledge by requiring a knower to hold his belief on the basis of an argument ultimately undefeated relative not just to the set of all truths, but also to the set of all socially sensitive truths. My proposal is:

S knows P if and only if S instantiates some argument A supporting P which is (1) ultimately undefeated relative to the set of all truths, and (2) ultimately undefeated relative to the set of all truths socially sensitive for S.

This proposal avoids both the Gettier problem and the social problems discussed by Harman. At this stage in history it would be rash to be very confident of any analysis of knowledge, but I put this forth tentatively as an analysis that seems to handle all of the known problems.

NOTES

1. See, for example, Michael Clark [1963].
2. See, for example, Brian Skyrms [1967].
3. The first defeasibility analysis was that of Keith Lehrer (1965). That was followed by Lehrer and

Thomas Paxson (1969), Peter Klein (1971, 1976, 1979, 1980), Lehrer (1974, 1979), Ernest Sosa (1974, 1980), and Marshall Swain (1981).

4. This is basically the analysis proffered by Klein (1971).

5. A good survey of the literature on the Gettier problem, going into much more detail than space permits here, can be found in Shope (1983).

6. This can be formulated in terms of defeaters and defeater defeaters. "Most of the things around here that look like barns are not barns" is a true reliability defeater, but there is no true defeater defeater. In particular, "That really is a barn," although true, does not restore your original justification—instead, it constitutes a new reason for believing that what you see is a barn.

7. See, for example, Alvin Goldman (1981), pp. 28–29.

8. See Harman (1968 and 1980). Harman credits Ernest Sosa (1964) with the original observation that social considerations play a role in knowledge.

REFERENCES

Clark, Michael. "Knowledge and Grounds: A Comment on Mr. Gettier's paper." *Analysis* 24 (1963): 46–48.

Goldman, Alvin. "The Internalist Conception of Justification." *Midwest Studies in Philosophy,* vol. 5, pp. 27–52. Minneapolis, 1981.

Harman, Gilbert. "Knowledge, Inference, and Explanation." *American Philosophical Quarterly* 5 (1968): 164–73.

———. "Reasoning and Explanatory Coherence." *American Philosophical Quarterly* 17 (1980): 151–58.

Klein, Peter. "Knowledge, Causality, and Defeasibility." *Journal of Philosophy* 73 (1976): 792–812.

———. "Misleading Evidence and the Restoration of Justification." *Philosophical Studies* 37 (1980): 81–89.

———. "Misleading 'Misleading Defeaters.' " *Journal of Philosophy* 76 (1979): 382–86.

———. "A Proposed Definition of Propositional Knowledge." *Journal of Philosophy* 68 (1971): 471–82.

Lehrer, Keith. "The Gettier Problem and the Analysis of Knowledge." In *Justification and Knowledge: New Studies in Epistemology,* ed. George Pappas, pp. 65–78. Dordrecht, 1979.

———. *Knowledge.* Oxford, 1974.

———. "Knowledge, Truth, and Evidence." *Analysis* 25 (1965): 168–75.

Lehrer, Keith, and Thomas Paxson. "Knowledge: Undefeated Justified True Belief." *Journal of Philosophy* 66 (1969): 225–37.

Shope, Robert K. *The Analysis of Knowing.* Princeton, N.J., 1983.

Skyrms, Brian. "The Explication of "X Knows That P." *Journal of Philosophy* 64 (1967): 373–89.

Sosa, Ernest. "The Analysis of "Knowledge That P." *Analysis* 25 (1964): 1–8.

———. "Epistemic Presupposition." In *Justification and Knowledge: New Studies in Epistemology,* ed. George Pappas. Dordrecht, 1980.

———. "How Do You Know?" *American Philosophical Quarterly* 11 (1974): 113–22.

Swain, Marshall. *Reasons and Knowledge.* Ithaca, N.Y., 1981.

THE ANALYSIS OF KNOWLEDGE: BIBLIOGRAPHY

Dretske, F. I. "Conclusive Reasons." *The Australasian Journal of Philosophy* 49 (1971): 1–22.

Goldman, A. "A Causal Theory of Knowing." *The Journal of Philosophy* 64 (1967): 357–72. Reprinted in *Essays on Knowledge and Justification,* ed. G. S. Pappas and M. Swain, pp. 67–86. Ithaca, N.Y., 1978.

———. "Discrimination and Perceptual Knowledge." *The Journal of Philosophy* 73 (1976): 771–91. Reprinted in *Essays on Knowledge and Justification,* pp. 120–45.

———. *Epistemology and Cognition.* Cambridge, Mass., 1986.

Harman, G. "Knowledge, Inference, and Explanation." *American Philosophical Quarterly* 5 (1968): 164–73.

———. "Knowledge, Reasons, and Causes." *The Journal of Philosophy* 67 (1970): 841–55.

———. "Reasoning and Evidence One Does Not

Possess." In *Midwest Studies in Philosophy, Vol. V: Studies in Epistemology*, ed. P. French et al., pp. 163–82. Minneapolis, 1980.

———. *Thought*, chapters 7–9. Princeton, N.J., 1973.

Klein, P. D. "Knowledge, Causality, and Defeasibility." *The Journal of Philosophy* 73 (1976): 792–812.

———. "A Proposed Definition of Propositional Knowledge." *The Journal of Philosophy* 68 (1971): 471–82.

———. "Misleading Evidence and the Restoration of Justification." *Philosophical Studies* 37 (1980): 81–89.

———. "Real Knowledge." *Synthese* 55 (1983): 143–64.

Lehrer, K. "The Gettier Problem and the Analysis of Knowledge." In *Justification and Knowledge*, ed. G. S. Pappas pp. 65–78. Dordrecht, 1979.

———. *Knowledge*, chapter 9. Oxford, 1974.

———. "Self-Profile." In *Keith Lehrer*, ed. R. Bogdan, pp. 3–104. Dordrecht, 1981.

———. *Theory of Knowledge*. Boulder, Col., 1990.

Moser, P. K. *Knowledge and Evidence*. Cambridge, Eng., 1989.

———. "Propositional Knowledge." *Philosophical Studies* 52 (1987): 91–114. Reprinted in *Knowledge and Justification*, Vol. 1, ed. E. Sosa, pp. 99–124. Aldershort, Eng., 1994.

———, ed. *The Oxford Handbook of Epistemology*. New York, 2003.

Roth, M. D., and L. Galis, eds. *Knowing: Essays in the Analysis of Knowledge*. New York, 1970.

Shope, R. K. *The Analysis of Knowing*. Princeton, N.J., 1983.

———. "Conditions and Analyses of Knowledge." In *The Oxford Handbook of Epistemology*, ed. P. K. Moser. New York, 2003.

———. "Knowledge and Falsity." *Philosophical Studies* 36 (1979), 389–405.

———. "Knowledge as Justified Belief in a True, Justified Proposition." *Philosophy Research Archives* 5 (1979): 1–36.

Slaght, Ralph. "Is Justified True Belief Knowledge? A Selective Critical Survey of Recent Work." *Philosophy Research Archives* 3 (1977), 1–135.

Sosa, E. "How Do You Know?" *American Philosophical Quarterly* 11 (1974): 113–22. Reprinted in *Essays on Knowledge and Justification*, ed. G. S. Pappas and M. Swain, pp. 184–205. Ithaca, N.Y., 1978.

———. "Epistemic Presupposition." In *Justification and Knowledge*, ed. G. S. Pappas, pp. 79–92 Dordrecht, 1979.

Swain, M. "Epistemic Defeasibility." *American Philosophical Quarterly* 11 (1974): 15–25. Reprinted in *Essays on Knowledge and Justification*, ed. G. S. Pappas and M. Swain, pp. 160–83. Ithaca, N.Y., 1978.

———. "Knowledge, Causality, and Justification." *The Journal of Philosophy* 69 (1972): 291–300. Reprinted in *Essays on Knowledge and Justification*, pp. 87–99.

———. *Reasons and Knowledge*. Ithaca, N.Y., 1981.

———. "Reasons, Causes, and Knowledge." *The Journal of Philosophy* 75 (1978): 229–49.

Thalberg, I. "In Defense of Justified True Belief." *The Journal of Philosophy* 66 (1969): 794–803.

A Priori Knowledge

Contemporary understanding of the general notion of a priori knowledge derives mainly from Kant's *Critique of Pure Reason*. The concept of a priori knowledge differs from the concept of what is (logically or metaphysically) necessarily true and the concept of what is true analytically, just in virtue of the meanings of a proposition's constituent terms. Kant's talk of a priori "modes of knowledge," in the *Critique of Pure Reason* (A2; eq B3), suggests a knowledge-oriented characterization of what is a priori. A priori knowledge is knowledge that does not depend on evidence from sensory experience. It *may* still be, however, that every proposition knowable a priori is either necessarily true or analytically true.

Many philosophers have assumed that a proposition is knowable a priori only if it is necessarily true, on the ground that if a proposition is possibly false, then it requires for its justification supporting evidence from sensory experience. Saul Kripke has argued that some contingently true propositions are knowable a priori. He cites one's knowledge that stick S is one meter long at a certain time, where stick S is the standard meter bar in Paris. If one uses stick S to "fix the reference" of the term "one meter," then, according to Kripke, one can know a priori that stick S is one meter long. The truth that stick S is one meter long is contingent rather than necessary, for S might not have been one meter long. (Application of considerable heat to S, for instance, would have changed its length.) Perhaps, then, contingent truths are knowable a priori, contrary to what many philosophers have assumed. This topic has generated controversy among contemporary philosophers, with some still contending that no contingently true proposition is knowable a priori.

A related philosophical controversy concerns whether any synthetic truth is knowable a priori. Kant held that some synthetic truths (e.g., those of geometry) have a kind of necessity that cannot come from experience and that they can be known a priori. Such synthetic truths, Kant maintained, can be known just on the basis of pure reason and pure understanding, independently of evidence from sensory experience. Kant's doctrine of synthetic a priori truths still generates controversy among philosophers, especially regarding such apparently synthetic propositions as "Nothing can be green and red all over" and "A straight line is the shortest path between two points."

Philosophers have offered a variety of accounts of propositions that can be known a priori. *Psychologism* about the a priori, advanced by Edmund Husserl, claims that a true proposition is knowable a priori by us if and only if our psychological constitution precludes our regarding that proposition as false. *Linguisticism* about the a priori, endorsed by A. J. Ayer and many other twentieth-century empiricists, states that a true proposition is knowable a priori by us if and only if our denying that proposition would violate rules of coherent language use. *Pragmatism* about the a priori, endorsed by Clarence Irving Lewis, claims that a true proposition is knowable a priori by a person if and only if it describes just that person's pragmatically guided intention to use a certain conceptual scheme of classification for the organizing of experiences. Lewis argued that pragmatic considerations regarding what suits one's needs guide the way in which one formulates a conceptual scheme. *Understanding-based apriorism*, supported by Roderick Chisholm and others, affirms that a true proposition is knowable a priori by us if and only if our understanding that proposition is all the evidence we need to see that the proposition in question is true. These are the most influential accounts of the a priori in circulation.

A full theory of a priori knowledge will identify the strengths and weakness of the aforementioned accounts. It must avoid confusing the notion of what is a priori with the notions of what is necessarily true, what is analytically true, what is innate, and what is certain.

In "A Pragmatic Conception of the A Priori," Clarence Irving Lewis defends a kind of pragmatism according to which a priori knowledge is knowledge of one's intent to use a certain conceptual scheme for classification of one's experience in an organized manner. Lewis maintains that pragmatic considerations about what suits one's needs influence the way in which one constructs such a conceptual scheme. Lewis argues that all knowledge has a pragmatic a priori component of the sort noted.

In "The Truths of Reason," Roderick Chisholm supports "the traditional" conception of the a priori according to which the following is one mark of an a priori proposition: Once we understand the proposition, we see that it is true. Chisholm's general view is that with regard to an a priori proposition, our understanding it is all the evidence we need to see that it is true. Chisholm discusses psychologism, linguisticism, and some relevant views of Leibniz, Kant, and Quine. Chisholm concludes that there is considerable support for the existence of synthetic a priori knowledge.

In "A Priori Knowledge, Necessity, and Contingency," Saul Kripke clarifies the notions of analyticity, necessity, and the a priori. Emphasizing that the notion of the a priori is epistemological, Kripke considers two questions: (a) Can we have a priori knowledge of contingent truths? (b) Is every necessarily true proposition knowable a priori by us? Kripke, as noted previously, argues that there can be a priori knowledge of contingent truths. In addition, Kripke contends that there are necessarily true propositions that must be known a posteriori if they are to be known at all. His main examples are true identity statements involving names, such as "Hesperus is Phosphorus." Kripke argues that such statements are necessarily true but that they could not have been known a priori.

23 / Clarence Irving Lewis (1883–1965)
A PRAGMATIC CONCEPTION OF THE A PRIORI

The conception of the a priori points to two problems which are perennial in philosophy: the part played in knowledge by the mind itself, and the possibility of "necessary truth" or of knowledge "independent of experience."

But traditional conceptions of the a priori have proved untenable. That the mind approaches the flux of immediacy with some godlike foreknowledge of principles which are legislative for experience, that there is any natural light

Reprinted by permission of the publisher from C. I. Lewis, "A Pragmatic Conception of the A Priori," *The Journal of Philosophy* 20 (1923), 169–77.

or any innate ideas, it is no longer possible to believe.

Nor shall we find the clues to the a priori in any compulsion of the mind to incontrovertible truth or any peculiar kind of demonstration which establishes first principles. All truth lays upon the rational mind the same compulsion to belief; as Mr. Bosanquet has pointed out, this character belongs to all propositions or judgments once their truth is established.

The difficulties of the conception are due, I believe, to two mistakes: whatever is a priori is necessary, but we have misconstrued the relation of necessary truth to mind; and the a priori is independent of experience, but in so taking it, we have misunderstood its relation to empirical fact. What is a priori is necessary truth not because it compels the mind's acceptance, but precisely because it does not. It is given experience, brute fact, the a posteriori element in knowledge which the mind must accept willy-nilly. The a priori represents an attitude in some sense freely taken, a stipulation of the mind itself, and a stipulation which might be made in some other way if it suited our bent or need. Such truth is necessary as opposed to contingent, not as opposed to voluntary. And the a priori is independent of experience not because it prescribes a form which the data of sense must fit, or anticipates some pre-established harmony of experience with the mind, but precisely because it prescribes nothing to experience. That is a priori which is true, no matter what. What it anticipates is not the given, but our attitude toward it: it concerns the uncompelled initiative of mind or, as Josiah Royce would say, our categorical ways of acting.

The traditional example of the a priori par excellence is the laws of logic. These cannot be derived from experience since they must first be taken for granted in order to prove them. They make explicit our general modes of classification. And they impose upon experience no real limitation. Sometimes we are asked to tremble before the spectre of the "alogical," in order that we may thereafter rejoice that we are saved from this by the dependence of reality upon mind. But the "alogical" is pure bogy, a word without a meaning. What kind of experience could defy the prin-

ciple that everything must either be or not be, that nothing can both be and not be, or that if x is y and y is z, then x is z? If anything imaginable or unimaginable could violate such laws, then the ever-present fact of change would do it every day. The laws of logic are purely formal; they forbid nothing but what concerns the use of terms and the corresponding modes of classification and analysis. The law of contradiction tells us that nothing can be both white and not-white, but it does not and cannot tell us whether black is not-white, or soft or square is not-white. To discover *what contradicts what* we must always consult the character of experience. Similarly the law of the excluded middle formulates our decision that whatever is not designated by a certain term shall be designated by its negative. It declares our purpose to make, for every term, a complete dichotomy of experience, instead—as we might choose—of classifying on the basis of a tripartite division into opposites (as black and white) and the middle ground between the two. Our rejection of such tripartite division represents only our penchant for simplicity.

Further laws of logic are of similar significance. They are principles of procedure, the parliamentary rules of intelligent thought and speech. Such laws are independent of experience because they impose no limitations whatever upon it. They are legislative because they are addressed to ourselves—because definition, classification, and inference represent no operations of the objective world, but only our own categorical attitudes of mind.

And further, the ultimate criteria of the laws of logic are pragmatic. Those who suppose that there is, for example, *a* logic which everyone would agree to if he understood it and understood himself are more optimistic than those versed in the history of logical discussion have a right to be. The fact is that there are several logics, markedly different, each self-consistent in its own terms and such that whoever using it, if he avoids false premises, will never reach a false conclusion. Mr. Russell, for example, bases *his* logic on an implication relation such that if twenty sentences be cut from a newspaper and put in a hat, and then two of these be drawn at random, one of them will certainly imply the other, and it is an even bet that the implication will be mutual. Yet upon a foundation so remote from ordinary modes of inference the whole structure of *Principia Mathematica* is built. This logic—and there are others even more strange—is utterly consistent and the results of it entirely valid. Over and above all questions of consistency, there are issues of logic which cannot be determined— nay, cannot even be argued—except on pragmatic grounds of conformity to human bent and intellectual convenience. That we have been blind to this fact, itself reflects traditional errors in the conception of the a priori.

We may note in passing one less important illustration of the a priori—the proposition "true by definition." Definitions and their immediate consequences, analytic propositions generally, are necessarily true, true under all possible circumstances. Definition is legislative because it is in some sense arbitrary. Not only is the meaning assigned to words more or less a matter of choice—that consideration is relatively trivial—but the manner in which the precise classifications which definition embodies shall be effected is something not dictated by experience. If experience were other than it is, the definition and its corresponding classification might be inconvenient, fantastic, or useless, but it could not be false. Mind makes classifications and determines meanings; in so doing it creates the a priori truth of analytic judgements. But that the manner of this creation responds to pragmatic considerations is so obvious that it hardly needs pointing out.

If the illustrations so far given seem trivial or verbal, that impression may be corrected by turning to the place which the a priori has in mathematics and in natural science. Arithmetic, for example, depends in toto upon the operation of counting or correlating a procedure which can be carried out at will in any world containing identifiable things—even identifiable ideas—regardless of the further characters of experience. Mill challenged this a priori character of arithmetic. He asked us to suppose a demon sufficiently powerful and maleficent so that every time two things were brought together with two other things, this demon should always introduce a fifth. The implication which he supposed to follow is that under such circumstances $2 + 2 = 5$ would be a universal law of arithmetic. But Mill was quite mistaken. In such a world we should be obliged to become a little clearer than is usual about the distinction between arithmetic and physics; that is all. If two black marbles were put in the same urn with two white ones, the demon could take his choice of colors, but it would be evident that there were more black marbles or more white ones than were put in. The same would be true of all objects in any wise identifiable. We should simply find ourselves in the presence of an extraordinary physical law, which we should recognize as universal in our world, that whenever two things were brought into proximity with two others, an additional and similar thing was always created by the process. Mill's world would be physically most extraordinary. The world's work would be enormously facilitated if hats or locomotives or tons of coal could be thus multiplied by anyone possessed originally of two pairs. But the laws of mathematics would remain unaltered. It is because this is true that arithmetic is a priori. Its laws prevent *nothing*; they are compatible with anything which happens or could conceivably happen in nature. They would be true in any possible world. Mathematical addition is not a physical transformation. Physical changes which result in an increase or decrease of the countable things involved are matters of everyday occurrence. Such physical processes present us with phenomena in which the purely mathematical has to be separated out by abstraction. Those laws and those laws only have necessary truth which we are prepared to maintain, no matter what. It is because we shall always separate out that part of the phenomenon not in conformity with arithmetic and designate it by some other category—physical change, chemical reaction, optical illusion—that arithmetic is a priori.

The a priori element in science and in natural law is greater than might be supposed. In the first place, all science is based upon definitive concepts. The formulation of these concepts is, indeed, a matter determined by the commerce between our intellectual or our pragmatic interests and the nature of experience. Definition is classification. The scientific search is for such classification as will make it possible to correlate appearance and behaviour, to discover law, to penetrate to the "essential nature" of things in order that behaviour may become predictable. In other words, if definition is unsuccessful, as early scientific definitions mostly have been, it is because the classification thus set up corresponds with no natural cleavage and does not correlate with any important uniformity of behaviour. A name itself must represent *some* uniformity in experience or it names nothing. What does not repeat itself or recur in intelligible fashion is not a thing. Where the definitive uniformity is a clue to other uniformities, we have successful scientific definition. Other definitions cannot be said to be false; they are merely useless. In scientific classification the search is, thus, for *things worth naming*. But the naming, classifying, defining activity is essentially prior to investigation. We cannot interrogate experience in general. Until our meaning is definite and our classification correspondingly exact, experience cannot conceivably answer our questions.

In the second place, the fundamental laws of any science—or those treated as fundamental—are a priori because they formulate just such definitive concepts or categorical tests by which alone investigation becomes possible. If the lightning strikes the railroad track at two places, *A* and *B,* how shall we tell whether these events are simultaneous?

We . . . require a definition of simultaneity such that this definition supplies us with the method by means of which . . . [we] can decide whether or not both the lightning strokes occurred simultaneously. As long as this requirement is not satisfied, I allow myself to be deceived as a physicist (and of course the same applies if I am not a physicist), when I imagine that I am able to attach a meaning to the statement of simultaneity. . . .

After thinking the matter over for some time you then offer the following suggestions with which to test simultaneity. By measuring along the rails, the connecting line *AB* should be measured up and an observer placed at the mid-point *M* of the distance *AB*. This observer should be supplied with an arrangement (e.g. two mirrors inclined at 90 degrees) which al-

lows him visually to observe both places *A* and *B* at the same time. If the observer perceives the two flashes at the same time, then they are simultaneous.

I am very pleased with this suggestion, but for all that I cannot regard the matter as quite settled, because I feel constrained to raise the following objection: "Your definition would certainly be right, if I only knew that the light by means of which the observer at *M* perceives the lightning flashes travels along the length *A—M* with the same velocity as along the length *B—M*. But an examination of this supposition would only be possible if we already had at our disposal the means of measuring time. It would thus appear as though we were moving here in a logical circle."

After further consideration you cast a somewhat disdainful glance at me—and rightly so—and you declare: "I maintain my previous definition, nevertheless, because in reality it assumes absolutely nothing about light. There is only *one* demand to be made of the definition of simultaneity, namely, that in every real case it must supply us with an empirical decision as to whether or not the conception which has to be defined is fulfilled. . . . That light requires the same time to traverse the path *A—M* as for the path *B—M* is in reality *neither a supposition nor a hypothesis* about the physical nature of light, but a *stipulation* which I can make of my own free will in order to arrive at a definition of simultaneity." . . . We are thus led also to a definition of "time" in physics.[1]

As this example from the theory of relativity well illustrates, we cannot even ask the questions which discovered law would answer until we have first by a priori stipulation formulated definitive criteria. Such concepts are not verbal definitions, nor classifications merely; they are themselves laws which prescribe a certain uniformity of behaviour to whatever is thus named. Such definitive laws are a priori; only so can we enter upon the investigation by which further laws are sought. Yet it should also be pointed out that such a priori laws are subject to abandonment if the structure which is built upon them does not succeed in simplifying our interpretation of phenomena. If, in the illustration given, the relation "simultaneous with," as defined, should not prove transitive—if event *A* should prove simultaneous with *B,* and *B* with *C,* but not *A* with *C*—this definition would certainly be rejected.

And thirdly, there is that a priori element in science—as in other human affairs—which constitutes the criteria of the real as opposed to the unreal in experience. An object itself is a uniformity. Failure to behave in certain categorical ways marks it as unreal. Uniformities of the type called "natural law" are the clues to reality and unreality. A mouse which disappears where no hole is, is no real mouse; a landscape which recedes as we approach is but illusion. As the queen remarked in the episode of the wishing-carpet: "If this were real, then it would be a miracle. But miracles do not happen. Therefore I shall wake presently." That the uniformities of natural law are the only reliable criteria of the real is inescapable. But such a criterion is *ipso facto* a priori. No conceivable experience could dictate the alteration of a law so long as failure to obey that law marked the content of experience as unreal.

This is one of the puzzles of empiricism. We deal with experience: what any reality may be which underlies experience, we have to learn. What we desire to discover is natural law, the formulation of those uniformities which obtain amongst the real. But experience as it comes to us contains not only the real but all the content of illusion, dream, hallucination, and mistake. The *given* contains both real and unreal, confusingly intermingled. If we ask for uniformities of this unsorted experience, we shall not find them. Laws which characterize all experience, of real and unreal both, are nonexistent and would in any case be worthless. What we seek are the uniformities of the *real*; but *until we have such laws, we cannot sift experience and segregate the real.*

The obvious solution is that the enrichment of experience, the separation of the real from the illusory or meaningless, and the formulation of natural law all grow up together. If the criteria of the real are a priori, that is not to say that no conceivable character of experience would lead to alteration of them. For example, spirits cannot be photographed. But if photographs of spiritistic phenomena, taken under properly guarded conditions, should become

sufficiently frequent, this a priori dictum would be called in question. What we should do would be to redefine our terms. Whether "spook" was spirit or matter, whether the definition of "spirit" or of "matter" should be changed—all this would constitute one interrelated problem. We should reopen together the question of definition or classification, of criteria for this sort of real, and of natural law. And the solution of one of these would mean the solution of all. Nothing could *force* a redefinition of spirit or of matter. A sufficiently fundamental relation to human bent, to human interests, would guarantee continuance unaltered even in the face of unintelligible and baffling experiences. In such problems, the mind finds itself uncompelled save by its own purposes and needs. I *may* categorize experience as I will; but *what* categorical distinctions will best serve my interests and objectify my own intelligence? What the mixed and troubled experience shall be—that is beyond me. But what I shall do with it—that is my own question, when the character of experience is sufficiently before me. I am coerced only by my own need to understand.

It would indeed be inappropriate to characterize as a priori a law which we are wholly prepared to alter in the light of further experience, even though in an isolated case we should discard as illusory any experience which failed to conform. But the crux of the situation lies in this: beyond such principles as those of logic, which we seem fully prepared to maintain no matter what, there must be further and more particular criteria of the real prior to any investigation of nature whatever. We cannot even interrogate experience without a network of categories and definitive concepts. And we must further be prepared to say what experimental findings will answer what questions, and how. Without tests which represent anterior principle, there is no question which experience could answer at all. Thus the most fundamental laws in any category—or those which we regard as most fundamental— are a priori, even though continued failure to render experience intelligible in such terms might result eventually in the abandonment of that category altogether. Matters so comparatively small as the behaviour of Mercury and of starlight passing the sun's limb may, if there be persistent failure to bring them within the field of previously accepted modes of explanation, result in the abandonment of the independent categories of space and time. But without the definitions, fundamental principles, and tests of the type which constitute such categories, no experience whatever could prove or disprove anything. And to that mind which should find independent space and time absolutely necessary conceptions, no possible experiment could prove the principles of relativity. "There must be some error in the experimental findings, or some law not yet discovered," represents an attitude which can never be rendered impossible. And the only sense in which it could be proved unreasonable would be the pragmatic one of comparison with another method of categorical analysis which more successfully reduced all such experience to order and law.

At the bottom of all science and all knowledge are categories and definitive concepts which represent fundamental habits of thought and deep-lying attitudes which the human mind has taken in the light of its total experience. But a new and wider experience may bring about some alteration of these attitudes, even though by themselves they dictate nothing as to the content of experience, and no experience can conceivably prove them invalid.

Perhaps some will object to this conception on the ground that only such principles should be designated a priori as the human mind *must* maintain, no matter what; that if, for example, it is shown possible to arrive at a consistent doctrine of physics in terms of relativity even by the most arduous reconstruction of our fundamental notions, then the present conceptions are by that fact shown not to be a priori. Such objection is especially likely from those who would conceive the a priori in terms of an absolute mind or an absolutely universal human nature. We should readily agree that a decision by popular approval or a congress of scientists or anything short of such a test as would bring to bear the full weight of human capacity and interest would be ill-considered as having to do with the a priori. But we wish to emphasize two facts: first, that in the field of those conceptions and principles which have altered in

human history, there are those which could neither be proved nor disproved by any experience, but represent the uncompelled initiative of human thought—that without this uncompelled initiative no growth of science, nor any science at all, would be conceivable; and second, that the difference between such conceptions as are, for example, concerned in the decision of relativity versus absolute space and time, and those more permanent attitudes such as are vested in the laws of logic, there is only a difference of degree. The dividing line between the a priori and the a posteriori is that between principles and definitive concepts which *can* be maintained in the face of all experience and those genuinely empirical generalizations which *might* be proven flatly false. The thought which both rationalism and empiricism have missed is that there are principles, representing the initiative of mind, which impose upon experience no limitations whatever, but that such conceptions are still subject to alteration on pragmatic grounds when the expanding boundaries of experience reveal their infelicity as intellectual instruments.

Neither human experience nor the human mind has a character which is universal, fixed, and absolute. "The human mind" does not exist at all save in the sense that all humans are very much alike in fundamental respects, and that the language habit and the enormously important exchange of ideas has greatly increased our likeness in those respects which are here in question. Our categories and definitions are peculiarly social products, reached in the light of experiences which have much in common, and beaten out, like other pathways, by the coincidence of human purposes and the exigencies of human co-operation. Concerning the a priori there need be neither universal agreement nor complete historical continuity. Conceptions, such as those of logic, which are least likely to be affected by the opening of new ranges of experience, represent the most stable of our categories; but none of them is beyond the possibility of alteration.

Mind contributes to experience the element of order, of classification, categories, and definition. Without such, experience would be unintelligible. Our knowledge of the validity of these is simply consciousness of our own fundamental ways of acting and our own intellectual intent. Without this element, knowledge is impossible, and it is here that whatever truths are necessary and independent of experience must be found. But the commerce between our categorical ways of acting, our pragmatic interests, and the particular character of experience is closer than we have realized. No explanation of any one of these can be complete without consideration of the other two.

Pragmatism has sometimes been charged with oscillating between two contrary notions: the one, that experience is "through and through malleable to our purpose"; the other,

that facts are "hard" and uncreated by the mind. We here offer a mediating conception: through all our knowledge runs the element of the a priori, which is indeed malleable to our purpose and responsive to our need. But throughout, there is also that other element of experience which is "hard," "independent," and unalterable to our will.

NOTE

1. Albert Einstein, *Relativity: The Special and General Theory,* trans. R. W. Lawson (New York, 1920), pp. 26–28; italics are the author's.

24 / Roderick M. Chisholm (1916–1999)
THE TRUTHS OF ·REASON

There are also two kinds of truths: those of reasoning and those of fact. The truths of reasoning are necessary, and their opposite is impossible. Those of fact, however, are contingent, and their opposite is possible. When a truth is necessary, we can find the reason by analysis, resolving the truth into simpler ideas and simpler truths until we reach those that are primary.

LEIBNIZ, *Monadology,* 33

I. A TRADITIONAL METAPHYSICAL VIEW

Reason, according to one traditional view, functions as a source of knowledge. This view, when it is clearly articulated, may be seen to involve a number of metaphysical presuppositions and it is, therefore, unacceptable to many contemporary philosophers. But the alternatives to this view, once *they* are clearly articulated, may be seen to be at least problematic and to imply an extreme form of scepticism.

According to this traditional view, there are certain *truths of reason* and some of these truths of reason can be known a priori. These truths pertain to certain abstract or eternal objects—things such as properties, numbers, and propositions or states of affairs, things that would exist even if there weren't any contingent things such as persons and physical objects. To present the traditional view, we will first illustrate such truths and then we will try to explain what is meant by saying that we know some of these truths a priori.

Some of the truths of reason concern what we might call relations of 'inclusion' and 'exclusion' that obtain among various properties.

The relation of *inclusion* among properties

From Roderick M. Chisholm, "The Truths of Reason," In *Theory of Knowledge,* 2d ed., © 1977, pp. 34–61. Reprinted by permission of Prentice-Hall, Inc., Englewood Cliffs, New Jersey.

is illustrated by these facts: The property of being square includes that of being rectangular, and that of being red includes that of being coloured. The relation of *exclusion* is exemplified by these facts: The property of being square excludes that of being circular, and that of being red excludes that of being blue. To say that one property excludes another, therefore, is to say more than that the one fails to include the other. Being red fails to include being heavy, but it does not exclude being heavy; if it excluded being heavy, as it excludes being blue, then nothing could be both red and heavy.[1]

Other examples of such inclusion and exclusion are these: Being both red and square includes being red and excludes being circular; being both red and warm-if-red includes being warm; being both non-warm and warm-if-red excludes being red.

These relations are all such that they hold *necessarily*. And they would hold, therefore, even if there weren't any contingent things.

One can formulate more general truths about the relations of inclusion and exclusion. For example, every property *F* and every property *G* is such that *F*'s excluding *G* includes *G*'s excluding *F; F*'s excluding *G* includes *F*'s including not-*G; F* excludes not-*F,* and includes *F*-or-*G*. And such truths as these are necessary.

States of affairs or propositions are analogous to properties.[2] Like properties, they are related by inclusion and exclusion; for example, "some men being Greeks" includes, and is included by, "some Greeks being men," and excludes "no Greeks being men." States of affairs, like properties, may be compound; for example, "some men being Greek and Plato being Roman"; "Socrates being wise or Xantippe being wise." The conjunctive state of affairs, "Socrates being a man and all men being mortal," includes "Socrates being mortal" and excludes "no men being mortal." Such truths about states of affairs are examples of truths of logic. And such truths, according to the traditional doctrine, are all necessary. They would hold even if there had been no Socrates or Greeks or men.

Other truths of reason are those of mathematics; for example, the truths expressed by "2 and 3 are 5" and "7 and 5 are 12."

2. NOT ALL KNOWLEDGE OF NECESSITY IS A POSTERIORI

When it is said that these truths of reason are known (or are capable of being known) a priori, what is meant may be suggested by contrasting them with what is known a posteriori. A single example may suggest what is intended when it is said that these truths may be known without being known a posteriori.

Corresponding to "Being red excludes being blue," which is a truth about properties, the following general statement is a truth about individual things: "Necessarily, every individual thing, past, present, or future, is such that if it is red then it is not blue." If the latter truth were known a posteriori, then it would be justified by some induction or inductions; our evidence presumably would consist in the fact that a great variety of red things and a great variety of non-blue things have been observed in the past, and that up to now, no red things have been blue. We might thus inductively confirm "Every individual thing, past, present, or future, is such that if it is red then it is not blue." Reflecting upon this conclusion, we may then go on to make still another step. We will proceed to the further conclusion, "Being red excludes being blue," and then deduce, "Necessarily, every individual thing, past, present, or future, is such that if it is red then it is not blue."

Thus, there might be said to be three steps involved in an inductive justification of "Necessarily, being red excludes being blue": (1) the accumulation of instances—"This red thing is not blue," "That blue thing is not red," and so on—along with the summary statement, "No red thing observed up to now has been blue"; (2) the inductive inference from these data to "Every individual thing, past, present, and future, is such that if it is red then it is not blue"; (3) the step from this inductive conclusion to "Being red excludes being blue," or "Necessarily, every individual thing, past, present, or future, is such that if it is red then it is not blue."

Why *not* say that such "truths of reason" are thus known a posteriori?

For one thing, some of these truths pertain

to properties that have never been exemplified. If we take "square,"; "rectangular," and "circular" in the precise way in which these words are usually interpreted in geometry, we must say that nothing is square, rectangular, or circular; things in nature, as Plato said, "fall short" of having such properties.[3] Hence, to justify "Necessarily, being square includes being rectangular and excludes being circular," we cannot even take the first of the three steps illustrated above; there being no squares, we cannot collect instances of squares that are rectangles and squares that are not circles.

For another thing, application of induction would seem to presuppose a knowledge of the "truths of reason." In setting out to confirm an inductive hypothesis, we must be able to recognize what its consequences would be. Ordinarily, to recognize these we must apply deduction; we take the hypothesis along with other things that we know and we see what is then implied. All of this, it would seem, involves apprehension of truths of reason—such truths as may be suggested by "For all states of affairs, p and q, the conjunctive state of affairs, composed of p and of either not-p or q, includes q," and "All As being B excludes some As not being B." Hence, even if we are able to justify some of the 'truths of reason' by inductive procedures, any such justification will presuppose others, and we will be left with some "truths of reason" which we have not justified by means of induction.[4]

And finally, the last of the three steps described above—the step from the inductive generalization "Every individual thing, past, present, and future, is such that if it is red then it is not blue" to "Being red excludes being blue," or "Necessarily, every individual thing, past, present, and future, is such that if it is red then it is not blue"—remains obscure.

How do we reach this final step? What justifies us in saying that *necessarily*, every individual thing, past, present, and future, is such that if it is red then it is not blue? The English philosopher, William Whewell, wrote that the mere accumulation of instances cannot afford the slightest ground for the necessity of a generalization upon those instances. "Experience," he said, can observe and record what has happened; but she cannot find, in any case, or in

any accumulation of cases, any reason for what *must* happen. She may see objects side by side, but she cannot see a reason why they must ever be side by side. She finds certain events to occur in succession; but the succession supplies, in its occurrence, no reasons for its recurrence; she contemplates external objects; but she cannot detect any internal bond, which indissolubly connects the future with the past, the possible with the real. To learn a proposition by experience, and to see it to be necessarily true, are two altogether different processes of thought. . . . If anyone does not clearly comprehend this distinction of necessary and contingent truths, he will not be able to go along with us in our researches into the foundations of human knowledge; nor indeed, to pursue with success any speculation on the subject.[5]

3. INTUITIVE INDUCTION

Plato suggested that in order to acquire a knowledge of necessity, we should turn away from "the twilight of becoming and perishing" and contemplate the world of "the absolute and eternal and immutable."[6] According to Aristotle, however, and to subsequent philosophers in the tradition with which we are here concerned, one way of obtaining the requisite intuition is to consider the particular things of this world.

As a result of perceiving a particular blue thing, or a number of particular blue things, we may come to know what it is for a thing to be blue, and thus, we may be said to know what the property of being blue is. And as a result of perceiving a particular red thing, or a number of particular red things, we may come to know what it is for a thing to be red, and thus, to know what the property of being red is. Then, having this knowledge of what it is to be red and of what it is to be blue, we are able to see that being red excludes being blue, and that this is necessarily so.

Thus, Aristotle tells us that as a result of perceiving Callias and a number of other particular men, we come to see what it is for a thing to have the property of being human. And then, by considering the property of being human, we come to see that being human includes being animal, and that this is necessarily so.[7]

Looking to these examples, we may distinguish four stages:

1. There is the perception of the individual things—in the one case, the perception of the particular red things and blue things, and in the other, the perception of Callias and the other particular men.
2. There is a process of abstraction—we come to see what it is for a thing to be red and for a thing to be blue, and we come to see what it is for a thing to be a man.
3. There is the intuitive apprehension of certain relations holding between properties—in the one case, apprehension of the fact that being red excludes being blue, and in the other, apprehension of the fact that being rational and animal includes being animal.
4. Once we have acquired this intuitive knowledge, then, *ipso facto,* we also know the truth of reason expressed by "Necessarily, everything is such that if it is red then it is not blue" and "Necessarily, everything is such that if it is human then it is animal."

Aristotle called this process 'induction'. But since it differs in essential respects from what subsequently came to be known as "induction," some other term, say, "intuitive induction," may be less misleading.[8]

If we have performed an "intuitive induction" in the manner described, then we may say that by contemplating the relation between properties we are able to know that being red excludes being blue and thus to know that *necessarily,* everything is such that if it is red then it is not blue. And we can say, therefore, that the universal generalization, as well as the proposition about properties, is known a priori. The order of justification thus differs from that of the enumerative induction considered earlier, where one attempts to justify the statement about properties by reference to a generalization about particular things.

There is a superficial resemblance between 'intuitive induction' and "induction by simple enumeration," since in each case, we start with particular instances and then proceed beyond them. Thus, when we make an induction by enumeration, we may proceed from "This *A* is *B*," "That *A* is *B*," and so on, to "In all probability, all *A*s are *B*s," or to "In all probability, the next *A* is *B*." But in an induction by enumeration, the function of the particular instances is to *justify* the conclusion. If we find subsequently that our perceptions of the particular instances were unveridical, say, that the things we took to be *A*s were not *A*s at all, then the inductive argument would lose whatever force it may have had. In an "intuitive induction," however, the particular perceptions are only incidental to the conclusion. This may be seen in the following way.

Let us suppose that the knowledge expressed by the two sentences "Necessarily, being red excludes being blue" and "Necessarily, being human includes being animal" is arrived at by intuitive induction; and let us suppose further that in each case, the process began with the perception of certain particular things. Neither conclusion depends for its *justification* upon the particular perceptions which led to the knowledge concerned. As Duns Scotus put it, the perception of the particular things is only the "occasion" of acquiring the knowledge. If we happen to find our perception was unveridical, this finding will have no bearing upon the result. "If the senses from which these terms were received were all false, or what is more deceptive, if some were false and others true, I still maintain that the intellect would not be deceived about such principles. . . ."[9] If what we take to be Callias is not a man at all, but only a clever imitation of a man, then, if the imitation is clever enough, our deceptive experience will still be an occasion for contemplating the property of being human—the property of being both rational and animal— and thus, for coming to know that being human includes being animal.

Leibniz thus observes: ". . . if I should discover any demonstrative truth, mathematical or other, while dreaming (as might in fact be), it would be just as certain as if I had been awake. This shows us how intelligible truth is independent of the truth of the existence outside of us of sensible and material things."[10]

It may be, indeed, that to perform an intuitive induction—i.e. to "abstract" a certain property, contemplate it, and then see what it includes and excludes—we need only to *think* of some individual thing as having that property. By thinking about a blue thing and a red thing, for example, we may come to see that being blue excludes being red. Thus, Ernst Mach spoke of "experiments in the imagination."[11] And E. Husserl, whose language may have been needlessly Platonic, said, "The Eidos, the *pure essence,* can be exemplified intuitively in the data of experience, data of perception, memory, and so forth, but just as readily *also in the mere data of fancy....*"[12]

According to this traditional account, then, once we have acquired some concepts (once we know, with respect to certain attributes, just *what* it is for something to have those attributes), we will also be in a position to know just *what* it is for a proposition or state of affairs to be necessary—to be necessarily such that it is true or necessarily such that it obtains. Then, by contemplating or reflecting upon certain propositions or states of affairs, we will be able to see that *they* are necessary.

This kind of knowledge has traditionally been called a priori.

4. AXIOMS

Speaking very roughly, we might say that one mark of an a priori proposition is this: once you understand it, you see that it is true. We might call this the traditional conception of the a priori. Thus Leibniz remarks: "You will find in a hundred places that the Scholastics have said that these propositions are evident, *ex terminis,* as soon as the terms are understood...."[13]

If we say an a priori proposition is one such that "once you understand it then you see that it is true," we must take the term "understand" in a somewhat rigid sense. You couldn't be said to "understand" a proposition, in the sense intended, unless you can grasp *what* it is for that proposition to be true. The properties or attributes that the proposition implies—those that would be instantiated if the proposition were true—must be properties or attributes that you can grasp in the sense that we have tried to

explicate. To "understand" a proposition, in the sense intended, then, it is not enough merely to be able to say what *sentence* in your language happens to express that proposition. The proposition must be one that you have contemplated and reflected upon.

One cannot *accept* a proposition, in the sense in which we have been using the word "accept," unless one also *understands* that proposition. We might say, therefore, that an a priori proposition is one such that, if you accept it, then it becomes certain for you. (For if you accept it, then you understand it, and as soon as you understand it, it becomes certain for you.) This account of the a priori, however, would be somewhat broad. We know some a priori propositions on the basis of others and these propositions are not themselves such that, once they are understood, then they are certain.

But let us begin by trying to characterize more precisely those a priori propositions which are not known on the basis of any *other* propositions.

Leibniz said that these propositions are the "first lights." He wrote: "The immediate apperception of our existence and of our thoughts furnishes us with the first truths a posteriori, or of fact, i.e. the *first experiences,* as the identical propositions contain the first truths a priori, or of reason, i.e. *the first lights.* Both are incapable of proof, and may be called *immediate....*"[14]

The traditional term for those a prior propositions which are "incapable of proof" is *axiom.* Thus Frege wrote: "Since the time of antiquity an axiom has been taken to be a thought whose truth is known without being susceptible to demonstration by a logical chain of reasoning."[15] In *one* sense, of course, every true proposition *h* is capable of proof, for there will always be other true propositions from which we can derive *h* by means of some principle of logic. What did Leibniz and Frege mean, then, when they said that an axiom is "incapable of proof"?

The answer is suggested by Aristotle. An axiom, or "basic truth," he said, is a proposition "which has no other proposition prior to it"; there is no proposition which is "better known" than it is.[16] We could say that if one proposition is "better known" than another, then accepting the one proposition is more reasonable than accepting the other. Hence, if an axiomatic proposition is one such that no other proposition is better known than it is, then it is one that is certain. (Let us say that a proposition *h* is *certain* for a person *S*, provided that *h* is evident for *S* and provided that there is no other proposition *i* which is such that it is *more* reasonable for *S* to accept *i* than it is for him to accept *h*.) Hence Aristotle said that an axiom is a "primary premiss." Its ground does not lie in the fact that it is seen to follow from *other* propositions. Therefore we cannot prove such a proposition by making use of any premisses that are "better known" than it is. (By "a proof," then, Aristotle, Leibniz, and Frege meant more than "a valid derivation from premisses that are true.")

Let us now try to say what it is for a proposition or state of affairs to be an *axiom:*

D3.1 *h* is an *axiom* = Df *h* is necessarily such that (i) it is true and (ii) for every *S*, if *S* accepts *h*, then *h* is certain for *S*.

The following propositions among countless others may be said to be axioms in our present sense of the term:

If some men are Greeks, then some Greeks are men.
If Jones is ill and Smith is away, then Jones is ill.
The sum of 5 and 3 is 8.
The product of 4 and 2 is 8.

For most of us, i.e. for those of us who really *do* consider them, they may be said to be *axiomatic* in the following sense:

D3.2 *h* is *axiomatic* for *S* = Df (i) *h* is an axiom and (ii) *S* accepts *h*.

We may assume that any conjunction of axioms is itself an axiom. But it does not follow from this assumption that any conjunction of propositions which are axiomatic for a subject *S* is itself axiomatic for *S*. If two propositions are axiomatic for *S* and if *S* does not accept their conjunction, then the conjunction is not axiomatic for *S*. (Failure to accept their conjunction need not be a sign that *S* is unreason-

able. It may be a sign merely that the conjunction is too complex an object for *S* to grasp.)

We have suggested that our knowledge of what is axiomatic is a subspecies of our a priori knowledge, that is to say, some of the things we know a priori are *not* axiomatic in the present sense. They are a priori but they are not what Aristotle called "primary premisses."

What would be an example of a proposition that is a priori for *S* but not axiomatic for *S*? Consider the last two axioms on our list above; i.e.

The sum of 5 and 3 is 8.
The product of 4 and 2 is 8.

Let us suppose that their conjunction is also an axiom and that *S* accepts this conjunction; therefore the conjunction is axiomatic for *S*. Let us suppose further that the following proposition is axiomatic for *S*.

If the sum of 5 and 3 is 8 and the product of 4 and 2 is 8, then the sum of 5 and 3 is the product of 4 and 2.

We will say that, if, in such a case, *S* accepts the proposition

The sum of 5 and 3 is the product of 4 and 2

then that proposition is a priori for *S*. Yet the proposition may not be one which is such that it is certain for anyone who accepts it. It may be that one can consider *that* proposition without thereby seeing that it is true.

There are various ways in which we might now attempt to characterize this broader concept of the a priori. Thus we might say: "You know a proposition a priori provided you accept it and it is implied by propositions that are axiomatic for you." But this would imply that *any* necessary proposition that you happen to accept is one that you know a priori to be true. (Any necessary proposition *h* is implied by an axiomatic proposition *e*. Indeed any necessary proposition *h* is implied by *any* proposition *e*— whether or not *e* is axiomatic and whether or not *e* is true or false. For if *h* is necessary, then, it is necessarily true that, for any proposition *e*, either *e* is false or *h* is true. And to say "*e* implies h" is to say it is necessarily true that either e is false or h is true.) *Some* of the necessary propositions that we accept may *not* be propositions that we know a priori. They may be such that, if we know them, we know them a posteriori—on the basis of authority. Or they may be such that we cannot be said to know them at all.

To capture the broader concept of the a priori, we might say that a proposition is known a priori provided it is axiomatic that the proposition follows from something that is axiomatic. But let us say, more carefully:

D3.3 h is known a priori by $S = $ Df There is an e such that (i) e is axiomatic for S, (ii) the proposition, e implies h, is axiomatic for S, and (iii) S accepts h.

We may add that a person knows a proposition a posteriori if he knows the proposition but doesn't know it a priori.[17]

We may assume that what is thus known a priori is evident. But the a priori, unlike the axiomatic, need not be certain. This accords with St Thomas's observation that "those who have knowledge of the principles [i.e. the axioms] have a more certain knowledge than the knowledge which is through demonstration."[18]

But is this account too restrictive? What if S derives a proposition from a set of axioms, not by means of one or two simple steps, but as a result of a complex proof, involving a series of interrelated steps? If the proof is formally valid, then shouldn't we say that S knows the proposition a priori?

I think that the answer is no. Complex proofs or demonstrations, as John Locke pointed out, have a certain limitation. They take time. The result is that the "evident lustre" of the early steps may be lost by the time we reach the conclusion: "In long deductions, and the use of many proofs, the memory does not always so readily retain." Therefore, he said, demonstrative knowledge "is more imperfect than intuitive knowledge."[19] Descartes also noted that memory is essential to demonstrative knowledge. He remarks in *Rules for the Direction of the Mind* that, if we can *remember* having deduced a certain conclusion step by step form a set of premises that are "known

by intuition," then even though we may not now recall each of the particular steps, we are justified in saying that the conclusion is "known by deduction."[20] But if, in the course of a demonstration, we must rely upon memory at various stages, thus using as premises contingent propositions about what we happen to remember, then, although we might be said to have "demonstrative knowledge" of our conclusion, in a somewhat broad sense of the expression "demonstrative knowledge," we cannot be said to have an a priori demonstration of the conclusion.

Of course, we may make mistakes in attempting to carry out a proof, just as we may make mistakes in doing simple arithmetic. And one might well ask: How can this be, if the propositions we are concerned with are known a priori? Sometimes, as the quotation from Locke suggests, there has been a slip of memory. Perhaps we are mistaken about just *what* the propositions are that we proved at an earlier step—just as, in doing arithmetic, we may mistakenly think we have carried the 2, or we may pass over some figure having thought that we included it, or we may inadvertently include something twice. And there are also occasions when we may just seem to get the a priori proposition wrong. In my haste I say to myself, "9 and 6 are 13," and then the result will come out wrong. But when I do this, I am not really considering the proposition that 9 and 6 are 13. I may just be considering the formula, "9 and 6 are 13," which sounds right at the time, and not considering at all the proposition that that formula is used to express.

We have said what it is for a proposition to be known a priori by a given subject. But we should note, finally, that propositions are sometimes said to be a priori even though they may not be known by anyone at all. Thus Kant held that "mathematical propositions, strictly so called, are always judgements a priori."[21] In saying this, he did not mean to be saying merely that mathematical propositions are necessarily true; he was saying something about their epistemic status and something about the way in which they could be known. Yet he could not have been saying that all mathematical propositions are known or even believed, by someone or other, to be true; for there are propositions of mathematics that no one knows to be true; and there are propositions of mathematics that no one has ever considered. What would it be, then, to say that a proposition might be a priori even though it has not been considered by anyone? I think the answer can only be that the proposition is one that *could* be known a priori. In other words;

> D3.4 *h* is a priori = Df It is possible that there is someone for whom *h* is a priori.

This definition allows us to say that a proposition may be "objectively a priori"—"objectively" in that it is a priori whether or not anyone knows it a priori.

Our definitions are in the spirit of several familiar dicta concerning the a priori. Thus, we may say, as Kant did, that necessity is a mark of the a priori—provided we mean by this that if a proposition is a priori then it is necessary.[22] For our definitions assure us that whatever is a priori is necessarily true.

The definitions also enable us to say, as St. Thomas did, that these propositions are "manifest through themselves."[23] For an axiomatic proposition is one such that, once it is reflected upon or considered, then it is certain. What a given person knows a priori may not *itself* be such that, once it is considered, it is certain. But our definition enables us to say that, if a proposition is one that is a priori for you, then you can see that it follows from a proposition that is axiomatic.

Kant said that our a priori knowledge, like all other knowledge, "begins with experience" but that, unlike our a posteriori knowledge, it does not "arise out of experience."[24] A priori knowledge may be said to "begin with experience" in the following sense. There is no a priori knowledge until some proposition is in fact contemplated and understood. Moreover, the acceptance of a proposition that is axiomatic is sufficient to make that proposition an axiom for whoever accepts it. But a priori knowledge does not "arise out of experience." For, if a proposition is axiomatic or a priori for us, then we have all the evidence we need to see that it is true. Understanding is enough; it is not necessary to make any further enquiry.

What Leibniz called "first truths a posteriori" coincide with what we have called the *directly evident*. And his "first truths a priori" coincide with what we have called the *axiomatic*. If we chose, we might say that both sets of truths are directly evident—in which case, our account of the directly evident in Chapter 2 of *Theory of Knowledge* could be said to be an account of what is *directly evident* a posteriori, and our account of what is axiomatic could be said to be an account of what is *directly evident* a priori.[25]

5. A PRIORI AND A POSTERIORI

Kant had said, as we have noted, that "necessity is a mark of the a priori." We may accept Kant's dictum, if we take it to mean that what is known a priori is necessary.

But is it possible to know a necessary proposition to be true and not to know this a priori? In other words, can we know some necessary propositions a posteriori?

A possible example of a proposition that is known a posteriori and is yet necessary might be a logical theorem which one accepts on the ground that reputable logicians assert it to be true. Whether there are in fact any such propositions depends upon two things, each of them somewhat problematic.

The first is that such a proposition cannot be said to be *known* to be true unless such testimonial evidence is sufficient for knowledge. And this is a question we cannot discuss in the present essay.[26]

The second is that such a proposition cannot be said to be known to be true unless it is one that the man *accepts*. But when a man, as we say, accepts a theorem on the basis of authority and not on the basis of demonstration, is it the theorem *itself* that he accepts or is it what Brentano calls a "surrogate" for the theorem?[27] If a man reads a logical text, finds there a formula which expresses a certain logical principle, and then, knowing that the author is reputable, concludes that the formula is true, it may well be that the man does *not* accept the logical principle. What he accepts is, rather, the contingent proposition to the effect that a certain formula in a book expresses a logical principle that is true.

But if we waive these difficulties, then perhaps we may say that there is an analytic a posteriori—or at least that some of the logical truths that we know are such that we know them only a posteriori.[28]

But even if some of the things we know a posteriori are logically true, there is at least this additional epistemic relation holding between the necessary and the a priori:

If a man knows—or someone once knew— a posteriori that a certain necessary proposition is true, then *someone* knows a priori that some necessary proposition is true. If the first man bases his knowledge on the testimony of authority, and if this authority in turn bases his knowledge upon the testimony of some other authority, then sooner or later there will be an "ultimate authority" who knows some proposition a priori.

6. SCEPTICISM WITH RESPECT TO THE A PRIORI

Let us now consider a sceptical objection to what we have been saying.

"You have said what it is for a proposition to be axiomatic for a person and you have given examples of propositions which, you say, are axiomatic for you and presumably for others. But how do you know that those propositions are axiomatic? How do you know that they satisfy the terms of your definitions?

"If you really do know that they are axiomatic, then you must have some *general principle* by means of which you can apply your definitions. There must be something about your experience that guarantees these propositions for you and you must *know* that it guarantees them. But what could the principle be?

"The most you can say, surely, is that such propositions just *seem* to be true, or that when you reflect on them you find you cannot doubt them and that you cannot help but accept them. But, as the history of science makes clear, such facts as these provide no guarantee that the propositions in question are true. Notoriously, there have been ever so many false propositions which reasonable people have found they couldn't doubt. And some of these may well

have been taken as axiomatic. Consider the logical paradoxes, for example. People found they couldn't help but believe certain propositions, and as a result they became entangled in contradictions."

The objection may be summarized as follows:

1. You cannot know that a given proposition is axiomatic for you unless the proposition is one such that, when you contemplate it, you have a kind of experience—say, a strong feeling of conviction—that provides you with a guarantee that the proposition is true. But

2. there is no experience which will provide such a guarantee. Therefore

3. you cannot really know, with respect to any proposition that it is one that is axiomatic.

Is this a valid argument? The conclusion certainly follows for the premises. And, knowing the history of human error, we can hardly question the second of the two premises. But what of the first premise? If we cannot find any reason to accept the first premise, then we do not need to accept the conclusion. How, then, would the sceptic defend his first premiss?

There is a certain more general principle to which the sceptic might appeal in the attempt to defend the first premiss. I will call this principle the *generalizability thesis* and formulate it as follows. "You cannot *know* that any given proposition *p* is true unless you also know two other things. The first of these things will be a certain more *general* proposition *q; q* will not imply *p* but it will specify the conditions under which propositions of a certain type are true. And the second thing will be a proposition *r*, which enables you to *apply* this general proposition to *p*. In other words, *r* will be a proposition to the effect that the first proposition *p* satisfies the conditions specified in the second proposition *q*."

But if the generalizability thesis is true, no one knows anything. Consider the application of the thesis to a single proposition *p*. According to the thesis, if we know *p*, then we know two further propositions—a general proposition *q* and a proposition *r* that applies *q* to *p*.

Applying the generalizability thesis to each of the two propositions, q and r, we obtain four more propositions; applying it to each of them, we obtain eight more propositions; . . . and so on *ad indefinitum*. The generalizability thesis implies, therefore, that we cannot know any proposition to be true unless we know all the members of such an infinite hierarchy of propositions. And therefore it implies that we cannot know any proposition to be true.

The sceptic may reply: "But in *objecting* to my general principle, you are presupposing that we *do* know something. And this begs the question." The proper rejoinder is: "But in *affirming* your general principle, you are presupposing that we *don't* know anything. And *that* begs the question."

The general reply to a scepticism that addresses itself to an entire area of knowledge can only be this: we do have the knowledge in question, and therefore, any philosophical theory implying that we do not is false. This way of looking at the matter may seem especially plausible in the present instance. It is tempting to say of scepticism, with respect to the truths of reasons, what Leonard Nelson said of scepticism, with respect to the truths of mathematics. The advocate of such a scepticism, Nelson said, has invited us to "sacrifice the clearest and most lucid knowledge that we possess—indeed, the *only* knowledge that is clear and lucid *per se*. I prefer to strike the opposite course. If a philosophy, no matter how attractive or plausible or ingenious it may be, brings me into conflict with mathematics, I conclude that not mathematics but my philosophy is on the wrong track."[29] There is certainly no *better* ground for scepticism with respect to our knowledge of the truths of reason than there is for scepticism with respect to our knowledge of physical things.[30]

And so what of the sceptic's question, "How do you know that the proposition that 2 and 4 are 6 is one that is axiomatic?" Let us recall what we said in connection with his question about self-presenting states.[31] The question was: "How do you know that seeming to have a headache is a self-presenting state?" In dealing with that question, we avoided falling into the sceptic's trap. We said that the only possible answer to such a question is that we *do*

know that seeming to have a headache is a self-presenting state. We should follow a similar course in the present case.

The sceptic may not be satisfied with this move and the result will be an impasse that is typical of philosophy and, in particular, of the theory of knowledge.

7. "PSYCHOLOGISM"

When the sceptic and the dogmatist thus fail to reach an agreement with respect to a given area of knowledge, it is well to ask whether there may not be a misunderstanding with respect to the propositions constituting the area of knowledge. I have said that the propositions in question are concerned with certain abstract entities or eternal objects, such as properties, numbers, and propositions or states of affairs. Is it possible to interpret them in another way?

Many attempts have been made to provide such a subject-matter.

Of the attempts that have been made to provide such an interpretation, the only ones worthy of consideration are, first, the view that came to be known in the nineteenth century as "psychologism," and second, its contemporary counterpart, which we might call "linguisticism." Much of what can be said in criticism of the one can also be said, *mutatis mutandis*, in criticism of the other.

Theodore Lipps wrote in 1880 that "logic is either a physics of thinking or it is nothing at all" and he tried to show that the truths of logic are, in fact, truths about the ways in which people think.[32] This is the view that was called "psychologism" and it was applied generally to the subject-matter of the truths of reason.

A psychologistic interpretation of "Necessarily, being red excludes being blue" might be: "Everyone is so constituted psychologically that if he thinks of a thing as being red, then he cannot also then think of it as being blue." And a psychologistic interpretation of the logical truth "For any propositions p and q, if p is true and p implies q, then q is true" might be: "Everyone is so constituted psychologically that if he believes that p is true, and if he believes that p implies q, then he cannot help but believe that q is true."

But obviously, these psychological sentences do not at all convey what is intended by the sentences they are supposed to translate. The psychological sentences are empirical generalizations about the ways in which people think, and as such, they can be supported only by extensive psychological investigation. Thus, Gottlob Frege said, in connection with the psychologistic interpretation of mathematics: "It would be strange if the most exact of all the sciences had to seek support from psychology, which is still feeling its way none too surely."[33] And being empirical generalizations, the psychological sentences are probable at best and are at the mercy of contrary instances. The existence somewhere of one unreasonable individual—one man who believed that some things are both red and blue, or one man who believed that a certain proposition p is true and also that p implies q, and who yet refused to believe that q is true—would be sufficient to ensure that the psychological sentence is false. And we know, all too well, that there are such men. Their existence, however, has no bearing upon the truths expressed by "Necessarily, being red excludes being blue" and "Necessarily, for any propositions p and q, if p is true and if p implies q, then q is true."

In the face of such difficulties, the proponent of psychologism is likely to modify his view. He will say of sentences expressing the laws of logic and the other truths of reason, that they really express *rules of thought*, and that they are not descriptive sentences telling us how people actually do think. But to see the hopelessness of this approach, we have only to consider the possible ways of interpreting the sentence, "The laws of logic are rules of thought."

1. One interpretation would be: "The laws of logic are ethical truths pertaining to our duties and obligations with respect to thinking." In this case, the problem of our knowledge of the laws of logic is transferred to the (more difficult) problem of our knowledge of the truths (if any) of ethics.

2. "The laws of logic are imperatives commanding us to think in certain ways—and imperatives are neither true nor false." This way of looking at the matter leaves us with the problem of distinguishing between valid and invalid imperatives. For there is a distinction between "Do not believe, with respect to any particular thing, both that it is red and that it is blue," and "Do not believe, with respect to any particular thing, that that thing is either red or not red." The former imperative, surely, is correct or valid, and the latter, incorrect or invalid. If we are not to fall back into scepticism, we must also say that the former is known to be valid and the latter is known to be invalid. Moreover, it is not possible to construe all of the statements of logic as imperatives. For the logician can also tell us non-imperatively such things as: If you believe that p, and if you believe that p implies q, and if you conform to the imperative, *modus ponens,* then you will also believe that q. This statement is a necessary truth. (A manual of chess, similarly, may give us certain rules in the form of imperatives: "Move the king only one square at a time." And possibly these imperatives are neither valid nor invalid. But whether or not they are valid, the chess manual will also contain true indicative sentences—sentences which are not themselves imperatives but which tell us what will happen when, in accordance with the imperatives that the manual lays down, we move the pieces into various positions. 'It is impossible, if white is in such and such a position, for black to win in less than seven moves.' And these statements are also necessary truths.)

3. "The laws of logic tell us which ways of believing will lead to truth and which will lead to falsehood." According to this interpretation, our two examples might be thought of as telling us respectively: "A necessary condition of avoiding false beliefs is to refrain from believing, with respect to any particular thing, both that that thing is red and also that it is blue," and "A necessary condition of avoiding false beliefs is to refrain from believing, at one and the same time, with respect to any proposition p and q, that p is true, that p implies q, and that q is false.' To see that this way of formulating psychologism leaves us with our problem, let us compare it with a similar psychologistic interpretation of some other subject-matter, say, astronomy. We may say, if we like, that what the statement "There are nine planets" really tells us is that if we wish to avoid error with respect to the number of planets, it is essential to refrain from believing that there are not nine

planets; it also tells us that if we wish to arrive at the truth about the number of planets, it is essential to believe that there *are* nine planets. It is not likely that in so spinning out what is conveyed by "There are nine planets," we can throw any light upon what the astronomer thinks he knows. In any case, our problem reappears when we compare our new versions of the statements of logic with those of the statements of astronomy. The former, but not the latter, can be prefixed by, "It is necessary that," and unless we give in to scepticism (which it was the point of psychologism to avoid), we must say that the result of such a prefixing is also a statement we can know to be true.[34]

8. "LINGUISTICISM"

A popular conception of the truths of reason at the present time is the linguistic analogue of psychologism. Versions of "linguisticism" may be obtained merely by altering our exposition of psychologism. We may replace the references to ways in which people *think* by references to ways in which they *use language*, replace the references to what people *believe* by references to what they *write* or *say*, replace "avoiding false belief" by "avoiding absurdity," and replace "rules of thought" by "rules of language." The result could then be criticized substantially, *mutatis mutandis*, as before.

Some of the versions of linguisticism, however, are less straightforward. It is often said, for example, that the sentences formulating the truths of logic are "true in virtue of the rules of language" and hence, that they are "true in virtue of the way in which we use words."[35] What could this possibly mean?

The two English sentences, "Being red excludes being blue" and "Being rational and animal includes being animal," could plausibly be said to "owe their truth," in part, to the way in which we use words. If we used "being blue" to refer to the property of being heavy, and not to that of being blue, then the first sentence (provided the other words in it had their present use) would be false instead of true. And if

we used the word "and" to express the relation of disjunction instead of conjunction, then the second sentence (again, provided that the other words in it had their present use) would also be false instead of true. But as W. V. Quine has reminded us, "even so factual a sentence as 'Brutus killed Caesar' owes its truth not only to the killing but equally to our using the component words as we do."[36] Had "killed," for example, been given the use that "was survived by" happens to have, then, other things being the same, "Brutus killed Caesar" would be false instead of true.

It might be suggested, therefore, that the truths of logic and other truths of reason stand in this peculiar relationship to language: they are true "solely in virtue of the rules of our language," or "solely in virtue of the ways in which we use words." But if we take the phrase "solely in virtue of" in the way in which it would naturally be taken, then the suggestion is obviously false.

To say of a sentence that it is true *solely* in virtue of the ways in which we use words, or that it is true *solely* in virtue of the rules of our language, would be to say that the only condition that needs to obtain in order for the sentence to be true is that we use words in certain ways or that there be certain rules pertaining to the way in which words are to be used. But let us consider what conditions must obtain if the English sentence "Being red excludes being blue" is to be true. One such condition is indicated by the following sentence which we may call *T*:

> The English sentence "Being blue excludes being red" is true if, and only if, being blue excludes being red.

Clearly, the final part of *T*, the part following the second "if," formulates a necessary condition for the truth of the English sentence "Being red excludes being blue"; but it refers to a relationship among properties and not to rules of language or ways in which we use words (to suppose otherwise would be to make the mistake, once again, of confusing use and mention in language). Hence, we cannot say that the only conditions that need to obtain in order for "Being red excludes being blue" to be true is that we use words in certain ways or that there be certain rules pertaining to the ways in which words are to be used; and therefore, the sentence cannot be said to be true solely in virtue of the ways in which we use words.

9. ANALYSING THE PREDICATE OUT OF THE SUBJECT

The terms "analytic" and "synthetic" were introduced by Kant in order to contrast two types of categorical judgement. It will not be inaccurate to interpret "judgement," in Kant's sense, to mean the same as what we mean by "proposition." The terms "analytic" and "synthetic" are used in much of contemporary philosophy to refer instead to the types of *sentence* that express the types of judgement to which Kant referred. And perhaps Kant's view is best expressed by reference to sentences: an analytic *judgement* or *proposition* is one that is expressible in a certain type of *sentence*. But what type of sentence?

An analytic judgement, according to Kant, is a judgement in which "the predicate adds nothing to the concept of the subject." If I judge that all squares are rectangles, then, in Kant's terminology, the concept of the subject of my judgement is the property of being square, and the concept of the predicate is the property of being rectangular. Kant uses the term "analytic," since, he says, the concept of the predicate helps to "break up the concept of the subject into those constituent concepts that have all along been thought in it."[37] Since being square is the conjunctive property of being equilateral and rectangular, the predicate of the judgement expressed by "All squares are rectangular" may be said to "analyse out" what is contained in the subject. An analytic judgement, then, may be expressed in the form of an explicit redundancy: e.g. "Everything is such that if it is both equilateral and rectangular then it is rectangular." To deny such an explicit redundancy would be to affirm a *contradictio in adjecto*, for it would be to judge that there are things which both have and do not have a certain property—in the present instance, that there is something that both is and

is not rectangular. Hence, Kant said that "the common principle of all analytic judgements is the law of contradiction."[38]

What might it mean to say, with respect to a sentence of the form "Everything that is an *S* is a *P*" that the predicate-term can be analysed out of the subject-term?

One thing that might be meant is this: that what the sentence expresses can *also* be expressed in a sentence in which the predicate-term is the same as the subject-term. Thus the predicate of "Everything that is a man is a rational animal" could be said to be analysed out of the subject, since what the sentence expresses can also be expressed by saying "Everything that is a rational animal is a rational animal." But not all of the traditional examples of propositions that are analytic may be expressed in sentences wherein the subject-term and the predicate-term are the same.

Consider the sentence:

1. All squares are rectangles.

What this sentence expresses may also be put as:

2. Everything that is an equilateral thing and a rectangle is a rectangle.

Sentence (2) provides us with a paradigm case of a sentence in which the predicate-term ("a rectangle") may be said to be analysed out of the subject-term ("an equilateral thing and a rectangle").

We may note that, in sentence (2), the predicate-term is *also* part of the subject-term. Shall we say, then, that the predicate of a sentence is *analysed out* of the subject if the predicate is the same as the subject or if the subject is a conjunction of two terms one of which is the predicate? This definition would be somewhat broad, for it would require us to say that in the following sentence the predicate is analysed out of the subject:

3. Everything that is a square and a rectangle is a rectangle.

But (3) does not exhibit the type of analysis that is to be found in (2). Thus in (3) the subject-term ("a square and a rectangle") is re-dundant (given "a square" in the subject we don't *need* to add "a rectangle"), but in (2) the subject-term ("an equilateral thing and a rectangle") is not redundant.

We could say, somewhat more exactly, that a predicate-term is *analysed out* of a subject-term provided the subject-term is such that either it is itself the predicate-term or it is a conjunction of independent terms one of which is the predicate-term. But what is it for two terms to be "independent"?

We may say, of certain pairs of terms in a given language, that one of the terms *logically implies* the other in that language. Thus in English "square" logically implies "rectangle," and "red thing" logically implies "coloured thing." These terms may be said to be such that in English they are *true of*, or *apply to*, certain things. And the English language is necessarily such that "rectangle" applies to everything that "square" applies to, and it is also necessarily such that "coloured thing" applies to everything that "red" applies to.[39] To say, then, "*T logically implies R* in language *L*" is to say this: *L* is necessarily such that *R* applies in *L* to all those things to which *T* applies in *L*.

Now we may say what it is for two terms to be *independent*—what it is for two terms to be logically independent of each other in a given language.

Two terms are *logically independent* of each other in a given language provided only that the terms and their negations are such that no one of them logically implies the other in that language.[40] Thus "red thing" and "square" are logically independent in English, for the four terms, "red thing," "square," "non-red thing," and "non-square" are such that no one of them implies the other in English.

We can now say, somewhat more exactly, what it is for the predicate-term *P*, of a sentence in a given language *L*, to be *analysed out* of the subject-term *S*. First of all, the sentence will be an "all *S* is *P*" sentence; that is to say, the sentence will be necessarily such that it is true in *L*, if and only if, for every *x*, if *S* applies to *x* in *L*, then *P* applies to *x* in *L*. And second, either the subject-term *S* is itself the same as *P* or it is a conjunction of logically independent terms one of which is *P*.

Finally, we may define the Kantian sense of "analytic proposition" as follows: A proposition is analytic provided only it may be expressed in a sentence in which the predicate-term is analysed out of the subject-term.

To see how the definitions may be applied, consider the following sentences, each of which may be said to express an analytic proposition, in the traditional sense of the term "analytic":

> All fathers are parents.
> No bachelors are married.
> All dogs are dogs or cats.

What these three sentences express in English may also be put as follows:

> Everything that is a male and a parent is a parent.
> Everything that is a male human and a thing that is unmarried is a thing that is unmarried.
> Everything that is (i) a dog or a cat and (ii) a dog or a non-cat is a dog or a cat.

The last three sentences are sentences in which the predicate is analysed out of the subject. And therefore the propositions expressed by the first sentences are all analytic.[41]

10. THE SYNTHETIC A PRIORI

Kant raised the question: Is there a synthetic a priori? Are there synthetic propositions that we know a priori to be true?

If we construe "analytic proposition" in the way in which we have tried to spell out (by reference to the predicate of a sentence being "analysed out of" the subject), and if, as many philosophers do, we take "synthetic proposition" to mean the same as "proposition which is not analytic," then Kant's question may not be particularly interesting. For, it would seem, there are many propositions which we know a priori and which are not analytic, in this restricted sense of the term "analytic." Among them are such propositions as:

> If there are more than 7 dogs, then there are more than 5 dogs.

If there are either dogs or cows but no cows, then there are dogs.

If all men are mortal and Socrates is a man, then Socrates is mortal.

But when philosophers ask whether there are synthetic propositions that we know a priori to be true, they are not usually thinking of such propositions as these. They are thinking rather of propositions which can be expressed naturally in English in the form "All *S* are *P*." Given what we have said about the nature of analytic propositions, we may put the question, "Is there a synthetic a priori?," somewhat more exactly as follows:

Are there any propositions which are such that: (i) they are known by us a priori; (ii) they can be expressed in English in the form "Everything which is *S* is *P*"; and yet (iii) they are *not* such that in English their predicate-terms can be analysed out of their subject-terms?

Let us consider, then, certain possible examples of "the synthetic a priori," so conceived.

1. One important candidate for the synthetic a priori is the knowledge that might be expressed by saying either "Being square includes being a shape" or "Necessarily, everything that is square is a thing that has a shape." The sentence "Everything that is square is a thing that has a shape" recalls our paradigmatic "Everything that is square is a rectangle." In the case of the latter sentence, we were able to "analyse the predicate out of the subject": We replaced the subject-term "square" with a conjunctive term, "equilateral thing and rectangle," and were thus able to express our proposition in the form:

Everything that is an *S* and a *P* is a *P*

where the terms replacing "*S*" and "*P*" are such that neither is implied by the other or by the negation of the other. But can we do this with "Everything that is square has a shape"?

The problem is to fill in the blank in the following sentence:

Everything that is a ___ and a thing that has a shape is a thing that has a shape

in the appropriate way. This means we should find a term such that: (i) the resulting sentence

will express what is expressed by "Everything that is square has a shape"; (ii) the term will neither imply nor be implied by "thing that has a shape"; and (iii) the negation of our term will neither imply nor be implied by "thing that has a shape." With what term, then, can we fill the blank?

We might try "either a square or a thing that does not have shape," thus obtaining "Everything that is (i) either a square or a thing that does not have a shape and (ii) a thing that has a shape is a thing that has a shape." But the sentence thus obtained is not one in which the predicate is analysed out of the subject. The two terms making up the subject, namely (i) "either a square or a thing that does not have a shape" and (ii) "a thing that has a shape," are such that, in our language, any negation of the second logically implies the first (i.e. "not such as to be a thing that has a shape" logically implies "either a square or a thing that does not have a shape"). We do not have a sentence, therefore, in which the predicate can be said to be analysed out of the subject; for the two terms making up the subject are not logically independent in our language.

What if we fill in the blank by "square," thus obtaining "Everything that is a square and a thing that has a shape is a thing that has a shape"? This will not help us, for the two terms making up the subject—"square" and "a thing that has a shape"—are such that, in our language, the first logically implies the second; hence they are not logically independent of each other; and therefore the sentence is not one in which the predicate is analysed out of the subject. And if we drop the second term from the subject, as we can without any loss, we will be back where we started.

And so we have not found a way of showing that "Everything that is square has a shape" is analytic. But the sentence expresses what we know a priori to be true. And therefore, it would seem, there is at last some presumption in favour of the proposition that there is a synthetic a priori.

There are indefinitely many other propositions presenting essentially the same difficulties as "Everything that is square has a shape." Examples are: "Everything red is coloured"; "Everyone who hears something in C-sharp minor hears a sound." The sentences express what is known a priori, but no one has been able to show that they are analytic.[42]

It has been suggested that the sentences giving rise to the problem of the synthetic a priori are really "postulates about the meanings of words," and therefore, that they do not express what is synthetic a priori. But if the suggestion is intended literally, then it would seem to betray the confusion between use and mention that we encountered earlier. A postulate about the meaning of the word "red," for example, or a sentence expressing such a postulate, would presumably mention the word "red." It might read, "The word 'red' may be taken to refer to a certain colour," or perhaps, "Let the word 'red' be taken to refer to a certain colour." But "Everything that is red is coloured," although it uses the words "red" and "coloured," doesn't mention them at all. Thus, there would seem to be no clear sense in which it could be said really to be a "meaning postulate" or to refer in any way to words and how they are used.

2. What Leibniz called the "disparates" furnish us with a second candidate for the synthetic a priori. These are closely related to the type of sentence just considered, but involve problems that are essentially different. An example of a sentence concerned with disparates would be our earlier "Being red excludes being blue" or (alternatively put) "Nothing that is red is blue."[43] Philosophers have devoted considerable ingenuity to trying to show that "Nothing that is red is blue" can be expressed as a sentence that is analytic, but so far as I have been able to determine, all of these attempts have been unsuccessful. Again, it is recommended that the reader try to re-express "Nothing that is red is blue" in such a way that the predicate may be "analysed out" of the subject in the sense we have described above.

3. It has also been held, not without plausibility, that certain ethical sentences express what is synthetic a priori. Thus, Leibniz, writing on what he called the "supersensible element" in knowledge, said: ". . . but to return to *necessary truths*, it is generally true that we know them only by this natural light, and not at all by the experience of the senses. For the senses can very well make known, in some sort, what is, but they cannot make known

what *ought to be* or what could not be otherwise."[44] Or consider the sentence, "All pleasures, as such, are intrinsically good, or good in themselves, whenever and wherever they may occur." If this sentence expresses something that is known to be true, then what it expresses must be synthetic a priori. To avoid this conclusion, some philosophers deny that sentences about what is intrinsically good, or good in itself, *can* be known to be true.[45]

II. AN UNTENABLE DUALISM?

But many philosophers now believe that the distinction between the analytic and the synthetic has been shown to be untenable; we should consider what reasons there might be for such a belief. Ordinarily, it is defended by reference to the following facts. (1) In drawing a distinction between analytic and synthetic sentences, one must speak of *necessity*, as we have done, or employ concepts, e.g. that of *synonymy*, that can be explicated only by reference to necessity. Thus we have spoken of a language being *necessarily* such that, if a given term applies to a thing in that language, then a certain other term also applies to that thing in that language. (2) There is no reliable way of telling, merely by observing a man's behavior, whether the language he then happens to be using is one which is *necessarily* such that if a given term applies to something in that language then a certain other term applies to that thing in that language. And (3) it is not possible, by reference merely to linguistic behaviour, to say what it is for a language to be *necessarily* such that, for two given terms, if the one applies to something in that language then the other also applies to that thing in that language.[46]

But these three propositions, even if they are true, are not sufficient to yield the conclusion (4) that the distinction between the analytic and the synthetic is untenable. If we attempt to formulate the additional premiss that would be needed to make the argument valid, we will see that it must involve a philosophical generalization—a generalization concerning what conditions must obtain if the distinction between the analytic and the synthetic is to be tenable. And how would the generalization be defended? This question should be considered in the light of what we have said about scepticism and the problem of the criterion. Of the philosophical generalizations that would make the above argument valid, none of them, so far as I know, has ever been defended. It is not accurate, therefore, to say that the distinction between the analytic and the synthetic has been *shown* to be untenable.

NOTES

1. "Being red excludes being blue" should not be taken to rule out the possibility of a thing being red in one part and blue in another; it tells us only that being red in one part at one time excludes being blue in exactly that same part at exactly that same time. The point might be put even more exactly by saying that it is necessarily true that anything that is red has a part that is not blue.
2. For the present, I will use "state of affairs" and "proposition" more or less interchangeably. Whenever we say of a state of affairs that it "occurs" or "obtains," we could say, instead, of a proposition that it is "true"; and conversely.
3. *Phaedo,* 75A.
4. Cf. Gottlob Frege, *The Foundations of Arithmetic* (Oxford, 1950), pp. 16–17; first published in 1884.
5. William Whewell, *Philosophy of the Inductive Sciences Founded upon Their History* (London, 1840), pp. 59–61.
6. *Republic,* 479, 508.
7. *Posterior Analytics,* 100ᵃ–100ᵇ.
8. This term was proposed by W. E. Johnson, *Logic* (London, 1921), pt. II, pp. 19 ff. Aristotle uses the term "induction" in the passages cited in the *Posterior Analytics*; cf. *The Nicomachean Ethics,* bk. VI, ch. 3, 1139ᵇ. Compare Franz Brentano, *The Origin of Our Knowledge of Right and Wrong* (London, 1969), pp. 111–13.
9. Philosophical Writings, ed. and trans. Alan Wolter (New York, 1962), p. 109; cf. p. 103.
10. *The Philosophical Works of Leibniz,* ed. G. M. Duncan (New Haven, Conn., 1908), p. 161.
11. *Erkenntnis und Irrtum* (Leipzig, 1905), pp. 180 ff.
12. E. Husserl, *Ideas: General Introduction to Phenomenology* (New York, 1931), p. 57.
13. G. W. Leibniz, *New Essays Concerning Human Understanding,* bk. IV, ch. 7 (Open Court edition), p. 462. Compare Alice Ambrose and Mor-

ris Lazerowitz, *Fundamentals of Symbolic Logic* (New York, 1962): "A proposition is said to be true a priori if its truth can be ascertained by examination of the proposition alone or if it is deducible from propositions whose truth is so ascertained, and by examination of nothing else. . . . Understanding the words used in expressing these propositions is sufficient for determining that they are true." p. 17.
14. *New Essays Concerning Human Understanding,* bk. IV, ch. 9, p. 499.
15. Gottlob Frege, *Kleine Schriften* (Hildesheim, 1967), p. 262.
16. *Posterior Analytics,* bk. I, ch. 2.
17. It should be noted that philosophers have used "a priori" and "a posteriori" in several different ways; it is not to be assumed that the present definitions are compatible with every such use. Compare David Benfield, "The A Priori-A Posteriori Distinction," *Philosophy and Phenomenological Research* 35 (1974), 151–66.
18. Thomas Aquinas, *Exposition of the Posterior Analytics of Aristotle,* trans. Pierre Conway, pt. II, lecture 20, no. 4 (Quebec, 1952).
19. *Essay Concerning Human Understanding,* bk. IV, ch. 2, sec. 7.
20. See *The Philosophical Works of Descartes,* ed. E. S. Haldane and G.R.T. Ross (London, 1934), p. 8. Some version of Descartes' principle should be an essential part of any theory of evidence. Compare Norman Malcolm's suggestion, "If a man previously had grounds for being sure that *p*, and now remembers that *p*, but does not remember what his grounds were," then he "*has* the same ground he previously had." *Knowledge and Certainty* (Englewood Cliffs, N.J., 1963), p. 230.
21. I. Kant, *Critique of Pure Reason,* trans. Norman Kemp Smith (London, 1933), p. 52.
22. Compare *Critique of Pure Reason,* B4 (Kemp Smith edition), p. 44. But we should not assume that if a proposition is necessary and known to be true, then it is a priori.
23. Thomas Aquinas, *Exposition of the Posterior Analytics of Aristotle,* pt. I, lecture 4, no. 10, p. 26.
24. *Critique of Pure Reason,* BI (Kemp Smith edition), p. 41.
25. This terminology is close to that of Franz Brentano. Compare his *The True and the Evident* (London, 1966), pp. 130 ff.
26. On the importance of testimony for the theory of evidence, cf. James F. Ross, Testimonial Evidence," in *Analysis and Metaphysics,* ed. Keith Lehrer (Dordrecht, 1975), pp. 35–55; and I. M. Bochenski, *Was ist Autorität?* (Freiburg im Breisgau, 1974).
27. Cf. Franz Brentano, *Grundzuge der Äshetik* (Bern: A. Franke, 1959), p. 167.

28. And so, given definition D3.4 above, the definition of the "objective" sense of a priori, we may seriously consider the possibility discussed by Bernard Bolzano: that a proposition "can be objectively a priori although it is subjectively only a posteriori." Bernard Bolzano, *Theory of Science*, trans. Rolf George (Oxford, 1972), p. 184.

29. Leonard Nelson, *Socratic Method and Critical Philosophy* (New Haven, Conn., 1949), p. 184.

30. "The preference of (say) seeing over understanding as a method of observation seems to me capricious. For just as an opaque body may be seen, so a concept may be understood and grasped." Alonzo Church, "Abstract Entities in Semantic Analysis," *Proceedings of the American Academy of Arts and Sciences* 80 (1951), 100–12; the quotation is on p. 104.

31. See Chisholm, *Theory of Knowledge*, 2nd ed. (Englewood Cliffs, N.J., 1977), ch. 2, sec. 8.

32. "Die Aufgabe der Erkenntnistheori," *Philosophische Monatshefte*, vol. XVI (1880); quoted by Husserl, in *Logical Investigations* (London, 1970), vol. I, p. 93. In his *Philosophie der Arithmetik* (Leipzig, 1891), Husserl defended a version of "psychologism," but he criticizes that view in *Logical Investigations*.

33. *The Foundations of Arithmetic*, p. 38; Frege's work was first published in 1884. Cf. Philip E. B. Jourdain, *The Philosophy of Mr. B*-rtr*-nd R*-ss*-ll* (London, 1918), p. 88: "The psychological founding of logic appears to be not without analogy with the surprising method of advocates of evolutionary ethics, who expect to discover what *is* good by inquiring what cannibals have *thought* good. I sometimes feel inclined to apply the historical method to the multiplication table. I should make a statistical inquiry among school-children, before their pristine wisdom has been biased by teachers. I should put down their answers to what 6 times 9 amounts to, I should work out the average of their answers to six places of decimals, and should then decide that, at the present stage of human development, this average is the value of 6 times 9."

34. Cf. the criticism of psychologism in Husserl's *Logical Investigations,* vol. i, pp. 90 ff., and Rudolf Carnap, *The Logical Foundations of Probability* (Chicago, 1950), pp. 37–42.

35. See Anthony Quinton, "The A Priori and the Analytic," in *Necessary Truth*, ed. Robert Sleigh (Englewood Cliffs, N.J., 1972), pp. 89–109.

36. W. V. Quine, "Carnap and Logical Truth," *The Philosophy of Rudolf Carnap,* ed. P. A. Schilpp (La Salle, Ill., 1963), p. 386.

37. *Critique of Pure Reason*, A7 (Kemp Smith edition), p. 48.

38. *Prolegomena to Any Future Metaphysics*, sec. 2.

39. And so we do not define "English language" in terms of the people who speak it or the lands wherein it is spoken. In our use of the word "English," we may say "English is necessarily such that in it 'red' applies to things that are red." But if we defined "English" as the language spoken, say, by Englishmen or in England, we could not say "English is *necessarily* such that in it 'red' applies to things that are red." Englishmen *could* have used "blue," or any other word, in the way in which, in fact, they used "red."

40. A term *T* may be said to be a *negation* of a term *S* in a given language *L* provided this condition holds: either *T* is part of *S*, or *S* is part of *T*; and *L* is necessarily such that, for every *x*, *T* is true of *x* in *L*, if and only if *S* is not true of *x* in *L*. Thus "non-square" is a negation of "square" in English (and "square" a negation of "non-square"), since one is part of the other and since English is necessarily such that "square" is true of any given thing if and only if "non-square" is not true of that thing.

41. If we define "father" as "male parent," and "mother" as "female parent," then we would have to say of a father who changes his sex that he becomes a mother. And analogously for a mother. Perhaps to accommodate our language to the possibility of sex change, we should define "father" not merely as male parent," but as "parent who was male at the time of procreation." And analogously for "mother."

42. Cf. C. H. Langford, "A Proof That Synthetic A Priori Propositions Exist," *Journal of Philosophy*, 46 (1949), 20–24.

43. Cf. John Locke, *Essay Concerning Human Understanding*, bk. IV ch. I, sec. 7; Franz Brentano, *Versuch über die Erkenntnis* (Leipzig, 1925), pp. 9–10.

44. Quoted from *The Philosophical Works of Leibniz*, p. 162.

45. Cf. the discussion of this question in chs. 5 and 6 in William Frankena, *Ethics*, 2nd ed. (Englewood Cliffs, N.J., 1973).

46. Cf. W. V. Quine, "Two Dogmas of Empiricism," in *From a Logical Point of View,* esp. pp. 20–37, and Morton White, "The Analytic and the Synthetic: An Untenable Dualism," in *Semantics and the Philosophy of Language,* ed. Leonard Linsky (Urbana, Ill., 1952), pp. 272–86.

25 / Saul A. Kripke
A PRIORI KNOWLEDGE, NECESSITY, AND CONTINGENCY

Philosophers have talked (and, of course, there has been considerable controversy in recent years over the meaningfulness of these notions) about various categories of truth, which are called "a priori," "analytic," "necessary"—and sometimes even "certain" is thrown into this batch. The terms are often used as if *whether* there are things answering to these concepts is an interesting question, but we might as well regard them all as meaning the same thing. Now, everyone remembers Kant (a bit) as making a distinction between "a priori" and "analytic." So maybe this distinction is still made. In contemporary discussion very few people, if any, distinguish between the concepts of statements being a priori and their being necessary. At any rate I shall *not* use the terms "a priori" and "necessary" interchangeably here.

Consider what the traditional characterizations of such terms as "a priori" and "necessary" are. First the notion of a prioricity is a concept of epistemology. I guess the traditional characterization from Kant goes something like: a priori truths are those which can be known independently of any experience. This introduces another problem before we get off the ground, because there's another modality in the characterization of "a priori," namely, it is supposed to be something which *can* be known independently of any experience. That means that in some sense it's *possible* (whether we do or do not in fact know it independently of any experience) to know this independently

of any experience. And possible for whom? For God? For the Martians? Or just for people with minds like ours? To make this all clear might involve a host of problems all of its own about what sort of possibility is in question here. It might be best therefore, instead of using the phrase "a priori truth," to the extent that one uses it at all, to stick to the question of whether a particular person or knower knows something a priori or believes it true on the basis of a priori evidence.

I won't go further too much into the problems that might arise with the notion of a prioricity here. I will say that some philosophers somehow change the modality in this characterization from *can* to *must*. They think that if something belongs to the realm of a priori knowledge, it couldn't possibly be known empirically. This is just a mistake. Something may belong in the realm of such statements that *can* be known a priori but still may be known by particular people on the basis of experience. To give a really common-sense example: anyone who has worked with a computing machine knows that the computing machine may give an answer to whether such and such a number is prime. No one has calculated or proved that the number is prime; but the machine has given the answer: this number is prime. We, then, if we believe that the number is prime, believe it on the basis of our knowledge of the laws of physics, the construction of the machine, and so on. We therefore do not believe this on the basis of purely a priori evidence. We believe it (if anything is a posteriori at all) on the basis of a posteriori evidence. Nevertheless, maybe this could be known a priori by someone who made the requisite calculations. So "*can* be known a priori" doesn't mean "*must* be known a priori."

The second concept which is in question is that of necessity. Sometimes this is used in an epistemological way and might then just mean a priori. And of course, sometimes it is used in a physical way when people distinguish between physical and logical necessity. But what I am concerned with here is a notion which is not a notion of epistemology but of metaphysics, in some (I hope) non-pejorative sense. We ask whether something might have been true, or might have been false. Well, if something is false, it's obviously not necessarily true. If it is true, might it have been otherwise? Is it possible that, in this respect, the world should have been different from the way it is? If the answer is "no," then this fact about the world is a necessary one. If the answer is "yes," then this fact about the world is a contingent one. This in and of itself has nothing to do with anyone's knowledge of anything. It's certainly a philosophical thesis, and not a matter of obvious definitional equivalence, either that everything a priori is necessary or that everything necessary is a priori. Both concepts may be vague. That may be another problem. But at any rate they are dealing with two different domains, two different areas, the epistemological and the metaphysical. Consider, say, Fermat's last theorem—or the Goldbach conjecture. The Goldbach conjecture says that an even number greater than 2 must be the sum of two prime numbers. If this is true, it is presumably necessary, and, if it is false, presumably necessarily false. We are taking the classical view of mathematics here and assuming that in mathematical reality it is either true or false.

If the Goldbach conjecture is false, then there is an even number, n, greater than 2, such that for no primes p_1 and p_2, both $< n$, does $n = p_1 + p_2$. This fact about n, if true, is verifiable by direct computation, and thus is necessary if the results of arithmetical computations are necessary. On the other hand, if the conjecture is true, then every even number exceeding 2 is the sum of two primes. Could it then be the case that, although in fact every such even number is the sum of two primes, there might have been such an even number which was not the sum of two primes? What would that mean? Such a number would have to be one of 4, 6, 8, 10, . . . ; and, by hypothesis, since we are assuming Goldbach's conjecture to be true, each of these can be shown, again by direct computation, to be the sum of two primes. Goldbach's conjecture, then, cannot be contingently true or false; whatever truth-value it has belongs to it by necessity.

But what we can say, of course, is that right now, as far as we know, the question can come out either way. So, in the absence of a mathematical proof deciding this question, none of us has any a priori knowledge about this question in either direction. We don't know whether Goldbach's conjecture is true or false. So right now we certainly don't know anything a priori about it.

Perhaps it will be alleged that we *can* in principle know a priori whether it is true. Well, maybe we can. Of course an infinite mind which can search through all the numbers can or could. But I don't know whether a finite mind can or could. Maybe there just is no mathematical proof whatsoever which decides the conjecture. At any rate this might or might not be the case. Maybe there is a mathematical proof deciding this question; maybe every mathematical question is decidable by an intuitive proof or disproof. Hilbert thought so; others have thought not; still others have thought the question unintelligible unless the notion of intuitive proof is replaced by that of formal proof in a single system. Certainly no one formal system decides all mathematical questions, as we know from Gödel. At any rate, and this is the important thing, the question is not trivial; even though someone said that it's necessary, if true at all, that every even number is the sum of two primes, it doesn't follow that anyone knows anything a priori about it. It doesn't even seem to me to follow without some further philosophical argument (it is an interesting philosophical question) that anyone *could* know anything a priori about it. The "could," as I said, involves some other modality. We mean that even if no one, perhaps even in the future, knows or will know a priori whether Goldbach's conjecture is right, in principle there is a way, which *could* have been used, of answering the question a priori. This assertion is not trivial.

The terms "necessary" and "a priori," then, as applied to statements, are *not* obvious synonyms. There may be a philosophical argument connecting them, perhaps even identifying them; but an argument is required, not simply the observation that the two terms are clearly interchangeable. (I will argue below that in fact they are not even coextensive—that necessary a posteriori truths, and probably contingent a priori truths, both exist.)

I think people have thought that these two things must mean the same for these reasons:

First, if something not only happens to be true in the actual world but is also true in all possible worlds, then, of course, just by running through all the possible worlds in our heads, we ought to be able with enough effort to see, if a statement is necessary, that it is necessary, and thus know it a priori. But really this is not so obviously feasible at all.

Second, I guess it's thought that, conversely, if something is known a priori it must be necessary, because it was known without looking at the world. If it depended on some contingent feature of the actual world, how could you know it without looking? Maybe the actual world is one of the possible worlds in which it would have been false. This depends on the thesis that there can't be a way of knowing about the actual world without looking that wouldn't be a way of knowing the same thing about every possible world. This involves problems of epistemology and the nature of knowledge; and of course it is very vague as stated. But it is not really *trivial* either. More important than any particular example of something which is alleged to be necessary and not a priori or a priori and not necessary, is to see that the notions are different, that it's not trivial to argue on the basis of something's being something which maybe we can only know a posteriori, that it's not necessary truth. It's not trivial, just because something is known in some sense a priori, that what is known is a necessary truth.

Another term used in philosophy is "ana-lytic." Here it won't be too important to get any clearer about this in this talk. The common examples of analytic statements, nowadays, are like "bachelors are unmarried." Kant (someone just pointed out to me) gives as an example "gold is a yellow metal," which seems to me an extraordinary one, because it's something I think that can turn out to be false. At any rate, let's just make it a matter of stipulation that an analytic statement is, in some sense, true by virtue of its meaning and true in all possible worlds by virtue of its meaning. Then something which is analytically true will be both necessary and a priori. (That's sort of stipulative.)

Another category I mentioned was that of certainty. Whatever certainty is, it's clearly not obviously the case that everything which is necessary is certain. Certainty is another epistemological notion. Something can be known, or at least rationally believed, a priori, without being quite certain. You've read a proof in the math book; and, though you think it's correct, maybe you've made a mistake. You often do make mistakes of this kind. You've made a computation, perhaps with an error.

. . . .

Let's use some terms quasi-technically. Let's call something a *rigid designator* if in every possible world it designates the same object, a *non-rigid* or *accidental designator* if that is not the case. Of course we don't require that the objects exist in all possible worlds. Certainly Nixon might not have existed if his parents had not gotten married, in the normal course of things. When we think of a property as essential to an object we usually mean that it is true of that object in any case where it would have existed. A rigid designator of a necessary existent can be called *strongly rigid*.

One of the intuitive theses I will maintain in these talks is that *names* are rigid designators. Certainly they seem to satisfy the intuitive test: although someone other than the US President in 1970 might have been the US President in 1970 (e.g. Humphrey might have), no one other than Nixon might have been Nixon. In the same way, a designator rigidly designates a certain object if it designates that object wherever the object exists; if, in addition, the object is a necessary existent, the designator can be called *strongly rigid*. For example, "the President of the US in 1970" designates a certain man, Nixon; but someone else (e.g. Humphrey) might have been the President in 1970, and Nixon might not have; so this designator is not rigid.

In these lectures I will argue, intuitively, that proper names are rigid designators, for although the man (Nixon) might not have been the President, it is not the case that he might not have been Nixon (though he might not have been *called* "Nixon"). Those who have argued that to make sense of the notion of rigid designator, we must antecedently make sense of "criteria of transworld identity" have precisely reversed the cart and the horse; it is *because* we can refer (rigidly) to Nixon, and stipulate that we are speaking of what might have happened to *him* (under certain circumstances), that "transworld identifications" are unproblematic in such cases.[1]

The tendency to demand purely qualitative descriptions of counterfactual situations has many sources. One, perhaps, is the confusion of the epistemological and the metaphysical, between a prioricity and necessity. If someone identifies necessity with a prioricity, and thinks that objects are named by means of uniquely identifying properties, he may think that it is the properties used to identify the object which, being known about it a priori, must be used to identify it in all possible worlds, to find out which object is Nixon. As against this, I repeat: (1) Generally, things aren't "found out" about a counterfactual situation, they are stipulated; (2) possible worlds need not be given purely qualitatively, as if we were looking at them through a telescope. And we will see shortly that the properties an object has in every counterfactual world have nothing to do with properties used to identify it in the actual world.

. . . .

Above I said that the Frege-Russell view that names are introduced by description could be taken either as a theory of the meaning of names (Frege and Russell seemed to take it this way) or merely as a theory of their reference. Let me give an example, not involving what

would usually be called a "proper name," to illustrate this. Suppose someone stipulates that 100 degrees centigrade is to be the temperature at which water boils at sea level. This isn't completely precise because the pressure may vary at sea level. Of course, historically, a more precise definition was given later. But let's suppose that this were the definition. Another sort of example in the literature is that one metre is to be the length of *S* where *S* is a certain stick or bar in Paris. (Usually people who like to talk about these definitions then try to make "the length of" into an "operational" concept. But it's not important.)

Wittgenstein says something very puzzling about this. He says: "There is one thing of which one can say neither that it is one metre long nor that it is not one metre long, and that is the standard metre in Paris. But this is, of course, not to ascribe any extraordinary property to it, but only to mark its peculiar role in the language game of measuring with a metre rule."[2] This seems to be a very "extraordinary property," actually, for any stick to have. I think he must be wrong. If the stick is a stick, for example, 39.37 inches long (I assume we have some different standard for inches), why isn't it one metre long? Anyway, let's suppose that he is wrong and that the stick is one metre long. Part of the problem which is bothering Wittgenstein is, of course, that this stick serves as a standard of length and so we can't attribute length to it. Be this as it may (well, it may not be), is the statement "Stick *S* is one metre long," a necessary truth? Of course its length might vary in time. We could make the definition more precise by stipulating that one metre is to be the length of *S* at a fixed time t_0. Is it then a necessary truth that stick *S* is one metre long at time t_0? Someone who thinks that everything one knows a priori is necessary might think: "This is the *definition* of a metre. By definition, stick *S* is one metre long at t_0. That's a necessary truth." But there seems to me to be no reason so to conclude, even for a man who uses the standard definition of "one metre." For he's using this definition not to *give the meaning* of what he called the "metre," but to *fix the reference*. (For such an abstract thing as a unit of length, the notion of reference may be unclear. But let's suppose it's clear enough for the present purposes.) He uses it to fix a reference. There is a certain length which he wants to mark out. He marks it out by an accidental property, namely that there is a stick of that length. Someone else might mark out the same reference by another accidental property. But in any case, even though he uses this to fix the reference of his standard of length, a metre, he can still say, "if heat had been applied to this stick S at t_o, then at t_o stick S would not have been one metre long."

Well, why can he do this? Part of the reason may lie in some people's minds in the philosophy of science, which I don't want to go into here. But a simple answer to the question is this: Even if this is the *only* standard of length that he uses,[3] there is an intuitive difference between the phrase "one metre" and the phrase "the length of S at t_o." The first phrase is meant to designate rigidly a certain length in all possible worlds, which in the actual world happens to be the length of the stick S at t_o. On the other hand "the length of S at t_o" does not designate anything rigidly. In some counterfactual situations the stick might have been longer and in some shorter, if various stresses and strains had been applied to it. So we can say of this stick, the same way as we would of any other of the same substance and length, that if heat of a given quantity had been applied to it, it would have expanded to such and such a length. Such a counterfactual statement, being true of other sticks with identical physical properties, will also be true of this stick. There is no conflict between that counterfactual statement and the definition of "one metre" as "the length of S at t_o," because the "definition," properly interpreted, does *not* say that the phrase "one metre" is to be *synonymous* (even when talking about counterfactual situations) with the phrase "the length of S at t_o," but rather that we have *determined the reference* of the phrase "one metre" by stipulating that "one metre" is to be a *rigid* designator of the length which is in fact the length of S at t_o. So this does *not* make it a necessary truth that S is one metre long at t_o. In fact, under certain circumstances, S would not have been one metre long. The reason is that one designator ("one metre") is rigid and the other designator ("the length of S at t_o") is not.

What then, is the *epistemological* status of the statement "Stick S is one metre long at t_o," for someone who has fixed the metric system by reference to stick S? It would seem that he knows it a priori. For if he used stick S to fix the reference of the term "one metre," then as a result of this kind of "definition" (which is not an abbreviative or synonymous definition), he knows automatically, without further investigation, that S is one metre long.[4] On the other hand, even if S is used as the standard of a metre, the *metaphysical* status of "S is one metre long" will be that of a contingent statement, provided that "one metre" is regarded as a rigid designator: under appropriate stresses and strains, heatings or coolings, S would have had a length other than one metre even at t_o. (Such statements as "Water boils at 100 degrees centigrade, at sea level" can have a similar status.) So in this sense, there are contingent a priori truths. More important for present purposes, though, than accepting this example as an instance of the contingent a priori, is its illustration of the distinction between 'definitions' which fix a reference and those which give a synonym.

In the case of names one might make this distinction too. Suppose the reference of a name is given by a description or a cluster of descriptions. If the name *means the same* as that description or cluster of descriptions, it will not be a rigid designator. It will not necessarily designate the same object in all possible worlds, since other objects might have had the given properties in other possible worlds, unless (of course) we happened to use essential properties in our descriptions. So suppose we say, "Aristotle is the greatest man who studied with Plato." If we used that as a *definition,* the name "Aristotle" is to mean "the greatest man who studied with Plato." Then of course in some other possible world that man might not have studied with Plato and some other man would have been Aristotle. If, on the other hand, we merely use the description to *fix the referent* then that man will be the referent of "Aristotle" in all possible worlds. The only use of the description will have been to pick out to which man we mean to refer. But then, when we say counterfactually "suppose Aristotle had never gone into philosophy at all," we need not mean "suppose a man who studied with Plato, and taught Alexander the Great, and wrote this and that, and so on, had never gone into philosophy at all," which might seem like a contradiction. We need only mean, "suppose that *that man* had never gone into philosophy at all."

It seems plausible to suppose that, in some cases, the reference of a name is indeed fixed *via* a description in the same way that the metric system was fixed. When the mythical agent first saw Hesperus, he may well have fixed his reference by saying, "I shall use 'Hesperus' as a name of the heavenly body appearing in yonder position in the sky." He then fixed the reference of "Hesperus" by its apparent celestial position. Does it follow that it is part of the *meaning* of the name that Hesperus has such and such position at the time in question? Surely not: if Hesperus had been hit earlier by a comet, it might have been visible at a different position at that time. In such a counterfactual situation we would say that Hesperus would not have occupied that position, but not that Hesperus would not have been Hesperus. The reason is that "Hesperus" rigidly designates a certain heavenly body and "the body in yonder position" does not—a different body, or no body might have been in that position, but no other body might have been Hesperus (though another body, not Hesperus, might have been *called* "Hesperus"). Indeed, as I have said, I will hold that names are always rigid designators.

. . . .

I guess the main thing I'll talk about now is identity statements between names. But I hold the following about the general case. First, that characteristic theoretical identifications like "Heat is the motion of molecules," are not contingent truths but necessary truths, and here of course I don't mean just physically necessary, but necessary in the highest degree—whatever that means. (Physical necessity *might* turn out to be necessity in the highest degree. But that's a question which I don't wish to prejudice. At least for this sort of example, it might be that when something's physically necessary, it always is necessary *tout court*.) Second, that the way in which these have turned out to be nec-

essary truths does not seem to me to be a way in which the mind-brain identities could turn out to be either necessary or contingently true. So this analogy has to go. It's hard to see what to put in its place. It's hard to see therefore how to avoid concluding that the two are actually different.

Let me go back to the more mundane case about proper names. This is already mysterious enough. There's a dispute about this between Quine and Ruth Barcan Marcus.[5] Marcus says that identities between names are necessary. If someone thinks that Cicero is Tully, and really uses "Cicero" and "Tully" as names, he is thereby committed to holding that his belief is a necessary truth. She uses the term "mere tag." Quine replies as follows, "We may tag the planet Venus, some fine evening, with the proper name 'Hesperus.' We may tag the same planet again, some day before sunrise, with the proper name 'Phosphorus.' When we discover that we have tagged the same planet twice our discovery is empirical. And not because the proper names were descriptions.[6] First, as Quine says when we discovered that we tagged the same planet twice, our discovery was empirical. Another example I think Quine gives in another book is that the same mountain seen from Nepal and from Tibet, or something like that, is from one angle called "Mt. Everest" (you've heard of that); from another it's supposed to be called "Gaurisanker." It can actually be an empirical discovery that Gaurisanker is Everest. (Quine says that the example is actually false. He got the example from Erwin Schrödinger. You wouldn't think the inventor of wave mechanics got things that wrong. I don't know where the mistake is supposed to come from. One could certainly imagine this situation as having been the case; and it's another good illustration of the sort of thing that Quine has in mind.)

What about it? I wanted to find a good quote on the other side from Marcus in this book but I am having trouble locating one. Being present at that discussion, I remember[7] that she advocated the view that if you really have names, a good dictionary should be able to tell you whether they have the same reference. So someone should be able, by looking in the dictionary, to say that Hesperus and Phosphorus are the same. Now this does not seem to be true. It does seem, to many people, to be a consequence of the view that identities between names are necessary. Therefore the view that identity statements between names are necessary has usually been rejected. Russell's conclusion was somewhat different. He did think there should never be any empirical question whether two names have the same reference. This isn't satisfied for ordinary names, but it is satisfied when you're naming your own sense datum, or something like that. You say, "Here, this, and that (designating the same sense datum by both demonstratives.)" So you can tell without empirical investigation that you're naming the same thing twice; the conditions are satisfied. Since this won't apply to ordinary cases of naming, ordinary "names" cannot be genuine names.

What should we think about this? First, it's true that someone can use the name "Cicero" to refer to Cicero and the name "Tully" to refer to Cicero also, and not know that Cicero is Tully. So it seems that we do not necessarily know a priori that an identity statement between names is true. It doesn't follow from this that the statement so expressed is a contingent one if true. This is what I've emphasized in my first lecture. There is a very strong feeling that leads one to think that, if you can't know something by a priori ratiocination, then it's got to be contingent: it might have turned out otherwise; but nevertheless I think this feeling is wrong.

Let's suppose we refer to the same heavenly body twice, as "Hesperus" and "Phosphorus." We say: Hesperus is that star over there in the evening; Phosphorus is that star over there in the morning. Actually, Hesperus is Phosphorus. Are there really circumstances under which Hesperus wouldn't have been Phosphorus? Supposing that Hesperus is Phosphorus, let's try to describe a possible situation in which it would not have been. Well, it's easy. Someone goes by and he calls two *different* stars "Hesperus" and "Phosphorus." It may even be under the same conditions as prevailed when we introduced the names "Hesperus" and "Phosphorus." But are those circumstances in which Hesperus is not Phosphorus or would

not have been Phosphorus? It seems to me that they are not.

Now, of course I'm committed to saying that they're not, by saying that such terms as "Hesperus" and "Phosphorus," when used as names, are rigid designators. They refer in every possible world to the planet Venus. Therefore, in that possible world too, the planet Venus is the planet Venus and it doesn't matter what any other person has said in this other possible world. How should *we* describe this situation? He can't have pointed to Venus twice, and in the one case called it "Hesperus" and in the other "Phosphorus," as we did. If he did so, then "Hesperus is Phosphorus" would have been true in that situation too. He pointed maybe neither time to the planet Venus—at least one time he didn't point to the planet Venus, let's say when he pointed to the body he called "Phosphorus." Then in that case we can certainly say that the name "Phosphorus" might not have referred to Phosphorus. We can even say that in the very position when viewed in the morning that we found Phosphorus, it might have been the case that Phosphorus was not there—that something else was there, and that even, under certain circumstances it would have been *called* "Phosphorus." But that still is not a case in which Phosphorus was not Hesperus. There might be a possible world in which, a possible counterfactual situation in which, "Hesperus" and "Phosphorus" weren't names of the things they in fact are names of. Someone, if he did determine their reference by identifying descriptions, might even have used the very identifying descriptions we used. But still that's not a case in which Hesperus wasn't Phosphorus. For there couldn't have been such a case, given that Hesperus is Phosphorus.

Now this seems very strange because in advance, we are inclined to say, the answer to the question whether Hesperus is Phosphorus might have turned out either way. So aren't there really two possible worlds—one in which Hesperus was Phosphorus, the other in which Hesperus wasn't Phosphorus—in advance of our discovering that these were the same? First, there's one sense in which things might turn out either way, in which it's clear that that doesn't imply that the way it finally turns out isn't necessary. For example, the four-colour theorem might turn out to be true and might turn out to be false. It might turn out either way. It still doesn't mean that the way it turns out is not necessary. Obviously, the "might" here is purely "epistemic"—it merely expresses our present state of ignorance, or uncertainty.

But it seems that in the Hesperus-Phosphorus case, something even stronger is true. The evidence I have before I know that Hesperus is Phosphorus is that I see a certain star or a certain heavenly body in the evening and call it "Hesperus," and in the morning and call it "Phosphorus." I know these things. There certainly is a possible world in which a man should have seen a certain star at a certain position in the evening and called it "Hesperus" and a certain star in the morning and called it "Phosphorus"; and should have concluded—should have found out by empirical investigations—that he names two different stars, or two different heavenly bodies. At least one of these stars or heavenly bodies was not Phosphorus, otherwise it couldn't have come out that way. But that's true. And so it's true that given the evidence that someone has antecedent to his empirical investigation, he can be placed in a sense in exactly the same situation, that is a qualitatively identical epistemic situation, and call two heavenly bodies "Hesperus" and "Phosphorus," without their being identical. So in that sense we can say that it might have turned out either way. Not that it might have turned out either way as to Hesperus's being Phosphorus. Though for all we knew in advance, Hesperus wasn't Phosphorus, that couldn't have turned out any other way, in a sense. But being put in a situation where we have exactly the same evidence, qualitatively speaking, it could have turned out that Hesperus was not Phosphorus; that is, in a counterfactual world in which "Hesperus" and "Phosphorus" were not used in the way that we use them, as names of this planet, but as names of some other objects, one could have had qualitatively identical evidence and concluded that "Hesperus" and "Phosphorus" named two different objects.[8] But we, using the names as we do right now, can say in advance, that if Hesperus and Phosphorus are one and the same, then in no other possible world can they be different. We use "Hesperus" as the name of a certain body and "Phosphorus" as the name of a certain body. We use them as names of those bodies in all possible worlds. If, in fact, they are the *same* body, then in any other possible world we have to use them as a name of that object. And so in any other possible world it will be true that Hesperus is Phosphorus. So two things are true: first, that we do not know a priori that Hesperus is Phosphorus, and are in no position to find out the answer except empirically. Second, this is so because we could have evidence qualitatively indistinguishable from the evidence we have and determine the reference of the two names by the positions of two planets in the sky, without the planets being the same.

Of course, it is only a contingent truth (not true in every other possible world) that the star seen over there in the evening is the star seen over there in the morning, because there are possible worlds in which Phosphorus was not visible in the morning. But that contingent truth shouldn't be identified with the statement that Hesperus is Phosphorus. It could only be so identified if you thought that it was a necessary truth that Hesperus is visible over there in the evening or that Phosphorus is visible over there in the morning. But neither of those are necessary truths even if that's the way we pick out the planet. These are the contingent marks by which we identify a certain planet and give it a name.

. . . .

We have concluded that an identity statement between names, when true at all, is necessarily true, even though one may not know it a priori. Suppose we identify Hesperus as a certain star seen in the evening and Phosphorus as a certain star, or a certain heavenly body, seen in the morning; then there may be possible worlds in which two different planets would have been seen in just those positions in the evening and morning. However, at least one of them, and maybe both, would not have been Hesperus, and then that would not have been a situation in which Hesperus was not Phosphorus. It might have been a situation in which the planet seen in this position in the evening was not the planet seen in this position in the morning; but that is not a situation in which Hesperus was not Phosphorus. It might also, if people gave the names "Hesperus" and "Phosphorus" to these planets, be a situation in which some planet other than Hesperus was called "Hesperus." But even so, it would not be a situation in which Hesperus itself was not Phosphorus.[9]

Some of the problems which bother people in these situations, as I have said, come from an identification, or as I would put it, a confusion, between what we can know a priori in advance and what is necessary. Certain statements—and the identity statement is a paradigm of such a statement on my view—if true at all must be necessarily true. One does know a priori, by philosophical analysis, that if such an identity statement is true it is necessarily true.

NOTES

1. Of course I don't imply that language contains a name for every object. Demonstratives can be used as rigid designators, and free variables can be used as rigid designators of unspecified objects. Of course when we specify a counterfactual situation, we do not describe the whole possible world, but only the portion which interests us.
2. *Philosophical Investigations*, sec. 50.
3. Philosophers of science may see the key to the problem in a view that "one metre" is a "cluster concept." I am asking the reader hypothetically to suppose that the "definition" given is the *only* standard used to determine the metric system. I think the problem would still arise.
4. Since the truth he knows is contingent, I choose *not* to call it "analytic," stipulatively requiring analytic truths to be both necessary and a priori.
5. Ruth Barcan Marcus, "Modalities and Intensional Languages" (comments by W. V. Quine, plus discussion), *Boston Studies in the Philosophy of Science* (Dordrecht, 1963), pp. 77–116.
6. P. 101.
7. P. 115.
8. There is a more elaborate discussion of this point in the third lecture, in *Naming and Necessity*, where its relation to a certain sort of counterpart theory is also mentioned.
9. Recall that we describe the situation in our language, not the language that the people in that situation would have used. Hence we must use the terms "Hesperus" and "Phosphorus" with the same reference as in the actual world. The fact that people in that situation might or might not have used these names for different planets is irrelevant. So is the fact that they might have done so using the very same descriptions as we did to fix their references.

A PRIORI KNOWLEDGE: BIBLIOGRAPHY

Benacerraf, P., and H. Putnam, eds. *Philosophy of Mathematics.* Englewood Cliffs, NJ, 1964.

Bennett, J. *Kant's Analytic.* Cambridge, Eng., 1966.

Blackburn, S, ed. *Meaning, Reference, and Necessity.* Cambridge, Eng., 1975.

BonJour, L. *In Defense of Pure Reason: A Rationalist Account of "A Priori" Justification.* New York, 1998.

Casullo, A., ed. *A Priori Knowledge.* Aldershot, Eng., 1999.

———. "A Priori Knowledge." In *The Oxford Handbook of Epistemology*, ed. P. K. Moser. New York, 2002.

———. "Actuality and the A Priori". *Australasian Journal of Philosophy* 66 (1988): 390–402.

———. "Necessity, Certainty, and the 'A Priori'." *Canadian Journal of Philosophy* 18 (1988): 43–66.

———. "Revisability, Reliabilism, and A Priori Knowledge." *Philosophy and Phenomenological Research* (1988): 187–213.

Harris, J. F., and R. H. Severens, eds. *Analyticity: Selected Readings.* Chicago, 1970.

Kitcher, P. *The Nature of Mathematical Knowledge.* New York, 1983.

———. "A Priori Knowledge." *The Philosophical Review* 76 (1980): 3–23.

———. "Apriority and Necessity." *Australasian Journal of Philosophy* 58 (1980): 89–101.

Kripke, S. A. *Naming and Necessity.* Cambridge, Mass., 1980.

———. "Identity and Necessity." In *Naming, Ne-*

cessity, and Natural Kinds, ed. by S. P. Schwartz, pp. 66–101. Ithaca, N.Y., 1977.

———. Wittgenstein on Rules and Private Language. Cambridge, Mass., 1982.

Lewis, C. I. An Analysis of Knowledge and Valuation, chaps. 3–6. La Salle, Ill., 1946.

———. Mind and the World Order, chaps. 7–9. New York, 1929.

———. "A Pragmatic Conception of the A Priori." The Journal of Philosophy 20 (1923), 169–77. Reprinted in Collected Papers of Clarence Irving Lewis, ed. by J. D. Goheen and J. L. Mothershead pp. 231–39 Stanford, 1970.

Moser, P. K., ed. A Priori Knowledge. Oxford, 1987.

———. ed. The Oxford Handbook of Epistemology. New York, 2003.

Pap, A. The A Priori in Physical Theory. New York, 1946.

———. Semantics and Necessary Truth. New Haven: Yale University Press, 1958.

Pasch, A. Experience and the Analytic: A Reconsideration of Empiricism. Chicago, 1958.

Price, H. H. Thinking and Experience, 2d ed. London, 1969.

Putnam, H. "The Analytic and the Synthetic." In Mind, Language, and Reality, Philosophical Papers, Vol. 2, pp. 33–69. Cambridge: Cambridge University Press, 1975.

———. "Analyticity and Apriority: Beyond Wittgenstein and Quine." In Midwest Studies in Philosophy, Vol. 4, ed P. French et al., pp. 432–41. Minneapolis, 1979.

———. "There Is At Least One A Priori Truth." Erkenntnis 13 (1978): 153–70. Reprinted in Putnam, Realism and Reason, Philosophical Papers, Vol. 3, pp. 98–114. Cambridge, 1983.

———. " 'Two Dogmas' Revisited." In Realism and Reason, Philosophical Papers, Vol. 3, pp. 87–97. Cambridge 1983.

Quine, W. V. "Carnap and Logical Truth." In Quine, The Ways of Paradox, pp. 100–125. New York, 1966.

———. "The Ground of Logical Truth." In Philosophy of Logic, chapter 7. Englewood Cliffs, NJ: Prentice Hall, 1970.

———. "Truth by Convention." In The Ways of Paradox, pp. 70–99. New York, 1966.

———. "Two Dogmas of Empiricism." In From a Logical Point of View, 2d ed. New York, 1963.

———. "Two Dogmas in Retrospect." Canadian Journal of Philosophy 21 (1991): 265–74.

Resnik, M. D. Frege and the Philosophy of Mathematics. Ithaca, N.Y., 1980.

Rosenthal, S. The Pragmatic A Priori: A Study in the Epistemology of C.I. Lewis. St. Louis, MO, 1976.

Sleigh, R. C., ed. Necessary Truth. Englewood Cliffs, N.J., 1972.

Steiner, M. Mathematical Knowledge. Ithaca, N.Y., 1975.

Wittgenstein, Ludwig. Remarks on the Foundations of Mathematics, 3d ed. Cambridge, Mass., 1978.

Justified Belief

The General Introduction outlined the regress problem concerning justification and the main contemporary positions on justified belief. This section focuses on the justification condition of knowledge, the condition that guarantees that the truth condition for knowledge is not accidentally related to the belief condition. One concern of the section is the conflict between foundationalism and coherentism: between the view that there are noninferentially justified beliefs that ultimately provide the justification for all inferentially justified beliefs, and the view that all justified beliefs are justified by their relations to other beliefs. Another concern of the section is whether the justification of a belief is a function solely of its reliability, that is, its being produced by a mechanism that tends to produce more true than false beliefs. Still another concern is what exactly our *concept* of epistemic justification involves.

In "Concepts of Epistemic Justification," William Alston surveys some prominent notions of epistemic justification. Alston distinguishes between deontological and nondeontological evaluative notions of justification. According to a deontological notion, one is justified in believing a proposition, *P*, if and only if no intellectual obligations concerning belief formation or belief sustenance are violated in one's believing that *P*. According to a nondeontological evaluative notion, one is justified in believing that *P* if and only if one's believing that *P*, as one now does, is a good thing from the epistemic point of view. Such a notion presupposes that there is a way of being good from the epistemic point of view that is not identical to one's being blameless regarding the violation of an intellectual obligation.

Alston defines the epistemic point of view in terms of the aim to maximize true belief and minimize false belief. He proposes that goodness relative to this aim consists in a belief's being true *as far as a believer can tell from what is available to him or her*. Such epistemic goodness requires *adequate evidence* for a belief, where adequate evidence is warrant that is sufficiently indicative of the truth of the belief in question. Alston argues that this nondeontological notion, rather than a deontological notion, is essential to our concept of empirical knowledge.

In "The Raft and the Pyramid: Coherence versus Foundations in the Theory of Knowledge," Ernest Sosa clarifies and assesses the dispute between the pyramid model of knowledge proposed by foundationalists and the raft model proposed by coherentists. Sosa characterizes substantive epistemic foundationalism as the view that "any piece of knowledge must be ultimately founded on beliefs that are not (inferentially) justified or warranted by other beliefs." Substantive epistemic coherentism, in contrast, is the view that "the ultimate sources of justification for any belief lie in relations among that belief and other beliefs of the subject: explanatory relations, perhaps, or relations of probability or logic."

Sosa observes that epistemic coherentism, like epistemic foundationalism, qualifies as a version of formal foundationalism, the view with respect to a normative property, *F*, that the conditions under which *F* would apply can be specified in general, perhaps in a recursive manner. Sosa supports formal foundationalism on the ground that normative properties generally are supervenient on non-normative properties, but opposes both substantive foundationalism and substantive coherentism. By way of an alternative to foundationalism and coherentism, Sosa sketches a version of epistemic reliabilism according to which (a) primary justification applies to intellectual virtues (that is, dispositions for belief acquisition) owing to their contribution toward the acquisition of truth, and (b) secondary justification applies to particular acts owing to their source in the intellectual virtues.

In "A Contextualist Theory of Epistemic Justification," David Annis develops a theory of justification that purportedly differs from foundationalism, coherentism, and reliabilism. The theory emphasizes the pragmatic and social (that is, contextual) factors in the acquisition of empirical knowledge. Annis bases his contextualism on the notions of an *issue-context* and an appropriate *objector-group*. The issue-context concerning a belief is merely the specific issue someone raises about the belief. The appropriate objector-group is the group of people qualified to make objections about the belief. According to Annis, a belief is *contextually basic* for a person at a particular time, relative to an appropriate objector-group, if and only if at that time the objector-group does not require the person in question to have any reasons for the belief. If, however, some member of the objector-group raises an objection to a belief, one will have to provide an appropriate response to support the belief. Given such a reason, the belief in question will not be contextually basic. On Annis's contextualism, however, a belief is epistemically justified if and only if it is itself contextually basic or is supported by reasons that are contextually basic beliefs. A key implication of Annis's account is that epistemology must be *naturalized*; for given contextualism, we cannot neglect the *actual* social practices and standards of justification of a group of inquirers.

In "Evidentialism," Richard Feldman and Earl Conee argue that the epistemic justification of a belief for a person is determined by the quality of that person's *evidence* for the belief. On their view, roughly speaking, a belief is justified for a person if and only if the belief *fits* the person's evidence. Feldman and Conee defend their view against the currently popular views that the justification of a belief depends on a person's cognitive capacities or on the cognitive processes that led to the belief. The latter views, they argue, neglect the crucial role of evidence in justification. Reliabilism, in particular, suffers from this kind of neglect of evidence.

In "Reflective Equilibrium, Analytic Epistemology and the Problem of Cognitive Diversity," Stephen Stich acknowledges and examines the phenomenon of cognitive diversity, diversity in ways of thinking. Human cognitive process, according to Stich, may resemble human language-processing abilities: "They may be acquired in ways that are deeply dependent on environmental variables, and they may differ quite radically from one individual or culture to another." Stich asks what might make one system of cognitive processes better than another, and considers the influential method of "reflective equilibrium" as a source of a likely answer. This method involves a process of bringing judgments about particular inferences and judgments about general principles into agreement.

Stich contends that a reflective-equilibrium approach fails to capture what we regard as justification, since obviously unreasonable beliefs can be in reflective equilibrium. In addition, Stich claims that "the evaluative epistemic concepts embedded in everyday thought and language are every bit as likely as the cognitive processes they evaluate to be culturally acquired and to vary from culture to culture." Stich faults analytic epistemologists, including Alvin Goldman, for assuming but failing to show that the notions of epistemic evaluation prominent in our own culture are better than the alternative evaluative notions in other cultures. The following question motivates Stich's essay: "In the absence of any reason to think that the locally prevailing notions of epistemic evaluation are superior to the alternatives, why should we care one whit whether the cognitive processes we use are sanctioned by those evaluative concepts?"

26 / William P. Alston
CONCEPTS OF EPISTEMIC JUSTIFICATION

I

Justification, or at least "justification," bulks large in recent epistemology. The view that knowledge consists of true-justified-belief (+ . . .) has been prominent in this century, and the justification of belief has attracted considerable attention in its own right. But it is usually not at all clear just what an epistemologist means by "justified," just what concept the term is used to express. An enormous amount of energy has gone into the attempt to specify conditions under which beliefs of one or another sort are justified; but relatively little has been done to explain *what it is* for a belief to be justified, what that is for which conditions are being sought.[1] The most common procedure has been to proceed on the basis of a number of (supposedly) obvious cases of justified belief, without pausing to determine what property it is of which these cases are instances. Now even if there were some single determinate concept that all these theorists have implicitly in mind, this procedure would be less than wholly satisfactory. For in the absence of an explicit account of the concept being applied, we lack the most fundamental basis for deciding between supposed intuitions and for evaluating proposed conditions of justification. And in any event, as philosophers we do not seek merely to speak the truth, but also to gain an explicit, reflective understanding of the matters with which we deal. We want to know not only when our beliefs are justified, but also what it is to enjoy that status. True, not every fundamental concept can be expli-

cated, but we shall find that much can be done with this one.

And since, as we shall see in this paper, there are several distinct concepts that are plausibly termed "concepts of epistemic justification," the need for analysis is even greater. By simply using "justified" in an unexamined, intuitive fashion the epistemologist is covering up differences that make important differences to the shape of a theory of justification. We cannot fully understand the stresses and strains in thought about justification until we uncover the most crucial differences between concepts of epistemic justification.

Not all contemporary theorists of justification fall under these strictures. Some have undertaken to give an account of the concept of justification they are using.[2] But none of them provide a map of this entire conceptual territory.

In this paper I am going to elaborate and interrelate several distinct concepts of epistemic justification, bringing out some crucial issues involved in choosing between them. I shall give reasons for disqualifying some of the contenders, and I shall explain my choice of a winner. Finally I shall vouchsafe a glimpse of the enterprise for which this paper is a propadeutic, that of showing how the differences between these concepts make a difference in what it takes for the justification of belief, and other fundamental issues in epistemology.

Before launching this enterprise we must clear out of the way a confusion between one's *being* justified in believing that *p*, and one's *justifying* one's belief that *p*, where the latter

Reprinted by permission from William Alston, "Concepts of Epistemic Justification," *The Monist* 68 (1985), 57–89. Copyright 1985, *The Monist*.

involves one's *doing* something to show that *p*, or to show that one's belief was justified, or to exhibit one's justification. The first side of this distinction, on the other hand, is a state or condition one is in, not anything one does or any upshot thereof. I might *be* justified in believing that there is milk on the table because I see it there, even though I have done nothing to show that there is milk on the table or to show that I am justified in believing there to be. It is amazing how often these matters are confused in the literature. We will be concentrating on the "be justified" side of this distinction, since that is of more fundamental epistemological interest. If epistemic justification were restricted to those cases in which the subject carries out a "justification" it would *obviously* not be a necessary condition of knowledge or even of being in a strong position to acquire knowledge. Most cases of perceptual knowledge, for example, involve no such activity.[3]

II

Let's begin our exploration of this stretch of conceptual territory by listing a few basic features of the concept that would seem to be common ground.

1. It applies to beliefs, or alternatively to a cognitive subject's having a belief. I shall speak indifferently of S's belief that *p* being justified and of S's being justified in believing that *p*. This is the common philosophical concept of belief, in which S's believing that *p* entails neither that S knows that *p* nor that S does not know that *p*. It is not restricted to conscious or occurent beliefs.

2. It is an evaluative concept, in a broad sense in which this is contrasted with "factual." To say that S is justified in believing that *p* is to imply that there is something all right, satisfactory, in accord with the way things should be, about the fact that S believes that *p*. It is to accord S's believing a positive evaluative status.

3. It has to do with a specifically *epistemic* dimension of evaluation. Beliefs can be evaluated in different ways. One may be more or less prudent, fortunate, or faithful in holding a

certain belief. Epistemic justification is different from all that. Epistemic evaluation is undertaken from what we might call the "epistemic point of view." That point of view is defined by the aim at maximizing truth and minimizing falsity in a large body of beliefs. The qualification "in a large body of beliefs" is needed because otherwise one could best achieve the aim by restricting one's belief to those that are obviously true. That is a rough formulation. How large a body of beliefs should we aim at? Is any body of beliefs of a given size, with the same truth-falsity ratio, equally desirable, or is it more important, epistemically, to form beliefs on some matters than others? And what relative weights should be assigned to the two aims at maximizing truth and minimizing falsity? We can't go into all that here; in any event, however these issues are settled it remains true that our central cognitive aim is to amass a large body of beliefs with a favorable truth-falsity ratio. For a belief to be epistemically justified is for it, somehow, to be awarded high marks relative to that aim.

4. It is a matter of degree. One can be more or less justified in believing that *p*. If, e.g., what justifies one is some evidence one has, one will be more or less justified depending on the amount and strength of the evidence. However in this paper I shall, for the sake of simplicity, treat justification as absolute. You may, if you like, think of this as the degree of justification required for some standard of acceptability.

III

Since any concept of epistemic justification is a concept of some condition that is desirable or commendable from the standpoint of the aim at maximizing truth and minimizing falsity, in distinguishing different concepts of justification we will be distinguishing different ways in which conditions can be desirable from this standpoint. As I see it, the major divide in this terrain has to do with whether believing, and refraining from believing, are subject to obligation, duty, and the like. If they are, we can think of the favorable evaluative status of a certain belief as consisting in the fact that in holding that belief one has fulfilled one's obligations, or refrained from violating one's obligations, to achieve the fundamental aim in question. If they are not so subject, the favorable status will have to be thought of in some other way.

I shall first explore concepts of the first sort, which I shall term "deontological,"[4] since they have to do with how one stands in believing that p, vis-à-vis duties or obligations. Most epistemologists who have attempted to explicate justification have set out a concept of this sort.[5] It is natural to set out a deontological concept on the model of the justification of behavior. Something I *did* was justified just in case it was *not in violation* of any relevant duties, obligations, rules, or regulations, and hence was not something for which I could rightfully be blamed. To say that my expenditures on the trip were justified is not to say that I was obliged to make those expenditures (e.g., for taxis), but only that it was all right for me to do so, that in doing so I was not in violation of any relevant rules or regulations. And to say that I was justified in making that decision on my own, without consulting the executive committee, is not to say that I was required to do it on my own (though that *may* also be true); it is only to say that the departmental by-laws permit the chairman to use his own discretion in matters of this kind. Similarly, to say that a belief was deontologically justified is not to say that the subject was obligated to believe this, but only that he was permitted to do so, that believing this did not involve any violation of relevant obligations. To say that I am justified in believing that salt is composed of sodium and chlorine, since I have been assured of this by an expert, is not to say that I am obligated to believe this, though this might also be true. It is to say that I am permitted to believe it, that believing it would not be a violation of any relevant obligation, e.g., the obligation to refrain from believing that p in the absence of adequate reasons for doing so. As Carl Ginet puts it, "One is *justified* in being confident that p if and only if it is not the case that one ought not to be confident that p; one could not be justly reproached for being confident that p."[6]

Since we are concerned specifically with the *epistemic* justification of belief, the concept in which we are interested is not that of *not violating obligations of any sort in believing*, but rather the more specific concept of *not violating "epistemic," "cognitive," or "intellectual" obligations in believing*. Where are such obligations to be found? If we follow out our earlier specification of the "epistemic point of view," we will think of our basic epistemic obligation as that of doing what we can to achieve the aim at maximizing truth and minimizing falsity within a large body of beliefs. There will then be numerous more specific obligations that owe their status to the fact that fulfilling them will tend to the achievement of that central aim. Such obligations might include *to refrain from believing that p in the absence of sufficient evidence* and *to accept whatever one sees to be clearly implied by something one already believes (or, perhaps, is already justified in believing).*[7] Of course other positions might be taken on this point.[8] One might suppose that there are a number of ultimate, irreducible intellectual duties that cannot be derived from any basic goal of our cognitive life. Or alternative versions of the central aim might be proposed. Here we shall think in terms of the basic aim we have specified, with more specific obligations derived from that.

Against this background we can set our first concept of epistemic justification as follows, using "d" for "deontological":

I. S is J_d in believing that p *iff* in believing that p S is not violating any epistemic obligations.

There are important distinctions between what we may call "modes" of obligation, justification, and other normative statuses. These distinctions are by no means confined to the epistemic realm. Let's introduce them in connection with moral norms for behavior. Begin with a statement of obligation in "objective" terms, a statement of the objective state of affairs I might be said to be obliged to bring about. For example, it is my obligation as a host to make *my guest, G, feel welcome*. Call that underlined state of affairs, "A." We may think of this as an *objective* conception of my obligation as a host. I have fulfilled that obligation *iff* G feels welcome.[9] But suppose I did what I sincerely believed would bring about A? In that case surely no one could blame me for dereliction of duty. That suggests a more *subjective* conception of my obligation as *doing what I believed was likely to bring about A*.[10] But perhaps I should not be let off so easily as that. "You should have realized that what you did was not calculated to make G feel welcome." This retort suggests a somewhat more stringent formulation of my obligation than the very permissive subjective conception just specified. It suggests that I can't fulfill my obligation by doing just anything I happen to believe will bring about A. I am not off the hook unless *I did what the facts available to me indicate will have a good chance of leading to A*. This is still a subjective conception in that what it takes to fulfill my obligation is specified from my point of view; but it takes my point of view to range over not all my beliefs, but only my justified beliefs. This we might call a *cognitive* conception of my obligation.[11] Finally, suppose that I did what I had adequate reason to suppose would produce A, and I did produce A, but I didn't do it for that reason. I was just amusing myself, and I would have done what I did even if I had known it would not make G feel welcome. In that case I might be faulted for moral irresponsibility, however well I rate in the other modes. This suggests what we may call a motivational conception of my obligation as *doing what I believed (or was justified in believing) would bring about A, in order to bring about A*.

We may sum up these distinctions as follows:

II. S has fulfilled his *objective* obligation *iff* S has brought about A.
III. S has fulfilled his *subjective* obligation *iff* S has done what he believed to be most likely to bring about A.
IV. S has fulfilled his *cognitive* obligation *iff* S did what he was justified in believing to be most likely to bring about A.
V. S has fulfilled his *motivational* obligation *iff* S has done what he did because he supposed it would be most likely to bring about A.

We can make analogous distinctions with respect to the justification of behavior or belief, construed as the absence of any violation of obligations.[12] Let's indicate how this works out for the justification of belief.

VI. S is *objectively* justified in believing that *p iff* S is not violating any objective obligation in believing that *p*.
VII. S *is subjectively* justified in believing that *p iff* S is not violating any subjective obligation in believing that *p*.
VIII. S is *cognitively* justified in believing that *p iff* S is not violating any cognitive obligation in believing that *p*.
IX. S is *motivationally* justified in believing that *p iff* S is not violating any motivational obligation in believing that *p*.

If we assume that only one intellectual obligation is relevant to the belief in question, viz., the obligation to believe that *p* only if one has adequate evidence for *p*, we can be a bit more concrete about this.

X. S is objectively justified in believing that *p iff* S has adequate evidence for *p*.[13]
XI. S is subjectively justified in believing that *p iff* S believes that he possesses adequate evidence for *p*.
XII. S is cognitively justified in believing that *p iff* S is justified in believing that he possesses adequate evidence for *p*.[14]
XIII. S is motivationally justified in believing that *p iff* S believes that *p* on the basis of adequate evidence, or, alternatively, on the basis of what he believed, or was justified in believing, was adequate evidence.

I believe that we can safely neglect XI. To explain why I will need to make explicit what it is to have adequate evidence for *p*. First a proposition, *q, is* adequate evidence for *p* provided they are related in such a way that if *q* is true then *p* is at least probably true. But I *have* that evidence only if I believe that *q*. Furthermore I don't "have" it in such a way as to thereby render my belief that *p* justified unless I know or am justified in believing that *q*. An unjustified belief that *q* wouldn't do it. If I believe that Begin has told the cabinet that he will resign, but only because I credited an unsubstantiated rumour, then even if Begin's having told the cabinet that he would resign is an adequate indication that he will resign, I will not thereby be justified in believing that he will resign.

Now I might very well *believe* that I have adequate evidence for q even though one or more of these conditions is not satisfied. This is an especially live possibility with respect to the first and third conditions. I might mistakenly believe that my evidence is adequate support, and I might mistakenly suppose that I am justified in accepting it. But, as we have just seen, if I am not justified in accepting the evidence for p then my believing it cannot render me justified in believing that p, however adequate that evidence. I would also hold, though this is perhaps more controversial, that if the evidence is not in fact adequate my having that evidence cannot justify me in believing that p. Thus, since my believing that I have adequate evidence is compatible with these nonjustifying states of affairs, we cannot take subjective justification, as defined in XI, to constitute epistemic justification.

That leaves us with three contenders. Here I will confine myself to pointing out that there is a strong tendency for J_d to be used in a cognitive rather than a purely objective form. J_d is, most centrally, a concept of freedom from blameworthiness, a concept of being "in the clear" so far as one's intellectual obligations are concerned. But even if I don't have adequate evidence for p, I could hardly be blamed for believing that p (even assuming, as we are in this discussion, that there is something wrong with believing in the absence of adequate evidence), provided I am justified in supposing that I have adequate evidence. So long as that condition holds I have done the right thing, or refrained from doing the wrong thing, so far as I am able to tell; and what more could be required of me? But this means that it is XII, rather than X, that brings out what it takes for freedom from blame, and so brings out what it takes for being J_d.[15]

What about the motivational form? We can have J_d in any of the first three forms with or without the motivational form. I can have ad-

equate evidence for p, and believe that p, (XI) whether or not my belief is based on that evidence; and so for the other two. But the motivational mode is parasitic on the other modes, in that the precise form taken by the motivational mode depends on the status of the (supposed) evidence on which the belief is based. This "unsaturated" character of the motivational mode is reflected in the threefold alternative that appears in our formulation of XIII. If S bases his belief that p on actually possessed adequate evidence, then XIII combines with X. If the evidence on which it is based is only believed to be adequate evidence, or only justifiably believed to be adequate evidence, then XIII combines with XI or XII. Of course, it may be based on actually possessed adequate evidence, which is justifiably believed to be such; in which case S is justified in all four modes. Thus the remaining question concerning J_d is whether a "motivational rider" should be put on XII. Is it enough for J_d that S be justified in believing that he has adequate evidence for p, or should it also be required that S's belief that p be based on that evidence? We will address this question in section V in the form it assumes for a quite different concept of justification.[16]

IV

We have explained *being J_d in believing that p as not violating any intellectual obligations in believing that p.* And, in parallel fashion, being J_d in refraining from believing that p would consist in not having violated any intellectual obligations in so doing. But if it is possible for me to violate an obligation in refraining from believing that p, it must be that I can be obliged, under certain conditions, to believe that p. And, by the same token, if I can violate obligations in believing that p then I can be obliged to refrain from believing that p. And this is the way we have been thinking of it. Our example of an intellectual obligation has been the obligation to refrain from believing that p in the absence of adequate evidence. On the other side, we might think of a person as being obliged to believe that p if confronted with conclusive evidence that p (where that includes the absence of sufficient overriding evidence to the contrary).

Now it certainly looks as if I can be obliged to believe or to refrain from believing, only if this is in my direct voluntary control; only if I can, here and now, believe that p or no just by willing (deciding, choosing . . .). And that is the way many epistemologists seem to construe the matter. At least many formulations are most naturally interpreted in this way. Think back, e.g., on Chisholm's formulation of our intellectual obligation (1977, p. 14), cited in n16. Chisholm envisages a person thinking of a certain proposition as a candidate for belief, considering what grounds there might be for belief or refraining from belief, and then effectively choosing belief or abstention on the basis of those considerations.[17] Let's call the version of J_d that presupposes direct voluntary control over belief (and thus thinks of an obligation to believe as an obligation to bring about belief here and now), "J_{dv}" ("v" for "voluntary").

I find this assumption of direct voluntary control over belief quite unrealistic. There are strong reasons for doubting that belief is usually, or perhaps ever, under direct voluntary control. First, think of the beliefs I acquire about myself and the world about me through experience—through perception, self-consciousness, testimony, and simple reasoning based on these data. When I see a car coming down the street I am not capable of believing or disbelieving this at will. In such familiar situations the belief-acquisition mechanism is isolated from the direct influence of the will and under the control of more purely cognitive factors.

Partisans of a voluntary control thesis will counter by calling attention to cases in which things don't appear to be so cut and dried: cases of radical underdetermination by evidence, as when a general has to dispose his forces in the absence of sufficient information about the position of enemy forces; or cases of the acceptance of a religious or philosophical position where there seem to be a number of equally viable alternatives. In such cases it can appear that one makes a decision as to what to believe and what not to believe. My view on these matters is that insofar as something is chosen voluntarily it is something other than a belief or abstention from belief. The general chooses to proceed on the working assumption that the enemy forces are disposed in such-and-such a way. The religious convert to whom it is not clear that the beliefs are correct has chosen to live a certain kind of life, or to selectively subject himself to certain influences. And so on. But even if I am mistaken about these kinds of cases, it is clear that for the vast majority of beliefs nothing like direct voluntary control is involved. And so J_{dv} could not possibly be a generally applicable concept of epistemic justification.

If I am right in rejecting the view that belief is, in general or ever, under direct voluntary control, are we foreclosed from construing epistemic justification as freedom from blameworthiness? Not necessarily. We aren't even prevented from construing epistemic justification as the absence of obligation-violations. We *will* have to avoid thinking of the relevant obligations as obligations to believe or refrain from believing, on the model of obligations to answer a question or to open a door, or to do anything else over which we have immediate voluntary control.[18] If we are to continue to think of intellectual obligations as having to do with believing it will have to be more on the model of the way in which obligations bear on various other conditions over which one lacks direct voluntary control but which one can influence by voluntary actions, such conditions as being overweight, being irritable, being in poor health, or having friends. I can't institute, nullify, or alter any of those conditions here and now just by deciding to do so. But I can do things at will that will influence those conditions; and in that way they may be to some extent under my indirect control. One might speak of my being obliged to be in good health or to have a good disposition, meaning that I am obliged to do what I can (or as much as could reasonably be expected of me) to institute and preserve those states of affairs. However since I think it less misleading to say exactly what I mean, I will not speak of our being obliged to weigh a certain amount or to have a good disposition, or to believe a proposition; I will rather speak of our having obligations to do what we can, or as much as can reasonably be expected of us, to influence those conditions.[19]

The things we can do to affect our believings can be divided into (1) activities that bring influences to bear, or withhold influences from, a particular situation, and (2) activities that affect our belief forming habits. (1) includes such activities as checking to see whether I have considered all the relevant evidence, getting a second opinion, searching my memory for analogous cases, and looking into the question of whether there is anything markedly abnormal about my current perceptual situation. (2) includes training myself to be more critical of gossip, talking myself into being either more or less subservient to authority, and practicing greater sensitivity to the condition of other people. Moreover it is plausible to think of these belief-influencing activities as being subject to intellectual obligations. We might, e.g., think of ourselves as being under an obligation to do what we can (or what could reasonably be expected of us) to make our belief-forming processes as reliable as possible.

All this suggests that we might frame a deontological conception of being epistemically justified in believing that p, in the sense that one's believing that p is not the result of one's failure to fulfill one's intellectual obligations vis-à-vis one's belief forming and maintaining activities. It would, again, be like the way in which one is or isn't to blame for other conditions that are not under direct voluntary control but which one can influence by one's voluntary activities. I am to blame for being overweight (being irritable, being in poor health, being without friends) only if that condition is in some way due to my own past failures to do what I should to limit my intake or to exercise or whatever. If I would still be overweight even if I had done everything I could and should have done about it, then I can hardly be blamed for it. Similarly, we may say that I am subject to reproach for believing that p, provided that I am to blame for being in that doxastic condition, in the sense that there are things I could and should have done, such that if I had done them I would not now be believing that p. If that is the case I am unjustified

in that belief. And if it is *not* the case, if there are no unfulfilled obligations the fulfilling of which would have inhibited that belief formation, then I am justified in the belief.

Thus we have arrived at a deontological concept of epistemic justification that does not require belief to be under direct voluntary control. We may label this concept "J_{di}" ("i" for "involuntary"). It may be more formally defined as follows:

XIV. S is J_{di} in believing that p at t *iff* there are no intellectual obligations that (1) have to do with the kind of belief-forming or sustaining habit the activation of which resulted in S's believing that p at t, or with the particular process of belief formation or sustenance that was involved in S's believing that p at t, and (2) which are such that:

A. S had those obligations prior to t.

B. S did not fulfill those obligations.

C. If S had fulfilled those obligations, S would not have believed that p at t.[20]

As it stands, this account will brand too many beliefs as unjustified, just because it is too undiscriminating in the counter-factual condition, C. There are ways in which the non-fulfillment of intellectual obligations can contribute to a belief acquisition without rendering the belief unjustified. Suppose that I fail to carry out my obligation to spend a certain period in training myself to observe things more carefully. I use the time thus freed up to take a walk around the neighborhood. In the course of this stroll I see two dogs fighting, thereby acquiring the belief that they are fighting. There was a relevant intellectual obligation I didn't fulfill, which is such that if I had fulfilled it I wouldn't have acquired that belief. But if that is a perfectly normal perceptual belief, it is surely not thereby rendered unjustified.

Here the dereliction of duty contributed to belief-formation simply by facilitating access to the data. That's not the kind of contribution we had in mind. The sorts of cases we were thinking of were those most directly suggested by the two sorts of intellectual obligations we distinguished: (a) cases in which the belief was acquired by the activation of a habit that we would not have possessed had we fulfilled our intellectual obligations; (b) cases in which we acquire, or retain, the belief only because we are sheltered from adverse considerations in a way we wouldn't be if we had done what we should have done. Thus we can avoid counterexamples like the above by reformulating C as follows:

C.   If S had fulfilled those obligations, then S's belief-forming habits would have changed, or S's access to relevant adverse considerations would have changed, in such a way that S would not have believed that p at t.

But even with this refinement J_{zi} does not give us what we expect of epistemic justification. The most serious defect is that it does not hook up in the right way with an adequate, truth-conducive ground. I may have done what could reasonably be expected of me in the management of cultivation of my doxastic life, and still hold a belief on outrageously inadequate grounds. There are several possible sources of such a discrepancy. First there is what we might call "cultural isolation." If I have grown up in an isolated community in which everyone unhesitatingly accepts the traditions of the tribe as authoritative, then if I have never encountered anything that seems to cast doubt on the traditions and have never thought to question them, I can hardly be blamed for taking them as authoritative. There is nothing I could reasonably be expected to do that would alter that belief-forming tendency. And there is nothing I could be expected to do that would render me more exposed to counterevidence. (We can suppose that the traditions all have to do with events distant in time and/or space, matters on which I could not be expected to gather evidence on my own.) I am J_{di} in believing these things. And yet the fact that it is the tradition of the tribe that p may be a very poor reason for believing that p.

Then there is deficiency in cognitive powers. Rather than looking at the extremer forms of this, let's consider a college student who just doesn't have what it takes to follow abstract philosophical reasoning, or exposition for that matter. Having read bk. IV of Locke's *Essay*, he believes that it is Locke's view that everything is a matter of opinion, that one person's opinion is just as good as another's, and that what is true for me may not be true for you. And it's not just that he didn't work hard enough on this particular point, or on the general abilities involved. There is nothing that he could and should have done such that had he done so, he would have gotten this straight. He is simply incapable of appreciating the distinction between "One's knowledge is restricted to one's own ideas" and "Everything is a matter of opinion." No doubt teachers of philosophy tend to assume too quickly that this description applies to some of their students, but surely there can be such cases—cases in which either no amount of time and effort would enable the student to get straight on the matter, or it would be unreasonable to expect the person to expend that amount of time or effort. And yet we would hardly wish to say that the student is justified in believing what he does about Locke.

Other possible sources of a discrepancy between J_{di} and epistemic justification are poor training that the person lacks the time or resources to overcome, and an incorrigible doxastic incontinence. ("When he talks like that I just can't help believing what he says.") What this spread of cases brings out is that J_{di} is not sufficient for epistemic justification; we may have done the best we can, or at least the best that could reasonably be expected of us, and still be in a very poor epistemic position in believing that p; we could, blamelessly, be believing p for outrageously bad reasons. Even though J_{di} is the closest we can come to a deontological concept of epistemic justification, if belief is not under direct voluntary control, it still does not give us what we are looking for.

V

Thus neither version of J_d is satisfactory. Perhaps it was misguided all along to think of epistemic justification as freedom from blame-worthiness. Is there any alternative, given the non-negotiable point that we are looking for a concept of epistemic evaluation? Of course there is. By no means all evaluation, even all evaluation of activities, states, and aspects of human beings, involves the circle of terms that includes "obligation," "permission," "right," "wrong," and "blame." We can evaluate a person's abilities, personal appearance, temperament, or state of health as more or less desirable, favorable, or worthwhile, without taking these to be within the person's direct voluntary control and so subject to obligation in a direct fashion (as with J_{dvi}), and without making the evaluation depend on whether the person has done what she should to influence these states (as with J_{di}). Obligation and blame need not come into it at all. This is most obvious when we are dealing with matters that are not even under indirect voluntary control, like one's basic capacities or bodily build. Here when we use positively evaluative terms like "gifted" or "superb," we are clearly not saying that the person has done all she could to foster or encourage the condition in question. But even where the condition is at least partly under indirect voluntary control, as with personal appearance or state of health, we need not be thinking in those terms when we take someone to present a pleasing appearance or to be in splendid health. Moreover, we can carry out these evaluations from a certain point of view. We can judge that someone has a fine bodily constitution from an athletic or from an aesthetic point of view, or that someone's manner is a good one from a professional or from a social point of view.

In like fashion one can evaluate S's believing that p as a good, favorable, desirable, or appropriate thing, without thinking of it as fulfilling or not violating an obligation, and without making this evaluation depend on whether the person has done what she could carry out belief-influencing activities. As in the other cases, it could simply be a matter of the possession of certain good-making characteristics. Furthermore, believings can be evaluated from various points of view, including the epistemic, which, as we have noted, is defined by the aim of maximizing truth and minimizing falsity. It

may be a good thing that S believes that p for his peace of mind, or from the standpoint of loyalty to the cause, or as an encouragement to the redoubling of his efforts. But none of this would render it a good thing for S to believe that p from the epistemic point of view. To believe that p because it gives peace of mind or because it stimulates effort may not be conducive to the attainment of truth and the avoidance of error.

All of this suggests that we can frame a concept of epistemic justification that is "evaluative," in a narrow sense of that term in which it contrasts with "deontological," with the assessment of conduct in terms of obligation, blame, right, and wrong. Let's specify an "evaluative" sense of epistemic justification as follows:

XV. S is J_e in believing that p iff S's believing that p, as S does, is a good thing from the epistemic point of view.

This is a way of being commendable from the epistemic point of view that is quite different from the subject's not being to blame for any violation of intellectual obligations.[21] The qualification "as S does" is inserted not to make it explicit that in order for S to be J_e in believing that p it need not be the case that any believing of p by S would be a good thing epistemically, much less any believing of p by anyone. It is rather that there are aspects of *this* believing of p by S that make it a good thing epistemically. There could conceivably be person-proposition pairs such that any belief in that proposition by that person would be a good thing epistemically; but this would be a limiting case and not typical of our epistemic condition.

Is there anything further to be said about this concept? Of course we should avoid building anything very substantive into the constitution of the concept. After all, it is possible for epistemologists to differ radically as to the conditions under which one or another sort of belief is justified. When this happens they are at least sometimes using the same concept of justification; otherwise they wouldn't be disagreeing over what is required for justification, though they could still disagree over which concept of justification is most fundamental or most useful. Both our versions of J_d are quite neutral in this way. Both leave it completely open as to what intellectual obligations we have, and hence as to what obligations must not be violated if one is to be justified. But while maintaining due regard for the importance of neutrality I believe that we can go beyond XV in fleshing out the concept.

We can get a start on this by considering the following question. If goodness from an epistemic point of view is what we are interested in, why shouldn't we identify justification with truth, at least extensionally? What could be better from that point of view than truth? If the name of the game is the maximization of truth and the minimization of falsity in our beliefs, then plain unvarnished truth is hard to beat. However this consideration has not moved epistemologists to identify justification with truth, or even to take truth as a necessary and sufficient condition for justification. The logical independence of truth and justification is a staple of the epistemological literature. But why should this be? It is obvious that a belief might be J_d without being true and vice versa; but what reason is there for taking J_e to be independent of truth?

I think the answer to this has to be in terms of the "internalist" character of justification. When we ask whether S is justified in believing that p, we are, as we have repeatedly been insisting, asking a question from the standpoint of an aim at truth; but we are not asking whether things are in fact as S believes. We are getting at something more "internal" to S's "perspective on the world." This internalist feature of justification made itself felt in our discussion of J_d when we pointed out that to be J_{dv} is to fail to violate any relevant intellectual obligations, *so far as one can tell*, to be J_{dv} in what we call the "cognitive" mode. With respect to J_e the analogous point is that although this is goodness vis-à-vis the aim at truth, it consists not in the beliefs fitting the way the facts actually are, but something more like the belief's being true "so far as the subject can tell from what is available to the subject." In asking whether S is J_e in believing that p we are asking whether the truth of p is strongly indicated by what S has to go on; whether, given what S had to go on, it is at least quite

likely that p is true. We want to know whether S had *adequate* grounds for believing that p, where *adequate* grounds are those sufficiently indicative to the truth of p.

If we are to make the notion of *adequate grounds* central for J_e we must say more about it. A belief has a certain ground, G, when it is "based on" G. What is it for a belief, B, to be *based on* G? That is a difficult question. So far as I know, there is no fully satisfactory general account in the literature, nor am I able to supply one. But we are not wholly at a loss. We do have a variety of paradigm cases; the difficulty concerns just how to generalize from them and just where to draw the line. When one infers p from q and *thereby* comes to accept p, this is a clear case of basing one belief on another. Again, when I come to believe that that is a tree because this visually appears to me to be the case, that is another paradigm; here my belief that that is a tree is based on my visual experience, or, if you prefer, on certain aspects of that experience. The main difficulties arise with respect to cases in which no conscious inference takes place but in which we are still inclined to say that one belief is based on another. Consider, for example, my forming the belief that you are angry on seeing you look and act in a certain way. I perform no conscious inference from a proposition about your demeanor and behavior to a proposition about your emotional state. Nevertheless it seems plausible to hold that I did learn about your demeanor and behavior through seeing it, and that the beliefs I thereby formed played a crucial role in my coming to believe that you are angry. More specifically it seems that the former beliefs gave rise to the latter belief; that if I hadn't acquired the former I would not have acquired the latter; and, finally, that if I am asked why I suppose that you are angry I would cite the behavior and demeanor as my reason (perhaps only as "the way he looked and acted"). How can we get this kind of case together with the conscious-inference cases into a general account? We might claim that they are all cases of inference, some of them being unconscious. But there are problems as to when we are justified in imputing unconscious inferences. We might take it that what lets in our problem cases is the subject's disposition to cite the one belief(s) as his reason for the other belief; and then make our general condition a disjunction of conscious inference from q and a tendency to cite q as the reason. But then what about subjects (small children and lower animals) that are too unsophisticated to be able to answer questions as to what their reasons are? Can't their beliefs be based on something when no conscious inference is performed? Moreover this disjunctive criterion will not include cases in which a belief is based on an experience, rather than on other beliefs. A third suggestion concerns causality. In all the cases mentioned thus far it is plausible to suppose that the belief that q was among the causes of the belief that p. This suggests that we might try to cut the Gordian knot by boldly identifying "based on" with "caused by." But this runs into the usual difficulties of simple causal theories. Many items enter into the causation of a belief, for example, various neuro-physiological happenings, that clearly don't qualify as even part of what the belief is based on. To make a causal account work we would have to beef it up into "caused by q in a certain way." And what way is that? Some way that is paradigmatically exemplified by our paradigms? But how to state this way in such a fashion that it applies equally to the non-paradigmatic cases?[22]

In the face of these perplexities our only recourse is to keep a firm hold on our paradigms, and work with a less than ideally determinate concept of a relationship that holds in cases that are "sufficiently like" the paradigms. That will be sufficient to do the job over most of the territory.[23]

Let's return to "grounds." What a belief is based on we may term the ground of the belief. A ground, in a more dispositional sense of the term, is the sort of item on which a belief can be based. We have already cited beliefs and experiences as possible grounds, and these would seem to exhaust the possibilities. Indeed, some epistemologists would find this too generous already, maintaining that beliefs can be based only on other beliefs. They would treat perceptual cases by holding that the belief that a tree is over there is based on the *belief that* there visually appears to me to be a tree over there rather than, as we are suggesting,

on the visual appearance itself. I can't accept that, largely because I doubt that all perceptual believers have such beliefs about their visual experience,[24] but I can't pause to argue the point. Suffice it to say that since my opponents' position is, to be as generous as possible, controversial, we do not want to build a position on this issue into the *concept* of epistemic justification. We want to leave open at least the *conceptual* possibility of *direct* or *immediate* justification by experience (and perhaps in other ways also), as well as *indirect* or *mediate* justification by relation to other beliefs (inferentially in the most explicit cases). Finally, to say that a subject *had adequate* grounds for her belief that p is to say that she has other justified beliefs, or experiences, on which the belief could be based and which are strongly indicative of the truth of the belief. The reason for the restriction to *justified* beliefs is that a ground shouldn't be termed adequate unless it can confer justification on the belief it grounds. But we noted earlier that if I infer my belief that p, by even impeccable logic, from an *unjustified* belief that q, the former belief is not thereby justified.[25]

To return to the main thread of the discussion, we are thinking of S's being J_e in believing that p as involving S's having adequate grounds for that belief. That is, we are thinking of the possession of those adequate grounds as constituting the goodness of the belief from the epistemic point of view. The next thing to note is that the various "modes" of J_d apply here as well.

Let's begin by noting an objective-subjective distinction. To be sure, in thinking of J_e as *having truth-indicative grounds within one's "perspective on the world,"* we are already thinking of it as more subjective than flat-out truth. But within that perspectival conception we can set the requirements as more objective or more subjective. There is more than one respect in which the possession of adequate grounds could be "subjectivized." First, there is the distinction between the existence of the ground and its adequacy. S is *objectively* J_e in believing that p if S does in fact have grounds that are in fact adequate grounds for that belief. A subjective version would require only that S *believe* one or the other part of this, or both; either (a) that there are (possible) grounds that are in fact adequate and he believes of those grounds that he has them; or (b) that he has grounds that he believes to be adequate; or the combination, (c) that he believes himself to have adequate grounds. Moreover, there are two ways in which the possession-of-grounds belief could go wrong. Confining ourselves to beliefs, one could mistakenly suppose oneself to believe that p, or one could mistakenly suppose one's belief that p to be justified. Lacking time to go into all these variations, I shall confine this discussion to the subjectivization of adequacy. So our first two modes will be:

XVI.   Objective—S does have adequate grounds for believing that p.

XVII. Subjective—S has grounds for believing that p and he believes them to be adequate.

And here too we have a "justified belief," or "cognitive" variant on the subjective version.

XVIII. Cognitive—S has grounds for believing that p and he is justified in believing them to be adequate.

We can dismiss XVII by the same arguments we brought against the subjective version of J_d. The mere fact that I believe, however unjustifiably or irresponsibly, that my grounds for believing that p are adequate could scarcely render me justified in believing that p. If I believe them to be adequate just because I have an egotistical penchant to overestimate my powers, that could hardly make it rational for me to believe that p. But here we will not find the same reason to favor XVIII over XVI. With J_d the cognitive version won out because of what it takes for blameworthiness. But whether one is J_e in believing that p has nothing to do with whether he is subject to blame. It depends rather on whether his believing that p is a *good thing* from the epistemic point of view. And however justifiably S believes that his grounds are adequate, if they are not then his believing that p on those grounds is not a good move in the truth-seeking game. Even if he isn't to blame for making that move it is a bad move nonetheless. Thus J_e is properly construed in the objective mode.

We are also confronted with the question of whether J_e should be construed "motivationally." Since we have already opted for an objective reading, the motivational version will take the following form:

XIX.   Motivational—S's belief that p is based on adequate grounds.

So our question is whether it is enough for justification that S *have* adequate grounds for his belief, whether used or not, or whether it is also required that the belief be based on those grounds. We cannot settle this question on the grounds that were available for J_{dvi}, since with J_e we are not thinking of the subject as being obliged to take relevant consideration into account in *choosing* whether to believe that p.

There is something to be said on both sides of this issue. In support of the first, source-irrelevant position (XVI without XIX), it can be pointed out that S's *having a justification* for believing that p is independent of whether S does believe that p; I can have adequate grounds for believing that p, and so *have* a justification, even though I do not in fact believe that p. Hence it can hardly be a requirement for having a justification for p that my non-existent belief have a certain kind of basis. Likewise my having adequate grounds for believing that p is sufficient for this being *a rational thing for me to believe*. But, says the opponent, suppose that S does believe that p. If simply having adequate grounds were sufficient for this belief to be justified, then, provided S does have the grounds, her belief that p would be justified however frivolous the source. But surely a belief that stems from wishful thinking would not be justified, however strong one's (unutilised) grounds for it.[26]

Now the first thing to say about this controversy is that both antagonists win, at least to the extent that each of them is putting forward a viable concept, and one that is actually used in epistemic assessment. There certainly is the concept of *having* adequate grounds for the belief that p, whether or not one does believe that p, and there equally certainly is the concept of one's belief being based on adequate grounds. Both concepts represent favorable epistemic statuses. *Ceteris paribus*, one is better off believing something for which one has adequate grounds than believing something for which one doesn't. And the same can be said for the contrast between having a belief that is based on adequate grounds and having one that isn't. Hence I will recognize that these are both concepts of epistemic justification, and I will resist the pressure to decide which is *the* concept.

Nevertheless we can seek to determine which concept is more fundamental to epistemology. On this issue it seems clear that the motivational concept is the richer one and thereby embodies a more complete account of a belief's being a good thing from the epistemic point of view. Surely there is something epistemically undesirable about a belief that is generated in an intellectually disreputable way, however adequate the unutilised grounds possessed by the subject. If, possessing excellent reasons for supposing that you are trying to discredit me professionally, I nevertheless believe this, not for those reasons but out of paranoia, in such a way that even if I didn't have those reasons I would have believed this just as firmly, it was undesirable from the point of view of the aim at truth for me to form that belief as I did. So if we are seeking the most inclusive concept of what makes a belief a good thing epistemically, we will want to include a consideration of what the belief is based on. Hence I will take XIX as the favored formulation of what makes a belief a good thing from the epistemic point of view.

I may add that XVI can be seen as derivative from XIX. To simply *have* adequate grounds is to be in such a position that *if* I make use of that position as a basis for believing that *p* I will thereby be justified in that belief. Thus XVI gives us a concept of a potential for XIX; it is a concept of having resources that are sufficient for believing justifiably, leaving open the question of whether those resources are used.

The next point to be noted is that XIX guarantees only prima facie justification. As often noted, it is quite possible for my belief that *p* to have been formed on the basis of evidence that in itself adequately supports *p*, even though the totality of the evidence at my disposal does not. Thus the evidence on which I came to believe that the butler committed the murder might strongly support that hypothesis, but when arriving at that belief I was ignoring other things I know or justifiably believe that tend to exculpate the butler; the total evidence at my disposal is not sufficient support for my belief. In that case we will not want to count my belief as justified all things considered, even though the grounds *on the basis of which* it was formed were themselves adequate. Their adequacy is, so to say, *overridden* by the larger perspectival context in which they are set. Thus XIX gives us prima facie justification, what will be justification provided it is not cancelled by further relevant factors. Unqualified justification requires an additional condition to the effect that S does not also have reasons that suffice to override the justification provided by the grounds on which the belief is based. Building that into XIX we get:

XX.   Motivational—S's belief that *p* is based on adequate grounds, and S lacks overriding reasons to the contrary.

Even though XX requires us to bring in the unused portions of the perspective, we cannot simplify the condition by ignoring the distinction between what provides the basis and what doesn't, and make the crucial condition something like "The totality of S's perspective provides adequate support." For then we would run up against the considerations that led us to prefer XIX to XVI.

We have distinguished two aspects of our evaluative concept of justification, the strictly evaluative portion—goodness from the epistemic point of view—and the very general statement of the relevant good making characteristic, *based on adequate grounds in the absence of overriding reasons to the contrary*. In taking the concept to include this second component we are opting for the view that this concept, though unmistakably evaluative rather than "purely factual" in character, is not so purely evaluative as to leave completely open the basis on which this evaluative status supervenes. I do not see how to justify this judgment by reference to any more fundamental considerations. It is just that in reflecting on epistemic justification, thought of in evaluative (as contrasted with deontological) terms, it seems clear to me that the range of possible bases for epistemic goodness is not left completely open by the concept, that it is part of what we mean in terming a belief justified, that the belief was based on adequate grounds (or, at least, that the subject had adequate grounds for it).[27] Though this means that J_c is not maximally neutral on the question of what it takes for justification, it is still quite close to that. It still leaves open whether there is immediate justification and if so on the basis of what, how strong a ground is needed for justification, what dimensions of strength there are for various kinds of grounds, and so on.

Let's codify our evaluative concept of justification as follows:

XXI.   S is J_{eg} in believing that p *iff* S's believing that p, as S did, was a good thing from the epistemic point of view, in that S's belief that p was based on adequate grounds and S lacked sufficient overriding reasons to the contrary.

In the subscript "g" stands for "grounds."

My supposition that all justification of belief involves adequate grounds may be contested. This does seem incontrovertible for beliefs based on other beliefs and for perceptual beliefs based on experience. But what about beliefs in self evident propositions where the self-evidence is what justifies me in the belief.[28] On considering the proposition that two quantities equal to the same quantity are equal to each other, this seems obviously true to me; and I shall suppose, though this is hardly uncontroversial, that in those circumstances I am justified in believing it. But where are the adequate grounds on which my belief is based? It is not that there are grounds here about whose adequacy we might well have doubts, it is rather that there seems to be nothing identifiable as grounds. There is nothing here that is distinguishable from my belief and the proposition believed, in the way evidence or reasons are distinct from that for which they are evidence or reasons, or in the way my sensory experience is distinct from the beliefs about the physical world that are based on it. Here I simply consider the proposition and straightaway accept it. A similar problem can be raised for

normal beliefs about one's own conscious states. What is the ground for a typical belief that one feels sleepy?[29] If one replies "One's being conscious of one's feeling of sleepiness," then it may be insisted, with some show of plausibility, that where one is consciously feeling sleepy there is no difference between one's feeling sleepy and one's being conscious that one is feeling sleepy.

This is a very large issue that I will not have time to consider properly. Suffice it to say that one may treat these as limiting cases in which the ground, though real enough, is minimally distinguishable either from the belief it is grounding or from the fact that makes the belief true. In the first person belief about one's own conscious state the ground coincides with the fact that makes the belief true. Since the belief is itself an experience of the subject, there need be nothing "between" the subject and the fact that serves as an indication of the latter's presence. The fact "reveals itself" directly. Self-evident propositions require separate treatment. Here I think that we can take the *way* the proposition appears to one, variously described as "obviously true," "self-evident," and "clear and distinct," as the ground on which the belief is based. I accept the proposition because it *seems* to me so obviously true. This is less distinct from the belief than an inferential or sensory experiential ground, since it has to do with how I am aware of the proposition. Nevertheless here is at least a minimal distinctness. I can form an intelligible conception of someone's failing to believe that p, where p seems obviously true. Perhaps this person has been rendered unduly sceptical by overexposure to the logical paradoxes.

VI

Let's go back to the idea that the "based on adequate grounds" part of J_{eg} is there because of the "internalist" character of justification. Contrasts between internalism and externalism have been popular in epistemology lately, but the contrast is not always drawn in the same way. There are two popular ways, both of which are distinct from what I have in mind.

First there is the idea that justification is internal in that it depends on what support is available for the belief from "within the subject's perspective," in the sense of what the subject knows or justifiably believes about the world.[30] This kind of internalism restricts justification to mediate or discursive justification, justification by reasons. Another version takes "the subject's perspective" to include whatever is "directly accessible" to the subject, accessible just on the basis of reflection; internalism on this version restricts justifiers to what is directly accessible to the subject.[31] This, unlike the first version, does not limit us to mediate justification, since experience can be taken to be at least as directly accessible as beliefs and knowledge.

In contrast to both these ways of drawing the distinction, what I take to be internal about justification is that whether a belief is justified depends on what it is based on (grounds); and grounds must be other psychological state(s) of the same subject. I am not absolutely certain that grounds are confined to beliefs and experiences, even if experiences are not confined to sensations and feelings but also include, e.g., the way a proposition seems obvious to one, and religious and aesthetic experiences; but these are the prime candidates, and any other examples must belong to some kind of which these are the paradigms. So in taking it to be conceptually true that one is justified in believing that p *iff* one's belief that p is based on an adequate ground, I take justification to be "internal" in that it depends on the way in which the belief stems from the believer's psychological states, which are "internal" to the subject in an obvious sense. What would be an externalist contrast with this kind of internalism? We shall see one such contrast in a moment, in discussing the relation of J_{eg} to reliabilism. Moreover, it contrasts with the idea that one can be justified in a certain belief just because of the status of the proposition believed (necessary, infallible). My sort of internalism is different from the first one mentioned above, in that experiences as well as beliefs can figure as grounds. And it is different from the second if, as I believe, what a belief is based on may not be directly accessible. This will be the case if, as seems plausible, much belief formation

goes on below the conscious level. It would seem, e.g., that, as we move about the environment, we are constantly forming short-term perceptual beliefs without any conscious monitoring of this activity.

The most prominent exponents of an explicitly non-deontological conception of epistemic justification have been realibilists, who have either identified justification with reliability [32] or have taken reliability to be an adequate criterion of justification.[33] The reliability that is in question here is the reliability of belief formation and sustenance.[34] To say that a belief was formed in a reliable way is, roughly, to say that it was formed in a way that can be depended on generally to form true rather than false beliefs, at least from inputs like the present one, and at least in the sorts of circumstances in which we normally find ourselves.[35] Thus if my visual system, when functioning as it is at present in yielding my belief that there is a tree in front of me, generally yields true beliefs about objects that are fairly close to me and directly in front of me, then my present belief that there is a tree in front of me was formed in a reliable manner.

Now it may be supposed that J_{eg}, as we have explained it, is just reliability of belief formation with an evaluative frosting. For where a belief is based on adequate grounds that belief has been formed in a reliable fashion. In fact, it is plausible to take reliability as a *criterion* for adequacy of grounds. If my grounds for believing that p are not such that it is generally true, they cannot be termed "adequate." Why do we think that wanting State to win the game is not an adequate reason for supposing that it has won, whereas the fact that a victory has been reported by several newspapers is an adequate reason? Surely it has something to do with the fact that beliefs like that when formed on the first sort of grounds are not *generally* true, while they are *generally* true when formed on grounds of the second sort. Considerations like this may lead us to suppose that J_{eg}, in effect, identifies justification with reliability.[36]

Nevertheless the internalist character of justification prevents it from being identified with reliability, and even blocks an extensional equivalence. Unlike justification, reliability of belief formation is not limited to cases in which a belief is based on adequate grounds within the subject's psychological states. A reliable mode of belief formation *may* work through the subject's own knowledge and experience. Indeed, it is plausible to suppose that all of the reliable modes of belief formation available to human beings are of this sort. But it is quite conceivable that there should be others. I might be so constituted that beliefs about the weather tomorrow which apparently just "pop into my mind" out of nowhere are in fact reliably produced by a mechanism of which we know nothing, and which does not involve the belief being based on anything. Here we would have reliably formed beliefs that are not based on adequate grounds from within my perspective, and so are not J_{eg}.

Moreover, even within the sphere of beliefs based on grounds, reliability and justification do not necessarily go together. The possibility of divergence here stems from another feature of justification embodied in our account, the way in which unqualified justification requires not only an adequate ground but also the absence of sufficient overriding reasons. This opens up the possibility of a case in which a belief is formed on the basis of grounds in a way that is in fact highly reliable, even though the subject has strong reasons for supposing the way to be unreliable. These reasons will (or may) override the prima facie justification provided by the grounds on which the belief was based. And so S will not be justified in the belief, even though it was reliably generated.

Consider, in this connection, a case presented by Alvin Goldman.

> Suppose that Jones is told on fully reliable authority that a certain class of his memory beliefs are almost all mistaken. His parents fabricate a wholly false story that Jones suffered from amnesia when he was seven but later developed *pseudo*-memories of that period. Though Jones listens to what his parents say and has excellent reasons to trust them, he persists in believing the ostensible memories from his seven-year-old past.[37]

Suppose that Jones, upon recalling his fifth birthday party, believes that he was given an

electric train for his fifth birthday because, as it seems to him, he remembers being given it.[38] By hypothesis, his memory mechanism is highly reliable, and so his belief about his fifth birthday was reliably formed. But this belief is not adequately supported by the *totality* of what he justifiably believes. His justifiable belief that he has no real memory of his first seven years overrides the support from his ostensible memory. Thus Jones is not J_{eg} in his memory belief, because the "lack of overriding reasons to the contrary" requirement is not satisfied. But reliability is subject to no such constraint. Just as reliable mechanisms are not restricted to those that work through the subject's perspective, so it is not a requirement on the reliability of belief-formation that the belief be adequately supported by the totality of the subject's perspective. However many and however strong the reasons Jones has for distrusting his memory, the fact remains that his memory beliefs are still reliably formed. Here is another way in which the class of beliefs that are J_{eg} and the class of reliably formed beliefs can fail to coincide.[39]

I would suggest that, of our candidates, J_{eg} most fully embodies what we are looking for under the heading of "epistemic justification." (1) Like its deontological competitors it is an evaluative concept, in a broad sense, a concept of a favorable status from an epistemic point of view. (2) Unlike J_{dv} it does not presuppose that belief is under direct voluntary control. (3) Unlike J_{di}, it implies that the believer is in a strong epistemic position in believing that *p*, i.e., that there is something about the way in which he believes that *p* that renders it at least likely that the belief is true. Thus it renders it intelligible that justification is something we should prize from an epistemic point of view. (4) Unlike the concept of a reliable mode of belief formation it represents this "truth-conducivity" as a matter of the belief's being based on an adequate ground within the subject's own cognitive states. Thus it recognizes the "internalist" character of justification; it recognizes that in asking whether a belief is justified we are interested in the prospects for the truth of the belief, given what the subject "has to go on." (5) Thus the concept provides broad guidelines for the specification of conditions of justification, but within those guide-lines there is ample room for disagreement over the precise conditions for one or another type of belief. The concept does not leave us totally at a loss as to what to look for. But in adopting J_{eg} we are not building answers to substantive epistemological questions into the concept. As the only candidate to exhibit all these desiderata, J_{eg} is clearly the winner.

VII

It may be useful to bring together the lessons we have learned from this conceptual exploration.

1. Justifying, an activity of showing or estab-lishing something, is much less central for epistemology than is "being justified," as a state or condition.
2. It is central to epistemic justification that *what justifies* is restricted to the subject's "perspective," to the subject's knowledge, justified belief, or experience.
3. Deontological concepts of justification are either saddled with an indefensible as-sumption of the voluntariness of belief (J_{dv}) or allow for cases in which one be-lieves that p without having any adequate ground for the belief (J_{di}).
4. The notion of one's belief being based on adequate grounds incorporates more of what we are looking for in a concept of epistemic justification than the weaker no-tion of having adequate grounds for belief.
5. Justification is closely related to reliability, but because of the perspectival character noted in 2., they do not completely coin-cide; much less can they be identified.
6. The notion of believing that p in a way that is good from an epistemic point of view in that the belief is based on adequate grounds (J_{eg}) satisfies the chief desiderata for a concept of epistemic justification.

VIII

The ultimate payoff of this conceptual explo-ration is the increased sophistication it gives us

in dealing with substantive epistemological is-sues. Putting our scheme to work is a very large enterprise, spanning a large part of epis-temology. In conclusion I will give one illus-tration of the ways in which our distinctions can be of help in the trenches. For this purpose I will restrict myself to the broad contrast be-tween J_{dv} and J_{eg}.

First, consider what we might term "higher-level requirements" for S's being justified in believing that p. I include under that heading all requirements that S know or justifiably be-lieve something *about* the epistemic status of p, or about the strength of S's grounds for p. This would include requirements that S be jus-tified in believing that:

1. R is an adequate reason for p (where R is alleged to justify S's belief that p).[40]
2. Experience e is an adequate indication that p (where e is alleged to justify S's belief that p).[41]

On J_{eg} there is no temptation to impose such requirements. If R *is* an adequate reason (e *is* an adequate indication), then if one believes that p on that basis, one is *thereby* in a strong position, epistemically; and the further knowl-edge, or justified belief, that the reason is ad-equate (the experience is an adequate indica-tion), though no doubt quite important and valuable for other purposes, will do nothing to improve the truth-conduciveness of one's be-lieving that p. But on J_{dv} we get a different story. If it's a question of being blameless in believing that p, it can be persuasively argued that this requires not only forming the belief on what is in fact an adequate ground, but do-ing so in the light of the realization that the ground is an adequate one. If I decide to be-lieve that p without knowing whether the ground is adequate, am I not subject to blame for proceeding irresponsibly in my doxastic be-havior, whatever the actual strength of the ground? If the higher-level requirements are plausible only if we are using J_{dv}, then the du-biousness of that concept will extend to those requirements.[42]

In the above paragraph we were considering whether S's being justified in believing that his ground is adequate is a *necessary* condition of justification. We can also consider whether it is sufficient. Provided that S is justified in believing that his belief that p is based on an adequate ground, G, does it make any difference, for his being justified in believing that p, whether the ground *is* adequate? Our two contenders will line up here as they did on the previous issue. For J_{eg} the mere fact that S is justified in supposing that G is adequate will cut no ice. What J_{eg} requires is that S *actually be* in an epistemically favorable position; and although S's being justified in supposing G to be adequate is certainly good evidence for that, it doesn't *constitute* being in such a position. Hence J_{eg} requires that the ground of the belief actually be an adequate one. As for J_{dv}, where it is a question of whether S is blameworthy in believing that p, what is decisive is how S's epistemic position appears within S's perspective on the world. If, so far as S could tell, G is an adequate ground, then S is blameless, i.e., J_{dv}, in believing that p on G. Nothing else could be required for justification in that sense. If S has chosen his doxastic state by applying the appropriate principles in the light of all his relevant knowledge and justified belief, then he is totally in the clear. Again the superior viability of J_{eg}, as over against J_{dv}, should tip the scales in favor of the more objective requirement of adequacy.[43]

NOTES

1. Of late a number of theorists have been driving a wedge between what it is to be "P" or what *property* "P" is, on the one hand, and what belongs to the *concept* of "P" or what is the meaning of "P" on the other. Thus it has been claimed (Kripke, 1972) that *what heat is* is determined by the physical investigation into the nature of heat, whether or not the results of that investigation are embodied in our *concept* of heat or in the meaning of "heat." I shall take it that no such distinction is applicable to epistemic justification, that here the only reasonable interpretation to be given to "what it is" is "what is involved in the concept" or "what the term means." If someone disagrees with this, that need not be a problem. Such a person can simply read "what concept of justification is being employed" for "what justification is taken to be."

2. I think especially Chisholm (1977), ch. 1; Ginet

(1975), ch. 3; Goldman (1979), (1980); Wolterstorff (1983).

3. It may be claimed that the activity concept is fundamental in another way, viz., by virtue of the fact that one is justified in believing that p only if one is *capable* of carrying out a justification of the belief. But if that were so we would be justified in far fewer beliefs than we suppose. Most human subjects are quite incapable of carrying out a justification of any perceptual or introspective beliefs.

4. I am indebted to Alvin Plantinga for helping me to see that this term is more suitable than the term "normative" that I had been using in earlier versions of this paper. The reader should be cautioned that "deontological" as used here does not carry the contrast with "teleological" that is common in ethical theory. According to that distinction a deontological ethical theory, like that of Kant's, does not regard principles of duty or obligation as owing their status to the fact that acting in the way they prescribe tends to realize certain desirable states of affairs. Whereas a teleological theory, like utilitarianism, holds that this is what renders a principle of obligation acceptable. The fact that we are not using "deontological" with this force is shown by the fact that we are thinking of epistemic obligations as owing their validity to the fact that fulfilling them would tend to lead to the realization of a desirable state of affairs, viz., a large body of beliefs with favorable truth-falsity ratio.

5. See Chisholm (1977), ch. 1; Ginet (1975), ch. 3; Wolterstorff (1983). An extended development of a deontological concept of epistemic justification is to be found in Naylor (1978). In my development of deontological concepts in this paper I have profited from the writing of all these people and from discussions with them.

6. (1975), p. 28. See also Ayer (1956), pp. 31–34; Chisholm (1977), p. 14; Naylor (1978), p. 8.

7. These examples are meant to be illustrative only; they do not necessarily carry the endorsement of the management.

8. Here I am indebted to Alvin Plantinga.

9. A weaker objective conception would be this. My obligation is to do what in fact is *likely* to bring out A. On this weaker conception I could be said to have fulfilled my obligation in (some) cases in which A is not forthcoming.

10. We could also subjectivize the aimed at result, instead of or in addition to subjectivizing what it takes to arrive at that result. In this way one would have subjectively fulfilled one's obligation if one had done what one believed to be one's obligation. Or, to combine the two moves to the subjective, one would have subjectively fulfilled one's obligation if one had done what one believed would lead to the fulfillment of

what one believed to be one's obligation. But sufficient unto the day is the distinction thereof.

11. I would call this "epistemic obligation," except that I want to make these same distinctions with respect to epistemic justification, and so I don't want to repeat the generic term for one of the species.

12. Since we are tacitly restricting this to epistemic justification, we will also be, tacitly, restricting ourselves to intellectual obligations.

13. Since this is all on the assumption that S does believe that p, we need not add that to the right hand side in order to get a sufficient condition.

14. Note that XI, XII, and some forms of XIII are in terms of higher-level beliefs about one's epistemic status vis-à-vis p. There are less sophisticated sorts of subjectivization. For example:

S is subjectively justified in believing that p *iff* S believes that q, and q is evidence for p.

(For the reason this does not count as having adequate evidence see the next paragraph in the text.)
Or even more subjectively:

S is subjectively justified in believing that p *iff* S believes that q and bases his belief that p on his belief that q.

The definitions presented in the text do not dictate what we should say in the case in which S does not have the higher level belief specified in XI and XIII, but satisfies either of the above conditions. A thorough treatment of modes of normative status would have to go into all of this.

15. We have been taking it that to be, e.g., subjectively or cognitively justified in believing that p is to not be violating any subjective or cognitive obligations in believing that p. That means that if we opt for cognitive justification we are committed to giving a correspondingly cognitive formula of what intellectual obligations one has. But that isn't the only way to do it. We could leave all the obligations in a purely objective form, and vary the function that goes from obligation to justification. That is, we could say that one is subjectively justified if one believes that one has not violated an (objective) obligation (or, perhaps believes something that is such that, given one's objective obligations, it implies that none of those obligations has been violated). And a similar move could be made for the other modes.

16. Here are a couple of examples of the attraction of XII for J_d. Chisholm (1977) presents an informal explanation of his basic term of epistemic evaluation, "more reasonable than" in terms of an "intellectual requirement." The explanation runs as follows.

One way, then, of re-expressing the locution "p is more reasonable than q for S at t" is to say this: S is so situated at t that his intellectual requirement, his responsibility as an intellectual being, is better fulfilled by p than by q. (14)

The point that is relevant to our present discussion is that Chisholm states our basic intellectual requirement in what I have called "cognitive" rather than "objective" terms; and with a motivational ride.

We may assume that every person is subject to a purely intellectual requirement—that of trying his best to bring it about that, for every proposition h that he considers, he accepts h if and only if h is true. (14)

The "requirement" is that one *try one's best* to bring this about, rather than that one do bring it about. I take it that to try my best to bring about a result, R, is to do what, so far as I can tell, will bring about R, insofar as that is within my power. (It might be claimed that so long as I do what I believe will bring about R I am trying my best, however irresponsible the belief. But it seems to me that so long as I am not acting on the best of the indications available to me I am not "trying my best.") The motivational rider comes in too, since unless I do what I do *because* I am taking it to (have a good chance to) lead to R, I am not trying at all to bring about R.

Of course, Chisholm is speaking in terms of fulfilling an intellectual obligation rather than, as we have been doing, in terms of not violating intellectual obligations. But we are faced with the same choice between our "modes" in either case.

For a second example I turn to Wolterstorff (1983). Wolterstorff's initial formulation of a necessary and sufficient condition of justification (or, as he says, "rationality") for an "eluctable" belief of S that P is: *S lacks adequate reasons for ceasing from believing that p* (164). But then by considerations similar to those we have just adduced, he recognizes that even if S does not in fact have adequate reason for ceasing to believe that p he would still be unjustified in continuing to hold the belief if he were "rationally obliged" to believe that he does have adequate reason to cease to believe that p. Moreover Wolterstorff recognizes that S would be justified in belief that p if, even though he does have adequate reason to cease from believing that p he is rationally justified in supposing that he doesn't. Both these qualifications amount to recognizing that what is crucial is not what reasons S has in fact, but what reasons S is justified in supposing himself to have. The final formulation, embodying these and other qualifications, runs as follows:

A person S is rational in his eluctable and innocently produced belief *Bp* if and only if S does believe *p* and either:

(i)   S neither has nor ought to have adequate reason to cease from believing *p*, and is not rationally obliged to believe that he *does* have adequate reason to cease; or

(ii) S does have adequate reason to cease from believing *p* but does not realize that he does, and is rationally justified in that. (168)

17. See also Ginet (1975), p. 36.
18. Note that I am not restricting the category of what is within my immediate voluntary control to "basic actions." Neither of the actions just mentioned would qualify for that title. The category includes both basic actions and actions that involve other conditions, where I can satisfy those other conditions, when I choose, just at the moment of choice. Thus my point about believing is not just that it is not a basic action, but that it is not even a non-basic action that is under my effective immediate control. Whatever is required for my believing that there will never be a nuclear war, it is not something that I can bring about immediately by choosing to do so; though, as I am about to point out, I can affect my believings and abstentions in a more long range fashion.
19. For other accounts of indirect voluntary control of beliefs see Naylor (1978), pp. 19–20; Wolterstorff (1983), pp. 153–55.
20. Our four "modes" can also be applied to J$_{di}$. Indeed, the possibilities for variation are even more numerous. For example, with respect to the *subjective* mode we can switch from the objective fact to the subject's belief with respect to (a) the circumstances of putative violation, (b) whether there was a violation, and (c) whether the violation was causally related to the belief-formation in question. We will leave all this as an exercise for the reader.
21. I must confess that I do not find "justified" an apt term for a favorable or desirable state or condition, when what makes it desirable is cut loose from considerations of obligation and blame. Nevertheless, since the term is firmly ensconced in the literature as the term to use for any concept that satisfies the four conditions set out in section II, I will stifle my linguistic scruples and employ it for a non-deontological concept.
22. There are also problems as to where to draw the line. What about the unconscious "use" of perceptual cues for the depth of an object in the visual field or for "size constancy"? And however we answer that particular question, just

where do we draw the line as we move farther and farther from our initial paradigms?

23. For some recent discussion on "based on" see Swain (1981), ch. 3, and Pappas (1979). One additional point I do need to make explicit is this. I mean "based on" to range over both what initially gave rise to the belief, and what sustains it while it continues to be held. To be precise one should speak of *what the belief is based on at time t*. If *t* is the time of acquisition one is speaking of what gave rise to the belief; if *t* is later than that one is speaking of what sustains it.
24. For an interesting discussion of this point see Quinton (1973), ch. 7. My opponent will be even more hard pressed to make out that beliefs about one's own conscious experience are based on other beliefs. His best move here would be either to deny that there are such beliefs or to deny that they are based on anything.
25. No such restriction would be required just for having grounds (of some sort). Though even here the word "ground" by itself carries a strong suggestion that what is grounded is, to some extent, supported. We need a term for anything a belief might be based on, however vainly. "Ground" carries too much positive evaluative force to be ideally suitable for this role.
26. For some recent discussion of this issue see Harman (1973), ch. 2; Lehrer (1974), ch. 6; Firth (1978); Swain (1981), ch. 3; Foley (1984).
27. Even though we have opted for the "based on" formulation as giving us the more fundamental concept of epistemic justification, we have also recognized the "has adequate grounds" formulation as giving us a concept of epistemic justification. Either of these will introduce a "basis of evaluative status" component into the concept.
28. This latter qualification is needed, because I might accept a self-evident proposition on authority. In that case I was not, so to say, taking advantage of its self-evidence.
29. We are not speaking here of a belief that one *is* sleepy. There a ground is readily identifiable— one's feeling of sleepiness.
30. See Bonjour (1980), Kornblith (1985), Bach (1985).
31. See Goldman (1980), Chisholm (1977), ch. 4, pp. 63–64; Ginet (1975), pp. 34–37.
32. Swain (1981), ch. 4.
33. Goldman (1979).
34. For simplicity I shall couch the ensuing formulations solely in terms of belief formation, but the qualification "or sustenance" is to be understood throughout.
35. These two qualifications testify to the difficulty of getting the concept of reliability in satisfactory shape; and there are other problems to be

dealt with, e.g., how to identify the general procedure of which the present belief formation is an instance.

36. An alternative to explicating "adequate" in terms of reliability would be to use the notion of conditional probability. G is an adequate ground for a belief that p just in case the probability of p on G is high. And since adequacy is closely related both to reliability and to conditional probability, they are presumably closely related to each other. Swain (1981), ch. 4, exploits this connection to explicate reliability in terms of conditional probability, though in a more complex fashion than is indicated by these brief remarks.

37. (1979), p. 18.

38. If you have trouble envisaging his trusting his memory in the fact of his parents' story, you may imagine that he is not thinking of that story at the moment he forms the memory belief.

39. In the article in which he introduces this example Goldman modifies the "reliability is a criterion of justification" view so that it will accommodate the example. The modified formulation runs as follows:

> If S's belief in p at t results from a reliable cognitive process, and there is no reliable or conditionally reliable process available to S which had it been used by S in addition to the process actually used, would have resulted in S's not believing p at t, then S's belief in p at t is justified. (p. 20).

On this revised formulation, being formed by a reliable process is sufficient for justification only if there is no other reliable process that the subject could have used and such that if he had used it he would not have come to believe that p. In the case cited there is such a reliable process, viz., taking account of the strong reasons for believing one's memory of pre-seven years old events to be unreliable. The revised reliability criterion yields the correct result in this case. However this move leaves unshaken the point that in this case Jones's belief *is* reliably formed but unjustified. That remains true, whatever is to be said about the revised criterion.

40. See, e.g., Armstrong (1973), p. 151; Skyrms (1967), p. 374.

41. See, e.g., Sellars (1963), pp. 168–69; Bonjour (1978), pp. 5–6; Lehrer (1974), pp. 103–5.

42. In my paper "What's Wrong with Immediate Knowledge?," *Synthese*, vol. 55, no. 2 (May 1983), pp. 73–95, I develop at much greater length this kind of diagnosis of Bonjour's deployment of a higher-level requirement in his argument against immediate knowledge (Bonjour, 1978).

43. Ancestors of this paper were presented at SUNY at Albany, SUNY at Buffalo, Calvin College, Cornell University, University of California at Irvine, Lehigh University, University of Michigan, University of Nebraska, Syracuse University, and the University of Western Ontario. I wish to thank members of the audience in all these institutions for their helpful comments. I would like to express special appreciation to Robert Audi, Carl Ginet, George Mavrodes, Alvin Plantinga, Fred Schmitt, and Nicholas Wolterstorff for their penetrating comments on earlier versions.

REFERENCES

Armstrong, D. M. *Belief, Truth, and Knowledge.* London, 1973.

Ayer, A. J. *The Problem of Knowledge.* London, 1956.

Bach, K. "A Rationale for Reliabilism," *The Monist* 68, (2) (1985).

Bonjour, L. "Can Empirical Knowledge Have a Foundation?," *Amer. Philos. Quart.* 15 (1978): 1–13.

Chisholm, R. M. *Theory of Knowledge*, 2nd ed. Englewood Cliffs, N.J., 1977.

Dretske, F. *Knowledge and the Flow of Information.* Cambridge, Mass., 1981.

Firth, R. "Are Epistemic Concepts Reducible to Ethical Concepts?" In A. I. Goldman and J. Kim, eds., *Values and Morals.* Dordrecht, 1978.

Foley, R. "Epistemic Luck and the Purely Epistemic." *American Philosophical Quarterly* 21 (1984): 113–24.

Ginet, C. *Knowledge, Perception, and Memory.* Dordrecht, 1975.

Goldman, A. I. "What Is Justified Belief?" in G. S. Pappas, ed., *Justification and Knowledge.* Dordrecht, 1979; "The Internalist Conception of Justification." *Midwest Studies in Philosophy* V (1980): 27–55.

Harman, G. *Thought.* Princeton, N.J., 1973.

Kornblith, H. "Ever Since Descartes." *The Monist* 68 (2) (1985).

Kripke, S. A. "Naming and Necessity." In *Semantics of Natural Language*, ed. D. Davidson and G. Harman. Dordrecht, 1972.

Lehrer, K. *Knowledge*. New York, 1974.

Naylor, M. B. "Epistemic Justification." Manuscript (1978).

Pappas, G. S. "Basing Relations." In G. S. Pappas, ed., *Justification and Knowledge*. Dordrecht, 1979.

Pollock, J. *Knowledge and Justification*. Princeton, N.J., 1974.

Quinton, A. *The Nature of Things*. London, 1973.

Sellars, W. *Science, Perception, and Reality*. London, 1963.

Skyrms, B. "The Explication of 'S Knows that P.' " *Journ. Philos.* 64 (1967): 373–89.

Swain, M. *Reasons and Knowledge*. Ithaca, N.Y., 1981.

Wolterstorff, N. "Can Belief in God Be Rational if It Has No Foundations?" In *Faith and Rationality*, ed. A. Plantinga and N. Wolterstorff. Notre Dame, Ind., 1983.

27 / Ernest Sosa

THE RAFT AND THE PYRAMID: COHERENCE VERSUS FOUNDATIONS IN THE THEORY OF KNOWLEDGE

Contemporary epistemology must choose between the solid security of the ancient foundationalist pyramid and the risky adventure of the new coherentist raft. Our main objective will be to understand, as deeply as we can, the nature of the controversy and the reasons for and against each of the two options. But first of all we take note of the two underlying assumptions.

1. Two Assumptions

(A1) Not everything believed is known, but nothing can be known without being at least believed (or accepted, presumed, taken for granted, or the like) in some broad sense. What additional requirements must a belief fill in order to be knowledge? There are surely at least the following two: (a) it must be true, and (b) it must be justified (or warranted, reasonable, correct, or the like).

(A2) Let us assume, moreover, with respect to the second condition A1(b): first, that it involves a normative or evaluative property; and, second, that the relevant sort of justification is that which pertains to knowledge: epistemic (or theoretical) justification. Someone seriously ill may have two sorts of justification for believing he will recover: the practical justification that derives from the contribution such belief will make to his recovery and the theoretical justification provided by the lab results, the doctor's diagnosis and prognosis, and so on. Only the latter is relevant to the question whether he knows.

2. Knowledge and Criteria (or Canons, Methods, or the Like)

a. There are two key questions of the theory of knowledge:

(i)   What do we know?
(ii)   How do we know?

The answer to the first would be a list of bits of knowledge or at least of types of knowledge: of the self, of the external world, of other minds, and so on. An answer to the second would give us criteria (or canons, methods, principles, or the like) that would explain how we know whatever it is that we do know.

b. In developing a theory of knowledge, we can begin either with a(i) or with a(ii). Particularism would have us begin with an answer to a(i) and only then take up a(ii) on the basis of that answer. Quite to the contrary, methodism would reverse that order. The particularist thus tends to be antiskeptical on principle. But the methodist is as such equally receptive to skepticism and to the contrary. Hume, for example, was no less a methodist than Descartes. Each accepted, in effect, that only the obvious and what is proved deductively on its basis can possibly be known.

c. What, then, is the obvious? For Descartes it is what we know by intuition, what is clear and distinct, what is indubitable and credible with no fear of error. Thus for Descartes basic knowledge is always an infallible belief in an indubitable truth. All other knowledge must stand on that basis through deductive proof. Starting from such criteria (canons, methods, etc.), Descartes concluded that knowledge extended about as far as his contemporaries believed.[1] Starting from similar criteria, however, Hume concluded that both science and common sense made claims far beyond their rightful limits.

d. Philosophical posterity has rejected Descartes's theory for one main reason: that it admits too easily as obvious what is nothing of the sort. Descartes's reasoning is beautifully simple: God exists; no omnipotent perfectly good being would descend to deceit; but if our common sense beliefs were radically false, that would represent deceit on His part. Therefore, our common sense beliefs must be true or at least cannot be radically false. But in order to buttress this line of reasoning and fill in details, Descartes appeals to various principles that appear something less than indubitable.

e. For his part, Hume rejects all but a miniscule portion of our supposed common sense knowledge. He establishes first that there is no way to prove such supposed knowledge on the basis of what is obvious at any given moment through reason or experience. And he concludes, in keeping with this methodism, that in point of fact there really is no such knowledge.

3. Two Metaphors: the Raft and the Pyramid

Both metaphors concern the body or system of knowledge in a given mind. But the mind is of course a more complex marvel than is sometimes supposed. Here I do not allude to the depths plumbed by Freud, nor even to Chomsky's. Nor need we recall the labyrinths inhabited by statesmen and diplomats, nor the rich patterns of some novels or theories. We need look no further than the most common, everyday beliefs. Take, for instance, the belief that driving tonight will be dangerous. Brief reflection should reveal that any of us with that belief will join to it several other closely related beliefs on which the given belief depends for its existence or (at least) its justification. Among such beliefs we could presumably find some or all of the following: that the road will be icy or snowy; that driving on ice or snow is dangerous; that it will rain or snow tonight; that the temperature will be below freezing; appropriate beliefs about the forecast and its reliability; and so on.

How must such beliefs be interrelated in order to help justify my belief about the danger of driving tonight? Here foundationalism and coherentism disagree, each offering its own metaphor. Let us have a closer look at this dispute, starting with foundationalism.

Both Descartes and Hume attribute to human knowledge an architectonic structure. There is a nonsymmetric relation of physical support such that any two floors of a building are tied by that relation: one of the two supports (or at least helps support) the other. And there is, moreover, a part with a special status: the foundation, which is supported by none of the floors while supporting them all.

With respect to a body of knowledge K (in someone's possession), foundationalism implies that K can be divided into parts K_1, K_2, ..., such that there is some nonsymmetric relation R (analogous to the relation of physical support) which orders those parts in such a way that there is one—call it F—that bears R to every other part while none of them bears R in turn to F.

According to foundationalism, each piece of knowledge lies on a pyramid such as the following:

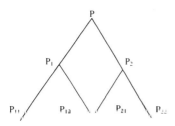

The nodes of such a pyramid (for a proposition P relative to a subject S and a time t) must obey the following requirements:

a. The set of all nodes that succeed (directly) any given node must serve jointly as a base that properly supports that node (for S at t).
b. Each node must be a proposition that S is justified in believing at t.
c. If a node is not self-evident (for S at t), it must have successors (that serve jointly as a base that properly supports that node).
d. Each branch of an epistemic pyramid must terminate.

For the foundationalist Descartes, for instance, each terminating node must be an indubitable proposition that S believes at t with no possi-

bility of error. As for the nonterminal nodes, each of them represents inferential knowledge, derived by deduction from more basic beliefs.

Such radical foundationalism suffers from a fatal weakness that is twofold:

(a) there are not so many perfectly obvious truths as Descartes thought; and
(b) once we restrict ourselves to what is truly obvious in any given context, very little of one's supposed common sense knowledge can be proved on that basis.

If we adhere to such radical foundationalism, therefore, we are just wrong in thinking we know so much.

In citing such a "fatal weakness" of radical foundationalism, we favor particularism as against the methodism of Descartes and Hume. For we reject the methods or criteria of Descartes and Hume when we realize that they plunge us in a deep skepticism. If such criteria are incompatible with our enjoyment of the rich body of knowledge that we commonly take for granted, then as good particularists we hold on to the knowledge and reject the criteria.

If we reject radical foundationalism, however, what are we to put in its place? Here epistemology faces a dilemma that different epistemologists resolve differently. Some reject radical foundationalism but retain some more moderate form of foundationalism. Others react more vigorously, however, by rejecting all forms of foundationalism in favor of a radically different coherentism. Coherentism is associated with idealism—of both the German and British variety—and has recently acquired new vigor and interest.

The coherentists reject the metaphor of the pyramid in favor of one that they owe to the positivist Neurath, according to whom our body of knowledge is a raft that floats free of any anchor or tie. Repairs must be made afloat, and though no part is untouchable, we must stand on some in order to replace or repair others. Not every part can go at once.

According to the new metaphor, what justifies a belief is not that it be an infallible belief with an indubitable object, nor that it have been proved deductively on such a basis, but that it cohere with a comprehensive system of beliefs.

4. A Coherentist Critique of Foundationalism

What reasons do coherentists offer for their total rejection of foundationalism? The argument that follows below summarizes much of what is alleged against foundationalism. But first we must distinguish between subjective states that incorporate a propositional attitude and those that do not. A propositional attitude is a mental state of someone with a proposition for its object: beliefs, hopes, and fears provide examples. By way of contrast, a headache does not incorporate any such attitude. One can of course be conscious of a headache, but the headache itself does not constitute or incorporate any attitude with a proposition for its object. With this distinction in the background, here is the antifoundationalist argument, which has two lemmas—a(iv) and b(iii)—and a principal conclusion.

a. (i)   If a mental state incorporates a propositional attitude, then it does not give us direct contact with reality, e.g., with pure experience, unfiltered by concepts or beliefs.

   (ii) If a mental state does not give us direct contact with reality, then it provides no guarantee against error.

  (iii) If a mental state provides no guarantee against error, then it cannot serve as a foundation for knowledge.

  (iv) Therefore, if a mental state incorporates a propositional attitude, then it cannot serve as a foundation for knowledge.

b. (i)   If a mental state does not incorporate a propositional attitude, then it is an enigma how such a state can provide support for any hypothesis, raising its credibility selectively by contrast with its alternatives. (If the mental state has no conceptual or propositional content, then what logical relation can it possibly bear to any hypothesis? Belief in a hypothesis would be a propositional attitude with the hypothesis itself as object. How can one depend logically for such a belief on an experience with no propositional content?)

  (ii) If a mental state has no propositional content and cannot provide logical support for any hypothesis, then it cannot serve as a foundation for knowledge.

  (iii) Therefore, if a mental state does not incorporate a propositional attitude, then it cannot serve as a foundation for knowledge.

c.   Every mental state either does or does not incorporate a propositional attitude.

d.   Therefore, no mental state can serve as a foundation for knowledge. (From a(iv), b(iii), and c.)

According to the coherentist critic, foundationalism is run through by this dilemma. Let us take a closer look.[2]

In the first place, what reason is there to think, in accordance with premise b(i), that only propositional attitudes can give support to their own kind? Consider practices—e.g., broad policies or customs. Could not some person or group be justified in a practice because of its consequences: that is, could not the consequences of a practice make it a good practice? But among the consequences of a practice may surely be found, for example, a more just distribution of goods and less suffering than there would be under its alternatives. And neither the more just distribution nor the lower degree of suffering is a propositional attitude. This provides an example in which propositional attitudes (the intentions that sustain the practice) are justified by consequences that are not propositional attitudes. That being so, is it not conceivable that the justification of belief that matters for knowledge be analogous to the objective justification by consequences that we find in ethics?

Is it not possible, for instance, that a belief that there is something red before one be justified in part because it has its origin in one's visual experience of red when one looks at an apple in daylight? If we accept such examples, they show us a source of justification that serves as such without incorporating a propositional attitude.

As for premise a(iii), it is already under suspicion from our exploration of premise b(i). A mental state M can be nonpropositional and hence not a candidate for so much as truth, much less infallibility, while it serves, in spite of that, as a foundation of knowledge. Leaving that aside, let us suppose that the relevant mental state is indeed propositional. Must it then be infallible in order to serve as a foundation of justification and knowledge? That is so far from being obvious that it seems more likely false when compared with an analogue in ethics. With respect to beliefs, we may distinguish between their being true and their being justified. Analogously, with respect to actions, we may distinguish between their being optimal (best of all alternatives, all things considered) and their being (subjectively) justified. In practical deliberation on alternatives for action, is it inconceivable that the most *eligible* alternatives *not* be objectively the best, all things considered? Can there not be another alternative—perhaps a most repugnant one worth little if any consideration—that in point of fact would have a much better total set of consequences and would thus be better, all things considered? Take the physician attending to Frau Hitler at the birth of little Adolf. Is it not possible that if he had acted less morally, that would have proved better in the fullness of time? And if that is so in ethics, may not its likeness hold good in epistemology? Might there not be justified (reasonable, warranted) beliefs that are not even true, much less infallible? That seems to me not just a conceivable possibility, but indeed a familiar fact of everyday life, where observational beliefs too often prove illusory but no less reasonable for being false.

If the foregoing is on the right track, then the antifoundationalist is far astray. What has led him there?

As a diagnosis of the antifoundationalist argument before us, and more particularly of its second lemma, I suggest that it rests on an Intellectualist Model of Justification.

According to such a model, the justification of belief (and psychological states generally) is parasitical on certain logical relations among propositions. For example, my belief (1) that the streets are wet, is justified by my pair of beliefs (2) that it is raining, and (3) that if it is raining, the streets are wet. Thus we have a structure such as this:

B(Q) is justified by the fact that B(Q) is grounded on (B(P), B($P \supset Q$)).

And according to an Intellectualist Model, this is parasitical on the fact that

P and ($P \supset Q$) together logically imply Q.

Concerning this attack on foundationalism I will argue (a) that it is useless to the coherentist, since if the antifoundationalist dilemma impales the foundationalist, a form of it can be turned against the coherentist to the same effect; (b) that the dilemma would be lethal not only to foundationalism and coherentism but also to the very possibility of substantive epistemology; and (c) that a form of it would have the same effect on normative ethics.

(a)   According to coherentism, what justifies a belief is its membership in a coherent and comprehensive set of beliefs. But whereas being grounded on B(P) and B($P \supset Q$) is a property of a belief B(Q) that yields immediately the logical implication of Q by P and ($P \supset Q$) as the logical source of that property's justificatory power, the property of being a member of a coherent set is not one that immediately yields any such implication.

It may be argued, nevertheless, (1) that the property of being a member of a coherent set would supervene in any actual instance on the property of being a member of a particular set a that is in fact coherent, and (2) that this would enable us to preserve our Intellectualist Model, since (3) the justification of the member belief B(Q) by its membership in a would then be parasitical on the logical relations among the beliefs in a which constitute the coherence of that set of beliefs, and (4) the justification of B(Q) by the fact that it is part of a coherent set would then be *indirectly* parasitical on logical relations among propositions after all.

But if such an indirect form of parasitism is allowed, then the experience of pain may perhaps be said to justify belief in its existence parasitically on the fact that *P* logically implies *P!* The Intellectualist Model seems either so trivial as to be dull, or else sharp enough to cut equally against both foundationalism and coherentism.

(b) If (1) only propositional attitudes can justify such propositional attitudes as belief, and if (2) to do so they must in turn be justified by yet other propositional attitudes, it seems clear that (3) there is no hope of constructing a complete epistemology, one which would give us, in theory, an account of what the justification of any justified belief would supervene on. For (1) and (2) would rule out the possibility of a finite regress of justification.

(c) If only propositional attitudes can justify propositional attitudes, and if to do so they must in turn be justified by yet other propositional attitudes, it seems clear that there is no hope of constructing a complete normative ethics, one which would give us, in theory, an account of what the justification of any possible justified action would supervene upon. For the justification of an action presumably depends on the intentions it embeds and the justification of these, and here we are already within the net of propositional attitudes from which, for the Intellectualist, there is no escape.

It seems fair to conclude that our coherentist takes his antifoundationalist zeal too far. His antifoundationalist argument helps expose some valuable insights but falls short of its malicious intent. The foundationalist emerges showing no serious damage. Indeed, he now demands equal time for a positive brief in defense of his position.

5. The Regress Argument

a. The regress argument in epistemology concludes that we must countenance beliefs that are justified in the absence of justification by other beliefs. But it reaches that conclusion only by rejecting the possibility in principle of an infinite regress of justification. It thus opts for foundational beliefs justified in some non-inferential way by ruling out a chain or pyramid of justification that has justifiers, and justifiers of justifiers, and so on *without end*. One may well find this too short a route to foundationalism, however, and demand more compelling reasons for thus rejecting an infinite regress as vicious. We shall find indeed that it is not easy to meet this demand.

b. We have seen how even the most ordinary of everyday beliefs is the tip of an iceberg. A closer look below the surface reveals a complex structure that ramifies with no end in sight. Take again my belief that driving will be dangerous tonight, at the tip of an iceberg, (1), that looks like this:

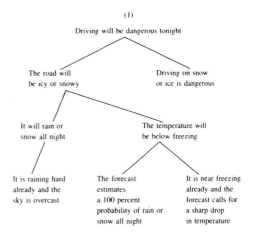

The immediate cause of my belief that driving will be hazardous tonight is the sound of raindrops on the windowpane. All but one or two members of the underlying iceberg are as far as they can be from my thoughts at the time. In what sense, then, do they form an iceberg whose tip breaks the calm surface of my consciousness?

Here I will assume that the members of (1) are beliefs of the subject, even if unconscious or subconscious, that causally buttress and thus justify his prediction about the driving conditions.

Can the iceberg extend without end? It may appear obvious that it cannot do so, and one may jump to the conclusion that any piece of knowledge must be ultimately founded on the beliefs that are *not* (inferentially) justified or warranted by other beliefs. This is a doctrine of *epistemic foundationalism*.

Let us focus not so much on the *giving* of justification as on the *having* of it. *Can* there be a belief that is justified in part by other beliefs, some of which are in turn justified by yet other beliefs, and so on without end? Can there be an endless regress of justification?

c.   There are several familiar objections to such a regress:

(i) *Objection*: "It is incompatible with human limitations. No human subject could harbor the required infinity of beliefs." *Reply*: It is mere presumption to fathom with such assurance the depths of the mind, and especially its unconscious and dispositional depths. Besides, our object here is the nature of epistemic justification in itself and not only that of such justification as is accessible to humans. Our question is not whether humans could harbor an infinite iceberg of justification. Our question is rather whether *any* mind, no matter how deep, could do so. Or is it ruled out *in principle* by the very nature of justification?

(ii) *Objection*: "An infinite regress is indeed ruled out in principle, for if justification were thus infinite how could it possibly end?" *Reply*: (i) If the end mentioned is *temporal*, then why must there be such an end? In the first place, the subject may be eternal. Even if he is not eternal, moreover, why must belief acquisition and justification occur seriatim? What precludes an infinite body of beliefs acquired at a single stroke? Human limitations may rule this out for humans, but we have yet to be shown that it is precluded in principle, by the very nature of justification. (ii) If the end mentioned is justificatory, on the other hand, then to ask how justification could possibly end is just to beg the question.

(iii) *Objection*: "Let us make two assumptions: first, that S's belief of q justifies his belief of

p only if it works together with a justified belief on his part that q provides good evidence for p; and, second, that if S is to be justified in believing p on the basis of his belief of q and is to be justified in believing q on the basis of his belief of r, then S must be justified in believing that r provides good evidence for p via q. These assumptions imply that an actual regress of justification requires belief in an infinite proposition. Since no one (or at least no human) can believe an infinite proposition, no one (no human) can be a subject of such an actual regress."[3]

Reply: Neither of the two assumptions is beyond question, but even granting them both, it may still be doubted that the conclusion follows. It is true that each finitely complex belief of the form "r provides good evidence for p via $q_1 \ldots q_n$" will *omit* how some members of the full infinite regress are epistemically tied to belief of p. But that seems irrelevant given the fact that for each member r of the regress, such that r is tied epistemically to belief of p, there *is* a finite belief of the required sort ("r provides good evidence for p via $q_1, \ldots, q_n$") that ties the two together. Consequently, there is no apparent reason to suppose—even granted the two assumptions—that an infinite regress will require a single belief in an infinite proposition, and not just an infinity of beliefs in increasingly complex finite propositions.

(iv) *Objection*: "But if it is allowed that justification extend infinitely, then it is too easy to justify any belief at all or too many beliefs altogether. Take, for instance, the belief that there are perfect numbers greater than 100. And suppose a mind powerful enough to believe every member of the following sequence:

(σ1)
There is at least one perfect number > 100
There are at least two perfect numbers > 100
      "   three   "

If such a believer has no other belief about perfect numbers save the belief that a perfect number is a whole number equal to the sum of its whole factors, then surely he is *not* justified in believing that there are perfect numbers greater than 100. He is quite unjustified in believing any of the members of sequence (σ1), in spite of the fact that a challenge to any can be met easily by appeal to its successor. Thus it cannot be allowed after all that justification extend infinitely, and an infinite regress is ruled out.'

Reply: We must distinguish between regresses of justification that are actual and those that are merely potential. The difference is *not* simply that an actual regress is composed of actual beliefs. For even if all members of the regress are actual beliefs, the regress may still be *merely potential* in the following sense: while it is true that *if* any member *were* justified then its predecessors *would* be, still none is in fact justified. Anyone with our series of beliefs about perfect numbers in the absence of any further relevant information on such numbers would presumably be the subject of such a merely potential justificatory regress.

(v) *Objection*: "But defenders of infinite justificatory regresses cannot distinguish thus between actual regresses and those that are merely potential. There is no real distinction to be drawn between the two. For if any regress ever justifies the belief at its head, then every regress must always do so. But obviously not every regress does so (as we have seen by examples), and hence no regress can do so."[4]

Reply: One can in fact distinguish between actual justificatory regresses and merely potential ones, and one can do so both abstractly and by examples. What an actual regress has that a merely potential regress lacks is the property of containing only justified beliefs as members. What they both share is the property of containing no member without successors that would jointly justify it.

Recall our regress about perfect numbers greater than 100: i.e., there is at least one, there are at least two; there are at least three; and so on. Each member has a successor that would justify it, but no member is justified (in the absence of further information external to the regress). That is therefore a merely potential infinite regress. As for an actual regress, I see no compelling reason why someone (if not a human, then some more powerful mind) could

not hold an infinite series of actually justified beliefs as follows:

(σ2)   There is at least one even number
          There are at least two even numbers
          "   three   "

It may be that no one could be the subject of such a series of justified beliefs unless he had a proof that there is a denumerable infinity of even numbers. But even if that should be so, it would not take away the fact of the infinite regress of potential justifiers, each of which is actually justified, and hence it would not take away the fact of the actual endless regress of justification.

The objection under discussion is confused, moreover, on the nature of the issue before us. Our question is *not* whether there can be an infinite potential regress, each member of which would be justified by its successors, such that the belief at its head is justified in virtue of its position there, at the head of such a regress. The existence and even the possibility of a single such regress with a belief at its head that was *not* justified in virtue of its position there would of course settle that question in the negative. Our question is, rather, whether there can be an actual infinite regress of justification, and the fact that a belief at the head of a potential regress might still fail to be justified despite its position does *not* settle this question. For even if there can be a merely potential regress with an unjustified belief at its head, that leaves open the possibility of an infinite regress, each member of which is justified by its immediate successors working jointly, where every member of the regress is in addition actually justified.

6. The Relation of Justification and Foundationalist Strategy

The foregoing discussion is predicated on a simple conception of justification such that a set of beliefs β conditionally justifies (*would* justify) a belief X iff, necessarily, if all members of β are justified then X is also justified (if it exists). The fact that on such a conception of justification actual endless regresses—such as (σ2)—seem quite possible blocks a straight-forward regress argument in favor of foundations. For it shows that an actual infinite regress cannot be dismissed out of hand.

Perhaps the foundationalist could introduce some relation of justification—presumably more complex and yet to be explicated—with respect to which it could be argued more plausibly that an actual endless regress is out of the question.

There is, however, a more straightforward strategy open to the foundationalist. For he *need not* object to the possibility of an endless regress of justification. His essential creed is the more positive belief that every justified belief must be at the head of a terminating regress. Fortunately, to affirm the universal necessity of a terminating regress is *not* to deny the bare possibility of a nonterminating regress. For a single belief can trail at once regresses of both sorts: one terminating and one not. Thus the proof of the denumerably infinite cardinality of the set of evens may provide for a powerful enough intellect a *terminating* regress for each member of the *endless* series of justified beliefs:

(σ2)   There is at least one even number
           There are at least two even numbers
              ″   three   ″

At the same time, it is obvious that each member of (σ2) lies at the head of an actual endless regress of justification, on the assumption that each member is conditionally justified by its successor, which is in turn actually justified.

"Thank you so much," the foundationalist may sneer, "but I really do not need that kind of help. Nor do I need to be reminded of my essential creed, which I know as well as anyone. Indeed my rejection of endless regresses of justification is only a means of supporting my view that every justified belief must rest ultimately on foundations, on a terminating regress. You reject that strategy much too casually, in my view, but I will not object here. So we put that strategy aside. And now, my helpful friend, just what do we put in its place?"

Fair enough. How then could one show the need for foundations if an endless regress is not ruled out?

7. Two Levels of Foundationalism

a.   We need to distinguish, first, between two forms of foundationalism: one *formal*, the other *substantive*. A type of *formal foundationalism* with respect to a normative or evaluative property φ is the view that the conditions (actual and possible) within which φ would apply can be specified in general, perhaps recursively. *Substantive foundationalism* is only a particular way of doing so, and coherentism is another.

Simple-minded hedonism is the view that:

(i)   every instance of pleasure is good.
(ii)   everything that causes something good is itself good, and
(iii) everything that is good is so in virtue of (i) or (ii) above.

Simple-minded hedonism is a type of formal foundationalism with respect to the good.

Classical foundationalism in epistemology is the view that:

(i)   every infallible, indubitable belief is justified.
(ii)   every belief deductively inferred from justified beliefs is itself justified, and
(iii) every belief that is justified is so in virtue of (i) or (ii) above.

Classical foundationalism is a type of formal foundationalism with respect to epistemic justification.

Both of the foregoing theories—simple-minded hedonism in ethics, and classical foundationalism in epistemology—are of course flawed. But they both remain examples of formal foundationalist theories.

b. One way of arguing in favor of formal foundationalism in epistemology is to formulate a convincing formal foundationalist theory of justification. But classical foundationalism in epistemology no longer has for many the attraction that it had for Descartes, nor has any other form of epistemic foundationalism won general acceptance. Indeed epistemic foundationalism has been generally abandoned and its advocates have been put on the defensive by the writings of Wittgenstein, Quine, Sellars,

Rescher, Aune, Harman, Lehrer, and others. It is lamentable that in our headlong rush away from foundationalism we have lost sight of the different types of foundationalism (formal vs. substantive) and of the different grades of each type. Too many of us now see it as a blur to be decried and avoided. Thus our present attempt to bring it all into better focus.

c. If we cannot argue from a generally accepted foundationalist theory, what reason is there to accept formal foundationalism? There is no reason to think that the conditions (actual and possible) within which an object is spherical are generally specifiable in nongeometric terms. Why should we think that the conditions (actual and possible) within which a belief is epistemically justified are generally specifiable in nonepistemic terms?

So far as I can see, the main reason for accepting formal foundationalist theory is the very plausible idea that epistemic justification is subject to the supervenience that characterizes normative and evaluative properties generally. Thus, if a car is a good car, then any physical replica of that car must be just as good. If it is a good car in virtue of such properties as being economical, little prone to breakdown, etc., then surely any exact replica would share all such properties and would thus be equally good. Similarly, if a belief is epistemically justified, it is presumably so in virtue of its character and its basis in perception, memory, or inference (if any). Thus any belief exactly like it in its character and its basis must be equally well justified. Epistemic justification is supervenient. The justification of a belief supervenes on such properties of it as its content and its basis (if any) in perception, memory, or inference. Such a doctrine of supervenience may itself be considered, with considerable justice, a grade of foundationalism. For it entails that every instance of justified belief is founded on a number of its nonepistemic properties, such as its having a certain basis in perception, memory, and inference, or the like.

But there are higher grades of foundationalism as well. There is, for instance, the doctrine that the conditions (actual and possible) within which a belief would be epistemically justified *can be specified* in general, perhaps recursively (and by reference to such notions as perception, memory, and inference).

A higher grade yet of formal foundationalism requires not only that the conditions for justified belief be specifiable, in general, but that they be specifiable by a simple, comprehensive theory.

d. Simple-minded hedonism is a formal foundationalist theory of the highest grade. If it is true, then in every possible world goodness supervenes on pleasure and causation in a way that is recursively specifiable by means of a very simple theory.

Classical foundationalism in epistemology is also a formal foundationalist theory of the highest grade. If it is true, then in every possible world epistemic justification supervenes on infallibility cum indubitability and deductive inference in a way that is recursively specifiable by means of a very simple theory.

Surprisingly enough, coherentism may also turn out to be formal foundationalism of the highest grade, provided only that the concept of coherence is itself both simple enough and free of any normative or evaluative admixture. Given these provisos, coherentism explains how epistemic justification supervenes on the nonepistemic in a theory of remarkable simplicity: a belief is justified if it has a place within a system of beliefs that is coherent and comprehensive.

It is a goal of ethics to explain how the ethical rightness of an action supervenes on what is not ethically evaluative or normative. Similarly, it is a goal of epistemology to explain how the epistemic justification of a belief supervenes on what is not epistemically evaluative or normative. If coherentism aims at this goal, that imposes restrictions on the notion of coherence, which must now be conceived innocent of epistemically evaluative or normative admixture. Its substance must therefore consist of such concepts as explanation, probability, and logical implication—with these conceived, in turn, innocent of normative or evaluative content.

e. We have found a surprising kinship between coherentism and substantive foundationalism, both of which turn out to be varieties of a deeper foundationalism. This deeper foundationalism is applicable to any normative or evaluative property ϕ, and it comes in three grades. The *first* or lowest is simply the supervenience of ϕ: the idea that whenever something has ϕ its having it is founded on certain others of its properties which fall into certain restricted sorts. The *second* is the explicable supervenience of ϕ: the idea that there are formulable principles that explain in quite general terms the conditions (actual and possible) within which ϕ applies. The *third* and highest is the easily explicable supervenience of ϕ: the idea that there is a *simple* theory that explains the conditions within which ϕ applies. We have found the coherentist and the substantive foundationalist sharing a primary goal: the development of a formal foundationalist theory of the highest grade. For they both want a simple theory that explains precisely how epistemic justification supervenes, in general, on the nonepistemic. This insight gives us an unusual viewpoint on some recent attacks against foundationalism. Let us now consider as an example a certain simple form of argument distilled from the recent antifoundationalist literature.[5]

8. Doxastic Ascent Arguments

Several attacks on foundationalism turn on a sort of "doxastic ascent" argument that calls for closer scrutiny.[6] Here are two examples:

A. A belief B is foundationally justified for S in virtue of having property F only if S is justified in believing (1) that most at least of his beliefs with property F are true, and (2) that B has property F. But this means that belief B is not foundational after all, and indeed that the very notion of (empirical) foundational belief is incoherent.

It is sometimes held, for example, that perceptual or observational beliefs are often justified through their origin in the exercise of one or more of our five senses in standard conditions of perception. The advocate of doxastic ascent would raise a vigorous protest, however, for in his view the mere fact of such sensory prompting is impotent to justify the belief prompted. Such prompting must be coupled with the further

belief that one's senses work well in the circumstances, or the like. For we are dealing here with *knowledge,* which requires not blind faith but *reasoned* trust. But now surely the further belief about the reliability of one's senses itself cannot rest on blind faith but requires its own backing of reasons, and we are off on the regress.

B. A belief B of proposition P is foundationally justified for S only if S is justified in believing that there are no factors present that would cause him to make mistakes on the matter of the proposition P. But, again, this means that belief B is not foundational after all and indeed that the notion of (empirical) foundational belief is incoherent.

From the vantage point of formal foundationalism, neither of these arguments seems persuasive. In the first place, as we have seen, what makes a belief foundational (formally) is its having a property that is nonepistemic (not evaluative in the epistemic or cognitive mode), and does not involve inference from other beliefs, but guarantees, via a necessary principle, that the belief in question is justified. A belief B is made foundational by having some such nonepistemic property that yields its justification. Take my belief that I am in pain in a context where it is caused by my being in pain. The property that my belief then has, of being a self-attribution of pain caused by one's own pain is, let us suppose, a nonepistemic property that yields the justification of any belief that has it. So my belief that I am in pain is in that context foundationally justified. Along with my belief that I am in pain, however, there come other beliefs that are equally well justified, such as my belief that someone is in pain. Thus I am foundationally justified in believing that I am in pain only if I am justified in believing that someone is in pain. Those who object to foundationalism as in A or B above are hence mistaken in thinking that their premises would refute foundationalism. The fact is that they would not touch it. For a belief is no less foundationally justified for having its justification yoked to that of another closely related belief.

The advocate of arguments like A and B must apparently strengthen his premises. He must apparently claim that the beliefs whose justification is entailed by the foundationally justified status of belief *B* must in some sense function as a *necessary source* of the justification of *B*. And this would of course preclude giving *B* foundationally justified status. For if the *being justified* of those beliefs is an *essential* part of the source of the justification of *B*, then it is ruled out that there be a wholly *nonepistemic* source of *B*'s justification.

That brings us to a second point about A and B, for it should now be clear that these cannot be selectively aimed at foundationalism. In particular, they seem neither more nor less valid objections to coherentism than to foundationalism, or so I will now argue about each of them in turn.

A'.   A belief *S* is justified for X in virtue of membership in a coherent set only if S is justified in believing (1) that most at least of his beliefs with the property of thus cohering are true, and (2) that *X* has that property.

Any coherentist who accepts A seems bound to accept A'. For what could he possibly appeal to as a relevant difference? But A' is a quicksand of endless depth. (How is he justified in believing A'(1)? Partly through justified belief that *it* coheres? And what would justify *this?* And so on. . . .)

B'.   A belief *X* is justified for S only if S is justified in believing that there are no factors present that would cause him to make mistakes on the subject matter of that belief.

Again, any coherentist who accepts B seems bound to accept B'. But this is just another road to the quicksand. (For S is justified in believing that there are no such factors only if . . . and so on.)

Why are such regresses vicious? The key is again, to my mind, the doctrine of supervenience. Such regresses are vicious because they would be logically incompatible with the supervenience of epistemic justification on such nonepistemic facts as the totality of a subject's beliefs, his cognitive and experiential history, and as many other nonepistemic facts as may seem at all relevant. The idea is that there is a set of such nonepistemic facts surrounding a justified belief such that no belief could possibly have been surrounded by those very facts without being justified. Advocates of A or B run afoul of such supervenience, since they are surely committed to the more general views derivable from either of A or B by deleting "foundationally" from its first sentence. In each case the more general view would then preclude the possibility of supervenience, since it would entail that the source of justification *always* includes an *epistemic* component.

9. Coherentism and Substantive Foundationalism

a. The notions of coherentism and substantive foundationalism remain unexplicated. We have relied so far on our intuitive grasp of them. In this section we shall consider reasons for the view that substantive foundationalism is superior to coherentism. To assess these reasons, we need some more explicit account of the difference between the two.

By "coherentism" we shall mean any view according to which the ultimate sources of justification for any belief lie in relations among that belief and other beliefs of the subject: explanatory relations, perhaps, or relations of probability or logic.

According to substantive foundationalism, as it is to be understood here, there are ultimate sources of justification other than relations among beliefs. Traditionally these additional sources have pertained to the special content of the belief or its special relations to the subjective experience of the believer.

b. The view that justification is a matter of relations among beliefs is open to an objection from alternative coherent systems or detachment from reality, depending on one's perspective. From the latter perspective the body of beliefs is held constant and the surrounding world is allowed to vary, whereas from the former perspective it is the surrounding world that is held constant while the body of beliefs is allowed to vary. In either case, according to the coherentist, there could be no effect on the justification for any belief.

Let us sharpen the question before us as follows. Is there reason to think that there is at least one system B', alternative to our actual system of beliefs B, such that B' contains a belief X with the following properties:

(i)   in our present nonbelief circumstances we would not be justified in having belief X even if we accepted along with that belief (as our total system of beliefs) the entire belief system B' in which it is embedded (no matter how acceptance of B' were brought about); and

(ii) that is so despite the fact that belief X coheres within B' at least as fully as does some actual justified belief of ours within our actual belief system B (where the justification of that actual justified belief is alleged by the coherentist to derive solely from its coherence within our actual body of beliefs B).

The coherentist is vulnerable to counterexamples of this sort right at the surface of his body of beliefs, where we find beliefs with minimal coherence, whose detachment and replacement with contrary beliefs would have little effect on the coherence of the body. Thus take my belief that I have a headache when I do have a splitting headache, and let us suppose that this *does* cohere with my present body of beliefs. (Thus I have no reason to doubt my present introspective beliefs, and so on. And if my belief does *not* cohere, so much the worse for coherentism, since my belief is surely justified.) Here then we have a perfectly justified or warranted belief. And yet such a belief may well have relevant relations of explanation, logic, or probability with at most a small set of other beliefs of mine at the time: say, that I am not free of headache, that I am in pain, that someone is in pain, and the like. If so, then an equally coherent alternative is not far to seek. Let everything remain constant, *including* the splitting headache, except for the following: replace the belief that I have a headache with the belief that I do *not* have a headache, the belief that I am in pain with the belief that I am *not* in pain, the belief that someone is in pain with the belief that someone is *not* in pain, and so on. I contend that my resulting hypothetical system of beliefs would cohere as fully as does my actual system of beliefs, and yet my hypothetical belief that I do *not* have a headache would not therefore be justified. What makes this difference concerning justification between my actual belief that I have a headache and the hypothetical belief that I am free of headache, each as coherent as the other within its own system, if not the actual splitting headache? But the headache is *not* itself a belief nor a relation among beliefs and is thus in no way constitutive of the internal coherence of my body of beliefs.

Some might be tempted to respond by alleging that one's belief about whether or not one has a headache is always *infallible*. But since we could devise similar examples for the various sensory modalities and propositional attitudes, the response given for the case of headache would have to be generalized. In effect, it would have to cover "peripheral" beliefs generally—beliefs at the periphery of one's body of beliefs, minimally coherent with the rest. These peripheral beliefs would all be said to be infallible. That is, again, a possible response, but it leads to a capitulation by the coherentist to the radical foundationalist on a crucial issue that has traditionally divided them: the infallibility of beliefs about one's own subjective states.

What is more, not all peripheral beliefs are about one's own subjective states. The direct realist is probably right that some beliefs about our surroundings are uninferred and yet justified. Consider my present belief that the table before me is oblong. This presumably coheres with such other beliefs of mine as that the table has the same shape as the piece of paper before me, which is oblong, and a different shape than the window frame here, which is square, and so on. So far as I can see, however, there is no insurmountable obstacle to replacing that whole set of coherent beliefs with an equally coherent set as follows: that the table before me is square, that the table has the same shape as the square window frame, and a different shape than the piece of paper, which is oblong, and so on. The important points are (a) that this replacement may be made without changing the rest of one's body of beliefs or any aspect of the world beyond, including one's present visual experience of something oblong, not square, as one looks at the table before one; and (b) that is so, in part, because of the fact

(c) that the subject need not have any beliefs about his present sensory experience.

Some might be tempted to respond by alleging that one's present experience is *self-intimating*, i.e., always necessarily taken note of and reflected in one's beliefs. Thus if anyone has visual experience of something oblong, then he believes that he has such experience. But this would involve a further important concession by the coherentist to the radical foundationalist, who would have been granted two of his most cherished doctrines: the infallibility of introspective belief and the self-intimation of experience.

10. The Foundationalist's Dilemma

The antifoundationalist zeal of recent years has left several forms of foundationalism standing. These all share the conviction that a belief can be justified not only by its coherence within a comprehensive system but also by an appropriate combination of observational content and origin in the use of the senses in standard conditions. What follows presents a dilemma for any foundationalism based on any such idea.

a. We may surely suppose that beings with observational mechanisms radically unlike ours might also have knowledge of their environment. (That seems possible even if the radical difference in observational mechanisms precludes overlap in substantive concepts and beliefs.)

b. Let us suppose that there is such a being, for whom experience of type ϕ (of which we have no notion) has a role with respect to his beliefs of type ϕ analogous to the role that our visual experience has with respect to our visual beliefs. Thus we might have a schema such as the following:

HUMAN	EXTRATERRESTRIAL BEING
Visual experience	ϕ experience
Experience of something red	Experience of something F
Belief that there is something red before one	Belief that there is something F before one

c. It is often recognized that our visual experience intervenes in two ways with respect to our visual beliefs: as cause and as justification. But these are not wholly independent. Presumably, the justification of the belief that something here is red derives at least in part from the fact that it originates in a visual experience of something red that takes place in normal circumstances.

d. Analogously, the extraterrestrial belief that something here has the property of being F might be justified partly by the fact that it originates in a ϕ experience of something F that takes place in normal circumstances.

e. A simple question presents the foundationalist's dilemma: regarding the epistemic principle that underlies our justification for believing that something here is red on the basis of our visual experience of something red, is it proposed as a fundamental principle or as a derived generalization? Let us compare the famous Principle of Utility of value theory, according to which it is best for that to happen which, of all the possible alternatives in the circumstances, would bring with it into the world the greatest balance of pleasure over pain, joy over sorrow, happiness over unhappiness, content over discontent, or the like. Upon this fundamental principle one may then base various generalizations, rules of thumb, and maxims of public health, nutrition, legislation, etiquette, hygiene, and so on. But these are all then derived generalizations which rest for their validity on the fundamental principle. Similarly, one may also ask, with respect to the generalizations advanced by our foundationalist, whether these are proposed as fundamental principles or as derived maxims or the like. This sets him face to face with a dilemma, each of whose alternatives is problematic. If his proposals are meant to have the status of secondary or derived maxims, for instance, then it would be quite unphilosophical to stop there. Let us turn, therefore, to the other alternative.

f. On reflection it seems rather unlikely that epistemic principles for the justification of observational beliefs by their origin in sensory experience could have a status more fundamental than that of derived generalizations. For by granting such principles fundamental status we would open the door to a multitude of equally basic principles with no unifying factor. There would be some for vision, some for hearing, etc., without even mentioning the corresponding extraterrestrial principles.

g. It may appear that there is after all an idea, however, that unifies our multitude of principles. For they all involve sensory experience and sensible characteristics. But what is a sensible characteristic? Aristotle's answer appeals to examples: colors, shapes, sounds, and so on. Such a notion might enable us to unify perceptual epistemic principles under some more fundamental principle such as the following:

> If σ is a sensible characteristic, then the belief that there is something with σ before one is (prima facie) justified if it is based on a visual experience of something with σ in conditions that are normal with respect to σ.

h. There are at least two difficulties with such a suggestion, however, and neither one can be brushed aside easily. First, it is not clear that we can have a viable notion of sensible characteristic on the basis of examples so diverse as colors, shapes, tones, odors, and so on. Second, the authority of such a principle apparently derives from contingent circumstances concerning the reliability of beliefs prompted by sensory experiences of certain sorts. According to the foundationalist, our visual beliefs are justified by their origin in our visual experience or the like. Would such beliefs be equally well justified in a world where beliefs with such an origin were nearly always false?

i. In addition, finally, even if we had a viable notion of such characteristics, it is not obvious that fundamental knowledge of reality would have to derive causally or otherwise from sensory experience of such characteristics. How could one impose reasonable limits on extraterrestrial mechanisms for noninferential acquisition of beliefs? Is it not possible that such mechanisms need not always function through sensory experience of any sort? Would such beings necessarily be denied any knowledge of their surroundings and indeed of any contingent spatio-temporal fact? Let us suppose them to possess a complex system of true beliefs concerning their surroundings, the structures

below the surface of things, exact details of history and geography, all constituted by concepts none of which corresponds to any of our sensible characteristics. What then? Is it not possible that their basic beliefs should all concern fields of force, waves, mathematical structures, and numerical assignments to variables in several dimensions? This is no doubt an exotic notion, but even so it still seems conceivable. And if it is in fact possible, what then shall we say of the noninferential beliefs of such beings? Would we have to concede the existence of special epistemic principles that can validate their noninferential beliefs? Would it not be preferable to formulate more abstract principles that can cover both human and extraterrestrial foundations? If such more abstract principles are in fact accessible, then the less general principles that define the human foundations and those that define the extraterrestrial foundations are both derived principles whose validity depends on that of the more abstract principles. In this the human and extraterrestrial epistemic principles would resemble rules of good nutrition for an infant and an adult. The infant's rules would of course be quite unlike those valid for the adult. But both would still be based on a more fundamental principle that postulates the ends of well-being and good health. What more fundamental principles might support both human and extraterrestrial knowledge in the way that those concerning good health and well-being support rules of nutrition for both the infant and the adult?

11. Reliabilism: an Ethics of Moral Virtues and an Epistemology of Intellectual Virtues

In what sense is the doctor attending Frau Hitler justified in performing an action that brings with it far less value than one of its accessible alternatives? According to one promising idea, the key is to be found in the rules that he embodies through stable dispositions. His action is the result of certain stable virtues, and there are no equally virtuous alternate *dispositions* that, given his cognitive limitations, he might have embodied with equal or better total consequences, and that would have led him to infanticide in the circumstances. The important move for our purpose is the stratification of justification. Primary justification attaches to virtues and other dispositions, to stable dispositions to act, through their greater contribution of value when compared with alternatives. Secondary justification attaches to particular acts in virtue of their source in virtues or other such justified dispositions.

The same strategy may also prove fruitful in epistemology. Here primary justification would apply to *intellectual* virtues, to stable dispositions for belief acquisition, through their greater contribution toward getting us to the truth. Secondary justification would then attach to particular beliefs in virtue of their source in intellectual virtues or other such justified dispositions.[7]

That raises parallel questions for ethics and epistemology. We need to consider more carefully the concept of a virtue and the distinction between moral and intellectual virtues. In epistemology, there is reason to think that the most useful and illuminating notion of intellectual virtue will prove broader than our tradition would suggest and must give due weight not only to the subject and his intrinsic nature but also to his environment and to his epistemic community. This is a large topic, however, to which I hope some of us will turn with more space, and insight, than I can now command.[8]

Summary

1. *Two assumptions.* (A1) that for a belief to constitute knowledge it must be (a) true and (b) justified; and (A2) that the justification relevant to whether or not one knows is a sort of epistemic or theoretical justification to be distinguished from its practical counterpart.

2. *Knowledge and criteria.* Particularism is distinguished from methodism: the first gives priority to particular examples of knowledge over general methods or criteria, whereas the second reverses that order. The methodism of Descartes leads him to an elaborate dogmatism whereas that of Hume leads him to a very simple skepticism. The particularist is, of course, antiskeptical on principle.

3. *Two metaphors: the raft and the pyramid.* For the foundationalist every piece of knowledge stands at the apex of a pyramid that rests on stable and secure foundations whose stability and security does not derive from the upper stories or sections. For the coherentist a body of knowledge is a free-floating raft every plank of which helps directly or indirectly to keep all the others in place, and no plank of which would retain its status with no help from the others.

4. *A coherentist critique of foundationalism.* No mental state can provide a foundation for empirical knowledge. For if such a state is propositional, then it is fallible and hence no secure foundation. But if it is *not* propositional, then how can it possibly serve as a foundation for belief? How can one infer or justify anything on the basis of a state that, having no propositional content, must be logically dumb? An analogy with ethics suggests a reason to reject this dilemma. Other reasons are also advanced and discussed.

5. *The regress argument.* In defending his position, the foundationalist often attempts to rule out the very possibility of an infinite regress of justification (which leads him to the necessity for a foundation.) Some of his arguments to that end are examined.

6. *The relation of justification and foundationalist strategy.* An alternative foundationalist strategy is exposed, one that does not require ruling out the possibility of an infinite regress of justification.

7. *Two levels of foundationalism.* Substantive foundationalism is distinguished from formal foundationalism, three grades of which are exposed: first, the supervenience of epistemic justification; second, its explicable supervenience; and, third, its supervenience explicable by means of a simple theory. There turns out to be a surprising kinship between coherentism and substantive foundationalism, both of which aim at a formal foundationalism of the highest grade, at a theory of the greatest simplicity that explains how epistemic justification supervenes on nonepistemic factors.

8. *Doxastic ascent arguments.* The distinction between formal and substantive foundationalism provides an unusual viewpoint on some recent attacks against foundationalism. We consider doxastic ascent arguments as an example.

9. *Coherentism and substantive foundationalism.* It is argued that substantive foundationalism is superior since coherentism is unable to account adequately for the epistemic status of beliefs at the "periphery" of a body of beliefs.

10. *The foundationalist's dilemma.* All foundationalism based on sense experience is subject to a fatal dilemma.

11. *Reliabilism.* An alternative to foundationalism of sense experience is sketched.

NOTES

1. But Descartes's methodism was at most partial. James Van Cleve has supplied the materials for a convincing argument that the way out of the Cartesian circle is through a particularism of basic knowledge. (See James Van Cleve, "Foundationalism, Epistemic Principles, and the Cartesian Circle," *The Philosophical Review* 88 (1979): 55–91.) But this is, of course, compatible with methodism on inferred knowledge. Whether Descartes subscribed to such methodism is hard (perhaps impossible) to determine, since in the end he makes room for all the kinds of knowledge required by particularism. But his language when he introduces the method of hyperbolic doubt, and the order in which he proceeds, suggest that he did subscribe to such methodism.

2. Cf. Laurence Bonjour, "The Coherence Theory of Empirical Knowledge," *Philosophical Studies* 30 (1976): 281–312; and especially, Michael Williams, *Groundless Belief* (New Haven, 1977); and L. Bonjour, "Can Empirical Knowledge Have a Foundation?" *American Philosophical Quarterly* 15 (1978): 1–15.

3. Cf. Richard Foley, "Inferential Justification and the Infinite Regress," *American Philosophical Quarterly* 15 (1978): 311–16.

4. Cf. John Post, "Infinite Regresses of Justification and Explanation," *Philosophical Studies* 38 (1980): 31–52.

5. The argument of this whole section is developed in greater detail in my paper "The Foundations of Foundationalism," *Noûs* 14 (1980): 547–64.

6. For some examples of the influence of doxastic ascent arguments, see Wilfrid Sellars's writing in epistemology: e.g., "Empiricism and the Philosophy of Mind," in *Science, Perception, and Reality* (London, 1963), especially section 8, and particularly p. 168. Also I. T. Oakley, "An Argument for Skepticism Concerning Justified Beliefs," *American Philosophical Quarterly* 13 (1976): 221–28; and Bonjour, "Can Empirical Knowledge Have a Foundation?"

7. This puts in a more traditional perspective the contemporary effort to develop a "causal theory of knowing." From our viewpoint, this effort is better understood not as an attempt to *define* propositional knowledge but as an attempt to formulate fundamental principles of justification.

   Cf. the work of D. Armstrong, *Belief, Truth and Knowledge* (London, 1973); and that of F. Dretske, A. Goldman, and M. Swain, whose relevant already published work is included in *Essays on Knowledge and Justification*, ed. G. Pappas and M. Swain (Ithaca and London, 1978). But the theory is still under development by Goldman and by Swain, who have reached general conclusions about it similar to those suggested here, though not necessarily—so far as I know—for the same reasons or in the same overall context.

8. I am indebted above all to Roderick Chisholm: for his writings and for innumerable discussions. The main ideas in the present paper were first presented in a seminar of 1976–77 at the University of Texas. I am grateful to Anthony Anderson, David and Jean Blumenfeld, Laurence Bonjour, and Martin Perlmutter, who made that seminar a valuable stimulus. Subsequent criticism by my colleague James Van Cleve has also been valuable and stimulating.

28 / David B. Annis
A CONTEXTUALIST THEORY OF EPISTEMIC JUSTIFICATION

I. FOUNDATIONALISM, COHERENTISM, AND CONTEXTUALISM

Foundationalism is the theory that every empirical statement which is justified ultimately must derive at least some of its justification from a special class of basic statements which have at least some degree of justification independent of the support such statements may derive from other statements. Such *minimal* foundationalism does not require certainty or incorrigibility; it does not deny the revisability of *all* statements, and it allows an important role for intrasystematic justification or coherence.[1] The main objections to foundationalism have been (a) the denial of the existence of basic statements and (b) the claim that even if such statements were not mythical, such an impoverished basis would never justify all the various statements we normally take to be justified.

Opposed to foundationalism has been the coherence theory of justification. According to coherentism a statement is justified if and only if it coheres with a certain kind of system of statements. Although there has been disagreement among coherentists in explaining what coherence is and specifying the special system of statements, the key elements in these explanations have been consistency, connectedness, and comprehensiveness. The chief objection to the theory has been that coherence within a consistent and comprehensive set of statements is not sufficient for justification.[2] Theorists of epistemic justification have tended to stress foundationalism and coherentism and in general have overlooked or ignored a third kind of theory, namely, *contextualism*. The contextualist denies that there are basic statements in the foundationalist's sense and that coherence is sufficient for justification. According to contextualism both theories overlook contextual parameters essential to justification. In what follows I develop a version of a contextualist theory.[3]

II. THE BASIC MODEL—MEETING OBJECTIONS

The basic model of justification to be developed here is that of a person's being able to meet certain objections. The objections one must meet and whether or not they are met are relative to certain goals. Since the issue is that of epistemic justification, the goals are epistemic in nature. With respect to one epistemic goal, accepting some statement may be reasonable, whereas relative to a different goal it may not be. Two of our epistemic goals are having true beliefs and avoiding having false beliefs. Other epistemic goals such as simplicity, conservation of existing beliefs, and maximization of explanatory power will be assumed to be subsidiary to the goals of truth and the avoidance of error.[4]

Given these goals, if a person S claims that

Reprinted from the *American Philosophical Quarterly* 15 (1978): 213–19, by permission of the author and the editor. Copyright 1978, *American Philosophical Quarterly*.

some statement h is true, we may object (A) that S is not in a position to know that h or (B) that h is false. Consider (A). Suppose we ask S how he knows that h and he responds by giving us various reasons $e_1, e_2 \ldots, e_n$ for the truth of h. We may object that one of his reasons $e_1 - e_n$ is false, $e_1 - e_n$ does not provide adequate support for h, S's specific reasoning from $e_1 - e_n$ and i does not provide adequate support for h. These objections may be raised to his reasons for $e_1 - e_n$ as well as to his responses to our objections.

There are also cases where a person is not required to give reasons for his claim that h is true. If S claims to see a brown book across the room, we usually do not require reasons. But we may still object that the person is not in a position to know by arguing, for example, that the person is not reliable in such situations. So even in cases where we do not in general require reasons, objections falling into categories (A) or (B) can be raised.

But it would be too strong a condition to require a person to be able to meet all *possible* objections falling into these categories. In some distant time new evidence may be discovered as the result of advances in our scientific knowledge which would call into question the truth of some statement h. Even though we do not in fact have that evidence now, it is logically possible that we have it, so it is a possible objection to h now. If the person had to meet the objection, he would have to be in a different and better epistemic position than the one he is presently in, that is, he would have to have new evidence in order to respond to the objection. The objectors also would have to be in a better position to raise the objection. But the objections to be raised and answered should not require the participants to be in a new epistemic position. What is being asked is whether the person in his present position is justified in believing h. Thus the person only has to answer *current* objections, that is, objections based on the current evidence available.

Merely uttering a question that falls into one of our categories does not make it an objection S must answer. To demand a response the objection must be an expression of a *real* doubt. According to Peirce, doubt is an uneasy and

dissatisfied state from which we struggle to free ourselves. Such doubt is the result of "some surprising phenomenon, some experience which either disappoints an expectation, or breaks in upon some habit of expectation."[5] As Dewey puts it, it is only when "jars, hitches, breaks, blocks . . . incidents occasioning an interruption of the smooth straight forward course of behavior" occur that doubt arises.[6] Thus for S to be held accountable for answering an objection, it must be a manifestation of a real doubt where the doubt is occasioned by a real life situation. Assuming that the subjective probabilities a person assigns reflect the person's actual epistemic attitudes and that these are the product of his confrontation with the world, the above point may be expressed as follows. S is not required to respond to an objection if in *general* it would be assigned a low probability by the people questioning S.

If an objection must be the expression of a real doubt caused by the jars of a real life situation, then such objections will be primarily *local* as opposed to *global*. Global objections call into question the totality of beliefs held at a certain time or a whole realm of beliefs, whereas local objections call into question a specific belief. This is not to say that a real situation might not occur that would prompt a global objection. If having experienced the nuclear radiation of a third world war, there were a sudden and dramatic increase in the error rate of perceptual beliefs of the visual sort, we would be more hesitant about them as a class.

It must be assumed that the objecting audience has the epistemic goals of truth and the avoidance of error. If they were not critical truth seekers, they would not raise appropriate objections. To meet an objection i, S must respond in such a way as to produce within the objecting group a general but not necessarily universal rejection of i or at least the general recognition of the diminished status of i as an objection. In the latter case S may, for example, point out that although i might be true, it only decreases the support of e_i (one of his reasons for believing h) a very small amount, and hence he is still justified in believing h. There are of course many ways in which S can handle an objection. He might indicate that it is not of the type (A) or (B) and so is not relevant. He may respond that it is just an *idle* remark not prompted by real doubt; that is, there is no reason for thinking that it is true. He may ask the objector for his reasons, and he can raise any of the objections of the type (A) or (B) in response. Again the give and take is based on real objections and responses.

III. THE SOCIAL NATURE OF JUSTIFICATION

When asking whether S is justified in believing *h*, this has to be considered relative to an *issue-context*. Suppose we are interested in whether Jones, an ordinary non-medically trained person, has the general information that polio is caused by a virus. If his response to our question is that he remembers the paper reporting that Salk said it was, then this is good enough. He has performed adequately given the issue-context. But suppose the context is an examination for the M.D. degree. Here we expect a lot more. If the candidate simply said what Jones did, we would take him as being very deficient in knowledge. Thus relative to one-issue-context a person may be justified in believing *h* but not justified relative to another context.

The issue-context is what specific issue involving *h* is being raised. It determines the level of understanding and knowledge that S must exhibit, and it determines an appropriate objector-group. For example in the context of the examination for the M.D. degree, the appropriate group is not the class of ordinary non-medically trained people, but qualified medical examiners.

The importance (value or utility) attached to the outcome of accepting *h* when it is false or rejecting *h* when it is true is a component of the issue-context. Suppose the issue is whether a certain drug will help cure a disease in humans without harmful effects. In such a situation we are much more demanding than if the question were whether it would help in the case of animals. In both cases the appropriate objector-group would be the same, namely, qualified researchers. But they would require quite a bit more proof in the former case. Re-

searchers do in fact strengthen or weaken the justificatory conditions in relation to the importance of the issue. If accepting *h* when *h* is false would have critical consequences, the researcher may increase the required significance level in testing *h*.

Man is a social animal, and yet when it comes to the justification of beliefs philosophers tend to ignore this fact. But this is one contextual parameter that no adequate theory of justification can overlook. According to the contextualist model of justification sketched above, when asking whether some person S is justified in believing *h*, we must consider this relative to some specific issue-context which determines the level of understanding and knowledge required. This in turn determines the appropriate objector-group. For S to be justified in believing *h* relative to the issue-context, S must be able to meet all current objections falling into (A) and (B) which express a real doubt of the qualified objector-group where the objectors are critical truth seekers. Thus social information—the beliefs, information, and theories of others—plays an important part in justification, for it in part determines what objections will be raised, how a person will respond to them, and what responses the objectors will accept.

Perhaps the most neglected component in justification theory is the *actual* social practices and norms of justification of a culture or community of people. Philosophers have looked for universal and a priori principles of justification. But consider this in the context of scientific inquiry. There certainly has been refinement in the methods and techniques of discovery and testing in science. Suppose that at a time *t* in accordance with the best methods then developed for discovery and testing in a scientific domain by critical truth seekers, S accepts theory *T*. It is absurd to say that S is not justified in accepting *T* since at a later time a refinement of those techniques would lead to the acceptance of a different theory. Thus relative to the standards at *t*, S is justified in accepting *T*.

The same conclusion follows if we consider a case involving two different groups existing at the same time instead of two different times as in the above example. Suppose S is an Earth physicist and accepts T on the basis of the best methods developed by Earth physicists at t. Unknown to us the more advanced physicists on Twin Earth reject T. S is still justified in accepting T.

To determine whether S is justified in believing h we must consider the actual standards of justification of the community of people to which he belongs. More specifically we determine whether S is justified in believing h by specifying an issue-context raised within a community of people G with certain social practices and norms of justification. This determines the level of understanding and knowledge S is expected to have and the standards he is to satisfy. The appropriate objector-group is a subset of G. To be justified in believing h, S must be able to meet their objections in a way that satisfies their practices and norms.

It follows that justification theory must be *naturalized*. In considering the justification of beliefs we cannot neglect the actual social practices and norms of justification of a group. Psychologists, sociologists, and anthropologists have started this study, but much more work is necessary.[7]

The need to naturalize justification theory has been recognized in recent philosophy of science. Positivists stressed the *logic* of science—the structure of theories, confirmation, explanation—in abstraction from science as actually carried on. But much of the main thrust of recent philosophy of science is that such an approach is inadequate. Science as *practiced* yields justified beliefs about the world. Thus the study of the actual practices, which have changed through time, cannot be neglected. The present tenor in the philosophy of science is thus toward a historical and methodological realism.[8]

From the fact that justification is relative to the social practices and norms of a group, it does not follow that they cannot be criticized nor that justification is somehow subjective. The practices and norms are epistemic and hence have as their goals truth and the avoidance of error. Insofar as they fail to achieve these goals they can be criticized. For example the Kpelle people of Africa rely more on the authority of the elders than we do. But this authority could be questioned if they found it led to too many false perceptual beliefs. An objection to a practice must of course be real; that is, the doubt must be the result of some jar or hitch in our experience of the world. Furthermore such objections will always be local as opposed to global. Some practice or norm and our experiences of the world yield the result that another practice is problematic. A real objection presupposes some other accepted practice. This however does not commit us to some form of subjectivism. Just as there is no theory-neutral observation language in science, so there is no standard-neutral epistemic position that one can adopt. But in neither case does it follow that objectivity and rational criticism are lost.[9]

IV. THE REGRESS ARGUMENT

Philosophers who have accepted foundationalism have generally offered a version of the infinite regress argument in support of it. Two key premises in the argument are the denial of a coherence theory of justification and the denial that an infinite sequence of reasons is sufficient to justify a belief. But there is another option to the conclusion of the argument besides foundationalism. A contextualist theory of the sort offered above stops the regress and yet does not require basic statements in the foundationalist's sense.

Suppose that the Joneses are looking for a red chair to replace a broken one in their house. The issue-context is thus not whether they can discern subtle shades of color. Nor is it an examination in physics where the person is expected to have detailed knowledge of the transmission of light and color perception. Furthermore nothing of great importance hinges on a correct identification. Mr. Jones, who has the necessary perceptual concepts and normal vision, points at a red chair a few feet in front of him and says "here is a red one." The appropriate objector-group consists of normal perceivers who have general knowledge about the standard conditions of perception and perceptual error. In such situations which we are all familiar with, generally, there will be no objections. His claim is accepted as justified.

But imagine that someone objects that there is a red light shining on the chair so it may not be red. If Jones cannot respond to this objection when it is real, then he is not in an adequate cognitive position. But suppose he is in a position to reply that he knows about the light and the chair is still red since he saw it yesterday in normal light. Then we will accept his claim.

A belief is *contextually basic* if, given an issue-context, the appropriate objector-group does not require the person to have reasons for the belief in order to be in a position to have knowledge. If the objector-group requires reasons, then it is not basic in the context. Thus in the first situation above Jones's belief that there is a red chair here is contextually basic, whereas it is not basic in the second situation.

Consider the case either where the objector-group does not require S to have reasons for his belief that h in order to be in a position to have knowledge and where they accept his claim, or the case where they require reasons and accept his claim. In either case there is no regress of reasons. If an appropriate objector-group, the members of which are critical truth seekers, have no real doubts in the specific issue-context, then the person's belief is justified. The belief has withstood the test of verifically motivated objectors.

V. OBJECTIONS TO THE THEORY

There are several objections to the contextualist theory offered, and their main thrust is that the conditions for justification imposed are too stringent. The objections are as follows. First according to the theory offered, to be justified in believing h one must be able to meet a restricted class of objections falling into categories (A) and (B). But this ignores the distinction between *being* justified and *showing* that one is justified. To be justified is just to satisfy the principles of justification. To show that one is justified is to demonstrate that one satisfies these principles, and this is much more demanding.[10] For example S might have evidence that justifies his belief that h even though he is not able to articulate the evidence. In this case

S would not be able to show that he was justified.

Second, if to be justified in believing h requires that one be able to meet the objection that h is false, then the theory ignores the distinction between truth and justification. A person can be justified in believing a statement even though it is false.

Finally the theory requires S to be in a position to answer all sorts of objections from a variety of perspectives. But this again is to require too much. For example assume that two scientists in different countries unaware of each other's work perform a certain experiment. The first scientist, S_1, gets one result and concludes that h. The second scientist, S_2, does not get the result (due to incorrect measurements). To require of S_1 that he be aware of S_2's experiment and be able to refute it is to impose an unrealistic burden on him in order for his belief to be justified. It is to build a *defeasibility* requirement into the justification condition. One approach to handling the Gettier problem has been to add the condition that in order to have knowledge, besides having justified true belief, the justification must not be defeated. Although there have been different characterizations of defeasibility, a core component or unrestricted version has been that a statement i defeats the justification evidence e provides h just in case i is true and the conjunction of i and e does not provide adequate support for h.[11] But according to the contextualist theory presented in order for S to be justified in believing h, he must be able to meet the objection that there is defeating evidence.

In reply to the first objection, the theory offered does not ignore the distinction between being justified and showing that one is justified. It is not required of S that he be able to state the standards of justification and demonstrate that he satisfies them. What is required is that he be able to meet real objections. This may *sometimes* require him to discuss standards, but not always. Furthermore the example given is not a counterexample since it is not a case of justified belief. Consider a case where relative to an issue-context we would expect S to have reasons for his belief that h. Suppose when asked how he knows or what his reasons are he is not able to say anything.

We certainly would not take him as justified in his belief. We may not be able to articulate all our evidence for *h*, but we are required to do it for some of the evidence. It is not enough that we have evidence for *h*; it must be *taken* by us as evidence, and this places us "in the logical space of reasons, of justifying and being able to justify what one says."[12]

The first point in response to the next objection is that *epistemic* justification makes a claim to knowledge. To be *epistemically* justified in believing *h* is to be in a position to know *h*. Furthermore if the goals of epistemic justification are truth and the avoidance of error, then one *ought not* accept false statements. From an epistemic point of view to do so is objectionable. Hence the falsity of *h* at least counts against the person's being justified.

However, the contextualist account offered does not ignore the distinction between truth and justification. Meeting an objection does not entail showing the objection is false. It only requires general agreement on the response. So the objection may still be true. Thus *S* may be justified in believing *h* since he can meet the objection when *h* is in fact false. Furthermore an objection in order to require a response has to be the expression of a real doubt. Since it is possible for verifically motivated objectors not to be aware of the falsity of *h*, this objection will not be raised, so *S* may be justified in believing *h* even though it is false.

The situation is complex, however, since there are cases where the falsity of *h* implies *S* is not justified in believing *h*. Suppose that Jones is at a party and wonders whether his friend Smith is there. Nothing of great importance hinges on his presence; he simply wonders whether he is there. Perhaps he would not mind a chat with Smith. He looks about and asks a few guests. They have not seen him there. In such a situation Jones is justified in believing Smith is not there.

Imagine now that Jones is a police officer looking for Smith, a suspected assassin, at the party. Merely looking about casually and checking with a few guests is certainly not adequate. If Smith turns out to be hiding in one of the closets, we will not conclude that Jones was justified in his belief only it turned out

false. He displayed gross negligence in not checking more thoroughly. There are cases where relative to an issue-context we require the person *S* to put himself in such an epistemic position that *h* will not turn out to be false. In this case the falsity of *h* is *non-excusable*. To be justified in believing *h* in non-excusable cases, *S* must be able to meet the objection that *h* is false. This is not required in excusable cases.

Assume that *h* is some very complicated scientific theory and *S* puts himself in the very best evidential position at the time. Even if the truth of *h* is very important, the falsity of *h* is excusable. The complexity of the issue and the fact that *S* put himself in the best position possible excuses *S* from the falsity of *h*, so he is still justified. But not all excusable cases involve a complex *h* nor being in the best position possible. Suppose that Smith has an identical twin brother but the only living person who knows this is the brother. Furthermore there are no records that there was a twin brother. If Jones returns a book to Smith's house and mistakenly gives it to the brother (where the issue-context is simply whether he returned the borrowed book and nothing of great importance hinges on to whom he gave it), he is still justified in his belief that he gave it to his friend Smith. Although Jones could have put himself in a better position (by asking questions about their friendship), there was no reason for him in the context to check further. People did not generally know about the twin brother, and Smith did not notice any peculiar behavior. Given the issue-context, members of the appropriate objector-group would not *expect* Jones to check further. So he evinces no culpability when his belief turns out to be false. Excusability thus depends on the issue-context and what the appropriate objector-group, given their standards of justification and the information available, expect of *S*.

Part of assimilating our epistemic standards, as is the case with both legal and moral standards, is learning the conditions of excusability. Such conditions are highly context-dependent, and it would be extremely difficult if not impossible to formulate rules to express them. In general we learn the conditions of excusability case by case. One need only consider moral and legal negligence to realize the full complexity of excuses, an area still to be studied despite Austin's well-known plea a number of years ago.

In response to the third objection it should be noted that epistemic justification is not to be taken lightly. Accepting *h* in part determines what other things I will believe and do. Furthermore I can infect the minds of others with my falsehoods and thus affect their further beliefs and actions. So to be epistemically justified requires that our claims pass the test of criticism. This point has motivated some philosophers to build a defeasibility requirement into the conditions of justification.

The contextualist theory presented above, however, does not do this. There may be a defeating statement *i*, but *S* need meet this objection only if the objector-group raises it. For them to raise it, *i* must be the expression of real doubt. But it is perfectly possible for verifically motivated people to be unaware of *i*.

Furthermore the concept of epistemic excusability applies to defeating evidence. Suppose there is defeating evidence *i*. *S* may still be justified in his belief that *h* in the issue-context, even though he is unable to meet the objection. Relative to the issue-context, the appropriate objector-group with their standards of justification and available information may not expect of *S* that he be aware of *i*. Perhaps the issue involving *h* is very complicated. Thus his failure to meet the defeating evidence is excusable.

In the experiment case we can imagine issue-contexts where we would expect the first scientist to know of the experiment of the other scientist. But not all issue-contexts demand this. Nevertheless we may still require that he be in a position to say something about the other experiment if informed about it. For example he might indicate that he knows the area well, has performed the experiment a number of times and gotten similar results, it was performed under carefully controlled conditions, so he has every reason for believing that the experiment is replicable with similar results. Thus there must be something wrong with the other experiment. Requiring the scientist to be

able to respond in the *minimal* way seems not to be overly demanding.

VI. SUMMARY

Contextualism is an alternative to the traditional theories of foundationalism and coherentism. It denies the existence of basic statements in the foundationalist's sense (although it allows contextually basic statements), and it denies that coherence as it traditionally has been explained is sufficient for justification. Both theories overlook contextual parameters essential to justification, such as the issue-context and thus the value of *h*, social information, and social practices and norms of justification. In particular, the social nature of justification cannot be ignored.

NOTES

1. For a discussion of minimal foundationalism see William P. Alston, "Has Foundationalism Been Refuted?"; James W. Cornman, "Foundationalism versus Nonfoundational Theories of Empirical Justification"; David B. Annis, "Epistemic Foundationalism."

2. Recent discussions of coherentism are found in Keith Lehrer, *Knowledge*, chaps. 7–8; Nicholas Rescher, "Foundationalism, Coherentism, and the Idea of Cognitive Systematization." and his *The Coherence Theory of Truth*. Criticism of Lehrer's coherence theory is to be found in Cornman, "Foundational Versus Nonfoundational Theories of Empirical Justification," and in my review of Lehrer in *Philosophia* 6 (1976): 209–13. Criticism of Rescher's version is found in Mark Pastin's "Foundationalism Redux," unpublished, an abstract of which appears in the *The Journal of Philosophy* 61 (1974): 709–10.

3. Historically the key contextualists have been Peirce, Dewey, and Popper. But contextualist hints, suggestions, and theories are also to be found in Robert Ackermann, *Belief and Knowledge*; Bruce Aune, *Knowledge, Mind and Nature*; John Austin *Sense and Sensibilia* (London, 1962); Isaac Levi, *Gambling with Truth* (New York, 1967); Stephen Toulmin, *The Uses of Argument* (London, 1958) and *Human Under-*

standing (Princeton, New Jersey, 1972); Carl Wellman, *Challenge and Response: Justification in Ethics* (Carbondale, Illinois, 1971); F. L. Will, *Induction and Justification*; Ludwig Wittgenstein, *Philosophical Investigations* (New York, 1953) and *On Certainty*.

4. For a discussion of epistemic goals see Levi, *Gambling with Truth*.
5. C. S. Peirce, *Collected Papers*, vol. 6, ed. Charles Hartshorne and Paul Weiss (Harvard, 1965), p. 469.
6. John Dewey, *Knowing and the Known* (Boston, 1949), p. 315. See also Wittgenstein's *On Certainty*.
7. See, for example, Michael Cole et al., *The Cultural Context of Learning and Thinking* (New York, 1971).
8. For a discussion of the need to naturalize justification theory in the philosophy of science, see

Frederick Suppe, "Afterword—1976" in the 2nd edition of his *The Structure of Scientific Theories* (Urbana, Illinois, 1977).
9. See Frederick Suppe's "The Search for Philosophic Understanding of Scientific Theories" and his "Afterword—1976" in *The Structure of Scientific Theories* for a discussion of objectivity in science and the lack of a theory-neutral observation language.
10. Alston discusses this distinction in "Has Foundationalism Been Refuted?" See also his "Two Types of Foundationalism," and "Self-Warrant: A Neglected Form of Privileged Access."
11. The best discussion of defeasibility is Marshall Swain's "Epistemic Defeasibility."
12. Wilfrid Sellars, *Science, Perception and Reality*, p. 13. Carl Ginet; "What Must Be Added to Knowing to Obtain Knowing That One Knows?," *Synthese* 21 (1970): 163–86.

29 / Richard Feldman and Earl Conee
EVIDENTIALISM

I

We advocate evidentialism in epistemology. What we call *evidentialism* is the view that the epistemic justification of a belief is determined by the quality of the believer's evidence for the belief. Disbelief and suspension of judgment also can be epistemically justified. The doxastic attitude that a person is justified in having is the one that fits the person's evidence. More precisely:

> EJ   Doxastic attitude D toward proposition p is epistemically justified for S at r if and only if having D toward p fits the evidence S has at t.[1]

We do not offer EJ as an analysis. Rather it serves to indicate the kind of notion of justification that we take to be characteristically epistemic—a notion that makes justification turn entirely on evidence. Here are three examples that illustrate the application of this notion of justification. First, when a physiologically normal person under ordinary circumstances looks at a plush green lawn that is directly in front of him in broad daylight, believing that there is something green before him is the attitude toward this proposition that fits his evidence. That is why the belief is epistemically justified. Second, suspension of judgment is the fitting attitude for each of us toward the proposition that an even number of ducks exists, since our evidence makes it equally likely that the number is odd. Neither belief nor disbelief is epistemically justified when our evidence is equally balanced. And third, when it comes to

From *Philosophical Studies* 48, no. 1 (1985). Copyright © 1985, D. Reidel Publishing Company. Reprinted by permission of the publisher and the authors.

the proposition that sugar is sour, our gustatory experience makes disbelief the fitting attitude. Such experiential evidence epistemically justifies disbelief.[2]

EJ is not intended to be surprising or innovative. We take it to be the view about the nature of epistemic justification with the most initial plausibility. A defense of EJ is now appropriate because several theses about justification that seem to cast doubt on it have been prominent in recent literature on epistemology. Broadly speaking, these theses imply that epistemic justification depends upon the cognitive capacities of people, or upon the cognitive processes of information-gathering practices that led to the attitude. In contrast, EJ asserts that the epistemic justification of an attitude depends only on evidence.

We believe that EJ identifies the basic concept of epistemic justification. We find no adequate grounds for accepting the recently discussed theses about justification that seem to cast doubt on EJ. In the remainder of this essay we defend evidentialism. Our purpose is to show that it continues to be the best view of epistemic justification.

II

In this section we consider two objections to EJ. Each is based on a claim about human limits and a claim about the conditions under which an attitude can be justified. One objection depends on the claim that an attitude can be justified only if it is voluntarily adopted, the other depends on the claim that an attitude toward a proposition or propositions can be justified for a person only if the ability to have that attitude toward the proposition or those propositions is within normal human limits.

Doxastic Voluntarism

EJ says that a doxastic attitude is justified for a person when that attitude fits the person's evidence. It is clear that there are cases in which a certain attitude toward a proposition fits a person's evidence, yet the person has no control over whether he forms that attitude to-

ward that proposition. So some involuntarily adopted attitudes are justified according to EJ. John Heil finds this feature of the evidentialist position questionable. He says that the fact that we "speak of a person's beliefs as being warranted, justified, or rational . . . makes it appear that . . . believing something can, at least sometimes, be under the voluntary control of the believer."[3] Hilary Kornblith claims that it seems "unfair" to evaluate beliefs if they "are not subject" to direct voluntary control.[4] Both Heil and Kornblith conclude that although beliefs are not under *direct* voluntary control, it is still appropriate to evaluate them because "they are not entirely out of our control either."[5] "One does have a say in the procedures one undertakes that lead to" the formation of beliefs.[6]

Doxastic attitudes need not be under any sort of voluntary control for them to be suitable for epistemic evaluation. Examples confirm that beliefs may be both involuntary and subject to epistemic evaluation. Suppose that a person spontaneously and involuntarily believes that the lights are on in the room, as a result of the familiar sort of completely convincing perceptual evidence. This belief is clearly justified, whether or not the person cannot voluntarily acquire, lose, or modify the cognitive process that led to the belief. Unjustified beliefs can also be involuntary. A paranoid man might believe without any supporting evidence that he is being spied on. This belief might be a result of an uncontrollable desire to be a recipient of special attention. In such a case the belief is clearly epistemically unjustified even if the belief is involuntary and the person cannot alter the process leading to it.

The contrary view that only voluntary beliefs are justified or unjustified may seem plausible if one confuses the topic of EJ with an assessment of the *person*.[7] A person deserves praise or blame for being in a doxastic state only if that state is under the person's control.[8] The person who involuntarily believes in the presence of overwhelming evidence that the lights are on does not deserve praise for this belief. The belief is nevertheless justified. The person who believes that he is being spied on as a result of an uncontrollable desire does not deserve to be blamed for that belief. But there is a fact about the belief's epistemic merit. It is epistemically defective—it is held in the presence of insufficient evidence and is therefore unjustified.

Doxastic Limits

Apart from the questions about doxastic voluntarism, it is sometimes claimed that it is inappropriate to set epistemic standards that are beyond normal human limits. Alvin Goldman recommends that epistemologists seek epistemic principles that can serve as practical guides to belief formation. Such principles, he contends, must take into account the limited cognitive capacities of people. Thus, he is led to deny a principle instructing people to believe all the logical consequences of their beliefs, since they are unable to have the infinite number of beliefs that following such a principle would require.[9] Goldman's view does not conflict with EJ, since EJ does not instruct anyone to believe anything. It simply states a necessary and sufficient condition for epistemic justification. Nor does Goldman think this view conflicts with EJ, since he makes it clear that the principles he is discussing are guides to action and not principles that apply the traditional concept of epistemic justification.

Although Goldman does not use facts about normal cognitive limits to argue against EJ, such an argument has been suggested by Kornblith and by Paul Thagard. Kornblith cites Goldman's work as an inspiration for his view that "having justified beliefs is simply doing the best one can in the light of the innate endowment one starts from. . . ."[10] Thagard contends that rational or justified principles of inference "should not demand of a reasoner inferential performance which exceeds the general psychological abilities of human beings."[11] Neither Thagard nor Kornblith argues against EJ, but it is easy to see how such an argument would go. A doxastic attitude toward a proposition is justified for a person only if having that attitude toward that proposition is within the normal doxastic capabilities of people. Some doxastic attitudes that fit a person's evidence are not within those capabilities. Yet EJ classifies them as justified. Hence, EJ is false.[12]

We see no good reason here to deny EJ. The argument has as a premise the claim that some attitudes beyond normal limits do fit someone's evidence. The fact that we are limited to a finite number of beliefs is used to support this claim. But this fact does not establish the premise. There is no reason to think that an infinite number of beliefs fit any body of evidence that anyone ever has. The evidence that people have under ordinary circumstances never makes it evident, concerning every one of an infinite number of logical consequences of that evidence, that it is a consequence. Thus, believing each consequence will not fit any ordinary evidence. Furthermore, even if there are circumstances in which more beliefs fit a person's evidence than he is able to have, all that follows is that he cannot have at one time all the beliefs that fit. It does not follow that there is any particular fitting belief which is unattainable. Hence, the premise of the argument that says that EJ classifies as justified some normally unattainable beliefs is not established by means of this example. There does not seem to be any sort of plausible evidence that would establish this premise. While some empirical evidence may show that people typically do not form fitting attitudes in certain contexts, or that some fitting attitudes are beyond some individual's abilities, such evidence fails to show that any fitting attitudes are beyond normal limits.

There is a more fundamental objection to this argument against EJ. There is no basis for the premise that what is epistemically justified must be restricted to feasible doxastic alternatives. It can be a worthwhile thing to help people to choose among the epistemic alternatives open to them. But suppose that there were occasions when forming the attitude that best fits a person's evidence was beyond normal cognitive limits. This would still be the attitude *justified* by the person's evidence. If the person had normal abilities, then he would be in the unfortunate position of being unable to do what is justified according to the standard for justification asserted by EJ. This is not a flaw in the account of justification. Some standards are met only by going beyond normal human limits. Standards that some teachers set for an "A" in a course are unattainable for most students. There are standards of artistic excellence that no one can meet, or at least standards that normal people cannot meet in any available circumstance. Similarly, epistemic justification might have been normally unattainable.

We conclude that neither considerations of doxastic voluntarism nor of doxastic limits provide any good reason to abandon EJ as an account of epistemic justification.

III

EJ sets an epistemic standard for evaluating doxastic conduct. In any case of a standard for conduct, whether it is voluntary or not, it is appropriate to speak of "requirements" or "obligations" that the standard imposes. The person who has overwhelming perceptual evidence for the proposition that the lights are on, epistemically ought to believe that proposition. The paranoid person epistemically ought not believe that he is being spied upon when he has no evidence supporting this belief. We hold the general view that one epistemically ought to have the doxastic attitudes that fit one's evidence. We think that being epistemically obligatory is equivalent to being epistemically justified.

There are in the literature two other sorts of view about epistemic obligations. What is epistemically obligatory, according to these other views, does not always fit one's evidence. Thus, each of these views of epistemic obligation, when combined with our further thesis that being epistemically obligatory is equivalent to being epistemically justified, yields results incompatible with evidentialism. We shall now consider how these proposals affect EJ.

Justification and the Obligation to Believe Truths

Roderick Chisholm holds that one has an "intellectual requirement" to try one's best to bring it about that, of the propositions one considers, one believes all and only the truths.[13] This theory of what our epistemic obligations are, in conjunction with our view that the justified attitudes are the ones we have an epistemic obligation to hold, implies the following principle:

CJ Doxastic attitude D toward proposition p is justified for person S at time t if and only if S considers p at t and S's having D toward p at t would result from S's trying his best to bring it about that S believe p at t iff p is true.

Evaluation of CJ is complicated by an ambiguity in "trying one's best." It might mean "trying in that way which will in fact have the best results." Since the goal is to believe all and only the truths one considers, the best results would be obtained by believing each truth one considers and disbelieving each falsehood one considers. On this interpretation, CJ implies that believing each truth and disbelieving each falsehood one considers is justified whenever believing and disbelieving in these ways would result from something one could try to do.

On this interpretation CJ is plainly false. We are not justified in believing every proposition we consider that happens to be true and which we could believe by trying for the truth. It is possible to believe some unsubstantiated proposition in a reckless endeavor to believe a truth and happen to be right. This would not be an epistemically justified belief.[14]

It might be contended that trying one's best to believe truths and disbelieve falsehoods really amounts to trying to believe and disbelieve in accordance with one's evidence. We agree that gaining the doxastic attitudes that fit one's evidence is the epistemically best way to use one's evidence in trying to believe all and only the truths one considers. This interpretation of CJ makes it nearly equivalent to EJ. There are two relevant differences. First, CJ implies that one can have justified attitudes only toward propositions one actually considers. EJ does not have this implication. CJ is also unlike EJ in implying that an attitude is justified if it would result from the *trying* to form the attitude that fits one's evidence. The attitude that is justified according to EJ is the one that as a matter of fact does fit one's evidence. This seems more plausible. What would happen if one tried to have a fitting attitude seems irrelevant—one might try but fail to form the fitting attitude.

We conclude that the doxastic attitudes that

would result from carrying out the intellectual requirement Chisholm identifies are not the epistemically justified attitudes.

Justification and Epistemically Responsible Action

Another view about epistemic obligations, proposed by Hilary Kornblith, is that we are obligated to seek the truth and gather evidence in a responsible way. Kornblith also maintains that the justification of a belief depends on how responsibly one carried out the inquiry that led to the belief.[15] We shall now examine how the considerations leading to this view affect EJ.

Kornblith describes a case of what he regards as "epistemically culpable ignorance." It is an example in which a person's belief seems to fit his evidence, and thus it seems to be justified according to evidentialism. Kornblith contends that the belief is unjustified because it results from epistemically irresponsible behavior. His example concerns a headstrong young physicist who is unable to tolerate criticism. After presenting a paper to his colleagues, the physicist pays no attention to the devastating objection of a senior colleague. The physicist, obsessed with his own success, fails even to hear the objection, which consequently has no impact on his beliefs, Kornblith says that after this, the physicist's belief in his own theory is unjustified. He suggests that evidentialist theories cannot account for this fact.

Crucial details of this example are left unspecified, but in no case does it provide a refutation of evidentialism. If the young physicist is aware of the fact that his senior colleague is making an objection, then this fact is evidence he has against his theory, although it is unclear from just this much detail how decisive it would be. So, believing his theory may no longer be justified for him according to a purely evidentialist view. On the other hand, perhaps he remains entirely ignorant of the fact that a senior colleague is objecting to his theory. He might be "lost in thought"—privately engrossed in proud admiration of the paper he has just given—and fail to understand what is going on in the audience. If this happens, and his evidence supporting his theory is just as it was prior to his presentation of the paper, then

believing the theory does remain justified for him (assuming that it was justified previously). There is no reason to doubt EJ in the light of this example. It may be true that the young physicist is an unpleasant fellow, and that he lacks intellectual integrity. This is an evaluation of the character of the physicist. It is supported by the fact that in this case he is not engaged in an impartial quest for the truth. But the physicist's character has nothing to do with the epistemic status of his belief in his theory.

Responsible evidence-gathering obviously has some epistemic significance. One serious epistemological question is that of how to engage in a thoroughgoing rational pursuit of the truth. Such a pursuit may require gathering evidence in responsible ways. It may also be necessary to be open to new ideas, to think about a variety of important issues, and to consider a variety of opinions about such issues. Perhaps it requires, as Bonjour suggests, that one "reflect critically upon one's beliefs."[16] But everyone has some justified beliefs, even though virtually no one is fully engaged in a rational pursuit of the truth. EJ has no implication about the actions one must take in a rational pursuit of the truth. It is about the epistemic evaluation of attitudes given the evidence one does have, however one came to possess that evidence.

Examples like that of the headstrong physicist show no defect in the evidentialist view. Justified beliefs can result from epistemically irresponsible actions.

Other Sorts of Obligation

Having acknowledged at the beginning of this section that justified attitudes are in a sense obligatory, we wish to forestall confusions involving other notions of obligations. It is not the case that there is always a *moral* obligation to believe in accordance with one's evidence. Having a fitting attitude can bring about disastrous personal or social consequences. Vicious beliefs that lead to vicious acts can be epistemically justified. This rules out any moral obligation to have the epistemically justified attitude.[17]

It is also false that there is always a *prudential* obligation to have each epistemically justified attitude. John Heil discusses the following example.[18] Sally has fairly good evidence that her husband Burt has been seeing another woman. Their marriage is in a precarious condition. It would be best for Sally if their marriage were preserved. Sally foresees that, were she to believe that Burt has been seeing another woman, her resulting behavior would lead to their divorce. Given these assumptions, EJ counts as justified at least some measure of belief by Sally in the proposition that Burt has been seeing another woman. But Sally would be better off if she did not have this belief, in light of the fact that she would be best served by their continued marriage. Heil raises the question of what Sally's prudential duty is in this case. Sally's *epistemic* obligation is to believe that her husband is unfaithful. But that gives no reason to deny what seems obvious here. Sally *prudentially* ought to refrain from believing her husband to be unfaithful. It can be prudent not to have a doxastic attitude that is correctly said by EJ to be justified, just as it can be moral not to have such an attitude.

More generally, the causal consequences of having an unjustified attitude can be more beneficial in *any* sort of way than the consequences of having its justified alternative. We have seen that it can be morally and prudentially best not to have attitudes justified according to EJ. Failing to have these attitudes can also have the best results for the sake of *epistemic* goals such as the acquisition of knowledge. Roderick Firth points out that a scientist's believing against his evidence that he will recover from an illness may help to effect a recovery and so contribute to the growth of knowledge by enabling the scientist to continue his research.[19] William James's case for exercising "the will to believe" suggests that some evidence concerning the existence of God is available only after one believes in God in the absence of justifying evidence. EJ does not counsel against adopting such beliefs for the sake of these epistemic ends. EJ implies that the beliefs would be unjustified when adopted. This is not to say that the believing would do no epistemic good.

We acknowledge that it is appropriate to speak of epistemic obligations. But it is a mistake to think that what is epistemically oblig-

atory, i.e., epistemically justified, is also morally or prudentially obligatory, or that it has the overall best epistemic consequences.

IV

Another argument that is intended to refute the evidentialist approach to justification concerns the ways in which a person can come to have an attitude that fits his evidence. Both Kornblith and Goldman propose examples designed to show that merely *having* good evidence for a proposition is not sufficient to make believing that proposition justified.[20] We shall work from Kornblith's formulation of the argument, since it is more detailed. Suppose Alfred is justified in believing p, and justified in believing if p then q. Alfred also believes q. EJ seems to imply that believing q is justified for Alfred, since that belief does seem to fit this evidence. Kornblith argues that Alfred's belief in q may still not be justified. It is not justified, according to Kornblith, if Alfred has a strong distrust of *modus ponens* and believes q because he likes the sound of the sentence expressing it rather than on the basis of the *modus ponens* argument. Similarly, Goldman says that a person's belief in q is not justified unless the belief is caused in some appropriate way.

Whether EJ implies that Alfred's belief in q is justified depends in part on an unspecified detail—Alfred's evidence concerning *modus ponens*. It is possible that Alfred has evidence against *modus ponens*. Perhaps he has just seen a version of the Liar paradox that seems to render *modus ponens* as suspect as the other rules and premises in the derivation. In the unlikely event that Alfred has such evidence, EJ implies that believing q is *not* justified for him. If rather, as we shall assume, his overall evidence supports *modus ponens* and q, then EJ does imply that believing q is justified for him.

When Alfred has strong evidence for q, his believing q is epistemically justified. This is the sense of "justified" captured by EJ. However, if Alfred's basis for believing q is not his evidence for it, but rather the sound of the sentence expressing q, then it seems equally clear that there is some sense in which this state of believing is epistemically "defective"—he did not arrive at the belief in the right way. The term "well-founded" is sometimes used to characterize an attitude that is epistemically both well-supported and properly arrived at. Well-foundedness is a second evidentialist notion used to evaluate doxastic states. It is an evidentialist notion because its application depends on two matters of evidence—the evidence one *has*, and the evidence one *uses* in forming the attitude. More precisely:

WF S's doxastic attitude D at t toward proposition p is well-founded if and only if
(i)   having D toward p is justified for S at t; and
(ii) S has D toward p on the basis of some body of evidence e, such that
   (a) S has e as evidence at t;
   (b) having D toward p fits e; and
   (c) there is no more inclusive body of evidence e' had by S at t such that having D toward p does not fit e'.[21]

Since the evidentialist can appeal to this notion of well-foundedness, cases in which a person has but does not use justifying evidence do not refute evidentialism. Kornblith and Goldman's intuitions about such cases can be accommodated. A person in Alfred's position *is* in an epistemically defective state—his belief in q is not well-founded. Having said this, it is reasonable also to affirm the other evidentialist judgment that Alfred's belief in q is in another sense epistemically right—it is justified.[22]

V

The theory of epistemic justification that has received the most attention recently is reliabilism. Roughly speaking, this is the view that epistemically justified beliefs are the ones that result from belief-forming processes that reliably lead to true beliefs.[23] In this section we consider whether reliabilism casts doubt on evidentialism.

Although reliabilists generally formulate their view as an account of epistemic justification, it is clear that in its simplest forms it is better regarded as an account of well-foundedness. In order for a belief to be favorably evaluated by the simple sort of reliabilism sketched above, the belief must actually be held, as is the case with WF. And just as with WF, the belief must be "grounded" in the proper way. Where reliabilism appears to differ from WF is over the conditions under which a belief is properly grounded. According to WF, this occurs when the belief is based on fitting evidence. According to reliabilism, a belief is properly grounded if it results from a belief-forming process that reliably leads to true beliefs. These certainly are *conceptually* different accounts of the grounds of well-founded beliefs.

In spite of this conceptual difference, reliabilism and WF may be extensionally equivalent. The question of equivalence depends on the resolution of two unclarities in reliabilism. One pertains to the notion of a belief-forming process and the other to the notion of reliability.

An unclarity about belief-forming processes arises because every belief is caused by a sequence of particular events which is an instance of many types of causal processes. Suppose that one evening Jones looks out his window and sees a bright shining disk-shaped object. The object is in fact a luminous frisbee, and Jones clearly remembers having given one of these to his daughter. But Jones is attracted to the idea that extraterrestrials are visiting the Earth. He manages to believe that he is seeing a flying saucer. Is the process that caused this belief reliable? Since the sequence of events leading to his belief is an instance of many types of process, the answer depends upon which of these many types is the relevant one. The sequence falls into highly general categories such as perceptually-based belief formation and visually-based belief formation. It seems that if these are the relevant categories, then his belief is indeed reliably formed, since these are naturally regarded as "generally reliable" sorts of belief-forming processes. The sequence of events leading to Jones's belief also falls into many relatively specific categories such as night-vision-of-a-nearby-object and vision-in-Jones's—precise—environmental—circumstances. These are not clearly reliable types. The sequence is also an instance of this contrived kind: process-leading-from-obviously - defeated - evidence - to - the - belief - that-one-sees-a-flying-saucer. This, presumably, is an unreliable kind of process. Finally, there is the maximally specific process that occurs only when physiological events occur that are exactly like those that led to Jones's belief that he saw a flying saucer. In all likelihood this kind of process occurred only once. Processes of these types are of differing degrees of reliability, no matter how reliability is determined. The implications of reliabilism for the case are rendered definite only when the kind of process whose reliability is relevant is specified. Reliabilists have given little attention to this matter, and those that have specified relevant kinds have not done so in a way that gives their theory an intuitively acceptable extension.[24]

The second unclarity in reliabilism concerns the notion of reliability itself. Reliability is fundamentally a property of kinds of belief-forming processes, not of sequences of particular events. But we can say that a sequence is reliable provided its relevant type is reliable. The problem raised above concerns the specification of relevant types. The current problem is that of specifying the conditions under which a kind of process is *reliable*. Among possible accounts is one according to which a kind of process is reliable provided most instances of that kind until now have led to true beliefs. Alternative accounts measure the reliability of a kind of process by the frequency with which instances of it produce true beliefs in the future as well as the past, or by the frequency with which its instances produce true beliefs in possible worlds that are similar to the world of evaluation in some designated respect, or by the frequency with which its instances produce true beliefs in all possible worlds.[25]

Because there are such drastically different ways of filling in the details of reliabilism the application of the theory is far from clear. The possible versions of reliabilism seem to include one that is extensionally equivalent to WF. It might be held that all beliefs are formed by one of two relevant kinds of belief-forming process. One kind has as instances all and only those sequences of events leading to a belief that is based on fitting evidence; the other is a kind of process that has as instances all and only those sequences leading to a belief that is not based on fitting evidence. If a notion of reliability can be found on which the former sort of process is reliable and the latter is not, the resulting version of reliabilism would be very nearly equivalent to WF.[26] We do not claim that reliabilists would favor this version of reliabilism. Rather, our point is that the fact that this *is* a version shows that reliabilism may not even be a rival to WF.[27]

Evaluation of reliabilism is further complicated by the fact that reliabilists seem to differ about whether they *want* their theory to have approximately the same extension as WF in fact has. The credibility of reliabilism and its relevance to WF depend in part on the concept reliabilists are really attempting to analyze. An example first described by Laurence Bonjour helps to bring out two alternatives.[28] Bonjour's example is of a person who is clairvoyant. As a result of his clairvoyance he comes to believe that the President is in New York City. The person has no evidence showing that he is clairvoyant and no other evidence supporting his belief about the President. Bonjour claims that the example is a counter-example to reliabilism, since the clairvoyant's belief is not justified (we would add: and therefore ill-founded), although the process that caused it is reliable—the person really is clairvoyant.

The general sort of response to this example that seems to be most commonly adopted by reliabilists is in effect to agree that such beliefs are not well-founded. They interpret or revise reliabilism with the aim of avoiding the counter-example.[29] An alternative response would be to argue that the reliability of clairvoyance shows that the belief *is* well-founded, and thus that the example does not refute reliabilism.[30]

We are tempted to respond to the second alternative—beliefs such as that of the clairvoyant in Bonjour's example really are well-founded—that this is so clear an instance of an ill-founded belief that any proponent of that view must have in mind a different concept from the one we are discussing. The clairvoyant has no reason for holding his belief about the President. The fact that the belief was caused by a process of a reliable kind—clairvoyance—is a significant fact about it. Such a belief may merit some favorable term of epistemic appraisal, e.g., "objectively probable." But the belief is not well-founded.

There are, however, two lines of reasoning that could lead philosophers to think that we must reconcile ourselves to the clairvoyant's belief turning out to be well-founded. According to one of these arguments, examples such as that of Alfred (discussed in Section IV above) show that the evidentialist account of epistemic merit is unsatisfactory and that epistemic merit must be understood in terms of the reliability of belief-forming processes.[31] Since the clairvoyant's belief is reliably formed, our initial inclination to regard it as ill-founded must be mistaken.

This argument is unsound. The most that the example about Alfred shows is that there is a concept of favorable epistemic appraisal other than justification, and that this other concept involves the notion of the *basis* of a belief. We believe that WF satisfactorily captures this other concept. There is no need to move to a reliabilist account, according to which some sort of causal reliability is *sufficient* for epistemic justification. The Alfred example does not establish that some version of reliabilism is correct. It does not establish that the clairvoyant's belief is well-founded.

The second argument for the conclusion that the clairvoyant's belief is well-founded makes use of the strong similarity between clairvoyance in Bonjour's example and normal perception. We claim that Bonjour's clairvoyant is not justified in his belief about the President because that belief does not fit his evidence. Simply having a spontaneous uninferred belief about the whereabouts of the President does not provide evidence for its truth. But, it might be asked, what better evidence is there for any ordinary perceptual belief, say, that one sees a book? If there is no relevant epistemological difference between ordinary perceptual beliefs and the clairvoyant's belief, then they should be evaluated similarly. The argument continues with the point that reliabilism provides an explanation of the crucial similarity between ordinary perceptual beliefs and the clairvoyant's

belief—both perception and clairvoyance *work*, in the sense that both are reliable. So beliefs caused by each process are well-founded on a reliabilist account. The fact that reliabilism satisfactorily explains this is to the theory's credit. On the other hand, in advocating evidentialism we have claimed that perceptual beliefs are well-founded and that the clairvoyant's belief is not. But there appears to be no relevant evidential difference between these beliefs. Thus, if the evidentialist view of the matter cannot be defended, then reliabilism is the superior theory and we should accept its consequence—the clairvoyant's belief is well-founded.

One problem with this argument is that reliabilism has no satisfactory explanation of *anything* until the unclarities discussed above are removed in an acceptable way: What shows that perception and clairvoyance are relevant and reliable types of processes? In any event, there *is* an adequate evidentialist explanation of the difference between ordinary perceptual beliefs and the clairvoyant's belief. On one interpretation of clairvoyance, it is a process whereby one is caused to have beliefs about objects hidden from ordinary view without any conscious state having a role in the causal process. The clairvoyant does not have the conscious experience of, say, seeming to see the President in some characteristic New York City setting, and on that basis form the belief that he is in New York. In this respect, the current version of clairvoyance is unlike ordinary perception, which does include conscious perceptual states. Because of this difference, ordinary perceptual beliefs are based on evidence—the evidence of these sensory states—whereas the clairvoyant beliefs are not based on evidence. Since WF requires that well-founded beliefs be based on fitting evidence, and typical clairvoyant beliefs on the current interpretation are not based on any evidence at all, the clairvoyant beliefs do not satisfy WF.

Suppose instead that clairvoyance does include visual experiences, though of remote objects that cannot stimulate the visual system in any normal way. Even if there are such visual experiences that could serve as a basis for a clairvoyant's beliefs, still there is a relevant epistemological difference between beliefs based on normal perceptual experience and the clairvoyant's belief in Bonjour's example. We have collateral evidence to the effect that when we have perceptual experience of certain kinds, external conditions of the corresponding kinds normally obtain. For example, we have evidence supporting the proposition that when we have the usual sort of experience of seeming to see a book, we usually do in fact see a book. This includes evidence from the coherence of these beliefs with beliefs arising from other perceptual sources, and it also includes testimonial evidence. This latter point is easily overlooked. One reason that the belief that one sees a book fits even a child's evidence when she has a perceptual experience of seeing a book is that children are taught, when they have the normal sort of visual experiences, that they are seeing a physical object of the relevant kind. This testimony, typically from people whom the child has reason to trust, provides evidence for the child. And of course testimony from others during adult life also gives evidence for the veridicality of normal visual experience. On the other hand, as Bonjour describes his example, the clairvoyant has no confirmation at all of his clairvoyant beliefs. Indeed, he has evidence against these beliefs, since the clairvoyant perceptual experiences do not cohere with his other experiences. We conclude, therefore, that evidentialists can satisfactorily explain why ordinary perceptual beliefs are typically well-founded and unconfirmed clairvoyant beliefs, even if reliably caused, are not. There is no good reason to abandon our initial intuition that the beliefs such as those of the clairvoyant in Bonjour's examples are not well-founded.

Again, reliabilists could respond to Bonjour's example either by claiming that the clairvoyant's belief is in fact well-founded or by arguing that reliabilism does not imply that it is well-founded. We turn now to the second of these alternatives, the one most commonly adopted by reliabilists. This view can be defended by arguing either that reliabilism can be reformulated so that it lacks this implication, or that as currently formulated it lacks this implication. We pointed out above that as a general approach reliabilism is sufficiently indefinite to allow interpretations under which it

does lack the implication in question. The only way to achieve this result that we know of that is otherwise satisfactory requires the introduction of evidentialist concepts. The technique is to specify the relevant types of belief-forming processes in evidentialist terms. It is possible to hold that the relevant types of belief-forming process are believing something on the basis of fitting evidence and believing not as a result of fitting evidence. This sort of "reliabilism" is a roundabout approximation of the straightforward evidentialist thesis, WF. We see no reason to couch the approximated evidentialist theory in reliabilist terms. Moreover, the reliabilist approximation is not exactly equivalent to WF, and where it differs it appears to go wrong. The difference is this: it seems possible for the process of believing on the basis of fitting evidence to be unreliable. Finding a suitable sort of reliability makes all the difference here. In various possible worlds where our evidence is mostly misleading, the frequency with which fitting evidence causes true belief is low. Thus, this type of belief-forming process is not "reliable" in such worlds in any straightforward way that depends on actual frequencies. Perhaps a notion of reliability that avoids this result can be found. We know of no such notion which does not create trouble elsewhere for the theory. So, the reliabilist view under consideration has the consequence that in such worlds beliefs based on fitting evidence are not well-founded. This is counterintuitive.[32]

In this section we have compared reliabilism and evidentialism. The vagueness of reliabilism makes it difficult to determine what implications the theory has and it is not entirely clear what implications reliabilists want their theory to have. If reliabilists want their theory to have approximately the same extension as WF, we see no better way to accomplish this than one which makes the theory an unnecessarily complex and relatively implausible approximation to evidentialism. If, on the other hand, reliabilists want their theory to have an extension which is substantially different from that of WF, and yet some familiar notion of "a reliable kind of process" is to be decisive for their notion of well-foundedness, then it becomes clear that the concept they are attempting to analyze is not one evidentialists seek to characterize. This follows from the fact that on this alternative they count as well-founded attitudes that plainly do not exemplify the concept evidentialists are discussing. In neither case, then, does reliabilism pose a threat to evidentialism.

use of a second evidentialist notion, well-foundedness. It does not, however, provide any good reason to think that EJ is false. Nor do we find reason to abandon evidentialism in favor of reliabilism. Evidentialism remains the most plausible view of epistemic justification.

VI

Summary and Conclusion

We have defended evidentialism. Some opposition to evidentialism rests on the view that a doxastic attitude can be justified for a person only if forming the attitude is an action under the person's voluntary control. EJ is incompatible with the conjunction of this sort of doxastic voluntarism and the plain fact that some doxastic states that fit a person's evidence are out of that person's control. We have argued that no good reason has been given for thinking that an attitude is epistemically justified only if having it is under voluntary control.

A second thesis contrary to EJ is that a doxastic attitude can be justified only if having that attitude is within the normal doxastic limits of humans. We have held that the attitudes that are epistemically justified according to EJ are within these limits, and that even if they were not, the fact would not suffice to refute EJ.

Some philosophers have contended that believing a proposition, *p*, is justified for *S* only when *S* has gone about gathering evidence about *p* in a responsible way, or has come to believe *p* as a result of seeking a meritorious epistemic goal such as the discovery of truth. This thesis conflicts with EJ, since believing *p* may fit one's evidence no matter how irresponsible one may have been in seeking evidence about *p* and no matter what were the goals that led to the belief. We agree that there is some epistemic merit in responsibly gathering evidence and in seeking the truth. But we see no reason to think that epistemic justification turns on such matters.

Another thesis conflicting with EJ is that merely having evidence is not sufficient to justify belief, since the believer might not make proper use of the evidence in forming the belief. Consideration of this claim led us to make

NOTES

1. EJ is compatible with the existence of varying strengths of belief and disbelief. If there is such variation, then the greater the preponderance of evidence, the stronger the doxastic attitude that fits the evidence.
2. There are difficult questions about the concept of fit, as well as about what it is for someone to *have* something as evidence, and of what kind of thing constitutes evidence. As a result, there are some cases in which it is difficult to apply EJ. For example, it is unclear whether a person has as evidence propositions he is not currently thinking of, but could recall with some prompting. As to what constitutes evidence, it seems clear that this includes both beliefs and sensory states such as feeling very warm and having the visual experience of seeing blue. Some philosophers seem to think that only beliefs can justify beliefs. (See, for example, Keith Lehrer, *Knowledge* (Oxford: Oxford University Press, 1974), 187–188.) The application of EJ is clear enough to do the work that we intend here—a defense of the evidentialist position.
3. See John Heil, "Doxastic Agency," *Philosophical Studies* 43 (1983): 355–364. The quotation is from p. 355.
4. See Hilary Kornblith, "The Psychological Turn," *Australasian Journal of Philosophy* 60 (1982): 238–253. The quotation is from p. 252.
5. Kornblith, op. cit., 253.
6. Heil, op. cit., p. 363.
7. Kornblith may be guilty of this confusion. He writes, "if a person has an unjustified belief, that person is epistemically culpable," op. cit., 243.
8. Nothing we say here should be taken to imply that any doxastic states are in fact voluntarily entered.
9. See Alvin I. Goldman, "Epistemics: The Regulative Theory of Cognition," *The Journal of Philosophy* 75 (1978): 509–523, esp. pp. 510 and 514. Reprinted in this volume.
10. Hilary Kornblith, "Justified Belief and Epistemically Responsible Action," *The Philosophical Review* 92 (1983): 33–48. The quotation is from p. 46.
11. Paul Thagard, "From the Descriptive to the Normative in Psychology and Logic," *Philosophy of*

Science 49 (1982): 24–42. The quotation is from p. 34.

12. Another version of this argument is that EJ is false because it classifies as justified for a person attitudes that are beyond *that person's* limits. This version is subject to similar criticisms.

13. See Roderick Chisholm, *Theory of Knowledge*, 2nd ed. (Englewood Cliffs, N.J.: Prentice-Hall, 1977), especially pp. 12–15.

14. Roderick Firth makes a similar point against a similar view in "Are Epistemic Concepts Reducible to Ethical Concepts," in *Values and Morals*, edited by A. I. Goldman and J. Kim (Dordrecht: D. Reidel, 1978), 215–229.

15. Kornblith defends this view in "Justified Belief and Epistemically Responsible Action." Some passages suggest that he intends to introduce a new notion of justification, one to be understood in terms of epistemically responsible action. But some passages, especially in Section II, suggest that the traditional analysis of justification is being found to be objectionable and inferior to the one he proposes.

16. Bonjour, "Externalist Theories of Empirical Knowledge." *Midwest Studies in Philosophy* 5 (1980): 63.

17. This is contrary to the view of Richard Gale, defended in "William James and the Ethics of Belief," *American Philosophical Quarterly* 17 (1980): 1–14, and of W. K. Clifford who said, "It is wrong always, everywhere, and for every one, to believe anything upon insufficient evidence" (quoted by William James in "The Will to Believe," reprinted in *Reason and Responsibility*, ed. J. Feinberg [Belmont, California: Wadsworth Publishing Co., 1981], 100).

18. See John Heil, "Believing What One Ought," *Journal of Philosophy* 80 (1983): 752–64.

19. See "Epistemic Merit, Intrinsic and Instrumental," *Proceedings and Addresses of The American Philosophical Association* 55 (1981): 5–6.

20. See Kornblith's "Beyond Foundationalism and the Coherence Theory," *The Journal of Philosophy* 77 (1980): 597–612, esp. pp. 601f., and Goldman's "What is Justified Belief?" in *Justification and Knowledge*, ed. George S. Pappas, (Dordrecht: D. Reidel, 1979), 1–24.

21. Clause (ii) of WF is intended to accommodate the fact that a well-founded attitude need not be based on a person's whole body of evidence. What seems required is that the person base a well-founded attitude on a justifying part of the person's evidence, and that he not ignore any evidence he has that defeats the justifying power of the evidence he does base his attitude on. It might be that his defeating evidence is itself defeated by a still wider body of his evidence. In such a case, the person's attitude is well-founded only if he takes the wider body into account.

22. Goldman uses this sort of example only to show that there is a causal element in the concept of justification. We acknowledge that there is an epistemic concept—well-foundedness—that appeals to the notion of basing an attitude on evidence, and this may be a causal notion. What seems to confer epistemic merit on basing one's belief on the evidence is that in doing so one *appreciates* the evidence. It is unclear whether one can appreciate the evidence without being caused to have the belief by the evidence. But in any event we see no such causal requirement in the case of justification.

23. The clearest and most influential discussion of reliabilism is in Goldman's "What Is Justified Belief?" One of the first statements of the theory appears in David Armstrong's *Belief, Truth and Knowledge* (London: Cambridge University Press, 1973). For extensive bibliographies on reliabilism, see Frederick Schmitt's "Reliability, Objectivity, and the Background of Justification," *Australasian Journal of Philosophy* 62 (1984): 1–15, and Richard Feldman's "Reliability and Justification," *The Monist* 68 (1985): 159–74.

24. For discussion of the problem of determining relevant kinds of belief-forming processes, see Goldman, "What is Justified Belief?" ; Schmitt, "Reliability, Objectivity, and the Background of Justification"; Feldman, "Reliability and Justification"; and Feldman, "Schmitt on Reliability, Objectivity, and Justification," *Australasian Journal of Philosophy* 63 (1985): 354–60.

25. In "Reliability and Justified Belief," *Canadian Journal of Philosophy* 14 (1984): 103–115, John Pollock argues that there is no account of reliability suitable for reliabilists.

26. This version of reliabilism will not be exactly equivalent to WF because it ignores the factors introduced by clause (ii) of WF.

27. It is also possible that versions of reliabilism making use only of natural psychological kinds of belief-forming processes are extensionally equivalent to WF. Goldman seeks to avoid evaluative epistemic concepts in his theory of epistemic justification, so he would not find an account of justification satisfactory unless it appealed only to such natural kinds. See "What is Justified Belief?," 6.

28. See Laurence Bonjour, "Externalist Theories of Empirical Knowledge," *Midwest Studies in Philosophy* 5 (1980): 62.

29. See Goldman, "What is Justified Belief?," 18–20; Kornblith, "Beyond Foundationalism and

the Coherence Theory," 609–611; and Frederick Schmitt, "Reliability, Objectivity, and the Background of Justification."

30. We know of no one who has explicitly taken this approach. It seems to fit most closely with the view defended by David Armstrong in *Belief, Truth and Knowledge*.

31. We know of no one who explicitly defends this inference. In "The Psychological Turn," 241f., Kornblith argues that these examples show that justification depends upon "psychological connections" and "the workings of the appropriate belief-forming process." But he clearly denies there that reliabilism is directly implied.

32. Stewart Cohen has made this point in "Justification and Truth." *Philosophical Studies* 46 (1984): 279–295. Cohen makes the point in the course of developing a dilemma. He argues that reliabilism has the sort of flaw that we describe above when we appeal to worlds where evidence is mostly misleading. Cohen also contends that reliabilism has the virtue of providing a clear explanation of how the epistemic notion of justification is connected with the notion of

truth. A theory that renders this truth connection inexplicable is caught on the second horn of Cohen's dilemma.

Although Cohen does not take up evidentialism as we characterize it, the second horn of his dilemma effects EJ and WF. They do not explain how having an epistemically justified or well-founded belief is connected to the truth of that belief. Evidentialists can safely say this much about the truth connection: evidence that makes believing p justified is evidence on which it is *epistemically* probable that p is true. Although there is this connection between justification and truth, we acknowledge that there may be no analysis of epistemic probability that makes the connection to truth as close, or as clear, as might have been hoped.

Cohen argues that there must be a truth connection. This shows no flaw in EJ or WF unless they are incompatible with there being such a connection. Cohen does not argue for this incompatibility and we know of no reason to believe that it exists. So at most Cohen's dilemma shows that evidentialists have work left to do.

30 / Stephen Stich
REFLECTIVE EQUILIBRIUM, ANALYTIC EPISTEMOLOGY AND THE PROBLEM OF COGNITIVE DIVERSITY

This is a paper about different ways of thinking—or cognitive diversity, as I shall sometimes say—and the problem of choosing among them. In the pages to follow I will defend a pair of claims. The first is that one influential proposal for solving the problem of cognitive diversity, a proposal that invokes the notion of reflective equilibrium, will not work.

The second is much more radical. What I propose to argue is that although some of the objections to the reflective equilibrium solution turn on details of that idea, the most serious objection generalizes into an argument against an entire epistemological tradition—the tradition that I shall call "analytic epistemology." Before attending to either of these claims, how-

Reprinted by permission of Kluwer Academic Publishers from *Synthese* 74 (1988), 391–413.

ever, I will have to say something about how I conceive of cognition and cognitive diversity.

1. COGNITION AND COGNITIVE DIVERSITY

Let me begin with a simplifying assumption that I hope you will not find wildly implausible. I shall assume that in humans and other higher animals there is a distinct category of mental states whose function it is to store information about the world. When the organisms in question are normal, adult humans in a culture not too remote from our own, folk psychology labels these states *beliefs*. Whether or not this folk label can be used appropriately for the belief-like states of animals, automata, young children and exotic folk is a question of considerable controversy.[1] For present purposes, however, it is a controversy best avoided. Thus I propose to adopt the term "cognitive state" as a broad cover term whose extension includes not only beliefs properly so-called, but also the belief-like information-storing mental states of animals, young children and those adult humans, if any there be, whose cognitive lives differ substantially from our own.

Our beliefs, and the cognitive states of other creatures, are in a constant state of flux. New ones are added and old ones removed as the result of perception, and as a result of various processes in which cognitive states interact with each other. In familiar cases, folk psychology provides us with labels like "thinking" and "reasoning" for these processes, though once again the propriety of these labels becomes controversial when the cognitive states being modified are those of children, animals or exotic folk. So I will use the term "cognitive processes" as a cover term whose extension includes our own reasoning processes, the updating of our beliefs as the result of perception, and the more or less similar processes that occur in other organisms.

Cognitive processes are biological processes; they are something that brains do. And, like other biological processes, they have been shaped by natural selection. Thus it is to be expected that our genes exert an important influence on the sorts of cognitive processes we have. It is also to be expected that the cognitive processes of other species with other needs and other natural environments will be in varying degrees different from those to be found among humans. But from the fact that genes inevitably exert a major influence on cognitive processes it does *not* follow that all of our cognitive processes are innate, or, indeed, that any of them are.

To see the point, we need only reflect on the case of language. My ability to speak English is a biological ability; processing English is something my brain does. Moreover, my genes are surely heavily implicated in the explanation of how I came to have a brain that could process English. Still, English is not innate. The ability to process English is an ability I acquired, and had I been raised in a different environment I might have acquired instead the ability to speak Korean or Lapp. This is not to deny that *something* relevant to language is innate. All normal human children have the ability to acquire the language spoken around them. And that is a very special ability. There is no serious evidence indicating that members of any other species can acquire human languages or anything much like them.

Now the point I want to stress is that, as far as we know, human cognitive processes may be like human language processing abilities. They may be acquired in ways that are deeply dependent on environmental variables, and they may differ quite radically from one individual or culture to another. Of course, it is also possible that human cognitive processes are much less plastic and much less under the influence of environmental variables. It is possible that cognition is more similar to digestion than to language. To make matters a bit messier, there is no reason a priori for all cognitive processes to be at the same point on this continuum. It may be that some of our cognitive processes are shared by all normal humans, while others are a part of our cultural heritage.[2] I am inclined to think that this last possibility is the most plausible one in the light of available evidence, and for the remainder of this paper I will take it for granted. But it must be admitted that the evidence is both fragmentary and very difficult to interpret.[3]

If we suppose that there is a fair amount of acquired diversity in human cognitive processes, and that patterns of reasoning or cognitive processing are to some substantial degree molded by cultural influences, it adds a certain urgency to one of the more venerable questions of epistemology. For if there are lots of different ways in which the human mind/brain can go about ordering and reordering its cognitive states, if different cultures could or do go about the business of reasoning in very different ways, *which of these ways should we use?* Which cognitive processes are the *good* ones? It is just here that the analogy with language breaks down in an illuminating way. Most of us are inclined to think that, at least to a first approximation, one language is as good as another. The one you should use is the one spoken and understood by the people around you.[4] By contrast, most of us are *not* inclined to accept this sort of thorough-going relativism about cognitive processes. If primitive tribesmen or pre-modern scientists or our own descendants think in ways that are quite different from the ways we think, few of us would be inclined to suggest that all of these ways are equally good. Some ways of going about the business of belief revision are better than others. But just what is it that makes one system of cognitive processes better than another, and how are we to tell which system of reasoning is best? In the remaining sections of this paper I want to consider one influential answer to this question. I shall argue that both the answer itself and the philosophical tradition it grows out of should be rejected.

2. REFLECTIVE EQUILIBRIUM AS A CRITERION FOR ASSESSING COGNITIVE PROCESSES

The answer I will disparage was first suggested about three decades ago when, in one of the more influential passages of twentieth century philosophy, Nelson Goodman described a process of bringing judgments about particular inferences and about general principles of inference into accord with one another. In the accord thus achieved, Goodman maintained, lay all the justification needed, and all the justification possible for the inferential principles that emerged. Other writers, most notably John Rawls, have adopted a modified version of Goodman's process as a procedure for justifying moral principles and moral judgments. To Rawls, too, we owe the term "reflective equilibrium" which has been widely used to characterize a system of principles and judgments that have been brought into coherence with one another in the way that Goodman describes.[5]

It is hard to imagine the notion of reflective equilibrium explained more eloquently than Goodman himself explains it.

> How do we justify a *de*duction? Plainly by showing that it conforms with the general rules of deductive inference. An argument that so conforms is justified or valid, even if its conclusion happens to be false. An argument that violates a rule is fallacious even if its conclusion happens to be true. . . . Analogously, the basic task in justifying an inductive inference is to show that it conforms to the general rules of *in*duction. . . .
>
> Yet, of course, the rules themselves must ultimately be justified. The validity of a deduction depends not upon conformity to any purely arbitrary rules we may contrive, but upon conformity with valid rules. When we speak of *the* rules of inference we mean the valid rules—or better, *some* valid rules, since there may be alternative sets of equally valid rules. But how is the validity of rules to be determined? Here . . . we encounter philosophers who insist that these rules follow from some self-evident axiom, and others who try to show that the rules are grounded in the very nature of the human mind. I think the answer lies much nearer to the surface. Principles of deductive inference are justified by their conformity with accepted deductive practice. Their validity depends upon accordance with the particular deductive inferences we actually make and sanction. If a rule yields unacceptable inferences, we drop it as invalid. Justification of general rules thus derives from judgments rejecting or accepting particular deductive inferences.

This looks flagrantly circular. I have said that deductive inferences are justified by their conformity to valid general rules, and that general rules are justified by their conformity to valid inferences. But this circle is a virtuous one. *A rule is amended if it yields an inference we are unwilling to accept; an inference is rejected if it violates a rule we are unwilling to amend.* The process of justification is the delicate one of making mutual adjustments between rules and accepted inferences; and in the agreement thus achieved lies the only justification needed for either.

All this applies equally well to induction. An inductive inference, too, is justified by conformity to general rules, and a general rule by conformity to accepted inductive inferences.[6]

There are three points in this passage that demand a bit of interpretation. First, Goodman claims to be explaining what justifies deductive and inductive inferences. However, it is not clear that, as he uses the term, *inference* is a cognitive process. It is possible to read Goodman as offering an account of the justification of principles of logic and of steps in logical derivations. Read in this way, Goodman's account of justification would be of no help in dealing with the problem of cognitive diversity unless it was supplemented with a suitable theory about the relation between logic and good reasoning. But as several authors have lately noted, that relation is much less obvious than one might suppose.[7] It is also possible to read Goodman as speaking directly to the question of how we should go about the business of reasoning,[8] and offering a solution to the problem of cognitive diversity. This is the reading I propose to adopt.

A second point that needs some elaboration is just what status Goodman would claim for the reflective equilibrium test he describes. It is clear Goodman thinks we can conclude that a system of inferential rules is justified if it passes the reflective equilibrium test. But it is not clear *why* we can conclude this. Two different sorts of answers are possible. According to one answer, the reflective equilibrium test is *constitutive* of justification or validity. For a system of inferential rules to be justified just *is* for them to be in reflective equilibrium. Another sort of answer is that if a set of inferential

principles passes the reflective equilibrium test, this counts as good *evidence* for them being valid or justified. But, on this second view, being in reflective equilibrium and being justified are quite different. One is not to be identified with the other. I am inclined to think that it is the former, constitutive view that best captures Goodman's intentions. But since my concern is to criticize a view and not an author, I don't propose to argue the point. Rather, I will simply stipulate that the constitutive reading is the one I'm stalking.[9]

The third point of interpretation concerns the status of the claim that reflective equilibrium is constitutive of justification. On this point, there are at least three views worth mentioning. The first is that the claim is a *conceptual truth*—that it follows from the meaning of "justification" or from the analysis of the concept of justification. Like other conceptual truths, it is both necessarily true and knowable a priori. If we adopt this view, the status of the claim that reflective equilibrium is constitutive of justification would be akin to the status of the claim that being a closed, three sided plane figure is constitutive of being a triangle, though the claim about justification is, of course, a much less obvious conceptual truth. A second view is that the claim is a non-conceptual necessary truth that is knowable only a posteriori. This would accord it much the same status that some philosophers accord to the claim that water is H_2O. Finally, it might be urged that the claim is being offered as a stipulative proposal. It is not telling us what our pre-existing concept of justification amounts to, nor what is essential to the referent of that concept. Rather, in a revisionary spirit, it is proposing a new notion of justification. Actually, the divide between the first and the last of these alternatives is not all that sharp, for one might start with an analysis of our ordinary notion and go on to propose modifications in an effort to tidy the notion up a bit here and there. As the changes proposed get bigger and bigger, this sort of "explication" gradually shades into pure stipulation. So long as the changes an explication urges in a pre-existing concept are motivated by considerations of simplicity and don't result in any radical departures from the ordinary concept, I'll count them as a kind of conceptual analysis. I think a good case can be made that Goodman took himself to be providing just such a conservative explication. But again, since it is a view rather than an author that I hope to refute, I will simply stipulate that the conceptual analysis or conservative explication interpretation is the one to be adopted here.

3. DOES THE REFLECTIVE EQUILIBRIUM ACCOUNT CAPTURE OUR NOTION OF JUSTIFICATION?

Goodman, as I propose to read him, offers us an account of what our concept of justified inference comes to. How can we determine whether his analysis is correct? One obvious strategy is to ask just what systems of inferential rules result from the process of mutual adjustment that Goodman advocates. If the inferential systems generated by the reflective equilibrium process strike us as systems that a rational person ought to invoke, this will count in favor of Goodman's analysis. If, on the other hand, the reflective equilibrium process generates what we take to be irrational or unjustified inferential rules or practices, this will cast doubt on Goodman's claim to have captured our concept of justification. Since we are viewing conceptual explication as a kind of analysis, we should not insist that Goodman's account coincide perfectly with our intuitive judgments. But if there are lots of cases in which Goodman's account entails that a system of inferential rules is justified and intuition decrees that it is not, this is a symptom that the analysis is in serious trouble.

In an earlier paper, Nisbett and I exploited the strategy just described to argue that the reflective equilibrium account does not capture anything much like our ordinary notion of justification.[10] On the basis of both controlled studies and anecdotal evidence, we argued that patently unacceptable rules of inference would pass the reflective equilibrium test for many people. For example, it appears likely that many people infer in accordance with some version of the gambler's fallacy when dealing with games of chance. These people infer that the likelihood of throwing a seven in a game

of craps increases each time a non-seven is thrown. What is more, there is every reason to think that the principle underlying their inference is in reflective equilibrium for them. When the principle is articulated and the subjects have had a chance to reflect upon it and upon their own inferential practice, they accept both. Indeed, one can even find some nineteenth century logic texts in which versions of the gambler's fallacy are explicitly endorsed. (In a delightful irony, one of these books was written by a man who held the same chair Goodman held when he wrote *Fact, Fiction and Forecast*.[11]) It can also be shown that many people systematically ignore the importance of base rates in their probabilistic reasoning, that many find the principle of regression to the mean to be highly counter-intuitive, that many judge the probability of certain sequences of events to be higher than the probability of components in the sequence, etc.[12] In each of these cases, and in many more that might be cited, it is very likely that, for some people at least, the principles that capture their inferential practice would pass the reflective equilibrium test. If this is right, it indicates there is something very wrong with the Goodmanian analysis of justification. For on that analysis, to be justified *is* to pass the reflective equilibrium test. But few of us are prepared to say that if the gambler's fallacy is in reflective equilibrium for a person, then his inferences that accord with that principle are justified.

Of course, each example of the infelicitous inferential principle that allegedly would pass the reflective equilibrium test is open to challenge. Whether or not the dubious principles that appear to guide many people's inferential practice would stand up to the reflective scrutiny Goodman's test demands is an empirical question. And for any given rule, a Goodmanian might protest that the empirical case has just not been made adequately. I am inclined to think that the Goodmanian who builds his defenses here is bound to be routed by a growing onslaught of empirical findings. But the issue need not turn on whether this empirical hunch is correct. For even the *possibility* that the facts will turn out as I suspect they will poses a serious problem for the Goodman's story. It is surely not an a priori fact that strange inferential principles will always fail the reflective equilibrium test for all subjects. And if it is granted, as surely it must be, that the gambler's fallacy (or any of the other inferential oddities that have attracted the attention of psychologists in recent years) could possibly pass the reflective equilibrium test for some group of subjects, this is enough to cast doubt on the view that reflective equilibrium is constitutive of justification as that notion is ordinarily used. For surely we are not at all inclined to say that a person is justified in using any inferential principle—no matter how bizarre it may be—simply because it accords with his reflective inferential practice.

Faced with this argument the friends of reflective equilibrium may offer a variety of responses. The one I have the hardest time understanding is simply to dig in one's heels and insist that if the gambler's fallacy (or some other curious principle) is in reflective equilibrium for a given person or group, then that principle is indeed justified for them. Although I have heard people advocate this line in conversation, I know of no one who has been bold enough to urge the view in print. Since no one else seems willing to take the view seriously, I won't either.

A very different sort of response is to urge that the notion of reflective equilibrium is itself in need of patching—that some bells and whistles must be added to the justificatory process Goodman describes. One idea along these lines is to shift from narrow Goodmanian reflective equilibrium to some analog of Rawls's "wide reflective equilibrium."[13] Roughly, the idea here is to broaden the scope of the judgments and convictions that are to be brought into coherence with one another. Instead of attending only to our assessments of inferential principles, wide reflective equilibrium also requires that our system of inferential rules is to cohere with our semantic, epistemological, metaphysical, or psychological views. Just how various philosophical or psychological convictions are supposed to constrain a person's inferential principles and practice has not been spelled out in much detail, though Norman Daniels, whose papers on wide reflective equilibrium are among the best around, gives us a hint when he suggests, by way of example, that Dum-

mett's views on logic are constrained by his semantic views.[14] It would also be plausible to suppose that the classical intuitionists in logic rejected certain inferential principles on epistemological grounds.

A rather different way of attempting to preserve a reflective equilibrium account of justification is to restrict the class of people whose reflective equilibrium is to count in assessing the justification of inferential principles. For example, Nisbett and I proposed that in saying an inferential principle is justified, what we are saying is that it would pass the (narrow) reflective equilibrium test for those people whom we regard as experts in the relevant inferential domain.[15]

A dubious virtue of both the wide reflective equilibrium and the expert reflective equilibrium accounts is that they make clear-cut counter-examples harder to generate. That is, they make it harder to produce actual examples of inferential rules which the analysis counts as justified and intuition does not. In the case of wide reflective equilibrium, counter-examples are hard to come by just because it is so hard to show that anything is in wide reflective equilibrium for anyone. ("Would she continue to accept that rule if she thought through her epistemological and metaphysical views and came to some stable equilibrium view?" Well, God knows.) In the case of the expert reflective equilibrium account, the dubious but reflectively self-endorsed inferential practice of the experimental subject or the Las Vegas sucker just don't count as counter-examples, since these people don't count as experts.

But though clear-cut cases involving actual people may be harder to find, each of these elaborations of the reflective equilibrium story falls victim to the argument from possible cases offered earlier. Consider wide reflective equilibrium first. No matter how the details of the wide reflective equilibrium test are spelled out, it is surely not going to turn out to be impossible for a person to reach wide reflective equilibrium on a set of principles and convictions that includes some quite daffy inferential rule. Indeed, one suspects that by allowing people's philosophical convictions to play a role in filtering their inferential principles, one is inviting such daffy principles, since many people are deeply attached to outlandish philosophical views. The expert reflective equilibrium move fares no better. For unless experts are picked out in a question begging way (e.g. those people whose inferential practices are in fact justified) it seems entirely possible for the expert community, under the influence of ideology, recreational chemistry, or evil demons, to end up endorsing some quite nutty set of rules.[16]

4. A "NEO-GOODMANIAN" PROJECT

At this point, if the friend of reflective equilibrium is as impressed by these arguments as I think he should be, he might head off to his study to work on some further variations on the reflective equilibrium theme that will do better at capturing our concept of justification. Despite a string of failures, he might be encouraged to pursue this project by a line of thought that runs something like the following. I'll call it the *neo-Goodmanian* line.

It can hardly be denied that we do *something* to assess whether or not an inferential practice is justified. Our decisions on these matters are certainly not made at random. Moreover, if there is some established procedure that we invoke in assessing justification, then it must surely be possible to describe this procedure. When we have succeeded at this we will have an account of what it is for an inferential practice to be justified. For, as Goodman has urged, to be justified just *is* to pass the tests we invoke in assessing an inferential practice. Our procedures for assessing an inferential practice are constitutive of justification. Granted, neither Goodman's narrow reflective equilibrium story nor the more elaborate stories told by others have succeeded in capturing the procedure we actually use in assessing justification. But that just shows we must work harder. The rewards promise to repay our efforts, since once we have succeeded in describing our assessment procedure, we will have taken a giant step forward in epistemology. We will have explained

what it is for a cognitive process to be justified. In so doing we will have at least begun to resolve the problem posed by cognitive diversity. For once we have a clear specification of what justification amounts to, we can go on to ask whether our own cognitive processes are justified or whether, perhaps, those of some other culture comes closer to the mark.

There is no doubt that this neo-Goodmanian line can be very appealing. I was myself under its sway for some years. However, I am now persuaded that the research program it proposes for epistemology is a thoroughly wrong-headed one. In the pages that follow I will try to say why. My case against the neo-Goodmanian project divides into two parts. First I shall raise some objections that are targeted more or less specifically on the details of the neo-Goodmanian program. Central to each of these objections is the fact that the neo-Goodmanian is helping himself to a healthy serving of empirical assumptions about the conceptual structures underlying our common-sense judgments of cognitive assessment, and each of these assumptions stands in some serious risk of turning out to be false. If one or more of them is false, then the project loses much of its initial attractiveness. In the following section I will set out a brief catalog of these dubious assumptions. The second part of my critique is much more general and I'll be after much bigger game. What I propose to argue is that neither the neo-Goodmanian program nor any alternative program that proposes to analyze or explicate our pre-systematic notion of justification will be of any help at all in resolving the problem posed by cognitive diversity. But here I am getting ahead of myself. Let me get back to the neo-Goodmanian and his dubious empirical presuppositions.

5. SOME QUESTIONABLE PRESUPPOSITIONS OF THE NEO-GOODMANIAN PROJECT

Let me begin with a fairly obvious point. The neo-Goodmanian, as I have portrayed him, retains his allegiance to the idea of reflective equilibrium. We last saw him heading back to his study to seek a more adequate elaboration of this notion. But nothing the neo-Goodmanian has said encourages us to expect that reflective equilibrium or anything much like it plays a role in our procedure for assessing the justification of a cognitive process. So even if it is granted that we have good reason to work hard at characterizing our justification-assessing procedure, we may find that the notion of reflective equilibrium is simply a nonstarter. Confronted with this objection, I think the only move open to the neo-Goodmanian is to grant the point and concede that in trying to patch the notion of reflective equilibrium he is simply playing a hunch. Perhaps it will turn out that something like reflective equilibrium plays a central role in our assessments of justification. But until we have an accurate characterization of the assessment process there can be no guarantees.

Two further assumptions of the neo-Goodmanian program are that we ordinarily invoke only *one* notion of justification for inferential processes, and that this is a *coherent* notion for which a set of necessary and sufficient conditions can be given. But once again these are not matters that can be known in advance. It might be that different people mean different things when they call a cognitive process "justified" because there are different notions of justification in circulation. These different meanings might cluster around a central core. But then again they might not. There are lots of normatively loaded terms that seem to be used in very different ways by different individuals or groups in society. I would not be at all surprised to learn that what I mean by terms like "morally right" and "freedom" is very different from what the followers of the Rev. Falwell or admirers of Col. Khadafi mean. And I wouldn't be much more surprised if terms of epistemic evaluation turned out to manifest similar interpersonal ambiguities.

Even discounting the possibility of systematic interpersonal differences, it might be that in assessing the justification of a cognitive process we use different procedures on different occasions, and that these procedures have different outcomes. Perhaps, for example, our intuitive notion of justification is tied to a number of prototypical exemplars, and that in deciding new cases we focus in some context sensitive way on one or another of these exemplars, making our decision about justification on the basis of how similar the case at hand is to the exemplar on which we are focusing. This is hardly a fanciful idea, since recent work on the psychological mechanisms underlying categorization suggests that in *lots* of cases our judgment works in just this way.[17] If it turns out that our judgments about the justification of cognitive processes are prototype or exemplar based, then it will be a mistake to look for a property or characteristic that all justified cognitive processes have. It will not be the case that there is any single test passed by all the cognitive processes we judge to be justified. I am partial to a reading of the later Wittgenstein on which this is just what he would urge about our commonsense notion of justification, and I am inclined to suspect that this Wittgensteinian story is right. But I don't pretend to have enough evidence to make a convincing case. For present purposes it will have to suffice to note that this *might* be how our commonsense concept of justification works. If it is, then the neo-Goodmanian program is in for some rough sledding.

A final difficulty with the neo-Goodmanian program is that it assumes, without any evidence, that the test or procedure we use for assessing the justification of cognitive processes exhausts our concept of inferential justification, and thus that we will have characterized the concept when we have described the test. But this is hardly a claim that can be assumed without argument. It might be the case that our procrustean concept of justification is an amalgam composed in part of folk epistemological theory specifying certain properties or characteristics that are essential to justification, and in part of a test or cluster of tests that folk wisdom holds to be indicative of those properties. Moreover, the tests proposed might not always (or ever) be reliable indicators of the properties.[18] I don't have any compelling reason to believe that our commonsense notion of justification will turn out like this. But I wouldn't be much surprised. Though our understanding of the mechanisms underlying commonsense concepts and judgments is still *very* primitive, as I read the literature it points to two important morals. First, the mental representation of concepts is likely to turn out to be a very messy business. Second, it is no easy job to separate commonsense concepts from the folk theories in which they are enmeshed. All of this bodes ill for the neo-Goodmanian who hopes that the analysis or explication of our concept of justification will yield some relatively straightforward elaboration of the reflective equilibrium test.

6. AGAINST ANALYTIC EPISTEMOLOGY

The problems posed in the previous section shared a pair of properties. They all turned on empirical assumptions about the nature of our ordinary concept of justification, and they were all targeted fairly specifically at the neo-Goodmanian project.[19] In the current section I want to set out a very different sort of argument, an argument which if successful will undermine not only reflective equilibrium theories but also the whole family of epistemological theories to which they belong.

To give some idea of the range of theories that are in the intended scope of my critique, it will be helpful to sketch a bit of the framework for epistemological theorizing suggested by Alvin Goldman in his recent book, *Epistemology and Cognition*.[20] Goldman notes that one of the major projects of both classical and contemporary epistemology has been to develop a theory of epistemic justification. The ultimate job of such a theory is to say which cognitive states are epistemically justified and which are not. Thus, a fundamental step in constructing a theory of justification will be to articulate a system of rules evaluating the justificatory status of beliefs and other cognitive states. These rules (Goldman calls them *justificational rules* or *J-rules*) will specify permissible ways in which a cognitive agent may go about the business of forming or updating his cognitive states. They "permit or prohibit beliefs, directly or indirectly, as a function of some states, relations, or processes of the cognizer."[21]

Of course, different theorists may have different views on which beliefs are justified or which cognitive processes yield justified beliefs, and thus they may urge different and incompatible sets of J-rules. It may be that there is more than one right system of justificational rules, but it is surely not the case that all systems are correct. So in order to decide whether a proposed system of J-rules is right, we must appeal to a higher criterion which Goldman calls a "criterion of rightness." This criterion will specify a "set of conditions that are necessary and sufficient for a set of J-rules to be right."[22]

But now the theoretical disputes emerge at a higher level, for different theorists have suggested very different criteria of rightness. Indeed, as Goldman notes, an illuminating taxonomy of epistemological theories can be generated by classifying theories or theorists on the basis of the sort of criterion of rightness they endorse. Coherence theories, for example, take the rightness of a system of J-rules to turn on whether conformity with the rules would lead to a coherent set of beliefs. Truth linked or reliability theories take the rightness of a set of J-rules to turn in one way or another on the truth of the set of beliefs that would result from conformity with the rules. Reflective equilibrium theories judge J-rules by how well they do on their favored version of the reflective equilibrium test. And so on. How are we to go about deciding among these various criteria of rightness? Or, to ask an even more basic question, just what does the correctness of a criterion of rightness come to; what makes a criterion right or wrong? On this point Goldman is not as explicit as one might wish. However, much of what he says suggests that, on his view, *conceptual analysis* or *conceptual explication* is the proper way to decide among competing criteria of rightness. The correct criterion of rightness is the one that comports with the conception of justifiedness that is "embraced by everyday thought or language."[23] To test a criterion we explore the judgments it would entail about specific cases, and we test these judgments against our "pretheoretic intuition." "A criterion is supported to the extent that implied judgments accord with such intuitions, and weakened to the extent that they do not."[24] Goldman is careful to note that there may be a certain amount of vagueness in our commonsense notion of justifiedness, and thus there may be no unique best criterion of rightness. But despite the vagueness, "there seems to be a common core idea of justifiedness" embedded in everyday thought and language, and it is this common core idea that Goldman tells us he is trying to capture in his own epistemological theorizing.[25]

The view I am attributing to Goldman on what it is for a criterion of rightness to itself be right is hardly an idiosyncratic or unfamiliar one. We saw earlier that a very natural reading of Goodman would have him offering the reflective equilibrium story as an explication or conceptual analysis of the ordinary notion of justification. And many other philosophers have explicitly or implicitly adopted much the same view. I propose to use the term *analytic epistemology* to denote any epistemological project that takes the choice between competing justificational rules or competing criteria of rightness to turn on conceptual or linguistic analysis. There can be little doubt that a very substantial fraction of the epistemological writing published in English in the last quarter of a century has been analytic epistemology.[26] However, it is my contention that if an analytic epistemological theory is taken to be part of the serious normative inquiry whose goal is to tell people which cognitive processes are good ones, or which ones they should use, then for most people it will prove to be an irrelevant failure.

I think the most intuitive way to see this point is to begin by recalling how the specter of culturally-based cognitive diversity lends a certain urgency to the question of which cognitive processes we should use. If patterns of inference are acquired from the surrounding culture, much as language or fashions or manners are, and if we can learn to use cognitive processes quite different from the ones we have inherited from our culture, then the question of whether our culturally inherited cognitive processes are good ones is of more than theoretical interest. If we *can* go about the business of cognition differently, and if others actually *do*, it is natural to ask whether there is any reason why we should continue to do it our way. Even

if we cannot change our cognitive processes once we've acquired them, it is natural to wonder whether those processes are good ones. Moreover, for many people the absence of a convincing affirmative answer can be seriously disquieting. For if we cannot say why our cognitive processes are any better than those prevailing elsewhere, it suggests that it is ultimately no more than an historical accident that we use the cognitive processes we do, or that we hold the beliefs that those processes generate, just as it is an historical accident that we speak English rather than Spanish and wear trousers rather than togas.

Consider now how the analytic epistemologist would address the problem that cognitive diversity presents. To determine whether our cognitive processes are good ones, he would urge, we must first *analyze* our concept of justification (or perhaps some other commonsense epistemic notion like rationality). If our commonsense epistemic notion is not too vague or ambiguous, the analysis will give us a criterion of rightness for J-rules (or perhaps a cluster of closely related criteria). Our next step is to investigate which sets of J-rules fit the criterion. Having made some progress there, we can take a look at our own cognitive processes and ask whether they do in fact accord with some right set of J-rules. If they do, we have found a reason to continue using those processes; we have shown that they are good ones because the beliefs they lead to are justified. If it turns out that our cognitive processes don't accord with a right set of J-rules, we can try to discover some alternative processes that do a better job, and set about training ourselves to use them.

It is my contention that something has gone very wrong here. For the analytic epistemologist's effort is designed to determine whether our cognitive states and processes accord with our commonsense notion of justification (or some other commonsense concept of epistemic evaluation). Yet surely the evaluative epistemic concepts embedded in everyday thought and language are every bit as likely as the cognitive processes they evaluate to be culturally acquired and to vary from culture to culture.[27] Moreover, the analytic epistemologist offers us no reason whatever to think that the notions of evaluation prevailing in our own language and culture are any better than the alternative evaluative notions that might or do prevail in other cultures. But in the absence of any reason to think that the locally prevailing notions of epistemic evaluation are superior to the alternatives, why should we care one whit whether the cognitive processes we use are sanctioned by those evaluative concepts? How can the fact that our cognitive processes are approved by the evaluative notions embraced in our culture alleviate the worry that our cognitive processes are no better than those of exotic folk, if we have no reason to believe that our evaluative notions are any better than alternative evaluative notions?

To put the point a bit more vividly, imagine that we have located some exotic culture that does in fact exploit cognitive processes very different from our own, and that the notions of epistemic evaluation embedded in their language also differ from ours. Suppose further that the cognitive processes prevailing in that culture accord quite well with *their* evaluative notions, while the cognitive processes prevailing in our culture accord quite well with *ours*. Would any of this be of any help at all in deciding which cognitive processes we should use? Without some reason to think that one set of evaluative notions was preferable to the other, it seems clear that it would be of no help at all.

In the philosophical literature there is a tradition, perhaps traceable to Wittgenstein, that would reject the suggestion that our evaluative notions should themselves be evaluated. Justifications, this tradition insists, must come to an end. And once we have shown that our practice accords with our evaluative concepts, there is nothing more to show. Our language game (or form of life) does not provide us with any way to go about evaluating our evaluative notions. There is no logical space in which questions like "should we hold justified beliefs?" or "should we invoke rational cognitive processes?" can be asked seriously. If a person did not recognize that the answers to these questions had to be affirmative, it would simply indicate that he did not understand the logical grammar of words like "should" and "justified" and "rational."

I am inclined to think that there is at least a kernel of truth in this "Wittgensteinian" stand. Justifications do ultimately come to an end. However, it is, I think, a disastrous mistake to think that they come to an end *here*. For there are *lots* of values that are both widely shared and directly relevant to our cognitive lives, though they are quite distinct from the "epistemic values" that lie behind our ordinary use of terms like "justified" and "rational." It is against the background of these non-epistemic values that our socially shared system of epistemic evaluation can itself be evaluated. Thus, for example, many people attach high value to cognitive states that foster happiness (their own or everyone's), and many people value cognitive states that afford them the power to predict and control nature. Some people share Mother Nature's concern that our cognitive lives should foster reproductive success. And, on a rather different dimension, many people care deeply that their beliefs be true.[28] Each of these values, along with many others that might be mentioned, affords a perspective from which epistemic values like justification and rationality can be evaluated. We can ask whether the cognitive states and processes endorsed by our notions of epistemic value foster happiness, or power, or accurate prediction, or reproductive success, or truth. More interestingly, we can ask whether the cognitive states and processes we actually have or use foster happiness, power, or the rest. And if they do not, we can explore alternatives that may do a better job, though there is of course no guarantee that all of these values can be maximized together.[29]

At this point, it might be protested that the values I am proposing to use in evaluating our socially shared notions of epistemic evaluation are themselves lacking any deeper justification. If someone can accept *these* as ultimate values, why couldn't someone do the same for justification or rationality? My reply is that of course someone could, but this is no objection to the view I am urging. There are many things that people might and do find ultimately or intrinsically valuable. Some of these values may be rooted more or less directly in our biological nature, and these we can expect to be widely shared. Other values, including intrinsic, life-shaping values, may be socially transmitted, and vary from society to society. Still others may be quite idiosyncratic. It is entirely possible for someone in our society to attach enormous value to having justified beliefs or inferential processes that fall within the extension of "justified" or "rational" as they are used in our language. Similarly, it is entirely possible for someone in another society to attach enormous value to having cognitive states that fall within the extension of the terms of cognitive evaluation current in that society. In each case the evaluation may be either instrumental or intrinsic. A person in our culture may value the states and processes that fall within the extension of "rational" or "justified" because he thinks they are likely to be true, to lead to happiness, etc., or he may value them for no further reason at all. And a person in another culture may have either sort of attitude in valuing what falls within the extension of his language's terms of cognitive evaluation. Where the value attached is instrumental, there is plenty of room for productive inquiry and dialogue. We can try to find out whether rational or justified cognitive processes do lead to happiness or power or truth, and if they do we can try to understand why. But where the value accorded to one or another epistemic virtue is intrinsic, there is little room for debate. If you value rationality for its own sake, and the native of another culture values some rather different cognitive characteristic ("shmashinality" as Hilary Putnam might put it) for *its* own sake, there is not much you can say to each other. Moreover, there is not much I can say to either of you, since on my view the fact that a cognitive process is sanctioned by the venerable standards embedded in our language of epistemic evaluation, or their's, is of no more interest than the fact that it is sanctioned by the venerable standards of a religious tradition or an ancient text—unless, of course, it can be shown that those standards correlate with something more generally valued.[30] But I do not pretend to have any arguments that will move the true epistemic xenophobe. If a person really does attach deep intrinsic value to the epistemic virtues favored by folk epistemology, then dialogue has come to an end.

Finally, let me say how all of this relates to analytic epistemology. The analytic epistemologist proposes to arbitrate between competing criteria of rightness by seeing which one accords best with the evaluative notions "embraced by everyday thought and language." However, it is my contention that this project is of no help whatever in confronting the problem of cognitive diversity unless one is an epistemic xenophobe. The program of analytic epistemology views conceptual analysis or explication as a stopping place in disputes about how we should go about the business of cognition. When we know that a certain cognitive process falls within the extension of our ordinary terms of epistemic evaluation—whatever the analysis of those terms may turn out to be—we know all that can be known that is relevant to the questions of how we should go about the business of reasoning. But as I see it, the only people who should take this information to be at all relevant to the question are the profoundly conservative people who find intrinsic value in having their cognitive processes sanctioned by culturally inherited standards, whatever those standards may be. Many of us care very much whether our cognitive processes lead to beliefs that are true, or give us power over nature, or lead to happiness. But only those with a deep and free-floating conservatism in matters epistemic will care whether their cognitive processes are sanctioned by the evaluative standards that happen to be woven into our language.[31]

NOTES

1. See Davidson (1982); Stich (1979); Routley (1981); Stich (1983), pp. 89–106; Stich (1984).
2. Nor are these the only alternatives. There are lots of characteristics which are innate (not part of our cultural heritage) though they differ substantially from one group to another. Sex, hair color, and blood type are three obvious examples.
3. See Cole and Scribner (1974); Cole and Means (1981).
4. Actually, the issue is not so straightforward if we compare languages at very different stages of development, or languages involving different

theoretical assumptions. It is only when the choice is between languages that are more or less intertranslatable with our own that we are inclined to judge that one is as good as another. Thanks to Paul Churchland for reminding me of this point.

5. Rawls (1971), pp. 20 ff.

6. Goodman (1965), pp. 66–67; emphasis is Goodman's.

7. Cherniak (1986, chap. 4); Harman (1986, chap. 2); Goldman (1986, sec. 5.1).

8. L. J. Cohen (1981) seems to read Goodman this way since he exploits Goodman's notion of reflective equilibrium in giving an account of good reasoning.

9. Well, I will argue it a little. Note first that according to Goodman the only justification needed for either rules or inferences "lies in" the agreement achieved by the reflective equilibrium process. This talk of justification *lying* in the agreement strongly suggests the constitutive reading. Moreover, on the non-constitutive reading, Goodman's doctrine would be an oddly incomplete one. It would present us with a test for justification without telling us why it was a test or giving us any account of what it is that is being tested for. On the constitutive reading, by contrast, no such problem arises. We have in one tidy package both an analysis of the notion of justification and an unproblematic explanation of the relation between justification and the process Goodman describes.

10. Stich and Nisbett (1980).

11. The writer was Henry Copée (1874). Here is a brief quote:

> Thus, in throwing dice, we cannot be sure that any single face or combination of faces will appear; but if, in very many throws, some particular face has not appeared, the chances of its coming up are stronger and stronger, until they approach very near to certainty. It must come; and as each throw is made and it fails to appear, the certainty of its coming draws nearer and nearer. [p. 162]

12. For an excellent survey of the literature in this area see Nisbett and Ross (1980); a number of important studies are collected in Kahneman, Slovic, and Tversky (1982).

13. Rawls (1974).

14. Daniels (1979, 1980 "Reflective Equilibrium" and 1980 "On Some Methods").

15. Stich and Nisbett (1980).

16. As Conee and Feldman (1983) point out, the situation is actually a bit worse for the version of the expert reflective equilibrium analysis that Nisbett and I offered. On that account, different groups may recognize different people as experts. And it is surely at least possible for a group of people to accept as an expert some guru who is as bonkers as he is charismatic. But we certainly don't want to say that the followers of such a guru would be rational to invoke whatever wild inferential principle might be in reflective equilibrium for their leader.

17. For a good review of the literature, see Smith and Medin (1981).

18. For some insightful observations on the potential complexity of commonsense concepts and the ways in which intuitive tests can fail to capture the extension of concepts, see Rey (1983).

19. Actually, the last three of my four objections might, with a bit of reworking, be generalized so as to apply to all of analytic epistemology, as it is defined below. But I don't propose to pursue them since, as we shall see, analytic epistemology has more pressing problems.

20. Goldman (1986).

21. Goldman, p. 60. For the reader who wants a more hands-on feel for Goldman's notion of a J-rule, the quote continues as follows:

> For example, J-rules might permit a cognizer to form a given belief because of some appropriate antecedent or current state. Thus, someone being "appeared to" in a certain way at t might be permitted to believe p at t. But someone else not in such a state would not be so permitted. Alternatively, the rules might focus on mental operations. Thus, if S's believing p at t is the result of a certain operation, or sequence of operations, then his belief is justified if the system of J-rules permits that operation or sequence of operations.

22. Goldman, p. 64.

23. Goldman, p. 58.

24. Goldman, p. 66.

25. Goldman, pp. 58–59.

26. For an extended review of part of this literature see Shope (1983). As Shope notes, relatively few of the philosophers who have tried their hands at constructing an "analysis" of knowledge (or of some other epistemic notion) have been explicit about their objectives (see pp. 34–44). However, absent indications to the contrary, I am inclined to think that if a philosophical project proceeds by offering definitions or "truth conditions," and testing them against our intuitions about real or imaginary cases, then the project should be viewed as an attempt at conceptual analysis or explication. Unless one has some pretty strange views about intuitions, it is hard to see what we could hope to gain from capturing them apart from some insight into the concepts that underlie them.

27. Evidence on this point, like evidence about cross-cultural differences in cognitive processes,

is hard to come by and hard to interpret. But there are some intriguing hints in the literature. Hallen and Sodipo (1986) studied the terms of epistemic evaluation exploited by the Yoruba, a west African people. It is their contention that the Yoruba do not have a distinction corresponding to our distinction between knowledge and (mere) true belief. They do, however, divide their beliefs into two other categories: those for which a person has immediate, eyewitness evidence, and those for which he does not. In the standard Yoruba-English dictionaries, the Yoruba term for the former set of belief, *mo*, is translated as "knowledge" while the term for the latter sort, *gbagbo*, is translated as "belief." However, Hallen and Sodipo argue that these translations are mistaken, since *mo* has a much narrower extension than "knowledge." Most of what we would classify as scientific knowledge, for example, would not count as *mo* for the Yoruba, because it is based on inference and secondhand report. Since the Yoruba do not draw the distinction between knowledge and (mere) true belief, they have no use for our notion of epistemic justification. Instead, the Yoruba presumably have another notion which they exploit in distinguishing *mo* from *gbagbo*. Hallen and Sodipo do not indicate whether the Yoruba have a single word for this notion, but if they do, it would be a mistake to translate the word as "(epistemic) justification." Clearly, if Hallen and Sodipo are right, the Yoruba categories of epistemic evaluation are significantly different from our own.

28. I should note, in passing, that I think it is a mistake to include truth on the list of intrinsically valuable features of one's cognitive life. But that is a topic for another paper (see Stich, in preparation), and I will ignore the point here.

29. The point I am making here is really just a generalization of a point made long ago by Salmon (1957), Skyrms (1975) and a number of other authors. Strawson (1952) argued that the rationality or reasonableness of inductive reasoning was easy to demonstrate, since being supported by inductive inference is part of what we *mean* when we say that an empirical belief is *reasonable*. To which Salmon replied that if Strawson is right about the meaning of "reasonable" it is not at all clear why anyone should *want* to be reasonable. What most of us do care about, Sal-

mon notes, is that our inferential methods be those that are "best suited to the attainment of our ends" (p. 41). "If we regard beliefs as reasonable simply because they are arrived at inductively and we hold that reasonable beliefs are valuable for their own sake, it appears that we have elevated inductive method to the place of an intrinsic good" (p. 42). The analytic epistemologist elevates being within the extension of our ordinary terms of epistemic evaluation to the place of an intrinsic good. In so doing, the analytic epistemologist embraces a system of value that few of us are willing to share.

30. Let me try to head off a possible misunderstanding. Some analytic epistemologists claim that our ordinary notions of epistemic evaluation are conceptually linked to truth. On Goldman's account, for example, the rightness of a set of J-rules is a function of how well the processes sanctioned by those rules do at producing truths. If this is right, then a person who attached intrinsic value to having true beliefs would, of course, have reason to be interested in whether his cognitive states and processes were sanctioned by the standards embedded in our language. But here it is the appeal to truth that is doing the work, not the appeal to traditional standards. For if Goldman is wrong in his conceptual analysis and "(epistemic) justification" is not conceptually tied to truth, the person who values truth will stay just as interested in whether his cognitive processes reliably lead to truth, though he may have no interest whatever in how traditional notions of epistemic evaluation judge his cognitive processes. Thanks to Steven Luper-Foy for the query that prompted this note.

31. This paper has been evolving for a long time. Earlier versions were presented in my seminars at the University of Sydney, the University of Maryland, and the University of California, San Diego, and in colloquia at the University of Adelaide, La Trobe University, the Australian National University, the University of Illinois at Chicago, the University of Vermont, Tulane University, the University of Southern California and the University of Colorado. Suggestions and criticisms from these varied audiences have led to more changes than I can remember or acknowledge. My thanks to all who helped, or tried. Special thanks are due to Philip Kitcher, David Stove and Joseph Tolliver.

REFERENCES

Cherniak, C. *Minimal Rationality*. Cambridge, Mass., 1986.

Cohen, L. J. "Can Human Irrationality Be Experimentally Demonstrated?" *Behavioral and Brain Sciences* 4 (1981): 317–70.

Cole, M., and B. Means. *Comparative Studies of How People Think*. Cambridge, Mass., 1981.

Cole, M., and S. Scribner: *Culture and Thought*. New York, 1974.

Conee, E., and R. Feldman. "Stich and Nisbett on Justifying Inference Rules." *Philosophy of Science* 50 (1983): 326–31.

Daniels, N. "On Some Methods of Ethics and Linguistics." *Philosophical Studies* 37 (1980): 21–36.

———. "Reflective Equilibrium and Archimedean Points." *Canadian Journal of Philosophy* 10 (1980): 83–103.

———. "Wide Reflective Equilibrium and Theory Acceptance in Ethics." *Journal of Philosophy* 76 (1979): 256–82.

Davidson, D. "Rational Animals." *Dialectica* 36 (1982): 317–27.

Goldman, A. *Epistemology and Cognition*. Cambridge, Mass. 1986.

Goodman, N. *Fact, Fiction, and Forecast*. Indianapolis, Ind., 1965.

Hallen, B., and J. O. Sodipo. *Knowledge, Belief, and Witchcraft*. London, 1986.

Harman, G. *Change of View*. Cambridge, Mass., 1986.

Kahneman, D., P. Slovic, and A. Tversky. eds., *Judgment Under Uncertainty*. Cambridge, Mass., 1982.

Nisbett, R., and L. Ross. *Human Inference: Strategies and Shortcomings of Social Judgment*. Englewood Cliffs, N.J., 1980.

Rawls, J. "The Independence of Moral Theory." *Proceedings and Addresses of the American Philosophical Association* 48 (1974): 4–22.

———. *A Theory of Justice*. Cambridge, Mass., 1971.

Rey, G. "Concepts and Stereotypes." *Cognition* 15 (1983): 237–62.

Routley, R. "Alleged Problems Attributing Beliefs, and Intentionality, to Animals." *Inquiry* 24 (1981).

Salmon, W. "Should We Attempt to Justify Induction?" *Philosophical Studies* 8 (1957): 33–48.

Skyrms, B. *Choice and Chance*. Belmont, Calif., 1975.

Smith, E., and D. Medin. *Concepts and Categories*. Cambridge, Mass., 1981.

Stich, S. "Do Animals Have Beliefs?" *Australasian Journal of Philosophy* 57 (1979): 15–28.

———. "Do You Really Care Whether Your Beliefs Are True?" (in preparation).

———. *From Folk Psychology to Cognitive Science*. Cambridge, Mass., 1983.

———. "Relativism, Rationality, and the Limits of Intentional Description." *Pacific Philosophical Quarterly* 65 (1984): 211–35.

Stich, S., and R. Nisbett. "Justification and the Psychology of Reasoning." *Philosophy of Science* 47 (1980): 188–202.

Strawson, P. *Introduction to Logical Theory*. New York, 1952.

BIBLIOGRAPHY: JUSTIFIED BELIEF

General

Alston, W. P. *Epistemic Justification*. Ithaca, N.Y., 1989.

———. "Meta-Ethics and Meta-Epistemology." In *Values and Morals*, ed. A. I. Goldman and J. Kim, pp. 275–97. Dordrecht, 1978.

———. *The Reliability of Sense Perception*. Ithaca, N.Y., 1993.

———. "The Role of Reason in the Regulation of Belief." In *Rationality in the Calvinian Tradition*, ed. N. Wolterstorff et al. pp. 135–70. Lanham, Md., 1983.

Antony, L., and C. Witt, eds. *A Mind of One's Own*. Boulder, Col., 1992.

Armstrong, D. M. *Belief, Truth, and Knowledge*. Cambridge, Eng., 1973.

Audi, R. *The Architecture of Reason*. New York, 2000.

———. *Epistemology*. London, 1998.

———. *The Structure of Justification*. Cambridge, 1993.

———. ed. *The Cambridge Dictionary of Philosophy*. Cambridge, 1995; 2d ed., 1999.

Axtell, G., ed. *Knowledge, Belief, and Character:*

Readings in Virtue Epistemology. Lanham, Md., 2000.

BonJour, L. *The Structure of Empirical Knowledge.* Cambridge, Mass., 1985.

Carruthers, P. *Human Knowledge and Human Nature.* Oxford 1992.

Chisholm, R. M. *The Foundations of Knowing.* Minneapolis, 1982.

———. *Perceiving: A Philosophical Study.* Ithaca, N.Y., 1957.

———. *Theory of Knowledge, 1st ed.* Englewood Cliffs, NJ, 1966; 2d ed., 1977; 3d ed., 1989.

Cornman, J. W. *Perception, Common Sense, and Science.* New Haven, Conn., 1975.

Craig, E. *Knowledge and the State of Nature.* Oxford, 1991.

Dancy, J., and E. Sosa, eds. *A Companion to Epistemology.* Oxford, 1992.

DePaul, M., and W. Ramsey, eds. *Rethinking Intuition.* Lanham, Md., 1998.

Firth, R. *In Defense of Radical Empiricism.* Edited by John Troyer. Lanham, Md., 1998.

Foley, R. *Intellectual Trust in Oneself and Others.* New York, 2001.

———. *The Theory of Epistemic Rationality.* Cambridge, Mass., 1987.

———. *Working Without a Net.* New York, 1993.

French, P. et al., eds. *Midwest Studies in Philosophy, Vol. V: Studies in Epistemology.* Minneapolis, 1980.

Fumerton, Richard. *Metaphysical and Epistemological Problems of Perception.* Lincoln, Nebr., 1985.

———. *Metaepistemology and Skepticism.* Lanham, Md., 1995.

Goldman, A. I. *Epistemology and Cognition.* Cambridge, Mass., 1986.

———. *Knowledge in a Social World.* New York, 1999.

———. *Liaisons.* Cambridge, Mass., 1992.

———. *Pathways of Knowledge.* New York, 2001.

Haack, S. *Evidence and Inquiry.* Oxford, 1994.

Harman, G. *Change In View.* Cambridge, Mass., 1986.

———. *Thought.* Princeton, N.J., 1973.

Hill, T. *Contemporary Theories of Knowledge.* New York, 1961.

Kvanvig, J. *The Intellectual Virtues and the Life of the Mind.* Lanham, Md., 1992.

———, ed. *Warrant in Contemporary Epistemology.* Lanham, Md., 1996.

Lehrer, K. *Knowledge.* Oxford, 1974.

———. *Self-Trust.* Oxford, 1997.

———. *Theory of Knowledge.* Boulder, Col., 1990.

Lewis, C. I. *An Analysis of Knowledge and Valuation.* LaSalle, Ill., 1946.

Lycan, W. *Judgment and Justification.* Cambridge, Eng., 1988.

Moser, P. K. *Empirical Justification.* Dordrecht, 1985.

———. *Knowledge and Evidence.* New York, 1989.

———. *Philosophy after Objectivity.* New York, 1993.

———, "Epistemology (1900—Present)." In *Routledge History of Philosophy, Vol. 10: Philosophy of the English Speaking World in the 20th Century*, ed. J. Canfield. London, 1996.

———, ed. *Empirical Knowledge, 2d ed.* Lanham, Md., 1996.

———, ed. *The Oxford Handbood of Epistemology.* New York, 2003.

———, ed. *Rationality in Action.* Cambridge, 1990.

Moser, Paul K., J. D. Trout, and D. H. Mulder. *The Theory of Knowledge.* New York, 1998.

Pappas, G. S., ed. *Justification and Knowledge.* Dordrecht, 1979.

Pappas, G. S., and M. Swain, eds. *Essays on Knowledge and Justification.* Ithaca, 1978.

Plantinga, A. *Warrant: The Current Debate.* Oxford, 1993.

———. *Warrant and Proper Function.* Oxford, 1993.

Pollock, J. L. *Contemporary Theories of Knowledge.* Lanham, Md., 1986; 2d ed. (with J. Cruz), 1999.

———. *Knowledge and Justification.* Princeton, 1974.

Schmitt, F. *Knowledge and Belief.* London, 1992.

Sellars, W. *Science, Perception, and Reality.* Atascadero, Calif., 1991.

———. *The Metaphysics of Epistemology.* Atascadero, Calif., 1989.

Sosa, E. *Knowledge in Perspective.* New York, 1991.

———, ed., *Knowledge and Justification.* Aldershort, Eng., 1994.

———, and J. Kim, eds. *Epistemology.* Malden, Mass., 2000.

Stich, S. *The Fragmentation of Reason.* Cambridge, Mass., 1990.

Stroud, B. *Understanding Human Knowledge: Philosophical Essays.* New York, 2000.

Tomberlin, J., ed. *Philosophical Perspectives, 2: Epistemology.* Atascadero, Calif., 1988.

———, ed. *Philosophical Perspectives, 13:Epistemology.* Cambridge, Mass., 1999.

Epistemic Foundationalism

Alston, W. P. *Epistemic Justification.* Ithaca, 1989.

———. "Plantinga's Religious Epistemology." In *Alvin Plantinga,* ed. J. E. Tomberlin and P. van Inwagen, pp. 287–309. Dordrecht, 1985.

———. "Some Remarks on Chisholm's Epistemology." *Noûs* 14 (1980): 565–86.

Annis, D. B. "Epistemic Foundationalism." *Philosophical Studies* 31 (1977): 345–52.

Armstrong, D. M. *Belief, Truth, and Knowledge.* Cambridge, Eng., 1973.

Audi, R. *The Structure of Justification.* Cambridge, Eng., 1993.

Ayer, A. J. "Basic Propositions." In *Philosophical Analysis,* ed. M. Black, pp. 60–74. Englewood Cliffs, NJ, 1950. Reprinted in Ayer, *Philosophical Essays* (London, 1965).

———. *The Foundations of Empirical Knowledge.* New York, 1940.

BonJour, L. "Externalist Theories of Empirical Knowledge." In *Midwest Studies in Philosophy, Vol. V: Studies in Epistemology,* ed. P. French et al., pp. 53–74. Minneapolis, 1980.

———. *The Structure of Empirical Knowledge.* Cambridge, Mass., 1985.

Chisholm, R. "The Directly Evident." In *Justification and Knowledge,* ed. G. S. Pappas, pp. 115–27. Dordrecht, 1979.

———. "On the Nature of Empirical Evidence." In *Essays on Knowledge and Justification,* ed. G. S. Pappas and M. Swain, pp. 253–78. Ithaca, N.Y., 1978.

———. *Theory of Knowledge, 1st ed.* Englewood Cliffs, NJ, 1966; 2d ed., 1977; 3d ed., 1989.

———. "Theory of Knowledge in America." In *The Foundations of Knowing,* pp. 109–96. Minneapolis, 1982.

———. "A Version of Foundationalism." In *The Foundations of Knowing,* pp. 3–32. Minneapolis, 1982.

Churchland, P. M. *Scientific Realism and the Plasticity of Mind,* chapter 2. Cambridge: 1979.

Cornman, James W. "Foundational versus Non-foundational Theories of Empirical Justification." *American Philosophical Quarterly* 14 (1977): 287–97. Reprinted in *Essays on Knowledge and Justification,* ed. G. S. Pappas and M. Swain, pp. 229–52. Ithaca, 1978.

———. *Skepticism, Justification, and Explanation.* Dordrecht, 1980.

DePaul, M., ed. *Resurrecting Old-Fashioned Foundationalism.* Lanham, Md., 2001.

Foley, R. *The Theory of Epistemic Rationality.* Cambridge, Mass., 1987.

———. *Working Without a Net.* Oxford, 1993.

Fumerton, R. *Metaepistemology and Skepticism.* Lanham, Md., 1995.

———. *Metaphysical and Epistemological Problems of Perception,* chapter 2. Lincoln, Nebr., 1985.

———. "Theories of Justification." In *The Oxford Handbook of Epistemology,* ed. P. K. Moser. New York, 2003.

Goldman, A. H. *Empirical Knowledge.* Berkeley, Calif., 1988.

———. "Epistemic Foundationalism and the Replaceability of Ordinary Language." *Journal of Philosophy* 79 (1982): 136–54.

Heidelberger, H. "Chisholm's Epistemic Principles." *Noûs* 3 (1969): 73–82.

Heil, J. "Foundationalism and Epistemic Rationality." *Philosophical Studies* 42 (1982): 179–88.

Kornblith, H. "Beyond Foundationalism and the Coherence Theory." *The Journal of Philosophy* 72 (1980): 597–612. Reprinted in *Naturalizing Epistemology,* ed. H. Kornblith, pp. 115–28. Cambridge, Mass., 1985.

Lehrer, K. *Theory of Knowledge.* Boulder, Col., 1990.

Lewis, C. I. *An Analysis of Knowledge and Valuation,* chapters 7 and 8. LaSalle, Ill., 1946.

———. "The Given Element in Empirical Knowledge." *The Philosophical Review* 61 (1952): 168–75.

———. *Mind and the World Order.* New York, 1929.

McGrew, T. *The Foundations of Knowledge.* Lanham, Md., 1995.

Moser, P. K. "A Defense of Epistemic Intuitionism." *Metaphilosophy* 15 (1984): 196–209.

———. *Empirical Justification,* chapters 4 and 5. Dordrecht, 1985.

———. *Knowledge and Evidence.* Cambridge, Eng., 1989.

———. *Philosophy after Objectivity.* Oxford, 1993.

————, ed. *The Oxford Handbook of Epistemology*. New York, 2003.

Pastin, M. "Lewis' Radical Foundationalism." *Noûs* 9 (1975): 407–20.

————. "Modest Foundationalism and Self-Warrant." In *American Philosophical Quarterly Monograph Series, No. 9: Studies in Epistemology*, ed. N. Rescher, pp. 141–49. Oxford, 1975. Reprinted in *Essays on Knowledge and Justification*, Ed. G. S. Pappas and M. Swain pp. 279–88. Ithaca N.Y., 1978.

Pollock, J. *Contemporary Theories of Knowledge*. Lanham, Md. 1986; 2d ed. (with J. Cruz), 1999.

————. *Knowledge and Justification*. Princeton, N.J., 1974.

————. "A Plethora of Epistemological Theories." in *Justification and Knowledge*, ed. G. S. Pappas pp. 93–113. Dordrecht, 1979.

Quinton, A. "The Foundations of Knowledge." In *British Analytic Philosophy*, ed. B. Williams and A. Montefiore pp. 55–86. London, 1966.

————. *The Nature of Things*, chapter 8. London, 1973.

Russell, B. *Human Knowledge: Its Scope and Limits*, Part 2. New York: Simon & Schuster, 1948.

————. *An Inquiry into Meaning and Truth*, chapters 9 and 10. New York, 1940.

————. "On Verification." *Proceedings of the Aristotelian Society* 38 (1937–38): 1–15.

Scheffler, I. *Science and Subjectivity, 2d ed.*, chapters 2 and 5. Indianapolis, 1982.

Sellars, W. "Does Empirical Knowledge Have a Foundation?," in "Empiricism and the Philosophy of Mind." In *Minnesota Studies in the Philosophy of Science*, Vol. 1, ed. H. Feigl and M. Scriven pp. 293–300. Minneapolis, 1956. Reprinted in Sellars, *Science, Perception, and Reality*. London, 1963.

Sosa, E. *Knowledge in Perspective*. Cambridge, Eng., 1991.

Strawson, P. F. "Does Knowledge Have Foundations?." In *Teorema, Mono. 1: Conocimiento y Creencia*, pp. 99–110. Universidad de Valencia, 1974.

Swain, M. "Cornman's Theory of Justification." *Philosophical Studies* 41 (1982): 129–48.

————. *Reasons and Knowledge*. Ithaca, N.Y., 1981.

Van Cleve, J. "Epistemic Supervenience and the Circle of Belief." *The Monist* 68 (1985): 90–104.

————. "Foundationalism, Epistemic Principles, and the Cartesian Circle." *The Philosophical Review* 88 (1979): 55–91.

Epistemic Coherentism

Audi, R. *The Structure of Justification*. Cambridge, Eng., 1993.

Bender, J., ed. *The Current State of the Coherence Theory*. Dordrecht, 1989.

Blanshard, B. *The Nature of Thought*, Vol. 2, chapters 25–27. London, 1939.

BonJour, L. "The Coherence Theory of Empirical Knowledge." *Philosophical Studies* 30 (1976): 281–312.

————. *The Structure of Empirical Knowledge*. Cambridge, Mass., 1985.

Dancy, J. *An Introduction to Contemporary Epistemology*, chapters 8 and 9. Oxford, 1985.

————. "On Coherence Theories of Justification: Can an Empiricist be a Coherentist?." *American Philosophical Quarterly* 21 (1984): 359–65.

Davidson, D. "A Coherence Theory of Truth and Knowledge." In *Kant oder Hegel*, ed. D. Henrich pp. 423–38. Stuttgart, 1983.

Firth, R. "Coherence, Certainty, and Epistemic Priority." *The Journal of Philosophy* 61 (1964): 545–57.

Harman, G. *Change In View*. Cambridge, Mass., 1986.

————. "Knowledge, Inference, and Explanation." *American Philosophical Quarterly* 5 (1968): 164–73.

————. "Knowledge, Reasons, and Causes." *The Journal of Philosophy* 67 (1970), 841–55.

————. *Thought*, chapter 8. Princeton, N.J., 1973.

Lehrer, K. "Justification, Explanation, and Induction." In *Induction, Acceptance, and Rational Belief*, ed. M. Swain, pp. 100–33. Dordrecht, 1970.

————. *Knowledge*, chapters 7 and 8. Oxford, 1974.

————. "The Knowledge Cycle." *Noûs* 11 (1977): 17–26.

————. "Knowledge, Truth, and Ontology." In *Language and Ontology: Proceedings of the 6th International Wittgenstein Symposium*, ed. W. Leinfellner et al., pp. 201–11. Vienna, 1982.

————. "Self-Profile." In *Keith Lehrer*, ed. R. J. Bogdan, pp. 3–104. Dordrecht, 1981.

———. *Theory of Knowledge.* Boulder, Col., 1990.

Lehrer, K., and S. Cohen. "Justification, Truth, and Coherence." *Synthese* 55 (1983): 191–208.

Lemos, N. "Coherence and Epistemic Priority." *Philosophical Studies* 41 (1982): 299–316.

Moser, P. K. *Empirical Justification,* chapter 3. Dordrecht, 1985.

———. *Knowledge and Evidence.* Cambridge, Eng., 1989.

———. ed. *The Oxford Handbook of Epistemology.* New York, 2003.

Pastin, M. "Social and Anti-Social Justification: A Study of Lehrer's Epistemology." In *Keith Lehrer,* pp. 205–22. Dordrecht, 1981.

Rescher, N. "Blanshard and the Coherence Theory of Truth." In *The Philosophy of Brand Blanshard,* ed. P. Schilpp, pp. 574–88. LaSalle, Ill. 1980.

———. *Cognitive Systematization.* Oxford, 1979.

———. *The Coherence Theory of Truth.* Oxford, 1973.

———. "Foundationalism, Coherentism, and the Idea of Cognitive Systematization." *The Journal of Philosophy* 71 (1974): 695–708.

———. *A System of Pragmatic Idealism,* 3 vols. Princeton, N.J., 1991–1994.

———. "Truth as Ideal Coherence." *The Review of Metaphysics* 38 (1985): 795–806.

Sellars, Wilfrid. "Epistemic Principles." In *Action, Knowledge, and Reality: Critical Studies in Honor of Wilfrid Sellars,* ed. H. N. Castaneda, pp. 332–48. Indianapolis 1975.

———. "Givenness and Explanatory Coherence." *The Journal of Philosophy* 70 (1973): 612–24.

———. "More on Givenness and Explanatory Coherence." In *Justification and Knowledge,* ed. G. S. Pappas, pp. 169–81. Dordrecht, 1979.

Sosa, E. "Circular Coherence and Absurd Foundations." In *A Companion to Inquiries into Truth and Interpretation,* ed E. Lepore. Oxford, 1985.

———. *Knowledge in Perspective.* Cambridge, Eng., 1991.

Epistemic Contextualism

Airaksinen, T. "Contextualism: A New Theory of Epistemic Justification." *Philosophia* 12 (1982): 37–50.

Annis, D. "The Social and Cultural Component of Epistemic Justification: A Reply." *Philosophia* 12 (1982): 51–55.

Morawetz, T. *Wittgenstein and Knowledge.* Amherst, Mass., 1978.

Moser, P. K. *Empirical Justification,* chapter 2. Dordrecht, 1985.

Rorty, R. *Philosophy and the Mirror of Nature,* chapter 7. Princeton, N.J., 1979.

———. "From Epistemology to Hermeneutics." In *Acta Philosophica Fennica, Vol. 30: The Logic and Epistemology of Scientific Change.* ed. I. Niiniluoto and R. Tuomela. Amsterdam, 1978.

Schmitt, F. ed. *Socializing Epistemology.* Lanham, Md., 1994.

Shiner, R. "Wittgenstein and the Foundations of Knowledge." *Proceedings of the Aristotelian Society* 78 (1977–78): 103–24.

Sosa, E. "On Groundless Belief." *Synthese* 43 (1979): 453–60.

Williams, Michael. "Coherence, Justification, and Truth." *The Review of Metaphysics* 34 (1980): 243–72.

———. *Groundless Belief.* Oxford, 1977; 2d ed., Princeton, N.J., 1999.

———. *Unnatural Doubts.* Oxford, 1991.

Wittgenstein, L. *On Certainty.* Ed. G.E.M. Anscombe and G. H. von Wright. Oxford, 1969.

Epistemic Reliabilism

Armstrong, D. M. *Belief, Truth, and Knowledge.* Cambridge, Eng., 1973.

———. "Self-Profile." In *D. M. Armstrong,* ed. R. Bogdan, pp. 30–37. Dordrecht, 1984.

Audi, R. *The Structure of Justification.* Cambridge, Eng., 1993.

BonJour, L. "Externalist Theories of Empirical Knowledge." In *Midwest Studies in Philosophy, Vol. V: Studies in Epistemology,* ed. P. French et al., pp. 53–73. Minneapolis, 1980.

Cohen, S. "Justification and Truth." *Philosophical Studies* 46 (1984): 279–95.

Dretske, F. I. "Conclusive Reasons." *The Australasian Journal of Philosophy* 49 (1971): 1–22. Reprinted in *Essays on Knowledge and Justification,* ed. G. S. Pappas and M. Swain, pp. 41–60: Ithaca, N.Y., 1978.

———. "The Pragmatic Dimension of Knowledge." *Philosophical Studies* 40 (1981): 363–78.

————. *Knowledge and the Flow of Information*, chapters 4 and 5. Cambridge, Mass., 1981.

————. "Precis of *Knowledge and the Flow of Information*." *The Behavioral and Brain Sciences* 6 (1983): 55–63.

Feldman, R. "Reliability and Justification." *The Monist* 68 (1985): 159–74.

————. "Schmitt on Reliability, Objectivity, and Justification." Forthcoming in *The Australasian Journal of Philosophy*.

Feldman, R., and E. Conee. "Evidentialism." *Philosophical Studies* 48 (1985): 15–34.

Firth, R. "Epistemic Merit, Intrinsic and Instrumental." In *Proceedings and Addresses of the American Philosophical Association* 55 (1981): 5–23.

Foley, R. "What's Wrong with Reliabilism?." *The Monist* 68 (1985): 188–202.

Friedman, M. "Truth and Confirmation." *The Journal of Philosophy* 76 (1979): 361–82. Reprinted in *Naturalizing Epistemology*, ed. H. Kornblith, pp. 147–68. Cambridge, Mass., 1985.

Ginet, C. "*Contra* Reliabilism." *The Monist* 68 (1985): 175–87.

Goldman, A. I. "Discrimination and Perceptual Knowledge." *The Journal of Philosophy* 73 (1976): 771–91. Reprinted in *Essays on Knowledge and Justification*, ed. G. S. Pappas and M. Swain, pp. 120–45. Ithaca, N.Y., 1978.

————. *Epistemology and Cognition*. Cambridge, Mass., 1986.

————. "The Internalist Conception of Justification." In *Midwest Studies in Philosophy, Vol. V: Studies in Epistemology*, ed. P. French et al., pp. 27–52. Minneapolis, 1980.

————. *Liaisons*. Cambridge, Mass., 1992.

————. "What is Justified Belief?." In *Justification and Knowledge*, ed. G. S. Pappas, pp. 1–23. Dordrecht, 1979.

Heil, J. "Reliability and Epistemic Merit." *The Australasian Journal of Philosophy* 62 (1984): 327–38.

Kornblith, H. "Beyond Foundationalism and the Coherence Theory." *The Journal of Philosophy* 72 (1980): 597–612.

————. "Ever Since Descartes." *The Monist* 68 (1985): 264–76.

————. "Justified Belief and Epistemically Responsible Action." *The Philosophical Review* 92 (1983): 33–48.

————. "The Psychological Turn." *The Australasian Journal of Philosophy* 60 (1982): 238–53. ed. *Naturalizing Epistemology*. Cambridge, Mass., 1994.

Kvanvig, J. *The Intellectual Virtues and the Life of the Mind*. Lanham, Md., 1992.

Lycan W. G. "Armstrong's Theory of Knowing." In *D. M. Armstrong*, ed. R. Bogdan, pp. 139–60. Dordrecht, 1984.

————. *Judgment and Justification*. Cambridge, Eng., 1988.

Montmarquet, J. *Epistemic Virtue and Doxastic Responsibility*. Lanham, Md., 1993.

Moser, P. K. *Empirical Justification*, chapter 4 and Appendix. Dordrecht, 1985.

————. "Knowledge Without Evidence." *Philosophia* 15 (1985): 109–16.

Nozick, R. *Philosophical Explanations*, chapter 3. Cambridge, Mass., 1981.

Pappas, G. S. "Non-Inferential Knowledge." *Philosophia* 12 (1982): 81–98.

Pastin, M. "Knowledge and Reliability: A Critical Study of D. M. Armstrong's *Belief, Truth, and Knowledge*." *Metaphilosophy* 9 (1978): 150–62.

————. "The Multi-perspectival Theory of Knowledge." In *Midwest Studies in Philosophy, Vol. V: Studies in Epistemology*, ed. P. French et al., pp. 97–111. Minneapolis, 1980.

Pollock, J. *Contemporary Theories of Knowledge*. Lanham, Md., 1986; 2d ed. (with J. Cruz), 1999.

————. "Reliability and Justified Belief." *The Canadian Journal of Philosophy* 14 (1984): 103–14.

Schmitt, F. F. "Justification as Reliable Indication or Reliable Process." *Philosophical Studies* 40 (1981): 409–17.

————. *Knowledge and Belief*. London, 1992.

————. "Knowledge as Tracking." *Topoi* 4 (1985): 73–80.

————. "Knowledge, Justification, and Reliability." *Synthese* 55 (1983): 209–29.

————. "Reliability, Objectivity, and the Background of Justification." *The Australasian Journal of Philosophy* 62 (1984): 1–15.

Shope, R. K. "Cognitive Abilities, Conditionals, and Knowledge: A Response to Nozick." *The Journal of Philosophy* 81 (1984): 29–47.

Sosa, E. *Knowledge in Perspective*. Cambridge, Eng., 1991.

Swain, M. "Justification and the Basis of Belief."

In *Justification and Knowledge*, ed. G. S. Pappas, pp. 25–49. Dordrecht, 1979.

———. "Justification and Reliable Belief." *Philosophical Studies* 40 (1981): 389–407.

———. "Justification, Reasons, and Reliability." *Synthese* 64 (1985): 69–92.

———. *Reasons and Knowledge*, chapter 4. Ithaca, N.Y., 1981.

Van Cleve, James. "Reliability, Justification, and the Problem of Induction." In *Midwest Studies in Philosophy, Vol. IX*, ed. P. French et al., pp. 555–67. Minneapolis, 1984.

Skepticism

The General Introduction drew some general distinctions regarding skepticism and outlined some influential arguments for skepticism. This section focuses on the threat of skeptical challenges to justification and knowledge, exploring various ways of replying to skepticism. The selections share an important assumption: Philosophers cannot simply ignore challenges from skeptics. Attention to skeptical challenges may yield significant lessons about reasons, doubt, justification, and knowledge.

In "Proof of an External World," G. W. Moore asks, "What sort of proof, if any, can be given of 'the existence of things outside of us'?" Focusing on Kant's treatment of the epistemological problem of the external world, Moore seeks to clarify the sense of the key phrase "things outside of us." Moore proposes that we can understand the latter phrase in terms of "whatever can be met with in space," and that we can prove various propositions regarding things outside of us. Moore relies on the following claims:

> . . . I can now give a large number of different proofs ["of the existence of things outside of us"], each of which is a perfectly rigorous proof. . . . I can prove now, for instance, that two human hands exist. How? By holding up my two hands, and saying, as I make a certain gesture with the right hand, "Here is one hand," and adding, as I make a certain gesture with the left, "and here is another."

Moore claims that his "proof" is "perfectly rigorous" and that it would be "absurd" to suggest that he did not actually know—but merely believed—that there were two hands in the places indicated by his gestures. Such is Moore's famous "proof" of the existence of external physical objects.

Moore claimed to prove, in addition, that there have been external objects in the past. Thus: "I held up two hands above this desk not very long ago; therefore two hands existed not very long ago; therefore at least two external objects have existed at some time in the past." Moore insists that he does know that he held up two hands in the past and thus that he has given a "perfectly conclusive proof that external objects have existed in the past."

Moore must face an objection. His "proofs" do not give us disproofs of either the claim that he is simply *dreaming* that he is holding up two hands or the claim that he is simply *misremembering* that he held up two hands. Moore replies that he cannot prove his claim that here is one hand and there another, but that this is no real problem. He finds it adequate that he has "conclusive evidence" for the previous claim and for the claim that he is not now dreaming or misremembering. We can have, on Moore's view, conclusive evidence for, and certain knowledge of, claims we cannot prove. Moore thus claims to have conclusive evidence that he is not dreaming, even though he cannot tell us what all that evidence is.

In "Cause and Effect: Intuitive Awareness," Ludwig Wittgenstein explores our common talk that seemingly presupposes intuitive awareness, and lack of doubt, of cause-and-effect relations. Wittgenstein considers the following position: "Doubting—I might say—has to come to an end somewhere. At some point we have to say—without doubting: *that* results from *this* cause." He replies as follows:

"The game can't start with doubting"—What we ought to say is: the game *doesn't* start with doubting.—Or else: the "can" has the same justification as it has in the assertion: "Street traffic can't begin with everybody doubting whether to go in this, or rather in that direction; in that case it would never amount to what we call 'traffic' and then we shouldn't call their hesitation 'doubting' either."

Wittgenstein adds a remark pertinent to the antiskeptical view of G. E. Moore: "A philosopher who protests, 'We KNOW there's a chair over there!' is simply describing a game."

Wittgenstein's talk of "games" is talk of "language games." He proposes that the origin of a language game is a reaction, a kind of action. More specifically: ". . . it is characteristic of our language that the foundation on which it grows consists in steady ways of living, regular ways of acting. . . . Its function is determined *above all* by action, which it accompanies." In other words: "The essence of the language game is a practical method (a way of acting)— not speculation, not chatter."

In "Skepticism, Naturalism and Transcendental Arguments," P. F. Strawson considers various kinds of attempts to answer traditional skepticism, including such attempts suggested by Moore, Carnap, Quine, and proponents of "transcendental arguments." Strawson's own position toward skepticism draws on similarities between Hume and Wittgenstein, particularly their shared view that "our 'beliefs' in the existence of body and . . . in the general reliability of induction are not grounded beliefs and at the same time are not open to serious doubt." The beliefs in question "define, or help to define, the area in which [our critical and rational] competence is exercised." Strawson's position aims "to represent skeptical arguments and rational counter-arguments as equally idle—not senseless, but idle—since what we have here are original, natural, inescapable commitments which we neither choose nor could give up." Transcendental arguments can elucidate connections among our beliefs, according to Strawson, but cannot settle traditional debates involving skepticism.

In "Philosophical Scepticism and Epistemic Circularity," Ernest Sosa defends an externalist, reliabilist theory of knowledge as the only way to avoid the skeptical conclusion that a fully general theory of knowledge is impossible. He rejects "internalism," the view that a belief can be justified only through the backing of reasons or arguments, on the ground that it gives us no way to refute the skepticism he mentions. He identifies three versions of "externalism," in the special sense of the word he uses. He finds that coherentism and foundationalism of the given both fail to offer a satisfactory general theory of knowledge that could refute skepticism. He defends a version of reliabilism while giving particular attention to the problem of circularity in epistemological theorizing. Sosa suggests that we are able to avoid skepticism by rejecting the demand for a fully general and *legitimating* philosophical understanding of all our knowledge. We must resign ourselves to a kind of circularity, according to Sosa, but it is not a philosophically destructive kind of circularity. Some epistemically circular arguments, he claims, can discriminate between reliable and unreliable doxastic practices. He concludes that philosophers such as Alston and Stroud have presented no good reason to accept philosophical skepticism.

In "Scepticism, 'Externalism', and the Goal of Epistemology," Barry Stroud responds to the previous essay by Sosa. He claims that scepticism is inescapable, but he uses the word "skepticism" to refer to a view different from the view Sosa intends with this term. Stroud calls "skepticism" the epistemological position that "nobody knows anything, or that nobody has any good reason to believe anything." He argues that the traditional epistemological project of explaining how we do in fact know the things we think we know should be rejected. Stroud adds: "I find the force and resilience of scepticism in the theory of knowledge to be so great, once the epistemological project is accepted, and I find its consequences to be so paradoxical, that I think the best thing to do now is to look much more closely and critically at the very enterprise of which scepticism or one of its rivals is the outcome: the task of the philosophical theory of knowledge itself." He claims that the circularity Sosa found to be unavoidable but philosophically acceptable renders the epistemological project itself and any possible answer to it thoroughly "dissatisfying." It is, he claims, the complete generality in a theory of knowledge demanded by the traditional epistemological project that compels us ultimately to be dissatisfied.

31 / G. E. Moore (1873–1958)
PROOF OF AN EXTERNAL WORLD

In the preface to the second edition of Kant's *Critique of Pure Reason* some words occur, which, in Professor Kemp Smith's translation, are rendered as follows:

> It still remains a scandal to philosophy . . . that the existence of things outside of us . . . must be accepted merely on *faith*, and that, if anyone thinks good to doubt their existence, we are unable to counter his doubts by any satisfactory proof.[1]

It seems clear from these words that Kant thought it a matter of some importance to give a proof of "the existence of things outside of us" or perhaps rather (for it seems to me possible that the force of the German words is better rendered in this way) of "the existence of *the* things outside of us"; for had he not thought it important that a proof should be given, he would scarcely have called it a "scandal" that no proof had been given. And it seems clear also that he thought that the giving of such a proof was a task which fell properly within the province of philosophy; for, if it did not, the fact that no proof had been given could not possibly be a scandal to *philosophy*.

Now, even if Kant was mistaken in both of these two opinions, there seems to me to be no doubt whatever that it is a matter of some importance and also a matter which falls properly within the province of philosophy, to discuss the question what sort of proof, if any, can be given of "the existence of things outside of us." And to discuss this question was my object when I began to write the present lecture. But I may say at once that, as you will find, I have only, at most, succeeded in saying a very small part of what ought to be said about it.

The words "it . . . remains a scandal to philosophy . . . that we are unable . . ." would, taken strictly, imply that, at the moment at which he wrote them, Kant himself was unable to produce a satisfactory proof of the point in question. But I think it is unquestionable that Kant himself did not think that he personally was at the time unable to produce such a proof. On the contrary, in the immediately preceding sentence, he has declared that he has, in the second edition of his *Critique*, to which he is now writing the Preface, given a 'rigorous proof' of this very thing; and has added that he believes this proof of his to be 'the only possible proof'. It is true that in this preceding sentence he does not describe the proof which he has given as a proof of "the existence of things outside of us" or of "the existence of the things outside of us," but describes it instead as a proof of "the objective reality of outer in-

Reprinted by permission of the publisher from *Proceedings of the British Academy* 25 (1939), 273–300.

tuition." But the context leaves no doubt that he is using these two phrases, "the objective reality of outer intuition" and "the existence of things (*or* 'the things') outside of us," in such a way that whatever is a proof of the first is also necessarily a proof of the second. We must, therefore, suppose that when he speaks as if *we* are unable to give a satisfactory proof, he does not mean to say that he himself, as well as others, is *at the moment* unable; but rather that, until he discovered the proof which he has given, both he himself and everybody else *were* unable. Of course, if he is right in thinking that he has given a satisfactory proof, the state of things which he describes came to an end as soon as his proof was published. As soon as that happened, anyone who read it was able to give a satisfactory proof by simply repeating that which Kant had given, and the "scandal" to philosophy had been removed once for all.

If, therefore, it were certain that the proof of the point in question given by Kant in the second edition is a satisfactory proof, it would be certain that at least one satisfactory proof can be given; and all that would remain of the question which I said I proposed to discuss would be, firstly, the question as to what *sort* of a proof this of Kant's is, and secondly the question whether (contrary to Kant's own opinion) there may not perhaps be other proofs, of the same or of a different sort, which are also satisfactory. But I think it is by no means certain that Kant's proof is satisfactory. I think it is by no means certain that he did succeed in removing once for all the state of affairs which he considered to be a scandal to philosophy. And I think, therefore, that the question whether it is possible to give *any* satisfactory proof of the point in question still deserves discussion.

But what is the point in question? I think it must be owned that the expression "things outside of us" is rather an odd expression, and an expression the meaning of which is certainly not perfectly clear. It would have sounded less odd if, instead of 'things outside of us' I had said "external things," and perhaps also the meaning of this expression would have seemed to be clearer; and I think we make the meaning of "external things" clearer still if we explain

that this phrase has been regularly used by philosophers as short for "things external to *our minds*." The fact is that there has been a long philosophical tradition, in accordance with which the three expressions "external things," "things external to *us*," and "things external to *our minds*" have been used as equivalent to one another, and have, each of them, been used as if they needed no explanation. The origin of this usage I do not know. It occurs already in Descartes; and since he uses the expressions as if they needed no explanation, they had presumably been used with the same meaning before. Of the three, it seems to me that the expression "external to *our minds*" is the clearest, since it at least makes clear that what is meant is not "external to *our bodies*"; whereas both the other expressions might be taken to mean this: and indeed there has been a good deal of confusion, even among philosophers, as to the relation of the two conceptions "external things" and "things external to *our bodies*." But even the expression "things external to our minds" seems to me to be far from perfectly clear; and if I am to make really clear what I mean by "proof of existence of things outside of us," I cannot do it by merely saying that by "outside of us" I mean "external to our minds."

There is a passage (*K.d.r.V.*, A 373) in which Kant himself says that the expression "outside of us" "carries with it an unavoidable ambiguity." He says that "sometimes it means something which exists *as a thing in itself* distinct from us, and sometimes something which merely belongs to external appearance"; he calls things which are "outside of us" in the first of these two senses "objects which might be called external in the transcendental sense," and things which are so in the second "empirically external objects"; and he says finally that, in order to remove all uncertainty as to the latter conception, he will distinguish empirically external objects from objects which might be called "external" in the transcendental sense, "by calling them outright things which are *to be met with in space*."

I think that this last phrase of Kant's "things which are to be met with in space," does indicate fairly clearly what sort of things it is with regard to which I wish to inquire what sort of proof, if any, can be given that there are any things of that sort. My body, the bodies of other men, the bodies of animals, plants of all sorts, stones, mountains, the sun, the moon, stars and planets, houses and other buildings, manufactured articles of all sorts—chairs, tables, pieces of paper, etc., are all of them "things which are to be met with in space." In short, all things of the sort that philosophers have been used to call "physical objects," "material things," or "bodies" obviously come under this head. But the phrase "things that are to be met with in space" can be naturally understood as applying also in cases where the names "physical object," "material thing," or "body" can hardly be applied. For instance, shadows are sometimes to be met with in space, although they could hardly be properly called "physical objects," "material things," or "bodies"; and although in one usage of the term "thing" it would not be proper to call a shadow a "thing," yet the phrase "things which are to be met within space" can be naturally understood as synonymous with "whatever can be met with in space," and this is an expression which can quite properly be understood to include shadows. I wish the phrase "things which are to be met with in space" to be understood in this wide sense; so that if a proof can be found that there ever have been as many as two different shadows it will follow at once that there have been at least two "things which were to be met with in space," and this proof will be as good a proof of the point in question as would be a proof that there have been at least two "physical objects" of no matter what sort.

The phrase "things which are to be met with in space" can, therefore, be naturally understood as having a very wide meaning—a meaning even wider than that of "physical object" or "body," wide as is the meaning of these latter expressions. But wide as is its meaning, it is not, in one respect, so wide as that of another phrase which Kant uses as if it were equivalent to this one; and a comparison between the two will, I think, serve to make still clearer what sort of things it is with regard to which I wish to ask what proof, if any, can be given that there are such things.

The other phrase which Kant uses as if it were equivalent to "things which are to be met

with in space" is used by him in the sentence immediately preceding that previously quoted in which he declares that the expression "things outside of us" "carries with it an unavoidable ambiguity" (A 373). In this preceding sentence he says that an "empirical object" "is called *external*, if it is presented (*vorgestellt*) *in space*." He treats, therefore, the phrase "presented in space" as if it were equivalent to "to be met with in space." But it is easy to find examples of "things," of which it can hardly be denied that they are "presented in space," but of which it could, quite naturally, be emphatically denied that they are "to be met with in space." Consider, for instance, the following description of one set of circumstances under which what some psychologists have called a "negative after-image" and others a "negative after-sensation" can be obtained. "If, after looking steadfastly at a white patch on a black ground, the eye be turned to a white ground, a grey patch is seen for some little time." (Foster's *Text-book of Physiology*, IV, iii, 3, p. 1266; quoted in Stout's *Manual of Psychology*, 3rd edition, page 280.) Upon reading these words recently, I took the trouble to cut out of a piece of white paper a four-pointed star, to place it on a black ground, to "look steadfastly" at it, and then to turn my eyes to a white sheet of paper: and I did find that I saw a grey patch for some little time—I not only saw a grey patch, but I saw it *on* the white ground, and also this grey patch was of roughly the same shape as the white four-pointed star at which I had "looked steadfastly" just before—it also was a four-pointed star. I repeated this simple experiment successfully several times. Now each of those grey four-pointed stars, one of which I saw in each experiment, was what is called an "after-image" or "after-sensation"; and can anybody deny that each of these after-images can be quite properly said to have been "presented in space"? I saw each of them on a real white background, and, if so, each of them was "presented" on a real white background. But though they were "presented in space" everybody, I think, would feel that it was gravely misleading to say that they were "to be met with in space." The white star at which I "looked steadfastly," the black ground on which I saw it, and the white ground on which

I saw the after-images, were, of course, "to be met with in space": they were, in fact, "physical objects" or surfaces of physical objects. But one important difference between them, on the one hand, and the *grey* after-images, on the other, can be quite naturally expressed by saying that the latter were *not* "to be met with in space." And one reason why this is so is, I think, plain. To say that so and so was at a given time "to be met with in space" naturally suggests that there are conditions such that *anyone* who fulfilled them might, conceivably, have "perceived" the "thing" in question—might have seen it, if it was a visible object, have felt it, if it was a tangible one, have heard it, if it was a sound, have smelt it, if it was a smell. When I say that the white four-pointed paper star, at which I looked steadfastly, was a "physical object" and was "to be met with in space," I am implying that *anyone*, who had been in the room at the time, and who had normal eyesight and a normal sense of touch, might have seen and felt it. But, in the case of those grey after-images which I saw, it is not conceivable that anyone besides myself should have seen any one of them. It is, of course, quite conceivable that other people, if they had been in the room with me at the time, and had carried out the same experiment which I carried out, would have seen grey after-images *very like* one of those which I saw. There is no absurdity in supposing even that they might have seen after-images *exactly* like one of those which I saw. But there is an absurdity in supposing even that they might have seen after-images *exactly* like one of those which I saw. But there is an absurdity in supposing that any one of the after-images which I saw could also have been seen by anyone else: in supposing that two different people can ever see the *very same* after-image. One reason, then, why we should say that none of those grey after-images which I saw was "to be met with in space," although each of them was certainly "presented in space" to me, is simply that none of them could conceivably have been seen by anyone else. It is natural so to understand the phrase "to be met with in space," that to say of anything which a man perceived that it was to be met with in space is to say that it might have

been perceived by *others* as well as by the man in question.

Negative after-images of the kind described are, therefore, one example of "things" which, though they must be allowed to be "presented in space," are nevertheless *not* "to be met with in space," and are *not* "external to our minds" in the sense with which we shall be concerned. And two other important examples may be given.

The first is this. It is well known that people sometimes see things double, an occurrence which has also been described by psychologists by saying that they have a "double image," or two "images," of some object at which they are looking. In such cases it would certainly be quite natural to say that each of the two "images" is "presented in space": they are seen, one in one place, and the other in another, in just the same sense in which each of those grey after-images which I saw was seen at a particular place on the white background at which I was looking. But it would be utterly unnatural to say that, when I have a double image, each of the two images is "to be met with in space." On the contrary it is quite certain that *both* of them are not "to be met with in space." If both were, it would follow that somebody else might see the *very same* two images which I see; and, though there is no absurdity in supposing that another person might see a pair of images exactly similar to a pair which I see, there is an absurdity in supposing that anyone else might see the *same identical pair*. In every case, then, in which anyone sees anything double, we have an example of at least one "thing" which, though "presented in space" is certainly not "to be met with in space."

And the second important example is this. Bodily pains can, in general, be quite properly said to be "presented in space." When I have a toothache, I feel it *in* a particular region of my jaw or *in* a particular tooth; when I make a cut on my finger smart by putting iodine on it, I feel the pain in a particular place in my finger; and a man whose leg has been amputated may feel a pain *in* a place where his foot might have been if he had not lost it. It is certainly perfectly natural to understand the phrase "presented in space" in such a way that if, in the sense illustrated, a pain is felt *in* a particular place, that pain is "presented in space." And yet of pains it would be quite unnatural to say that they are "to be met with in space," for the same reason as in the case of after-images or double images. It is quite conceivable that another person should feel a pain exactly like one which I feel, but there is an absurdity in supposing that he could feel *numerically the same* pain which I feel. And pains are in fact a typical example of the sort of "things" of which philosophers say that they are *not* "external" to our minds, but "within" them. Of any pain which *I* feel they would say that it is necessarily *not* external to my mind but *in* it.

And finally it is, I think, worth while to mention one other class of "things," which are certainly not "external" objects and certainly not "to be met with in space," in the sense with which I am concerned, but which yet some philosophers would be inclined to say are "presented in space," though they are not "presented in space" in quite the same sense in which pains, double images, and negative after-images of the sort I described are so. If you look at an electric light and then close your eyes, it sometimes happens that you see, for some little time, against the dark background which you usually see when your eyes are shut, a bright patch similar in shape to the light at which you have just been looking. Such a bright patch, if you see one, is another example of what some psychologists have called "after-images" and others "after-sensations"; but, unlike the negative after-images of which I spoke before, it is seen when your eyes are shut. Of such an after-image, seen with closed eyes, some philosophers might be inclined to say that this image too was "presented in space," although it is certainly not "to be met with in space." They would be inclined to say that it is "presented in space," because it certainly is presented as at some little distance from the person who is seeing it: and how can a thing be presented as at some little distance from me, without being "presented in space"? Yet there is an important difference between such after-images, seen with closed eyes, and after-images of the sort I previously described—a

difference which might lead other philosophers to deny that these after-images, seen with closed eyes, are "presented in space" at all. It is a difference which can be expressed by saying that when your eyes are shut, you are not seeing any part of *physical* space at all—of the space which is referred to when we talk of "things which are to be met with in *space*." An after-image seen with closed eyes certainly is presented in *a* space, but it may be questioned whether it is proper to say that it is presented in *space*.

It is clear, then, I think, that by no means everything which can naturally be said to be "presented in space" can also be naturally said to be "a thing which is to be met with in space." Some of the "things," which are presented in space, are very emphatically *not* to be met with in space: or, to use another phrase, which may be used to convey the same notion, they are emphatically *not* "physical realities" at all. The conception "presented in space" is therefore, in one respect, much wider than the conception "to be met with in space": many "things" fall under the first conception which do not fall under the second—many after-images, one at least of the pair of "images" seen whenever anyone sees double, and most bodily pains, are "presented in space," though none of them are to be met with in space. From the fact that a "thing" is presented in space, it by no means follows that it is to be met with in space. But just as the first conception is, in one respect, wider than the second, so, in another, the second is wider than the first. For there are many "things" to be met with in space, of which it is not true that they are presented in space. From the fact that a "thing" is to be met with in space, it by no means follows that it is presented in space. I have taken "to be met with in space" to imply, as I think it naturally may, that a "thing" *might be* perceived; but from the fact that a thing *might* be perceived, it does not follow that is *is* perceived; and if it is not actually perceived, then it will not be presented in space. It is characteristic of the sorts of "things," including shadows, which I have described as "to be met with in space," that there is no absurdity in supposing with regard to any one of them which *is*, at a given time, perceived, both (1) that it might have existed at that very time, without being perceived; (2) that it might have existed at another time, without being perceived at that other time; and (3) that during the whole period of its existence, it need not have been perceived at any time at all. There is, therefore, no absurdity in supposing that many things, which were at one time to be met with in space, never were "presented" at any time at all, and that many things which *are* to be met with in space now, are not now "presented" and also never were and never will be. To use a Kantian phrase, the conception of "things which are to be met with in space" embraces not only objects of actual experience, but also objects of *possible* experience; and from the fact that a thing is or was an object of *possible* experience, it by no means follows that it either was or is or will be "presented" at all.

I hope that what I have now said may have served to make clear enough what sorts of "things" I was originally referring to as "things outside us" or "things external to our minds." I said that I thought that Kant's phrase "things that are to be met with in space" indicated fairly clearly the sorts of "things" in question; and I have tried to make the range clearer still, by pointing out that this phrase only serves the purpose, if (*a*) you understand it in a sense, in which many "things," e.g. after images, double images, bodily pains, which might be said to be "presented in space," are nevertheless *not* to be reckoned as "things that are to be met with in space," and (*b*) you realize clearly that there is no contradiction in supposing that there have been and are "to be met with in space" things which never have been, are not now, and never will be perceived, nor in supposing that among those of them which have at some time been perceived many existed at times at which they were not being perceived. I think it will now be clear to everyone that, since I do not reckon as "external things" after-images, double images, and bodily pains, I also should not reckon as "external things," any of the "images" which we often "see with the mind's eye" when we are awake, nor any of those which we see when we are asleep and dreaming; and also that I was so using the expression "external" that from the fact that a man was at a given time

having a visual hallucination, it will follow that he was seeing at that time something which was *not* "external" to his mind, and from the fact that he was at a given time having an auditory hallucination, it will follow that he was at the time hearing a sound which was *not* "external" to his mind. But I certainly have not made my use of these phrases, "external to our minds" and "to be met with in space," so clear that in the case of every kind of "thing" which might be suggested, you would be able to tell at once whether I should or should not reckon it as "external to our minds" and "to be met with in space." For instance, I have said nothing which makes it quite clear whether a reflection which I see in a looking-glass is or is not to be regarded as "a thing that is to be met with in space" and "external to our minds," nor have I said anything which makes it quite clear whether the sky is or is not to be so regarded. In the case of the sky, everyone, I think, would feel that it was quite inappropriate to talk of it as "a thing that is to be met with in space"; and most people, I think, would feel a strong reluctance to affirm, without qualification, that reflections which people see in looking-glasses are "to be met with in space." And yet neither the sky nor reflections seen in mirrors are in the same position as bodily pains or after-images in the respect which I have emphasized as a reason for saying of these latter that they are *not* to be met with in space—namely that there is an absurdity in supposing that *the very same* pain which I feel could be felt by someone else or that *the very same* after-image which I see could be seen by someone else. In the case of reflections in mirrors we should quite naturally, in certain circumstances, use language which implies that another person may see the same reflection which we see. We might quite naturally say to a friend: "Do you see that reddish reflection in the water there? I can't make out what it's a reflection of," just as we might say, pointing to a distant hill-side: "Do you see that white speck on the hill over there? I can't make out what it is." And in the case of the sky, it is quite obviously *not* absurd to say that other people see it as well as I.

It must, therefore, be admitted that I have not made my use of the phrase "things to be met with in space," nor therefore that of "external to our minds," which the former was used to explain, so clear that in the case of every kind of "thing" which may be mentioned, there will be no doubt whatever as to whether things of that kind are or are not "to be met with in space" or "external to our minds." But this lack of a clear-cut definition of the expression "things that are to be met with in space," does not, so far as I can see, matter for my present purpose. For my present purpose it is, I think, sufficient if I make clear, in the case of many kinds of things, that I am so using the phrase "things that are to be met with in space," that, in the case of each of these kinds, from the proposition that there are things of that kind it *follows* that there are things to be met with in space. And I have, in fact, given a list (though by no means an exhaustive one) of the kinds of things which are related to my use of the expression "things that are to be met with in space" in this way. I mentioned among others the bodies of men and of animals, plants, stars, houses, chairs, and shadows; and I want now to emphasize that I am so using "things to be met with in space" that, in the case of each of these kinds of "things," from the proposition that there are "things" of that kind it *follows* that there are things to be met with in space: e.g. from the proposition that there are plants or that plants exist it *follows* that there are things to be met with in space, from the proposition that shadows exist, it *follows* that there are things to be met with in space, and so on, in the case of all the kinds of "things" which I mentioned in my first list. That this should be clear is sufficient for my purpose, because, if it is clear, then it will also be clear that, as I implied before, if you have proved that two plants exist, or that a plant and a dog exist, or that a dog and a shadow exist, etc. etc., you will *ipso facto* have proved that there are things to be met with in space: you will not require *also* to give a separate proof that from the proposition that there are plants it *does* follow that there are things to be met with in space.

Now with regard to the expression "things that are to be met with in space" I think it will readily be believed that I may be using it in a sense such that no proof is required that from "plants exist" there follows "there are things to

be met with in space"; but with regard to the phrase "things external to our minds" I think the case is different. People may be inclined to say: "I can see quite clearly that from the proposition 'At least two dogs exist at the present moment' there *follows* the proposition 'At least two things are to be met with in space at the present moment,' so that if you can prove that there are two dogs in existence at the present moment you will *ipso facto* have proved that two things at least are to be met with in space at the present moment. I can see that you do not also require a separate proof that from 'Two dogs exist' 'Two things are to be met with in space ' *does* follow; it is quite obvious that there couldn't be a dog which wasn't to be met with in space. But it is not by any means so clear to me that if you can prove that there are two dogs or two shadows, you will *ipso facto* have proved that there are two things *external to our minds*. Isn't it possible that a dog, though it certainly must be 'to be met with in space', might *not* be an external object—an object external to our minds? Isn't a separate proof required that anything that is to be met with in space must be external to our minds? Of course, if you are using 'external' as a mere synonym for 'to be met with in space', no proof will be required that dogs are external objects: in that case, if you can prove that two dogs exist, you will *ipso facto* have proved that there are some external things. But I find it difficult to believe that you, or anybody else, do really use 'external' as a mere synonym for 'to be met with in space'; and if you don't, isn't some proof required that whatever is to be met with in space must be external to our minds?"

Now Kant, as we saw, asserts that the phrases "outside of us" or "external" are in fact used in two very different senses; and with regard to one of these two senses, that which he calls the "transcendental" sense, and which he tries to explain by saying that it is a sense in which "external" means "existing *as a thing in itself* distinct from us," it is notorious that he himself held that things which are to be met with in space are *not* "external" in that sense. There is, therefore, according to him, *a* sense of "external," a sense in which the word has been commonly used by philosophers—such that, if "external" be used in that sense, then from the proposition "Two dogs exist" it will *not* follow that there are some external things. What this supposed sense is I do not think that Kant himself ever succeeded in explaining clearly; nor do I know of any reason for supposing that philosophers ever have used "external" in a sense, such that in *that* sense things that are to be met with in space are *not* external. But how about the other sense, in which, according to Kant, the word "external" has been commonly used—that which he calls "empirically external"? How is this conception related to the conception "to be met with in space"? It may be noticed that, in the passage which I quoted (A 373), Kant himself does not tell us at all clearly what he takes to be the proper answer to this question. He only makes the rather odd statement that, in order to remove all uncertainty as to the conception "empirically external," he will distinguish objects to which it applies from those which might be called "external" in the transcendental sense, by "calling them outright things which are *to be met with in space*." These odd words certainly suggest, as one possible interpretation of them, that in Kant's opinion the conception "empirically external" is *identical* with the conception "to be met with in space"—that he does think that "external," when used in this second sense, is a mere synonym for "to be met with in space." But, if this is his meaning, I do find it very difficult to believe that he is right. Have philosophers, in fact, ever used "external" as a mere synonym for "to be met with in space"? Does he himself do so?

I do not think they have, nor that he does himself; and, in order to explain how they have used it, and how the two conceptions "external to our minds" and "to be met with in space" are related to one another, I think it is important expressly to call attention to a fact which hitherto I have only referred to incidentally: namely the fact that those who talk of certain things as "external to" our minds, do, in general, as we should naturally expect, talk of other "things," with which they wish to contrast the first, as "in" our minds. It has, of course, been often pointed out that when "in" is thus used, followed by "my mind," "your mind," "his mind," etc., "in" is being used

metaphorically. And there are some metaphorical uses of "in," followed by such expressions, which occur in common speech, and which we all understand quite well. For instance, we all understand such expressions as "I had you in mind, when I made that arrangement" or "I had you in mind, when I said that there are some people who can't bear to touch a spider." In these cases "I was thinking of you" can be used to mean the same as "I had you in mind." But it is quite certain that this particular metaphorical use of "in" is not the one in which philosophers are using it when they contrast what is 'in' my mind with what is "external" to it. On the contrary, in their use of "external," you will be external to my mind even at a moment when I have you in mind. If we want to discover what this peculiar metaphorical use of "*in* my mind" is, which is such that nothing, which is, in the sense we are now concerned with, "external" to my mind, can ever be "in" it, we need, I think, to consider instances of the sort of "things" which they would say are "in" my mind in this special sense. I have already mentioned three such instances, which are, I think, sufficient for my present purpose: any bodily pain which I feel, any after-image which I see with my eyes shut, and any image which I "see" when I am asleep and dreaming, are typical examples of the sort of "thing" of which philosophers have spoken as "*in* my mind." And there is no doubt, I think, that when they have spoken of such things as my body, a sheet of paper, a star—in short "physical objects" generally—as "external," they have meant to emphasize some important difference which they feel to exist between such things as these and such "things" as a pain, an after-image seen with closed eyes, and a dream-image. But *what* difference? What difference do they feel to exist between a bodily pain which I feel or an after-image which I see with closed eyes, on the one hand, and my body itself, on the other—what difference which leads them to say that whereas the bodily pain and the after-image are "in" my mind, my body itself is *not* "in" my mind—not even when I am feeling it and seeing it or thinking of it? I have already said that one difference which there is between the two, is that my body is to be met with in space, whereas the bodily pain and the after-image are not. But I think it would be quite wrong to say that this is *the* difference which has led philosophers to speak of the two latter as "in" my mind, and of my body as *not* "in" my mind.

The question what the difference is which has led them to speak in this way, is not, I think, at all an easy question to answer; but I am going to try to give, in brief outline, what I *think* is a right answer.

It should, I think, be noted, first of all, that the use of the word "mind," which is being adopted when it is said that any bodily pains which I feel are "in my mind," is one which is not quite in accordance with any usage common in ordinary speech, although we are very familiar with it in philosophy. Nobody, I think, would say that bodily pains which I feel are "in my mind," unless he was also prepared to say that it is *with* my mind that I feel bodily pains; and to say this latter is, I think, not quite in accordance with common non-philosophic usage. It is natural enough to say that it is with my mind that I remember, and think, and imagine, and feel *mental* pains—e.g. disappointment, but not, I think, quite so natural to say that it is with my mind that I feel *bodily* pains, e.g. a severe headache; and perhaps even less natural to say that it is with my mind that I see and hear and smell and taste. There is, however, a well-established philosophical usage according to which seeing, hearing, smelling, tasting, and having a bodily pain are just as much *mental* occurrences or processes as are remembering, or thinking, or imagining. This usage was, I think, adopted by philosophers, because they saw a real resemblance between such statements as "I saw a cat," "I heard a clap of thunder," "I smelt a strong smell of onions," "My finger smarted horribly," on the one hand, and such statements as "I remembered having seen him," "I was thinking out a plan of action," "I pictured the scene to myself," "I felt bitterly disappointed," on the other—a resemblance which puts all these statements in one class together, as contrasted with other statements in which "I" or "my" is used, such as, e.g., "I was less than four feet high," "I was lying on my back," "My hair was very long." What is the resemblance in question? It is a resemblance which might be ex-

pressed by saying that all the first eight statements are the sort of statements which furnish data for psychology, while the three latter are not. It is also a resemblance which may be expressed, in a way now common among philosophers, by saying that in the case of all the first eight statements, if we make the statement more specific by adding a date, we get a statement such that, if it is true, then it *follows* that I was "having an experience" at the date in question, whereas this does not hold for the three last statements. For instance, if it is true that I saw a cat between 12 noon and 5 minutes past, today, it *follows* that I was "having some experience" between 12 noon and 5 minutes past, today; whereas from the proposition that I was less than four feet high in December 1877, it does not *follow* that I had any experiences in December 1877. But this philosophic use of "having an experience" is one which itself needs explanation, since it is not identical with any use of the expression that is established in common speech. An explanation, however, which is, I think, adequate for the purpose, can be given by saying that a philosopher, who was following this usage, would say that I was at a given time "having an experience" if and only if either (1) I was conscious at the time or (2) I was dreaming at the time or (3) something else was true of me at the time, which resembled what is true of me when I am conscious and when I am dreaming, in a certain very obvious respect in which what is true of me when I am dreaming resembles what is true of me when I am conscious, and in which what would be true of me, if at any time, for instance, I had a vision, would resemble both. This explanation is, of course, in some degree vague; but I think it is clear enough for our purpose. It amounts to saying that, in this philosophic usage of "having an experience," it would be said of me that I was, at a given time, having *no* experience, if I was at the time neither conscious nor dreaming nor having a vision nor *anything else of the sort*; and, of course, this is vague in so far as it has not been specified what else would be *of the sort*: this is left to be gathered from the instances given. But I think this is sufficient: often at night when I am asleep, I am neither conscious nor dreaming nor having a vision nor *anything else of the sort*—that is to say, I am having no experiences. If this explanation of this philosophic usage of "having an experience" is clear enough, then I think that what has been meant by saying that any pain which I feel or any after-image which I see with my eyes closed is "*in* my mind," can be explained by saying that what is meant is neither more nor less than that there would be a contradiction in supposing *that very same pain* or *that very same after-image* to have existed at a time at which I was having no experience; or, in other words, that from the proposition, with regard to any time, that *that* pain or *that* after-image existed at that time, it *follows* that I was having some experience at the time in question. And if so, then we can say that the felt difference between bodily pains which I feel and after-images which I see, on the one hand, and my body on the other, which had led philosophers to say that any such pain or after-image is "*in* my mind," whereas my body *never* is but is always "outside of" or "external to" my mind, is just this, that whereas there is a contradiction in supposing a pain which I feel or an after-image which I see to exist at a time when I am having no experience, there is no contradiction in supposing my body to exist at a time when I am having no experience; and we can even say, I think, that just this and nothing more is what they have meant by these puzzling and misleading phrases "in my mind" and "external to my mind."

But now, if to say of anything, e.g. my body, that it is external to *my* mind, means merely that from a proposition to the effect that it existed at a specified time, there in no case follows the further proposition that *I* was having an experience at the time in question, then to say of anything that is external to *our* minds, will mean similarly that from a proposition to the effect that it existed at a specified time, it in no case follows that any of *us* were having experiences at the time in question. And if by *our* minds be meant, as is, I think, usually meant, the minds of human beings living on the earth, then it will follow that any pains which animals may feel, any after-images they may see, any experiences they may have, though not external to *their* minds, yet are external to *ours*. And this at once makes plain

how different is the conception "external to our minds" from the conception "to be met with in space"; for, of course, pains which animals feel or after-images which they see are no more to be met with in space than are pains which *we* feel or after-images which *we* see. From the proposition that there are external objects—objects that are not in any of *our* minds, it does *not* follow that there are things to be met with in space; and hence "external to our minds" is not a mere synonym for "to be met with in space": that is to say, "external to our minds" and "to be met with in space" are two different conceptions. And the true relation between these conceptions seems to me to be this. We have already seen that there are ever so many kinds of "things," such that, in the case of each of these things, from the proposition that there is at least one thing of that kind there *follows* the proposition that there is at least one thing to be met with in space: e.g. this follows from "There is at least one star," from "There is at least one human body," from "There is at least one shadow," etc. And I think we can say that of every kind of thing of which this is true, it is also true that from the proposition that there is at least one "thing" of that kind there *follows* the proposition that there is at least one thing external to our minds: e.g. from "There is at least one star" there follows not only "There is at least one thing to be met with in space" but also "There is at least one external thing," and similarly in all other cases. My reason for saying this is as follows. Consider any kind of thing, such that anything of that kind, if there is anything of it, must be "to be met with in space": e.g. consider the kind "soap-bubble." If I say of anything which I am perceiving, "That is a soap-bubble," I am, it seems to me, certainly implying that there would be no contradiction in asserting that it existed before I perceived it and that it will continue to exist, even if I cease to perceive it. This seems to me to be part of what is meant by saying that it is a real soap-bubble, as distinguished, for instance, from an hallucination of a soap-bubble. Of course, it by no means follows, that if it really is a soap-bubble, it did in fact exist before I perceived it or will continue to exist after I cease to perceive it: soap-bubbles are an example of a kind of "physical object" and "thing to be met with in space," in the case of which it is notorious that particular specimens of the kind often do exist only so long as they are perceived by a particular person. But a thing which I perceive would not be a soap-bubble unless its existence at any given time were *logically independent* of my perception of it at that time; unless that is to say, from the proposition, with regard to a particular time, that it existed at that time, it *never* follows that I perceived it at that time. But, if it is true that it would not be a soap-bubble, unless it *could* have existed at any given time without being perceived by me at that time, it is certainly also true that it would not be a soap-bubble, unless it *could* have existed at any given time, without its being true that I was having any experience of any kind at the time in question: it would not be a soap-bubble, unless, whatever time you take, from the proposition that it existed at that time it does *not* follow that I was having any experience at that time. That is to say, from the proposition with regard to anything which I am perceiving that it is a soap-bubble, there *follows* the proposition that it is external to *my* mind. But if, when I say that anything which I perceive is a soap-bubble, I am implying that it is external to *my* mind, I am, I think, certainly also implying that it is also external to all other minds: I am implying that it is not a thing of a sort such that things of that sort *can* only exist at a time when somebody is having an experience. I think, therefore, that from any proposition of the form "There's a soap-bubble!" there does really *follow* the proposition "There's an external object!" "There's an object external to *all* our minds!" And, if this is true of the kind "soap-bubble," it is certainly also true of any other kind (including the kind "unicorn") which is such that, if there are any things of that kind, it follows that there are *some* things to be met with in space.

I think, therefore, that in the case of all kinds of "things," which are such that if there is a pair of things, both of which are of one of these kinds, or a pair of things one of which is of one of them and one of them of another, then it will follow at once that there are some things to be met with in space, it is true also that if I can prove that there are a pair of things, one of which is of one of these kinds and another

of another, or a pair both of which are of one of them, then I shall have proved *ipso facto* that there are at least two "things outside of us." That is to say, if I can prove that there exist now both a sheet of paper and a human hand, I shall have proved that there are now "things outside of us"; if I can prove that there exist now both a shoe and sock, I shall have proved that there are now "things outside of us"; etc.; and similarly I shall have proved it, if I can prove that there exist now two sheets of paper, or two human hands, or two shoes, or two socks, etc. Obviously, then, there are thousands of different things such that, if, at any time, I can prove any one of them, I shall have proved the existence of things outside of us. Cannot I prove any of these things?

It seems to me that, so far from its being true, as Kant declares to be his opinion, that there is only one possible proof of the existence of things outside of us, namely the one which he has given, I can now give a large number of different proofs, each of which is a perfectly rigorous proof; and that at many other times I have been in a position to give many others. I can prove now, for instance, that two human hands exist. How? By holding up my two hands, and saying, as I make a certain gesture with the right hand, "Here is one hand," and adding, as I make a certain gesture with the left, "and here is another." And if, by doing this, I have proved *ipso facto* the existence of external things, you will see that I can also do it now in numbers of other ways: there is no need to multiply examples.

But did I prove just now that two human hands were then in existence? I do want to insist that I did; that the proof which I gave was a perfectly rigorous one; and that it is perhaps impossible to give a better or more rigorous proof of anything whatever. Of course, it would not have been a proof unless three conditions were satisfied; namely (1) unless the premiss which I adduced as proof of the conclusion was different from the conclusion I adduced it to prove; (2) unless the premiss which I adduced was something which I *knew* to be the case, and not merely something which I believed but which was by no means certain, or something which, though in fact true, I did not know to be so; and (3) unless the conclusion did really follow from the premiss. But all these three conditions were in fact satisfied by my proof. (1) The premiss which I adduced in proof was quite certainly different from the conclusion, for the conclusion was merely "Two human hands exist at this moment"; but the premiss was something far more specific than this—something which I expressed by showing you my hands, making certain gestures, and saying the words "Here is one hand, and here is another." It is quite obvious that the two were different, because it is quite obvious that the conclusion might have been true, even if the premiss had been false. In asserting the premiss I was asserting much more than I was asserting in asserting the conclusion. (2) I certainly did at the moment *know* that which I expressed by the combination of certain gestures with saying the words "There is one hand and here is another." I *knew* that there was one hand in the place indicated by combining a certain gesture with my first utterance of "here" and that there was another in the different place indicated by combining a certain gesture with my second utterance of "here." How absurd it would be to suggest that I did not know it, but only believed it, and that perhaps it was not the case! You might as well suggest that I do not know that I am now standing up and talking— that perhaps after all I'm not, and that it's not quite certain that I am! And finally (3) it is quite certain that the conclusion did follow from the premiss. This is as certain as it is that if there is one hand here and another here *now*, then it follows that there are two hands in existence *now*.

My proof, then, of the existence of things outside of us did satisfy three of the conditions necessary for a rigorous proof. Are there any other conditions necessary for a rigorous proof, such that perhaps it did not satisfy one of them? Perhaps there may be; I do not know; but I do want to emphasize that, so far as I can see, we all of us do constantly take proofs of this sort as absolutely conclusive proofs of certain conclusions—as finally settling certain questions, as to which we were previously in doubt. Suppose, for instance, it were a question whether there were as many as three misprints on a certain page in a certain book. A says there are, B is inclined to doubt it. How could

A prove that he is right? Surely he *could* prove it by taking the book, turning to the page, and pointing to three separate places on it, saying "There's one misprint here, another here, and another here": surely that is a method by which it *might* be proved! Of course, A would not have proved, by doing this, that there were at least three misprints on the page in question, unless it was certain that there was a misprint in each of the places to which he pointed. But to say that he *might* prove it in this way, is to say that it *might* be certain that there was. And if such a thing as that could ever be certain, then assuredly it was certain just now that there was one hand in one of the two places I indicated and another in the other.

I did, then, just now, give a proof that there were *then* external objects; and obviously, if I did, I could *then* have given many other proofs of the same sort that there were external objects *then*, and could now give many proofs of the same sort that there are external objects *now*.

But, if what I am asked to do is to prove that external objects have existed *in the past*, then I can give many different proofs of this also, but proofs which are in important respects of a different *sort* from those just given. And I want to emphasize that, when Kant says it is a scandal not to be able to give a proof of the existence of external objects, a proof of their existence in the past would certainly *help* to remove the scandal of which he is speaking. He says that, if it occurs to anyone to question their existence, we ought to be able to confront him with a satisfactory proof. But by a person who questions their existence, he certainly means not merely a person who questions whether any exist at the moment of speaking, but a person who questions whether any have *ever* existed; and a proof that some have existed in the past would certainly therefore be relevant to *part* of what such a person is questioning. How then can I prove that there have been external objects in the past? Here is one proof. I can say: "I held up two hands above this desk not very long ago; therefore two hands existed not very long ago; therefore at least two external objects have existed at some time in the past, Q.E.D." This is a perfectly good proof, provided I *know* what is asserted in the premiss. But I *do* know that I held up two hands above this desk not very long ago. As a matter of fact, in this case you all know it too. There's no doubt whatever that I did. Therefore I have given a perfectly conclusive proof that external objects have existed in the past; and you will all see at once that, if this is a conclusive proof, I could have given many others of the same sort, and could now give many others. But it is also quite obvious that this sort of proof differs in important respects from the sort of proof I gave just now that there were two hands existing *then*.

I have, then, given two conclusive proofs of the existence of external objects. The first was a proof that two human hands existed at the time when I gave the proof; the second was a proof that two human hands had existed at a time previous to that at which I gave the proof. These proofs were of a different sort in important respects. And I pointed out that I could have given, then, many other conclusive proofs of both sorts. It is also obvious that I could give many others of both sorts now. So that, if these are the sort of proof that is wanted, nothing is easier than to prove the existence of external objects.

But now I am perfectly well aware that, in spite of all that I have said, many philosophers will still feel that I have not given any satisfactory proof of the point in question. And I want briefly, in conclusion, to say something as to why this dissatisfaction with my proofs should be felt.

One reason why, is, I think, this. Some people understand "proof of an external world" as including a proof of things which I haven't attempted to prove and haven't proved. It is not quite easy to say *what* it is that they want proved—*what* it is that is such that unless they got a proof of it, they would not say that they had a proof of the existence of external things; but I can make an approach to explaining what they want by saying that if I had proved the propositions which I used as *premisses* in my two proofs, then they would perhaps admit that I had proved the existence of external things, but, in the absence of such a proof (which, of course, I have neither given nor attempted to give), they will say that I have not given what they mean by a proof of the existence of ex-

ternal things. In other words, they want a proof of what I assert *now* when I hold up my hands and say "Here's one hand and here's another"; and, in the other case, they want a proof of what I assert *now* when I say "I did hold up two hands above this desk just now." Of course, what they really want is not merely a proof of these two propositions, but something like a general statement as to how *any* propositions of this sort may be proved. This, of course, I haven't given; and I do not believe it can be given: if this is what is meant by proof of the existence of external things, I do not believe that any proof of the existence of external things is possible. Of course, in some cases what might be called a proof of propositions which seem like these can be got. If one of you suspected that one of my hands was artificial he might be said to get a proof of my proposition "Here's one hand, and here's another," by coming up and examining the suspected hand close up, perhaps touching and pressing it, and so establishing that it really was a human hand. But I do not believe that any proof is possible in nearly all cases. How am I to prove now that "Here's one hand, and here's another"? I do not believe I can do it. In order to do it, I should need to prove for one thing, as Descartes pointed out, that I am not now dreaming. But how can I prove that I am not? I have, no doubt, conclusive reasons for asserting that I am not now dreaming; I have conclusive evidence that I am awake: but that is a very different thing from being able to prove it. I could not tell you what all my evidence is; and I should require to do this at least, in order to give you a proof.

But another reason why some people would feel dissatisfied with my proofs is, I think, not merely that they want a proof of something which I haven't proved, but that they think that, if I cannot give such extra proofs, then the proofs that I have given are not conclusive proofs at all. And this, I think, is a definite mistake. They would say: "If you cannot prove your premiss that here is one hand and here is another, then you do not know it. But you yourself have admitted that, if you did not know it, then your proof was not conclusive. Therefore your proof was not, as you say it was, a conclusive proof." This view that, if I cannot prove such things as these, I do not know them, is, I think, the view that Kant was expressing in the sentence which I quoted at the beginning of this lecture, when he implies that so long as we have no proof of the existence of external things, their existence must be accepted merely on *faith*. He means to say, I think, that if I cannot prove that there is a hand here, I must accept it merely as a matter of faith—I cannot know it. Such a view, though it has been very common among philosophers, can, I think, be shown to be wrong— though shown only by the use of premisses which are not known to be true, unless we do know of the existence of external things. I can know things, which I cannot prove; and among things which I certainly did know, even if (as

I think) I could not prove them, were the premisses of my two proofs. I should say, therefore, that those, if any, who are dissatisfied with these proofs merely on the ground that I did not know their premisses, have no good reason for their dissatisfaction.

NOTES

1. B xxxix, note: Kemp Smith, p. 34. The German words are *"so bleibt es immer ein Skandal der Philosophie . . . , das Dasein der Dinge ausser uns . . . bloss auf* Glauben *annehmen zu müssen, und wenn es jemand einfällt es zu bezweifeln, ihm keinen genugtuenden Beweis entgegenstellen zu können."*

32 / Ludwig Wittgenstein (1889–1951)
CAUSE AND EFFECT: INTUITIVE AWARENESS

If someone says: "I am frightened, because he looks so threatening"—this looks as if it were a case of recognizing a cause immediately without repeated experiments.

Russell said that before recognizing something as a cause through repeated experience, we would have to recognize something as a cause by intuition.[1]

Isn't that like saying: Before recognizing something as 2m long by measuring it, we have to recognize something as 1m long by intuition?

For what if that intuition is contradicted by repeated experiments? Who is right then?

And what does the intuition tell us about the experience which we recognize as the cause? Is there anything more to it than a reaction of ours to the object: the cause?

Don't we recognize immediately that the pain is produced by the blow we have received? Isn't this the cause and can there be any doubt about it?—But isn't it quite possible to suppose that in certain cases we are deceived about this? And later recognize the deception? It seems as though something hits us and at the same time we feel a pain. (Sometimes we think we are causing a sound by making a certain movement and then realize that it is quite independent of us.)

Certainly there is in such cases a genuine experience which can be called "experience of the cause." But not because it infallibly shows us the cause; rather because *one* root of the cause-effect language-game is to be found here, in our looking out for a cause.

We react to the cause.

Calling something "the cause" is like pointing and saying: "*He's* to blame!"

English translation by Peter Winch. Reprinted by permission from *Philosophia* 6 (1976).

We instinctively get rid of the cause if we don't want the effect. We instinctively look from what has been hit to what has hit it. (I am assuming that we do this.)

Now suppose I were to say that when we speak of cause and effect we always have in mind a comparison with impact; that this is the prototype of cause and effect? Would this mean that we had *recognized* impact as a cause? Imagine a language in which people always said "impact" instead of "cause."

Think of two different kinds of plant, A and B, both of which yield seeds; the seeds of both kinds look exactly the same and even after the most careful investigation we can find no difference between them. But the seeds of an A-plant always produce more A-plants, the seeds of a B-plant, more B-plants. In this situation we can predict what sort of plant will grow out of such a seed only if we know which plant it has come from.—Are we to be satisfied with this; or should we say: "There *must* be a difference in the seeds themselves, otherwise they *couldn't* produce different plants; their previous histories on their own *can't* cause their further development unless their histories have left traces in the seeds themselves"?

But now what if we don't discover any difference between the seeds? And the fact is: It wasn't from the peculiarities of either seed that we made the prediction but from its previous history.—If I say: the history can't be the cause of the development, then this doesn't mean that I can't predict the development from the previous history, since that's what I do. It means rather that we don't call *that* a "causal connection," that this isn't a case of predicting the effect from the cause.

And to protest: "There *must* be a difference in the seeds, even if we don't discover it," doesn't alter the facts, it only shows what a powerful urge we have to see everything in terms of cause and effect.[2]

When people talk about graphology, physiognomics and suchlike they constantly say: ". . . clearly character must be expressed in handwriting *somehow* . . ." "Must": that means we are going to apply this picture come what may.

(One might even say that philosophy is the grammar of the words "must" and "can," for that is how it shows what is a priori and what a posteriori.)

And then you can imagine that the seed of a plant A produces a plant B and that the seed of this, which is exactly like that of the first, produces an A-plant, and so on alternately—although we don't know *"why,"* etc.

And now suppose that in the foregoing example someone had at last succeeded in discovering a difference between the seed of an A-plant and the seed of a B-plant: he would no doubt say: "There, you see, it just isn't possible for *one seed* to grow into two different plants." What if I were to retort: "How do you know that the characteristic you have discovered is not completely irrelevant? How do you know *that* has anything to do with which of the two plants grows out of the seed?"

On cause and effect, intuitive awareness:

A sound seems to come from over there, even before I have investigated its (physical) source. In the cinema the sound of speech seems to come from the mouth of the figures on the screen.

What does this experience consist in? Perhaps in the fact that we involuntarily look towards a particular spot—the apparent source of the sound—when we hear a sound. And in the cinema no one looks towards where the microphone is.

The basic form of our game must be one in which there is no such thing as doubt.—What makes us sure of this? It can't surely be a matter of historical certainty.

"The basic form of the game can't include doubt." What we are doing here above all is to *Imagine* a basic form: a possibility, indeed a *very important* possibility. (We very often confuse what is an important possibility with historical reality.)

"Doubting"—I might say—"has to come to an end somewhere." At some point we have to say—without doubting: *"that* results from *this* cause."

Similarly: we say: "Take this chair" and it doesn't occur to us that we might be mistaken, that perhaps it isn't really a chair, that later experience may show us something different. Here one game is played that does not include the possibility of a mistake, and another more complicated one which does include it.

Isn't this how it is: It is very fundamental to the game we play that we utter certain words and regularly *act* according to them.

Doubt is a moment of hesitation and is, *essentially*, an exception to the rule.

We might say: It is essential to street traffic that in the great majority of cases a car, or a pedestrian, travels in a constant line towards a destination and does *not* move about like somebody who is changing his mind at every moment, going first from A towards B, then turning round and taking a few steps back, then turning round again, and so on . . . —And to say "This is an essential feature of street traffic" means: it is an important and characteristic feature; if this were different, then a tremendous amount would change.

So what does it mean to say: at first the game has to start without including doubt; doubt can only come into it subsequently? Why *shouldn't* doubting be there right from the start? But wait a minute—what does doubting look like? The point is—whatever it feels like or however it is expressed, its *surroundings* are quite different from those we are familiar with. (For, since doubt is an exception, the rule is its environment.) (Do these eyes have any expression if they are not part of a face?)

As things are, the *reasons* for doubting are reasons for leaving a familiar track.

Our world looks quite different if we surround it with different possibilities.

We teach a child: "*That's* a chair." Could we teach him right at the start to doubt whether this is a chair? Someone will say: "That's impossible. He must first know what a chair is if he is to be in a position to doubt whether this is one." But isn't it conceivable that the child should learn right from the start to say: "That looks like a chair—but is it really one?—" Or at any rate that he should learn from the beginning to say in a doubting tone of voice: "I *think* there's a chair here" and not in an affirmative tone: "There's a chair here."

Now what about this remark: "We can't begin with doubting"? A "can't" of this sort is always fishy.

We may say: Doubting can't be a *necessary* element without which the game is obviously incomplete and incorrect. For in your game the criteria for justifying a doubt aren't applied any *differently* than the criteria for the opposite. And the game which includes doubt is simply a more complicated one than a game which does not.

It is easy to think: only the game which includes doubt is *true to nature*.

(If the same fare were charged for both long and short railway journeys—would that be an obviously unjust, absurd arrangement?)

"We can't know whether somebody is in pain? Oh yes we *can*, we can *know* it!"—But that is not to say: "We have 'intuitive knowledge' of these pains." It is simply a—justified—objection against those who say: "We can't *know* . . ." But it isn't to claim the existence of a natural capacity which the others deny.

"The game can't start with doubting"—What we ought to say is: the game *doesn't* start with doubting.—Or else: the "can" has the same justification as it has in the assertion: "Street traffic can't begin with everybody doubting whether to go in this, or rather in that direction; in that case it would never amount to what we call 'traffic' and then we shouldn't call their hesitation 'doubting' either."

A philosopher who protests, "We *KNOW* there's a chair over there!" is simply describing a game. But he *seems* to be saying that I am moved by feelings of unshakeable conviction if I say to someone: "Fetch me that chair."

The game doesn't begin with doubting whether someone has a toothache, because that doesn't—as it were—fit the game's biological function in our life. In its most primitive form it is a reaction to somebody's cries and gestures, a reaction of sympathy or something of the sort. We comfort him, try to help him. We may think that because doubt is a refinement, and in a certain sense too an improvement of the game, the correct thing would surely be to start straight off with doubt. (Just as we may think that, because it is often good to give the reasons for a judgement, the complete justification of a judgement would have to extend the chain of reasons to infinity.)

Let us imagine that doubt and conviction, instead of being expressed in a language, are expressed rather through actions, gestures, demeanour. It might be like this with very primitive people, or with animals. So imagine a mother whose child is crying and holding his cheek. *One* kind of reaction to this is for the mother to try and comfort her child and to nurse him in some way or other. In this case there is nothing corresponding to a doubt whether the child is really in pain. Another case would be this: The usual reaction to the child's complaints is as just described, but under some circumstances the mother behaves sceptically. Perhaps she shakes her head suspiciously, stops comforting and nursing her child—even expresses annoyance and lack of sympathy. But now imagine a mother who is sceptical right from the very beginning: If her child cries, she shrugs her shoulders and shakes her head; sometimes she looks at him inquiringly, examines him; on exceptional occasions she also makes vague attempts to comfort and nurse him.—Were we to encounter such behaviour, we definitely wouldn't call it scepticism; it would strike us as queer and crazy.—"The game can't begin with doubting" means: we shouldn't call it "doubting," if the game began with it.

Consider this question: "Can a match *start* with one of the players winning (or losing) and the game going on from there?" Why shouldn't a procedure that looks like a game start with what usually happens when a game is won or lost? For instance, one of the participants is paid money, congratulated on his success, and so on. However, we won't call this "winning the game" and perhaps we won't call the whole thing a "game." If we were to meet such a practice, it would be "incomprehensible" to us and we should probably not say: "these people win and lose at the *start* of the game."

"*Can* that happen?!—Certainly. Just describe it in detail and you will then see that the procedure you describe can perfectly well be imagined, although you will clearly not apply such and such expressions to it.

"Could the rhyme in a poem come at the beginning of the lines instead of at the end?"

"All right, doubting doesn't have any place in your simple game—but does that mean it is *certain* that he has toothache?" *That* is the game,—And you can, if you want, gather from it how the word "toothache" is being used: what it means.

"What if he is shamming?" But he can't be shamming if the way he acts doesn't count as *shamming* in the game.

"So is it certain there's a chair here?"—Well, don't I have two alternatives: to be certain or to doubt? Doesn't it depend on whether I count something as justifying doubt?

If something doesn't happen as we expected we say: we have *made a mistake*, a wrong assumption. The mistake is a fault; we are reproached for it, reproach ourselves.

Compare that with the following: We determine the mid-point between two places A and B, by making repeated estimates in this way: we say

A   C C'   B
X———————————————————————X

"I assume it lies near C" and I make a mark more or less near the centre.—Then we take the length $\overline{AC}$ starting at B and get point C'. The procedure is then repeated, taking a point roughly halfway between C and C'.—Was the first assumption a mistake? You can call it that if you like—but here this "mistake" is not treated as a fault.

If we don't doubt, we regard this as a mistake, something stupid—doubting is a deeper insight into the nature of the matter: or so it seems.

Representing people (etc.) in perspective strikes us as correct compared with the Egyptian way of drawing them. Of course; after all, people don't really look that!—But must this count as an argument? Who says I want people on paper to look the way they do in reality?

"Anyone who doesn't doubt is simply overlooking the possibility that things might be otherwise!"—Not in the least—if this possibility doesn't exist in his language. (Just as someone who gives or asks for the same wages for long and short periods of work needn't be overlooking anything.) "But then he is just not paying for the work performed!" That's how it *is*.

Why do we call what we recognize immediately by the same name as the one we apply to what we learn from repeated experience of conjunctions? To what extent *is* it the same? (Knowledge which flows from a different source is different knowledge.)

"There are two ways of becoming aware of the existence of a mechanism: first, by *seeing* it, secondly by seeing its effects." Might we not say: the assertion "there is a mechanism of such and such a sort here" is used in two different ways (a) if such a mechanism can be seen—(b) if effects can be discerned of a kind which such a mechanism would produce.

There is reaction which can be called "reacting to the cause."—We also speak of "tracing" the cause; a simple case would be, say, following a string to see who is pulling at it. If I then find him—how do I know that he, his pulling, is the cause of the string's moving? Do I establish this by a series of experiments?

Someone has followed the string and has found who is pulling at it: does he make a further step in concluding: so that was the cause—or did he not just want to discover if someone, and if so who, was pulling at it? Let's imagine once more a language-game simpler than the one we play with the word "cause."

Consider two procedures: in the first somebody who feels a tug on a string, or has some similar sort of experience, follows the string— the mechanism—in this sense finds the *cause*, and perhaps removes it. He may also ask: "Why is this string moving?," or something of the sort. The second case is this: He has noticed that, since his goats have been grazing on that slope, they give less milk. He shakes his head, asks "Why?"—and then makes some experiments. He finds that such and such a fodder is the cause of the phenomenon.

"But aren't these cases both of the same kind: after all he could have made some experiments to determine whether the man who is pulling at the string is really the cause of the movement, whether *he* is not really being moved by the string and this in its turn by some other cause!"—He could have made experiments—but I'm assuming that he does *not*. *This* is the game he plays.

Now what is it I constantly do in such cases? Reason—I feel like saying—presents itself to us as the gauge *par excellence* against which everything that we do, all our language games, measure and judge themselves. We may say: we are so exclusively preoccupied by contemplating a yardstick that we can't allow our gaze

to *rest* on certain phenomena or patterns. We are used, as it were, to "dismissing" these as irrational, as corresponding to a low state of intelligence, etc. The yardstick rivets our attention and keeps distracting us from these phenomena, as it were, making us look beyond. Suppose a certain style of building or behaviour captivates us to such an extent that we can't focus our attention *directly* on another one, but can only glance at it obliquely. (Connected with this: a nice remark of Eddington's about the demonstration of the law of inertia.)

In one case "*He* is the cause" simply means: *he* pulled the string. In the other case it means roughly: those are the conditions that I would have to change in order to get rid of this phenomenon.

"But then how did he come by the idea— how was it even possible to come by the idea— of altering a condition *in order to* get rid of such and such a phenomenon? Surely that presupposes that he first of all senses there is some connection. Thinks there may be a connection: where no connection is to be seen. So he must already have got the idea of such a causal connection." Yes, we can say it presupposes that he looks round for a cause; that he doesn't attend to this phenomenon—but to *another* one.

Intuition. Knowing the cause by intuition. What game is being played with the word "Intuition"? What sort of feat is it supposed to achieve?

The underlying idea is this: Knowing this state of affairs is a state of mind; and *how* this state of mind has come about is irrelevant if all that interests us is that somebody *knows* such and such. Just as headaches can be caused in all sorts of ways, so too with knowing. That such a state should interest us at all in a logical investigation is certainly remarkable. Why should such states concern us? Remember the question "*When* does a man know that (e.g.) someone is in the next room?"—While he is thinking the thought? And if he does think it: throughout all the phases (words) of the thought?

If I say: "I know there is someone in the room" and it turns out that I have made a mistake, then I didn't *know* it—have I made a mistake in introspecting my state of mind then? I looked inside and took something to be a *knowing* when it wasn't.—Or can't I *really* know something like that, but only such facts as: "I see something red," "I am in pain," and the like? That is, we are supposed to use the word "know" only in situations where nobody does use it; in other words, where "I know that p" means nothing, unless perhaps it means the same as "p," and the expression "I don't know that p" is nonsense.

Whatever you do, don't look at the actual use of the words "I know . . ." just look at the words and speculate what might be a fitting use of them.

How does the language-game work then—when do we say we *"know"?* Is it really when we ascertain that we are in a certain state of mind? Isn't it when we have evidence of a certain sort? And then it's a matter of the evidence, without which it isn't knowing.

What is intuition then? Is it a way of experiencing things so as to attain knowledge which we are familiar with in common life? Or is it a chimera, which we make use of only in philosophy? Is the belief that intuition is involved in such and such circumstances comparable to the belief that such and such an illness is produced by an insect sting? (This belief may be true or false, but anyway we are familiar with kinds of case produced like that). Or is this a case where we can say:

Denn eben wo Begriffe fehlen,
Da stellt ein Wort zur rechten Zeit sich ein.[3]

(One could imagine a use of language in which people say: "Mr. Unknown did it" instead of: "It isn't known who did this"—so that they don't have to say there is something they don't know.)

What do we know about intuition? What idea have we of it? It's presumably supposed to be a sort of seeing, recognition at a *single* glance; I wouldn't know what more to say.—"So you do after all know what an intuition is!"—Roughly in the same way as I know what it means "to see a body from all sides at once." I don't want to say that one cannot apply this expression to some process or other, for some good reason or other—but do I therefore know what it means?

"Knowing the cause intuitively" means: *somehow or other* knowing the cause, (experiencing it in a way different from the usual one).—All right, somebody knows it—but what's the good of that,—if his knowing doesn't *prove its worth* in the usual way in the course of time? But then he's no different from someone who has somehow *correctly guessed* the cause. That is: We don't have any concept of this special *knowing* of the cause. We can certainly imagine someone saying, with signs of inspiration, that now he *knows* the cause; but this doesn't prevent us from testing whether what he claims to know is right.

Knowing interests us only within the game.

(It is just as if somebody claimed to have knowledge of human anatomy by intuition; and we say: "We don't doubt it; but if you want to be a doctor, you must pass all the examinations like anybody else.")

Why is it that "doubt must come to an end somewhere"?—Is it because the game would never get started if it were to begin with doubt?

But suppose it began with someone's racking his brains about what the cause is of something or other. How should we have to conceive this brain-racking, these reflections? Well, quite simply. It's just a matter of *searching* for, and eventually finding some object (the cause). So what's the point of saying that the game can't begin with doubt?

Doubt has to have some physiognomy. If someone doubts, the question is: what does his doubt look like? What, e.g., does the inquiry that he initiates look like?—Do you merely want to say: the game can't begin with someone's saying: "We can never *know* what the cause of something is"?—But why shouldn't he say *that* too; as long as he confidently makes the next step? But in that case there's no need to speak of the *beginnings* of the game, and we can say: The game of "looking for the cause" *consists* above all in a certain practice, a certain method. Within it something that we call doubt and uncertainty plays a role, but this is a second-order feature. In an analogous way it is characteristic of how a sewing machine functions that its parts may wear out and get bent, and its axles may wobble in their bearings, but still this is a second-order characteristic compared with the normal working of the machine.

Imagine this strange possibility: up to now we have always made a mistake in calculating 12×12. Yes, it's quite incomprehensible how it could happen, but that's how it is. So everything that we've calculated like that is wrong!—But what does it matter? It doesn't matter at all!—So there must be something wrong here in the idea we have of the truth and falsity of arithmetical propositions.

The origin and the primitive form of the language game is a reaction; only from this can more complicated forms develop.

Language—I want to say—is a refinement. *im Anfang war die Tat.**

First there must be firm, hard stone for building, and the blocks are laid rough-hewn one on another. *Afterwards* it's certainly important that the stone can be trimmed, that it's not *too* hard.

The primitive form of the language game is certainty, not uncertainty. For uncertainty could never lead to action.

I want to say: it is characteristic of our language that the foundation on which it grows consists in steady ways of living, regular ways of acting.

Its function is determined *above all* by action, which it accompanies.

We have an idea of which ways of living are primitive, and which could only have developed out of these. We believe that the simplest plough existed before the complicated one.

The simple form (and that is the prototype) of the cause-effect game is determining the cause, not doubting.

("... At some point we have to say—without doubting—: *that* happens because of *this* cause.")[4] As opposed to *what* for instance? As opposed surely to never *tightening* the knot, but remaining constantly uncertain what the cause of the phenomenon really is; as if it made sense to say: strictly speaking no one could ever *know* the cause with certainty. So that it would correspond most strictly to the

truth *not* to settle the question. This idea is based on a total misunderstanding of the role played by exactitude and doubt.

The basic form of the game must be one in which we act.

"How could the concept of 'cause' be set up if we were always doubting?"

"Originally the cause must be something palpable."

Isn't the real point this: we can't start with *philosophical speculation?*

If I never knew the cause of anything how would I ever have arrived at this concept? But that means: how could I ever have wondered what was the cause of this or that event if I hadn't already seen the cause of something? But, don't forget, this "could" has to be taken in a logical sense,—because otherwise one might start thinking of all sorts of possible explanations. Whereas the point is simply: When you give a description of this "wondering," take care that you really are describing something.

The essence of the language game is a practical method (a way of acting)—not speculation, not chatter.

.   .   .   .

The machine (its structure) as symbol of its mode of operating:[5] The machine I might start by saying—already seems to have its mode of operating within itself. What does this mean?

According to our knowledge of the machine, all the rest, that is, the movements it will make, seem already to be completely determined.

"We talk as though these parts *could* move only in this way, as though they couldn't do anything different."

How is that—are we forgetting the possibility that they may bend, break off, melt, etc.? *Yes;* in *many* cases we don't think of that at all. We use a machine, or the picture of a machine, as a symbol for a particular mode of operation. For example, we give someone this picture and assume he will conclude from it

---

*"In the beginning was the deed."

how the parts will move. (Just as we can give someone a number by telling him it's the twenty-fifth in the series 1, 4, 9, 16 . . .).

"The machine already seems to have its mode of operating within it" means: You are inclined to compare the details of the machine's movements with objects which are already in a drawer and which we then take out.

But we don't talk like that when what interests us is predicting the actual behaviour of a machine; then we don't usually forget that it's possible for the parts to get deformed, etc.

On the other hand this is what we may do if we are wondering how we can use the machine as a symbol of a way of moving— since it may after all in fact move quite *differently.*

Well, we might say that the machine, or its picture, is the first member of a series of pictures which we've learnt to derive from it.

But if we reflect that the machine could have behaved differently, we easily get the impression that the machine as symbol contains its own mode of operation much more determinately than does the real machine. In that case we're not satisfied that the movements should be those which experience has taught us to expect; on the contrary we feel they must really—in a mysterious sense—already be *present* in the machine. And it's quite true: the operation of the machine symbol is predetermined in a different way from that of some real machine.

But in all these cases the difficulty comes from confusing "is" and "is called."

We say: "It is hard to know whether this medicine helps or not, because we don't know if the cold would have lasted longer or got worse if we hadn't taken it." If we really have no evidence concerning this, is it simply hard to know?

Suppose I have invented a medicine and say: *Every* man who takes this medicine for a few months will have his life extended by one month. If he hadn't taken it, he would have died a month earlier. "We can't *know* whether it was really the medicine; or whether he

wouldn't have lived just as long without it." Isn't this a misleading way to speak? Wouldn't it be better to say: "It is meaningless to say this medicine prolongs life, if testing the claim is ruled out in this way"? In other words, we are indeed dealing with a correct English sentence constructed on the analogy of sentences which are in common use, but you are not clear about the *fundamental* difference in the use of these sentences. It isn't easy to have a clear view of this use. The sentence is there before your eyes, but not a clear overall representation of its use.

So to say "It is meaningless . . ." is to point out that perhaps you are being misled by these words, that they make you imagine a use which they do not have. They do perhaps evoke an idea (the prolongation of life, etc.), but the game with the sentence is so arranged that it doesn't have the essential point which makes useful the game with similarly constructed sentences. (As the "race between the hare and the hedgehog" looks like a race, but isn't one.)

You must ask yourself: what does one accept as a criterion for a medicine's helping one? There are various cases. In which cases do we say: "It is hard to say whether it has helped"? In what cases should we reject as senseless the expression: "Of course we can never be certain whether it was the medicine that helped"?

When do we say that two bodies weigh the same? If we have weighed them or whilst we are weighing them?

Suppose weighing were our sole criterion of something's weight;—if a body registers a greater weight at one weighing than at the previous one, *when* did its weight change? It might be established usage to say: the body weighs so and so much until a new weighing gives a different result. We answer the question: "When did its weight change?," by giving the time of this weighing. Or: we say it's impossible for us to know when it changes its weight, we only know that it has one weight at the first weighing and another at the second. Or: "It's senseless to ask when it changed its weight, we can only ask when the change in weight was registered."

"Still, the body had *some* weight at any given time, so the right answer was: we *don't know* when it changed."

And what if we said that a body doesn't have any weight at all except when it is being registered somehow, or that it doesn't have any *definite* weight, except when it is being measured? Couldn't we play this game too?

Imagine we sell some material "by weight" and the custom is as follows: we weigh the material every five minutes and then calculate the price according to the result of the last weighing. Or another custom: we calculate the price in this way only if the weight is the same when the material is weighed after the sale; if it has changed, we calculate the price according to the arithmetic mean of the two weights. Which way of fixing the price is the more correct?

(If the price of a commodity has changed between yesterday and today, *when* did it change? How much was it at midnight when nobody was buying?)

Conclusion: The expressions "the body now has a weight of . . .", "the body now weighs roughly . . .", "I don't know how much it weighs now," aren't connected quite straightforwardly with the results of the weighing, but this depends on a variety of circumstances; we can easily imagine different roles which weighing could play among the institutions within which we live and different roles for the expressions which accompany the game of weighing.

TRANSLATOR'S NOTES

1. "The Limits of Empiricism" by Bertrand Russell, in *Proceedings of the Aristotelian Society, 1935–36*, p. 149:

    > When I am hurt and cry out, I can perceive not only the hurt and the cry, but the fact that the one 'produces' the other. When I perceive three events in a time order, I can perceive that preceding is transitive—a general truth of which an instance is contained in the present sense-datum. . . . If we can sometimes *perceive* relations which are analogous to causation, we do not depend wholly upon enumerations of instances in the proof of causal laws. . . .

    p. 137:

    > If I say: 'I said "cat" because I saw a cat,' I am saying more than is warranted. One should say: 'I willed to say "cat" because there was a visual appearance which I classified as feline.' This statement, at any rate, isolates the 'because' as much as possible. What I am maintaining is that we can know this statement in the same way in which we know that there was a feline appearance, and that, if we could not, there would be no verbal empirical knowledge. I think that the word 'because' in this sentence must be understood as expressing a more or less causal relation, and that this relation must be *perceived*, not merely inferred from frequent concomitance.

2. Variation: how powerful the cause-effect schema is in us.
3. "For where concepts are lacking, we shall always find a word in good time."
4. See above, p. 412.
5. Cf. *Remarks on the Foundations of Mathematics*, pt. I, sec. 122.

33 / P. F. Strawson
SKEPTICISM, NATURALISM AND TRANSCENDENTAL ARGUMENTS

1. INTRODUCTORY REMARKS

The term "naturalism" is elastic in its use. The fact that it has been applied to the work of philosophers having as little in common as Hume and Spinoza is enough to suggest that there is a distinction to be drawn between varieties of naturalism. In later chapters, I shall myself draw a distinction between two main varieties, within which there are subvarieties. Of the two main varieties, one might be called *strict* or *reductive* naturalism (or, perhaps, *hard* naturalism). The other might be called *catholic* or *liberal* naturalism (or, perhaps, *soft* naturalism). The words "catholic" and "liberal" I use here in their comprehensive, not in their specifically religious or political, senses; nothing I say will have any direct bearing on religion or the philosophy of religion or on politics or political philosophy.

Each of these two general varieties of naturalism will be seen by its critics as liable to lead its adherents into intellectual aberration. The exponent of some subvarieties of strict or reductive naturalism is liable to be accused of what is pejoratively known as scientism, and of denying evident truths and realities. The soft or catholic naturalist, on the other hand, is liable to be accused of fostering illusions or propagating *myths*. I do not want to suggest that a kind of intellectual cold war between the two is inevitable. There is, perhaps, a possibility of compromise or détente, even of reconciliation. The soft or catholic naturalist, as his

name suggests, will be the readier with proposals for peaceful coexistence.

My title seems to speak of varieties of skepticism as well as varieties of naturalism. An exponent of some subvariety of reductive naturalism in some particular area of debate may sometimes be seen, or represented, as a kind of skeptic in that area: say, a moral skeptic or a skeptic about the mental or about abstract entities or about what are called "intensions." I shall explore some of these areas later on; and it is only then that the distinction between hard and soft naturalism will come into play.

For the present, I shall not need any such distinction and I shall not make any such slightly deviant or extended applications of the notion of skepticism. To begin with, I shall refer only to some familiar and standard forms of philosophical skepticism. Strictly, skepticism is a matter of doubt rather than of denial. The skeptic is, strictly, not one who denies the validity of certain types of belief, but one who questions, if only initially and for methodological reasons, the adequacy of our grounds for holding them. He puts forward his doubts by way of a challenge—sometimes a challenge to himself—to show that the doubts are unjustified, that the beliefs put in question are justified. He may conclude, like Descartes, that the challenge can successfully be met; or, like Hume, that it cannot (though this view of Hume's was importantly qualified). Traditional targets of philosophic doubt include the existence of the external world, i.e. of physical ob-

Reprinted by permission of the publisher from P. F. Strawson, *Skepticism and Naturalism: Some Varieties*, pp. 1–29. New York: Columbia University Press, 1985.

jects or bodies, our knowledge of other minds; the justification of induction; the reality of the past. Hume concerned himself most with the first and third of these—body and induction; and I shall refer mainly, though not only, to the first.

I shall begin by considering various different kinds of attempts to meet the challenge of traditional skepticism by argument; and also various replies to these attempts, designed to show that they are unsuccessful or that they miss the point. Then I shall consider a different kind of response to skepticism—a response which does not so much attempt to meet the challenge as to pass it by. And this is where I shall first introduce an undifferentiated notion of Naturalism. The hero of this part of the story is Hume: he appears in the double role of arch-skeptic and arch-naturalist. Other names which will figure in the story include those of Moore, Wittgenstein, Carnap and, among our own contemporaries, Professor Barry Stroud. This part of the story is the theme of the present chapter. It is an old story, so I shall begin by going over some familiar ground. In the remaining chapters I shall tackle a number of different topics— viz. morality, perception, mind and meaning— and it is only in connection with these that I shall introduce and make use of the distinction between hard and soft naturalism.

2. TRADITIONAL SKEPTICISM

To begin, then, with G. E. Moore. It will be remembered that in his famous *A Defence of Common Sense*[1] Moore asserted that he, and very many other people as well, knew with certainty a number of propositions regarding which some philosophers had held that they were not, and could not be, known with certainty. These propositions included the proposition that the earth had existed for a great many years; that on it there had been, and were now, many bodies, or physical objects, of many different kinds; that these bodies included the bodies of human beings who, like Moore himself, had had, or were having, thoughts and feelings and experiences of many different kinds. If Moore was right in holding that such

propositions are widely known, with certainty, to be true, then it seems to follow that certain theses of philosophical skepticism are false: e.g. the thesis that it cannot be known with certainty that material objects exist, and the thesis that no one can know with certainty of the existence of any minds other than his own or, to put it a little more bluntly, that no one can know with certainty that there are other people. Again, the first of these two skeptical theses is implicitly challenged, indeed denied, by Moore in yet another famous paper called *Proof of an External World*.[2] He claimed, in delivering this paper, to prove that two human hands exist, hence that external things exist, by holding up first one hand, then another and saying, as he did so, "Here is one hand and here is another." The proof was rigorous and conclusive, he claimed, since he knew for certain that the premise was true and it was certain that the conclusion followed from the premise.

It was hardly to be expected that Moore's "Defence" or his "Proof" would be universally accepted as settling the questions to which they were addressed. Rather, it was felt by some philosophers that the point of philosophical skepticism about, say, the existence of external things, of the physical world, was somehow being missed. A recent expression of this feeling is given by Professor Barry Stroud in an article called "The Significance of Scepticism."[3] At its most general, the skeptical point concerning the external world seems to be that subjective experience could, logically, be just the way it is without its being the case that physical or material things actually existed. (Thus Berkeley, for example, embraced a different hypothesis—that of a benevolent deity as the cause of sense-experiences—and we can find in Descartes the suggestion, though not, of course, the endorsement, of another—that of a malignant demon; while the consistent phenomenalist questions the need for any external source of sense-experience at all.) So if Moore, in making the claims he made, was simply relying on his own experience being just the way it was, he was missing the skeptical point altogether; and if he was not, then, since he issues his knowledge claims without any further argument, all he has done is simply to issue a dogmatic denial of the skeptical thesis. But simple dogmatism settles nothing in philosophy. Stroud, at the end of his article, suggests that we ought to try to find some way of *defusing* skepticism. He does not mean, some way of establishing or proving that we do know for certain what the skeptic denies we know for certain, for he does not appear to think that this is possible; but, rather, some way of *neutralizing* the skeptical question, rendering it philosophically *impotent*. These expressions are not very clear, but I doubt if Stroud intended them to be.

Stroud mentions one attempt to neutralize the skeptical question, an attempt which he finds unsatisfactory. The attempt is Carnap's.[4] Carnap distinguished two ways in which the words "There are or exist external or physical things" might be taken. On one interpretation these words simply express a proposition which is an obvious truism, a trivial consequence of hosts of propositions, like Moore's "Here are two hands," which are ordinarily taken, and in a sense correctly taken, to be empirically verified, to be established by and in sense-experience. On this interpretation, Moore's procedure is perfectly in order. Nevertheless Carnap would agree with Stroud that Moore's procedure is powerless to answer the *philosophical* question whether there really are physical things, powerless to establish the *philosophical* proposition that there really are such things. For Carnap accepts the point that, as the skeptic understands, or, more precisely, as he claims to understand, the words "There exist physical things," Moore's experience, or any experience, could be just the way it is without these words expressing a truth; and hence that no course of experience could establish the proposition these words are taken by the skeptic to express; that it is in principle unverifiable in experience. But the conclusion that Carnap draws is not the skeptical conclusion. The conclusion he draws is that the words, so taken, express no proposition at all; they are deprived of meaning so that the question whether the proposition they express is true or false does not arise. There is no theoretical issue here. There is indeed a practical issue: whether or not to adopt, or persist in, a certain convention, to make, or persist in, the choice of the physical-thing language or framework of con-

cepts for the organization of experience. Given that the choice is made, the convention is adopted, or persisted in, then we have, internally to the adopted framework, a host of empirically verifiable thing-propositions and hence, internally to the framework, the trivial truth that there exist physical things. But the *external*, philosophical question, which the skeptic tries to raise, viz. whether the framework in general *corresponds to reality*, has no verifiable answer and hence makes no sense.

Moore, then, according to Stroud, either misses the point of the skeptical challenge or has recourse to an unacceptable dogmatism, a dogmatic claim to knowledge. Carnap, again according to Stroud, does not altogether miss the point, but seeks to smother or extinguish it by what Stroud finds an equally unacceptable verificationist dogmatism. It is all very well, says Stroud, to declare the philosophical question to be meaningless, but it does *seem* to be meaningless; the skeptical challenge, the skeptical question, *seem* to be intelligible. We should at least need more argument to be convinced that they were not.

Many philosophers would agree with Stroud, as against Carnap, on this point; and would indeed go further and contend both that the skeptical challenge is perfectly intelligible, perfectly meaningful, and that it can be met and answered by rational argument. Descartes was one such; though his appeal to the veracity of God to underwrite, or guarantee the reliability of, our natural inclination to believe in the existence of the physical world no longer seems very convincing; if it ever did. More popular today is the view that the assumption of the existence of a physical world, of physical things having more or less the characteristics and powers which our current physical theory represents them as having, provides a far better *explanation* of the course of our sensory experience than any alternative hypothesis. Such an assumption puts us in the way of a non-arbitrary, full, detailed, coherent causal account of that experience to an extent which no alternative story comes anywhere near rivalling. It can therefore be judged rational to accept it by the same criteria of rationality as govern our assessment of explanatory theories framed in natural scientific enquiry or empirical inquiries generally. I shall return to this answer later.

Stroud does not discuss this approach in quite the form I have given it; but he does discuss a near relation of it, viz. Quine's suggestion of what he calls a "naturalised epistemology," which would address itself to the empirical question of how, from the meager data available to us in experience, we come to form the elaborate structure of our ordinary and scientific beliefs about the world.[5] Stroud acknowledges that such an enquiry is perfectly legitimate in itself; but, he contends, it leaves the skeptical challenge completely untouched. If it were seen as an attempted *answer* to the philosophical question, it would be, he maintains, in no better position than Moore's commonsense assertion; merely a "scientific" version or analogue of the latter. We may in the end be convinced that Quine's legitimate naturalistic question is the only substantial one that confronts us; but if we are to be satisfied that this is so, it must first be shown that there is something radically faulty, radically misconceived, about the skeptical challenge, about regarding what Carnap called the external question as raising a genuine issue. But this, says Stroud, has not so far been shown, either by Carnap, though he asserted it, or anyone else.

It is at this point that Stroud acknowledges the appeal of a kind of argument which he calls "transcendental." Such arguments typically take one of two forms. A philosopher who advances such an argument may begin with a premise which the skeptic does not challenge, viz. the occurrence of self-conscious thought and experience; and then proceed to argue that a necessary condition of the possibility of such experience is, say, knowledge of the existence of external objects or of states of mind of other beings. Or he may argue that the skeptic could not even raise his doubt unless he knew it to be unfounded; i.e. he could have no use for the concepts in terms of which he expresses his doubt unless he were able to know to be true at least some of the propositions belonging to the class all members of which fall within the scope of the skeptical doubt. Stroud remains dubious of the success of such arguments; presumably for the same reasons as he expounded in an earlier article entitled "Transcendental Arguments."[6] There he confronts the propounder of such arguments with a dilemma. *Either* these arguments, in their second form, are little more than an elaborate and superfluous screen behind which we can discern a simple reliance on a simple form of verification principle *or* the most that such arguments can establish is that in order for the intelligible formulation of skeptical doubts to be possible or, generally, in order for self-conscious thought and experience to be possible, we must take it, or *believe*, that we have knowledge of, say, external physical objects or other minds; but to establish this falls short of establishing that these beliefs are, or must be, true.

The second horn of the dilemma is perhaps the more attractive in that it at least allows that transcendental argument may demonstrate something about the use and interconnection of our concepts. But if the dilemma is sound, the skeptic's withers are unwrung in any case. (Stroud seems to assume without question that the point of transcendental argument in general is an antiskeptical point; but the assumption may be questioned, as I shall later suggest. In either case, according to Stroud, the skeptic is unshaken because he does not deny that we do, and need not deny that we must, employ and apply the concepts in question in experiential conditions which we take to warrant or justify their application. His point is, and remains, that the fulfillment of those conditions is consistent with the falsity of all the propositions we then affirm; and hence that—failing further argument to the contrary—we cannot be said really to *know* that any such propositions are true.

3. HUME: REASON AND NATURE

Is there any other way with skepticism which is not a variant on those I have referred to, i.e. is neither an attempt directly to refute it by rational argument drawing on commonsense or theological or quasi-scientific considerations nor an attempt indirectly to refute it by showing that it is in some way unintelligible or self-defeating? I think there is another way. There is nothing new about it, since it is at least as old as Hume; and the most powerful latter-day exponent of the closely related position is Wittgenstein. I shall call it the way of naturalism; though this name is not to be understood in the sense of Quine's "naturalized epistemology."

In a famous sentence in Book II of the *Treatise* Hume limits the pretensions of reason to determine the ends of action.[7] In a similar spirit, towards the end of Book I, he limits the pretensions of reason to determine the formation of beliefs concerning matters of fact and existence. He points out that all arguments in *support* of the skeptical position are totally inefficacious; and, by the same token, all arguments *against* it are totally idle. His point is really the very simple one that, whatever arguments may be produced on one side or the other of the question, we simply *cannot help* believing in the existence of body, and *cannot help* forming beliefs and expectations in general accordance with the basic canons of induction. He might have added, though he did not discuss this question, that the belief in the existence of other people (hence other minds) is equally inescapable. Hume regularly expresses his point by reference to Nature, which leaves us no option in these matters but "by absolute and uncontrollable necessity" determines us "to judge as well as to breathe and feel." Speaking of that total skepticism which, arguing from the fallibility of human judgment, would tend to undermine all belief and opinion, he says: "Whoever has taken the pains to refute the cavils of this total scepticism has really disputed without an antagonist and endeavoured by arguments to establish a faculty which Nature has antecedently implanted in the mind and rendered unavoidable."[8] He goes on to point out that what holds for total skepticism holds also for skepticism about the existence of body. Even the professed skeptic "*must assent* to the principle concerning the existence of body, though he cannot pretend by any arguments of philosophy to maintain its veracity"; for "nature has not left this to his choice, and has doubtless esteemed it an affair of too great importance to be entrusted to our uncertain reasonings and speculations." Hence " 'tis vain to ask Whether there be body or not? That is a point which we must take for granted in all our reasonings."[9]

Here I interpolate some remarks which are not strictly to the present purpose but which are very much to the purpose if one is considering the question of Hume himself. Hume contrasts the vain question, *Whether there be body or not?* with a question he says "we may well ask," viz. *What causes induce us to believe in the existence of body?*—thus seeming to anticipate Quine's program for a naturalized epistemology. But there follows, in Hume, what seems to be a striking inconsistency between principle and practice. For, having said that the existence of body is a point which we must take for granted in *all* our reasonings, he then conspicuously does *not* take it for granted in the reasonings which he addresses to the causal question. Indeed those reasonings famously point to a skeptical conclusion. So, as he himself is the first to acknowledge,[10] there is an unresolved tension in Hume's position (a tension which may be found reminiscent in some ways of the tension between Kant's empirical realism and his transcendental idealism). One might speak of two Humes: Hume the skeptic and Hume the naturalist; where Hume's naturalism, as illustrated by the passages I quoted, appears as something like a refuge from his skepticism. An exponent of a more thoroughgoing naturalism could accept the question, *What causes induce us to believe in the existence of body?* as one we may well ask, as one that can be referred to empirical psychology, to the study of infantile development; but would do so in the justified expectation that answers to it would in fact take for granted the existence of body.

Hume, then, we may say, is ready to accept and to tolerate a distinction between two levels of thought: the level of philosophically critical thinking which can offer us no assurances against skepticism; and the level of everyday empirical thinking, at which the pretensions of critical thinking are completely overriden and suppressed by Nature, by an inescapable natural commitment to belief: to belief in the existence of body and inductively based expectations. (I hinted at a parallel with Kant; and a parallel there is, though it is only a loose one. There is a parallel in that Kant also recognizes two levels of thought: the empirical level at which we justifiably claim knowledge of an external world of causally related objects in space; and the critical level at which we recognize that this world is only appearance, appearance of an ultimate reality of which we can have no positive knowledge at all. The parallel, however, is only a loose one. Where Hume refers to an inescapable *natural disposition* to belief, Kant produces *argument* [transcendental argument] to show that what, at the empirical level, is rightly reckoned as empirical knowledge of an external world of law-governed objects is a necessary condition of self-awareness, of knowledge of our own inner states; and—a yet more striking difference—where, at the critical level, Hume leaves us with unrefuted skepticism, Kant offers us his own brand of idealism.)

Here I end my digression concerning the complex tensions in Hume's thought and the parallels with Kant; and return to a consideration of Hume as naturalist, leaving on one side Hume the skeptic. According to Hume the naturalist, skeptical doubts are not to be met by argument. They are simply to be neglected (except, perhaps, in so far as they supply a harmless amusement, a mild diversion to the intellect). They are to be neglected because they are *idle*; powerless against the force of nature, of our naturally implanted disposition to belief. This does not mean that Reason has no part to play in relation to our beliefs concerning matters of fact and existence. It has a part to play, though a subordinate one: as Nature's lieutenant rather then Nature's commander. (Here we may recall and adapt that famous remark about Reason and the passions). Our inescapable natural commitment is to a general frame of belief and to a general style (the inductive) of belief-formation. But *within* that frame and style, the requirement of Reason, that our beliefs should form a consistent and coherent system, may be given full play. Thus, for example, though Hume did not think that a rational justification of induction in general was either necessary or possible, he could quite consistently proceed to frame "rules for judging of cause and effect." Though it is Nature which commits us to inductive belief-formation in general, it is Reason which leads us to refine and elaborate our inductive canons and procedures and, in their light, to

criticize, and sometimes to reject, what in detail we find ourselves naturally inclined to believe.

4. HUME AND WITTGENSTEIN

In introducing this way with skepticism, I associated the name of Wittgenstein with that of Hume. I have in mind primarily Wittgenstein's notes *On Certainty*.[11] Like Hume, Wittgenstein distinguishes between those matters—those propositions—which are up for question and decision in the light of reason and experience and those which are not, which are, as he puts it, "exempt from doubt." Of course there are differences between Hume and Wittgenstein. We do not, for example, find in Wittgenstein any explicit repetition of Hume's quite explicit appeal to Nature. But, as we shall see, the resemblances, and even the echoes, are more striking than the differences. Above all, there is, in Wittgenstein's work, as in Hume's, the distinction between "what it is vain" to make a matter of inquiry, what "we must take for granted in all our reasonings," as Hume puts it, on the one hand, and what is genuinely matter for inquiry on the other.

Wittgenstein has a host of phrases to express this antithesis. Thus he speaks of a kind of conviction or belief as "*beyond being justified or unjustified*; as it were, as something *animal*" (359);[12] and here we may find an echo of Hume's appeal to Nature and, even more, of Hume's remark that "belief is more properly an act of the sensitive than of the cogitative part of our nature."[13] Again, Wittgenstein says that "certain propositions seem to *underlie* all questions and all thinking" (415); that "some propositions are *exempt from doubt*" (341); that "certain things are *in deed* [in der Tat, in practice] not doubted" (342); he speaks of "belief that is not founded" (253) but "in the entire system of our language-games *belongs to the foundation*" (411). Again, he speaks of "propositions which have *a peculiar logical role* in the system [of our empirical propositions]" (136); which belong to our "*frame of reference*" (83); which "*stand fast or solid*" (151);

which constitute the "world-picture" which is "the *substratum* of all my enquiring and asserting" (162) or "the *scaffolding* of our thoughts" (211) or "the element in which arguments have their life" (105). This world-picture, he says, is not something he has because he has satisfied himself of its correctness. "No: it is the inherited background against which I distinguish between true and false" (94). He compares the propositions describing this world-picture to the rules of a game which "can be learned purely practically without learning any explicit rules" (95).

Though the general tendency of Wittgenstein's position is clear enough, it is not easy to extract a wholly clear consecutive statement of it from the mass of figures or metaphors which I have illustrated. Evidently his aim, at least in part, is to give a realistic account or description of how it actually is with our human systems or bodies of belief. Evidently, too, he distinguishes, as I have said, between those propositions, or actual or potential elements in our belief-systems, which we treat as subject to empirical confirmation or falsification, which we consciously incorporate in our belief-system (when we do) for this or that *reason* or on the basis of this or that *experience*, or which we actually treat as matter for inquiry or doubt—and, on the other hand, those elements of our belief-system which have a quite different character, alluded to by the figures of scaffolding, framework, background, substratum, etc. (The metaphors include that of foundations; but it is quite clear that Wittgenstein does not regard these propositions, or elements of the belief-system, as foundations in the traditional empiricist sense, i.e. as basic reasons, themselves resting on experience, for the rest of our beliefs. The metaphor of a scaffolding or framework, within which the activity of building or modifying the structure of our beliefs goes on, is a better one.)

Wittgenstein does not represent this distinction between two kinds of element in our belief-systems as sharp, absolute, and unchangeable. On the contrary. And this is just as well in view of some of his examples of propositions of the second class, i.e. of propositions which are "exempt from doubt." (Writ-ing in 1950–51, he gives as one example the proposition that no one has been very far [e.g. as far as the moon] from the surface of the earth.) It would have been helpful, though probably contrary to his inclinations, if he had drawn distinctions, or indicated a *principle* of distinction, *within* this class. An indication that there are such distinctions to be drawn comes at the end of an extended metaphor (96–99) in which he compares those propositions which are subject to empirical test to the waters moving in a river and those which are not so subject to the bed or banks of the river. The situation is not unchangeable in that there may sometimes be shifts of the bed or even of the bank. But, he concludes, "The bank of that river consists partly of hard rock, *subject to no alteration or only to an imperceptible one*, partly of sand which now in one place now in another gets washed away or deposited."

But how close, really, is Wittgenstein to Hume? There are points at which he may seem closer to Carnap. These are the points at which he seems disposed to express his sense of the difference between those propositions which are subject to empirical test and those which form the scaffolding, framework, foundations etc. of our thought (the hard rock of the river bank) by denying to the latter the status of propositions at all—comparing them, as we have seen, to rules "which can be learned purely practically." Thus he writes at one point: "No such proposition as 'There are physical objects' can be formulated" (36); and even that " 'There are physical objects' is nonsense" (35). But he is not very close to Carnap. Carnap speaks of a practical issue, a choice—a decision to adopt, or to persist in the use of, a certain framework. There is nothing of this in Wittgenstein. "It is not," he says, "as if we *chose* the game" (317). And elsewhere, though he is dissatisfied with the expression, we find: "I want to say: propositions of the form of empirical propositions, and not only propositions of logic, form the foundation of all operating with thoughts (with language)" (401). (There is here an evident allusion to the *Tractatus*.) Later, straightforwardly enough, we find: "certain propositions seem to underlie all questions and all thinking." The apparent shilly-shallying over "proposition" is perhaps palliated by the remarks at 319–20, where he speaks of a lack of sharpness in the boundary between rule and empirical proposition and adds that the concept "proposition" is itself not a sharp one.[14]

To sum up now the relations between Hume and Wittgenstein. Hume's position seems much the simpler. All that is explicitly mentioned by him as constituting the framework of all inquiry—what is to be "taken for granted in all our reasoning"—amounts to two things: acceptance of the existence of body and of the general reliability of inductive belief-formation. This is the groundwork; and its source is unambiguously identified. These unavoidable natural convictions, commitments or prejudices are ineradicably implanted in our minds by Nature. Wittgenstein's position is, as we have seen, at least superficially more complicated. First, the propositions or crypto-propositions of the framework, though they may be taken to include the two Humean elements, are presumptively more various. Second, the framework is, up to a point at least, dynamically conceived: what was at one time part of the framework may change its status, may assume the character of a hypothesis to be questioned and perhaps falsified—some of what we would now regard as assumptions about supernatural agents or powers presumably come into this category—whereas other parts of the framework remain fixed and unalterable. Finally, and connectedly, Wittgenstein does not speak, as Hume does, of one exclusive source, viz. Nature, for these *préjugés*. Rather, he speaks of our learning, from childhood up, an activity, a practice, a social practice—of making judgments, of forming beliefs—to which the crypto-propositions have the special relation he seeks to illuminate by the figures of framework, scaffolding, substratum etc.; that is, they are not judgments we actually make or, in general, things we explicitly learn or are taught in the course of that practice, but rather reflect the general character of the practice itself, form a frame within which the judgments we actually make hang together in a more or less coherent way.

In spite of the greater complication of Wittgenstein's position, we can, I think, at least as far as the general skeptical questions are concerned, discern a profound community between him and Hume. They have in common the view that our "beliefs" in the existence of body and, to speak roughly, in the general reliability of induction are not grounded beliefs and at the same time are not open to serious doubt. They are, one might say, outside our critical and rational competence in the sense that they define, or help to define, the area in which that competence is exercised. To attempt to confront the professional skeptical doubt with arguments in support of these beliefs, with rational justifications, is simply to show a total misunderstanding of the role they actually play in our belief-systems. The correct way with the professional skeptical doubt is not to attempt to rebut it with argument, but to point out that it is idle, unreal, a pretense; and then the rebutting arguments will appear as equally idle; the reasons produced in those arguments to justify induction or belief in the existence of body are not, and do not become, *our* reasons for these beliefs; there is no such thing as *the reasons for which we hold* these beliefs. We simply cannot help accepting them as defining the areas within which the questions come up of what beliefs we should rationally hold on such-and-such a matter. The point may be underlined by referring again to some attempts to rebut skepticism by argument.

Perhaps the best skepticism-rebutting argument in favor of the existence of body is the quasi-scientific argument I mentioned earlier: i.e., that the existence of a world of physical objects having more or less the properties which current science attributes to them provides the best available explanation of the phenomena of experience, just as accepted theories within physical science supply the best available explanations of the physical phenomena they deal with. But the implicit comparison with scientific theory simply proclaims its own weakness. We accept or believe the scientific theories (when we do) just because we believe they supply the best available explanations of the phenomena they deal with. That is our reason for accepting them. But no one accepts the existence of the physical world *because* it supplies the best available explanation, etc. That is no one's reason for accepting it. Anyone who claimed it was his reason would be pretending. It is, as Hume declared, a point we are naturally bound to take for granted in all our reasonings and, in particular, in all those reasonings which underlie our acceptance of particular physical theories.

Similarly, the best argument against other-minds skepticism is, probably, that, given the non-uniqueness of one's physical constitution and the general uniformity of nature in the biological sphere as in others, it is in the highest degree improbable that one is unique among members of one's species in being the enjoyer of subjective states, and of the kind of subjective states one does enjoy in the kind of circumstances in which one enjoys them. But, again, this is no one's reason for believing in the existence of other minds, of other people, subjects of just such a range of sensations, emotions, and thoughts as he is aware of in himself. We simply react to others as to other *people*. They may puzzle us at times; but that is part of so reacting. Here again we have something which we have no option but to take for granted in all our reasoning.

5. "ONLY CONNECT": THE ROLE OF TRANSCENDENTAL ARGUMENTS

Suppose we accept this naturalist rejection both of skepticism and of skepticism-rebutting arguments as equally idle—as both involving a misunderstanding of the role in our lives, the place in our intellectual economy, of those propositions or crypto-propositions which the skeptic seeks to place in doubt and his opponent in argument seeks to establish. How, in this perspective, should we view arguments of the kind which Stroud calls "transcendental"? Evidently not as supplying the reasoned rebuttal which the skeptic perversely invites. Our naturalism is precisely the rejection of that invitation. So, even if we have a tenderness for transcendental arguments, we shall be happy to accept the criticism of Stroud and others that either such arguments rely on an unacceptably simple verificationism or the most they can establish is a certain sort of interdependence of conceptual capacities and beliefs: e.g., as I put

it earlier, that in order for the intelligible formulation of skeptical doubts to be possible or, more generally, in order for self-conscious thought and experience to be possible, we must take it, or *believe*, that we have knowledge of external physical objects or other minds. The fact that such a demonstration of dependence would not refute the skeptic does not worry our naturalist, who repudiates any such aim. But our naturalist might well take satisfaction in the demonstration of these connections—if they can indeed be demonstrated—for their own sake. For repudiation of the project of wholesale validation of types of knowledge-claim does not leave the naturalist without philosophical employment. E. M. Forster's motto—"only connect"—is as valid for the naturalist at the moral and personal level. That is to say, having given up the unreal project of wholesale validation, the naturalist philosopher will embrace the real project of investigating the connections between the major structural elements of our conceptual scheme. If connections as tight as those which transcendental arguments, construed as above, claim to offer are really available, so much the better.

Of course, it is often disputed, both in detail and in general, that arguments of this kind do or can achieve even as much as the most that Stroud allowed them. Typically, a transcendental argument, as now construed, claims that one type of exercise of conceptual capacity is a necessary condition of another (e.g., that taking some experiences to consist in awareness of objects in physical space is a necessary condition of the self-ascription of subjective states as ordered in time or that being equipped to identify some states of mind in others is a necessary condition of being able to ascribe any states of mind to ourselves). I am not now concerned with the general character of the criticisms to which they are typically subject. Typically, the criticism is that what is claimed to be a necessary condition has not been shown to be so and could not be shown to be so without eliminating all possible (or candidate) alternatives, a task which is not attempted. The transcendental arguer is always exposed to the charge that even if *he* cannot conceive of alternative ways in which conditions of the possibility of a certain kind of experience or exercise of conceptual capacity might be fulfilled, this inability may simply be due to lack of imagination on his part—a lack which makes him prone to mistake sufficient for necessary conditions.

It is not my present purpose to inquire how successfully arguments of the kind in question (on the present relatively modest construal of their aims) survive these criticisms; to inquire, that is, whether some or any of them are strictly valid. I am inclined to think that at least some are (e.g. self-ascription implies the capacity for other ascription), though I must admit that few, if any, have commanded universal assent among the critics. But whether or not they are strictly valid, these arguments, or weakened versions of them, will continue to be of interest to our naturalist philosopher. For even if they do not succeed in establishing such tight or rigid connections as they initially promise, they do at least indicate or bring out conceptual connections, even if only of a looser kind; and, as I have already suggested, to establish the connections between the major structural features or elements of our conceptual scheme—to exhibit it, not as a rigidly deductive system, but as a coherent whole whose parts are mutually supportive and mutually dependent, interlocking in an intelligible way—to do this may well seem to our naturalist the proper, or at least the major, task of analytical philosophy. As indeed it does to me. (Whence the phrase, "descriptive [as opposed to validatory or revisionary] metaphysics.")

6. THREE QUOTATIONS

Vis-à-vis traditional skepticism, then, I am proposing that we adopt, at least provisionally (and everything in philosophy is provisional), the naturalist position. Or, perhaps, since we have yoked Wittgenstein to Hume in characterizing and illustrating the position, we should qualify the name and, since where Hume speaks only of Nature, Wittgenstein speaks of the language-games we learn from childhood up, i.e. in a social context, should call it, not simply "naturalism," but "social naturalism." Whatever the name, I can perhaps illustrate the

break that adoption of it constitutes with other attitudes with the help of two quotations: the first from the greatest of modern philosophers, the second from a philosopher whose title to respect is less considerable, but who nevertheless seems to me to be on the right side on this point.

In the Preface to the second edition of *The Critique of Pure Reason* (B xi) Kant says: "it remains a scandal to philosophy and to human reason in general that the existence of things outside us . . . must be accepted merely on *faith* and that if anyone thinks good to doubt their existence, we are unable to counter his doubts by any satisfactory proof."

In *Being and Time* (1.6) Heidegger ripostes: "The 'scandal of philosophy' is not that this proof has yet to be given, but that *such proofs are expected and attempted again and again*."

To complete this short series of quotations, here is one, from Wittgenstein again, that neatly sums things up from the naturalist, or social naturalist, point of view: "It is so difficult to find the *beginning*. Or better: it is difficult to begin at the beginning. And not to try to go further back." (471)

To try to meet the skeptic's challenge, in whatever way, by whatever style of argument, is to try to go further back. If one is to begin at the beginning, one must refuse the challenge as our naturalist refuses it.

7. HISTORICISM AND THE PAST

But now, as Wittgenstein's first thought—as opposed to what he calls the better thought—in that quotation suggests, the question arises: Where exactly is the beginning? In other words, what are those structural features of our conceptual scheme, the framework features, which must be regarded as equally beyond question and beyond validation, but which offer themselves, rather, for the kind of philosophical treatment which I have suggested and which might be called "connective analysis"? Hume, in Book I of the *Treatise*, concentrates, as we saw, on two such features: the habit of induction and the belief in the existence of body, of the physical world. Wittgenstein seems to offer, or suggest, a more miscellaneous collection, though he mitigates the miscellaneousness by the dynamic element in his picture, the provision for change: some things which at some time, or in some context or relation, may have the status of framework features, beyond question or test, may at another time, or in another context or relation, become open to question or even be rejected; others are fixed and unalterable. Part, though not the whole, of the explanation of what may seem cloudy or unsatisfactory in Wittgenstein's treatment in *On Certainty* is that he is fighting on more than one front. He is not concerned only with the common framework of human belief-systems at large. He is also concerned to indicate what a realistic picture of *individual* belief-systems is like; and in such a picture room must be found for, as it were, local and idiosyncratic propositions (like "My name is Ludwig Wittgenstein") as elements in someone's belief-system which are, for him, neither grounded nor up for question. But, obviously, no such proposition as that forms part of the common framework of human belief-systems at large.

But now it might be suggested that—even setting aside the point about individual belief-systems—Wittgenstein's admission of a dynamic element in the *collective* belief-system puts the whole approach in question. Earlier on, the unfortunate example, of the conviction that no one has been as far from the surface of the earth as the moon, was mentioned. One can think of more far-reaching beliefs. Surely the geocentric view of the universe—or at least of what we now call the solar system—at one time formed part of the framework of human thinking at large. Or, again, some form of creation-myth. Or some form of animism. If our "frame of reference," to use Wittgenstein's phrase, can undergo such radical revolutions as the Copernican (the real, not the Kantian, Copernican revolution), why should we assume that anything in it is "fixed and unalterable"? And if we drop that assumption, must we not be content to cast our metaphysics for a more modest—a historical or historicist—role; somewhat in the spirit of Collingwood,[15] who declared that metaphysics was indeed an essentially historical study, the attempt to elicit

what he called the "absolute presuppositions" of the science of the day? Metaphysical truth would thus be relativized to historical periods. Derelativization could be achieved only by explicitly assigning a system of presuppositions to its historical place. ("At such-and-such a period it *was* absolutely presupposed that . . ." or "As of now, it *is* absolutely presupposed that . . .").

In fact, there is no reason why metaphysics should tamely submit to historicist pressure of this kind. The human world-picture is of course subject to change. But it remains a *human world-picture*: a picture of a world of physical objects (bodies) in space and time including human observers capable of action and of acquiring and imparting knowledge (and error) both of themselves and each other and of whatever else is to be found in nature. So much of a constant conception, of what, in Wittgenstein's phrase, is "not subject to alteration or only to an imperceptible one," is given along with the very idea of historical alteration in the human world-view.

It is all of a piece with Wittgenstein's extreme aversion, in his later work, from any systematic treatment of issues, that he never attempted to specify which aspects of our world-picture, our frame of reference, are "not subject to alteration or only to an imperceptible one"; to which aspects our human or natural commitment is so profound that they stand fast, and may be counted on to stand fast, through all revolutions of scientific thought or social development. So far only those aspects have been specifically mentioned, or dwelt on to any extent, which have a relevance to—or show the irrelevance of—certain traditional skeptical problems: concerning the existence of body, knowledge of other minds and the practice of induction. I shall not attempt now to compile a list, or to engage in the connective metaphysical task of exhibiting the relations and interdependences of the elements of the general structure. But, before I pass on to a different, though related, set of questions, I want to mention now one further aspect of our thought which seems to have a similarly inescapable character; and I choose it because of its relevance to some current discussions.

It is to be remembered that the point has

been, not to offer a rational justification of the belief in external objects and other minds or of the practice of induction, but to represent skeptical arguments and rational counter-arguments as equally idle—not senseless, but idle—since what we have here are original, natural, inescapable commitments which we neither choose nor could give up. The further such commitment which I now suggest we should acknowledge is the commitment to belief in the reality and determinateness of the past. This is worth mentioning at the moment, not because it is a topic of traditional skeptical challenge, but because it is currently a topic of challenge from a certain kind of limited or moderate anti-realism, based on a particular, quasi-verificationist theory of meaning.[16] Of course, it *could* be a topic of skeptical challenge, a challenge, e.g., taking a form which Russell once toyed with: i.e. "We have no guarantee, no certain knowledge, that the world didn't come into existence just five minutes ago; all our current experience, including our apparent memories, could be just as it is consistently with this being the case." But the current challenge is different. Roughly speaking (some of the challengers would probably say this is a good deal too rough), it allows, with respect to questions about the past, that there is a determinate fact of the matter in those cases to which our memories or conclusively confirming or falsifying evidence extend (or it is known could be brought to extend), but no determinate fact of the matter in any other cases. Only those questions about the past which we can answer (or bring ourselves into a position to answer) *have* answers, true or false. (One casualty of this view, evidently, is standard logic—which is deprived of the law of excluded middle.) Much subtlety of argument can be devoted to advancing this view and to opposing it. But my present concern is not to meet it with argument, but to suggest, again, that arguments on both sides are idle, since belief in the reality and determinateness of the past is as much part of that general framework of beliefs to which we are inescapably committed as is belief in the existence of physical objects and the practice of inductive belief-formation. Indeed, it would be hard to separate the conception of objects which we have and

our acceptance of inductively formed beliefs from that conception of the past. All form part of our mutually supportive natural meta-physics. We are equally happy to acknowledge, with the poet, that full many a flower is born to blush unseen and, with the naturalist meta-physician, that full many a historical fact is destined to remain unverified and unverifiable by subsequent generations.

NOTES

1. In J. H. Muirhead, ed. *Contemporary British Philosophy*, 2d series (London, 1925); repr. in G. E. Moore, *Philosophical Papers* (London, 1959).
2. *Proceedings of the British Academy* vol. 25, (1939); repr. in Moore, *Philosophical Papers*.
3. In P. Bieri, R. P. Horstmann, and L. Kruger, eds., *Trancendental Arguments and Science* (Dordrecht, 1979).
4. Carnap, "Empiricism, Semantics and Ontology," *Revue Internationale de Philosophie* vol. 11, (1950); repr. in L. Linsky, eds., *Semantics and the Philosophy of Language* (Champaign, Ill., 1952).
5. W. V. Quine, "Epistemology Naturalized." In *Ontological Relativity* (New York, 1969); see also *The Roots of Reference* (La Salle, Ill., 1973).
6. *Journal of Philosophy* (1968); repr. in T. Penelham and J. J. MacIntosh, eds., *The First Critique* (Belmont, Calif.: 1969) and in Walker, ed., *Kant on Pure Reason* (Oxford, 1982).
7. "Reason is and ought only to be the slave of the passions and can never pretend to any other office than to serve and obey them." *Treatise of Human Nature*, Selby-Bigge, ed., bk. 2, sec. 3, p. 415.
8. *Ibid.*, p. 183.
9. *Ibid.*, p. 187.
10. *Ibid.*, bk. 1, pt. 4, sec. 7, *passim*.
11. Wittgenstein, *On Certainty* (Oxford, 1969).
12. Each quoted phrase is followed by its paragraph number in the text of *On Certainty*. Italics are generally mine.
13. *Treatise*, bk. 1, pt. 4, sec. 1, p. 183, another Humean echo is found at para. 135: "But we do not simply follow the principle that what has always happened will happen again (or something like it). What does it mean to follow this principle? Do we really *introduce* it into our reasoning? Or is it merely the *natural law* which our inferring apparently follows? This latter it may be. It is not an item in our considerations."

14. The restrictions which Wittgenstein is conspic-uously inclined to place on the concept of knowledge, on the use of the verb "to know," reflect, and more emphatically, the inclination to restrict the application of the concept of a prop-osition. Only what are clearly propositions sub-ject to empirical testing are, he consistently im-plies, proper objects of the verb "to know"; just as only they can be genuinely objects of doubt.

15. Collingwood, *An Essay on Metaphysics*. London, 1940.

16. Cf. Michael Dummett, "The Reality of the Past," in *Truth and Other Enigmas*. London, 1978.

34 / Ernest Sosa
PHILOSOPHICAL SCEPTICISM AND EPISTEMIC CIRCULARITY

Epistemic circularity has dogged epistemology from the time of the Greek sceptics, through Descartes's circle and Hegel's serpent biting its tail, to serve finally as a source of today's rel-ativism and scepticism—an important source, though of course only one of several. 'Since there is no way to justify one's overall practical or theoretical stance without clarity,' we are told, 'all justification must be ultimately rela-tive to one's basic commitments, conceived perhaps as arbitrary creatures of the will. In comparing overall systems, anyhow, especially when these are equally coherent and self-supportive, there is no way to privilege one's own except arbitrarily, irrationally or aration-ally, perhaps by adopting a frank and honest ethnocentrism.' That is today a widespread at-titude. This paper aims to expose questionable assumptions on which it rests.

We shall consider the following thesis and its supporting argument.

Philosophical Scepticism. There is no way to attain full philosophical understanding of our knowledge. A fully general theory of knowl-edge is impossible.

The Radical Argument (RA)

A1. Any theory of knowledge must be inter-nalist or externalist.

A2. A fully general internalist theory is impossible.

A3. A fully general externalist theory is impossible.

C. From A1–A3, *philosophical scepticism* follows.

In discussing these, first it will be convenient to define some terminology. 'Formal internal-ism'—or 'internalism' for short—shall stand for the doctrine that a belief can be justified and amount to knowledge only through the backing of reasons or arguments. This is of course a special sense of the word, but inter-nalism in this sense today enjoys substantial support. Here are some representative pas-sages, drawn from the writings of Donald Da-vidson, Richard Rorty, Laurence BonJour, and Michael Williams.

> [Nothing] . . . can count as a reason for holding a belief except another belief . . . [And it] . . . will promote matters at this point to review very hastily some of the reasons for abandon-

Reprinted by courtesy of the Editor of the Aristotelian Society from *Proceedings of the Aristotelian Society*, Supplementary Volume 68 (1994), pp. 263–290. © 1994.

ing the search for a basis of knowledge outside the scope of our beliefs. By 'basis' I mean here specifically an epistemological basis, a source of justification.[1]

[It] . . . is absurd to look for . . . something outside [our beliefs] . . . which we can use to test or compare with our beliefs.[2]

[Nothing] . . . counts as justification unless by reference to what we already accept, and there is no way to get outside our beliefs and our language so as to find some test other than coherence.[3]

[We] can think of knowledge as a relation to propositions, and thus of justification as a relation between the propositions in question and other propositions from which the former may be inferred. Or we may think of both knowledge and justification as privileged relations to the objects those propositions are about. If we think in the first way, we will see no need to end the potentially infinite regress of propositions-brought-forward-in-defense-of-other-propositions. It would be foolish to keep conversation going on the subject once everyone, or the majority, or the wise, are satisfied, but of course we *can*. If we think of knowledge in the second way, we will want to get behind reasons to causes, beyond argument to compulsion from the object known, to a situation in which argument would be not just silly but impossible . . . To reach that point is to reach the foundations of knowledge.[4]

To accept the claim that there is no standpoint outside the particular historically conditioned and temporary vocabulary we are presently using from which to judge this vocabulary is to give up on the idea that there can be reasons for using languages as well as reasons within languages for believing statements. This amounts to giving up the idea that intellectual or political progress is rational, in any sense of 'rational' which is neutral between vocabularies.[5]

[The] notion of a [foundational] 'theory of knowledge' will not make sense unless we have confused causation and justification in the manner of Locke.[6]

If we let φ represent the feature or characteristic, whatever it may be, which distinguishes basic empirical beliefs from other empirical beliefs, then in an acceptable foundationalist account a particular empirical belief could qualify as basic only if the premises of the following justificatory argument were adequately justified:

(1)   B has feature φ.
(2)   Beliefs with feature φ are highly likely to be true.

Therefore, B is highly likely to be true.

. . . But if all this is correct, we get the disturbing result that B is not basic after all, since its justification depends on that of at least one other empirical belief.[7]

Only a legitimating account of our beliefs about the world will give an understanding of our knowledge of the world. This means that an account of our knowledge of the world must trace it to something that is *ours*, and that is *knowledge*, but that is not *knowledge of the world*.[8]

'Formal externalism' shall stand for the denial of formal internalism. And, again, for short we shall drop the qualifier, and speak simply of 'externalism'.

A very wide and powerful current of thinking would sweep away externalism root and branch. This torrent of thought in one way or another encompasses much of contemporary philosophy, both on the Continent and in the Anglophone sphere, as may be seen in the Continental rejection of presence to the mind as well as in the analytic rejection of the given. The Continentals have been led by Heidegger, Gadamer, Habermas, Foucault, and Derrida to a great variety of anti-foundationalisms, ranging from consensualism and hermeneutics to relativism and contextualism. The tide against the given on this side of the Channel is no less powerful and is illustrated by the passages already cited. Having also rejected the given and presence to the mind, others settle into an irresolvable frustration that recognizes the problems but denies the possibility of any satisfactory solution.[9] Many who now object to externalism in such terms offer little by way of support. Barry Stroud and William Alston are exceptional in spelling out the deep reasons why, in their view, externalism will leave us ultimately dissatisfied.[10] They have made as persuasive a case as can be made for the unacceptability in principle of any externalist circles in epistemology, and have done so on a very simple *a priori* basis grounded in what seemed to be demands inherent in the traditional epistemological project itself. What follows will focus on their case against such externalism, but much of it applies *mutatis mutandis* to the reasoning, such as it is, offered by other thinkers as well.[11] Though the issue before us is phrased in the terms of analytic epistemology, it is a wellspring of main currents of thought that reach beyond analysis and epistemology. Yet the issue and its options, rarely faced directly, are very ill-understood.

One thing is already clear. Given our definition of externalism as simply the denial of internalism, premise A1 is trivially true and amounts to *p or not-p*.

Note further that an acceptable *internalist* epistemological account of all one's knowledge in some domain D would be, in the following sense, a 'legitimating' account of such knowledge.

A is a legitimating account of one's knowledge in domain D IFF D is a domain of one's beliefs that constitute knowledge and are hence justified (and more), and A specifies the sorts of inferences that justify one's beliefs in D, without circularity or endless regress.

But such an account cannot be attained for all one's knowledge:

The impossibility of general, legitimating, philosophical understanding of all one's knowledge: It is impossible to attain a legitimating account of absolutely all one's own knowledge; such an account admits only justification provided by inference or argument and, since it rules out circular or endlessly regressive inferences, such an account must stop with premises that it supposes or 'presupposes' that one is justified in accepting, without explaining how one is justified in accepting them in turn.

Accordingly, premise A2 of argument RA seems clearly right. And it all comes down to premise A3. If we are to resist philosophical scepticism we cannot accept that premise. What then are the prospects for a formal externalist epistemology?

The formal externalist has, it seems to me,

three main choices today, concerning how a belief attains the status of knowledge, how it acquires the sort of epistemic justification (or aptness or warrant, or anyhow the positive epistemic status) required if it is to amount to knowledge. These three choices are:

E1. *Coherentism.* When a belief is epistemically justified, it is so in virtue of its being part of a coherent body of beliefs (or at least of one that is sufficiently coherent and appropriately comprehensive).

E2. *Foundationalism of the given.* When a belief is epistemically justified, it is so in virtue of being either the taking of the given, the mere recording of what is present to the mind of the believer, or else by being inferred, appropriately from such foundations.

E3. *Reliabilism.* When a belief is epistemically justified, it is so in virtue of deriving from an epistemically, truth-conducively reliable process or faculty or intellectual virtue of belief acquisition.

E1. There is a lot to be said about coherentism, but I lack the space to say much of it here. Suffice it to say that the most comprehensive coherence accompanied by the truth of what one believes will not yet amount to knowledge. The New Evil Demon problem establishes this as follows. Consider the victim of Descartes' evil demon. In fact, suppose we are now such victims. Could that affect whether or not we are *epistemically justified* in believing what we believe? If we are justified as we are, we would *seem* equally justified, in some appropriate sense, so long as nothing changed within our whole framework of experiences and beliefs. However, if by sheer luck one happened to be right in the belief that one faces a fire, one's being *both* thus justified *and* right still would fall short of one's knowing about the fire. So whatever is to be said for coherence, or even for comprehensive coherence, one thing seems clear: none of that will be enough just on its own to explain fully what a true belief needs in order to be knowledge. One's beliefs can be comprehensively coherent without amounting to knowledge, and the same goes for one's beliefs and experiences together. So the sense of 'epistemic justification' in play here is one that will not capture fully the epistemic status required in a true belief if it is to constitute knowledge.

E2. What of foundationalism of the given? *Cogito ergo sum* exclaimed Descartes, as he at last found a good apple off the tree of knowledge. By that time many other apples had already been judged defective, or at least not clearly enough undefective. Our perceptual beliefs had not qualified, since we could so easily be fooled into believing something false on the basis of sensory experience. For example, one could fall victim to illusion or hallucination, and, more dramatically, to an evil demon or a mad scientist who manipulated one's soul or one's brain directly, thus creating systematically the sorts of experiences that one would normally take to be indicative of a normal environment. None of this will affect the *cogito*, however, since even while hallucinating or while manipulated by evil demon or mad scientist, we must still exist and we must still be thinking, if we are to be fooled into thinking something incorrectly. One thought that could never be incorrect is the thought that one exists, and another is the thought that one is thinking.

What is the feature of the *cogito* that explains its special assurance? Consider the proposition (a) that I am now standing. This proposition is true but only contingently so, since I might have been sitting now. In contrast, it is not only true but necessarily true (b) that either I am standing or I am not standing. Is it the necessity of (b) that accounts for its special certainty as compared with (a)? Not entirely. For much is necessary without being certain, and much is certain without being necessary. And, in any case, it cannot be the necessity of 'I think' or 'I exist' that gives such propositions their special epistemic status. For in itself the *cogito*, the proposition that I am thinking, is only true and not necessarily true: I might have been unconscious, or even dead, in which case I would not have been thinking. What is not just contingently true, what is necessarily true, is the fact that *if* I am thinking that I think, *then* I am right: no-one can think that they think without being right. Is it *this*, then, that distinguishes the *cogito* and makes it a legitimately known contingent truth, of which we can properly be assured?

No, that one must be right in believing something does not entail that one is justified in doing so. Take the proposition that there is no largest prime. Since that proposition is necessarily true, we could not possibly go wrong in believing it. Nevertheless, we are not justifiably assured in believing it if we are just guessing the right and have seen no proof. That a belief could not be wrong is hence not enough to make it apt, nor is a belief necessarily apt just because even the Cartesian demon could not fool one into holding it incorrectly. A groundless belief is one that we hold in the absence of supporting reasons or arguments. Some such beliefs seem far superior to others: some amount to knowledge of the obvious, while others are no better than superstition or dogma. We are now after distinguishing properties or features that will help explain which groundless beliefs might qualify as knowledge and which could never do so, and for some account of why these properties or features can make such a difference.

A second main source of apt, groundless beliefs, according to the epistemological tradition, is presence to the mind, or what is given in sensory and other experience. What is involved in one's aptly believing something about the character of one's present sensory experience? It is required by the tradition that one be reporting simply how it is in one's experience itself. One must be reporting on the intrinsic, qualitative character of some experience.

But here again a similar problem arises. Suppose one eyes a well-lit surface with a medium-sized white triangle against a black background. In that case, assuming one is normally sighted, one would have visual experience of a certain distinctive sort, as if one saw a white triangle against a black background. Introspectively, then, one could easily come to know that one was then having experience of that sort: viz, that one was presented with a white triangular image, or the like. What now is the relevant feature of one's introspective belief, what is the feature that makes one's belief apt, makes it indeed a bit of knowledge? Is it simply that one is just reporting what is directly present to one's mind, what is given in one's experience?

No, that something is thus present to one's

mind or given in one's experience is not enough to make it something of which one can be legitimately assured. Take that same situation and change the white image projected on the black surface from a triangle to a dodecagon. And suppose you believe yourself to be presented with a white dodecagon on a black surface, all other conditions remaining as before. Are you then properly assured about the character of your experience so that your introspective belief can then count as apt belief, and indeed as knowledge? What of someone poor at reporting dodecagons in visual experience, who often confuses them with decagons, but who now happens by luck to be right? Such a belief could hardly count as knowledge or even as apt belief.

What Descartes needs in order to explain the special status of the *cogito* is not just that one cannot incorrectly believe that one thinks, but rather that one could not possibly answer incorrectly the question whether one thinks (at least not sincerely and *in foro interno*). And how can one explain this special status enjoyed by that proposition? Descartes's explanation is of course that even a powerful evil demon could not fool one into thinking incorrectly that one thinks. For if the demon gets one to *think* that one thinks—and how else could he fool one into *thinking* incorrectly that one thinks?—then of course inevitably one *does* think and one is bound to be right.

However, that does only half the job. It explains only how one must be right if one thinks that one thinks. It does not explain why it is that one would never think that one does *not* think. Of course Descartes does *claim* that the proposition that one thinks is not only one with regard to which one is infallible, such that if one accepts it one must be right. He also thinks that it is an *indubitable* proposition. But whereas he explains incontestably why one must be right in thinking that one thinks, he does little or nothing to explain why it is that the *cogito* and other similarly simple, clear, distinct propositions are for us indubitable.

What of the doctrine of the given or of presence to the mind? Here the proposal would be that one aptly introspects P iff P describes a present state of one's own consciousness and while considering attentively and with a clear mind the question whether P is the case, one

believes P. It is held to be very unlikely that one would ever opt wrong on such a proposition when in such circumstances.

By reflecting on how the doctrine of the given must be formulated in order to meet certain objections, we have arrived at a reliabilist version of foundationalism. What matters is not that one attend to the contents of one's mind, to one's experiences or beliefs or other states of mind, nor is what matters that one attend to simple necessary truths. For simplicity is a relative matter: what is simple for an experienced mathematician is far from it to the schoolchild learning arithmetic. It is important rather that the subject be reliable on the object of knowledge, and unlikely to go wrong on such subject matter.

E3. So we are down to the third and last of the options open to the formal externalist. But I view generic reliabilism as a *very* broad category indeed, one capacious enough to include thinkers as diverse as Descartes and Alvin Goldman. If we are to resist philosophical scepticism it would appear that here we must make a stand. For, remember, if A3 cannot be defeated, then philosophical scepticism seems the inevitable consequence. So let us consider some objections to generic reliabilism. Here we turn to the promised arguments by Barry Stroud and William Alston.

According to Stroud, 'we need some reason to accept a theory of knowledge if we are going to rely on that theory to understand how our knowledge is possible. That is what . . . no form of 'externalism' can give a satisfactory account of.'[12] Against Descartes, for example, and against the 'externalist' in general he objects on the basis of the following *metaepistemic requirement*:

MR   In order to understand one's knowledge satisfactorily one must see oneself as having some reason to accept a theory that one can recognize would explain one's knowledge if it were true.

And how is MR to be defended? From the assumptions: (a) that understanding something is a matter of having good reason to accept something that would be an explanation if it were true, and (b) that, as a generality-thirsty theorist of knowledge, one wants to understand how one knows the things one thinks one knows.[13] But MR does not follow from these assumptions. From these assumptions it follows only that in order to understand one's knowledge one must in fact *have* good reason or at least justification to accept some appropriate explanation. Why must one also *see oneself as having* such reason?

Far from being just an isolated slip, MR represents rather a deeply held intuition that underlies a certain way of thinking about epistemology. We have seen already several passages that fit this intuition. According to such 'anti-externalism,' as Stroud might label it, what is important in epistemology is justification; and the justification of any given belief requires appeal to *other* beliefs that constitute one's reasons for holding the given belief. Of course, when one combines this with rejection of circularity, the case for scepticism is very strong, assuming that for limited humans an infinite regress of reasons or justifications is out of the question.

The 'externalist' therefore wants to allow some *other* way for a belief to acquire the epistemic status required for it to be knowledge, some way *other* than the belief's being based on some justification, argument, or reason. Note, moreover, how very broad this sense of 'externalism' is. Even arch-internalist Descartes is an 'externalist' in our present sense. We distinguish our present externalism as '*formal* externalism,' it will be recalled, which induces a corresponding type of internalism, 'formal internalism.' Formal internalism holds that there is only one way a belief can have the positive epistemic status required for knowledge, namely by having the backing of reasons or arguments. Note the connection with the requirements that a philosophically satisfactory account of how one knows must be a *legitimating* account, one that specifies the reasons favouring one's belief. Obviously, a formal internalist will believe that for *every* belief that amounts to knowledge there must be such a legitimating account, and that only once we have such an account can we understand what makes that belief knowledge.[14]

Consider now the naturalist, externalist epistemologist. Will he be able to understand how people know the things they do? He will only

if he knows or has some reason to believe his scientific account of the world around him. According to Stroud, this dooms our epistemologist:

If his goal was, among other things, to explain our scientific knowledge of the world around us, he will have an explanation of such knowledge only if he can see himself as possessing some knowledge in that domain. In studying other people, that presents no difficulty. It is precisely by knowing what he does about the world that he explains how others know what they do about the world. But if he had started out asking how anyone knows anything at all about the world, he would be no further along towards understanding how any of it is possible if he had not understood how he himself knows what he has to know about the world in order to have any explanation at all. He must understand himself as knowing or having some reason to believe that his theory is true.[15]

But it is again unclear why the epistemologist needs to *see himself as having* justification for his theory, or as knowing his theory, in order for it to give him understanding of how he and others know the things they know, either in general or in the domain in question. Why is it not enough that he in fact *have good reason to accept his theory* or perhaps even *know his theory to be true*? This is different from his knowing that he has good reason to believe his epistemologically explanatory theory, or even knowing that he knows his theory to be true. To this the response is as follows.

[The externalist epistemologist] . . . is at best in the position of someone who has good reason to believe his theory if that theory is in fact true, but has no such reason to believe it if some other theory is true instead. He can see what he *would* have good reason to believe if the theory he believes were true, but he cannot see or understand himself as knowing or having good reason to believe what his theory says.[16]

[Even] . . . if it is true that you can know something without knowing that you know it, the philosophical theorist of knowledge cannot simply insist on the point and expect to find acceptance of an 'externalist' account of knowledge fully satisfactory. If he could, he would be in the position of someone who says: 'I don't know whether I understand human knowledge or not. If what I believe about it is true and my beliefs about it are produced in what my theory says is the right way, I do know how human knowledge comes to be, so in that sense I do understand. But if my beliefs are not true, or not arrived at in that way, I do not. I wonder which it is. I wonder whether I understand human knowledge or not.' That is not a satisfactory position to arrive at in one's study of human knowledge—or of anything else.[17]

But again it is hard to see why the externalist theorist of knowledge must be in that position. Suppose that, as suggested earlier, he does *not* have to say or believe that he does know his theory of knowledge. Suppose he does not after all need to satisfy MR. Must he then say or believe that he does not know his theory of knowledge? Must he begin to wonder *whether* his theory of knowledge is true, or whether he does really understand human knowledge or not?

Here the dialectic is given a further twist. It is replied that the sort of understanding of our knowledge of the external that we want in philosophy is not just understanding by dumb luck. What we want is rather *knowledgeable* understanding. And this we will never have until we are in a good position to accept our view of our own faculties (of perception or memory, for example), a view which properly underlies our trust in their reliability. But this view we will never be able to justify without relying in turn on already attained knowledge of the external. And this precludes our ever attaining a philosophically satisfactory understanding of all our knowledge in that domain.[18]

The demands introduced by this drive for *knowledgeable* philosophical understanding are different from those deriving from the twofold assumption that (a) epistemic justification is required for knowledge, and (b) reasons and arguments are universally required for epistemic justification. This twofold assumption—formal internalism—leads, as we have seen, to the impossibility of any fully general, legitimating, philosophical understanding of one's knowledge (and indeed to the impossibility of one's knowledge altogether). The new demands do

not derive simply from such formal internalism. They derive rather from a distinctively epistemic circularity that came to philosophical consciousness long ago.

The dialectic of the diallelus is about as ancient as philosophy itself. Nor is Stroud the *only* philosopher today who argues extensively on the basis of epistemic circularity. Recent books by William Alston, for example, contain extensive discussion of these issues, and feature the following main theme:

> *if sense-perception is reliable*, a track-record argument will suffice to show that it is. Epistemic circularity does not in and of itself disqualify the argument. But even granting that point, the argument will not do its job unless we *are* justified in accepting its premises; and that is the case only if sense perception is in fact reliable. And this is to offer a stone instead of bread. We can say the same of any belief-forming practice whatever, no matter how disreputable. We can just as well say of crystalball gazing that if it *is* reliable, we can use a track record argument to show that it is reliable. But when we ask whether one or another source of belief is reliable, we are interested in *discriminating* those that can reasonably be trusted from those that cannot. Hence merely showing that *if* a given source is reliable it can be shown by its record to be reliable, does nothing to indicate that the source belongs with the sheep rather than with the goats. I have removed an allegedly crippling disability, but I have not given the argument a clean bill of health.[19]

Both in that book and in more recent work[20] Alston is forthright in his statement of the problem of circularity that he sees, and in his response to that perceived problem:

> Hence I shall disqualify epistemically circular arguments on the grounds that they do not serve to discriminate between reliable and unreliable doxastic practices.[21]

> Hence, when we reflect on our epistemic situation, we can hardly turn our backs *on our inability to give a satisfactory demonstration of SP and other doxastic practices . . .* [22]

In response to this, Alston argues instead that it is 'practically rational' for us to engage in our firmly rooted doxastic practices,[23] such as our 'sense perceptual practice,' SP, 'our customary ways of forming beliefs about the external environment on the basis of sense perception.'[24] And he believes that 'in showing it to be rational to engage in SP,' he has thereby, 'not shown SP to be reliable, but shown it to be rational to suppose SP to be reliable.'[25] This is so in the sense that it would be irrational for one to judge that SP is rational and deny that SP is reliable, or even to abstain from judging that SP is reliable if the question arises. So in accepting that SP is rational one 'pragmatically implies' and thereby 'commits oneself' to its being the case that SP is reliable.

Just how is it shown that it is 'rational' (or 'reasonable') to engage in SP? Here the argument begins by drawing from Thomas Reid the following claim:

1. The 'only (noncircular) basis we have for trusting rational intuition and introspection is that they are firmly established doxastic practices, so firmly established that we cannot help [doing so] . . . ; and we have exactly the same basis for trusting sense perception, memory, nondeductive reasoning, and other sources of belief for which Descartes and Hume were demanding an external validation.'[26]

And it continues as follows:

2. [Even if] we could adopt some basic way of forming beliefs about the physical environment other than SP, or some basic way of forming beliefs about the past other than memory, . . . why should we?'[27]
3. 'The same factors that prevent us from establishing the reliability of SP, memory, and so on without epistemic circularity would operate with the same force in these other cases.'[28]
4. 'These considerations seem to me to indicate that it is eminently *reasonable* for us to form beliefs in the ways we standardly do,'[29] such as SP.

This is presented as an argument for the practical rationality (or reasonableness) of using SP, one which avoids the 'epistemic circularity' that cripples track-record and other arguments

for the *reliability* of SP. Where exactly is the circularity, and just how does it do its damage? The answer considers the use of a track-record argument, an argument that appeals to our past cognitive success through using SP:

[If] I were to ask myself why I should accept the premises, I would, if I pushed the reflection far enough, have to make the claim that sense perception is reliable. For if I weren't prepared to make that claim on reflection, why should I, as a rational subject, countenance perceptual beliefs? Since this kind of circularity involves a commitment to the conclusion as a presupposition of our supposing ourselves to be *justified* in holding the premises, we can properly term it 'epistemic circularity'.[30]

However, consider again the earlier argument in favour of the conclusion that it is *rational* (or reasonable) to use SP, the argument presented above as 1–4. If we push reflection far enough with regard to why we should accept the premises of *this* argument, don't we find ourselves appealing precisely to *its* conclusion? And, if so, then is not this argument just as circular, and in a similar way, as the track-record argument in favour of the reliability of SP?

Epistemological reflection therefore leads to a situation that does seem 'fairly desperate' after all. We wonder whether we really know what we take ourselves to know. We wonder how we know whatever it is that we know. We hope that our way of forming beliefs—with its characteristic elements of memory, introspection, perception, and reason—does give us knowledge and explains how we know. But how can we be sure?

Suppose W is our total way of forming beliefs. If we believe that W is reliable, R(W), our belief B:R(W) is itself formed by W. And if a belief is justified iff formed in a reliable way, then our B:R(W) is justified iff W is reliable (given that it is formed by W). B:R(W) is justified, therefore, iff W *is* reliable.

Yet we must sympathize with the critics of 'externalism,' who argue that this is to 'give us a stone instead of bread,' and that the externalist 'is at best in the position of someone who . . . can see what he *would* have good reason to believe if the theory he believes were true.' Let us consider carefully what they have to say.

Alston, in his recent book, argues as follows.

Consider our sense-perceptual doxastic practice SP, (our total way of forming beliefs based on sense perception). The reliability of SP can be inferred, let us suppose, by relying on the deliverances of SP itself. Hence, assuming our reasoning is otherwise unobjectionable, belief B:R(SP) is justified if SP is reliable. But using the deliverances of SP to argue for B:R(SP) would be unacceptably circular.

Here, again, is how he puts it.

[When] we ask whether one or another source of belief is reliable, we are interested in *discriminating* those that can reasonably be trusted from those that cannot. Hence merely showing that *if* a given source is reliable it can be shown by its record to be reliable, does nothing to indicate that the source belongs with the sheep rather than with the goats. I have removed an allegedly crippling disability, but I have not given the argument a clean bill of health. Hence I shall disqualify epistemically circular arguments on the grounds that they do not serve to discriminate between reliable and unreliable doxastic practices.[31]

But what exactly is the problem for the justification of B:R(SP)? And, even more generally, what exactly is the problem for the justification of B:R(W), where W is our total way of forming beliefs (of which SP would be only one among several components)?

Justification can be either a matter of one's internal rationality and coherence, or it can go beyond that to encompass some broader (or just different) state pertinent to whether one knows. Thus the victim of Descartes's evil demon may have internal justification for believing that there is a fire before him, but would still lack knowledge even if *by accident* he is right. Similarly, the hopelessly myopic Mr. Magoo may have internal justification for believing that it is safe to step ahead, but would still lack knowledge even if the board over the precipice does by accident still lie ahead.

For now let us focus just on internal justifi-

cation or rational coherence. Are we bound to fall short of rational coherence if we form our belief that W is reliable—B:R(W)—through W itself? Alston suggests that we do fall short, in *some* way, since in asking whether one or another source of belief is reliable, we wish to *discriminate* sources that we can trust with good reason. Therefore, to show that *if* a given source is reliable it can be shown by its own use to be reliable does nothing to discriminate it from the many other possible sources equally able to pass that test.

We are thus offered the following view of the matter. We have before us a menu of sources, of ways of forming beliefs: W1, . . . , Wn. And we would like to discriminate the reliable from the unreliable. About Wi we discover that it has this much to be said for it: if one uses Wi to form beliefs, then by Wi one can form the belief B:R(Wi), the belief that Wi is reliable. And *if* Wi *is* reliable, then B: R(Wi) will itself of course be justified. When a way of forming beliefs, Wi, has this feature relative to a subject S in circumstances C, let us say that Wi is self-supportive for S in C: i.e., for S in C, Wi will deliver the belief on the part of S *that* Wi is itself reliable—B:R(Wi).

Here then is Alston's point about the feature of being self-supportive relative to oneself and one's circumstances: *several* (indefinitely many) ways of forming beliefs might well have this feature relative to oneself and one's circumstances, but many of these are palpably unacceptable. Indeed they might well be inconsistent in such a way that most by far are bound to be *unreliable*. Therefore, even once we reach the conclusion that Wi is self-supportive relative to us and our circumstances, that by itself does *not* enable us to conclude that it is acceptable, that it is a sheep, not a goat.

That much is surely right. But there is more. There is also the further proposal that if a way of forming beliefs W (a doxastic practice) is 'firmly established' for us, then we *can* conclude that it is *practically* acceptable, that we are practically rational in accepting it.[32] Presumably this feature of a doxastic practice of its being FE (firmly established) is thought to have an advantage over the feature of a doxastic practice of its being R (reliable), with regard to the dialectic above. But it is hard to see how it can possibly enjoy any such advantage. For in order to reach the belief that our total way of forming beliefs W is firmly established—B:FE(W)—we could hardly avoid using W itself. And it is not hard to see that indefinitely many crazy ways W* of forming beliefs might (conceivably) be equally effective, if used by one in one's circumstances, in leading to the belief—B:FE(W*)—that W* is firmly established for us, even though W* is still clearly unacceptable. What is more, it is also conceivable that there be a way W* that might *in fact* become firmly established, even though W* remained unacceptable (by our present lights, of course). Conclusion: It is hard to see the advantage in moving from reliability to firm establishment and practical reasonableness. True, even if using W to settle whether W is reliable would yield a positive verdict, that is not enough to lift W above its many competitors with an analogous feature. But, similarly, even if using W to settle whether W is firmly established would yield a positive verdict, that is not enough to lift W above its similar competitors *either*. It might be answered that we needn't *see W as firmly established* in order for its firm establishment to lend us practical justification for using it. But then why need we *see W as reliable* in order for its reliability to lend us epistemic justification for using it?

Again, suppose we use way W, and that the use of W assures us that W itself *is* reliable. Indeed, consider our situation in the very *best conceivable outcome*. Suppose:

(a)   W *is* reliable (and suppose even that, given our circumstances and fundamental nature, it is the *most* reliable overall way we could have).

(b)   We are *right* in our description of W: it *is* exactly W that we use in forming beliefs, and it is of course (therefore) W that we use in forming the belief that W is our way of forming beliefs.

(c)   We *believe* that W *is* reliable (correctly so, given *a* above), and this belief, too, is formed by means of W.

Now what? Are we still in a 'desperate situation'? What could possibly be missing? How could we possibly improve our epistemic situation?

It might be suggested that perhaps we could still search for some argument that would not be flawed by epistemic circularity. But is such circularity necessarily vicious? After all, what does an argument *ever* accomplish? Suppose you are given argument A with premises P and conclusion C and you correctly accept it as evidently valid. What this gives you in the first instance is the conviction that P entails C. And, unless you go back on this conviction, you are now *restricted* in the combinations of coherent attitudes that are open to you. But that is all that the argument by itself does: i.e., that is all you can derive from its validity. As far as the argument goes, its relevant deliverance is your belief that P entails C, and this justifies your believing C, given that you believe P, only by contrast with believing P and either disbelieving or consciously withholding on C. But it does not justify your believing C, given that you believe P, by contrast with many other optional attitudes: e.g., disbelieving C and disbelieving P. N.B.: it is a kind of intrinsic coherence that lifts the preferable attitudes over the lesser ones: once we have **(a) B:[P entails C]**, we need to avoid **(b) B:P and D:C,** and **(c) B:P and Wh:C**—where D:P means B: ~P, and Wh:P means consciously or deliberately withholding on whether P or ~P. Many other combinations of attitudes remain open options, of course, but so long as we retain (a), both (b) and (c) are to be avoided. Why so? Because they do not cohere well. There is some evident lack of fittingness or harmony in each of them. Here I won't try to spell out the exact nature of the incoherence that attaches not only to (a) & (b) but also to (a) & (c). I'll assume we can agree that it is here, whatever its nature. In fact, it is not really necessary to say anything that strong. A comparative judgment is enough. Consider: **(d) B:P and B:C.** All we need is the judgment that (a) & (d) is more coherent than either of (a) & (b) or (a) & (c). Given (a), which results from our supposed argument above, (d) is lifted over each of (b) and (c) in respect of coherence.

The upshot: all that (the validity of) an argument ever does is to raise some combinations of attitudes (to premises and conclusion respectively) above others in respect of coherence.

But now suppose that by using way W of forming beliefs (which may and probably will include the use of argument) we arrive at the conviction that W is our way of forming beliefs. Now, so long as we do not go back on that conviction, does that not restrict our coherent combinations of attitudes? Take: **(e) B: [W is my overall way of forming beliefs].** And compare **(f) B:[W is reliable], (g) D:[W is reliable]** and **(h) Wh:[W is reliable].** Is it not evident that (e) & (f) would be more satisfyingly coherent than either of (e) & (g) or (e) & (h)?

If so, the question arises: Just how would any further argument provide a fundamentally different and superior source of justification or rationality for our accepting the reliability of our overall way W of forming beliefs, as compared with what we are provided already by our conviction that W is indeed that overall way of ours?

The answer might come back: 'But once we had an argument A for W being reliable from premises already accepted, we would embed our faith in W's reliability within a more comprehensively coherent whole that would include the premises of our argument A.' And it must be granted that such an argument *would* bring that benefit. However: we know that such an argument would *have* to be epistemically circular, since its premises can only qualify as beliefs of ours through the use of way W. That is to say, a correct and full response to rational pressure for disclosure of what justifies one in upholding the premises must circle back down to the truth of the conclusion. *Necessarily* such an argument must be epistemically circular—that much seems clear enough. To rue that fact at this stage is hence like pining for a patron saint of modesty (who blesses all and only those who do not bless themselves), once we have seen that there could not possibly be such a saint.

Perhaps the dissatisfaction emphasized by Alston and Stroud, and many others, has a different source than any we have considered. Perhaps it arises from the following reasoning:

If we justify our belief in the reliability of our W—B:R(W)—by noting that W itself yields B:

R(W), then anyone with a rival but self-supporting method W* would be able to attain an equal measure of justification through parallel reasoning. They would justify their belief B:R(W*) by noting that W* itself yields B: R(W*). So are we not forced to conclude that someone clever enough could attain a measure of rational justification equal to ours so long as their way of forming beliefs, W*, turned out to be, to the same extent, coherently and comprehensively self-supporting?

If *this* is the source of the discomfort, then it is discomfort we must learn to tolerate—though in time reason should be able to dispel it, just as it would dispel any desire to meet the saint who blesses all and only the nonself-blessed. After all, discursive, inferential reason is not our only faculty; and logical brilliance does not even ensure sanity. In light of this, I see no sufficient argument why we must settle, at the end of the day, for any irresolvable theoretical frustration.

We need to distinguish the internal justification that amounts to rational coherence, or even to rational coherence plus rational intuition, from the broader intellectual virtue required for knowledge. In order to know that p, one's belief must not fail the test of rational, internal coherence. But it must be tested in other ways as well: it must be true, for one thing. And, more than that, it must be *apt*: it must be a belief that manifests overall intellectual virtue, and is not flawed essentially by vice. (Mr. Magoo can infer brilliantly and a belief of his can manifest *that* virtue, while it is still flawed by epistemic vice and fails to manifest overall virtue.) Finally, if it is to amount to knowledge a belief must be such that, in the circumstances it *would* be held by that subject iff it were true, and this in virtue of its being apt in the way that it is apt, in virtue of deriving from the complex of virtues that form it and sustain it.

Suppose we are rationally justified in accepting the reliability of our way of forming beliefs W, and suppose our justification derives from the way that very belief coheres within our overall body of beliefs. Then we do of course commit ourselves to the consequence that anyone intelligent enough to secure an equal measure of coherence for their body of beliefs would attain thereby a comparable degree of rational justification for their belief in the reliability of their way of forming beliefs (a belief we may assume to be already part of their corpus). And this remains so even if their way amounts on the whole to madness! For in granting them logical coherence we need not grant thereby that there is *no* epistemically pertinent distinction between them and us. There are faculties other than reason, surely, and there is plenty of scope for madness and other vices beyond the ability to spin a coherent story.

To sum up: We can legitimately and with rational justification arrive at a belief that a certain set of faculties or doxastic practices are those that we employ *and* are reliable. That remains so, even though someone mad can weave a system of comparable internal coherence and can thereby attain a comparable degree of internal justification. But in granting this we must not grant that such coherently rational belief need only be true in order to be knowledge. A coherently rational belief can fail to be apt, surely, and can even be mad if formed by a mind that is brilliantly logical though deranged in its social and physical perception and perhaps also in its memory. (A rationally coherent belief *can* also be apt, of course, and can thereby amount to knowledge as well.) Anyhow, the point remains; there is no obstacle in principle to our conceivably attaining rationally coherent belief in some general account of our own epistemic faculties and their reliability. This would be bread, not a stone (or a sheep, not a goat). Why could we not conceivably attain thereby a general understanding of how we know whatever we do know?

We have also felt the attraction of Stroud's reasoning, however: his brief for a very general and fundamental doubt against our ever conceivably attaining any such general understanding.

Stroud's reasoning, and that of many others along the historical length and contemporary breadth of philosophy, may perhaps return us to an assumption that seems questionable: the questionable assumption that a satisfyingly general philosophical account of human knowledge would have to be a legitimating account that would reveal how all such knowledge can be traced back to some epistemically prior knowledge from which it can be shown to be derived (without logical or epistemic circularity).[33] There is no good reason to make this assumption, especially when it is evident that no such general account of all our knowledge could conceivably be obtained.

The desire for a fully general, legitimating, philosophical understanding of all our knowledge is unfulfillable. It is unfulfillable for simple, demonstrable logical reasons. In this respect it is like the desire to find the saint who blesses all and only the nonselfblessed. A trek through the Himalayas may turn up likely prospects each of whom eventually is seen to fall short, until someone in the expedition reflects that there could not possibly be such a saint, and this for evident, logical reasons. How should they all respond to this result? They may of course be very unhappy to have been taken in by a project now clearly defective, and this may leave them frustrated and dissatisfied. But is it reasonable for them to insist that somehow the objective is still worthy, even if unfortunately it turns out to be incoherent? Is this a sensible response? How would we respond if we found ourselves in that situation? Would it not be a requirement of good sense or even of sanity to put that obviously incoherent project behind us, to just forget about it and to put our time to better use? And is that not what we must do with regard to the search for fully general, legitimating, philosophical accounts of our knowledge?

If it does not just return us to that questionable assumption, however, then what can be the basis for the objection to a general theory of knowledge, indeed to one so general that it encompasses not only all of our knowledge of the external but all of our knowledge in general? Suppose one's belief in one's theory takes the following form:

T A belief X amounts to knowledge if and only if it satisfies conditions C.

It would not be long before a philosopher would wonder in virtue of what T itself is a piece of knowledge, and if T is held as an explanatory theory for all of our knowledge, then the answer would not be far to seek: T is a piece of knowledge because T itself meets conditions C. And how do we know that T meets conditions C? Well, of course, *that* belief itself must meet conditions C in turn. And so on, without end. Is there any unacceptability in principle here, is there any unavoidable viciousness? Compare the following three things.

E   A belief B in a general epistemological account of when beliefs are justified (or apt) that applies to B itself and explains in virtue of what it, too, is justified (apt).
G   A statement S of a general account of when statements are grammatical (or a sentence S stating when sentences are grammatical) that applies to S itself and explains in virtue of what it, too, is grammatical.
P   A belief B in a general psychological account of how one acquires the beliefs one holds, an account that applies to B itself and explains why it, too, is held.

Why should E be any more problematic than G or P? Why should there be any more of a problem for a general epistemology than there would be for a general grammar the grammaticality of whose statement is explained in turn by itself, or for a general psychology belief in which is explained by that very psychology?

It must be granted that what we want is a sort of explanation that would in principle enable us to understand how we have any knowledge at all. Question: "Why are there chickens?" Answer: "They come from eggs." "And why are there eggs?" "They come from chickens." This exchange could not provide a complete answer to a child's question, if the question is, more fully, that of why there are chickens *at all, ever*. To answer this question we need appeal to divine creation, or evolution, or anyhow to something entirely other than chickens. Consider now the analogous question about knowledge, about the sources of the epistemic status of our knowledgeable beliefs (and not now about the causal sources of their existence). A complete answer for this question must appeal to something other than beliefs claimed already to enjoy the status of knowl-

edge. For we want an explanation of how beliefs *ever* attain that status *at all*.

It is important to avert a confusion. We shall never be able really to *have* an explanation of anything without our *having* some knowledge, the knowledge that constitutes our having the explanation, knowledge like

K   X is the case in virtue of such and such.

Though we must have such knowledge if we are to understand why X is the case, however, there is no need to include any attribution of knowledge in the explanans of K, in the 'such and such.' The concept of knowledge need not be part of that explanans. Compare again our general theory of knowledge schema:

T   A belief X amounts to knowledge if and only if it satisfies conditions C.

T is something we must *know* if it is to give us real understanding, and in offering it we are perhaps, in some sense, 'presupposing' that we know it. This does not mean that our theory must be less than fully general. Our theory T may still be fully general so long as no epistemic status—e.g., knowledge, or justification—plays any role in the 'conditions C' that constitute the explanans of T.

It is true that in epistemology we want *knowledgeable* understanding, and not just 'understanding by dumb luck' (which, in the relevant sense, is incoherent anyhow, and hence not to be had). But there is no apparent reason why we cannot have it with a theory such as T, without compromising the full generality of our account. Of course in explaining how we know theory T, whether to the sceptic or to ourselves, we have to appeal to theory T itself, given the assumptions of correctness and full generality that we are making concerning T. Given those assumptions there seems no way of correctly answering such a sceptic except by 'begging the question' and 'arguing circularly' against him. But, once we understand this, what option is left to us except to go ahead and 'beg' that question against *such* a sceptic (though 'begging the question' and 'arguing circularly' may now be misnomers for what we do, since it is surely no fallacy, not if it constitutes correct and legitimate intellectual procedure). Nor are we, in proceeding thus, by means of a self-supporting argument, assuming that *all self-supporting arguments are on a par.* This would be a serious mistake. It is not just *in virtue of being self-supporting* that our belief in T would acquire its epistemic status required for knowledge. Rather it would be in virtue of meeting conditions C.[34] And conditions C must not yield that a belief for a system of beliefs has the appropriate positive epistemic status provided simply that it is self-supporting. For this would obviously be inadequate. Therefore, our belief in T *would* be self-supporting, as had better be any successful and general theory of knowledge, but it would not amount to knowledge or even to a belief with the appropriate epistemic status, *simply in virtue of being self-supporting.*

In all our reflection and in all our discussion of objections to externalism we have found no good argument for the view that epistemically circular arguments must be disqualified globally as ineffectual in making discriminations between reliable and unreliable doxastic practices. Nor have we been able to find any good reason to yield to the sceptic or to reject externalist theories of knowledge globally and antecedently as theories that could not possibly give us the kind of understanding of human knowledge in general that is a goal of epistemology. And so we have found no good reason to accept *philosophical scepticism,* the main target thesis of this paper. As for any desperate retreat to relativism or ethnocentrism, finally, that now seems ill-conceived and imperceptive.[35] I mean the retreat into relativism that sees no way of adjudicating through reason among clashing, equally coherent systems. The recoil to ethnocentrism (or the like) betrays a rationalist *malgré lui* with no objective way to adjudicate except reason.[36] Who but a philosopher could expect so much from reason?[37] What privileges our positions, if anything does, cannot be that it is self-supportive, as we have seen; *but nor can it possibly be just that it is ours.* Our position would be privileged rather by deriving from cognitive virtues, from the likes of perception and cogent thought, and not from derangement or superstition or their ilk.[38]

NOTES

1. Donald Davidson, 'A Coherence Theory of Truth and Knowledge,' in *Kant oder Hegel,* ed. Dieter Henrich (Stuttgart: Klett-Cotta, 1983), pp. 423–438; p. 426.
2. *Ibid.,* p. 431.
3. Richard Rorty, *Philosophy and the Mirror of Nature* (Princeton, N.J.: Princeton University Press, 1979), p. 178.
4. *Ibid.,* p. 159.
5. Richard Rorty, *Contingency, Irony, and Solidarity* (Cambridge, UK: Cambridge University Press, 1989), p. 48. Note the ambiguity between 'reasons for using languages' that one *has* and adduces, versus reasons that there are whether or not one has them or adduces them. And note also the assumption that only what is based on reasonings from adduced reasons can be assessed as 'rational.' (One might of course yield the vocabulary of the 'rational' in the face of such uninhibited assumptions, for the sake of the conversation, so long as one could still distinguish among beliefs, and even among 'choices of vocabulary,' those that are 'apt,' in some apt sense, from those that are not.)
6. Rorty, *Philosophy and the Mirror of Nature,* p. 152.
7. Laurence BonJour, *The Structure of Empirical Knowledge* (Cambridge, MA: Harvard Univ. Press, 1985), p. 31.
8. Michael Williams, 'Epistemological Realism and the Basis of Scepticism,' *Mind* 97 (1988), p. 246. (This paper sketches a view developed and defended in his *Unnatural Doubts* (Oxford: Blackwell Publishers, 1992).) Here Williams is attributing a view to Stroud. But in his paper (and in his book) he evidently agrees that if there were a way of attaining a general philosophical understanding of our knowledge of the world, it would have to be in terms of a legitimating account; and he does not take seriously the possibility of a substantially externalist account.
9. Such overreaction against objective foundations may drive even someone brilliant to unfortunate excesses. Compare the writings of Paul Feyerabend. Moreover, the sort of internalism that enforces capitulation to 'circularity'-wielding relativists is not confined to the *avant-garde* we have already consulted. For just one example, earlier in the century, in an otherwise most illuminating paper, Alan Gewirth had this to say: 'Consequently, it is circular to say that the basic principles of science are themselves cognitive; for it is these principles or norms which determine whether anything else is to be called cognitive. Moreover, these principles are a selection

from among other possible principles—possible, that is, in the sense that they are espoused by people who claim to have "science" or "knowledge" by methods which are in important respects different from those grounded in inductive and deductive logic. These other methods include those of Christian Science, astrology, phrenology, tribal medicine-men, and many others. Each of these other methods has its own way of defining what is to be meant by "fact," "knowledge," and so forth. Hence, if any of these latter is to be called "noncognitive," it will be by reference not to *its* norms or principles but to those of *some* other way of viewing "science" or "knowledge." To claim that any of those is "absolutely" non-cognitive is to ignore the relativity of all claims of cognitiveness to norms or principles which define what is to be meant by "cognitive." . . . Hence, strictly speaking, the choice among different conceptions of "knowledge" or "science" cannot itself be said to be made by cognitive means.' (From A. Gewirth, 'Positive "Ethics" and Normative "Science",' *The Philosophical Review* LXIX (1960); the passage quoted comes from the thirteenth paragraph.) Here again, we might well yield the vocabulary of 'choices made by cognitive means,' so long as we could keep a distinction between choices or commitments that are 'apt' and those that are not, where this is not just something 'relative' to raw or brute or 'arbitrary' commitments.

10. Alston is among those who settle into irresolvable frustration, insofar as he accepts externalism at the cost of a freely avowed dissatisfaction, which, as we shall see, he takes to be inherent in the human *theoretical* condition. Insofar as he tries to struggle against this, it is by conceding the theoretical frustration, and turning to a kind of practical reasonability, in a way we shall consider.

11. The position on these issues of my *Knowledge in Perspective* (Cambridge, UK: Cambridge University Press, 1991), has repeatedly drawn an objection (as detailed in notes 19 and 33 below) that we shall consider in what follows.

12. Barry Stroud, 'Understanding Human Knowledge in General,' in *Knowledge and Scepticism*, ed. by Marjorie Clay and Keith Lehrer ((Boulder: Westview, 1989), p. 43.

13. Compare p. 44, *ibid*.: '[Descartes is] . . . a theorist of knowledge. He wants to understand how he knows the things he thinks he knows. And he cannot satisfy himself on that score unless he can see himself as having some reason to accept the theory that he (and all the rest of us) can recognize would explain his knowledge if it were true. That is not because knowing implies knowing that you know. It is because having an

explanation of something in the sense of understanding it is a matter of having good reason to accept something that would be an explanation if it were true.'

14. Compare here again the passages from Davidson and Rorty cited earlier, and the consequences drawn by Rorty not only for theory but also for praxis.

15. *Ibid.*, p. 45.

16. *Ibid.*, p. 46.

17. *Ibid.*, p. 47.

18. Compare Stroud on this: 'We want witting, not unwitting, understanding. That requires knowing or having some reason to accept the scientific story you believe about how people know the things they know. And in the case of knowledge of the world around us, that would involve already knowing or having some reason to believe something in the domain in question. Not all the knowledge in that domain would thereby be explained.' (*Ibid.*, p. 48.) Also: 'The demand for completely general understanding of knowledge in a certain domain requires that we see ourselves at the outset as not knowing anything in that domain and then coming to have such knowledge on the basis of some independent and in that sense prior knowledge or experience . . . [When] we try to explain how we know . . . things [in a domain we are interested in] we find we can understand it only by assuming that we have got some knowledge in the domain in question. And that is not philosophically satisfying. We have lost the prospect of explaining and therefore understanding all of our knowledge with complete generality.' (*Ibid.*, pp. 48–9.)

19. W. P. Alston, *Perceiving God: The Epistemology of Religious Experience* (Ithaca: Cornell University Press, 1991), p. 148. In a review of my *Knowledge in Perspective*, in *Mind* 102 (1993): 199–203, Alston adds that 'it is plausible to suppose that we cannot give an impressive argument for the reliability of sense perception without making use of what we have learned from sense perception. This problem affects Sosa's view as much as it does any other form of externalism that requires for justification or knowledge that the source of a belief is truth-conducive. To apply Sosa's view we would have to determine which belief forming habits are intellectual virtues, i.e., which can be depended on to yield mostly true beliefs. Doesn't epistemic circularity attach to these enterprises, by his own showing? What does he have to say about that?'

20. W. P. Alston, *The Reliability of Sense Perception* (Ithaca: Cornell University Press, 1993).

21. *Ibid.*, p. 17. The problem is supposed to arise from the fact that the data on the basis of which

a track-record argument reaches the conclusion that a certain doxastic practice DP is reliable, are data that derive (at some remove, if not immediately) from the use of that very practice DP.

22. *Ibid.*, p. 120. My emphasis.
23. *Ibid.*, p. 130.
24. *Ibid.*, p. 7.
25. *Ibid.*, p. 131.
26. *Ibid.*, p. 127.
27. *Ibid.*, p. 125.
28. *Ibid.*
29. *Ibid.*, p. 126.
30. *Ibid.*, p. 15.
31. *Ibid.*, p. 17.
32. I will use 'firmly established' here as short for 'firmly established in the way described more fully by Alston and proposed by him as sufficient for practical reasonableness or rationality'.
33. See p. 6 above. And compare Paul Moser's statement of the difficulty as he sees it (Paul Moser, Review of *Knowledge in Perspective*, in *Canadian Philosophical Reviews* XI (1991): 425–7): 'What . . . can effectively justify one's meta-belief in the virtue of memory? What can effectively justify the claim that "the products of such faculties are likely to be true"? These questions . . . ask what, if anything, can provide a cogent defense of the alleged reliability of memory against familiar sceptical queries . . . The . . . questions ask not for absolute proof, but for a non-questionbegging reason supporting the alleged reliability of memory, a reason that does not beg a key question against the sceptic. It is doubtful that we can deliver such a reason; coherence of mere beliefs will surely not do the job' T. F. Wilkerson also joins the broad consensus against the supposed 'circularity' in externalism: 'How can I know that I am intellectually virtuous, that I have a settled ability or disposition to arrive at the truth? Indeed, how do I know that I have arrived at the truth? As Sosa points out, it is no good to answer that my beliefs are true in so far as they are justified by

other beliefs: that way lies *either* old-fashioned foundationalism *or* coherentism. Nor presumably is it any good to say that they are justified because they have been acquired in an intellectually virtuous way: the circle seems swift and unbreakable.' (Review of *Knowledge in Perspective*, in *Philosophical Books* 33(1992): 159–61.)

34. This seems the key to an answer for Alston's charge that epistemically circular arguments 'do not serve to discriminate between reliable and unreliable doxastic practices,' cited earlier. One can make such discriminations with epistemically circular arguments (ones with premises that are in fact true and justified, etc.) even if it is not the circular character of the reasoning that by itself effects the discrimination.

35. And a similar objection can be lodged, based on similar reflections, on the analogous retreat in moral and political philosophy.

36. About other views that are in some way 'relativist' I remain silent.

37. And, besides, the irrationalist cannot be answered nonquestionbeggingly *anyhow*, not if our answer presupposes the validity of reason. When thought through, the requirement of nonquestionbegging defensibility against all conceivable comers is ill-advised, and indeed incoherent. But once we see why that is so, we should see also that reason cannot plausibly be held above perception or memory as a proper source of epistemic status.

38. 'But that bare assertion is so empty! Which are these virtues? What means this cogency? What else is involved?' To this reaction the response would have to be a very long story, if told in full, one that turns now longer, now shorter, with every advance in our understanding of ourselves and our thought and our environment and our origins, and the relations among all these. One's epistemic perspective is joined indispensably to one's broader worldview.

35 / BARRY STROUD
SCEPTICISM, 'EXTERNALISM', AND THE GOAL OF EPISTEMOLOGY

Scepticism has been different things at different times in the history of philosophy, and has been put to different uses. In this century it has been understood primarily as a position—or threat—within the theory of knowledge. It says that nobody knows anything, or that nobody has good reason to believe anything. That view must be of central significance in epistemology, given that the goal of the enterprise is to explain how we know the things we think we do. It would seem that any satisfying positive theory of knowledge should imply the falsity of scepticism.

Scepticism need not always be taken as completely general. It has more typically been restricted to this or that particular kind of alleged knowledge or reasonable belief: we have no reason to believe anything about the future, for example, even if we know a great deal about the past and the present; we know nothing about the world around us, although we know what the course of our own experience is like; or I know what the physical world and my own thoughts and experiences are like, but I know nothing about the minds of other persons. Scepticism is most illuminating when restricted to particular areas of knowledge in this way because it then rests on distinctive and problematic features of the alleged knowledge in question, not simply on some completely general conundrum in the notion of knowledge itself, or in the very idea of reasonable belief. It is meant to be a theory about human beings as they actually are, and about the knowledge

we think we actually have in the circumstances in which we find ourselves.

Scepticism in the theory of knowledge involves much more than the bare assertion that no one knows anything or has any reason to believe anything of a particular kind. If all animate life were suddenly (or even gradually) wiped off the face of the earth no one would then know anything or have any reason to believe anything about the world, but that would not make scepticism about the external world true. A philosophical theorist wants to understand human knowledge as it is as human beings and the world they live in actually are. But again not just any denial of human knowledge in a certain domain counts as philosophical scepticism. Human beings as they are right now do not know the causes of many kinds of cancer, or of AIDS, or the fundamental structure of matter. But universal ignorance in a particular domain does not make scepticism true of that domain. Scepticism holds that people as they actually are fail to know or have good reason to believe the sorts of things we all think we already know right now. Anti-scepticism, or a positive theory of knowledge, holds the opposite. It would explain how human beings, equipped as they are and living in the world they live in, do in fact know the sorts of things they think they do.

Theories of knowledge which conflict in this way nevertheless typically share many assumptions about human beings and their cognitive and perceptual resources. It is agreed on all

Reprinted by courtesy of the Editor of the Aristotelian Society from *Proceedings of the Aristotelian Society*, Supplementary Volume 68 (1994), pp. 291–307. © 1994.

sides, for example, that if human beings know things about the world around them, they know them somehow on the basis of what they perceive by means of the senses. The dispute then turns on whether and how what the senses provide can give us knowledge or good reason to believe things about the world. Knowledge of matters which go beyond perception to the independent world is seen, at least temporarily, as problematic. A successful positive theory of knowledge would explain how the problem is solved so that we know the things we think we know about the world after all.

It must be admitted, I think, that what many philosophers have said about perceptual knowledge is pretty clearly open to strong sceptical objections. That is, *if* the way we know things about the world is the way many philosophers have said it is, *then* a good case can be made for the negative sceptical conclusion that we do not really know such things after all. That is why scepticism remains such a constant threat. If you don't get your description of the human condition right, if you describe human perception and cognition and reasoning in certain natural but subtly distorted ways, you will leave human beings as you describe them incapable of the very knowledge you are trying to account for. A sceptical conclusion will be derivable from the very description which serves to pose the epistemological problem. Thus did the ancient sceptics argue, conditionally, against the Stoics: "if human knowledge is arrived at in the way you say it is, there could be no such thing as human knowledge at all." Even if true, that does not of course show that scepticism is correct. It shows at most that human knowledge or the human condition must be understood in some other way. The threat of scepticism is what keeps the theory of knowledge going.

The point is that scepticism and its competitors among more positive theories of knowledge are all part of the same enterprise. They offer conflicting answers to what is for all of them a common question or set of questions. The task is to understand all human knowledge of a particular kind, or all reasonable belief concerning a certain kind of matter of fact. Scepticism is one possible outcome of that task. In that sense, scepticism, like its rivals, is

a general theory of human knowledge. But it is not a satisfactory theory or outcome. It is paradoxical. It represents us as having none of the knowledge or good reasons we ordinarily think we've got. No other theory or answer is satisfactory either if it does not meet and dispel the threat of scepticism. I think many philosophical theories of knowledge have failed to do that, despite what their defenders have claimed for them.

In fact, I find the force and resilience of scepticism in the theory of knowledge to be so great, once the epistemological project is accepted, and I find its consequences to be so paradoxical, that I think the best thing to do now is to look much more closely and critically at the very enterprise of which scepticism or one of its rivals is the outcome: the task of the philosophical theory of knowledge itself. Its goal is not just any understanding of human knowledge; it seeks to understand knowledge in a certain way. Both scepticism and its opposites claim to understand human knowledge in that special way, or from that special philosophical point of view. I would like to inquire what that way of understanding ourselves and our knowledge is, or is supposed to be. I wonder whether there is a coherent point of view from which we could get a satisfactory understanding of ourselves of the kind we apparently aspire to. Many would dismiss scepticism as absurd on the grounds that there is no such point of view, or that we could never get ourselves into the position of seeing that it is true if it were true. But to adopt a more positive theory of knowledge instead is still to offer a description of the human condition from that same special position or point of view. If we cannot get into that position and see that scepticism is true, can we be sure that we can get into it and see that scepticism is false?

The coherence and achievability of what we aspire to in the epistemological enterprise tends to be taken for granted, or left unexplored. But that question is prior to the question whether scepticism or one or another of its positive competitors is the true theory of human knowledge. What does a true theory of knowledge do? What does a philosophical theorist of knowledge seek?

These are large and complicated questions

to which we obviously cannot hope to get a definitive answer today. Distinguishing them from the question of the relative merits of scepticism and its competitors might nonetheless help to locate the target of Ernest Sosa's opposition to something he calls 'scepticism'. He gives that label to the view that "there is no way to attain full philosophical understanding of our knowledge" or that "a fully general theory of knowledge is impossible."[1] That is obviously not what I have just called 'scepticism', which is itself a fully general theory of knowledge. Sosa considers a two-step argument for the view he has in mind which would show exhaustively that any general theory of knowledge possessing a certain feature would be what he calls "impossible," and that any general theory lacking that feature would be "impossible" too. So there couldn't be a fully general theory of knowledge. The conclusion certainly does follow from those two premisses, but Sosa doubts the second premiss. He thinks some theories which lack the feature in question have not been shown to be defective in the way the original argument was meant to show. The surviving theories are what he calls 'externalist'.

Theories of the first type hold that a belief acquires the status of knowledge only by "being based on some justification, argument, or reason."[2] That requirement is what makes them "impossible," according to Sosa, because in order to succeed they would have to show that our acceptance of the things we think we know is justified in each case by good inferences or arguments which are not circular or infinitely regressive. That is what it would take to 'legitimate' those beliefs, and that cannot be done. Every inference has to start from something, so without circular or regressive reasoning there must always be something whose acceptance by us is left unsupported by inference, and so cannot be accounted for as knowledge by theories of this type. But a fully general theory of knowledge must account for everything we know. Sosa concludes that there could be no fully "general, legitimating, philosophical understanding of all one's knowledge."[3] This is equivalent, I believe, to saying that no such theory avoids the conclusion that we know nothing. What he is saying of theo-

ries of this first type is that if, in order to know things, we had to satisfy what those theories say are conditions of knowledge, then we would not know anything, since we cannot satisfy those conditions. So theories of the first type depict us as knowing nothing. They cannot be distinguished, in their consequences, from the view that I (but not Sosa) have called 'scepticism'.

I take it to be the main point of Sosa's paper to show that certain "externalist, reliabilist" theories escape that fate. They can be fully general and still succeed where theories of other kinds fail. He thinks there is "a very wide and powerful current of thinking [which] would sweep away externalism root and branch,"[4] and he wants to resist that "torrent of thought".[5] He concentrates here on the reasons he thinks William Alston and I have given for thinking that, as he puts it, "externalism will leave us ultimately dissatisfied."[6] He appears to equate that charge with what he calls the "unacceptability in principle"[7] of 'externalism'.

What exactly are these objections? For my part, I do think there is a way in which 'externalism' would leave us "ultimately dissatisfied" as an answer to the completely general philosophical question of how any knowledge of the world is possible. I tried to indicate what I have in mind in the paper that Sosa refers to and discusses.[8] But I do not suggest that 'externalism' is unsatisfying because it cannot avoid depicting us as knowing nothing about the world and so is indistinguishable from the view that I call 'scepticism'. Nor would I argue that it is inconsistent or viciously circular or internally deficient in some other way which prevents it in principle from being true or acceptable. Sosa says the objections are "grounded in what seem to be demands inherent to the traditional epistemological project itself,"[9] and I think his efforts to meet the objections are intended to defend not only 'externalist' theories but also by implication that very epistemological project as well. My own doubts about 'externalism' could perhaps be said to be grounded in or at least connected with demands inherent to that project, but that is because they are doubts not only about 'externalism' but about the coherence or feasibility of the general epistemological project itself. That question is what I think should be our primary target, not just one or another of the answers offered to it. We need to examine more critically what we want or hope for from the traditional epistemological project of understanding human knowledge in general.

Alston's objections might well have a different source. I suspect that in opposing externalism as he does he is working towards what he sees as a more adequate theory of knowledge, perhaps one which would recognize some beliefs as evident or *prima facie* justified in a way that externalism cannot explain. But to support a theory that competes with pure externalism as the right answer to the philosophical question is not to bring that whole philosophical project itself into question. Although I think there are many points on which we would agree, I shall therefore leave Alston to one side. That leaves me with the question: does Sosa's defence of externalism show that it does not have that feature which I think means it must always leave us dissatisfied, and so by implication that the goal of epistemology must always leave us dissatisfied as well, or does he really accept the point and not regard it as a deficiency in his externalist theory?

The question is complicated because Sosa sees opposition to externalism as coming from some competing philosophical conception or theory of knowledge. His defence amounts to arguing that any theory from which the objections could come must be a theory of his first general type, and so can be discredited "for simple, demonstrable logical reasons."[10] If it is a conflict between competing theories of knowledge, 'externalism' must win, since it does not have the fatal defect those other theories have. In order to bring out my doubts about the kind of satisfaction offered by 'externalism' I can grant that point. I would like to reveal something that I think remains unsatisfying about 'externalism' even if it is the best philosophical theory of knowledge there is or could be. I do not want to put a better theory in its place; I want to ask what a philosophical theory of knowledge is supposed to be, even at its best. Revealing the unsatisfactoriness of even the best answer to the philosophical question can perhaps help draw attention to its unsatisfiable demands.

We aspire in philosophy to see ourselves as knowing all or most of the things we think we know and to understand how all that knowledge is possible. We want an explanation, not just of this or that item or piece of knowledge, but of knowledge, or knowledge of a certain kind, *in general*. Take all our knowledge of the world of physical objects around us, for example. A satisfactory theory or explanation of that knowledge must have several features. To be satisfyingly positive it must depict us as knowing all or most of the things of that sort that we think we know. It must explain, given what it takes to be the facts of human perception, how we nonetheless know the sorts of things we think we know about the world. To say simply that we see, hear, and touch the things around us and in that way know what they are like, would leave nothing even initially problematic about that knowledge. Rather than explaining how, it would simply state that we know. There is nothing wrong with that; it is true, but it does not explain how we know even in those cases in which (as we would say) we are in fact seeing or hearing or touching an object. That is what we want in a philosophical explanation of our knowledge. How, given what perception provides us with even in such cases, do we thereby know what the objects in question are like? What needs explanation is the connection between our perceiving what we do and our knowing the things we do about the physical objects around us. How does the one lead to, or amount to, the other?

Suppose there is an 'externalist, reliabilist' theory of the kind Sosa has in mind which accounts for this. I mean suppose there are truths about the world and the human condition which link human perceptual states and cognitive mechanisms with further states of knowledge and reasonable belief, and which imply that human beings acquire their beliefs about the physical world through the operation of belief-forming mechanisms which are on the whole reliable in the sense of giving them mostly true beliefs. Let us not pause over details of the formulation of such truths, although they are of course crucial and have not to this day been put right by anybody, as far as I know. If there are truths of this kind, although no one has discovered them yet, that fact alone obviously will do us no good as theorists who want to understand human knowledge in this philosophical way. At the very least we must believe some such truths; their merely being true would not be enough to give us any illumination or satisfaction. But our merely happening to believe them would not be enough either. We seek understanding of certain aspects of the human condition; so we seek more than just a set of beliefs about it; we want to know or have good reason for thinking that what we believe about it is true. This is why I say, as Sosa quotes me: "we need some reason to accept a theory of knowledge if we are going to rely on that theory to understand how our knowledge is possible."[11]

Sosa does not dispute that as a condition of success for understanding human knowledge. He disputes my going on to say that "no form of 'externalism' can give a satisfactory account"[12] of our having such a reason to accept it and so understanding our knowledge of the world in purely 'externalist' terms. He thinks my only support for that second claim comes from what he calls a *metaepistemic requirement*[13] which does not follow from the conditions of success admitted so far. It comes, he thinks, from "a deeply held intuition that underlies a certain way of thinking about epistemology."[14] He thinks I have an 'anti-externalist' conception of knowledge according to which 'what is important in epistemology is justification,' which in turn requires "appeal to *other* beliefs that constitute one's reasons for holding the given belief."[15] That is what can only lead in a circle or down an infinite regress, and so in Sosa's terms it is an "impossible" theory of knowledge. Without that requirement, he thinks, the objection vanishes.

Now I want to say that I do not accept any of that. As far as I know, I do not hold an 'anti-externalist' theory of knowledge with which I seek to oppose 'externalism'. I do not think that everything a person knows requires justification which involves appeal to other beliefs, and so on. I think that what I am drawing attention to about 'externalism' is something that can be recognized by anyone who has a good idea of what the general epistemological project is after. Of course, it could be that I am unwittingly imposing the 'anti-externalist' requirement that Sosa's diagnosis says I am. He

thinks I must be; I don't think I am. But rather than searching my soul, which I am sure would be of limited general interest, let me again present for public assessment the way I think 'externalism' must leave us dissatisfied. I find in any case that Sosa has not really considered the reasons I actually gave.

We agree that an "externalist" theorist of knowledge must know or have good reason to believe that his explanation of our knowledge of the physical world around us is correct in order to understand in that way how that knowledge is possible. How will he know or have good reason to believe that? Well, his theory is in part a theory of the conditions under which people in fact know or have good reasons to believe things about the world. If that theory is true in particular of the theorist's own acceptance of that theory, then the theorist has what his own theory says is knowledge of or reasonable belief in the truth of that theory. I believe this is the situation Sosa is describing when he says: "We can legitimately and with rational justification arrive at a belief that a certain set of faculties or doxastic practices are those that we employ *and* are reliable."[16] He thinks there is "no obstacle in principle"[17] to our achieving such a state. I do not disagree with that.

That Sosa thinks the resistance to 'externalism' must be based on some such obstacle in principle is suggested by his immediately going on to ask "why could we not conceivably attain thereby a general understanding of how we know whatever we do know?"[18] It is clear that his question at that point is rhetorical. His idea is that if we can have what an 'externalist' theory calls good reason to believe our 'externalist' theory, it could thereby give us a satisfactory general understanding of our knowledge. For me his question is not rhetorical. I think we can see why, even with what counts for an 'externalist' as good reason to believe his theory, there would remain something ineliminably unsatisfactory about the position a theorist would then be in for gaining a philosophical understanding of his knowledge of the physical world in general.

The difficulty I have in mind does not show up in understanding the knowledge which other people, not myself, have about the world.

I understand others' knowledge by connecting their beliefs in the right way with what I know to be true in the world they live in. I can discover that others get their beliefs through the operation of belief-forming mechanisms which I can see to be reliable in the sense of producing beliefs which are largely true. But each of us as theorists of knowledge is also a human being to whom our theory of knowledge is meant to apply, so we must understand ourselves as knowers, just as we understand others. *All* human knowledge of the world is what we want to understand.

If I ask of my own knowledge of the world around me how it is possible, I can explain it along 'externalist' lines by showing that it is a set of beliefs I have acquired through perception by means of belief-forming mechanisms which are reliable. Suppose that is what I believe about the connection between my perceptions and the beliefs I acquire about the world. As we saw, my merely happening to believe such a story would not be enough for me to be said to understand in that way how that knowledge is possible. I must know or have good reason to believe that that story is true of me. As a good 'externalist', I do of course believe that I do. I think that I acquired my belief in my 'externalist' explanation of human knowledge by means of perception and of the operation of the same reliable belief forming mechanisms which give me and others all our other knowledge of the world around us. So I think I do know or have good reason to believe my theory; I believe that I fulfil the conditions which that very theory says are sufficient for knowing or having good reason to believe it. Do I now have a satisfactory understanding of my knowledge of the world? Have I answered to my own satisfaction the philosophical question of how my knowledge of the world is possible? I want to say No.

It is admittedly not easy to describe the deficiency in a few words. It is not that there is some internal defect or circularity in the 'externalist' theory that I believe. Nor is there any obstacle to my believing that theory or even to my having good reasons in the 'externalist' sense to believe it. *If* the theory is true, and *if* I did acquire my belief in it in the way I think

I did, *then* I do know or have a good reason to believe it to be true. To appreciate what I still see as a deficiency, or as less than what one aspires to as a philosophical theorist of knowledge, let us consider the merits of a different and conflicting, but still 'externalist', account of our knowledge of the world.

I have in mind a fictional 'externalist' whom I shall call "Descartes." The theory of our knowledge of the world which he accepts says that there is a beneficent, omnipotent, and omniscient God who guarantees that whatever human beings carefully and clearly and distinctly perceive to be true is true. The real René Descartes held a closely similar theory, but he tried to prove demonstratively that it is true. He was accused of arguing in a circle. My 'externalist' Descartes offers no proofs. He believes that when people carefully and clearly and distinctly perceive things to be true, they are true; God makes sure of that. That is how people come to know things. He also acknowledges that what he himself needs in order to know or have good reason to believe his own theory of knowledge is to fulfil the conditions it says are sufficient for knowing or having good reason to believe something: to acquire belief in it by carefully and clearly and distinctly perceiving it to be true while God guarantees that it is true. Suppose he examines the origins of his own theory and carefully and clearly and distinctly perceives that he did acquire his belief in it in just that way. Does he now have a satisfactory understanding of his knowledge of the world? Has he got what he can see to be a satisfactory answer to the philosophical question of how his knowledge of the world is possible? I want to say No.

Your seeing and sharing my reservations about the adequacy of 'externalism' and so about the feasibility of the epistemological project depend on your finding the position of this 'externalist' Descartes unsatisfactory in a certain way as an understanding of his knowledge. The question is what is wrong with it. I think most of us will say first that what is wrong is that his theory is simply not true; there is no divine guarantor of the truth of even our most carefully arrived-at beliefs, and he is therefore wrong to think that he acquired his belief in his theory in that way. Even if that is so, is it the only deficiency in his position? I think it is not.

We cannot deny that he does believe his explanation of human knowledge, and does believe that he came to believe that theory by a procedure which his theory says is reliable, so we have to admit that *if* his theory and his account of how he came to believe it were true, *then* he would know or have good reason to believe his explanation of knowledge. But if we say that the falsity of his theory is the only deficiency in his position we would have to admit that if his theory and his belief about how he came to believe it were true, then he would have a satisfactory understanding of all of his knowledge of the world. That implies that whether he understands how his knowledge is possible or not depends only on whether the theory which he holds about how he came to believe it is true or not. If it is true, he does understand his knowledge; if it is not, he does not. An 'externalist' theorist of this fictional kind who reflects on his position could still always ask: "I wonder whether I understand how my knowledge of the world is possible? I have a lot of beliefs about it. If what I believe about it is true, I do; if it is not, I don't. Of course, I believe all of it is true, so I believe that I do understand my knowledge. But I wonder whether I do." I think anyone who can get into only that position with respect to his alleged knowledge of the world has not achieved the kind of satisfaction which the traditional epistemological project aspires to. He has not got into a position from which he can see all of his knowledge of the world all at once in a way that accounts for it as reliable or true.

Sosa's 'externalist, reliabilist', I believe, can get himself into no better position for understanding himself. If what distinguishes his position from that of my 'externalist' Descartes is only that his theory is in fact true while that fictional character's theory is false, then he too will be in a position to say no more about himself than "If what I believe about my knowledge is true, I do understand it; if it is not, I do not. I think I do, but I wonder whether I understand my knowledge or not?" This is where the difficulty of describing the deficiency in his position comes in. It will not be true to say simply that although he believes his theory, he has no reason to believe it. If we imagine that his 'externalist' theory and his account of how he came to believe it are in fact true, as I have been conceding, then in that sense he does have good reason to believe his explanation of human knowledge. But still his own view of his position can look no better to him than the fictional 'externalist' Descartes's position looks to him.

It would be to no avail at this point for him to try to improve his position by asking himself whether he knows or has good reason to believe that he does know or have good reason to believe his theory. Answering that question would be a matter of coming by what he believes is a procedure that his theory says is reliable to the belief that he knows or has good reason to believe his theory. Again, if he did come to believe that in that way, and his theory is in fact true, he will in fact know or have good reason to believe a second-order claim about the goodness of his reasons for believing his theory. But still he could then make only the same sort of conditional assertion about his position one level up, as it were, as he made earlier. The 'externalist' Descartes could do the same. He could carefully and clearly and distinctly perceive that he came to believe his theory to be true of himself by what that very theory says is a way of coming to know or have good reason to believe. He could then come to a similarly true conditional verdict about his position. Both he and Sosa's 'externalist' could say at most: "If the theory I hold is true, I do know or have good reason to believe that I know or have good reason to believe it, and I do understand how I know the things I do.' I think that in each case we can see a way in which the satisfaction the theorist seeks in understanding his knowledge still eludes him. Given that all of his knowledge of the world is in question, he will still find himself able to say only "I might understand my knowledge, I might not. Whether I do or not all depends on how things in fact are in the world I think I've got knowledge of."

Those of us who are inclined to think that

Sosa's 'externalist's' theory is in fact true and the fictional Descartes's theory false will say that he does know and perhaps that he does understand his knowledge and that the fictional Descartes does not. But that does not show that that theorist's position gives him a satisfactory understanding of his own knowledge. As I said, the difficulty does not show up in one's understanding all of someone else's knowledge of the world; it is only when each of us seeks to understand our own knowledge of the world in general that we reach this unsatisfactory position.

If we do recognize a certain ineliminable dissatisfaction in any such 'externalist' attempt at self-understanding, I do not think it is because of hidden attachment to an opposing 'internalist' theory which requires that everything we know must be justified by reasonable inference from something else we believe. We can be 'externalists' and still reach at best what I think is an unsatisfactory position, even if we do in fact have what 'externalism' regards as knowledge of or reasonable belief in that 'externalist' theory. I think the dissatisfaction, if we recognize it, is felt to come from the demands of the epistemological project itself, or perhaps we could say from the complete generality of the project. Whatever we seek, and what the theorists I have imagined appear to lack, is something that 'externalism' alone seems unable to explain or to account for.

Sosa grants that the epistemological goal can never be reached if the successful theory is expected to provide what he calls a "legitimating" account. He means by that an account which "specifies the reasons favouring one's beliefs,"[19] and he thinks no theory that is 'internalist' in his sense can do that without circularity or regress. But surely the goal of understanding how we know what we do does require that the successful account be legitimating at least in the sense of enabling us to understand that what we have got *is* knowledge of, or reasonable belief in, the world's being a certain way. We should be able to see that the view that I call 'scepticism' is not true of us, and we want to understand how we get the knowledge we can see that we've got. 'Externalism' implies that *if* such-and-such is true in the world, *then* human beings do know things

about what the world is like. Applying that conditional proposition to ourselves, to our own knowledge of the world, to our own knowledge of how that knowledge is acquired, and so on, even when the antecedent and so the consequent are in fact both true, still leaves us always in the disappointingly second-best position I have tried to illustrate, however far up we go to higher and higher levels of reiterated knowledge or reasonable belief. We want to be in a position knowingly to detach that consequent about ourselves, and at the same time to know and so to understand how any or all of that knowledge of the world comes to be. And that would require appealing to or relying on part of our knowledge of the world in the course of explaining to ourselves how we come to have any knowledge of the world at all.

There are indications that Sosa acknowledges and accepts the situation I have tried to describe. Believing that our belief-forming mechanisms are reliable when they are in fact reliable, and coming by what are in fact those very mechanisms to believe that they are reliable, he says, is "the very best conceivable outcome"[20] of the epistemological project. "How could we possibly improve our epistemic situation?" he asks.[21] The thought that someone else could find his own 'epistemic situation' equally good on the basis of a competing theory of knowledge, he admits, might cause some dissatisfaction or discomfort, but he thinks that is "discomfort we must learn to tolerate."[22] He concedes that in explaining, even to ourselves, how we know our 'externalist' theory of knowledge to be true, we must appeal to that very theory, and so cannot avoid, as he puts it, "begging the question" or "arguing circularly"[23] in our attempts to account for our knowledge. But again, he asks, "once we understand this, what option is left to us except to go ahead and 'beg' that question?"[24] I think his thought is that without doing that, we would have no chance of answering the epistemological question at all. We have to "tolerate" the "discomfort" of relying on a "self-supporting argument"[25] for our theory simply because we could not arrive at a "successful and general theory of knowledge"[26] in any other way.

Here, perhaps, we approach something that Sosa and I can agree about. What I have tried to identify as a dissatisfaction that the epistemological project will always leave us with is for him something that simply has to be accepted if we are going to have a fully general theory of knowledge at all. He appears to think, as I do, that it is endemic to the epistemological project itself. We differ in what moral we draw from that thought.

I want to conclude that we should therefore re-examine the source of, and so perhaps find ourselves able to resist, the not-fully-satisfiable demand embodied in the epistemological question. I think its source lies somewhere within the familiar and powerful line of thinking by which all of our alleged knowledge of the world gets even temporarily split off all at once from what we get in perception, so we are presented with a completely general question of how perception so understood gives us knowledge of anything at all in the physical world. If that manoeuvre cannot really be carried off successfully, we have no completely general question about our knowledge of the world to answer. We could still ask how we know one sort of thing about the physical world, given that we know certain other things about it, but there would be no philosophical problem about all of our knowledge of the world in general. What then would 'externalism' or any other fully general theory of knowledge be trying to do?

Sosa wants his 'externalism', even with its admitted "discomfort," to serve as a bulwark against the 'relativism', 'contextualism', and 'scepticism' which he sees as rampant in our culture. I share his dark view of our times, but if those widely-invoked 'isms' are thought of as competing answers to a fully general question about our "epistemic situation" in the world, I think the resistance has to start farther back. It is what all such theories purport to be about, and what we expect or demand that any such theory should say about the human condition, that we should be examining, not just which one of them comes in first in the traditional epistemological sweepstake. In that tough competition, it still seems to me, scepticism will always win going away.

NOTES

1. Sosa, 'Philosophical Scepticism and Epistemic Circularity', this volume.
2. Sosa, op. cit.
3. Sosa, op. cit.
4. Sosa, op. cit.
5. Sosa, op. cit.
6. Sosa, op. cit.
7. Sosa, op. cit.
8. 'Understanding Human Knowledge in General', in *Knowledge and Scepticism*, ed. M. Clay & K. Lehrer (Boulder, Colorado: Westview, 1989).
9. Sosa, op. cit.
10. Sosa, op. cit.
11. Sosa, op. cit. quoting from Clay & Lehrer (ed.), p. 43.
12. Clay & Lehrer (ed.), p. 43.
13. Sosa, 'Philosophical Scepticism and Epistemic Circularity' this volume.
14. Sosa, op. cit.
15. Sosa, op. cit.
16. Sosa, op. cit.
17. Sosa, op. cit.
18. Sosa, op. cit.
19. Sosa, op. cit.
20. Sosa, op. cit.
21. Sosa, op. cit.
22. Sosa, op. cit.
23. Sosa, op. cit.
24. Sosa, op. cit.
25. Sosa, op. cit.
26. Sosa, op. cit.

SKEPTICISM: BIBLIOGRAPHY

Amico, R. *The Problem of the Criterion*. Lanham, Md., 1993.

Brueckner, A. L. "Skepticism and Epistemic Closure." *Philosophical Topics* 13 (1985): 89–117.

Burnyeat, M., ed. *The Skeptical Tradition*. Berkeley, Calif., 1983.

Butchvarov, P., *Skepticism about the External World*. New York, 1998.

Chisholm, R. M. "The Problem of the Criterion."

In *The Foundations of Knowing*, pp. 61–75. Minneapolis: University of Minnesota Press, 1982.

Clay, M., and K. Lehrer, eds. *Knowledge and Skepticism*. Boulder, Col., 1989.

Cornman, J. W. *Skepticism, Justification, and Explanation*. Dordrecht, 1980.

Dancy, J. *An Introduction to Contemporary Epistemology*, chapter 1. Oxford, 1985.

DeRose, K., and T. Warfield, eds. *Skepticism*. New York, 1999.

Floridi, L. *Scepticism and the Foundation of Epistemology*. Leiden, 1996.

Fogelin, R. *Pyrrhonian Reflections on Knowledge and Justification*. Oxford, 1994.

Foley, R. *Working Without a Net*. Oxford, 1993.

———. Review of Peter Klein's *Certainty: A Refutation of Scepticism*. *Philosophy & Phenomenological Research* 4 (1984).

Fumerton, R. *Metaepistemology and Skepticism*. Lanham, Md., 1995.

Greco, J. *Putting Skeptics in their Place*. New York, 2000.

Hilpinen, R. "Skepticism and Justification." *Synthese* 55 (1983): 165–74.

Huemer, M. *Skepticism and the Veil of Perception*. Lanham, Md., 2001.

Johnson, O. "Ignorance and Irrationality: A Study in Contemporary Skepticism." *Philosophy Research Archives* 5 (1979): 368–417.

———. *Skepticism and Cognitivism*. Berkeley, Calif., 1978.

Klein, P. D. *Certainty: A Refutation of Scepticism*. Minneapolis, 1981.

———. "Real Knowledge." *Synthese* 55 (1983): 143–64.

———. "Skepticism." In *The Oxford Handbook of Epistemology*, ed. P. K. Moser New York, 2003.

Lehrer, K. *Knowledge*, chapter 10. Oxford, 1974.

———. "The Problem of Knowledge and Skepticism." In J. Cornman, K. Lehrer, and G. Pappas, *Philosophical Problems and Arguments: An Introduction, 3d ed.*, chapter 2. New York, 1982.

———. *Theory of Knowledge*. Boulder, Col., 1990.

———. "Why Not Scepticism?" *The Philosophical Forum* 2 (1971): 283–98. Reprinted in *Essays on Knowledge and Justification*, pp. 346–63.

Luper-Foy, S, ed. *The Possibility of Knowledge: Nozick and his Critics*. Lanham, Md., 1986.

Moser, P. K. "Justified Doubt Without Certainty." *The Pacific Philosophical Quarterly* 65 (1984): 97–104.

———. *Knowledge and Evidence*. Cambridge, Eng., 1989.

———. *Philosophy After Objectivity*. Oxford, 1993.

———. "Skepticism Undone?" In *The Philosophy of Ernest Sosa*, ed. John Greco. Cambridge, Mass., 2002.

———, ed. *The Oxford Handbook of Epistemology*. New York, 2003.

Naess, A. *Skepticism*. London, 1969.

Nozick, R. *Philosophical Explanations*, chapter 3. Cambridge, Mass., 1981.

Oakley, I. T. "An Argument for Skepticism Concerning Justified Belief." *American Philosophical Quarterly* 13 (1976): 221–28.

Odegard, D. "Chisholm's Approach to Scepticism." *Metaphilosophy* 12 (1981): 7–12.

———. *Knowledge and Skepticism*. Totowa, NJ: Rowman & Littlefield, 1983.

Pappas, G. "Some Forms of Epistemological Skepticism." In *Essays on Knowledge and Justification*, ed. G. Pappas and M. Swain, pp. 309–16. Ithaca, N.Y., 1978.

Rescher, N. *Scepticism: A Critical Reappraisal*. Oxford, 1979.

Roth, M. D., and G. Ross, eds. *Doubting*. Dordrecht, 1990.

Slote, M. *Reason and Scepticism*. New York, 1970.

Sosa, E., and E. Villanueva, eds. *Skepticism*. Cambridge, Mass., 2000.

Strawson, P. F. *Skepticism and Naturalism*. New York, 1985.

Stroud, B. *The Significance of Philosophical Scepticism*. Oxford, 1984.

———. "The Significance of Scepticism." In *Transcendental Arguments and Science*. ed. P. Bieri et al. Dordrecht, 1979.

———. "Skepticism and the Possibility of Knowledge." *The Journal of Philosophy* 81 (1984): 545–51.

Unger, Peter. "A Defense of Skepticism." *The Philosophical Review* 80 (1971): 198–218. Reprinted in *Essays on Knowledge and Justification*, ed. G. Pappas and M. Swain, pp. 317–36 Ithaca, N.Y., 1978.

———. *Ignorance*. Oxford, 1976.

————. "Two Types of Scepticism." *Philosophical Studies* 25 (1974): 77–96.

Vinci, T. Critical Notice of Peter Klein's *Certainty: A Refutation of Scepticism. The Canadian Journal of Philosophy* 14 (1984): 125–45.

Watkins, J. *Science and Scepticism*. Princeton, N.J., 1984.

Williams, M. *Unnatural Doubts*. Oxford, 1991.

Wittgenstein, L. *On Certainty*. Edited by G.E.M. Anscombe and G. H. von Wright. Oxford, 1969.

Woods, M. "Scepticism and Natural Knowledge." *Proceedings of the Aristotelian Society* 54 (1980): 231–48.

Epistemology and Psychology

This section focuses on the significance of empirical psychological investigations to the resolution of epistemological problems. Since the beginning of the twentieth century, it had been typical of philosophers working on epistemology to ignore empirical cognitive studies by psychologists. Recently, however, there has been a move among epistemologists toward interaction with the empirical work of cognitive psychologists, specifically the psychological work on the nature of belief, perception, intelligence, and rationality. The selections in this section comment on, or at least represent, such a move.

In "Epistemology Naturalized," W. V. Quine defends the bold proposal that since we cannot justify our empirical beliefs in any foundational way (i.e., on the basis of immediate experience), we should dispense with traditional epistemology and settle for empirical psychology instead. Quine sees no hope of success in the once-popular effort to achieve certainty by reducing all of our empirical beliefs to beliefs about immediate sensory experience.

Many philosophers would object that the reliance on empirical psychology to settle epistemological questions involves circular reasoning. Quine finds that such worries about circularity are misguided, especially if we abandon the goal of deriving all of our knowledge from immediate sensory experience. On Quine's view, we can plausibly replace epistemology with psychology once we give up the attempt to justify our knowledge of the external world via sensory foundations. Quine concludes with a brief account of observation sentences to show that his view does not commit one to the "epistemological nihilism" suggested by such philosophers of science as Thomas Kuhn and N. R. Hanson.

In "Why Reason Can't be Naturalized," Hilary Putnam opposes several attempts to naturalize the fundamental notions of epistemology, notions such as that of justification or rationality. For instance, Putnam opposes (a) proponents of "evolutionary epistemology," (b) reliabilists such as Alvin Goldman (see his essay in the section on justified belief), (c) "cultural relativists" such as Richard Rorty, and (d) "positivists" such as W. V. Quine (see his essay "Epistemology Naturalized").

Putnam construes Quine's "Epistemology Naturalized" as proposing that we simply eliminate the normative notions of justification, good reason, warranted assertion, etc. Putnam claims that such a proposal is incoherent if we construe "truth" in a correspondence sense, for, according to Putnam, the relevant notions needed to explain such truth (e.g., the notion of causality) presuppose the normative notions being eliminated. Putnam argues, furthermore, that the elimination of normative notions altogether leads to "mental suicide" inasmuch as it leads to an untenable "solipsism of the present moment." Putnam concludes, therefore, that there is no eliminating the normative and that epistemology cannot be naturalized.

In "Epistemic Folkways and Scientific Epistemology," Alvin Goldman calls our common-sense epistemic concepts and norms *epistemic folkways* and proposes that one proper task of epistemology is to elucidate such epistemic folkways. He holds that lessons from cognitive science are crucial for the understanding of epistemic folkways. Goldman claims, in addition, that cognitive science can contribute to "transcending" epistemic folkways, at least by offering a detailed, empirically based characterization of psychological mechanisms. He recommends a kind of *scientific epistemology* that has descriptive and normative branches. Such epistemology, according to Goldman, should preserve continuity with epistemic folkways and use reliability, question-answering power, and question-answering speed as bases for epistemic evaluation. Goldman illustrates how cognitive science can inform scientific epistemology in a variety of ways.

In "Quine as Feminist: The Radical Import of Naturalized Epistemology," Louise Antony argues that we need epistemology to be sensitive to the insights of feminism. Feminist epistemology need not, she adds, reject all existing epistemological paradigms. Naturalized epistemology can contribute significantly to the goals of a feminist epistemology. She claims that feminists, in criticizing traditional epistemology and contemporary analytic epistemology, have seriously misunderstood both. Naturalized epistemology, according to Antony, benefits feminism by providing criticisms of the epistemic ideal of complete impartiality while also showing how to condemn bad, or harmful, epistemic biases. Its criticisms of the ideal of impartiality are, in fact, more radical than many of the criticisms coming from outside contemporary analytic epistemology, according to Antony. Naturalized epistemology supports the claim that all human knowledge is "biased," in the sense that it must start from some perspective containing presuppositions, but it also allows us to identify the "good biases" as those that facilitate the search for truth (in a realist sense) and the "bad biases" as those that impede the search for truth. Which biases facilitate the search for truth is an empirical matter. Antony argues that many feminists have misunderstood traditional epistemology because they have failed to appreciate the importance of the distinction between empiricist and rationalist theories of knowledge and of the mind. They have focussed on a notion of objectivity as impartiality that received support only from empiricist philosophers. They have also failed to represent accurately recent analytic epistemology, for they have failed to appreciate its radical critique of neo-empiricism, especially the empiricism of the Logical Positivists. Feminists' wholesale rejection of analytic epistemology, including naturalized epistemology, harms them in many ways, according to Antony.

36 / W. V. Quine (1908–2000)
EPISTEMOLOGY NATURALIZED

Epistemology is concerned with the foundation of science. Conceived thus broadly, epistemology includes the study of the foundations of mathematics as one of its departments. Specialists at the turn of the century thought that their efforts in this particular department were achieving notable success: mathematics seemed to reduce altogether to logic. In a more recent perspective this reduction is seen to be better describable as a reduction to logic and set theory. This correction is a disappointment epistemologically, since the firmness and obviousness that we associate with logic cannot be claimed for set theory. But still the success achieved in the foundations of mathematics remains exemplary by comparative standards, and we can illuminate the rest of epistemology somewhat by drawing parallels to this department.

Studies in the foundations of mathematics divide symmetrically into two sorts, conceptual and doctrinal. The conceptual studies are concerned with meaning, the doctrinal with truth. The conceptual studies are concerned with clarifying concepts by defining them, some in terms of others. The doctrinal studies are concerned with establishing laws by proving them, some on the basis of others. Ideally the obscurer concepts would be defined in terms of the clearer ones so as to maximize clarity, and the less obvious laws would be proved from the more obvious ones so as to maximize certainty. Ideally the definitions would generate all the concepts from clear and distinct ideas, and the proofs would generate all the theorems from self-evident truths.

The two ideals are linked. For, if you define all the concepts by use of some favored subset of them, you thereby show how to translate all theorems into these favored terms. The clearer these terms are, the likelier it is that the truths couched in them will be obviously true, or derivable from obvious truths. If in particular the concepts of mathematics were all reducible to the clear terms of logic, then all the truths of mathematics would go over into truths of logic; and surely the truths of logic are all obvious or at least potentially obvious, i.e., derivable from obvious truths by individually obvious steps.

This particular outcome is in fact denied us, however, since mathematics reduces only to set theory and not to logic proper. Such reduction still enhances clarity, but only because of the interrelations that emerge and not because the end terms of the analysis are clearer than others. As for the end truths, the axioms of set theory, these have less obviousness and certainty to recommend them than do most of the mathematical theorems that we would derive from them. Moreover, we know from Gödel's work that no consistent axiom system can cover mathematics even when we renounce self-evidence. Reduction in the foundations of mathematics remains mathematically and philosophically fascinating, but it does not do what the epistemologist would like of it: it does not reveal the ground of mathematical knowledge, it does not show how mathematical certainty is possible.

Still there remains a helpful thought, regarding epistemology generally, in that duality of structure which was especially conspicuous in the foundations of mathematics. I refer to the bifurcation into a theory of concepts, or meaning, and a theory of doctrine, or truth; for this applies to the epistemology of natural knowledge no less than to the foundations of mathematics. The parallel is as follows. Just as mathematics is to be reduced to logic, or logic and set theory, so natural knowledge is to be based somehow on sense experience. This means explaining the notion of body in sensory terms; here is the conceptual side. And it means justifying our knowledge of truths of nature in sensory terms; here is the doctrinal side of the bifurcation.

Hume pondered the epistemology of natural knowledge on both sides of the bifurcation, the conceptual and the doctrinal. His handling of the conceptual side of the problem, the explanation of body in sensory terms, was bold and simple: he identified bodies outright with the sense impressions. If common sense distinguishes between the material apple and our sense impressions of it on the ground that the apple is one and enduring while the impressions are many and fleeting, then, Hume held, so much the worse for common sense; the notion of its being the same apple on one occasion and another is a vulgar confusion.

Nearly a century after Hume's *Treatise*, the same view of bodies was espoused by the early American philosopher Alexander Bryan Johnson.[1] "The word iron names an associated sight and feel," Johnson wrote.

What then of the doctrinal side, the justification of our knowledge of truths about nature? Here, Hume despaired. By his identification of bodies with impressions he did succeed in construing some singular statements about bodies as indubitable truths, yes; as truths about impressions, directly known. But general statements, also singular statements about the future, gained no increment of certainty by being construed as about impressions.

On the doctrinal side, I do not see that we are further along today than where Hume left us. The Humean predicament is the human predicament. But on the conceptual side there has been progress. There the crucial step forward was made already before Alexander Bryan Johnson's day, although Johnson did not emulate it. It was made by Bentham in his theory of fictions. Bentham's step was the recognition of contextual definition, or what he called paraphrasis. He recognized that to explain a term we do not need to specify an object for it to refer to, nor even to specify a synonymous word or phrase; we need only show, by whatever means, how to translate all the whole sentences in which the term is to be used. Hume's and Johnson's desperate measure of identifying bodies with impressions ceased to be the only conceivable way of making sense of talk of bodies, even granted that impressions were the only reality. One could undertake to explain talk of bodies in terms of talk of impressions by translating one's whole sentences about bodies into whole sentences about impressions, without equating the bodies themselves to anything at all.

This idea of contextual definition, or recognition of the sentence as the primary vehicle of meaning, was indispensable to the ensuing developments in the foundations of mathematics. It was explicit in Frege, and it attained its full flower in Russell's doctrine of singular descriptions as incomplete symbols.

Contextual definition was one of two resorts that could be expected to have a liberating effect upon the conceptual side of the epistemology of natural knowledge. The other is resort to the resources of set theory as auxiliary concepts. The epistemologist who is willing to eke out his austere ontology of sense impressions with these set-theoretic auxiliaries is suddenly rich; he has not just his impressions to play with, but sets of them, and sets of sets, and so on up. Constructions in the foundations of mathematics have shown that such set-theoretic aids are a powerful addition; after all, the entire glossary of concepts of classical mathematics is constructible from them. Thus equipped, our epistemologist may not need either to identify bodies with impressions or to settle for contextual definition; he may hope to find in some subtle construction of sets upon sets of sense impressions a category of objects enjoying just the formula properties that he wants for bodies.

The two resorts are very unequal in epistemological status. Contextual definition is unassailable. Sentences that have been given meaning as wholes are undeniably meaningful, and the use they make of their component terms is therefore meaningful, regardless of whether any translations are offered for those terms in isolation. Surely Hume and A. B. Johnson would have used contextual definition with pleasure if they had thought of it. Recourse to sets, on the other hand, is a drastic ontological move, a retreat from the austere ontology of impressions. There are philosophers who would rather settle for bodies outright than accept all these sets, which amount, after all, to the whole abstract ontology of mathematics.

This issue has not always been clear, however, owing to deceptive hints of continuity between elementary logic and set theory. This is why mathematics was once believed to reduce to logic, that is, to an innocent and unquestionable logic, and to inherit these qualities. And this is probably why Russell was content to resort to sets as well as to contextual definition when in *Our Knowledge of the External World* and elsewhere he addressed himself to the epistemology of natural knowledge, on its conceptual side.

To account for the external world as a logical construct of sense data—such, in Russell's terms, was the program. It was Carnap, in his *Der logische Aufbau der Welt* of 1920, who came nearest to executing it.

This was the conceptual side of epistemology; what of the doctrinal? There the Humean predicament remained unaltered. Carnap's constructions, if carried successfully to completion, would have enabled us to translate all sentences about the world into terms of sense data, or observation, plus logic and set theory. But the mere fact that a sentence is *couched* in terms of observation, logic, and set theory does not mean that it can be *proved* from observation sentences by logic and set theory. The most modest of generalizations about observable traits will cover more cases than its utterer can have had occasion actually to observe. The hopelessness of grounding natural science upon immediate experience in a firmly logical way was acknowledged. The Cartesian quest for certainty had been the remote motivation of epistemology, both on its conceptual and its doctrinal side; but that quest was seen as a lost cause. To endow the truths of nature with the full authority of immediate experience was as forlorn a hope as hoping to endow the truths of mathematics with the potential obviousness of elementary logic.

What then could have motivated Carnap's heroic efforts on the conceptual side of epistemology, when hope of certainty on the doctrinal side was abandoned? There were two good reasons still. One was that such construction could be expected to elicit and clarify the sensory evidence for science, even if the inferential steps between sensory evidence and scientific doctrine must fall short of certainty. The other reason was that such constructions would deepen our understanding of our discourse about the world, even apart from questions of evidence; it would make all cognitive discourse as clear as observation terms and logic and, I must regretfully add, set theory.

It was sad for epistemologists, Hume and others, to have to acquiesce in the impossibility of strictly deriving the science of the external world from sensory evidence. Two cardinal tenets of empiricism remained unassailable, however, and so remain to this day. One is that whatever evidence there *is* for science *is* sensory evidence. The other, to which I shall recur, is that all inculcation of meanings of words must rest ultimately on sensory evidence. Hence the continuing attractiveness of the idea of a *logischer Aufbau* in which the sensory content of discourse would stand forth explicitly.

If Carnap had successfully carried such a construction through, how could he have told whether it was the right one? The question would have had no point. He was seeking what he called a *rational reconstruction*. Any construction of physicalistic discourse in terms of sense experience, logic, and set theory would have been seen as satisfactory if it made the physicalistic discourse come out right. If there is one way there are many, but any would be a great achievement.

But why all this creative reconstruction, all this make-believe? The stimulation of his sensory receptors is all the evidence anybody has had to go on, ultimately, in arriving at his picture of the world. Why not just see how this construction really proceeds? Why not settle for psychology? Such a surrender of the epistemological burden to psychology is a move that was disallowed in earlier times as circular reasoning. If the epistemologist's goal is validation of the grounds of empirical science, he defeats his purpose by using psychology or other empirical science in the validation. However, such scruples against circularity have little point once we have stopped dreaming of deducing science from observations. If we are out simply to understand the link between observation and science, we are well advised to use any available information, including that provided by the very science whose link with observation we are seeking to understand.

But there remains a different reason, unconnected with fears of circularity, for still favoring creative reconstruction. We should like to be able to *translate* science into logic and observation terms and set theory. This would be a great epistemological achievement, for it would show all the rest of the concepts of science to be theoretically superfluous. It would legitimize them—to whatever degree the concepts of set theory, logic, and observation are themselves legitimate—by showing that everything done with the one apparatus could in principle be done with the other. If psychology itself could deliver a truly translational reduction of this kind, we should welcome it; but certainly it cannot, for certainly we did not grow up learning definitions of physicalistic language in terms of a prior language of set theory, logic, and observation. Here, then, would be good reason for persisting in a rational reconstruction: we want to establish the essential innocence of physical concepts, by showing them to be theoretically dispensable.

The fact is, though, that the construction which Carnap outlined in *Der logische Aufbau der Welt* does not give translation reduction either. It would not even if the outline were filled in. The crucial point comes where Carnap is explaining how to assign sense qualities to positions in physical space and time. These assignments are to be made in such a way as to fulfill, as well as possible, certain desiderata which he states, and with growth of experience the assignments are to be revised to suit. This plan, however illuminating, does not offer any key to *translating* the sentences of science into terms of observation, logic, and set theory.

We must despair of any such reduction. Carnap had despaired of it by 1936, when, in "Testability and Meaning,"[2] he introduced so-called *reduction forms* of a type weaker than definition. Definitions had shown always how to translate sentences into equivalent sentences. Contextual definition of a term showed how to translate sentences containing the term into equivalent sentences lacking the term. Reduction forms of Carnap's liberalized kind, on the other hand, do not in general give equivalences; they give implications. They explain a new term, if only partially, by specifying some sentences which are implied by sentences containing the term, and other sentences which imply sentences containing the term.

It is tempting to suppose that the countenancing of reduction forms in this liberal sense is just one further step of liberalization comparable to the earlier one, taken by Bentham, of countenancing contextual definition. The former and sterner kind of rational reconstruction might have been represented as a fictitious history in which we imagined our ancestors introducing the terms of physicalistic discourse on a phenomenalistic and set-theoretic basis by a succession of contextual definitions. The new and more liberal kind of rational reconstruction is a fictitious history in which we imagine our ancestors introducing those terms by a succession rather of reduction forms of the weaker sort.

This, however, is a wrong comparison. The fact is rather that the former and sterner kind of rational reconstruction, where definition reigned, embodied no fictitious history at all. It was nothing more nor less than a set of directions—or would have been, if successful—for accomplishing everything in terms of phenomena and set theory that we now accomplish in terms of bodies. It would have been a true reduction by translation, a legitimation by elimination. *Definire est eliminare*. Rational reconstruction by Carnap's later and looser reduction forms does none of this.

To relax the demand for definition, and settle

for a kind of reduction that does not eliminate, is to renounce the last remaining advantage that we supposed rational reconstruction to have over straight psychology; namely, the advantage of translation reduction. If all we hope for is a reconstruction that links science to experience in explicit ways short of translation, then it would seem more sensible to settle for psychology. Better to discover how science is in fact developed and learned than to fabricate a fictitious structure to a similar effect.

The empiricist made one major concession when he despaired of deducing the truths of nature from sensory evidence. In despairing now even of translating those truths into terms of observation and logico-mathematical auxiliaries, he makes another major concession. For suppose we hold, with the old empiricist Peirce, that the very meaning of a statement consists in the difference its truth would make to possible experience. Might we not formulate, in a chapter-length sentence in observational language, all the difference that the truth of a given statement might make to experience, and might we not then take all this as the translation? Even if the difference that the truth of the statement would make to experience ramifies indefinitely, we might still hope to embrace it all in the logical implications of our chapter-length formulation, just as we can axiomatize an infinity of theorems. In giving up hope of such translation, then, the empiricist is conceding that the empirical meanings of typical statements about the external world are inaccessible and ineffable.

How is this inaccessibility to be explained? Simply on the ground that the experiential implications of a typical statement about bodies are too complex for finite axiomatization, however lengthy? No; I have a different explanation. It is that the typical statement about bodies has no fund of experiential implications it can call its own. A substantial mass of theory, taken together, will commonly have experiential implications; this is how we make verifiable predictions. We may not be able to explain why we arrive at theories which make successful predictions, but we do arrive at such theories.

Sometimes also an experience implied by a theory fails to come off; and then, ideally, we declare the theory false. But the failure falsifies only a block of theory as a whole, a conjunction of many statements. The failure shows that one or more of those statements is false, but it does not show which. The predicted experiences, true and false, are not implied by any one of the component statements of the theory rather than another. The component statements simply do not have empirical meanings, by Peirce's standard; but a sufficiently inclusive portion of theory does. If we can aspire to a sort of *logischer Aufbau der Welt* at all, it must be to one in which the texts slated for translation into observational and logico-mathematical terms are mostly broad theories taken as wholes, rather than just terms or short sentences. The translation of a theory would be a ponderous axiomatization of all the experiential difference that the truth of the theory would make. It would be a queer translation, for it would translate the whole but none of the parts. We might better speak in such a case not of translation but simply of observational evidence for theories; and we may, following Peirce, still fairly call this the empirical meaning of the theories.

These considerations raise a philosophical question even about ordinary unphilosophical translation, such as from English to Arunta or Chinese. For, if the English sentences of a theory have their meaning only together as a body, then we can justify their translation into Arunta only together as a body. There will be no justification for pairing of the component English sentences with component Arunta sentences, except as these correlations make the translation of the theory as a whole come out right. Any translations of the English sentences into Arunta sentences will be as correct as any other, so long as the net empirical implications of the theory as a whole are preserved in translation. But it is to be expected that many different ways of translating the component sentences, essentially different individually, would deliver the same empirical implications for the theory as a whole: deviations in the translation of one component sentence could be compensated for in the translation of another component sentence. Insofar, there can be no ground for saying which of two glaringly unlike translations of individual sentences is right.[3]

For an uncritical mentalist, no such indeterminacy threatens. Every term and every sentence is a label attached to an idea, simple or complex, which is stored in the mind. When on the other hand we take a verification theory of meaning seriously, the indeterminacy would appear to be inescapable. The Vienna Circle espoused a verification theory of meaning but did not take it seriously enough. If we recognize with Peirce that the meaning of a sentence turns purely on what would count as evidence for its truth, and if we recognize with Duhem that theoretical sentences have their evidence not as single sentences but only as larger blocks of theory, then the indeterminacy of translation of theoretical sentences is the natural conclusion. And most sentences, apart from observation sentences, are theoretical. This conclusion, conversely, once it is embraced, seals the fate of any general notion of propositional meaning or, for that matter, state of affairs.

Should the unwelcomeness of the conclusion persuade us to abandon the verification theory of meaning? Certainly not. The sort of meaning that is basic to translation, and to the learning of one's own language, is necessarily empirical meaning and nothing more. A child learns his first words and sentences by hearing and using them in the presence of appropriate stimuli. These must be external stimuli, for they must act both on the child and on the speaker from whom he is learning.[4] Language is socially inculcated and controlled; the inculcation and control turn strictly on the keying of sentences to shared stimulation. Internal factors may vary *ad libitum* without prejudice to communication as long as the keying of language to external stimuli is undisturbed. Surely one has no choice but to be an empiricist so far as one's theory of linguistic meaning is concerned.

What I have said of infant learning applies equally to the linguist's learning of a new language in the field. If the linguist does not lean on related languages for which there are previously accepted translation practices, then obviously he has no data but the concomitances of native utterance and observable stimulus situation. No wonder there is indeterminacy of translation—for of course only a small fraction of our utterances report concurrent external stimulation. Granted, the linguist will end up with unequivocal translations of everything;

but only by making many arbitrary choices—arbitrary even though unconscious—along the way. Arbitrary? By this I mean that different choices could still have made everything come out right that is susceptible in principle to any kind of check.

Let me link up, in a different order, some of the points I have made. The crucial consideration behind my argument for the indeterminacy of translation was that a statement about the world does not always or usually have a separable fund of empirical consequences that it can call its own. That consideration served also to account for the impossibility of an epistemological reduction of the sort where every sentence is equated to a sentence in observational and logico-mathematical terms. And the impossibility of that sort of epistemological reduction dissipated the last advantage that rational reconstruction seemed to have over psychology.

Philosophers have rightly despaired of translating everything into observational and logico-mathematical terms. They have despaired of this even when they have not recognized, as the reason for this irreducibility, that the statements largely do not have their private bundles of empirical consequences. And some philosophers have seen in this irreducibility the bankruptcy of epistemology. Carnap and the other logical positivists of the Vienna Circle had already pressed the term "metaphysics" into pejorative use, as connoting meaninglessness; and the term "epistemology" was next. Wittgenstein and his followers, mainly at Oxford, found a residual philosophical vocation in therapy: in curing philosophers of the delusion that there were epistemological problems.

But I think that at this point it may be more useful to say rather that epistemology still goes on, though in a new setting and a clarified status. Epistemology, or something like it, simply falls into place as a chapter of psychology and hence of natural science. It studies a natural phenomenon, viz., a physical human subject. This human subject is accorded a certain experimentally controlled input—certain patterns of irradiation in assorted frequencies, for instance—and in the fullness of time the subject delivers as output a description of the three-dimensional external world and its history. The relation between the meager input

and the torrential output is a relation that we are prompted to study for somewhat the same reasons that always prompted epistemology; namely, in order to see how evidence relates to theory, and in what ways one's theory of nature transcends any available evidence.

Such a study could still include, even, something like the old rational reconstruction, to whatever degree such reconstruction is practicable; for imaginative constructions can afford hints of actual psychological processes, in much the way that mechanical stimulations can. But a conspicuous difference between old epistemology and the epistemological enterprise in this new psychological setting is that we can now make free use of empirical psychology.

The old epistemology aspired to contain, in a sense, natural science; it would construct it somehow from sense data. Epistemology in its new setting, conversely, is contained in natural science, as a chapter of psychology. But the old containment remains valid too, in its way. We are studying how the human subject of our study posits bodies and projects his physics from his data, and we appreciate that our position in the world is just like his. Our very epistemological enterprise, therefore, and the psychology wherein it is a component chapter, and the whole of natural science wherein psychology is a component book—all this is our own construction or projection from stimulations like those we were meting out to our epistemological subject. There is thus reciprocal containment, though containment in different senses: epistemology in natural science and natural science in epistemology.

This interplay is reminiscent again of the old threat of circularity, but it is all right now that we have stopped dreaming of deducing science from sense data. We are after an understanding of science as an institution or process in the world, and we do not intend that understanding to be any better than the science which is its object. This attitude is indeed one that Neurath was already urging in Vienna Circle days, with his parable of the mariner who has to rebuild his boat while staying afloat in it.

One effect of seeing epistemology in a psychological setting is that it resolves a stubborn old enigma of epistemological priority. Our retinas are irradiated in two dimensions, yet we see things as three-dimensional without conscious inference. Which is to count as observation—the unconscious two-dimensional reception or the conscious three-dimensional apprehension? In the old epistemological context the conscious form had priority, for we were out to justify our knowledge of the external world by rational reconstruction, and that demands awareness. Awareness ceased to be demanded when we gave up trying to justify our knowledge of the external world by rational reconstruction. What to count as observation now can be settled in terms of the stimulation of sensory receptors, let consciousness fall where it may.

The Gestalt psychologists' challenge to sensory atomism, which seemed so relevant to epistemology forty years ago, is likewise deactivated. Regardless of whether sensory atoms or Gestalten are what favor the forefront of our consciousness, it is simply the stimulations of our sensory receptors that are best looked upon as the input to our cognitive mechanism. Old paradoxes about unconscious data and inference, old problems about chains of inference that would have to be completed too quickly—these no longer matter.

In the old anti-psychologistic days the question of epistemological priority was moot. What is epistemologically prior to what? Are Gestalten prior to sensory atoms because they are noticed, or should we favor sensory atoms on some more subtle ground? Now that we are permitted to appeal to physical stimulation, the problem dissolves; *A* is epistemologically prior to *B* if *A* is causally nearer than *B* to the sensory receptors. Or, what is in some ways better, just talk explicitly in terms of causal proximity to sensory receptors and drop the talk of epistemological priority.

Around 1932 there was debate in the Vienna Circle over what to count as observation sentences, or *Protokollsätze*.[5] One position was that they had the form of reports of sense impressions. Another was that they were statements of an elementary sort about the external world, e.g., "A red cube is standing on the table." Another, Neurath's, was that they had the form of reports of relations between percipients and external things: "Otto now sees a red cube on the table." The worst of it was that there seemed to be no objective way of settling the matter: no way of making real sense of the question.

Let us now try to view the matter unreservedly in the context of the external world. Vaguely speaking, what we want of observation sentences is that they be the ones in closest causal proximity to the sensory receptors. But how is such proximity to be gauged? The idea may be rephrased this way: observation sentences are sentences which, as we learn language, are most strongly conditioned to concurrent sensory stimulation rather than to stored collateral information. Thus let us imagine a sentence queried for our verdict as to whether it is true or false; queried for our assent or dissent. Then the sentence is an observation sentence if our verdict depends only on the sensory stimulation present at the time.

But a verdict cannot depend on present stimulation to the exclusion of stored information. The very fact of our having learned the language evinces much storing of information, and of information without which we should be in no position to give verdicts on sentences however observational. Evidently then we must relax our definition of observation sentence to read thus: a sentence is an observation sentence if all verdicts on it depend on present sensory stimulation and on no stored information beyond what goes into understanding the sentence.

This formulation raises another problem: how are we to distinguish between information that goes into understanding a sentence and information that goes beyond? This is the problem of distinguishing between analytic truth which issues from the mere meanings of words, and synthetic truth, which depends on more than meanings. Now I have long maintained that this distinction is illusory. There is one step toward such a distinction, however, which does make sense: a sentence that is true by mere meanings of words should be expected, at least if it is simple, to be subscribed to by all fluent speakers in the community. Perhaps the controversial notion of analyticity can be dispensed with, in our definition of observation sentence, in favor of this straightforward attribute of community-wide acceptance.

This attribute is of course no explication of analyticity. The community would agree that there have been black dogs, yet none who talk of analyticity would call this analytic. My rejection of the analyticity notion just means drawing no line between what goes into the mere understanding of the sentences of a language and what else the community sees eye-to-eye on. I doubt that an objective distinction can be made between meaning and such collateral information as is community-wide.

Turning back then to our task of defining observation sentences, we get this: an observation sentence is one on which all speakers of the language give the same verdict when given the same concurrent stimulation. To put the point negatively, an observation sentence is one that is not sensitive to differences in past experience within the speech community.

This formulation accords perfectly with the traditional role of the observation sentence as the court of appeal of scientific theories. For by our definition the observation sentences are the sentences on which all members of the community will agree under uniform stimulation. And what is the criterion of membership in the same community? Simple general fluency of dialogue. This criterion admits of degrees, and indeed we may usefully take the community more narrowly for some studies than for others. What count as observation sentences for a community of specialists would not always so count for a larger community.

There is generally no subjectivity in the phrasing of observation sentences, as we are now conceiving them; they will usually be about bodies. Since the distinguishing trait of an observation sentence is intersubjective agreement under agreeing stimulation, a corporeal subject matter is likelier than not.

The old tendency to associate observation sentences with a subjective sensory subject matter is rather an irony when we reflect that observation sentences are also meant to be the intersubjective tribunal of scientific hypotheses. The old tendency was due to the drive to base science on something firmer and prior in the subject's experience; but we dropped that project.

The dislodging of epistemology from its old status of first philosophy loosed a wave, we saw, of epistemological nihilism. This mood is reflected somewhat in the tendency of Polányi, Kuhn, and the late Russell Hanson to belittle

the role of evidence and to accentuate cultural relativism. Hanson ventured even to discredit the idea of observation, arguing that so-called observations vary from observer to observer with the amount of knowledge that the observers bring with them. The veteran physicist looks at some apparatus and sees an x-ray tube. The neophyte, looking at the same place, observes rather "a glass and metal instrument replete with wires, reflectors, screws, lamps, and pushbuttons."[6] One man's observation is another man's closed book or flight of fancy. The notion of observation as the impartial and objective source of evidence for science is bankrupt. Now my answer to the x-ray example was already hinted a little while back: what counts as an observation sentence varies with the width of community considered. But we can also always get an absolute standard by taking in all speakers of the language, or most.[7] It is ironical that philosophers, finding the old epistemology untenable as a whole, should react by repudiating a part which has only now moved into clear focus.

Clarification of the notion of observation sentence is a good thing, for the notion is fundamental in two connections. These two correspond to the duality that I remarked upon early in this lecture: the duality between concept and doctrine, between knowing what a sentence means and knowing whether it is true. The observation sentence is basic to both enterprises. Its relation to doctrine, to our knowledge of what is true, is very much the traditional one: observation sentences are the repository of evidence for scientific hypotheses. Its relation to meaning is fundamental too, since observation sentences are the ones we are in a position to learn to understand first, both as children and as field linguists. For observation sentences are precisely the ones that we can correlate with observable circumstances of the occasion of utterance or assent, independently of variations in the past histories of individual informants. They afford the only entry to a language.

The observation sentence is the cornerstone of semantics. For it is, as we just saw, fundamental to the learning of meaning. Also, it is where meaning is firmest. Sentences higher up in theories have no empirical consequences they can call their own; they confront the tribunal of sensory evidence only in more or less inclusive aggregates. The observation sentence, situated at the sensory periphery of the body scientific, is the minimal verifiable aggregate; it has an empirical content all its own and wears it on its sleeve.

The predicament of the indeterminacy of translation has little bearing on observation sentences. The equating of an observation sentence of our language to an observation sentence of another language is mostly a matter of empirical generalization; it is a matter of identity between the range of stimulations that would prompt assent to the one sentence and the range of stimulations that would prompt assent to the other.[8]

It is no shock to the preconceptions of old Vienna to say that epistemology now becomes semantics. For epistemology remains centered as always on evidence, and meaning remains centered as always on verification; and evidence is verification. What is likelier to shock preconceptions is that meaning, once we get beyond observation sentences, ceases in general to have any clear applicability to single sentences; also that epistemology merges with psychology, as well as with linguistics.

This rubbing out of boundaries could contribute to progress, it seems to me, in philosophically interesting inquiries of a scientific nature. One possible area is perceptual norms. Consider, to begin with, the linguistic phenomenon of phonemes. We form the habit, in hearing the myriad variations of spoken sounds, of treating each as an approximation to one or another of a limited number of norms—around thirty altogether—constituting so to speak a spoken alphabet. All speech in our language can be treated in practice as sequences of just those thirty elements, thus rectifying small deviations. Now outside the realm of language also there is probably only a rather limited alphabet of perceptual norms altogether, toward which we tend unconsciously to rectify all perceptions. These, if experimentally identified, could be taken as epistemological building blocks, the working elements of experience. They might prove in part to be culturally variable, as phonemes are, and in part universal.

Again there is the area that the psychologist Donald T. Campbell calls evolutionary epistemology.[9] In this area there is work by Hüseyin Yilmaz, who shows how some structural traits of color perception could have been predicted from survival value.[10] And a more emphatically epistemological topic that evolution helps to clarify is induction, now that we are allowing epistemology the resources of natural science.[11]

NOTES

1. A. B. Johnson, *A Treatise on Language* (New York, 1836; Berkeley, 1947).
2. *Philosophy of Science* 3 (1936): 419–471; 4 (1937): 1–40.
3. See W. V. Quine, *Ontological Relativity and Other Essays* (New York, 1969), 2 ff.
4. See Quine, *Ontological Relativity*, 28.
5. Carnap and Neurath in *Erkenntis* 3 (1932): 204–228.
6. N. R. Hanson. "Observation and Interpretation," in S. Morgenbesser, ed., *Philosophy of Science Today* (New York: Basic Books, 1966).
7. This qualification allows for occasional deviants such as the insane or the blind. Alternatively, such cases might be excluded by adjusting the level of fluency of dialogue whereby we define sameness of language. (For prompting this note and influencing the development of this paper also in more substantial ways I am indebted to Burton Dreben.)
8. Cf. Quine, *Word and Object*. (Cambridge, Mass., 1960), 31–46, 68.
9. D. T. Campbell, "Methodological Suggestions from a Comparative Psychology of Knowledge Processes." *Inquiry* 2 (1959): 152–182.
10. Hüseyin Yilmaz, "On Color Vision and a New Approach to General Perception," in E. E. Bernard and M. R. Kare, eds., *Biological Prototypes and Synthetic Systems* (New York: Plenum, 1962): "Perceptual Invariance and the Psychophysical Law," *Perception and Psychophysics* 2 (1967): 533–538.
11. See Quine, "Natural Kinds," Chap. 5 in *Ontological Relativity and Other Essays*.

37 / Hilary Putnam
WHY REASON CAN'T BE NATURALIZED

Elsewhere I have described the failure of contemporary attempts to "naturalize" metaphysics.[1] In the present essay I shall examine
attempts to naturalize the fundamental notions
of the theory of knowledge, for example the
notion of a belief's being *justified* or *rationally
acceptable*.

While the two sorts of attempts are alike in
that they both seek to reduce "intentional" or
mentalistic notions to materialistic ones, and
thus are both manifestations of what Peter
Strawson[2] has described as a permanent tension in philosophy, in other ways they are quite
different. The materialist metaphysician often
uses such traditional metaphysical notions as
causal power and *nature* quite uncritically. (I
have even read papers in which one finds the
locution "realist truth," as if everyone understood this notion except a few fuzzy anti-
realists.) The "physicalist" generally doesn't
seek to *clarify* these traditional metaphysical
notions, but just to show that science is progressively verifying the *true* metaphysics. That
is why it seems just to describe *his* enterprise
as "natural metaphysics," in strict analogy to
the "natural theology" of the eighteenth and
nineteenth centuries. Those who raise the slogan "epistemology naturalized," on the other
hand, generally *disparage* the traditional enterprises of epistemology. In this respect, moreover, they do not differ from philosophers of a
less reductionist kind; the criticisms they voice
of traditional epistemology—that it was in the
grip of a "quest for certainty," that it was unrealistic in seeking a "foundation" for knowledge as a whole, that the "foundation" it

claimed to provide was by no means indubitable in the way it claimed, that the whole
"Cartesian enterprise" was a mistake, etc.,—
are precisely the criticisms one hears from philosophers of all countries and types. Hegel already denounced the idea of an "Archimedean
point" from which epistemology could judge
all of our scientific, legal, moral, religious, etc.
beliefs (and set up standards for all of the special subjects). It is true that Russell and Moore
ignored these strictures of Hegel (as they ignored Kant), and revived "foundationalist epistemology"; but today that enterprise has few
defenders. The fact that the naturalized epistemologist is trying to reconstruct what he can
of an enterprise that few philosophers of any
persuasion regard as unflawed is perhaps the
explanation of the fact that the naturalistic tendency in epistemology expresses itself in so
many incompatible and mutually divergent
ways, while the naturalistic tendency in metaphysics appears to be, and regards itself as, a
unified movement.

Evolutionary Epistemology

The simplest approach to the problem of giving
a naturalistic account of reason is to appeal to
Darwinian evolution. In its crudest form, the
story is familiar: reason is a capacity we have
for discovering truths. Such a capacity has survival value; it evolved in just the way that any
of our physical organs or capacities evolved. A
belief is rational if it is arrived at by the exercise of this capacity.

This approach assumes, at bottom, a meta-

From *Realism and Reason*, vol. 3 of *Philosophical Papers* (Cambridge: Cambridge University Press, 1983),
229–47. Copyright © 1983, Cambridge University Press. Reprinted by permission of the author and the
publisher.

physically "realist" notion of truth: truth as "correspondence to the facts" or something of that kind. And this notion, as I have argued in *Realism and Reason*, is incoherent. We don't have notions of the "existence" of things or of the "truth" of statements that are independent of the versions we construct and of the procedures and practices that give sense to talk of "existence" and "truth" within those versions. Do *fields* "exist" as physically real things? Yes, fields really exist: relative to one scheme for describing and explaining physical phenomena; relative to another there are particles, plus "virtual" particles plus "ghost" particles, plus . . . Is it true that *brown* objects exist? Yes, relative to a common-sense version of the world: although one cannot give a necessary and sufficient condition for an object to be brown,[3] (one that applies to all objects, under all conditions) in the form of a finite closed formula in the language of physics. Do *dispositions* exist? Yes, in our ordinary way of talking (although disposition talk is just as recalcitrant to translation into physicalistic language as counterfactual talk, and for similar reasons). We have many irreducibly different but legitimate ways of talking, and true "existence" statements in all of them.

To postulate a set of "ultimate" objects, the furniture of the world, or what you will, whose "existence" is *absolute*, not relative to our discourse at all, and a notion of truth as "correspondence" to these ultimate objects is simply to revive the whole failed enterprise of traditional metaphysics. I show *how* unsuccessful attempts to revive *that* enterprise have been in the twelfth chapter of *Realism and Reason*.

Truth, in the only sense in which we have a vital and working notion of it, is rational acceptability (or, rather, rational acceptability under sufficiently good epistemic conditions; and which conditions are epistemically better or worse is relative to the type of discourse in just the way rational acceptability itself is). But to substitute this characterization of truth into the formula "reason is a capacity for discovering truths" is to see the emptiness of that formula at once: "reason is a capacity for discovering what is (or would be) rationally acceptable" is *not* the most informative statement a philosopher might utter. The evolutionary epistemologist must either presuppose a "realist" (i.e., a metaphysical) notion of truth or see his formula collapse into vacuity.

Roderick Firth[4] has argued that, in fact, it collapses into a kind of epistemic vacuity on *any* theory of rational acceptability (*or* truth). For, he points out, whatever we take the correct epistemology (or the correct theory of truth) to be, we have no way of *identifying* truths except to posit that the statements that are currently rationally acceptable (by our lights) are true. Even if these beliefs are false, even if our rational beliefs contribute to our survival for some reason *other* than the truth, the way "truths" are identified *guarantees* that reason will seem to be a "capacity for discovering truths." This characterization of reason has thus no real empirical content.

The evolutionary epistemologist could, I suppose, try using some notion *other* than the notion of "discovering truths." For example, he might try saying that "reason is a capacity for arriving at beliefs which *promote our survival*" (or our "inclusive genetic fitness"). But this would be a loser! Science itself, and the methodology which we have developed since the seventeenth century for constructing and evaluating theories, has *mixed* effects on inclusive genetic fitness and all too uncertain effects on survival. If the human race perishes in a nuclear war, it may well be (although there will be no one alive to say it) that scientific beliefs did *not*, in a sufficiently long time scale, promote "survival". Yet that will not have been because the scientific theories were not rationally acceptable, but because our *use* of them was irrational. In fact, if rationality were measured by survival value, then the proto-beliefs of the cockroach, who has been around for tens of millions of years longer than we, would have a far higher claim to rationality than the sum total of human knowledge. But such a measure would be cockeyed; there is no contradiction in imagining a world in which people have utterly irrational beliefs which for some reason enable them to survive, or a world in which the most rational beliefs quickly lead to extinction.

If the notion of "truth" in the characterization of rationality as a "capacity for discovering truths" is problematic, so, almost equally, is the notion of a "capacity." In one sense of the term, *learning* is a "capacity" (even, a "capacity for discovering truths"), and *all* our beliefs are the product of *that* capacity. Yet, for better or worse, not all our beliefs are rational.

The problem here is that there are no sharp lines in the brain between one "capacity" and another (Chomskians to the contrary). Even seeing includes not just the visual organs, the eyes, but the whole brain; and what is true of seeing is certainly true of *thinking* and *inferring. We* draw lines between one "capacity" and another (or build them into the various versions we construct); but a sharp line at one level does not usually correspond to a sharp line at a lower level. The table at which I write, for example, is a natural unit at the level of everyday talk; I am aware that the little particle of food sticking to its surface (I must do something about that!) is not a "part" of the table; but at the physicist's level, the decision to consider that bit of food to be outside the boundary of the table is not natural at all. Similarly, "believing" and "seeing" are quite different at the level of ordinary language psychology (and usefully so); but the corresponding brain-processes interpenetrate in complex ways which can only be separated by looking outside the brain, at the environment and at the output behavior *as structured by our interests and saliencies.* "Reason is a capacity" is what Wittgenstein called a "grammatical remark"; by which he meant (I think) not an analytic truth, but simply the sort of remark that philosophers often *take* to be informative when in fact it tells us nothing useful.

None of this is intended to deny the obvious scientific facts: that we would not be able to reason if we did not have brains, and that those *brains* are the product of evolution by natural selection. What is wrong with evolutionary epistemology is not that the scientific facts are wrong, but that they don't answer any of the philosophical questions.

The Reliability Theory of Rationality

A more sophisticated recent approach to these matters, proposed by Professor Alvin Goldman,[5] runs as follows: let us call a *method* (as opposed to a single belief) *reliable* if the method leads to a high frequency (say, 95%) of *true* beliefs in a long run series of representative applications (or *would* lead to such a high truth-frequency in such a series of applications). Then (the proposal goes) we can define a *rational* belief to be one which is *arrived at by using a reliable method.*

This proposal does not avoid the first objection we raised against evolutionary epistemology: it too presupposes a metaphysical notion of truth. Forgetting that rational acceptability does the lion's share of the work in fixing the notion of "truth," the reliability theorist only pretends to be giving an analysis of rationality in terms that do not presuppose it. The second objection we raised against evolutionary epistemology, namely, the notion of a "capacity" is hopelessly vague and general, is met, however, by replacing that notion with the notion of an arbitrary method for generating true or false statements, and then restricting the class to those methods (in this sense) whose reliability (as defined) is high. "Learning" may be a method for generating statements, but its *reliability* is not high enough for every statement we "learn" to count as rationally acceptable, on this theory. Finally, *no* hypothesis is made as to whether the reliable methods we employ are the result of biological evolution, cultural evolution, or what: this is regarded as no part of the theory of what rationality is, in this account.

This account is vulnerable to many counter-examples, however. *One* is the following: suppose that Tibetan Buddhism is, in fact, *true,* and that the Dalai Lama is, in fact, *infallible* on matters of faith and morals. Anyone who believes in the Dalai Lama, and who invariably believes any statement the Dalai Lama makes on a matter of faith or morals, follows a method which is 100% reliable; thus, if the reliability theory of rationality were correct, such a person's beliefs on faith and morals would all be rational *even if his argument for his belief that the Dalai Lama is never wrong is "the Dalai Lama says so."*

Cultural Relativism

I have already said that, in my view, truth and rational acceptability—a claim's being right and someone's being in a position to make it—are relative to the sort of language we are using and the sort of context we are in. "That weighs one pound" may be true in a butcher shop, but the same sentence would be understood very differently (as demanding four decimal places of precision, perhaps) if the same object were being weighed in a laboratory. This does not mean that a claim is right *whenever* those who employ the language in question would accept it as right in its context, however. There are two points that must be *balanced*, both points that have been made by philosophers of many different kinds: (1) talk of what is "right" and "wrong" in any area only makes sense against the background of an *inherited tradition*; but (2) traditions themselves can be *criticized*. As Austin[6] says, remarking on a special case of this, "superstition and error and fantasy of all kinds do become incorporated in ordinary language and even sometimes stand up to the survival test (only, when they do, why should we not detect it?)."

What I am saying is that the "standards" accepted by a culture or a subculture, either explicitly or implicitly, cannot *define* what reason is, even in context, because they *presuppose* reason (reasonableness) for their interpretation. On the one hand, there is no notion of reasonableness at all *without* cultures, practices, procedures; on the other hand, the cultures, practices, procedures we inherit are not an algorithm to be slavishly followed. As Mill said, commenting on his own inductive logic, there is no rule book which will not lead to terrible results "if supposed to be conjoined with universal idiocy." Reason is, in this sense, both immanent (not to be found outside of concrete language games and institutions) and transcendent (a regulative idea that we use to criticize the conduct of *all* activities and institutions).

Philosophers who lose sight of the immanence of reason, of the fact that reason is always relative to context and institution, become lost in characteristic philosophical fantasies. "The ideal language," "inductive logic," "the empiricist criterion of significance"—these are the fantasies of the positivist, who would replace the vast complexity of human reason with a kind of intellectual Wal-

den II. "The absolute idea": this is the fantasy of Hegel, who, without ignoring that complexity, would have us (or, rather, "spirit") reach an endstage at which we (it) could comprehend it all. Philosophers who lose sight of the transcendence of reason become cultural (or historical) relativists.

I want to talk about cultural relativism, because it is one of the most influential—perhaps the most influential—forms of naturalized epistemology extant, although not usually recognized as such.

The situation is complicated, because cultural relativists usually *deny* that they are cultural relativists. I shall count a philosopher as a cultural relativist for our purposes if I have not been able to find anyone who can explain to me why he *isn't* a cultural relativist. Thus I count Richard Rorty as a cultural relativist, because his explicit formulations are relativist ones (he identifies truth with right assertibility by the standards of one's cultural peers, for example), and because his entire attack on traditional philosophy is mounted on the basis that the nature of reason and representation are non-problems, because the only kind of truth it makes sense to seek is to convince one's cultural peers. Yet he himself *tells* us that relativism is self-refuting.[7] And I count Michel Foucault as a relativist because his insistence on the determination of beliefs by language is so overwhelming that it is an incoherence on his part not to apply his doctrine to his *own* language and thought. Whether Heidegger ultimately escaped something very much like cultural, or rather historical, relativism is an interesting question.

Cultural relativists are not, in their own eyes, scientistic or "physicalistic." They are likely to view materialism and scientism as just the hangups of one particular cultural epoch. If I count them as "naturalized epistemologists" it is because their doctrine is, none the less, a product of the same deference to the claims of nature, the same desire for harmony with the world version of some science, as physicalism. The difference in style and tone is thus explained: the physicalist's paradigm of science is a *hard* science, *physics* (as the term "physicalism" suggests); the cultural relativist's paradigm is a *soft* science: anthropology, or linguistics, or psychology, or history, as the case may be. That reason is whatever the norms of the local culture determine it to be is a naturalist view inspired by the *social* sciences, including history.

There is something which makes cultural relativism a far more dangerous cultural tendency than materialism. At bottom, there is a deep irrationalism to cultural relativism, a denial of the possibility of *thinking* (as opposed to making noises in counterpoint or in chorus). An aspect of this which is of special concern to philosophy is the suggestion, already mentioned, that the deep questions of philosophy are not deep at all. A corollary to this suggestion is that philosophy, as traditionally understood, is a *silly* enterprise. But the questions *are* deep, and it is the easy answers that are silly. Even seeing that relativism is inconsistent is, if the knowledge is taken seriously, seeing something important about a deep question. Philosophers *are* beginning to talk about the great issues again, and to feel that something can be *said* about them, even if there are no grand or ultimate solutions. There is an excitement in the air. And if I react to Professor Rorty's book[8] with a certain sharpness, it is because one more "deflationary" book, one more book telling us that the deep questions aren't deep and the whole enterprise was a mistake, is just what we *don't* need right now. Yet I am grateful to Rorty all the same, for his work has the merit of addressing profound questions head-on.

So, although we all know that cultural relativism is inconsistent (or say we do) I want to take the time to say again that it is inconsistent. I want to point out one reason that it is: not one of the quick, logic-chopping refutations (although every refutation of relativism teaches us something about reason) but a somewhat messy, somewhat "intuitive," reason.

I shall develop my argument in analogy with a well-known argument against "methodological solipsism." The "methodological solipsist"— one thinks of Carnap's *Logische Aufbau* or of Mach's *Analyse der Empfindungen*—holds that *all* our talk can be reduced to talk about experiences and logical constructions out of experiences. More precisely, he holds that everything he can conceive of is identical (in the

ultimate logical analyses of his language) with one or another complex of his *own* experiences. What makes him a *methodological* solipsist as opposed to a real solipsist is that he kindly adds that *you*, dear reader, are the "I" of this construction when *you* perform it: he says *everybody* is a (methodological) solipsist.

The trouble, which should be obvious, is that his two stances are ludicrously incompatible. His solipsist stance implies an enormous asymmetry between persons: my body is a construction out of my experiences, in the system, but *your* body isn't a construction out of *your* experiences. It's a construction out of *my* experiences. And your experiences—viewed from within the system—are a construction out of your bodily behavior, which, as just said, is a construction out of *my* experiences. My experiences are different from everyone else's (within the system) in that they are what *everything* is constructed from. But his transcendental stance is that it's all symmetrical: the "you" he addresses his higher-order remark to cannot be the *empirical* "you" of the system. But if it's really true that the "you" of the system is the only "you" he can *understand*, then the transcendental remark is *unintelligible*. Moral: don't be a methodological solipsist unless you are a *real* solipsist!

Consider now the position of the cultural relativist who says, "When I say something is *true*, I mean that it is correct according to the norms of *my* culture." If he adds, "When a member of a different culture says that something is true, what he means (whether he knows it or not) is that it is in conformity with the norms of *his* culture," then he is in exactly the same plight as the methodological solipsist.

To spell this out, suppose R. R., a cultural relativist, says

> When Karl says "Schnee ist weiss," what Karl means (whether he knows it or not) is that snow is white *as determined by* the norms of Karl's culture

(which we take to be German culture).

Now the sentence "Snow is white as determined by the norms of German culture" is itself one which R. R. has to *use*, not just mention, to say what Karl says. On his own account, what R. R. means by *this* sentence is

"Snow is white as determined by the norms of German culture" is true by the norms of R. R.'s culture

(which we take to be American culture).

Substituting this back into the first displayed utterance, (and changing to indirect quotation) yields:

> When Karl says "Schnee ist weiss," what he means (whether he knows it or not) is that it is true as determined by the norms of American culture that it is true as determined by the norms of German culture that snow is white.

In general, if R. R. understands *every* utterance *p* that *he* uses as meaning "it is true by the norms of American culture that *p*," then he must understand his own hermeneutical utterances, the utterances he uses to interpret others, the same way, no matter how many qualifiers of the "according to the norms of German culture" type or however many footnotes, glosses, commentaries on the cultural differences, or whatever, he accompanies them by. Other cultures become, so to speak, logical constructions out of the procedures and practices of American culture. If he now attempts to add "the situation is reversed from the point of view of the *other* culture" he lands in the predicament the methodological solipsist found himself in: the transcendental claim of a *symmetrical* situation cannot be *understood* if the relativist doctrine is right. And to say, as relativists often do, that the other culture has "incommensurable" concepts is no better. This is just the transcendental claim in a special jargon.

Stanley Cavell[9] has written that skepticism about other minds can be a significant problem because we don't, in fact, always fully acknowledge the reality of others, their equal *validity* so to speak. One might say that the methodological solipsist is led to his transcendental observation that everyone is equally the "I" of the construction by his praiseworthy desire to *acknowledge* others in this sense. But you *can't* acknowledge others in this sense, which involves recognizing that the situation *really is* symmetrical, if you think they are really constructions out of *your* sense data. Nor can you acknowledge others in this sense if you think that the *only* notion of truth there is for *you* to

understand is "truth-as-determined-by-the-norms-of-*this*-culture."

For simplicity, I have discussed relativism with respect to truth, but the same discussion applies to relativism about rational acceptability, justification, etc.; indeed, a relativist is unlikely to be a relativist about one of these notions and not about the others.

Cultural Imperialism

Just as the methodological solipsist can become a *real* solipsist, the cultural relativist can become a cultural imperialist. He can say, "Well then, truth—the only notion of truth I understand—is defined by the norms of *my* culture." ("After all," he can add, "which norms should I rely on? The norms of *somebody else's* culture?") Such a view is no longer relativist at all. It postulates an *objective* notion of truth, although one that is said to be a product of our culture, and to be defined by our culture's criteria (I assume the cultural imperialist is one of *us*). In this sense, just as consistent solipsism becomes indistinguishable from realism (as Wittgenstein said in the *Tractatus*), consistent cultural relativism also becomes indistinguishable from realism. But cultural imperialist realism is a special *kind* of realism.

It is realist in that it accepts an objective difference between what is true and what is merely thought to be true. (Whether it can consistently *account for* this difference is another question.)

It is not a *metaphysical* or transcendental realism, in that truth cannot go beyond right assertibility, as it does in metaphysical realism. But the notion of right assertibility is fixed by "criteria," in a positivistic sense: something is rightly assertible only if the norms of the culture specify that it is; these norms are, as it were, an *operational definition* of right assertibility, in this view.

I don't know if any philosopher holds such a view, although several philosophers have let themselves fall into talking at certain times as if they did. (A philosopher in this mood is likely to say, "*X* is *our* notion," with a certain petulance, where *X* may be *reason, truth, justification, evidence*, or what have you.)

This view is, however, self-refuting, at least in our culture. I have discussed this elsewhere; [10] the argument turns on the fact that our culture, unlike totalitarian or theocratic cultures, does not have "norms" which decide *philosophical* questions. (Some philosophers have thought it does; but they had to postulate a "depth grammar" accessible only to *them*, and not describable by ordinary linguistic or anthropological investigation.) Thus the philosophical statement:

> A statement is true (rightly assertible) only if it is assertible according to the norms of modern European and American culture

is itself neither assertible nor refutable in a way that requires assent by everyone who does not deviate from the norms of modern European and American culture. So, if this statement is true, it follows that it is not true (not rightly assertible). Hence it is not true. QED. (I believe that *all* theories which identify truth or right assertibility with what people agree with, or with what they would agree with in the long run, or with what educated and intelligent people agree with, or with what educated and intelligent people would agree with in the long run, are contingently self-refuting in this same way.)

Cultural imperialism would not be contingently self-refuting in this way if, as a matter of contingent fact, our culture were a totalitarian culture which erected its own cultural imperialism into a required dogma, a culturally normative belief. But it would still be wrong. For every culture has norms which are vague, norms which are unreasonable, norms which dictate inconsistent beliefs. We have all become aware how many inconsistent beliefs about *women* were culturally normative until recently, and are still strongly operative, not only in subcultures, but in all of us to some extent; and examples of inconsistent but culturally normative beliefs could easily be multiplied. Our task is not to mechanically *apply* cultural norms, as if they were a computer program and we were the computer, but to interpret them, to criticize them, to bring them and the ideals which inform them into reflective equilibrium. Cavell has aptly described this as "confronting the culture with itself, along the lines in which it meets in me." And he adds,[11] "This seems to me a task that warrants the name of Philosophy." In this sense, we are called to be philosophers to a greater or lesser extent.

The culturalist, relativist or imperialist, like the historicist, has been caught up in the fascination of something really fascinating; but caught up in a sophomorish way. Traditions, cultures, history, deserve to be emphasized, as they are not by those who seek Archimedean points in metaphysics or epistemology. It is true that we speak a public language, that we inherit versions, that talk of truth and falsity only make sense against the background of an "inherited tradition," as Wittgenstein says. But it is also true that we constantly remake our language, that we make new versions out of old ones, and that we have to use reason to do all this, and, for that matter, even to understand and apply the norms we do not alter or criticize. Consensus definitions of reason do not work, because consensus among grown-ups *presupposes* reason rather than defining it.

Quinian Positivism

The slogan "epistemology naturalized" is the title of a famous paper by Quine.[12] If I have not discussed that paper up to now, it is because Quine's views are much more subtle and much more elaborate than the disastrously simple views we have just reviewed, and it seemed desirable to get the simpler views out of the way first.

Quine's philosophy is a large continent, with mountain ranges, deserts, and even a few Okefenokee Swamps. I do not know how all of the pieces of it can be reconciled, if they can be; what I shall do is discuss two different strains that are to be discerned in Quine's epistemology. In the present section I discuss the positivistic strain; the next section will discuss "epistemology naturalized."

The positivist strain, which occurs early and late, turns on the notion of an *observation sentence*. In his earliest writings, Quine gave this a phenomenalistic interpretation but, since the 1950s at least, he has preferred a definition in neurological and cultural terms. First, a preliminary notion: The *stimulus meaning* of a sentence is defined to be the set of stimulations (of "surface neurons") that would "prompt assent" to the sentence. It is thus supposed to be a *neurological* correlate of the sentence. A sentence may be called "stimulus-true" for a speaker if the speaker is actually experiencing a pattern of stimulation of his surface neurons that lie in its stimulus meaning; but one should be careful to remember that a stimulus-true sentence is not necessarily true *simpliciter*. If you show me a life-like replica of a duck, the sentence, "That's a duck," may be stimulus-true for me, but it isn't true. A sentence is defined to be an *observation* sentence for a community if it is an occasioned sentence (one whose truth value is regarded as varying with time and place, although this is not the Quinian definition) and it has the *same* stimulus meaning for all speakers. Thus "He is a bachelor" is not an observation sentence, since different stimulations will prompt you to assent to it than will prompt me (we know different people); but "That's a duck" is (nearly enough) an observation sentence. Observe that the criterion is supposed to be entirely physicalistic. The key idea is that observation sentences are distinguished among occasioned sentences by being keyed to the same stimulations *intersubjectively.*

Mach held that talk of unobservables, including (for him) material objects, is justified only for reasons of "economy of thought." The business of science is *predicting regularities in our sensations*; we introduce "objects" other than sensations only as needed to get theories which neatly predict such regularities.

Quine[13] comes close to a "physicalized" version of Mach's view. Discussing the question, whether there is more than one correct "system of the world," he gives his criteria for such a system: (1) it must predict a certain number of stimulus-true observation sentences,[14] (2) it must be finitely axiomatized; (3) it must contain nothing unnecessary to the purpose of predicting stimulus-true observation sentences and conditionals. In the terminology Quine introduces in this paper, the theory formulation must be a "tight fit"[15] over the relevant set of stimulus-true observation conditionals. (This is a formalized version of Mach's "economy of thought.")

If this were all of Quine's doctrine, there would be no problem. It is reconciling what Quine says here with what Quine says elsewhere that is difficult and confusing. I am *not* claiming that it is impossible however; a lot, if not all, of what Quine says *can* be reconciled. What I claim is that Quine's position is much more complicated than is generally realized.

For example, what is the *status* of Quine's ideal "systems of the world"? It is tempting to characterize the sentences in one of Quine's ideal "theory formulations" as *truths* (relative to that language and that choice of a formulation from among the equivalent-but-incompatible-at-face-value formulations of what Quine would regard as the *same* theory) and as *all* the truths (relative to the same choice of language and formulation), but this would conflict with *bivalence*, the principle that *every* sentence, in the ideal scientific language Quine envisages, is true or false.

To spell this out: Quine's ideal systems of the world are *finitely axiomatizable theories*, and contain standard mathematics. Thus Gödel's celebrated result applies to them: there are sentences in them which are neither provable nor refutable on the basis of the system. If being *true* were just being a theorem in the system, such sentences would be neither true nor false, since neither they nor their negations are theorems. But Quine[16] holds to bivalence.

If Quine were a metaphysical realist there would again be no problem: the ideal system would contain everything that could be *justified* (from a very idealized point of view, assuming knowledge of all observations that *could* be made, and logical omniscience); but, Quine could say, the undecidable sentences are still determinately true or false—only we can't tell which. But the rejection of metaphysical realism, of the whole picture of a determinate "copying" relation between words and a noumenal world, is at the heart of Quine's philosophy. And, as we shall see in the next section, "justification" is a notion Quine is leery of. So what *is* he up to?[17]

I hazard the following interpretation: bivalence has *two* meanings for Quine: a "first-order" meaning, a meaning as viewed *within* the system of science (including its Tarskian metalanguage) and a "second-order" meaning, a meaning as viewed by the philosopher. In effect, I am claiming that Quine too allows himself a "transcendental" standpoint which is different from the "naive" standpoint that we get by just taking the system at face value. (I am not claiming that this is *inconsistent* however; some philosophers feel that such a move is *always* an inconsistency, but taking this line would preclude using *any* notion in science which one would explain away as a useful fiction in one's commentary on one's first-order practice. There was an inconsistency in the case of the methodological solipsist, because he claimed his first-order system reconstructed the *only* way he could understand the notion of another mind; if he withdraws that claim, then his position becomes perfectly consistent: it merely loses all philosophical interest.)

From *within* the first-order system, "*p* is true or *p* is false" is simply true; a derivable consequence of the Tarskian truth definition, given standard propositional calculus. From *outside*, from the meta-metalinguistic point of view Quine occupies, there is no unique "world," no unique "intended model." Only *structure* matters; every model of the ideal system (I assume there is just one ideal theory, and we have fixed a formulation) is an intended model. Statements that are provable are true in *all* intended models; undecidable statements are true or false in each intended model, but not *stably* true or false. Their truth value varies from model to model.

If *this* is Quine's view, however, then there is still a problem. For Quine, what the philosopher says from the "transcendental" standpoint is subject to the same methodological rules that govern ordinary first-order scientific work. Even mathematics is subject to the same rules. Mathematical truths, too, are to be certified as such by showing they are theorems in a system which we need to predict sensations (or rather, stimulus-true observation conditionals), given the physics which we are constructing as we construct the mathematics. More precisely, the *whole system of knowledge* is justified *as a whole* by its utility in predicting observations. Quine emphasizes that there is no room in this view for a special status for philosophical utterances. There is no "first philosophy" above or apart from science, as he puts it.

Consider, now the statement:

A statement is *rightly assertible* (true in all models) just in case it is a theorem of the relevant "finite formulation," and that formulation is a "tight fit" over the appropriate set of stimulus-true observation conditionals.

This statement, like most philosophical statements, does not imply *any* observation conditionals, either by itself or in conjunction with physics, chemistry, biology, etc. Whether we say that some statements which are undecidable in the system are really rightly assertible or deny it does not have any effects (that one can foresee) on prediction. Thus, *this* statement *cannot* itself be rightly assertible. In short, *this* reconstruction of Quine's positivism makes it *self-refuting*.

The difficulty, which is faced by all versions of positivism, is that positivist exclusion principles are always self-referentially inconsistent. In short, *positivism produced a conception of rationality so narrow as to exclude the very activity of producing that conception*. (Of course, it also excluded a great many other kinds of rational activity.) The problem is especially sharp for Quine, because of his explicit rejection of the analytic/synthetic distinction, his rejection of a special status for philosophy, etc.

It may be, also, that I have just got Quine wrong. Quine would perhaps reject the notions of "right assertibility," "intended model," and so on. But then I just don't know *what* to make of this strain in Quine's thought.

"Epistemology Naturalized"

Quine's paper "Epistemology Naturalized" takes a very different tack. "Justification" has failed. (Quine considers the notion only in its strong "Cartesian" setting, which is one of the things that makes his paper puzzling.) Hume taught us that we *can't* justify our knowledge claims (in a foundational way). Conceptual reduction has also failed (Quine reviews the failure of phenomenalism as represented by Carnap's attempt in the *Logische Aufbau*.) So,

Quine urges, let us give up epistemology and "settle for psychology."

Taken at face value, Quine's position is sheer epistemological eliminationism: we should just *abandon* the notions of justification, good reason, warranted assertion, etc., and *reconstrue* the notion of "evidence" (so that the "evidence" becomes the sensory stimulations that *cause us* to have the scientific beliefs we have). In conversation, however, Quine has repeatedly said that he didn't mean to "rule out the normative"; and this is consistent with his recent interest in such notions as the notion of a "tight fit" (an economical finitely axiomatized system for predicting observations).

Moreover, the expression "naturalized epistemology" is being used today by a number of philosophers who explicitly consider themselves to *be* doing normative epistemology, or at least methodology. But the paper "Epistemology Naturalized" really does rule all that out. So it's all *extremely* puzzling.

One way to reconcile the conflicting impulses that one sees at work here might be to replace justification theory by reliability theory in the sense of Goldman; instead of saying that a belief is justified if it is arrived at by a reliable method, one might say that the notion of justification should be *replaced* by the notion of a verdict's being the product of a reliable method. This is an *eliminationist* line in that it does not try to reconstruct or analyze the traditional notion; that was an intuitive notion that we now perceive to have been defective from the start, such a philosopher might say. Instead, he proposes a *better* notion (by his lights).

While some philosophers would, perhaps, move in this direction, Quine would not for a reason already given: Quine rejects metaphysical realism, and the notion of reliability presupposes the notion of *truth*. Truth is, to be sure, an acceptable notion for Quine, if defined à la Tarski, but so defined, it cannot serve as the primitive notion of epistemology or of methodology. For Tarski simply defines "true" so that "*p* is true" will come out equivalent to "*p*"; so that, to cite the famous example, *"Snow is white" is true* will come out equivalent to "Snow is white." What the procedure does is to define "true" so that saying that a statement is true is equivalent to *assenting* to the statement; truth, as defined by Tarski, is not a *property* of statements at all, but a syncategorematic notion which enables us to "ascend semantically," i.e., to talk about sentences instead of about objects.[18]

I will assent to "*p* is true" whenever I assent to *p*; therefore, I will accept a method as reliable whenever it *yields verdicts I would accept*. I believe that, in fact, this is what the "normative" becomes for Quine: the search for methods that yield verdicts that one oneself would accept.

Why We Can't Eliminate the Normative

I shall have to leave Quine's views with these unsatisfactory remarks. But why not take a full blown eliminationist line? Why *not* eliminate the normative from our conceptual vocabulary? Could it be a superstition that there is such a thing as reason?

If one abandons the notions of justification, rational acceptability, warranted assertibility, right assertibility, and the like, completely, then "true" goes as well, except as a mere device for "semantic ascent," that is, a mere mechanism for switching from one level of language to another. The mere introduction of a Tarskian truth predicate cannot define for a language any notion of *rightness* that was not already defined. To reject the notions of justification and right assertibility while *keeping a metaphysical realist notion of truth* would, on the other hand, not only be peculiar (what ground could there be for regarding truth, in the "correspondence" sense, as *clearer* than right assertibility?), but incoherent; for the notions the naturalistic metaphysician uses to explain truth and reference, for example the notion of causality (explanation) and the notion of the *appropriate type* of causal chain, depend on notions which presuppose the notion of reasonableness.

But if *all* notions of rightness, both epistemic and (metaphysically) realist are eliminated, then what are our statements but noisemakings? What are our thoughts but *mere* subvocalizations? The elimination of the normative is attempted mental suicide.

The notions, "verdict I accept" and "method that leads to verdicts I accept" are of little help. If the *only* kind of rightness any statement has that I can understand is "being arrived at by a method which yields verdicts *I* accept," than I am committed to a solipsism of the present moment. To solipsism, because this *is* a methodologically solipsist substitute for assertibility ("verdicts I accept"), and we saw before that the methodological solipsist is only consistent if he is a real solipsist. And to solipsism of the present moment because this is a *tensed* notion (a substitute of warranted assertibility at *a time*, not for assertibility in the best conditions); and if the *only* kind of rightness my present "subvocalizations" have is *present* assertibility (however defined); if there is no notion of a *limit* verdict, however fuzzy; then there is no sense in which my "subvocalizations" are *about* anything that goes beyond the present moment. (Even the thought "there is a future" is "right" only in the sense of being *assertible at the present moment*, in such a view.)

One could try to overcome this last defect by introducing the notion of "a verdict I would accept *in the long run*," but this would at once involve one with the use of counterfactuals, and with such notions as "similarity of possible worlds." But it is pointless to make further efforts in this direction. Why should we expend our mental energy in convincing ourselves that we aren't thinkers, that our thoughts aren't really *about* anything, noumenal *or* phenomenal, that there is *no* sense in which any thought is *right* or *wrong* (including the thought that no thought is right or wrong) beyond being the verdict of the moment, and so on? This is a self-refuting enterprise if there ever was one! Let us recognize that one of our fundamental self-conceptualizations, one of our fundamental "self-descriptions," in Rorty's phrase, is that we are *thinkers*, and that *as* thinkers we are committed to there being *some* kind of truth, some kind of correctness which is substantial and not merely "disquotational." That means that there is no eliminating the normative.

If there is no eliminating the normative, and no possibility of reducing the normative to our favorite science, be it biology, anthropology, neurology, physics, or whatever, then where are we? We might try for a grand theory of the normative in its *own* terms, a formal epistemology, but that project seems decidedly overambitious. In the meantime, there is a great deal of philosophical work to be done, and it will be done with fewer errors if we free ourselves of the reductionist and historicist hangups that have marred so much recent philosophy. If reason is both transcendent and immanent, then philosophy, as culture-bound reflection and argument about eternal questions, is both in time and eternity. We don't have an Archimedean point; we always speak the language of a time and place; but the rightness and wrongness of what we say is not *just* for a time and a place.

NOTES

1. See Hilary Putnam, "Why There Isn't a Ready-Made World," in *Realism and Reason* (Cambridge, Eng., 1983), 205–28.
2. P. F. Strawson, "Universals," *Midwest Studies in Philosophy* IV (1979): 3–10.
3. I chose brown because brown is not a spectral color. But the point also applies to spectral colors: if being a color were purely a matter of reflecting light of a certain wavelength, then the objects we see would change color a number of times a day (and would all be black in total darkness). Color depends on background conditions, edge effects, reflectancy, relations to amount of light etc. Giving a description of all of these would only define *perceived* color: to define the "real" color of an object one also needs a notion of "standard conditions": traditional philosophers would have said that the color of a red object is a power (a disposition) to look red to normal observers under normal conditions. This, however, requires a counterfactual conditional (whenever the object is *not* in normal conditions) and the attempt to define counterfactuals in "physical" terms has failed. What makes color terms physically undefinable is not that color is subjective but that it is *subjunctive*. The common idea that there is some one molecular structure (or whatever) common to all objects which look red "under normal conditions" has no foundation: consider the difference between the physical structure of a red star and a red book (and the difference in what we count as "normal conditions" in the two cases).
4. This argument appears in Firth's Presidential Address to the Eastern Division of the American Philosophical Association (29 December 1981),

titled "Epistemic Merit, Intrinsic and Instrumental." Firth does not specifically refer to evolutionary epistemology, but rather to "epistemic utilitarianism"; however, his argument applies as well to evolutionary epistemology of the kind I describe.

5. A. Goldman, "What Is Justified Belief?" in G. S. Pappas, ed., *Justification and Knowledge* (Dordrecht, 1979).

6. J. L. Austin, "A Plea for Excuses," in his *Philosophical Papers* (Oxford, 1961), 175–204.

7. R. Rorty, "Pragmatism, Relativism and Irrationalism," *Proceedings and Addresses of the American Philosophical Association* 53 (1980).

8. R. Rorty, *Philosophy and the Mirror of Nature* (Oxford, 1980).

9. S. Cavell, *Must We Mean What We Say* (New York, 1969).

10. H. Putnam, *Reason, Truth and History* (Cambridge, Engl. 1981).

11. S. Cavell, *The Claim of Reason* (Oxford, 1979), 86–125.

12. W. V. Quine, "Epistemology Naturalized," in *Ontological Relativity and Other Essays* (New York, 1969). Reprinted in this volume.

13. Quine, "On Empirically Equivalent Systems of the World," *Erkenntnis* 9 (1975): 313–28.

14. Quine actually requires that a "system of the world" predict that certain "pegged observation sentences" be true. I have oversimplified in the text by writing "observation sentence" for

"pegged observation sentence." Also the "stimulus meaning" of an observation sentence includes a specification of conditions under which the speaker *dissents*, as well as the conditions under which he assents. The details are in Quine's paper cited in note 13.

15. A theory is a "tight fit" if it is interpretable in every axiomatizable theory, which implies the observation conditionals (conditionals whose antecedent and consequent are pegged observation sentences) in question in a way that holds the pegged observation sentences fixed. To my knowledge, no proof exists that a "tight fit" even exists, apart from the trivial case in which the observation conditionals can be axiomatized *without* going outside of the observation vocabulary.

16. Quine, "What Price Bivalence?" *Journal of Philosophy* 78 (1981), 90–95. Reprinted in his *Theories and Things* (Cambridge, Mass., 1981).

17. Quine *rejected* the interpretation I offer below (discussion at Heidelberg in 1981), and opted for saying that our situation is "asymmetrical": he is a "realist" with respect to his *own* language but not with respect to other languages.

18. Quine himself puts this succinctly, "Whatever we affirm, after all, we affirm as a statement within our aggregate theory of nature as we now see it: and to call a statement true is just to reaffirm it." (Quine, "On Empirically Equivalent Systems of the World," 327.)

38 / Alvin I. Goldman
EPISTEMIC FOLKWAYS AND SCIENTIFIC EPISTEMOLOGY

I

What is the mission of epistemology, and what is its proper methodology? Such meta-epistemological questions have been prominent in recent years, especially with the emergence of various brands of "naturalistic" epistemology. In this paper, I shall reformulate and expand upon my own meta-epistemological conception (most fully articulated in Goldman

From Alvin I. Goldman, *Liasons: Philosophy Meets the Cognitive and Social Sciences*, pp. 155–75. Cambridge, Mass: M.I.T. Press, 1992. Reprinted by permission.

1986), retaining many of its former ingredients while reconfiguring others. The discussion is by no means confined, though, to the meta-epistemological level. New substantive proposals will also be advanced and defended.

Let us begin, however, at the meta-epistemological level, by asking what role should be played in epistemology by our ordinary epistemic concepts and principles. By some philosophers' lights, the sole mission of epistemology is to elucidate commonsense epistemic concepts and principles: concepts like knowledge, justification, and rationality, and principles associated with these concepts. By other philosophers' lights, this is not even part of epistemology's aim. Ordinary concepts and principles, the latter would argue are fundamentally naive, unsystematic, and uninformed by important bodies of logic and/or mathematics. Ordinary principles and practices, for example, ignore or violate the probability calculus, which ought to be the cornerstone of epistemic rationality. Thus, on the second view, proper epistemology must neither *end* with naive principles of justification or rationality, nor even *begin* there.

My own stance on this issue lies somewhere between these extremes. To facilitate discussion, let us give a label to our commonsense epistemic concepts and norms; let us call them our *epistemic folkways*. In partial agreement with the first view sketched above, I would hold that *one* proper task of epistemology is to elucidate our epistemic folkways. Whatever else epistemology might proceed to do, it should at least have its roots in the concepts and practices of the folk. If these roots are utterly rejected and abandoned, by what rights would the new discipline call itself 'epistemology' at all? It may well be desirable to reform or transcend our epistemic folkways, as the second of the views sketched above recommends. But it is essential to preserve continuity; and continuity can only be recognized if we have a satisfactory characterization of our epistemic folkways. Actually, even if one rejects the plea for continuity, a description of our epistemic folkways is in order. How would one know what to criticize, or what needs to be transcended, in the absence of such a de-

scription? So a first mission of epistemology is to describe or characterize our folkways.

Now a suitable description of these folk concepts, I believe, is likely to depend on insights from cognitive science. Indeed, identification of the semantic contours of many (if not all) concepts can profit from theoretical and empirical work in psychology and linguistics. For this reason, the task of describing or elucidating folk epistemology is a *scientific* task, at least a task that should be informed by relevant scientific research.

The second mission of epistemology, as suggested by the second view above, is the formulation of a more adequate, sound, or systematic set of epistemic norms, in some way(s) transcending or naive epistemic repertoire. How and why these folkways might be transcended, or improved upon, remains to be specified. This will partly depend on the contours of the commonsense standards that emerge from the first mission. On my view, epistemic concepts like knowledge and justification crucially invoke psychological faculties or processes. Our folk understanding, however, has a limited and tenuous grasp of the processes available to the cognitive agent. Thus, one important respect in which epistemic folkways should be transcended is by incorporating a more detailed and empirically based depiction of psychological mechanisms. Here too epistemology would seek assistance from cognitive science.

Since both missions of epistemology just delineated lean in important respects on the deliverances of science, specifically cognitive science, let us call our conception of epistemology *scientific epistemology*. Scientific epistemology, we have seen, has two branches: *descriptive* and *normative*. While descriptive scientific epistemology aims to describe our ordinary epistemic assessments, normative scientific epistemology continues the practice of making epistemic judgments, or formulating systematic principles for such judgments.[1] It is prepared to depart from our ordinary epistemic judgments, however, if and when that proves advisable. (This overall conception of epistemology closely parallels the conception of metaphysics articulated in chapters 2 and 3.

The descriptive and normative branches of scientific epistemology are precise analogues of the descriptive and prescriptive branches of metaphysics, as conceptualized there.) In the remainder of this paper, I shall sketch and defend the particular forms of descriptive and normative scientific epistemology that I favor.

II

Mainstream epistemology has concentrated much of its attention on two concepts (or terms): knowledge and justified belief. The preceding essay primarily illustrates the contributions that cognitive science can make to an understanding of the former; this essay focuses on the latter. We need not mark this concept exclusively by the phrase 'justified belief'. A family of phrases pick out roughly the same concept: "well-founded belief," "reasonable belief," "belief based on good grounds," and so forth. I shall propose an account of this concept that is in the reliabilist tradition, but departs at a crucial juncture from other versions of reliabilism. My account has the same core idea as Ernest Sosa's *intellectual virtues* approach, but incorporates some distinctive features that improve its prospects.[2]

The basic approach is, roughly, to identify the concept of justified belief with the concept of belief obtained through the exercise of intellectual virtues (excellences). Beliefs acquired (or retained) through a chain of "virtuous" psychological processes qualify as justified; those acquired partly by cognitive "vices" are derogated as unjustified. This, as I say, is a *rough* account. To explain it more fully, I need to say things about the psychology of the epistemic evaluator, the possessor and deployer of the concept in question. At this stage in the development of semantical theory (which, in the future, may well be viewed as part of the "dark ages" of the subject), it is difficult to say just what the relationship is between the meaning or "content" of concepts and the form or structure of their mental representation. In the present case, however, I believe that an account of the form of representation can contribute to our understanding of the content, although I am unable to formulate these matters in a theoretically satisfying fashion.

The hypothesis I wish to advance is that the epistemic evaluator has a mentally stored set, or list, of cognitive virtues and vices. When asked to evaluate an actual or hypothetical case of belief, the evaluator considers the processes by which the belief was produced, and matches these against his list of virtues and vices. If the processes match virtues only, the belief is classified as justified. If the processes are matched partly with vices, the belief is categorized as unjustified. If a belief-forming scenario is described that features a process not on the evaluator's list of either virtues or vices, the belief may be categorized as neither justified nor unjustified, but simply *non*justified. Alternatively (and this alternative plays an important role in my story), the evaluator's judgment may depend on the (judged) *similarity* of the novel process to the stored virtues and vices. In other words, the "matches" in question need not be perfect.

This proposal makes two important points of contact with going theories in the psychology of concepts. First, it has some affinity to the *exemplar* approach to concept representation (cf. Medin and Schaffer 1978; Smith and Medin 1981; Hintzman 1986). According to that approach, a concept is mentally represented by means of representations of its positive instances, or perhaps types of instances. For example, the representation of the concept *pants* might include a representation of a particular pair of faded blue jeans and/or a representation of the type *blue jeans*. Our approach to the concept of justification shares the spirit of this approach insofar as it posits a set of examples of virtues and vices, as opposed to a mere abstract characterization—e.g., a definition—of (intellectual) virtue or vice. A second affinity to the exemplar approach is in the appeal to a similarity, or matching, operation in the classification of new target cases. According to the exemplar approach, targets are categorized as a function of their similarity to the positive exemplars (and dissimilarity to the foils). Of course, similarity is invoked in many other approaches to concept deployment as well (see E. E. Smith 1990). This makes our account of justification consonant with the psychological literature generally, whether or not it meshes specifically with the exemplar approach.

Let us now see what this hypothesis predicts for a variety of cases. To apply it, we need to make some assumptions about the lists of virtues and vices that typical evaluators mentally store. I shall assume that the virtues include belief formation based on sight, hearing, memory, reasoning in certain "approved" ways, and so forth. The vices include intellectual processes like forming beliefs by guesswork, wishful thinking, and ignoring contrary evidence. *Why* these items are placed in their respective categories remains to be explained. As indicated, I plan to explain them by reference to reliability. Since the account will therefore be at bottom, a reliabilist type of account, it is instructive to see how it fares when applied to well-known problem cases for standard versions of reliabilism.

Consider first the demon-world case. In a certain possible world, a Cartesian demon gives people deceptive visual experiences, which systematically lead to false beliefs. Are these vision-based beliefs justified? Intuitively, they are. The demon's victims are presented with the same sorts of visual experiences that we are, and they use the same processes to produce corresponding beliefs. For most epistemic evaluators, this seems sufficient to induce the judgment that the victims' beliefs are justified. Does our account predict this result? Certainly it does. The account predicts that an epistemic evaluator will match the victims' vision-based processes to one (or more) of the items on his list of intellectual virtues, and therefore judge the victims' beliefs to be justified.

Turn next to Laurence BonJour's (1985) cases in which hypothetical agents are assumed to possess a perfectly reliable clairvoyant faculty. Although these agents form their beliefs by this reliable faculty, BonJour contends that the beliefs are not justified; and apparently most (philosophical) evaluators agree with that judgment. This result is not predicted by simple forms of reliabilism.[3] What does our present theory predict? Let us consider the four

cases in two groups. In the first three cases (Samantha, Casper, and Maud), the agent has contrary evidence that he or she ignores. Samantha has a massive amount of apparently cogent evidence that the president is in Washington, but she nonetheless believes (through clairvoyance) that the president is in New York City. Casper and Maude each has large amounts of ostensibly cogent evidence that he/she has no reliable clairvoyant power, but they rely on such a power nonetheless. Here our theory predicts that the evaluator will match these agents' belief-forming processes to the vice of ignoring contrary evidence. Since the processes include a vice, the beliefs will be judged to be unjustified.

BonJour's fourth case involves Norman, who has a reliable clairvoyant power but no reasons for or against the thesis that he possesses it. When he believes, through clairvoyance, that the president is in New York City, while possessing no (other) relevant evidence, how should this belief be judged? My own assessment is less clear in this case than the other three cases. I am tempted to say that Norman's belief is *non*justified, not that it is thoroughly *un*justified. (I construe unjustified as "having negative justificational status," and nonjustified as "lacking positive justificational status.") This result is also readily predicted by our theory. On the assumption that I (and other evaluators) do not have clairvoyance on my list of virtues, the theory allows the prediction that the belief would be judged neither justified nor unjustified, merely nonjustified. For those evaluators who would judge Norman's belief to be *un*justified, there is another possible explanation in terms of the theory. There is a class of putative faculties, including mental telepathy, ESP, telekinesis, and so forth that are scientifically disreputable. It is plausible that evaluators view any process of basing beliefs on the supposed deliverances of such faculties as vices. It is also plausible that these evaluators judge the process of basing one's belief on clairvoyance to be *similar* to such vices. Thus, the theory would predict that they would view a belief acquired in this way as unjustified.[4]

Finally, consider Alvin Plantinga's (1988) examples that feature disease-triggered or mind-malfunctioning processes. These include processes engendered by a brain tumor, radiation-caused processes, and the like. In each case Plantinga imagines that the process is reliable, but reports that we would not judge it to be justification conferring. My diagnosis follows the track outlined in the Norman case. At a minimum, the processes imagined by Plantinga fail to match any virtue on a typical evaluator's list. So the beliefs are at least non-justified. Furthermore, evaluators may have a prior representation of pathological processes as examples of cognitive vices. Plantinga's cases might be judged (relevantly) similar to these vices, so that the beliefs they produce would be declared unjustified.

In some of Plantinga's cases, it is further supposed that the hypothetical agent possesses countervailing evidence against his belief, which he steadfastly ignores. As noted earlier, this added element would strengthen a judgment of unjustifiedness according to our theory, because ignoring contrary evidence is an intellectual vice. Once again, then, our theory's predictions conform with reported judgments.

Let us now turn to the question of how epistemic evaluators acquire their lists of virtues and vices. What is the basis for their classification? As already indicated, my answer invokes the notion of reliability. Belief-forming processes based on vision, hearing, memory and ("good") reasoning are deemed virtuous because they (are deemed to) produce a high ratio of true beliefs. Processes like guessing, wishful thinking, and ignoring contrary evidence are deemed vicious because they (are deemed to) produce a low ratio of true beliefs.

We need not assume that each epistemic evaluator chooses his/her catalogue of virtues and vices by direct application of the reliability test. Epistemic evaluators may partly inherit their lists of virtues and vices from other speakers in the linguistic community. Nonetheless, the hypothesis is that the selection of virtues and vices rests, ultimately, on assessments of reliability.

It is not assumed, of course, that all speakers have the same lists of intellectual virtues and vices. They may have different opinions about the reliability of processes, and therefore differ in their respective lists.[5] Or they may belong to different subcultures in the linguistic community, which may differentially influence their lists. Philosophers sometimes seem to assume great uniformity in epistemic judgments. This assumption may stem from the fact that it is mostly the judgments of philosophers themselves that have been reported, and they are members of a fairly homogeneous subculture. A wider pool of "subjects" might reveal a much lower degree of uniformity. That would conform to the present theory, however, which permits individual differences in catalogues of virtues and vices, and hence in judgments of justifiedness.

If virtues and vices are selected on the basis of reliability and unreliability, respectively, why doesn't a hypothetical case introducing a novel reliable process induce an evaluator to add that process to his list of virtues, and declare the resulting belief justified? Why, for example, doesn't he add clairvoyance to his list of virtues, and rule Norman's beliefs to be justified?

I venture the following explanation. First, people seem to have a trait of *categorical conservatism*. They display a preference for "entrenched" categories, in Nelson Goodman's (1955) phraseology, and do not lightly supplement or revise their categorial schemes. An isolated single case is not enough. More specifically, merely imaginary cases do not exert much influence on categorial structures. People's cognitive systems are responsive to live cases, not purely fictional ones. Philosophers encounter this when their students or nonphilosophers are unimpressed with science fiction-style counterexamples. Philosophers become impatient with this response because they presume that possible cases are on a par (for counterexample purposes) with actual ones. This phenomenon testifies, however, to a psychological propensity to take an invidious attitude toward purely imaginary cases.

To the philosopher, it seems both natural and inevitable to take hypothetical cases seriously, and if necessary to restrict one's conclusions about them to specified "possible worlds." Thus, the philosopher might be inclined to hold, "If reliability is the standard of intellectual virtue, shouldn't we say that clairvoyance is a virtue *in the possible worlds* of BonJour's examples, if not a virtue in general?" This is a natural thing for philosophers to say, given their schooling, but there is no evidence that this is how people naturally think about the matter. There is no evidence that "the folk" are inclined to relativize virtues and vices to this or that possible world.

I suspect that concerted investigation (not undertaken here) would uncover ample evidence of conservatism, specifically in the normative realm. In many traditional cultures, for example, loyalty to family and friends is treated as a cardinal virtue.[6] This view of loyalty tends to persist even through changes in social and organizational climate, which undermine the value of unqualified loyalty. Members of such cultures, I suspect, would continue to view personal loyalty as a virtue even in *hypothetical* cases where the trait has stipulated unfortunate consequences.

In a slightly different vein, it is common for both critics and advocates of reliabilism to call attention to the relativity of reliability to the domain or circumstances in which the process is used. The question is therefore raised, what is the relevant domain for judging the reliability of a process? A critic like John Pollock (1986, pp. 118–19), for example, observes that color vision is reliable on earth but unreliable in the universe at large. In determining the reliability of color vision, he asks, which domain should be invoked? Finding no satisfactory reply to this question, Pollock takes this as a serious difficulty for reliabilism. Similarly, Sosa (1988 and 1991) notes that an intellectual structure or disposition can be reliable with respect to one field of propositions but unreliable with respect to another, and reliable in one environment but unreliable in another. He does not view this as a difficulty for reliabilism, but concludes that any talk of intellectual virtue must be relativized to field and environment.

Neither of these conclusions seems apt, however, for purposes of *description* of our epistemic folkways. It would be a mistake to suppose that ordinary epistemic evaluators are sensitive to these issues. It is likely—or at least plausible—that our ordinary apprehension of the intellectual virtues is rough, unsystematic, and insensitive to any theoretical desirability of relativization to domain or environment. Thus, as long as we are engaged in the description

of our epistemic folkways, it is no criticism of the account that it fails to explain what domain or environment is to be used. Nor is it appropriate for the account to introduce relativization where there is no evidence of relativization on the part of the folk.

Of course, we do need an explanatory story of how the folk arrive at their selected virtues and vices. And this presumably requires some reference to the domain in which reliability is judged. However, there may not be much more to the story than the fact that people determine reliability scores from the cases they personally "observe." Alternatively, they *may* regard the observed cases as a sample from which they infer a truth ratio in some wider class of cases. It is doubtful, however, that they have any precise conception of the wider class. They probably don't address this theoretical issue, and don't do (or think) anything that commits them to any particular resolution of it. It would therefore be wrong to expect descriptive epistemology to be fully specific on this dimension.

A similar point holds for the question of process individuation. It is quite possible that the folk do not have highly principled methods for individuating cognitive processes, for "slicing up" virtues and vices. If that is right, it is a mistake to insist that descriptive epistemology uncover such methods. It is no flaw in reliabilism, considered as descriptive epistemology, that it fails to unearth them. It may well be desirable to develop sharper individuation principles for purposes of normative epistemology (a matter we shall address in section III). But the missions and requirements of descriptive and normative epistemology must be kept distinct.

This discussion has assumed throughout that the folk have lists of intellectual virtues and vices. What is the evidence for this? In the moral sphere ordinary language is rich in virtues terminology. By contrast, there are few common labels for intellectual virtues, and those that do exist—"perceptiveness," "thoroughness," "insightfulness," and so forth—are of limited value in the present context. I propose to identify the relevant intellectual virtues (at least those relevant to *justification*) with the belief-forming capacities, faculties, or processes that would be accepted as answers to the question "How does X know?" In answer to this form of question, it is common to reply, "He saw it," "He heard it," "He remembers it," "He infers it from such-and-such evidence," and so forth. Thus, basing belief on seeing, hearing, memory, and (good) inference are in the collection of what the folk regard as intellectual virtues. Consider, for contrast, how anomalous it is to answer the question "How does X know?" with "By guesswork," "By wishful thinking," or "By ignoring contrary evidence." This indicates that *these* modes of belief formation—guessing, wishful thinking, ignoring contrary evidence—are standardly regarded as intellectual *vices*. They are not ways of obtaining knowledge, nor ways of obtaining justified belief.

Why appeal to "knowledge"-talk rather than "justification"-talk to identify the virtues? Because "know" has a greater frequency of occurrence than "justified," yet the two are closely related. Roughly, justified belief is belief acquired by means of the same sort of capacities, faculties, or processes that yield knowledge in favorable circumstances (i.e., when the resulting belief is true and there are no Gettier complications, or no relevant alternatives).

To sum up the present theory, let me emphasize that it depicts justificational evaluation as involving two stages. The first stage features the acquisition by an evaluator of some set of intellectual virtues and vices. This is where reliability enters the picture. In the second stage, the evaluator applies his list of virtues and vices to decide the epistemic status of targeted beliefs. At this stage, there is no direct consideration of reliability.

There is an obvious analogy here to rule utilitarianism in the moral sphere. Another analogy worth mentioning is Saul Kripke's (1980) theory of *reference-fixing*. According to Kripke, we can use one property to fix a reference to a certain entity, or type of entity; but once this reference has been fixed, that property may cease to play a role in identifying the entity across various possible worlds. For example, we can fix a reference to heat as the phenomenon that causes certain sensations in people. Once heat has been so picked out, this

property is no longer needed, or relied upon, in identifying heat. A phenomenon can count as heat in another possible world where it doesn't cause those sensations in people. Similarly, I am proposing, we initially use reliability as a test for intellectual quality (virtue or vice status). Once the quality of a faculty or process has been determined, however, it tends to retain that status in our thinking. At any rate, it isn't reassessed each time we consider a fresh case, especially a purely imaginary and bizarre case like the demon world. Nor is quality relativized to each possible world or environment.

The present version of the virtues theory appears to be a successful variant of reliabilism, capable of accounting for most, if not all, of the most prominent counterexamples of earlier variants of reliabilism.[7] The present approach also makes an innovation in naturalistic epistemology. Whereas earlier naturalistic epistemologists have focused exclusively on the psychology of the epistemic agent, the present paper (along with the preceding essay) also highlights the psychology of the epistemic evaluator.

III

Let us turn now to *normative* scientific epistemology. It was argued briefly in section I that normative scientific epistemology should preserve continuity with our epistemic folkways. At a minimum, it should rest on the same types of evaluative criteria as those on which our commonsense epistemic evaluations rest. Recently, however, Stephen Stich (1990) has disputed this sort of claim. Stich contends that our epistemic folkways are quite idiosyncratic and should not be much heeded in a reformed epistemology. An example he uses to underline his claim of idiosyncracy is the notion of justification as rendered by my "normal worlds" analysis in Goldman 1986. With hindsight, I would agree that that particular analysis makes our ordinary notion of justification look pretty idiosyncratic. But that was the fault of the analysis, not the analysandum. On the present rendering, it looks as if the folk notion of justification is keyed to dispositions to produce a high ratio of true beliefs in the actual world, not in "normal worlds"; and there is nothing idiosyncratic about that. Furthermore, there seem to be straightforward reasons for thinking that true belief is worthy of positive valuation, if only from a pragmatic point of view, which Stich also challenges. The pragmatic utility of true belief is best seen by focusing on a certain subclass of beliefs, viz., beliefs about one's own *plans of action*. Clearly, true beliefs about which courses of action would accomplish one's ends will help secure these ends better than false beliefs. Let proposition $P=$"Plan N will accomplish my ends" and proposition $P'=$"Plan N' will accomplish my ends." If P is true and P' is false, I am best off believing the former and not believing the latter. My belief will guide my choice of a plan, and belief in the true proposition (but not the false one) will lead me to choose a plan that *will* accomplish my ends. Stich has other intriguing arguments that cannot be considered here, but it certainly appears that true belief is a perfectly sensible and stable value, not an idiosyncratic one.[8] Thus, I shall assume that normative scientific epistemology should follow in the footsteps of folk practice and use reliability (and other truth-linked standards) as a basis for epistemic evaluation.

If scientific epistemology retains the fundamental standard(s) of folk epistemic assessment, how might it diverge from our epistemic folkways? One possible divergence emerges from William Alston's (1988) account of justification. Although generally sympathetic with reliabilism, Alston urges a kind of constraint not standardly imposed by reliabilism (at least not process reliabilism.) This is the requirement that the processes from which justified beliefs issue must have as their input, or basis, a state of *which the cognizer is aware* (or can easily become aware). Suppose that Alston is right about this as an account of our folk conception of justification. It may well be urged that this ingredient needn't be retained in a scientifically sensitive epistemology. In particular, it may well be claimed that one thing to be learned from cognitive science is that only a small proportion of our cognitive processes operate on consciously accessible inputs. It could therefore be argued that a reformed conception of intellectually virtuous processes should dispense with the "accessibility" requirement.

Alston aside, the point of divergence I wish to examine concerns the psychological units that are chosen as virtues or vices. The lay epistemic evaluator uses casual, unsystematic, and largely introspective methods to carve out the mental faculties and processes responsible for belief formation and revision. Scientific epistemology, by contrast, would utilize the resources of cognitive science to devise a more subtle and sophisticated picture of the mechanisms of belief acquisition. I proceed now to illustrate how this project should be carried out.

An initial phase of the undertaking is to sharpen our conceptualization of the types of cognitive units that should be targets of epistemic evaluation. Lay people are pretty vague about the sorts of entities that qualify as intellectual virtues or vices. In my description of epistemic folkways, I have been deliberately indefinite about these entities, calling them variously "faculties," "processes," "mechanisms," and the like. How should systematic epistemology improve on this score?

A first possibility, enshrined in the practice of historical philosophers, is to take the relevant units to be cognitive *faculties*. This might be translated into modern parlance as *modules*, except that this term has assumed a rather narrow, specialized meaning under Jerry Fodor's (1983) influential treatment of modularity. A better translation might be (cognitive) *systems*, e.g., the visual system, long-term memory, and so forth. Such systems, however, are also suboptimal candidates for units of epistemic analysis. Many beliefs are the outputs of two or more systems working in tandem. For example, a belief consisting in the visual classification of an object ("That is a chair") may involve matching some information in the visual system with a category stored in long-term memory. A preferable unit of analysis, then, might be a *process*, construed as the sort of entity depicted by familiar flow charts of cognitive activity. This sort of diagram depicts a sequence of operations (or sets of parallel operations), ultimately culminating in a belief-like output. Such a sequence may span several cognitive systems. This is the sort of entity I had in mind in previous publications (especially Goldman 1986) when I spoke of "cognitive processes."

Even this sort of entity, however, is not a fully satisfactory unit of analysis. Visual classification, for example, may occur under a variety of degraded conditions. The stimulus may be viewed from an unusual orientation; it may be partly occluded, so that only certain of its parts are visible; and so forth. Obviously, these factors can make a big difference to the reliability of the classification process. Yet it is one and the same process that analyzes the stimulus data and comes to a perceptual "conclusion." So the same process can have different degrees of reliability depending on a variety of parameter values. For purpose of epistemic assessment, it would be instructive to identify the parameters and parameter values that are critically relevant to degrees of reliability. The virtues and vices might then be associated not with processes per se, but with processes operating *with specified parameter values*. Let me illustrate this idea in connection with visual perception.

Consider Irving Biederman's (1987, 1990) theory of object recognition, recognition-by-components (RBC). The core idea of Biederman's theory is that a common concrete object like a chair, a giraffe, or a mushroom is mentally represented as an arrangement of simple primitive volumes called *geons (geometrical ions)*. These geons, or primitive "components" of objects, are typically symmetrical volumes lacking sharp concavities, such as blocks, cylinders, spheres, and wedges. A set of twenty-four types of geons can be differentiated on the basis of dichotomous or trichotomous contrasts of such attributes as curvature (straight versus curved), size variation (constant versus expanding), and symmetry (symmetrical versus asymmetrical). These twenty-four types of geons can then be combined by means of six relations (e.g., top-of, side-connected, larger-than, etc.) into various possible multiple-geon objects. For example, a cup can be represented as a cylindrical geon that is side-connected to

a curved, handle-like geon, whereas a pail can be represented as the same two geons bearing a different relation: the curved, handle-like geon is at the top of the cylindrical geon.

Simplifying a bit, the RBC theory of object recognition posits five stages of processing. (1) In the first stage, low-level vision extracts edge characteristics, such as L's, Y-vertices, and arrows. (2) On the basis of these edge characteristics, viewpoint-independent attributes are detected, such as curved, straight, size-constant, size-expanding, etc. (3) In the next stage, selected geons and their relations are activated. (4) Geon activation leads to the activation of object models, that is, familiar models of simple types of objects, stored in long-term memory. (5) The perceived entity is then "matched" to one of these models, and thereby identified as an instance of that category or classification. (In this description of the five stages, all processing is assumed to proceed bottom-up, but in fact Biederman also allows for elements of top-down processing.)

Under what circumstances, or what parameter values, will such a sequence of processing stages lead to *correct*, or *accurate*, object identification? Biederman estimates that there are approximately 3,000 common basic-level, or entry-level, names in English for familiar concrete objects. However, people are probably familiar with approximately ten times that number of object models because, among other things, some entry-level terms (such as *lamp* and *chair*) have several readily distinguishable object models. Thus, an estimate of the number of familiar object models would be on the order of 30,000.

Some of these object models are simple, requiring fewer than six components to appear complete; others are complex, requiring six to nine components to appear complete. Nonetheless, Biederman gives theoretical considerations and empirical results suggesting that an arrangement of only *two* or *three* geons almost always suffices to specify a simple object and even most complex ones. Consider the number of possible two-geon and three-geon objects. With twenty-for possible geons, Biederman says, the variations in relations can produce 186,624 possible two-geon objects. A third geon with its possible relations to another geon yields over 1.4 billion possible three-geon objects. Thus, if the 30,000 familiar object models were distributed homogeneously throughout the space of possible object models, Biederman reasons, an arrangement of two or three geons would almost always be sufficient to specify any object. Indeed, Biederman puts forward a *principle of geon recovery:* If an arrangement of two or three geons can be recovered from the image, objects can be quickly recognized even when they are occluded, rotated in depth, novel, extensively degraded, or lacking in customary detail, color, and texture.

The principle of three-geon sufficiency is supported by the following empirical results. An object such as an elephant or an airplane is complex, requiring six or more geons to appear complete. Nonetheless, when only three components were displayed (the others being occluded), subjects still made correct identifications in almost 80 percent of the nine-component objects and more than 90 percent of the six-component objects. Thus, the reliability conferred by just three geons and their relations is quite high. Although Biederman doesn't give data for recovery of just one or two geons of complex objects, presumably the reliability is much lower. Here we presumably have examples of parameter values—(1) number of components in the complete object, and (2) number of recovered components—that make a significant difference to reliability. The same process, understood as an instantiation of one and the same flow diagram, can have different levels of reliability depending on the values of the critical parameters in question. Biederman's work illustrates how research in cognitive science can identify both the relevant flow of activity and the crucial parameters. The quality (or "virtue") of a particular (token) process of belief-acquisition depends not only on the flow diagram that is instantiated, but on the parameter values instantiated in the specific tokening of the diagram.

Until now reliability has been my sole example of epistemic quality. But two other dimensions of epistemic quality—which also invoke truth or accuracy—should be added to our evaluative repertoire. These are *question-answering power* and *question-answering speed.* (These are certainly reflected in our epistemic folkways, though not well reflected in the concepts of knowledge or justification.) If a person asks himself a question, such as "What kind of object is that?" or "What is the solution to this algebra problem?," there are three possible outcomes: (A) he comes up with *no answer* (at least none that he believes), (B) he forms a belief in an answer which is *correct,* and (C) he forms a belief in an answer which is *incorrect.* Now reliability is the ratio of cases in category (B) to cases in categories (B) and (C), that is, the proportion of true beliefs to beliefs. Question-answering *power,* on the other hand, is the ratio of (B) cases to cases in categories (A), (B), and (C). Notice that it is possible for a system to be highly reliable but not very powerful. An object-recognition system that never yields outputs in category (C) is perfectly reliable, but it may not be very powerful, since most of its outputs could fall in (A) and only a few in (B). The human (visual) object-recognition system, by contrast, is very powerful as well as quite reliable. In general, it is power and not just reliability that is an important epistemic desideratum in a cognitive system or process.

Speed introduces another epistemic desideratum beyond reliability and power. This is another dimension on which cognitive science can shed light. It might have been thought, for example, that correct identification of complex objects like an airplane or an elephant requires more time than simple objects such as a flashlight or a cup. In fact, there is no advantage for simple objects, as Biederman's empirical studies indicate. This lack of advantage for simple objects could be explained by the geon theory in terms of parallel activation: geons are activated in parallel rather than through a serial trace of the contours of the object. Whereas more geons would require more processing time under a serial trace, this is not required under parallel activation.

Let us turn now from perception to learning, especially language learning. Learnability theory (Gold 1967; Osherson, Stob, and Weinstein 1985) uses a criterion of learning something like our notion of power, viz., the ability or inability of the learning process to arrive at a correct hypothesis after some fixed period of time. This is called *identification in the limit*. In language learning, it is assumed that the child is exposed to some information in the world, e.g., a set of sentences parents utter, and the learning task is to construct a hypothesis that correctly singles out the language being spoken. The child is presumed to have a learning strategy: an algorithm that generates a succession of hypotheses in response to accumulating evidence. What learning strategy might lead to success? *That* children learn their native language is evident to common sense. But *how* they learn it—what algorithm they possess that constitutes the requisite intellectual virtue—is only being revealed through research in cognitive science.

We may distinguish two types of evidence that a child might receive about its language (restricting attention to the language's grammar): positive evidence and negative evidence. Positive evidence refers to information about which strings of words *are* grammatical sentences in the language, and negative evidence refers to information about which strings of words are *not* grammatical sentences. Interestingly, it appears that children do not receive (much) negative evidence. The absence of negative evidence makes the learning task much harder. What algorithm might be in use that produces success in this situation?

An intriguing proposal is advanced by Robert Berwick (1986; cf. Pinker 1990). In the absence of negative evidence, the danger for a learning strategy is that it might hypothesize a language that is a superset of the correct language, i.e., one that includes all grammatical sentences of the target language plus some additional sentences as well. Without negative evidence, the child will be unable to learn that the "extra" sentences are incorrect, i.e., don't belong to the target language. A solution is to avoid ever hypothesizing an overly general hypothesis. Hypotheses should be *ordered* in such a way that the child always guesses the narrowest possible hypothesis or language at each step. This is called the *subset principle*. Berwick finds evidence of this principle at work in a number of domains, including concepts,

sound systems, and syntax. Here, surely, is a kind of intellectual disposition that is not dreamed of by the "folk."

IV

We have been treating scientific epistemology from a purely reliabilist, or veritistic (truth-linked), vantage point. It should be stressed, however, that scientific epistemology can equally be pursued from other evaluative perspectives. You need not be a reliabilist to accept the proposed role of cognitive science in scientific epistemology. Let me illustrate this idea with the so-called *responsibilist* approach, which characterizes a justified or rational belief as one that is the product of epistemically responsible action (Kornblith 1983; Code 1987), or perhaps epistemically responsible processes (Talbot 1990). Actually, this conception of justification is approximated by my own *weak* conception of justification, as presented in chapter 7. Both depict a belief as justified as long as its acquisition is *blameless* or *nonculpable*. Given limited resources and limited information, a belief might be acquired nonculpably even though its generating processes are not virtuous according to the reliabilist criterion.

Let us start with a case of Hilary Kornblith. Kornblith argues that the justificational status of a belief does not depend exclusively on the *reasoning* process that produces that belief. Someone might reason perfectly well from the evidence he possesses, but fail to be epistemically responsible because he neglects to acquire certain further evidence. Kornblith gives the case of Jones, a headstrong young physicist eager to hear the praise of his colleagues. After Jones presents a paper, a senior colleague makes an objection. Unable to tolerate criticism, Jones pays no attention to the objection. The criticism is devastating, but it makes no impact on Jones's beliefs because he does not even hear it. Jones's conduct is epistemically irresponsible. But his reasoning process from the evidence he actually possesses—which does not include the colleague's evidence—may be quite impeccable.

The general principle suggested by Kornblith's example seems to be something like this. Suppose that an agent (1) believes *P*, (2) does not believe *Q*, and (3) would be unjustified in believing *P* if he did believe *Q*. If, finally, he is *culpable* for failing to believe *Q* (for being ignorant of *Q*), then he is unjustified in believing *P*. In Kornblith's case, *P* is the physics thesis that Jones believes. *Q* consists in the criticisms of this thesis presented by Jones's senior colleague. Jones does not believe *Q*, but if he did believe *Q*, he would be unjustified in believing *P*. However, although Jones does not believe *Q*, he is culpable for failing to believe it (for being ignorant of these criticisms), because he *ought* to have paid attention to his colleague and acquired belief in *Q*. Therefore, Jones's belief in *P* is unjustified.

The provision that the agent be *culpable* for failing to believe *Q* is obviously critical to the principle in question. If the criticisms of Jones's thesis had never been presented within his hearing, nor published in any scientific journal, then Jones's ignorance of *Q* would not be culpable. And he might well be justified in believing *P*. But in Kornblith's version of the case, it seems clear that Jones *is* culpable for failing to believe *Q*, and that is why he is unjustified in believing *P*.

Under what circumstances is an agent culpable for failing to believe something? That is a difficult question. In a general discussion of culpable ignorance, Holly Smith (1983) gives an example of a doctor who exposes an infant to unnecessarily high concentrations of oxygen and thereby causes severe eye damage. Suppose that the latest issue of the doctor's medical journal describes a study establishing this relationship, but the doctor hasn't read this journal. Presumably his ignorance of the relationship would be culpable; he *should* have read his journal. But suppose that the study had appeared in an obscure journal to which he does not subscribe, or had only appeared one day prior to this particular treatment. Is he still culpable for failing to have read the study by the time of the treatment?

Smith categorizes her example of the doctor as a case of *deficient investigation*. The question is (both for morals and for epistemology), What amounts and kinds of investigation are, in general, sufficient or deficient? We may distinguish two types of investigation: (1) investigation into the physical world (including statements that have been made by other agents), and (2) investigation into the agent's own storehouse of information, lodged in long-term memory. Investigation of the second sort is particularly relevant to questions about the role of cognitive science, so I shall concentrate here on this topic. Actually, the term "investigation" is not wholly apt when it comes to long-term memory. But it is adequate as a provisional delineation of the territory.

To illustrate the primary problem that concerns me here, I shall consider two examples drawn from the work of Amos Tversky and Daniel Kahneman. The first example pertains to their study of the "conjunction fallacy" (Tversky and Kahneman 1983). Suppose that a subject assigns a higher probability to a conjunction like "Linda is a bank teller and is active in the feminist movement" than to one of its own conjuncts, "Linda is a bank teller." According to the standard probability calculus, no conjunction can have a higher probability than one of its conjuncts. Let us assume that the standard probability calculus is, in some sense, "right." Does it follow that a person is irrational, or unjustified, to make probability assignments that violate this calculus? This is subject to dispute. One might argue that it does not follow, in general, from the fact that *M* is an arbitrary mathematical truth, that anyone who believes something contrary to *M* is ipso facto irrational or unjustified. After all, mathematical facts are not all so transparent that it would be a mark of irrationality (or the like) to fail to believe any of them. However, let us set this issue aside. Let us imagine the case of a subject who has studied probability theory and learned the conjunction rule in particular. Let us further suppose that this subject would retract at least one of his two probability assignments if he recognized that they violate the conjunction rule. (This is by no means true of all subjects that Tversky and Kahneman studied.) Nonetheless, our imagined subject fails to think of the conjunction rule in connection with the Linda example. Shall we say that the failure to recover the conjunction rule from long-term memory is a *culpable omission*, one that makes his maintenance of his probability judgments unjustified? Is this like the example of Jones who culpably fails to learn of his senior colleague's criticism? Or is it a case of nonculpable nonrecovery of a relevant fact, a fact that is, in some sense "within reach," but legitimately goes unnoticed?

This raises questions about when a failure to recover or activate something from long-term memory is culpable, and that is precisely a problem that invites detailed reflection on mechanisms of memory retrieval. This is not a matter to which epistemologists have devoted much attention, partly because little has been known about memory retrieval until fairly recently. But now that cognitive science has at least the beginnings of an understanding of this phenomenon, normative epistemology should give careful attention to that research. Of course, we cannot expect the issue of culpability to be resolved directly by empirical facts about cognitive mechanisms. Such facts are certainly relevant, however.

The main way that retrieval from memory works is by *content addressing* (cf. Potter 1990). Content addressing means starting retrieval with part of the content of the to-be-remembered material, which provides an "address" to the place in memory where identical or similar material is located. Once a match has been made, related information laid down by previously encoded associations will be retrieved, such as the name or appearance of the object. For example, if you are asked to think of a kind of bird that is yellow, a location in memory is addressed where "yellow bird" is located. "Yellow bird" has previously been associated with "canary," so the latter information is retrieved. Note, however, that there are some kinds of information that cannot be used as a retrieval address, although the information is in memory. For example, what word for a family relationship (e.g., *grandmother*) ends with *w?* Because you have probably never encoded that piece of information explicitly, you may have trouble thinking of the word (hint: not *niece*). Although it is easy to move from the word in question *(nephew)* to "word for a family relationship ending with *w*," it is not easy to move in the opposite direction.

Many subjects who are given the Linda ex-

ample presumably have not established any prior association between such pairs of propositions ("Linda is a bank teller and is active in the feminist movement" and "Linda is a bank teller") and the conjunction rule. Furthermore, in some versions of the experiment, subjects are not given these propositions adjacent to one another. So it may not occur to the subject even to *compare* the two probability judgments, although an explicit comparison would be more likely to address a location in memory that contains an association with the conjunction rule. In short, it is not surprising, given the nature of memory retrieval, that the material provided in the specified task does not automatically yield retrieval of the conjunction rule for the typical subject.

Should the subject deliberately search memory for facts that might retrieve the conjunction rule? Is omission of such deliberate search a culpable omission? Perhaps, but how much deliberate attention or effort ought to be devoted to this task? (Bear in mind that agents typically have numerous intellectual tasks on their agendas, which vie for attentional resources.) Furthermore, what form of search is obligatory? Should memory be probed with the question, "Is there any rule of probability theory that my (tentative) probability judgments violate?" This is a plausible search probe for someone who has already been struck by a thought of the conjunction rule and its possible violation, or whose prior experiences with probability experiments make him suspicious. But for someone who has not already retrieved the conjunction rule, or who has not had experiences with probability experiments that alert him to such "traps," what reason is there to be on the lookout for violations of the probability calculus? It is highly questionable, then, that the subject engaged in "deficient investigation" in failing to probe memory with the indicated question.

Obviously, principles of culpable retrieval failure are not easy to come by. Any principles meriting our endorsement would have to be sensitive to facts about memory mechanisms.

A similar point can be illustrated in connection with the so-called *availability heuristic,* which was formulated by Tversky and Kahneman (1973) and explored by Richard Nisbett and Lee Ross (1980). A cognizer uses the availability heuristic when he estimates the frequency of items in a category by the instances he can *bring to mind* through memory retrieval, imagination, or perception. The trouble with this heuristic, as the abovementioned researchers indicate, is that the instances one brings to mind are not necessarily well correlated with objective frequency. Various *biases* may produce discrepancies: biases in initial sampling, biases in attention, or biases in manner of encoding or storing the category instances.

Consider some examples provided by Nisbett and Ross: one hypothetical example and one actual experimental result. (1) (Hypothetical example) An Indiana businessman believes that a disproportionate number of Hoosiers are famous. This is partly because of a bias in initial exposure, but also because he is more likely to notice and remember when the national media identify a famous person as a Hoosier. (2) (Actual experiment) A group of subjects consistently errs in judging the relative frequency of words with *R* in first position versus words with *R* in third position. This is an artifact of how words are encoded in memory (as already illustrated in connection with *nephew*). We don't normally code words by their third letters, and hence words having *R* in the third position are less "available" (from memory) than words beginning with *R*. But comparative availability is not a reliable indicator of actual frequency.

Nisbett and Ross (p. 23) view these uses of the availability heuristic as normative errors. "An indiscriminate use of the availability heuristic," they write, "clearly can lead people into serious judgmental errors." They grant, though, that in many contexts perceptual salience, memorability, and imaginability may be relatively unbiased and well correlated with true frequency or causal significance. They conclude: "The normative status of using the availability heuristic . . . thus depend[s] on the judgmental domain and context. People are not, of course, totally unaware that simple availability criteria must sometimes be discounted. For example, few people who were asked to estimate the relative number of moles versus cats in their neighborhood would conclude 'there must be more cats because I've seen several of them

but I've never seen a mole.' Nevertheless, as this book documents, people often fail to distinguish between legitimate and superficially similar, but illegitimate, uses of the availability heuristic."

We can certainly agree with Nisbett and Ross that the availability heuristic can often lead to incorrect estimates of frequency. But does it follow that uses of the heuristic are often *illegitimate* in a sense that implies the epistemic *culpability* of the users? One might retort, "These cognizers are using all the evidence that they possess, at least *consciously* possess. Why are they irresponsible if they extrapolate from this evidence?" The objection apparently lurking in Nisbett and Ross's minds is that these cognizers *should* be aware that they are using a systematically biased heuristic. This is a piece of evidence that they *ought* to recognize. And their failure to recognize it, and/or their failure to take it into account, makes their judgmental performance culpable. Nisbett and Ross's invocation of the cat/mole example makes the point particularly clear. If someone can appreciate that the relative number of cats and moles *he has seen* is not a reliable indicator of the relative number of cats and moles in the neighborhood, surely he can be expected to appreciate that the relative number of famous Hoosiers *he can think of* is not a reliable indicator of the proportion of famous people who are Hoosiers!

Is it so clear that people *ought* to be able to appreciate the biased nature of their inference pattern in the cases in question? Perhaps it seems transparent in the mole and Hoosier cases; but consider the letter *R* example. What is (implicitly) being demanded here of the cognizer? First, he must perform a feat of metacognitive analysis: he must recognize that he is inferring the relative proportion of the two types of English words from his own constructed samples of these types. Second, he must notice that his construction of these samples depends on the way words are encoded in memory. Finally, he must realize that this implies a bias in ease of retrieval. All these points may seem obvious in hindsight, once pointed out by researchers in the field. But how straightforward or obvious are these matters if they haven't already been pointed out to the subject? Of course, we currently have no "metric" of straightforwardness or obviousness. That is precisely the sort of thing we need, however, to render judgments of culpability in this domain. We need a systematic account of how difficult it is, starting from certain information and preoccupations, to generate and apprehend the truth of certain relevant hypotheses. Such an account clearly hinges on an account of the inferential and hypothesis-generating strategies that are natural to human beings. This is just the kind of thing that cognitive science is, in principle, capable of delivering. So epistemology must work hand in hand with the science of the mind. The issues here are not purely scientific, however. Judgments of justifiedness and unjustifiedness, on the responsibilist conception, require assessments of culpability and nonculpability. Weighing principles for judgments of culpability is a matter for philosophical attention. (One question, for example, is how much epistemic culpability depends on voluntariness.) Thus, a mix of philosophy and psychology is needed to produce acceptable principles of justifiedness.

NOTES

I wish to thank Tom Senor, Holly Smith, and participants in a conference at Rice University for helpful comments on earlier versions of this paper.

1. Normative scientific epistemology corresponds to what I elsewhere call *epistemics* (see Goldman 1986). Although epistemics is not restricted to the assessment of *psychological* processes, that is the topic of the present paper. So we are here dealing with what I call *primary epistemics.*

2. Sosa's approach is spelled out most fully in Sosa 1985, 1988, and 1991.

3. My own previous formulations of reliabilism have not been so simple. Both "What Is Justified Belief?" (chapter 6 of this volume) and *Epistemology and Cognition* (Goldman 1986) had provisions—e.g., the non-undermining provision of *Epistemology and Cognition*—that could help accommodate BonJour's examples. It is not entirely clear, however, how well these qualifications succeeded with the Norman case, described below.

4. Tom Senor presented the following example to his philosophy class at the University of Arkansas. Norman is working at his desk when out of the blue he is hit (via clairvoyance) with a very distinct and vivid impression of the president at the Empire State Building. The image is phenomenally distinct from a regular visual impression but is in some respects similar and of roughly equal force. The experience is so overwhelming that Norman just can't help but form the belief that the president is in New York. About half of Senor's class judged that in this case Norman justifiably believes that the president is in New York. Senor points out, in commenting on this paper, that their judgments are readily explained by the present account, because the description of the clairvoyance process makes it sufficiently similar to vision to be easily "matched" to that virtue.

5. Since some of these opinions may be true and others false, people's lists of virtues and vices may have varying degrees of accuracy. The "real" status of a trait as a virtue or vice is independent of people's opinions about that trait. However, since the enterprise of descriptive epistemology is to describe and explain evaluators' judgments, we need to advert to the traits that they *believe* to be virtues or vices, i.e., the ones on their mental lists.

6. Thanks to Holly Smith for this example. She cites Riding 1989 (chap. 6) for relevant discussion.

7. It should be noted that this theory of justification is intended to capture what I call the *strong* conception of justification.

8. For further discussion of Stich, see Goldman 1991.

REFERENCES

Alston, W. "An Internalist Externalism." *Synthese* 74 (1988): 265–283.

Berwick, R. "Learning from Positive-Only Examples: The Subset Principle and Three Case Studies." In R. S. Michalski, J. G. Carbonell, and T. M. Mitchell, eds., *Machine Learning:* *An Artificial Intelligence Approach,* vol. 2. Los Altos, Calif., 1986.

Biederman, I. "Higher-Level Vision." In D. Osherson, S. M. Kosslyn, and J. M. Hollerbach, eds., *Visual Cognition and Action: An Invitation to Cognitive Science.* Cambridge, Mass., 1990.

————. "Recognition-By-Components: A Theory of Human Image Understanding." *Psychological Review* 94 (1987): 115–47.

BonJour, L. *The Structure of Empirical Knowledge.* Cambridge, Mass., 1985.

Code, L. *Epistemic Responsibility.* Hanover, N.H., 1987.

Fodor, J. *The Modularity of Mind.* Cambridge, Mass., 1983.

Gold, E. M. "Language Identification in the Limit." *Information and Control* 10 (1967): 447–74.

Goldman, A. I. *Epistemology and Cognition.* Cambridge, Mass., 1986.

————. "Review of S. Stich, *The Fragmentation of Reason.*" *Philosophy and Phenomenological Research* 51 (1991): 189–93.

Goodman, N. *Fact, Fiction, and Forecast.* Cambridge, Mass., 1955.

Hintzman, D. "'Schema Abstraction' in a Multiple-Trace Memory Model." *Psychological Review* 93 (1986): 411–28.

Kornblith, H. "Justified Belief and Epistemically Responsible Action." *Philosophical Review* 92 (1983): 33–48.

Kripke, S. *Naming and Necessity.* Cambridge, Mass., 1980.

Medin, D. L., and M. M. Schaffer. "A Context Theory of Classification Learning." *Psychological Review* 85 (1978): 207–38.

Nisbett, R., and L. Ross. *Human Inference: Strategies and Shortcomings of Social Judgment.* Englewood Cliffs, N.J., 1980.

Osherson, D., M. Stob, and S. Weinstein. *Systems That Learn.* Cambridge, Mass., 1985.

Pinker, S. "Language Acquisition." In D. N. Osherson and H. Lasnik, eds., *Language: An Invitation to Cognitive Science.* Cambridge, Mass., 1990.

Plantinga, A. "Positive Epistemic Status and Proper Function." In J. Tomberlin, ed., *Philosophical Perspectives,* vol. 2, Atascadero, Calif., 1988.

Pollock, J. *Contemporary Theories of Knowledge.* Totowa, N.J., 1986.

Potter, M. "Remembering." In D. N. Osherson and E. E. Smith, eds., *Thinking: An Invitation to Cognitive Science.* Cambridge, Mass., 1990.

Riding, A. *Distant Neighbors: A Portrait of the Mexicans.* New York, 1989.

Smith, E. E. "Categorization." In D. Osherson and E. Smith, eds., *Thinking: An Invitation to Cognitive Science.* Cambridge, Mass., 1990.

Smith, E. E., and M. Medin. *Categories and Concepts.* Cambridge, Mass., 1981.

Smith, H. "Knowledge and Intellectual Virtue." *The Monist* 68 (1983): 226–63.

Sosa, E. "Beyond Skepticism, to the Best of Our Knowledge." *Mind* 97 (1988): 153–88.

————. "Reliabilism and Intellectual Virtue." In Sosa, *Knowledge in Perspective.* Cambridge, Eng., 1991.

Stich, S. *The Fragmentation of Reason.* Cambridge, Mass., 1990.

Talbott, W. *The Reliability of the Cognitive Mechanism: A Mechanist Account of Empirical Justification.* New York, 1990.

Tversky, A., and D. Kahneman. "Availability: A Heuristic for Judging Frequency and Probability." *Cognitive Psychology* 5 (1973): 207–32.

————. "Extensional Versus Intuitive Reasoning: The Conjunction Fallacy in Probability Judgment." *Psychological Review* 90 (1983): 293–315.

39 / Louise M. Antony
QUINE AS FEMINIST: THE RADICAL IMPORT OF NATURALIZED EPISTEMOLOGY

The truth is always revolutionary.

—Antonio Gramsci

I. INTRODUCTION

Do we need a feminist epistemology? This is a very complicated question. Nonetheless it has a very simple answer: yes and no.

Of course, what I should say (honoring a decades-old philosophical tradition) is that a great deal depends on what we *mean* by "feminist epistemology." One easy—and therefore tempting—way to interpret the demand for a feminist epistemology is to construe it as nothing more than a call for more theorists *doing* epistemology. On this way of viewing things, calls for "feminist political science," "feminist organic chemistry," and "feminist finite mathematics" would all be on a par, and the need for any one of them would be justified in exactly the same way, viz., by arguing for the general need for an infusion of feminist consciousness into the academy.

Construed in this way, an endorsement of "feminist epistemology" is perfectly neutral with respect to the eventual content of the epistemological theories that feminists might devise. Would it turn out, for example, that feminists as a group reject individualism or foundationalism? Would they favor empiricism over rationalism? Would they endorse views that privileged intuition over reason or the subjective over the objective? We'd just have to wait and see. It must even be left open, at least at the outset, whether a feminist epistemology would be discernibly and systematically different from epistemology as it currently exists, or whether there would instead end up being exactly the same variety among feminists as there is now among epistemologists in general.

Now it might appear that the project of developing a feminist epistemology in this sense is one that we can all happily sign on to, for who could object to trying to infuse the disciplines with feminist consciousness? But now I must honor a somewhat newer philosophical tradition than the one I honored earlier, and ask, "We, who?" For though the determined neutrality of this way of conceiving feminist epistemology—let me call it "bare proceduralism"—may give it the superficial appearance of a consensus position, it is in fact quite a partisan position. Even setting aside the fact that there are many people—yes, even some philosophers—who would rather be infused with bubonic plague than with feminist consciousness, it's clear that not everyone is going to like bare proceduralism. And ironically, it is its very neutrality that makes this an unacceptable reading of many, if not most, of the theorists who are currently calling for a feminist epistemology.[1]

To see the sticking point, consider the question of whether we should, as feminists, have an obligation to support *any* project whose participants represent themselves as feminists. Should we, for example, support the development of a "feminist sociobiology" or a "feminist military science" on the grounds that it's always a good idea to infuse a discipline, or a theory, with feminist consciousness, or on the grounds that there are people who are engaged in such projects who regard themselves as feminists and therefore have a claim on our sympathies? The answer to these questions, arguably, is no. Some projects, like the rationalization of war, may simply be *incompatible* with feminist goals; and some theories, like those with biological determinist presuppositions, may be *inconsistent* with the results of feminist inquiry to date.

Bare proceduralism, with its liberal, all-purpose, surely-there's-something-we-can-all-agree-on ethos, both obscures and begs the important question against those who believe that not all epistemological frameworks cohere—or cohere equally well—with the insights and aims of feminism. Specifically, it presupposes something that many feminist philosophers are at great pains to deny, namely the *prima facie* adequacy, from a feminist point of view, of those epistemological theories currently available within mainstream Anglo-American philosophy. At the very least, one who adopts the bare proceduralist standpoint with respect to feminist epistemology is making a substantive presupposition about where we currently stand in the process of feminist theorizing. To allow even that a feminist epistemology *might* utilize certain existing epistemological frameworks is to assert that feminist theorizing has not yet issued in substantive results regarding such frameworks.[2] Such a view, if not forthrightly expressed and explicitly defended, is disrespectful to the work of those feminists who claim to have already shown that those very epistemological theories are incompatible with feminism.

So we can't simply interpret the question, "Do we need a feminist epistemology?" in the bare proceduralist way and nod an enthusiastic assent. If we do, we'll be obscuring or denying the existence of substantive disagreements among feminists about the relation between feminism and theories of knowledge. One natural alternative to the bare proceduralist interpretation would be to try to give feminist epistemology a *substantive* sense—that is, take it to refer to a particular kind of epistemology or to a particular theory within epistemology, one that is specifically feminist.

But this won't work either, for two good reasons. First, there simply is no substantive consensus position among feminists working in epistemology, so that it would be hubris for anyone to claim that his or her epistemology was *the* feminist one.[3] Second, many feminists would find the idea that there *should* be such a single "feminist" position repellent. Some would dislike the idea simply for its somewhat totalitarian, "PC" ring. (Me, I'm not bothered by that—it seems to me that one should strive to be correct in all things, including politics.) Some theorists would argue that variety in feminist philosophical positions is to be expected at this point in the development of feminist consciousness, and that various intra- and inter-theoretic tensions in philosophical inquiry reflect unprocessed conflicts among deeply internalized conceptions of reality, of ourselves as human beings, and of ourselves as women.[4] Still others would see the expectation or hope that there will *ever* be a single, comprehensive, "true" feminist position as nothing but a remnant of outmoded, patriarchal ways of thinking.[5]

Thus, while individual feminist theorists may be advertising particular epistemological theories as feminist theories, general calls for the development of a feminist epistemology cannot be construed as advocacy for any particular one of these. But recognition of this fact does not throw us all the way back to the bare proceduralist notion. It simply means that in order to decide on the need for a feminist epistemology, we need to look at details—both with respect to the issues that feminism is supposed to have raised for the theory of knowledge and with respect to the specific epistemological theories that have been proffered as answering to feminist needs.

This is where the yes-and-no comes in. If we focus on the existence of what might be called a "feminist agenda" in epistemology— that is, if the question, "Do we need a feminist epistemology?" is taken to mean, "Are there specific questions or problems that arise as a result of feminist analysis, awareness, or experience that any adequate epistemology must accommodate?"—then I think the answer is clearly yes. But if, taking for granted the existence of such an agenda, the question is taken to be, "Do we need, in order to accommodate these questions, insights, and projects, a specifically feminist alternative to currently available epistemological frameworks?" then the answer, to my mind, is no.

Now it is on this point that I find myself in disagreement with many feminist philosophers. For despite the diversity of views within contemporary feminist thought, and despite the disagreements about even the desiderata for a genuinely feminist epistemology, one theoretical conclusion shared by almost all those feminists who explicitly advocate the development of a feminist epistemology is that existing epistemological paradigms—particularly those available within the framework of contemporary analytic philosophy—are fundamentally unsuited to the needs of feminist theorizing.

It is this virtual unanimity about the inadequacy of contemporary analytic epistemology that I want to challenge. There is an approach to the study of knowledge that promises enormous aid and comfort to feminists attempting to expose and dismantle the oppressive intellectual ideology of a patriarchal, racist, class-stratified society, and it is an approach that lies squarely within the analytic tradition. The theory I have in mind is Quine's "naturalized epistemology"—the view that the study of knowledge should be treated as the empirical investigation of knowers.

It's both unfortunate and ironic that Quine's work has been so uniformly neglected by feminists interested in the theory of knowledge, because although naturalized epistemology is nowadays as mainstream a theory as there is, Quine's challenges to logical positivism were radical in their time, and still retain an untapped radical potential today. His devastating critique of epistemological foundationalism bears many similarities to contemporary feminist attacks on "modernist" conceptions of objectivity and scientific rationality, and his positive views on the holistic nature of justification provide a theoretical basis for pressing the kinds of critical questions feminist critics are now raising.

Thus my primary aim in this essay is to highlight the virtues, from a feminist point of view, of naturalized epistemology. But—as is no doubt quite clear—I have a secondary, polemical aim as well. I want to confront head-on the charges that mainstream epistemology is irremediably phallocentric, and to counter the impression, widespread among progressives both within and outside of the academy, that there is some kind of natural antipathy between radicalism on the one hand and the methods and aims of analytic philosophy on the other. I believe that this impression is quite false, and its promulgation is damaging not only to individual feminists—especially women—working within the analytic tradition, but also to the prospects for an adequate feminist philosophy.

The "Bias" Paradox

I think the best way to achieve both these aims—defending the analytic framework in general and showcasing naturalized epistemology in particular—is to put the latter to work on a problem that is becoming increasingly important within feminist theory. The issue I have in mind is the problem of how properly to conceptualize *bias*. There are several things about this issue that make it particularly apt for my purposes.

In the first place, the issue provides an example of the way in which feminist analysis can generate or uncover serious epistemological questions, for the problem about bias that I want to discuss will only be recognized as a problem by individuals who are critical, for one reason or another, of one standard conception of objectivity. In the second place, because of the centrality of this problem to feminist theory, the ability of an epistemological theory to provide a solution offers one plausible desideratum of a theory's adequacy as a feminist epistemology. Last of all, because the notions of bias and partiality figure so prominently in feminist critiques of mainstream analytic epistemology, discussion of this issue will enable me to address directly some of the charges that have led some feminist theorists to reject the analytic tradition.

But what is the problem? Within certain theoretical frameworks, the analysis of the notion of "bias" is quite straightforward. In particular, strict empiricist epistemology concurs with liberal political theory in analyzing bias as the mere possession of belief or interest prior to investigation. But for anyone who wishes to criticize the liberal/empiricist ideal of an "open mind," the notion of bias is enormously problematic and threatens to become downright paradoxical.

Consider feminist theory: On the one hand, it is one of the central aims of feminist scholarship to expose the male-centered assumptions and interests—the male *biases*, in other words—underlying so much of received "wisdom." But on the other hand, there's an equally important strain of feminist theory that seeks to challenge the ideal of pure objectivity by emphasizing both the ubiquity and the value of certain kinds of partiality and interestedness. Clearly, there's a tension between those feminist critiques that accuse science or philosophy of displaying male bias and those that reject the ideal of impartiality.

The tension blossoms into paradox when critiques of the first sort are applied to the concepts of objectivity and impartiality themselves. According to many feminist philosophers, the flaw in the ideal of impartiality is supposed to be that the ideal itself is biased: Critics charge either that the concept of "objectivity" serves to articulate a masculine or patriarchal viewpoint (and possibly a pathological one),[6] or that it has the ideological function of protecting the rights of those in power, especially men.[7] But how is it possible to criticize the partiality of the concept of objectivity without presupposing the very value under attack? Put baldly: If we don't think it's good to be *im*partial, then how can we object to men's being *partial*?

The critiques of "objectivity" and "impartiality" that gives rise to this paradox represent the main source of feminist dissatisfaction with existing epistemological theories. It's charged that mainstream epistemology will be forever unable to either acknowledge or account for the partiality and locatedness of knowledge, because it is wedded to precisely those ideals of objective or value-neutral inquiry that ultimately and inevitably subserve the interests of the powerful. The valorization of impartiality within mainstream epistemology is held to perform for the ruling elite the critical ideological function of *denying the existence of partiality itself*.[8]

Thus Lorraine Code, writing in the *APA Newsletter on Feminism and Philosophy*,[9] charges that mainstream epistemology (or what she has elsewhere dubbed "malestream" epistemology[10]) has "defined 'the epistemological project' so as to make it illegitimate to ask questions about the identities and specific circumstances of these knowers." It has accomplished this, she contends, by promulgating a view of knowers as essentially featureless and interchangeable, and by donning a "mask of objectivity and value-neutrality." The transformative potential of a feminist—as opposed to a malestream—epistemology lies in its ability to tear off this mask, exposing the "complex power structure of vested interest, dominance, and subjugation" that lurks behind it.

But not only is it not the case that contemporary analytic epistemology is committed to such a conception of objectivity, it was analytic epistemology that was largely responsible for initiating the critique of the empiricistic notions Code is attacking. Quine, Goodman, Hempel, Putnam, Boyd, and others within the analytic tradition have all argued that a certain received conception of objectivity is untenable as an ideal of epistemic practice. The detailed critique of orthodox empiricism that has developed within the analytic tradition is in many ways more pointed and radical than the charges that have been leveled from without.

Furthermore, these philosophers, like many feminist theorists, have emphasized not only the *ineliminability* of bias but also the *positive value* of certain forms of it. As a result, the problems that arise for a naturalized epistemology are strikingly similar to those that beset the feminist theories mentioned above: Once we've acknowledged the necessity and legitimacy of partiality, *how do we tell the good bias from the bad bias*?

What kind of epistemology is going to be able to solve a problem like this? Code asserts that the specific impact of feminism on epistemology has been "to move the question '*Whose* knowledge are we talking about?' to a central place in epistemological discussion,"[11] suggesting that the hope lies in finding an epistemological theory that assigns central importance to consideration of the nature of the subjects who actually do the knowing. I totally agree: No theory that abjures empirical study of the cognizer, or of the actual processes by which knowledge develops, is ever going to yield insight on this question.

But more is required than this. If we as feminist critics are to have any bias for distinguishing the salutary from the pernicious forms of bias, we can't rest content with a *description* of the various ways in which the identity and social location of a subject make a difference to her beliefs. We need, in addition, to be able to make *normative* distinctions among various processes of belief-fixation as well. Otherwise, we'll never escape the dilemma posed by the bias paradox: either endorse pure impartiality or give up criticizing bias.[12]

It is here that I think feminist philosophy stands to lose the most by rejecting the analytic tradition. The dilemma will be impossible to escape, I contend, for any theory that eschews the notion of *truth*—for any theory, that is, that tries to steer some kind of middle course between absolutism and relativism. Such theories inevitably leave themselves without resources for making the needed normative distinctions, because they deprive themselves of any conceptual tools for distinguishing the grounds of a statement's truth from the explanation of a statement's acceptance.

Naturalized epistemology has the great advantage over epistemological frameworks outside the analytic tradition (I have in mind specifically standpoint and postmodern epistemologies) in that it permits an appropriately realist conception of truth, viz., one that allows a conceptual gap between epistemology and metaphysics, between the world as we see it and the world as it is.[13] Without appealing to at least this minimally realist notion of truth, I see no way to even state the distinction we ultimately must articulate and defend. Quite simply, an adequate solution to the paradox must enable us to say the following: What makes the *good* bias good is that it facilitates the search for truth, and what makes the *bad* bias bad is that it impedes it.

Now that my absolutist leanings are out in the open, let me say one more thing about truth that I hope will forestall a possible misunderstanding of my project here. I do believe in truth, and I have *never* understood why people concerned with justice have given it such a bad rap. Surely one of the goals of feminism is to *tell the truth* about women's lives and women's experience. Is institutionally supported discrimination not a *fact*? Is misogynist violence not a *fact*? And isn't the existence of ideological denial of the first two facts *itself* a fact? What in the world else could we be doing when we talk about these things, *other* than asserting that the world actually *is* a certain way?

Getting at the truth is complicated, and one of the things that complicates it considerably is that powerful people frequently have strong motives for keeping less powerful people from getting at the truth. It's one job of a critical epistemology, in my view, to expose this fact, to make the mechanisms of such distortions transparent. But if we, as critical epistemologists, lose sight of what we're after, if we concede that there's nothing at stake other than the matter of whose "version" is going to prevail, then our projects become as morally bankrupt and baldly self-interested as Theirs.

This brings me to the nature of the current discussion. I would like to be clear that in endorsing the project of finding a "feminist epistemology," I do not mean to be advocating the construction of a serviceable epistemological ideology "for our side." And when I say that I think naturalized epistemology makes a good feminist epistemology, I don't mean to be suggesting that the justification for the theory is instrumental. A good *feminist* epistemology must be, in the first place, a good epistemology, and that means being a theory that is likely to be *true*. But of course I would not think that naturalized epistemology was likely to be true unless I also thought it explained the facts. And among the facts I take to be central are the long-ignored experiences and wisdom of women.

In the next section, I will explain in more detail the nature of the charges that have been raised by feminist critics against contemporary analytic epistemology. I'll argue that the most serious of these charges are basically misguided—that they depend on a misreading of the canonical figures of the Enlightenment as well as of contemporary epistemology. In the last section, I'll return to the bias paradox and try to show why a naturalized approach to the study of knowledge offers some chance of a solution.

II. WHAT IS MAINSTREAM EPISTEMOLOGY AND WHY IS IT BAD?

One difficulty that confronts anyone who wishes to assess the need for a "feminist alternative" in epistemology is the problem of finding out exactly what such an epistemology would be an alternative to. What is "mainstream" epistemology anyway? Lorraine Code is more forthright than many in her willingness to name the enemy. According to her, "mainstream epistemology," the proper object of feminist critique, is "post-positivist empiricist epistemology: the epistemology that still dominates in Anglo-American philosophy, despite the best efforts of socialist, structuralist, hermeneuticist, and other theorists of knowledge to deconstruct or discredit it."[14]

By the "epistemology that still dominates in Anglo-American philosophy," Code would have to be referring to the set of epistemological theories that have developed within the analytic paradigm, for analytic philosophy has been, in fact, the dominant philosophical paradigm in the English-speaking academic world since the early twentieth century.[15] This means, at the very least, that the agents of sexism within academic philosophy—the individuals who have in fact been the ones to discriminate against women as students, job applicants, and

colleagues—have been, for the most part, analytic philosophers, a fact that on its own makes the analytic paradigm an appropriate object for feminist scrutiny.

But this is not the main reason that Code and others seek to "deconstruct or discredit" analytic epistemology. The fact that the analytic paradigm has enjoyed such an untroubled hegemony within this country during the twentieth century—the period of the most rapid growth of American imperial power—suggests to many radical social critics that analytic philosophy fills an ideological niche. Many feminist critics see mainstream analytic philosophy as the natural metaphysical and epistemological complement to liberal political theory, which, by obscuring real power relations within the society, makes citizens acquiescent or even complicit in the growth of oppression, here and abroad.

What is it about analytic philosophy that would enable it to play this role? Some have argued that analytic or "linguistic" philosophy, together with its cognate fields (such as formal linguistics and computationalist psychology), is inherently male, "phallogecentric."[16] Others have argued that the analytic paradigm, because of its emphasis on abstraction and formalization and its valorization of elite skills, may be an instrument of cognitive control, serving to discredit the perspectives of members of nonpriviliged groups.[17]

But most of the radical feminist critiques of "mainstream" epistemology (which, as I said, must denote the whole of analytic epistemology) are motivated by its presumed allegiance to the conceptual structures and theoretical commitments of the Enlightenment, which provided the general philosophical background to the development of modern industrialized "democracies."[18] By this means, "mainstream" epistemology becomes identified with "traditional" epistemology, and this traditional epistemology becomes associated with political liberalism. Feminist theorists like Alison Jaggar and Sandra Harding, who have both written extensively about the connection between feminist political analysis and theories of knowledge, have encouraged the idea that acceptance of mainstream epistemological paradigms is tantamount to endorsing liberal feminism. Jaggar contends that the connection lies in the radically individualistic conception of human nature common to both liberal political theory and Enlightenment epistemology. In a chapter entitled "Feminist Politics and Epistemology: Justifying Feminist Theory," she writes:

> Just as the individualistic conception of human nature sets the basic problems for the liberal political tradition, so it also generates the problems for the tradition in epistemology that is associated historically and conceptually with liberalism. This tradition begins in the 17th century with Descartes, and it emerges in the 20th century as the analytic tradition. Because it conceives humans as essentially separate individuals, this epistemological tradition views the attainment of knowledge as a project for each individual on her or his own. The task of epistemology, then, is to formulate rules to enable individuals to undertake this project with success.[19]

Harding, in a section of her book called "A Guide to Feminist Epistemologies," surveys what she sees as the full range of epistemological options open to feminists. She imports the essentially conservative political agenda of liberal feminism, which is focused on the elimination of formal barriers to gender equality, into mainstream epistemology, which she labels "feminist empiricism": "*Feminist empiricism* argues that sexism and androcentrism are social biases correctable by stricter adherence to the existing methodological norms of scientific inquiry."[20] Harding takes the hallmark of feminist empiricism (which on her taxonomy is the only alternative to the feminist standpoint and postmodernist epistemologies) to be commitment to a particular conception of objectivity, which, again, is held to be part of the legacy of the Enlightenment. In her view, acceptance of this ideal brings with it faith in the efficacy of "existing methodological norms of science" in correcting biases and irrationalities within science, in the same way that acceptance of the liberal ideal of impartiality brings with it faith in the system to eliminate political and social injustice.

In Harding's mind, as in Jaggar's, this politically limiting conception of objectivity is one that can be traced to traditional conceptions of the knowing subject, specifically to Enlightenment conceptions of "rational man." The message, then, is that mainstream epistemology, because it still operates with this traditional conception of the self, functions to limit our understanding of the real operations of power, and of our place as women within oppressive structures. A genuine feminist transformation in our thinking therefore requires massive overhaul, if not outright repudiation, of central aspects of the tradition.

This is clearly the message that political scientist Jane Flax gleans from her reading of feminist philosophy; she argues that feminist theory, ought properly to be viewed as a version of postmodern thought, since postmodern theorists and feminist theorists are so obviously engaged in a common project:

> Postmodern philosophers seek to throw into radical doubt beliefs still prevalent in (especially American) culture but derived from the Enlightenment . . . ;[21] feminist notions of the self, knowledge and truth are too contradictory to those of the Enlightenment to be contained within its categories. The way to feminist future(s) cannot lie in reviving or appropriating Enlightenment concepts of the person or knowledge.[22]

But there are at least two serious problems with this argument. The first is that the "tradition" that emerges from these critiques is a gross distortion and oversimplification of the early modern period. The critics' conglomeration of all classical and Enlightenment views into a uniform "traditional" epistemology obscures the enormous amount of controversy surrounding such notions as knowledge and the self during the seventeenth and eighteenth centuries, and encourages crude misunderstandings of some of the central theoretical claims. Specifically, this amalgamation makes all but invisible a debate that has enormous relevance to discussions of bias and objectivity, viz., the controversy between rationalists and empiricists about the extent to which the structure of the mind might constrain the development of knowledge.[23]

The second problem is that the picture of analytic epistemology that we get once it's allied with this oversimplified "traditional" epistemology is downright cartoonish. When we look at the actual content of the particular conceptions of objectivity and scientific method that the feminist critics have culled from the modern period, and which they subsequently attach to contemporary epistemology, it turns out that these conceptions are precisely the ones that have been the focus of *criticism* among American analytic philosophers from the 1950s onward. The feminist critics' depiction of "mainstream" epistemology utterly obscures this development in analytic epistemology, and in glossing over the details of the analytic critique of positivism, misses points that are of crucial relevance to any truly radical assault on the liberal ideology of objectivity.[24]

The second problem is partly a consequence of the first. The feminist critics, almost without exception, characterize mainstream epistemology as "empiricist." But one of the chief accomplishments of the analytic challenge to positivism was the demonstration that a strictly empiricistic conception of knowledge is untenable. As a result, much of analytic epistemology has taken a decidedly rationalistic turn. Neglect of the rationalist/empiricist debate and misunderstanding of rationalist tenets make the critics insensitive to these developments and blind to their implications.

But the misreading of contemporary epistemology is also partly just a matter of the critics' failure to realize the extent to which analytic philosophy represents a *break* with tradition. I do not mean to deny that there were *any* important theoretical commitments common to philosophers of the early modern period. One such commitment, shared at least by classical rationalists and empiricists, and arguably by Kant, was an epistemological metahypothesis called "externalism." This is the view that the proper goal of epistemological theory is the rational *vindication* of human epistemic practice. But if externalism is regarded as the hallmark of "traditional epistemology," then the identification of analytic epistemology with traditional epistemology becomes all the more spurious.

It was the main burden of Quine's critique of positivism to demonstrate the impossibility of an externalist epistemology, and his suggested replacement, "naturalized epistemol-

ogy," was meant to be what epistemology could be once externalist illusions were shattered. As a result of the analytic critique of externalism, the notions of objectivity and rationality available to contemporary analytic epistemologists are necessarily more complicated than the traditional conceptions they replace. This is so even for epistemologists who would not identify themselves as partisans of naturalized epistemology.

In what follows, I'll discuss in turn these two problems: first, the mischaracterization of the tradition, and then the caricature of contemporary analytic epistemology.

Rationalism v. Empiricism: The Importance of Being Partial

What I want to show first is that the "traditional epistemology" offered us by Jaggar and Flax grafts what is essentially a rationalist (and in some respects, specifically Cartesian) theory of *mind* onto what is essentially an empiricist conception of *knowledge*. This is a serious error. Although Jaggar and Flax claim that there are deep connections between the one and the other, the fact of the matter is that they are solidly opposed. The conception of objectivity that is ultimately the object of radical critique— perfect impartiality—is only supportable as an epistemic ideal on an empiricist conception of *mind*. Thus, I'll argue, the rationalistic conception of the self attacked by Jaggar and Flax as unsuitable or hostile to a feminist point of view actually provides the basis for a critique of the view of knowledge they want ultimately to discredit.

Much of what is held to be objectionable in "traditional epistemology" is supposed to derive from the tradition's emphasis on *reason*. But different traditional figures emphasized reason in different ways. Only the rationalists and Kant were committed to what I'll call "cognitive essentialism," a feature of the "traditional" conception of mind that comes in for some of the heaviest criticism. I take cognitive essentialism to be the view (1) that there are certain specific properties the possession of which is both distinctive of and universal among human beings, (2) that these properties are cognitive in nature, (3) that our possession of these properties amounts to a kind of innate knowledge, and (4) that our status as moral agents is connected to the possession of these properties. Empiricists denied all these claims—in particular, they denied that reason had anything but a purely instrumental role to play in either normative or nonnormative activity, and tended to be opposed to any form of essentialism, cognitive or otherwise.

Although the purely instrumental conception of reason is also criticized by feminist scholars, cognitive essentialism is the focus of one specific set of feminist concerns. It is held to be suspect on the grounds that such a doctrine could easily serve to legitimate the arrogant impulses of privileged Western white men: first to canonize their own culture-and time-bound speculations as revelatory of the very norms of human existence, and then simultaneously to deny the very properties deemed "universal" to the majority of human beings on the planet.

Here's how it is supposed to work: Cognitive essentialism is supposed to engender a kind of fantasy concerning actual human existence and the actual prerequisites of knowledge. Because of its emphasis on *cognitive* characteristics, it's argued, the view permits privileged individuals to ignore the fact of their embodiment, and with that, the considerable material advantages they enjoy in virtue of their class, gender, and race.[25] To the extent that the characteristics they find in themselves are the result of their particular privileges instead of a transcendent humanity, the fantasy provides a basis for viewing less-privileged people—who well may lack such characteristics—as inherently less human. But since these characteristics have been lionized as forming the essence of moral personhood, the fantasy offers a rationale for viewing any differences between themselves and others as negative deviations from a moral norm.

Recall, for example, that the particular elements of Enlightenment thought that Flax finds inimical to feminist theory and praxis are the alleged universality, transcendence, and abstractness assigned to the faculty of reason:

> The notion that reason is divorced from "merely contingent" existence still predominates in contemporary Western thought and now appears to mask the embeddedness and dependence of the self upon social relations, as well as the partiality and historical specificity of this self's existence. . . .

In fact, feminists, like other postmodernists, have begun to suspect that all such transcendental claims reflect and reify the experience of a few persons—mostly White, Western males.[26]

But moreover, cognitive essentialism is supposed to lead to what Jaggar calls "individualism,"[27] the view that individual human beings are epistemically self-sufficient, that human society is unnecessary or unimportant for the development of knowledge. If the ideal "man of reason" is utterly without material, differentiating features, then the ideal knower would appear to be *pure* rationality, a mere calculating mechanism, a person who has been stripped of all those particular aspects of self that are of overwhelming human significance. Correlatively, as it is precisely the features "stripped off" the self by the Cartesian method that "traditional" epistemology denigrates as distorting influences, the ideally objective cognizer is also the man of reason. Knowledge is then achieved, it appears, not by active engagement with one's world and with the people in it, but by a pristine transcendence of the messy contingencies of the human condition.[28]

Lending support to Lorraine Code's grievance against "traditional" epistemology, Jaggar thus insists that it is this abstract and detached individualism that underwrites a solipsistic view of the construction of knowledge and precludes assigning any epistemological significance to the situation of the knower.

> Because it conceives humans as essentially separate individuals, this epistemological tradition views the attainment of knowledge as a project for each individual on his or her own. The task of epistemology, then, is to formulate rules to enable individuals to undertake this project with success.[29]

It is here that the link is supposed to be forged between the Cartesian/Kantian conception of the self and the particular conception of objectivity—objectivity as pure neutrality—that is thought to be pernicious.

But the individualism Jaggar takes to unite

rationalists and empiricists is not in fact a view that *anyone* held. She derives it from a fairly common—indeed, almost canonical—misreading of the innate ideas debate. Significantly, Jaggar acknowledges the existence of disagreements within the early modern period, but avers that such issues as divided rationalists from empiricists are differences that make no difference. Both were foundationalists, she points out, and though the foundation for rationalists was self-evident truths of reason and the foundation for empiricists was reports of sensory experience, "in either case, . . . the attainment of knowledge is conceived as essentially a solitary occupation that has no necessary social preconditions."[30]

The reading, in other words, is that whereas the empiricists thought all knowledge came from experience, the rationalists thought *all knowledge came from reason*. But the second element of this interpretation is simply wrong. It was no part of Descartes's project (much less Kant's) to assert the self-sufficiency of reason. Note that a large part of the goal of the exercise of hyperbolic doubt in the *Meditations* was to establish the reliability of sensory experience, which Descartes took to be essential to the development of adequate knowledge of the world. And although he maintained the innateness of many ideas, including sensory ideas, he carefully and repeatedly explained that he meant by this only that human beings were built in such a way that certain experiences would trigger these ideas and no others.[31]

Furthermore, Descartes himself explicitly endorses two of the very epistemic values his position is supposed to preclude. Not only does he clearly reject the sort of epistemic individualism Jaggar deplores, but he strongly upholds the necessity of acquainting oneself with the variety of human experience in order to form a just conception of the world. Expressing his contempt for the contradictions and sophistries of his learned and cloistered teachers, he recounts how, as soon as he was old enough to "emerge from the control of [his] tutors," he "entirely quitted the study of letters."

> And resolving to seek no other science than that which could be found in myself, *or at least in the great book of the world* [my emphasis],

I employed the rest of my youth in travel, in seeing courts and armies, in intercourse with men of diverse temperaments and conditions, in collecting varied experiences, in proving myself in the various predicament in which I was placed by fortune, and under all circumstances bringing my mind to bear on the things which came before it, so that I might derive some profit from my experience.[32]

And far from recommending the divestiture of one's particular concerns as sound epistemic practice, Descartes affirms the importance of concrete engagement in finding the truth, pointing to the degradation of knowledge that can result from disinterestedness.

> For it seemed to me that I might meet with much more truth in the reasonings that each man makes on the matters that specifically concern him, and the issue of which would very soon punish him if he made a wrong judgment, than in the case of those made by a man of letters in his study touching speculations which lead to no result, and which bring about no other consequences to himself expecting that he will be all the more vain the more they are removed from common sense, since in this case it proves him to have employed so much the more ingenuity and skill in trying to make them seem probable.[33]

The bottom line is that rationalists, Descartes especially, did not hold the view that experience was inessential or even that it was unimportant; nor did they hold the view that the best epistemic practice is to discount one's own interests. The misreading that saddles Descartes with such views stems from a popular misconception about the innate ideas debate.

The disagreement between rationalists and empiricists was not simply about the existence of innate ideas. Both schools were agreed that the mind was natively structured and that that structure partially determined the shape of human knowledge. What they disagreed about was the *specificity* of the constraints imposed by innate mental structure. The rationalists believed that native structure placed quite specific limitations on the kinds of concepts and hypotheses the mind could form in response to experience, so that human beings were, in effect, natively *biased* toward certain ways of conceiving the world. Empiricists, on the other hand, held that there were relatively few native constraints on how the mind could organize sensory experience, and that such constraints as did exist were *domain-general* and *content-neutral*.

According to the empiricists, the human mind was essentially a mechanism for the manipulation of sensory data. The architecture of the mechanism was supposed to ensure that the concepts and judgments constructed out of raw sense experience accorded with the rules of logic. This did amount to a minimal constraint on the possible contents of human thought—they had to be logical transforms of sensory primitives—but it was a highly general one, applying to every subject domain in precisely the same way. Thus, on this model, any one hypothesis should be as good as any other as far as the mind is concerned, as long as both hypotheses are logically consistent with the sensory evidence.[34] This strict empiricist model of mind, as it turns out, supports many of the elements of epistemology criticized by Code, Jaggar, and others (e.g., a sharp observation/theory distinction, unmediated access to a sensory "given," and an algorithmic view of justification). I'll spell this out in detail in the next section. For present purposes, however, the thing to note is that the model provides clear warrant for the particular conception of the ideal of objectivity—perfect neutrality—that is the main concern of Jaggar and the others and that is supposed to follow from cognitive essentialism. Here's how.

Because the mind itself, on the empiricist model, makes no substantive contribution to the contents of thought, knowledge on this model is *entirely* experience-driven: All concepts and judgments are held to reflect regularities in an individual's sensory experience. But one individual cannot see everything there is to see—one's experience is necessarily limited, and there's always the danger that the regularities that form the basis of one's own judgments are not general regularities, but only artifacts of one's limited sample. (There is, in other words, a massive restriction-of-range problem for empiricists.) The question then arises how one can tell whether the patterns one perceives are present in nature generally, or are just artifacts of one's idiosyncratic perspective.

The empiricists' answer to this question is that one can gauge the general validity of one's judgments by the degree to which they engender reliable expectations about sensory experience. But although this answer addresses the problem of how to tell whether one's judgments are good or bad, it doesn't address the problem of how to get good judgments in the first place. Getting good judgments means getting good data—that is, exposing oneself to patterns of sensations that are representative of the objective distribution of sensory qualities throughout nature.

This idea immediately gives rise to a certain ideal (some would say fantasy) of epistemic location—the best spot from which to make judgments would be that spot which is *least particular*. Sound epistemic practice then becomes a matter of constantly trying to maneuver oneself into such a location—trying to find a place (or at least come as close as one can) where the regularities in one's own personal experience match the regularities in the world at large. A knower who could be somehow stripped of all particularities and idiosyncrasies would be the best possible knower there is.

This is not, however, a fantasy that would hold any particular appeal for a rationalist, despite the image of detachment evoked by a cursory reading of the *Meditations*. The rationalists had contended all along that sensory experience *by itself* was insufficient to account for the richly detailed body of knowledge that human beings manifestly possessed, and thus that certain elements of human knowledge—what classical rationalists called *innate ideas*—must be natively present, a part of the human essence.

Because the rationalists denied that human knowledge was a pure function of the contingencies of experience, they didn't need to worry nearly as much as the empiricists did about epistemic location. If it is the structure of mind, rather than the accidents of experience, that largely determines the contours of human concepts, then we can relax about at least the broad parameters of our knowledge. We don't have to worry that idiosyncratic features of our epistemic positions will seriously distort our worldviews, because the development of our knowledge is not dependent upon the patterns that happen to be displayed in our particular experiential histories. The regularities we "perceive" are, in large measure, regularities that we're *built* to perceive.

"Pure" objectivity—if that means giving equal weight to every hypothesis consistent with the data, or if it means drawing no conclusions beyond what can be supported by the data—is thus a nonstarter as an epistemic form from a rationalist's point of view. The rationalists were in effect calling attention to the *value* of a certain kind of partiality: if the mind were not natively biased—i.e., disposed to take seriously certain kinds of hypotheses and to disregard or fail to even consider others—then knowledge of the sort that human beings possess would itself be impossible. There are simply too many ways of combining ideas, too many different abstractions that could be performed, too many distinct extrapolations from the same set of facts, for a pure induction machine to make much progress in figuring out the world.

The realization that perfect neutrality was not necessarily a good thing, and that bias and partiality are potentially salutary, is thus a point that was strongly present in the early modern period, *pace* Jaggar and Flax. There was no single "traditional" model of mind; the model that can properly be said to underwrite the conceptions of rationality and objectivity that Jaggar brings under feminist attack is precisely a model to which Descartes and the other rationalists were *opposed*, and, ironically, the one that, on the face of it, assigns the most significance to experience. And although it is the cognitive essentialists who are charged with deflecting attention away from epistemically significant characteristics of the knower, it was in fact these same essentialists, in explicit opposition to the empiricists, who championed the idea that human knowledge was necessarily "partial."

Hume, Quine, and the Break with Tradition

Let me turn now to the second serious problem with the feminist criticisms of "mainstream" epistemology: To the extent that there really is

a "tradition" in epistemology, it is a tradition that has been explicitly rejected by contemporary analytic philosophy.

If the rationalists solved one problem by positing innate ideas; it was at the cost of raising another. Suppose that there are, as the rationalists maintained, innate ideas that perform the salutary function of narrowing down to a manageable set the hypotheses that human minds have to consider when confronted with sensory data. That eliminates the problem faced by the empiricists of filtering out idiosyncratic "distortions." But now the question is, How can we be sure that these biases—so helpful in getting us to *a* theory of the world—are getting us to the *right* theory of the world? What guarantees that our minds are inclining us in the right direction? Innate ideas lead us somewhere, but do they take us where we want to go?

The rationalists took this problem very seriously. A large part of their project was aimed at validating the innate constraints, at showing that these mental biases did not lead us astray. Descartes's quest for "certainty" needs to be understood in this context: The method of hyperbolic doubt should be viewed not as the efforts of a paranoid to free himself forever from the insecurity of doubt, but as a theoretical exercise designed to show that the contours imposed on our theories by our own minds were proper reflections of the topography of reality itself.

It is at this point that we're in a position to see what rationalists and empiricists actually had in common—not a conception of mind, not a theory of how knowledge is constructed, but a theory of *theories* of knowledge. If there is a common thread running through Enlightenment epistemologies, it is this: a belief in the possibility of providing a *rational* justification of the processes by which human beings arrive at theories of the world. For the empiricists, the trick was to show how the content of all knowledge could be reduced to pure reports of sensory experience; for the rationalists, it was showing the indubitability of the innate notions that guided and facilitated the development of knowledge. Philosophers in neither group were really on a quest for certainty—all the wanted was a reliable map of its boundaries.

But if one of the defining themes of the

modern period was the search for an externalist justification of epistemic practice, then *Hume* must be acknowledged to be the first postmodernist. Hume, an empiricist's empiricist discovered a fatal flaw in his particular proposal for justifying human epistemic practice. He realized that belief in the principle of induction—the principle that says that the future will resemble the past or that similar things will behave similarly—could not be rationally justified. It was clearly not a truth of reason, since its denial was not self-contradictory. But neither could it be justified by experience: Any attempt to do so would be circular, because the practice of using past experience as evidence about the future is itself only warranted if one accepts the principle of induction.

Hume's "skeptical solution" to his own problem amounted to an abandonment of the externalist hopes of his time. Belief in induction, he concluded, was a *custom*, a tendency of mind ingrained by nature, one of "a species of natural instincts, which no reasoning or process of the thought and understanding is able, either to produce or to prevent."[35] For better or worse, Hume contended, we're stuck with belief in induction—we are constitutionally incapable of doubting it and conceptually barred from justifying it. The best we can do is to *explain* it.

Hume's idea was thus to offer as a replacement for the failed externalist project of rational justification of epistemic practice, the *empirical* project of characterizing the cognitive nature of creatures like ourselves, and then figuring out how such creatures, built to seek knowledge in the ways we do, could manage to survive and flourish. In this way, he anticipated to a significant degree the "postmodernist" turn taken by analytic philosophy in the twentieth century as the result of Quine's and others' critiques of externalism's last gasp—logical positivism.

Before fast-forwarding into the twentieth century, let me summarize what I take to be the real lessons of the modern period—lessons that, I've argued, have been missed by many feminist critiques of "traditional" epistemology. First, there is the essentially rationalist insight that perfect objectivity is not only impossible but undesirable, that certain kinds of "bias" or "partiality" are necessary to make our epistemic tasks tractable. Second, there is Hume's realization that externalism won't work, that we can never manage to offer a justification of epistemic norms without somehow presupposing the very norms we wish to justify. See this, if you will, as the beginning of the postmodern recognition that theory always proceeds from an "embedded" location, that there is no transcendent spot from which we can inspect our own theorizing.

The rationalist lesson was pretty much lost and the import of Hume's insight submerged by the subsequent emergence and development of neo-empiricist philosophy. This tradition, which involved primarily the British empiricists Mill and Russell, but also Wittgenstein and the Vienna Circle on the Continent, culminated in the school of thought known as logical positivism.[36] The positivists' project was, in some ways, an externalist one. They hoped to develop criteria that would enforce a principled distinction between empirically significant and empirically meaningless sentences. In the minds of some positivists (Schlick, arguably, and Ayer), this criterion would help to vindicate scientific practice by helping to distinguish science from "metaphysics," which was for positivists, a term of abuse.

The positivists were perfectly well aware of Hume's dilemma about the status of the principle of induction—similar problems about even more fundamental principles of logic and mathematics had come to light since his time. But the positivists in effect attempted to rehabilitate epistemological externalism by means of a bold move. They took all the material that was needed to legitimize scientific practice but that could not be traced directly to sensory experience, and relegated it to the *conventions* of human language. This tack had, at least *prima facie*, some advantages over Hume's nativist move: If our epistemic norms are a matter of convention, then (1) there's no longer any question of explaining how we got them—they're there because we *put* them there; and (2) there's no need to justify them because the parameter of evaluation for conventions is not truth but *utility*.

The positivists thus embarked on a program they called "rational reconstruction"—they wanted to show, in detail, how any empirically meaningful claim could be reduced, by the successive application of semantic and logical rules, to statements purely about sensory experience. If such reconstructions could be shown to be possible at least in principle, then all theoretical disagreements could be shown to be susceptible to resolution by appeal to the neutral court of empirical experience. And in all of this, the positivists were committed to basically the same series of assumptions that warranted the view of objectivity that I earlier associated with classical empiricism.

But there were two things absolutely essential to the success of this project. First, there had to be a viable distinction that could be drawn between statements whose truth depended on empirical contingencies (the contentful claims of a theory that formed the substance of the theory) and statements that were true "by convention" and thus part of the logical/semantic structure of the theory. Second, it would have to be shown that the reduction of empirically contentful statements to specific sets of claims about sensory experience could be carried out. But in the early 1950s, Quine (together with Hempel, Goodman, Putnam, and others) began producing decisive arguments against precisely these assumptions.[37] The ensuing changes in analytic epistemology were nothing short of radical.

Quine's main insight was that individual statements do not have any specific consequences for experience if taken individually— that it is only in conjunction with a variety of other claims that experiential consequences can even be derived. It follows from this that no single experience or observation can decisively refute any theoretical claim or resolve any theoretical dispute, and that all experimental tests of hypotheses are actually tests of *conjunctions* of hypotheses. The second insight—actually a corollary of the first point—was that no principled distinction can be drawn among statements on the basis of the grounds of their truth—there can be no distinction between statements made true or false by experience and those whose truth value depends entirely on semantic or logical conventions.

The implications of these two insights were far-reaching. Quine's arguments against the "two dogmas of empiricism" entailed, in the first place, that the confirmation relation could not be hierarchical, as the foundationalist picture required, but must rather be holistic. Because theories have to face "the tribunal of sensory experience as a corporate body" (to use Quine's military-industrial metaphor), there can be no evidentially foundational set of statements that asymmetrically confirm all the others—every statement in the theory is linked by some justificatory connections to every other.

It also meant that responses at the theoretical level to the acquisition of empirical data were not fully dictated by logic. If experimental tests were always tests of *groups* of statements, then if the prediction fails, logic will tell us only that *something* in the group must go, but not *what*. If logic plus data don't suffice to determine how belief is modified in the face of empirical evidence, then there must be, in addition to logic and sensory evidence, *extra-empirical* principles that partially govern theory selection. The "justification" of these principles can only be pragmatic—we are warranted in using them just to the extent that they work.[38]

But to say this is to say that epistemic norms—a category that must include any principle that in fact guides theory selection—are themselves subject to empirical disconfirmation. And indeed, Quine embraces this consequence, explicitly extending the lesson to cover not only pragmatic "rules of thumb," but to rules of logic and language as well. In short, any principle that facilitates the development of knowledge by narrowing down our theoretical options becomes itself a part of the theory, and a part that must be defended on the same basis as any other part. So much for the fact/value distinction.

The reasoning above represents another of the many routes by which Quine's attack on foundationalism can be connected with his critique of the analytic/synthetic distinction, so central to positivist projects. With the demonstration that any belief, no matter how apparently self-evident, could in principle be rejected on the basis of experience, Quine effectively destroyed the prospects for any "first philosophy"—any Archimedean fixed point from which we could inspect our own epistemic practice and pronounce it sound.

But his critique also pointed the way (as Hume's "skeptical solution" did to the problem of induction) to a different approach to the theory of knowledge. Epistemology, according to Quine, had to be "naturalized," transformed into the empirical study of the actual processes—not "rational reconstructions" of those processes—by which human cognizers achieve knowledge.[39] If we accept this approach, several consequences follow for our understanding of knowledge and of the norms that properly govern its pursuit.

The first lesson is one that I believe may be part of what the feminist critics are themselves pointing to in their emphasis on the essential locatedness of all knowledge claims. The lesson is that all theorizing *takes some knowledge for granted*. Theorizing about theorizing is no exception. The decision to treat epistemology as the empirical study of the knower requires us to presume that we can, at least for a class of clear cases, distinguish epistemic success from epistemic failure. The impossibility of the externalist project shows us that we cannot expect to learn *from our philosophy* what counts as knowledge and how much of it we have; rather, we must begin with the assumption that we know certain things and figure out how that happened.

This immediately entails a second lesson. A naturalized approach to knowledge requires us to give up the idea that our own epistemic practice is transparent to us—that we can come to understand how knowledge is obtained either by *a priori* philosophizing or by casual introspection. It requires us to be open to the possibility that the processes that we actually rely on to obtain and process information about the world are significantly different from the ones our philosophy told us had to be the right ones.

Let me digress to point out a tremendous irony here, much remarked upon in the literature on Quine's epistemology and philosophy of mind. Despite his being the chief evangelist of the gospel that everything is empirical, Quine's own philosophy is distorted by his a prioristic commitment to a radically empiricistic, instrumentalist theory of psychology, namely psychological behaviorism. Quine's commitment to this theory—which holds that human behavior can be adequately explained without any reference to mental states or processes intervening between environmental

stimuli and the organism's response—is largely the result of his philosophical antipathy to intentional objects, together with a residual sympathy for the foundationalist empiricism that he himself was largely responsible for dismantling.

Chomsky, of course, was the person most responsible for pointing out the in-principle limitations of behaviorism, by showing in compelling detail the empirical inadequacies of behaviorist accounts of the acquisition of language.[40] Chomsky also emphasized the indefensibility of the a prioristic methodological constraints that defined empiricistic accounts of the mind, appealing to considerations that Quine himself marshaled in his own attacks on instrumentalism in nonpsychological domains.[41]

Chomsky's own theory of language acquisition did not differ from the behaviorist account only, or even primarily, in its mentalism. It was also rationalistic: Chomsky quite self-consciously appealed to classical rationalistic forms of argument about the necessity of mental partiality in establishing the empirical case for his strong nativism. Looking at the actual circumstances of language acquisition, and then at the character of the knowledge obtained in those circumstances, Chomsky argued that the best explanation of the whole process is one that attributes to human beings a set of innate biases limiting the kinds of linguistic hypotheses available for their consideration as they respond to the welter of data confronting them.[42]

Chomsky can thus be viewed, and is viewed by many, as a naturalized epistemologist *par excellence*. What his work shows is that a naturalized approach to epistemology—in this case, the epistemology of language—yields an *empirical* vindication of rationalism. Since Chomsky's pathbreaking critique of psychological behaviorism, and the empiricist conception of mind that underlies it, nativism in psychology has flourished, and a significant degree of rationalism has been imported into contemporary epistemology.

A casual student of the analytic scene who has read only Quine could, of course, be forgiven for failing to notice this, given Quine's adamant commitment to an empiricist conception of mind; this may explain why so many of the feminist critics of contemporary epistemology seem to identify analytic epistemology with empiricism and to ignore the more rationalistic alternatives that have developed out of the naturalized approach. But I think, too, that the original insensitivity to the details of the original rationalist/empiricist controversy plays a role. Anyone who properly appreciates the import of the rationalist defense of the value of partiality will, I think, see where Quine's rejection of externalism is bound to lead.

So let's do it. I turn now to the feminist critique of objectivity and the bias paradox.

III. QUINE AS FEMINIST: WHAT NATURALIZED EPISTEMOLOGY CAN TELL US ABOUT BIAS

I've argued that much of the feminist criticism of "mainstream" epistemology depends on a misreading of both contemporary analytic philosophy, and of the tradition from which it derives. But it's one thing to show that contemporary analytic philosophy is not what the feminist critics think it is, and quite another to show that the contemporary analytic scene contains an epistemology that can serve as an adequate *feminist* epistemology. To do this, we must return to the epistemological issues presented to us by feminist theory and see how naturalized epistemology fares with respect to them. I want eventually to show how a commitment to a naturalized epistemology provides some purchase on the problem of conceptualizing bias, but in order to do that, we must look in some detail at those feminist arguments directed against the notion of objectivity.

Capitalist Science and the Ideal of Objectivity

As we've seen, one of the most prominent themes in feminist epistemology and feminist philosophy of science concerns the alleged ide-

ological function of a certain conception of objectivity. Many feminist critics see a connection between radical (i.e., nonliberal) critiques of science and feminist critiques of "received" epistemology. Such critics take as their starting point the observation that science, as it has developed within industrialized capitalist societies like the United States, is very much an instrument of oppression: Rather than fulfilling its Enlightenment promise as a liberatory and progressive force, institutionalized science serves in fact to sustain and even to enhance existing structures of inequality and domination.[43]

Although all feminists agree that part of the explanation of this fact must be that modern science has been distorted by the sexist, racist, and classist biases it inherits from the society in which it exists, feminist theorists divide on the issue of whether some "deeper" explanation is required. Alison Jaggar's "liberal feminists" and Sandra Harding's "feminist empiricists" hold that society and science are both potentially self-correcting—that more equitable arrangements of power and more scrupulous enforcement of the rules of fairness would turn science back to its natural progressive course.

But Harding and Jaggar, together with Lorraine Code and Evelyn Fox Keller, disagree with this liberal analysis. They contend that the modern scientific establishment has not simply inherited its oppressive features from the inequitable society that conditions it. Rather, they claim, a large part of the responsibility for societal injustices lies deep within science itself, in the conception of knowledge and knowers that underlies "scientific method." These critics charge that the very ideals to which Western science has traditionally aspired—particularly rationality and objectivity—serve to sanction and promote a form of institutionalized inquiry uniquely suited to the needs of patriarchy. Thus, it's argued, feminist critique must not stop at exposing cases in which science has broken its own rules; it must press on to expose the androcentric bias inherent in the rules themselves.

Thus Evelyn Fox Keller claims that any critique that does not extend to the rules of scientific method allies itself with political liberalism in virtue of its epistemology. Any such critique, she argues, "can still be accommodated within the traditional framework by the simple argument that the critiques, if justified, merely reflect the fact that [science] is not sufficiently scientific." In contrast, there is "the truly radical critique that attempts to locate androcentric bias . . . in scientific ideology itself. The range of criticism takes us out of the liberal domain and requires us to question the very assumptions of rationality that underlie the scientific enterprise."[44]

All this seems to set a clear agenda for feminist philosophers who wish to be part of the struggle for a genuinely radical social transformation: If one's going to go deeper politically and criticize the presuppositions of liberal political theory, then one must coordinately go deeper *conceptually* and criticize the presuppositions of the epistemology and metaphysics that underwrite the politics.

But does this argument work? I think that it doesn't. To see why, we need to look more closely at the epistemological position that the feminist critics take to be allied with liberalism and look in more detail at the argument that is supposed to show that such a view of knowledge is oppressive.

The "traditional" epistemology pictured in the work of Flax, Code, and Jaggar, I've argued, is an unvigorous hybrid of rationalist and empiricist elements, but the features that are supposed to limit it from the point of view of feminist critique of science all derive from the empiricist strain. Specifically, the view of knowledge in question contains roughly the following elements:

(1) it is strongly foundationalist: It is committed to the view that there is a set of epistemically privileged beliefs, from which all knowledge is in principle derivable.

(2) it takes the foundational level to be constituted by reports of sensory experience, and views the mind as a mere calculating device, containing no substantive contents other than what results from experience.

(3) as a result of its foundationalism and its

empiricism, it is committed to a variety of sharp distinctions: observation/theory, fact/value, context of discovery/context of justification.

This epistemological theory comes very close to what Hempel has termed "narrow inductivism,"[45] but I'm just going to call it the "Dragnet" theory of knowledge. To assess the "ideological potential" of the Dragnet theory, let's look first at some of the epistemic values and attitudes the theory supports.

To begin with, because of its empiricistic foundationalism, the view stigmatizes both inference and theory. On this view, beliefs whose confirmation depends upon logical relations to other beliefs bear a less direct, less "objective" connection to the world than reports of observations, which are supposed to provide us transparent access to the world. To "actually see" or "directly observe" is better, on this conception, than to infer, and an invidious distinction is drawn between the "data" or "facts" (which are incontrovertible) on the one hand and "theories" and "hypotheses" (unproven conjectures) on the other.

Second, the view supports the idea that any sound system of beliefs can, in principle, be rationally reconstructed. That is, a belief worth having is either itself a fact or can be assigned a position within a clearly articulated confirmational hierarchy erected on fact. With this view comes a denigration of the epistemic role of hunches and intuitions. Such acts of cognitive impulse can be difficult to defend "rationally" if the standards of defense are set by a foundationalist ideal. When a hunch can't be defended, but the individual persists in believing it anyway, that's *ipso facto* evidence of irresponsibility or incompetence. Hunches that happen to pay off are relegated to the context of discovery and are viewed as inessential to the justification of the ensuing belief. The distinction between context of discovery and context of justification itself follows from foundationalism: As long as it's possible to provide a rational defense of a belief *ex post facto* by demonstrating that it bears the proper inferential relation to established facts, we needn't give any thought to the circumstances that actually gave rise to that belief. Epistemic location becomes, to that extent, evidentially irrelevant.

Finally, the Dragnet theory is going to lead to a certain conception of how systematic inquiry ought to work. It suggests that good scientific practice is relatively mechanical: that data gathering is more or less passive and random, that theory construction emerges from the data in a relatively automatic way, and that theory testing is a matter of mechanically deriving predictions and then subjecting them to decisive experimental tests. Science (and knowledge-seeking generally) will be good *to the extent that* its practitioners can conform to the ideal of objectivity.

This ideal of objective method requires a good researcher, therefore, to put aside all prior beliefs about the outcome of the investigation, and to develop a willingness to be carried wherever the facts may lead. But other kinds of discipline are necessary, too. Values are different in kind from facts, on this view, and so are not part of the confirmational hierarchy. Values (together with the emotions and desires connected with them) become, at best, epistemically irrelevant and, at worst, disturbances or distortions. Best to put them aside, and try to go about one's epistemic business in as calm and disinterested a way as possible.

In sum, the conception of ideal epistemic practice yielded by the Dragnet theory is precisely the conception that the feminist critics disdain. Objectivity, on this view (I'll refer to it from now on as "Dragnet objectivity"), is the result of complete divestiture—divestiture of theoretical commitments, of personal goals, of moral values, of hunches and intuitions. We'll get to the truth, sure as taxes, provided everyone's willing to be rational and to play by the (epistemically relevant) rules. Got an especially knotty problem to solve? Just the facts, ma'am.

Now let's see how the Dragnet theory of knowledge, together with the ideal of objectivity it supports, might play a role in the preservation of oppressive structures.

Suppose for the sake of argument that the empirical claims of the radical critics are largely correct. Suppose, that is, that in contemporary U.S. society institutionalized inquiry does function to serve the specialized needs of a powerful ruling elite (with trickle-down social goods permitted insofar as they generate profits or at least don't impede the fulfillment of ruling-class objectives). Imagine also that such inquiry is very costly, and that the ruling elite strives to socialize those costs as much as possible.

In such a society, there will be a great need to obscure this arrangement. The successful pursuit of the agendas of the ruling elite will require a quiescent—or, as it's usually termed, "stable"—society, which would surely be threatened if the facts were known. Also required is the acquiescence of the scientists and scholars, who would like to view themselves as autonomous investigators serving no masters but the truth and who would deeply resent the suggestion (as anyone with any self-respect would) that their honest intellectual efforts subserve any baser purpose.

How can the obfuscation be accomplished? One possibility would be to promote the idea that science is organized for the sake of *public* rather than *private* interests. But the noble lie that science is meant to make the world a better place is a risky one. It makes the public's support for science contingent upon science's producing tangible and visible public benefits (which may not be forthcoming) and generates expectations of publicity and accountability that might lead to embarrassing questions down the road.

An altogether more satisfactory strategy is to promote the idea that science is *value-neutral*—that it's organized for the sake of *no* particular interests at all! Telling people that science serves only the truth is safer than telling people that science serves *them*, because it not only hides the truth about who benefits, but deflects public attention away from the whole question. Belief in the value-neutrality of science can thus serve the conservative function of securing *unconditional* public support for what are in fact ruling-class initiatives. Any research agenda whatsoever—no matter how pernicious—can be readily legitimated on the grounds that it is the natural result of the self-justifying pursuit of truth, the more or less inevitable upshot of a careful look at the facts.

It will enhance the lie that science is objective, to augment it with the lie that scientists as individuals are especially "objective," either by nature or by dint of their scientific training. If laypersons can be brought to believe this, then the lie that scientific practice can transcend its compromised setting becomes somewhat easier to swallow. And if *scientists* can be brought to embrace this gratifying self-image, then the probability of *their* acquiescence in the existing system will be increased. Scientists will find little cause for critical reflection on their own potential biases (since they will believe that they are more able than others to put aside their own interests and background beliefs in the pursuit of knowledge), and no particular incentive to ponder the larger question of who actually is benefiting from their research.[46]

Now in such a society, the widespread acceptance of a theory of knowledge like the Dragnet theory would clearly be a good thing from the point of view of the ruling elite. By fostering the epistemic attitudes it fosters, the Dragnet theory helps confer special authority and status on science and its practitioners and deflects critical attention away from the material conditions in which science is conducted. Furthermore, by supporting Dragnet objectivity as an epistemic ideal, the theory prepares the ground for reception of the ideology of the objectivity of science.

In a society in which people have a reason to believe that science is successful in yielding knowledge, the Dragnet theory and the ideology of objectivity will in fact be mutually reinforcing. If one believes that science must be objective to be good, then if one independently believes that science is good, one must also believe that science *is objective!* The Dragnet theory, taken together with propagandistic claims that science is value-neutral, etc., offers an *explanation* of the fact that science leads to knowledge. Against the background belief that knowledge is actually structured the way the Dragnet theory says it is, the *success* of science seems to confirm the ideology.

We can conclude from all this that the Dragnet theory, along with the ideal of objectivity it sanctions, has clear ideological value, in the sense that their acceptance may play a causal role in people's acceptance of the ideology of scientific objectivity.

But we cannot infer from this fact either that the Dragnet theory is false or that its ideals are flawed. Such an inference depends on conflating what are essentially *prescriptive* claims (claims about how science ought to be conducted) with *descriptive* claims (claims about how science is in fact conducted). It's one thing to embrace some particular ideal of scientific method and quite another to accept ideologically useful assumptions about the satisfaction of that ideal within existing institutions.[47]

Note that in a society such as the one I've described, the ideological value of the Dragnet theory depends crucially on how successfully it can be promulgated *as a factual characterization* of the workings of the intellectual establishment. It's no use to get everyone to believe simply that it would be a good thing if scientists *could* put aside their prior beliefs and their personal interests; people must be brought to believe that scientists largely *succeed* in such divestitures. The ideological cloud of Dragnet objectivity thus comes not so much from the belief that science *ought* to be value-free, as from the belief that it *is* value-free. And of course it's precisely the fact that science is *not* value-free in the way it's proclaimed to be that makes the ideological ploy necessary in the first place.

If science as an institution fails to live up to its own ideal of objectivity, then the character of existing science entails nothing about the value of the ideal, nor about the character of some imagined science which *did* live up to it. In fact, notice that the more we can show that compromised science is *bad* science (in the sense of leading to false results), the less necessary we make it to challenge the Dragnet theory itself. A good part of the radical case, after all, is made by demonstrating the ways in which scientific research has been *distorted* by some of the very factors a Dragnet epistemologist would cite as inhibitors of epistemic progress: prejudiced beliefs, undefended hunches, material desires, ideological commitments.

There's no reason, in short, why a Dragnet theorist couldn't come to be convinced of the radical analysis of the material basis of science. Such a person might even be expected to experience a special kind of outrage at discovering the way in which the idea of objectivity is ideologically exploited in the service of special interests, much the way many peace activists felt when they first learned of some of the realities masked by U.S. officials' pious avowals of their commitment to "human rights" and "democracy."

A materialist analysis of institutionalized science leads to awareness of such phenomena as the commoditization of knowledge, the "rationalization" of scientific research, and the proletarianization of scientists. Such phenomena make the limits of liberal reformism perfectly clear: Not even the most scrupulous adherence to prescribed method on the part of individual scientists could by itself effect the necessary transformations. But it's possible for even a Dragnet theorist to acknowledge these limits, and to do so without giving up the ideal of neutral objectivity.

I began by considering the claim, defended by several feminist theorists, that "traditional" epistemology limits the possibilities for exposing the machinations of the elite because it endorses the rules of the elite's game. On the contrary, I've argued; since a big part of the lie that needs exposing is the fact that capitalist science *doesn't follow* its own rules, the task of exposing the ideology of scientific objectivity needn't change the rules. A radical critique of science and society, *even if* it implicates certain ideals, *does not require repudiation of those ideals*.

Naturalized Epistemology and the Bias Paradox

What I think I've shown so far is that if our only desideratum on an adequate critical epistemology is that it permits us to expose the real workings of capitalist patriarchy, then the Dragnet theory will do just fine, *pace* its feminist critics. But I certainly do not want to defend that theory; nor do I want to defend as an epistemic ideal the conception of objectivity as neutrality. In fact, I want to join feminist critics in rejecting this ideal. But I want to be clear about the proper basis for criticizing it.

There are, in general, two strategies that one can find in the epistemological literature for challenging the ideal of objectivity as impar-

tiality. (I leave aside for the moment the question of why one might want to challenge an epistemic ideal, though this question will figure importantly in what follows.) The first strategy is to prove the *impossibility* of satisfying the ideal—this involves pointing to the *ubiquity* of bias. The second strategy is to try to demonstrate the *undesirability* of satisfying the ideal— this involves showing the *utility* of bias. The second strategy is employed by some feminist critics, but often the first strategy is thought to be sufficient, particularly when it's pursued together with the kind of radical critique of institutionalized science discussed above. Thus Jaggar, Code, and others emphasize the essential locatedness of every individual knower, arguing that if all knowledge proceeds from some particular perspective, then the transcendent standpoint suggested by the ideology of objectivity is unattainable. All knowledge is conditioned by the knower's location, it is claimed; if we acknowledge that, then we cannot possibly believe that anyone is "objective" in the requisite sense.

But the appeal to the *de facto* partiality of all knowledge is simply not going to justify rejecting the ideal of objectivity, for three reasons. In the first place, the wanted intermediate conclusion—that Dragnet objectivity is impossible—does not follow from the truism that all knowers are located. The Dragnet conception of impartiality is perfectly compatible with the fact that all knowers start from some particular place. The Dragnet theory, like all empiricist theories, holds that knowledge is a strict function of the contingencies of experience. It therefore entails that differences in empirical situation will lead to differences in belief, and to that extent validates the intuition that all knowledge is partial.[48] Thus the neutrality recommended by the Dragnet theory does not enjoin cognizers to abjure the particularities of their own experience, only to honor certain strictures in drawing conclusions from that experience. Impartiality is not a matter of where you are, but rather how well you do from where you sit.

In the second place, even if it could be shown to be impossible for human beings to achieve perfect impartiality, that fact in itself would not speak against Dragnet objectivity *as an ideal.* Many ideals—particularly moral ones—are unattainable but that does not make them useless, or reveal them to be inadequate as ideals.[49] The fact—and I have no doubt that it is a fact—that no one can fully rid oneself of prejudices, neurotic impulses, selfish desires, and other psychological detritus does not impugn the moral or the cognitive value of attempting to do so. Similarly, the fact that no one can fully abide by the cognitive strictures imposed by the standards of strict impartiality doesn't entail that one oughtn't to try. The real test of the adequacy of a norm is not whether it can be realized, but (arguably) whether we get closer to what we want if we try to realize it.

But the third and the most serious problem with this tack is that it is precisely the one that is going to engender the bias paradox. Notice that the feminist goal of exposing the structures of interestedness that constitute patriarchy and other forms of oppression requires doing more than just demonstrating that particular interests are being served. It requires criticizing that fact, showing that there's something wrong with a society in which science selectively serves the interests of one dominant group. And it's awfully hard to see how such a critical stand can be sustained without some appeal to the value of impartiality.

A similar problem afflicts the variation on this strategy that attempts to base a critique of the norm of objectivity on the androcentric features of its *source*. Even if it could be established that received epistemic norms originated in the androcentric fantasies of European white males (and I meant to give some reason to question this in section II), how is that fact supposed to be elaborated into a *critique* of those norms? All knowledge is partial—let it be so. How then does the particular partiality of received conceptions of objectivity diminish their worth?

The question that must be confronted by anyone pursuing this strategy is basically this: If bias is ubiquitous and ineliminable, then what's the good of exposing it? It seems to me that the whole thrust of feminist scholarship in this area has been to demonstrate that androcentric biases have distorted science and, indeed, distorted the search for knowledge generally. But if biases are distorting, and if we're all biased in one way or another, then it seems there could be no such thing as an *undistorted* search for knowledge. So what are we complaining about? Is it just that we want it to be distorted in *our* favor, rather than in theirs? We must say something about the badness of the biases we expose or our critique will carry no normative import at all.

We still have to look at the second of the two strategies for criticizing the ideal of objectivity, but this is a good place to pick up the question I bracketed earlier on: *Why* might one want to challenge an epistemic ideal? If my arguments have been correct up to this point, then I have shown that many of the arguments made against objectivity are not only unsound but ultimately self-defeating. But by now the reader must surely be wondering why we need *any* critique of the notion of objectivity as neutrality. If radical critiques of the ideology of scientific objectivity are consistent with respect for this ideal, and if we need some notion of objectivity anyway, why not this one?

The short answer is this: because the best empirical theories of knowledge and mind do not sanction pure neutrality as sound epistemic policy.

The fact is that the Dragnet theory is *wrong*. We know this for two reasons: First, the failure of externalism tells us that its foundationalist underpinnings are rotten, and second, current work in empirical psychology tells us that its empiricist conception of the mind is radically incorrect. But if the Dragnet theory is wrong about the structure of knowledge and the nature of the mind, then the main source of warrant for the ideal of epistemic neutrality is removed. It becomes an open question whether divestiture of emotions, prior beliefs, and moral commitments hinders, or aids, the development of knowledge.

The fact that we find ourselves wondering about the value of a proposed epistemic ideal is itself a consequence of the turn to a naturalized epistemology. As I explained in section II, Quine's critique of externalism entailed that epistemic norms themselves were among the presuppositions being subjected to empirical test in the ongoing process of theory confirmation. This in itself authorizes the project of *criticizing* norms—it makes coherent and gives point to a project which could be nothing but an exercise in skepticism, to an externalist's way of thinking.

Naturalized epistemology tells us that there is no presuppositionless position from which to assess epistemic practice, that we must take some knowledge for granted. The only thing to do, then, is to begin with whatever it is we think we know, and try to figure out how we came to know it: Study knowledge by studying the knower. Now if, in the course of such study, we discover that much of human knowledge is possible only because our knowledge seeking does not conform to the Dragnet model, then we will have good empirical grounds for rejecting perfect objectivity as an epistemic ideal. And so we come back to the second of the two strategies I outlined for challenging the ideal of objectivity. Is there a case to be made against the desirability of epistemic neutrality? Indeed there is, on the grounds that a genuinely open mind, far from leading us closer to the truth, would lead to epistemic chaos.

As I said in section II, empirical work in linguistics and cognitive science is making it increasingly clear how seriously mistaken the empiricist view of the mind actually is. From Chomsky's groundbreaking research on the acquisition of language, through David Marr's theory of the computational basis of vision, to the work of Susan Carey, Elizabeth Spelke, Barbara Landau, Lila Gleitman, and others in developmental psychology, the evidence is mounting that inborn conceptual structure is a crucial factor in the development of human knowledge.[50]

Far from being the streamlined, uncluttered logic machine of classical empiricism, the mind now appears to be much more like a bundle of highly specialized modules, each natively fitted for the analysis and manipulation of a particular body of sensory data. General learning strategies of the sort imagined by classical empiricists, if they are employed by the mind at all, can apply to but a small portion of the cognitive tasks that confront us. Rationalism vindicated.

But if the rationalists have turned out to be right about the structure of the mind, it is because they appreciated something that the empiricists missed—the value of partiality for human knowers. Whatever might work for an ideal mind, operating without constraints of time or space, it's clear by now that complete neutrality of the sort empiricists envisioned would not suit human minds in human environments. A completely "open mind," confronting the sensory evidence we confront, could never manage to construct the right systems of knowledge we construct in the short time we take to construct them. From the point of view of an *unbiased* mind, the human sensory flow contains both too much information and too little: too much for the mind to generate *all* the logical possibilities, and too little for it to decide among even the relatively few that *are* generated.

The problem of paring down the alternatives is the defining feature of the human epistemic condition. The problem is partly solved, I've been arguing, by one form of "bias"—native conceptual structure. But it's important to realize that this problem is absolutely endemic to human knowledge seeking, whether we're talking about the subconscious processes by which we acquire language and compute sensory information, or the more consciously accessible processes by which we explicitly decide what to believe. The everyday process of forming an opinion would be grossly hampered if we were really to consider matters with anything even close to an "open mind."

This point is one that Quine has emphasized over and over in his discussions of the underdetermination of theory by data. If we had to rely on nothing but logic and the contingencies of sensory experience, we could never get anywhere in the process of forming an opinion, because we would have *too many choices*. There are an infinite number of distinct and incompatible hypotheses consistent with any body of data, never mind that there are always more data just around the corner, and never mind that we're logically free to reinterpret the "data" to save our hypotheses. If we really had to approach data gathering and theory building with a perfectly open mind, we wouldn't get anywhere.

This insight is also borne out by the history of science. As Thomas Kuhn has pointed out, science is at its least successful during the periods in its history when it most closely resembles the popular models of scientific objectivity. During a discipline's "pre-paradigm" phase, when there is no consensus about fundamental principles, nor even about what to count as the central phenomena, research is anarchic and unproductive. But progress accelerates dramatically when a discipline enters its mature period, marked by the emergence of a theory—a paradigm—capable of organizing the phenomena in a compelling enough way that it commands near-universal acceptance.

Kuhn emphasizes that one of the chief benefits a paradigm brings with it is a degree of closure about foundational issues, instilling in members of the community a principled and highly functional unwillingness to reconsider basic assumptions. The paradigm not only settles important empirical controversies, but also decides more methodological matters—what are the acceptable forms of evidence, what is the right vocabulary for discussing things, what are the proper standards for judging research. The fact is that all of these matters are disputable in principle—but a paradigm relieves its adherents of the considerable burden of having constantly to dispute them.

But what this means is that the practice and attitudes of scientists working within a paradigm will systematically deviate from the popular ideal of scientific objectivity: They will approach their research with definite preconceptions, and they will be reluctant to entertain hypotheses that conflict with their own convictions. Kuhn's point, however, is that the existence of such closed-mindedness among working scientists—what he calls "the dogmatism of mature science"—is not to be regretted; that it is actually beneficial to the course of scientific development: "Though preconception and resistance to innovation could very easily choke off scientific progress, their omnipresence is nonetheless symptomatic of characteristics upon which the continuing vitality of research depends."[51]

Once we appreciate these aspects of mature science, we can explain a great deal about how a fantasy of the pure objectivity of science can take hold independently of any ideological purposes such a fantasy might serve. (This is important if we want a serious, nuanced story about how ideologies work.) The fact that certain tenets of theory are, for all practical purposes, closed to debate can render invisible their actual status as hypotheses. Deeply entrenched theoretical principles, like the laws of thermodynamics or the principle of natural selection, become established "facts."[52] Similarly, the high degree of theoretical background required to translate various numbers and images into observations or data is forgotten by people accustomed to performing the requisite inferences on a daily basis.

Consensus and uniformity thus translate into objectivity. The more homogeneous an epistemic community, the more objective it is likely to regard itself, and, if its inquires are relatively self-contained, the more likely it is to be viewed as objective by those outside the community. This suggests one fairly obvious explanation for the general perception that the physical sciences are more objective than the social sciences: Sociology, political sciences, economics, and psychology are disciplines that still lack paradigms in Kuhn's technical sense. Because there is still public debate in these fields about basic theoretical and methodological issues, there can be no credible pretense by any partisan of having hold of the unvarnished truth.

The kind of bias that Kuhn is here identifying is, of course, different in several important respects from the kinds of biases that classical rationalists and contemporary cognitive psychologists are concerned with. For one thing, the biases that come with belief in a paradigm are acquired rather than innate; for another, there is an important social component in one case but not in the other. The lesson, however, is still the same: Human beings would know less, not more, if they were to actualize the Dragnet ideal.

What all this means is that a naturalized approach to knowledge provides us with *empirical* grounds for rejecting pure neutrality as an epistemic ideal, and for valuing those kinds of "biases" that serve to trim our epistemic jobs to manageable proportions. But it also seems to mean that we have a new route to the bias paradox—if biases are now not simply ineliminable, but downright *good*, how is it that *some* biases are *bad?*

I'm going to answer this question, honest, but first let me show how bad things really are. It's possible to see significant analogies between the function of a paradigm within a scientific community, and what is sometimes called a "worldview" within other sorts of human communities. Worldviews confer some of the same cognitive benefits as paradigms, simplifying routine epistemic tasks, establishing an informal methodology of inquiry, etc., and they also offer significant social benefits, providing a common sense of reality and fostering a functional sense of normalcy among members of the community.

But what about those outside the community? A shared language, a set of traditions and mores, a common sense of what's valuable and why—the very things that bind some human beings together in morally valuable ways—function simultaneously to exclude those who do not share them. Moreover, human communities are not homogeneous. In a stratified community, where one group of people dominates others, the worldview of the dominant group can become a powerful tool for keeping those in the subordinate groups in their places.

The real problem with the liberal conceptions of objectivity and neutrality begins with the fact that while they are unreliable, it's possible for those resting comfortably in the center of a consensus to find that fact invisible. Members of the dominant group are given no reason to question their own assumptions: Their worldview acquires, in their minds, the status of established fact. Their opinions are transformed into what "everybody" knows.[53] Furthermore, these privileged individuals have the power to promote and elaborate their own worldview in public forums while excluding all others, tacitly setting limits to the range of "reasonable" opinion.[54]

Because of the familiarity of its content, the "objectivity" of such reportage is never challenged. If it were, it would be found woefully lacking *by liberal standards*. That's because

the liberal ideal of objectivity is an *unreasonable* one; it is not just unattainable, but unattainable by a long measure. But because the challenge is *only* mounted against views that are aberrant, it is *only* such views that will ever be demonstrated to be "non-objective," and thus *only* marginal figures that will ever be charged with bias.[55]

Lorraine Code makes a similar point about the unrealistic stringency of announced standards for knowledge.[56] She rightly points out that most of what we ordinarily count as knowledge wouldn't qualify as such by many proposed criteria. I would go further and say that as with all unrealistically high standards, they tend to support the status quo—in this case, received opinion—by virtue of the fact that they will only be invoked in "controversial" cases, i.e., in case of challenge to familiar or received or "expert" opinion. Since the standards are unreasonably high, the views tested against them will invariably be found wanting; since the only views so tested will be unpopular ones, their failure to pass muster serves to add additional warrant to prevailing prejudices, as well as a patina of moral vindication to the holders of those prejudices, who can self-righteously claim to have given "due consideration" to the "other side."

But what are we anti-externalist, naturalized epistemologists to say about this? We can't simply condemn the members of the dominant class for their "bias," for their lack of "open-mindedness" about our point of view. To object to the hegemony of ruling-class opinion on this basis would be to tacitly endorse the discredited norm of neutral objectivity. "Biased" they are, but then, in a very deep sense, so are we. The problem with ruling-class "prejudices" cannot be the fact that they are deeply held beliefs, or beliefs acquired "in advance" of the facts—for the necessity of such *kinds* of belief is part of the human epistemic condition.

The real problem with the ruling-class worldview is not that it is biased; it's that it is false. The epistemic problem with ruling-class people is not that they are closed-minded; it's that they hold too much power. The recipe for radical epistemological action then becomes simple: Tell the truth and get enough power so that people have to listen. Part of telling the truth, remember, is telling the truth about how knowledge is actually constructed—advocates of feminist epistemology are absolutely correct about that. We do need to dislodge those attitudes about knowledge that give unearned credibility to elements of the ruling-class worldview, and this means dislodging the hold of the Dragnet theory of knowledge. But we must be clear: The Dragnet theory is not false because it's pernicious; it's pernicious because it is false.

Whether we are talking in general about the ideology of scientific objectivity, or about particular sexist and racist theories, we must be willing to talk about truth and falsity. If we criticize such theories primarily on the basis of their ideological function, we risk falling prey to the very illusions about objectivity that we are trying to expose. I think this has happened to some extent within feminist epistemology. Because so much of feminist criticism has been oblivious to the rationalistic case that can be made against the empiricistic conception of mind at work in the Dragnet theory, empiricistic assumptions continue to linger in the work of even the most radical feminist epistemologists. This accounts, I believe, for much of the ambivalence about Dragnet objectivity expressed even by those feminist critics who argue most adamantly for its rejection.

This ambivalence surfaces, not surprisingly, in discussions about what to do about bad biases, where positive recommendations tend to fall perfectly in line with the program of liberal reformism. Lorraine Code's discussion of stereotypical thinking provides a case in point.[57] Code emphasizes, quite correctly, the degree to which stereotypical assumptions shape the interpretation of experience, both in science and in everyday life. But despite her recognition of the "unlikelihood of pure objectivity,"[58] the "unattainability of pure theory-neutrality,"[59] and her acknowledgment of the necessary role of background theory *in science*, her recommendations for reforming everyday epistemic practice are very much in the spirit of liberal exhortations to open-mindedness. She sees a difference between a scientist's reliance on his or her paradigm, and ordinary dependence on stereotypes:

It is not possible for practitioners to engage in normal science without paradigms to guide their recognition of problems, and their problem-solving endeavours. Stereotype-governed thinking is different in this respect, for it is both possible and indeed desirable to think and to know in a manner *not* governed by stereotypes.[60]

But it's by no means clear that it *is* possible. I sense that Code has not appreciated the depth of human reliance on theories that cannot be shown to be "derived from the facts alone." In characterizing certain kinds of background belief and certain forms of "hasty generalization" *as stereotypes*, she is presupposing a solution to the very problem that must be solved: viz., telling which of the background theories that we routinely bring to bear on experience are *reliable* and which ones are not.

The liberal epistemological fantasy, still somewhat at work here, is that there will be formal marks that distinguish good theories from bad. The empiricist version of this fantasy is that the formal mark consists in a proper relation between theory and "fact." In this case, the good theories are supposed to be the ones that derive in the proper way from the data, whereas the bad ones—the biases, the prejudices, the stereotypes—are the ones that antedate the data. But once we realize that theory infects observation and that confirmation is a multidirectional relation, we must also give up on the idea that the good theories are going to look different from the bad theories. They can't be distinguished on the basis of their formal relation to the "facts," because (1) there are no "facts" in the requisite sense, and (2) there are too many good biases whose relation to the data will appear as tenuous as those of the bad ones.

But what's the alternative?

A naturalized approach to knowledge, because it requires us to give up *neutrality* as an epistemic ideal, also requires us to take a different attitude toward bias. We know that human knowledge requires biases; we also know that we have no possibility of getting *a priori* guarantees that our biases incline us in the right direction. What all this means is that the "biasedness" of biases drops out as a parameter of epistemic evaluation. There's only one thing to do, and it's the course always counseled by a naturalized approach: *We must treat the goodness or badness of particular biases as an empirical question.*

A naturalistic study of knowledge tells us biases are good when and to the extent that they facilitate the gathering of *knowledge*— that is, when they lead us to the truth. Biases are bad when they lead us *away* from the truth. One important strategy for telling the difference between good and bad biases is thus to evaluate the overall theories in which the biases figure. This one point has important implications for feminist theory in general and for feminist attitudes about universalist or essentialist theories of human nature in particular.

As we saw in section II, much of the feminist criticism raised against cognitive essentialism focused on the fact that rationalist and Kantian theories of the human essence were all devised by men, and based, allegedly, on exclusively male experience. Be that so—it would still follow from a naturalized approach to the theory of knowledge that it is an *empirical* question whether or not 'androcentrism' of that sort leads to bad theories. Partiality does not in general compromise theories; as we feminists ourselves have been insisting, all theorizing proceeds from *some* location or other. We must therefore learn to be cautious of claims to the effect that particular forms of partiality will inevitably and systematically influence the outcome of an investigation. Such claims must be treated as empirical hypotheses, subject to investigation and challenge, rather than as enshrined first principles.

So what about universalist or essentialist claims concerning human nature? I have argued that there really are no grounds for regarding such claims as antipathetic to feminist aspirations or even to feminist insights regarding the importance of embodiment or the value of human difference. Suggestions that essentialist theories reify aspects of specifically male experience, I argued, involve a serious misunderstanding of the rationalist strategy. But notice that even if such charges were true, the real problem with such theories should be their *falseness*, rather than their androcentrism. A theory that purports to say what human beings

are like essentially must apply to *all human beings*; if it does not, it is wrong, whatever its origins.

In fact, I think there is excellent evidence for the existence of a substantial human nature and virtually no evidence for the alternative, the view that there is no human essence. But what's really important is to recognize that the latter view is as much a substantive empirical thesis as the Cartesian claim that we are essentially rational language-users. We need to ask ourselves *why* we ought to believe that human selves are, at the deepest level, "socially constructed"—the output of a confluence of contingent factors.[61]

Another thing that a naturalized approach to knowledge offers us is the possibility of *an empirical theory of biases*. As we've already seen, there are different kinds of biases—some are natively present, some are acquired. An empirical study of biases can refine the taxonomy and possibly tell us something about the reliability and the corrigibility of biases of various sorts. It may turn out that we can on this basis get something like a principled sorting of biases into good ones and bad ones, although it will be more likely that we'll learn that even a "good" bias can lead us astray in certain circumstances.[62]

One likely upshot of an empirical investigation of bias is a better understanding of the processes by which human beings design research programs. What we decide to study and how we decide to study it are matters in which unconscious biases—tendencies to see certain patterns rather than others, to attend to certain factors rather than others, to act in accordance with certain interests rather than others—play a crucial role. We can't eliminate the biases— we shouldn't want to, for we'd have no research programs left if we did—but we can identify the particular empirical presuppositions that lie behind a particular program of research so that we can subject them, if necessary, to empirical critique.

One important issue is the *saliency* of certain properties. Every time a study is designed, a decision is made, tacitly or explicitly, to pay attention to some factors and to ignore others. These "decisions" represent tacit or explicit hypotheses about the likely connection between various aspects of the phenomena under study, hypotheses that can be subjected to empirical scrutiny.

Imagine a study purporting to investigate the development of human language by examining a sample of two hundred preschoolers. Must the sample, to be a valid basis for extrapolation, contain boys and girls? Must it be racially mixed? How one answers these questions will depend on the empirical assumptions one makes about the likely connection between parameters like gender and race, on the one hand, and the language faculty on the other. To think that gender or race must be controlled for in such studies is to make a substantive empirical conjecture—in this case, it is to deny the rationalistic hypothesis that human beings' biological endowment includes a brain structured in a characteristic way, and to make instead the assumption that cognitive development is sensitive to the kinds of differences that we *socially* encode as gender and race.

Such an assumption, laid out this baldly, seems pretty dubious. Indeed, it's hard to see what such an assumption is doing other than reflecting sexist, racist, and classist beliefs to the effect that social groupings are determined by biological groupings. Realizing this is a necessary first step to countering the genuinely pernicious "essentialist" theories of Jensen, Herrnstein, and the human sociobiologists and to exposing the racism and sexism inherent in their programs of "research." Such "research" is precisely at odds with rationalist methodology, which only invokes human essences as a way of explaining human *commonalities*—and then, only when such commonalties cannot plausibly be explained by regularities in the environment.

Consider, for example, the claims that blacks are "innately" less intelligent than whites.[63] In the first place, we must point out, as we do, that race is not a biological kind, but rather a *social* kind. That is to say that while there may be a biological explanation for the presence of each of the characteristics that constitute racial criteria—skin color, hair texture, and the like— the *selection of those characteristics as criteria* of membership in some category is *conventionally* determined. Here is where the empiricist notion of "nominal essence" has some

work to do: race, in contrast to some other categories, *is* socially constructed.

The second step is to point out that if such classifications as race fail to reflect deep regularities in human biology, and reflect instead only historically and culturally specific interests, then there is no reason, *apart from racist ones*, to investigate the relation between race and some presumably biological feature of human beings. Again, it takes an extreme form of empiricism to believe that brute correlations between one arbitrary selected characteristic and another constitutes *science*—but even from such a perspective it must be an arbitrary choice to investigate one set of such correlations rather than another. Why intelligence and *race?* Why not intelligence and number of hair follicles?

It is this point that really gives the lie to Herrnstein's repugnant invocation of "scientific objectivity" in defense of his racist undertakings.[64] The fact that there is no empirical grounding for the selection of race as a theoretical parameter in the study of intelligence utterly defeats the disingenuous defense that such "science" as Herrnstein is engaged in is simply detached fact gathering—callin' 'em like he sees 'em. The decision to use race as an analytical category betrays a host of substantive assumptions that would be exceedingly hard to defend once made explicit. How could one defend the proposition that race and intelligence are connected without confronting the embarrassing fact that there's no biologically defensible definition of "race"? And how could one defend the proposition that human "mating strategies" will receive their explanation at the biological level, without having to explicitly argue against the wealth of competing explanations available at the social and personal/intentional levels?[65]

In sum, a naturalized approach to knowledge requires us, as feminists and progressives, to be critical of the saliency such categories as gender and race have *for us*. The fact that such parameters have been egregiously overlooked in cases where they are demonstrably relevant shouldn't make us think automatically that they are always theoretically significant. The recognition that selection of analytical categories is an empirical matter, governed by both background theory and consideration of the facts, is in itself part of the solution to the paradox of partiality.

The naturalized approach proceeds by showing the empirical inadequacy of the theory of mind and knowledge that makes perfect neutrality seem like a good thing. But at the same time that it removes the warrant for one epistemic ideal, it gives support for new norms, ones that will enable us to criticize some biases without presupposing the badness of bias in general. The naturalized approach can therefore vindicate all of the insights feminist theory has produced regarding the ideological functions of the concept of objectivity without undercutting the critical purpose of exposing androcentric and other objectionable forms of bias, when they produce oppressive falsehoods.

IV. THE END

I began this essay by asking whether we need a "feminist" epistemology, and I answered that we did, as long as we understood that need to be the need for an epistemology informed by feminist insight, and responsive to the moral imperatives entailed by feminist commitments. But I've argued that we do not necessarily need a conceptual transformation of epistemological theory in order to get a feminist epistemology in this sense. We need, in the first instance, a *political* transformation of the society in which theorizing about knowledge takes place. We've got to stop the oppression of women, eliminate racism, redistribute wealth, and *then* see what happens to our collective understanding of knowledge.

My bet? That some of the very same questions that are stimulating inquiry among privileged white men, right now in these sexist, racist, capitalist-imperialist times, are *still* going to be exercising the intellects and challenging the imaginations of women of color, gay men, physically handicapped high school students, etc.

I'm not saying that we should stop doing epistemology until after the revolution. That would of course be stupid, life being short. What I am saying is that those of us who think

we know what feminism is, must guard constantly against the presumptuousness we condemn in others, of claiming as Feminist the particular bit of ground upon which we happen to be standing. We need to remember that part of what unites philosophers who choose to characterize their own work as "feminist" is the conviction that philosophy ought to matter—that it should make a positive contribution to the construction of a more just, humane, and nurturing world than the one we currently inhabit.

I have argued that contemporary analytic philosophy is capable of making such a contribution and that it is thus undeserving of the stigma "malestream" philosophy. But there's more at stake here than the abstract issue of mischaracterization. Attacks on the analytic tradition as "androcentric," "phallogocentric," or "male-identified" are simultaneously attacks on the feminist credentials of those who work within the analytic tradition. And the stereotyping of contemporary analytic philosophy— the tendency to link it with views (like the Dragnet theory) to which it is in fact antipathetic—has turned feminists away from fruitful philosophical work, limiting our collective capacity to imagine genuinely novel and transformative philosophical strategies.

I acknowledge both the difficulty and the necessity of clarifying the implications of feminist theory for other kinds of endeavors. It's important, therefore, for feminist theorists to continue to raise critical challenges to particular theories and concepts. But surely this can be done without the caricature, without the throwaway refutations, in a way that is more respectful of philosophical differences.

Let's continue to argue with each other by all means. But let's stop arguing about which view is more feminist, and argue instead about which view is more likely to be true. Surely we can trust the dialectical process of feminists discussing these things with other feminists to yield whatever "feminist epistemology" we need.[66]

NOTES

1. A possible exception may be Jean Grimshaw, who comes closer than any other thinker I've

encountered to endorsing what I'm calling a "bare proceduralist" conception of feminist philosophy: "There is no particular view, for example, of autonomy, of morality, of self, no one characterisation of women's activities which can be appealed to in any clear way as the woman's (or feminist) view. But I think nevertheless that feminism makes a difference to philosophy. The difference it makes is that women, in doing philosophy, have often raised new problems, problematised issues in new ways and moved to the centre questions which have been marginalised or seen as unimportant or at the periphery." From Grimshaw, *Philosophy and Feminist Thinking* (Minneapolis: University of Minnesota Press, 1986), p. 260.

2. Naomi Scheman made this point in a letter to members of the Committee on the Status of Women of the American Philosophical Association in 1988, when she and I were serving on the committee. Her letter was partly a response to a letter of mine raising questions about whether our charge as a committee should include the promotion of "feminist philosophy."

3. For discussions of epistemological frameworks available to feminists, see Sandra Harding, *The Science Question in Feminism*, (Ithaca, N.Y.: Cornell University Press, 1986), especially pp. 24–29; Mary Hawkesworth, "Feminist Epistemology: A Survey of the Field," *Women and Politics* 7 (1987): 112–124; and Hilary Rose, "Hand, Brain, and Heart: A Feminist Epistemology for the Natural Sciences," *Signs* 9, 11 (1983): 73–90.

4. See Mary E. Hawkesworth, "Knowers, Knowing, Known: Feminist Theory and Claims of Truth," *Signs* 14, 3 (1989): 533–557.

5. See, for example, Sandra Harding: "I have been arguing for open acknowledgement, even enthusiastic appreciation, of certain tensions that appear in the feminist critiques. I have been suggesting that these reflect valuable alternative social projects which are in opposition to the coerciveness and regressiveness of modern science. . . . [S]table and coherent theories are not always the ones to be most highly desired; there are important understandings to be gained in seeking the social origins of instabilities and incoherences in our thoughts and practices—understandings that we cannot arrive at if we repress recognition of instabilities and tensions in our thought" (*Science Question in Feminism*, pp. 243–244).

6. See Naomi Scheman, "Othello's Doubt/Desdemona's Death: The Engendering of Skepticism," in *Power, Gender, Values*, ed. Judith Genova (Edmonton, Alberta: Academic Printing and Publishing, 1987). See also Evelyn Fox Keller, "Cognitive Repression in Physics," *American* *Journal of Physics* 47 (1979): 718–721; and "Feminism and Science," in *Sex and Scientific Inquiry*, ed. S. Harding and J. O'Barr (Chicago: University of Chicago Press, 1987), pp. 233–246, reprinted in *The Philosophy of Science*, ed. by Richard Boyd, Philip Gaspar, and John Trout (Cambridge, Mass.: MIT Press, 1991).

7. For example, see Catharine A. MacKinnon, *Towards a Feminist Theory of the State* (Cambridge, Mass.: Harvard University Press, 1989).

8. This is not quite right—the ideology of 'objectivity' is perfectly capable of charging those *outside* the inner circle with partiality, and indeed, such charges are also crucial to the preservation of the status quo. More on this below.

9. Lorraine Code, "The Impact of Feminism on Epistemology," *APA Newsletter on Feminism and Philosophy*, ed. by Morwenna Griffiths and Margaret Whitford (Bloomington: Indiana University Press, 1988), p. 189ff.

10. Lorraine Code, "Experience, Knowledge, and Responsibility," in *Feminist Perspectives in Philosophy*, ed. by Morwenna Griffiths and Margaret Whitford (Bloomington: Indiana University Press, 1988), pp. 189ff.

11. Code, "Impact of Feminism on Epistemology," p. 25.

12. It might be objected that there is a third option—that we could criticize those biases that are biases against our interests and valorize those that promote our interests. But if we are in fact left with only this option, then we are giving up on the possibility of any medium of social change other than power politics. This is bad for two reasons: (1) as moral and political theory, egoism should be repugnant to any person ostensibly concerned with justice and human well-being; and (2) as tactics, given current distributions of power, it's really stupid.

13. I have defended a kind of non-realist conception of truth, but one which maintains this gap. See my "Can Verificationists Make Mistakes?" *American Philosophical Quarterly* 24, 3 (July 1987): 225–236. For a defense of a more robustly realist conception of truth, see Michael Devitt, *Realism and Truth* (Princeton, N.J.: Princeton University Press, 1984). (A new edition is in press.)

14. Code, "Impact of Feminism on Epistemology," p. 25.

15. Significantly, these theories are not all empiricist, and the theories that are most "postpositivist" are the least empiricist of all. I'll have much more to say about this in what follows.

16. See, e.g., Helen Cixous, "The Laugh of the Medusa," tr. by Keith Cohen and Paula Cohen, *Signs* 1, 4 (1976): 875–893; Luce Irigaray, "Is the Subject of Science Sexed?" tr. by Carol Mastrangelo Bove, *Hypatia* 2, 3 (Fall 1987):

65–87; and Andrea Nye, "The Inequalities of Semantic Structure: Linguistics and Feminist Philosophy," *Metaphilosophy* 18, 3–4 (July/October 1987): 222–240. I must say that for the sweepingness of Nye's claims regarding "linguistics" and "semantic theory," her survey of work in these fields is, to say the least, narrow and out-of-date.

17. See, e.g., Ruth Ginzberg, "Feminism, Rationality, and Logic" and "Teaching Feminist Logic," *APA Newsletter on Feminism and Philosophy* 88, 2 (March 1989): 34–42 and 58–65.

18. Note that the term "Enlightenment" itself does not have any single, precise meaning, referring in some contexts to only the philosophers (and *philosophes*) of eighteenth-century France, in other contexts to any philosopher lying on the trajectory of natural-rights theory in politics, from Hobbes and Locke through Rousseau, and in still other contexts to all the canonical philosophical works of the seventeenth and eighteen centuries, up to and including Kant. I shall try to use the term "early modern philosophy" to denote seventeenth-century rationalism and empiricism, but I may slip up.

19. In Alison Jaggar, *Feminist Politics and Human Nature* (Totowa, N.J.: Rowman and Allenheld, 1983), p. 355.

20. In Harding, *Science Question in Feminism*, p. 24.

21. Jane Flax, "Postmodernism and Gender Relations in Feminist Theory," *Signs* 12, 4 (Summer 1987): 624.

22. Ibid., p. 627.

23. Never mind Kant, who, apart from this note, I'm going to pretty much ignore. Virtually nothing that Flax cites as constitutive of the Enlightenment legacy can be easily found in Kant. He was not a dualist, at least not a Cartesian dualist; his opinions regarding the possible existence of a mind-independent reality were complicated (to say the least), but he clearly thought that it would be impossible for human beings to gain knowledge of such a world if it *did* exist; and the reading of the Categorical Imperative—how does it go? "Treat others as ends-in-themselves, never merely as means"?—that has Kant coming out as ignorant or neglectful of human difference seems to me to be positively Orwellian.

24. Harding is an exception, since she acknowledges Quine, though nothing after Quine. Code does allude to there being some changes in mainstream epistemology since the heyday of positivism, but she says that the changes are not of the right nature to license the questions she thinks are central to feminist epistemology. The only contemporary analytic epistemologist Code ever cites in either of her two books is Alvin Goldman, whom she does not discuss.

This is ironic, because Goldman has been one of the chief advocates of a version of epistemology called reliabilism, that makes the actual circumstances of belief production an essential part of their justification. See his *Epistemology and Cognition* (Cambridge, Mass.: Harvard University Press, 1986). It is also terribly unfair. Goldman takes it to be a truism that knowledge has a social component and that the study of knowledge requires consideration of the social situation of the knower: "Most knowledge is a cultural product, channeled through language and social communication. So how could epistemology *fail* to be intertwined with studies of culture and social systems?" I do not believe Goldman deserves the opprobrium Code heaps upon him.

Jaggar, too, acknowledges that positivism has lost favor, but says nothing about the shape of the theories that have succeeded it. See Jaggar, *Feminist Politics*.

25. Cognitive essentialism generally gets associated with another thesis singled out for criticism—namely, dualism, the view that the mind is separate from the body and that the self is to be identified with the mind. Although dualism is not exclusively a rationalist view (Locke is standardly classified as a dualist), it is most closely associated with Descartes, and it is Descartes's *a priori* argument for dualism in the *Meditations* that seems to draw the most fire. Cartesian dualism is seen as providing a metaphysical rationale for dismissing the relevance of material contingencies to the assessment of knowledge claims, because it separates the knowing subject from the physical body, and because it seems to assert the sufficiency of disembodied reason for the attainment of knowledge.

In fact, dualism is a red herring. It's an uncommon view in the history of philosophy. Many people classically characterized as dualists, like Plato, were surely not Cartesian dualists. And on top of that, the dualism does not work. Being a dualist is neither necessary nor sufficient for believing that the human essence is composed of cognitive properties.

26. Flax, "Postmodernism," p. 262.

27. "Individualism" as Jaggar uses it is rather a term of art. It has a variety of meanings within philosophical discourse, but I don't know of any standard use within epistemology that matches Jaggar's. In the philosophy of mind, the term denotes the view that psychological states can be individuated for purposes of scientific psychology, without reference to objects or states outside the individual. This use of the term has *nothing* to do with debates in political theory about such issues as individual rights or individual autonomy. A liberal view

of the moral/political individual can work just as well (or as poorly) on an anti-individualist psychology (such as Hilary Putnam's or Tyler Burge's) as on an individualist view like Jerry Fodor's.

28. See also Naomi Scheman's essay in *A Mind of One's Own* (Westview, 1993).
29. Jaggar, "Postmodernism," p. 355.
30. Ibid.
31. See, for example, the excerpts from *Notes Directed against a Certain Program*, in Margaret Wilson, ed., *The Essential Descartes* (New York: Mentor Press, 1969).
32. Ibid., p. 112.
33. Ibid. One passage from one work should, of course, not be enough to convince anyone, and Descartes is clearly fictionalizing his own history to some extent (like who doesn't?). I do not have the space here to provide a full defense of my interpretation, but I invite you to read the *Discourse* on your own.
34. A little qualification is necessary here: The empiricist's requirement that all concepts be reducible to sensory simples does count as a substantive restriction on the possible contents of thought, but it's one which is vitiated by the reductionist semantic theory favored by empiricists, which denies the meaningfulness of any term which cannot be defined in terms of sensory primitives. See the discussion of this point in Jerry Fodor, *Modularity of Mind: An Essay on Faculty Psychology* (Cambridge, Mass.: MIT Press, 1983).

Also, the empiricists did allow a kind of "bias" in the form of innate standards of similarity, which would permit the mind to see certain ideas as inherently resembling certain others. This innate similarity metric was needed to facilitate the operation of *association*, which as the mechanism for generating more complex and more abstract ideas out of the sensory simples. But the effects of a bias such as this were vitiated by the fact that associations could also be forged by the contiguity of ideas in experience, with the result once more that no effective, substantive limits were placed on the ways in which human beings could analyze the data presented them by sensory experience.

35. David Hume, *An Enquiry Concerning Human Understanding* (Indianapolis: Hackett, 1977), p. 30. For a different assessment of Hume's potential contributions to a feminist epistemology, see Annette Baier's essay in *A Mind of One's Own*.
36. I have been much chastised by serious scholars of early-twentieth-century analytic philosophy (specifically Warren Goldfarb, Neil Tennant, and Philip Kitcher) for here reinforcing the myth that logical positivism was a uniform "school of

thought." I guess I should thank them. The view that I am labeling "positivism" is the usual received view of the movement, but it may have belonged to only some of the more flatfooted and marginal members of the group (like A. J. Ayer) and certainly was not the view of the most important philosopher in the movement, Rudolf Carnap.

Still, the version of positivism I am outlining is the version that Quine attributed to his predecessors, and the version that he was reacting against. Moreover, even if Carnap was not an externalist in the sense of seeking a metaphysical vindication of scientific practice (as Michael Friedman argues in "The Re-evaluation of Logical Positivism," *Journal of Philosophy* 88, 10 [October 1991]: 505–519), he still was committed to a sharp separation between contentful and merely analytic statements, which is enough to generate the kinds of difficulties that I'm claiming beset positivism generally. My thanks to Marcia Homiak for calling my attention to the Friedman article.

37. Here are some of the most important works: W.V.O. Quine, "Two Dogmas of Empiricism," reprinted in Quine, *From a Logical Point of View* (Cambridge, Mass.: Harvard University Press 1953); Carl G. Hempel, "Problems and Changes in the Empiricist Criterion of Meaning," *Revue Internationale de Philosophie* 11 (1950): 41–63, and "Empiricist Criteria of Cognitive Significance: Problems and Changes," in Hempel, *Aspects of Scientific Explanation and Other Essays in the Philosophy of Science* (New York: Free Press, 1965); Nelson Goodman, *Fact, Fiction, and Forecast* (Cambridge, Mass.: Harvard University Press, 1955); and Hilary Putnam, "What Theories Are Not," reprinted in Putnam, *Mathematics, Matter, and Method: Philosophical Papers, Vol. I* (Cambridge: Cambridge University Press, 1975).
38. Quine and J. S. Ullian catalog these principles—which they refer to as the "virtues" of hypotheses—in an epistemological primer called *The Web of Belief* (New York: Random House, 1970). Quine and Ullian employ a strikingly Humean strategy in trying to explain the epistemological value of the virtues.
39. W.V.O. Quine, "Epistemology Naturalized," in Quine, *Ontological Relativity and Other Essays* (New York: Columbia University Press, 1969), pp. 69–90.
40. See Noam Chomsky, "Review of B. F. Skinner's *Verbal Behavior*," *Language* 35, 1 (1959): 53–68.
41. See Noam Chomsky, "Quine's Empirical Assumptions," in *Words and Objections: Essays on the Work of W. V. Quine*, ed. by D. Davidson and J. Hintikka (Dordrecht: D. Reidel, 1969). See

also Quine's response to Chomsky in the same volume.

I discuss the inconsistency between Quine's commitment to naturalism and his *a prioristic* rejection of mentalism and nativism in linguistics in "Naturalized Epistemology and the Study of Language," in *Naturalistic Epistemology: A Symposium of Two Decades*, ed. by Abner Shimony and Debra Nails (Dordrecht: D. Reidel, 1987), pp. 235–257.

42. For an extremely helpful account of the Chomskian approach to the study of language, see David Lightfoot's *The Language Lottery: Toward a Biology of Grammars* (Cambridge, Mass.: MIT Press, 1984).

43. I take this to be an established fact. There's a mountainous body of scholarship on this issue, much of it the result of feminist concerns about specific ways in which women have been excluded from and damaged by institutionalized science. The whole area of biological determinist theorists provides an excellent case study of the ways in which science both supports and is distorted by social stratification. *Genes and Gender II*, ed. by Ruth Hubbard and Marian Lowe (New York: Gordion Press, 1979), is a collection of now classic articles critically examining alleged biological and ethological evidence for the genetic basis of gender differences. For a more current analysis of similar research in neurophysiology and endocrinology, see Helen Longino, *Science as Social Knowledge* (Princeton, N.J.: Princeton University Press, 1990), ch. 6. Two excellent general discussions of the interactions among politics, economics, ideology, and science as exemplified by the growth of biological determinist theories are Stephen Jay Gould, *The Mismeasure of Man* (New York: W. W. Norton, 1981); and R. C. Lewontin, Steven Rose, and Leon J. Kamin, *Not in Our Genes* (New York: Pantheon Books, 1984).

44. Evelyn Fox Keller, "Feminism and Science," in Boyd, Gaspar, and Trout, eds., *Philosophy of Science*, p. 281. In this passage, Keller is also remarking on the tendency of (what she views as) the liberal critiques to focus on the "softer" biological and social sciences, and to leave alone the "harder" sciences of math and physics.

45. Carl R. Hempel, *Philosophy of Natural Science* (Englewood Cliffs, N.J.: Prentice-Hall, 1966). See especially pp. 10–18.

46. There's a good case to be made that scientists actually have *disincentives* to ponder such questions. The structure of incentives in academia necessitates rapid generation and publication of research, and research requires securing long-term funding, usually from a government agency or a private corporate foundation. Scientific research is thus heavily compromised at the outset, whatever the ideals and values of the individual scientists. For a detailed discussion of the ways in which academic and economic pressures systematically erode "objectivity" in science, see William Broad and Nicholas Wade, *Betrayers of the Truth: Fraud and Deceit in the Halls of Science* (New York: Simon and Schuster, 1982).

47. This follows from a general point emphasized by Georges Rey in personal conversation: It's important in general to distinguish people's theories of human institutions from the actual character of those institutions.

48. This despite the fact that the Dragnet theory supports a strong context of discovery/context of justification distinction. On empiricist theories, the justification of an individual's belief is ultimately a relation between the belief and the sensory experience of that individual. Location matters, then, because the same belief could be justified for one individual and unjustified for another, precisely because of the differences in their experiences.

49. This is not to say that there are no puzzling issues about moral ideals that are in some sense humanly unattainable. One such issue arises with respect to the ideals of altruism and supererogation, ideals which it would be, arguably, *unhealthy* for human beings to fully realize. See Larry Blum, Marcia Homiak, Judy Housman, and Naomi Scheman, "Altruism and Women's Oppression," in *Women and Philosophy*, ed. by Carol C. Gould and Marx W. Wartofsky (New York: G. P. Putnam, 1980), pp. 222–247. On the question of whether it would be good for human beings to fully realize *any* moral ideal, see Susan Wolf, "Moral Saints," *The Journal of Philosophy* 79, 8 (August 1982): 419–439.

50. Jerry Fodor, *Modularity of Mind* (Cambridge, Mass.: MIT Press, 1983); Noam Chomsky, *Reflections on Language* (New York: Random House, 1975); David Marr, *Vision: A Computational Investigation Into the Human Representation and Processing of Visual Information* (San Francisco: W. H. Freeman, 1982); Susan Carey, *Conceptual Change in Childhood* (Cambridge, Mass.: MIT Press, 1985); Elizabeth Spelke, "Perceptual Knowledge of Objects in Infancy," in J. Mehler, E.C.T. Walker, and M. Garrett, eds., *Perspectives on Mental Representations* (Hillsdale, N.Y.: Erlbaum, 1982); Barbara Landau and Lila Gleitman, *Language and Experience: Evidence from the Blind Child* (Cambridge, Mass.: Harvard University Press, 1985); Steven Pinker, *Learnability and Cognition: The Acquisition of Argument Structure* (Cambridge, Mass.: MIT Press, 1989).

51. Thomas S. Kuhn, "The Function of Dogma in

Scientific Research," (1963), reprinted in Janet A. Kourany, ed., *Scientific Knowledge* (Belmont, Calif.: Wadsworth, 1987), pp. 253–265. Quotation is from p. 254.

52. This phenomenon affects even as sensitive and sophisticated a critic of science as Stephen Jay Gould. Responding to creationist charges that evolution is "just a theory," Gould insists: "Well, evolution *is* a theory. It is also a fact. And facts and theories are different things, not rungs in a hierarchy of increasing certainty. Facts are the world's data. Theories are structures of ideas that explain and interpret facts. Facts do not go away while scientists debate rival theories for explaining them . . . [H]uman beings evolved from apelike ancestors whether they did so by Darwin's proposed mechanism or by some other, yet to be discovered." Stephen Jay Gould, "Evolution as Fact and Theory," *Hen's Teeth and Horse's Toes* (New York: W. W. Norton, 1980), pp. 253–262. Quotation from p. 254.

   Gould's point, I believe, is that the world is as it is independently of our ability to understand it—a position I share. But if facts are part of the mind-independent world, they cannot also be "the world's data." "*Data*" is the name we give to that *part* of our theory about which we can achieve a high degree of interpersonal and intertheoretic agreement; however, there can be as much contention about "the data" as about "the theory." Gould concedes as much in the next paragraph when he writes: "Moreover, 'fact' does not mean 'absolute certainty.' . . . In science, 'fact' can only mean 'confirmed to such a degree that it would be perverse to withhold provisional assent.' " If *that's* what "facts" are, then they can and do sometimes "go away while scientists debate rival theories for explaining them." Ibid., p. 255.

53. Notice that we don't have to assume here that anyone is knowingly telling lies. Clearly, in the real world, members of the ruling elite *do* consciously lie, and they do it a lot. But here I'm trying to point out that some of the mechanisms that can perpetuate oppressive structures are epistemically legitimate.

54. See Edward Herman and Noam Chomsky, *Manufacturing Consent* (New York: Pantheon, 1988); Noam Chomsky, *Necessary Illusions: Thought Control in Democratic Society* (Boston: South End Press, 1989), esp. ch. 3 ("The Bounds of the Expressible"); and Martin A. Lee and Norman Solomon, *Unreliable Sources: A Guide to Detecting Bias in News Media* (New York: Carol Publishing Group, 1990).

55. This explains some of what's going on in the so-called "debate" about so-called "political correctness." Most of what's going on involves pure dishonesty and malice, but to the extent that there are some intelligent and relatively fair-minded people who find themselves worrying about such issues as the "politicization" of the classroom, or about "ideological biases" among college professors, these people are reacting to the *unfamiliarity* of progressive perspectives. Those foundational beliefs that are very common within the academy—belief in a (Christian) god, in the benignity of American institutions, in the viability of capitalism—generally go without saying and are thus invisible. *Our* worldviews are unfamiliar, and so must be articulated and acknowledged. Precisely because we are willing and able to do that, while our National Academy of Scholars colleagues are not, we become open to the charge of being "ideological."

   It's the very fact that there are so *few* leftist, African-Americans, Hispanic, openly gay, feminist, female persons in positions of academic authority that accounts for all this slavish nonsense about our "taking over."

56. Lorraine Code, "Credibility: A Double Standard," in *Feminist Perspectives*, ed. Code, Mullett, and Overall, pp. 65–66.

57. Ibid.

58. Ibid., p. 71.

59. Ibid., p. 73.

60. Ibid., p. 72.

61. Ironically, the preference among many feminist theorists for "thin" theories of the self, like postmodernist constructivist theories, is itself a vestige of an incompletely exorcised empiricism in contemporary feminist thought. It is a specifically empiricist position that the groupings of objects into kinds effected by human cognition are not keyed to "real essences," but are rather reflections of superficial regularities in experience that persist only because of their pragmatic utility.

62. We know, for example, that some of the built-in rules that make it possible for the human visual system to pick out objects from their backgrounds—so-called structure from motion rules—also make us subject to certain specific kinds of visual illusions. See A. L. Yuille and S. Ullman, "Computational Theories of Low-Level Vision," in *Visual Cognition and Action*, ed. by Daniel N. Osherson, Stephen M. Kosslyn, and John M. Hollerbach, vol. 2 of *An Invitation to Cognitive Science*, ed. by Daniel N. Osherson (Cambridge, Mass.: MIT Press, 1990), pp. 5–39.

63. I am here reiterating the arguments Chomsky mounted against Hernstein's apologia for Jensen's theory of race and intelligence. See Noam Chomsky, "Psychology and Ideology," reprinted in Chomsky, *For Reasons of State* (New York: Random House, 1973), pp. 318–369; excerpted and reprinted as "The Fallacy of Richard Herrn-

stein's IQ," in *The IQ Controversy*, ed. by Ned Block and Gerald Dworkin (New York: Random House, 1976), pp. 285–298.

64. See Herrnstein's reply to Chomsky, "Whatever Happened to Vaudeville?" in Block and Dworkin, eds., *IQ Controversy*, esp. pp. 307–309.

65. These considerations also help defeat the charge, hurled against critics of biological determinist theories, that we progressives are the ones guilty of "politicizing" the debate about nature and nurture. The Herrnsteins and E. O. Wilsons of this world like to finesse the meticulously arrayed empirical criticisms of their work by accusing their critics of the most pathetic kind of wishful thinking—"Sorry if you don't *like* what my utterly objective and bias-free research has proven beyond a shadow of a doubt. You must try to be big boys and girls and learn to cope with the unpleasant truth." For examples, see Herrnstein, "Whatever Happened to Vaudeville?" in Block and Dworkin, eds., *IQ Controversy*; and E. O. Wilson, "Academic Vigilantism and the Political Significance of Sociobiology," reprinted in *The Sociobiology Debate*, ed. by Arthur L. Caplan (New York: Harper and Row, 1978), pp. 291–303.

66. Much of the preliminary work for this essay was done during a fellowship year at the National Humanities Center, and I wish to thank both the center and the Andrew J. Mellon Foundation for this support. The essay is based on a presentation I gave at the Scripps College Humanities Institute Conference, "Thinking Women: Feminist Scholarship in the Humanities," in March 1990. I want to thank the institute, especially Norton Batkin, for the invitation to think about these issues. I also want to thank my co-participants at the conference, especially Naomi Scheman, to whom I owe a special debt. I have enjoyed an enormous amount of stimulating and challenging conversation and correspondence with Naomi about all the issues in this essay. It's a tribute to her sense of intellectual fairness and her commitment to feminist praxis that she and I have managed to conduct such an extended dialogue about these issues, given the intensity of our disagreements. I also want to make it clear that while I had the benefit of reading Naomi's essay before completing my own, I did not finish mine in time for her to react to any of the points I raise here.

Many other people have helped me with this essay. I want to thank Judith Ferster, Suzanne Graver, Charlotte Gross, Sally Haslanger, Barbara Metcalf, and Andy Reath for hours of valuable conversation. Marcia Homiak, Alice Kaplan, and Georges Rey supplied extremely useful comments on earlier drafts; David Auerbach did all that *and* extricated me from an eleventh-hour computer crisis, and I thank them heartily. Very special thanks to my co-editor, Charlotte Witt, for her excellent philosophical and editorial advice and for her abundant patience and good sense. I cannot express my thanks to Joe Levine for all he's done, intellectually and personally, to help me complete this project. Thanks as well to my children, Paul and Rachel, for their patience during all the times I was out consorting with my muse.

EPISTEMOLOGY AND PSYCHOLOGY: BIBLIOGRAPHY

Almeder, R. *Harmless Naturalism*. Chicago, 1998.

———. "On Naturalizing Epistemology." *American Philosophical Quarterly* 27 (1990): 263–79.

Bogen, J. "Traditional Epistemology and Naturalistic Replies to its Skeptical Critics." *Synthese* 64 (1985): 195–223.

Boyd, R. "Scientific Realism and Naturalistic Epistemology." In *PSA* 80 (1982), Vol. 2. East Lansing, Mich.

Devitt, M. *Realism and Truth*, chapter 5. Princeton, N.J., 1984; 2d ed., 1991.

Gardner, H. *The Mind's New Science*. New York, 1985.

Goldman, A. I. *Epistemology and Cognition*. Cambridge, Mass., 1986.

———. "Epistemology and the Psychology of Belief." *The Monist* 61 (1978): 525–35.

———. "Epistemology and the Theory of Problem Solving." *Synthese* 55 (1983): 21–48.

———. *Liaisons*. Cambridge, Mass., 1992.

———. "The Relation between Epistemology and Psychology." *Synthese* 64 (1985): 29–68.

———. "The Sciences and Epistemology." In *The Oxford Handbook of Epistemology*, ed. P. K. Moser New York, 2003.

———. "Varieties of Cognitive Appraisal." *Noûs* 13 (1979): 23–38.

Haack, S. "The Relevance of Psychology to Epistemology." *Metaphilosophy* 6 (1975): 161–76.

Kitcher, P. "The Naturalists Return." *Philosophical Review* 101 (1992): 53–114.

Kornblith, H. ed. *Naturalizing Epistemology.* Cambridge, Mass., 1985; 2d ed., 1994.

Lycan, W. G. "Epistemic Value." *Synthese* 64 (1985): 137–64.

Moser, P. K., and D. Yandell. "Against Naturalizing Rationality." In *The Contextualization of Rationality*, ed. G. Preyer and G. Peter, pp. 81–94. Paderborn, 2000.

Nisbett, R., and L. Ross. *Human Inference.* Englewood Cliffs, N.J., 1980.

Putnam, H. "Why Reason Can't Be Naturalized." In *Realism and Reason: Philosophical Papers, Vol. 3*, pp. 229–47. Cambridge, Eng., 1983.

Quine, W. V. "The Nature of Natural Knowledge." In *Mind and Language: Wolfson College Lectures*, ed. S. Guttenplan, pp. 67–81. Oxford, 1975.

Rorty, R. *Philosophy and the Mirror of Nature*, chapter 5. Princeton, 1979.

Siegel, H. "Empirical Psychology, Naturalized Epistemology, and First Philosophy." *Philosophy of Science* 51 (1984): 667–676.

———. "Justification, Discovery, and the Naturalizing of Epistemology." *Philosophy of Science* 47 (1980): 297–321.

———. "Naturalism, Instrumental Rationality, and the Normativity of Epistemology." In *The Contextualization of Rationality*, ed. G. Preyer and G. Peter, pp. 95–107. Paderborn, 2000.

Sosa, E. "Nature Unmirrored, Epistemology Naturalized." *Synthese* 55 (1983): 49–72.

Stroud, Barry. "The Significance of Naturalized Epistemology." In *Midwest Studies in Philosophy, Vol. VI: Analytic Philosophy*, ed. P. French et al., pp. 455–71. Minneapolis, 1981. Reprinted in *Naturalizing Epistemology*, ed. H. Kornblith, pp. 71–89. Cambridge, Mass., 1985.

———. *The Significance of Philosophical Scepticism*, chapter 6. Oxford, 1984.

Swain, M. "Epistemics and Epistemology." *The Journal of Philosophy* 75 (1978): 523–25.

Name Index

Subject Index